college
accounting
a practical
approach

jeffrey slater
NORTH SHORE COMMUNITY COLLEGE

brian zwicker
GRANT MACEWAN UNIVERSITY (INSTRUCTOR EMERITUS)

canadian eleventh edition

Pearson Canada
Toronto

Library and Archives Canada Cataloguing in Publication

Slater, Jeffrey, 1947-
    College accounting : a practical approach / Jeffrey Slater, Brian Zwicker. – Canadian 11th ed.

Includes index.
ISBN 978-0-13-511132-1

    1. Accounting —Textbooks. I. Zwicker, Brian, 1944- II. Title.

F5636.S53 2011   657'.044   C2010-905657-4

ISBN 978-0-13-511132-1

Vice-President, Editorial Director: Gary Bennett
Editor-in-Chief Editor: Nicole Lukach
Marketing Manager: Cas Shields
Developmental Editor: Darryl Kamo
Project Manager: Sarah Lukaweski
Production Editor: Heather Sangster (Strong Finish), Gail Copeland
Copy Editor: Kathy White, Strong Finish
Proofreader: Deborah Cooper-Bullock
Compositor: Nelson Gonzalez
Photo and Permissions Researcher: Beth McAuley
Art Director: Julia Hall
Cover and Interior Designer: Jennifer Stimson
Cover Image: Alamy

3 4 5   15 14 13 12

Printed and bound in the Unites States of America.

For Darien and Laura

Brief Contents

PREFACE xv

CHAPTER 1 Accounting Concepts and Procedures: An Introduction   1

CHAPTER 2 Debits and Credits: Analyzing and Recording Business Transactions   46

CHAPTER 3 Beginning the Accounting Cycle: Journalizing, Posting, and the Trial Balance   91

CHAPTER 4 The Accounting Cycle Continued: Preparing Worksheets and Financial Statements   137

CHAPTER 5 The Accounting Cycle Completed: Adjusting, Closing, and Post-Closing Trial Balance   182

CHAPTER 6 Special Journals: The Basics   246

CHAPTER 7 Banking Procedures and Control of Cash   310

CHAPTER 8 Payroll Procedures: The Employees' Perspective   364

CHAPTER 9 The Employer's Tax Responsibilities: Principles and Procedures   412

CHAPTER 10 Special Journals with Taxes   447

CHAPTER 11 The Synoptic (Combined) Journal   510

CHAPTER 12 Preparing a Worksheet for a Merchandising Company   541

CHAPTER 13 Completion of the Accounting Cycle for a Merchandising Company   573

CHAPTER 14 Accounting for Bad Debts   614

CHAPTER 15 Accounting for Property, Plant, Equipment, and Intangible Assets   640

CHAPTER 16 Statement of Cash Flows   679

INDEX 703

Contents

◆ **PREFACE**   xv

◆ **CHAPTER 1   ACCOUNTING CONCEPTS AND PROCEDURES: AN INTRODUCTION   1**

The Big Picture   1
Categories of Business Organization   3
Classifying Organizations by Activity   4
Learning Unit 1-1: The Accounting Equation   6
Assets, Liabilities, and Equities   6
Learning Unit 1-2: The Balance Sheet   11
Points to Remember in Preparing a Balance Sheet   12
Learning Unit 1-3: The Accounting Equation Expanded: Revenue, Expenses, and Withdrawals   14
Key Terms in the Accounting Equation   14
Expanded Accounting Equation   15
Learning Unit 1-4: Preparing Financial Reports   20
The Income Statement   20
The Statement of Owner's Equity   21
The Balance Sheet   22
Main Elements of the Income Statement, the Statement of Owner's Equity, and the Balance Sheet   22
Subway: A Fresh Start   26
Chapter Assignments   27
Summary of Key Points   30
Key Terms   31
Blueprint of Financial Reports   33
Questions, Classroom Demonstration Exercises, Exercises, and Problems   33
Continuing Problem   45

◆ **CHAPTER 2   DEBITS AND CREDITS: ANALYZING AND RECORDING BUSINESS TRANSACTIONS   46**

The Big Picture   46
Learning Unit 2-1: The T Account   47
Balancing an Account   49
Learning Unit 2-2: Recording Business Transactions: Debits and Credits   50
T Account Entries for Accounting in the Accounting Equation   50
The Accounting Analysis: Five Steps   52
Applying the Transaction Analysis to Catherine Hall's Law Practice   53
Summary of Transactions for Catherine Hall   59
Learning Unit 2-3: The Trial Balance and Preparation of Financial Statements   62
The Trial Balance   62

Preparing Financial Statements   63
Subway: Debits on the Left   68
Chapter Assignments   69
Summary of Key Points   73
Blueprint for Preparing Financial Statements from a Trial Balance   75
Questions, Classroom Demonstration Exercises, Exercises, and
   Problems   75
Continuing Problem   90

◆ **CHAPTER 3   BEGINNING THE ACCOUNTING CYCLE:
               JOURNALIZING, POSTING, AND THE TRIAL
               BALANCE   91**

The Big Picture   91
**Learning Unit 3-1: Analyzing and Recording Business Transactions in a
   Journal: Steps 1 and 2 of the Accounting Cycle**   92
The General Journal   92
**Learning Unit 3-2: Posting to the Ledger: Step 3 of the Accounting
   Cycle**   101
Posting   101
**Learning Unit 3-3: Preparing the Trial Balance: Step 4 of the Accounting
   Cycle**   109
What to Do If a Trial Balance Doesn't Balance   110
Some Common Mistakes   110
Making a Correction Before Posting   110
Making a Correction After Posting   111
Correcting an Entry Posted to the Wrong Account   111
Chapter Assignments   114
Summary of Key Points   118
Key Terms   119
Blueprint of First Four Steps of the Accounting Cycle   120
Questions, Classroom Demonstration Exercises, Exercises, and
   Problems   121
Continuing Problem   134
Computer Workshops   136

◆ **CHAPTER 4   THE ACCOUNTING CYCLE CONTINUED:
               PREPARING WORKSHEETS AND FINANCIAL
               STATEMENTS   137**

The Big Picture   137
**Learning Unit 4-1: Step 5 of the Accounting Cycle:
   Preparing a Worksheet**   138
The Trial Balance Section   139
The Adjustments Section   139
The Adjusted Trial Balance Section   145
The Income Statement Section   148
The Balance Sheet Section   149
**Learning Unit 4-2: Step 6 of the Accounting Cycle: Preparing the Financial
   Statements from the Worksheet**   152
Preparing the Income Statement   152
Preparing the Statement of Owner's Equity   152
Preparing the Balance Sheet   154
Subway: Where the Dough Goes   158
Chapter Assignments   159
Summary of Key Points   162
Key Terms   163
Blueprint of Steps 5 and 6 of the Accounting Cycle   164

Questions, Classroom Demonstration Exercises, Exercises, and
   Problems   164
Continuing Problem   180
Computer Workshops   181

◆ CHAPTER 5   THE ACCOUNTING CYCLE COMPLETED:
                ADJUSTING, CLOSING, AND POST-CLOSING TRIAL
                BALANCE   182

The Big Picture   182
Learning Unit 5-1: Journalizing and Posting Adjusting Entries:
   Step 7 of the Accounting Cycle   183
Recording Journal Entries from the Worksheet   183
Learning Unit 5-2: Journalizing and Posting the Closing Entries:
   Step 8 of the Accounting Cycle   187
How to Journalize Closing Entries   188
Learning Unit 5-3: The Post-Closing Trial Balance: Step 9 of the Accounting
   Cycle and the Accounting Cycle Reviewed   198
Preparing a Post-Closing Trial Balance   198
The Account Cycle Reviewed   199
Subway: Closing Time   202
Chapter Assignments   203
Summary of Key Points   211
Key Terms   212
Blueprint of the Closing Process from the Worksheet   213
Questions, Classroom Demonstration Exercises, Exercises, and
   Problems   213
Continuing Problem   228
Mini Practice Set   229
Computer Workshops   245

◆ CHAPTER 6   SPECIAL JOURNALS: THE BASICS   246

The Big Picture   246
Learning Unit 6-1: Chou's Toy Shop: Seller's View of a Merchandising
   Company   247
Gross Sales   247
Sales Returns and Allowances   248
Sales Discount   249
Learning Unit 6-2: The Sales Journal and Accounts Receivable
   Subsidiary Ledger   250
Special Journals   250
Subsidiary Ledgers   251
The Sales Journal   252
Learning Unit 6-3: The Credit Memorandum   255
Journalizing, Recording, and Posting the Credit Memorandum   256
Learning Unit 6-4: Cash Receipts Journal and Schedule of Accounts
   Receivable   259
Journalizing, Recording, and Posting from the Cash Receipts Journal   261
Schedule of Accounts Receivable   262
Learning Unit 6-5: Chou's Toy Shop: Buyer's View of a Merchandising
   Company   264
Purchases   264
Purchases Returns and Allowances   265
Purchases Discounts   266
Learning Unit 6-6: Steps Taken in Purchasing Merchandise and Recording
   Purchases   268

Steps Taken by Art's Wholesale When Ordering Goods   268
The Purchases Journal and Accounts Payable Subsidiary Ledger   270
The Debit Memorandum   270
Learning Unit 6-7: The Cash Payments Journal and Schedule of Accounts Payable   275
Journalizing, Posting, and Recording from the Cash Payments Journal to the Accounts Payable Subsidiary Ledger and the General Ledger   278
Chapter Assignments   282
Summary of Key Points   286
Key Terms   288
Blueprint of Sales and Cash Receipts Journals   291
Questions, Classroom Demonstration Exercises, Exercises, and Problems   292
Continuing Problem   307
Computer Workshops   309

◆ CHAPTER 7   BANKING PROCEDURES AND CONTROL OF CASH   310

The Big Picture   310
Learning Unit 7-1: Bank Procedures, Chequing Accounts, and Bank Reconciliation   311
Opening a Chequing Account   312
Cheque Endorsement   312
The Chequebook   314
Monthly Recordkeeping: The Bank's Statement of Account and In-Company Records   316
The Bank Reconciliation Process   316
Trends in Banking   319
Learning Unit 7-2: The Establishment of Petty Cash and Change Funds   329
Setting Up the Petty Cash Fund   329
Making Payments from the Petty Cash Fund   330
How to Replenish the Petty Cash Fund   331
Setting up a Change Fund and Insight into Cash Short and Over   333
Subway: Counting Down the Cash   337
Chapter Assignments   338
Summary of Key Points   338
Key Terms   338
Blueprint of a Bank Reconciliation   340
Questions, Classroom Demonstration Exercises, Exercises, and Problems   340
Continuing Problem   360
Computer Workshops   363

◆ CHAPTER 8   PAYROLL PROCEDURES: THE EMPLOYEES' PERSPECTIVE   364

The Big Picture   364
Learning Unit 8-1: Important Laws and How They Affect Payroll   365
Minimum Wage Laws   366
Federal and Provincial Income Tax   366
Canada or Quebec Pension Plan   371
Employment Insurance Plan   372
CPP and EI: Some Additional Information   372
Workers' Compensation Plans   372
Various Union Agreements   372
Other Deductions   372

Learning Unit 8-2: A Typical Payroll 374
The Payroll Summary in Detail 374
Learning Unit 8-3: Recording and Payment 376
Last Step Directly Affecting Employees 377
Employee Earnings Record 378
Subway: Payroll Records: A Full-Time Job 382
Chapter Assignments 383
Summary of Key Points 383
Key Terms 384
Blueprint for Recording, Posting, and Paying the Payroll 386
Questions, Classroom Demonstration Exercises, Exercises, and
    Problems 387
Continuing Problem 396
Appendices: Employee Payroll Deductions (Extracted):
    Income Taxes, CPP, EI 398
        Appendix 8-1F—Federal Taxes 398
        Appendix 8-1P—Ontario Tax Tables 403
        Appendix 8-2—Simulated Canada Pension Plan Contributions 408
        Appendix 8-3—Employment Insurance Premium Calculations 410

◆ **CHAPTER 9   THE EMPLOYER'S TAX RESPONSIBILITIES:
                PRINCIPLES AND PROCEDURES   412**

The Big Picture 412
Learning Unit 9-1: Employer's Expenses Associated with Payroll 413
How to Calculate Employer's Remittance 414
Learning Unit 9-2: Completing the Monthly Remittance Form 418
Learning Unit 9-3: Employer's Annual T4 Summary 422
Workers' Compensation Insurance 424
Subway: Hold the Lettuce, Withhold the Taxes 426
Chapter Assignments 427
Summary of Key Points 427
Key Terms 427
Blueprint of the Tax Calendar 428
Questions, Classroom Demonstration Exercises, Exercises, and
    Problems 429
Continuing Problem 444
Mini Practice Set 445

◆ **CHAPTER 10   SPECIAL JOURNALS WITH TAXES   447**

The Big Picture 447
Introduction to GST and HST 448
**Learning Unit 10-1: Chou's Toy Shop: Seller's View of a Merchandising
    Company** 449
Provincial Sales Tax Collected 449
The Credit Memorandum with Provincial Sales Tax (PST) 451
How Companies Record GST and HST 452
GST/HST Collected on Sales 452
GST/HST and the Credit Memorandum 454
Provincial Sales Tax with GST/HST 455
Sales Invoice with PST and GST/HST 455
Credit Memorandum with PST and GST/HST 456
**Learning Unit 10-2: Cash Receipts Journal and Schedul of Accounts
    Receivable** 459
Journalizing, Recording, and Posting from the Cash Receipts Journal 460
Schedule of Accounts Receivable 462
Learning Unit 10-3: GST/HST Paid on Purchases 465

Overview   465
Recording Purchases with GST/HST   466
The Debit Memorandum   468
Chapter Assignments   475
Summary of Key Points   480
Key Terms   482
Blueprint of Sales and Cash Receipts Journals   483
Blueprint of Purchases and Cash Payments Journals   484
Questions, Classroom Demonstration Exercises, Exercises, and
    Problems   485
Continuing Problem   507
Computer Workshops   509

◆ **CHAPTER 11   THE SYNOPTIC (COMBINED) JOURNAL   510**

The Big Picture   510
**Learning Unit 11-1: Synoptic Journal: A Modified Cash System for a Service
    Company**   512
Chart of Accounts   512
Recording Transactions in the Synoptic Journal   514
Posting the Synoptic Journal   515
Recording Payroll Deductions and Employer's Payroll Tax Expense   515
**Learning Unit 11-2: Synoptic Journal for Art's Wholesale Clothing
    Company**   518
Recording and Posting the Synoptic Journal   519
Chapter Assignments   524
Summary of Key Points   524
Key Terms   524
Blueprint of a Typical Chart of Accounts for a Lawyer Using a Modified Cash
    Basis (Including Payroll)   525
Questions, Classroom Demonstration Exercises, Exercises, and
    Problems   525
Continuing Problem   540

◆ **CHAPTER 12   PREPARING A WORKSHEET FOR A
                MERCHANDISING COMPANY   541**

The Big Picture   541
**Learning Unit 12-1: Adjustments for Merchandise Inventory and Unearned
    Rent**   542
Adjustment for Merchandise Inventory   543
Adjustment for Unearned Rent   544
Learning Unit 12-2: Completing the Worksheet   545
Chapter Assignments   555
Summary of Key Points   555
Key Terms   555
Blueprint of a Worksheet for a Merchandising Company   556
Questions, Classroom Demonstration Exercises, Exercises and
    Problems   557
Continuing Problem   571

◆ **CHAPTER 13   COMPLETION OF THE ACCOUNTING CYCLE FOR A
                MERCHANDISING COMPANY   573**

The Big Picture   573
Learning Unit 13-1: Preparing Financial Statements   574
The Income Statement   574
Statement of Owner's Equity   577

The Balance Sheet   577
Learning Unit 13-2: Journalizing and Posting Adjusting and Closing Entries; Preparing the Post-Closing Trial Balance   581
Journalizing and Posting Adjusting Entries   581
Journalizing and Posting Closing Entries   584
The Post-Closing Trial Balance   584
Learning Unit 13-3: Reversing Entries (Optional Section)   587
Chapter Assignments   590
Summary of Key Points   590
Key Terms   590
Blueprint of Financial Statements   591
Questions, Classroom Demonstration Exercises, Exercises, and Problems   593
Continuing Problem   607
Mini Practice Set   608

◆ **CHAPTER 14   ACCOUNTING FOR BAD DEBTS   614**

The Big Picture   614
Learning Unit 14-1: Accrual Accounting and Recording Bad Debts   615
Writing Off an Account Deemed Uncollectible   616
Learning Unit 14-2: The Allowance Method: Two Approaches to Estimating the Amount of Bad Debts Expense   618
The Income Statement Approach   618
The Balance Sheet Approach   619
Aging the Accounts Receivables   620
Learning Unit 14-3: Writing Off Uncollectible Accounts   622
Writing Off an Account Using the Allowance for Doubtful Accounts   622
The Direct Write-Off Method   623
Insight into Income Tax Regulations   624
Chapter Assignments   626
Summary of Key Points   626
Key Terms   628
Questions, Classroom Demonstration Exercises, Exercises, and Problems   628
Continuing Problem   639

◆ **CHAPTER 15   ACCOUNTING FOR PROPERTY, PLANT, EQUIPMENT, AND INTANGIBLE ASSETS   640**

The Big Picture   640
Learning Unit 15-1: Cost of Property, Plant, and Equipment   641
Land and Land Improvements   642
Buildings   642
Learning Unit 15-2: Amortization Methods   644
Straight-Line Method   644
Units-of-Production Method   645
Double-Declining-Balance Method   645
Optional Section: Sum-of-the-Years'-Digits Method   646
Amortization for Partial Years   647
Amortization for Tax Purposes: Capital Cost Allowance   647
Learning Unit 15-3: Capital and Revenue Expenditures and Disposal of Plant Assets   652
Capital Expenditures   653
Revenue Expenditures   653
Disposal of Plant Assets   654
Learning Unit 15-4: Natural Resources and Intangible Assets   659

Intangible Assets and the Concept of Impairment   659
Learning Unit 15-5: Complex Cases in Accounting for Capital Assets   661
Site Restoration Costs   661
Assets Acquired by Lease   661
Writing Down Goodwill   662
Impairment of Tangible Long-Term Assets   662
Self-Constructed Capital Assets   662
Final Thoughts   663
Chapter Assignments   664
Summary of Key Points   664
Key Terms   666
Blueprint of Key Accounts   667
Questions, Classroom Demonstration Exercises, Exercises, and
  Problems   668

◆ **CHAPTER 16   STATEMENT OF CASH FLOWS   679**

The Big Picture   679
Learning Unit 16-1: Statement of Cash Flows: Indirect Method   680
Cash Flows from Operating Activities: Indirect Method   681
Cash Flows from Investing Activities   683
Cash Flows from Financing Activities   684
Learning Unit 16-2: Statement of Cash Flows: Direct Method   686
Chapter Assignments   690
Summary of Key Points   690
Key Terms   690
Blueprint of Statement of Cash Flows   692
Questions, Classroom Demonstration Exercises, Exercises, and
  Problems   693

◆ **INDEX   703**

AVAILABLE ON *MYACCOUNTINGLAB.COM*

◆ **CHAPTER 10 APPENDIX:** What Special Journals Would Look Like in a
                          Perpetual Accounting System

◆ **CHAPTER 12 APPENDIX:** A Worksheet for Art's Wholesale Clothing
                          Company Using a Perpetual Inventory System

◆ **AUXILIARY CHAPTER 17:** Analyzing Financial Statements

◆ **AUXILIARY CHAPTER 18:** Notes Receivable and Notes Payable

◆ **AUXILIARY CHAPTER 19:** Accounting for Merchandise Inventory

◆ **AUXILIARY CHAPTER 20:** Partnerships and Corporations

◆ **AUXILIARY CHAPTER 21:** Corporations—Bonds Payable

◆ **AUXILIARY CHAPTER 22:** The Voucher System

◆ **AUXILIARY CHAPTER 23:** Departmental Accounting

◆ **AUXILIARY CHAPTER 24:** Manufacturing Accounting

◆ **APPENDIX A:** How Companies Record Credit Card Sales in Their Special
                  Journals

Preface

Welcome to the Canadian Eleventh Edition of *College Accounting: A Practical Approach* by Jeffrey Slater and Brian Zwicker. In this edition, we introduce several important changes that will greatly enhance the student learning experience while allowing for highly organized and efficient class leadership. In most revisions, even one of the changes we have included in this edition would be a standout event, but several very positive alterations make the Canadian Eleventh Edition the most significant regeneration in the long and respected history of *College Accounting*. At the same time, we have maintained the many features that have helped make *College Accounting* a classroom favourite for more than 20 years.

New to the Canadian Eleventh Edition

Introducing MyAccountingLab! By any reasonable measure, the addition of MyAccountingLab (MAL) eclipses all the other changes combined. The MAL platform—an online homework presentation and assessment tool—is new to this edition of *College Accounting* but has been designed, tested, and used in various textbooks published by Pearson in North America for many years. The addition of MAL to any text is a carefully considered venture mainly because of the effort required by all involved. The result is well worth the investment because MAL provides student and instructor access to a considerable set of resources that will greatly expand and enhance the teaching and learning of accounting. Through MAL, instructors integrate technology into their course design and students gain a valuable supplemental resource. MAL can also be used in the student assessment process, if desired. However, the biggest benefit may well be the large quantity and high quality of review material available to students who need additional practice and assistance in the learning of accounting.

Revised Chapter Order. A new and improved chapter order makes its debut in the Canadian Eleventh Edition. In previous editions, the topic of special journals was covered in Chapters 9 (Sales and Receipts) and 10 (Purchases and Payments). While this was in many ways logical, it did present some challenges in chapter organization and was really not ideal from the standpoint of student learning. Starting with this edition, a new Chapter 6 covers all four major special journals, without the complexities of involving taxes such as PST, GST, or HST. This new placement follows on quite logically from the completion of the accounting cycle in Chapter 5, and students should find it an easy transition. Chapter 10 now includes all four major special journals but also adds in a realistic way the topic of various taxes so that students who are asked to complete the chapter will enter the workplace with confidence and some added marketable skills.

On the way to creating this significant change to the textbook, a strange thing happened. As usual, we contacted a number of reviewers as step one in our revision plan. Many of the reviewers let it be known (in various ways, to be sure) that there might be a better way to cover this material. That feedback led to the proposed change in chapter order, but it was such a fundamental alteration that it was deemed wise to seek additional feedback from a selected additional group of reviewers. These individuals were given the revised Chapters 6 and 10, and to the astonishment of all involved, their response was unanimous—the change was excellent! In the 20-plus years of seeking feedback from various adopters or potential adopters, this had never happened before, so of course the revision plan was approved, including this chapter rearrangement.

New "Need Help?" Feature. Many of our reviewers pointed out that students needed more explanation and practice material with the basics. The new "Need Help?" feature is our major response to these requests. The first five chapters now include the "Need Help?" sections, with each of the self-review quizzes near the end of each learning unit. It is like having a private tutoring session with the authors, as student questions are anticipated and step-by-step guidance is given as the solution is laid out in logical order. This feature should greatly extend student retention, especially for those students who benefit from detailed and exacting repetition.

Several reviewers also called for additional explanatory material on the subject of debits and credits, mentioning that some students just do not "get it" the first (or, indeed, the second) time around. This edition also includes a "Need Help?" feature on debits and credits, drawing on material used for decades by the Canadian author in classroom settings. While there is no objective evidence that it helps with understanding this sometimes troublesome topic, the number of smiles around the classroom following the "nautical" example does suggest that it works—sometimes very well. This new feature is included, logically enough, in Chapter 2.

Major Features Maintained and Expanded

In addition to the above major additions and changes, the Canadian Eleventh Edition has retained and in many cases improved upon the pedagogy that has made *College Accounting* a classic. Here are some details:

Includes 24 chapters! In a major revamping of the book's content, in the last edition the number of chapters was increased from 16 to 24. We have maintained this expanded material for the Canadian Eleventh Edition. In addition to the 16 chapters published in the text itself, eight additional chapters are available from MyAccountingLab for those institutions that need to incorporate them into their course design. The additional chapters are:

- Chapter 17—Analyzing Financial Statements. Updated from an earlier edition of *College Accounting*
- Chapter 18—Notes Receivable and Payable. Updated from an earlier edition of *College Accounting*
- Chapter 19—Accounting for Merchandise Inventory. Adapted with minor changes from the ninth edition of *College Accounting*
- Chapter 20—Partnerships and Corporations. Adapted with minor changes from the ninth edition of *College Accounting*
- Chapter 21—Corporate Bonds Payable. Canadianized version of a similar chapter from the tenth U.S. edition of *College Accounting*
- Chapter 22—The Voucher System. Canadianized version of a similar chapter from the tenth U.S. edition of *College Accounting*
- Chapter 23—Departmental Accounting. Canadianized version of a similar chapter from the tenth U.S. edition of *College Accounting*
- Chapter 24—Manufacturing Accounting. Canadianized version of a similar chapter from the tenth U.S. edition of *College Accounting*

These auxiliary chapters will assist instructors who need to extend their students' education while keeping the text's price under control. In general, the chapters continued from an earlier Canadian edition retain many of the features adopters have come to appreciate (there are C-type problems, and a computer workshop for Auxiliary Chapter 19), while the four U.S. edition chapters, while Canadianized, do not have all the features of the (former) Canadian edition chapters. However, because they are adapted from a high-quality source, they will still be of considerable assistance in selected circumstances.

Expanded Coverage of Banking Trends. This material was already the best available in Canada but has been further upgraded to allow coverage at an enhanced level, including aspects of modern banking realities in Canada. Additional problem material has been developed and will be appreciated by any instructor who aims to provide students with plenty of practice in this vital area.

Outstanding Computer Workshops on MyAccountingLab. Use of computers to process accounting transactions and conduct ebusiness is taken for granted in many businesses today. *College Accounting* helps students learn and integrate these skills by infusing the tried-and-true Slater/Zwicker system with real-world applications. Continuing with the Canadian Eleventh Edition is the inclusion of computer workshops on MyAccountingLab. These carefully crafted computer workshops (at the end of Chapters 3, 4, 5, 6, 7, and 10) greatly increase the practice and instruction available to assign to students and will be appreciated by instructors dealing with large class sizes and/or multiple sections. Workshops are available in two different formats: Simply Accounting® Pro 2010 and QuickBooks® Premier 2010. These two accounting software packages represent the best available in Canada and are the most popular, based on total sales.

We continue to accompany each workshop with a detailed, step-by-step guide accompanied by screen grabs to allow most students to complete the workshops in the minimum time and with the fewest errors. Some other details:

a. Completely Revised Computer Workshops. Since their introduction, the workshops been altered very little. Now that this feature is being used more generally throughout the system, it was deemed essential to completely update them. Four files were created for each of the workshops—an instruction file, the opening data set, the detailed instruction file, and the completed data set. Almost half of the new workshops were created by the Canadian author, and most of these were then used by assistants who thereby had a quality example to work from. The workshops at the end of Chapter 6 are completely new to this edition, created by the author, and carefully crafted to enhance the new material in that chapter.

b. Relocating the Computer Workshop Material. Moving the computer workshop material to MyAccountingLab has made it possible to add selected material to the text without dropping any chapters. Where an instructor deems it inappropriate to focus on computer accounting in the introductory accounting course, this is now easier than ever to accomplish.

c. Simply Accounting® Pro and QuickBooks® Premier. In all cases, the data sets and detailed explanatory material have been updated to include current dates and screen captures. The data sets themselves will be upgraded to 2011 and 2012 versions of these software programs as they become available.

d. Software Available! At the time of publication, the "Professional" version of both of these award-winning applications continues to be offered to students free of charge by the software companies. Some educational entities have one or both of the software packages available for students to use in computer labs, but where students are expected to use their own laptops, it is easier than ever to obtain free versions to use with classroom material, such as the computer workshops.

e. Step-by-Step Guides to Computer Workshops. Detailed guides lead students through the entire process of completing computer workshops. Fully illustrated, including many appropriate screen captures, this excellent feature has proven popular with all students but may be of special interest to the increasing proportion of students who approach their education through distance education courses. The detailed guide to half of the workshops in each chapter is included free to all students on MyAccountingLab. Detailed guides to the other workshops are made available for use at the instructors's discretion. This permits instructors to use selected workshops as examination or quiz material, if appropriate.

Chapter Openers Refreshed. Several new or revised chapter opening vignettes introduce students to business realities and accounting. These opening scenarios are interesting, easy to read, and mostly based on businesses in Canada. All readers should appreciate the creativity and appropriateness these short introductions provide.

Continuing Problem. A continuing problem runs through Chapters 1 through 14, asking students to apply skills to the business scenario set in the Big Picture. It is based on the Precision Computer Centre. Reviewers have reported success in having some, or all, of the continuing problem completed using accounting software.

Payroll Chapters. Chapter 8 and 9 (formerly 7 and 8) have been rewritten where necessary to reflect the latest laws and taxation deduction rules in effect in Canada, and updated forms are shown as well. At the request of a number of reviewers, a special comprehensive payroll problem has been added near the end of Chapter 9. This should provide an excellent resource for courses that stress the complete knowledge of the payroll process.

GST and HST Accounting. These taxes are a reality in Canada. The essential details of how to account for GST and HST are covered in Chapter 10. This chapter has been designed to accommodate instructors who choose to emphasize this topic, and textbook examples and problem material using HST have been strengthened. This seems especially logical now that BC and Ontario have joined the ranks of those that charge and collect HST in Canada. Plenty of material using PST still exists in the text for those situations where HST is not yet a marketplace reality.

Special Journal Coverage Continued. Considerable investigation of Canadian needs dictated that we maintain coverage of this worthwhile material in the main text. As already mentioned, however, we changed the order of presentation so that the elements are covered in (new) Chapter 6 while the more complex material relating to special journals is now part of Chapter 10. This decision was based on the thought that a detailed description of special journals in manual form will greatly assist students when they first encounter the realities of computer accounting.

Subway Boxes. The real-world accounting issues facing franchise owners and corporate staff are presented in boxed features based on research of the internationally known company. Discussion questions tie the boxes to chapter concepts.

Check Figures. Brief mention of key amounts or other hints in the margins continue to provide quick feedback for students to monitor progress in all A, B, and C problems.

Coverage of Perpetual Inventory. Both merchandise inventory and special journals are discussed. An appendix uses the general journal approach to teach entries for a merchandise company using perpetual inventory, while an appendix to Chapter 10 available on MyAccountingLab shows how all the special journals in Chapters 6 and 10 would look in a perpetual system. The related appendix to Chapter 12, also available on MyAccountingLab, shows how a worksheet for a merchandise company would look in a perpetual inventory system. Auxiliary Chapter 19 extends this coverage in a very complete way, where the bulk of the material is directed to perpetual inventory issues.

Chapter on Partnerships and Corporations. Canadian students appreciate having a chapter that covers the essentials of these two alternative forms of business activity. Revised for the Canadian business environment, this chapter proved to be a popular and useful addition. It is included with the auxiliary chapters in MyAccountingLab.

Extensive End-of-Chapter Framework. Each chapter offers extensive learning aids, including:

- Discussion Questions/Classroom Demonstration Exercises
- Mini Exercises
- Exercises
- Problem sets A, B, and C (D problems are also available, but are supplied separately)
- Exploring E-Biz Internet exercises that put your students on the Web, now moved to MyAccountingLab, based on feedback from reviewers
- Continuing Problem: a cumulative problem that runs through Chapters 1 to 14, asking students to work through the entire business cycle for Precision Computer Centre
- Simulations available in selected chapters: students will benefit from completing the extended and realistic cases presented at the end of Chapters 5, 9, and 13

The Slater/Zwicker Package

The text is just the starting point. Because the needs of Canadian instructors are very high on our priority list, we have taken certain other steps designed to maximize instructor effectiveness and efficiency. These steps include the provision of an Instructor's Resource Manual, Instructor's Solution Manual, and Pearson Canada TestGen (a computerized test bank available online and on the Instructor's Resource CD-ROM). We also offer the complete Canadianization of the *Study Guide with Working Papers*. We invested many hours to ensure the highest quality possible, and we hope it shows in increased clarity, accuracy, and consistency.

Instructor's Supplements

Instructor's Resource CD-ROM. This resource CD-ROM brings together all the materials that facilitate and augment each instructor's special skills, strengths, and experience. The IRCD includes the following instructor supplements:

- **Instructor's Solutions Manual.** This manual provides answers to discussion questions and solutions to exercises, mini exercises, problems, practice problems, classroom demonstration exercises, and a guide to discussion of ethical issues.

  To ensure accurate solutions, each page of the Solutions Manual was carefully reviewed by Laurence P. Hanchard, C.A. His exacting review will be appreciated by all instructors using this package.

- **Instructor's Resource Manual.** The Instructor's Resource Manual (IRM) includes Class Quizzes and Class Activities, both designed to reinforce key points introduced in the text; Lesson Outlines designed for a variety of classroom situations; Typical Student Misconceptions that identify common errors gathered from almost 50 years of combined teaching experience; and Teaching Tips to help students remember and absorb textbook material. In addition, Lecture Notes provide a useful check to ensure nothing critical is overlooked during classroom preparation, and Business-World Notes take students beyond the accounting textbook by providing a glimpse of what takes place in the real world. The IRM is also available online as a download.

- **Pearson TestGen.** The Pearson TestGen provides testing software that enables instructors to view and edit existing questions, add questions, generate tests, and distribute those tests in a variety of formats. Powerful search and sort functions make it easy to locate questions and arrange them in any order desired. TestGen also enables instructors to administer tests on a local area network, have the tests graded electronically, and have the results prepared in electronic or printed reports. TestGen is compatible with Windows and Macintosh operating systems and is available online for download. The question content has been significantly expanded as well to provide a larger set of questions from which to choose tests and quizzes, etc.

- **Computer Workshop Guides/Solutions.** The computer workshops have been newly customized for both Simply Accounting® Pro and QuickBooks® Premier. Students are provided with a detailed, step-by-step guide to completing one of the workshops at the end of selected chapters, and in addition to this detailed guide for students on MyAccountingLab, the instructor's resources include a detailed guide for a second workshop at the end of selected chapters. This allows instructors to control this important feature and ensure they are used appropriately—i.e., not as a substitute for learning. Naturally, a solution data set is provided (in the instructor's area of MyAccountingLab) for each of the computer workshops. This provides all instructors with a starting point for providing feedback to students who complete them.

- **Type D Problems.** Like the C-type problems in the text, these problems are slightly more challenging than the A or B problems. Solutions are provided (also in the Instructor's Resource Manual) so these new problems can be used in interesting ways—such as for extra-challenging work for students or on quizzes or examinations. The headings for most of the C-type problems in the *Study Guide with Working Papers* have been deliberately omitted (at the request of a number of instructors). This means these forms can be used for the D-type problems as well, if convenient. The D-type problems are available in the instructor's area of MyAccountingLab.

CourseSmart for Instructors. CourseSmart goes beyond traditional expectations—providing instant, online access to the textbooks and course materials you need at a lower cost for students. And even as students save money, you can save time and hassle with a digital eTextbook that allows you to search for the most relevant content at the very moment you need it. Whether it's evaluating textbooks or creating lecture notes to help students with difficult concepts, CourseSmart can make life a little easier. See how when you visit **www.coursesmart.com/instructors**.

Technology Specialists. Pearson's Technology Specialists work with faculty and campus course designers to ensure that Pearson technology products, assessment tools, and online course materials are tailored to meet your specific needs. This highly qualified team is dedicated to helping schools take full advantage of a wide range of educational resources, by assisting in the integration of a variety of instructional materials and media formats. Your local Pearson Canada sales representative can provide you with more details on this service program.

For Students

Study Guide with Working Papers. This publication has undergone all necessary revisions and enhancements. It contains forms for the quiz at the end of each learning unit in the chapter, for all exercises and mini exercises, for the problems (A, B, and C) at the end of each chapter, and for the practice-set problems that follow Chapters 5, 9, and 13. In addition, all worksheets are treated as foldouts—an appreciated enhancement by all accounts. At the end of each chapter of the *Study Guide with Working Papers*, there is a summary practice test designed to prepare students for in-class exams. It consists of fill-in-the-blank questions, a matching question, and true/false questions. Like previous editions, the *Study Guide with Working Papers* is a completely Canadian publication. Many changes have been made to help ensure that each student's experience is as effective and efficient as possible.

MyAccountingLab with Online Study Guide and Simply Accounting® Pro and QuickBooks® Premier Data Sets. Our exciting new feature MyAccountingLab includes a comprehensive online study guide that presents students with numerous review exercises and research tools. There is a detailed review of key concepts for every chapter, and practice tests with true/false and multiple-choice questions, completion exercises, and accounting problems. Students obtain instant feedback for questions and exercises, and they may view full solutions to problems. A page reference to the text is supplied with every answer, while destinations and search tools facilitate further research into key organizations and topics discussed in the text. MyAccountingLab also provides the instruction files as well as data sets for the computer workshops in the text, and the data sets will be updated each year as new versions of the software are released.

The Accountant's Toolbox. Pearson Canada is proud to present The Accountant's Toolbox, a portal to the best accounting websites on the Internet, which is included as part of MyAccountingLab. Whether you are a student or an instructor, The Accountant's Toolbox will give you access to the latest information from the world of accounting.

Using The Accountant's Toolbox drop-down menu on Pearson Canada's AccountingCentral home page, you can link to dozens of websites grouped into the following broad categories: International, Careers, Firms, Resources, Tax, Software, and Humour. You can access The Accountant's Toolbox by visiting **www.pearsoned.ca/accounting**. And don't forget to check out *AccountingCentral* frequently for new features and updates!

CourseSmart for Students. CourseSmart provides instant, online access to the textbooks and course materials you need at a lower cost. With instant access from any computer and the ability to search your text, you'll find the content you need quickly, no matter where you are. See all the benefits at **www.coursesmart.com/ students**.

Acknowledgments

The task of publishing a Canadian edition of any textbook is a challenging venture. In this case it helped to be working from an outstanding original and with an outstanding team.

Thanks are certainly due to the many helpful folks at Pearson Canada, including Editor in Chief Nicole Lukach, Developmental Editor Darryl Kamo, Project Manager Sarah Lukaweski, and Freelance Production Editor Heather Sangster of Strong Finish. Special thanks to copy editor Kathy White of Strong Finish for her diligence and hard work. Gail Copeland also used her talents in this aspect of quality control.

Thanks are also due to the following reviewers who provided valuable criticism and suggestions during the development of the manuscript: Allan Bray, Saskatchewan Institute of Applied Science and Technology; Carmen Burt, Okanagan College; Tina M. Dean, College of the North Atlantic; Imelda Engels, College of the Rockies; Ken Hartford, St. Clair College; Pat Humphreys, Medicine Hat College; Michael Malkoun, St. Clair College; Joe Mariani, Algonquin College; and Don Woolridge, College of the North Atlantic.

The *Study Guide with Working Papers* as well as the Solutions Manual were created by Pat Tuttle, whose skills with the software used are substantial. Pat cheerfully took on several other tasks as well and generally made the whole process run quite smoothly.

A special thanks to Imelda Engels, who very kindly allowed the use (with modifications) of the comprehensive payroll project she used very successfully with her students at the College of the Rockies in Cranbrook, B.C.

Four individuals worked on the project creating the many aspects of the computer workshops for this edition. Cassie Chen, Tina Wang, Brandon Baker, and Gloria Shewchuk each took on their duties with enthusiasm and dedication. A few mistakes that escaped their attention were caught and corrected before the workshops were declared "final."

My final thanks go to Laurie Hanchard, who, once again, not only carried out his assigned duties of reviewing the text, the *Study Guide with Working Papers*, and the Solutions Manual with remarkable care and attention, but also took it as a personal goal to add substantial value to the overall package. The text—indeed, most aspects of this project—is much improved because of Laurie's caring and thoughtful review.

Despite the best efforts of so many talented people, it is inevitable that a few errors will persist. I accept responsibility for them and would appreciate your help in identifying them so that they can be totally eliminated in future printings. With so much material now available online, it is possible to update many important documents without waiting for a revised printing, so please take the time to contact me if you spot anything that needs to be improved.

Brian Zwicker
Edmonton, Alberta
email me at: brian@bzwicker.ca

Testimonial

As requested, I have read the first-pass pages of *College Accounting*, Canadian Eleventh Edition, by Slater and Zwicker, Chapters 1 to 24. I have also read the pages of the *Study Guide with Working Papers* and the Solutions Manual for *College Accounting*. I checked the arithmetic and logic in all three books with respect to the worked examples and exhibits in the proofed copies. I also ensured that the references to these examples and exhibits within the text were accurate.

Laurence P. Hanchard, C.A.

1 Accounting Concepts and Procedures

An Introduction

THE BIG PICTURE

In October 2008, shares in the Royal Bank of Canada sold for over $50.00 each on the Toronto Stock Exchange. Within six months, the same shares were selling for less than $30.00. It is true that the bank reported that its profits per share had fallen somewhat during this time (and before and after as well), but much of the reason for the 40% decline is thought to be the general decline in stock prices caused by the worldwide recession of 2009.

All Canadian banks performed very well (compared to others around the world) during the global crisis, and many analysts now see our Canadian banking system as a good model. Most stock prices of publicly traded companies declined more than the bank shares did, and some say that a worldwide financial collapse was avoided by the narrowest of margins. Students who are more interested in the global recession of 2009–10 will have plenty of material to study, as even a quick look at available articles on the Internet (using, for example, Google) will reveal.

What decides the price of a share? This is really a big question, with potentially thousands of answers, but in simple terms, stock exchanges exist in most countries and provide a facility where buyers and sellers of shares can do business. The share price for Royal Bank, then, is set by what buyers are willing to pay, and this matches a price sellers are willing to accept.

Many factors determine the price of a share. Important ones include economic forecasts, the skills of those who manage a company, recent mergers and acquisitions, the history of dividend payments, and especially the worldwide economic situation. Most analysts agree that the most important factor in a stock's price is the company's periodic accounting reports.

Accounting has been referred to as the language of business, and for a very good reason. Investors everywhere buy and sell shares in thousands of companies, and in order to make good decisions, they rely on systems of financial reporting that are clear, accurate, current, understandable, and reliable. Accounting is the best system we have to generate and communicate this vital information.

But the need for accounting is not by any means restricted to large companies that sell their shares through stock markets worldwide. Smaller businesses, as well as all other kinds of entities in our society, need accounting reports to help make good decisions. Religious organizations, charities, government agencies, neighbourhood associations, artistic societies, and other similar groups need to manage their affairs in an orderly and systematic manner. Accounting produces the records and reports that allow all of these entities to manage their affairs appropriately.

This textbook is for those who want to know how the basics of accounting work. While becoming an accountant may not be your current career goal, most members of society will benefit from knowing the elements of accounting, and not just because they might someday be called on to do some basic accounting. Knowing the basics will make you a much better decision-maker while you serve, for example, on the board of a sports association, church, local charity, or other not-for-profit entity. It will also enable you to make better financial decisions for yourself and your family.

As I write this (spring 2010), share prices for the Royal Bank have risen to more than double their low of February 2009. Where will they go from here? I wish I knew the answer to that question, but all that can be said with certainty is that at this period in history, both buyers and sellers of Royal Bank shares think the shares are worth just about $60.00. There is no doubt that accounting will play an important role in determining where that price will go in the future.

1 Defining and listing the functions of accounting (p. 5)
2 Recording transactions in the basic accounting equation (p. 7)
3 Seeing how revenue, expenses, and withdrawals expand the basic accounting equation (p. 14)
4 Preparing an income statement, a statement of owner's equity, and a balance sheet (p. 20)

During the past few years, you could pick up almost any newspaper and read stories about financial scandals. In the United States, the events related to WorldCom and Enron are good examples, while here in Canada, Nortel Networks Corporation has created headlines. Were these companies "cooking the books"? With jail sentences of up to 25 years for some of the corporate officers convicted of unlawful activities, the answer is clearly—yes! In the United States, a federal statute called the **Sarbanes-Oxley Act** was passed into law to help prevent future attempts to defraud the public. In Canada, the Ontario Securities Commission has created National Policies (Numbers 58-102—which gave birth to the Canadian Public Accountability Board—and 58-201) that cover much the same thing. Both countries are attempting to increase the focus on internal controls, the role and responsibility of auditors, and increased penalties for business fraud in order to improve the accuracy and reliability of published accounting reports.

> Many corporate executives feel that Sarbanes-Oxley is too strict and costly to implement. In Canada, our new legislation is seen as less objectionable—possibly because our laws did not require as much of a change as in the United States.

Accounting is the language of business; it provides information to managers, owners, investors, governmental agencies, and others inside and outside the organization. Accounting provides answers and insights to questions like these:

◆ Should I invest in Amazon.com?

◆ Is Subway's cash balance sufficient?

◆ Will Internet companies show a good return in the future?

◆ Can General Motors Canada pay its debt obligations?

◆ What percentage of IBM's marketing budget is for e-business? How does this compare with the competition? What is the overall financial condition of IBM?

Smaller businesses also need answers to their financial questions:

◆ Did business increase enough over the last year to warrant hiring a new assistant?

◆ Should we spend more money to design, produce, and send out new brochures in an effort to create more business?

◆ What role should the Internet play in our business?

> The Internet is creating many new opportunities and challenges for all forms of business organizations.

Accounting is as important to individuals as it is to businesses; it answers questions like:

◆ Should I take out a loan for a new car or wait until I can afford to pay cash?

◆ Would my money work better in a chartered bank or in a credit union savings plan?

Accounting is the process that analyzes, records, classifies, summarizes, reports, and interprets financial information for decision-makers—whether individuals, small businesses, large corporations, or governmental agencies—in a timely fashion. It is important that students understand the "whys" of the accounting process. Just knowing the mechanics is not enough.

TABLE 1-1 Types of Business Organization

	Sole Proprietorship	Partnership	Corporation
Ownership	Business owned by one person	Business owned by more than one person	Business owned by shareholders
Formation	Easy to form	Easy to form	More difficult to form
Liability	Owner could lose personal assets to meet obligations of business	Partners could lose personal assets to meet obligations of partnership	Limited personal risk; shareholders' loss is usually limited to their investment in the company
Closing	Ends with death of owner or closing of business	Ends with death of a partner or exit of a partner	Can continue indefinitely

CATEGORIES OF BUSINESS ORGANIZATION

There are three main categories of business organization: (1) sole proprietorship, (2) partnership, and (3) corporation. Let's define each of them and look at their advantages and disadvantages. This information also appears in Table 1-1 and is more extensively discussed in one of the auxiliary chapters now appearing on the MyAccountingLab at www.myaccountinglab.com.

Sole Proprietorship

A **sole proprietorship** is a business that has one owner. That person is both the owner and the manager of the business. One advantage of a sole proprietorship is that the owner makes all the decisions for the business. One disadvantage is that if the business cannot pay its obligations, the business owner must pay them. This means that the owner could lose some personal assets (e.g., house or savings).

Sole proprietorships are easy to form. They end if the business closes or when the owner dies.

Partnership

A **partnership** is a form of business ownership that has at least two owners (partners). Each partner acts as an owner of the company. This is an advantage because the partners can share the decision-making and the risks of the business. A disadvantage is that, as in a sole proprietorship, the partners' personal assets could be lost if the partnership cannot meet its obligations.

Partnerships are easy to form. They end when a partner dies or leaves the partnership.

Corporation

eBay is an example of a corporation.

A **corporation**, such as Canadian Tire, is a business owned by shareholders. The corporation may have only a few shareholders or it may have many shareholders. The shareholders are not personally liable for the corporation's debts, and they usually do not have input into the business decisions.

Corporations are more difficult to form than sole proprietorships or partnerships. Corporations can exist indefinitely.

CLASSIFYING ORGANIZATIONS BY ACTIVITY

Whether we are looking at a sole proprietorship, a partnership, or a corporation, the business can be classified by what the business does to earn money. Companies are categorized as service, merchandising, or manufacturing businesses (see Table 1-2 for examples of each type).

TABLE 1-2 Examples of Service, Merchandising, and Manufacturing Businesses

Service Businesses	Merchandising Businesses	Manufacturing Businesses
eBay	Sears	Mattel
Jane's Painting Co.	Eddie Bauer	General Motors
Dr. Wheeler, M.D.	The Bay	Intel
H&R Block	Amazon.com	Bombardier

CAREERS IN ACCOUNTING

There are many career opportunities in accounting. They vary according to the amount of education and experience required. You should note that while a lot of routine accounting work is now done using computers, this has not lessened the need for all kinds of accounting personnel.

Accounting Clerks: Accounting clerks perform most of a business's record-keeping functions. Sometimes, accounting clerks perform specific functions and are given a title that relates to these functions. *Payroll clerk* and *accounts payable clerk* are examples of such titles. Accounting clerks may perform their work manually or by computer.

Accounting clerks generally are required to have completed at least a one-semester accounting course and have some computer skills.

Bookkeepers: Bookkeepers are sometimes called "general bookkeepers" or "full-charge bookkeepers." That is because they do general accounting work, perform some summarizing and analyzing of accounting information, and supervise the accounting clerks. In some companies, they also may help managers and owners interpret accounting information. The size of the company determines the bookkeeper's responsibility.

Usually, bookkeepers need one or two years of accounting training and experience as an accounting clerk. Some computer knowledge is necessary too.

Accountants: Accountants plan, summarize, analyze, report, and interpret accounting information. Other responsibilities include assisting the owners and managers of the business in making financial decisions and supervising other accounting personnel.

Generally, accountants need a college diploma in accounting. They also may need additional professional credentials.

Accountants fall into three general classifications: public accountants, private accountants, and non-profit accountants. (The opportunities in these categories are discussed in the following sections for each classification.)

A local cab company is a good example of a **service company** because it provides a service. The first part of this book focuses on service businesses.

Stores like Sears and Eddie Bauer sell products. They are called merchandising companies. **Merchandising companies** can either make and sell their own products or sell products that are made by other suppliers. Companies like Intel and General Motors that only make products and sell to wholesalers are called **manufacturing companies.**

Definition of Accounting

1 Defining and listing the functions of accounting

Accounting (also called the **accounting process**) is a system that measures the activities of a business in financial terms. It provides reports and financial statements that show how the various transactions the business undertook (e.g., buying and selling goods) affected the business. It does this by performing the following functions:

- **Analyzing:** Looking at what happened and how the business was affected
- **Recording:** Putting the information into the accounting system
- **Classifying:** Grouping all of the same activities (e.g., all purchases) together
- **Summarizing:** Creating totals by category and/or date, which are used in the next two functions
- **Reporting:** Issuing the reports that tell the results of the previous functions
- **Interpreting:** Examining the reports to determine how the various pieces of information they contain relate to each other

The system communicates the reports and financial statements to people who are interested in the information, such as the business's decision-makers, investors, creditors, governmental agencies (e.g., Canada Revenue Agency), and so on.

As you can see, a lot of people use these reports. A set of procedures and guidelines exists to make sure that everyone prepares and interprets the reports the same way.

Canadian accountants rely on a set of **generally accepted accounting principles** (abbreviated as GAAP) to guide them in the process of preparing financial reports for business entities. To study these in detail usually takes a complete course, but a list and brief description is included in a later chapter.

Types of Accountants

Public Accountants: Public accountants provide services to clients for a fee. They may work alone or work for an accounting firm. Two professional accounting bodies are chiefly concerned with public accounting in Canada: the Certified General Accountants Association and the Canadian Institute of Chartered Accountants. (All professional groups have provincial identities as well.) Membership is restricted to those who have passed a challenging set of qualifying examinations and who have served a period of training in various accounting positions. These professional accountants perform many accounting tasks, but they also provide advice on taxation, perform audits, and consult on many aspects of business operations.

Private Accountants (Managerial Accountants): The main difference between public accountants and private accountants is that most private accountants work for a single business. A business may employ one accountant or it may have many.

Private accountants who pass an examination prepared by the Society of Management Accountants of Canada will become Certified Management Accountants (CMAs). Those who pass the exam given by the Institute of Internal Auditors can become Certified Internal Auditors (CIAs).

There are many opportunities in private accounting. Private accountants may manage the accounting system, prepare reports and financial statements, prepare budgets, or determine certain costs (e.g., the cost of producing a new product). Some large firms have their own tax accountants and internal auditors.

Non-profit (Governmental) Accountants: Non-profit accounting is used by governmental agencies and non-profit agencies such as religious organizations, hospitals, and charitable organizations. These entities use accountants to prepare budgets and keep records.

It is important to know that some non-profit agencies do make money. These agencies can keep their non-profit classifications if they keep the profit in the agency. Also, accounting procedures are very similar to procedures for profit-seeking businesses.

International Accounting Rules Come to Canada

Companies that have their shares listed on stock exchanges must now adhere to a set of international accounting rules for financial years beginning in 2010. **International Financial Reporting Standards (IFRS)** have been adopted by a large number of countries, and Canada has joined their ranks. The United States has yet to adopt the IFRS but may well do so in the next few years. The important thing to know is that only Canada's largest companies need to pay attention to the IFRS, because small- and medium-sized companies are exempt (although any company can use the new rules if it chooses to do so). Furthermore, Canadian accounting standards were already very advanced, and because of that fact, in many detailed areas, Canada's rules were already in agreement with the international ones.

Most students who use this textbook should not worry too much about IFRS. Just be aware that the new rules exist, and if ever you decide to pursue a career in accounting, it is only then that you will need to become closely involved in how IFRS really work and how they are applied.

Difference Between Bookkeeping and Accounting

Confusion often arises concerning the difference between bookkeeping and accounting. **Bookkeeping** is the recording (record-keeping) function of the accounting process; a bookkeeper enters accounting information in the company's books. An accountant takes that information and prepares the financial reports that are used to analyze the company's financial position. Accounting involves many complex activities. Often, it includes the preparation of tax and financial reports, budgeting, and analyses of financial information.

Today, computers are used for routine bookkeeping operations that used to take weeks or months to complete. This text explains how the advantages of the computer can be applied to a manual accounting system by using hands-on knowledge of how accounting works. Basic accounting knowledge is needed even though computers can help with routine tasks.

Learning Unit 1-1
The Accounting Equation

ASSETS, LIABILITIES, AND EQUITIES

Let's begin our study of accounting concepts and procedures by looking at a small business: Catherine Hall's law practice. Catherine decided to open her practice at the end of August 2013. She consulted her accountant Todd Amark before she made her decision. Todd told her some important things before she made this decision. First, he told her the new business would be considered a separate **business entity** whose finances had to be kept separate and distinct from Catherine's personal finances. The accountant went on to say that all transactions can be analyzed using the basic accounting equation: Assets = Liabilities + Owner's Equity.

Catherine had never heard of the basic accounting equation. She listened carefully as Todd explained the terms used in the equation and how the equation works.

Assets

Cash, land, supplies, office equipment, buildings, and other properties of value *owned* by a firm are called **assets.**

Equities

The rights or financial claims to the assets are called **equities**. Equities belong to those who supply the assets. If you are the only person to supply assets to the firm, you have the sole right or financial claim to them. For example, if you supply the law firm with $5,000 in cash and $4,000 in office equipment, your equity in the firm is $9,000.

Relationship Between Assets and Equities

The relationship between assets and equities is:

$$\textbf{Assets} \quad = \quad \textbf{Equities}$$
(Total value of items *owned* by a business)   (Total claims *against* the assets)

The total dollar value of the assets of the law firm will be equal to the total dollar value of the financial claims to those assets; that is, equal to the total dollar value of the equities.

The total dollar value is broken down on the left-hand side of the equation to show the specific items of value owned by the business and on the right-hand side to show the types of claims against the assets owned.

Liabilities

A firm may have to borrow money to buy more assets; when this occurs, it means the firm is *buying assets on account* (buy now, pay later). Suppose Catherine's law firm purchases a desk for $400 on account from Joe's Stationery, and the store is willing to wait 10 days for payment. The law firm has created a **liability**: an obligation to pay that comes due in the future. Joe's Stationery is called the **creditor**. This liability—the amount owed to Joe's Stationery—gives the store the right, or the financial claim, to $400 of the law firm's assets. When Joe's Stationery is paid, the store's rights to the assets of the law firm will end since the obligation has been paid off.

Basic Accounting Equation

To better understand the various claims to a business's assets, accountants divide equities into two parts. The claims of creditors—outside persons or businesses—are labelled *liabilities*. The claims of the business's owner are labelled **owner's equity**. Let's see how the accounting equation looks now. It can be rewritten as follows:

$$\textbf{Assets} = \qquad\qquad\qquad \textbf{Equities}$$

1. Liabilities: rights of creditors
2. Owner's equity: rights of owner

$$\textbf{Assets} = \textbf{Liabilities} + \textbf{Owner's Equity}$$

2 Recording transactions in the basic accounting equation

The total value of all the assets of a firm equals the combined total value of the financial claims of the creditors (liabilities) and the claims of the owner (owner's equity). This is known as the **basic accounting equation**. The basic accounting equation provides a basis for understanding the conventional accounting system of a business. The equation is used to record business transactions in a logical and orderly way that shows their impact on the company's assets, liabilities, and owner's equity.

Importance of Creditors

Another way of presenting the basic accounting equation is:

Assets – Liabilities = Owner's Equity

This form of the equation stresses the importance of creditors. The owner's rights to the business's assets are determined after the rights of the creditors are subtracted. In other words, creditors have first claim on assets. If a firm has no liabilities—and therefore no creditors—the owner has the total rights to assets. Another term for the owner's current investment, or equity, in the business's assets is **capital.**

As Catherine Hall's law firm engages in business transactions (paying bills, serving clients, and so on), changes will take place in the assets, liabilities, and owner's equity (capital). Let's analyze some of these transactions.

> The term *cash* in accounting includes currency and cheques on hand and bank accounts also. In this textbook, *cash account* will usually mean the balance in the company's bank account.

Transaction A: Aug. 26: Catherine invests $7,000 in cash and $800 worth of office equipment into the business.

On August 26, Catherine withdraws $7,000 from her personal bank account and deposits the money in the law firm's newly opened bank account. She also invests $800 worth of office equipment in the business. She plans to be open for business on September 1. With the help of her accountant, Catherine begins to prepare the accounting records for the business. We put this information into the basic accounting equation as follows:

> In our analyses, assume that any number without a sign in front of it is a + amount.

ASSETS		= LIABILITIES	+ OWNER'S EQUITY
Cash + **Office Equipment**	=		**C. Hall, Capital**
$7,000 + $800	=		$7,800
	$7,800 = $7,800		

> *Note:* Capital is part of owner's equity; it is not an asset.

Note that the total value of the assets, cash, and office equipment—$7,800—is equal to the combined total value of liabilities (none, so far) and owner's equity ($7,800). Remember, Catherine Hall has supplied all the cash and office equipment, so she has the sole financial claim to the assets. Note that the heading "C. Hall, Capital" is written under the owner's equity heading. The $7,800 is Catherine's investment, or equity, in the firm's assets.

Transaction B: Aug. 27: Law practice buys office equipment for cash, $900.

From the initial investment of $7,000 cash, the law firm buys $900 worth of office equipment (such as a desk). **Equipment** lasts a long time, while **supplies** (such as pens) tend to be used up relatively quickly.

	ASSETS		= LIABILITIES	+ OWNER'S EQUITY
	Cash + **Office Equipment**	=		**C. Hall, Capital**
BEGINNING BALANCE	$7,000 + $ 800	=		$7,800
TRANSACTION	−900 + 900			
ENDING BALANCE	6,100 + $1,700	=		$7,800
	$7,800 = $7,800			

Shift in Assets

As a result of the last transaction, the law office has less cash but has increased its amount of office equipment. This is called a **shift in assets**—the makeup of the assets has changed, but the total of the assets remains the same.

Suppose you go food shopping at the supermarket with $100 and spend $60. Now you have two assets, food and money. The composition of the assets has been *shifted*—you have more food and less money than you did—but the *total* of the assets has not increased or decreased. The total value of the food, $60, plus the cash, $40, is still $100. When you borrow money from the bank, on the other hand, you have an increase in cash (an asset) and an increase in liabilities; overall there is an increase in assets, not just a shift.

An accounting equation can remain in balance even if only one side is affected. The key point to remember is that the left-hand-side total of assets must always equal the right-hand-side total of liabilities and owner's equity.

Transaction C: **Aug. 30: Business buys additional office equipment on account, $400.**

The law firm purchases an additional $400 worth of chairs and desks from Wilmington Company. Instead of demanding cash right away, Wilmington agrees to deliver the equipment and to allow up to 60 days for the law practice to pay the invoice (bill).

This liability, or obligation to pay in the future, has some interesting effects on the basic accounting equation. Wilmington Company has accepted as payment a partial claim against the assets of the law practice. This claim exists until the law firm pays the bill. This unwritten promise to pay the creditor is a liability called **accounts payable.**

	ASSETS		= LIABILITIES	+ OWNER'S EQUITY
	Cash	+ Office Equipment	= Accounts Payable	C. Hall, Capital
BEGINNING BALANCE	$6,100	+ $1,700	=	$7,800
TRANSACTION		+400	= +$400	
ENDING BALANCE	$6,100	+ $2,100	= $ 400	+ $7,800
		$8,200	= $8,200	

When this information is analyzed, we can see that the law practice has increased what it owes (accounts payable) as well as what it owns (office equipment) by $400. The law practice gains $400 in an asset but has an obligation to pay Wilmington Company at a future date.

The owner's equity remains unchanged. This transaction results in an increase of total assets from $7,800 to $8,200.

Finally, note that after each transaction, the basic accounting equation remains in balance.

LEARNING UNIT 1-1 REVIEW

AT THIS POINT you should be able to:

◆ List the functions of accounting. (pp. 2, 4–5)

◆ Define and explain the differences between sole proprietorships, partnerships, and corporations. (p. 3)

◆ Compare and contrast bookkeeping and accounting. (p. 6)

◆ Explain the role of the computer as an accounting tool. (p. 6)

◆ State the purpose of the accounting equation. (pp. 7–8)

◆ Explain the difference between liabilities and owner's equity. (p. 7)

◆ Define capital. (p. 8)

◆ Explain the difference between a shift in assets and an increase in assets. (p. 9)

To test your understanding of this material, complete Self-Review Quiz 1-1. The blank forms you need are in the *Study Guide with Working Papers* for Chapter 1. The solution to the quiz follows the quiz here in the text. If you have difficulty doing the problems, review Learning Unit 1-1 and the solution to the quiz. You might also check the text's website for helpful student aids. Your instructor will provide details.

Keep in mind that learning accounting is like learning to type—the more you practise, the better you become. You will not be an expert in one day. Be patient. It will all come together.

Self-Review Quiz 1-1

(The blank forms you need are on page 1-1 of the *Study Guide with Working Papers*.)

Record the following transactions in the basic accounting equation:

1. Gracie Ryan invests $17,000 to begin a real estate office.
2. The real estate office buys $600 worth of computer equipment for cash.
3. The real estate office buys $500 worth of additional computer equipment on account.

Solution to Self-Review Quiz 1-1

	ASSETS		=	LIABILITIES	+	OWNER'S EQUITY
	Cash	+ Computer Equipment	=	Accounts Payable	+	Gracie Ryan, Capital
1.	+$17,000					+$17,000
BALANCE	17,000		=			17,000
2.	−600	+$600				
BALANCE	16,400 +	600	=			17,000
3.		500		+$500		
ENDING BALANCE	$16,400 +	$ 1,100	=	$500	+	$17,000
		$17,500 = $17,500				

NEED HELP?

Let's review first: The left side of the accounting equation shows what is owned by the business and the right side of the equation shows you who supplied those assets to a business. Now let's look at the transactions in the solution:

Transaction 1: In your head you must say to yourself, "What did the business get and how did it get it?" The business is getting or increasing its cash by $17,000 and that cash is being supplied by Gracie Ryan. Think of Gracie as increasing her rights in the business since she is supplying cash. Keep in mind that capital does not mean cash. Instead it is what the owner supplies to the business. (Gracie may in the future supply other items to the business.)

So the end result is to put $17,000 on the left side of the equation under cash and put $17,000 under Gracie Ryan, Capital, on the right side. The sum of the left side must equal the sum on the right side.

Transaction 2: Here we are NOT looking at the personal finances of Gracie. You must focus on the business. What did the business get and who supplied it to the business?

In this transaction the business is getting $600 of computer equipment by using some of its cash. IT IS SHIFTING ITS ASSETS: MORE EQUIPMENT FOR LESS CASH. Note that capital is not affected since Gracie has not supplied anything new to the business. Note that the right side of the equation is not touched, but the equation still remains in balance. We are just rearranging the composition of the assets.

Transaction 3: Now the business is getting more equipment but is not paying cash. The equipment is being supplied by a creditor called Accounts Payable. Hopefully in the future the business will be able to pay the creditor back the $500 that it owes. The end result is that the business now has $1,100 in equipment. Note that capital is not affected since no new investments were made by Gracie into the business.

SUMMARY

At the end of these three transactions this company is made up of two assets, Cash $16,400 and Computer Equipment $1,100. The total of the assets was supplied by creditors $500 and the owner, Gracie Ryan, Capital, $17,000. The sum of the left side must equal the sum of the right side.

Learning Unit 1-2
The Balance Sheet

> The balance sheet shows the company's financial position as of a particular date. (In our example, that date is at the end of August.)

In the first learning unit, the transactions for Catherine Hall's law office were recorded in the accounting equation. The transactions we recorded occurred before the law firm opened for business. A report, called a **balance sheet** or **statement of financial position**, can show the position of the company before it started operating. The balance sheet is a formal report that presents the information from the ending balances of both sides of the accounting equation. Think of the balance sheet as a snapshot of the business's financial position as of a particular date.

Let's look at the balance sheet of Catherine Hall's law practice for August 31, 2013, shown in Figure 1-1. The figures in the balance sheet come from the ending balances of the accounting equation for the law practice as shown in Learning Unit 1-1.

Note in Figure 1-1 that the assets owned by the law practice appear on the left-hand side and that liabilities and owner's equity appear on the right-hand side. Both

Figure 1-1
The Balance Sheet

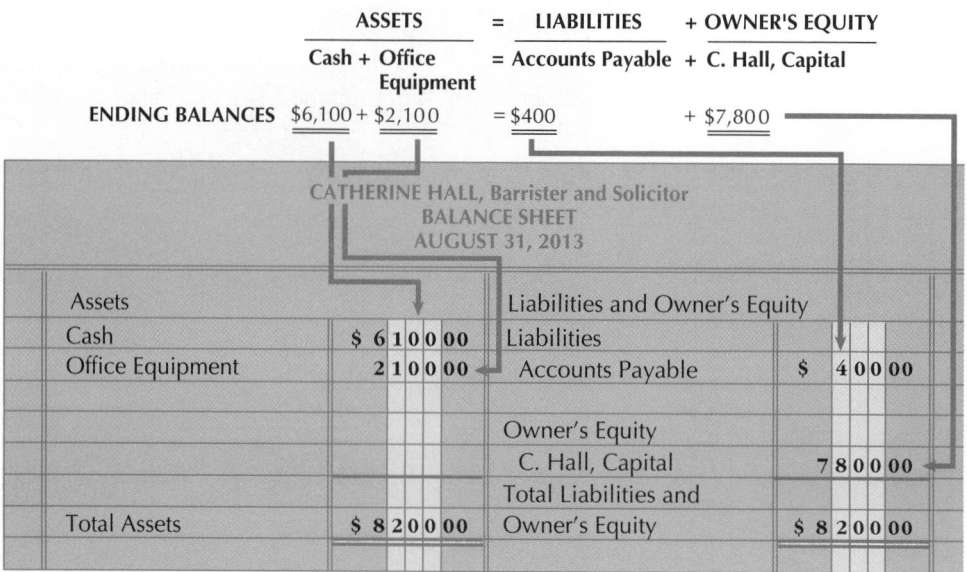

			ASSETS	=	LIABILITIES	+ OWNER'S EQUITY

sides equal $8,200. This *balance* between left and right gives the balance sheet its name. In later chapters, we will be looking at other ways to set up a balance sheet.

POINTS TO REMEMBER IN PREPARING A BALANCE SHEET

The Heading

> Do you remember the three elements that make up a balance sheet? They are assets, liabilities, and owner's equity.

The heading of the balance sheet provides the following information:

- ◆ The company name: Catherine Hall, Barrister and Solicitor
- ◆ The name of the report: Balance Sheet
- ◆ The date for which the report is prepared: August 31, 2013

Use of the Dollar Sign

Note that the dollar sign is not repeated every time a figure appears. As shown in the balance sheet for Catherine Hall's law practice, it is usually placed to the left of each column's top figure and to the left of the column's total.

Distinguishing the Total

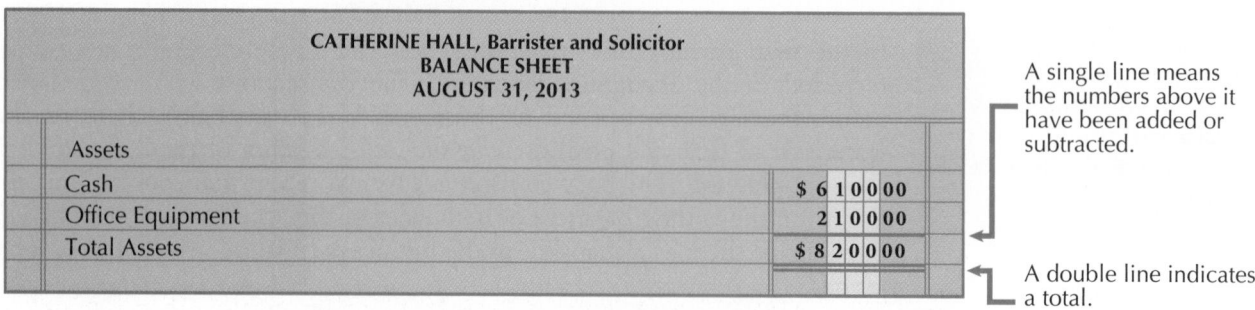

When adding numbers down a column, use a single line before the total and a double line beneath it. A single line means that the numbers above it have been added or subtracted. A double line indicates a total. It is important to align the numbers in the column; many errors occur because these figures are not lined up. These rules are the same for all accounting reports.

This balance sheet gives Catherine the information she needs to see the law firm's financial position before it opens for business. This information does not tell her, however, whether the firm will make a profit.

LEARNING UNIT 1-2 REVIEW

AT THIS POINT you should be able to:
- Define and state the purpose of a balance sheet. (p. 11)
- Identify and define the elements making up a balance sheet. (p. 12)
- Show the relationship between the accounting equation and the balance sheet. (p. 12)
- Prepare a balance sheet in proper form from information provided. (p. 12)
- Place dollar signs correctly in a formal report. (p. 12)

Self-Review Quiz 1-2

(The blank forms you need are on page 1-2 of the *Study Guide with Working Papers*.)

The date is November 30, 2013. Use the following information to prepare in proper form a balance sheet for Janning Company:

Accounts Payable	$30,000
Cash	8,000
A. Janning, Capital	9,000
Office Equipment	31,000

Quiz Tip

The heading of a balance sheet answers the questions *Who, What,* and *When.* November 30, 2013 is the particular date.

Solution to Self-Review Quiz 1-2

JANNING COMPANY
BALANCE SHEET
NOVEMBER 30, 2013

Assets		Liabilities and Owner's Equity	
Cash	$ 8 0 0 00	Liabilities	
Office Equipment	31 0 0 00	Accounts Payable	$ 30 0 0 0 00
		Owner's Equity	
		A. Janning, Capital	9 0 0 0 00
		Total Liabilities and	
Total Assets	$ 39 0 0 0 00	Owner's Equity	$ 39 0 0 0 00

Capital does not mean cash. The capital amount is the owner's current investment of assets in the business.

NEED HELP?

Let's review first: A photo of your family as of a particular date is like a balance sheet. It gives you a history of your family as of a particular date. The balance sheet is a formal report that lists assets, liabilities, and owner's equity for a business as of a particular date.

Before making the report, identify whether each title is an asset, liability, or owner's equity. Accounts payable is a liability. Ideally the business will be able to pay. Cash is an asset, or something of value owned by the business. A. Janning, Capital, is owner's equity, or what the owner is supplying to the business.

The heading of a balance sheet answers three questions:

Who? Janning Company

What report? Balance Sheet

When? November 30, 2013

The left side of the balance sheet lists the assets: cash, and office equipment.

The right side lists who supplies the assets to the business: creditors (accounts payable) or the owner, A. Janning, Capital. Use single rules to add and double rules for totals. The sum of the left side must equal the sum of the right side.

Learning Unit 1-3

The Accounting Equation Expanded: Revenue, Expenses, and Withdrawals

3 Seeing how revenue, expenses, and withdrawals expand the basic accounting equation

As soon as Catherine Hall's office opened, she began performing legal services for her clients and earning revenue for the business. At the same time, as a part of doing business, she incurred various expenses, such as rent. See Figure 1-2 for an example of how these activities affect owner's equity.

When Catherine asked her accountant how these transactions fitted into the accounting equation, he began by defining some terms.

KEY TERMS IN THE ACCOUNTING EQUATION

When revenue is earned, it is recorded as an increase in owner's equity and an increase in assets.

Revenue A service company earns **revenue** when it provides services to its clients. Catherine's law firm earned revenue when she provided legal services to her clients for legal fees. When revenue is earned, owner's equity is increased. In effect, revenue is a subdivision of owner's equity.

Assets are increased. The increase is in the form of cash if the client pays right away. If the client promises to pay in the future, the increase is called **accounts receivable**. When revenue is earned, the transaction is recorded as an increase in revenue and an increase in assets (either as cash and/or as accounts receivable, depending on whether it was paid right away or will be paid in the future).

Accounts receivable is an asset. The law firm expects to receive amounts owed by clients at a later date.

Expenses A business's **expenses** are the costs the company incurs in carrying on operations in its effort to create revenue. Expenses are also a subdivision of owner's equity; when expenses are incurred, they *decrease* owner's equity. Expenses can be paid for in cash or they can be charged.

Figure 1-2
Owner's Equity

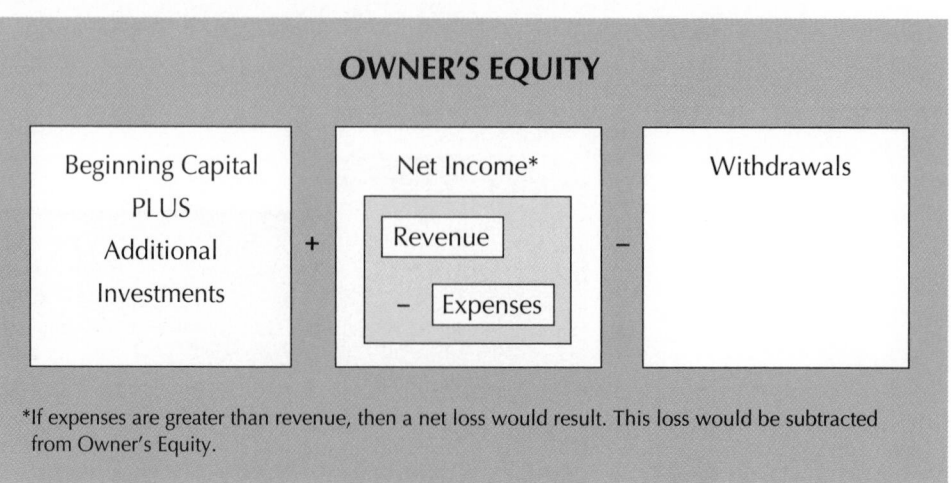

OWNER'S EQUITY

| Beginning Capital PLUS Additional Investments | + | Net Income* Revenue − Expenses | − | Withdrawals |

*If expenses are greater than revenue, then a net loss would result. This loss would be subtracted from Owner's Equity.

Remember: Accounts receivable results from earning revenue when cash is not yet received.

Record an expense when it is incurred, whether it is paid then or is to be paid later.

Withdrawals are not the same as salary. Catherine's law firm is not incorporated and hence cannot pay her a salary.

Net Income/Net Loss   When revenue totals more than expenses, **net income** is the result; when expenses total more than revenue, **net loss** is the result.

Withdrawals   At some point, Catherine Hall may need to withdraw cash or other assets from the business to pay living or other personal expenses that do not relate to the business. We will record these transactions in an account called **withdrawals**. Sometimes this account is called the *owner's drawing account*. The withdrawals account is a subdivision of owner's equity that records personal expenses not related to the business. Withdrawals decrease owner's equity.

It is important to remember the difference between expenses and withdrawals. Expenses relate to business operations; withdrawals are the result of personal needs outside the normal operations of the business.

Now let's analyze the September transactions for Catherine Hall's law firm using an **expanded accounting equation** that includes withdrawals, revenues, and expenses.

EXPANDED ACCOUNTING EQUATION

Transaction D: Sept. 1–30: Provided legal services for cash, $3,000.

Transactions A, B, and C were discussed earlier when the law office was being formed in August. See Learning Unit 1-1.

In the law firm's first month of operation, a total of $3,000 in cash was received for legal services performed. In the accounting equation, the asset Cash is increased by $3,000. Revenue is also increased by $3,000, resulting in an increase in owner's equity.

	ASSETS			= LIABILITIES	+		OWNER'S EQUITY		
	Cash	+ Accts. Rec.	+ Office Equip.	= Accts. Pay.		+ C. Hall, Capital	– C. Hall, Withdr.	+ Revenue	– Expenses
BAL. FWD.	$6,100		+$ 2,100 =	$ 400		+$7,800			
TRANS.	+3,000							+ $3,000	
END. BAL.	$9,100		+$ 2,100 =	$ 400		+$7,800		+ $3,000	
			$11,200 =	$11,200					

A revenue column was added to the basic accounting equation. Amounts are recorded in the revenue column when they are earned. They are also recorded in the assets columns, under Cash and/or under Accounts Receivable. Do not think of revenue as an asset. It is part of owner's equity. It is the revenue that creates an inward flow of cash and accounts receivable.

Transaction E: Sept. 1–30: Provided legal services on account, $4,000.

	ASSETS			= LIABILITIES	+		OWNER'S EQUITY	
	Cash	+ Accts. Rec.	+ Office Equip.	= Accts. Pay.	+ C. Hall, Capital	– C. Hall, Withdr.	+ Revenue	– Expenses
BAL. FWD.	$9,100		+ $ 2,100 =	$ 400	+ $7,800		+ $3,000	
TRANS.		+ $4,000					+ 4,000	
END. BAL.	$9,100	+ $4,000	+ $ 2,100 =	$ 400	+ $7,800		+ $7,000	
			$15,200 =	$ 15,200				

Catherine's law practice performed legal work on account for $4,000. Her firm did not receive the cash for these earned legal fees; it accepted an unwritten promise from these clients that payment would be made in the future.

During September, some of Catherine's clients who had received services and promised to pay in the future decided to reduce what they owed the practice by $700 when their bills came due. This is shown as follows on the expanded accounting equation.

Transaction F: Sept. 1–30: Received $700 cash as partial payment of previous services performed on account.

	ASSETS			=	LIABILITIES +		OWNER'S EQUITY			
	Cash	+ Accts. Rec.	+ Office Equip.	=	Accts. Pay.	+ C. Hall, Capital	– C. Hall, Withdr.	+ Revenue	– Expenses	
BAL. FWD.	$9,100	+ $4,000	+ $2,100	=	$ 400	+ $7,800		+ $7,000		
TRANS.	+700	−700								
END. BAL.	$9,800	+ $3,300	+ $2,100	=	$ 400	+ $7,800		+ $7,000		
			$15,200	=	$15,200					

The law firm increased the asset Cash by $700 and decreased another asset, Accounts Receivable, by $700. The *total* of assets does not change. The right-hand side of the expanded accounting equation has not been touched because the total on the left-hand side of the equation has not changed. The revenue was recorded when it was earned, and the *same revenue cannot be recorded twice.* This transaction analyzes the situation *after* the revenue has been previously earned and recorded. Transaction F shows a shift in assets—increased cash and reduced accounts receivable.

Transaction G: Sept. 1–30: Paid salaries expense, $600.

	ASSETS			=	LIABILITIES +		OWNER'S EQUITY			
	Cash	+ Accts. Rec.	+ Office Equip.	=	Accts. Pay.	+ C. Hall, Capital	– C. Hall, Withdr.	+ Revenue	– Expenses	
BAL. FWD.	$9,800	+ $3,300	+ $ 2,100	=	$ 400	+ $7,800		+ $7,000		
TRANS.	−600								+$600	
END. BAL.	$9,200	+ $3,300	+ $ 2,100	=	$ 400	+ $7,800		+ $7,000	− $600	
			$14,600	=	$14,600					

As expenses increase, they decrease owner's equity. This incurred expense of $600 reduces the cash by $600. Although the expense was paid, the total of our expenses to date has *increased* by $600. Keep in mind that owner's equity decreases as expenses increase, so the accounting equation remains in balance.

	ASSETS			=	LIABILITIES +		OWNER'S EQUITY			
	Cash	+ Accts. Rec.	+ Office Equip.	=	Accts. Pay.	+ C. Hall, Capital	− C. Hall, Withdr.	+ Revenue	− Expenses	
BAL. FWD.	$9,200	+ $3,300	+ $ 2,100	=	$ 400	+$7,800		+ $7,000	− $ 600	
TRANS.	−700								+700	
END. BAL.	$8,500	+ $3,300	+ $ 2,100	=	$ 400	+$7,800		+ $7,000	− $1,300	
		$13,900		=	$13,900					

During September, the practice incurred rent expenses of $700. This rent was not paid in advance; it was paid when it came due. The payment of rent reduces the asset Cash by $700 and increases the expenses of the firm, resulting in a decrease in owner's equity. The firm's expenses are now $1,300.

	ASSETS			=	LIABILITIES +		OWNER'S EQUITY			
	Cash	+ Accts. Rec.	+ Office Equip.	=	Accts. Pay.	+ C. Hall, Capital	− C. Hall, Withdr.	+ Revenue	− Expenses	
BAL. FWD.	$8,500	+ $3,300	+ $ 2,100	=	$ 400	+$7,800		+ $7,000	− $1,300	
TRANS.					+300				+300	
END. BAL.	$8,500	+ $3,300	+ $ 2,100	=	$ 700	+$7,800		+ $7,000	− $1,600	
		$13,900		=	$13,900					

Catherine ran an ad in the local newspaper and incurred an expense of $300. This increase in expenses caused a corresponding decrease in owner's equity. Since Catherine has not paid the newspaper for the advertising yet, her firm owes $300. Thus the firm's liabilities (Accounts Payable) increase by $300. Eventually, when the bill comes in and is paid, both Cash and Accounts Payable will be decreased.

	ASSETS			=	LIABILITIES +		OWNER'S EQUITY			
	Cash	+ Accts. Rec.	+ Office Equip.	=	Accts. Pay.	+ C. Hall, Capital	− C. Hall, Withdr.	+ Revenue	− Expenses	
BAL. FWD.	$8,500	+ $3,300	+ $ 2,100	=	$ 700	+ $7,800		+ $7,000	− $1,600	
TRANS.	−200						+$200			
END. BAL.	$8,300	+ $3,300	+ $ 2,100	=	$ 700	+ $7,800	− $200	+ $7,000	− $1,600	
		$13,700		=	$13,700					

By taking $200 for personal use, Catherine has *increased* her withdrawals from the business by $200 and decreased the asset Cash by $200. Note that, as withdrawals increase, the owner's equity will *decrease*. Keep in mind that a withdrawal is *not* a business expense. It is a subdivision of owner's equity that records money or other assets an owner withdraws from the business for *personal* use.

Subdivision of Owner's Equity

Take a moment to review the subdivisions of owner's equity:

◆ As capital increases, owner's equity increases (see transaction A).
◆ As withdrawals increase, owner's equity decreases (see transaction J).
◆ As revenue increases, owner's equity increases (see transaction D).
◆ As expenses increase, owner's equity decreases (see transaction G).

Catherine Hall's Expanded Accounting Equation

The following is a summary of the expanded accounting equation for Catherine Hall's law firm. The + or − sign in front of a transaction indicates whether the account is increased or decreased by that transaction.

Catherine Hall
Barrister and Solicitor
Expanded Accounting Equation: A Summary

	ASSETS			= LIABILITIES +		OWNER'S EQUITY			
	Cash	+ Accts. Rec.	+ Office Equip.	= Accts. Pay.	+ C. Hall, Capital	− C. Hall, Withdr.	+ Revenue	− Expenses
A.	$7,000		+ $800 =		+$7,800			
BALANCE	7,000		+ 800 =		7,800			
B.	−900		+900					
BALANCE	6,100		+ 1,700 =		7,800			
C.			+400	+$400				
BALANCE	6,100		+ 2,100 =	400	+ 7,800			
D.	+3,000						+$3,000	
BALANCE	9,100		+ 2,100 =	400	+ 7,800		+ 3,000	
E.		+$4,000					+4,000	
BALANCE	9,100	+ 4,000	+ 2,100 =	400	+ 7,800		+ 7,000	
F.	+700	−700						
BALANCE	9,800	+ 3,300	+ 2,100 =	400	+ 7,800		+ 7,000	
G.	−600							+$600
BALANCE	9,200	+ 3,300	+ 2,100 =	400	+ 7,800		+ 7,000	− 600
H.	−700							+700
BALANCE	8,500	+ 3,300	+ 2,100 =	400	+ 7,800		+ 7,000	− 1,300
I.				+300				+300
BALANCE	8,500	+ 3,300	+ 2,100 =	700	+ 7,800		+ 7,000	− 1,600
J.	−200					+$200		
END. BAL.	$8,300	+ $ 3,300	+ $2,100 =	$700	+ $ 7,800	− $200	+ $7,000	− $1,600
		$13,700		=		$13,700		

LEARNING UNIT 1-3 REVIEW

AT THIS POINT you should be able to:
◆ Define and explain the difference between revenue and expenses. (p. 14)
◆ Define and explain the difference between net income and net loss. (p. 15)
◆ Explain the subdivision of owner's equity. (pp. 16–18)
◆ Explain the effects of withdrawals, revenue, and expenses on owner's equity. (pp. 16–17)
◆ Record transactions in an expanded accounting equation and balance the basic accounting equation as a means of checking the accuracy of your calculations. (p. 18)

(The blank forms you need are on page 1-2 of the *Study Guide with Working Papers*.)

Record the following transactions in the expanded accounting equation for the Bing Company. Note that all titles have a beginning balance.

1. Received cash revenue, $4,000.
2. Billed customers for services rendered, $6,000.
3. Received a bill for telephone expenses (to be paid next month), $125.
4. Bob Bing withdrew cash for personal use, $500.
5. Received $1,000 from customers in partial payment for services performed in transaction 2.

> **Quiz Tip**
>
> Think of expenses and withdrawals as *increasing*. As they increase, they will reduce the owner's rights. For example, in transaction 4, withdrawals increased by $500, resulting in total withdrawals increasing from $800 to $1,300. This represents a decrease in owner's equity.

Solution to Self-Review Quiz 1-3

	ASSETS			= LIABILITIES +		OWNER'S EQUITY			
	Cash	+ Accts. Rec.	+ Cleaning Equip.	= Accts. Pay.	+ B. Bing, Capital	− B. Bing, Withdr.	+ Revenue	− Expenses
BEG. BAL.	$ 9,000	+ $ 2,500	+ $6,500	= $1,000	+ $11,800	− $ 800	+ $ 8,000	− $2,000
1.	+4,000						+4,000	
BALANCE	13,000	+ 2,500	+ 6,500	= 1,000	+ 11,800	− 800	+ 12,000	− 2,000
2.		+6,000					+6,000	
BALANCE	13,000	+ 8,500	+ 6,500	= 1,000	+ 11,800	− 800	+ 18,000	− 2,000
3.				+125				+125
BALANCE	13,000	+ 8,500	+ 6,500	= 1,125	+ 11,800	− 800	+ 18,000	− 2,125
4.	−500					+500		
BALANCE	12,500	+ 8,500	+ 6,500	= 1,125	+ 11,800	− 1,300	+ 18,000	− 2,125
5.	+1,000	−1,000						
END. BAL.	$13,500	+ $ 7,500	+ $6,500	= $1,125	+ $11,800	− $ 1,300	+ $18,000	− $2,125
	$27,500			=		$27,500		

NEED HELP?

Let's review first: You record revenue only when it is earned. What can the business get? Cash, of course, but also customers' promises to pay later, which are called Accounts Receivable. Revenue is not an asset but does provide an inward flow of assets into the business. Revenue is part of owner's equity. Think of expenses as always increasing in a business. The end result will be a decrease in owner's equity. Expenses are recorded when they happen and can be paid for by cash or charged as Accounts Payable.

Withdrawals work just like expenses, but they represent personal withdrawals by the owner. Expenses and withdrawals are not recorded together. Each has a separate title.

Transaction 1: The company has done the work. It now records revenue of $4,000 in the revenue column (put numbers in this column only when we do the work). This time the inward flow from the revenue is all in the form of cash of $4,000.

Transaction 2: This time the company does the work but is not getting the cash. It is receiving promises that it will be paid in the future. You record the $6,000 in the revenue column because you did the work. The inward flow from this revenue is not cash but promises called Accounts Receivable. Thus, the Accounts Receivable column is increased by $6,000.

Transaction 3: An expense has happened and should be recorded whether money is paid or not. The expenses for telephone have INCREASED by $125, resulting in the total expenses rising to $2,125. As expenses in a business rise, the end result is a reduction in owner's equity.

Since the expense was charged, the $125 is recorded under Accounts Payable because the expense will be paid in the future. At this point this telephone expense has created a liability. Remember that an expense is not a liability.

Transaction 4: This transaction relates to a personal transaction and does not affect any expenses in the business. Bob Bing takes $500 cash from the business. Think of Bob as gaining the $500, but in reality his owner's rights will be reduced. This is shown by a $500 gain under withdrawals, which now results in a total of $1,300 (a reduction to owner's equity) and a decrease to cash. Note that expenses are not affected since this is a personal transaction.

Transaction 5: No new work is done, so we do not record any new revenue. Here customers are paying part of what they owe. The result is that company cash increased by $1,000 and Accounts Receivable is reduced by $1,000. This is a shift in assets: more cash, less accounts receivable.

SUMMARY

Note the four subdivisions of owner's equity: Capital, Withdrawals, Revenues, and Expenses. As capital and revenue increases, owner's equity will increase. As expenses and withdrawals increase, owner's equity will decrease. Revenue is not an asset. Rather, it provides assets in the form of cash and/or accounts receivable. Record revenue only when work is done. Record expenses only when they happen, whether or not cash is received.

Learning Unit 1-4
Preparing Financial Reports

4 Preparing an income statement, a statement of owner's equity, and a balance sheet

Catherine Hall would like to be able to find out whether her firm is making a profit, so she asks her accountant whether he can measure the firm's financial performance on a monthly basis. Her accountant replies that there are a number of financial reports that he can prepare, such as the income statement, which shows how well the law firm has performed over a specific period of time. The accountant can use the information in the income statement to prepare other reports.

THE INCOME STATEMENT

The income statement is prepared from data found in the revenue and expense columns of the expanded accounting equation.

An **income statement** is an accounting report that shows business results in terms of revenue and expenses. If revenues are greater than expenses, the report shows net income. If expenses are greater than revenues, the report shows net loss. An income statement can cover any number of months up to 12. It does not usually cover more than one year. The report shows the result of all revenues and expenses throughout the entire period and not just as of a specific date. The income statement for Catherine Hall's law firm is shown in Figure 1-3.

Points to Remember in Preparing an Income Statement

Heading   The heading of an income statement tells the same three things as all other accounting reports: the company's name, the name of the report, and the period of time the report covers (or the date prepared).

Locate the dollar signs used in the Income Statement. They are shown at the top of each column and in the total.

The Set-Up   As you can see on the income statement, the inside column of numbers ($600, $700, and $300) is used to subtotal all expenses ($1,600) before subtracting them from revenue ($7,000 − $1,600 = $5,400).

Operating expenses may be listed in alphabetical order, in order of largest amounts to smallest, or in a set order established by the accountant.

Figure 1-3
The Income Statement

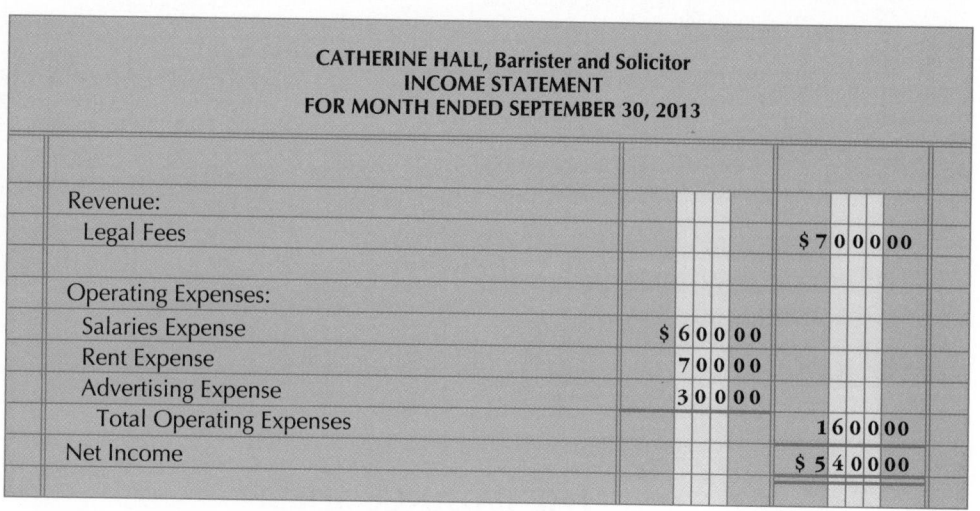

CATHERINE HALL, Barrister and Solicitor INCOME STATEMENT FOR MONTH ENDED SEPTEMBER 30, 2013			
Revenue:			
Legal Fees			$ 7 0 0 0 0 0
Operating Expenses:			
Salaries Expense	$ 6 0 0 0 0		
Rent Expense	7 0 0 0 0		
Advertising Expense	3 0 0 0 0		
Total Operating Expenses		1 6 0 0 0 0	
Net Income		$ 5 4 0 0 0 0	

> Note that withdrawals are not shown in the Income Statement. They are not an expense.

THE STATEMENT OF OWNER'S EQUITY

As we said, the income statement is a business report that shows business results in terms of revenue and expenses. However, how does net income or net loss affect owner's equity? To find that out, we have to look at another category of report, the statement of owner's equity.

The **statement of owner's equity** shows for a certain period of time what changes occurred in Catherine Hall, Capital. The statement of owner's equity is shown in Figure 1-4.

The capital of Catherine Hall can be

> If this statement of owner's equity is omitted, the information will be included in the owner's equity section of the balance sheet.

Increased by: Owner Investment
Net Income (Revenue greater than Expenses)

Decreased by: Owner Withdrawals
Net Loss (Expenses greater than Revenue)

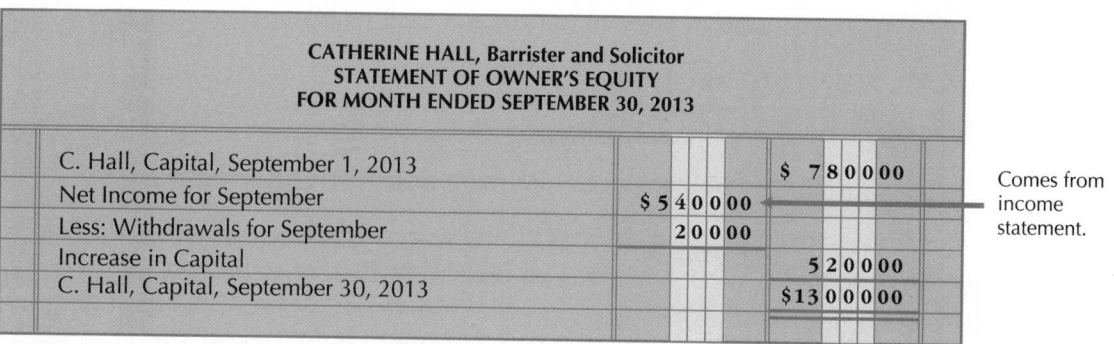

CATHERINE HALL, Barrister and Solicitor STATEMENT OF OWNER'S EQUITY FOR MONTH ENDED SEPTEMBER 30, 2013			
C. Hall, Capital, September 1, 2013			$ 7 8 0 0 0 0
Net Income for September	$ 5 4 0 0 0 0		
Less: Withdrawals for September	2 0 0 0 0		
Increase in Capital		5 2 0 0 0 0	
C. Hall, Capital, September 30, 2013		$13 0 0 0 0 0	

Comes from income statement.

Figure 1-4   Statement of Owner's Equity

Remember, a withdrawal is *not* a business expense and thus is not involved in the calculation of net income or net loss on the income statement. It appears on the statement of owner's equity. The statement of owner's equity summarizes the effects of all the subdivisions of owner's equity (revenue, expenses, withdrawals) on beginning capital. The ending capital figure ($13,000) will be the beginning figure in the next statement of owner's equity.

Suppose that Catherine's law firm had operated at a loss in the month of September. Instead of net income, there was a net loss and an additional investment of $700 was made on September 15. The statement on the next page shows how it would look if this had happened.

CATHERINE HALL, Barrister and Solicitor
STATEMENT OF OWNER'S EQUITY
FOR MONTH ENDED SEPTEMBER 30, 2013

C. Hall, Capital, September 1, 2013		$7 8 0 0 00
Additional Investment, September 15, 2013		7 0 0 00
		$8 5 0 0 00
Less: Net Loss for September	$4 0 0 00	
Withdrawals for September	2 0 0 00	
Decrease in Capital		6 0 0 00
C. Hall, Capital, September 30, 2013		$7 9 0 0 00

THE BALANCE SHEET

Now let's look at how to prepare a balance sheet from the expanded accounting equation (see Figure 1-5). As you can see, the asset accounts (Cash, Accounts Receivable, and Office Equipment) appear on the left side of the balance sheet. Accounts Payable and C. Hall, Capital, appear on the right side. Notice that the $13,000 of capital can be calculated within the accounting equation or read from the statement of owner's equity.

MAIN ELEMENTS OF THE INCOME STATEMENT, THE STATEMENT OF OWNER'S EQUITY, AND THE BALANCE SHEET

In this chapter, we have discussed three financial reports: the income statement, the statement of owner's equity, and the balance sheet. (There is a fourth report, called the cash flow statement, that is covered in Chapter 16 of this textbook.) Let us review the elements of the expanded accounting equation that go into each report and the usual order in which the reports are prepared. Figure 1-5 presents a diagram of the balance sheet and the accounting equation. Table 1-3 summarizes what information goes on each report.

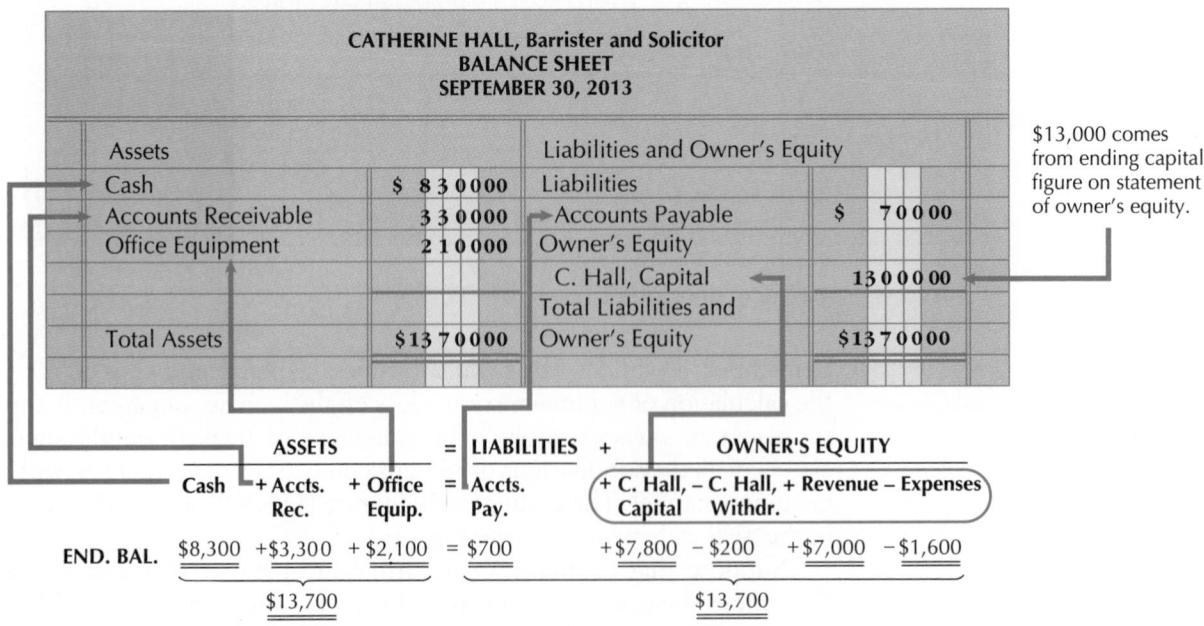

Figure 1-5   The Balance Sheet and the Accounting Equation

- The income statement is prepared first; it includes revenues and expenses and shows net income or net loss. This net income or net loss is used to update the next report, the statement of owner's equity.
- The statement of owner's equity is prepared second; it includes beginning capital and any additional investments, the net income or net loss shown on the income statement, withdrawals, and the total, which is the **ending capital**.
- The balance sheet is prepared last; it includes the final balances of each of the elements listed in the accounting equation under Assets and Liabilities. The balance in Capital comes from the statement of owner's equity.

TABLE 1-3 What Goes on Each Financial Report

	Income Statement	Statement of Owner's Equity	Balance Sheet
Assets			X
Liabilities			X
Capital (beginning)		X	
Additional Investments		X	
Capital (ending)		X	X
Withdrawals		X	
Revenues	X		
Expenses	X		
Net Income (Loss)	X	X	

LEARNING UNIT 1-4 REVIEW

AT THIS POINT you should be able to:

- Define and state the purpose of the income statement, the statement of owner's equity, and the balance sheet. (pp. 20–22)
- Discuss why the income statement should be prepared first. (p. 23)
- Calculate a new figure for capital on the statement of owner's equity and balance sheet. (pp. 21–22)
- Compare and contrast these three financial reports. (pp. 22–23)
- Show what happens on a statement of owner's equity if there is a net loss. (p. 22)

Self-Review Quiz 1-4

(The blank forms you need are on pages 1-3 and 1-4 of the *Study Guide with Working Papers*.)

From the following balances for Rusty Realty, prepare:

1. Income statement for month ended November 30, 2014
2. Statement of owner's equity for the month ended November 30, 2014
3. Balance sheet as of November 30, 2014

Cash	$40,000	R. Rusty, Withdrawals	1,000
Accounts Receivable	13,700	Commissions Earned	15,000
Office Furniture	14,900	Rent Expense	2,000
Accounts Payable	9,000	Advertising Expense	1,500
R. Rusty, Capital,		Salaries Expense	900
November 1, 2014	$50,000		

Solution to Self-Review Quiz 1-4

Quiz Tip

Note that the inside column is used only for subtotalling.

RUSTY REALTY
INCOME STATEMENT
FOR MONTH ENDED NOVEMBER 30, 2014

Revenue:		
Commissions Earned		$ 15 00 000
Operating Expenses:		
Rent Expense	$ 2 00 000	
Advertising Expense	1 50 000	
Salaries Expense	90 000	
Total Operating Expenses		4 40 000
Net Income		$ 10 60 000

Subtotal Columns

Quiz Tip

The Net Income from the income statement is used to help build the statement of owner's equity.

RUSTY REALTY
STATEMENT OF OWNER'S EQUITY
FOR MONTH ENDED NOVEMBER 30, 2014

R. Rusty, Capital, November 1, 2014		$ 5 0 00 000
Net Income for November	$ 10 60 000	
Less: Withdrawals for November	1 00 000	
Increase in Capital		9 60 000
R. Rusty, Capital, November 30, 2014		$ 59 60 000

Quiz Tip

The new figure for Capital, from the statement of owner's equity, is used as the Capital figure on the balance sheet.

RUSTY REALTY
BALANCE SHEET
NOVEMBER 30, 2014

Assets		Liabilities and Owner's Equity	
Cash	$ 40 00 000	Liabilities	
Accounts Receivable	13 70 000	Accounts Payable	$ 9 00 000
Office Furniture	14 90 000		
		Owner's Equity	
		R. Rusty, Capital	59 60 000
		Total Liabilities and	
Total Assets	$ 68 60 000	Owner's Equity	$ 68 60 000

Let's review first: The first formal report is the income statement, which is made up of only revenues and expenses. This report shows how a company is performing for a specific period of time. The second report is the statement of the owner's equity. This report shows how capital has changed from its beginning balance. The net income is added to the beginning balance less any personal withdrawals resulting in a new figure for capital, which will be placed in the balance sheet. This third report, the balance sheet, is made up of assets, liabilities, and the new figure for capital. The balance sheet shows the history of the company as of a particular date.

The Income Statement: Commissions earned is the revenue for Rusty Realty. It is entered to the right since it is the only revenue. The inside column is used for a subtotal if there is more than one revenue.

Rent, Advertising, and Salaries are expenses that are listed on the income statement. Note that we use the inside column to subtotal them and then list the final figure as total operating expenses of $4,400 in the right column. The difference between revenue ($15,000) and the total operating expenses ($4,400) results in a net income of $10,600. Keep in mind that net income is not cash. Remember that some revenue may not have resulted in cash and some of the expenses may not have been paid for in cash.

Statement of Owner's Equity: The beginning balance of R. Rusty, Capital is $50,000. We place this to the right because it is one number. We then use the inside column to add net income from the income statement ($10,600) and subtract any withdrawals ($1,000) to get an increase in capital of $9,600, which is placed in the right column. This figure is then added to beginning capital to arrive at R. Rusty, Capital (ending) of $59,600.

Balance Sheet: All the assets are listed on the left (cash, accounts receivable, and office furniture), for a total of $68,600. The liability of $9,000 for accounts payable is listed on the right and will be added to the new figure for R. Rusty, Capital of $59,600 from the statement of owner's equity.

SUMMARY

The income statement lists out revenue and expenses. No withdrawals are found on this report. The statement of owner's equity will show how capital changes by net income, net loss, and/or withdrawals. The balance shows the new history of the company's assets, liabilities, and a new figure for capital.

"Hey, Stan the man!" a loud voice boomed. "I never thought I'd see you making sandwiches!" Stan Hernandez stopped layering lettuce in a foot-long submarine sandwich and grinned at his old college buddy, Ron.

"Neither did I. But then again," said Stan, "I never thought I'd own a profitable business either." That night, catching up on their lives over dinner, Stan told Ron how he became the proud owner of a Subway sandwich restaurant. "After working like crazy at Xellent Media for five years and *finally* making it to marketing manager, then wham . . . I got laid off," said Stan. "That very day I was having my lunch at the local Subway as usual, when . . . "

"Hmmm, wait a minute! I did notice you've lost quite a bit of weight," Ron interrupted and began to compare him to Jared Fogle, the young man who lost weight on a diet of Subway sandwiches.

"Right!" Stan quipped, "Not only was I laid off, but I was 'downsizing!' *Anyway*, I was eating a Sweet Onion Chicken Teriyaki sub when I opened up an *Entrepreneur* magazine someone had left on the table—right to the headline 'Subway Named #1 Franchise in All Categories for 17th Time in 23 Years.'"

To make a foot-long submarine sandwich story short, Stan realized his long-time dream of being his own boss by owning a business with a proven product and highly successful business model. When you look at Stan's restaurant, you are really seeing two businesses. While Stan is the sole proprietor of his business, he operates under an agreement with Subway head office. Subway supplies the business know-how and support (like training at Subway University, national advertising, and gourmet bread recipes). Stan supplies capital (his $15,000 investment fee) and his food preparation, management, and elbow grease. Subway and Stan operate interdependent businesses, and both rely on accounting information for their success.

Subway, in business since 1965, has grown dramatically over the years and now has over 33,000 locations in 92 countries. It has even surpassed McDonald's in the number of locations in

SUBWAY

A FRESH START

Preparing Financial Statements ❹ (20 min)

the United States and Canada. To manage this enormous service business requires very careful control of each of its stores.

At a Subway regional office, Mariah Washington, a field consultant for Stan's territory, monitors Stan's restaurant closely. In addition to making monthly visits to check whether Stan is complying with Subway's model in everything from décor to uniforms to food quality and safety, she also looks closely at Stan's weekly sales and inventory reports. When Stan's sales go up, Subway's do too, because each Subway franchisee, like Stan, pays Subway, the franchiser, a percentage of sales in the form of royalties.

Why does headquarters require accounting reports? Accounting reports give the information both Stan and the company need to make business decisions in a number of vital areas. For example:

◆ Before Stan could buy his Subway restaurant, the company needed to know how much cash Stan had, the value of his assets, and the amount of his liabilities (such as credit card debt). Stan prepared a personal balance sheet to give them this information.

◆ Stan must have the right amount of supplies on hand. If he has too few, he can't make the sandwiches. If he has too much for the amount he expects to sell, items like sandwich meats and bread dough may spoil. The inventory report tells Mariah what supplies are on hand. In combination with the sales report, it also alerts Mariah to potential red flags. If Stan is reporting that he is using far too much bread dough for the number of sandwiches he is selling, then there is a problem.

◆ Although Subway does not require its restaurant owners to report operating costs and profit information, Subway gives them the option and most franchisees choose to report. Information on profitability helps Mariah and Stan make decisions like whether and when to remodel or buy new equipment.

So that its restaurant owners can make business decisions in a timely manner, Subway requires them to submit the weekly sales and inventory report to headquarters electronically every Thursday by 2 p.m. Stan has his latest report in mind as he makes a move to pay the bill for his dinner with Ron. "We had a great week. Let me get this," he says. "Thanks, Stan the Man. I'm going to keep in touch because I may just be ready for a business opportunity of my own!"

DISCUSSION QUESTIONS

1. What makes Stan a sole proprietor?
2. Why are Stan and Subway interdependent businesses?
3. Why did Stan have to share his personal balance sheet with Subway? Do you think most interdependent businesses do this?
4. What does Subway learn from Stan's weekly sales and inventory reports?

Chapter Assignments

DEMONSTRATION PROBLEM

Michael Brown opened his law office on June 1, 2013. During the first month of operations, Michael conducted the following transactions:

(The blank forms you need are on pages 1-5 and 1-6 of the *Study Guide with Working Papers*.)

1. Invested $6,000 in cash into the law practice.
2. Paid $600 for office equipment.
3. Purchased additional office equipment on account, $1,000.
4. Received cash for performing legal services for clients, $2,000.
5. Paid part-time salaries, $800.
6. Performed legal services for clients on account, $1,000.
7. Paid rent, $1,200.
8. Withdrew $500 from his law practice for personal use.
9. Received $500 from clients in partial payment for legal services performed, transaction 6.

Assignment

Record these transactions in the expanded accounting equation.

Prepare the financial statements at June 30 for Michael Brown, Barrister and Solicitor.

Solution to Demonstration Problem

	ASSETS			= LIABILITIES +		OWNER'S EQUITY		
A.	Cash	+ Accts. Rec.	+ Office Equip.	= Accts. Pay.	+ M. Brown, Capital	− M. Brown, Withdr.	+ Legal Fees	− Expenses
1.	+ $6,000				+ $6,000			
BAL.	6,000			=	6,000			
2.	− 600		+ $ 600					
BAL.	5,400		+ 600 =		6,000			
3.			+ 1,000	+ $1,000				
BAL.	5,400		+ 1,600 =	1,000	+· 6,000			
4.	+ 2,000						+ $2,000	
BAL.	7,400		+ 1,600 =	1,000	+ 6,000		+ 2,000	
5.	− 800							+ $800
BAL.	6,600		+ 1,600 =	1,000	+ 6,000		+ 2,000	− 800
6.		+ $1,000					+ 1,000	
BAL.	6,600 +	1,000 +	1,600 =	1,000	+ 6,000		+ 3,000	− 800
7.	− 1,200							+ 1,200
BAL.	5,400 +	1,000 +	1,600 =	1,000	+ 6,000		+ 3,000	− 2,000
8.	− 500					+ $500		
BAL.	4,900 +	1,000 +	1,600 =	1,000	+ 6,000	− 500	+ 3,000	− 2,000
9.	+ 500 −	500						
END. BAL.	$5,400 +	$ 500 +	$1,600 =	$1,000	+ $6,000	− $500	+ $3,000	− $2,000

$$\$7,500 = \$7,500$$

Solution Tips to Expanded Accounting Equation

◆ **Transaction 1:** The business increased its Cash by $6,000. Owner's Equity (capital) increased when Michael supplied the cash to the business.

◆ **Transaction 2:** A shift in assets occurred when the equipment was purchased. The business lowered its Cash by $600, and a new column—Office Equipment—was increased for the $600 of equipment that was bought. The amount of capital is not touched because the owner did not supply any new funds.

◆ **Transaction 3:** When creditors supply $1,000 of additional equipment, the business Accounts Payable shows the debt. The business had increased what it owes the creditors.

◆ **Transaction 4:** Legal Fees, a subdivision of Owner's Equity, is increased when the law firm provides a service even if no money is received. The service provides an inward flow of $2,000 to Cash, an asset. Remember that Legal Fees are not an asset. As Legal Fees increase, Owner's Equity increases.

◆ **Transaction 5:** The salary paid by Michael's law office shows an $800 increase in Expenses and a corresponding decrease in Owner's Equity as well as a decrease in Cash.

◆ **Transaction 6:** Michael did the work and earned the $1,000. That $1,000 is recorded as revenue. This time the Legal Fees create an inward flow of assets called Accounts Receivable for $1,000. Remember that Legal Fees are not an asset. They are a subdivision of Owner's Equity.

◆ **Transaction 7:** The $1,200 rent expense reduces Owner's Equity as well as Cash.

◆ **Transaction 8:** Withdrawals are for personal use. Here the business decreases Cash by $500 while Michael's withdrawals increase $500. Withdrawals decrease the Owner's Equity.

◆ **Transaction 9:** This transaction does not reflect new revenue in the form of Legal Fees. It is only a shift in assets: more Cash and less Accounts Receivable.

Solution Tips to Financial Statements

B-1. The income statement lists only revenues and expenses for a period of time. The inside column is for subtotalling. Withdrawals are not listed here.

B-2. The statement of owner's equity takes the net income figure of $1,000 and adds it to beginning capital less any withdrawals. This new capital figure of $6,500 will go on the balance sheet. This statement shows changes in capital for a period of time.

B-3. The $5,400, $500, $1,600, and $1,000 came from the totals of the expanded accounting equation. The capital figure of $6,500 came from the statement of owner's equity. This balance sheet reports assets, liabilities, and a new figure for capital at a specific date.

B-1.

MICHAEL BROWN, BARRISTER AND SOLICITOR
INCOME STATEMENT
FOR MONTH ENDED JUNE 30, 2013

Revenue:		
Legal Fees		$3,000
Operating Expenses:		
Salaries Expense	$ 800	
Rent Expense	1,200	
Total Operating Expenses		2,000
Net Income		$1,000

B-2.

MICHAEL BROWN, BARRISTER AND SOLICITOR
STATEMENT OF OWNER'S EQUITY
FOR MONTH ENDED JUNE 30, 2013

Michael Brown, Capital, June 1, 2013		$6,000
Net income for June	$1,000	
Less withdrawls for June	500	
Increase in Capital		500
Michael Brown, Capital, June 30, 2013		$6,500

B-3.

MICHAEL BROWN, BARRISTER AND SOLICITOR
BALANCE SHEET
JUNE 30, 2013

Assets		Liabilities and Owner's Equity	
Cash	$5,400	Liabilities	
Accounts Receivable	500	Accounts Payable	$1,000
Office Equipment	1,600	Owner's Equity	
		M. Brown, Capital	$6,500
Total Assets	$7,500	Total Liabilities and Owner's Equity	$7,500

SUMMARY OF KEY POINTS

Learning Unit 1-1

1. The functions of accounting involve analyzing, recording, classifying, summarizing, reporting, and interpreting financial information.
2. A sole proprietorship is a business owned by one person. A partnership is a business owned by two or more persons. A corporation is a business owned by shareholders.
3. Bookkeeping is the recording part of accounting.
4. The computer is a tool to use in the accounting process.
5. Assets = Liabilities + Owner's Equity is the basic accounting equation that helps in analyzing business transactions.
6. Liabilities represent amounts owed to creditors, while capital represents what is invested by the owner.
7. Capital does not mean cash. Capital is the owner's current investment. The owner could have invested in equipment that was purchased before the new business was started.
8. In a shift of assets, the composition of assets changes, but the total value of assets does not change. For example, if a bill is paid by a customer, the firm increases cash (an asset) but decreases accounts receivable (an asset), so there is no overall increase in assets; total assets remain the same. When you borrow money from a bank, you have an increase in cash (an asset) and an increase in liabilities; overall there is an increase in assets, not just a shift.

Learning Unit 1-2

1. The balance sheet is a report written as of a particular date. It lists the assets, liabilities, and owner's equity of a business. The heading of the balance sheet answers the questions *Who, What,* and *When* (as of a specific date).
2. The balance sheet is a formal report of a financial position.

Learning Unit 1-3

1. Revenue generates an inward flow of assets. Expenses generate an outward flow of assets or a potential outward flow. Revenue and expenses are subdivisions of owner's equity. Revenue is not an asset.
2. When revenue totals more than expenses, net income is the result; when expenses total more than revenue, net loss is the result.
3. Owner's equity can be subdivided into four elements: capital, withdrawals, revenue, and expenses.
4. Withdrawals decrease owner's equity; revenue increases owner's equity; expenses decrease owner's equity. A withdrawal is not a business expense; it is for personal use.

Learning Unit 1-4

1. The income statement is a report written for a specific period of time that lists earned revenue and expenses incurred to produce the earned revenue. The net income or net loss will be used in the statement of owner's equity.
2. The statement of owner's equity reveals the causes of a change in capital. This report lists additional investments in the company, net income (or net loss), and withdrawals. The ending figure for capital will be used on the balance sheet.

3. The balance sheet uses the ending balances of assets and liabilities from the accounting equation and the capital from the statement of owner's equity.

4. The income statement should be prepared first because the information on it relating to net income or net loss is used to prepare the statement of owner's equity, which in turn provides information about capital for the balance sheet. In this way, one builds upon the previous information and it begins with the income statement.

KEY TERMS

Accounting A system that measures a business's activities in financial terms, provides written reports and financial statements about those activities, and communicates these reports to decision-makers and others (p. 5)

Accounting process See *Accounting* (p. 5)

Accounts payable Amounts owed to creditors that result from the purchase of goods or services on account; a liability (p. 9)

Accounts receivable Amounts to be paid by customers resulting from sales of goods and/or services on credit; an asset (p. 14)

Assets Properties (resources) of value owned by a business (cash, supplies, equipment, land, and so on) (p. 7)

Balance sheet A report, as of a particular date, that shows the amount of assets owned by a business as well as the amount of claims (liabilities and owner's equity) against these assets (p. 11)

Basic accounting equation Assets = Liabilities + Owner's Equity (p. 7)

Bookkeeping The recording function of the accounting process (p. 6)

Business entity In accounting, it is assumed that a business is separate and distinct from the personal assets of the owner. Each unit or entity requires separate accounting functions. (p. 6)

Capital The owner's investment of equity in the company (p. 8)

Corporation A type of business organization that is owned by shareholders. Usually, shareholders are not personally liable for the corporation's debts. (p. 3)

Creditor Someone who has a claim to assets (p. 7)

Ending capital Beginning Capital + Additional Investments + Net Income − Withdrawals = Ending Capital. *Or:* Beginning Capital + Additional Investments − Net Loss − Withdrawals = Ending Capital (p. 23)

Equipment Assets acquired to be used in business activities, usually with an expected life of from two to ten years (p. 8)

Equities The financial claim of creditors (liabilities) and owners (owner's equity) who supply the assets and expenses to a firm (p. 7)

Expanded accounting equation Assets = Liabilities + Capital − Withdrawals + Revenue − Expenses (p. 15)

Expense Cost incurred in running a business by consuming goods or services in producing revenue; a subdivision of owner's equity. When expenses increase, there is a decrease in owner's equity. (p. 14)

Generally accepted accounting principles (GAAP) The procedures and guidelines that must be followed during the accounting process (p. 5)

Income statement An accounting report that details the performance of a firm (revenue minus expenses) for a specific period of time (p. 20)

International Financial Reporting Standards (IFRS) Adopted in Canada effective January 1, 2010, for companies listing their shares on a stock exchange. May be adapted by other Canadian companies as well, but is optional (p. 6)

Liability An obligation that comes due in the future. A liability increases the financial rights or claims of creditors to assets. (p. 7)

Manufacturing companies Businesses that make a product and sell it to their customers; they may also make and sell their own products (p. 5)

Merchandising companies Businesses that buy a product from a manufacturing company, distributor, or wholesaler to sell to their customers (p. 5)

Net income When revenue totals more than expenses, the result is net income. (p. 15)

Net loss When expenses total more than revenue, the result is net loss. (p. 15)

Owner's equity Rights or financial claims to the assets of a business by the owner (in the accounting equation, assets minus liabilities) (p. 7)

Partnership A form of business organization that has at least two owners. The partners are usually personally liable for the partnership's debts. (p. 3)

Revenue An amount earned by performing services for customers or selling goods to customers. Revenue increases cash and/or accounts receivable. It is a subdivision of owner's equity—as revenue increases, owner's equity increases. (p. 14)

Sarbanes-Oxley Act Legislation passed in the United States that attempts to prevent false or misleading financial statements by public companies (p. 2)

Service company Business that provides a service (p. 4)

Shift in assets A shift that occurs when the composition of the assets has changed, but the total of the assets remains the same (p. 9)

Sole proprietorship A business that has one owner. The owner is personally liable for paying the business's debts. (p. 3)

Statement of financial position Another name for a balance sheet (p. 11)

Statement of owner's equity A financial report that reveals the change in capital. The ending figure for capital is then placed on the balance sheet. (p. 21)

Supplies One type of asset acquired by a firm. A supply item is temporarily treated as an asset until it is consumed, when it is transferred to expense. Sometimes if it is not a significant amount it is treated as an expense when purchased—both treatments are possible. (p. 8)

Withdrawals A subdivision of owner's equity that records money or other assets an owner withdraws from a business for personal use (p. 15)

BLUEPRINT OF FINANCIAL REPORTS

❶ Income Statement

Measuring performance

Revenue		XXX
Less: Operating expenses:		
Expense 1	XXX	
Expense 2	XX	
Expense 3	XX	XXX
Net Income		XXX

❷ Statement of Owner's Equity

Calculating new figure for Capital

Beginning Capital		XXX
Additional Investments		XXX
Total Investments		XXX
Net Income (or Loss)	XXX	
Less: Withdrawals	XXX	
Change in Capital		XXX
Ending Capital		XXX

❸ Balance Sheet

Showing where we now stand

Assets		Liabilities and Owner's Equity	
	XXX	Liabilities	XXX
	XXX	Owner's Equity	
	XXX	Ending Capital	XXX
		Total Liabilities +	
Total Assets	XXX	Owner's Equity	XXX

QUESTIONS, CLASSROOM DEMONSTRATION EXERCISES, EXERCISES, AND PROBLEMS

Discussion Questions and Critical Thinking/Ethical Case

1. What are the functions of accounting?
2. Define, compare, and contrast sole proprietorships, partnerships, and corporations.
3. How are businesses classified?
4. What is the relationship of bookkeeping to accounting?
5. List the three elements of the basic accounting equation.
6. Define capital.
7. The total of the left-hand side of the accounting equation must equal the total of the right-hand side. True or false? Please explain.
8. A balance sheet tells a company where it is going and how well it will perform. True or false? Please explain.
9. Revenue is an asset. True or false? Please explain.
10. Into what categories is owner's equity subdivided?

11. A withdrawal is a business expense. True or false? Please explain.

12. As expenses increase, they cause owner's equity to increase. Defend or reject.

13. What does an income statement show?

14. The statement of owner's equity calculates only ending withdrawals. True or false? Please explain.

15. Paul Kloss, accountant for Lowe & Co., travelled to Vancouver on company business. His total expenses came to $350. Paul felt that since the trip extended over the weekend, he could pad his expense account with an additional $100 of expenses. After all, weekends represent his own time, not the company's. What would you do? Write your specific recommendations to Paul.

MyAccountingLab

Make the grade with MyAccountingLab! The exercises and problems marked in green can be found on MyAccountingLab at www.myaccountinglab.com. You can practise them as often as you want, and many of them feature step-by-step guided solutions to help you find the right answer. You can also find working papers for selected problems in the Multimedia Library on MyAccountingLab.

Classroom Demonstration Exercises

(The blank forms you need are on page 1-7 of the *Study Guide with Working Papers*.)

Set A

Classifying Accounts

Preparing to record transactions ② (5 min)

1. Classify each of the following items as an asset (A), liability (L), or part of owner's equity (OE).

   a. Apple iPod   _____
   b. Accounts Receivable   _____
   c. Accounts Payable   _____
   d. Cash   _____
   e. B. James, Capital   _____
   f. Kodak Digital Camera   _____

The Accounting Equation

Accounting equation details ② (5 min)

2. Complete:

   a. _____: rights of the creditors.
   b. _____ are the total value of items owned by a business.
   c. _____ _____ is an unwritten promise to pay the creditor.

Shift Versus Increase in Assets

Recording transactions in the basic accounting equation ② (5 min)

3. Identify which transaction below results in a shift in assets (S) and which transaction causes an increase in assets (I).

   a. Jay's Internet Cafe bought computer equipment on account _____.
   b. Eastern Tile Co. bought office equipment for cash _____.

The Balance Sheet

Preparing a balance sheet
2 4 (5 min)

4. From the following, calculate what would be the total of assets on the balance sheet.

B. Fleese, Capital	$18,000
Computer Equipment	4,000
Accounts Payable	6,000
Cash	12,000

The Accounting Equation Expanded

Expanding the basic accounting equation
3 (5 min)

5. Identify with a ✓ which of the following are subdivisions of owner's equity.

a. Vehicles	_____	**e.** Accounts Receivable	_____
b. J. Penny, Capital	_____	**f.** Advertising Expense	_____
c. Accounts Payable	_____	**g.** Taxi Fees Earned	_____
d. J. Penny, Withdrawals	_____	**h.** Computer Equipment	_____

Identifying Assets

Steps in the recording of transactions 2 (5 min)

6. Identify with a ✓ which of the following are *not* assets.

a. DVD Player _____
b. Accounts Receivable _____
c. Accounts Payable _____
d. Grooming Fees Earned _____

The Accounting Equation Expanded

Revenue and expenses expand the basic accounting equation 3 (5 min)

7. Which of the following statements are false?

a. _____ Revenue provides only outward flows of cash.
b. _____ Revenue is a subdivision of assets.
c. _____ Revenue provides an inward flow of cash and/or accounts receivable.
d. _____ Expenses are part of total assets.

Preparing Financial Statements

Expanded accounting equation details are used to prepare financial statements
4 (5 min)

8. Indicate whether the following items would appear on the income statement (IS), statement of owner's equity (OE), or balance sheet (BS).

a. _____ Tutoring Fees Earned
b. _____ Office Equipment
c. _____ Accounts Receivable
d. _____ Supplies on Hand
e. _____ Legal Fees Earned
f. _____ Advertising Expense
g. _____ J. Earl, Capital (Beginning)
h. _____ Accounts Payable

Preparing Financial Statements

Financial statements
4 (5 min)

9. Indicate next to each statement whether it refers to the income statement (IS), statement of owner's equity (OE), or balance sheet (BS).

   a. _____ Withdrawals found on it
   b. _____ Lists total of all assets
   c. _____ Statement that is prepared last
   d. _____ Statement listing net income

Set B

Classifying Accounts

Preparing to record transactions 2 (5 min)

1. Classify each of the following items as an asset (A), liability (L), or part of owner's equity (OE).

   a. Salaries Payable _____
   b. Accounts Payable _____
   c. J. Free, Capital _____
   d. Supplies on Hand _____
   e. Cash _____
   f. Canon Digital Camera _____

The Accounting Equation

Accounting equation details
2 (5 min)

2. Complete:

   a. A(n) _____ _____ _____ results when the total of the assets remains the same, but the makeup of the assets has changed.
   b. Assets – _____ = Owner's Equity.
   c. Capital does not mean _____.

Shift Versus Increase in Assets

Recording transactions in the basic accounting equation
2 (5 min)

3. Identify which transaction below results in a shift in assets (S) and which transaction causes an increase in assets (I).

   a. Ace Jewellery bought computer equipment for cash _____.
   b. Jake's Appliances bought office equipment on account _____.

The Balance Sheet

Preparing a balance sheet
2 4 (5 min)

4. From the following, calculate what would be the total of assets on the balance sheet.

B. Bryan, Capital	$15,000
Desktop Publishing Equipment	2,000
Accounts Payable	8,000
Cash	14,000

The Accounting Equation Expanded

Expanding the basic accounting equation
3 (5 min)

5. Identify with a ✓ which of the following are subdivisions of owner's equity.

   a. Land _____   e. Accounts Payable _____
   b. M. Kaminsky, Capital _____   f. Rent Expense _____
   c. Accounts Receivable _____   g. Office Equipment _____
   d. M. Kaminsky, Withdrawals _____ h. Hair Salon Fees Earned _____

Identifying Assets

Steps in the recording of transactions ❷ (5 min)

6. Identify with a ✓ which of the following are *not* assets.

  a. Fax Machines _____

  b. Accounts Payable _____

  c. Legal Fees Earned _____

  d. Accounts Receivable _____

The Accounting Equation Expanded

Revenue and withdrawals expand the basic accounting equation ❸ (5 min)

7. Which of the following statements are false?

  a. _____ Revenue is an asset.

  b. _____ Revenue is a subdivision of owner's equity.

  c. _____ Revenue provides an inward flow of cash and/or accounts receivable.

  d. _____ Withdrawals are part of total assets.

Preparing Financial Statements

Prepare financial statements using details from the expanded accounting equation ❹ (5 min)

8. Indicate whether the following items would appear on the income statement (IS), statement of owner's equity (OE), or balance sheet (BS).

  a. _____ B. Clo, Withdrawals

  b. _____ Supplies on Hand

  c. _____ Accounts Payable

  d. _____ Computer Equipment

  e. _____ Commission Fees Earned

  f. _____ Salaries Expense

  g. _____ B. Clo, Capital (Beginning)

  h. _____ Accounts Receivable

Preparing Financial Statements

Financial statements ❹ (5 min)

9. Indicate next to each statement whether it refers to the income statement (IS), statement of owner's equity (OE), or balance sheet (BS).

  a. _____ Calculate new figure for Capital

  b. _____ Prepared as of a particular date

  c. _____ Statement that is prepared first

  d. _____ Report listing revenues and expenses

Exercises

(The forms you need are on pages 1-8 and 1-9 of the *Study Guide with Working Papers*.)

The accounting equation ❷ (5 min)

1-1. Complete the following table:

	Assets	=	Liabilities	+	Owner's Equity
a.	$19,000	=	?	+	$4,000
b.	?	=	$6,000	+	$9,000
c.	$10,000	=	$4,000	+	?

1-2. Record the following transactions in the basic accounting equation:

$$\text{Assets} = \text{Liabilities} + \text{Owner's Equity}$$

Treat each transaction separately.

a. Ralph invests $8,000 in his company.

b. The company buys equipment for cash, $600.

c. The company buys equipment on account, $900.

1-3. From the following, prepare a balance sheet for Range Co.'s Cleaners at the end of November 2013: Cash, $50,000; Equipment, $7,000; Accounts Payable, $14,000; B. Range, Capital.

1-4. Record the following transactions in the expanded accounting equation. The running balance may be omitted for simplicity.

ASSETS			= LIABILITIES +		OWNER'S EQUITY			
Cash	+ Accounts Receivable	+ Computer Equipment	= Accounts Payable	+ B. Bell, Capital	− B. Bell, Withdrawals	+ Revenue	− Expenses

a. B. Bell invested $60,000 in Bell's Computer Company.

b. Bought computer equipment on account, $7,000.

~~**c.**~~ Paid personal telephone bill from company bank account, $200.

~~**d.**~~ cash for services rendered, $14,000.

~~**e.**~~ tomers for services rendered for the month, $30,000.

f. Paid current rent expense, $4,000.

g. Paid supplies expense, $1,500.

1-5. From the following account balances for June 2013, prepare in proper form (a) an income statement, (b) a statement of owner's equity, and (c) a balance sheet for French Realty.

Cash	$3,310	S. French, Withdrawals	40
Accounts Receivable	1,490	Professional Fees	2,900
Office Equipment	6,700	Salaries Expense	500
Accounts Payable	2,000	Utilities Expense	360
S. French, Capital, June 1, 2013	8,000	Rent Expense	500

Group A Problems

(The forms you need are on pages 1-10 to 1-16 of the *Study Guide with Working Papers*.)

1A-1. Mia Anabelle, who lives in Winnipeg, decided to open Mia's Nail Spa. Mia completed the following transactions:

A. Invested $20,000 cash from her personal bank account into the business.

B. Bought equipment for cash, $4,000.

C. Bought additional equipment on account, $6,000.

D. Paid $1,000 cash to reduce what was owed from Transaction C.

Based on the above information, record these transactions in the basic accounting equation.

Preparing a balance sheet
2 **4** **(15 min)**

Check Figure

Total Assets $52,000

1A-2. Bill See is the accountant for See's Internet Service. His task is to construct a balance sheet from the following information, as of September 30, 2014, in proper form. Could you help him?

Building	$20,000	Cash	18,000
Accounts Payable	15,000	Equipment	14,000
B. See, Capital	37,000		

Recording transactions in the expanded accounting equation **3** **(20 min)**

Check Figure

Total Assets $17,340

1A-3. At the end of November, Rick Fox of Corner Brook decided to open his own desktop publishing business. Analyze the following transactions he completed by recording their effects in the expanded accounting equation.

A. Invested $12,000 in his desktop publishing business.
B. Bought new office equipment on account, $4,000.
C. Received cash for desktop publishing services rendered, $500.
D. Performed desktop publishing services on account, $2,100.
E. Paid part-time secretary's salary, $650.
F. Paid office supplies expense for the month, $210.
G. Rent expense for office due but not yet paid, $900.
H. Rick Fox withdrew cash for personal use, $400.

Preparing the income statement, statement of owner's equity, and balance sheet **4** **(30 min)**

Check Figure

Total Assets $3,385

1A-4. Jane West, owner of West's Stencilling Service in Grande Prairie, has requested that you prepare from the following balances **a.** an income statement for June 2014, **b.** a statement of owner's equity for June, and **c.** a balance sheet as of June 30, 2014.

Cash	$2,300	Stencilling Fees	3,000
Accounts Receivable	400	Advertising Expense	110
Equipment	685	Repair Expense	25
Accounts Payable	310	Travel Expense	250
J. West, Capital, June 1, 2014	1,200	Supplies Expense	190
J. West, Withdrawals	300	Rent Expense	250

Comprehensive problem
2 **3** **4** **(45 min)**

Check Figure

Total Assets Nov. 30 $12,915

1A-5. Jill Martin of Regina opened Martin's Catering Service. As her accountant, analyze the transactions listed below and present in proper form:

1. The analysis of the transactions by utilizing the expanded accounting equation
2. A balance sheet showing the position of the firm before opening on November 1, 2013
3. An income statement for the month of November
4. A statement of owner's equity for November
5. A balance sheet as of November 30, 2013

2013

Oct. 28 Jill Martin invested $8,000 in the catering business from her personal savings account.

29 Bought equipment for cash from Munroe Co., $900.

30 Bought additional equipment on account from Ryan Co., $1,800.

31 Paid $1,000 to Ryan Co. as partial payment of the October 30 transaction.

(You should now prepare your balance sheet as of October 31, 2013.)

Nov.	1	Catered a graduation and immediately collected cash, $2,900.
	4	Paid salaries of employees, $720.
	8	Prepared desserts for customers on account, $300.
	11	Received $100 cash as partial payment of November 8 transaction.
	15	Paid telephone bill, $75.
	18	Jill paid her home electricity bill from the company's bank account, $90.
	19	Catered a wedding and received cash, $1,800.
	25	Bought additional equipment on account, $400.
	28	Rent expense due but not yet paid, $600.
	29	Paid supplies expense, $400.

Group B Problems

(The forms you need are on pages 1-10 to 1-16 of the *Study Guide with Working Papers*.)

The accounting equation
2 (15 min)

Check Figure

Total Assets $16,700

1B-1. Mia Anabelle of Winnipeg began a new business called Mia's Nail Spa. The following transactions resulted:

A. Mia invested $16,000 cash from her personal bank account into the salon.
B. Bought equipment on account, $1,500.
C. Paid $800 cash to reduce what was owed from Transaction B.
D. Purchased additional equipment for cash, $3,000.

Record these transactions in the basic accounting equation.

Preparing a balance sheet
2 4 (15 min)

Check Figure

Total Assets $84,000

1B-2. Bill See has asked you to prepare a balance sheet as of September 30, 2014, for See's Internet Service of Halifax. Assist Bill.

B. See, Capital	$24,000
Accounts Payable	60,000
Equipment	40,000
Building	28,000
Cash	16,000

Recording transactions in the expanded accounting equation 3 (20 min)

Check Figure

Total Assets $14,505

1B-3. Rick Fox of Corner Brook decided to open his own desktop publishing company at the end of November. Analyze the following transactions by recording their effects in the expanded accounting equation.

A. Rick Fox invested $9,000 in the desktop publishing business.
B. Purchased new office equipment on account, $3,000.
C. Received cash for desktop publishing services rendered, $1,290.
D. Paid part-time secretary's salary, $625.
E. Billed customers for desktop publishing services rendered, $2,690.
F. Paid rent expense for the month, $500.
G. Rick withdrew cash for personal use, $350.
H. Advertising expense due but not yet paid, $100.

1B-4. Jane West, owner of West's Stencilling Service in Grande Prairie, has requested that you prepare from the following balances **a.** an income statement for June 2014, **b.** a statement of owner's equity for June, and **c.** a balance sheet as of June 30, 2014.

Cash	$2,043	Stencilling Fees	1,098
Accounts Receivable	1,140	Advertising Expense	135
Equipment	540	Repair Expense	45
Accounts Payable	45	Travel Expense	90
J. West, Capital, June 1, 2014	3,720	Supplies Expense	270
J. West, Withdrawals	360	Rent Expense	240

1B-5. Jill Martin of Regina opened Martin's Catering Service. As her accountant, analyze the transactions listed below and present the following information in proper form:

1. The analysis of the transactions using the expanded accounting equation
2. A balance sheet showing the financial position of the firm before opening on November 1, 2013
3. An income statement for the month of November
4. A statement of owner's equity for November
5. A balance sheet as of November 30, 2013

2013

Oct. 28 Jill Martin invested $9,500 in the catering business.
     29 Bought equipment on account from Munroe Co., $1,200.
     30 Bought equipment for cash from Ryan Co., $1,500.
     31 Paid $600 to Munroe Co. as partial payment of the October 29 transaction.

Nov. 1 Catered a business luncheon and immediately collected cash, $2,400.
     4 Paid salaries of employees, $580.
     8 Provided catering services to Northwest Community College on account, $4,500.
     11 Received from Northwest Community College $2,000 cash as partial payment of November 8 transaction.
     15 Paid telephone bill, $95.
     18 Jill paid her home mortgage with a company cheque, $825.
     19 Provided catering services and received cash, $1,800.
     25 Bought additional equipment on account, $500.
     28 Rent expense due but not yet paid, $750.
     29 Paid supplies expense, $600.

Group C Problems

(The forms you need are on pages 1-17 to 1-23 of the *Study Guide with Working Papers*.)

1C-1. Robbie James began a new business called RJ Graphics, located in Moncton. The following transactions resulted:

A. Robbie invested $14,000 cash from her personal bank account in the graphics company.
B. Bought computer equipment on account, $3,500.
C. Paid $2,000 cash to reduce what was owed from Transaction B.
D. Purchased software for cash, $4,300.

Record these transactions in the basic accounting equation.

Preparing a balance sheet
2 **4** (15 min)

Check Figure

Total Assets $76,000

Recording transactions in the expanded accounting equation **3** (25 min)

Check Figure

Total Assets $19,908

Preparing an income statement, statement of owner's equity, and balance sheet **4** (35 min)

Check Figure

Total Assets $8,776

Comprehensive problem
2 **3** **4** (50 min)

Check Figure

Total Assets May 31 $27,722

1C-2. Dave Chan has asked you to prepare a balance sheet as of April 30, 2013, for Chan's Database Service of Orillia.

Dave Chan, Capital	$49,000	Building	34,000
Accounts Payable	27,000	Cash	16,000
Equipment	26,000		

1C-3. Ray Owens of Vancouver decided to open his own training services company at the end of October. Analyze the following transactions by recording their effects in the expanded accounting equation.

A. Ray invested $12,000 in the company.
B. Purchased new office equipment on account, $4,500.
C. Received cash for services rendered, $2,350.
D. Paid secretary's salary, $800.
E. Billed customers for training services rendered, $3,650.
F. Paid rent expense for the month, $600.
G. Ray withdrew cash for personal use, $1,000.
H. Advertising expense was due but as yet unpaid, $400.
I. Repair to office equipment paid, $192.

1C-4. Jennifer Pace, owner of Jennifer's Fashion Service (located in Dorval), has requested that you prepare from the following balances **a.** an income statement for July 2013, **b.** a statement of owner's equity for July, and **c.** a balance sheet as of July 31, 2013.

Cash	$1,524	Advertising Expense	635
Accounts Receivable	3,672	Repair Expense	387
Equipment	3,580	Travel Expense	1,690
Accounts Payable	1,830	Supplies Expense	262
Jennifer Pace, Capital, July 1, 2013	6,430	Rent Expense	440
Jennifer Pace, Withdrawals	710	Office Expenses	175
Consulting Fees Earned	4,815		

1C-5. Howard McGraw of Windsor opened First City Surveying Service. As his accountant, analyze the transactions listed and present to Howard the following information, in proper form:

1. The analysis of the transactions using the expanded accounting equation
2. A balance sheet showing the financial position of the firm before opening on May 1, 2013
3. An income statement for the month of May
4. A statement of owner's equity for May
5. A balance sheet as of May 31, 2013

2013
April 23 Howard invested $17,000 in the surveying business.
26 Bought equipment on account from Chapman & Co., $4,750.
29 Bought equipment for cash from Majestic Co., $2,895.
30 Paid $2,375 to Chapman & Co. as partial payment of the April 26 transaction.
May 2 Surveyed a new business location and immediately collected cash, $2,350.
3 Paid salaries of employees, $975.
10 Provided surveying services to City Community College on account, $4,950.
13 Received from City Community College $2,500 cash as partial payment of the May 10 transaction.
14 Paid telephone bill, $104.

May	17	Howard paid his home mortgage from the company's bank account, $1,043.
	21	Provided surveying services and received cash, $1,825.
	24	Bought additional equipment on account from Jensen Bros., $2,415.
	27	Paid rent expense for the month, $825.
	28	Paid supplies expense, $246.
	31	Advertising bill received but not yet paid, $410.

On-the-Job Training

(The forms you need are on pages 1-24 to 1-25 of the *Study Guide with Working Papers.*)

Recording and reporting transactions ③ ④ (20 min)

T-1. You have just been hired to prepare, if possible, an income statement for the year ended December 31, 2012, for Roger's Window Washing Company. The problem is that Roger kept only the following records (on the back of a piece of cardboard).

Assume that Roger's Window Washing Company records all revenues when earned and all expenses when incurred.

You feel that it is part of your job to tell Roger how to organize his records better. What would you tell him?

> *Money in:*
>
> | *Window cleaning* | *$11,376* |
> |---|---|
> | *My investment* | *1,200* |
> | *Loan from brother-in-law* | *4,000* |
>
> *Money out:*
>
> | *Salaries* | *$5,080* |
> |---|---|
> | *Withdrawals* | *6,200* |
> | *Supplies expense* | *1,400* |
>
> *What I owe or they owe me*
> *A. People that work for me but I still owe salaries to $1,800*
> *B. Owe bank interest of $300*
> *C. Work done but clients still owe me $2,900*
> *D. Advertising bill due but not paid $95*

T-2. While Jon Lune was on a business trip, he asked Abby Slowe, the book-keeper for Lune Co., to try to complete a balance sheet for the year ended December 31, 2013. Abby, who had been on the job only two months, submitted the following:

LUNE CO. FOR THE YEAR ENDED DECEMBER 31, 2013				
Building	$44 600 00	Accounts Payable	$127 604 00	
Land	72 935 00	Accounts Receivable	104 337 00	
Notes Payable	75 328 00	Auto	14 268 00	
Cash	10 016 00	Desks	6 825 00	
J. Lune, Capital	?	Total Equity	$250 034 00	

1. Help Abby fix as well as complete the balance sheet.
2. What written recommendations would you make about the bookkeeper? Should she be retained?
3. Suppose that (a) Jon Lune invested an additional $20,000 in cash as well as additional desks with a value of $8,000 and (b) Lune Co. bought an auto for $6,000 that was originally marked $8,000, paying $2,000 down and issuing a note for the balance. Prepare an updated balance sheet. Assume that these two transactions occurred on January 4.

CONTINUING PROBLEM

Preparing financial statements
from the expanded
accounting equation
3 4 (45 min)

The following problem will continue from one chapter to the next, carrying
the balances forward from month to month. Each chapter will focus on the
learning experience of the chapter and add additional information as the business
grows. The necessary forms are provided on pages 1-26 to 1-28 of the
Study Guide with Working Papers.

Assignment

1. Set up an expanded accounting equation spreadsheet using the following
accounts:

Assets	Liabilities	Owner's Equity
Cash	Accounts Payable	T. Freedman, Capital
Supplies		T. Freedman, Withdrawals
Computer Shop		Service Revenue
Equipment		Expenses (notate type)
Office Equipment		

2. Analyze and record each transaction in the expanded accounting equation.

3. Prepare the financial statements for Precision Computer Centre for the
period ending May 31.

Tony Freedman decided to begin his own computer service business on May 2,
2013. He named the business the Precision Computer Centre. During the
month of May, Tony conducted the following business transactions:

(a) Invested $4,500 of his savings into the business.

(b) Paid $1,200 (cheque No. 201) for a computer from Multi Systems, Inc.

(c) Paid $600 (cheque No. 202) for office equipment from Office Furniture,
Inc.

(d) Set up a new account with Staples and purchased $250 in office supplies
on credit.

(e) Paid May rent, $400 (cheque No. 203).

(f) Repaired a system for a customer; collected $250.

(g) Collected $200 for system upgrade labour charge from a customer.

(h) Electric bill due at May 31 but unpaid, $85.

(i) Received $1,200 for services performed on Taylor Golf computers.

(j) Tony withdrew $100 (cheque No. 204) to take his wife Carol out in celebration of opening the new business. **Note:** The business is too small to
worry about GST (or HST) and PST is not applicable either. Tony's
company may on occasion pay some GST or HST, but these details are
not set forth in any transactions until Chapter 10.

Debits and Credits

Analyzing and Recording Business Transactions

THE BIG PICTURE

What would you sacrifice to see your dreams come true? Would you invest every penny of your savings, sleep under your desk, and eat a constant diet of canned beans and macaroni?

Albertans Evan and Shane Chrapko and their former business partner Valerian Pappes know what it's like to sacrifice to make their dream a success. While it took only 19 months to take the DocSpace Company, a Toronto-based technology startup, to a value of more than $800 million, the personal and financial sacrifices began years earlier. The trio gave up many comforts to make their business succeed: their office furniture was salvaged, home was a futon under the desk, and dinner was far from extravagant.

Their commitment led to one of the fastest and greatest successes in Canadian e-business history. In March 2000, less than two years after DocSpace was founded, the company was purchased by Critical Path, a California dot-com, for a whopping C$811 million.

The three entrepreneurs were fortunate to sell at the height of dot-com madness, benefiting from an inflated technology market. But their success had more to do with sound business principles than with merely being in the right place at the right time.

The partners decided early on to operate as a business—protecting their technology with patent applications and keeping a close eye on their bottom line. They resisted throwing money around and gathered a strong workforce, many of whom received some or all of their compensation in the form of shares rather than cash. While their would-be competitors were offering products for free, DocSpace established reasonable market prices and sought out paying customers.

The strategy worked. By the time Critical Path made its offer, the partners had considered and declined three offers that would have made them—and many loyal employees—millionaires. However, with a clear idea of the value of their technology, the young Canadians held out until they received a bid that represented the value of their creation.

In this chapter, you learn the steps that go into generating a financial statement. When you analyze a business transaction, you decide not only which accounts change in value, but also whether they increase or decrease. You'll see how to use a *T Account* to write the value of a transaction as a debit or credit in a standard format and total the account at any time. You'll use the ending balances on every T account to prepare a *trial balance*, a test of the equality of debits and credits in all your accounts. You can then use the account balances to generate financial statements that you can compare month to month. By comparing financial statements, you can estimate how the financials will look in the future.

This chapter won't teach you how to turn your ideas and dreams into a multimillion-dollar company. However, if $811 million ever happens your way, at least you'll know how to record the transaction in the proper T account!

1 Recording transactions in T accounts according to the rules of debit and credit (p. 51)
2 Setting up and organizing a chart of accounts (p. 51)
3 Preparing a trial balance (p. 62)
4 Preparing financial statements from a trial balance (pp. 63–64)

In Chapter 1, we used the expanded accounting equation to document the financial transactions performed by Catherine Hall's law firm. Remember how long it was: the cash column had a long list of pluses and minuses, and there was no quick system of recording and summarizing the increases and decreases of cash or other items. Can you imagine the problem Canadian Tire or Tim Hortons would have if they used the expanded accounting equation to track the thousands of business transactions they do each day?

Let's look at the problem a little more closely. Every business transaction is recorded in the accounting equation under a specific **account**. There are different accounts for each of the subdivisions of the accounting equation—there are asset accounts, liability accounts, expense accounts, revenue accounts, and so on. What is needed is a way to record the increases and decreases in specific account *categories* and yet keep them together in one place. The answer is the **standard account** form (see Figure 2-1). A standard account is a formal account that includes columns for date, explanation, posting reference (PR), debit, and credit. Each account has a separate form and all transactions affecting that account are recorded on the form. All the business's account forms (which often are referred to as *ledger accounts*) are then placed in a **ledger**. Each page of the ledger contains one account. The ledger may be in the form of a bound or a loose-leaf book. If computers are used, the ledger may be part of a computer printout. For simplicity's sake, in this chapter, we will use the **T account** form, which got its name because it looks like the letter T. Generally, T accounts are used for classroom demonstration purposes.

Figure 2-1
The Standard Account Form

Account Title							Account No.	
Date	Item	PR	Debit	Date	Item	PR	Credit	

The standard account form is the source of the T account's shape.

Learning Unit 2-1

The T Account

Each T account contains three basic parts:

1 **Title of Account**

2 **Left side** | **Right side** 3

Debit defined

1. The *left* side of any T account
2. An amount entered on the left side of any account is said to be *debited* to an account.

Credit defined

1. The *right* side of any T account
2. An amount entered on the right side of an account is said to be *credited* to an account.

All T accounts have this structure. In accounting, the left side of any T account is called the **debit** side.

At this point, for you, the word *debit* in accounting means a position, the left side of an account. Don't think of it as good (+) or bad (−).

| Left side |
| Dr. (debit) |

Amounts entered on the left side of any account are said to be *debited* to an account. The word *debit* is from the Latin *debere*; the abbreviation for debit is Dr.

The right side of any T account is called the **credit** side.

| | Right side |
| | Cr. (credit) |

Amounts entered on the right side of an account are said to be *credited* to an account. The word *credit* is from the Latin *credere*; the abbreviation for credit is Cr.

At this point, do not associate the definitions of debit and credit with the words *increase* and *decrease*. Think of debit or credit as indicating only a *position* (left side or right side) of a T account.

NEED HELP?

Most of the jobs or professions in society use a terminology that includes unique terms. This is true for many of our non-business tasks as well. Take golf, for example. There are many unique golf terms in constant use, such as "par," "eagle," and (all too often) "bogie," and you only need to listen to a televised golf competition to hear them.

Many people enjoy sailing as a hobby, and there are thousands of mariners who work in the shipping industry. As you might expect, these people have developed certain terms or abbreviations that have a distinct meaning for them.

If during a sailing competition a sailor shouts, "Hard to port!" it does not mean turn around and head for shore, and it certainly has nothing to do with an expensive, sweet, strong wine! In the context of sailing, "port" simply means "left." If a right turn is wanted, you say, "Starboard." This same terminology has been adopted in the airline industry as well.

So it has always been a puzzle why some accounting students have difficulty with the terms "debit" and "credit." There should be no puzzle here; the terms are used in a manner unique to bookkeeping, and all students of accounting need to familiarize themselves with what the terms mean and how they are used. This should not take long, but possibly because the words do have a more general meaning in society, it can be confusing at first. But if you want to get a good foothold in this field, it is essential to quickly master the use of these terms.

This chapter explains the terms clearly, and students should make an effort to ensure they know what each term means. It might help to remember that, just as in sailing, "port" means "left" and so it is with bookkeeping. "Debit" also means "left" ("on the left," actually). And also, just as "starboard" means "right" in sailing, "credit" also means "right" ("on the right"). While it is true that the word "credit" has other meanings, these should be ignored when you are learning about bookkeeping and accounting.

Good luck with mastering these two terms!

BALANCING AN ACCOUNT

No matter which individual account is being balanced, the procedure will be the same.

	Dr.	Cr.
Entries	4,000	300
	500	400
Footings	4,500	700
Ending Balance	3,800	

In the "real" world, the T account would also include the date of the transaction. The date would appear to the left of the entry, as shown below.

Note that on the debit (left) side, the amounts add up to $4,500. On the credit (right) side, the amounts add up $700. The $4,500 and the $700 written in small type are called **footings**. Footings help in calculating the new (or ending) balance. The **ending balance** ($3,800) is placed on the debit or left side, since the total of the debit side is greater than that of the credit side.

		Dr.	Cr.	
	4/2	4,000	300	4/3
	4/20	500	400	4/25
Footings		4,500	700	
Balance		3,800		

Remember, the ending balance does not tell us anything about increase or decrease. It tells us only that we have an ending balance of $3,800 on the debit side.

LEARNING UNIT 2-1 REVIEW

AT THIS POINT you should be able to:

◆ Define ledger. (p. 47)
◆ State the purpose of a T account. (p. 47)
◆ Identify the three parts of a T account. (p. 47)
◆ Define debit. (p. 48)
◆ Define credit. (p. 48)
◆ Explain footings and calculate the balance of an account. (p. 49)

Self-Review Quiz 2-1

(The blank forms you need are on page 2-1 of the *Study Guide with Working Papers*.)

Respond True or False to the following:

1.

Dr.	Cr.
3,000	200
200	600

The balance of the account is $2,400 Cr.

2. A credit always means increase.

3. A debit is the left side of any account.

4. A ledger can be prepared manually or by computer.
5. Footings replace the need for debits and credits.

Solutions to Self-Review Quiz 2-1

1. False   2. False   3. True   4. True   5. False

NEED HELP?

Let's review first: Debit does not mean good or bad. Instead, it represents a position, the left side of any account. Credit does not mean good or bad either. It represents a position, the right side of any account.

1. It is false because if you add the two debits of 3,000 and 200 you get 3,200 on the debit, or left side. A Dr. + Dr. = Debit balance. Now if you add the credit side of 200 and 600 you get a balance of 800 on the credit side. A Cr. + Cr. = Credit balance. To find the ending balance we take 3,200 less the 800 to arrive at a balance that is still larger on the DEBIT side by 2,400.

2. A credit is a position. It is the right side of any account.

3. Yes, the debit is always the left-hand side of any account. It does not mean good or bad.

4. Years ago the ledger, a group of accounts, was prepared manually; however, today most ledgers are updated by computer software.

5. Footings are used to total the debits and total the credits. The smaller total is deducted from the larger total to arrive at a new balance. Think of footings as the totals of a column.

Learning Unit 2-2
Recording Business Transactions: Debits and Credits

Can you get a queen in checkers? Is there a fourth down in the CFL? In a baseball game, does a runner rounding first base skip second base and run over the pitcher's mound to get to third? No—most of us don't do such things because we follow the rules of the game. Usually we learn the rules first and reflect on the reasons for them afterward. The same is true in accounting.

Instead of first trying to understand all the rules of debit and credit and how they were developed in accounting, it will be easier to learn the rules by "playing the game."

T ACCOUNT ENTRIES FOR ACCOUNTING IN THE ACCOUNTING EQUATION

Have patience. Learning the rules of debit and credit is like learning to play any game—the more you play, the easier it becomes. Table 2-1 shows the rules for the side on which you enter an increase or a decrease for each of the separate accounts in the accounting equation. For example, an increase is entered on the debit side in the asset account but on the credit side for a liability account.

Be sure to follow the rules of debit and credit when recording accounts. They were designed to keep the accounting equation in balance.

1 Recording transactions in T accounts according to the rules of debit and credit

TABLE 2-1 Rules of Debit and Credit

Account Category	Increase (Normal Balance)	Decrease
Assets	Debit	Credit
Liabilities	Credit	Debit
Owner's Equity:		
Capital	Credit	Debit
Withdrawals	Debit	Credit
Revenue	Credit	Debit
Expenses	Debit	Credit

It might be easier to visualize these rules of debit and credit if we look at them in the T account form, using + to show increase and − to show decrease.

ASSETS = LIABILITIES + OWNER'S EQUITY

ASSETS		LIABILITIES		Capital	−	Withdrawals	+	Revenue	−	Expenses
Dr. | Cr.	=	Dr. | Cr.	+	Dr. | Cr.		Dr. | Cr.		Dr. | Cr.		Dr. | Cr.
+ | −		− | +		− | +		+ | −		− | +		+ | −

Rules for Assets Work in the Opposite Direction to Those for Liabilities

When you look at the equation, you can see that the rules for assets work in the opposite direction to those for liabilities. That is, for assets, the increases appear on the debit side and the decreases are shown on the credit side; the opposite is true for liabilities. As for owner's equity, the rules for withdrawals and expenses, which *decrease* owner's equity, work in the opposite direction to the rules for capital and revenue, which *increase* owner's equity.

Assets	+	Withdrawals	+	Expenses	=	Liabilities	+	Capital	+	Revenue
Dr. | Cr.		Dr. | Cr.		Dr. | Cr.		Dr. | Cr.		Dr. | Cr.		Dr. | Cr.
+ | −		+ | −		+ | −		− | +		− | +		− | +

This setup may help you understand that the rules for withdrawals and expenses are just the opposite of the rules for capital and revenue.

A **normal balance of an account** is the side that increases by the rules of debit and credit. For example, the balance of cash is a debit balance because an asset is increased by a debit. We will discuss normal balances further in Chapter 3.

Normal Balance

Dr.	Cr.
Assets	Liabilities
Expenses	Capital
Withdrawals	Revenue

Balancing the Equation

It is important to remember that any amount(s) entered on the debit side of a T account or accounts also must be on the credit side of another T account or accounts. This ensures that the total amount added to the debit side will equal the total amount added to the credit side, thereby keeping the accounting equation in balance.

The chart of accounts aids in locating and identifying accounts quickly.

2 Setting up and organizing a chart of accounts

Chart of Accounts

Our job is to analyze Catherine Hall's business transactions—the transactions we looked at in Chapter 1—using a system of accounts guided by the rules of debits and credits that will summarize increases and decreases of individual accounts in the ledger. The goal is to prepare an income statement, statement of owner's equity, and balance sheet for Catherine Hall. Sound familiar? If this system works, the rules of debits and credits and the use of accounts will give us the same answers as in Chapter 1 but with greater ease, and faster, too!

TABLE 2-2 Chart of Accounts for Catherine Hall, Barrister and Solicitor

Balance Sheet Accounts

Assets
111 Cash
112 Accounts Receivable
121 Office Equipment

Liabilities
211 Accounts Payable

Owner's Equity
311 Catherine Hall, Capital
312 Catherine Hall, Withdrawals

Income Statement Accounts

Revenue
411 Legal Fees

Expenses
511 Salaries Expense
512 Rent Expense
513 Advertising Expense

Balance Sheet Accounts

Catherine's accountant developed what is called a **chart of accounts**. The chart of accounts is a numbered list of all of the business's accounts. It allows accounts to be located quickly. In Catherine's business, for example, 100s are assets, 200s are liabilities, and so on. As you can see in Table 2-2, each separate asset and liability has its own number. Note that the chart may be expanded as the business grows.

> Large companies may have four digits assigned to each title, and sometimes up to 24 or more digits (e.g., Exxon).

THE ACCOUNTING ANALYSIS: FIVE STEPS

We will analyze the transactions in Catherine Hall's law firm using a teaching device called a *transaction analysis chart*. (Keep in mind that the transaction analysis chart is not a part of any formal accounting system.) There are five steps in analyzing each business transaction:

Step 1: Determine which accounts are affected. *Examples:* cash, accounts payable, rent expense. A transaction always affects at least two accounts.

Step 2: Determine which categories the accounts belong to—assets, liabilities, capital, withdrawals, revenue, or expenses. *Example:* Cash is an asset.

Step 3: Determine whether the accounts increase or decrease. *Example:* If you receive cash, that account is increasing.

Step 4: What do the rules of debits and credits say (Table 2-1)?

Step 5: What does the T account look like? Place amounts in the accounts on either the left or right side depending on the rules in Table 2-1.

> Steps to analyze and record transactions. Steps 1 and 2 will come from the chart of accounts. Remember the rules of debit and credit tell us only on which side to place information. Whether the debit or credit represents increases or decreases depends on the account category:
>
> * Assets, Expenses, and Withdrawals, which are increased with a debit
> * Liabilities, Owner's Equity, and Revenue, which are increased with a credit
>
> Think of a business transaction as an exchange—you get something and you give up or part with something.

This is how the five-step analysis looks in chart form:

1 Accounts Affected	2 Category	3 ↓ or ↑ (decrease) (increase)	4 Rules of Dr. and Cr.	5 Appearance of T Accounts

Let us emphasize a major point: *Do not try to debit or credit an account until you have gone through the first four steps of the transaction analysis.*

Note that in column 3 of the chart, there can be any combination of arrows, as long as the sum of the debits equals the sum of the credits in the T accounts in column 5.

APPLYING THE TRANSACTION ANALYSIS TO CATHERINE HALL'S LAW PRACTICE

Transaction A: **Aug. 26: Catherine Hall invests $7,000 cash and $800 worth of office equipment in the business.**

1 Accounts Affected	2 Category	3 ↓ ↑	4 Rules of Dr. and Cr.	5 Appearance of T Accounts
Cash	Asset	↑	Dr.	**Cash 111** (A) 7,000
Office Equipment	Asset	↑	Dr.	**Office Equipment 121** (A) 800
C. Hall, Capital	Owner's Equity	↑	Cr.	**C. Hall, Capital 311** 7,800 (A)

Note again that every transaction affects at least two T accounts, and the total amount added to the debit side(s) must equal the total amount added to the credit side(s) of the T accounts for each transaction.

Analysis of Transaction A

Step 1: Which accounts are affected? The law firm receives cash and office equipment, so three accounts are involved: cash, office equipment, and C. Hall, Capital. These account titles come from the chart of accounts.

Step 2: Which categories do these accounts belong to? Cash and office equipment are assets; C. Hall, Capital, is owner's equity.

Step 3: Are the accounts increasing or decreasing? The cash and office equipment, both assets, are increasing in the business. The rights or claims of C. Hall, Capital, are also increasing since Catherine invested money and office equipment in the business.

Step 4: What do the rules say? According to the rules of debit and credit, an increase in assets (cash and office equipment) is a debit. An increase in capital is a credit. Note that the total dollar amount of debits will equal the total dollar amount of credits when the T accounts are updated in column 5.

Step 5: What does the T account look like? The amount for cash and office equipment is entered on the debit side. The amount for C. Hall, Capital, goes on the credit side.

A transaction that involves more than one credit or more than one debit is called a **compound entry**. This first transaction of Catherine Hall's law firm is a compound entry; it involves a debit of $7,000 to Cash and a debit of $800 to Office Equipment (as well as a credit of $7,800 to C. Hall, Capital).

There is a name for this double-entry analysis of transactions, where two or more accounts are affected and the total of debits equals the total of credits. It is called **double-entry bookkeeping**. This double-entry system helps in checking the recording of business transactions.

As we continue, the explanations will be brief, but do not forget to apply the five steps in analyzing and recording each business transaction.

Double-entry bookkeeping system: The total of all debits is equal to the total of all credits.

Transaction B:	Aug. 27: Law practice bought office equipment for cash, $900.

1 Accounts Affected	2 Category	3 ↓	↑	4 Rules of Dr. and Cr.	5 T Account Update
Office Equipment	Asset		↑	Dr.	**Office Equipment 121** (A) 800 (B) 900
Cash	Asset	↓		Cr.	**Cash 111** (A) 7,000 | 900 (B)

Analysis of Transaction B

Step 1: The law firm paid cash for the office equipment it received. The accounts involved in the transaction are Cash and Office Equipment.

Step 2: The accounts belong to these categories: Office Equipment is an asset account; Cash is an asset account.

Step 3: The asset account Office Equipment is increasing. The asset account Cash is decreasing—it is being reduced in order to buy the office equipment.

Step 4: An increase in the asset account Office Equipment is a debit; a decrease in the asset account Cash is a credit.

Step 5: When the amounts are placed in the T accounts, the amount for office equipment goes on the debit side and the amount for cash on the credit side.

Transaction C:	Aug. 30: Bought more office equipment on account, $400.

1 Accounts Affected	2 Category	3 ↓	↑	4 Rules of Dr. and Cr.	5 T Account Update
Office Equipment	Asset		↑	Dr.	**Office Equipment 121** (A) 800 (B) 900 (C) 400
Accounts Payable	Liability		↑	Cr.	**Accounts Payable 211** | 400 (C)

Analysis of Transaction C

Step 1: The law firm receives office equipment by promising to pay in the future. An obligation or liability account, Accounts Payable, is created.

Step 2: Office Equipment is an asset. Accounts Payable is a liability.

Step 3: The asset account Office Equipment is increasing; the liability account Accounts Payable is increasing because the law firm is increasing what it owes.

Step 4: An increase in the asset account, Office Equipment, is a debit. An increase in the liability account, Accounts Payable, is a credit.

Step 5: Enter the amount for office equipment on the debit side of the T account. The amount for accounts payable goes on the credit side.

Transaction D: Sept. 1–30: Provided legal services for cash, $3,000.

1 Accounts Affected	2 Category	3 ↓ ↑	4 Rules of Dr. and Cr.	5 T Account Update
Cash	Asset	↑	Dr.	**Cash 111** (A) 7,000 | 900 (B) (D) 3,000 |
Legal Fees	Revenue	↑	Cr.	**Legal Fees 411** | 3,000 (D)

Analysis of Transaction D

Step 1: The firm has earned revenue from legal services and receives $3,000 in cash.

Step 2: Cash is an asset account. Legal fees are revenue.

Step 3: Cash, an asset account, is increasing. Legal fees, or revenue, is also increasing.

Step 4: An increase in cash, an asset, is debited. An increase in legal fees, or revenue, is credited.

Step 5: Enter the amount for cash on the debit side of the T account. Enter the amount for legal fees on the credit side.

Transaction E: Sept. 1–30: Provided legal services on account, $4,000.

1 Accounts Affected	2 Category	3 ↓ ↑	4 Rules of Dr. and Cr.	5 T Account Update
Accounts Receivable	Asset	↑	Dr.	**Accounts Receivable 112** (E) 4,000 |
Legal Fees	Revenue	↑	Cr.	**Legal Fees 411** | 3,000 (D) | 4,000 (E)

Analysis of Transaction E

Step 1: The law practice has earned revenue but has not yet received payment (cash). The amounts owed by these clients are called *accounts receivable*. Revenue is earned at the time the legal services are provided, whether payment is received then or will be received sometime in the future.

Step 2: Accounts Receivable is an asset account. Legal Fees is a revenue account.

Step 3: The Accounts Receivable account is increasing because the law practice has increased the amount owed to it for legal fees that have been earned but not paid. The Legal Fees account, or revenue, is increasing.

Step 4: An increase in the asset account, Accounts Receivable, is a debit. An increase in revenue is a credit.

Step 5: Enter the amount for Accounts Receivable on the debit side of the T account. The amount for Legal Fees goes on the credit side.

Transaction F: Sept. 1–30: Received $700 cash from clients for services rendered previously on account.

1 Accounts Affected	2 Category	3 ↓ ↑	4 Rules of Dr. and Cr.	5 T Account Update
Cash	Asset	↑	Dr.	**Cash 111**
				(A) 7,000 900 (B) (D) 3,000 (F) 700
Accounts Receivable	Asset	↓	Cr.	**Accounts Receivable 112**
				(E) 4,000 700 (F)

Analysis of Transaction F

Step 1: The law firm collects $700 in cash from previous revenue earned. Since the revenue is recorded at the time it is earned and not when the payment is made, in this transaction, we are concerned only with the payment, which affects the Cash and Accounts Receivable accounts.

Step 2: Cash is an asset account. Accounts Receivable is an asset account.

Step 3: Since clients are paying what is owed, cash (asset) is increasing and the amount owed (accounts receivable) is decreasing (the total amount owed by clients to Catherine Hall is going down). This transaction results in a shift in assets, more cash for less accounts receivable.

Step 4: An increase in the Cash account, an asset, is a debit. A decrease in the Accounts Receivable account, an asset, is a credit.

Step 5: Enter the amount for Cash on the debit side of the T account. The amount for Accounts Receivable goes on the credit side.

Transaction G: Sept. 1–30: Paid salaries expense, $600.

1 Accounts Affected	2 Category	3 ↓ ↑	4 Rules of Dr. and Cr.	5 T Account Update
Salaries Expense	Expense	↑	Dr.	**Salaries Expense 511**
				(G) 600
Cash	Asset	↓	Cr.	**Cash 111**
				(A) 7,000 900 (B) (D) 3,000 600 (G) (F) 700

Analysis of Transaction G

Step 1: The law firm pays $600 worth of salaries expense by cash.

Step 2: Salaries Expense is an expense account. Cash is an asset account.

Step 3: The salaries expense of the law firm is increasing, which results in a decrease in cash available.

Step 4: An increase in Salaries Expense, an expense account, is a debit. A decrease in Cash, an asset account, is a credit.

Step 5: Enter the amount for Salaries Expense on the debit side of the T account. The amount for Cash goes on the credit side.

Transaction H: Sept. 1–30: Paid rent expense, $700.

1 Accounts Affected	2 Category	3 ↓ ↑	4 Rules of Dr. and Cr.	5 T Account Update
Rent Expense	Expense	↑	Dr.	**Rent Expense 512** (H) 700 |
Cash	Asset	↓	Cr.	**Cash 111** (A) 7,000 | 900 (B) (D) 3,000 | 600 (G) (F) 700 | 700 (H)

Analysis of Transaction H

Step 1: The law firm's rent expenses are paid in cash.

Step 2: Rent is an expense. Cash is an asset.

Step 3: The rent expense increases the expenses, and the payment for the rent expense decreases the cash.

Step 4: An increase in Rent Expense, an expense account, is a debit. A decrease in Cash, an asset account, is a credit.

Step 5: Enter the amount for Rent Expense on the debit side of the T account. Place the amount for Cash on the credit side.

Transaction I: Sept. 1–30: Received a bill for advertising expense (to be paid next month), $300.

1 Accounts Affected	2 Category	3 ↓ ↑	4 Rules of Dr. and Cr.	5 T Account Update
Advertising Expense	Expense	↑	Dr.	**Advertising Expense 513** (I) 300 |
Accounts Payable	Liability	↑	Cr.	**Accounts Payable 211** | 400 (C) | 300 (I)

Analysis of Transaction I

Step 1: The advertising bill has come in and payment is due but has not yet been made. Therefore, the accounts involved here are Advertising Expense and Accounts Payable; the expense has created a liability.

Step 2: Advertising Expense is an expense account. Accounts Payable is a liability account.

Step 3: Both the expense and the liability are increasing.

Step 4: An increase in an expense is a debit. An increase in a liability is a credit.

Step 5: Enter the amount for the Advertising Expense account on the debit side of the T account. Enter the amount for the Accounts Payable account on the credit side.

Transaction J: Sept. 1–30: Hall withdrew cash for personal use, $200.

1 Accounts Affected	2 Category	3 ↓ ↑	4 Rules of Dr. and Cr.	5 T Account Update
C. Hall, Withdrawals	Owner's Equity (Withdrawals)*	↑	Dr.	C. Hall, Withdrawals 312 (J) 200 |
Cash	Asset	↓	Cr.	Cash 111 (A) 7,000 900 (B) (D) 3,000 600 (G) (F) 700 700 (H) 200 (J)

*Withdrawals are actually a subcategory of Owner's Equity and act as a contra account—that is, as the Withdrawals account increases the Owner's Equity account decreases.

Analysis of Transaction J

Withdrawals are always increased by debits.

Step 1: Catherine Hall withdraws cash from the business for *personal* use. This withdrawal is not a business expense.

Step 2: This transaction affects the Withdrawals and Cash accounts.

Step 3: Catherine has increased what she has withdrawn from the business for personal use. The business cash has been decreased.

Step 4: An increase in withdrawals is a debit. A decrease in cash is a credit. (*Remember:* Withdrawals go on the statement of owner's equity; expenses go on the income statement.)

Step 5: Enter the amount for C. Hall, Withdrawals, on the debit side of the T account. The amount for Cash goes on the credit side.

SUMMARY OF TRANSACTIONS FOR CATHERINE HALL

ASSETS	=	LIABILITIES	+	CAPITAL	−	WITHDRAWALS	+	REVENUE	−	EXPENSES

Cash 111 = **Accounts Payable 211** + **C. Hall, Capital 311** − **C. Hall, Withdrawals 312** + **Legal Fees 411** − **Salaries Expense 511**

Cash 111		Accounts Payable 211	C. Hall, Capital 311	C. Hall, Withdrawals 312	Legal Fees 411	Salaries Expense 511
(A) 7,000	900 (B)	400 (C)	7,800 (A)	(J) 200	3,000 (D)	(G) 600
(D) 3,000	600 (G)	300 (I)			4,000 (E)	
(F) 700	700 (H)					
	200 (J)					

Accounts Receivable 112

Accounts Receivable 112		Rent Expense 512
(E) 4,000	700 (F)	(H) 700

Office Equipment 121

Office Equipment 121	Advertising Expense 513
(A) 800	(I) 300
(B) 900	
(C) 400	

LEARNING UNIT 2-2 REVIEW

AT THIS POINT you should be able to:

- State the rules of debit and credit. (p. 51)
- List the five steps of a transaction analysis. (p. 52)
- Show how to fill out a transaction analysis chart. (p. 53)
- Explain double-entry bookkeeping. (p. 53)

Self-Review Quiz 2-2

(The blank forms you need are on pages 2-1 and 2-2 of the *Study Guide with Working Papers*.)

King Company uses the following accounts from its chart of accounts: Cash (111), Accounts Receivable (112), Equipment (121), Accounts Payable (211), Jamie King, Capital (311), Jamie King, Withdrawals (312), Professional Fees (411), Utilities Expense (511), and Salaries Expense (512).

Record the following transactions in transaction analysis charts.

A. Jamie King invested $1,000 cash and equipment worth $700 from his personal assets into the business.

B. Billed clients for services rendered, $12,000.

C. Utilities bill due but as yet unpaid, $150.

D. Jamie King withdrew cash for personal use, $120.

E. Paid salaries expense, $250.

Solution to Self-Review Quiz 2-2

A.

1 Accounts Affected	2 Category	3 ↓ ↑	4 Rules of Dr. and Cr.	5 T Account Update
Cash	Asset	↑	Dr.	Cash 111 (A) 1,000 |
Equipment	Asset	↑	Dr.	Equipment 121 (A) 700 |
Jamie King, Capital	Capital	↑	Cr.	Jamie King, Capital 311 | 1,700 (A)

B.

1 Accounts Affected	2 Category	3 ↓ ↑	4 Rules of Dr. and Cr.	5 T Account Update
Accounts Receivable	Asset	↑	Dr.	Accounts Receivable 112 (B) 12,000 |
Professional Fees	Revenue	↑	Cr.	Professional Fees 411 | 12,000 (B)

C.

1 Accounts Affected	2 Category	3 ↓ ↑	4 Rules of Dr. and Cr.	5 T Account Update
Utilities Expense	Expense	↑	Dr.	Utilities Expense 511 (C) 150 |
Accounts Payable	Liability	↑	Cr.	Accounts Payable 211 | 150 (C)

D.

1 Accounts Affected	2 Category	3 ↓ ↑	4 Rules of Dr. and Cr.	5 T Account Update
Jamie King, Withdrawals	Owner's Equity (Withdrawals)	↑	Dr.	Jamie King, Withdrawals 312 (D) 120 |
Cash	Asset	↓	Cr.	Cash 111 (A) 1,000 | 120 (D)

E.

1 Accounts Affected	2 Category	3 ↓ ↑	4 Rules of Dr. and Cr.	5 T Account Update
Salaries Expense	Expense	↑	Dr.	**Salaries Expense 512** (E) 250 |
Cash	Asset	↓	Cr.	**Cash 111** (A) 1,000 | 120 (D) | 250 (E)

NEED HELP?

Let's review first: Make up a note card of the rules of debit and credit from Table 2.1. You will notice that assets, withdrawals, and expenses increase when you put amounts on the left, or debit, side of these accounts. The accounting system balances because liabilities, capital, and revenue increase when you put amounts on the right, or credit, side of these accounts. The increase side of any account will represent its normal balance. Think of a chart of accounts as a roadmap to all account titles a company will use. ALL ACCOUNTS AFFECTED MUST COME FROM THE CHART OF ACCOUNTS.

Transaction A: In column 1 all titles must come from the chart of accounts. The order listed does not matter as long as the sum of the left side equals the sum of the right side. In this transaction we see that accounts affected include cash, equipment, and Jamie King, Capital. Cash and equipment are assets, while capital is categorized as capital. Remember that the six category choices are as follows:

assets

liabilities

capital

withdrawals

revenue

expenses

The cash and equipment in the business are increasing (thus arrows up), and because the owner, Jamie King, supplied them Capital rights are increasing. Assets are increased by putting amounts on the debit side and capital is increased by putting amounts on the credit side.

Transaction B: Here we do the work but do not get the money. We see from the chart of accounts that revenue is called Professional Fees and customers owing money are called Accounts Receivable. Revenue for King Co. is going up and customers owe the company more money. Increase in an asset is a debit and increase in revenue is a credit.

Transaction C: Here we record utilities expense before it is paid. The expenses have increased for King Co., and it has increased what it owes the utility company. An increase in an expense is a debit and an increase in a liability is a credit. Here an expense has created a liability.

Transaction D: This is not a business expense since this is a personal withdrawal of cash by the owner, King. Withdrawals are increasing since King is taking the withdrawal but the business is lowering its cash from the withdrawal. An increase in withdrawal is a debit and a decrease in cash is a credit. Note the "dr" in the middle of "withdrawal." A withdrawal always increases by a debit.

Transaction E: In this transaction the business has another expense increasing and is paying for it in cash. The end result is that expenses increase on the debit side and cash, which is an asset, decreases on the credit side. Remember that we record expenses when they happen whether they are paid or not. Here they were paid. In transaction C they were not paid.

Learning Unit 2-3

The Trial Balance and Preparation of Financial Statements

Let us look at all the transactions we have discussed for Catherine Hall's business, arranged by T account and recorded using the rules of debit and credit.

ASSETS	=	LIABILITIES	+	CAPITAL	−	WITHDRAWALS	+	REVENUE	−	EXPENSES

Cash 111 = **Accounts Payable 211** + **C. Hall, Capital 311** − **C. Hall, Withdrawals 312** + **Legal Fees 411** − **Salaries Expense 511**

Cash 111		Accounts Payable 211		C. Hall, Capital 311	C. Hall, Withdrawals 312	Legal Fees 411		Salaries Expense 511
(A) 7,000	900 (B)		400 (C)	7,800 (A)	(J) 200		3,000 (D)	(G) 600
(D) 3,000	600 (G)		300 (I)				4,000 (E)	
(F) 700	700 (H)		700				7,000	
	200 (J)							
10,700	2,400	←Footings						
8,300		←Ending Balance						

Rent Expense 512

(H) 700	

Accounts Receivable 112

(E) 4,000	700 (F)
3,300	

Advertising Expense 513

(I) 300	

Office Equipment 121

(A) 800	
(B) 900	
(C) 400	
2,100	

3 Preparing a trial balance

Footings are used to indicate or obtain the balance of any T account. They are not needed if there is only one entry in the account.

This grouping of accounts is much easier to use than the expanded accounting equation because all of the transactions that affect a particular account are in one place.

As we saw in Learning Unit 2-2, when all the transactions are recorded in the accounts, the total of all the debits should be equal to the total of all the credits. (If they are not equal, the accountant must go back and find the error by checking the numbers and adding every column again.)

THE TRIAL BALANCE

Footings are used to indicate or obtain the balance of any T account that has more than one entry. If all entries in the account are on one side, the total *is* the footing. If there are entries on both sides of the account, the balance is obtained by subtracting the smaller total (footing) from the larger. For example, look at the Cash account above. The footing for the debit side is $10,700 and the footing for the credit side is $2,400. Since the debit side is larger, we subtract $2,400 from $10,700 to arrive at an *ending balance* of $8,300. Now look at the Rent Expense account. There is no need for a footing because there is only one entry. The amount itself is the ending balance. When the ending balance has been found for every

Figure 2-2
Trial Balance for
Catherine Hall's Law Firm

CATHERINE HALL, Barrister and Solicitor TRIAL BALANCE SEPTEMBER 30, 2013	Dr.	Cr.
Cash	8 3 0 0 00	
Accounts Receivable	3 3 0 0 00	
Office Equipment	2 1 0 0 00	
Accounts Payable		7 0 0 00
C. Hall, Capital		7 8 0 0 00
C. Hall, Withdrawals	2 0 0 00	
Legal Fees		7 0 0 0 00
Salaries Expense	6 0 0 00	
Rent Expense	7 0 0 00	
Advertising Expense	3 0 0 00	
Totals	15 5 0 0 00	15 5 0 0 00

Since this is not a formal report, there is no need to use dollar signs; however, the single and double lines under subtotals and final totals are still used for clarity.

account, we should be able to show that the total of all debits equals the total of all credits.

The ending balances are used to prepare a **trial balance**. The trial balance is not a financial report, although it is used to prepare financial reports. The trial balance lists all of the accounts with their balances in the same order as they appear in the chart of accounts. It proves the accuracy of the ledger.

As mentioned earlier, the ending balance of cash, $8,300, is a *normal balance* because it is on the side that increases the asset account.

In the ideal situation, businesses would take a trial balance every day. The large number of transactions most businesses conduct each day makes this impractical. Instead, trial balances are prepared periodically.

Keep in mind that the figure for capital might not be the beginning figure if any additional investment has taken place during the period. You can tell this by looking at the capital account in the ledger.

Only the ending balance of each account is listed.

A more detailed discussion of the trial balance will be provided in the next chapter. For now, notice the heading, how the accounts are listed, the debits in the left column, the credits in the right, and the fact that the total of debits is equal to the total of credits.

A trial balance for Catherine Hall's firm's accounts is shown in Figure 2-2.

PREPARING FINANCIAL STATEMENTS

4 Preparing financial statements from a trial balance

The trial balance is used to prepare the financial statements. The diagram in Figure 2-3 shows how financial statements can be prepared from a trial balance. Financial statements do not have debit or credit columns. The left column in the income statement and the statement of owner's equity is used only to subtotal numbers. If there were more than one liability, we would have two columns on the right-hand side of the balance sheet, one to subtotal the liabilities (inside column) and the total of the liabilities in the right column.

CATHERINE HALL, Barrister and Solicitor
INCOME STATEMENT
FOR MONTH ENDED SEPTEMBER 30, 2013

Revenue:		
Legal Fees		$7 0 0 0 00
Operating Expenses:		
Salaries Expense	$6 0 0 00	
Rent Expense	7 0 0 00	
Advertising Expense	3 0 0 00	
Total Operating Expenses		1 6 0 0 00
Net Income		$5 4 0 0 00

CATHERINE HALL, Barrister and Solicitor
TRIAL BALANCE
SEPTEMBER 30, 2013

	Dr.	Cr.
Cash	8 3 0 0 00	
Accounts Receivable	3 3 0 0 00	
Office Equipment	2 1 0 0 00	
Accounts Payable		7 0 0 00
C. Hall, Capital		7 8 0 0 00
C. Hall, Withdrawals	2 0 0 00	
Legal Fees		7 0 0 0 00
Salaries Expense	6 0 0 00	
Rent Expense	7 0 0 00	
Advertising Expense	3 0 0 00	
Totals	15 5 0 0 00	15 5 0 0 00

CATHERINE HALL, Barrister and Solicitor
STATEMENT OF OWNER'S EQUITY
FOR MONTH ENDED SEPTEMBER 30, 2013

C. Hall, Capital		
September 1, 2013		$7 8 0 0 00
Net Income for September	$5 4 0 0 00	
Less: Withdrawals		
for September	2 0 0 00	
Increase in Capital		5 2 0 0 00
C. Hall, Capital		
September 30, 2013		$1 3 0 0 0 00

CATHERINE HALL, Barrister and Solicitor
BALANCE SHEET
SEPTEMBER 30, 2013

Assets		Liabilities and Owner's Equity	
Cash	$8 3 0 0 00	Liabilities	
Accounts Receivable	3 3 0 0 00	Accounts Payable	$7 0 0 00
Office Equipment	2 1 0 0 00	Owner's Equity	
		C. Hall, Capital	1 3 0 0 0 00
		Total Liab. and	
Total Assets	$13 7 0 0 00	Owner's Equity	$13 7 0 0 00

Figure 2-3 Steps in Preparing Financial Statements from a Trial Balance

LEARNING UNIT 2-3 REVIEW

AT THIS POINT you should be able to:

◆ Explain the role of footings. (p. 62)

◆ Prepare a trial balance from a set of accounts. (p. 62)

◆ Prepare financial statements from a trial balance. (p. 64)

Self-Review Quiz 2-3

(The blank forms you need are on pages 2-2 to 2-4 of the *Study Guide with Working Papers*.)

As the bookkeeper of Pam's Hair Salon, you are to prepare from the following accounts on June 30, 2014: (1) a trial balance as of June 30; (2) an income statement for the month ended June 30; (3) a statement of owner's equity for the month ended June 30; and (4) a balance sheet as of June 30, 2014.

Cash 111		Accounts Payable 211		Salon Fees 411
4,500	300	300	700	3,500
2,000	100		400	1,000
1,000	1,200			4,500
300	1,300			
	2,600			
7,800	5,500			
2,300				

Accounts Receivable 121		Pam Jay, Capital 311	Rent Expense 511
1,000	300	4,000*	1,200
700			

Salon Equipment 131	Pam Jay, Withdrawals 321	Salon Supplies Expense 521
700	100	1,300

	Salaries Expense 531
	2,600

*No additional investments.

Solution to Self-Review Quiz 2-3

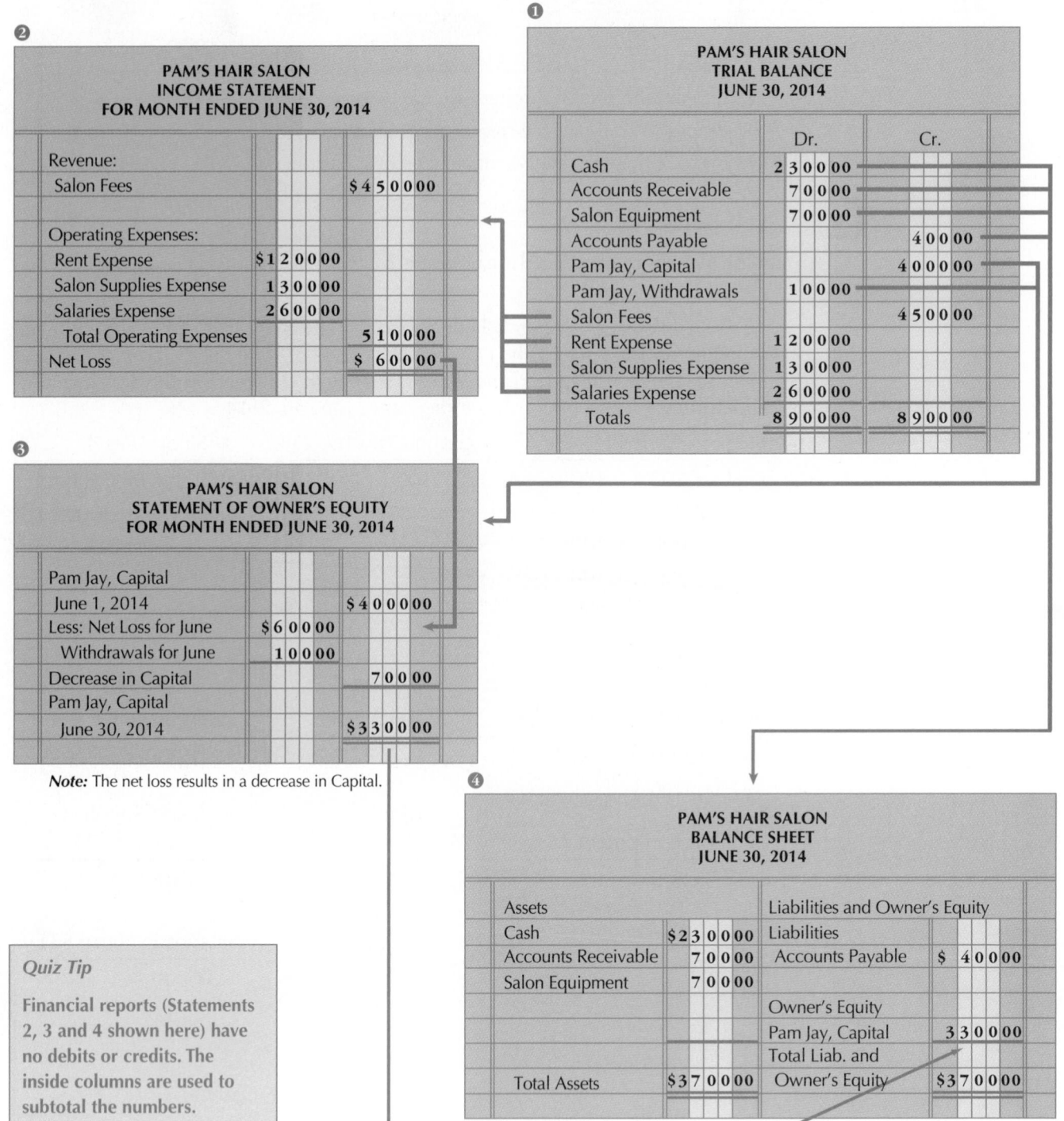

❷

PAM'S HAIR SALON
INCOME STATEMENT
FOR MONTH ENDED JUNE 30, 2014

Revenue:			
Salon Fees		$4 5 0 0 00	
Operating Expenses:			
Rent Expense	$1 2 0 0 00		
Salon Supplies Expense	1 3 0 0 00		
Salaries Expense	2 6 0 0 00		
Total Operating Expenses		5 1 0 0 00	
Net Loss		$ 6 0 0 00	

❶

PAM'S HAIR SALON
TRIAL BALANCE
JUNE 30, 2014

	Dr.	Cr.
Cash	2 3 0 0 00	
Accounts Receivable	7 0 0 00	
Salon Equipment	7 0 0 00	
Accounts Payable		4 0 0 00
Pam Jay, Capital		4 0 0 0 00
Pam Jay, Withdrawals	1 0 0 00	
Salon Fees		4 5 0 0 00
Rent Expense	1 2 0 0 00	
Salon Supplies Expense	1 3 0 0 00	
Salaries Expense	2 6 0 0 00	
Totals	8 9 0 0 00	8 9 0 0 00

❸

PAM'S HAIR SALON
STATEMENT OF OWNER'S EQUITY
FOR MONTH ENDED JUNE 30, 2014

Pam Jay, Capital			
June 1, 2014		$4 0 0 0 00	
Less: Net Loss for June	$6 0 0 00		
Withdrawals for June	1 0 0 00		
Decrease in Capital		7 0 0 00	
Pam Jay, Capital			
June 30, 2014		$3 3 0 0 00	

Note: The net loss results in a decrease in Capital.

Quiz Tip

Financial reports (Statements 2, 3 and 4 shown here) have no debits or credits. The inside columns are used to subtotal the numbers.

❹

PAM'S HAIR SALON
BALANCE SHEET
JUNE 30, 2014

Assets		Liabilities and Owner's Equity	
Cash	$2 3 0 0 00	Liabilities	
Accounts Receivable	7 0 0 00	Accounts Payable	$ 4 0 0 00
Salon Equipment	7 0 0 00		
		Owner's Equity	
		Pam Jay, Capital	3 3 0 0 00
		Total Liab. and	
Total Assets	$3 7 0 0 00	Owner's Equity	$3 7 0 0 00

Let's review first: The trial balance is a list of accounts and their ending balances. Each account will have either a debit or credit balance (but not both). When a trial balance is complete the total of all the debits must equal the total of all the credits. When preparing a trial balance you list out assets, liabilities, capital, withdrawals, revenue, and expenses.

Trial balance: After you have taken the balance of the Cash account in the ledger, it has a debit balance of 2,300 (we added the debits, we added the credits, and we took the difference between them, which resulted in 2,300 more on the left side). For Accounts Receivable 1,000 less 300 leaves us with a 700 debit balance. Salon Equipment has one number so that is the balance (700 debit). Once Accounts Payable is balanced it is 400 larger on the credit side (700–300). The only other title that needs footing is Salon Fees, so the 3,500 and 1,000 are added together for a credit balance of 4,500. Once each balance is listed, the sum on the left (8,900) does indeed equal the sum on the right (8,900). Each ending balance for Pam's Hair Salon ends up on the normal balance side.

	Dr.	Cr.
Cash	x	
Acc. Rec.	x	
Salon Equip.	x	
Acc. Pay.		x
Pam Jay, Cap.		x
Pam Jay, Withd.	x	
Salon Fees		x
Rent Exp.	x	
Salon Supp. Exp.	x	
Salaries Exp.	x	

Note that titles on the trial balance are not indented.

Income Statement: Once the trial balance is complete, the first report to make is the income statement, which is made up of only revenue and expense. Remember that there are no debits or credits on financial reports. All we are taking are the ending balances of each title from the trial balance. For the income statement, we list salon fees as the revenue and then list the three expense titles in the inside column. Total operating expenses are then subtracted from the salon fees to arrive at a net loss. Here revenue is less than operating expenses ($4,500–$5,100).

Statement of Owner's Equity: The second report to prepare is the statement of owner's equity, which shows how to calculate a new figure for capital. Note that in this case, the net loss of $600 is ADDED to the $100 of withdrawals, resulting in a decrease of $700 to capital. The new figure for capital is $3,300 ($4,000–$700).

Balance Sheet: The third report is the balance sheet, which lists out each asset, liability, and the new figure for capital. This report shows that as of June 30 total assets is $3,700 and total liabilities and owner's equity is $3,700. Remember that the ending figure for capital comes from the statement of owner's equity.

SUMMARY

The trial balance is a list of ending balances of ledger accounts. These balances are used to prepare the three financial reports. Financial reports have no debits or credits. The inside columns are used to subtotal numbers. Revenue and expenses go on the income statement. Withdrawals and either net income or net loss go on the statement of owner's equity to calculate a new figure for capital. The balance sheet is a list of assets, liabilities, and the new amount for ending capital. Remember that the trial balance has debit or credits, not the financial reports.

When Stan took the big leap from being an employee to a Subway owner, the thing that terrified him most was not the part about managing people—that was one of his strengths as a marketing manager. Why, at Xellent Media, 40 sales reps reported to him! No, Stan was terrified of having to manage the accounts. Subway restaurant owners have so many accounts to deal with—food costs, payroll, rent, utilities, supplies, advertising, promotion, and, biggest of all, cash. It's critical for them to keep debits and credits straight. If not, both they and Subway could lose a lot of money, quickly.

While Stan got some intense training in accounting and bookkeeping at Subway University, he still felt shaky about doing his own books. When he confided his fears to Mariah Washington, his field consultant, she suggested he hire an accountant. "You need to play to your strengths," said Mariah. "More and more owners are using accountants, and almost all owners of multiple franchises do. In fact, some accountants actually specialize in handling Subway accounts for these multi-restaurant owners."

Even though Stan decided to hire his cousin, Lila, to do his accounting, he still needs to feed her the right data so she can calculate his T accounts. Like many small business owners, Stan enters data

DEBITS ON THE LEFT

Recording transactions accurately **2** (20 min)

into an accounting software program such as QuickBooks® or Simply Accounting®, which he then uploads to his accountant, who edits it and reviews it for accuracy. Several times in the beginning, Stan mistakenly debited both cash and supplies when he paid for orders of paper cups, bread dough, and other supplies.

Lila urged Stan to review the rules for recording debits and credits. She even told him to practise for a while using a paper ledger. "On the computer, debits and credits are not as visible as they are with your paper system. Since you enter only the payables, the computer does the other side of the balance sheet. So you have to bone up on debits and credits to ensure that your QuickBooks® data is correct."

DISCUSSION QUESTIONS

1. Why is the cash account so important in Stan's business?
2. Why do you think that most owners of the larger shops use accountants to do their books instead of doing the books themselves?
3. Is the difference between debits and credits important to Subway restaurant owners who don't do their own books?

DEMONSTRATION PROBLEM

The chart of accounts of Mel's Delivery Service includes the following: Cash, 111; Accounts Receivable, 112; Office Equipment, 121; Delivery Trucks, 122; Accounts Payable, 211; Mel Free, Capital, 311; Mel Free, Withdrawals, 312; Delivery Fees Earned, 411; Advertising Expense, 511; Gas Expense, 512; Salaries Expense, 513; and Telephone Expense, 514. The following transactions resulted for Mel's Delivery Service during the month of July 2014:

A. Mel invested $10,000 in the business from his personal savings account.

B. Bought delivery truck on account, $17,000.

C. Advertising bill received but unpaid, $700.

D. Bought office equipment for cash, $1,200.

E. Received cash for delivery services rendered, $15,000.

F. Paid salaries expense, $3,000.

G. Paid gas expense for company trucks, $1,250.

H. Billed customers for delivery services rendered, $4,000.

I. Paid telephone bill, $300.

J. Received $3,000 as partial payment of transaction H.

K. Mel paid home telephone bill from company chequebook, $150.

Assignment

As Mel's newly employed accountant, you must do the following:

1. Set up T accounts in a ledger.
2. Record transactions in the T accounts. (Place the letter of the transaction next to the entry.)
3. Foot and take the balance of each account where appropriate.
4. Prepare a trial balance at the end of July.
5. Prepare from the trial balance, in proper form, **a.** an income statement for the month of July, **b.** a statement of owner's equity, and **c.** a balance sheet as of July 31, 2014.

Solution to Demonstration Problem

1, 2, 3.   **GENERAL LEDGER**

Cash 111				Accounts Payable 211			Advertising Expense 511	
(A) 10,000	1,200	(D)			17,000	(B)	(C) 700	
(E) 15,000	3,000	(F)			700	(C)		
(J) 3,000	1,250	(G)			17,700			
	300	(I)						
	150	(K)						
28,000	5,900							
22,100								

Accounts Receivable 112		Mel Free, Capital 311		Gas Expense 512	
(H) 4,000	3,000 (J)		10,000 (A)	(G) 1,250	
1,000					

Office Equipment 121		Mel Free, Withdrawals 312		Salaries Expense 513	
(D) 1,200		(K) 150		(F) 3,000	

Delivery Trucks 122		Delivery Fees Earned 411		Telephone Expense 514	
(B) 17,000			15,000 (E)	(I) 300	
			4,000 (H)		
			19,000		

Solution Tips to Recording Transactions

A.	Cash	A	↑	Dr.
	Mel Free, Capital	Cap.	↑	Cr.

F.	Salaries Expense	Exp.	↑	Dr.
	Cash	A	↓	Cr.

B.	Delivery Trucks	A	↑	Dr.
	Accts. Payable	L	↑	Cr.

G.	Gas Expense	Exp.	↑	Dr.
	Cash	A	↓	Cr.

C.	Advertising Expense	Exp.	↑	Dr.
	Accts. Payable	L	↑	Cr.

H.	Accts. Receivable	A	↑	Dr.
	Del. Fees Earned	Rev.	↑	Cr.

D.	Office Equipment	A	↑	Dr.
	Cash	A	↓	Cr.

I.	Tel. Expense	Exp.	↑	Dr.
	Cash	A	↓	Cr.

E.	Cash	A	↑	Dr.
	Del. Fees Earned	Rev.	↑	Cr.

J.	Cash	A	↑	Dr.
	Accts. Receivable	A	↓	Cr.

K.	Mel Free, Withdr.	Withdr.	↑	Dr.
	Cash	A	↓	Cr.

4.

Mel's Delivery Service
Trial Balance
July 31, 2014

	Dr.	Cr.
Cash	22,100	
Accounts Receivable	1,000	
Office Equipment	1,200	
Delivery Trucks	17,000	
Accounts Payable		17,700
Mel Free, Capital		10,000
Mel Free, Withdrawals	150	
Delivery Fees Earned		19,000
Advertising Expense	700	
Gas Expense	1,250	
Salaries Expense	3,000	
Telephone Expense	300	
Totals	46,700	46,700

Solution Tips to Taking the Balance of an Account and Preparation of a Trial Balance

3. Footings: Cash   Add left side, $28,000.
                                              Add right side, $5,900.
                                            Take difference, $22,100, and stay on side that is larger.

                   Accounts Payable   Add $17,000 + $700 and stay on same side. Total is $17,700.

4. Trial balance is a list of the ledger's ending balances. The list is in the same order as the chart of accounts. Each title has only one number listed, either as a debit or credit balance.

Figure 2-4 **5(a)**
Financial Reports

MEL'S DELIVERY SERVICE
INCOME STATEMENT
FOR MONTH ENDED JULY 31, 2014

Revenue:		
Delivery Fees Earned		$19 000 00
Operating Expenses:		
Advertising Expense	$ 7 00 00	
Gas Expense	1 2 5 0 00	
Salaries Expense	3 0 0 0 00	
Telephone Expense	3 0 0 00	
Total Operating Expenses		5 2 5 0 00
Net Income		$13 7 5 0 00

(b)

MEL'S DELIVERY SERVICE
STATEMENT OF OWNER'S EQUITY
FOR MONTH ENDED JULY 31, 2014

Mel Free, Capital		
July 1, 2014		$10 0 0 0 00
Net Income for July	$13 7 5 0 00	
Less Withdrawals for July	1 5 0 00	
Increase in Capital		$13 6 0 0 00
Mel Free, Capital		
July 31, 2014		$23 6 0 0 00

(c)

MEL'S DELIVERY SERVICE
BALANCE SHEET
JULY 31, 2014

Assets		Liabilities and Owner's Equity	
Cash	$22 1 0 0 00	Liabilities	
Accounts Receivable	1 0 0 0 00	Accounts Payable	$17 7 0 0 00
Office Equipment	1 2 0 0 00		
Delivery Trucks	17 0 0 0 00		
		Owner's Equity	
		Mel Free, Capital	23 6 0 0 00
		Total Liab. and	
Total Assets	$41 3 0 0 00	Owner's Equity	$41 3 0 0 00

Solution Tips to Preparing Financial Statements from a Trial Balance

			Trial Balance	
			Dr.	**Cr.**
Balance Sheet	<	Assets	X	
		Liabilities		X
Statement of Equity	<	Capital		X
		Withdrawals	X	
Income Statement	<	Revenues		X
		Expenses	X	
			XX	XX

Net income of $13,750 on the income statement goes on the statement of owner's equity.

Ending capital of $23,600 on the statement of owner's equity goes on the balance sheet as the new figure for capital.

Note: Financial statements do not show debits or credits. The inside column is used for subtotalling.

SUMMARY OF KEY POINTS

Learning Unit 2-1

1. A T account is a simplified version of a standard account.
2. A ledger is a group of accounts.
3. A debit is the left-hand position (side) of an account and a credit is the right-hand position (side) of an account.
4. A footing is the total of one side of an account. The ending balance is the difference between the footings on the left and right sides.

Learning Unit 2-2

1. A chart of accounts for a company lists the account titles and their numbers.
2. The transaction analysis chart is a teaching device, not to be confused with standard accounting procedures.
3. A compound entry is a transaction involving more than one debit or credit.

Learning Unit 2-3

1. In double-entry bookkeeping, the recording of each business transaction affects two or more accounts, and the total of debits equals the total of credits.
2. A trial balance is a list of the ending balances of all accounts, listed in the same order as on the chart of accounts.
3. Any additional investments during the period will result in having a figure for capital in the trial balance different from the beginning figure for capital in the statement of owner's equity.
4. There are *no* debit or credit columns on the three financial statements.

KEY TERMS

Account An accounting device used in bookkeeping to record increases and decreases of business transactions relating to individual assets, liabilities, capital, withdrawals, revenue, and expenses (p. 47)

Chart of accounts A numbering system of accounts that lists the account titles and account numbers to be used by a company (p. 52)

Compound entry A transaction involving more than one debit or credit (p. 53)

Credit The right-hand side of any account. A number entered on the right side of any account is said to be credited to that account. (p. 48)

Debit The left-hand side of any account. A number entered on the left side of any account is said to be debited to that account. (p. 48)

Double-entry bookkeeping An accounting system in which the recording of each transaction affects two or more accounts, and the total of the debits is equal to the total of the credits (p. 53)

Ending balance The difference between footings in a T account (p. 49)

Footings The totals of each of the two sides of a T account (p. 49)

Ledger A group of accounts that records data from business transactions (p. 47)

Normal balance of an account The side of an account that increases by the rules of debit and credit (p. 51)

Standard account A formal account that includes columns for date, explanation, posting reference, debit, and credit amounts (p. 47)

T account A skeleton version of a standard account, used for demonstration purposes (p. 47)

Trial balance A list of the ending balances of all the accounts in a ledger. The total of the debits should equal the total of the credits. (p. 63)

BLUEPRINT FOR PREPARING FINANCIAL STATEMENTS FROM A TRIAL BALANCE

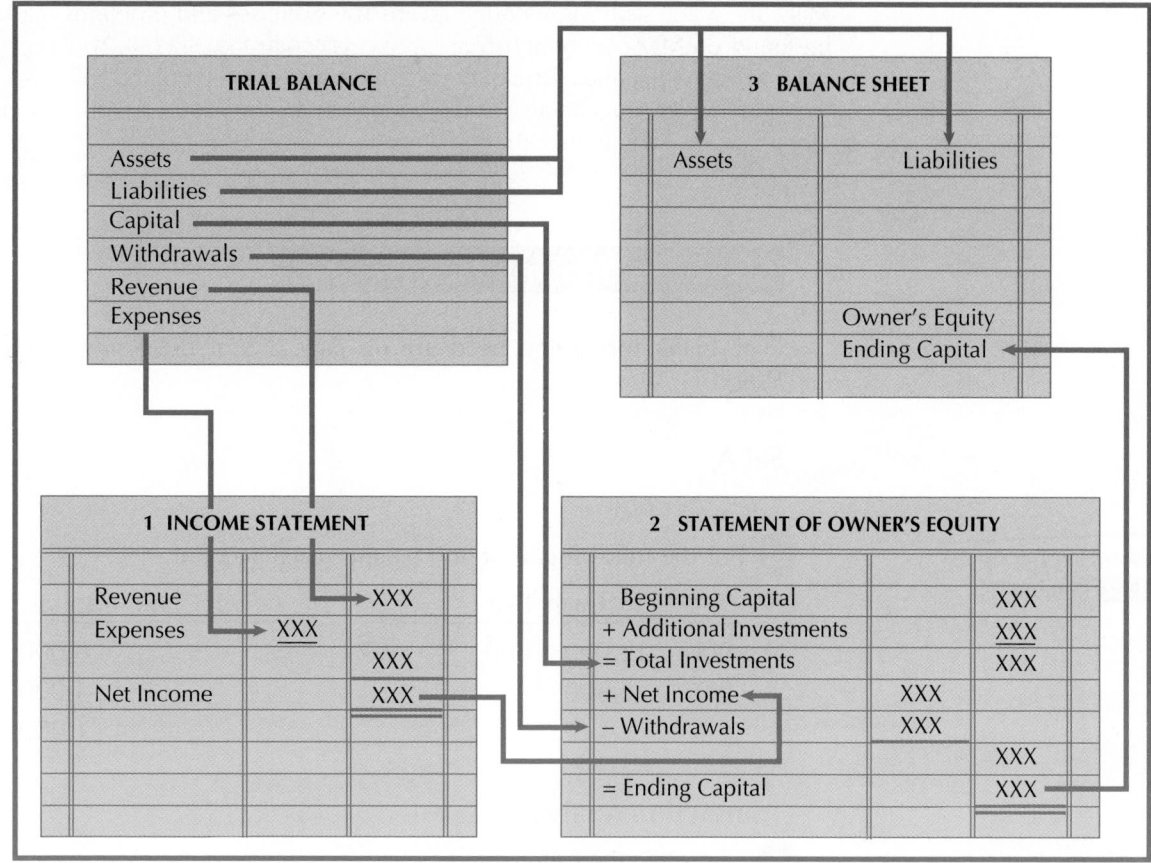

QUESTIONS, CLASSROOM DEMONSTRATION EXERCISES, EXERCISES, AND PROBLEMS

Discussion Questions and Critical Thinking/Ethical Case

1. Define a ledger.
2. Why is the left-hand side of an account called a debit?
3. Footings are used in balancing all accounts. True or false? Please explain.
4. What is the end product of the accounting process?
5. What do we mean when we say that a transaction analysis chart is a teaching device?
6. What are the five steps of the transaction analysis chart?
7. Explain the concept of double-entry bookkeeping.
8. A trial balance is a formal report. True or false? Please explain.
9. Why are there no debit or credit columns on financial reports?
10. Compare the financial statements prepared from the expanded accounting equation with those prepared from a trial balance.
11. Audrey Flet, the bookkeeper of ALN Co., was scheduled to leave on a three-week vacation at 5:00 on Friday. She couldn't get the company's trial balance to balance. At 4:30, she decided to put in fictitious figures to make it balance. Audrey told herself she would fix it when she got back from her vacation. Was Audrey right or wrong to do this? Why?

MyAccountingLab

Make the grade with MyAccountingLab! The exercises and problems marked in green can be found on MyAccountingLab at **www.myaccountinglab.com**. You can practise them as often as you want, and many of them feature step-by-step guided solutions to help you find the right answer. You can also find working papers for selected problems in the Multimedia Library on MyAccountingLab.

Classroom Demonstration Exercises

(The blank forms you need are on page 2-8 of the *Study Guide with Working Papers*.)

Set A

The T Account

Balancing T accounts
❶❷ (5 min)

1. For the following, foot and balance each account.

Cash 110			
9/5	12,000	800	9/7
9/9	6,000		

C. Clark, Capital 311	
6,000	6/9
4,000	9/3
1,000	9/7

Transaction Analysis

Analyzing transactions
❶ (5 min)

2. Complete the following:

Account	Category	↑	↓	Normal Balance
A. Accounts Payable	Liability	Cr.	Dr.	Cr.
B. Taxable Fees Earned				
C. Accounts Receivable				
D. M. Blanc, Capital				
E. M. Blanc, Withdrawals				
F. Prepaid Advertising				
G. Rent Expense				

Transaction Analysis

Analyzing and recording
transactions
2 (5 min)

3. Record the following transaction in the transaction analysis chart: Provided bookkeeping services for $2,500, receiving $600 cash with the remainder to be paid next month.

Accounts Affected	Category	↓	↑	Rules of Dr. and Cr.	T Accounts

Trial Balance

Preparing a trial balance
3 (5 min)

4. Rearrange the following titles in the order in which they would appear in a trial balance:

J. Joy, Withdrawals   Hair Salon Fees Earned
Accounts Receivable   Utility Expense
Cash   Salary Expense
J. Joy, Capital   Advertising Expense
Office Equipment   Accounts Payable

Trial Balance/Financial Statements

Preparing financial statements
from a trial balance
4 (10 min)

5. For the following trial balance, identify the statement in the following list in which each title will appear:

◆ Income Statement (IS)
◆ Statement of Owner's Equity (OE)
◆ Balance Sheet (BS)

Bernie Co.
Trial Balance
November 20, 2012

		Dr.	Cr.
A. _____	Cash	500	
B. _____	Accounts Receivable	200	
C. _____	Computer Equipment	600	
D. _____	Accounts Payable		900
E. _____	L. Bernard, Capital		240
F. _____	L. Bernard, Withdrawals	250	
G. _____	Legal Fees Earned		1,000
H. _____	Director's Fees Earned		500
I. _____	Wage Expense	300	
J. _____	Supplies Expense	700	
K. _____	Internet Advertising Expense	90	
	TOTALS	2,640	2,640

Set B

The T Account

Balancing T accounts
①② (5 min)

1. For the following, foot and balance each account.

Cash 110					C. Clark, Capital 311	
5/8	3,000	1,000	5/11		8,000	4/9
5/12	9,000				4,000	4/12
					9,000	5/2

Transaction Analysis

Analyzing transactions
② (5 min)

2. Complete the following:

Account	Category	↑	↓	Normal Balance
A. Digital Cameras	Asset	Dr.	Cr.	Dr.
B. Prepaid Rent				
C. Accounts Payable				
D. A. Sung, Capital				
E. A. Sung, Withdrawals				
F. Legal Fees Earned				
G. Salary Expense				

Transaction Analysis

Analyzing and recording transactions
② (5 min)

3. Record the following transaction in the transaction analysis chart: Provided legal services for $4,000, receiving $3,000 cash with the remainder to be paid next month.

Accounts Affected	Category	↓	↑	Rules of Dr. and Cr.	T Accounts

Trial Balance

4. Rearrange the following titles in the order in which they would appear in a trial balance:

Salaries Expense   Legal Fees Earned
Accounts Receivable   D. Cope, Withdrawals
Accounts Payable   Rent Expense
D. Cope, Capital   Advertising Expense
Computer Equipment   Cash

Trial Balance/Financial Statements

Preparing financial statements
from a trial balance
4 (10 min)

5. For the following trial balance, identify the statement in the following list in which each title will appear:

◆ Income Statement (IS)
◆ Statement of Owner's Equity (OE)
◆ Balance Sheet (BS)

Logan Co.
Trial Balance
September 30, 2012

		Dr.	Cr.
A. _____	Cash	390	
B. _____	Supplies	100	
C. _____	Office Equipment	200	
D. _____	Accounts Payable		100
E. _____	D. Logan, Capital		450
F. _____	D. Logan, Withdrawals	160	
G. _____	Hair Salon Fees		290
H. _____	Cosmetic Sales		300
I. _____	Salaries Expense	130	
J. _____	Rent Expense	120	
K. _____	Advertising Expense	40	
	TOTALS	1,140	1,140

Exercises

(The blank forms you need are on pages 2-9 and 2-10 of the *Study Guide with Working Papers*.)

2-1. From the following titles, prepare a chart of accounts using the same numbering system as used in this chapter.

Panasonic HD Television   Legal Fees
Salary Expense   L. Jones, Capital
Accounts Payable   Cash
Accounts Receivable   Advertising Expense
Repair Expense   L. Jones, Withdrawals

2-2. Record the following transaction in the transaction analysis chart: Sandy Pointer bought a new piece of computer equipment for $19,000, paying $3,000 down and agreeing to pay the balance in 30 days.

2-3. Complete the following table. For each account listed on the left, indicate the category to which it belongs, whether increases and decreases in the account are marked on the debit or credit side, and in which financial report the account appears. A sample is provided.

Accounts Affected	Category	↑	↓	Appears on Which Financial Report
Supplies	Asset	Dr.	Cr.	Balance Sheet
Legal Fees Earned				
P. Rey, Withdrawals				
Accounts Payable				
Salaries Expense				
Auto				

2-4. Given the following accounts, complete the table by inserting the appropriate number next to each individual transaction to indicate which account is debited and which account is credited.

1. Cash
2. Accounts Receivable
3. Equipment
4. Accounts Payable
5. B. Baker, Capital

6. B. Baker, Withdrawals
7. Plumbing Fees Earned
8. Salaries Expense
9. Advertising Expense
10. Supplies Expense

Transaction	Rules	
	Dr.	Cr.
A. Paid salaries expense.	8	1
B. Bob paid personal utilities bill from company bank account.		
C. Advertising bill was received but not yet paid.		
D. Received cash from plumbing fees.		
E. Paid supplies expense.		
F. Bob invested additional equipment in the business.		
G. Billed customers for plumbing services rendered.		
H. Received one-half the balance from transaction G.		
I. Bought equipment on account.		

2-5. From the following trial balance of Hall's Cleaners, prepare the following:
◆ Income statement
◆ Statement of owner's equity
◆ Balance sheet

HALL'S CLEANERS TRIAL BALANCE JULY 31, 2013		
	Dr.	Cr.
Cash	5 5 0 00	
Equipment	6 9 2 00	
Accounts Payable		4 5 5 00
J. Hall, Capital		8 0 0 00
J. Hall, Withdrawals	1 9 8 00	
Cleaning Fees		4 5 8 00
Salaries Expense	1 6 0 00	
Utilities Expense	1 1 3 00	
Totals	1 7 1 3 00	1 7 1 3 00

Group A Problems

(The forms you need are on pages 2-11 to 2-16 of the *Study Guide with Working Papers.*)

Using a transaction analysis chart
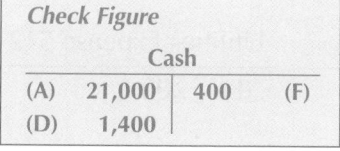
❶ (20 min)

2A-1. The following transactions occurred in the opening and operation of Bills's Delivery Service of Charlottetown:

A. Bill O'Brien opened the delivery service by investing $21,000 from his personal savings account.

B. Purchased used delivery trucks on account, $9,000.

C. Rent expense was due but unpaid, $900.

D. Received cash for services rendered, $1,400.

E. Billed a client on account, $150.

F. Bill withdrew cash for his personal use, $400.

Check Figure

Cash		
(A)	21,000	400	(F)
(D)	1,400		

Complete the transaction analysis chart in the *Study Guide with Working Papers.* The chart of accounts includes Cash; Accounts Receivable; Delivery; Accounts Payable; Bill O'Brien, Capital; Bill O'Brien, Withdrawals; Delivery Fees Earned; and Rent Expense.

Recording transactions in ledger accounts
❶ (20 min)

2A-2. Bernie Pillows opened a consulting company in Fairview and the following transactions resulted:

A. Bernie invested $20,000 in the consulting business.

B. Bought office equipment on account, $5,000.

C. Received cash for consulting work that it completed for a client, $900.

D. Bernie paid a personal bill from the company bank account, $90.

E. Paid advertising expense for the month, $400.

F. Rent expense for the month was due but not yet paid, $1,400.

G. Paid $1,000 as partial payment of what was owed from the transaction in **B.**

Check Figure

Cash		
(A)	20,000	90	(D)
(C)	900	400	(E)
		1,000	(G)

As Bernie's accountant, analyze and record the transactions in T account form. Set up the T accounts on the basis of the chart of accounts on page 82. Enter each transaction in the appropriate T account and label it with the letter of the transaction.

Chart of Accounts

Assets
Cash 111
Office Equipment 121

Liabilities
Accounts Payable 211

Owner's Equity
Bernie Pillows, Capital 311
Bernie Pillows, Withdrawals 312

Revenue
Consulting Fees Earned 411

Expenses
Advertising Expense 511
Rent Expense 512

Preparing a trial balance from the T accounts
3 (20 min)

2A-3. From the following T accounts of Barry's Cleaning Service of Yarmouth, **a.** record and foot the balances on the appropriate pages in the *Study Guide with Working Papers*, and **b.** prepare a trial balance in proper form for May 31, 2013.

Cash 111			
(A)	7,000	200	(D)
(G)	3,500	200	(E)
		400	(F)
		200	(H)
		900	(I)

Accounts Payable 211			
(D)	200	1,300	(C)

Fees Earned 411	
8,000	(B)

Check Figure

Trial Balance Total $16,100

Accounts Receivable 112			
(B)	8,000	3,500	(G)

Barry Joy, Capital 311	
7,000	(A)

Rent Expense 511	
(F) 400	

Office Equipment 121	
(C)	1,300
(H)	200

Barry Joy, Withdrawals 312	
(I) 900	

Utilities Expense 512	
(E) 200	

Preparing financial reports from the trial balance
4 (40 min)

2A-4. From the trial balance of Grace Lantz, Barrister and Solicitor, of Winnipeg, prepare **a.** an income statement for the month of May, **b.** a statement of owner's equity for the month ended May 31, and **c.** a balance sheet as of May 31, 2014.

Check Figure

Total Assets $6,400

GRACE LANTZ, Barrister and Solicitor
TRIAL BALANCE
MAY 31, 2014

	Dr.	Cr.
Cash	5 000 00	
Accounts Receivable	6 5 0 00	
Office Equipment	7 5 0 00	
Accounts Payable		4 3 0 0 00
Salaries Payable		6 7 5 00
G. Lantz, Capital		1 2 7 5 00
G. Lantz, Withdrawals	3 0 0 00	
Revenue from Legal Fees		2 3 5 0 00
Utilities Expense	3 0 0 00	
Rent Expense	4 5 0 00	
Salaries Expense	1 1 5 0 00	
Totals	8 6 0 0 00	8 6 0 0 00

82   CHAPTER 2

2A-5. The chart of accounts for Angel's Delivery Service of Flin Flon is as follows:

Chart of Accounts

Assets	**Revenue**
Cash 111	Delivery Fees Earned 411
Accounts Receivable 112	
Office Equipment 121	**Expenses**
Delivery Trucks 122	Advertising Expense 511
	Gas Expense 512
Liabilities	Salaries Expense 513
Accounts Payable 211	Telephone Expense 514

Owner's Equity
Alice Angel, Capital 311
Alice Angel, Withdrawals 312

Check Figure

Trial Balance Total $38,100

Angel's Delivery Service completed the following transactions during the month of March 2013:

A. Alice Angel invested $16,000 in the delivery service from her personal savings account.

B. Bought delivery trucks on account, $18,000.

C. Bought office equipment for cash, $600.

D. Paid advertising expense, $250.

E. Collected cash for delivery services rendered, $2,600.

F. Paid drivers' salaries, $900.

G. Paid gas expense for trucks, $1,200.

H. Performed delivery services for a customer on account, $800.

I. Telephone expense was due but not yet paid, $700.

J. Received $300 as partial payment of transaction H.

K. Alice Angel withdrew cash for personal use, $300.

As Alice's newly employed accountant, you must:

1. Set up T accounts in a ledger.

2. Record transactions in the T accounts. (Place the letter of the transaction next to the entry.)

3. Foot the T accounts where appropriate.

4. Prepare a trial balance at the end of March 2013.

5. Prepare from the trial balance, in proper form, **a.** an income statement for the month of March, **b.** a statement of owner's equity for the month of March, and **c.** a balance sheet as of March 31, 2013.

(The forms you need are on pages 2-11 to 2-16 of the *Study Guide with Working Papers.*)

Using a transaction analysis chart

2 (20 min)

Check Figure

Cash

2,500	275
1,200	

2B-1. Bill O'Brien decided to open a delivery service in Charlottetown. Record the following transactions in the transaction analysis charts:

- **A.** Bill invested $2,500 in the delivery service from his personal savings account.
- **B.** Purchased a delivery truck on account, $900.
- **C.** Rent expense was due but unpaid, $250.
- **D.** Performed delivery services for cash, $1,200.
- **E.** Billed clients for deliveries rendered, $700.
- **F.** Bill paid his home heating bill using a company cheque, $275.

The chart of accounts for the delivery service includes Cash; Accounts Receivable; Delivery Truck; Accounts Payable; Bill O'Brien, Capital; Bill O'Brien, Withdrawals; Fees Earned; and Rent Expense.

Recording transactions in ledger accounts

1 (20 min)

Check Figure

Cash

(A)	20,000	200	(D)
(C)	1,200	600	(E)
		400	(G)

2B-2. Bernie Pillows established a new consulting company in Fairview. Record the following transactions for Bernie in T account form. Label each entry with the letter of the transaction.

- **A.** Bernie invested $20,000 in the consulting business from his personal bank account.
- **B.** Bought office equipment on account, $6,000.
- **C.** Company rendered consulting to Jensen Corp. and received cash, $1,200.
- **D.** Bernie withdrew cash for personal use, $200.
- **E.** Paid advertising expense, $600.
- **F.** Rent expense was due but not yet paid, $500.
- **G.** Paid $400 in partial payment of transaction B.

The chart of accounts includes Cash, 111; Office Equipment, 121; Accounts Payable, 211; Bernie Pillows, Capital, 311; Bernie Pillows, Withdrawals, 312; Consulting Fees Earned, 411; Advertising Expense, 511; and Rent Expense, 512.

Preparing a trial balance from the T accounts

3 (20 min)

Check Figure

Trial Balance Total $20,000

2B-3. From the following T accounts of Barry's Cleaning Service of Yarmouth, **a.** record and foot the balances on the appropriate pages in the *Study Guide with Working Papers,* and **b.** prepare a trial balance for May 31, 2013.

Cash 111			Accounts Receivable 112		Office Equipment 121	
(A) 10,000	4,000 (C)	(G) 2,000		(B) 2,000	
(F) 4,000	310 (D)			(C) 4,000	
(G) 2,000	50 (E)				
	600 (H)				

Accounts Payable 211	Barry Joy, Capital 311	Barry Joy, Withdrawals 312
2,000 (B)	10,000 (A)	(H) 600

Fees Earned 411	Rent Expense 511	Utilities Expense 512
4,000 (F)	(D) 310	(E) 50
4,000 (G)		

Preparing financial statements
from the trial balance

4 (40 min)

2B-4. From the trial balance of Grace Lantz, Barrister and Solicitor of Winnipeg, prepare **a.** an income statement for the month of May, **b.** a statement of owner's equity for the month ended May 31, and **c.** a balance sheet as of May 31, 2014.

GRACE LANTZ, Barrister and Solicitor TRIAL BALANCE MAY 31, 2014	Dr.	Cr.
Cash	6 0 0 0 00	
Accounts Receivable	2 4 0 0 00	
Office Equipment	2 4 0 0 00	
Accounts Payable		2 0 0 00
Salaries Payable		6 0 0 00
G. Lantz, Capital		4 0 0 0 00
G. Lantz, Withdrawals	2 0 0 0 00	
Revenue from Legal Fees		9 8 0 0 00
Utilities Expense	1 0 0 00	
Rent Expense	3 0 0 00	
Salaries Expense	1 4 0 0 00	
Totals	14 6 0 0 00	14 6 0 0 00

Check Figure

Total Assets $10,800

Comprehensive problem

1 **3** **4** (60 min)

2B-5. The chart of accounts of Angel's Delivery Service of Flin Flon includes the following: Cash, 111; Accounts Receivable, 112; Office Equipment, 121; Delivery Trucks, 122; Accounts Payable, 211; Alice Angel, Capital, 311; Alice Angel, Withdrawals, 312; Delivery Fees Earned, 411; Advertising Expense, 511; Gas Expense, 512; Salaries Expense, 513; and Telephone Expense, 514. The following transactions resulted from Angel's Delivery Service during the month of March 2013:

A. Alice invested $40,000 in the business from her personal savings account.

B. Bought delivery trucks on account, $25,000.

C. Advertising bill was received but not yet paid, $800.

D. Bought office equipment for cash, $2,500.

E. Received cash for delivery services rendered, $13,000.

F. Paid salaries expense, $1,850.

G. Paid gas expense for company trucks, $750.

H. Billed customers for delivery services rendered, $5,500.

I. Paid telephone bill, $400.

J. Received $1,600 as partial payment of transaction H.

K. Alice paid her home telephone bill with a company cheque, $88.

As Alice's newly employed accountant, you must:

1. Set up T accounts in a ledger.
2. Record transactions in the T accounts. (Place the letter of the transaction next to the entry.)
3. Foot the T accounts where appropriate.
4. Prepare a trial balance at the end of March 2013.

Check Figure

Trial Balance Total $84,300

5. Prepare from the trial balance, in proper form, **a.** an income statement for the month of March, **b.** a statement of owner's equity for the month ended March 31, and **c.** a balance sheet as of March 31, 2013.

Group C Problems

(The forms you need are on pages 2-17 to 2-21 of the *Study Guide with Working Papers.*)

Using a transaction analysis chart

1 (20 min)

2C-1. Janis Evans decided to open an editing service in Vernon. Record the following transactions in the transaction analysis charts:

    A. Janis invested $3,000 in the editing service from her personal savings account.

    B. Purchased office equipment on account, $1,875.

    C. Rent expense was due but not yet paid, $425.

    D. Performed editing services for cash, $2,100.

    E. Billed clients for editing services provided, $1,490.

    F. Janis paid a home repair bill from the company bank account, $160.

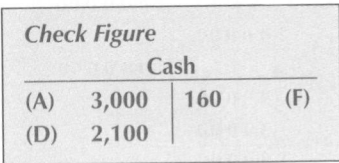

The chart of accounts for the business includes Cash; Accounts Receivable; Office Equipment; Accounts Payable; Janis Evans, Capital; Janis Evans, Withdrawals; Editing Fees Earned; and Rent Expense.

Recording transactions in ledger accounts

1 (20 min)

2C-2. Tom Caper of Halifax established a graphics company. Record the following transactions for Tom in T account form. Label each entry with the letter of the transaction.

    A. Tom Caper invested $14,000 in the business from his personal bank account.

    B. Bought computer equipment on account, $5,800.

    C. Business rendered service to Portias Corp. and received cash, $3,250.

    D. Tom Caper withdrew cash for personal use, $364.

    E. Paid advertising expense, $725.

    F. Rent expense was due but not yet paid, $615.

    G. Paid $2,900 in partial payment of transaction B.

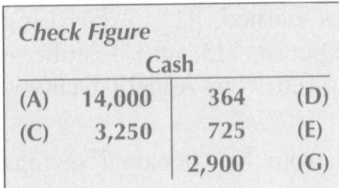

The chart of accounts includes Cash, 111; Office Equipment, 121; Accounts Payable, 211; Tom Caper, Capital, 311; Tom Caper, Withdrawals, 312; Graphics Fees Earned, 411; Advertising Expense, 511; and Rent Expense, 512.

Preparing a trial balance from the T accounts
3 (20 min)

2C-3. From the following T accounts of Carl's Consulting Service of Taber, **a.** record and foot the balances on the appropriate pages in the *Study Guide with Working Papers*, and **b.** prepare a trial balance for October 31, 2014.

Check Figure

Trial Balance Total $14,500

Cash 111				Accounts Receivable 112		Equipment 121	
(A) 6,000	4,000 (B)			(G) 1,000		(B) 4,000	
(F) 4,000	340 (D)					(C) 500	
(G) 3,000	150 (E)						
	800 (H)						

Accounts Payable 211		Carl Tyrell, Capital 311		Carl Tyrell, Withdrawals 312	
	500 (C)		6,000 (A)	(H) 800	

Fees Earned 411		Rent Expense 511		Utilities Expense 512	
	4,000 (F)	(D) 340		(E) 150	
	4,000 (G)				

Preparing financial statements from the trial balance
4 (40 min)

2C-4. From the trial balance shown below for Glenda Shaver, an architect from Peterborough, prepare **a.** an income statement for the month of June, **b.** a statement of owner's equity for the month ended June 30, and **c.** a balance sheet as of June 30, 2014.

Check Figure

Total Assets $9,740

GLENDA SHAVER, Architect TRIAL BALANCE JUNE 30, 2014	Dr.	Cr.
Cash	2 2 0 0 00	
Accounts Receivable	1 0 7 5 00	
Supplies	2 6 5 00	
Equipment	6 2 0 0 00	
Accounts Payable		6 2 0 00
Glenda Shaver, Capital		5 6 0 0 00
Glenda Shaver, Withdrawals	9 5 0 00	
Fees Earned		6 7 1 5 00
Rent Expense	1 2 0 0 00	
Advertising Expense	4 8 0 00	
Utilities Expense	5 6 5 00	
Totals	1 2 9 3 5 00	1 2 9 3 5 00

2C-5. The chart of accounts of Clara's Design Service of Montreal includes the following: Cash, 111; Accounts Receivable, 112; Office Equipment, 121; Design Equipment, 122; Accounts Payable, 211; Clara Benson, Capital, 311; Clara Benson, Withdrawals, 312; Design Fees Earned, 411; Advertising Expense, 511; Repair Expense, 512; Salaries Expense, 513; and Telephone Expense, 514. The following transactions occurred for Clara's Design Service during the month of March 2014:

A.   Clara invested $33,000 in the business from her personal savings account.

B.   Bought design equipment on account, $14,000.

C.   Advertising bill was received but not yet paid, $1,150.

D.   Bought office equipment for cash, $3,300.

E.   Received cash for design services rendered, $5,900.

F.   Paid salaries expense, $1,720.

G.   Paid repair expense for design equipment, $320.

H.   Billed customers for design services rendered, $4,300.

I.   Paid telephone bill, $150.

J.   Received $2,000 as partial payment of transaction H.

K.   Clara paid home telephone bill from company bank account, $66.

L.   Paid $700 on the bill received in transaction C.

As Clara's newly employed accountant, your task is to:

1. Set up T accounts in a ledger.

2. Record transactions in the T accounts. (Place the letter of the transaction next to the entry.)

3. Foot the T accounts where appropriate.

4. Prepare a trial balance for the end of March 2014.

5. Prepare from the trial balance, in proper form, **a.** an income statement for the month of March, **b.** a statement of owner's equity for the month ended March 31, and **c.** a balance sheet as of March 31, 2014.

(The forms you need are on pages 2-22 and 2-23 of the *Study Guide with Working Papers*.)

Preparing a trial balance from accurate transactions

❸ (20 min)

T-1. Andy Leaf is a careless bookkeeper. He is having a terrible time getting his trial balance to balance. Andy has asked for your assistance in preparing a correct trial balance. The following is the incorrect trial balance.

RANCH COMPANY
TRIAL BALANCE
JUNE 30, 2014

	Dr.	Cr.
Cash	5 1 0 00	
Accounts Receivable		6 3 5 00
Office Equipment	2 6 0 00	
Accounts Payable	1 0 00	
Wages Payable	1 0 00	
H. Clo, Capital	6 3 5 00	
H. Clo, Withdrawals	1 4 4 0 00	
Professional Fees		2 2 4 0 00
Rent Expense		2 4 0 00
Advertising Expense	2 5 00	
Totals	2 8 9 0 00	3 1 1 5 00

Facts you have discovered:

◆ Debits to the Cash account were $2,640; credits to the Cash account were $2,150.

◆ Amy Hall paid $15, but this was not updated in Accounts Receivable.

◆ A purchase of office equipment for $105 on account was never recorded in the ledger.

◆ Revenue was understated in the ledger by $180.

Show how the trial balance will indeed balance once these are corrected.

Tell Ranch Company how it can avoid this problem in the future. Write out your recommendations.

Preparing accurate transaction records ensures the trial balance will be correct

❸ (20 min)

T-2. Cookie Mejias, owner of Mejias Company, asked her bookkeeper how each of the following situations will affect the totals of the trial balance and individual ledger accounts.

◆ An $850 payment for a desk was recorded as a debit to Office Equipment, $85, and a credit to Cash, $85.

◆ A payment of $300 to a creditor was recorded as a debit to Accounts Payable, $300, and a credit to Cash, $100.

◆ An Accounts Receivable collection of $400 was recorded as a debit to Cash, $400, and a credit to C. Mejias, Capital, $400.

◆ The payment of a liability of $400 was recorded as a debit to Accounts Payable, $40, and a credit to Supplies, $40.

◆ A purchase of equipment for $800 was recorded as a debit to Supplies, $800, and a credit to Cash, $800.

◆ A payment of $95 to a creditor was recorded as a debit to Accounts Payable, $95, and a credit to Cash, $59.

What did the bookkeeper tell Cookie? Which accounts were overstated and which were understated? Which were correct? Explain in writing how mistakes can be avoided in the future.

CONTINUING PROBLEM

The Precision Computer Centre created its chart of accounts as follows:

Chart of Accounts
as of May 1, 2013

Assets
1000	Cash
1020	Accounts Receivable
1025	Prepaid Rent
1030	Supplies
1080	Computer Shop Equipment
1090	Office Equipment

Liabilities
2000	Accounts Payable

Owner's Equity
3000	T. Freedman, Capital
3010	T. Freedman, Withdrawals

Revenue
4000	Service Revenue

Expenses
5010	Advertising Expense
5020	Rent Expense
5030	Utilities Expense
5040	Phone Expense
5050	Supplies Expense
5060	Insurance Expense
5070	Postage Expense

You will use this chart of accounts to complete the Continuing Problem.

The following problem continues from Chapter 1. The balances as of May 31 have been brought forward in your *Study Guide with Working Papers* on pages 2-24 to 2-25. Additional transactions in June were:

(k) Received the phone bill for the month of May, $155

(l) Paid $150 (cheque No. 205) for insurance for the month

(m) Paid $200 (cheque No. 206) of the amount due from transaction (d) in Chapter 1

(n) Paid advertising expense for the month, $1,400 (cheque No. 207)

(o) Billed a client (Jeannine Sparks) for services rendered, $850

(p) Collected $900 for services rendered—a cash sale

(q) Paid the electric bill in full for the month of May (cheque No. 208—transaction (h), Chapter 1), $85

(r) Paid cash (cheque No. 209) for $50 in stamps

(s) Purchased $200 worth of supplies from Computer Connection on account

Assignment

1. Set up T accounts in a ledger.
2. Record the transactions (k) through (s) in the appropriate T accounts.
3. Foot the T accounts where appropriate.
4. Prepare a trial balance at the end of June 2013.
5. From the trial balance, prepare an income statement, a statement of owner's equity, and a balance sheet for the two months ending June 30, 2013.

THE BIG PICTURE

When you take your next vacation, will you buy your airline ticket online or visit a travel agency? Chances are good that, even if you don't book online, you'll compare prices or check out hotels on your computer.

Travel companies know that an Internet presence is increasingly important to customers. In a tough Canadian market, smart companies are doing everything they can to maintain and grow their customer base.

For a generation of students who have grown up with online shopping, it may come as a surprise to know that just over 10 years ago ticket sales on WestJet's website accounted for less than 2% of bookings. Nowadays, the majority of tickets are purchased this way, and passengers routinely use the site to check in for their flight 24 hours beforehand. Some airlines are now allowing passengers with modern cell phones to display a boarding-pass code on their phone screens that can be read at the departure gate, thus saving some time before take-off.

But WestJet understands that, while having a strong Web presence is essential, nothing beats old-fashioned customer service. The airline revolutionized the way Canadians fly, staffing its flights with casually dressed flight attendants who generally treat everyone and everything in a casual manner—everything, that is, except for the pre-flight safety messages.

WestJet keeps its maintenance and training costs low by using only one type of aircraft—the Boeing 737 Next Generation series—and maximizes the use of its fleet, flying to 69 destinations with only 88 aircraft. This policy alone results in lower costs for the company, a goal that is further boosted by insisting that each aircraft is fitted with up-to-date engines and other parts to lower the operating cost per kilometre for what is probably the lowest in the industry.

Whatever the future holds for the Canadian airline industry, companies will continue to look at ways to combine high-tech services with a personal touch. In this, they are like savvy accountants who hope to thrive in the new economy. Most likely, you will accomplish all the activities in the *accounting cycle* on the computer. Yet, in order to help your client or company—let's say it's a local travel company—you'll need to be familiar with every step so you can explain results and correct any errors. Doing accounting steps manually while you are learning is the best way to prepare for this.

In this chapter, you'll learn how to perform the first activities in the accounting cycle: keeping a *journal* of business transactions, transferring journal information to a *general ledger*, and preparing a *trial balance*. Whether you do this manually or on a computer, the first step of the accounting cycle is the same: Business transactions occur and generate source documents. At WestJet, customers pay online with credit cards or in person with credit cards, cash, or debit cards. Source documents for such transactions will run the gamut from credit card receipts to cash register receipts, as well as electronic transaction summaries and deposit slips. All of these business transactions must be recorded accurately, either in a computerized journal or with ink in a traditional journal. Accuracy is extremely important because errors will throw off the rest of the accounting cycle.

Sources: Based on Paul Knowles, "The Little Airline That Could," *Tourist*, September 2001; information from Industry Canada, "Success Stories: WestJet Airlines," Electronic Commerce in Canada website, www.e-com.ic.gc.ca; WestJet Airlines website, www.westjet.com.

1 Journalizing—analyzing and recording business transactions into a journal (p. 92)
2 Posting—transferring information from a journal to a ledger (p. 101)
3 Preparing a trial balance (p. 109)

The normal accounting procedures that are performed over a period of time are called the **accounting cycle**. The accounting cycle takes place in a period of time called an **accounting period**. An accounting period is the period of time covered by the income statement. Although it can be any time period up to one year (e.g., one month or three months), most businesses use a one-year accounting period. The year can be either a **calendar year** (January 1 through December 31) or a fiscal year.

A **fiscal year** is an accounting period that runs for any 12 consecutive months, so it can be the same as a calendar year. A business can choose any fiscal year that is convenient. For example, some retailers may decide to end their fiscal year when inventories and business activity are at a low point, such as after the Christmas season. This is called a **natural business year**. Using a natural business year allows the business to count its year-end inventory when it is easiest to do so.

Businesses would not be able to operate successfully if they prepared financial statements only at the end of their calendar or fiscal year. That is why most businesses prepare **interim reports** on a monthly, quarterly, or semiannual basis and companies whose shares are traded on stock exchanges are required to produce these reports quarterly for reporting on stock exchanges.

In this chapter, as well as in Chapters 4 and 5, we will follow Brenda Clark's new business, Clark's Desktop Publishing Services. We will follow the normal accounting procedures that the business performs over a period of time. Clark has chosen to use a fiscal period of January 1 to December 31.

> This chapter covers steps 1 to 4 of the accounting cycle.

> 1 Journalizing—analyzing and recording business transactions into a journal

Learning Unit 3-1

Analyzing and Recording Business Transactions in a Journal: Steps 1 and 2 of the Accounting Cycle

THE GENERAL JOURNAL

> A business uses a journal to record transactions in chronological order. A ledger accumulates information from a journal. The journal and the ledger are in two different books.

Chapter 2 taught us how to analyze and record business transactions in T accounts, or ledger accounts. However, recording a debit in an account on one page of the ledger and recording the corresponding credit on a different page of the ledger can make it difficult to find errors. It would be much easier if all of the business's transactions were located in the same place. That is the function of the **journal** or **general journal**. Transactions are entered in the journal in chronological order (January 1, 8, 15, etc.) and then this recorded information is used to update the ledger accounts. In computerized accounting, a journal may be recorded on disk or in cloud computing, the accounting files may be stored off site.

> Journal—book of original entry
> Ledger—book of final entry

We will use a general journal, the simplest form of a journal, to record the transactions of Clark's Desktop Publishing Services. A transaction (debit[s] + credit[s]) that has been analyzed and recorded in a journal is called a **journal entry**. The process of recording the journal entry in the journal is called **journalizing**.

> Journal—from the French word *jour: day* (chronological)

The journal is called the **book of original entry** since it contains the first formal information about the business transactions. The ledger is known as the **book of final entry** because the information it contains has been transferred from the journal. Like the ledger, the journal may be a bound or loose-leaf book. Each of the journal pages looks like the one in Figure 3-1. The pages of the journal are

Figure 3-1
The General Journal

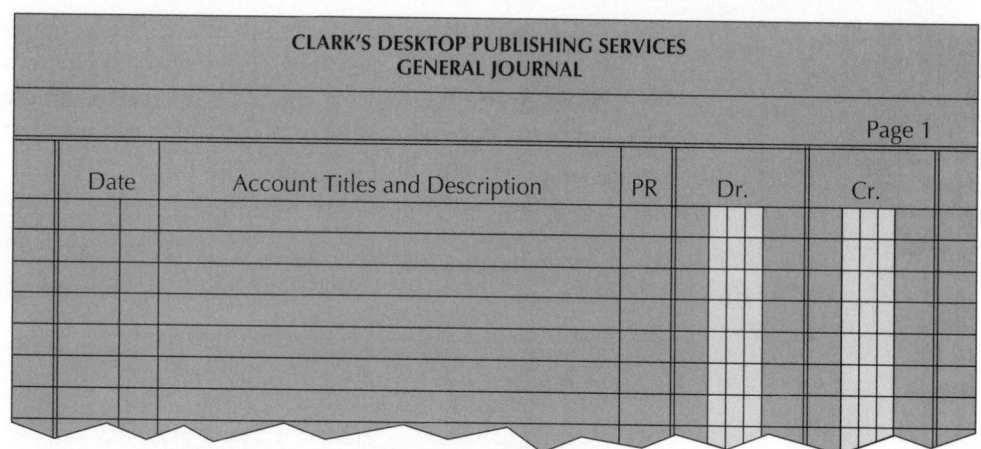

numbered consecutively from page 1. Keep in mind that the journal and the ledger are separate books. Also note that both journals and ledgers exist in computerized accounting although they may look different from the manual formats.

Relationship Between the Journal and the Chart of Accounts

The accountant must refer to the business's chart of accounts for the account name that is to be used in the journal. Every company has its own "unique" chart of accounts.

The chart of accounts for Clark's Desktop Publishing Services appears below. By the end of Chapter 5, we will have discussed each of these accounts.

Note that we will continue to use transaction analysis charts as a teaching aid in the journalizing process.

Journalizing the Transactions of Clark's Desktop Publishing Services

Certain formalities must be followed in making journal entries: The date of the transaction must be recorded. The debit portion of the transaction is always recorded first. The credit portion of a transaction is indented about 1 centimetre and placed below the debit portion. The explanation of the journal entry follows

---

Clark's Desktop Publishing Services
Chart of Accounts

Assets (100–199)
111 Cash
112 Accounts Receivable
114 Office Supplies
115 Prepaid Rent
121 Desktop Publishing Equipment
122 Accumulated Amortization,
       Desktop Publishing Equipment

Liabilities (200–299)
211 Accounts Payable
212 Salaries Payable

Owner's Equity (300–399)
311 Brenda Clark, Capital
312 Brenda Clark, Withdrawals
313 Income Summary

Revenue (400–499)
411 Desktop Publishing Fees

Expenses (500–599)
511 Office Salaries Expense
512 Advertising Expense
513 Telephone Expense
514 Office Supplies Expense
515 Rent Expense
516 Amortization Expense,
       Desktop Publishing Equipment

---

immediately after the credit and about 2 centimetres from the date column. A one-line space follows each transaction and explanation. This makes the journal easier to read, and there is less chance of mixing transactions. Finally, as always, the total amount of debits must equal the total amount of credits. The same format is used for each of the entries in the journal.

May 1, 2013: Brenda Clark began the business by investing $10,000 in cash.

1 Accounts Affected	2 Category	3 ↑ ↓	4 Rules of Dr. and Cr.
Cash	Asset	↑	Dr.
Brenda Clark, Capital	Owner's Equity	↑	Cr.

CLARK'S DESKTOP PUBLISHING SERVICES
GENERAL JOURNAL

Page 1

Date		Account Titles and Description	PR	Dr.	Cr.
2013 May	1	Cash		10 00 00 0	
		Brenda Clark, Capital			10 00 0 00
		Initial investment of cash by owner			

For now the PR (posting reference) column is blank; we will discuss it later.

Let's now look at the structure of this journal entry. The entry contains the following information:

1. Year of the journal entry   2013
2. Month of the journal entry   May
3. Day of the journal entry   1
4. Name(s) of account(s) debited   Cash
5. Name(s) of account(s) credited   Brenda Clark, Capital
6. Explanation of transaction   Initial investment of cash by owner
7. Amount of debit(s) $10,000
8. Amount of credit(s) $10,000

May 1: Purchased desktop publishing equipment from Ben Co. for $6,000, paying $1,000 and promising to pay the balance within 30 days.

1 Accounts Affected	2 Category	3 ↑ ↓	4 Rules of Dr. and Cr.
Desktop Publishing Equipment	Asset	↑	Dr.
Cash	Asset	↓	Cr.
Accounts Payable	Liability	↑	Cr.

Note that in this compound entry we have one debit and two credits—but the total amount of debits equals the total amount of credits.

A journal entry that includes three or more accounts is called a compound journal entry.

This transaction affects three accounts. When a journal entry has more than two accounts, it is called a **compound journal entry**.

1	Desktop Publishing Equipment		6 0 0 0 00		
	Cash			1 0 0 0 00	
	Accounts Payable			5 0 0 0 00	
	Purchase of equipment from Ben Co.				

In this entry, only the day is entered in the date column. That is because the year and month were entered at the top of the page from the first transaction. There is no need to repeat this information until a new page is needed or a change of month occurs.

May 1: Rented office space, paying $1,200 in advance for the first three months.

1 Accounts Affected	2 Category	3 ↑ ↓	4 Rules of Dr. and Cr.
Prepaid Rent	**Asset**	↑	**Dr.**
Cash	**Asset**	↓	**Cr.**

Rent paid in advance is an asset.

In this transaction, Clark gains an asset called prepaid rent and gives up an asset, cash. The prepaid rent does not become an expense until it expires.

1	Prepaid Rent		1 2 0 0 00		
	Cash			1 2 0 0 00	
	Rent paid in advance (3 months)				

May 3: Purchased office supplies from Norris Co. on account, $600.

1 Accounts Affected	2 Category	3 ↑ ↓	4 Rules of Dr. and Cr.
Office Supplies	**Asset**	↑	**Dr.**
Accounts Payable	**Liability**	↑	**Cr.**

Supplies become an expense when used up.

Remember, supplies are an asset when they are purchased. Once they are used up or consumed in the operation of business, they become an expense.

3	Office Supplies		6 0 0 00		
	Accounts Payable			6 0 0 00	
	Purchase of supplies on account				
	from Norris Co.				

May 7: Completed sales promotion pieces for a client and immediately collected $3,000.

1 Accounts Affected	2 Category	3 ↑ ↓	4 Rules of Dr. and Cr.
Cash	Asset	↑	Dr.
Desktop Publishing Fees	Revenue	↑	Cr.

	7	Cash		3 0 0 0 00	
		Desktop Publishing Fees			3 0 0 0 00
		Cash received for services rendered			

May 10: Paid office salaries, $650.

1 Accounts Affected	2 Category	3 ↑ ↓	4 Rules of Dr. and Cr.
Office Salaries Expense	Expense	↑	Dr.
Cash	Asset	↓	Cr.

	10	Office Salaries Expense		6 5 0 00	
		Cash			6 5 0 00
		Payment of office salaries			

> Remember, expenses are recorded when they are incurred, no matter when they are paid.

May 17: Bill received from Al's News Co. but not paid.

1 Accounts Affected	2 Category	3 ↑ ↓	4 Rules of Dr. and Cr.
Advertising Expense	Expense	↑	Dr.
Accounts Payable	Liability	↑	Cr.

	17	Advertising Expense		2 5 0 00	
		Accounts Payable			2 5 0 00
		Bill received but not paid from			
		Al's News Co.			

May 20: Paid personal mortgage instalment, $625.

1 Accounts Affected	2 Category	3 ↑ ↓	4 Rules of Dr. and Cr.
Brenda Clark, Withdrawals	Owner's Equity (Withdrawals)	↑	Dr.
Cash	Asset	↓	Cr.

	20	Brenda Clark, Withdrawals		625 00	
		Cash			625 00
		Personal withdrawal of cash			

May 22: Billed Morris Company for a sophisticated desktop publishing job, $5,000.

1 Accounts Affected	2 Category	3 ↑ ↓	4 Rules of Dr. and Cr.
Accounts Receivable	Asset	↑	Dr.
Desktop Publishing Fees	Revenue	↑	Cr.

	22	Accounts Receivable		5000 00	
		Desktop Publishing Fees			5000 00
		Billed Morris Co. for fees earned			

May 24: Paid office salaries, $650.

1 Accounts Affected	2 Category	3 ↑ ↓	4 Rules of Dr. and Cr.
Office Salaries Expense	Expense	↑	Dr.
Cash	Asset	↓	Cr.

Note: Since we are on page 2 of the journal, the year and month are repeated.

CLARK'S DESKTOP PUBLISHING SERVICES
GENERAL JOURNAL

Page 2

Date		Account Titles and Description	PR	Dr.	Cr.
2013 May	24	Office Salaries Expense		650 00	
		Cash			650 00
		Payment of office salaries			

May 28: Paid half the amount owed for desktop publishing equipment purchased May 1 from Ben Co., $2,500.

1 Accounts Affected	2 Category	3 ↑ ↓	4 Rules of Dr. and Cr.
Accounts Payable	Liability	↓	Dr.
Cash	Asset	↓	Cr.

	28	Accounts Payable		2 500 00	
		Cash			2 500 00
		Paid half the amount owed Ben Co.			

May 29: Received and paid telephone bill, $220.

1 Accounts Affected	2 Category	3 ↑ ↓	4 Rules of Dr. and Cr.
Telephone Expense	Expense	↑	Dr.
Cash	Asset	↓	Cr.

	29	Telephone Expense		220 00	
		Cash			220 00
		Paid telephone bill			

This concludes the journal transactions of Clark's Desktop Publishing Services. (See pages 104 and 105 for a summary of all the transactions.)

LEARNING UNIT 3-1 REVIEW

AT THIS POINT you should be able to:

♦ Explain the purpose of the accounting cycle. (p. 92)

♦ Define and explain the relationship of the accounting period to the income statement. (p. 92)

♦ Compare and contrast a calendar year and a fiscal year. (p. 92)

♦ Explain the term "natural business year." (p. 92)

♦ Explain the function of interim reports. (p. 92)

♦ Define and state the purpose of a journal. (p. 92)

♦ Compare and contrast a book of original entry and a book of final entry. (p. 92)

♦ Differentiate between a chart of accounts and a journal. (p. 93)

♦ Explain a compound entry. (p. 94–95)

♦ Journalize business transactions. (p. 94)

Self-Review Quiz 3-1

(The blank forms you need are on pages 3-1 and 3-2 of the *Study Guide with Working Papers.*)

The following are the transactions of Lowe's Repair Service. Journalize the transactions in proper form. The chart of accounts includes Cash; Accounts Receivable; Prepaid Rent; Repair Supplies; Repair Equipment; Accounts Payable; A. Lowe, Capital; A. Lowe, Withdrawals; Repair Fees Earned; Salaries Expense; Advertising Expense; and Supplies Expense.

2012

June 1 A. Lowe invested $7,000 cash and $5,000 worth of repair equipment in the business.

 1 Paid two months' rent in advance, $1,200.

 4 Bought repair supplies from Melvin Co. on account, $600. (These supplies have not yet been consumed or used up.)

 15 Performed repair work, received $600 in cash, and had to bill Doe Co. for remaining balance of $300.

 18 A. Lowe paid his home telephone bill, $50, using a company cheque.

 22 Advertising bill for $400 from Jones Co. was received, but payment was not due yet. (Advertising has already appeared in the newspaper.)

 25 Paid salaries, $1,400.

Solution to Self-Review Quiz 3-1

Quiz Tip

All titles for the debits and credits come from the chart of accounts. Debits are against the date column and credits are indented. The description is indented further. The PR column is left blank in the journalizing process.

LOWE'S REPAIR SERVICE
GENERAL JOURNAL

Page 1

Date			Account Titles and Description	PR*	Dr.	Cr.
2012 June	1		Cash		7 0 0 0 00	
			Repair Equipment		5 0 0 0 00	
			A. Lowe, Capital			1 2 0 0 0 00
			Owner investment			
	1		Prepaid Rent		1 2 0 0 00	
			Cash			1 2 0 0 00
			Rent paid in advance (2 months)			
	4		Repair Supplies		6 0 0 00	
			Accounts Payable			6 0 0 00
			Purchase of supplies on account			
	15		Cash		6 0 0 00	
			Accounts Receivable		3 0 0 00	
			Repair Fees Earned			9 0 0 00
			Performed repairs			
	18		A. Lowe, Withdrawals		5 0 00	
			Cash			5 0 00
			Personal withdrawal			
	22		Advertising Expense		4 0 0 00	
			Accounts Payable			4 0 0 00
			Advertising bill			
	25		Salaries Expense		1 4 0 0 00	
			Cash			1 4 0 0 00
			Paid salaries			

*Note that the PR column is left blank in the journalizing process.

NEED HELP?

Let's review first: When recording transactions into a general journal the debit(s) will be against the date column and the credit(s) will be indented. These titles will come from the chart of accounts. The explanation line will then be indented below the last credit entry. The sum of the left side (Dr.) must equal the sum of the right side (Cr.) for each transaction.

Here are the mind process charts for each transaction. Be sure to remember that the accounts affected come from the chart of accounts. You have six categories: assets, liabilities, capital, withdrawals, revenues, and expenses. You must ask yourself what the company is getting and how it is getting it. Remember to think of expenses and withdrawals as increasing, resulting in a decrease to owner's equity.

June 1	Cash	Asset	↑	Dr.
	Repair Equip.	Asset	↑	Dr.
	A. Lowe, Cap.	Capital	↑	Cr.

Debits are listed first against the date column and credits are indented. This is an investment by the owner. The month is written because the month starts a new page.

1	Prepaid Rent	Asset	↑	Dr.
	Cash	Asset	↓	Cr.

This is a shift in assets, more rent paid in advance by cash. Note that the month is not repeated.

4	Repair Supplies	Asset	↑	Dr.
	Accounts Pay.	Liability	↑	Cr.

This is an example of buy now and pay later. Supplies will not be an expense until they are used up.

15	Cash	Asset	↑	Dr.
	Acc. Receiv.	Asset	↑	Dr.
	Rep. Fees Earn.	Revenue	↑	Cr.

Here we did the work and got some money as well as a promise that the customer will pay later. Note how the two debits are against the date column and the credit is indented.

18	A. Lowe, Withdr.	Withdr.	↑	Dr.
	Cash	Asset	↓	Cr.

The owner increases her withdrawals for personal use and the end result is that the business has less cash.

22	Advertising Exp.	Expense	↑	Dr.
	Accounts Pay.	Liability	↑	Cr.

An expense has been incurred but is not paid for. This expense has created a liability. Think of expenses as always increasing.

25	Salaries Exp.	Expense	↑	Dr.
	Cash	Asset	↓	Cr.

Here the expense is increasing and it is being paid for in cash.

Learning Unit 3-2

Posting to the Ledger: Step 3 of the Accounting Cycle

2 Posting—transferring information from a journal to a ledger

The **general journal** serves a particular purpose: it puts every transaction that the business makes in one place. There are things it cannot do, however. For example, if you were asked to find the balance of the Cash account from the general journal, you would have to go through the entire journal and look for only the cash entries. Then you would have to add up the debits and the credits for the Cash account (separately) and determine the difference between the two totals.

What we really need to do to find balances of accounts is transfer the information from the journal to the **general ledger**. This is called **posting**. In the general ledger, we will accumulate an ending balance for each account so that we can prepare financial statements.

POSTING

Footings are not needed in three-column accounts.

In Chapter 2, we used the T account form to make our ledger entries. T accounts are very simple, but they are not used in the real business world. They are used only for demonstration purposes. In practice, accountants often use a **three-column account** form that includes a column for each account's running balance. Figure 3-2 shows a standard three-column account (all the details are made up).

Figure 3-2
Three-Column Account

GENERAL LEDGER

Accounts Payable   Account No. 211

Date 2013		Explanation	Post. Ref.	Debit	Credit	DR or CR	Balance
May	1		GJ1		5 0 0 0 00	CR	5 0 0 0 00
	3		GJ1		6 0 0 00	CR	5 6 0 0 00
	17		GJ1		2 5 0 00	CR	5 8 5 0 00
	28		GJ2	2 5 0 0 00		CR	3 3 5 0 00

We will use that format in the text from now on to illustrate general ledger accounts.

Now let's look at how to post the transactions of Clark's Desktop Publishing Services from its journal. The diagram in Figure 3-3 shows how to post the cash line from the journal to the ledger. The steps in the posting process are numbered and illustrated in the figure.

Step 1: In the Cash account in the ledger, record the date (May 1, 2013) and the amount of the entry ($10,000).

Step 2: Record the page number of the journal "GJ1" in the posting reference (PR) column of the Cash account.

Step 3: Calculate the new balance of the account. You keep a running balance in each account as you would in your chequebook. To do this, you take the present balance in the account on the previous line and add or subtract the transaction as necessary to arrive at your new balance.

Step 4: Record the account number of Cash (111) in the posting reference (PR) column of the journal. This is called **cross-referencing**.

The same sequence of steps occurs for each line in the journal. In a manual system like Clark's, the debits and credits in the journal may be posted in the order in which they were recorded, or all the debits may be posted first and then all the credits. If Clark used a computer system, the program would post at the press of a menu button.

Using Posting References

The posting references (PR) are very helpful. In the journal, the PR column tells us which transactions have or have not been posted and also to which accounts they have been posted. In the ledger, the posting reference leads us back to the original transaction in its entirety so that we can see why the debit or credit was recorded and what other accounts were affected. (It leads us back to the original transaction by identifying the journal and the page in the journal from which the information came.)

Figure 3-3
How to Post from
Journal to Ledger

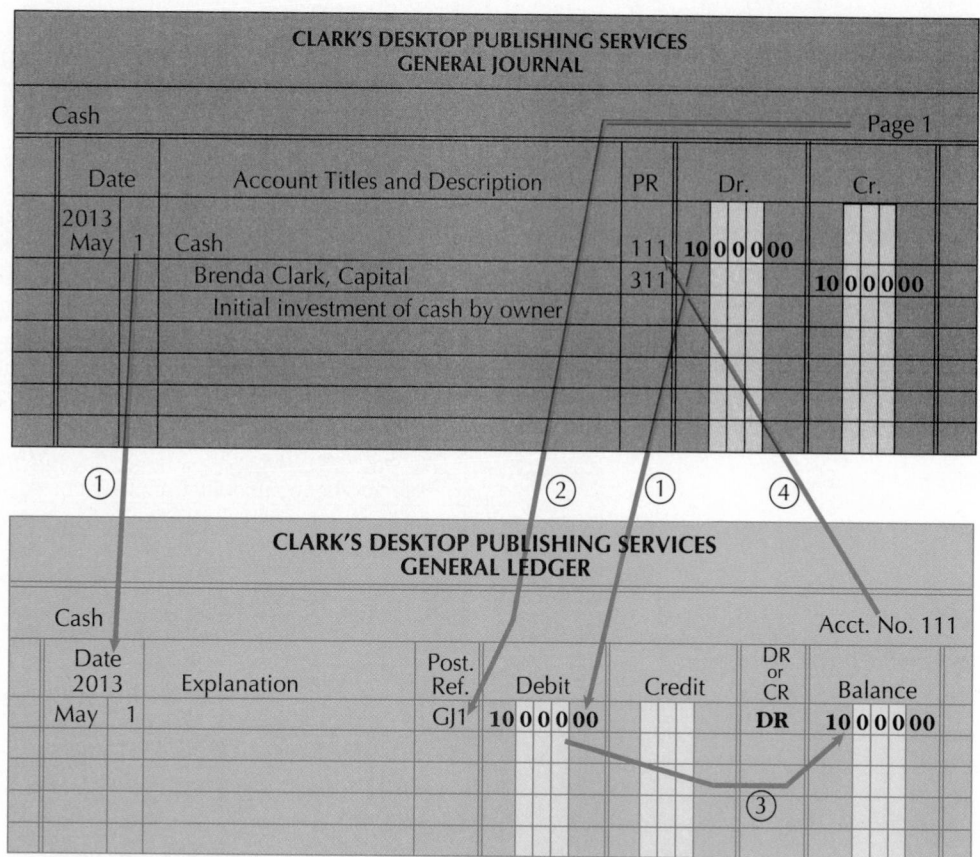

LEARNING UNIT 3-2 REVIEW

AT THIS POINT you should be able to:

◆ State the purpose of posting. (p. 101)

◆ Discuss the advantages of the three-column account. (p.101)

◆ Identify the elements to be posted. (p. 102)

◆ From journalized transactions, post to the general ledger. (p. 102)

Self-Review Quiz 3-2

(The forms you need are on pages 3-3 to 3-6 of the *Study Guide with Working Papers.*)

The following are the journalized transactions of Clark's Desktop Publishing Services. Your task is to post information to the ledger. The ledger in your workbook has all the account titles and numbers that were used from the chart of accounts.

CLARK'S DESKTOP PUBLISHING SERVICES
GENERAL JOURNAL

Page 1

Date			Account Titles and Description	PR	Dr.	Cr.
2013 May	1		Cash		10 0 0 0 00	
			Brenda Clark, Capital			10 0 0 0 00
			Initial investment of cash by owner			
	1		Desktop Publishing Equipment		6 0 0 0 00	
			Cash			1 0 0 0 00
			Accounts Payable			5 0 0 0 00
			Purchase of equipment from Ben Co.			
	1		Prepaid Rent		1 2 0 0 00	
			Cash			1 2 0 0 00
			Rent paid in advance (3 months)			
	3		Office Supplies		6 0 0 00	
			Accounts Payable			6 0 0 00
			Purchase of supplies on account from			
			Norris Co.			
	7		Cash		3 0 0 0 00	
			Desktop Publishing Fees			3 0 0 0 00
			Cash received for services rendered			
	10		Office Salaries Expense		6 5 0 00	
			Cash			6 5 0 00
			Payment of office salaries			
	17		Advertising Expense		2 5 0 00	
			Accounts Payable			2 5 0 00
			Bill received but not paid from			
			Al's News Co.			
	20		Brenda Clark, Withdrawals		6 2 5 00	
			Cash			6 2 5 00
			Personal withdrawal of cash			
	22		Accounts Receivable		5 0 0 0 00	
			Desktop Publishing Fees			5 0 0 0 00
			Billed Morris Co. for fees earned			

CLARK'S DESKTOP PUBLISHING SERVICES
GENERAL JOURNAL

Page 2

Date		Account Titles and Description	PR	Dr.	Cr.
2013 May	24	Office Salaries Expense		65000	
		Cash			65000
		Payment of office salaries			
	28	Accounts Payable		250000	
		Cash			250000
		Paid half the amount owed Ben Co.			
	29	Telephone Expense		22000	
		Cash			22000
		Paid telephone bill			

Solution to Self-Review Quiz 3-2

Posting references

CLARK'S DESKTOP PUBLISHING SERVICES
GENERAL JOURNAL

Page 1

Remember: The PR column remains empty until the entries have been posted.

Date		Account Titles and Description	PR	Dr.	Cr.
2013 May	1	Cash	111	1000000	
		Brenda Clark, Capital	311		1000000
		Initial investment of cash by owner			
	1	Desktop Publishing Equipment	121	600000	
		Cash	111		100000
		Accounts Payable	211		500000
		Purchase of equipment from Ben Co.			
	1	Prepaid Rent	115	120000	
		Cash	111		120000
		Rent paid in advance (3 months)			
	3	Office Supplies	114	60000	
		Accounts Payable	211		60000
		Purchase of supplies on account from Norris Co.			
	7	Cash	111	300000	
		Desktop Publishing Fees	411		300000
		Cash received for services rendered			
	10	Office Salaries Expense	511	65000	
		Cash	111		65000
		Payment of office salaries			

				PR	Dr.	Cr.
	17	Advertising Expense		512	2 5 0 00	
		Accounts Payable		211		2 5 0 00
		Bill received from Al's News Co. but				
		not paid				
	20	Brenda Clark, Withdrawals		312	6 2 5 00	
		Cash		111		6 2 5 00
		Personal withdrawal of cash				
	22	Accounts Receivable		112	5 0 0 0 00	
		Desktop Publishing Fees		411		5 0 0 0 00
		Billed Morris Co. for fees earned				

CLARK'S DESKTOP PUBLISHING SERVICES
GENERAL JOURNAL

Page 2

Date		Account Titles and Description	PR	Dr.	Cr.
2013 May	24	Office Salaries Expense	511	6 5 0 00	
		Cash	111		6 5 0 00
		Payment of office salaries			
	28	Accounts Payable	211	2 5 0 0 00	
		Cash	111		2 5 0 0 00
		Paid half the amount owed Ben Co.			
	29	Telephone Expense	513	2 2 0 00	
		Cash	111		2 2 0 00
		Paid telephone bill			

Posting to ledger accounts

CLARK'S DESKTOP PUBLISHING SERVICES
PARTIAL GENERAL LEDGER

Cash   Acct. No. 111

Date 2013		Explanation	Post. Ref.	Debit	Credit	DR or CR	Balance
May	1		GJ1	1 0 0 0 0 00		DR	1 0 0 0 0 00
	1		GJ1		1 0 0 0 00	DR	9 0 0 0 00
	1		GJ1		1 2 0 0 00	DR	7 8 0 0 00
	7		GJ1	3 0 0 0 00		DR	1 0 8 0 0 00
	10		GJ1		6 5 0 00	DR	1 0 1 5 0 00
	20		GJ1		6 2 5 00	DR	9 5 2 5 00
	24		GJ2		6 5 0 00	DR	8 8 7 5 00
	28		GJ2		2 5 0 0 00	DR	6 3 7 5 00
	29		GJ2		2 2 0 00	DR	6 1 5 5 00

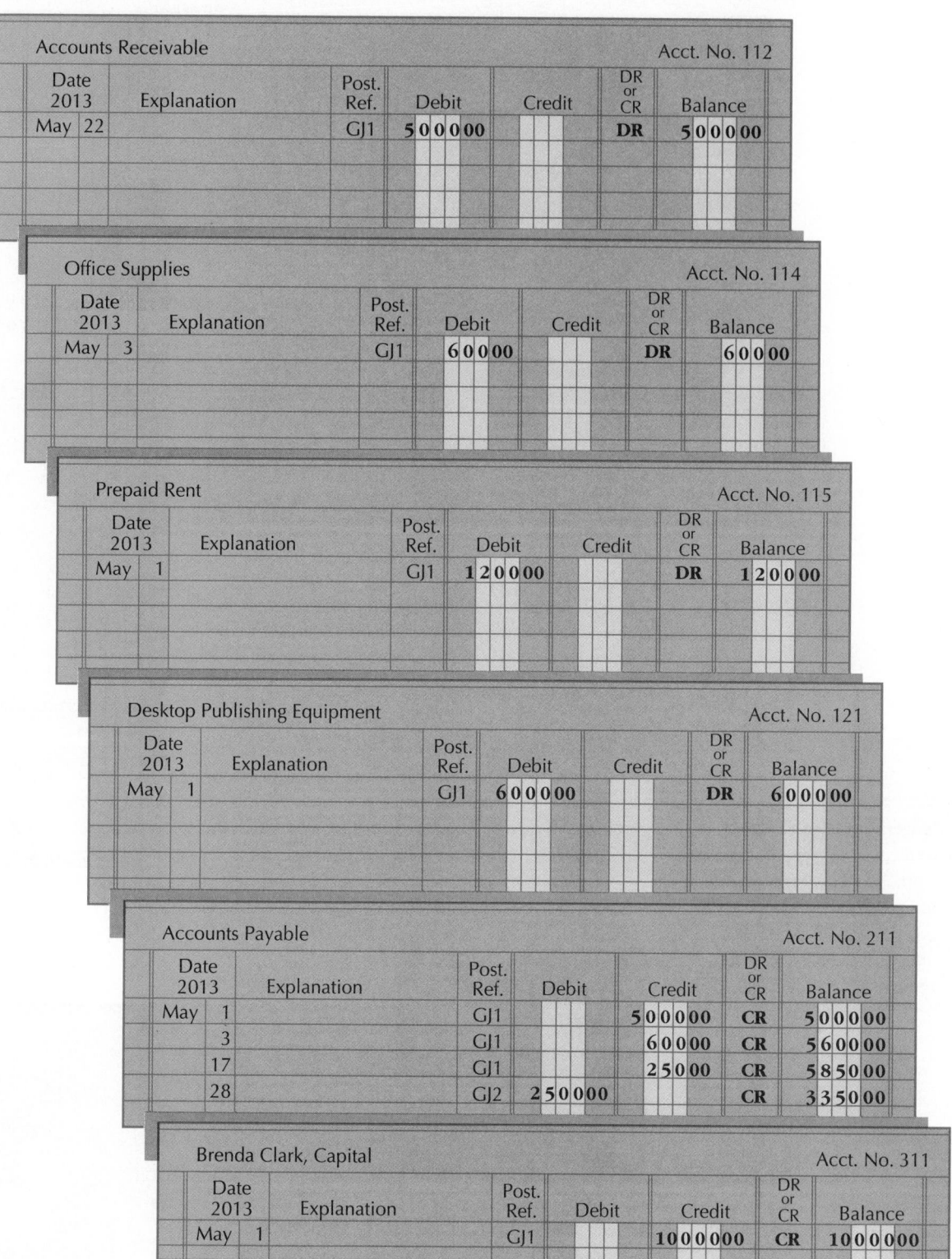

Accounts Receivable — Acct. No. 112

Date 2013		Explanation	Post. Ref.	Debit	Credit	DR or CR	Balance
May	22		GJ1	5 0 0 0 00		DR	5 0 0 0 00

Office Supplies — Acct. No. 114

Date 2013		Explanation	Post. Ref.	Debit	Credit	DR or CR	Balance
May	3		GJ1	6 0 0 00		DR	6 0 0 00

Prepaid Rent — Acct. No. 115

Date 2013		Explanation	Post. Ref.	Debit	Credit	DR or CR	Balance
May	1		GJ1	1 2 0 0 00		DR	1 2 0 0 00

Desktop Publishing Equipment — Acct. No. 121

Date 2013		Explanation	Post. Ref.	Debit	Credit	DR or CR	Balance
May	1		GJ1	6 0 0 0 00		DR	6 0 0 0 00

Accounts Payable — Acct. No. 211

Date 2013		Explanation	Post. Ref.	Debit	Credit	DR or CR	Balance
May	1		GJ1		5 0 0 0 00	CR	5 0 0 0 00
	3		GJ1		6 0 0 00	CR	5 6 0 0 00
	17		GJ1		2 5 0 00	CR	5 8 5 0 00
	28		GJ2	2 5 0 0 00		CR	3 3 5 0 00

Brenda Clark, Capital — Acct. No. 311

Date 2013		Explanation	Post. Ref.	Debit	Credit	DR or CR	Balance
May	1		GJ1		1 0 0 0 0 00	CR	1 0 0 0 0 00

Brenda Clark, Withdrawals — Acct. No. 312

Date 2013	Explanation	Post. Ref.	Debit	Credit	DR or CR	Balance
May 20		GJ1	6 2 5 00		DR	6 2 5 00

Desktop Publishing Fees — Acct. No. 411

Date 2013	Explanation	Post. Ref.	Debit	Credit	DR or CR	Balance
May 7		GJ1		3 0 0 0 00	CR	3 0 0 0 00
22		GJ1		5 0 0 0 00	CR	8 0 0 0 00

Office Salaries Expense — Acct. No. 511

Date 2013	Explanation	Post. Ref.	Debit	Credit	DR or CR	Balance
May 10		GJ1	6 5 0 00		DR	6 5 0 00
24		GJ2	6 5 0 00		DR	1 3 0 0 00

Advertising Expense — Acct. No. 512

Date 2013	Explanation	Post. Ref.	Debit	Credit	DR or CR	Balance
May 17		GJ1	2 5 0 00		DR	2 5 0 00

Telephone Expense — Acct. No. 513

Date 2013	Explanation	Post. Ref.	Debit	Credit	DR or CR	Balance
May 29		GJ2	2 2 0 00		DR	2 2 0 00

Quiz Tip

The Post. Ref. column in the ledger tells from which part of the journal the information came. The PR column in the journal (the last to be filled in) tells to what account number in the ledger the information was posted.

NEED HELP?

Let's review first: The PR column of the journal will show to which account information has been posted. The PR column in the ledger accounts shows from which page of the journal the information came. When updating ledger accounts, two debits added equals a debit balance. Two credits added would be a credit balance. If you have a debit and a credit, take the difference between them; whichever side is larger is the balance (be it a debit or credit).

Partial General Ledger:

Cash: There are nine postings from the journal to the cash account. GJ1 means that posting came from the general journal, page 1. In the second line the credit of 1,000 is subtracted from the debit balance in line 1 (10,000) to show a new balance of 9,000 in line 2. In line 3 the 1,200 credit is then subtracted from the 9,000 debit for a current balance of 7,800. Normally the balance is on the side that causes it to increase. Thus cash is normally a debit balance.

Accounts Payable: In this account, the first three postings were credits from the general journal. Note that the month is written only once. Since all three are credits, we add them together, arriving at a credit balance of 5,850. On May 28 a debit of 2,500 is posted and we take the difference between a 5,850 credit balance and a 2,500 debit balance to arrive at a 3,350 ending credit balance.

Learning Unit 3-3

Preparing the Trial Balance: Step 4 of the Accounting Cycle

3   Preparing a trial balance

Did you notice in Self-Review Quiz 3-2 that each account had a running balance figure? Did you know the normal balance of each account in Clark's ledger? As we discussed in Chapter 2, the list of the individual accounts with their balances taken from the ledger is called a **trial balance**.

The trial balance shown in Figure 3-4 was developed from the ledger accounts of Clark's Desktop Publishing Services that were posted and balanced in Self-Review Quiz 3-2. If the information is journalized or posted incorrectly, the trial balance will not be correct.

There are some things the trial balance will not show:

The totals of a trial balance can balance and yet be incorrect.

◆   The capital figure on the trial balance may not be the beginning capital figure. For instance, if Brenda Clark had made additional investments during the period, the additional investment would have been journalized and posted to the capital account. The only way to tell whether the capital balance on the trial balance is the original balance is to check the ledger capital account to see whether any additional investments were made. This will be important when we make financial reports.

CLARK'S DESKTOP PUBLISHING SERVICES TRIAL BALANCE MAY 31, 2013	Debit	Credit
Cash	6 1 5 5 00	
Accounts Receivable	5 0 0 0 00	
Office Supplies	6 0 0 00	
Prepaid Rent	1 2 0 0 00	
Desktop Publishing Equipment	6 0 0 0 00	
Accounts Payable		3 3 5 0 00
Brenda Clark, Capital		10 0 0 0 00
Brenda Clark, Withdrawals	6 2 5 00	
Desktop Publishing Fees		8 0 0 0 00
Office Salaries Expense	1 3 0 0 00	
Advertising Expense	2 5 0 00	
Telephone Expense	2 2 0 00	
Totals	21 3 5 0 00	21 3 5 0 00

The trial balance lists the accounts in the same order as in the ledger. The $6,155 figure for cash came from the ledger.

Figure 3-4 The Trial Balance

♦ There is no guarantee that transactions have been properly recorded. For example, the following errors would remain undetected: (1) a transaction that may have been omitted in the journalizing process; (2) a transaction incorrectly analyzed and recorded in the journal; (3) a journal entry journalized or posted twice; and (4) a journal entry posted to an incorrect account.

WHAT TO DO IF A TRIAL BALANCE DOESN'T BALANCE

The trial balance of Clark's Desktop Publishing Services shows that the total of debits is equal to the total of credits. However, what happens if the trial balance is in balance, but the correct amount is not recorded in each ledger account? Accuracy in the journalizing and posting process will help ensure that no errors are made.

Even if there is an error, the first rule is "Don't panic." Everyone makes mistakes and there are accepted ways of correcting them. Once an entry has been made in ink, correcting an error must always show that the entry has been changed and who changed it. Sometimes the change has to be explained.

SOME COMMON MISTAKES

Correcting the trial balance: what to do if your trial balance doesn't balance.

Did you clear your adding machine?

If the trial balance does not balance, the cause could be something relatively simple. Here are some common errors and how they can be fixed:

♦ If the difference (the amount you are off) is 10, 100, 1,000, and so on, there probably is a mathematical error.
♦ If the difference is equal to an individual account balance in the ledger, the amount could have been omitted. It is also possible that the figure was not posted from the general journal.
♦ Divide the difference by 2; then check to see if a debit should have been a credit and vice versa in the ledger or the trial balance. *Example:* $150 difference ÷ 2 = $75. This means that you may have placed $75 as a debit to an account instead of a credit or vice versa.
♦ If the difference is evenly divisible by 9, a slide or a transposition may have occurred. A **slide** is an error resulting from adding or deleting zeros in writing numbers. For example, $4,175.00 may have been copied as $41.75. A **transposition** is the accidental rearrangement of the digits of a number. For example, $4,175 might have been accidentally written as $4,157.
♦ Compare the balances in the trial balance with the ledger accounts to check for copying errors.
♦ Recompute balances in each ledger account.
♦ Trace all postings from journal to ledger.

If you cannot find the error after you have done all of this, take a break. Then start all over again.

MAKING A CORRECTION BEFORE POSTING

Before posting, error correction is straightforward. Simply draw a line through the incorrect entry in the journal, write the correct information above the line, and write your initials near the change.

Correcting an Error in an Account Title The following illustration shows an error and its correction in an account title:

	1	Desktop Publishing Equipment	6 0 0 0 00	
		Cash		1 0 0 0 00
		~~Accounts Payable~~ *amp*		
		~~Accounts Receivable~~		5 0 0 0 00
		Purchase of equipment from Ben Co.		

Correcting a Numerical Error Numbers are handled the same way as account titles, as the next change, from 520 to 250, shows:

	17	Advertising Expense	2 5 0 00	
		Accounts Payable		*amp* 2 5 0 00 ~~5 2 0 00~~
		Bill from Al's News		

Correcting an Entry Error If a number has been entered in the wrong column, a straight line is drawn through it, and the number is then written in the correct column:

	1	Desktop Publishing Equipment	6 0 0 0 00	
		Cash		1 0 0 0 00
		Accounts Payable	*amp* ~~5 0 0 0 00~~	5 0 0 0 00
		Purchase of equipment from Ben Co.		

MAKING A CORRECTION AFTER POSTING

It is also possible to correct an amount that is correctly entered in the journal but posted incorrectly to the ledger of the proper account. The first step is to draw a line through the error and write the correct figure above it. The next step is to change the running balance to reflect the corrected posting. Here, too, a line is drawn through the balance and the corrected balance is written above it. Both changes must be initialled.

Desktop Publishing Fees							Acct. No. 411
Date 2013		Explanation	Post. Ref.	Debit	Credit	DR or CR	Balance
May	7		GJ1		3 0 0 0 00	CR	3 0 0 0 00
	22		GJ1		*amp* 5 0 0 0 00 ~~2 5 0 00~~	CR	8 0 0 0 00 ~~3 5 0 00~~ *amp*

CORRECTING AN ENTRY POSTED TO THE WRONG ACCOUNT

Drawing a line through an error and writing the correction above it is possible when a mistake has occurred within the proper account, but when an error involves a posting to the wrong account, the journal must include a correction accompanied by an explanation. In addition, the correct information must be posted to the appropriate ledger accounts.

Suppose, for example, that as a result of tracing postings from journal entries to ledger accounts, you find that a $180 telephone bill was incorrectly debited as an advertising expense. The following illustration shows how this is done.

Step 1: The error is corrected by making a new entry in the journal, dated with the date when the correction is entered, and the correction is explained.

GENERAL JOURNAL					Page 3
Date 2013	Account Titles and Description	PR	Dr.	Cr.	
May 29	Telephone Expense	513	18000		
	Advertising Expense	512		18000	
	To correct error in which				
	Advertising Expense was debited				
	for charges to Telephone Expense				

Step 2: The Advertising Expense ledger account is also corrected, by posting the new entry.

Advertising Expense						Acct. No. 512
Date 2013	Explanation	Post. Ref.	Debit	Credit	DR or CR	Balance
May 17			17500		DR	17500
23			18000		DR	35500
29	Correcting entry	GJ3		18000	DR	17500

Step 3: The Telephone Expense ledger is corrected.

Telephone Expense						Acct. No. 513
Date 2013	Explanation	Post. Ref.	Debit	Credit	DR or CR	Balance
May 29		GJ3	18000		DR	18000

LEARNING UNIT 3-3 REVIEW

AT THIS POINT you should be able to:

◆ Prepare a trial balance from a ledger, which uses three-column accounts. (p. 109)

◆ Analyze and correct a trial balance that doesn't balance. (p. 110)

◆ Correct journal and posting errors. (pp. 111–113)

Self-Review Quiz 3-3

(The blank forms you need are on page 3-7 of the *Study Guide with Working Papers*.)

1.

```
                                Interoffice Memo

To:    Al Vincent
From:  Professor Jones
Re:    Trial Balance
You have submitted to me an incorrect trial balance. Could you please rework and
turn it in to me before next Friday?
Note: Individual amounts look okay.
```

A. RICE TRIAL BALANCE OCTOBER 31, 2014	Dr.	Cr.
Cash		8 0 6 0 00
Operating Expenses		1 7 0 0 00
A. Rice, Withdrawals		4 0 0 00
Service Revenue		5 4 0 0 00
Equipment	5 0 0 0 00	
Accounts Receivable	3 5 4 0 00	
Accounts Payable	2 0 0 0 00	
Supplies	3 0 0 00	
A. Rice, Capital		11 6 0 0 00

2. An $8,000 debit to Office Equipment was mistakenly journalized and posted on June 9, 2014, to Office Supplies. Prepare the appropriate journal entry to correct this error.

Solution to Self-Review Quiz 3-3

1.

A. RICE TRIAL BALANCE OCTOBER 31, 2014	Dr.	Cr.
Cash	8 0 6 0 00	
Accounts Receivable	3 5 4 0 00	
Supplies	3 0 0 00	
Equipment	5 0 0 0 00	
Accounts Payable		2 0 0 0 00
A. Rice, Capital		11 6 0 0 00
A. Rice, Withdrawals	4 0 0 00	
Service Revenue		5 4 0 0 00
Operating Expenses	1 7 0 0 00	
Totals	19 0 0 0 00	19 0 0 0 00

Quiz Tip

Items in a trial balance are listed in the same order as in the ledger or the chart of accounts. Expect each account to have its normal balance (either debit or credit).

2.

GENERAL JOURNAL					Page 4	
Date		Account Titles and Description	PR	Dr.	Cr.	
2014 June	9	Office Equipment		8 0 0 0 0 0		
		Office Supplies			8 0 0 0 0 0	
		To correct error in which Office Supplies				
		was debited for purchase of				
		Office Equipment				

NEED HELP?

Let's review first: Items in a trial balance are listed in the same order as in the ledger or the chart of accounts. Expect each account to have its normal balance (either a debit or a credit). No title in the trial balance can have both a debit and credit balance.

List the ending balance of each ledger account (last number listed in the balance columns) and list them in the order of the ledger. They should follow this pattern:

Assets	Dr.
Liabilities	Cr.
Capital	Cr.
Withdrawals	Dr.
Revenues	Cr.
Expenses	Dr.

When complete, the total of all debits will equal the total of the credits. In this case the total is 19,000.

SUMMARY

The trial balance lists the accounts in the same order as the ledger. Be sure to refer to the learning unit for what to do if the trial balance does not balance. It could be a posting mistake or just a math error.

Chapter Assignments

DEMONSTRATION PROBLEM: STEPS 1–4 OF THE ACCOUNTING CYCLE

(The blank forms you need are on pages 3-8 to 3-10 of the *Study Guide with Working Papers.*)

In March, Abby's Employment Agency had the following transactions:

2013
March   1   Abby Todd invested $5,000 cash in the new employment agency.
          4   Bought equipment for cash, $200.
          5   Earned employment fee commission, $200, but payment from Blue Co. will not be received until June.
          7   Paid wages expense, $300.
          8   Abby paid her home utility bill from the company chequebook, $75.
       11   Placed Rick Wool at DVD Corporation, receiving $1,200 cash.
       15   Paid cash for supplies, $200.

28 Telephone bill received but not paid, $180.
29 Advertising bill received but not paid, $400.

The chart of accounts includes Cash, 111; Accounts Receivable, 112; Supplies, 131; Equipment, 141; Accounts Payable, 211; A. Todd, Capital, 311; A. Todd, Withdrawals, 321; Employment Fees Earned, 411; Wage Expense, 511; Telephone Expense, 521; and Advertising Expense, 531.

Your task is to:

a. Set up a ledger based on the chart of accounts.
b. Journalize (all page 1) and post transactions.
c. Prepare a trial balance for March 31.

Solution to Demonstration Problem

a.

Figure 3-5
General Ledger

Cash   111

Date		PR	Dr.	Cr.	Balance Dr.	Cr.
2013 Mar	1	GJ1	5,000		5,000	
	4	GJ1		200	4,800	
	7	GJ1		300	4,500	
	8	GJ1		75	4,425	
	11	GJ1	1,200		5,625	
	15	GJ1		200	5,425	

Accounts Receivable   112

Date		PR	Dr.	Cr.	Balance Dr.	Cr.
2013 Mar	5	GJ1	200		200	

Supplies   131

Date		PR	Dr.	Cr.	Balance Dr.	Cr.
2013 Mar	15	GJ1	200		200	

Equipment   141

Date		PR	Dr.	Cr.	Balance Dr.	Cr.
2013 Mar	4	GJ1	200		200	

Accounts Payable   211

Date		PR	Dr.	Cr.	Balance Dr.	Cr.
2013 Mar	28	GJ1		180		180
	29	GJ1		400		580

A. Todd, Capital   311

Date		PR	Dr.	Cr.	Balance Dr.	Cr.
2013 Mar	1	GJ1		5,000		5,000

A. Todd, Withdrawals   321

Date		PR	Dr.	Cr.	Balance Dr.	Cr.
2013 Mar	8	GJ1	75		75	

Employment Fees Earned   411

Date		PR	Dr.	Cr.	Balance Dr.	Cr.
2013 Mar	5	GJ1		200		200
	11	GJ1		1,200		1,400

Wage Expense   511

Date		PR	Dr.	Cr.	Balance Dr.	Cr.
2013 Mar	7	GJ1	300		300	

Telephone Expense   521

Date		PR	Dr.	Cr.	Balance Dr.	Cr.
2013 Mar	28	GJ1	180		180	

Advertising Expense   531

Date		PR	Dr.	Cr.	Balance Dr.	Cr.
2013 Mar	29	GJ1	400		400	

b.

Figure 3-6
Journal Entries and Post
References

	Date		Account Titles and Description	PR	Dr.	Cr.
	2013 Mar	1	Cash	111	5 0 0 0 00	
			A. Todd, Capital	311		5 0 0 0 00
			Owner investment			
		4	Equipment	141	2 0 0 00	
			Cash	111		2 0 0 00
			Bought equipment for cash			
		5	Accounts Receivable	112	2 0 0 00	
			Employment Fees Earned	411		2 0 0 00
			Fees on account from Blue Co.			
		7	Wage Expense	511	3 0 0 00	
			Cash	111		3 0 0 00
			Paid wages			
		8	A. Todd, Withdrawals	321	7 5 00	
			Cash	111		7 5 00
			Personal withdrawals			
		11	Cash	111	1 2 0 0 00	
			Employment Fees Earned	411		1 2 0 0 00
			Cash fees			
		15	Supplies	131	2 0 0 00	
			Cash	111		2 0 0 00
			Bought supplies for cash			
		28	Telephone Expense	521	1 8 0 00	
			Accounts Payable	211		1 8 0 00
			Telephone bill owed			
		29	Advertising Expense	531	4 0 0 00	
			Accounts Payable	211		4 0 0 00
			Advertising bill received			

ABBY'S EMPLOYMENT AGENCY — Page 1

Solution Tips to Journalizing

1. When journalizing, the PR column is not filled in.
2. Write the name of the debit against the date column. Indent credits and list them below debits. Be sure total debits for each transaction equal total credits.
3. Skip a line after each transaction.

| March 1 | Cash | A | ↑ | Dr. | $5,000 |
| | A. Todd, Capital | O.E. | ↑ | Cr. | $5,000 |

| 4 | Equipment | A | ↑ | Dr. | $ 200 |
| | Cash | A | ↓ | Cr. | $ 200 |

| 5 | Accts. Receivable | A | ↑ | Dr. | $ 200 |
| | Empl. Fees Earned | Rev. | ↑ | Cr. | $ 200 |

| 7 | Wages Expense | Exp. | ↑ | Dr. | $ 300 |
| | Cash | A | ↓ | Cr. | $ 300 |

| 8 | A. Todd, Withdrawals | O.E. | ↑ | Dr. | $ 75 |
| | Cash | A | ↓ | Cr. | $ 75 |

| 11 | Cash | A | ↑ | Dr. | $1,200 |
| | Empl. Fees Earned | Rev. | ↑ | Cr. | $1,200 |

| 15 | Supplies | A | ↑ | Dr. | $ 200 |
| | Cash | A | ↓ | Cr. | $ 200 |

| 28 | Telephone Expense | Exp. | ↑ | Dr. | $ 180 |
| | Accounts Payable | L | ↑ | Cr. | $ 180 |

| 29 | Advertising Expense | Exp. | ↑ | Dr. | $ 400 |
| | Accounts Payable | L | ↑ | Cr. | $ 400 |

Solution Tips to Posting

The PR column in the ledger cash account tells you from which page journal information came. After the ledger cash account is posted, account number 111 is put in the PR column of the journal for cross-referencing.

Note how we keep a running balance in the cash account. A $5,000 debit balance and a $200 credit entry result in a new debit balance of $4,800.

Figure 3-7   c.

ABBY'S EMPLOYMENT AGENCY TRIAL BALANCE MARCH 31, 2013	Dr.	Cr.
Cash	5 4 2 5 00	
Accounts Receivable	2 0 0 00	
Supplies	2 0 0 00	
Equipment	2 0 0 00	
Accounts Payable		5 8 0 00
A. Todd, Capital		5 0 0 0 00
A. Todd, Withdrawals	7 5 00	
Employment Fees Earned		1 4 0 0 00
Wage Expense	3 0 0 00	
Telephone Expense	1 8 0 00	
Advertising Expense	4 0 0 00	
Totals	6 9 8 0 00	6 9 8 0 00

Solution Tip to Trial Balance

The trial balance lists the ending balance of each title in the order in which they appear in the ledger. The total of 6,980 on the left equals 6,980 on the right.

SUMMARY OF KEY POINTS

Learning Unit 3-1

1. The accounting cycle is a sequence of accounting procedures that are usually performed during an accounting period.
2. An accounting period is the time period for which the income statement is prepared. The time period can be any period up to one year.
3. A calendar year is from January 1 to December 31. The fiscal year is any 12-month period. A fiscal year could be a calendar year but does not have to be.
4. Interim reports are statements that are usually prepared for a portion of the business's calendar or fiscal year (e.g., a month or a quarter).
5. A general journal is a book that records transactions in chronological order. Here debits and credits are shown together on one page. It is the book of original entry.
6. The ledger is a collection of accounts where information is accumulated from the postings of the journal. The ledger is the book of final entry.
7. Journalizing is the process of recording journal entries.
8. The chart of accounts provides the specific titles of accounts to be entered in the journal.
9. When journalizing, the posting reference (PR) column is left blank.
10. A compound journal entry occurs when more than two accounts are affected in the journalizing process of a business transaction.

1. Posting is the process of transferring information from the journal to the ledger.
2. The journal and ledger contain the same information but in a different form.
3. The three-column ledger account keeps a running balance of an account.
4. The normal balance of an account will be located on the side that increases according to the rules of debits and credits. For example, the normal balances of liabilities occur on the credit side.
5. The mechanical process of posting requires care in accurately transferring dates, posting references, titles, and amounts.

1. A trial balance is a list of the individual accounts with their balances.
2. A trial balance can balance but be incorrect. For example, an entire journal entry may not have been posted.
3. If a trial balance doesn't balance, check for errors in addition, omission of postings, slides, transpositions, copying errors, and so on.
4. Specific procedures should be followed in making corrections in journals and ledgers.

KEY TERMS

Accounting cycle For each accounting period, the process that begins with the analyzing and recording of business transactions into a journal and ends with the completion of a post-closing trial balance (to be described in Chapter 5) (p. 92)

Accounting period The period of time for which an income statement is prepared (p. 92)

Book of final entry A ledger that receives information about business transactions from a book of original entry—a journal (p. 92)

Book of original entry Book that records the first formal information about business transactions—a journal (p. 92)

Calendar year January 1 to December 31 (p. 92)

Compound journal entry A journal entry that affects more than two accounts (p. 94)

Cross-referencing Adding the account number of the ledger account that was updated to the PR column of the journal, and inserting the journal page on the ledger account (p. 102)

Fiscal year The 12-month period a business chooses for its accounting year (p. 92)

General journal The simplest form of a journal, which records information from transactions in chronological order as they occur. This journal links the debit and credit parts of transactions. (pp. 92, 101)

General ledger A collection of accounts that includes all those needed to contain the individual balances that show up on any of the financial statements (asset accounts, liability and equity accounts, revenue accounts, and expense accounts) (p. 101)

Interim reports Financial reports that are prepared for a month, quarter, or some other portion of the fiscal year (p. 92)

Journal   A listing of business transactions in chronological order. The journal links the debit and credit parts of transactions on one page. (p. 92)

Journal entry   The transaction (debits and credits) that is recorded in a journal once it is analyzed (p. 92)

Journalizing   The process of recording a transaction entry in the journal (p. 92)

Natural business year   A business's fiscal year that ends at the same time as a slow seasonal period begins (p. 92)

Posting   The transferring, copying, or recording of information from a journal to a ledger (p. 101)

Slide   The error of adding or deleting zeros when a number is written; for example, 79,200 → 7,920 (p. 110)

Three-column account   A running balance account that records debits and credits, has a column for an ending balance (debit or credit), and replaces the standard two-column account we used earlier (p. 101)

Transposition   The accidental rearrangement of the digits of a number; for example, 152 for 125 (p. 110)

Trial balance   An informal listing of the ledger accounts and their balances that aids in proving the equality of debits and credits (p. 109)

BLUEPRINT OF FIRST FOUR STEPS
OF THE ACCOUNTING CYCLE

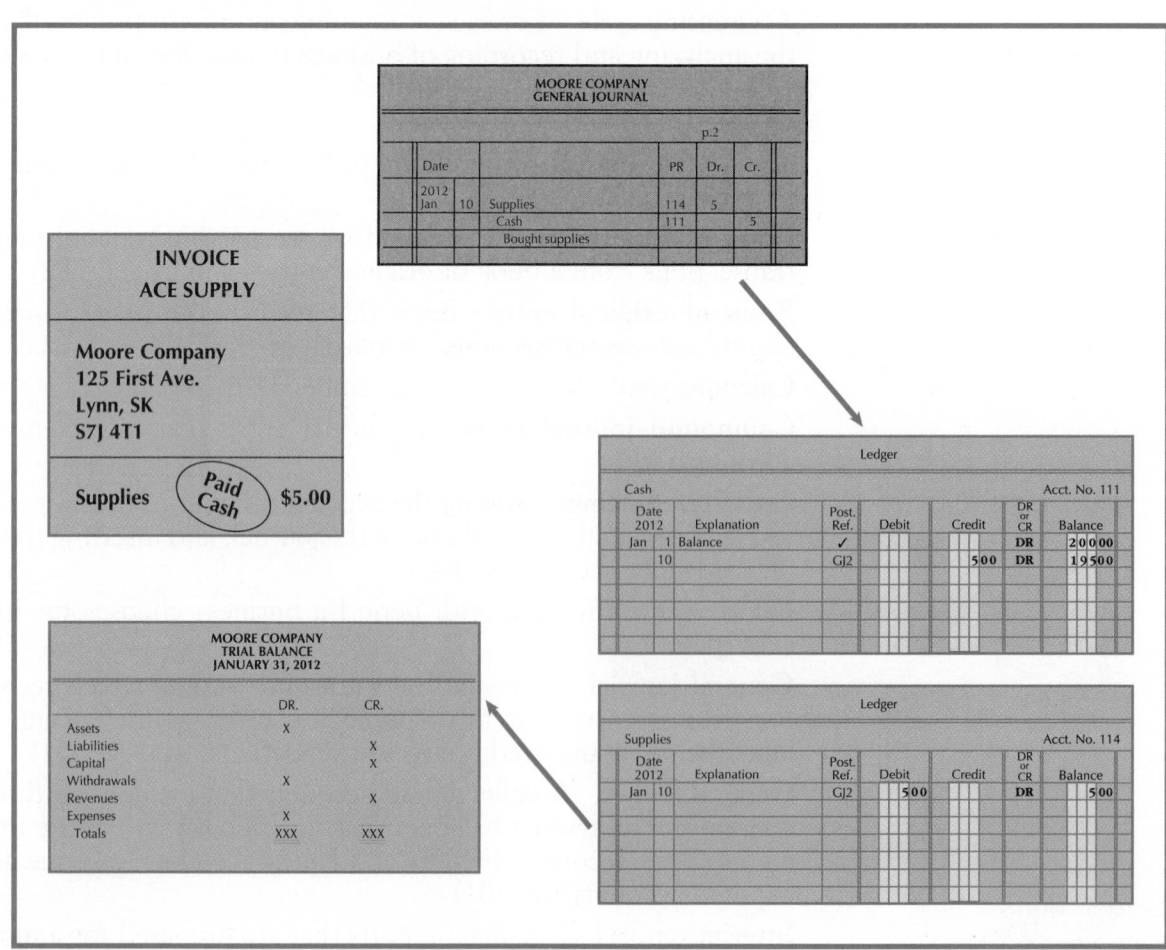

QUESTIONS, CLASSROOM DEMONSTRATION EXERCISES, EXERCISES, AND PROBLEMS

Discussion Questions and Critical Thinking/Ethical Case

1. Explain the concept of the accounting cycle.
2. An accounting period is based on the balance sheet. Agree or disagree.
3. Compare and contrast a calendar year versus a fiscal year.
4. What are interim reports?
5. Why is the ledger called the book of final entry?
6. How do transactions get "linked" in a general journal?
7. What is the relationship of the chart of accounts to the general journal?
8. What is a compound journal entry?
9. Posting means updating the journal. Agree or disagree. Please comment.
10. The side that decreases an account is the normal balance. True or false?
11. The PR column of a general journal is the last item to be filled in during the posting process. Agree or disagree.
12. Discuss the concept of cross-referencing.
13. What is the difference between a transposition and a slide?
14. Jay Simons, the accountant of See Co., wanted to buy a new computer software package for his general ledger. He couldn't do it because all funds were frozen for the rest of the fiscal period. Jay called his friend at Joor Industries and asked whether he could copy its software. Why should or shouldn't Jay do that?

MyAccountingLab

Make the grade with MyAccountingLab! The exercises and problems marked in green can be found on MyAccountingLab at www.myaccountinglab.com. You can practise them as often as you want, and many of them feature step-by-step guided solutions to help you find the right answer. You can also find working papers for selected problems in the Multimedia Library on MyAccountingLab.

Classroom Demonstration Exercises

(The blank forms you need are on page 3-11 of the *Study Guide with Working Papers.*)

Set A

General Journal

Analyzing the general journal
1 (5 min)

1. Complete the following from the general journal of Moore Company.

		MOORE COMPANY GENERAL JOURNAL				Page 1	
Date		Account Titles and Descriptions	PR	Dr.		Cr.	
2012 Nov.	19	Cash		9 0 0 0 00			
		Equipment		10 0 0 0 00			
		B. Moore, Capital				19 0 0 0 00	
		Initial investment by owner					

a. Year of journal entry
b. Month of journal entry
c. Day of journal entry
d. Name(s) of account(s) debited
e. Name(s) of account(s) credited
f. Explanation of transaction
g. Amount of debit(s)
h. Amount of credit(s)
i. Page of journal

General Journal

Explanation of transactions
① (5 min)

2. Provide the explanation for each of these general journal entries.

		GENERAL JOURNAL				Page 4	
Date		Account Titles and Descriptions	PR	Debit		Credit	
2012 June	11	Cash		17 0 0 0 00			
		Office Equipment		26 0 0 0 00			
		B. Blue, Capital				43 0 0 0 00	
		(A)					
	15	Cash		4 0 00			
		Accounts Receivable		7 0 00			
		Legal Fees Earned				1 1 0 00	
		(B)					
	22	Salary Expense		4 0 00			
		Cash				4 0 00	
		(C)					

Posting and Balancing

Balancing general ledger accounts
② (5 min)

3. Balance this three-column account. What function does the Post. Ref. column serve? When will Account 111 be used in the journalizing and posting process?

Name: Cash						Account No. 111	
Date 2012		Explanation	Post. Ref.	Debit	Credit	DR or CR	Balance
May	1		GJ1	1 9 00			
	4		GJ1	9 00			
	11		GJ2		6 00		
	14		GJ3	2 0 00			

The Trial Balance

Preparing an accurate trial balance

3️⃣ (15 min)

4. The following trial balance was prepared *incorrectly*.

Lee Company
Trial Balance
October 31, 2014

	Dr.	Cr.
D. Lee, Capital	30	
Equipment	112	
Rent Expense		17
Advertising Expense		3
Accounts Payable		108
Taxi Fare Income	16	
Cash	17	
D. Lee, Withdrawals		5
Totals	**175**	**133**

a. Rearrange the accounts in proper order.

b. Calculate the total of the trial balance. (Small numbers are used intentionally so that you can do the calculations in your head.) Assume that each account has a normal balance.

Correcting Entry

When a trial balance does not balance

3️⃣ (5 min)

5. On June 2, 2014, a telephone expense for $210 was debited to Repair Expense. On July 11, 2014, this error was found. Prepare the correcting journal entry. When would a correcting entry *not* be needed?

Set B

General Journal

Analyzing the general journal

1️⃣ (5 min)

1. Complete the following from the general journal of Ranger Company.

RANGER COMPANY GENERAL JOURNAL						Page 1
Date		Account Titles and Descriptions	PR	Dr.	Cr.	
2012 Aug.	17	Cash		6 0 0 0 00		
		Equipment		4 0 0 00		
		B. Ranger, Capital			6 4 0 0 00	
		Initial investment by owner				

a. Year of journal entry

b. Month of journal entry

c. Day of journal entry

d. Name(s) of account(s) debited

e. Name(s) of account(s) credited

f. Explanation of transaction

g. Amount of debit(s)

h. Amount of credit(s)

i. Page of journal

2. Provide the explanation for each of these general journal entries.

	Date		Account Titles and Descriptions	PR	Debit	Credit
	2012 July	10	Cash		8 00 00	
			Office Equipment		5 00 00	
			J. Walsh, Capital			13 00 00
			(A)			
		16	Cash		30 00	
			Accounts Receivable		60 00	
			Hair Fees Earned			90 00
			(B)			
		20	Advertising Expense		40 00	
			Accounts Payable			40 00
			(C)			

GENERAL JOURNAL — Page 4

Posting and Balancing

3. Balance this three-column account. What function does the Post. Ref. column serve? When will Account 111 be used in the journalizing and posting process?

Name: __Cash__   Account No. __111__

Date 2012		Explanation	Post. Ref.	Debit	Credit	DR or CR	Balance
June	1		GJ1	15 00			
	6		GJ1	6 00			
	11		GJ2		4 00		
	12		GJ3	1 0 0			

The Trial Balance

4. The following trial balance was prepared *incorrectly*.

   a. Rearrange the accounts in proper order.

   b. Calculate the total of the trial balance. (Small numbers are used intentionally so that you can do the calculations in your head.) Assume that each account has a normal balance.

Lee Company
Trial Balance
October 31, 2014

	Dr.	Cr.
D. Lee, Capital	17	
Equipment	12	
Rent Expense		4
Advertising Expense		3
Accounts Payable		8
Taxi Fare Income	16	
Cash	17	
D. Lee, Withdrawals		5
Totals	**62**	**20**

Correcting Entry

5. On May 2, 2014, a telephone expense for $180 was debited to Repair Expense. On June 13, 2014, this error was found. Prepare the correcting journal entry. When would a correcting entry *not* be needed?

Exercises

(The forms you need are on pages 3-12 to 3-16 of the *Study Guide with Working Papers.*)

3-1. Prepare journal entries for the following transactions that occurred during October:

2014
Oct.   3   Janet Wills invested $70,000 cash and $6,000 worth of equipment in her new business.
6   Purchased building for $40,000 on account.
13   Purchased a truck from Lowell Co. for $16,000 cash.
17   Bought supplies from Lee Co. on account, $900.

3-2. Record the following in the general journal of Reggie's Auto Repair Shop.

2013
Jan.   4   Reggie Long invested $16,000 cash in the auto repair shop.
7   Paid $7,000 for auto repair equipment.
8   Bought auto repair equipment for $6,000 on account from Lowell Co.
15   Received $900 for repair fees earned.
18   Billed Sullivan Co. $900 for services rendered.
22   Reggie withdrew $300 for personal use.

3-3. Post the following transactions to the ledger of King Company. The partial ledger of King Company includes Cash, 111; Equipment, 121; Accounts Payable, 211; and A. King, Capital, 311. Please use three-column accounts in the posting process.

Date 2012			PR	Dr.	Cr.
April	6	Cash		15 00 0 00	
		A. King, Capital			15 00 0 00
		Cash investment			
	13	Equipment		9 00 0 00	
		Cash			4 00 0 00
		Accounts Payable			5 00 0 00
		Purchase of equipment			

Page 4

Journalizing, posting, and
preparing a trial balance
① ② ③ (20 min)

3-4. From the following transactions for Lowe Company for the month of July, **a.** prepare journal entries (assume that it is page 1 of the journal), **b.** post to the ledger (use three-column account style), and **c.** prepare a trial balance.

2014

July	4	Joan Lowe invested $6,000 in the business.
	7	Bought equipment on account, $800 from Lax Co.
	15	Billed Friend Co. for services rendered, $4,000.
	18	Received $5,000 cash for services rendered.
	25	Paid salaries expense, $1,800.
	28	Joan withdrew $400 for personal use.

A partial chart of accounts includes: Cash, 111; Accounts Receivable, 112; Equipment, 121; Accounts Payable, 211; J. Lowe, Capital, 311; J. Lowe, Withdrawals, 312; Fees Earned, 411; Salaries Expense, 511.

3-5. You have been hired to correct the following trial balance that has been recorded improperly from the ledger to the trial balance.

SUN CO.
TRIAL BALANCE
MARCH 31, 2012

	Dr.	Cr.
Accounts Payable	2 0 0 0 00	
A. Sun, Capital		6 5 0 0 00
A. Sun, Withdrawals		3 0 0 00
Services Earned		4 7 0 0 00
Concessions Earned	2 5 0 0 00	
Rent Expense	4 0 0 00	
Salaries Expense	2 5 0 0 00	
Miscellaneous Expense		1 3 0 0 00
Cash	10 0 0 0 00	
Accounts Receivable		1 2 0 0 00
Totals	17 4 0 0 00	14 0 0 0 00

3-6. On February 5, 2013, Mike Sullivan made the following journal entry to record the purchase of office equipment priced at $1,400 on account. This transaction had not yet been posted when the error was discovered. Make the appropriate correction.

GENERAL JOURNAL

Date			Account Titles and Description	PR	Dr.	Cr.
2013 Feb.	5		Office Equipment		9 0 0 00	
			Accounts Payable			9 0 0 00
			Purchase of office equipment on account			

(The forms you need are on pages 3-17 to 3-26 of the *Study Guide with Working Papers*.)

Journalizing
1 (30 min)

3A-1. Jack Lang operates Jack's Cleaning Service in Victoria. As the bookkeeper, you have been requested to journalize the following transactions:

2013
Aug.
1 Paid rent for two months in advance, $9,000.
6 Purchased cleaning equipment on account from Ryan's Supply House, $4,000.
12 Purchased cleaning supplies from Lee's Wholesale for $900 cash.
15 Received $1,900 cash from cleaning fees earned.
19 Jack withdrew $900 for his personal use.
22 Advertising bill was received from *Sagnicton News* but was still unpaid, $400.
23 Paid hydro expense, $90.
26 Paid salaries expense, $700.
29 Performed cleaning services for $2,100; however, payment will not be received until October.
29 Paid Ryan's Supply House half the amount owed from August 6 transaction.

Check Figure

November 22
Dr. Advertising Expense $400
Cr. Accounts Payable $400

Your task is to journalize the above transactions. The chart of accounts for Jack's Cleaning Service is as follows:

Chart of Accounts

Assets	**Owner's Equity**
111 Cash	311 Jack Lang, Capital
112 Accounts Receivable	312 Jack Lang, Withdrawals
114 Prepaid Rent	
116 Cleaning Supplies	
120 Office Equipment	**Revenue**
121 Cleaning Equipment	411 Cleaning Fees Earned
Liabilities	**Expenses**
211 Accounts Payable	511 Advertising Expense
	512 Hydro Expense
	514 Salaries Expense

Comprehensive problem:
journalizing, posting, and
preparing a trial balance
①②③ (45 min)

3A-2. On June 2, 2014, Betty Rice opened Betty's Art Studio in Toronto. The following transactions occurred in June:

2014
June   2   Betty Rice invested $12,000 in the art studio.
         3   Paid three months' rent in advance, $1,200.
         4   Purchased $600 worth of equipment from Astor Co. on account.
         6   Received $900 cash for art training workshop for teachers.
         9   Purchased $400 worth of art supplies for cash.
      10   Billed Lester Co. $2,100 for group art lessons for its employees.
      10   Paid salaries of assistants, $600.
      16   Betty withdrew $200 from the business for her personal use.
      27   Paid electrical expense, $140.
      30   Paid telephone bill for June, $210.

Required

a. The ledger is already set up for you based on the Chart of Accounts.
b. Journalize (using journal page 1) and post the June transactions.
c. Prepare a trial balance as of June 30, 2014.

The chart of accounts for Betty's Art Studio is as follows:

Check Figure

Trial Balance Total $15,600

Chart of Accounts

Assets	**Owner's Equity**
111 Cash	311 Betty Rice, Capital
112 Accounts Receivable	312 Betty Rice, Withdrawals
114 Prepaid Rent	
121 Art Supplies	**Revenue**
131 Equipment	411 Art Fees Earned
Liabilities	**Expenses**
211 Accounts Payable	511 Electrical Expense
	521 Salaries Expense
	531 Telephone Expense

Comprehensive problem:
journalizing, posting, and
preparing a trial balance
①②③ (45 min)

3A-3. The following transactions occurred in June 2012 for A. French Placement Agency of Fredericton:

2012
June   1   A. French invested $9,000 cash in the placement agency.
        1   Bought equipment on account from Hook Co., $2,000.
        4   Earned placement fees of $1,600, but payment will not be received until July.
        5   A. French withdrew $100 for his personal use.
        8   Paid wages expense, $300.
     11   Placed a client on a local TV show, receiving $600 cash.
     15   Bought supplies on account from Lyon Co., $500.
     28   Paid telephone bill for June, $160.
     29   Advertising bill from Shale Co. was received but not yet paid, $900.

Check Figure

Trial Balance Total $14,600

The chart of accounts for A. French Placement Agency is as follows:

Chart of Accounts

Assets	Owner's Equity
111 Cash	311 A. French, Capital
112 Accounts Receivable	321 A. French, Withdrawals
131 Supplies on Hand	
141 Equipment	**Revenue**
	411 Placement Fees Earned
Liabilities	
211 Accounts Payable	**Expenses**
	511 Wages Expense
	521 Telephone Expense
	531 Advertising Expense

Required

a. The ledger is already set up for you based on the Chart of Accounts.
b. Journalize (page 1) and post the June transactions.
c. Prepare a trial balance as of June 30, 2012.

Group B Problems

(The forms you need are on pages 3-17 to 3-26 of the *Study Guide with Working Papers.*)

Journalizing
 (30 min)

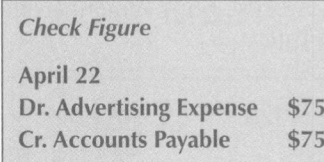 In April 2013, Jack Lang opened a new cleaning service in Victoria. Please assist him by journalizing the following business transactions:

2013
April   1   Jack Lang invested $6,000 worth of cleaning equipment as well as $3,000 cash in the new business.
        2   Purchased cleaning supplies on account from Rex Co., $500.
        9   Purchased office equipment on account from Ross Stationery, $400.
      12   Jack paid his home telephone bill from the company bank account, $60.
      19   Received $600 cash for cleaning services performed.
      22   Advertising bill was received but not yet paid, $75.
      23   Hydro bill was received but not yet paid, $90.
      26   Performed cleaning services for Eastgate School, $700; however, payment will not be received until May.
      29   Paid salaries expense, $400.
      30   Paid Ross Stationery half the amount owed from April 9 transaction.

The chart of accounts for Jack's Cleaning Service includes: Cash, 111; Accounts Receivable, 112; Prepaid Rent, 114; Cleaning Supplies, 116; Office Equipment, 120; Cleaning Equipment, 121; Accounts Payable, 211; Jack Lang, Capital, 311; Jack Lang, Withdrawals, 312; Cleaning Fees Earned, 411; Advertising Expense, 511; Hydro Expense, 512; and Salaries Expense, 514.

> **Check Figure**
>
> April 22
> Dr. Advertising Expense $75
> Cr. Accounts Payable $75

Comprehensive problem:
journalizing, posting, and
preparing a trial balance
①②④ (45 min)

3B-2. In June, the following transactions occurred for Betty's Art Studio of Toronto:

2014

June
2 Betty Rice invested $6,000 in the art studio.
2 Paid four months' rent in advance, $1,200.
3 Purchased art supplies on account from A.J.K., $700.
6 Purchased equipment on account from Reese Company, $900.
9 Received $1,300 cash for art training program provided to Northwest Community College.
10 Billed Long Co. for art lessons provided, $600.
13 Betty withdrew $400 from the art studio to buy a new power saw for her home.
16 Paid salaries expense, $400.
27 Paid telephone bill, $118.
30 Electricity bill was received but not yet paid, $120.

Required

a. The ledger is already set up for you based on the Chart of Accounts.
b. Journalize (all page 1) and post the June transactions.
c. Prepare a trial balance as of June 30, 2014.

Chart of accounts includes: Cash, 111; Accounts Receivable, 112; Prepaid Rent, 114; Art Supplies, 121; Equipment, 131; Accounts Payable, 211; Betty Rice, Capital, 311; Betty Rice, Withdrawals, 312; Art Fees Earned, 411; Electrical Expense, 511; Salaries Expense, 521; Telephone Expense, 531.

Comprehensive problem:
journalizing, posting, and
preparing a trial balance
①②③ (45 min)

3B-3. In June, A. French Placement Agency of Fredericton had the following transactions:

2012

June
1 A. French invested $6,000 in the new placement agency.
4 Bought equipment for cash, $350.
5 Earned placement fee commission, $2,100, but payment from Avon Co. will not be received until July.
8 Paid wages expense, $400.
11 A. French paid his home utility bill using a company cheque, $69.
12 Placed Jay Diamond on a national TV show, receiving $900 cash.
15 Paid cash for supplies, $350.
28 Telephone bill was received but not yet paid, $185.
29 Advertising bill was received but not yet paid, $200.

The chart of accounts includes: Cash, 111; Accounts Receivable, 112; Supplies, 131; Equipment, 141; Accounts Payable, 211; A. French, Capital, 311; A. French, Withdrawals, 321; Placement Fees Earned, 411; Wages Expense, 511; Telephone Expense, 521; Advertising Expense, 531.

Required

a. The ledger is already set up for you based on the Chart of Accounts.
b. Journalize (all page 1) and post transactions.
c. Prepare a trial balance for June 30, 2012.

(The forms you need are on pages 3-27 to 3-36 of the *Study Guide with Working Papers*.)

Journalizing
❶ (40 min)

3C-1. In March, Etta Standforth opened a financial planning centre in downtown Calgary. Please assist her by journalizing the following business transactions:

2012
Mar. 2 Etta Standforth invested $4,100 worth of computer equipment as well as $10,500 cash in the new business.
      6 Purchased computer supplies on account from Carry Co., $355.
      9 Purchased office equipment on account from A-One Stationery, $1,895.
     13 Etta paid her home telephone bill from the company bank account, $55.
     20 Received $875 cash for financial planning services performed.
     21 Advertising bill was received but not yet paid, $450.
     23 Cleaning bill was received but not yet paid, $95.
     27 Performed financial planning services for Harriet Corp., $2,725; however, payment will not be received until April.
     28 Paid salaries expense, $2,100.
     29 Paid A-One Stationery half the amount owed from March 9 transaction, $947.50.
     30 Received bill for repairs on equipment, $250—to be paid in April.

The chart of accounts for the company includes: Cash, 111; Accounts Receivable, 112; Prepaid Rent, 114; Computer Supplies, 116; Office Equipment, 120; Computer Equipment, 121; Accounts Payable, 211; Etta Standforth, Capital, 311; Etta Standforth, Withdrawals, 312; Planning Fees Earned, 411; Advertising Expense, 511; Salaries Expense, 512; Repairs Expense, 513; and Cleaning Expense, 514.

Comprehensive problem: journalizing, posting, and preparing a trial balance
❶❷❸ (50 min)

3C-2. In July, the following transactions occurred for Andy's Fitness Training Studio of Sydney:

2014
July 2 Andy James invested $17,600 in the studio.
      3 Paid three months' rent in advance, $1,650.
      4 Purchased supplies on account from Marlin Supplies, $640.
      7 Purchased equipment on account from Brinkley Company, $5,800.
      8 Received $2,100 cash for fitness training program provided to Anne Webber Dance Group.
     11 Billed Short Co. for lessons provided, $1,400.
     14 Andy withdrew $759 from the studio to buy a new stereo for his apartment.
     15 Paid salaries expense, $1,500.
     28 Paid telephone bill for studio, $160.
     29 Electricity bill was received but not yet paid, $150.
     31 Advertising bill was received from *City Newspaper* but not yet paid, $325.

< start>
Required

a. The ledger is already set up for you based on the Chart of Accounts.

b. Journalize (all page 1) and post the July transactions.

c. Prepare a trial balance as of July 31, 2014.

Chart of accounts includes: Cash, 111; Accounts Receivable, 112; Prepaid Rent, 114; Supplies, 121; Equipment, 131; Accounts Payable, 211; Andy James, Capital, 311; Andy James, Withdrawals, 321; Fees Earned, 411; Advertising Expense, 511; Electrical Expense, 515; Salaries Expense, 521; Telephone Expense, 531.

Comprehensive problem: journalizing, posting, and preparing a trial balance
❶❷❸ (50 min)

3C-3. In June, Matt Nepoose Investigative Agency of Thunder Bay had the following transactions:

2013

June	3	Matt Nepoose invested $15,000 in the new agency.
	4	Bought equipment for cash, $5,100.
	7	Earned investigative fee, $3,200, but payment from client will not be received until later.
	10	Matt paid his home water and gas bill from the company bank account, $107.
	11	Located missing spouse, received $975 cash.
	14	Paid cash for supplies, $270.
	18	Paid wages expense, $1,100.
	25	Received half of the fee earned on June 7, $1,600.
	27	Telephone bill was received but not yet paid, $130.
	28	Advertising bill was received but not yet paid, $525.

Check Figure

Trial Balance total $19,830

The chart of accounts includes: Cash, 111; Accounts Receivable, 112; Supplies, 131; Equipment, 141; Accounts Payable, 211; M. Nepoose, Capital, 311; M. Nepoose, Withdrawals, 321; Investigative Fees Earned, 411; Wages Expense, 511; Telephone Expense, 521; Advertising Expense, 531.

Required

a. The ledger is already set up for you based on the Chart of Accounts.

b. Journalize (all page 1) and post transactions.

c. Prepare a trial balance for June 30, 2013.

On-the-job Training

(The forms you need are on pages 3-37 to 3-38 of the *Study Guide with Working Papers*.)

Correcting the trial balance
❸ (30 min)

T-1. Paul Regan, bookkeeper of Hampton Co., has been up half the night trying to get his trial balance to balance. His results are on page 133.

Ken Small, the accountant, compared Paul's amounts in the trial balance with those in the ledger, recomputed each account balance, and compared postings. Ken found the 10 errors listed on page 133.

HAMPTON CO. TRIAL BALANCE JUNE 30, 2013				
		Dr.		Cr.
Office Sales				5 7 2 0 00
Cash		3 2 6 0 00		
Accounts Receivable		5 6 6 0 00		
Office Equipment		8 4 0 0 00		
Accounts Payable				4 1 6 0 00
D. Hole, Capital				11 5 6 0 00
D. Hole, Withdrawals				7 0 0 00
Wages Expense		2 6 0 0 00		
Rent Expense		9 4 0 00		
Utilities Expense		2 6 00		
Office Supplies		1 2 0 00		
Prepaid Rent		1 8 0 00		

1. A $200 debit to D. Hole, Withdrawals, was posted as a credit.
2. D. Hole, Withdrawals, was listed on the trial balance as a credit.
3. A Note Payable account with a credit balance of $2,400 was not listed on the trial balance.
4. The pencilled footings for Accounts Payable were debits of $5,320 and credits of $8,800.
5. A debit of $180 to Prepaid Rent was not posted.
6. The entry for office supplies bought for $60 was posted as a credit to Supplies.
7. A debit of $120 to Accounts Receivable was not posted.
8. A cash payment of $420 was credited to Cash for $240.
9. The pencilled footing of the credits to Cash was overstated by $400.
10. The Utilities Expense of $260 was listed in the trial balance as $26.

Assist Paul Regan by preparing a correct trial balance. What advice could you give Ken about Paul? Explain the situation to Paul. Put your answers in writing.

Errors in recording transactions and their relationship to the trial balance

❸ (20 min)

T-2. Lauren Oliver, an accountancy lab tutor, is having a debate with some of her assistants. They are trying to find out how each of the following five unrelated situations would affect the trial balance:

1. A $5 debit to Cash in the ledger was not posted.
2. A $10 debit to Computer Supplies was debited to Computer Equipment.
3. An $8 debit to Wages Expense was debited twice to the account.
4. A $4 debit to Computer Supplies was debited to Computer Sales.
5. A $35 credit to Accounts Payable was posted as a $53 credit.

Indicate to Lauren the effect that each situation will have on the trial balance. If a situation will have no effect, indicate that fact. Put in writing how each of these situations could be avoided in the future.

CONTINUING PROBLEM

Preparing financial statements after journalizing, posting, and preparing a trial balance ❶❷❸ (45 min)

Tony's computer centre is picking up in business, so he has decided to expand his bookkeeping system to a general journal/ledger system. The balances from June have been forwarded to the ledger accounts.

The forms are in the *Study Guide with Working Papers*, pages 3-39 to 3-44.

Assignment

1. Use the chart of accounts provided in Chapter 2 (page 90) to record the transactions illustrated by the following documents.

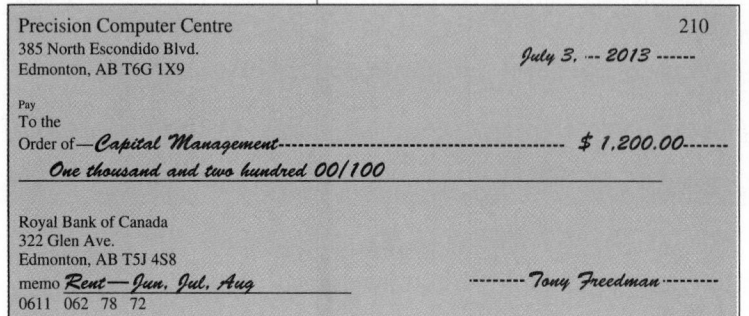

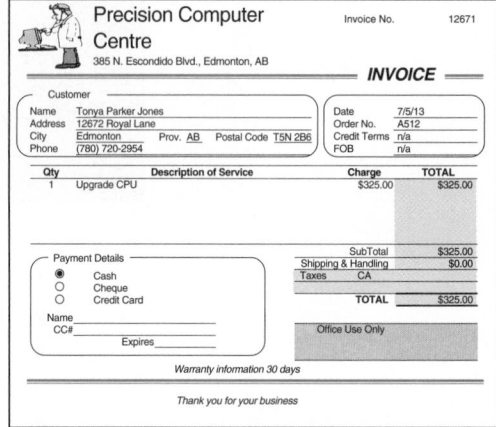

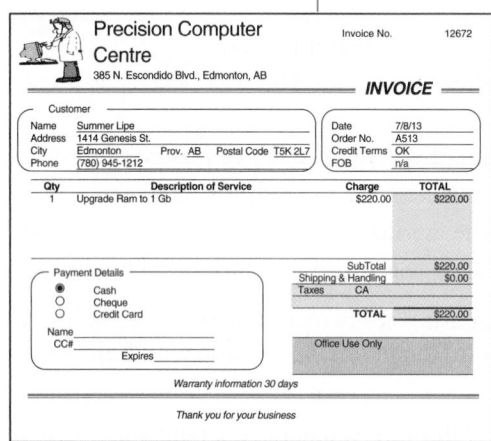

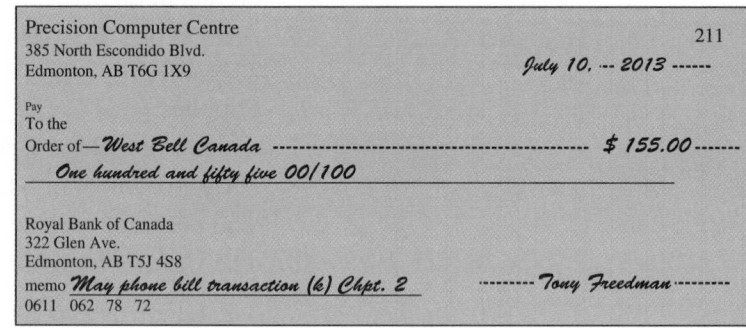

Refer back to Chapter 2, transaction (k).

Refer back to Chapter 2, transaction (o).

Refer back to Chapter 2, transaction (s).

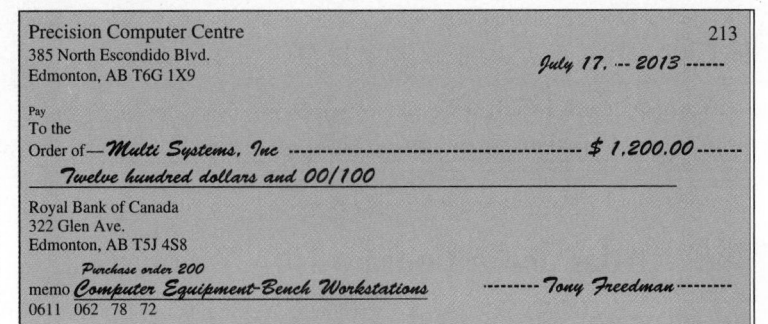

Purchased computer shop equipment.

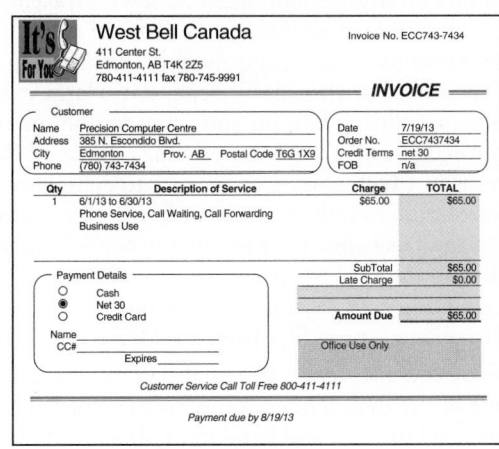

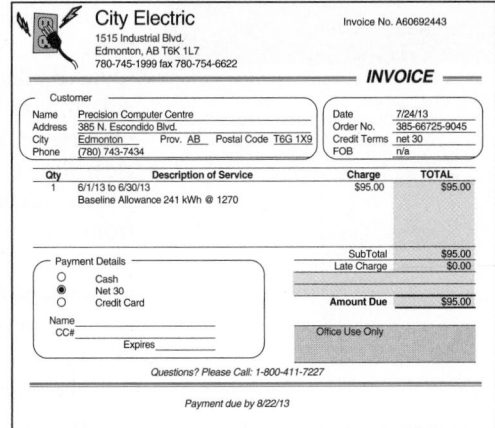

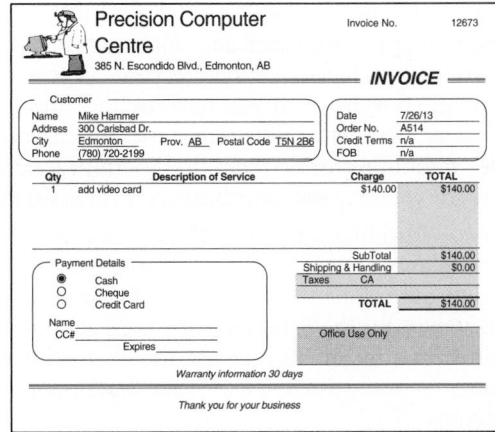

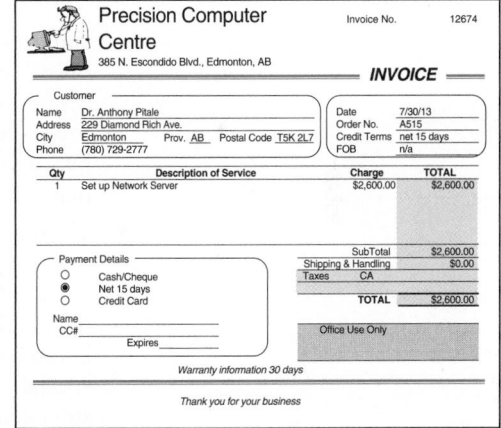

2. Post all transactions to the general ledger accounts (the Prepaid Rent account No. 1025 has been added to the chart of accounts).
3. Prepare a trial balance for July 31, 2013.
4. Prepare the financial statements for the three months ended July 31, 2013.

Instructions and data files for completing this Computer Workshop assignment can be found in the Multimedia Library on MyAccountingLab at **www.myaccountinglab.com**.

Computer Workshops

Atlas and Altinora

Depending on the goals your instructor has set for the course you are taking, you may be asked to complete one or more of the computer workshops created especially for Chapter 3. If you are completing any of the workshops, you will obtain all necessary details from the Multimedia Library on MyAccountingLab at **www.myaccountinglab.com**.

There are a total of four workshops available. For each company, Atlas and Altinora, there are two versions—one using Simply Accounting Pro® and the other using QuickBooks Premier®. The choice will depend to a large extent on which software is available to you in your college's lab, on your own laptop, or other computer, as well as the preference, knowledge, and experience of your instructor. Before beginning, be sure to get clear directions as to which workshop you are to complete. Please note that special, time-limited versions of both Simply Accounting® and QuickBooks® are available at no charge from each company's website. Your instructor might handle this for you, but it is easy to obtain the software and set it up yourself by visiting www.intuit.ca (QuickBooks®) or www.simplyaccounting.com (Simply Accounting®).

You need to obtain several files from the MyAccountingLab website before you begin:

- First there are the instruction files that describe the company, details of its fiscal year, and a listing of the transactions you need to record. This set of files also sets forth the reports you need to print and hand in to obtain a grade on your work.

- Second are the data sets that have been carefully crafted for you so you may begin each workshop with minimal bother. You will find that each data set is downloaded in a compressed format to save space and time, and this means that you need to "uncompress," or restore, each data set before you can use it. Details will be found on the MyAccountingLab website, or you may use the "Restore" command that each of the programs offers. You will get an error message if you try to run these compressed backup files without restoring them first. Both programs also have Help files that you may refer to, or you may ask your instructor for assistance.

- Third are two Word files (one for each program) that set forth in great detail the step-by-step keystrokes you need to make to complete the Atlas assignment. These files are complete with full-colour screen captures that will be of great assistance to you. The help files that exist for the Altinora workshops are not usually available for student use because instructors might want to use the alternative workshop for a quiz, exam, or special project. Some instructors may make the Altinora help files available to you under strict conditions.

As you complete the workshop, please pay close attention to making periodic backups. This does use a bit of your hard drive space but may save you considerable time if and when you make an error. The step-by-step files do cover making a backup, however, you may want to make yourself a backup copy more often than mentioned there. This is a lot more important in later chapters where the number of transactions is greater than those found in the Atlas (and Altinora) workshops.

The Accounting Cycle Continued

THE BIG PICTURE

What is the largest reporting entity in Canada? Put another way, where would you look if you wanted to see the country's largest dollar figures on a set of financial statements?

For an answer, check out www.fin.gc.ca. As you may have guessed, the Government of Canada easily qualifies as the largest Canadian fiscal entity. It is not a business, of course, so it does not have sales revenue, but it does take in well over $200 billion every year.

All accounting students in Canada should visit this site and review Canada's financial position. Lots of people may have the impression that the federal government's financial statements are too complex to bother with. Well, it is true that the numbers are really large, and 2002 introduced some important changes in the way the government reports its financial affairs, but the statements are surprisingly understandable to most Canadians.

Up until 2001, the government used the cash basis of accounting (modified somewhat) for preparing its financial statements. This means that no accruals were used in calculating the numbers shown in the financial statements—tax revenue, for example, was simply the amount of tax received by the government in its fiscal year, not the amount of tax the vari-

ous taxpayers in Canada owed in that year. One other really important aspect of this cash-based approach is that the majority of funds expended on assets were simply written off. If the federal government spent a few million on an upgrade to an airport, for instance, that expenditure just showed up as an expense in the year it happened.

Starting in 2002, the federal government based its financial statements on the accrual basis of accounting, much as it asks all businesses in Canada to do. This meant a substantial increase in the number of adjustments the government departments made in their financial records.

This chapter introduces you to the process of adjustments. You will discover that, rather than recording only the cash in and out, really useful accounting reports are prepared only after a number of adjustments are calculated and recorded in the entity's accounting records. Now, Canada's largest government does the same—and the results dramatically change the details of what our federal government reports to Canadians.

Keep watching Canada's largest fiscal entity. You will learn a lot about accounting, and be a much better informed voter besides!

In the accompanying diagram, steps 1–4 show the steps of the accounting cycle that were completed for Clark's Desktop Publishing Services in the last chapter. This chapter continues the cycle with steps 5 and 6, the preparation of a worksheet and the three financial statements.

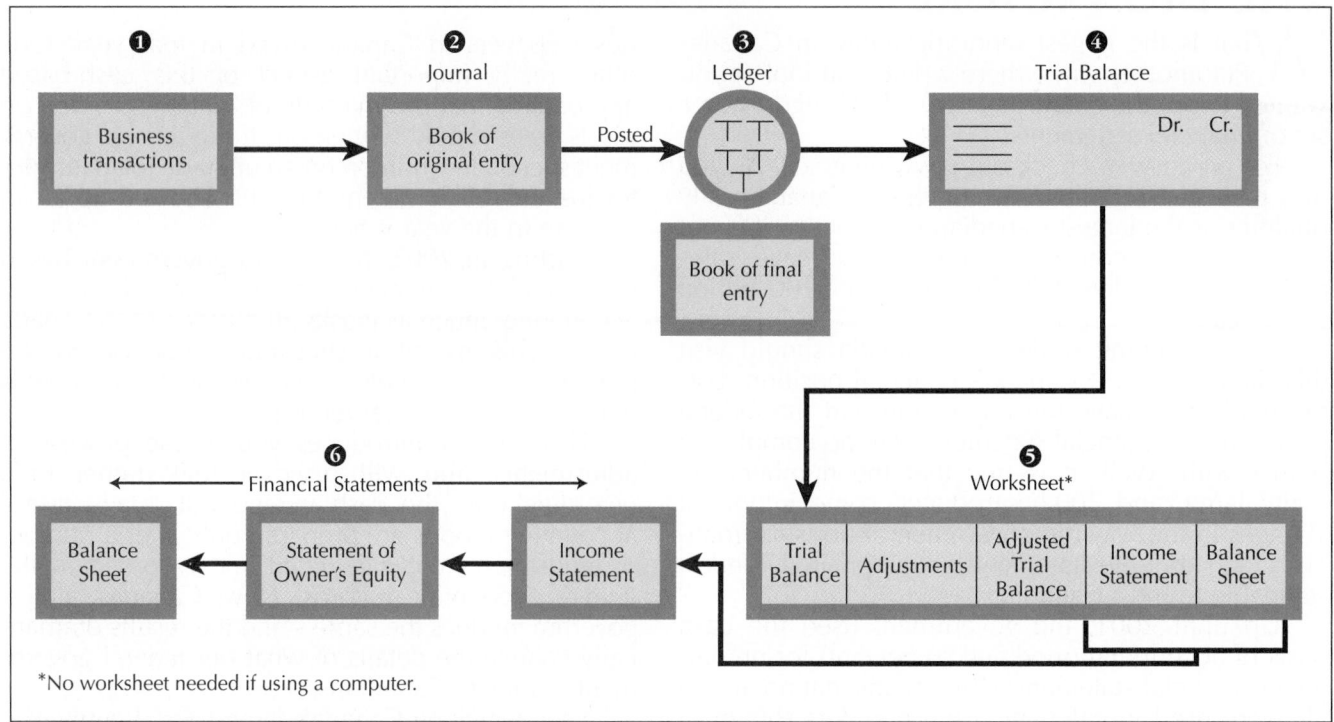

*No worksheet needed if using a computer.

The worksheet is not a formal report, so no dollar signs appear on it. Because it is a ruled form, there are no commas either.

An accountant uses a **worksheet** to organize and check data before preparing the financial reports necessary to complete the accounting cycle. The most important function of the worksheet is to allow the accountant to find and correct errors before financial statements are prepared. In a way, a worksheet acts as the accountant's scratch pad. No one sees the worksheet once the formal reports are prepared. The beginning of a sample worksheet is shown in Figure 4-1.

Learning Unit 4-1

Step 5 of the Accounting Cycle: Preparing a Worksheet

The accounts listed on the far left of the worksheet are taken from the ledger. The rest of the worksheet has five sections: trial balance, adjustments, adjusted trial balance, income statement, and balance sheet. Each of these sections is divided into debit and credit columns. Refer often to the special overlays in Figure 4-5 (see page 148b) as you

CLARK'S DESKTOP PUBLISHING SERVICES
WORKSHEET
FOR MONTH ENDED MAY 31, 2013

Account Titles	Trial Balance Dr.	Trial Balance Cr.	Adjustments Dr.	Adjustments Cr.	Adjusted Trial Balance Dr.	Adjusted Trial Balance Cr.	Income Statement Dr.	Income Statement Cr.
Cash	6 1 5 5 00							
Accounts Receivable	5 0 0 0 00							
Office Supplies	6 0 0 00							
Prepaid Rent	1 2 0 0 00							
Desktop Publishing Equipment	6 0 0 0 00							
Accounts Payable		3 3 5 0 00						
Brenda Clark, Capital		10 0 0 0 00						
Brenda Clark, Withdrawals	6 2 5 00							
Desktop Publishing Fees		8 0 0 0 00						
Office Salaries Expense	1 3 0 0 00							
Advertising Expense	2 5 0 00							
Telephone Expense	2 2 0 00							
	21 3 5 0 00	21 3 5 0 00						

Figure 4-1 Sample Worksheet—Started, with Trial Balance

study this learning unit. The transparencies illustrating the completion of a worksheet can be very useful to your understanding of the process.

THE TRIAL BALANCE SECTION

We discussed how to prepare a trial balance in Chapter 3. Some companies prepare a separate trial balance; others, such as Clark's Desktop Publishing Services, prepare the trial balance directly on the worksheet. Every account in the ledger that has a balance is entered in the trial balance. Additional titles from the ledger are added as they are needed. (We will show this later.)

THE ADJUSTMENTS SECTION

Chapters 1 to 3 discussed transactions that occurred with outside suppliers and companies. In a real business, inside transactions also occur during the accounting cycle. These transactions must be recorded too. At the end of the worksheet process, the accountant will have all of the business's accounts up to date and ready to be used to prepare the formal financial statements. By analyzing each of Clark's accounts on the worksheet, the accountant will be able to identify specific accounts that must be **adjusted** to bring them up to date. The accountant for Clark's Desktop Publishing Services needs to adjust the following accounts:

    A. Office Supplies   C. Desktop Publishing Equipment

    B. Prepaid Rent   D. Office Salaries Expense

Let's look at how to analyze and adjust each of these accounts.

A. Adjusting the Office Supplies Account

On May 31, the accountant found out that the company had only $100 worth of office supplies on hand. When the company originally purchased the $600 worth of office supplies, they were considered an asset. However, as the supplies were used up, they became an expense.

◆ Office supplies available, $600
◆ Office supplies left or on hand as of May 31, $100
◆ Office supplies used up in the operation of the business for the month of May, $500

As a result, the asset Office Supplies on the trial balance is too high (it should be $100, not $600). At the same time, if we don't show the additional expense of supplies used, the company's *net income* will be too high.

If Clark's accountant does not adjust the trial balance to reflect the change, the company's net income would be too high on the income statement and both sides (assets and owner's equity) of the balance sheet also would be too high.

Now let's look at the adjustment for office supplies in terms of the transaction analysis chart.

Will go on income statement.

Accounts Affected	Category	↑ ↓	Rules
Office Supplies Expense	Expense	↑	Dr.
Office Supplies	Asset	↓	Cr.

Will go on balance sheet.

The Office Supplies Expense account comes from the Chart of Accounts on page 93. Since it is not listed in the trial balance account titles, it must be listed below the trial balance. Let's see how we enter this adjustment on the worksheet.

Place $500 in the debit column of the adjustments section on the same line as Office Supplies Expense. Place $500 in the credit column of the adjustments section on the same line as Office Supplies. The numbers in the adjustment column show what is used, *not* what is on hand.

The adjustment for supplies deals with the amount of supplies used up.

Adjustments affect both the income statement and the balance sheet.

Office Supplies Expense 514

| 500 | |

This is supplies used up.

Office Supplies 114

| 600 | 500 |
| 100 | |

This is supplies on hand.

For our discussion, the letter A is used to code the Office Supplies adjustment because it is the first adjustment.

Note: All accounts listed below the trial balance will be *increasing*.

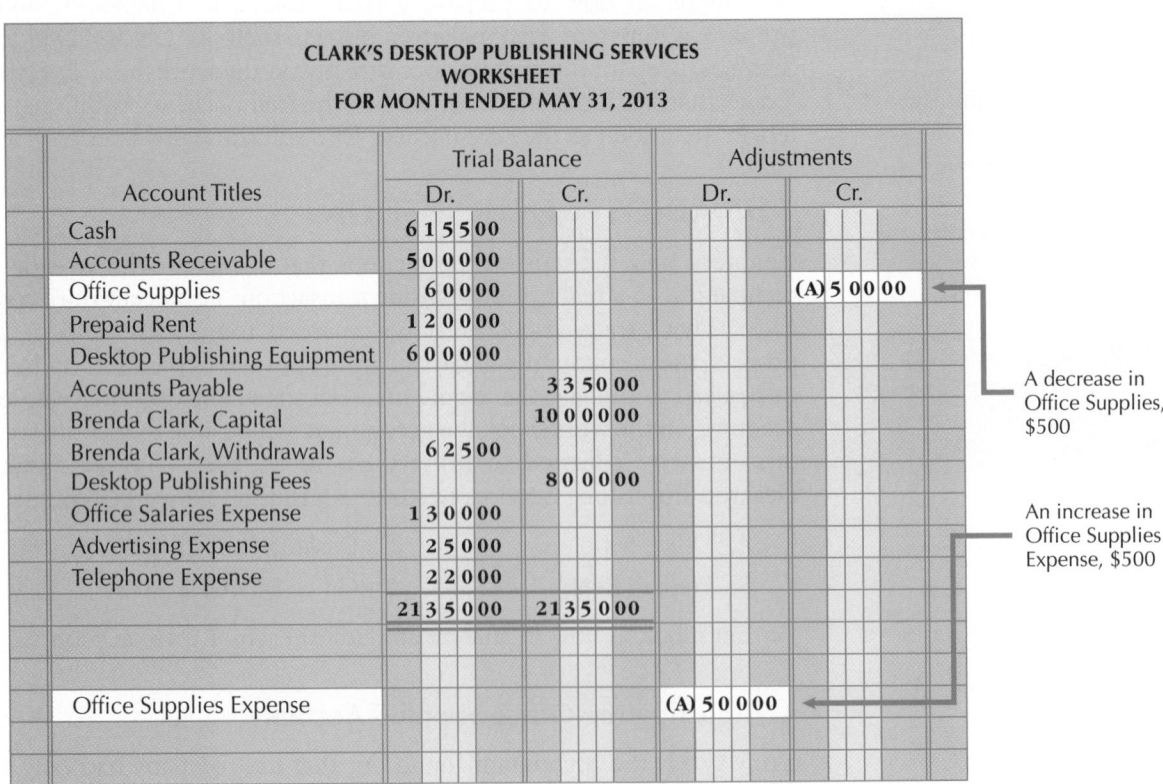

CLARK'S DESKTOP PUBLISHING SERVICES
WORKSHEET
FOR MONTH ENDED MAY 31, 2013

Account Titles	Trial Balance Dr.	Trial Balance Cr.	Adjustments Dr.	Adjustments Cr.
Cash	6 1 5 5 00			
Accounts Receivable	5 0 0 0 00			
Office Supplies	6 0 0 00			(A) 5 0 0 00
Prepaid Rent	1 2 0 0 00			
Desktop Publishing Equipment	6 0 0 0 00			
Accounts Payable		3 3 50 00		
Brenda Clark, Capital		10 0 0 0 00		
Brenda Clark, Withdrawals	6 2 5 00			
Desktop Publishing Fees		8 0 0 0 00		
Office Salaries Expense	1 3 0 0 00			
Advertising Expense	2 5 0 00			
Telephone Expense	2 2 0 00			
	21 3 5 0 00	21 3 5 0 00		
Office Supplies Expense			(A) 5 0 0 00	

A decrease in Office Supplies, $500

An increase in Office Supplies Expense, $500

B. Adjusting the Prepaid Rent Account

The Office Supplies Expense account (on page 140) indicates the amount of supplies used up. It is listed below other trial balance accounts since it was not on the original trial balance.

A debit will increase the account Office Supplies Expense; a credit will reduce the asset account Office Supplies.

Adjusting Prepaid Rent: On page 109 the trial balance showed a figure for Prepaid Rent of $1,200. The amount of rent *expired* is the adjustment figure used to update Prepaid Rent and Rent Expense.

Rent Expense 515

400	

Prepaid Rent 115

1,200	400
800	

Back on May 1, Clark's Desktop Publishing Services paid three months' rent in advance. The accountant realized that the rent expense would be $400 per month ($1,200 ÷ 3 months = $400).

Remember, when rent expense is paid in advance, it is considered an asset called *prepaid rent.* When the asset, prepaid rent, begins to expire or be used up, it becomes an expense. Now it is May 31, and one month's prepaid rent has become an expense.

How is this handled? Should the account be $1,200, or is there really only $800 of prepaid rent left as of May 31? What do we need to do to bring prepaid rent to the "true" balance? The answer is that we must increase Rent Expense by $400 and decrease Prepaid Rent by $400.

Without this adjustment, the expenses for Clark's Desktop Publishing Services for May will be too low, and the asset Prepaid Rent will be too high. If unadjusted amounts were used in the formal reports, the net income shown on the income statement would be too high, and both sides (assets and owner's equity) would be too high on the balance sheet.

In terms of our transaction analysis chart, the adjustment would look like this:

Will go on income statement.

Accounts Affected	Category	↑ ↓	Rules
Rent Expense	**Expense**	↑	**Dr.**
Prepaid Rent	**Asset**	↓	**Cr.**

Will go on balance sheet.

Like the Office Supplies Expense account, the Rent Expense account comes from the chart of accounts on page 93.

The worksheet on page 142 shows how to enter an adjustment to Prepaid Rent.

C. Adjusting the Desktop Publishing Equipment Account for Amortization

Take this one slowly.

Original cost of $6,000 for desktop publishing equipment remains *unchanged* after adjustments.

The life of the asset affects how it is adjusted. The two accounts we discussed above, Office Supplies and Prepaid Rent, involved things that are used up relatively quickly. Equipment—like desktop publishing equipment—is expected to last much longer. Also, it is expected to help produce revenue over a longer period. That is why accountants treat it differently. The balance sheet reports the **historical cost**, or original cost, of the equipment. The original cost also is reflected in the ledger. The adjustment shows how the cost of the equipment is allocated (spread) to the income statement over its expected useful life. This spreading is called **amortization**. To amortize the equipment, we have to figure out how much of its value goes down each month. Then we have to keep a running total of how that amortization mounts up over time. Canada Revenue Agency has a specific set of rules (called **Capital Cost Allowance** rules), which tell how businesses in Canada may amortize their assets for tax purposes. For accounting reports, however, different methods can be used to calculate amortization. We will use the simplest method—straight-line amortization—to calculate the amortization of Clark's Desktop Publishing Services' equipment. Under the straight-line method, equal amounts are taken over successive periods of time. Chapter 15 includes many detailed examples and illustrations of amortization, but for now, only a very simple example is being used.

The Rent Expense is the second account to be adjusted. We label it B as a reference for our discussion.

Rent Expense is listed below other trial balance accounts since it was not on the original trial balance.

Again, note that accounts listed below the trial balance are always increasing.

CLARK'S DESKTOP PUBLISHING SERVICES
WORKSHEET
FOR MONTH ENDED MAY 31, 2013

Account Titles	Trial Balance Dr.	Trial Balance Cr.	Adjustments Dr.	Adjustments Cr.
Cash	6 1 5 5 00			
Accounts Receivable	5 0 0 0 00			
Office Supplies	6 0 0 00			(A) 5 0 0 00
Prepaid Rent	1 2 0 0 00			(B) 4 0 0 00
Desktop Publishing Equipment	6 0 0 0 00			
Accounts Payable		3 3 5 0 00		
Brenda Clark, Capital		1 0 0 0 0 00		
Brenda Clark, Withdrawals	6 2 5 00			
Desktop Publishing Fees		8 0 0 0 00		
Office Salaries Expense	1 3 0 0 00			
Advertising Expense	2 5 0 00			
Telephone Expense	2 2 0 00			
	2 1 3 5 0 00	2 1 3 5 0 00		
Office Supplies Expense			(A) 5 0 0 00	
Rent Expense			(B) 4 0 0 00	

A decrease in Prepaid Rent, $400

An increase in Rent Expense, $400

The calculation of amortization for the year for Clark's Desktop Publishing Services is as follows:

$$\frac{\text{Cost of Equipment} - \text{Residual Value}}{\text{Estimated Years of Usefulness}}$$

Assume equipment has a five-year life.

Desktop Publishing equipment has an expected life of approximately five years. At the end of that time, the property's value is called its "residual value." Think of **residual value** as the estimated value of the equipment at the end of the fifth year. For Clark, the equipment has an estimated residual value of $1,200.

Clark's will record $960 of amortization each year.

$$\frac{\$6,000 - \$1,200}{5 \text{ Years}} = \frac{\$4,800}{5} = \$960 \text{ amortization per year}$$

Our trial balance is for one month, so we must determine the adjustment for that month:

$$\frac{\$960}{12 \text{ Months}} = \$80 \text{ amortization per month}$$

Amortization is an expense reported on the income statement.

This $80 is known as *Amortization Expense* and will be shown on the income statement.

Next, we have to create a new account that can keep a running total of the amortization amount apart from the original cost of the equipment. That account is called **Accumulated Amortization**.

Accumulated Amortization	
Dr.	Cr.
–	+

is a contra-asset account found on the balance sheet.

The Accumulated Amortization account shows the amount of amortization that has been taken or accumulated over a period of time. This is a **contra-asset account**; it has a normal balance opposite that of an asset such as equipment. Accumulated Amortization will summarize, accumulate, or build up the amount of amortization that is taken on the desktop publishing equipment over its estimated useful life.

This is how it would look on a partial balance sheet of Clark's Desktop Publishing Services.

❶ Historical cost of $6,000 for equipment is not changed.

❷ Amount of accumulated amortization is $80.

❸ This shows the remaining portion of the historical cost of the equipment that may be amortized in future periods of time. This figure, the cost of the asset less its accumulated amortization, is often termed **book value** or carrying value.

CLARK'S DESKTOP PUBLISHING SERVICES
BALANCE SHEET
MAY 31, 2013

Assets

		XXXX
Desktop Publishing Equipment	$6,000	
Less: Accumulated Amortization	80	5,920

Let's summarize the key points before going on to enter the adjustment on the worksheet:

1. Amortization Expense goes on the income statement, which results in:
   a. An increase in total expenses
   b. A decrease in net income

2. Accumulated amortization is a contra-asset account found on the balance sheet next to its related equipment account.
3. The original cost of equipment is not reduced; it stays the same until the equipment is sold or retired.
4. Each month, the amount in the Accumulated Amortization account grows larger, while the cost of the equipment remains the same.
5. Businesses may reduce their income tax expense by deducting Capital Cost Allowance (CCA). This CCA is similar to amortization, and some smaller businesses may use CCA values for their amortization expense. Chapter 15 has further details.

Now, let's analyze the adjustment on the transaction analysis chart.

Will go on income statement.

Accounts Affected	Category	↑ ↓	Rules
Amortization Expense, Desktop Publishing Equipment	**Expense**	↑	**Dr.**
Accumulated Amortization, Desktop Publishing Equipment	**Asset (Contra)**	↑	**Cr.**

Will go on balance sheet.

Remember, the original cost of the equipment never changes: the equipment account is not included among the affected accounts because the original cost of equipment remains the same. When the Accumulated Amortization increases (as a credit), the equipment's **book value** decreases.

The worksheet on page 144 shows how we enter the adjustment for amortization of desktop publishing equipment.

CLARK'S DESKTOP PUBLISHING SERVICES
WORKSHEET
FOR MONTH ENDED MAY 31, 2013

Account Titles	Trial Balance Dr.	Trial Balance Cr.	Adjustments Dr.	Adjustments Cr.
Cash	6 1 5 5 00			
Accounts Receivable	5 0 0 0 00			
Office Supplies	6 0 0 00			(A) 5 0 0 00
Prepaid Rent	1 2 0 0 00			(B) 4 0 0 00
Desktop Publishing Equipment	6 0 0 0 00			
Accounts Payable		3 3 5 0 00		
Brenda Clark, Capital		10 0 0 0 00		
Brenda Clark, Withdrawals	6 2 5 00			
Desktop Publishing Fees		8 0 0 0 00		
Office Salaries Expense	1 3 0 0 00			
Advertising Expense	2 5 0 00			
Telephone Expense	2 2 0 00			
	21 3 5 0 00	21 3 5 0 00		
Office Supplies Expense			(A) 5 0 0 00	
Rent Expense			(B) 4 0 0 00	
Amortization Exp., DTP Equip.			(C) 8 0 00	
Acc. Amortization, DTP Equip.				(C) 8 0 00

An increase in Amortization Expense, Desktop Publishing Equipment

An increase in Accumulated Amortization, Desktop Publishing Equipment

Accumulated Amortization

Dr.	Cr.
	History of amount of amortization taken to date

Because this is a new business, neither account had a previous balance. Therefore, neither is listed in the account titles of the trial balance. We need to list both accounts below Rent Expense in the account titles section. On the worksheet, put $80 in the debit column of the adjustments section on the same line as Amortization Expense, DTP Equipment, and put $80 in the credit column of the adjustments section on the same line as Accumulated Amortization, DTP Equipment.

Next month, on June 30, a further $80 would be entered under Amortization Expense, and Accumulated Amortization would show a balance of $160. Remember, Clark's was a new company in May, so no previous amortization was taken.

Now let's look at the last adjustment for Clark's Desktop Publishing Services.

D. Adjusting the Accrued Salaries Account

Clark's Desktop Publishing Services paid $1,300 in Office Salaries Expense (see the trial balance of any previous worksheet in this chapter). The last salary cheques for the month were paid on May 25. How can we update this account to show the salary expense as of May 31?

John Murray worked for Clark's on May 28, 29, 30, and 31, but his next paycheque is not due until June 8. John earned $350 for these four days. Is the $350 an expense to Clark's in May, when it was earned, or in June when it is due and is paid?

May						
S	M	T	W	T	F	S
		1	2	3	4	5
6	7	8	9	10	11	12
13	14	15	16	17	18	19
20	21	22	23	24	25	26
27	28	29	30	31		

Think back to Chapter 1 when we first discussed revenue and expenses. We noted then that revenue is recorded when it is earned, not when the payment is received, and expenses are recorded when they are incurred, not when they are actually paid. This principle will be discussed further in a later chapter; for now, it is enough to remember that we record revenue and expenses when they occur because we want to match earned revenue with the expenses that resulted in earning those revenues. In this case, by working those four days, John Murray created some revenue for Clark's in May. Therefore, the office salaries expense must be shown in May—the month in which the revenue was earned.

The results are:

◆ Office Salaries Expense is increased by $350. This unpaid and unrecorded expense for salaries for which payment is not yet due is called **accrued salaries**. Sometimes, accrued salaries is also called **Salaries Payable**. In effect, we now show the true expense for salaries ($1,650 instead of $1,300):

Office Salaries Expense
1,300	
350	

◆ The second result is that accrued salaries is increased by $350. Clark's has created a liability called Accrued Salaries, meaning that the firm owes money for salaries. When the firm pays John Murray, it will reduce its liability, Accrued Salaries, as well as decrease its cash.

In terms of the transaction analysis chart, the following would be done:

Accounts Affected	Category	↑ ↓	Rules
Office Salaries Expense	Expense	↑	Dr.
Accrued Salaries	Liability	↑	Cr.

How the adjustment for accrued salaries is entered on the worksheet is shown at the top of page 146.

The account Office Salaries Expense is already listed in the account titles, so $350 is placed in the debit column of the adjustments section on the same line as Office Salaries Expense. However, because the Accrued Salaries is not listed in the account titles, the account title Accrued Salaries is added below the trial balance, below Accumulated Amortization, DTP Equipment. Also, $350 is placed in the credit column of the adjustments section on the same line as Accrued Salaries.

Now that we have finished all the adjustments that we intended to make, we total the adjustments section, as shown in Figure 4-2.

THE ADJUSTED TRIAL BALANCE SECTION

The adjusted trial balance is the next section on the worksheet. To fill it out, we must summarize the information in the trial balance and adjustments sections, as shown in Figure 4-3.

Note that when the numbers are brought across from the trial balance to the adjusted trial balance, two debits will be added together and two credits will be added together. If the numbers include a debit and a credit, take the difference between the two and place it on the side that has the larger figure. The total debits should equal the total credits on the adjusted trial balance.

Now that we have completed the adjustments and adjusted trial balance sections of the worksheet, it is time to move on to the income statement and the balance sheet sections. Before we do that, however, look at the chart shown in Table 4-1 on page 148. This table should be used as a reference to help you fill out the next two sections of the worksheet.

The Accrued Salaries account is coded D because it is the fourth account to be adjusted.

Remember, all accounts added below the trial balance are increasing.

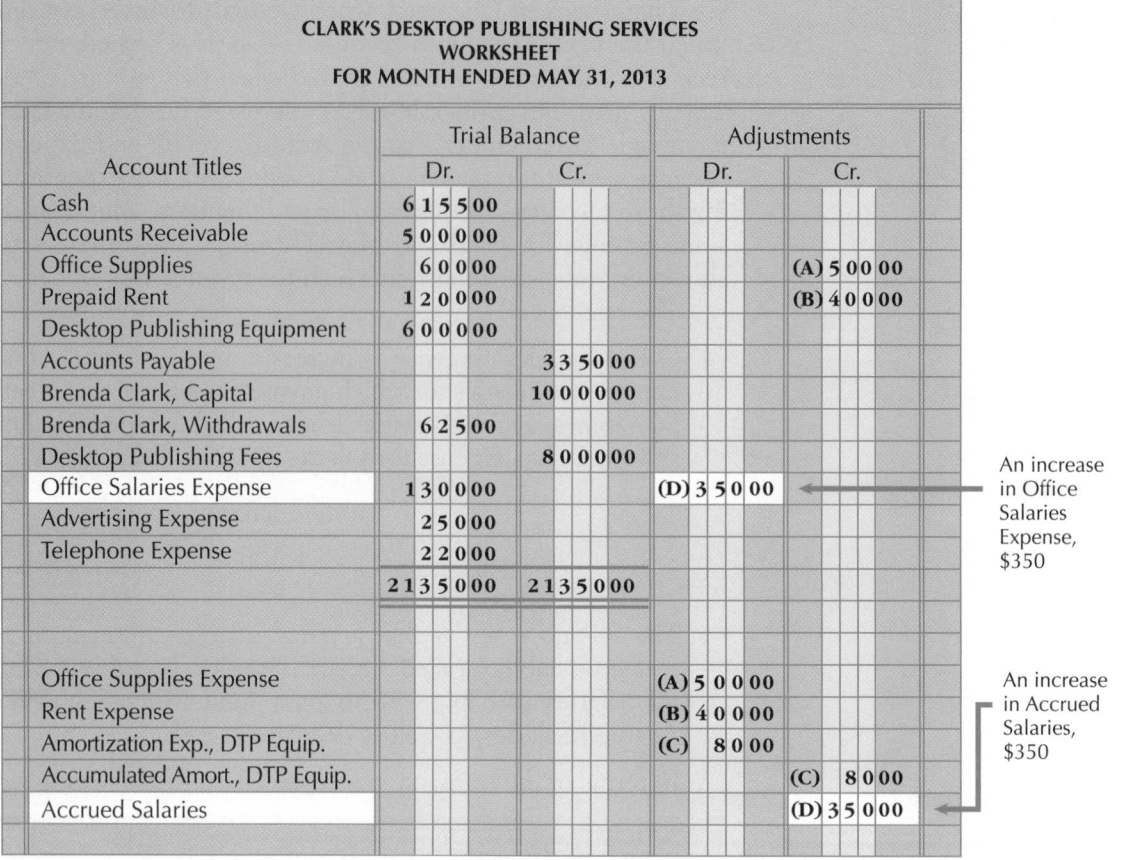

CLARK'S DESKTOP PUBLISHING SERVICES
WORKSHEET
FOR MONTH ENDED MAY 31, 2013

Account Titles	Trial Balance Dr.	Trial Balance Cr.	Adjustments Dr.	Adjustments Cr.
Cash	6 1 5 5 00			
Accounts Receivable	5 0 0 0 00			
Office Supplies	6 0 0 00			(A) 5 00 00
Prepaid Rent	1 2 0 0 00			(B) 4 0 0 00
Desktop Publishing Equipment	6 0 0 0 00			
Accounts Payable		3 3 5 0 00		
Brenda Clark, Capital		10 0 0 0 00		
Brenda Clark, Withdrawals	6 2 5 00			
Desktop Publishing Fees		8 0 0 0 00		
Office Salaries Expense	1 3 0 0 00		(D) 3 5 0 00	
Advertising Expense	2 5 0 00			
Telephone Expense	2 2 0 00			
	21 3 5 0 00	21 3 5 0 00		
Office Supplies Expense			(A) 5 0 0 00	
Rent Expense			(B) 4 0 0 00	
Amortization Exp., DTP Equip.			(C) 8 0 00	
Accumulated Amort., DTP Equip.				(C) 8 0 00
Accrued Salaries				(D) 3 5 0 00

An increase in Office Salaries Expense, $350

An increase in Accrued Salaries, $350

Figure 4-2
The Adjustments Section of the Worksheet

CLARK'S DESKTOP PUBLISHING SERVICES
WORKSHEET
FOR MONTH ENDED MAY 31, 2013

Account Titles	Trial Balance Dr.	Trial Balance Cr.	Adjustments Dr.	Adjustments Cr.
Cash	6 1 5 5 00			
Accounts Receivable	5 0 0 0 00			
Office Supplies	6 0 0 00			(A) 5 0 0 00
Prepaid Rent	1 2 0 0 00			(B) 4 0 0 00
Desktop Publishing Equipment	6 0 0 0 00			
Accounts Payable		3 3 5 0 00		
Brenda Clark, Capital		10 0 0 0 00		
Brenda Clark, Withdrawals	6 2 5 00			
Desktop Publishing Fees		8 0 0 0 00		
Office Salaries Expense	1 3 0 0 00		(D) 3 5 0 00	
Advertising Expense	2 5 0 00			
Telephone Expense	2 2 0 00			
	21 3 5 0 00	21 3 5 0 00		
Office Supplies Expense			(A) 5 0 0 00	
Rent Expense			(B) 4 0 0 00	
Amortization Expense, DTP Equip.			(C) 8 0 00	
Accum. Amort., DTP Equip.				(C) 8 0 00
Accrued Salaries				(D) 3 5 0 00
			1 3 3 0 00	1 3 3 0 00

CLARK'S DESKTOP PUBLISHING SERVICES
WORKSHEET
FOR MONTH ENDED MAY 31, 2010

Account Titles	Trial Balance Dr.	Trial Balance Cr.	Adjustments Dr.	Adjustments Cr.	Adjusted Trial Balance Dr.	Adjusted Trial Balance Cr.
Cash	6 1 5 5 00				6 1 5 5 00	
Accounts Receivable	5 0 0 0 00				5 0 0 0 00	
Office Supplies	6 0 0 00			(A) 5 0 0 00	1 0 0 00	
Prepaid Rent	1 2 0 0 00			(B) 4 0 0 00	8 0 0 00	
Desktop Publishing Equipment	6 0 0 0 00				6 0 0 0 00	
Accounts Payable		3 3 5 0 00				3 3 5 0 00
Brenda Clark, Capital		10 0 0 0 00				10 0 0 0 00
Brenda Clark, Withdrawals	6 2 5 00				6 2 5 00	
Desktop Publishing Fees		8 0 0 0 00				8 0 0 0 00
Office Salaries Expense	1 3 0 0 00		(D) 3 5 0 00		1 6 5 0 00	
Advertising Expense	2 5 0 00				2 5 0 00	
Telephone Expense	2 2 0 00				2 2 0 00	
	21 3 5 0 00	21 3 5 0 00				
Office Supplies Expense			(A) 5 0 0 00		5 0 0 00	
Rent Expense			(B) 4 0 0 00		4 0 0 00	
Amortization Exp., DTP Equip.			(C) 8 0 00		8 0 00	
Accum. Amort., DTP Equip.				(C) 8 0 00		8 0 00
Accrued Salaries				(D) 3 5 0 00		3 5 0 00
			1 3 3 0 00	1 3 3 0 00	21 7 8 0 00	21 7 8 0 00

Annotations:

If no adjustment is made, just carry over the amount from the trial balance on same side.

Supplies were $600, but we used up $500, leaving us with a $100 balance in supplies. *Note:* If there is a debit and a credit, take the *difference* between the two and place it on the side that has the larger figure.

Note: Equipment is *not* adjusted here.

Two debits are added together. If there were two credits, they also would have been added together and shown in the credit column.

Carry these amounts over to adjusted trial balance in the same positions.

Note: The total of the left (debit) must equal the total of the right (credit) ($21,780).

Figure 4-3 The Adjusted Trial Balance Section of the Worksheet

TABLE 4-1　Normal Balances and Account Categories

Account Title	Category	Normal Balance on Adjusted Trial Balance	Income Statement Dr.	Income Statement Cr.	Balance Sheet Dr.	Balance Sheet Cr.
Cash	Asset	Dr.			X	
Accounts Receivable	Asset	Dr.			X	
Office Supplies	Asset	Dr.			X	
Prepaid Rent	Asset	Dr.			X	
Desktop Publishing Equipment	Asset	Dr.			X	
Accounts Payable	Liability	Cr.				X
Brenda Clark, Capital	Owner's Equity	Cr.				X
Brenda Clark, Withdrawals	Owner's Equity	Dr.			X	
Desktop Publishing Fees	Revenue	Cr.		X		
Office Salaries Expense	Expense	Dr.	X			
Advertising Expense	Expense	Dr.	X			
Telephone Expense	Expense	Dr.	X			
Office Supplies Expense	Expense	Dr.	X			
Rent Expense	Expense	Dr.	X			
Amortization Expense, DTP Equipment	Expense	Dr.	X			
Accumulated Amortization, DTP Equipment	Asset (Contra)	Cr.				X
Accrued Salaries	Liability	Cr.				X

Keep in mind that the numbers from the adjusted trial balance are carried over to one of the last four columns of the worksheet before the net income or net loss can be calculated.

THE INCOME STATEMENT SECTION

3 Completing the income statement and balance sheet sections of the worksheet

In the worksheet, net income is placed in the debit column of the income statement. Net loss goes in the credit column.

The difference between $3,100 Dr. and $8,000 Cr. indicates a net income of $4,900. Do not think of the Net Income as a Dr. or Cr. The $4,900 is placed in the debit column to balance the two columns at $8,000. Actually, the credit side is larger by $4,900.

As shown in Figure 4-4, the income statement section lists only revenue and expenses from the adjusted trial balance. Note that Accumulated Amortization and Accrued Salaries do not go on the income statement. Accumulated Amortization is a contra-asset account found on the balance sheet. Accrued Salaries is a liability account found on the balance sheet.

The revenue ($8,000) and all the individual expenses are listed in the income statement section. The revenue is placed in the credit column of the income statement section because it has a credit balance. The expenses have debit balances, so they are placed in the debit column of the income statement section. The following steps must be taken after the debits and credits are placed in the correct columns:

Step 1: Total the debits and the credits.

Step 2: Calculate the difference between the totals of the debit and credit columns and place this difference on the side with the smaller total.

Step 3: Total the two columns again.

The worksheet in Figure 4-4 shows that the label "Net Income" is added in the account title column on the same line as $4,900. When there is a net income, it will be placed in the debit column of the income statement section of the worksheet. If there is a net loss, it is placed in the credit column. The $8,000 total indicates that the two columns are in balance.

Account Titles	Adjusted Trial Balance Dr.	Adjusted Trial Balance Cr.	Income Statement Dr.	Income Statement Cr.
Cash	6 1 5 5 00			
Accounts Receivable	5 0 0 0 00			
Office Supplies	1 0 0 00			
Prepaid Rent	8 0 0 00			
Desktop Publishing Equipment	6 0 0 0 00			
Accounts Payable		3 3 50 00		
Brenda Clark, Capital		10 0 0 0 00		
Brenda Clark, Withdrawals	6 2 5 00			
Desktop Publishing Fees		8 0 0 0 00		8 0 0 0 00
Office Salaries Expense	1 6 5 0 00		1 6 5 0 00	
Advertising Expense	2 5 0 00		2 5 0 00	
Telephone Expense	2 2 0 00		2 2 0 00	
Office Supplies Expense	5 0 0 00		5 0 0 00	
Rent Expense	4 0 0 00		4 0 0 00	
Amortization Expense, DTP Equipment	8 0 00		8 0 00	
Accumulated Amortization, DTP Equipment		8 0 00		
Accrued Salaries		3 5 0 00		
	21 7 8 0 00	21 7 8 0 00	3 1 0 0 00	8 0 0 0 00
Net Income			4 9 0 0 00	
			8 0 0 0 00	8 0 0 0 00

CLARK'S DESKTOP PUBLISHING SERVICES
WORKSHEET
FOR MONTH ENDED MAY 31, 2013

8,000
− 3,100
4,900 → Net Income

Figure 4-4   The Income Statement Section of the Worksheet

Remember: The ending figure for capital is *not* on the worksheet.

To see whether additional investments occurred for the period, you must check the capital account in the ledger.

The amounts come from the adjusted trial balance except the $4,900, which was carried over from the income statement section.

THE BALANCE SHEET SECTION

To fill out the balance sheet section of the worksheet, the following are carried over from the adjusted trial balance section: assets, contra-assets, liabilities, capital, and withdrawals. The net income is brought over to the credit column of the balance sheet so the two columns balance. This net income will be added to the figure for capitalization on the statement of owner's equity.

Let's now look at the completed worksheet in Figure 4-5 to see how the balance sheet section is completed. The base worksheet here provides the trial balance. When Overlay No. 1 is placed over the base worksheet, we can see all the adjustments and the adjusted trial balance. Overlay No. 2 provides the income statement items and also the balance sheet items. Finally, Overlay No. 3 totals the income statement and balance sheet columns, determines the difference, enters the difference appropriately in each statement, and totals the columns again. Note how the net income of $4,900 is brought over to the credit column of the worksheet. The figure for capital is also in the credit column, while the figure for withdrawals is in the debit column. By placing the net income in the credit column, both sides total $18,680. If a net loss were to occur, it would be placed in the debit column of the balance sheet.

Now that we have completed the worksheet, we can go on to the three financial statements. But let's summarize our progress first.

CLARK'S DESKTOP PUBLISHING SERVICES
WORKSHEET
FOR MONTH ENDED MAY 31, 2013

Account Titles	Trial Balance Dr.	Trial Balance Cr.	Adjustments Dr.	Adjustments Cr.	Adjusted Trial Balance Dr.	Adjusted Trial Balance Cr.	Income Statement Dr.	Income Statement Cr.	Balance Sheet Dr.	Balance Sheet Cr.
Cash	6 1 5 5 00									
Accounts Receivable	5 0 0 0 00									
Office Supplies	6 0 0 00									
Prepaid Rent	1 2 0 0 00									
Desktop Publishing Equipment	6 0 0 0 00									
Accounts Payable		3 3 5 0 00								
Brenda Clark, Capital		10 0 0 0 00								
Brenda Clark, Withdrawals	6 2 5 00									
Desktop Publishing Fees		8 0 0 0 00								
Office Salaries Expense	1 3 0 0 00									
Advertising Expense	2 5 0 00									
Telephone Expense	2 2 0 00									
	21 3 5 0 00	21 3 5 0 00								

Figure 4-5 Sample Worksheet

Flip to Overlay No. 1—Adjustments A, B, C, and D

LEARNING UNIT 4-1 REVIEW

AT THIS POINT you should be able to:

◆ Define and explain the purpose of a worksheet. (p. 138)
◆ Explain the need as well as the process for adjustments. (p. 139)
◆ Explain the concept of amortization. (p. 141)
◆ Explain the difference between amortization expense and accumulated amortization. (p. 142)
◆ Prepare a worksheet from a trial balance and adjustment data. (p. 145)

Self-Review Quiz 4-1

From the accompanying trial balance and adjustment data, complete a worksheet for P. Logan Company for the month ended December 31, 2012. (You can use a blank foldout worksheet located at the end of the *Study Guide with Working Papers.*)

Note: The numbers used in this quiz may seem impossibly small, but we have done that on purpose, so that at this point you don't have to worry too much about arithmetic, just about preparing the worksheet correctly.

P. LOGAN COMPANY TRIAL BALANCE DECEMBER 31, 2012	Dr.	Cr.
Cash	15 00	
Accounts Receivable	3 00	
Prepaid Insurance	3 00	
Store Supplies	5 00	
Store Equipment	6 00	
Accumulated Amortization, Store Equipment		4 00
Accounts Payable		2 00
P. Logan, Capital		14 00
P. Logan, Withdrawals	3 00	
Revenue from Clients		25 00
Rent Expense	2 00	
Salaries Expense	8 00	
	45 00	45 00

Adjustment Data

a. Amortization Expense, Store Equipment, $1
b. Insurance expired, $2
c. Supplies on hand, $1
d. Salaries owed but not paid to employees, $3

Solution to Self-Review Quiz 4-1

Don't adjust this line! Store Equipment always contains the historical cost.

Quiz Tip

The adjustment for supplies worth $4 represents the amount *used up*. The *on-hand* amount of $1 ends up on the adjusted trial balance.

P. LOGAN COMPANY
WORKSHEET
FOR MONTH ENDED DECEMBER 31, 2012

Account Titles	Trial Balance Dr.	Trial Balance Cr.	Adjustments Dr.	Adjustments Cr.	Adjusted Trial Balance Dr.	Adjusted Trial Balance Cr.	Income Statement Dr.	Income Statement Cr.	Balance Sheet Dr.	Balance Sheet Cr.
Cash	15 00				15 00				15 00	
Accounts Receivable	3 00				3 00				3 00	
Prepaid Insurance	3 00			(B) 2 00	1 00				1 00	
Store Supplies	5 00			(C) 4 00	1 00				1 00	
Store Equipment	6 00				6 00				6 00	
Accumulated Amortization, Store Equipment		4 00		(A) 1 00		5 00				5 00
Accounts Payable		2 00				2 00				2 00
P. Logan, Capital		14 00				14 00				14 00
P. Logan, Withdrawals	3 00				3 00				3 00	
Revenue from Clients		25 00				25 00		25 00		
Rent Expense	2 00				2 00		2 00			
Salaries Expense	8 00		(D) 3 00		11 00		11 00			
	45 00	45 00								
Amortization Expense, Store Equipment			(A) 1 00		1 00		1 00			
Insurance Expense			(B) 2 00		2 00		2 00			
Supplies Expense			(C) 4 00		4 00		4 00			
Accrued Salaries				(D) 3 00		3 00				3 00
			10 00	10 00	49 00	49 00	20 00	25 00	29 00	24 00
Net Income							5 00			5 00
							25 00	25 00	29 00	29 00

Note that Accumulated Amortization is listed in the trial balance since this is not a new company. Store Equipment has already been amortized $4 from an earlier period.

NEED HELP?

Let's review first: When completing a worksheet we list the original trial balance, add adjustments, complete an adjusted trial balance, and then decide which titles go on the income statement and balance sheet. Since we do not have columns for statement of owner's equity, withdrawals and net income will be placed on the balance sheet columns to arrive at a new figure for capital. Remember, it is the old figure for capital that is placed on the worksheet.

Account title column: Any item not listed on the original trial balance will be listed below the trial balance. This will happen when we make adjustments. Note that when we list each title below the trial balance, it will be increasing in value.

Adjustment column: Amortization

A. Amortization:

In this adjustment Accumulated Amortization is already listed on the trial balance so we only have to add Amortization Expense below the trial balance. Here is the mind process chart for this adjustment:

Amort. Expense, St. Equip.	Expense	↑	Dr. $1
Acc. Amort., St. Equip.	Contra-asset	↑	Cr. $1

Note that the original cost of Store Equipment of $6 is not touched.

B. Insurance Expired:

In this adjustment Prepaid Insurance is already listed on the trial balance, so we only have to add Insurance Expense below the trial balance. Here is the mind process chart for this adjustment:

Insurance Expense	Expense	↑	Dr. $2
Prepaid Insurance	Asset	↓	Cr. $2

Expired means used up and thus we use the amount of $2.

C. Supplies On Hand:

In this adjustment we have to calculate the amount of supplies used up. We take the beginning amount of supplies of $5 less the amount on hand of $1 to equal the amount used up of $4. This is the amount of the adjustment. Since we have Office Supplies listed on the trial balance, we only have to add Supplies Expense below the trial balance. Here is the mind process chart for this adjustment:

Supplies Expense	Expense	↑	Dr. $4
Office Supplies	Asset	↓	Cr. $4

D. Salaries Owed:

In this adjustment, we have Salaries Expense already listed on the trial balance. Here we have to add Accrued Salaries below the trial balance. The following mind process chart shows the new expense that has been incurred but has not been paid:

Salaries Expense	Expense	↑	Dr. $3
Accrued Salaries	Liability	↑	Cr. $3

The sum of all the debits on the adjustments equals the sum of the credits.

Adjusted Trial Balance Columns: Accounts that were not adjusted or added below the trial balance have their balances carried over to the adjusted trial balance. Accounts that were adjusted will have their combined balances carried over to the adjusted trial balance.

For example, Salaries Expense is adjusted by adding the debit balance of $8 and the adjustment of $3 to equal an $11 debit balance on the adjusted trial balance. Every account in the adjusted trial balance will end up on the Income Statement or Balance Sheet columns of the worksheet.

Income Statement Columns: From the adjusted trial balance all revenues and expenses Accounts are listed. Note that when we total the debit and credit columns, they do not equal each other until we calculate the difference between revenues and expenses. In this case, the

($5) difference will be added to the debit column of the income statement section so both columns will total $25.

Balance Sheet Columns: From the adjusted trial balance, assets and withdrawals will end up in the debit column. The old figures for capital, liabilities, and contra-assets are in the credit column. Note that the totals of the columns will not balance until a net income of $5 is placed under the $24. This is done because we use the old figure for capital on the worksheet, and there is no column on the worksheet for the statement of owner's equity.

SUMMARY

On the worksheet, accounts listed below the trial balance are increasing. Adjustments must be made for supplies used up. The original cost of equipment is never touched in the adjustment process. Capital is the old balance on the worksheet. Net income is the difference between revenue and expenses and is carried over to the credit column of the balance sheet. Net losses would be in opposite columns. Income Statement Columns and Balance Sheet Columns will be out of balance by amount of Net Income.

Learning Unit 4-2

Step 6 of the Accounting Cycle: Preparing the Financial Statements from the Worksheet

4 Preparing financial statements from the worksheet

The formal financial statements can be prepared from the worksheet completed in Learning Unit 4-1. Before beginning, we must check that the entries on the worksheet are correct and in balance. To do this, we have to be sure that (1) all entries are recorded in the appropriate columns, (2) the correct amounts are entered in the proper places, (3) the addition is correct across the columns (i.e., from the trial balance to the adjusted trial balance to the financial reports), and (4) the columns are added correctly.

PREPARING THE INCOME STATEMENT

The first statement to be prepared for Clark's Desktop Publishing Services is the income statement. When preparing the income statement, it is important to remember that:

1. Every figure on the formal report is on the worksheet. Figure 4-6 shows where each of these figures goes on the income statement.
2. There are no debit or credit columns on the formal report.
3. The inside column on financial reports is used for subtotalling.
4. Withdrawals do not go on the income statement; they go on the statement of owner's equity.

Take a moment to look at the income statement in Figure 4-6. Note which items go where from the income statement section of the worksheet onto the formal report.

PREPARING THE STATEMENT OF OWNER'S EQUITY

Figure 4-7 is the statement of owner's equity for Clark's. The figure shows where on the worksheet the information comes from. It is important to remember that if there were additional investments, the figure on the worksheet for capital would not be the beginning figure for capital. Checking the ledger account for capital will

Figure 4-6 From Worksheet to Income Statement

Worksheet — Income Statement columns

Account Titles	Dr.	Cr.
Cash		
Accounts Receivable		
Office Supplies		
Prepaid Rent		
Desktop Publishing Equipment		
Accounts Payable		
Brenda Clark, Capital		
Brenda Clark, Withdrawals		
Desktop Publishing Fees		8 0 0 0 00
Office Salaries Expense	1 6 5 0 00	
Advertising Expense	2 5 0 00	
Telephone Expense	2 2 0 00	
Office Supplies Expense	5 0 0 00	
Rent Expense	4 0 0 00	
Amort. Expense, DTP Equip.	8 0 00	
Accumulated Amort., DTP Equip.		
Accrued Salaries		
	3 1 0 0 00	8 0 0 0 00
Net Income	4 9 0 0 00	
	8 0 0 0 00	8 0 0 0 00

CLARK'S DESKTOP PUBLISHING SERVICES
INCOME STATEMENT
FOR MONTH ENDED MAY 31, 2013

Revenue:		
Desktop Publishing Fees		$ 8 0 0 0 00
Operating Expenses:		
Office Salaries Expense	$ 1 6 5 0 00	
Advertising Expense	2 5 0 00	
Telephone Expense	2 2 0 00	
Office Supplies Expense	5 0 0 00	
Rent Expense	4 0 0 00	
Amortization Expense, DTP Equipment	8 0 00	
Total Operating Expenses		3 1 0 0 00
Net Income		$ 4 9 0 0 00

CLARK'S DESKTOP PUBLISHING SERVICES
STATEMENT OF OWNER'S EQUITY
FOR MONTH ENDED MAY 31, 2013

Brenda Clark, Capital, May 1, 2013		$ 10 0 0 0 00
Net Income for May	$ 4 9 0 0 00	
Less: Withdrawals for May	6 2 5 00	
Increase in Capital		4 2 7 5 00
Brenda Clark, Capital, May 31, 2013		$ 14 2 7 5 00

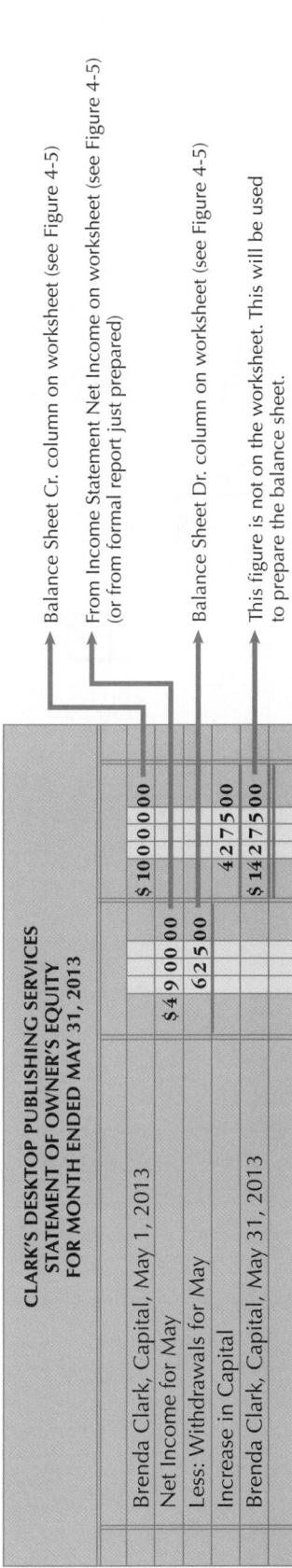

- Balance Sheet Cr. column on worksheet (see Figure 4-5)
- From Income Statement Net Income on worksheet (see Figure 4-5) (or from formal report just prepared)
- Balance Sheet Dr. column on worksheet (see Figure 4-5)
- This figure is not on the worksheet. This will be used to prepare the balance sheet.

Figure 4-7 Completing a Statement of Owner's Equity

tell you whether the amount is correct. Note how net income and withdrawals aid in calculating the new figure for capital.

PREPARING THE BALANCE SHEET

In preparing the balance sheet (page 155), remember that the balance sheet section totals on the worksheet ($18,680) do *not* usually match the totals on the formal balance sheet ($17,975). This occurs because information is grouped differently on the formal report. First, in the formal report, Accumulated Amortization ($80) is subtracted from Desktop Publishing Equipment, reducing the balance. Second, Withdrawals ($625) are subtracted from Owner's Equity, reducing the balance further. These two reductions (–$80 + [–$625] = –$705) represent the difference between the worksheet and the formal version of the balance sheet ($17,975 – $18,680 = –$705). Figure 4-8 (page 155) shows how to prepare the balance sheet from the worksheet.

LEARNING UNIT 4-2 REVIEW

AT THIS POINT you should be able to:

- ◆ Prepare the three financial statements from a worksheet. (pp. 152, 154)
- ◆ Explain why totals of the formal balance sheet don't match totals of balance sheet columns on the worksheet. (p. 154)

Self-Review Quiz 4-2

(The forms you need are located on pages 4-1 to 4-3 of the *Study Guide with Working Papers*.)

From the worksheet on page 150 for P. Logan, prepare (1) an income statement for December, (2) a statement of owner's equity, and (3) a balance sheet for December 31, 2012. No additional investments took place during the period.

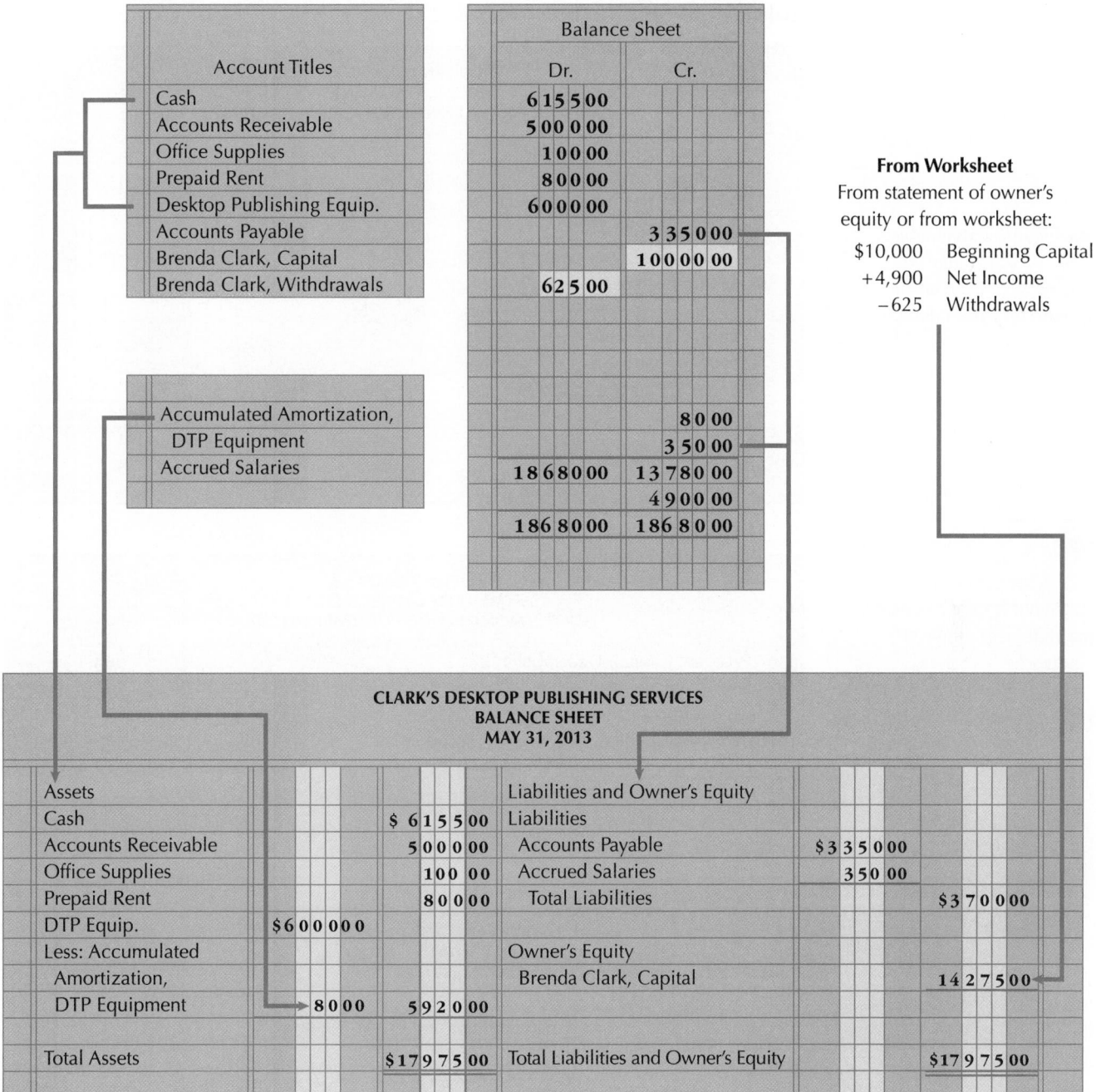

Figure 4-8 From Worksheet to Balance Sheet

Solution to Self-Review Quiz 4-2

Quiz Tip

The income statement is made up of revenue and expenses. Use the inside column for subtotalling.

P. LOGAN COMPANY
INCOME STATEMENT
FOR THE MONTH ENDED DECEMBER 31, 2012

Revenue:			
Revenue from Clients			$ 25 00
Operating Expenses:			
Rent Expense	$ 2 00		
Salaries Expense	11 00		
Amortization Expense, Store Equipment	1 00		
Insurance Expense	2 00		
Supplies Expense	4 00		
Total Operating Expenses		20 00	
Net Income		$ 5 00	

Quiz Tip

The $5 on the income statement is used to update the statement of owner's equity.

Quiz Tip

The ending capital figure on the statement of owner's equity ($16) is used as the capital figure on the balance sheet.

P. LOGAN COMPANY
STATEMENT OF OWNER'S EQUITY
FOR THE MONTH ENDED DECEMBER 31, 2012

P. Logan, Capital, December 1, 2012		$ 14 00
Net Income for December	$ 5 00	
Less: Withdrawals for December	3 00	
Increase in Capital		2 00
P. Logan, Capital, December 31, 2012		$ 16 00

P. LOGAN COMPANY
BALANCE SHEET
DECEMBER 31, 2012

Assets			Liabilities and Owner's Equity		
Cash		$ 15 00	Liabilities		
Accounts Receivable		3 00	Accounts Payable	$ 2 00	
Prepaid Insurance		1 00	Accrued Salaries	3 00	
Store Supplies		1 00	Total Liabilities		$ 5 00
Store Equipment	$ 6 00		Owner's Equity		
Less Accumulated			P. Logan, Capital		16 00
Amortization,					
Store Equipment	5 00	1 00	Total Liabilities and		
Total Assets		$ 21 00	Owner's Equity		$ 21 00

NEED HELP?

Let's review first: There are no debits or credits on the formal financial statements. The three financial statements are made from the last four columns of the worksheet.

Income Statement: The income statement is made up of revenues and expenses. Use the inside column for subtotalling. All numbers found on the income statement are also found on the worksheet.

Statement of Owner's Equity: The net income of $5 is used from the income statement to update the statement of owner's equity. Note that $14 is the old figure from the worksheet. The increase in capital of $2 is not found on the worksheet. Logan's ending figure of $16 is not found on the worksheet.

Balance Sheet: Logan's ending figure of $16 from the statement of owner's equity is used as the capital figure on the balance sheet. Note under assets how the inside column is used to calculate store equipment less accumulated amortization. Note that the totals of $21 from the balance sheet are not found on the worksheet. When the financial report is prepared there are no debits or credits.

SUMMARY

The worksheet was prepared in terms of debits and credits, not the formal financial statements. The inside column of the financial statements is for subtotalling. The worksheet used the old figure for Capital while the balance sheet uses the figure from the statement of owner's equity for the new figure of Capital. Many of the numbers on the statement of owner's equity and balance sheet will not be found on the worksheet since there are no debits or credits on formal financial statements.

No matter how harried Stan Hernandez feels as the owner of his own Subway restaurant, the aroma of his fresh-baked gourmet breads always perks him up. However, the sales generated by Subway's line of gourmet seasoned breads perk Stan up even more. Subway restaurants introduced freshly baked bread in 1983, a practice that made it stand out from other fast-food chains and helped build its reputation for made-to-order freshness. Since then, Subway franchisees have introduced many types of gourmet seasoned breads—such as Hearty Italian or Monterey Cheddar—according to a schedule determined by headquarters.

Stan was one month into the "limited-time promotion" for the chain's new Roasted Garlic seasoned bread when his bake oven started faltering. "The temperature controls just don't seem quite right," said his employee and sandwich artist, Rashid. "It's taking incrementally longer to bake the bread."

"This couldn't happen at a worse time," moaned Stan. "We're baking enough Roasted Garlic bread to keep a whole town of vampires away, but if we don't get it out of the oven fast enough, we'll keep our customers away!"

That very day Stan called his field consultant, Mariah, to discuss what to do about his bake oven. Mariah reminded Stan that his oven trouble illustrated the flip side of buying an existing store from a retired franchisee—having to repair or replace worn or old equipment. After receiving a rather expensive repair estimate and considering the age of the oven, Stan ultimately decided it would make sense for him to purchase a new one. Mariah concurred, saying, "At the rate your sales are going,

Stan, you're going to need that roomier new model."

"Wow, do you realize how much this new bake oven is going to cost me?—$3,000!" Stan exclaimed while meeting with his cousin-turned-Subway-accountant, Lila Hernandez. "Yes, it's a lot to lay out, Stan," said Lila, "but you'll be amortizing the cost over a period of 10 years, which will help you at tax time. Let's do the adjustment on your worksheet so that you can see it."

The two of them were sitting in Stan's small office behind the Subway kitchen, and they pulled up this month's worksheet on Stan's QuickBooks® program. Lila laughed, "I'm sure glad you started entering your worksheets on QuickBooks® again! The figures on those old ones were so doodled over and crossed out that I could barely decipher them! We may need your worksheets at tax time."

"Anything for you, *mi prima*," Stan said. "I may amortize my bake oven, but my gratitude for your accounting skills only appreciates with time!"

DISCUSSION QUESTIONS

1. If you are using a straight-line method of amortization and Stan's bake oven has a residual value of $1,000, how much amortization will he account for each year, and what would be the adjustment for each month?
2. Where does Lila get the information on the useful life of Stan's bake oven and the estimate for its residual value? Why do you think she gets her information from this particular source?
3. Why is a clean worksheet helpful even after that month's statements have been prepared?

DEMONSTRATION PROBLEM: STEPS 5 AND 6 OF THE ACCOUNTING CYCLE

(The blank forms you need are on pages 4-4 and 4-5 of the *Study Guide with Working Papers*.)

From the following trial balance and additional data, complete (1) a worksheet and (2) the three financial statements (numbers are intentionally small so you can concentrate on the theory).

Frost Company
Trial Balance
December 31, 2014

	Dr.	Cr.
Cash	14	
Accounts Receivable	4	
Prepaid Insurance	5	
Plumbing Supplies	3	
Plumbing Equipment	7	
Accumulated Amortization, Plumbing Equipment		5
Accounts Payable		1
J. Frost, Capital		12
J. Frost, Withdrawals	3	
Plumbing Fees		27
Rent Expense	4	
Salaries Expense	5	
Totals	45	45

Adjustment Data

a. Insurance expired, $3
b. Plumbing supplies on hand, $1
c. Amortization Expense, Plumbing Equipment, $1
d. Salaries owed but not paid to employees, $2

Solution Tips for Building a Worksheet

1. Adjustments

a.

Insurance Expense	Expense	↑	Dr.	$3
Prepaid Insurance	Asset	↓	Cr.	$3

Expired means used up.

b.

Plumbing Supplies Expense	Expense	↑	Dr.	$2
Plumbing Supplies	Asset	↓	Cr.	$2

$3 − $1 = $2 *used up*

c.

Amortization Expense, Plumbing Equipment	Expense	↑	Dr.	$1
Accumulated Amortization, Amortization Plumbing Equipment	Contra-Asset	↑	Cr.	$1

The original cost of equipment of $7 is not "touched."

d.

Salaries Expense	Expense	↑	Dr.	$2
Accrued Salaries	Liability	↑	Cr.	$2

2. Last four columns of worksheet are prepared from adjusted trial balance.
3. Capital of $12 is the old figure. Net income of $10 (revenue − expenses) is brought over to same side as capital on the balance sheet Cr. column to balance columns.

Frost Company
Income Statement
for Month Ended December 31, 2014

Revenue:		
Plumbing Fees		$27
Operating Expenses:		
Rent Expense	$4	
Salaries Expense	7	
Insurance Expense	3	
Plumbing Supplies Expense	2	
Amortization Expense, Plumbing Equipment	1	
Total Operating Expenses		17
Net Income		$10

Frost Company
Statement of Owner's Equity
for Month Ended December 31, 2014

J. Frost, Capital, December 1, 2014		$12
Net Income for December	$10	
Less: Withdrawals for December	3	
Increase in Capital		7
J. Frost, Capital, December 31, 2014		$19

Frost Company
Balance Sheet
December 31, 2014

Assets			Liabilities and Owner's Equity		
Cash		$14	Liabilities:		
Accounts Receivable		4	Accounts Payable	$1	
Prepaid Insurance		2	Accrued Salaries	2	
Plumbing Supplies		1	Total Liabilities		$3
Plumbing Equipment	$7				
Less: Accum. Amort.	6	1	Owner's Equity:		
			J. Frost, Capital		19
			Total Liabilities and		
Total Assets		$22	Owner's Equity		$22

FROST COMPANY
WORKSHEET
FOR MONTH ENDED DECEMBER 31, 2014

Annotations: "Original cost not adjusted" · "used up" · "on hand"

Account Titles	Trial Balance Dr.	Trial Balance Cr.	Adjustments Dr.	Adjustments Cr.	Adjusted Trial Balance Dr.	Adjusted Trial Balance Cr.	Income Statement Dr.	Income Statement Cr.	Balance Sheet Dr.	Balance Sheet Cr.
Cash	14 00				14 00				14 00	
Accounts Receivable	4 00				4 00				4 00	
Prepaid Insurance	5 00			(A) 3 00	2 00				2 00	
Plumbing Supplies	3 00			(B) 2 00	1 00				1 00	
Plumbing Equipment	7 00				7 00				7 00	
Accumulated Amortization, Plumbing Equipment		5 00		(C) 1 00		6 00				6 00
Accounts Payable		1 00				1 00				1 00
J. Frost, Capital		12 00				12 00				12 00
J. Frost, Withdrawals	3 00				3 00				3 00	
Plumbing Fees		27 00				27 00		27 00		
Rent Expense	4 00				4 00		4 00			
Salaries Expense	5 00		(D) 2 00		7 00		7 00			
	45 00	45 00								
Insurance Expense			(A) 3 00		3 00		3 00			
Plumbing Supplies Expense			(B) 2 00		2 00		2 00			
Amortization Expense, Plumbing Equipment			(C) 1 00		1 00		1 00			
Accrued Salaries				(D) 2 00		2 00				2 00
			8 00	8 00	48 00	48 00	17 00	27 00	31 00	21 00
Net Income							10 00			10 00
							27 00	27 00	31 00	31 00

Solution Tips for Preparing Financial Statements from a Worksheet

Inside columns of the three financial statements are used for subtotalling. No debits or credits appear on the formal statements.

Statement

Income statement	From Income Statement columns of worksheet for revenue and expenses.
Statement of Owner's Equity	Beginning figure for Capital from Balance Sheet worksheet Cr. column. Net Income from Income Statement. Withdrawal figure from Balance Sheet worksheet Dr. column.
Balance Sheet	Assets from Balance Sheet worksheet Dr. column. Liabilities and Accumulated Amortization from Balance Sheet worksheet Cr. Column. New figure for Capital from statement of owner's equity.

Note how Plumbing Equipment $7 and Accumulated Amortization $6 are rearranged on the formal balance sheet. The Total Assets of $22 is not on the worksheet. Remember, no debits or credits appear on formal statements.

SUMMARY OF KEY POINTS

Learning Unit 4-1

1. The worksheet is not a formal statement.

2. Adjustments update certain accounts so that they will be up to their latest balance before financial reports are prepared. Adjustments are the result of internal transactions.

3. Adjustments will affect both the income statement and the balance sheet.

4. Accounts listed *below* the account titles on the trial balance of the worksheet are *increasing*.

5. The original cost of a piece of equipment is not adjusted; historical cost is not lost.

6. Amortization is the process of spreading the original cost of the asset over its expected useful life.

7. Accumulated amortization is a contra-asset on the balance sheet that summarizes, accumulates, or builds up the amount of amortization that an asset has accumulated.

8. Book value is the original cost less accumulated amortization.

9. Accrued salaries are unpaid and unrecorded expenses that are accumulating but for which payment is not yet due.

10. Revenue and expenses go on income statement sections of the worksheet. Assets, contra-assets, liabilities, capital, and withdrawals go on balance sheet sections of the worksheet.

1. The formal statements prepared from a worksheet do not have debit or credit columns.

2. Revenue and expenses go on the income statement. Beginning capital plus net income less withdrawals (or beginning capital minus net loss, less withdrawals) goes on the statement of owner's equity. Be sure to check the capital account in the ledger to see if any additional investments took place. Assets, contra-assets, liabilities, and the new figure for capital go on the balance sheet.

KEY TERMS

Accrued salaries   A liability account that records salaries that are earned by employees but are unpaid and unrecorded (and thus need to be recorded by an adjustment) and will not come due for payment until the next accounting period (p. 145)

Accumulated Amortization   A contra-asset account that summarizes or accumulates the amount of amortization that has been taken on an asset (p. 142)

Adjusting   The process of calculating the latest up-to-date balance of each account at the end of an accounting period (p. 139)

Amortization   The allocation (spreading) of the cost of an asset (such as an auto or equipment) over its expected useful life (p. 141)

Book value   Cost of equipment less accumulated amortization (p. 143)

Capital Cost Allowance   Another term for amortization as defined in law by the *Income Tax Act* and administered by the Canada Revenue Agency (p. 141)

Contra-asset account   An account that causes another related account to be restated or revalued. Its normal balance is a credit, which reduces the net asset value. (p. 142)

Historical cost   The actual cost of an asset at time of purchase (p. 141)

Residual value   Book value of an asset after all the allowable amortization has been deducted. Also, an estimate of disposal value at the end of an asset's useful life (p. 142)

Salaries Payable   Sometimes used as an alternative term for accrued salaries. It is not as precise because, even though employees may have earned wages at the year (or month) end date, the amounts are often not actually payable until the next period. (p. 145)

Worksheet   A columnar device used by accountants to aid them in completing the accounting cycle. It is not a formal statement. (p. 138)

BLUEPRINT OF STEPS 5 AND 6 OF THE ACCOUNTING CYCLE

Prepare worksheet.

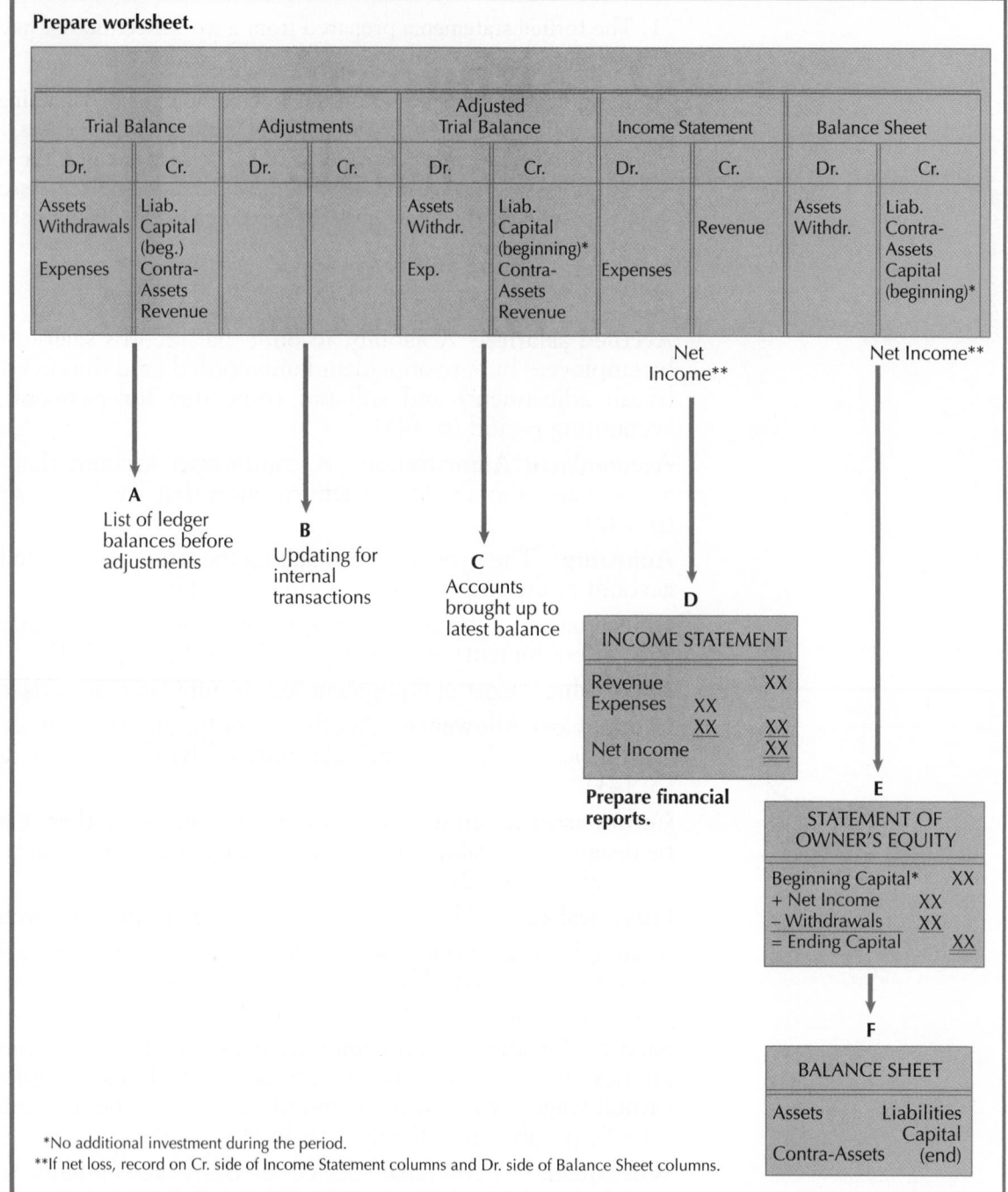

	Trial Balance		Adjustments		Adjusted Trial Balance		Income Statement		Balance Sheet	
	Dr.	Cr.	Dr.	Cr.	Dr.	Cr.	Dr.	Cr.	Dr.	Cr.
	Assets Withdrawals Expenses	Liab. Capital (beg.) Contra-Assets Revenue			Assets Withdr. Exp.	Liab. Capital (beginning)* Contra-Assets Revenue	Expenses	Revenue	Assets Withdr.	Liab. Contra-Assets Capital (beginning)*

Net Income**

Net Income**

A
List of ledger balances before adjustments

B
Updating for internal transactions

C
Accounts brought up to latest balance

D

INCOME STATEMENT

Revenue		XX
Expenses	XX	
	XX	XX
Net Income		XX

Prepare financial reports.

E

STATEMENT OF OWNER'S EQUITY

Beginning Capital*		XX
+ Net Income	XX	
– Withdrawals	XX	
= Ending Capital		XX

F

BALANCE SHEET

Assets	Liabilities
	Capital
Contra-Assets	(end)

*No additional investment during the period.
**If net loss, record on Cr. side of Income Statement columns and Dr. side of Balance Sheet columns.

QUESTIONS, CLASSROOM DEMONSTRATION EXERCISES, EXERCISES, AND PROBLEMS

Discussion Questions and Critical Thinking/Ethical Case

1. Worksheets are required in every company's accounting cycle. Please agree or disagree and explain why.

2. What is the purpose of adjusting accounts?

3. What is the relationship of internal transactions to the adjusting process?

4. Explain how an adjustment can affect both the income statement and balance sheet. Please give an example.

5. Why do we need the accumulated amortization account?

6. Amortization expense goes on the balance sheet. True or false? Why?

7. Each month the cost of accumulated amortization grows while the cost of equipment goes up. Agree or disagree. Defend your position.

8. Define accrued salaries.

9. Why don't the formal financial statements contain debit or credit columns?

10. Explain how the financial statements are prepared from the worksheet.

11. Janet Fox, President of Angel Co., went to a tax seminar. One of the speakers at the seminar advised the audience to put off showing expenses until next year because doing so would allow them to take advantage of a new tax law. When Janet returned to the office, she called in her accountant, Frieda O'Riley. She told Frieda to forget about making any adjustments for salaries in the old year so more expenses could be shown in the new year. Frieda told her that putting off these expenses would not follow generally accepted accounting principles. Janet said she should do it anyway. You make the call. Write your specific recommendations to Frieda.

MyAccountingLab

Make the grade with MyAccountingLab! The exercises and problems marked in green can be found on MyAccountingLab at **www.myaccountinglab.com**. You can practise them as often as you want, and many of them feature step-by-step guided solutions to help you find the right answer. You can also find working papers for selected problems in the Multimedia Library on MyAccountingLab.

Classroom Demonstration Exercises

(The blank forms you need are on pages 4-6 and 4-7 of the *Study Guide with Working Papers*.)

Set A

Adjustment for Supplies

Making adjustments for supplies
① (5 min)

1. Before adjustment:

Office Supplies	Office Supplies Expense
700	

Given

At year-end, an inventory of supplies shows $50.

Required

a. How much is the adjustment for office supplies?
b. Draw a transaction analysis box for this adjustment.
c. What will be the balance of office supplies on the adjusted trial balance?

Adjustment for Prepaid Rent

2. Before adjustment:

Prepaid Rent		Rent Expense
1,200		

Given

At year-end, rent expired is $700.

Required

a. How much is the adjustment for Prepaid Rent?

b. Draw a transaction analysis box for this adjustment.

c. What will be the balance of Prepaid Rent on the adjusted trial balance?

Adjustment for Amortization

3. Before adjustment:

Equipment	Accumulated Amortization, Equipment	Amortization Expense, Equipment
9,000	2,000	

Given

For the current year, amortization on equipment is $2,000.

Required

a. Which of the three T accounts is not affected?

b. Which title is a contra-asset?

c. Draw a transaction analysis box for this adjustment.

d. What will be the balance of each of these three accounts on the adjusted trial balance?

Adjustment for Accrued Salaries

4. Before adjustment:

Salaries Expense		Accrued Salaries
1,400		

Given

Accrued Salaries, $300

Required

a. Draw a transaction analysis box for this adjustment.

b. What will be the balances of these two accounts on the adjusted trial balance?

Worksheet

5. From the following adjusted trial balance (ATB) titles on a worksheet of a lawyer, identify in which column each account will be listed in the last four columns of the worksheet.

(ID) Income statement, Dr. column

(IC) Income statement, Cr. column

(BD) Balance sheet, Dr. column

(BC) Balance sheet, Cr. column

ATB	ID	IC	BD	BC
a. Legal Fees	___	___	___	___
b. Accounts Payable	___	___	___	___
c. Cash	___	___	___	___
d. Prepaid Advertising	___	___	___	___
e. Accrued Salaries	___	___	___	___
f. Amortization Expense	___	___	___	___
g. V., Capital	___	___	___	___
h. V., Withdrawals	___	___	___	___
i. Computer Supplies	___	___	___	___
j. Rent Expense	___	___	___	___
k. Supplies Payable	___	___	___	___
l. Advertising Expense	___	___	___	___
m. Accumulated Amortization	___	___	___	___
n. Accrued Wages	___	___	___	___

Preparing financial statements from the worksheet
3 4 (15 min)

6. From the following balance sheet (which was made from the worksheet and other financial statements), explain why the lettered numbers were not found on the worksheet. *Hint:* There are no debits or credits on the formal financial statements.

Laze Co.
Balance Sheet
December 31, 2012

Assets			Liabilities and Owner's Equity		
Cash		$ 6	Liabilities		
Accounts Receivable		2	Accounts Payable	$2	
Supplies		2	Accrued Salaries	1	
Equipment	$10		Total Liabilities		$ 3 (B)
Less: Accumulated			Owner's Equity		
Amortization	4	6 (A)	H. Wells, Capital		13
			Total Liabilities and		
Total Assets		$16	Owner's Equity		$16

Set B

Adjustment for Supplies

Making adjustments for supplies
1 (5 min)

1. Before adjustment:

Computer Supplies	Computer Supplies Expense
700	

Given

At year-end, an inventory of computer supplies shows $100.

Required

a. How much is the adjustment for computer supplies?
b. Draw a transaction analysis box for this adjustment.
c. What will the balance of computer supplies be on the adjusted trial balance?

Adjustment for Prepaid Rent

Making adjustments for prepaid rent
1 (10 min)

2. Before adjustment:

Prepaid Rent	Rent Expense
700	

Given

At year-end, rent expired is $300.

Required

a. How much is the adjustment for Prepaid Rent?
b. Draw a transaction analysis box for this adjustment.
c. What will be the balance of Prepaid Rent on the adjusted trial balance?

Adjustment for Amortization

3. Before adjustment:

Equipment	Accumulated Amortization, Equipment	Amortization Expense, Equipment
6,000	1,000	

Making adjustments for amortization
1 (10 min)

Given

For the current year, amortization on equipment is $800.

Required

a. Which of the three T accounts is not affected?
b. Which title is a contra-asset?
c. Draw a transaction analysis box for this adjustment.
d. What will be the balance of each of these three accounts on the adjusted trial balance?

Adjustment for Accrued Salaries

Making adjustments for accrued salaries
1 (10 min)

4. Before adjustment:

Salaries Expense	Accrued Salaries
900	

Given

Accrued Salaries, $200

Required

a. Draw a transaction analysis box for this adjustment.
b. What will be the balances of these two accounts on the adjusted trial balance?

Worksheet

Preparing worksheet sections
2 3 (15 min)

5. From the following adjusted trial balance (ATB) titles on a worksheet, identify in which column each account will be listed in the last four columns of the worksheet.

(ID) Income statement, Dr. column
(IC) Income statement, Cr. column
(BD) Balance sheet, Dr. column
(BC) Balance sheet, Cr. column

ATB		ID	IC	BD	BC
a.	Supplies				
b.	Accounts Receivable				
c.	Cash				
d.	Prepaid Rent				
e.	Equipment				
f.	Accumulated Amortization				
g.	B., Capital				
h.	B., Withdrawals				
i.	Taxi Fare Income				
j.	Advertising Expense				
k.	Office Supplies Expense				
l.	Rent Expense				
m.	Amortization Expense				
n.	Accrued Salaries				

Preparing financial statements from worksheets

3 4 (15 min)

6. From the following balance sheet (which was made from the worksheet and other financial statements), explain why the lettered numbers were not found on the worksheet. *Hint:* There are no debits or credits on the formal financial statements.

H. Wells
Balance Sheet
December 31, 2012

Assets			Liabilities and Owner's Equity		
Cash		$ 6	Liabilities		
Accounts Receivable		2	Accounts Payable	$2	
Supplies		2	Accrued Salaries	1	
Equipment	$10		Total Liabilities		$ 3 (B)
Less: Accumulated			Owner's Equity		
Amortization	4	6	H. Wells, Capital		13 (C)
			Total Liabilities and		
Total Assets		$16 (A)	Owner's Equity		$16 (D)

Exercises

(The blank forms you need are on pages 4-8 and 4-9 of the *Study Guide with Working Papers*.)

Categorizing accounts
4 **(5 min)**

4-1. Complete the following table.

Account	Category	Normal Balance	Found on Which Financial Statement(s)
Accounts Payable			
Prepaid Rent			
Office Equipment			
Amortization Expense			
B. Reel, Capital			
B. Reel, Withdrawals			
Office Supplies			
Accumulated Amortization			

Reviewing adjustments and the transaction analysis charts
1 **(10 min)**

4-2. Use transaction analysis charts to analyze the following adjustments:

a. Amortization on equipment, $600

b. Rent expired, $400

Recording adjusting entries
1 **(10 min)**

4-3. From the following adjustment data, calculate the adjustment amount and record appropriate debits or credits:

a. Supplies purchased, $700; Supplies on hand, $200

b. Store equipment, $12,000; Accumulated amortization before adjustment, $900; Amortization expense, $200

Preparing a worksheet
2 **3** **(20 min)**

4-4. From the following trial balance and adjustment data, complete a worksheet for J. Trent as of December 31, 2014:

a. Amortization expense, store equipment, $2.00

b. Insurance expired, $1.00

c. Store supplies on hand, $4.00

d. Wages owed but not paid, $5.00 (they are an expense in the old year)

J. TRENT
TRIAL BALANCE
DECEMBER 31, 2014

	Dr.	Cr.
Cash	9 00	
Accounts Receivable	2 00	
Prepaid Insurance	7 00	
Store Supplies	6 00	
Store Equipment	7 00	
Accumulated Amortization, Store Equipment		2 00
Accounts Payable		4 00
J. Trent, Capital		17 00
J. Trent, Withdrawals	6 00	
Revenue from Clients		24 00
Rent Expense	4 00	
Wage Expense	6 00	
	47 00	47 00

Preparing financial statements
from a worksheet
④ (20 min)

4-5. From the completed worksheet in Exercise 4-4, prepare:

  a. An income statement for December

  b. A statement of owner's equity for December

  c. A balance sheet as of December 31, 2014

Group A Problems

(The blank forms you need are on pages 4-10 and 4-11 of the *Study Guide with Working Papers.*)

Completing a partial worksheet
up to the adjusted trial balance
① ② (15 min)

4A-1. The following is the trial balance for Jill's Fitness Centre of Etobicoke for December 31, 2013.

JILL'S FITNESS CENTRE
TRIAL BALANCE
DECEMBER 31, 2013

	Debit	Credit
Cash	1 00 0 0 00	
Accounts Receivable	6 0 0 0 00	
Fitness Supplies	5 4 0 0 00	
Fitness Equipment	9 2 0 0 00	
Accumulated Amortization, Fitness Equipment		7 0 0 0 00
J. Walsh, Capital		14 3 5 0 00
J. Walsh, Withdrawals	3 0 0 0 00	
Fitness Fees		13 3 0 0 00
Rent Expense	9 0 0 00	
Advertising Expense	1 5 0 00	
	34 6 5 0 00	34 6 5 0 00

Given

The following adjustment data on December 31:

  a. Fitness supplies on hand, $900

  b. Amortization taken on fitness equipment, $700

Complete a partial worksheet up to the adjusted trial balance.

4A-2. The trial balance below is for Ling's Landscaping Service of Merritt for December 31, 2012.

LING'S LANDSCAPING SERVICE TRIAL BALANCE DECEMBER 31, 2012		
	Dr.	Cr.
Cash	4 0 0 0 00	
Accounts Receivable	7 0 0 00	
Prepaid Rent	8 0 0 00	
Landscaping Supplies	7 4 2 00	
Landscaping Equipment	1 4 0 0 00	
Accumulated Amortization, Landscaping Equipment		1 0 6 0 00
Accounts Payable		8 3 6 00
A. Ling, Capital		3 2 5 0 00
Landscaping Revenue		4 3 5 6 00
Heat Expense	4 0 0 00	
Advertising Expense	2 0 0 00	
Wages Expense	1 2 6 0 00	
	9 5 0 2 00	9 5 0 2 00

Adjustment data to update the trial balance:

a. Rent expired, $600

b. Landscaping supplies on hand (remaining), $200

c. Amortization expense, landscaping equipment, $300

d. Wages earned by workers but not paid and not due until January, $400

Required

Prepare a worksheet for Ling's Landscaping Service for the month of December.

4A-3. The following is the trial balance for Kevin's Moving Co. of Dartmouth.

KEVIN'S MOVING CO. TRIAL BALANCE OCTOBER 31, 2014		
	Dr.	Cr.
Cash	5 0 0 0 00	
Prepaid Insurance	2 5 0 0 00	
Moving Supplies	1 2 0 0 00	
Moving Truck	1 1 0 0 0 00	
Accumulated Amortization, Moving Truck		9 0 0 0 00
Accounts Payable		2 7 6 8 00
K. Hoff, Capital		5 4 4 2 00
K. Hoff, Withdrawals	1 4 0 0 00	
Revenue from Moving		9 0 0 0 00
Wages Expense	3 7 1 2 00	
Rent Expense	1 0 8 0 00	
Advertising Expense	3 1 8 00	
	2 6 2 1 0 00	2 6 2 1 0 00

Adjustment data to update trial balance:

a. Insurance expired, $700

b. Moving supplies on hand, $900

c. Amortization on moving truck, $500

d. Wages earned but unpaid, $250

Required

1. Complete a worksheet for Kevin's Moving Co. for the month of October.
2. Prepare an income statement for October, a statement of owner's equity for October, and a balance sheet as of October 31, 2014.

Comprehensive problem ❶❷❸❹ (60 min)

4A-4. The following is a trial balance for Dick's Repair Service of Moose Jaw.

DICK'S REPAIR SERVICE TRIAL BALANCE NOVEMBER 30, 2013		
	Dr.	Cr.
Cash	3 2 0 0 00	
Prepaid Insurance	4 0 0 0 00	
Repair Supplies	4 6 0 0 00	
Repair Equipment	3 0 0 0 00	
Accumulated Amortization, Repair Equipment		7 0 0 00
Accounts Payable		5 5 7 0 00
D. Horn, Capital		3 8 0 0 00
Revenue from Repairs		7 0 0 0 00
Wages Expense	1 8 0 0 00	
Rent Expense	3 6 0 00	
Advertising Expense	1 1 0 00	
	1 7 0 7 0 00	1 7 0 7 0 00

Check Figure

Net Income $1,830

Adjustment data to update the trial balance:

a. Insurance expired, $700
b. Repair supplies on hand, $3,000
c. Amortization on repair equipment, $200
d. Wages earned but not yet paid, $400

Required

1. Complete a worksheet for Dick's Repair Service for the month of November.
2. Prepare an income statement for November, a statement of owner's equity for November, and a balance sheet as of November 30, 2013.

Group B Problems

(The blank forms you need are on pages 4-10 and 4-11 of the *Study Guide with Working Papers.*)

Completing a partial worksheet up to adjusted trial balance ❶❷ (15 min)

4B-1. For Jill's Fitness Centre of Etobicoke, complete a partial worksheet up to the adjusted trial balance using the following adjustment data and trial balance:

a. Fitness supplies on hand, $3,000
b. Amortization taken on fitness equipment, $500

JILL'S FITNESS CENTRE TRIAL BALANCE DECEMBER 31, 2013		
	Dr.	Cr.
Cash	6 0 0 0 00	
Accounts Receivable	2 0 0 0 00	
Fitness Supplies	4 2 0 0 00	
Fitness Equipment	8 0 0 0 00	
Accumulated Amortization, Fitness Equipment		4 7 0 0 00
J. Walsh, Capital		16 0 0 0 00
J. Walsh, Withdrawals	1 0 0 0 00	
Fitness Fees		1 4 0 0 00
Rent Expense	8 0 0 00	
Advertising Expense	1 0 0 00	
	22 1 0 0 00	22 1 0 0 00

Check Figure

Total, Adjusted Trial Balance
$22,600

Completing a worksheet
❶❷❸ (30 min)

4B-2. Given the following trial balance and adjustment data for Ling's Landscaping Service of Merritt, prepare a worksheet for the month of December.

LING'S LANDSCAPING SERVICE TRIAL BALANCE DECEMBER 31, 2012		
	Dr.	Cr.
Cash	3 9 6 00	
Accounts Receivable	2 8 4 00	
Prepaid Rent	4 0 0 00	
Landscaping Supplies	3 1 0 00	
Landscaping Equipment	1 0 0 0 00	
Accumulated Amortization, Landscaping Equipment		2 0 0 00
Accounts Payable		3 4 6 00
A. Ling, Capital		4 5 6 00
Landscaping Revenue		4 6 8 0 00
Heat Expense	6 3 2 00	
Advertising Expense	1 2 0 0 00	
Wages Expense	1 4 6 0 00	
Total	5 6 8 2 00	5 6 8 2 00

Check Figure

Net Income $673

Adjustment Data

a. Landscaping supplies on hand, $60
b. Rent expired, $150
c. Amortization on landscaping equipment, $200
d. Wages earned but unpaid, $115

Comprehensive problem
❶❷❸❹ (60 min)

4B-3. Using the following trial balance and adjustment data for Kevin's Moving Co. of Dartmouth, prepare:

1. A worksheet for the month of October
2. An income statement for October, a statement of owner's equity for October, and a balance sheet as of October 31, 2014

Adjustment Data

a. Insurance expired, $600
b. Moving supplies on hand, $310

c. Amortization on moving truck, $580

d. Wages earned but unpaid, $410

KEVIN'S MOVING CO. TRIAL BALANCE OCTOBER 31, 2014		
	Dr.	Cr.
Cash	3 9 20 00	
Prepaid Insurance	3 2 88 00	
Moving Supplies	1 4 00 00	
Moving Truck	10 6 58 00	
Accumulated Amortization, Moving Truck		3 66 0 00
Accounts Payable		1 3 12 00
K. Hoff, Capital		17 4 82 00
K. Hoff, Withdrawals	4 2 40 00	
Revenue from Moving		8 16 2 00
Wages Expense	5 7 12 00	
Rent Expense	1 0 80 00	
Advertising Expense	3 18 00	
	30 6 16 00	30 6 16 00

Check Figure

Net Loss $1,628

Comprehensive problem
① ② ③ ④ (60 min)

4B-4. As the bookkeeper of Dick's Repair Service in Moose Jaw, use the information that follows to prepare:

1. A worksheet for the month of November

2. An income statement for November, a statement of owner's equity for November, and a balance sheet as of November 30, 2013

DICK'S REPAIR SERVICE TRIAL BALANCE NOVEMBER 30, 2013		
	Dr.	Cr.
Cash	3 2 0 4 00	
Prepaid Insurance	4 0 0 0 00	
Repair Supplies	7 7 0 00	
Repair Equipment	3 1 0 6 00	
Accumulated Amortization, Repair Equipment		6 5 0 00
Accounts Payable		1 9 0 4 00
D. Horn, Capital		6 2 5 8 00
Revenue from Repairs		5 6 3 4 00
Wages Expense	1 6 0 0 00	
Rent Expense	1 5 6 0 00	
Advertising Expense	2 0 6 00	
	14 4 4 6 00	14 4 4 6 00

Check Figure

Net Income $1,012

Adjustment Data

a. Insurance expired, $300

b. Repair supplies on hand, $170

c. Amortization on repair equipment, $250

d. Wages earned but unpaid, $106

(The forms you need are on pages 4-12 and 4-13 of the *Study Guide with Working Papers*.)

Completing a partial worksheet up to adjusted trial balance
① ② (15 min)

4C-1. Please complete a partial worksheet up to the adjusted trial balance for Bannister Rescue Service of Banff, using the following adjustment data and trial balance:

    a. Supplies on hand, $1,605

    b. Amortization taken on equipment, $340

Check Figure

Total, Adjusted Trial Balance
$20,881

BANNISTER RESCUE SERVICE TRIAL BALANCE DECEMBER 31, 2014		
	Dr.	Cr.
Cash	1 2 1 0 0 00	
Accounts Receivable	1 3 7 0 00	
Supplies	2 1 7 0 00	
Rescue Equipment	2 4 7 5 00	
Accumulated Amortization, Rescue Equipment		1 2 2 5 00
Amos Bannister, Capital		15 4 1 6 00
Amos Bannister, Withdrawals	7 0 0 00	
Fees Earned		3 9 0 0 00
Rent Expense	9 0 0 00	
Advertising Expense	3 7 0 00	
Utilities Expense	4 5 6 00	
Totals	20 5 4 1 00	20 5 4 1 00

Completing a worksheet
① ② ③ (30 min)

4C-2. Given the following trial balance and adjustment data for Laura's Screen Printing Service of Richmond, your task is to prepare a worksheet for the month of November, the first month of operations in a new fiscal year.

Check Figure

Net Income $3,915.33

LAURA'S SCREEN PRINTING SERVICE TRIAL BALANCE NOVEMBER 30, 2012		
	Dr.	Cr.
Cash	3 8 1 3 00	
Accounts Receivable	2 8 2 0 00	
Prepaid Rent	8 5 0 00	
Screen Printing Supplies	9 2 1 00	
Screen Printing Equipment	6 5 8 0 00	
Accumulated Amortization, Screen Printing Equipment		2 4 4 0 00
Accounts Payable		1 7 8 8 00
Laura Bailey, Capital		5 8 2 8 00
Screen Printing Revenue		7 9 6 6 00
Advertising Expense	5 1 0 00	
Utilities Expense	2 7 8 00	
Wages Expense	2 2 5 0 00	
Totals	18 0 2 2 00	18 0 2 2 00

Adjustment Data

    a. Screen printing supplies on hand, $680.

    b. Prepaid rent represents the first and last months' rent on a new office lease signed November 1, 2012.

c. Amortization on screen printing equipment is based on straight-line, five-year life and a residual value of $480.

d. Wages earned but unpaid amounted to 24.5 hours at $10 per hour.

Comprehensive problem
①②③④ (60 min)

4C-3. Using the following trial balance and adjustment data for Vivian's Repair Co. of Windsor, prepare:

1. A worksheet for October

2. An income statement for October, a statement of owner's equity for October, and a balance sheet as of October 31, 2013

Adjustment Data

a. One-quarter of the prepaid insurance has expired.

b. Repair supplies on hand, $795.

c. Amortization on repair equipment is based on the straight-line approach, with a 10-year life and a residual value of $1,200.

d. Amortization on building is also straight-line, 50-year life, and no residual value.

e. Wages earned but unpaid amounted to 76 hours at $14 per hour at month-end.

Check Figure

Net Income $13,553.92

VIVIAN'S REPAIR CO. TRIAL BALANCE OCTOBER 31, 2013	Dr.	Cr.
Cash	3 3 2 6 00	
Prepaid Insurance	1 3 8 9 00	
Repair Supplies	1 1 4 8 00	
Repair Equipment	8 4 6 0 00	
Building	50 0 0 0 00	
Accumulated Amortization, Repair Equipment		3 9 5 2 00
Accumulated Amortization, Building		12 5 0 0 00
Accounts Payable		2 7 24 00
Vivian Hunter, Capital		43 0 85 00
Vivian Hunter, Withdrawals	13 4 0 0 00	
Repair Fees Revenue		28 6 85 00
Wages Expense	10 8 9 0 00	
Utilities Expense	8 4 1 00	
Advertising Expense	1 4 9 2 00	
Totals	90 9 46 00	90 9 46 00

Comprehensive problem
①②③④ (60 min)

4C-4. As the bookkeeper of Maritime Internet Access Service of Amherst, use the information that follows to prepare:

1. A worksheet for August, the end of the first quarter in the current fiscal year

2. An income statement for August, a statement of owner's equity for August, and a balance sheet as of August 31, 2012

Adjustment Data

a. Two-thirds of the prepaid insurance remains prepaid at month-end.

b. Computer supplies on hand, $268.

c. Amortization on computer equipment is based on the straight-line method, a four-year life, and residual value of $1,400.

d. Wages earned but unpaid amounted to 64 hours at $15 per hour at month-end.

e. Advertising bill received, not yet paid, $245.

MARITIME INTERNET ACCESS SERVICE TRIAL BALANCE AUGUST 31, 2012	Dr.	Cr.
Cash	7 0 8 00	
Prepaid Insurance	1 0 5 0 00	
Computer Supplies	4 2 6 00	
Computer Equipment	11 4 8 0 00	
Accumulated Amortization, Computer Equipment		4 2 0 0 00
Accounts Payable		8 4 0 00
Lucy Northwest, Capital		2 8 8 7 00
Lucy Northwest, Withdrawals	1 4 7 8 00	
Revenue from Services Provided		14 3 8 5 00
Wages Expense	4 7 6 0 00	
Rent Expense	1 4 8 5 00	
Advertising Expense	9 2 5 00	
Totals	22 3 1 2 00	22 3 1 2 00

Check Figure

Net Income $5,292.00

On-the-job Training

(The blank forms you need are on pages 4-14 to 4-15 of the *Study Guide with Working Papers*.)

Preparing adjustments

1 (20 min)

T-1.

> To: Hal Hogan, Bookkeeper
>
> From: Pete Tennant, V. P.
>
> Re: Adjustments for year ended December 31, 2013
>
> Hal, here is the information you requested. Please supply me with the adjustments needed ASAP. Also, please put in writing why we need to do these adjustments.
>
> Thanks

Attached to memo:

a. Insurance data:

Policy No.	Date of Policy Purchase	Policy Length	Cost
100	November 1 of previous year	4 years	$480
200	May 1 of current year	2 years	600
300	September 1 of current year	1 year	240

b. Rent data: Prepaid rent had a $500 balance at beginning of year. An additional $400 in rent was paid in advance in June. At year-end, $200 in rent had expired.

c. Revenue data: Accrued storage fees of $500 were earned but uncollected and unrecorded at year-end.

T-2.

Hint: Unearned rent is a liability on the balance sheet.

On Friday, Harry Swag's boss asks him to prepare a special report that is due on Monday at 8 a.m. Harry gathers the following material in his briefcase:

		December 31	
		2013	2014
Prepaid Advertising		$300	$600
Accrued Interest		150	350
Unearned Rent		500	300
Cash paid for:	Advertising	$1,900	
	Interest	1,500	
Cash received for:	Rent	2,300	

As his best friend, you want to help Harry show the amounts that are to be reported on the 2014 income statement for **a.** Advertising Expense, **b.** Interest Expense, and **c.** Rent Fees Earned. Please explain in writing why unearned rent is considered a liability.

Comprehensive problem
①②③④ (45 min)

At the end of July, Tony took a complete inventory of his supplies and found the following:

5 dozen ¼″ screws at a cost of $8 a dozen

2 dozen ½″ screws at a cost of $5 a dozen

2 cartons of computer inventory paper at a cost of $14 a carton

3 metres of coaxial cable at a cost of $4 per metre

After speaking to his accountant, he found that a reasonable amortization amount for each of his long-term assets is as follows:

Computer purchased May 6, 2013	Amortization $33 a month
Office equipment purchased	
May 16, 2013, 2010	Amortization $10 a month
Computer workstations purchased	
July 17, 2013	Amortization $20 a month

Tony uses the straight-line method of amortization and declares no salvage value for any of the assets. If any long-term asset is purchased in the first 15 days of the month, he will charge amortization for the full month. If an asset is purchased on the 16th of the month, or later, he will not charge amortization in the month it was purchased.

July's rent has now expired.

Assignment

Use your trial balance from the completed problem in Chapter 3 and the above adjusting information to complete the worksheet for the three months ended July 31, 2013. From the worksheets, prepare the financial statements. (See pages 4-16 to 4-19 in your *Study Guide with Working Papers*.)

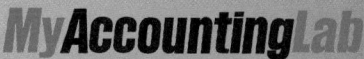

Instructions and data files for completing this Computer Workshop assignment can be found in the Multimedia Library on MyAccountingLab at **www.myaccountinglab.com**.

Computer Workshops

Zell and Zadich

Depending on the goals your instructor has set for the course you are taking, you may be asked to complete one or more of the computer workshops created especially for Chapter 4. If you need to complete any of the workshops, you will obtain all necessary details from the Multimedia Library on MyAccountingLab.com at www.myaccountinglab.com.

There are a total of four workshops available. For each company, Zell and Zadich, there are two versions—one using Simply Accounting Pro® and the other using QuickBooks Premier®. The choice will depend to a large extent on which software is available to you in your college's lab, on your own laptop, or other computer, as well as the preference, knowledge, and experience of your instructor. Before beginning, be sure to get clear directions as to which workshop you are to complete. Please note that special, time-limited versions of both Simply Accounting® and QuickBooks® are available at no charge from each company's website. Your instructor might handle this for you, but it is easy to obtain the software and set it up yourself by visiting www.intuit.ca (QuickBooks®) or www.simplyaccounting.com (Simply Accounting®).

You need to obtain several files from the MyAccountingLab website before you begin.

1. The instruction files that describe each company and the details of the assignment.

2. Data sets that have been carefully crafted for you so you may begin each workshop with minimal bother. All are in compressed format, and will need to be uncompressed with the "Restore" feature built into the software before they can be used. You will get an error message if your try to use the downloaded files without first restoring them. (Compressing files saves storage space on the servers, and also greatly speeds up the download process for each student.) The instruction and guide files on the MyAccountingLab website provide details to assist you. You may also want to reread the section on page 136 at the end of Chapter 3 for additional information.

3. A Word file that sets forth in detail the step-by-step instructions you need to complete the Zell assignment. There is a separate file for each software package. Help files also exist for the Zadich workshops, but these are available for student use only if they are provided by your instructor.

5 The Accounting Cycle Completed

THE BIG PICTURE

Warren Beesley is probably not a name that many accounting students would recognize, but you may get to know more about him and his company in the future. Warren's company, Beesley Exhibitions Inc., is the brains behind Canada's Financial Technology Show, held in Toronto in 2010 and Vancouver in 2012.

Each of the shows brings together most of Canada's accounting software firms to demonstrate their products' capabilities to hundreds of professional accountants. It is a kind of "one-stop" event where accountants can go to discover solutions for accounting problems they or, more usually, their companies face. The show's website (www.financial-technologyshow.com) stated proudly that if you cannot find a solution for your accounting needs at the show, then a solution probably does not exist.

Those are strong words, to be sure, but does the show actually deliver? Judging by the list of exhibitors—a virtual "who's who" of accounting software providers—one would have to say yes! If that is not enough, the show's co-sponsors include *The Bottom Line*, Canada's accounting newspaper, which has been keeping the accounting profession informed and up to date for three decades. Many other top companies are also proud to be associated with the show.

Warren once worked for *The Bottom Line* and still contributes an article or two as time permits. But for the past eight years, he has been devoting most of his attention to ensuring the success of his two shows. Is he having fun yet? There are anxious moments, of course, but he really would not want to be doing anything else. Being the go-to guy for Canada's top show in accounting technology has its own rewards, and the future seems very bright indeed.

If you ever need details of how you can complete the accounting cycle and close your company's books, you could do worse than attend one of Warren's shows. But you will definitely want to complete this chapter first.

Remember: For ease of presentation, we are using a month as the accounting cycle for Clark's. In the business world, the cycle can be any time period but is usually one year.

In Chapters 3 and 4, we completed these steps of the manual accounting cycle for Clark's Desktop Publishing Services:

Step 1: Business transactions occurred and generated source documents.

Step 2: Business transactions were analyzed and recorded in a journal.

Step 3: Information was posted or transferred from journal to ledger.

Step 4: A trial balance was prepared.

Step 5: A worksheet was completed.

Step 6: Financial statements were prepared.

This chapter covers the following steps, which will complete Clark's accounting cycle for the month of May:

Step 7: Journalizing and posting adjusting entries

Step 8: Journalizing and posting closing entries

Step 9: Preparing a post-closing trial balance

Learning Unit 5-1

Journalizing and Posting Adjusting Entries: Step 7 of the Accounting Cycle

1 Journalizing and posting adjusting entries

Purpose of adjusting entries

At this point, many ledger accounts are *not up to date.*

RECORDING JOURNAL ENTRIES FROM THE WORKSHEET

The information in the worksheet is up to date. The financial statements prepared from that information can give the business's management and other interested parties a good idea of where the business stands as of a particular date. The problem is that the worksheet is an informal report. The information concerning the adjustments has not been placed in the journal or posted to the ledger accounts. This means that the books are not up to date and ready for the next accounting cycle to begin. For example, the ledger shows $1,200 of prepaid rent (page 105), but the balance sheet we prepared in Chapter 4 shows an $800 balance. Essentially, the worksheet is a tool for preparing financial statements. Now we must use the adjustment columns of the worksheet as a basis for bringing the ledger up to date. We do this by **adjusting journal entries** (see Figure 5-1). Again, the updating must be done before the next accounting period starts. For Clark's Desktop Publishing Services, the next period begins on June 1.

Figure 5-1 shows the adjusting journal entries for Clark's taken from the adjustments section of the worksheet (see Figure 5-2). Once the adjusting journal entries are posted to the ledger, the accounts making up the financial statements that were prepared from the worksheet will correspond with the updated ledger. (Keep in mind that this is the same journal we have been using.) Let's look at some simplified T accounts to show how Clark's ledger looked before and after the adjustments were posted (see adjustments A to D on page 185).

Figure 5-1
Adjusting Journal Entries

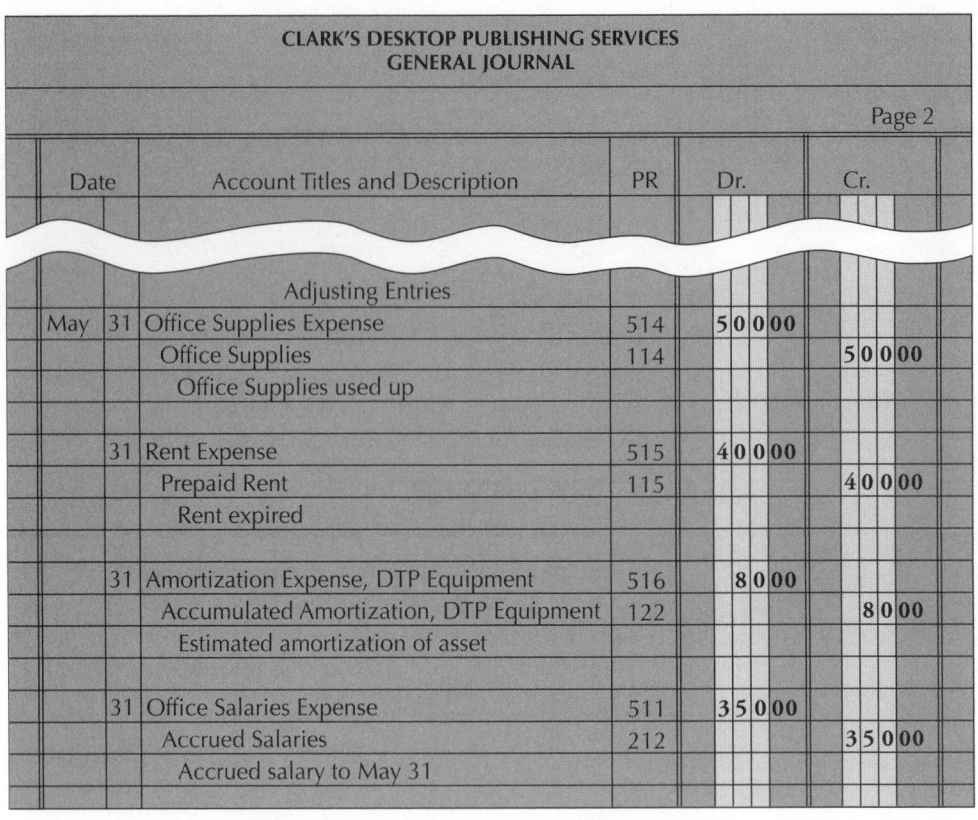

CLARK'S DESKTOP PUBLISHING SERVICES
GENERAL JOURNAL

Page 2

Date		Account Titles and Description	PR	Dr.	Cr.
		Adjusting Entries			
May	31	Office Supplies Expense	514	5 0 0 00	
		Office Supplies	114		5 0 0 00
		Office Supplies used up			
	31	Rent Expense	515	4 0 0 00	
		Prepaid Rent	115		4 0 0 00
		Rent expired			
	31	Amortization Expense, DTP Equipment	516	8 0 00	
		Accumulated Amortization, DTP Equipment	122		8 0 00
		Estimated amortization of asset			
	31	Office Salaries Expense	511	3 5 0 00	
		Accrued Salaries	212		3 5 0 00
		Accrued salary to May 31			

Figure 5-2
Journalizing and Posting Adjustments from the Adjustments Section of the Worksheet

Account Titles	Trial Balance		Adjustments	
	Dr.	Cr.	Dr.	Cr.
Cash	6 1 5 5 00			
Accounts Receivable	5 0 0 0 00			
Office Supplies	6 0 0 00			(A) 5 0 0 00
Prepaid Rent	1 2 0 0 00			(B) 4 0 0 00
Desktop Publishing Equipment	6 0 0 0 00			
Accounts Payable		3 3 5 0 00		
Brenda Clark, Capital		1 0 0 0 0 00		
Brenda Clark, Withdrawals	6 2 5 00			
Desktop Publishing Fees		8 0 0 0 00		
Office Salaries Expense	1 3 0 0 00		(D) 3 5 0 00	
Advertising Expense	2 5 0 00			
Telephone Expense	2 2 0 00			
	2 1 3 5 0 00	2 1 3 5 0 00		
Office Supplies Expense			(A) 5 0 0 00	
Rent Expense			(B) 4 0 0 00	
Amortization Expense, DTP Equipment			(C) 8 0 00	
Accumulated Amortization, DTP Equipment				(C) 8 0 00
Accrued Salaries				(D) 3 5 0 00
			1 3 3 0 00	1 3 3 0 00

Adjustment A

Before posting:

Office Supplies 114	Office Supplies Expense 514
600	

After posting:

Office Supplies 114	Office Supplies Expense 514
600 | 500	500 |

Adjustment B

Before posting:

Prepaid Rent 115	Rent Expense 515
1,200	

After posting:

Prepaid Rent 115	Rent Expense 515
1,200 | 400	400 |

Adjustment C

Before posting:

Desktop Publishing Equipment 121	Amortization Expense, DTP Equipment 516	Accumulated Amortization, DTP Equipment 122
6,000 |		

After posting:

Desktop Publishing Equipment 121	Amortization Expense, DTP Equipment 516	Accumulated Amortization, DTP Equipment 122
6,000 |	80 |	| 80

This last adjustment shows the same balances for Amortization Expense and Accumulated Amortization. However, in subsequent adjustments, the Accumulated Amortization balance will keep getting larger, but the debit to Amortization Expense and the credit to Accumulated Amortization will be the same. We will see why in a moment.

Adjustment D

Before posting:

Office Salaries Expense 511	Accrued Salaries 212
650 |	
650 |	

After posting:

Office Salaries Expense 511	Accrued Salaries 212
650 |	| 350
650 |	
350 |	

LEARNING UNIT 5-1 REVIEW

AT THIS POINT you should be able to:

◆ Define and state the purpose of adjusting entries. (p. 183)
◆ Journalize adjusting entries from the worksheet. (p. 184)
◆ Post journalized adjusting entries to the ledger. (p. 184)
◆ Compare specific ledger accounts before and after posting of the journalized adjusting entries. (p. 185)

Self-Review Quiz 5-1

(The blank forms you need are on pages 5-1 and 5-2 of the *Study Guide with Working Papers.*)

Turn to the worksheet of P. Logan Company (p. 150) and (1) journalize and post the adjusting entries and (2) compare the adjusted ledger accounts before and after the adjustments are posted. T accounts with beginning balances are provided in your *Study Guide.*

Solution to Self-Review Quiz 5-1

Quiz Tip

These journal entries come from the adjustments column of the worksheet.

	Date		Account Titles and Description	PR	Dr.		Cr.	
			Adjusting Entries					
	Dec.	31	Amortization Expense, Store Equipment	511	1	00		
			Accumulated Amortization, Store Equipment	122			1	00
			Estimated amortization of equipment					
		31	Insurance Expense	516	2	00		
			Prepaid Insurance	116			2	00
			Insurance expired					
		31	Supplies Expense	514	4	00		
			Store Supplies	114			4	00
			Store Supplies used					
		31	Salaries Expense	512	3	00		
			Accrued Salaries	212			3	00
			Accrued salaries payable					

Page 2

PARTIAL LEDGER

Before Posting		After Posting	

Before Posting

Amortization Expense, Store Equipment 511

Accumulated Amortization, Store Equipment 122
| 4

Prepaid Insurance 116
3 |

Insurance Expense 516

Store Supplies 114
5 |

Supplies Expense 514

Salaries Expense 512
8 |

Accrued Salaries 212

After Posting

Amortization Expense, Store Equipment 511
1 |

Accumulated Amortization, Store Equipment 122
| 4
| 1

Prepaid Insurance 116
3 | 2

Insurance Expense 516
2 |

Store Supplies 114
5 | 4

Supplies Expense 514
4 |

Salaries Expense 512
8 |
3 |

Accrued Salaries 212
| 3

NEED HELP?

Let's review first: Once the financial statements are prepared from the worksheet, our ledger is still not up to date. Information about the adjustments on the worksheet have not been journalized or posted to the ledger.

How to update the ledger with adjustments on the worksheet: Using the worksheet of Logan Company, go to the adjustments column and journalize the four adjusting entries. Once the adjustments are journalized, they must be posted to the ledger. When the postings are complete, the titles for amortization expense, accumulated amortization, insurance expense, prepaid insurance, supplies expense, store supplies, accrued salaries, and salaries expense will have the latest, up-to-date balances.

SUMMARY

The ending balances in the ledger after posting adjustments will be the same amounts that were found on the adjusted trial balance.

Learning Unit 5-2

Journalizing and Posting Closing Entries: Step 8 of the Accounting Cycle

2 Journalizing and posting closing entries

To make recording of the next fiscal year's transactions easier, a mechanical step, called **closing**, is taken by the accountant at Clark's. Closing is used to end—or close off—the revenue, expense, and withdrawal accounts at the end of the fiscal year. The information needed to complete closing entries will be found in the income statement and balance sheet sections of the worksheet.

To make it easier to understand this process, we will first look at the difference between temporary (nominal) accounts and permanent (real) accounts.

Here is the expanded accounting equation that we used in an earlier chapter:

Assets = Liabilities + Capital – Withdrawals + Revenues – Expenses

Permanent accounts are found on the balance sheet.

Three of the items in that equation—assets, liabilities, and capital—are known as **real** or **permanent accounts** because their balances are carried over from one fiscal year to another. The other three items—withdrawals, revenue, and expenses—are called **nominal** or **temporary accounts** because their balances are not carried over from one fiscal year to another. Instead, their balances are set to zero at the beginning of each fiscal year. This allows us to accumulate new data about revenue, expenses, and withdrawals in the new fiscal year. The process of closing summarizes the effects of the temporary accounts on capital for that period by using **closing journal entries** and by posting them to the ledger. When the closing process is complete, the accounting equation will be reduced to:

Assets = Liabilities + Ending Capital

If you look back at page 153 in Chapter 4, you will see that we have calculated the new capital on the balance sheet for Clark's Desktop Publishing Services to be $14,275. However, before the mechanical closing procedures are journalized and posted, the capital account of Brenda Clark in the ledger is only $10,000 (Chapter 3, page 107). Let's look now at how to journalize and post closing entries.

HOW TO JOURNALIZE CLOSING ENTRIES

There are four steps to be performed in journalizing closing entries:

Step 1: Clear the revenue balances and transfer them to Income Summary. **Income Summary** is a temporary account in the ledger needed for closing. At the end of the closing process, there will be no balance in Income Summary.

Revenue → Income Summary

Step 2: Clear the individual expense balances and transfer them to Income Summary.

Expenses → Income Summary

Step 3: Clear the balance in Income Summary and transfer it to Capital.

Income Summary → Capital

Step 4: Clear the balance in Withdrawals and transfer it to Capital.

Withdrawals → Capital

Figure 5-3 is a visual representation of these four steps. Keep in mind that this information must first be journalized and then posted to the appropriate ledger accounts. The worksheet presented in Figure 5-4 contains all the figures we will need for the closing process.

Step 1: Clear Revenue Balances and Transfer to Income Summary

Here is what is in the ledger before closing entries are journalized and posted:

Desktop Publishing Fees 411	Income Summary 313
	8,000		

The income statement section on the worksheet on page 189 shows that the Desktop Publishing Fees account has a credit balance of $8,000. To close or clear this to zero in the ledger, a debit of $8,000 is needed. However, if we add an amount to the debit side, we must also add a credit—so we add $8,000 on the credit side of the Income Summary account.

After all closing entries are journalized and posted to the ledger, all temporary accounts have a zero balance in the ledger. Closing is a step-by-step process.

An Income Summary is a temporary account located in the chart of accounts under Owner's Equity. It does not have a normal balance of a debit or a credit.

Sometimes, closing the accounts is referred to as "clearing the accounts."

Don't forget two goals of closing:

1. Clear all temporary accounts in the ledger.
2. Update Capital to a new balance that reflects a summary of all the temporary accounts.

All numbers used in the closing process can be found on the worksheet in Figure 5-4. Note that the *account* Income Summary is *not* on the worksheet.

Figure 5-3
Four Steps in Journalizing
Closing Entries

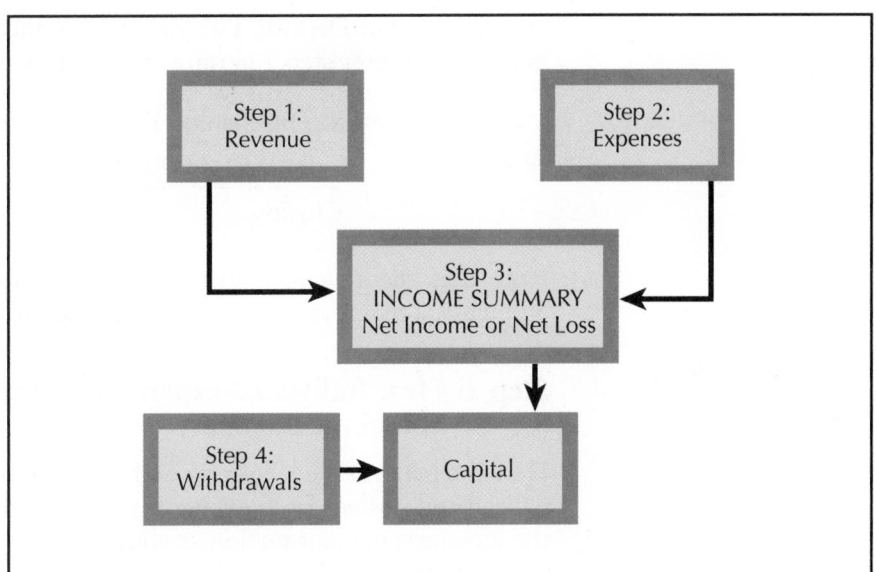

Figure 5-4
Closing Figures on the
Worksheet

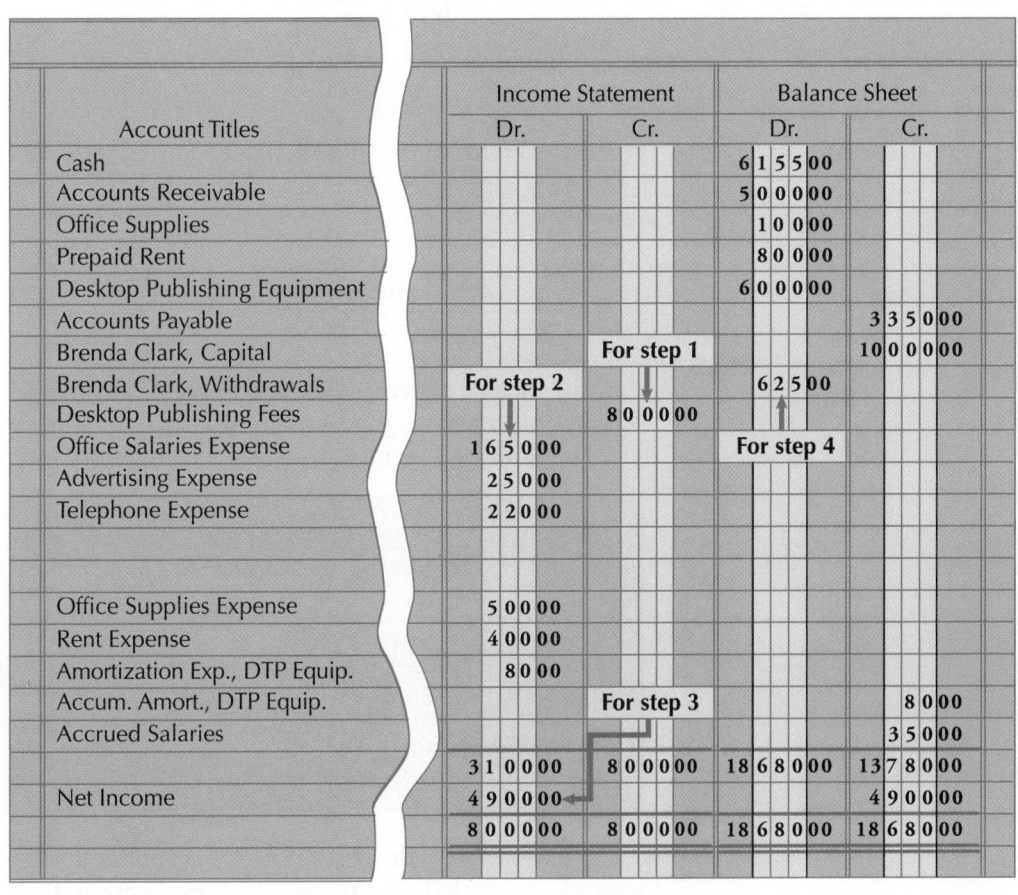

Account Titles	Income Statement Dr.	Income Statement Cr.	Balance Sheet Dr.	Balance Sheet Cr.
Cash			6 1 5 5 00	
Accounts Receivable			5 0 0 0 00	
Office Supplies			1 0 0 00	
Prepaid Rent			8 0 0 00	
Desktop Publishing Equipment			6 0 0 0 00	
Accounts Payable				3 3 5 0 00
Brenda Clark, Capital		For step 1		1 0 0 0 0 00
Brenda Clark, Withdrawals	For step 2		6 2 5 00	
Desktop Publishing Fees		8 0 0 0 00		
Office Salaries Expense	1 6 5 0 00		For step 4	
Advertising Expense	2 5 0 00			
Telephone Expense	2 2 0 00			
Office Supplies Expense	5 0 0 00			
Rent Expense	4 0 0 00			
Amortization Exp., DTP Equip.	8 0 00			
Accum. Amort., DTP Equip.		For step 3		8 0 00
Accrued Salaries				3 5 0 00
	3 1 0 0 00	8 0 0 0 00	18 6 8 0 00	13 7 8 0 00
Net Income	4 9 0 0 00			4 9 0 0 00
	8 0 0 0 00	8 0 0 0 00	18 6 8 0 00	18 6 8 0 00

The following is the journalized closing entry for step 1:

	2013					
	May	31	Desktop Publishing Fees	411	8 0 0 0 00	
			Income Summary	313		8 0 0 0 00
			To close income account			

This is what Desktop Publishing Fees and Income Summary should look like in the ledger after step 1 closing entries are journalized and posted:

Desktop Publishing Fees 411			Income Summary 313	
8,000	8,000			8,000
	Closing			Revenue

Note that the revenue balance is cleared to zero and transferred to Income Summary, a temporary account also located in the ledger.

Step 2: Clear Individual Expense Balances and Transfer the Total to Income Summary

Here is what is in the ledger for each expense before step 2 closing entries are journalized and posted. Each expense is listed on the worksheet in the debit column of the income statement section as above.

Office Salaries Expense 511		Advertising Expense 512	
650		250	
650			
350			

Telephone Expense 513		Office Supplies Expense 514	
220		500	

Rent Expense 515		Amortization Expense, DTP Equipment 516	
400		80	

The income statement section of the worksheet lists all the expenses as debits. If we want to reduce each expense to zero, each one must be credited.
The following is the journalized closing entry for step 2:

> The $3,100 is the total of the expenses on the worksheet.

	31	Income Summary	313	3 1 0 0 00	
		Office Salaries Expense	511		1 6 5 0 00
		Advertising Expense	512		2 5 0 00
		Telephone Expense	513		2 2 0 00
		Office Supplies Expense	514		5 0 0 00
		Rent Expense	515		4 0 0 00
		Amortization Expense, DTP Equipment	516		8 0 00
		To close expense accounts			

This is what individual expense accounts and the Income Summary should look like in the ledger after step 2 closing entries are journalized and posted:

Office Salaries Expense 511		Advertising Expense 512	
650	Closing 1,650	250	Closing 250
650			
350			

Telephone Expense 513		Office Supplies Expense 514	
220	Closing 220	500	Closing 500

Rent Expense 515		Amortization Expense 516	
400	Closing 400	80	Closing 80

Income Summary 313	
Expenses	Revenue
Step 2 3,100	8,000 Step 1

Remember: The worksheet is a tool. The accountant realizes that the information about the total of the expenses will be transferred to Income Summary.

Step 3: Clear Balance in Income Summary (Net Income) and Transfer It to Capital

This is how the Income Summary and Brenda Clark, Capital, accounts look before step 3:

Income Summary 313		Brenda Clark, Capital 311	
3,100	8,000		10,000
	4,900		

Note that the balance of Income Summary (Revenue minus Expenses, or $8,000 − $3,100) is $4,900. That is the amount we must clear from the Income Summary account and transfer to the Brenda Clark, Capital, account.

The opposite would take place if the business had a net loss.

In order to transfer the balance of $4,900 from Income Summary (check the bottom of the debit column of the income statement section on the worksheet; see Figure 5-4) to Capital, it will be necessary to debit Income Summary for $4,900 (the difference between the revenue and the expenses) and credit or increase Capital of Brenda Clark with $4,900.

This is the journalized closing entry for step 3:

	31	Income Summary	313	4 9 0 0 00	
		Brenda Clark, Capital	311		4 9 0 0 00
		Net income closed to capital			

At the end of these three steps, Income Summary has a zero balance. If we had a net loss, the end result would be to decrease capital. The entry would be to debit Capital and credit Income Summary for the loss.

This is what the Income Summary and Brenda Clark, Capital, accounts will look like in the ledger after step 3 closing entries are journalized and posted:

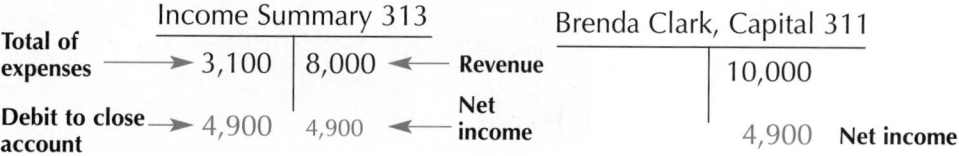

Today's accounting software handles the closing process easily. However, accountants usually have to do step 4 separately.

Step 4: Clear the Withdrawals Balance and Transfer It to Capital

Next, we must close the Withdrawals account. The Brenda Clark, Withdrawals, and Brenda Clark, Capital, accounts now look like this:

Brenda Clark, Withdrawals 312		Brenda Clark, Capital 311	
625			10,000
			4,900

Note that the $10,000 is a beginning balance since no additional investments were made during the period.

To bring the Withdrawals account to a zero balance and summarize its effect on Capital, we must credit Withdrawals and debit Capital.

Remember, withdrawals are a non-business expense and thus not transferred to Income Summary. The closing entry is journalized as follows:

	31	Brenda Clark, Capital	311	6 2 5 00	
		Brenda Clark, Withdrawals	312		6 2 5 00
		Close withdrawals into capital			

At this point, the Brenda Clark, Withdrawals, and Brenda Clark, Capital, accounts would look like this in the ledger:

Brenda Clark, Withdrawals 312	
625	Closing 625

Brenda Clark, Capital 311	
→ 625	10,000 ↖
Withdrawals	**Beginning balance**
	4,900 ↖
	Net income

The four steps in closing the books

CLARK'S DESKTOP PUBLISHING SERVICES
GENERAL JOURNAL

Date 2013		Account Title and Description	Post. Ref.	Dr.	Cr.
May	31	Desktop Publishing Fees	411	8 0 0 0 00	
		Income Summary	313		8 0 0 0 00
		To close income account			
	31	Income Summary	313	3 1 0 0 00	
		Office Salaries Expense	511		1 6 5 0 00
		Advertising Expense	512		2 5 0 00
		Telephone Expense	513		2 2 0 00
		Office Supplies Expense	514		5 0 0 00
		Rent Expense	515		4 0 0 00
		Amortization Expense, DTP Equipment	516		8 0 00
		To close expense accounts			
	31	Income Summary	313	4 9 0 0 00	
		Brenda Clark, Capital	311		4 9 0 0 00
		Net income closed to capital			
	31	Brenda Clark, Capital	311	6 2 5 00	
		Brenda Clark, Withdrawals	312		6 2 5 00
		Transfer withdrawals to capital			

Now let's look at a summary of the closing entries. The complete ledger for Clark's Desktop Publishing Services is shown in Figure 5-5 beginning on the next page. Note that the word "adjusting" or "closing" is written in the explanation column of individual ledgers, as, for example, in the one for Office Supplies. If the goals of closing have been achieved, only permanent accounts will have balances carried to the next fiscal year. All temporary accounts should have zero balances.

Figure 5-5
Complete Ledger

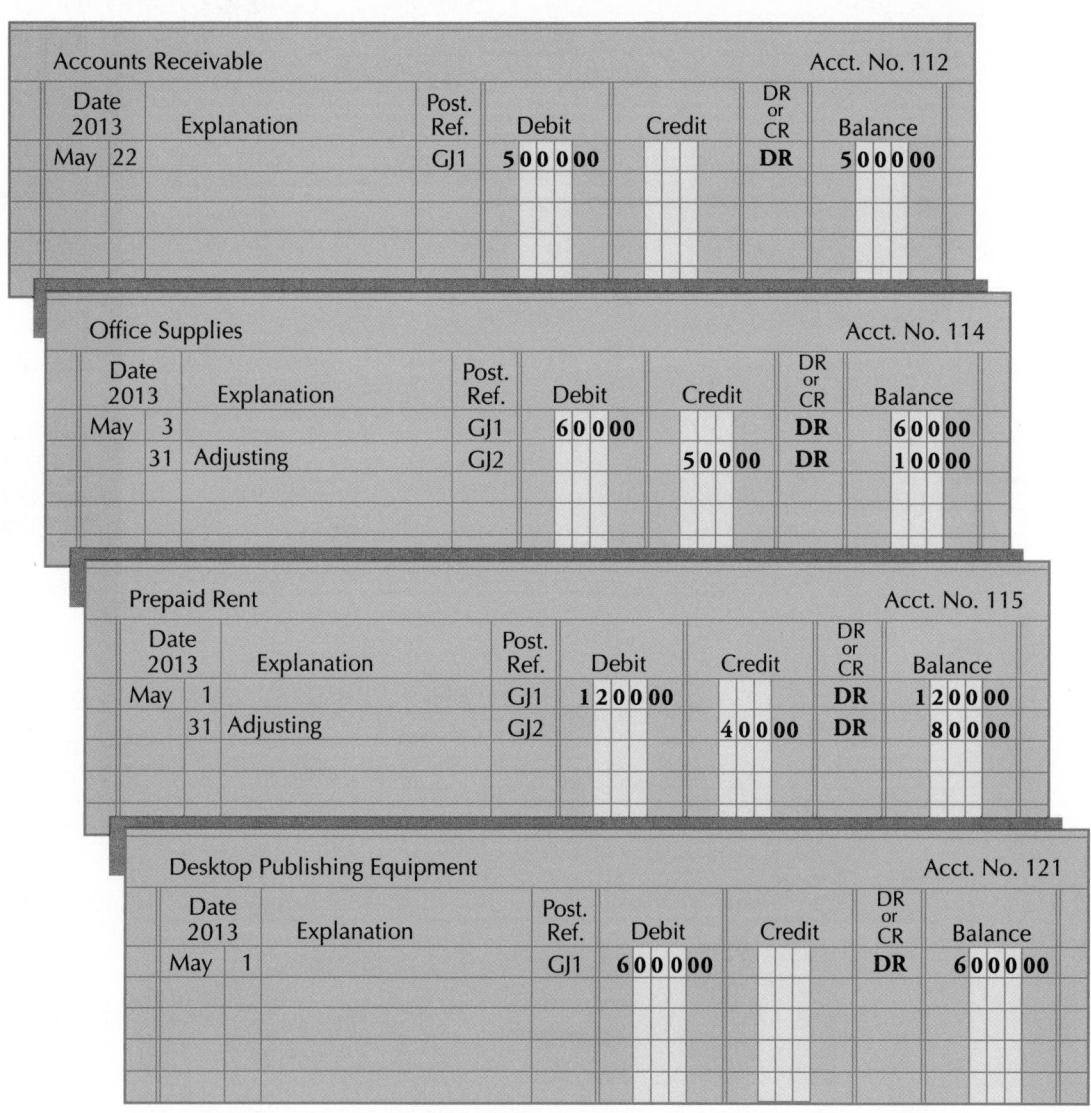

CLARK'S DESKTOP PUBLISHING SERVICES
GENERAL LEDGER

Cash   Account No. 111

Date 2013	Explanation	Post. Ref.	Debit	Credit	DR or CR	Balance
May 1		GJ1	10000 00		DR	10000 00
1		GJ1		1000 00	DR	9000 00
1		GJ1		1200 00	DR	7800 00
7		GJ1	3000 00		DR	10800 00
10		GJ1		650 00	DR	10150 00
20		GJ1		625 00	DR	9525 00
24		GJ2		650 00	DR	8875 00
28		GJ2		2500 00	DR	6375 00
29		GJ2		220 00	DR	6155 00

Accounts Receivable   Acct. No. 112

Date 2013	Explanation	Post. Ref.	Debit	Credit	DR or CR	Balance
May 22		GJ1	5000 00		DR	5000 00

Office Supplies   Acct. No. 114

Date 2013	Explanation	Post. Ref.	Debit	Credit	DR or CR	Balance
May 3		GJ1	600 00		DR	600 00
31	Adjusting	GJ2		500 00	DR	100 00

Prepaid Rent   Acct. No. 115

Date 2013	Explanation	Post. Ref.	Debit	Credit	DR or CR	Balance
May 1		GJ1	1200 00		DR	1200 00
31	Adjusting	GJ2		400 00	DR	800 00

Desktop Publishing Equipment   Acct. No. 121

Date 2013	Explanation	Post. Ref.	Debit	Credit	DR or CR	Balance
May 1		GJ1	6000 00		DR	6000 00

Figure 5-5 (continued)

Accumulated Amortization, Desktop Publishing Equipment — Acct. No. 122

Date 2013		Explanation	Post. Ref.	Debit	Credit	DR or CR	Balance
May	31	Adjusting	GJ2		8000	CR	8000

Accounts Payable — Acct. No. 211

Date 2013		Explanation	Post. Ref.	Debit	Credit	DR or CR	Balance
May	1		GJ1		500000	CR	500000
	3		GJ1		60000	CR	560000
	17		GJ1		25000	CR	585000
	28		GJ2	250000		CR	335000

Accrued Salaries — Acct. No. 212

Date 2013		Explanation	Post. Ref.	Debit	Credit	DR or CR	Balance
May	31	Adjusting	GJ2		35000	CR	35000

Brenda Clark, Capital — Acct. No. 311

Date 2013		Explanation	Post. Ref.	Debit	Credit	DR or CR	Balance
May	1		GJ1		1000000	CR	1000000
	31	Closing (Net Income)	GJ2		490000	CR	1490000
	31	Closing (Withdrawals)	GJ2	62500		CR	1427500

Note that this is the same ending balance as on page 153.

Brenda Clark, Withdrawals — Acct. No. 312

Date 2013		Explanation	Post. Ref.	Debit	Credit	DR or CR	Balance
May	20		GJ1	62500		DR	62500
	31	Closing	GJ2		62500		–0–

Income Summary — Acct. No. 313

Date 2013		Explanation	Post. Ref.	Debit	Credit	DR or CR	Balance
May	31	Closing (Revenue)	GJ2		800000	CR	800000
	31	Closing (Expense)	GJ2	310000		CR	490000
	31	Closing (Net Income)	GJ2	490000			–0–

Desktop Publishing Fees   Acct. No. 411

Date 2013		Explanation	Post. Ref.	Debit	Credit	DR or CR	Balance
May	7		GJ1		3 0 0 0 00	CR	3 0 0 0 00
	22		GJ1		5 0 0 0 00	CR	8 0 0 0 00
	31	Closing	GJ2	8 0 0 0 00			– 0 –

Office Salaries Expense   Acct. No. 511

Date 2013		Explanation	Post. Ref.	Debit	Credit	DR or CR	Balance
May	10		GJ1	6 5 0 00		DR	6 5 0 00
	24		GJ2	6 5 0 00		DR	1 3 0 0 00
	31	Adjusting	GJ2	3 5 0 00		DR	1 6 5 0 00
	31	Closing	GJ2		1 6 5 0 00		– 0 –

Advertising Expense   Acct. No. 512

Date 2013		Explanation	Post. Ref.	Debit	Credit	DR or CR	Balance
May	17		GJ1	2 5 0 00		DR	2 5 0 00
	31	Closing	GJ2		2 5 0 00		– 0 –

Telephone Expense   Acct. No. 513

Date 2013		Explanation	Post. Ref.	Debit	Credit	DR or CR	Balance
May	29		GJ2	2 2 0 00		DR	2 2 0 00
	31	Closing	GJ2		2 2 0 00		– 0 –

Office Supplies Expense   Acct. No. 514

Date 2013		Explanation	Post. Ref.	Debit	Credit	DR or CR	Balance
May	31	Adjusting	GJ2	5 0 0 00		DR	5 0 0 00
	31	Closing	GJ2		5 0 0 00		– 0 –

Figure 5-5 (continued)

Rent Expense						Acct. No. 515	
Date 2013	Explanation	Post. Ref.	Debit	Credit	DR or CR	Balance	
May 31	Adjusting	GJ2	4 0 0 00		DR	4 0 0 00	
31	Closing	GJ2		4 0 0 00		– 0 –	

Amortization Expense, Desktop Publishing Equipment						Acct. No. 516	
Date 2013	Explanation	Post. Ref.	Debit	Credit	DR or CR	Balance	
May 31	Adjusting	GJ2	8 0 00		DR	8 0 00	
31	Closing	GJ2		8 0 00		– 0 –	

LEARNING UNIT 5-2 REVIEW

AT THIS POINT you should be able to:

- ◆ Define closing. (p. 187)
- ◆ Differentiate between temporary (nominal) and permanent (real) accounts. (p. 188)
- ◆ List the four mechanical steps of closing. (p. 188)
- ◆ Explain the role of the Income Summary account. (p. 188)
- ◆ Explain the role of the worksheet in the closing process. (p. 188)

Self-Review Quiz 5-2

(The blank forms you need are on pages 5-2 and 5-3 of the *Study Guide with Working Papers.*)

Go to the worksheet for P. Logan on page 150. Then (1) journalize and post the closing entries and (2) calculate the new balance for P. Logan, Capital.

Solution to Self-Review Quiz 5-2

QUIZ Tip

Revenue closed to Income Summary

Each expense closed to Income Summary

Net Income closed to Capital

Withdrawals closed to Capital

				Dr		Cr	
		Closing Entries					
Dec.	31	Revenue from Clients	410	25	00		
		Income Summary	312			25	00
		To close income account					
	31	Income Summary	312	20	00		
		Rent Expense	518			2	00
		Salaries Expense	512			11	00
		Amortization Expense, Store Equipment	510			1	00
		Insurance Expense	516			2	00
		Supplies Expense	514			4	00
		To close expense accounts					
	31	Income Summary	312	5	00		
		P. Logan, Capital	310			5	00
		Transfer net income to Capital accounts					
	31	P. Logan, Capital	310	3	00		
		P. Logan, Withdrawals	311			3	00
		Transfer withdrawals to Capital accounts					

PARTIAL LEDGER

P. Logan, Capital 310			Revenue from Clients 410			Supplies Expense 514	
	3	14	25	25		4	4
		5					
		16					

P. Logan, Withdrawals 311		Amortization Expense, Store Equipment 510		Insurance Expense 516	
3	3	1	1	2	2

Income Summary 312		Salaries Expense 512		Rent Expense 518	
20	25	11	11	2	2
5	5				

P. Logan, Capital		$14
Net Income	$5	
Less: Withdrawals	3	
Increase in Capital		2
P. Logan, Capital (ending)		$16

Quiz Tip

No calculations are needed in the closing process. All numbers come from the worksheet. Income Summary is a temporary account in the ledger.

NEED HELP?

Let's review first: Why are closing entries necessary? In the ledger, we need to get the new balance in the Capital account. When financial statements were prepared, the ledger for Capital had only the old balance. Also, to get ready for the next accounting period, we must close all temporary accounts to zero so they will be ready to collect new data regarding revenues, expenses, and withdrawals. Without the closing process each year, financial statements would run into the next period and financial analysis would be difficult. Keep in mind that the Income Summary account that will be used in the closing process is a temporary account (I like to call it a storage area for revenues and expenses).

Why use the four steps to closing?

The four steps to closing when journalized and posted will do the following:

1. Clear all temporary accounts to zero.

2. Update the Capital account in the ledger to its new balance.

Steps to closing:

1. Close revenue account(s) to Income Summary.

2. Close each INDIVIDUAL expense to Income Summary.

3. Remove the balance in Income Summary (net income or net loss) and transfer it to the Capital account.

4. Close any withdrawals directly to Capital.

All the closing entries can be journalized directly from the last four columns of the worksheet. Each individual expense, along with the total of expenses, is found on the worksheet. Once these four closing entries are journalized and posted, all temporary accounts have a zero balance and P. Logan, Capital, now has an ending balance of $16. This is same amount of ending capital that was used to make the formal balance sheet.

SUMMARY

If you look at the T account in the solution you will see four numbers in Income Summary. Can you explain them?
20...this represents the total of all the expenses.
25...this represents the total revenue of all the revenues.
5 on the credit side...this is net income (25 − 20).
5 on the debit side...this comes from the third closing entry, which transfers the balance in Income Summary to Capital.

Learning Unit 5-3

The Post-Closing Trial Balance: Step 9 of the Accounting Cycle and the Accounting Cycle Reviewed

3 Preparing a post-closing trial balance

The post-closing trial balance helps prove the accuracy of the adjusting and closing process. It contains the true ending figure for capital.

PREPARING A POST-CLOSING TRIAL BALANCE

The last step in the accounting cycle is the preparation of a **post-closing trial balance** (sometimes called an opening trial balance), which lists only permanent accounts in the ledger and their balances after adjusting and closing entries have been posted. This post-closing trial balance aids in checking whether the ledger is in balance. It is important to do this checking because so many new postings go to the ledger from the adjusting and closing process.

The procedure for taking a post-closing trial balance is the same as for a trial balance except that since closing entries have closed all temporary accounts, the post-closing trial balance will contain only permanent accounts (balance sheet). Keep in mind, however, that adjustments have occurred.

THE ACCOUNTING CYCLE REVIEWED

Table 5-1 lists the steps that we completed in the manual accounting cycle for Clark's Desktop Publishing Services for the month of May.

Insight: Most companies journalize and post adjusting and closing entries only at the end of their fiscal year. A company that prepares interim reports may complete only the first six steps of the cycle. Worksheets allow the preparation of interim reports without the formal adjusting and closing of the books.

TABLE 5-1   Steps of the Manual Accounting Cycle

Step	Explanation
1. Business transactions occur and generate source documents.	Source documents are cash register tapes, sales tickets, bills, cheques, payroll cards, etc.
↓	↓
2. Analyze and record business transactions into a journal.	Called journalizing.
↓	↓
3. Post or transfer information from journal to ledger.	Copying the debits and credits of the journal entries into the ledger accounts.
↓	↓
4. Prepare a trial balance.	Summarizing each individual ledger account and listing these accounts and their balances to test for mathematical accuracy in recording transactions.
↓	↓
5. Prepare a worksheet.	A multicolumn form that summarizes accounting information to complete the accounting cycle.
↓	↓
6. Prepare financial statements.	Income statement, statement of owner's equity, and balance sheet.
↓	↓
7. Journalize and post adjusting entries.	Use figures in the adjustment columns of the worksheet.
↓	↓
8. Journalize and post closing entries.	Use figures in the income statement and balance sheet sections of worksheet.
↓	↓
9. Prepare a post-closing trial balance.	Prove the mathematical accuracy of the adjusting and closing process of the accounting cycle.

Insight: To prepare a financial report for April, the data needed can be obtained by subtracting the worksheet accumulated totals for the end of March from the worksheet prepared at the end of April. In this chapter, we chose a month that would show the completion of an entire cycle for Clark's Desktop Publishing Services.

LEARNING UNIT 5-3 REVIEW

AT THIS POINT you should be able to:
- Prepare a post-closing trial balance. (p. 198)
- Explain the relationship of interim reports to the accounting cycle. (p. 199)

Self-Review Quiz 5-3

(The blank forms you need are on page 5-3 of the *Study Guide with Working Papers*.)

From the ledger on pages 193–196, prepare a post-closing trial balance.

Solution to Self-Review Quiz 5-3

QUIZ Tip

The post-closing trial balance contains only permanent accounts because all temporary accounts have been closed. All temporary accounts are summarized in the Capital account.

CLARK'S DESKTOP PUBLISHING SERVICES
POST-CLOSING TRIAL BALANCE
MAY 31, 2013

	Dr.	Cr.
Cash	6 1 5 5 00	
Accounts Receivable	5 0 0 0 00	
Office Supplies	1 0 0 00	
Prepaid Rent	8 0 0 00	
Desktop Publishing Equipment	6 0 0 0 00	
Accumulated Amortization, Desktop Publishing Equipment		8 0 00
Accounts Payable		3 3 5 0 00
Accrued Salaries		3 5 0 00
Brenda Clark, Capital		14 2 7 5 00
Totals	18 0 5 5 00	18 0 5 5 00

NEED HELP?

Let's review first: The post-closing trial balance contains only permanent accounts because all temporary accounts have been closed. All temporary accounts are summarized in the Capital account. Remember that Income Summary is a temporary account.

Post-Closing Trial Balance: Once all the closing entries have been journalized and posted we can then prepare a post-closing trial balance. Since only permanent accounts are left after closing, the structure of the post-closing trial balance should look as follows:

Assets ....Dr.

Contra-Assets ....Cr.

Liabilities ....Cr.

Ending Capital ....Cr.

SUMMARY

To begin the next accounting cycle, only permanent accounts with balances are brought forward. In the new cycle, transactions will be journalized and posted. Adjustments will be made and new financial statements will be prepared. By the end of the cycle, all temporary accounts will be closed to get a new ending figure for capital in the ledger. The end result will be to prepare a new post-closing trial balance.

"You wait and see," Stan told his new sandwich artist Wanda Kurtz. "Everything will fall into place soon." Wanda had a tough time serving customers quickly enough, and Stan was in the middle of giving her a pep talk when the phone rang.

"I'll let the machine pick it up," Stan reassured Wanda, as he proceeded to train her in some crucial POS touch-screen manoeuvres.

"Stan!" an urgent voice came over the answering machine. "I think you've forgotten something!" Stan picked up the phone and said, "Lila, can I get back to you tomorrow? I'm in the middle of an important talk with Wanda." One of Stan's strong points as an employer was his ability to focus 100% on his employees' concerns. Yet, Lila simply would not wait.

"Stan," Lila said impatiently, "you absolutely must get me your worksheet by 12 noon tomorrow so that I can close your books," she insisted. "Tomorrow's the 31st of March and we close on the last day of the month!"

"*Ay caramba!*" Stan sighed. "Looks like I'm going to be up till the wee hours," he confided to Wanda when he put down the phone.

Although Subway company policy doesn't require a closing every month, closing the books is a key part of their accounting training for all new franchisees. By closing their books, business owners can clearly measure their net profit and loss for each period, separate from all other periods. This makes activities such as budgeting and comparing performance with similar businesses (or performance over time) possible.

At 9 a.m. the next day, an exhausted Stan opened the restaurant and emailed his worksheet to Lila. He was feeling quite pleased with himself—that is, until he heard Lila's urgent-sounding voice coming over the answering machine 10 minutes later.

"I've been over and over this," said Lila after Stan picked it up, "and I can't get it to balance. I

SUBWAY

CLOSING TIME

Closing and balancing the books

②③ (20 min)

know it's hard for you to do this during working hours, but I need you to go back over the figures."

Stan opened up QuickBooks® and pored over his worksheets. Errors are hard to find when closing the books and, unfortunately, there is no set way to detect errors and even no set place to start. Stan chose payroll because it is one of the largest expenses and because of the new hire.

At 11:45 he called Lila, who sounded both exasperated and relieved to hear from him. "I think I've got it! It looks like I messed up on adjusting the Salaries Expense account. I looked at the Payroll Register and compared the total of the Accrued Salaries account. It didn't match! When I hired Wanda Kurtz on the 26th, I should have increased both the Salaries Expense and the Accrued Salaries lines because she has accrued wages."

"Yes," said Lila. "Salaries Expense is a debit and Accrued Salaries is a credit and you skipped the payable. Great! With this adjusting entry in the general journal, the worksheet will balance."

Stan's sigh of relief turned into a big yawn and they both laughed. "I guess I just find it easier to hire people and train them than to account for them," said Stan.

DISCUSSION QUESTIONS

1. How would the adjustment be made if Wanda Kurtz received $7 per hour and worked 25 additional hours? Where do you place her accrued wages?
2. Stan bought three new Subway aprons and hats for Wanda Kurtz for $20 each but forgot to post it to the Uniforms account. How much will the closing balance be off? In what way will it be off?
3. Put yourself in Stan's shoes: What is the value of doing a monthly closing, no matter how much—or little—business you do?

DEMONSTRATION PROBLEM: REVIEWING THE ACCOUNTING CYCLE

(The blank forms you need are on pages 5-4 to 5-10 of the *Study Guide with Working Papers*.)

From the following transactions for Rolo Company, complete the entire accounting cycle. The chart of accounts includes:

Assets
111 Cash
112 Accounts Receivable
114 Prepaid Rent
115 Office Supplies
121 Office Equipment
122 Accumulated Amortization, Office Equipment

Liabilities
211 Accounts Payable
212 Accrued Salaries

Owner's Equity
311 R. Kern, Capital
312 R. Kern, Withdrawals
313 Income Summary

Revenue
411 Fees Earned

Expenses
511 Salaries Expense
512 Advertising Expense
513 Rent Expense
514 Office Supplies Expense
515 Amortization Expense, Office Equipment

We will use unusually small numbers to simplify the calculations and to emphasize the theory.

2013
Jan. 2 Rolo Kern invested $1,200 cash and $100 worth of office equipment to open Rolo Co.
      2 Paid rent for three months in advance, $300.
      3 Purchased office equipment on account, $50.
      4 Bought office supplies for cash, $40.
      8 Collected $400 for services rendered.
      11 Rolo paid his home electric bill from the company bank account, $20.
      14 Provided $100 worth of services to clients who will not pay until next month.
      15 Paid salaries, $60.
      18 Advertising bill for $70 was received but will not be paid until next month.

Adjustment Data on January 31

a. Supplies on Hand, $6
b. Rent Expired, $100
c. Amortization, Office Equipment, $20
d. Salaries Accrued, $50

Solutions to Demonstration Problem

Journalizing Transactions and Posting to Ledger, Rolo Company

General Journal					Page 1
Date	Account Titles and Description	PR	Dr.	Cr.	
2013 Jan. 2	Cash	111	1 2 0 0 00		
	Office Equipment	121	1 0 0 00		
	R. Kern, Capital	311		1 3 0 0 00	
	Initial investment				
2	Prepaid Rent	114	3 0 0 00		
	Cash	111		3 0 0 00	
	Rent paid in advance—3 months				
3	Office Equipment	121	5 0 00		
	Accounts Payable	211		5 0 00	
	Purchased equipment on account				
4	Office Supplies	115	4 0 00		
	Cash	111		4 0 00	
	Supplies purchased for cash				
8	Cash	111	4 0 0 00		
	Fees Earned	411		4 0 0 00	
	Services rendered				
11	R. Kern, Withdrawals	312	2 0 00		
	Cash	111		2 0 00	
	Personal payment of a bill				
14	Accounts Receivable	112	1 0 0 00		
	Fees Earned	411		1 0 0 00	
	Services rendered on account				
15	Salaries Expense	511	6 0 00		
	Cash	111		6 0 00	
	Paid salaries				
18	Advertising Expense	512	7 0 00		
	Accounts Payable	211		7 0 00	
	Advertising bill, but not paid				

Solution Tips to Journalizing and Posting Transactions

	Cash	Asset	↑	Dr.	$1,200
Jan. 2	Office Equipment	Asset	↑	Dr.	$ 100
	R. Kern, Capital	Capital	↑	Cr.	$1,300

Jan. 2	Prepaid Rent	Asset	↑	Dr.	$ 300
	Cash	Asset	↓	Cr.	$ 300

Jan. 3	Office Equipment	Asset	↑	Dr.	$ 50
	Accounts Payable	Liability	↑	Cr.	$ 50

Jan. 4	Office Supplies	Asset	↑	Dr.	$ 40
	Cash	Asset	↓	Cr.	$ 40

Jan. 8	Cash	Asset	↑	Dr.	$ 400
	Fees Earned	Revenue	↑	Cr.	$ 400

Jan. 11	R. Kern, Withdrawals	Owner's Equity (Withdr.)	↑	Dr.	$ 20
	Cash	Asset	↓	Cr.	$ 20

Jan. 14	Accounts Receivable	Asset	↑	Dr.	$ 100
	Fees Earned	Revenue	↑	Cr.	$ 100

Jan. 15	Salaries Expense	Expense	↑	Dr.	$ 60
	Cash	Asset	↓	Cr.	$ 60

Jan. 18	Advertising Expense	Expense	↑	Dr.	$ 70
	Accounts Payable	Liability	↑	Cr.	$ 70

Note: All account titles come from the chart of accounts. When journalizing, the PR column of the general journal is blank. It is in the posting process that we update the ledger. The PR columns in the ledger accounts tell us from which journal page the information came. After posting to the account in the ledger, we fill in the PR column of the journal, which tells us to what account number the information was transferred.

COMPLETING THE WORKSHEET
See the worksheet on page 206.

Solution Tips to the Trial Balance and Completion of the Worksheet

After the posting process from the journal to the ledger is complete, we take the ending balance in each account and prepare a trial balance on the worksheet. If an account title has no balance, it is not listed on the trial balance. New titles on the worksheet will be added below the trial balance as needed.

ROLO COMPANY
WORKSHEET
FOR MONTH ENDED JANUARY 31, 2013

Account Titles	Trial Balance Dr.	Trial Balance Cr.	Adjustments Dr.	Adjustments Cr.	Adjusted Trial Balance Dr.	Adjusted Trial Balance Cr.	Income Statement Dr.	Income Statement Cr.	Balance Sheet Dr.	Balance Sheet Cr.
Cash	118000				118000				118000	
Accounts Receivable	10000				10000				10000	
Prepaid Rent	30000			(B) 10000	20000				20000	
Office Supplies	4000			(A) 3400	600				600	
Office Equipment	15000				15000				15000	
Accounts Payable		12000				12000				12000
R. Kern, Capital		130000				130000				130000
R. Kern, Withdrawals	2000				2000				2000	
Fees Earned		50000				50000		50000		
Salaries Expense	6000		(D) 5000		11000		11000			
Advertising Expense	7000				7000		7000			
	192000	192000								
Office Supplies Expense			(A) 3400		3400		3400			
Rent Expense			(B) 10000		10000		10000			
Amort. Expense, Office Equip.			(C) 2000		2000		2000			
Accum. Amort., Office Equip.				(C) 2000		2000				2000
Accrued Salaries				(D) 5000		5000				5000
			20400	20400	199000	199000	33400	50000	165600	149000
Net Income							16600			16600
							50000	50000	165600	165600

206 CHAPTER 5

The amount of office supplies on hand ($6) is *not* the adjustment. The amount used up needs to be calculated.	**Office Supplies Expense** **Office Supplies**	Expense Asset	↑ ↓	Dr. Cr.	$ 34 $ 34	($40 − $6)
Expired	**Rent Expense** **Prepaid Rent**	Expense Asset	↑ ↓	Dr. Cr.	$100 $100	
Do not touch original cost of equipment.	**Amort. Exp., Office Equip.** **Accum. Amort., Office Equip.**	Expense Asset (Contra)	↑ ↓	Dr. Cr.	$ 20 $ 20	
Owed but not paid	**Salaries Expense** **Accrued Salaries**	Expense Liability	↑ ↑	Dr. Cr.	$ 50 $ 50	

Note: This information is on the worksheet but has *not* been updated in the ledger. (This will occur when we journalize and post adjustments at the end of the cycle.)

Note that the last four columns of the worksheet come from numbers on the adjusted trial balance.

We move Net Income of $166 to the balance sheet credit column since the capital figure is the old one on the worksheet.

PREPARING THE FORMAL FINANCIAL STATEMENTS

ROLO COMPANY
INCOME STATEMENT
FOR MONTH ENDED JANUARY 31, 2013

Revenue:		
Fees Earned		$ 5 0 0 00
Operating Expenses:		
Salaries Expense	$ 1 1 0 00	
Advertising Expense	7 0 00	
Office Supplies Expense	3 4 00	
Rent Expense	1 0 0 00	
Amortization Expense, Office Equipment	2 0 00	
Total Operating Expenses		3 3 4 00
Net Income		$ 1 6 6 00

ROLO COMPANY
STATEMENT OF OWNER'S EQUITY
FOR MONTH ENDED JANUARY 31, 2013

R. Kern, Capital, January 1, 2013		$ 1 3 0 0 00
Net Income for January	$ 1 6 6 00	
Less: Withdrawals for January	2 0 00	
Increase in Capital		1 4 6 00
R. Kern, Capital, January 31, 2013		$ 1 4 4 6 00

ROLO COMPANY BALANCE SHEET JANUARY 31, 2013								
Assets				**Liabilities and Owner's Equity**				
Cash			$1 1 8 0 00	Liabilities:				
Accounts Receivable			1 0 0 00	Accounts Payable	$ 1 2 0 00			
Prepaid Rent			2 0 0 00	Accrued Salaries	5 0 00			
Office Supplies			6 00	Total Liabilities			$ 1 7 0 00	
Office Equipment	$ 1 5 0 00			Owner's Equity:				
Less: Acc. Amort.	2 0 00		1 3 0 00	R. Kern, Capital			1 4 4 6 00	
				Total Liabilities and				
Total Assets			$1 6 1 6 00	Owner's Equity			$1 6 1 6 00	

Solution Tips to Preparing the Financial Statements

The statements are prepared from the worksheet. (Many of the ledger accounts are not up to date.) The income statement lists revenue and expenses. The net income figure of $166 is used to update the statement of owner's equity. The statement of owner's equity calculates a new figure for Capital, $1,446 (Beginning Capital + Net Income – Withdrawals). This new figure is then listed on the balance sheet (Assets, Liabilities, and a new figure for Capital).

JOURNALIZING AND POSTING ADJUSTING AND CLOSING ENTRIES

See the journal at the top of page 209.

Solution Tips to Journalizing and Posting Adjusting and Closing Entries

ADJUSTMENTS

The adjustments from the worksheet are journalized (same journal) and posted to the ledger. Now ledger accounts will be brought up to date. Remember, we have already prepared the financial reports from the worksheet. Our goal now is to get the ledger up to date.

CLOSING

Note: Income Summary is a temporary account located in the ledger.

Goals

Where do I get my information for closing?

1. Adjust all temporary accounts in the ledger to zero balances.
2. Determine a new figure for capital in the ledger.

	Date		Account Titles and Description	PR	Dr.	Cr.

General Journal — Page 2

	Date		Account Titles and Description	PR	Dr.	Cr.
	2013		**Adjusting Entries**			
	Jan.	31	Office Supplies Expense	514	34 00	
			Office Supplies	115		34 00
			Supplies used			
		31	Rent Expense	513	100 00	
			Prepaid Rent	114		100 00
			Rent expired			
		31	Amortization Expense, Office Equipment	515	20 00	
			Accumulated Amortization, Office Equip.	122		20 00
			Estimated Amortization			
		31	Salaries Expense	511	50 00	
			Accrued Salaries	212		50 00
			Accrued salaries			
			Closing Entries			
Step 1 →		31	Fees Earned	411	500 00	
			Income Summary	313		500 00
			To close income accounts			
Step 2 →		31	Income Summary	313	334 00	
			Salaries Expense	511		110 00
			Advertising Expense	512		70 00
			Office Supplies Expense	514		34 00
			Rent Expense	513		100 00
			Amortization Expense, Office Equipment	515		20 00
			To close expense accounts			
Step 3 →		31	Income Summary	313	166 00	
			R. Kern, Capital	311		166 00
			Net income closed to capital			
Step 4 →		31	R. Kern, Capital	311	20 00	
			R. Kern, Withdrawals	312		20 00
			Close withdrawals into capital			

Closing { Step 1, Step 2, Step 3, Step 4 }

Steps in the Closing Process

Step 1: Close revenue to Income Summary.

Step 2: Close individual expenses to Income Summary.

Step 3: Close balance of Income Summary to Capital. (This really is the net income figure on the worksheet.)

Step 4: Close balance of Withdrawals to Capital.

All the journal closing entries are posted. (No new calculations are needed since all figures are on the worksheet.) The result in the ledger is that all temporary accounts have a zero balance.

GENERAL LEDGER

Cash — Acct. No. 111

Date 2013	Explanation	Post. Ref.	Debit	Credit	DR or CR	Balance
Jan. 2		GJ1	120000		DR.	120000
2		GJ1		30000	DR.	90000
4		GJ1		4000	DR.	86000
8		GJ1	40000		DR.	126000
11		GJ1		2000	DR.	124000
15		GJ1		6000	DR.	118000

Accounts Receivable — Acct. No. 112

Date 2013	Explanation	Post. Ref.	Debit	Credit	DR or CR	Balance
Jan. 14		GJ1	10000		DR.	10000

Prepaid Rent — Acct. No. 114

Date 2013	Explanation	Post. Ref.	Debit	Credit	DR or CR	Balance
Jan. 2		GJ1	30000		DR.	30000
31	Adjustment	GJ2		10000	DR.	20000

Office Supplies — Acct. No. 115

Date 2013	Explanation	Post. Ref.	Debit	Credit	DR or CR	Balance
Jan. 4		GJ1	4000		DR.	4000
31	Adjustment	GJ2		3400	DR.	600

Office Equipment — Acct. No. 121

Date 2013	Explanation	Post. Ref.	Debit	Credit	DR or CR	Balance
Jan. 2		GJ1	10000		DR.	10000
3		GJ1	5000		DR.	15000

Accumulated Amortization, Office Equipment — Acct. No. 122

Date 2013	Explanation	Post. Ref.	Debit	Credit	DR or CR	Balance
Jan. 31	Adjustment	GJ2		2000	CR.	2000

Accounts Payable — Acct. No. 211

Date 2013	Explanation	Post. Ref.	Debit	Credit	DR or CR	Balance
Jan. 3		GJ1		5000	CR.	5000
18		GJ1		7000	CR.	12000

Accrued Salaries — Acct. No. 212

Date 2013	Explanation	Post. Ref.	Debit	Credit	DR or CR	Balance
Jan. 31	Adjustment	GJ2		5000	CR.	5000

R. Kern, Capital — Acct. No. 311

Date 2013	Explanation	Post. Ref.	Debit	Credit	DR or CR	Balance
Jan. 2		GJ1		130000	CR.	130000
31	Closing	GJ2		16600	CR.	146600
31	Closing	GJ2	2000		CR.	144600

R. Kern, Withdrawals — Acct. No. 312

Date 2013	Explanation	Post. Ref.	Debit	Credit	DR or CR	Balance
Jan. 12		GJ1	2000		DR.	2000
31	Closing	GJ2		2000		-0-

Income Summary — Acct. No. 313

Date 2013	Explanation	Post. Ref.	Debit	Credit	DR or CR	Balance
Jan. 31	Closing	GJ2		50000	CR.	50000
31	Closing	GJ2	33400		CR.	16600
31	Closing	GJ2	16600			-0-

Fees Earned — Acct. No. 411

Date 2013	Explanation	Post. Ref.	Debit	Credit	DR or CR	Balance
Jan. 8		GJ1		40000	CR.	40000
14		GJ1		10000	CR.	50000
31	Closing	GJ2	50000			-0-

Salaries Expense — Acct. No. 511

Date 2013	Explanation	Post. Ref.	Debit	Credit	DR or CR	Balance
Jan. 15		GJ1	6000		DR.	6000
31	Adjusting	GJ2	5000		DR.	11000
31	Closing	GJ2		11000		-0-

Advertising Expense — Acct. No. 512

Date 2013	Explanation	Post. Ref.	Debit	Credit	DR or CR	Balance
Jan. 18		GJ1	7000		DR.	7000
31	Closing	GJ2		7000		-0-

Rent Expense — Acct. No. 513

Date 2013	Explanation	Post. Ref.	Debit	Credit	DR or CR	Balance
Jan. 31	Adjusting	GJ2	10000		DR.	10000
31	Closing	GJ2		10000		-0-

Office Supplies Expense — Acct. No. 514

Date 2013	Explanation	Post. Ref.	Debit	Credit	DR or CR	Balance
Jan. 31	Adjusting	GJ2	3400		DR.	3400
31	Closing	GJ2		3400		-0-

Amortization Expense, Office Equipment — Acct. No. 515

Date 2013	Explanation	Post. Ref.	Debit	Credit	DR or CR	Balance
Jan. 31	Adjusting	GJ2	2000		DR.	2000
31	Closing	GJ2		2000		-0-

ROLO CO.
POST-CLOSING TRIAL BALANCE
JANUARY 31, 2013

	Dr.	Cr.
Cash	1 1 8 0 00	
Accounts Receivable	1 0 0 00	
Prepaid Rent	2 0 0 00	
Office Supplies	6 00	
Office Equipment	1 5 0 00	
Accumulated Amortization, Office Equipment		2 0 00
Accounts Payable		1 2 0 00
Accrued Salaries		5 0 00
R. Kern, Capital		1 4 4 6 00
Total	1 6 3 6 00	1 6 3 6 00

Solution Tips for the Post-Closing Trial Balance

The post-closing trial balance is a list of the ledger balances *after* adjusting and closing entries have been completed. Note the figure for capital $1,446 is the new figure.

Beginning Capital	$1,300
+ Net Income	166
− Withdrawals	20
= Ending Capital	$1,446

Next accounting period, we will enter new amounts in the Revenues, Expenses, and Withdrawals accounts. For now, the post-closing trial balance is made up only of permanent accounts.

SUMMARY OF KEY POINTS

Learning Unit 5-1

1. After formal financial reports have been prepared, the ledger still has not been brought up to date.

2. Information for journalizing adjusting entries comes from the adjustments section of the worksheet.

Learning Unit 5-2

1. Closing is a mechanical process that is completed before the accountant can record transactions for the next fiscal year.

2. Assets, Liabilities, and Capital are permanent (real) accounts; their balances are carried over from one fiscal year to another. Withdrawals, Revenue, and Expenses are nominal (temporary) accounts; their balances are *not* carried over from one fiscal year to another.

3. Income Summary is a temporary account in the general ledger and does not have a normal balance. It will summarize revenue and expenses and transfer the balance to capital. Withdrawals do not go into Income Summary because they are *not* business expenses.

4. All information for closing can be obtained from the worksheet.

5. When closing is complete, all temporary accounts in the ledger will have a zero balance, and all this information will be updated in the Capital account.

6. Closing entries are usually done only at year-end. Interim reports can be prepared from worksheets that are prepared monthly, quarterly, and so on.

Learning Unit 5-3

1. The post-closing trial balance is prepared from the ledger accounts after the adjusting and closing entries have been posted.

2. The accounts on the post-closing trial balance are all permanent accounts.

KEY TERMS

Adjusting journal entries   Journal entries that are needed in order to update specific ledger accounts to reflect correct balances at the end of an accounting period (p. 183)

Closing   The process of bringing the balances of all revenue, expense, and withdrawal accounts to zero, ready for a new fiscal year (p. 187)

Closing journal entries   Journal entries that are prepared to (a) reduce or clear all temporary accounts to a zero balance and (b) update capital to a new closing balance (p. 188)

Income Summary   A temporary account in the ledger that summarizes revenue and expenses and transfers its balance (net income or net loss) to capital. It does not have a normal balance. (p. 188)

Nominal accounts   See *Temporary accounts* (p. 188)

Permanent accounts   Balances of accounts that are carried over to the next fiscal year; examples: assets, liabilities, capital (p. 187)

Post-closing trial balance   The final step in the accounting cycle that lists only permanent accounts in the ledger and their balances after adjusting and closing entries have been posted (p. 198)

Real accounts   See *Permanent accounts* (p. 187)

Temporary accounts   Balances of accounts at the end of a fiscal year that are not carried over to the next fiscal year. These accounts—Revenue, Expenses, Withdrawals—help to provide a new or ending figure for capital to begin the next fiscal year. Keep in mind that Income Summary is also a temporary account. (p. 188)

BLUEPRINT OF THE CLOSING PROCESS FROM THE WORKSHEET

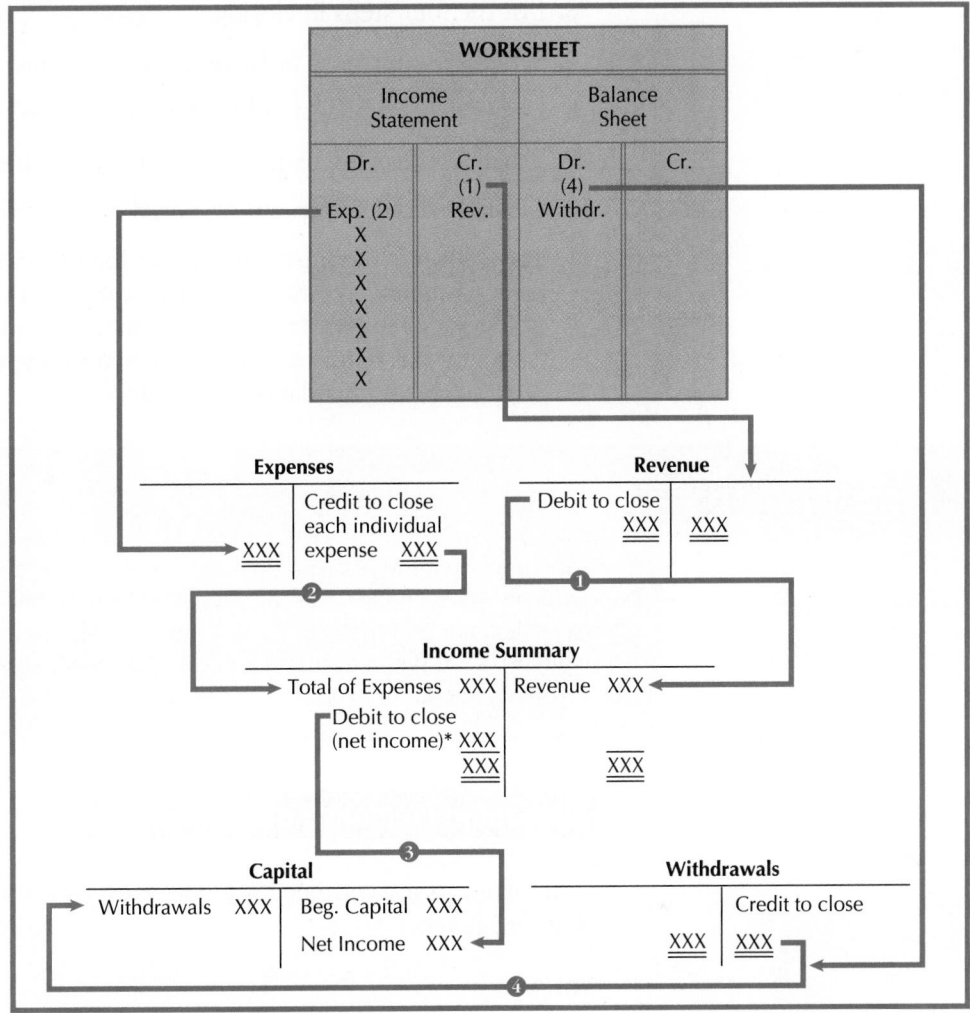

*If a net loss, it would require a credit to close.

The Closing Steps
1. Close revenue balances to Income Summary.
2. Close each *individual* expense and transfer the *total* of all expenses to Income Summary.
3. Transfer the balance in Income Summary (Net Income or Net Loss) to Capital.
4. Close Withdrawals to Capital.

QUESTIONS, CLASSROOM DEMONSTRATION EXERCISES, EXERCISES, AND PROBLEMS

Discussion Questions and Critical Thinking/Ethical Case

1. When a worksheet is completed, what balances are found in the general ledger?

2. Why must adjusting entries be journalized even though the formal reports have already been prepared?

3. "Closing slows down the recording of next year's transactions." Defend or reject this statement with supporting evidence.

4. What is the difference between temporary and permanent accounts?

5. What are the two major goals of the closing process?

6. List the four steps in closing.

7. What is the purpose of Income Summary and where is it located?

8. How can a worksheet aid the closing process?

9. What accounts are usually listed on a post-closing trial balance?

10. Closing entries are always prepared once a month. Agree or disagree. Why?

11. Todd Silver is the purchasing agent for Moore Company. One of his suppliers, Gem Company, offers Todd a free vacation to France if he buys at least 75% of Moore's supplies from Gem Company. Todd, who is angry because Moore Company has not given him a raise in over a year, is considering the offer. Write out your recommendation to Todd.

MyAccountingLab

Classroom Demonstration Exercises

(The blank forms you need are on pages 5-11 and 5-12 of the *Study Guide with Working Papers*.)

Set A

Journalizing and Posting Adjusting Entries

Posting adjusting entries
1 (5 min)

1. Enter the beginning balances in the *Study Guide with Working Papers*. Post the following adjusting entries (be sure to cross-reference back to the journal) that came from the Adjustment columns of the worksheet.

General Journal					Page 3	
Date 2012		Account Titles and Description	PR	Dr.	Cr.	
Dec.	31	Insurance Expense		6 00		
		Prepaid Insurance			6 00	
		Insurance expired				
	31	Supplies Expense		4 00		
		Store Supplies			4 00	
		Supplies used				
	31	Amortization Expense, Store Equipment		9 00		
		Accum. Amortization, Store Equipment			9 00	
		Estimated amortization				
	31	Salaries Expense		5 00		
		Accrued Salaries			5 00	
		Accrued salaries				

LEDGER ACCOUNTS BEFORE ADJUSTING ENTRIES POSTED

Prepaid Insurance 115	Insurance Expense 510
18	

Store Supplies 116	Amortization Expense, Store Equipment 512
17	

Accumulated Amortization, Store Equipment 119	Supplies Expense 514
13	

Accrued Salaries 210	Salaries Expense 516
	9

Closing Steps and Journalizing Closing Entries

Steps in the closing process
2 (10 min)

2. Explain the four steps of the closing process given the following Dec. 31 ending balances, before closing:

Fees Earned	$200
Rent Expense	100
Advertising Expense	60
J. Rice, Capital	3,000
J. Rice, Withdrawals	15

Journalizing Closing Entries

Journalizing the closing entries from T accounts
2 (15 min)

3. From the following accounts, journalize the closing entries (assume that December 31 is the closing date).

Mel Blanc, Capital 310	Gas Expense 510
40	8

Mel Blanc, Withdrawals 312	Advertising Expense 512
7	12

Income Summary 314	Amortization Expense, Taxi 516
	8

Taxi Fare Income 410	
39	

Posting to Income Summary

The Income Summary account
2 (10 min)

4. Draw a T account of Income Summary and post to it all entries from question 3 that affect it. Is Income Summary a temporary or permanent account?

Posting to Capital

The capital account
2 (10 min)

5. Draw a T account for Mel Blanc, Capital, and post to it all entries from question 3 that affect it. What is the final balance of the capital account?

Set B

Journalizing and Posting Adjusting Entries

1. Enter the beginning balances in the *Study Guide with Working Papers*. Post the following adjusting entries (be sure to cross-reference back to the journal) that came from the Adjustment columns of the worksheet.

General Journal						Page 3
Date 2012		Account Titles and Description	PR	Dr.	Cr.	
Dec.	31	Insurance Expense		4 00		
		Prepaid Insurance			4 00	
		Insurance expired				
	31	Supplies Expense		3 00		
		Store Supplies			3 00	
		Supplies used				
	31	Amortization Expense, Store Equipment		7 00		
		Accum. Amortization, Store Equipment			7 00	
		Estimated amortization				
	31	Salaries Expense		4 00		
		Accrued Salaries			4 00	
		Accrued salaries				

LEDGER ACCOUNTS BEFORE ADJUSTING ENTRIES POSTED

Prepaid Insurance 115
12 |

Insurance Expense 510
|

Store Supplies 116
15 |

Amortization Expense, Store Equipment 512
|

Accumulated Amortization, Store Equipment 119
| 12

Supplies Expense 514
|

Accrued Salaries 210
|

Salaries Expense 516
7 |

Closing Steps and Journalizing Closing Entries

Steps in the closing process
2 (10 min)

2.

```
                    Worksheet

          IS                    BS

  Dr.     Cr.          Dr.          Cr.
  (2)     Revenue (1)  Withdrawals  (4)
  E
  X
  P
  E
  N
  S
  E
  S
  _____   _____

  NI (3)
```

Goals of Closing

1. Temporary accounts in the ledger should have a zero balance.
2. New figure for capital is determined in closing.

Note: All closing can be done from the worksheet. Income Summary is a temporary account in the ledger.

From the above worksheet, explain the four steps of closing. Keep in mind that each *individual* expense normally would be listed in the closing process.

Journalizing Closing Entries

Journalizing the closing entries from T accounts
2 (15 min)

3. From the following accounts, journalize the closing entries (assume that December 31 is the closing date).

Mel Blanc, Capital 310	Gas Expense 510
	30	5	

Mel Blanc, Withdrawals 312	Advertising Expense 512
6		4	

Income Summary 314	Amortization Expense, Taxi 516
		6	

Taxi Fare Income 410	
	18	

Posting to Income Summary

The Income Summary account
2 (10 min)

4. Draw a T account of Income Summary and post to it all entries from question 3 that affect it. Is Income Summary a temporary or permanent account?

Posting to Capital

The capital account
2 (10 min)

5. Draw a T account for Mel Blanc, Capital, and post to it all entries from question 3 that affect it. What is the final balance of the capital account?

(The blank forms you need are on pages 5-13 and 5-14 of the *Study Guide with Working Papers.*)

Journalizing adjusting entries
1 (1 min)

5-1. From the adjustments section of a worksheet presented here, prepare adjusting journal entries for the end of December.

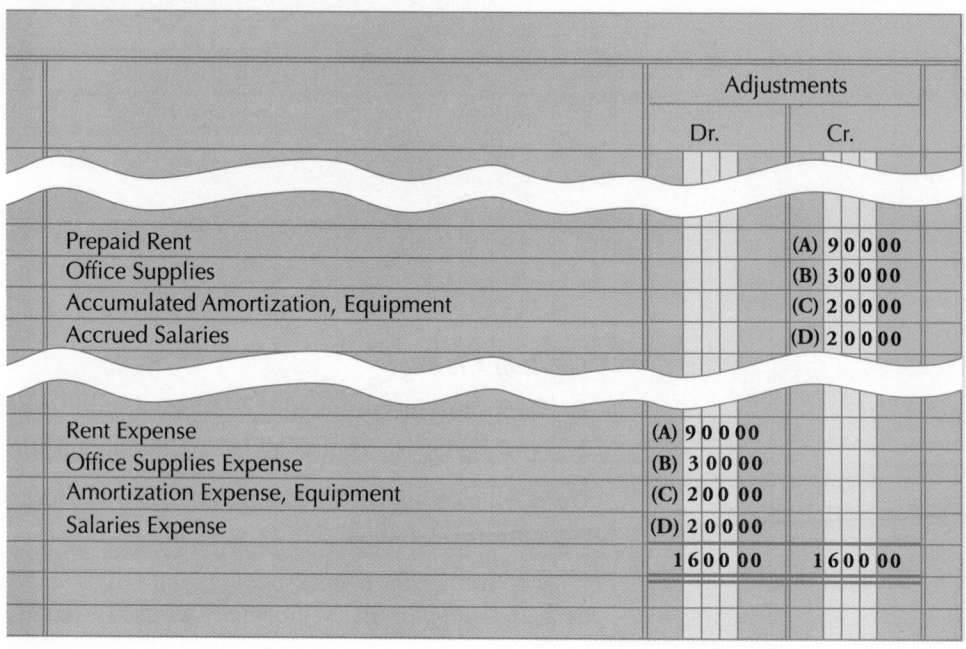

	Adjustments	
	Dr.	Cr.
Prepaid Rent		(A) 9 0 0 00
Office Supplies		(B) 3 0 0 00
Accumulated Amortization, Equipment		(C) 2 0 0 00
Accrued Salaries		(D) 2 0 0 00
Rent Expense	(A) 9 0 0 00	
Office Supplies Expense	(B) 3 0 0 00	
Amortization Expense, Equipment	(C) 2 0 0 00	
Salaries Expense	(D) 2 0 0 00	
	1 6 0 0 00	1 6 0 0 00

Temporary versus permanent accounts
1 2 (10 min)

5-2. Complete this table by placing an X in the correct column for each item.

	Temporary	Permanent	Will Be Closed
Example: **Accounts Receivable**		X	
1. Income Summary			
2. Jen Rich, Capital			
3. Salary Expense			
4. Jen Rich, Withdrawals			
5. Fees Earned			
6. Accounts Payable			
7. Cash			

Closing entries
2 (5 min)

5-3. From the following T accounts, journalize the four closing entries on December 31, 2012.

J. King, Capital		Rent Expense	
	14,000	5,000	

J. King, Withdrawals		Wages Expense	
4,000		7,000	

Income Summary		Insurance Expense	
		1,200	

Fees Earned		Amortization Expense, Office Equipment	
	33,000	900	

5-4. From the following posted T accounts, reconstruct the closing journal entries for December 31, 2014.

M. Foster, Capital			Insurance Expense	
Withdrawals 100	2,000 (Dec. 1)		50	Closing 50
	Net Income 700			

M. Foster, Withdrawals			Wages Expense	
100	Closing 100		100	Closing 100

Income Summary			Rent Expense	
Expenses 600	Revenue 1,300		200	Closing 200
700				

Salon Fees			Amortization Expense, Equipment	
Closing 1,300	1,300		250	Closing 250

5-5. From the following accounts (not in order), prepare a post-closing trial balance for Wey Co. on December 31, 2015. ***Note:*** These balances are *before* closing.

Accounts Receivable	18,875	P. Wey, Capital	63,450
Legal Library	14,250	P. Wey, Withdrawals	1,500
Office Equipment	59,700	Legal Fees Earned	12,000
Repair Expense	2,850	Accounts Payable	45,000
Salaries Expense	1,275	Cash	22,000

Group A Problems

(The blank forms you need are on pages 5-15 to 5-30 of the *Study Guide with Working Papers*.)

Review of preparing a worksheet
and journalizing adjusting and
closing entries
1 **2** (40 min)

5A-1. The following data is given for Debbie's Dance Studio of Vernon:

Check Figure

Net Income $14,600

DEBBIE'S DANCE STUDIO TRIAL BALANCE JUNE 30, 2014		
	Dr.	Cr.
Cash	4 0 0 0 0 0	
Accounts Receivable	7 0 0 0 0 0	
Prepaid Insurance	4 0 0 0 0	
Dance Supplies	1 5 0 0 0 0	
Dance Equipment	13 0 0 0 0 0	
Accumulated Amortization, Dance Equipment		11 9 0 0 0 0
Accounts Payable		21 0 0 0 0 0
D. Dee, Capital		13 2 0 0 0 0
D. Dee, Withdrawals	8 0 0 0 0	
Dance Fees Earned		19 8 0 0 0 0
Salaries Expense	1 6 0 0 0 0	
Telephone Expense	1 0 0 0 0 0	
Advertising Expense	6 0 0 0 0	
	65 9 0 0 0 0	65 9 0 0 0 0

Adjustment Data

a. Insurance expired, $300

b. Dance supplies on hand, $700

c. Amortization on dance equipment, $500

d. Salaries earned by employees but not to be paid until July, $400

Required

1. Prepare a worksheet.

2. Journalize adjusting and closing entries.

5A-2. As the bookkeeper for Potter Cleaning Service, **a.** from the trial balance columns of the worksheet on page 221, enter the beginning balance of each account before adjustments in your working papers, **b.** journalize and post adjusting entries, **c.** journalize and post closing entries, and **d.** from the ledger (after all posting is complete), prepare a post-closing trial balance at March 31, 2013.

5A-3. As the bookkeeper of Pete's Plowing of Fredericton, you have been asked to complete the entire accounting cycle for Pete from the following information (see the chart of accounts on page 222):

2012

Jan.		
	3	Pete invested $7,000 cash and $6,000 worth of snow equipment in the plowing company.
	3	Paid rent in advance for garage space, $2,000.
	5	Purchased office equipment on account from Ling Corp., $7,200.
	6	Purchased snow supplies for $700 cash.
	9	Collected $15,000 from plowing local shopping centres.
	12	Pete Mack withdrew $1,000 from the business for personal use.
	20	Plowed North East Co. parking lots, payment not to be received until March, $5,000.
	26	Paid salaries to employees, $1,800.
	27	Paid Ling Corp. one-half amount owed for office equipment.
	30	Advertising bill was received from Bush Co. but will not be paid until March, $900.
	31	Paid telephone bill, $210.

Adjustment Data

a. Snow supplies on hand, $400

b. Rent expired, $600

c. Amortization on office equipment, $120

($7,200 ÷ 5 yr. → $\frac{\$1,440}{12 \text{ mo.}} = \$120$)

d. Amortization on snow equipment,

$100 ($6,000 ÷ 5 yr. → $\frac{\$1,200}{12 \text{ mo.}} = \$100$)

e. Accrued salaries, $190

Journalizing and posting adjusting and closing entries and preparing a post-closing trial balance

① ② ③ (35 min)

Check Figure (5A-2)

Post-Closing Trial Balance total $3,504

Comprehensive review of the entire accounting cycle, Chapters 1–5

① ② ③ (150 min)

Check Figure

Net Income $15,780

POTTER CLEANING SERVICE
WORKSHEET
FOR MONTH ENDED MARCH 31, 2013

Account Titles	Trial Balance Dr.	Trial Balance Cr.	Adjustments Dr.	Adjustments Cr.	Adjusted Trial Balance Dr.	Adjusted Trial Balance Cr.	Income Statement Dr.	Income Statement Cr.	Balance Sheet Dr.	Balance Sheet Cr.
Cash	40000				40000				40000	
Prepaid Insurance	52000			(A) 18000	34000				34000	
Cleaning Supplies	14400			(B) 10000	4400				4400	
Auto	272000				272000				272000	
Accum. Amortization, Auto		86000		(C) 15000		101000				101000
Accounts Payable		22400				22400				22400
B. Potter, Capital		54000				54000				54000
B. Potter, Withdrawals	46000				46000				46000	
Cleaning Fees		468000				468000		468000		
Salaries Expense	144000		(D) 16000		160000		160000			
Telephone Expense	26400				26400		26400			
Advertising Expense	19600				19600		19600			
Gas Expense	16000				16000		16000			
	630400	630400								
Insurance Expense			(A) 18000		18000		18000			
Cleaning Supplies Expense			(B) 10000		10000		10000			
Amortization Expense, Auto			(C) 15000		15000		15000			
Accrued Salaries				(D) 16000		16000				16000
			59000	59000	661400	661400	265000	468000	396400	193400
Net Income							203000			203000
							468000	468000	396400	396400

Pete's Plowing
Chart of Accounts

Assets
111 Cash
112 Accounts Receivable
114 Prepaid Rent
115 Snow Supplies
121 Office Equipment
122 Accumulated Amortization,
    Office Equipment
123 Snow Equipment
124 Accumulated Amortization,
    Snow Equipment

Liabilities
211 Accounts Payable
212 Accrued Salaries

Owner's Equity
311 Pete Mack, Capital
312 Pete Mack, Withdrawals
313 Income Summary

Revenue
411 Plowing Fees

Expenses
511 Salaries Expense
512 Advertising Expense
513 Telephone Expense
514 Rent Expense
515 Snow Supplies Expense
516 Amortization Expense,
    Office Equipment
517 Amortization Expense,
    Snow Equipment

Group B Problems

(The blank forms you need are on pages 5-15 to 5-30 of the *Study Guide with Working Papers.*)

Review of preparing a worksheet and journalizing and closing entries
1 2 (40 min)

5B-1.

To:	Matt Kamimsk
From:	Abbey Ellen
Re:	Accounting Needs

Please prepare ASAP from the following information (attached) (1) a worksheet, along with (2) journalized adjusting and closing entries.

Check Figure

Net Income $3,530

DEBBIE'S DANCE STUDIO TRIAL BALANCE JUNE 30, 2014		
	Dr.	Cr.
Cash	10 15 0 00	
Accounts Receivable	5 0 0 0 00	
Prepaid Insurance	7 0 0 00	
Dance Supplies	3 0 0 00	
Dance Equipment	12 9 5 0 00	
Accumulated Amortization, Dance Equipment		4 0 0 0 00
Accounts Payable		5 7 5 0 00
D. Dee, Capital		15 15 0 00
D. Dee, Withdrawals	4 0 0 00	
Dance Fees Earned		5 2 0 0 00
Salaries Expense	4 5 0 00	
Telephone Expense	7 0 00	
Advertising Expense	8 0 00	
	30 10 0 00	30 10 0 00

Adjustment Data

a. Insurance expired, $100
b. Dance supplies on hand, $20
c. Amortization on dance equipment, $200
d. Salaries earned by employees but not due to be paid until July, $490

Journalizing and posting adjusting and closing entries, and preparing a post-closing trial balance

 (35 min)

Check Figure (5B-2)

Post-Closing Trial Balance $3,294

5B-2. As the bookkeeper for Potter Cleaning Service, **a.** from the trial balance columns of the worksheet on page 224, enter the beginning balance of each account in your working papers, **b.** journalize and post adjusting entries, **c.** journalize and post closing entries, and **d.** from the ledger (after all posting is complete), prepare a post-closing trial balance at March 31, 2013.

5B-3. From the following transactions as well as additional data, complete the entire accounting cycle for Pete's Plowing of Fredericton (use the chart of accounts on page 222).

Comprehensive review of entire accounting cycle, Chapters 1–5

 (150 min)

Check Figure

Net Income $9,610

2012
Jan. 3 To open the business, Pete invested $8,000 cash and $9,600 worth of snow equipment.
3 Paid rent for five months in advance, $3,000.
5 Purchased office equipment on account from Russell Co., $6,000.
6 Bought snow supplies, $350.
9 Collected $7,000 for plowing during winter storm emergency.
12 Pete paid his home telephone bill using a company cheque, $70.
20 Billed Eastern Freight Co. for plowing fees earned but not to be received until March, $6,500.
23 Advertising bill was received from Jones Co. but will not be paid until next month, $350.
26 Paid salaries to employees, $1,800.
30 Paid Russell Co. one-half of amount owed for office equipment.
31 Paid telephone bill of company, $165.

Adjustment Data

a. Snow supplies on hand, $200
b. Rent expired, $600
c. Amortization on office equipment ($6,000 ÷ 4 yr. → $1,500 ÷ 12 = $125), $125
d. Amortization on snow equipment ($9,600 ÷ 2 yr. → $4,800 ÷ 12 = $400), $400
e. Salaries accrued, $300

Group C Problems

(The forms you need are on pages 5-31 to 5-47 of the *Study Guide with Working Papers*.)

Review of preparing a worksheet and journalizing adjusting and closing entries

1 2 (40 min)

Check Figure

Net Income $16,308.75

5C-1.

To: Peter George

From: Janine Martins

Re: Accounting Procedures

Please prepare from the following information (attached), (1) a worksheet, along with (2) journalized adjusting and closing entries for the year ending May 31, 2014.

POTTER CLEANING SERVICE
WORKSHEET
FOR MONTH ENDED MARCH 31, 2013

Account Titles	Trial Balance Dr.	Trial Balance Cr.	Adjustments Dr.	Adjustments Cr.	Adjusted Trial Balance Dr.	Adjusted Trial Balance Cr.	Income Statement Dr.	Income Statement Cr.	Balance Sheet Dr.	Balance Sheet Cr.
Cash	1724 00				1724 00				1724 00	
Prepaid Insurance	350 00			(A) 200 00	150 00				150 00	
Cleaning Supplies	800 00			(B) 600 00	200 00				200 00	
Auto	1220 00				1220 00				1220 00	
Accumulated Amortization, Auto		660 00		(C) 150 00		810 00				810 00
Accounts Payable		674 00				674 00				674 00
B. Potter, Capital		2480 00				2480 00				2480 00
B. Potter, Withdrawals	600 00				600 00				600 00	
Cleaning Fees		3700 00				3700 00		3700 00		
Salaries Expense	2000 00		(D) 175 00		2175 00		2175 00			
Telephone Expense	284 00				284 00		284 00			
Advertising Expense	276 00				276 00		276 00			
Gas Expense	260 00				260 00		260 00			
	7514 00	7514 00								
Insurance Expense			(A) 200 00		200 00		200 00			
Cleaning Supplies Expense			(B) 600 00		600 00		600 00			
Amortization Expense, Auto			(C) 150 00		150 00		150 00			
Accrued Salaries				(D) 175 00		175 00				175 00
			1125 00	1125 00	7839 00	7839 00	3945 00	3700 00	3894 00	4139 00
Net Loss								245 00	245 00	
							3945 00	3945 00	4139 00	4139 00

Adjustment Data

a. Insurance expired, $510.75

b. Disposal supplies on hand, $723

c. Amortization for the year on disposal equipment is based on the straight-line method, 12-year life, and a residual value of $850.

d. Amortization for the year on building is also straight-line, 20-year life, and a residual value of $25,000.

e. Wages earned by employees but not due to be paid until June amounted to 36 hours at $18/hour plus 30 hours at $24/hour.

ECO DOCUMENT DISPOSAL COMPANY TRIAL BALANCE MAY 31, 2014	Debit	Credit
Cash	22 460 00	
Accounts Receivable	1 200 00	
Prepaid Insurance	68 1 00	
Disposal Supplies	1 542 00	
Disposal Equipment	11 740 00	
Accumulated Amortization, Disposal Equipment		7 260 00
Building	48 000 00	
Accumulated Amortization, Building		20 700 00
Accounts Payable		4 66 0 00
J. Martin, Capital		48 681 00
J. Martin, Withdrawals	16 742 00	
Disposal Fees Revenue		52 720 00
Wages Expense	28 240 00	
Utilities Expense	2 544 00	
Advertising Expense	8 72 00	
Totals	134 021 00	134 021 00

Journalizing and posting adjusting and closing entries, and preparing a post-closing trial balance

①②③ (35 min)

5C-2. Refer to the worksheet for Tran's Computer Repair Service of Brandon on page 226. The beginning balances (from the trial balance column) in each account are already entered in your working papers. **a.** Journalize and post adjusting and closing entries to each account in the ledger, and **b.** prepare from the ledger a post-closing trial balance at the end of November.

5C-3. From the following transactions as well as additional data, please complete the entire accounting cycle for Mike's Plumbing of Prince Albert (use a chart of accounts similar to the one on page 222).

Check Figure (5C-2)

Post-Closing Trial Balance
$30,815.63

Comprehensive review of the entire accounting cycle, Chapters 1–5

①②③ (175 min)

2013

May		
	1	To open the business, Mike Quinlan invested $10,000 cash and $7,400 worth of plumbing equipment.
	1	Paid rent for four months in advance, $1,980.
	3	Purchased office equipment on account from MacKenzie Co., $3,800.
	7	Bought plumbing supplies, $1,645.
	8	Collected $3,600 for plumbing services provided.
	9	Mike paid his home utility bill with a company cheque, $122.
	10	Billed Western Construction Co. for plumbing fees earned but not to be received until later, $9,600.
	14	Advertising bill was received from ABCD Radio Co. but is not to be paid until next month, $420.
	21	Received cheque from Western Construction Co. in partial payment of transaction dated May 10, $4,800.

TRAN'S COMPUTER REPAIR SERVICE
WORKSHEET
NOVEMBER 30, 2012

Account Titles	Trial Balance Dr.	Trial Balance Cr.	Adjustments Dr.	Adjustments Cr.	Adjusted Trial Balance Dr.	Adjusted Trial Balance Cr.	Income Statement Dr.	Income Statement Cr.	Balance Sheet Dr.	Balance Sheet Cr.
Cash	236648			(A) 3684	232964				232964	
Prepaid Insurance	71456			(C) 23819	47637				47637	
Accounts Receivable	527742				527742				527742	
Repair Parts and Supplies	159747			(D) 54027	105720				105720	
Van	2167500				2167500				2167500	
Accumulated Amortization, Van		810365		(B) 34740		845105				845105
Accounts Payable		377260		(F) 24300		401560				401560
Megan Tran, Capital		1366358				1366358				1366358
Megan Tran, Withdrawals	260000				260000				260000	
Repair Revenue		1645870				1645870		1645870		
Advertising Expense	71438		(F) 24300		95738		95738			
Automotive Expense	234551				234551		234551			
Cleaning Expense	37500				37500		37500			
Miscellaneous Expense	17814				17814		17814			
Postage and Office Expense	28417				28417		28417			
Salaries Expense	387040		(E) 42000		429040		429040			
	4199853	4199853								
Insurance Expense			(C) 23819		23819		23819			
Bank Charges Expense			(A) 3684		3684		3684			
Amortization Expense, Van			(B) 34740		34740		34740			
Accrued Salaries				(E) 42000		42000				42000
Supplies Expense			(D) 54027		54027		54027			
			182570	182570	4300893	4300893	959330	1645870	3341563	2655023
Net Income							686540			686540
							1645870	1645870	3341563	3341563

May	28	Paid MacKenzie Co. one-half of amount owed for office equipment, $1,900.
	31	Paid telephone bill of company, $184.
	31	Received bill from George's Cleaning to be paid in June, $215.
	31	Paid salaries to employees, $4,100.

Adjusting Data

a. Plumbing supplies remaining at month-end were $328.

b. One month's rent expired in May.

c. Amortization on office equipment uses the straight-line method, a life of five years, and a residual value of $500.

d. Amortization of plumbing equipment also uses the straight-line method, a life of three years, and zero residual value.

e. Salaries accrued amounted to 20% of the salaries paid on May 31.

Check Figure

Net Income $5,388.44

On-the-job Training

(The forms you need are on page 5-48 of the *Study Guide with Working Papers*.)

Analyzing financial information and completing the accounting cycle
2 (15 min)

T-1. Carol Miller needs a loan from her local bank to help finance her business. She has submitted the following unadjusted trial balance to the bank. As the loan officer, you will be meeting with Carol tomorrow. Could you make some specific written suggestions to Carol regarding her loan report?

Cash in Bank	770	
Accounts Receivable	1,480	
Office Supplies	3,310	
Equipment	7,606	
Accounts Payable		684
C. Miller, Capital		8,000
Service Fees		17,350
Salaries	11,240	
Utilities Expense	842	
Rent Expense	360	
Insurance Expense	280	
Advertising Expense	146	
Totals	26,034	26,034

Closing entries
2 (15 min)

T-2. Janet Smother is the new bookkeeper who replaced Dick Burns, owing to his sudden illness. Janet finds a note on her desk requesting that she close the books and supply the ending capital figure. Janet is upset since she can find only the following:

a. Revenue and expense accounts were all zero balance.

b. Income Summary

14,360	19,300

c. Owner withdrew $8,000.

d. Owner's beginning capital was $34,400.

Could you help Janet accomplish her assignment? What written suggestions should Janet make to her supervisor so that this situation will not happen again?

CONTINUING PROBLEM

Comprehensive problem:
journalizing and posting
adjusting and closing entries; and
preparing a post-closing trial
balance
①②③ (60 min)

Tony has decided to end the Precision Computer Centre's first year as of July 31, 2013. Below is an updated chart of accounts.

Assets

1000	Cash
1020	Accounts Receivable
1025	Prepaid Rent
1030	Supplies
1080	Computer Shop Equipment
1081	Accumulated Amortization, Computer Shop Equipment
1090	Office Equipment
1091	Accumulated Amortization, Office Equipment

Liabilities

2000	Accounts Payable

Owner's Equity

3000	T. Freedman, Capital
3010	T. Freedman, Withdrawals
3020	Income Summary

Revenue

4000	Service Revenue

Expenses

5010	Advertising Expense
5020	Rent Expense
5030	Utilities Expense
5040	Phone Expense
5050	Supplies Expense
5060	Insurance Expense
5070	Postage Expense
5080	Amortization Expense, Computer Shop Equipment
5090	Amortization Expense, Office Equipment

Assignment

(See pages 5-49 to 5-54 in your *Study Guide with Working Papers*.)

1. Journalize the adjusting entries from Chapter 4.

2. Post the adjusting entries to the ledger.

3. Journalize the closing entries.

4. Post the closing entries to the ledger.

5. Prepare a post-closing trial balance.

Sullivan Realty
Reviewing the Accounting Cycle Twice

This comprehensive review problem requires you to complete the accounting cycle for Sullivan Realty twice. This will allow you to review Chapters 1 to 5 while reinforcing the relationships among all parts of the accounting cycle. By completing two cycles, you will see how the ending June balances in the ledger are used to accumulate data in July. (The blank forms you need are on pages 5-58 to 5-74 of the *Study Guide with Working Papers.*)

On June 1, John Sullivan opened a real estate office in Hamilton called Sullivan Realty. The following transactions were completed for the month of June. Note that facsimile documents have been provided to illustrate these events:

2013

#1, p. 230 → June   3   John Sullivan invested $20,000 cash in the real estate agency, along with $4,000 worth of office equipment.

#2, p. 230 ———→   3   Rented office space and paid three months' rent in advance, $3,000, cheque No. 601.

Sullivan Realty
Chart of Accounts

Assets
111	Cash
112	Accounts Receivable
114	Prepaid Rent
115	Office Supplies
121	Office Equipment
122	Accumulated Amortization, Office Equipment
123	Automobile
124	Accumulated Amortization, Automobile

Liabilities
211	Accounts Payable
212	Accrued Salaries

Owner's Equity
311	John Sullivan, Capital
312	John Sullivan, Withdrawals
313	Income Summary

Revenue
411	Commissions Earned

Expenses
511	Rent Expense
512	Salaries Expense
513	Gas Expense
514	Repairs Expense
515	Telephone Expense
516	Advertising Expense
517	Office Supplies Expense
518	Amortization Expense, Office Equipment
519	Amortization Expense, Automobile
524	Miscellaneous Expense

1.

CURRENT ACCOUNT DEPOSIT SLIP	PLEASE LIST FOREIGN CHEQUES ON A SEPARATE DEPOSIT SLIP			
ROYAL BANK	VISA AND CHEQUES		DETAILS	CASH (INCL COUPONS)
		VISA VOUCHER TOTAL		
	Sullivan	20,000:00	X 5	
June 3, 2013			X 10	
DATE			X 20	
			X 50	
DEPOSITOR'S INITIALS / TELLER'S INITIALS			X 100	
JS / PRL			X	
CREDIT ACCOUNT OF			COIN	
			CANADIAN CASH TOTAL	
SULLIVAN REALTY		20,000:00	VISA & CHQS	20,000:00
	U.S. CHQS.		RATE	
	U.S. CASH		RATE	
			NET DEPOSIT	20,000:00

I: 05337 123'498'6   51

COMPARED WITH ORIGINAL DEPOSIT SLIP AS TO TOTAL ONLY

2.

```
                                                                    601
  S        SULLIVAN REALTY
           485 KING STREET WEST
           HAMILTON, ONTARIO  L9H 6W3              June 3   20 13
           PHONE (905) 527-1223

  PAY TO    Hamilton One Property Management Co.        $ 3,000
  THE ORDER OF
  ~~~~~~~~ Three thousand ~~~~~~~~~~~~~~~~~~~~~       00/100 DOLLARS

  THE ROYAL BANK OF CANADA
         MAIN BRANCH
     204 KING STREET WEST              SULLIVAN REALTY
     HAMILTON, ONTARIO L9H 4Z9

  FOR  Rent – June-August 2013         PER    John Sullivan

       II"000601 I: 05337     123'498'6
```

2013

#3a & b, **p. 231**	→ June	4	Bought a company automobile. Cheque No. 602, $14,000.00
#4a & b, **pp. 231 & 232**	→	4	Purchased office supplies. Wrote cheque No. 603, $300.
#5, **p. 232**	→	5	Purchased additional office supplies on account, $150.
#6a & b, **pp. 232 & 233**	→	6	Sold a house and collected a $6,000 commission.
#7, **p. 233**	→	7	Paid gas bill for car, $22. Cheque No. 604.
#8, **p. 233**	→	14	Paid the salary of the part-time office secretary, $350. Cheque No. 605.
#9, **p. 233**	→	18	Sold a building lot and earned a commission, $6,500. Payment is to be received on July 9.
#10, **p. 234**	→	21	John Sullivan withdrew $1,000 from the business to pay personal expenses. Cheque No. 606.
#11a & b, **p. 234**	→	21	Sold a house and collected a $3,500 commission.
#12, **p. 235**	→	24	Paid gas bill for car. $25. Cheque No. 607.
#13a & b, **p. 235**	→	25	Paid $600 to repair automobile. Cheque No. 608.
#14, **p. 236**	→	28	Paid the salary of the part-time office secretary, $350. Cheque No. 609.
#15a & b, **p. 236**	→	28	Paid the June telephone bill, $510. Cheque No. 610.
#16, **p. 237**	→	28	Received advertising bill for June, $1,200. The bill is to be paid by July 5.

3a.

AUTO CITY WEST

2674 King Street West
Hamilton, Ontario L9H 1A1
Phone (905) 527-9755; Fax (905) 527-9756

INVOICE

INVOICE NO. WEA1097

DATE: June 4/13

TERMS: Cash

To:
Sullivan Realty
485 King Street West
Hamilton, Ontario L9H 6W3

Ship To:

June 4/13

Pickup

QUANTITY	DESCRIPTION		UNIT PRICE	AMOUNT
1	ONLY	2008 Z75 4-Door Automatic	14,000	$14,000

	SUBTOTAL	14,000
Make all cheques payable to Auto City West	FREIGHT	
PAYMENT RECEIVED - Cheque #602 - Thank you	TAX	
	TOTAL DUE	$14,000

THANK YOU FOR YOUR BUSINESS!

3b.

SULLIVAN REALTY
485 KING STREET WEST
HAMILTON, ONTARIO L9H 6W3
PHONE (905) 527-1223

602

June 4 20 13

PAY TO
THE ORDER OF   *Auto City West* $ 14,000.00

~~~~ *Fourteen thousand* ~~~~~~~~~~~~~~~~~~~~~~~   00 /100 DOLLARS

THE ROYAL BANK OF CANADA
MAIN BRANCH
204 KING STREET WEST
HAMILTON, ONTARIO L9H 4Z9

SULLIVAN REALTY

FOR *Automobile – Inv. WEA1097*   PER   *John Sullivan*

⑈′000602 ⑆: 05337   123′498′6

4a.

Office Depot

#53 Niagara Mall
Hamilton, Ontario L9H 1B1
Phone (905) 527-1233, Fax (905) 527-1234

INVOICE

DATE: Jun 4/13
NUMBER: D198795
TERMS: Cash

SOLD TO:
Sullivan Realty
485 King Street West
Hamilton, Ontario L9H 6W3

SHIPPED TO:
Sullivan Realty
485 King Street West

DATE	DESCRIPTION	UNIT PRICE	AMOUNT
Jun 4/13	Office supplies PAYMENT RECEIVED - CHQ #603 - THANK YOU		$300.00
		Subtotal	300.00
		Total	$300.00

Business Number: 115555559

	PLEASE PAY THE ABOVE

THANK YOU FOR YOUR BUSINESS

4b.

S **SULLIVAN REALTY** 485 KING STREET WEST HAMILTON, ONTARIO L9H 6W3 PHONE (905) 527-1223	**603** _June 4_ 20**13**

PAY TO THE ORDER OF ___Office Depot_____ $ 300.00

~~~~ _Three hundred_ ~~~~~~~~~~~~~~~~~ 00 /100 DOLLARS

THE ROYAL BANK OF CANADA
MAIN BRANCH
204 KING STREET WEST
HAMILTON, ONTARIO L9H 4Z9

SULLIVAN REALTY

FOR ___Office supplies_____ PER ___John Sullivan_____

II″000603 I: 05337 123′498′6

5.

Office Depot   INVOICE

#53 Niagara Mall
Hamilton, Ontario L9H 1B1
Phone (905) 527-1233, Fax (905) 527-1234

DATE: Jun 5/13
NUMBER: D198825
TERMS: net 30

SOLD TO:	SHIPPED TO:
Sullivan Realty 485 King Street West Hamilton, Ontario L9H 6W3	Sullivan Realty 485 King Street West

DATE	DESCRIPTION	UNIT PRICE	AMOUNT
Jun 5/13	Office supplies		$150.00
		Subtotal	150.00
		Total	$150.00

Business Number: 115555559

PLEASE PAY
THE ABOVE

THANK YOU FOR YOUR BUSINESS

6a.

CURRENT ACCOUNT
DEPOSIT SLIP
ROYAL BANK

June 6, 2013
DATE

DEPOSITOR'S INITIALS	TELLER'S INITIALS
JS	MG

CREDIT ACCOUNT OF

SULLIVAN REALTY

PLEASE LIST FOREIGN CHEQUES ON A SEPARATE DEPOSIT SLIP

VISA AND CHEQUES		DETAILS	CASH (INCL COUPONS)
	VISA VOUCHER TOTAL		
H. Penchant	6,000 00	X 5	
		X 10	
		X 20	
		X 50	
		X 100	
		X	
		COIN	
		CANADIAN CASH TOTAL	
	6,000 00	VISA & CHQS	6,000 00
U.S. CHQS.		RATE	
U.S. CASH		RATE	
	NET DEPOSIT		6,000 00

COMPARED WITH ORIGINAL DEPOSIT
SLIP AS TO TOTAL ONLY

I: 05337 123′498′6   51

6b.

SULLIVAN REALTY				
COMMISSION REPORT			*Date* June 6, 2013	
Name:	Mr. and Mrs. Harold Penchant			
Date	*Sales Description*	*Sales No.*	*Commission Amount*	
Jun 6/13	*Home at 44 Brookhaven Crescent*	*A1001*	$6,000.00	*Paid in full.*
C001			*Remarks:*	

7.

```
S        SULLIVAN REALTY                              604
         485 KING STREET WEST
         HAMILTON, ONTARIO  L9H 6W3
         PHONE (905) 527-1223               June 7   20 13

PAY  TO   Anderson Petroleum Ltd.              $ 22.00
THE ORDER OF
          ~~~~ Twenty-two ~~~~~~~~~~          00/100 DOLLARS

THE ROYAL BANK OF CANADA
     MAIN BRANCH
     204 KING STREET WEST
     HAMILTON, ONTARIO L9H 4Z9           SULLIVAN REALTY

FOR   Gas bill - June 7             PER    John Sullivan

        II"000604 I: 05337      123'498'6
```

8.

```
S        SULLIVAN REALTY                              605
         485 KING STREET WEST
         HAMILTON, ONTARIO  L9H 6W3
         PHONE (905) 527-1223               June 14  20 13

PAY  TO   Pamela Dawson                        $ 350.00
THE ORDER OF
          ~~~~ Three hundred fifty ~~~~~~~~~~  00 /100 DOLLARS

THE ROYAL BANK OF CANADA
     MAIN BRANCH
     204 KING STREET WEST
     HAMILTON, ONTARIO  L9H 4Z9          SULLIVAN REALTY

FOR   Salary - June 1-14             PER    John Sullivan

        II"000605 I: 05337      123'498'6
```

9.

SULLIVAN REALTY				
COMMISSION REPORT			*Date* June 18, 2013	
Name:	East End Land Developers			
Date	*Sales Description*	*Sales No.*	*Commission Amount*	
Jun 18/13	*Lot at 999 King Street East*	*A1002*	$6,500.00	
C002			*Remarks:* Payment due July 9, 2013	

10.

S **SULLIVAN REALTY** 485 KING STREET WEST HAMILTON, ONTARIO L9H 6W3 PHONE (905) 527-1223	606

June 21 20 *13*

PAY TO THE ORDER OF   *John Sullivan* $ *1,000.00*

~~~~ *One thousand* ~~~~~~~~~~~~~~~~~~~~~~   *00* /100 DOLLARS

THE ROYAL BANK OF CANADA
MAIN BRANCH
204 KING STREET WEST
HAMILTON, ONTARIO L9H 4Z9

SULLIVAN REALTY

FOR   *Withdrawal*   PER   *John Sullivan*

⑈000606 ⑊: 05337   123'498'6

11a.

CURRENT ACCOUNT DEPOSIT SLIP **ROYAL BANK**				
	PLEASE LIST FOREIGN CHEQUES ON A SEPARATE DEPOSIT SLIP			
	VISA AND CHEQUES		DETAILS	CASH (INCL COUPONS)
		VISA VOUCHER TOTAL		
	L. Harrison	3,500 00	X 5	
June 21, 2013 DATE			X 10	
			X 20	
			X 50	
			X 100	
DEPOSITOR'S INITIALS / TELLER'S INITIALS			X	
PD / *AS*			COIN	
CREDIT ACCOUNT OF			CANADIAN CASH TOTAL	
SULLIVAN REALTY		3,500 00	VISA & CHQS	3,500 00
	U.S. CHQS.		RATE	
	U.S. CASH		RATE	
		NET DEPOSIT		3,500 00
			COMPARED WITH ORIGINAL DEPOSIT SLIP AS TO TOTAL ONLY	

⑊: 05337 123'498'6   51

11b.

SULLIVAN REALTY

COMMISSION REPORT   *Date* June 21, 2013

Name: Ms Laura Harrison

Date	*Sales Description*	*Sales No.*	*Commission Amount*	
Jun 21/13	*Home at 842 Alder Road*	*A1003*	*$3,500.00*	*Paid in full.*
C003			*Remarks:*	

12.

SULLIVAN REALTY
485 KING STREET WEST
HAMILTON, ONTARIO L9H 6W3
PHONE (905) 527-1223

607

June 24 20 13

PAY TO THE ORDER OF ___Anderson Petroleum Ltd.___ $ 25.00

~~~ Twenty-five ~~~~~~~   00/100 DOLLARS

THE ROYAL BANK OF CANADA
MAIN BRANCH
204 KING STREET WEST
HAMILTON, ONTARIO L9H 4Z9

SULLIVAN REALTY

FOR ___Gas bill – June 24___   PER ___John Sullivan___

11"000607 1: 05337   123'498'6

13a.

AUTO CITY WEST

2674 King Street West
Hamilton, Ontario L9H 1A1
Phone (905) 527-9755; Fax (905) 527-9756

INVOICE

INVOICE NO. WES3750

DATE: June 25/13

TERMS: Cash

To:
Sullivan Realty
485 King Street West
Hamilton, Ontario L9H 6W3

Ship To:
Pickup

QUANTITY	DESCRIPTION	UNIT PRICE	AMOUNT
1	Only Z75 Air conditioning repair		$ 600.00

Make all cheques payable to Auto City West

PAYMENT RECEIVED - Cheque #608 - Thank you

THANK YOU FOR YOUR BUSINESS!

SUBTOTAL	600.00
FREIGHT	
TAX	
TOTAL DUE	$ 600.00

13b.

SULLIVAN REALTY
485 KING STREET WEST
HAMILTON, ONTARIO L9H 6W3
PHONE (905) 527-1223

608

June 25 20 13

PAY TO THE ORDER OF ___Auto City West___ $ 600.00

~~~ Six hundred ~~~~~~~   00 /100 DOLLARS

THE ROYAL BANK OF CANADA
MAIN BRANCH
204 KING STREET WEST
HAMILTON, ONTARIO L9H 4Z9

SULLIVAN REALTY

FOR ___Automobile repairs – Inv WES3750___   PER ___John Sullivan___

11"000608 1: 05337   123'498'6

14.

SULLIVAN REALTY
485 KING STREET WEST
HAMILTON, ONTARIO L9H 6W3
PHONE (905) 527-1223

609

June 28 20 **13**

PAY TO THE ORDER OF *Pamela Dawson* $ 350.00

~~~ Three hundred fifty ~~~~~~~~~~~~~~~~~~   00 /100 DOLLARS

THE ROYAL BANK OF CANADA
MAIN BRANCH
204 KING STREET WEST
HAMILTON, ONTARIO L9H 4Z9

SULLIVAN REALTY

FOR *Salary – June 16-30*   PER *John Sullivan*

11″000609 1: 05337   123′498′6

15a.

Phones Ontario

#2110 Steel Place
Hamilton, Ontario L9G 4B4
Phone (905) 529-7190
Fax (905) 529-0063

Your Statement

In Account with   SULLIVAN REALTY
485 KING STREET WEST
HAMILTON ON L9H 6W3

Account #09444 710-190

Billing Period: June 1 to June 30

Payments/Adjustments/Deposits Details
Opened account June 3, 2013. Thank you.

Payment received July 2, 2013
Phones Ontario

                                                  $0.00

Monthly rental and changes to service   510.00

Amount now. due
Payment due after July 10, 2013 $522.75   **Total Due** $510.00

15b.

SULLIVAN REALTY
485 KING STREET WEST
HAMILTON, ONTARIO L9H 6W3
PHONE (905) 527-1223

610

June 28 20 **13**

PAY TO THE ORDER OF *Phones Ontario* $ 510.00

~~~ Five hundred ten ~~~~~~~~~~~~   00/100 DOLLARS

THE ROYAL BANK OF CANADA
MAIN BRANCH
204 KING STREET WEST
HAMILTON, ONTARIO L9H 4Z9

SULLIVAN REALTY

FOR *June phone bill*   PER *John Sullivan*

11″000610 1: 05337   123′498′6

16.

City News

85 Main Street, Hamilton, Ontario L9H 0C0
Phone (905) 527-1030   Fax (905) 527-1031

I N V O I C E

SOLD TO:	Sullivan Realty	Invoice No.:	4879
	485 King Street West	Date:	June 28, 2013
	Hamilton ON L9H 6W3	Due Date:	July 5, 2013

DATE	DESCRIPTION		AMOUNT
June 25/13	Advertising in City News during June 2013		$1,200.00
		SUBTOTAL	1,200.00
Business Number 944122338		TOTAL	$1,200.00

MAKE ALL CHEQUES PAYABLE TO CITY NEWS.

Required Work for June

1. Journalize transactions and post to ledger accounts.
2. Prepare a trial balance in the first two columns of the worksheet and complete the worksheet using the following adjustment data:
   a. One month's rent had expired
   b. An inventory shows $50 worth of office supplies remaining
   c. Amortization on office equipment, $100
   d. Amortization on automobile, $200
3. Prepare a June income statement, statement of owner's equity, and balance sheet.
4. From the worksheet, journalize and post adjusting and closing entries (page 3 of journal).
5. Prepare a post-closing trial balance.
   During July, Sullivan Realty completed these transactions:

		2013	
#17, p. 238	→	July 2	Paid for June office supplies purchased on account, $150. Cheque No. 611.
#18, p. 238	→	2	Purchased additional office supplies on account, $700.
#19, p. 238	→	2	Paid advertising bill for June. Cheque No. 612.
#20a & b, p. 239	→	4	Sold a house and collected a commission, $6,600.
#21, p. 239	→	5	Paid for gas for car, $29. Cheque No. 613.
#22, p. 240	→	9	Collected commission from sale of building lot on June 18.
#23, p. 240	→	12	Paid $300 to send employees to realtor's workshop. Cheque No. 614.
#24, p. 240	→	15	Paid the salary of the part-time office secretary, $350. Cheque No. 615.
#25, p. 241	→	16	Sold a house and earned a commission of $2,400. Commission to be received August 11.
#26a & b, p. 241	→	19	Sold a building lot and collected a commission of $7,000.
#27, p. 242	→	23	Sent a cheque for $40 to help sponsor a local road race to aid the poor. (This is not to be considered an advertising expense, but it is a business expense.) Cheque No. 616.
#28a & b, p. 242	→	26	Paid for repairs to automobile, $590. Cheque No. 617.
#29, p. 243	→	29	John Sullivan withdrew $1,800 from the business to pay personal expenses. Cheque No. 618.

#30, p. 243

31 Paid the salary of the part-time office secretary, $350. Cheque No. 619.

#31a & b, pp. 243 & 244 July 31 Paid the July telephone bill, $236. Cheque No. 620.

#32, p. 244 31 Advertising bill for July was received, $1,400. The bill is to be paid in August.

17.

SULLIVAN REALTY
485 KING STREET WEST
HAMILTON, ONTARIO L9H 6W3
PHONE (905) 527-1223

611

July 2 20 **13**

PAY TO THE ORDER OF *Office Depot* $ 150.00

~~~ *One hundred fifty* ~~~~~~~~ 00 /100 DOLLARS

THE ROYAL BANK OF CANADA
MAIN BRANCH
204 KING STREET WEST
HAMILTON, ONTARIO L9H 4Z9

SULLIVAN REALTY

FOR *Invoice #D198825* PER *John Sullivan*

II‴000611 I: 05337   123'498'6

18.

Office Depot

#53 Niagara Mall
Hamilton, Ontario L9H 1B1
Phone (905) 527-1233, Fax (905) 527-1234

INVOICE

DATE: July 2/13
NUMBER: D1996035
TERMS: Cash

SOLD TO:	SHIPPED TO:
Sullivan Realty 485 King Street West Hamilton, Ontario L9H 6W3	Sullivan Realty 485 King Street West

DATE	DESCRIPTION	UNIT PRICE	AMOUNT
July 2/13	Office supplies		$700.00
		Subtotal	700.00
		Total	$700.00

Business Number: 115555559

THANK YOU FOR YOUR BUSINESS

PLEASE PAY THE ABOVE

19.

SULLIVAN REALTY
485 KING STREET WEST
HAMILTON, ONTARIO L9H 6W3
PHONE (905) 527-1223

612

July 2 20 **13**

PAY TO THE ORDER OF *City News* $ 1,200.00

~~~ *One thousand two hundred* ~~~~~~~ 00 /100 DOLLARS

THE ROYAL BANK OF CANADA
MAIN BRANCH
204 KING STREET WEST
HAMILTON, ONTARIO L9H 4Z9

SULLIVAN REALTY

FOR *Invoice #4879* PER *John Sullivan*

II‴000612 I: 05337   123'498'6

20a.

SULLIVAN REALTY					
COMMISSION REPORT				*Date* July 4, 2013	
Name:	Mr. and Mrs. Andrew Tran				
Date	*Sales Description*	*Sales No.*	*Commission Amount*		
July 4/13	*Home at 1014 Cedar Lane*	*A1004*	*$6,600.00*	*Paid in full.*	
C004			*Remarks:*		

20b.

CURRENT ACCOUNT
DEPOSIT SLIP

ROYAL BANK

July 4, 2013
DATE

DEPOSITOR'S INITIALS	TELLER'S INITIALS
PD	MG

CREDIT ACCOUNT OF

SULLIVAN REALTY

PLEASE LIST FOREIGN CHEQUES ON A SEPARATE DEPOSIT SLIP

VISA AND CHEQUES		DETAILS	CASH (INCL COUPONS)
	VISA VOUCHER TOTAL		
A. Tran	6,6000 00	X 5	
		X 10	
		X 20	
		X 50	
		X 100	
		X	
		COIN	
		CANADIAN CASH TOTAL	
	6,600 00	VISA & CHQS	6,600 00
U.S. CHQS.		RATE	
U.S. CASH		RATE	
	NET DEPOSIT		6,600 00

I: 05337 123'498'6   51

COMPARED WITH ORIGINAL DEPOSIT SLIP AS TO TOTAL ONLY

21.

SULLIVAN REALTY
485 KING STREET WEST
HAMILTON, ONTARIO L9H 6W3
PHONE (905) 527-1223

613

July 5 20 13

PAY TO THE ORDER OF _Anderson Petroleum Ltd._ $ 29.00

~~~ Twenty-nine ~~~~~~~   00/100 DOLLARS

THE ROYAL BANK OF CANADA
MAIN BRANCH
204 KING STREET WEST
HAMILTON, ONTARIO L9H 4Z9

SULLIVAN REALTY

FOR _Gas bill – July 5_   PER _John Sullivan_

II"000613 I: 05337   123'498'6

22.

CURRENT ACCOUNT DEPOSIT SLIP **ROYAL BANK**		PLEASE LIST FOREIGN CHEQUES ON A SEPARATE DEPOSIT SLIP		
		VISA AND CHEQUES	DETAILS	CASH (INCL COUPONS)
		VISA VOUCHER TOTAL		
		East End	X 5	
		Land	X 10	
July 9, 2013 DATE		Developers 6,500.00	X 20	
			X 50	
DEPOSITOR'S INITIALS	TELLER'S INITIALS		X 100	
PD	MG		X	
CREDIT ACCOUNT OF			COIN	
			CANADIAN CASH TOTAL	
SULLIVAN REALTY		6,500 00	VISA & CHQS	6,500 00
		U.S. CHQS.	RATE	
		U.S. CASH	RATE	
		NET DEPOSIT		6,500 00
			COMPARED WITH ORIGINAL DEPOSIT SLIP AS TO TOTAL ONLY	

I: 05337 123'498'6   51

23.

SULLIVAN REALTY
485 KING STREET WEST
HAMILTON, ONTARIO L9H 6W3
PHONE (905) 527-1223

614

July 12 20 13

PAY TO THE ORDER OF   Hamilton Realtors' Association $ 300.00

~~~~ Three hundred ~~~~~~~~~~~~~~~~~~~~   00 /100 DOLLARS

THE ROYAL BANK OF CANADA
MAIN BRANCH
204 KING STREET WEST
HAMILTON, ONTARIO L9H 4Z9

SULLIVAN REALTY

FOR   Workshop registration   PER   John Sullivan

II⌐000614 I: 05337   123'498'6

24.

SULLIVAN REALTY
485 KING STREET WEST
HAMILTON, ONTARIO L9H 6W3
PHONE (905) 527-1223

615

July 15 20 13

PAY TO THE ORDER OF   Pamela Dawson $ 350.00

~~~~ Three hundred fifty ~~~~~~~~~~~~~~~~   00 /100 DOLLARS

THE ROYAL BANK OF CANADA
MAIN BRANCH
204 KING STREET WEST
HAMILTON, ONTARIO L9H 4Z9

SULLIVAN REALTY

FOR   Salary – July 1–15   PER   John Sullivan

II⌐000615 I: 05337   123'498'6

25.

SULLIVAN REALTY				
COMMISSION REPORT			*DATE* July 14, 2013	
Name: Mr. Hans Hollemeyer				
Date	*Sales Description*	*Sales No.*	*Commission Amount*	
July 16/13	*Home at RR2, Site 3*	*A1010*	*$2,400.00*	
C005		*Remarks:* Payment due August 11, 2013		

26a.

CURRENT ACCOUNT DEPOSIT SLIP	PLEASE LIST FOREIGN CHEQUES ON A SEPARATE DEPOSIT SLIP			
ROYAL BANK	VISA AND CHEQUES		DETAILS	CASH (INCL COUPONS)
		VISA VOUCHER TOTAL		
	B. Game	7,000.00	X 5	
July 19, 2013			X 10	
DATE			X 20	
DEPOSITOR'S INITIALS / TELLER'S INITIALS			X 50	
PD / PRL			X 100	
			X	
CREDIT ACCOUNT OF			COIN	
			CANADIAN CASH TOTAL	
SULLIVAN REALTY		7,000.00	VISA & CHQS	7,000.00
	U.S. CHQS.		RATE	
	U.S. CASH		RATE	
		NET DEPOSIT		7,000.00
I: 05337 123'498'6 51			COMPARED WITH ORIGINAL DEPOSIT SLIP AS TO TOTAL ONLY	

26b.

SULLIVAN REALTY				
COMMISSION REPORT			*Date* July 19, 2013	
Name: Mr. and Mrs. Benjamin Game				
Date	*Sales Description*	*Sales No.*	*Commission Amount*	
July 19/13	*Building lot at 5004 King St. E*	*A1005*	*$7,000.00*	*Paid in full.*
C006		*Remarks:*		

27.

SULLIVAN REALTY
485 KING STREET WEST
HAMILTON, ONTARIO L9H 6W3
PHONE (905) 527-1223

616

July 23 20 *13*

PAY TO
THE ORDER OF   *Mustard Seed Ministries* $ 40.00

~~~ *Forty* ~~~~~~~~~~~~~~~~   00/100 DOLLARS

THE ROYAL BANK OF CANADA
MAIN BRANCH
204 KING STREET WEST
HAMILTON, ONTARIO L9H 4Z9   SULLIVAN REALTY

FOR   *Aid to the poor*   PER   *John Sullivan*

II"000616 I: 05337   123'498'6

28a.

AUTO
CITY
WEST

2674 King Street West
Hamilton, Ontario L9H 1A1
Phone (905) 527-9755; Fax (905) 527-9756

INVOICE

INVOICE NO. WES3945

DATE: July 26/13

TERMS: Cash

To:
Sullivan Realty
485 King Street West
Hamilton, Ontario L9H 6W3

Ship To:

Pickup

QUANTITY	DESCRIPTION	UNIT PRICE	AMOUNT
	Z75 75,000 km maintenance		$ 590.00

	SUBTOTAL	590.00
Make all cheques payable to Auto City West	FREIGHT	
PAYMENT RECEIVED - Cheque #617 - Thank you	TAX	
	TOTAL DUE	$ 590.00

THANK YOU FOR YOUR BUSINESS!

28b.

SULLIVAN REALTY
485 KING STREET WEST
HAMILTON, ONTARIO L9H 6W3
PHONE (905) 527-1223

617

July 26 20 *13*

PAY TO
THE ORDER OF   *Auto City West* $ 590.00

~~~ *Five hundred ninety* ~~~~~~~~~~   00 /100 DOLLARS

THE ROYAL BANK OF CANADA
MAIN BRANCH
204 KING STREET WEST
HAMILTON, ONTARIO L9H 4Z9   SULLIVAN REALTY

FOR *Automobile repairs – Inv. WES3945*   PER   *John Sullivan*

II"000617 I: 05337   123'498'6

29.

S SULLIVAN REALTY 485 KING STREET WEST HAMILTON, ONTARIO L9H 6W3 PHONE (905) 527-1223	**618** _July 29_ 20 **13**

PAY TO THE ORDER OF _John Sullivan_   **$ 1,800.00**

~~~ _One thousand eight hundred_ ~~~~~~~ **00** /100 DOLLARS

THE ROYAL BANK OF CANADA
MAIN BRANCH
204 KING STREET WEST
HAMILTON, ONTARIO L9H 4Z9

SULLIVAN REALTY

FOR _Withdrawal_   PER _John Sullivan_

⑈000618 ⑆: 05337   123'498'6

30.

S SULLIVAN REALTY 485 KING STREET WEST HAMILTON, ONTARIO L9H 6W3 PHONE (905) 527-1223	**619** _July 31_ 20 **13**

PAY TO THE ORDER OF _Pamela Dawson_   **$ 350.00**

~~~ _Three hundred fifty_ ~~~~~~~ **00**/100 DOLLARS

THE ROYAL BANK OF CANADA
MAIN BRANCH
204 KING STREET WEST
HAMILTON, ONTARIO L9H 4Z9

SULLIVAN REALTY

FOR _Salary – July 16–31_   PER _John Sullivan_

⑈000619 ⑆: 05337   123'498'6

31a.

Phones Ontario

#2110 Steel Place
Hamilton, Ontario L9G 4B4
Phone (905) 529-7190
Fax (905) 529-0063

Your Statement

In Account with   SULLIVAN REALTY
485 KING STREET WEST
HAMILTON ON L9H 6W3

Account #09444 710-190

Payment received July 31, 2013
Phones Ontario

Billing Period: July 1 to July 31

Payments/Adjustments/Deposits Details	$510.00
Payment Received July 2. Thank you.	-510.00
Monthly rental and services	236.00
	————
Total Due	$236.00

Amount now due
Payment due after August 9, 2013 $241.90

31b.

```
                                                                          620
  ┌─────┐    SULLIVAN REALTY
  │  S  │    485 KING STREET WEST
  └─────┘    HAMILTON, ONTARIO L9H 6W3           July 31  20 13
             PHONE (905) 527-1223
                                                   $ 236.00
  PAY TO    Phones Ontario
  THE ORDER OF
      ~~~ Two hundred thirty-six ~~~~~~~~~~~~~       00 /100 DOLLARS

  THE ROYAL BANK OF CANADA
        MAIN BRANCH
     204 KING STREET WEST
   HAMILTON, ONTARIO  L9H 4Z9              SULLIVAN REALTY

  FOR   July phone bill              PER    John Sullivan

         II"000620 I: 05337      123'498'6
```

32.

City News

85 Main Street, Hamilton, Ontario L9H 0C0
Phone (905) 527-1030   Fax (905) 527-1031

I N V O I C E

SOLD TO: Sullivan Realty   Invoice No.:   5400
            485 King Street West   Date: July 30, 2013
            Hamilton ON L9H 6W3   Due Date: August 7, 2013

DATE	DESCRIPTION		AMOUNT
July 30/13	Advertising in City News during July 2013		$1,400.00
		SUBTOTAL	1,400.00
Business Number 944122338		TOTAL	$1,400.00

MAKE ALL CHEQUES PAYABLE TO CITY NEWS.

Required Work for July

1. Journalize transactions in a general journal (pages 4 and 5) and post to ledger accounts.
2. Prepare a trial balance in the first two columns of the worksheet and complete the worksheet using the following adjustment data:
   a. One month's rent had expired.
   b. An inventory shows $90 worth of office supplies remaining.
   c. Amortization on office equipment, $100
   d. Amortization on automobile, $200
3. Prepare a July income statement, statement of owner's equity, and balance sheet. June/July
4. From the worksheet, journalize and post adjusting and closing entries (page 6 of journal).
5. Prepare a post-closing trial balance.

MyAccountingLab

Computer Workshops

Sullivan and Sunny

Depending on the goals your instructor has set for the course you are taking, you may be asked to complete one or more of the computer workshops created especially for Chapter 5. If you need to complete any of the workshops, you will obtain all necessary details from the Multimedia Library on the MyAccountingLab website.

There are a total of four workshops available. For each company, Sullivan and Sunny, there are two versions—one using Simply Accounting Pro® and the other using QuickBooks Premier®. The choice will depend to a large extent on which software is available to you in your college's lab, your own laptop, or other computer, as well as the preference, knowledge, and experience of your instructor. Before beginning, be sure to get clear directions as to which workshop you are to complete. Please note that special, time-limited versions of both Simply Accounting® and QuickBooks® are available at no charge from each company's website. Your instructor might handle this for you, but it is easy to obtain the software and set it up yourself by visiting www.intuit.ca (QuickBooks®) or www.simply-accounting.com (Simply Accounting®).

You need to obtain several files from the MyAccountingLab website before you begin. (Please also see the added details on page 134 at the end of Chapter 3.)

1. The instruction files that describe each company and the details of the assignment.

2. Data sets that have been carefully crafted for you so you may begin each workshop with minimal bother. All of these data sets are downloaded in compressed format, and will need to be restored by the software before you can work on them. Details can be found in the detailed guide documents.

3. A Word file that sets forth in detail the step-by-step instructions you need to complete the Sullivan assignment. Help files also exist for the Sunny workshops, but these are available for student use only if they are provided by your instructor.

6 Special Journals

The Basics

THE BIG PICTURE

Canadian e-tailers are mostly exempt from charging provincial sales tax to their customers in provinces other than where they are based. Out-of-country e-tailers dealing with intellectual property (such as software) do not charge any taxes at all when the customer is Canadian. While it is true that the GST or HST is collected on most physical goods entering Canada, overall, these online merchandising companies enjoy an advantage over their brick-and-mortar counterparts. And this difference is getting wider as e-commerce expands.

Still, traditional stores do have some important advantages over their electronic competitors—at least in theory. Usually they will have the product their customers want in stock, so not waiting for delivery can be an important incentive to buy locally, even if GST/PST or HST needs to be paid. Another advantage is the personal approach and ability to discuss a product's features (or lack of same). For these advantages to work, however, the business must keep adequate stock on hand and employ qualified and well-trained sales staff. It also helps to feature local service availability instead of the dreadful experience many consumers face when forced to call India or the Philippines to initiate a service call.

If you decide to purchase your iPod from an e-tailer, there is an additional cost factor to consider: shipping and handling (S&H). Probably the S&H cost to get you an iPod from a Canadian source is between $10 and $20, depending on how fast you

want it. Naturally, the speedier forms of shipping cost the most. If you do the math properly, you probably discover that your tax savings are wiped out by the shipping costs.

As an accounting student, you also need to see this issue from the standpoint of the merchandising companies. For them, S&H costs are an expense—often a significant one. In this chapter, you will discover that their shipping and handling costs are considered "F.O.B. shipping point," which means that the customer pays these costs.

As a brief but interesting aside, you should ask whether merchandising companies should treat the S&H fees they charge to their customers as revenue or a "negative cost." If Amazon.ca sells you an iPod for $200, and then adds $15 for S&H, does the company have revenue of $200 or $215? A complicated but complete answer to this question is provided in more advanced accounting textbooks, but the short answer here is that the accounting gurus have decided that companies should treat the entire amount as revenue, and then show the actual cost of S&H as an expense.

Despite any possible controversies, this chapter shows how merchandising companies account for the purchase and sale of the goods they sell. The chapter also discusses how special journals are used to facilitate the recording process. A fuller discussion of how to record taxes is deferred until Chapter 10.

Learning Objectives

1 Recording Sales, Sales Returns, and Sales Discounts–an overview (p. 247)

2 Entering transactions into the Sales Journal, and recording to the Accounts Receivable sub-ledger (p. 252)

3 Generating, recording, and posting a credit memorandum (p. 255)

4 Entering transactions into the Cash Receipts Journal, recording to the AR sub-ledger, posting to the General Ledger accounts, and preparing a schedule of Accounts Receivable (p. 259)

5 Recording Purchases, Purchase Returns and Purchase Discounts—an overview (p. 264)

6 Using Purchase Requisitions, Purchase Orders, recording Purchase Invoices and Purchase Returns (the debit memorandum) into the Purchases Journal and General Journal, and recording these events to the AP sub-ledger as well as posting to the General Ledger (p. 268)

7 Entering transactions into the Cash Payments Journal, recording to the AP sub-ledger, posting to the General Ledger accounts, and preparing a schedule of Accounts Payable (p. 275)

This chapter looks at how merchandise companies operate. The first part focuses on sellers of goods; towards the end of the chapter, we discuss buyers. In both cases, companies do not keep continual track of their inventory. This is called a *periodic inventory system*. A company simply takes an inventory of what is left at the end of its accounting period. The appendices at the end of Chapter 12 look at how a company keeps continual track of its inventory. This system is called a *perpetual inventory system*.

Let's first look at Chou's Toy Shop to get an overview of merchandise terms and journal entries. After that, we will take an in-depth look at how Art's Wholesale Clothing Company keeps its books. Remember that we will first look at the periodic inventory system (no continual track of inventory).

Learning Unit 6-1

Chou's Toy Shop: Seller's View of a Merchandising Company

1 Recording Sales, Sales Returns and Sales Discounts—an overview

Chou's Toy Shop is a **retailer**. It buys toys, games, bikes, and so on from manufacturers and **wholesalers** and resells these goods (or **merchandise**) to its customers. The shelving, display cases, and so on are called "fixtures" or "equipment." These items are not for resale.

GROSS SALES

Gross sales: revenue earned from the sale of merchandise to customers

Each cash or charge sale made at Chou's Toy Shop is rung up at the cash register. Suppose the shop had $3,000 in sales on July 18. Of that amount, sales worth $1,800 were cash sales and $1,200 worth of sales were charged. This is how the account that recorded those sales would look:

Sales (Gross)	
Dr.	Cr.
	3,000 ← Revenue account with a credit balance

This account is a revenue account with a credit balance and will be found on the income statement. Here is the journal entry for the day. *Note:* We will discuss provincial sales tax and GST/HST in Chapter 10.

Accounts Affected	Category	↑↓	Rules	T Account Update
Cash	Asset	↑	Dr.	**Cash** 1,800 |
Accounts Receivable	Asset	↑	Dr.	**Accounts Receivable** 1,200 |
Sales	Revenue	↑	Cr.	**Sales** | 3,000

July	18	Cash		1 8 0 0 00		
		Accounts Receivable		1 2 0 0 00		
		Sales			3 0 0 0 00
		Sales for July 18			

SALES RETURNS AND ALLOWANCES

It would be great for Chou if all the customers were completely satisfied, but that is rarely the case. On July 19, Michelle Reese brought back a doll she bought on account for $50. She told Chou that the doll was defective and she wanted either a price reduction or a new doll. They agreed on a $10 price reduction. Michelle now owes Chou $40. The account called **Sales Returns and Allowances** would record this information.

Contra-revenue account with a debit balance

Sales Returns and Allowances

Dr.	Cr.
10	

This account is a contra-revenue account with a debit balance. It will be recorded on the income statement. This is how the journal entry would look:

Accounts Affected	Category	↑↓	Rules	T Account Update
Sales Returns and Allowances	Revenue (Contra)	↑	Dr.	**Sales Returns & Allowances** Dr. | Cr. 10 |
Accounts Receivable	Asset	↓	Cr.	**Accounts Receivable** Dr. | Cr. 1,200 | 10

Look at how the sales returns and allowances increase:

July	19	Sales Returns and Allowances		1 0 00		
		Accounts Receivable, Michelle Reese			1 0 00
		Issued credit memorandum			

SALES DISCOUNT

Chou gives a 2% **sales discount** to customers who pay their bills early. He wanted his customers to know about this policy, so he posted the following sign at the cash register:

Sales Discount Policy	
2/10, n/30	2% discount is allowed off price on bill if paid within the first 10 days, or full amount is due within 30 days.
n/10, EOM	No discount. Full amount of bill is due within 10 days after the end of the month.

Note that the **discount period** is the time during which a discount is granted. The discount period is shorter than the **credit period**, which is the length of time allowed to pay the amount owed on the bill.

If Michelle pays her $40 bill early, she will get an $0.80 discount. This is the account that records this information:

Contra-revenue account with a debit balance

Sales Discount

Dr.	Cr.
0.80	

This is how Michelle's discount is calculated:

$$0.02 \times \$40 = \$0.80$$

Michelle pays her bill on July 24. She is entitled to the discount because she paid her bill within 10 days. Let's look at how Chou would record this on the company's books.

Accounts Affected	Category	↑↓	Rules	T Account Update
Cash	Asset	↑	Dr.	**Cash** Dr. 39.20 | Cr.
Sales Discounts	Revenue (Contra)	↑	Dr.	**Sales Discounts** Dr. 0.80 | Cr.
Accounts Receivable	Asset	↓	Cr.	**Accounts Receivable** Dr. 1,200 | Cr. 10 | 40

July	24	Cash					3 9 20			
		Sales Discounts					80			
		Accounts Receivable, Michelle Reese							4 0 00	

Although Michelle pays $39.20, her account receivable is credited for the full amount, $40. ***Note:*** The actual or **net sales** for Chou would be gross sales less sales returns and allowances and less any sales discounts.

In Chapter 10, we will show you how to record a credit memorandum with sales tax and GST/HST.

LEARNING UNIT 6-1 REVIEW

AT THIS POINT you should be able to:

◆ Explain the purpose of a contra-revenue account. (p. 248)

◆ Explain how to calculate net sales. (p. 249)

◆ Define, journalize, and explain gross sales, sales returns and allowances, and sales discounts. (pp. 247–249)

Self-Review Quiz 6-1

(The forms you need are on page 6-1 of the *Study Guide with Working Papers*.)

Which of the following statements are false?

1. Sales Returns and Allowances is a contra-asset account.

2. Sales Discounts has a normal balance of a debit.

3. Sales Discounts is a contra-asset.

4. Credit terms are standard in all industries.

Quiz Tip	
Sales	Revenue ↑ Cr.
Sales Returns and Allowances (Contra)	Revenue ↑ Dr.
Sales Discounts	Revenue ↑ Dr.
	(Contra)

Solution to Self-Review Quiz 6-1

Numbers 1, 3, and 4 are false.

Learning Unit 6-2

The Sales Journal and Accounts Receivable Subsidiary Ledger

SPECIAL JOURNALS

Now let's examine how Art's Wholesale Clothing Company keeps its books. Art's business conducts many transactions. The following partial general journal shows the journal entries that Art's must make for sales on account transactions.

ART'S WHOLESALE CLOTHING COMPANY GENERAL JOURNAL					
April	2	Accounts Receivable, Hal's		80000	
		Sales			80000
		Sales on account			
	6	Accounts Receivable, Bevans		160000	
		Sales			160000
		Sales on account			
	19	Accounts Receivable, Roe		200000	
		Sales			200000
		Sales on account			

This method is not very efficient. However, if Art's Wholesale Clothing Company kept a **special journal** for each type of transaction conducted, the number of postings required for each transaction would be reduced. In addition, when a company grows larger, special journals permit several accounting clerks to work on the company's books at the same time. If the general journal is used alone, only one person can enter transactions and this results in slow data entry. After carefully looking at the situation with his accountant, Art has decided to use the following special journals:

For a discussion of the recording of credit cards in special journals, see Appendix A on MyAccountingLab at www.myaccountinglab.com.

Special Journal Type	What It Records	
Sales journal (SJ)	Sale of merchandise on account	} Covered in this Learning Unit
Cash receipts journal (CRJ)	Receiving cash from any source	
Purchases journal (PJ)	Buying merchandise or other items on account	} Covered in Learning Unit 6-6
Cash payments journal (CPJ) (cash disbursements journal)	Payment of cash for any purpose	

SUBSIDIARY LEDGERS

In the same way that Art's Wholesale Clothing Company needs more than just a general journal, the business needs more than just a general ledger. For example, so far in this text, the only title we have used for recording amounts owed to the seller has been Accounts Receivable. Art could have replaced the Accounts Receivable title in the general ledger with the following list of customers who owe him money:

◆ Account Receivable, Bevans Company
◆ Account Receivable, Hal's Clothing
◆ Account Receivable, Mel's Department Store
◆ Account Receivable, Roe Company

As you can see, this would not be manageable if Art had 1,000 or more credit customers. To solve this problem, Art sets up a separate **accounts receivable subsidiary ledger**. Such a special ledger, often simply called a **subsidiary ledger**, contains a single type of account, such as "on account" customers. A page is opened for each customer and the pages are usually arranged alphabetically by customer name.

The general ledger is *not* in the same book as the accounts receivable subsidiary ledger.

Figure 6-1 shows how the accounts receivable subsidiary ledger fits in with the general ledger. To clarify the difference in updating the general ledger versus the subsidiary ledger, we will *post* to the general ledger and *record* in the subsidiary ledger. The word "post" refers to information that is moved from the journal to the general ledger; the word "record" refers to information that is transferred from the journal into the individual customer's account in the subsidiary ledger.

The accounts receivable subsidiary ledger or any other subsidiary ledger can be in the form of a card file, a binder notebook, or computer files on disks. It probably will not have page numbers, but each account may have a unique number to help identify it. The accounts receivable subsidiary ledger is organized alphabetically by customer name and address; new customers can be added and inactive customers deleted.

Making sure that the total of all customer accounts agrees with the controlling account is often called reconciliation.

When using an accounts receivable subsidiary ledger, Accounts Receivable in the general ledger is called the **controlling account** since it summarizes or controls the accounts receivable subsidiary ledger. At the end of the month, the total of the individual accounts in the accounts receivable ledger must equal the ending balance in Accounts Receivable in the general ledger.

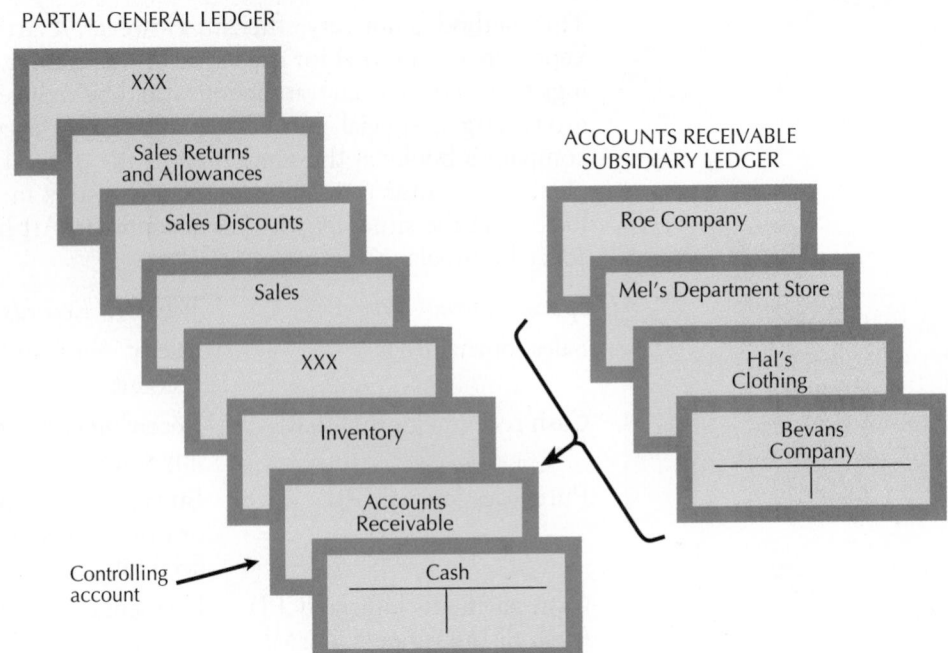

PARTIAL GENERAL LEDGER

ACCOUNTS RECEIVABLE
SUBSIDIARY LEDGER

XXX
Sales Returns and Allowances
Sales Discounts
Sales
XXX
Inventory
Accounts Receivable
Cash

Controlling account

Roe Company
Mel's Department Store
Hal's Clothing
Bevans Company

> *Proving:* At the end of the month, the sum of the accounts receivable subsidiary ledger balances will equal the ending balance in Accounts Receivable, the controlling account in the general ledger.

Art's Wholesale Clothing Company will use the following subsidiary ledgers:

Accounts receivable subsidiary ledger   Records money owed by credit customers

Accounts payable subsidiary ledger   Records money owed to creditors

Let's now look more closely at the sales journal, general ledger, and subsidiary ledger for Art's Wholesale Clothing Company to see how transactions are recorded in the special journal as well as posted and recorded to specific ledger accounts.

THE SALES JOURNAL

The **sales journal** for Art's Wholesale Clothing Company records all sales made on account to customers. Figure 6-2 shows the sales journal at the end of the first month of operation, along with the recordings in the accounts receivable ledger and posting to the general ledger. Keep in mind that the reason the balances in the accounts receivable subsidiary ledger are *debit* balances is that the customers listed *owe* Art's Wholesale money. For some companies, a sales journal would have multiple revenue account columns.

Look at the first transaction listed in the sales journal. It shows that on April 2, Art's Wholesale Clothing Company sold merchandise on account to Hal's Clothing for $800. The bill or **sales invoice** for this sale is shown in Figure 6-3 on page 254.

Recording from the Sales Journal to the Accounts Receivable Subsidiary Ledger

As shown on the first line of the sales journal in Figure 6-2, the information on the invoice is recorded in the sales journal. However, *the PR column is left blank.* As soon as possible, we now update the accounts receivable subsidiary ledger. To do this, we pull out the Hal's Clothing file card and update it: The debit side must show the $800 owed to Art along with the date (April 2) and page of the sales journal (SJ1). Once that is done, place a ✔ in the posting reference column of the sales journal. The accounts receivable subsidiary ledger shows us Hal's outstanding balance at any moment in time. We do not have to go through all the invoices. Note that the sales journal needs only one line instead of the three lines that would have been required in a general journal.

---

2   Entering transactions into the Sales Journal, and recording to the Accounts Receivable sub-ledger

Recording in the accounts receivable subsidiary ledger occurs daily.

Hal's Clothing

Dr.	Cr.
4/2 SJ1 800	

✓ in the journal means accounts receivable subsidiary ledger has been updated.

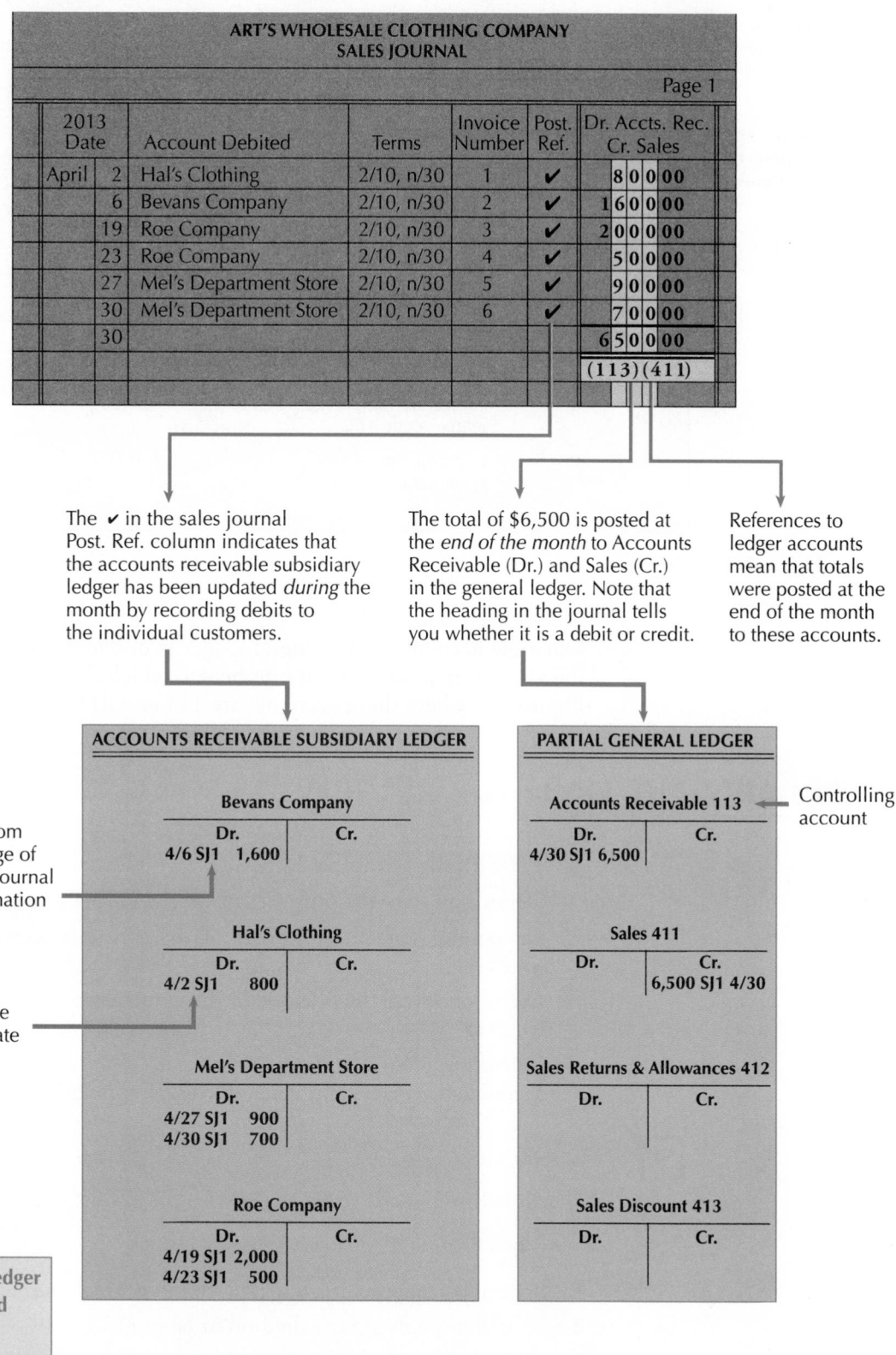

Figure 6-2
Sales Journal
Recording and Postings

The ✔ in the sales journal Post. Ref. column indicates that the accounts receivable subsidiary ledger has been updated *during* the month by recording debits to the individual customers.

The total of $6,500 is posted at the *end of the month* to Accounts Receivable (Dr.) and Sales (Cr.) in the general ledger. Note that the heading in the journal tells you whether it is a debit or credit.

References to ledger accounts mean that totals were posted at the end of the month to these accounts.

Tells us from which page of the sales journal the information comes.

Tells us the invoice date

Controlling account

Recording to the general ledger occurs at end of month and uses the journal total:

Accounts Receivable 113

Dr.	Cr.
SJ1 4/30 6,500	

Sales 411

Dr.	Cr.
	6,500 4/30 SJ1

Posting at the End of the Month from the Sales Journal to the General Ledger

The sales journal is totalled ($6,500) at the end of the month. Looking above, you can see that one heading of Art's sales journal is a debit to accounts receivable and a credit to sales. Therefore, at the end of the month, the $6,500 total is posted to Accounts Receivable (debit) *and* to Sales (credit) in the general ledger. In the general ledger, we record the date (4/30), the initials of the journal (SJ), the page of the sales journal (1), and the appropriate debit or credit ($6,500).

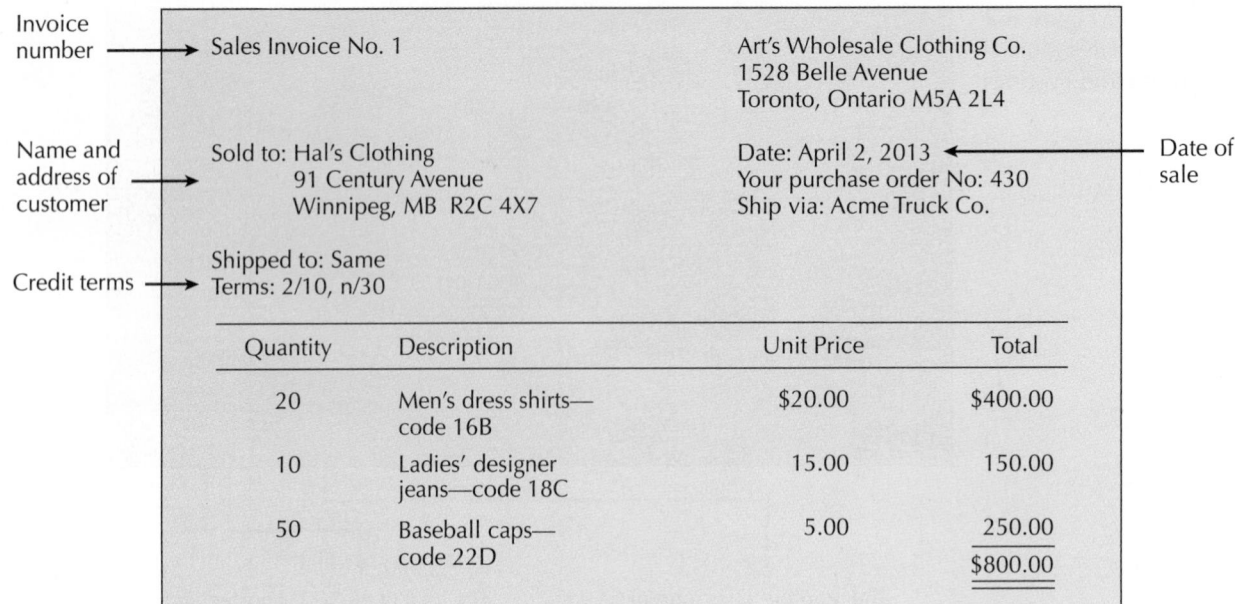

Invoice number → Sales Invoice No. 1

Art's Wholesale Clothing Co.
1528 Belle Avenue
Toronto, Ontario M5A 2L4

Name and address of customer → Sold to: Hal's Clothing
91 Century Avenue
Winnipeg, MB R2C 4X7

Date: April 2, 2013 ← Date of sale
Your purchase order No: 430
Ship via: Acme Truck Co.

Shipped to: Same
Credit terms → Terms: 2/10, n/30

Quantity	Description	Unit Price	Total
20	Men's dress shirts—code 16B	$20.00	$400.00
10	Ladies' designer jeans—code 18C	15.00	150.00
50	Baseball caps—code 22D	5.00	250.00
			$800.00

Figure 6-3 Sales Invoice

Once the account in the general ledger is updated, we place below the totals in the sales journal the account numbers to which the information was posted (as in Figure 6-2, where these accounts are 113 and 411).

LEARNING UNIT 6-2 REVIEW

AT THIS POINT you should be able to:

◆ Define and state the purposes of special journals. (p. 250)

◆ Define and state the purposes of the accounts receivable subsidiary ledger. (p. 251)

◆ Define and state the purpose of the controlling account, Accounts Receivable. (p. 251)

◆ Journalize, record, and post sales on account to a sales journal and its related accounts receivable and general ledgers. (pp. 252–253)

Self-Review Quiz 6-2

(The forms you need are on page 6-1 of the *Study Guide with Working Papers.*)

Which of the following statements are false?

1. Special journals completely replace the general journal.
2. Special journals aid the division of labour.
3. The subsidiary ledger makes the general ledger less manageable.
4. The subsidiary ledger is separate from the general ledger.
5. The controlling account is located in the accounts receivable subsidiary ledger.
6. The total(s) of a sales journal is (are) posted to the general ledger at the end of the month.
7. The accounts receivable subsidiary ledger is arranged in alphabetical order.
8. Transactions recorded into a sales journal are recorded only weekly to the accounts receivable subsidiary ledger.

Quiz Tip

The normal balance of each account in the accounts receivable subsidiary ledger is a debit.

Numbers 1, 3, 5, and 8 are false.

Learning Unit 6-3
The Credit Memorandum

At the beginning of this chapter, we introduced the Sales Returns and Allowances account. Merchandising businesses often use this account to handle transactions involving goods that have already been sold to customers on account. For example, if a customer returns the goods he has bought, his account will be credited for the amount charged for the goods returned; if a customer gets an allowance because the goods she purchased were damaged, her account will be credited for the amount of the allowance. In both of these examples, the company's net sales revenue decreases. That is why the account is called a contra-revenue account: The sales revenue decreases and its normal balance is a debit.

> A credit memorandum *reduces* accounts receivable.

Companies usually handle sales returns and allowances by means of a **credit memorandum**. Credit memoranda inform customers that the amount of the goods returned or the amount allowed for damaged goods has been subtracted from (credited to) the customer's ongoing account with the company.

A sample credit memorandum from Art's Wholesale Clothing Company appears in Figure 6-4. It shows that on April 12, credit memo No. 1 was issued to Bevans Company for defective merchandise that had been returned. (Figure 6-2 on page 253 shows that Art's Wholesale Clothing Company sold Bevans Company $1,600 worth of merchandise on April 6.)

Sales Returns and Allowances	
Dr.	Cr.
+	−
A contra-revenue account	

Let's assume that Art's Wholesale has high-quality goods and does not expect many sales returns and allowances. On this assumption, no special journal for sales returns and allowances will be needed. Instead, any returns and allowances will be recorded in the general journal, and all postings and recordings will be done when journalized. Let's look at a transaction analysis chart before we journalize, record, and post this transaction.

Figure 6-4
Credit Memorandum

> End result is that Bevans owes Art's Wholesale less money.

Art's Wholesale Clothing Company
1528 Belle Avenue
Toronto, ON M5A 2L4

Credit Memorandum No. 1

Date: April 12, 2013

Credit to: Bevans Company
110 Aster Road
Amherst, NS B4H 3A5

We credit your account as follows:
Merchandise returned 60 model 8B men's dress gloves—$600

> Note that the Sales Returns and Allowances account is increasing, which in turn reduces sales revenue and reduces the amount owed by the customer (accounts receivable).

Accounts Affected	Category	↑↓	Rules
Sales Returns and Allowances	Revenue (Contra)	↑	Dr.
Accounts Receivable, Bevans Co.	Asset	↓	Cr.

Remember, sales discounts are *not* taken on returns.

JOURNALIZING, RECORDING, AND POSTING THE CREDIT MEMORANDUM

The credit memorandum results in two postings to the general ledger and one recording in the accounts receivable subsidiary ledger (see Figure 6-5).

Note in the PR column next to Accounts Receivable, Bevans Co., that there is a diagonal line with the account number 113 above and a ✔ below. This is to show that the amount of $600 has been credited to Accounts Receivable, the controlling account in the general ledger, *and* credited to the account of Bevans Company in the accounts receivable subsidiary ledger.

Figure 6-5
Postings and Recordings for the Credit Memorandum in the Subsidiary and General Ledgers

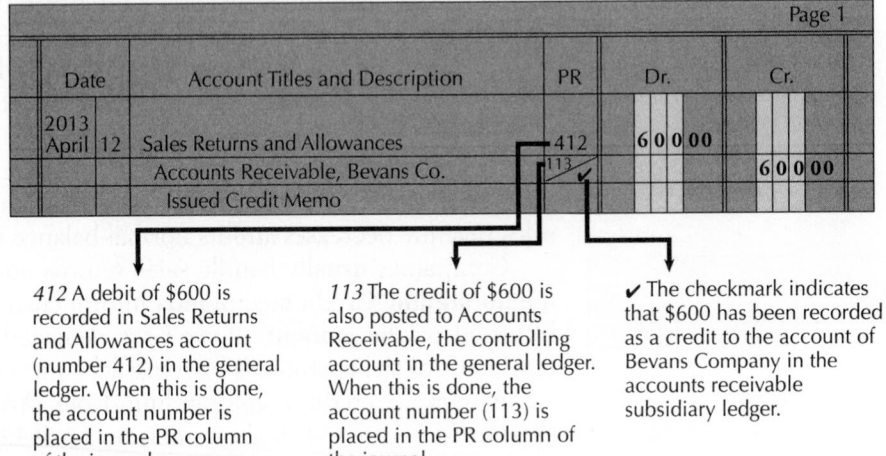

412 A debit of $600 is recorded in Sales Returns and Allowances account (number 412) in the general ledger. When this is done, the account number is placed in the PR column of the journal.

113 The credit of $600 is also posted to Accounts Receivable, the controlling account in the general ledger. When this is done, the account number (113) is placed in the PR column of the journal.

✔ The checkmark indicates that $600 has been recorded as a credit to the account of Bevans Company in the accounts receivable subsidiary ledger.

If the accountant for Art's Wholesale Clothing Company decided to develop a special journal for sales returns and allowances, the entry for a credit memorandum such as the one we've been discussing would look like this:

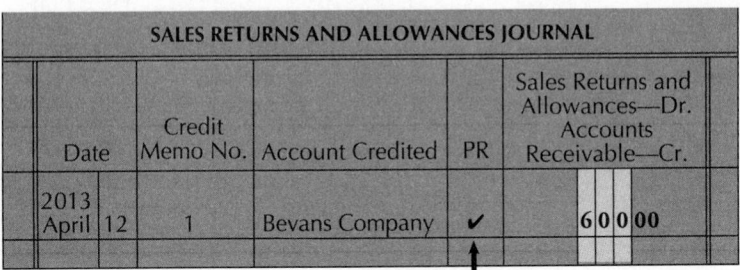

During the month, the subsidiary ledger is updated.

LEARNING UNIT 6-3 REVIEW

AT THIS POINT you should be able to:

◆ Explain, journalize, post, and record a credit memorandum without provincial sales tax. (pp. 255–256)

Self-Review Quiz 6-3

(The forms you need are on pages 6-1 to 6-3 of the *Study Guide with Working Papers*.)

Journalize the following transactions in the sales journal or general journal for Moss Company. Record in the accounts receivable subsidiary ledger and post to general ledger accounts as appropriate. Use the same journal headings that we used for Art's Wholesale Clothing Company. (All sales carry credit terms of 2/10, n/30.)

2012

May 1 Sold merchandise on account to Jane Company, invoice No. 1, $600.

4 Sold merchandise on account to Ralph Company, invoice No. 2, $2,500.

18 Issued credit memo No. 1 to Jane Company for $200 for defective merchandise returned.

Solution to Self-Review Quiz 6-3

Quiz Tip

Total of accounts receivable subsidiary ledger, $400 + $2,500, does indeed equal the balance ($2,900) in the controlling account, Accounts Receivable, at the end of the month in the general ledger.

MOSS COMPANY
SALES JOURNAL

Page 1

Date		Account Debited	Terms	Invoice No.	Post. Ref.	Dr. Accts. Rec. Cr. Sales
2012 May	1	Jane Company	2/10, n/30	1	✔	6 00 00
	4	Ralph Company	2/10, n/30	2	✔	2 50 00 00
	31					3 10 0 00
						(112) (411)

MOSS COMPANY
GENERAL JOURNAL

Page 1

Date		Account Titles and Description	PR	Dr.	Cr.
2012 May	18	Sales Returns and Allowances	412	2 0 0 00	
		Accounts Receivable, Jane Company	112 ✔		2 0 0 00
		Issued credit memo #1			

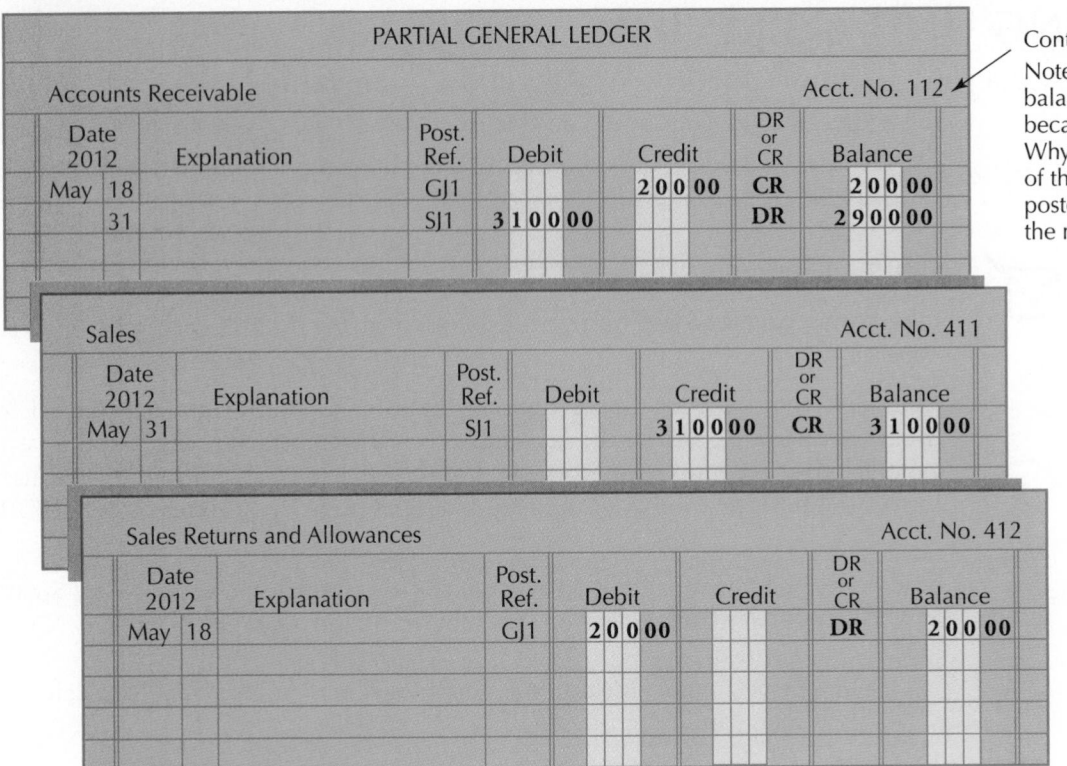

PARTIAL GENERAL LEDGER

Accounts Receivable   Acct. No. 112

Date 2012	Explanation	Post. Ref.	Debit	Credit	DR or CR	Balance
May 18		GJ1		200 00	CR	200 00
31		SJ1	3 100 00		DR	2 900 00

Sales   Acct. No. 411

Date 2012	Explanation	Post. Ref.	Debit	Credit	DR or CR	Balance
May 31		SJ1		3 100 00	CR	3 100 00

Sales Returns and Allowances   Acct. No. 412

Date 2012	Explanation	Post. Ref.	Debit	Credit	DR or CR	Balance
May 18		GJ1	200 00		DR	200 00

Controlling Account. Note the unusual balance of $200 (Cr.) because of the return. Why? Because the total of the sales journal is not posted until the end of the month.

ACCOUNTS RECEIVABLE LEDGER

NAME Jane Company
ADDRESS 1218 Broadview Avenue, Toronto, ON M5X 2A1

Date 2012	Explanation	Post. Ref.	Debit	Credit	DR Balance
May 1		SJ1	600 00		600 00
18		GJ1		200 00	400 00

NAME Ralph Company
ADDRESS 1300 Marine Drive, West Vancouver, BC V6P 9B6

Date 2012	Explanation	Post. Ref.	Debit	Credit	DR Balance
May 4		SJ1	2 500 00		2 500 00

Customers owe Moss money and thus each account has a debit balance.

Cash Receipts Journal and Schedule of Accounts Receivable

Besides the sales journal, another special journal often used in a merchandising operation is the cash receipts journal. The **cash receipts journal** records the receipt of cash (or cheques) from any source. The number of columns a cash receipts journal will have depends on how frequently certain types of transactions occur. For example, in the cash receipts journal for Art's Wholesale, the accountant has developed the headings shown in Figure 6-6. Below each heading is a description of the purpose of that column and when to update the accounts receivable ledger as well as the general ledger.

The following transactions occurred in April for Art's Wholesale and affected the cash receipts journal:

2013

April	1	Art Newner invested $8,000 in the business.
	5	Received cheque from Hal's Clothing for payment of invoice No. 1 less discount.
	15	Cash sales for first half of April, $900.
	16	Received cheque from Bevans Company in settlement of invoice No. 2 less returns and discount.
	22	Received cheque from Roe Company for payment of invoice No. 3 less discount.
	26	Sold store equipment, $500.
	30	Cash sales for second half of April, $1,200.

Figure 6-6   Cash Receipts Journal

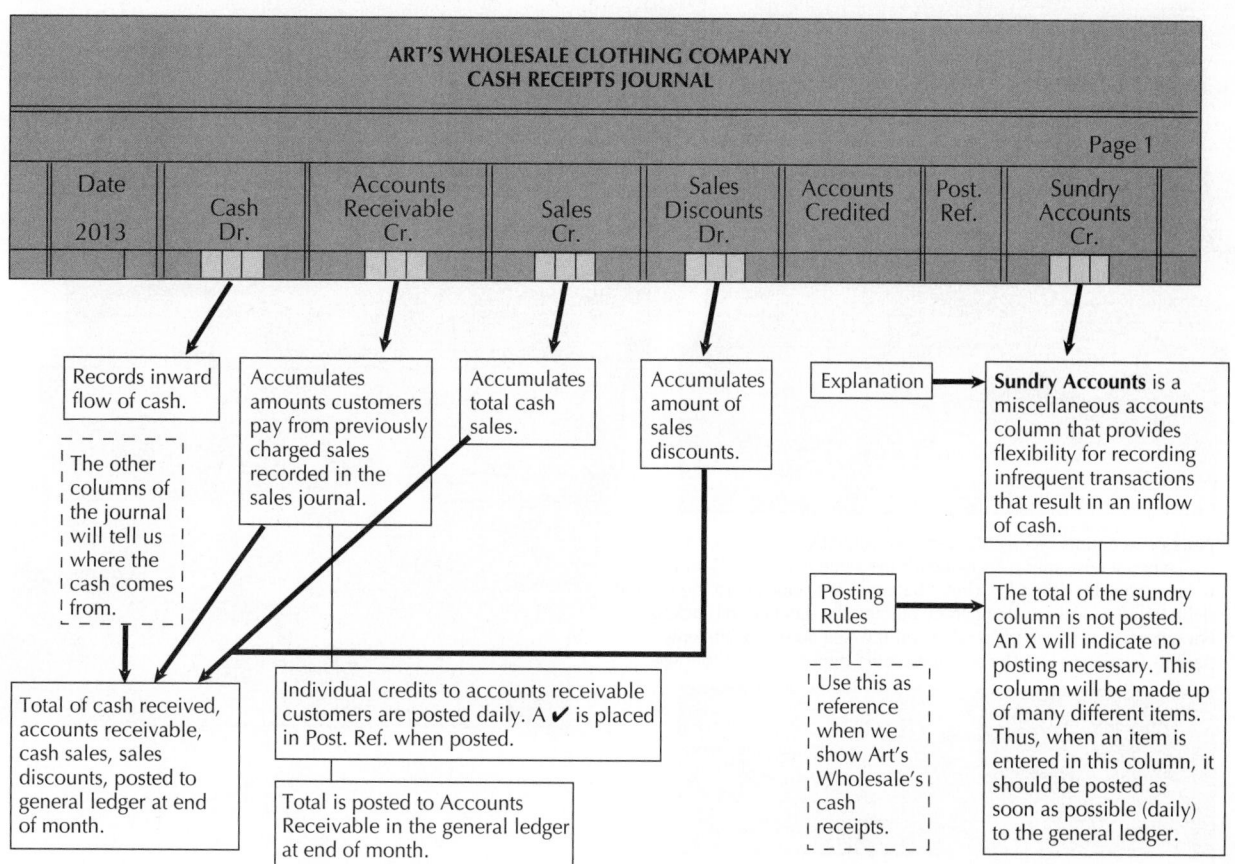

Figure 6-7 shows the cash receipts journal for the end of April, along with the recordings to the accounts receivable ledger and posting to the general ledger. Study the diagram; we will review it in a moment.

Figure 6-7 Cash Receipts Journal and Posting

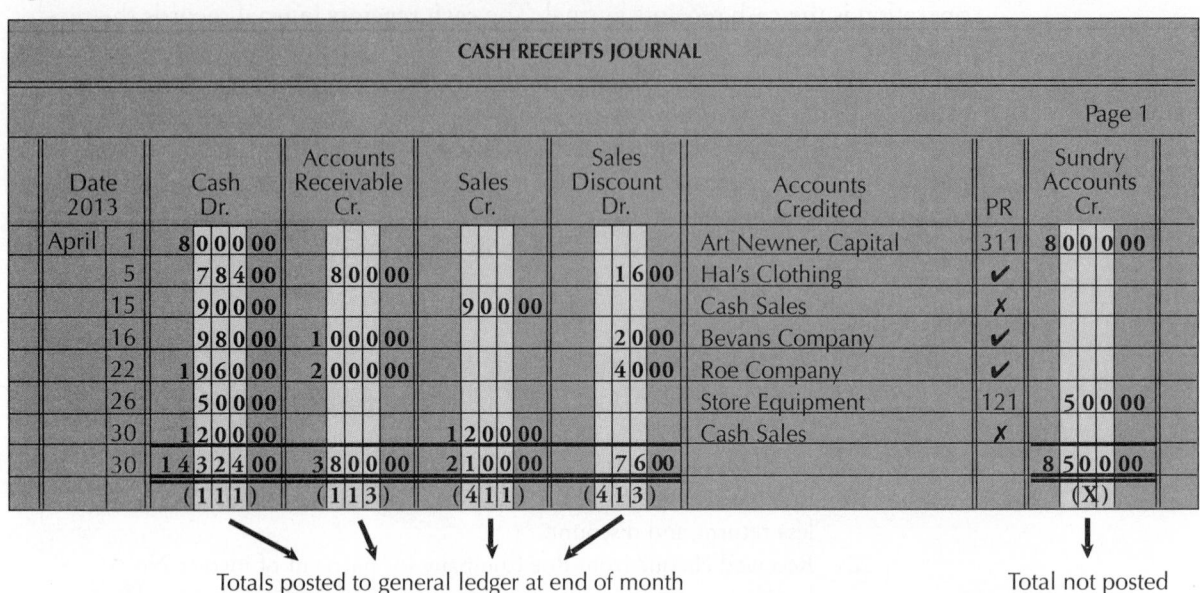

Note on accounts receivable: Very occasionally (because of an error, e.g., when a customer pays twice for the same invoice), a credit balance may be called for. Credit balances are opposite to the normal debit balance and are signified by placing the balance in brackets. For example, suppose that Hal's Clothing (see above) mistakenly paid its invoice twice. The account would then appear as follows:

JOURNALIZING, RECORDING, AND POSTING FROM THE CASH RECEIPTS JOURNAL

On April 5, Art's Wholesale received a cheque from Hal's Clothing for payment of invoice No. 1 less discount. Remember, it was in the sales journal that this transaction was first recorded (Figure 6-2). At that time, we updated the accounts receivable ledger, indicating that Hal's Clothing owed Art $800. Since Hal's Clothing is paying within the 10-day discount period, Art's Wholesale offers a $16 sales discount ($800 × 0.02). (Remember, all credit sales carried terms of 2/10, n/30.)

Now, when payment is received, Art's Wholesale updates the cash receipts journal (see page 260) by entering the date (April 5), cash debit of $784, sales discounts debit of $16, credit to accounts receivable of $800, and which account name (Hal's Clothing) is to be credited. The terms of sale indicate that Hal's Clothing is entitled to the discount and no longer owes Art's Wholesale the $800 balance. *As soon as this line is entered into the cash receipts journal, Art's Wholesale will update the ledger account of Hal's Clothing.* Note, in the accounts receivable ledger of Hal's Clothing, how the date (April 5), posting reference (CRJ1), and credit amount ($800) are recorded. The balance in the accounts receivable ledger is zero. The last step of this transaction is to go back to the cash receipts journal and put a ✔ in the posting reference column.

In studying this cash receipts journal, note that:

1. All totals of cash receipts in the journal columns except sundry were posted to the general ledger at the end of the month.

2. Art Newner, Capital, and Store Equipment were posted to the general ledger when entered in the sundry column. It is assumed that the equipment account had a beginning balance of $4,000 in the general ledger.

3. The cash sales were not posted when entered (hence the X to show no posting is needed). The sales and cash totals are posted at the end of the month.

4. A ✔ means information was recorded daily to the accounts receivable ledger.

5. The Accounts Credited column describes each transaction.

We can prove the accuracy of recording transactions of the cash receipts journal by totalling the columns with debit balances and the columns with credit balances. This process, called **cross-footing**, is done before the totals are posted. Also, if a bookkeeper were using more than one page for the cash receipts journal, the balances on the bottom of one page would be brought forward to the top of the next page. This verifying of totals would result in less work when trying to find journalizing or posting errors at a later date. Let's see how to cross-foot the cash receipts journal of Art's Wholesale (Figure 6-7).

Debit Columns	=	Credit Columns		
Cash + Sales Discounts	=	**Accounts Receivable +**	**Sales**	**+ Sundry**
$14,324 + $76	=	$3,800	+ $2,100	+ $8,500
$14,400	=	$14,400		

> The last step is to put a checkmark in the PR column of the cash receipts journal to show the accounts receivable ledger is up to date.

> Proving the cash receipts journal

SCHEDULE OF ACCOUNTS RECEIVABLE

From Figure 6-7, let's list the customers that have an ending balance in the accounts receivable ledger of Art's Wholesale. This listing is called a **schedule of accounts receivable**. The balance of the controlling account, Accounts Receivable ($2,100), in the general ledger (see p. 260) does indeed equal the sum of the individual customer balances in the accounts receivable ledger ($2,100), as shown below in the schedule of accounts receivable. The schedule of accounts receivable can help forecast potential cash inflows as well as possible credit and collection decisions.

Schedule is listed in alphabetical order.

Art's Wholesale Clothing Company Schedule of Accounts Receivable April 30, 2013	
Mel's Department Store	$1600.00
Roe Company	500.00
Total Accounts Receivable	$2100.00

LEARNING UNIT 6-4 REVIEW

AT THIS POINT you should be able to:

- Journalize, record, and post, transactions using a cash receipts journal. (p. 261)
- Prepare a schedule of accounts receivable. (p. 262)

Self-Review Quiz 6-4

(The forms you need are on pages 6-4 to 6-6 of the *Study Guide with Working Papers*.)

Journalize, cross-foot, record, and post when appropriate, the following transactions into the cash receipts journal of Moore Co. Use the same headings as for Art's Wholesale.

Accounts Receivable Ledger

Name	Balance	Invoice No.
Irene Welch	$500	1
Chantel Simard	200	2

Partial General Ledger

Account	Account No.	Balance
Cash	110	$600
Accounts Receivable	120	700
Store Equipment	130	600
Sales	410	700
Sales Discounts	420	—

2013

May 3 Received cheque from Irene Welch for invoice No. 1 less 2% discount.

7 Cash sales collected, $400.

14 Received cheque from Chantel Simard for invoice No. 2 less 2% discount.

20 Sold store equipment at cost, $300.

Solution to Self-Review Quiz 6-4

MOORE COMPANY
CASH RECEIPTS JOURNAL

Page 2

Date 2013	Cash Dr.	Accounts Receivable Cr.	Sales Cr.	Sales Discounts Dr.	Description of Receipt	Post. Ref.	Sundry Accounts Cr.
May 3	490 00	500 00		10 00	Irene Welch	✔	
7	400 00		400 00		Cash Sales	✗	
14	196 00	200 00		4 00	Chantel Simard	✔	
20	300 00				Store Equipment	130	300 00
31	1386 00	700 00	400 00	14 00			300 00
	(110)	(120)	(410)	(420)			(X)

Cross-footing: $1,400.00 = $1,400.00

PARTIAL GENERAL LEDGER

Quiz Tip

The total of the Sundry column is not posted; only individual amounts are posted to the general ledger.

Quiz Tip

Sum of all debits equals sum of all credits.

Cash   Acct. No. 110

Date 2013	Explanation	Post. Ref.	Debit	Credit	DR or CR	Balance
May 1	Balance	✔			DR.	600 00
31		CRJ2	1386 00		DR.	1986 00

Accounts Receivable   Acct. No. 120

Date 2013	Explanation	Post. Ref.	Debit	Credit	DR or CR	Balance
May 1	Balance	✔			DR.	700 00
31		CRJ2		700 00		–0–

Store Equipment   Acct. No. 130

Date 2013	Explanation	Post. Ref.	Debit	Credit	DR or CR	Balance
May 1	Balance	✔			DR.	600 00
20		CRJ2		300 00	DR.	300 00

Sales   Acct. No. 410

Date 2013	Explanation	Post. Ref.	Debit	Credit	DR or CR	Balance
May 1	Balance	✔			CR.	7 0 0 00
31		CRJ2		4 0 0 00	CR.	1 1 0 0 00

Sales Discounts   Acct. No. 420

Date 2013	Explanation	Post. Ref.	Debit	Credit	DR or CR	Balance
May 31		CRJ2	1 4 00		DR.	1 4 00

ACCOUNTS RECEIVABLE LEDGER

NAME Irene Welch
ADDRESS 10 Rong Road, Timmins, ON P4N 4M3

Date 2013	Explanation	Post. Ref.	Debit	Credit	Dr. Balance
May 1	Balance	✔			5 0 0 00
3		CRJ2		5 0 0 00	– 0 –

NAME Chantel Simard
ADDRESS 9017 Robitaille Road, Montreal, QC H1K 4R3

Date 2013	Explanation	Post. Ref.	Debit	Credit	Dr. Balance
May 1	Balance	✔			2 0 0 00
14		CRJ2		2 0 0 00	– 0 –

Learning Unit 6-5

Chou's Toy Shop: Buyer's View of a Merchandising Company

5 Recording Purchases, Purchase Returns and Purchase Discounts—an overview

PURCHASES

Chou brings merchandise into his toy store for resale to customers. The account that records the cost of this merchandise is called **Purchases**. Suppose that Chou buys $4,000 worth of Barbie dolls on account from Mattel Manufacturing on July 6. The Purchases account records all merchandise bought for resale. Here's how this would be recorded if special journals were not used.

Purchases is a cost.
The rules work just as if it were an expense.

	Purchases			Accounts Payable	
	Dr.	Cr.		Dr.	Cr.
	4,000				4,000

This account has a debit balance and is classified as a cost. Purchases represent costs that are directly related to bringing merchandise into the store for resale to customers. The July 6 entry would be analyzed and journalized as follows:

Accounts Affected	Category	↑ ↓	Rules	T Account Update
Purchases	Expense	↑	Dr.	**Purchases** Dr. | Cr. 4,000 |
Accounts Payable, Mattel	Liability	↑	Cr.	**Accounts Payable** | **Mattel Account** Dr. | Cr. | | 4,000 | 4,000 | |

	July	6	Purchases		4 0 0 0 00		
			Accounts Payable, Mattel			4 0 0 0 00	
			Purchases on account				

Keep in mind that we would have to record a liability to Mattel in the accounts payable subsidiary ledger. We will talk about the subsidiary ledger in Learning Unit 6-6.

PURCHASES RETURNS AND ALLOWANCES

Chou noticed that some of the dolls he received were not as ordered, and he notified the manufacturer of this fact. On July 9, Mattel issued a debit memorandum,* indicating that Chou would get a $500 reduction from the original selling price. Chou then agreed to keep the dolls. The account that records a decrease in a buyer's cost is a contra-expense account called **Purchases Returns and Allowances**. This account lowers the cost of purchases.

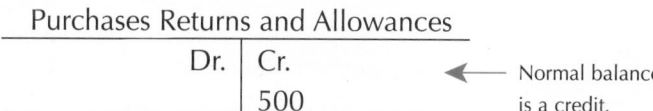

Purchases Returns and Allowances
Dr. | Cr.
     | 500   ← Normal balance is a credit.

Let's analyze this reduction to cost and prepare a general journal entry.

Accounts Affected	Category	↑ ↓	Rules	T Account Update
Accounts Payable, Mattel	Liability	↓	Dr.	**Accounts Payable** | **Mattel Account** Dr. | Cr. | 500 | 4,000 500 | 4,000 | |
Purchases Returns and Allowances	Expense (Contra)	↑	Cr.	**Purchases, Returns & Allowances** Dr. | Cr. | 500

	July	9	Accounts Payable, Mattel		5 0 0 00		
			Purchases Returns and Allowances			5 0 0 00	
			To record debit memorandum				

When posting to the general ledger accounts and recording in the accounts payable subsidiary ledger for Mattel have been completed, the records show that Chou's Toy Shop owes $500 less.

*Technically, Mattel would issue a *credit* memorandum. This is explained later in the chapter.

PURCHASES DISCOUNTS

Remember: For Mattel, this is a sales discount; for Chou, this is a purchases discount.

Now let's look at the analysis and journal entry when Chou pays Mattel. Mattel offers a 2% cash discount to customers that pay their invoices within 10 days. To take advantage of this cash discount, Chou sent a company cheque to Mattel on July 15. The discount is taken after the allowance.

$$\begin{aligned} &\$4,000 \\ -\ &\underline{\ \ 500}\ \text{allowance} \\ &\$3,500 \times 0.02 = \$70\ \text{purchases discount} \end{aligned}$$

The account that records this discount is called **Purchases Discounts**. It, too, is a contra-expense account because it lowers the cost of purchases.

Remember: Purchases are debits; purchases discounts are credits.

Purchases Discounts

Dr.	Cr.
	70

← Normal balance is a credit.

Let's analyze and prepare a general journal entry:

Accounts Affected	Category	↑↓	Rules	T Account Update
Accounts Payable, Mattel	Liability	↓	Dr.	Accounts Payable / Mattel Account — Dr. 500, 3,500 / Cr. 4,000, 3,500 — Mattel: Dr. 500 / 4,000, 3,500
Purchases Discounts	Expense (Contra)	↑	Cr.	Purchases Discounts — Dr. / Cr. 70
Cash	Asset	↓	Cr.	Cash — Dr. / Cr. 3,430

July	15	Accounts Payable, Mattel	3 5 0 0 00		
		Purchases Discounts			7 0 00
		Cash			3 4 3 0 00
		Paid Mattel balance owed			

After the journal entry is posted and recorded to Mattel, the result will show that Chou saved $70 and totally paid what his company owed to Mattel. The actual or net cost of his purchase is $3,430, calculated as follows:

Purchases	$4,000
− Purchases Returns and Allowances	500
− Purchases Discounts	70
= Net Purchases	$3,430

Freight charges are not taken into consideration in calculating net purchases. Still, they are very important. If the seller is responsible for paying the shipping cost until the goods reach its destination, the freight charges are **F.O.B. destination**. For example, if a seller located in Winnipeg sold goods F.O.B. destination to a buyer in Edmonton, the seller would have to pay the cost of shipping the goods to the buyer.

If the buyer is responsible for paying the shipping costs, the freight charges are **F.O.B. shipping point**. In this situation, the seller sometimes will prepay the freight charges as a matter of convenience and will add it to the invoice of the purchaser.

F.O.B. stands for "free on board" the carrier.

F.O.B. Destination: Seller pays freight to the point of destination.

F.O.B. Shipping Point: Buyer pays freight from the seller's shipping point.

Example

Bill amount ($800 + $80 prepaid freight)	$880
Less 5% cash discount (0.05 × $800)	40
Amount to be paid by buyer	$840

Purchases discounts are not taken on freight.

If the seller ships goods F.O.B. shipping point, legal ownership (title) passes to the buyer *when the goods are shipped.* If goods are shipped by the seller F.O.B. destination, title will change *when goods have reached their destination.*

> When does title to goods shipped change?

LEARNING UNIT 6-5 REVIEW

AT THIS POINT you should be able to:

◆ Explain and calculate purchases, purchases returns and allowances, and purchases discounts. (pp. 264–266)

◆ Calculate net purchases. (p. 266)

◆ Explain why purchases discounts are not taken on freight. (p. 266)

◆ Compare and contrast F.O.B. destination with F.O.B. shipping point. (p. 266)

Self-Review Quiz 6-5

(The forms you need are on page 6-7 of the *Study Guide with Working Papers.*)

Which of the following statements are false?

1. Net Purchases = Purchases − Purchases Returns and Allowances − Purchases Discounts.
2. Purchases are a contra-expense.
3. F.O.B. destination means the seller covers the shipping cost and retains title until the goods reach their destination.
4. Purchases discounts are not taken on freight.
5. Purchases Discounts is a contra-expense account.

Solution to Self-Review Quiz 6-5

Number 2 is false.

Quiz Tip						
	Buyer				*Seller*	
Purchase	Dr.	Cost		Sale	Cr.	Revenue
PRA	Cr.	Contra-cost		SRA	Dr.	Contra-revenue
PD	Cr.	Contra-cost		SD	Dr.	Contra-revenue

Learning Unit 6-6

Steps Taken in Purchasing Merchandise and Recording Purchases

6 Using Purchase Requisitions, Purchase Orders, recording Purchase Invoices and Purchase Returns (the debit memorandum) into the Purchases Journal and General Journal, and recording these events to the AP sub-ledger as well as posting to the General Ledger

Merchandising companies must take specific steps when they purchase goods for resale. Let's look at the steps Art's Wholesale Clothing Company took when it ordered goods from Abby Blake Company on April 1.

STEPS TAKEN BY ART'S WHOLESALE WHEN ORDERING GOODS

Step 1: Prepare a Purchase Requisition at Art's Wholesale

The inventory clerk notes a low inventory level of ladies' jackets for resale, so he sends a **purchase requisition** to the purchasing department. A duplicate copy is sent to the accounting department. A third copy remains with the department that initiated the request to allow follow-up on any late or missing shipments.

Authorized personnel initiate purchase requisitions. No example is shown here because this is strictly an internal form.

Step 2: Purchasing Department of Art's Wholesale Prepares a Purchase Order

After checking various price lists and suppliers' catalogues, the purchasing department fills out a form called a **purchase order**. This form gives Abby Blake Company the authority to ship the ladies' jackets ordered by Art's Wholesale Clothing Company (see Figure 6-8). Note that purchase orders do not result in any formal entries on the issuer's books. Most accounting software (such as Simply Accounting®) can easily handle the issuance of purchase orders. Purchase orders are usually pre-numbered so that they are easy to keep track of.

There are four copies of the purchase order: (1) (original) goes to supplier; (2) is sent to accounting department; (3) goes to department that initiated purchase requisition; (4) is filed in purchasing department.

Step 3: Sales Invoice Prepared by Abby Blake Company

Abby Blake Company receives the purchase order and prepares a sales invoice. The sales invoice for the seller is the **purchase invoice** for the buyer. A sales invoice is shown in Figure 6-9.

The invoice shows that the goods will be shipped F.O.B. Quebec City. This means that Art's Wholesale Clothing Company must pay the shipping costs. The sales invoice shows this freight charge. This means that Abby Blake prepaid the

Figure 6-8
Purchase Order

Most accounting software can easily create, print, and manage purchase orders. Even in programs such as *Simply Accounting®*, no accounts are debited or credited when a P.O. is created.

Purchase Order No. 41
Art's Wholesale Clothing Company
1528 Belle Avenue
Toronto, Ontario M5A 2L4

Purchased From: Abby Blake Company
12 Foster Road
Quebec City, QC G1M 4H3

Date: April 1, 2013
Shipped Via: Freight truck
Terms: 2/10, n/60
FOB: Quebec City

Quantity	Description	Unit Price	Total
100	Ladies' Jackets Code 14-0	$50	$5,000

Art's Wholesale
By: Bill Joy

Purchase order number must appear on all invoices.

Figure 6-9
Sales Invoice

```
                    Sales Invoice No. 228
                    Abby Blake Company
                      12 Foster Road
                  Quebec City, QC G1M 4H3
```

Sold to: Art's Wholesale   Date: April 1, 2013
         Clothing Co.   Shipped Via: Freight truck
         1528 Belle Avenue   Terms: 2/10, n/60
         Toronto, ON   Your Order No.: 41
         M5A 2L4   FOB: Quebec City

Quantity	Description	Unit Price	Total
100	Ladies' Jackets Code 14-0	$50	$5,000
	Freight		50
			$5,050

shipping costs as a matter of convenience. Art's Wholesale will repay the freight charges when it pays the invoice.

Step 4: Receiving the Goods

When goods are received, Art's Wholesale inspects the shipment and completes a **receiving report**. The receiving report verifies that the exact merchandise that was ordered was received in good condition.

Step 5: Verifying the Numbers

Before the invoice is approved for recording and payment, the accounting department must check the purchase order, invoice, and receiving report to make sure that all are in agreement and that no steps have been omitted. The form used for checking and approval is an **invoice approval form** (see Figure 6-10).

Remember that Art's Wholesale Clothing Company does not record this purchase in its accounting records until the *invoice is approved for recording and payment.* However, Abby Blake Company records this transaction in its records when the sales invoice is prepared.

Figure 6-10
Invoice Approval Form

```
                INVOICE APPROVAL FORM

Purchase order #                        _____

Requisition check                       _____

Purchase order check                    _____

Receiving report check                  _____

Invoice check                           _____

Approved for payment                    _____
```

This can be rubber-stamped on invoices in some companies.

THE PURCHASES JOURNAL AND ACCOUNTS PAYABLE SUBSIDIARY LEDGER

Let's look at how Art's Wholesale Clothing Company journalizes, posts, and records to the accounts payable subsidiary ledger. We will also look at the **purchases journal**, a multicolumn special journal that Art's Wholesale uses to record the buying of merchandise or other items on account, and the **accounts payable subsidiary ledger**, an alphabetical record of the amounts owed to creditors from purchases on account.

For example, on April 2, Art's Wholesale Clothing Company records the following in its purchases journal:

- ◆ Date: April 2, 2013
- ◆ Account Credited: Abby Blake Company
- ◆ Date of Invoice: April 1
- ◆ Invoice Number: 228
- ◆ Terms: 2/10, n/60
- ◆ Accounts payable: $5,050; Purchases: $5,000; Freight-in, $50

See Figure 6-11 for a complete purchases journal.

As soon as the information is journalized in the purchases journal (see Figure 6-11), you should:

1. Record in the Abby Blake Co. account in the accounts payable subsidiary ledger to indicate that the amount owed is now $5,050. When this is complete, place a ✔ in the PR column of the purchases journal.
2. Post to Freight-In, account No. 514, in the general ledger right away. When this is complete, record 514 in the PR column under Sundry in the purchases journal.

Note that the normal balance in the accounts payable subsidiary ledger is a credit.

The posting and recording rules are similar to those shown previously in this chapter, but here we are looking at the buyer rather than the seller.

THE DEBIT MEMORANDUM

Earlier in this chapter (page 256), Art's Wholesale Clothing Company had to handle returned goods as a seller. It did this by issuing credit memoranda to customers who returned goods or received an allowance on the price. In this part of the chapter, Art's must handle returns as a buyer. It does this by using debit memoranda. A **debit memorandum** is a piece of paper issued by a customer to a seller, which indicates that a return or allowance is required.

Suppose that, on April 6, Art's Wholesale had purchased men's hats for $800 from Thorpe Company (see Figure 6-11). On April 9, 20 hats valued at $200 were found to have defective brims. Art's issued a debit memorandum to Thorpe Company, as shown in Figure 6-12. At some point in the future, Thorpe will issue Art's a credit memorandum. Let's look at how Art's Wholesale Clothing Company handles such a transaction in its accounting records.

Journalizing and Posting the Debit Memo

First, let's look at a transaction analysis chart.

Result of debit memo: debits or reduces Accounts Payable. On seller's books, accounts affected would include Sales Returns and Allowances and Accounts Receivable.

Accounts Affected	Category	↑ ↓	Rules
Accounts Payable	Liability	↓	Dr.
Purchases Returns and Allowances	Expense (Contra)	↑	Cr.

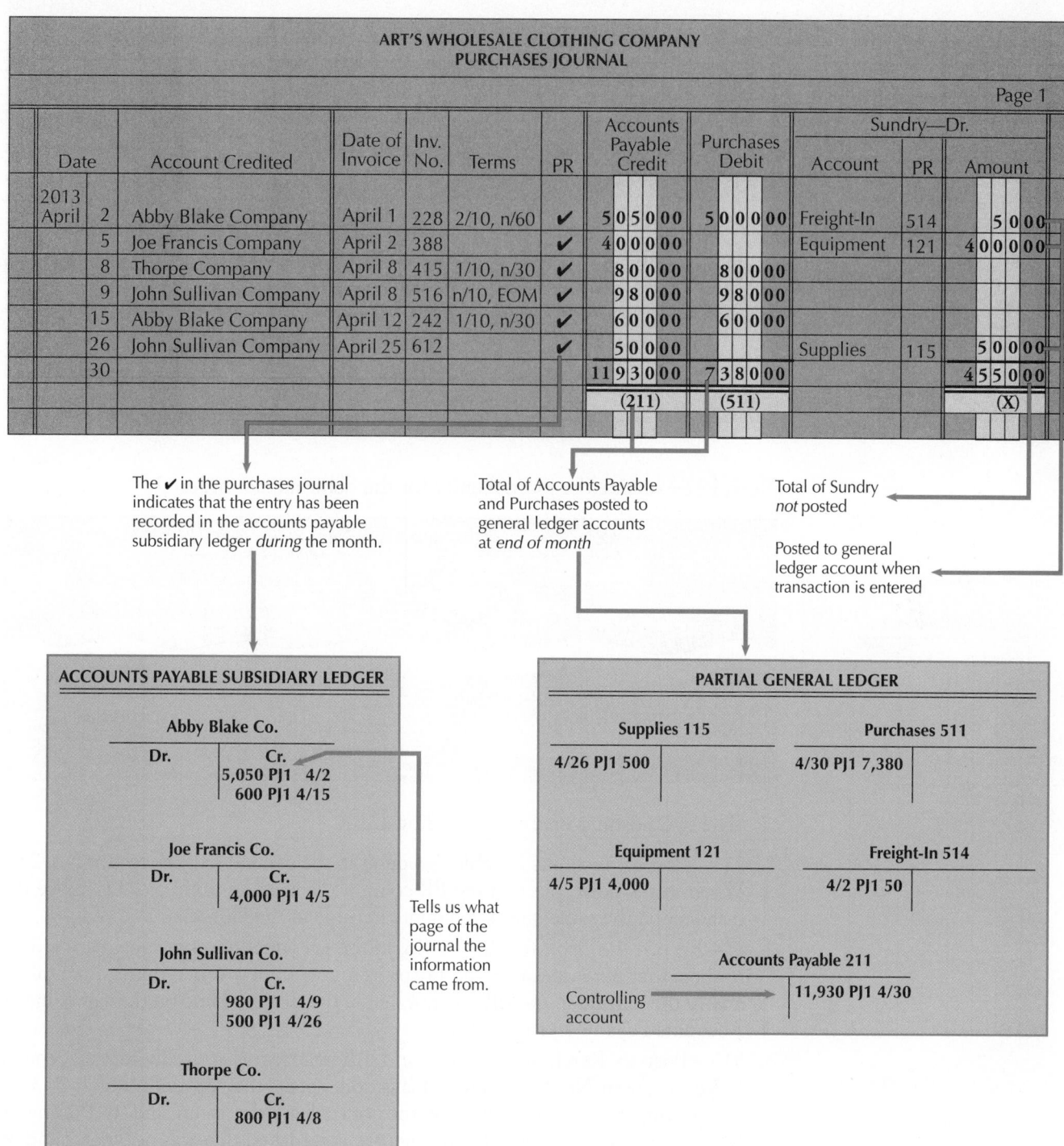

Figure 6-11 Purchases Journal

Figure 6-12
Debit Memorandum

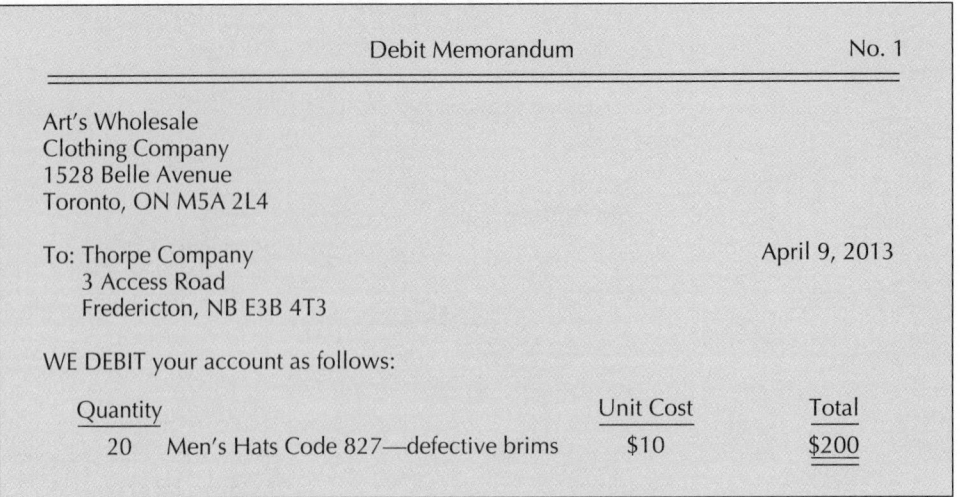

Next, let's examine the journal entry for the debit memorandum:

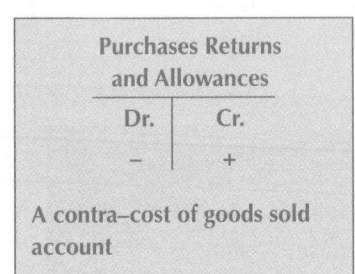

Purchases Returns and Allowances

Dr.	Cr.
–	+

A contra–cost of goods sold account

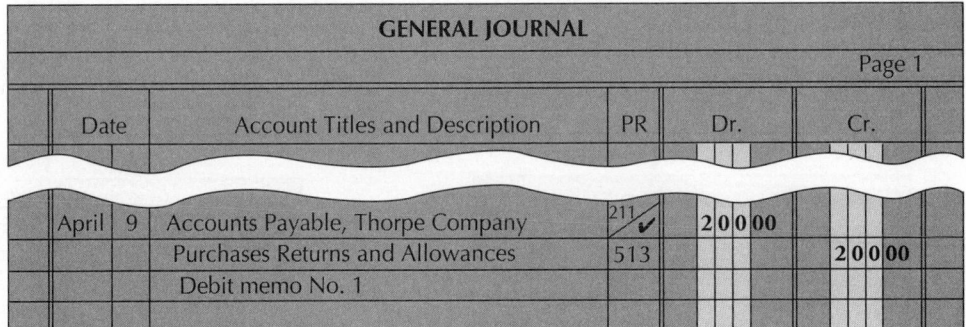

The two postings and one recording are:

1. 211—Post to Accounts Payable as a debit in the general ledger account No. 211. When this is done, place in the PR column the account number, 211, above the diagonal on the same line as Accounts Payable in the journal.

2. ✔—Record the debit to Thorpe Co. in the accounts payable subsidiary ledger to show that Art's doesn't owe Thorpe as much money. When this is done, place a ✔ in the journal in the PR column below the diagonal line on the same line as Accounts Payable in the journal.

3. 513—Post to Purchases Returns and Allowances as a credit in the general ledger (account No. 513). When this is done, place the account number, 513, in the posting reference column of the journal on the same line as Purchases Returns and Allowances. (If equipment was returned that was not merchandise for resale, we would credit Equipment and not Purchases Returns and Allowances.)

LEARNING UNIT 6-6 REVIEW

AT THIS POINT you should be able to:

◆ Explain the relationship between a purchase requisition, a purchase order, and a purchase invoice. (p. 268)

◆ Explain why a typical invoice approval form may be used. (p. 269)

◆ Journalize transactions in a purchases journal. (pp. 270 and 271)

◆ Explain how to record the accounts payable subsidiary ledger and post to the general ledger from a purchases journal. (p. 271)

◆ Explain a debit memorandum and be able to journalize an entry resulting from its issuance. (pp. 270 and 272)

Self-Review Quiz 6-6

(The forms you need are on pages 6-7 to 6-9 of the *Study Guide with Working Papers*.)

Journalize the following transactions in the purchases journal or general journal for Munroe Co. Record in the accounts payable subsidiary ledger and post to general ledger accounts as appropriate. Use the same journal headings that we used for Art's Wholesale Clothing Company.

2014

May   5   Bought merchandise on account from Flynn Co., invoice No. 512, dated May 2, terms 1/10, n/30, $900.

        6   Bought merchandise from John Butler Company, invoice No. 403, dated May 5, terms n/10, EOM, $1,000.

      13   Issued debit memo No. 1 to Flynn Co. for merchandise returned, $300, from invoice No. 512.

      16   Purchased $400 worth of equipment on account from John Butler Company, invoice No. 413, dated May 15.

Solution to Self-Review Quiz 6-6

Quiz Tip	
Buyer	*Seller*
Issues Debit Memo	Receives Debit Memo
Receives Credit Memo	Issues Credit Memo
Dr. Accounts Payable	Dr. SRA
Cr. PRA	Cr. Accounts Receivable

MUNROE CO. PURCHASES JOURNAL

Page 2

Date		Account Credited	Date of Invoice	Inv. No.	Terms	PR	Accounts Payable Credit	Purchases Debit	Sundry—Dr. Account	PR	Amount
2014 May	5	Flynn Co.	May 2	512	1/10, n/30	✔	90000	90000			
	6	John Butler	May 5	403	n/10, EOM	✔	100000	100000			
	16	John Butler	May 15	413		✔	40000		Equip.	121	40000
	31						230000	190000			40000
							(212)	(512)			(X)

MUNROE CO. GENERAL JOURNAL

Page 1

Date		Account Titles and Description	PR	Dr.	Cr.
2014 May	13	Accounts Payable, Flynn Co.	212 ✔	30000	
		Purchases Returns and Allowances	513		30000
		Debit memo #1			

ACCOUNTS PAYABLE SUBSIDIARY LEDGER

JOHN BUTLER COMPANY
18 REED ROAD
WINNIPEG, MB R2B 8G6

Date 2014		Explanation	Post. Ref.	Debit	Credit	CR. Balance
May	6		PJ2		100000	100000
	16		PJ2		40000	140000

FLYNN COMPANY
15 FOSS AVENUE
QUEBEC CITY, QC G1L 2W4

Date 2014		Explanation	Post. Ref.	Debit	Credit	CR. Balance
May	5		PJ2		90000	90000
	13		GJ1	30000		60000

PARTIAL GENERAL LEDGER

Equipment   Acct. No. 121

Date 2014	Explanation	Post. Ref.	Debit	Credit	DR or CR	Balance
May 16		PJ2	4 00 00		DR.	4 00 00

Accounts Payable   Acct. No. 212

Date 2014	Explanation	Post. Ref.	Debit	Credit	DR or CR	Balance
May 13		GJ1	3 00 00		DR.	3 00 00
31		PJ2		2 3 00 00	CR.	2 00 00

Purchases   Acct. No. 512

Date 2014	Explanation	Post. Ref.	Debit	Credit	DR or CR	Balance
May 31		PJ2	1 90 0 00		DR.	1 90 0 00

Purchases Returns and Allowances   Acct. No. 513

Date 2014	Explanation	Post. Ref.	Debit	Credit	DR or CR	Balance
May 13		GJ1		3 00 00	CR.	3 00 00

Learning Unit 6-7

The Cash Payments Journal and Schedule of Accounts Payable

7   Entering transactions into the Cash Payments Journal, recording to the AP sub-ledger, posting to the General Ledger accounts, and preparing a schedule of Accounts Payable

Art's Wholesale Clothing Company will record all payments made by cheque in a **cash payments journal** (also called a *cash disbursements journal*). In many ways, the structure of this journal resembles that of the cash receipts journal discussed earlier in this chapter. Now, however, we are looking at the outward flow of cash instead of the inward flow.

Art's Wholesale conducted the following cash transactions in April:

2013
April   2   Issued cheque No. 101 to Pete Blum for insurance paid in advance, $900.

        5   Issued cheque No. 102 to Joe Francis Company in payment of its April 2 invoice No. 388.

        9   Issued cheque No. 103 to Rick Flo Co. for merchandise purchased for cash, $800.

      12   Issued cheque No. 104 to Thorpe Company in payment of its April 5 invoice No. 415 less the return and discount.

      26   Issued cheque No. 105, $700, for salaries paid.

The diagram in Figure 6-13 shows the cash payments journal for the end of April, along with the recordings in the accounts payable subsidiary ledger and postings to the general ledger. Study the diagram; we will review it in a moment.

Figure 6-13
Cash Payments Journal
Recording and Posting

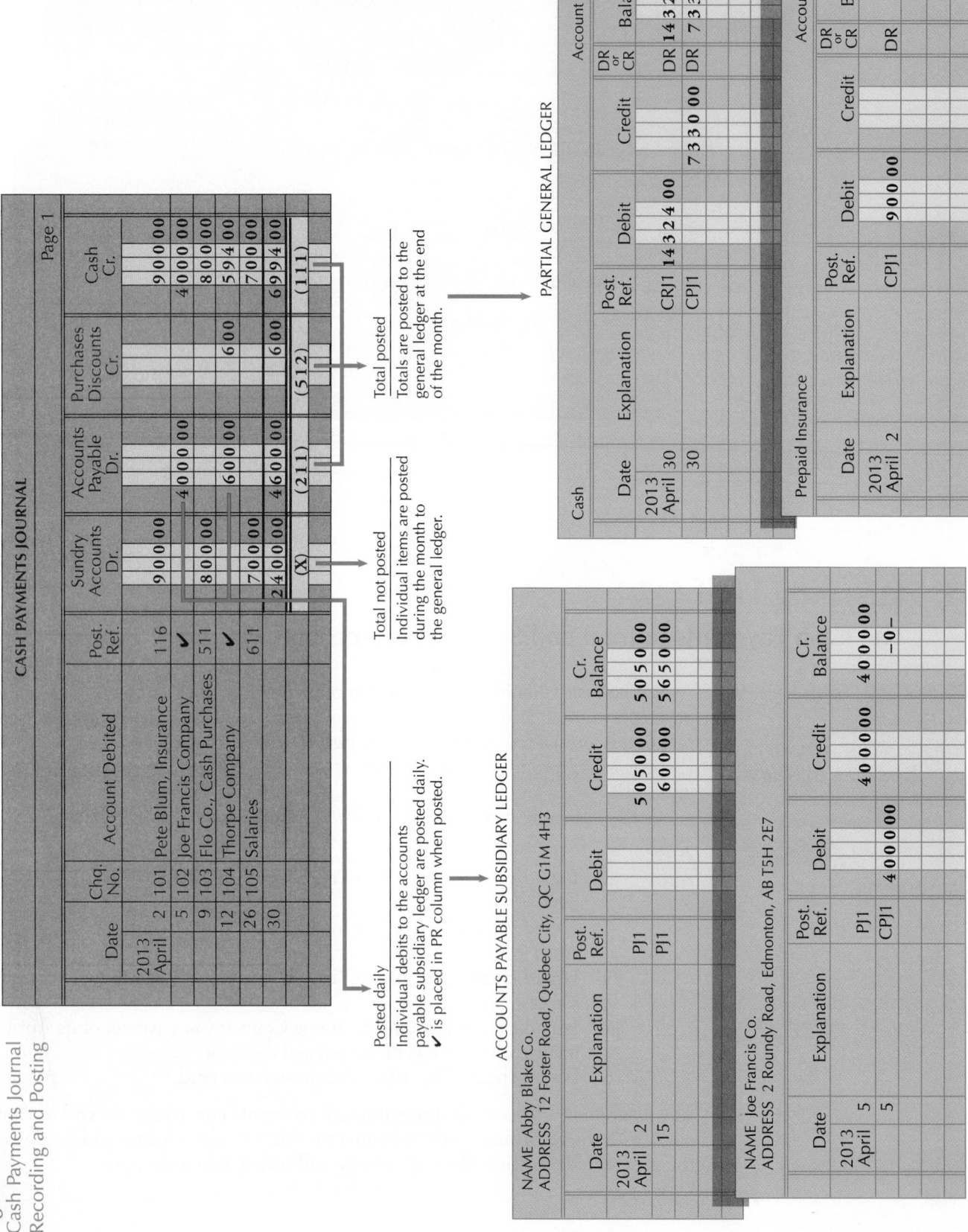

Figure 6-13 (continued)

Controlling Account →

Accounts Payable — Account No. 211

Date	Explanation	Post. Ref.	Debit	Credit	DR or CR	Balance
2013 April 9		GJ1	20000		DR	20000
30		PJ1		1193000	CR	1173000
30		CPJ1	460000		CR	713000

Purchases — Account No. 511

Date	Explanation	Post. Ref.	Debit	Credit	DR or CR	Balance
2013 April 9		CPJ1	80000	.	DR	80000
30		PJ1	738000		DR	818000

Purchases Discounts — Account No. 512

Date	Explanation	Post. Ref.	Debit	Credit	DR or CR	Balance
2013 April 30		CPJ1		600	CR	600

Salaries Expense — Account No. 611

Date	Explanation	Post. Ref.	Debit	Credit	DR or CR	Balance
2013 April 26		CPJ1	70000		DR	70000

NAME John Sullivan Co.
ADDRESS 18 Print Street, Regina, SK S4P 2A6

Date	Explanation	Post. Ref.	Debit	Credit	Cr. Balance
2013 April 9		PJ1		98000	98000
26		PJ1		50000	148000

NAME Thorpe Co.
ADDRESS 3 Access Road, Fredericton, NB E3B 4T3

Date	Explanation	Post. Ref.	Debit	Credit	Cr. Balance
2013 April 8		PJ1		80000	80000
9		GJ1	20000		60000
12		CPJ1	60000		-0-

NAME Joe Francis Co.
ADDRESS 2 Roundy Road, Edmonton, AB T5H 2E7

Date	Explanation	Post. Ref.	Debit	Credit	Cr. Balance
2013 April 4		PJ1		400000	400000
5		CPJ1	400000		-0-
15		GJ4	40000		(40000)

Note on Accounts Payable balance: Very occasionally (perhaps because of the return of defective goods after they have been paid for), a debit balance may be called for in Accounts Payable. Debit balances are opposite to the normal credit balance and are signified by placing the balance in brackets. For example, suppose we get a credit note from Joe Francis Co. for $400 after we have paid off its account completely. The account would then appear as follows:

JOURNALIZING, POSTING, AND RECORDING FROM THE CASH PAYMENTS JOURNAL TO THE ACCOUNTS PAYABLE SUBSIDIARY LEDGER AND THE GENERAL LEDGER

Figure 6-13 shows how Art's Wholesale Clothing Company recorded the payment of cash on April 12 to Thorpe Company. The purchases journal (page 271) shows that Art's purchased $800 worth of merchandise from Thorpe on account on April 8. The amount Art's owes is discounted 1%. The amount paid ($800 – $200 returns) is recorded in the accounts payable subsidiary ledger as soon as the entry is made in the cash payments journal. The payment reduces the balance owing to Thorpe to zero. Art's Wholesale Clothing Company receives a $6 purchases discount.

At the end of the month, the totals of the Cash, Purchases Discounts, and Accounts Payable accounts are posted to the general ledger. The total of Sundry is *not* posted. The accounts Prepaid Insurance, Purchases, and Salaries Expense are posted to the general ledger at the time the entry is put in the journal.

The cash payments journal of Art's Wholesale Clothing Company can be cross-footed as follows:

$$\text{Debit Columns} = \text{Credit Columns}$$

Sundry	+	Accounts Payable	=	Purchases Discounts	+	Cash
$2,400	+	$4,600	=	$6	+	$6,994

$$\$7,000 = \$7,000$$

Schedule of Accounts Payable

Now let's prove that the sum of the accounts payable subsidiary ledger at the end of the month is equal to the controlling account, Accounts Payable, at the end of April for Art's Wholesale Clothing Company. To do this, creditors with an ending balance in Art's Wholesale's accounts payable subsidiary ledger must be listed in the schedule of accounts payable (see Figure 6-14). At the end of the month, the total owed ($7,130) in Accounts Payable, the **controlling account** in the general ledger, should equal the sum of what is owed the individual creditors who are listed on the schedule of accounts payable. If it doesn't, the journalizing, posting, and recording must be checked to ensure that they are complete. Also, the balance of each account should be checked.

Trade Discounts

Trade discounts are reductions from the purchase price. Usually, they are given to customers who buy items to resell or use to produce other saleable goods.

$$\text{Amount of Trade Discount} = \text{List Price} - \text{Net Price}$$

Different trade discounts are available to different classes of customers. Often, trade discounts are listed in catalogues that contain the list price and the amount of trade discount available. Such catalogues usually are updated by discount sheets.

ART'S WHOLESALE CLOTHING COMPANY
SCHEDULE OF ACCOUNTS PAYABLE
APRIL 30, 2013

Abby Blake Co.	$5 6 5 0 00
John Sullivan Co.	1 4 8 0 00
Total Accounts Payable	$7 1 3 0 00

Figure 6-14
Schedule of Accounts Payable

Trade discounts have *no relationship* to whether a customer is paying a bill early. Trade discounts and list prices are not shown in the accounts of either the purchaser or the seller. Cash discounts are not taken on the amount of trade discount.

For example, look at the following:

- List price, $800
- 30% trade discount
- 5% cash discount
- *Thus:* Invoice cost of $560 ($800 − $240) less the cash discount of $28 ($560 × 0.05) results in a final cost of $532 if the cash discount is taken.

The purchaser as well as the seller would record the invoice amount at $560.

LEARNING UNIT 6-7 REVIEW

AT THIS POINT you should be able to:

- Journalize, post, and record transactions utilizing a cash payments journal. (pp. 275–277)
- Prepare a schedule of accounts payable. (p. 278)
- Compare and contrast a cash discount with a trade discount. (p. 278)

Self-Review Quiz 6-7

(The forms you need are on pages 6-9 and 6-10 of the *Study Guide with Working Papers.*)

Given the following information, journalize, cross-foot, and, when appropriate, record and post the transactions of Melissa Company. Use the same headings as used for Art's Wholesale. All purchases discounts are 2/12, n/30. The cash payments journal is page 2.

Accounts Payable Subsidiary Ledger

Name	Balance	Invoice No.
Bob Finkelstein	$300	488
Al Jeep	200	410

Partial General Ledger

Account No.	Balance
Cash 110	$700
Accounts Payable 210	500
Purchases Discounts 511	—
Advertising Expense 610	—

2012
June 1 Issued cheque No. 15 to Al Jeep in payment of its May 25 invoice No. 410, less purchases discount.

7 Issued cheque No. 16 to Moss Advertising Co. to pay advertising bill due, $75, no discount.

8 Issued cheque No. 17 to Bob Finkelstein in payment of his May 28 invoice No. 488, less purchases discounts.

Solution to Self-Review Quiz 6-7

MELISSA COMPANY
CASH PAYMENTS JOURNAL

Page 2

Date		Chq. No.	Account Debited	Post. Ref.	Sundry Accounts Dr.	Accounts Payable Dr.	Purchases Discounts Cr.	Cash Cr.
2012 June	1	15	Al Jeep	✔		200 00	4 00	196 00
	7	16	Advertising Expense	610	75 00			75 00
	8	17	Bob Finkelstein	✔		300 00	6 00	294 00
					75 00	500 00	10 00	565 00
					(X)	(210)	(511)	(110)

$$\$75 + \$500 = \$10 + \$565$$
$$\underline{\$575 = \$575}$$

ACCOUNTS PAYABLE SUBSIDIARY LEDGER

NAME Bob Finkelstein
ADDRESS 112 Flying Highway, Montreal, QC H1K 2H7

Date		Explanation	Post. Ref.	Debit	Credit	Cr. Balance
2012 June	1	Balance	✔			300 00
	8		CPJ2	300 00		–0–

NAME Al Jeep
ADDRESS 118 Wang Road, London, ON N5X 2Y3

Date		Explanation	Post. Ref.	Debit	Credit	Cr. Balance
2012 June	1	Balance	✔			200 00
	1		CPJ2	200 00		–0–

Quiz Tip

The balance of the accounts payable subsidiary ledger is zero.

PARTIAL GENERAL LEDGER

Cash   Acct. No. 110

Date 2012		Explanation	Post. Ref.	Debit	Credit	DR or CR	Balance
June	1	Balance	✔			DR	7 0 0 00
	30		CPJ2		5 6 5 00	DR	1 3 5 00

Accounts Payable   Acct. No. 210 ← Controlling account

Date 2012		Explanation	Post. Ref.	Debit	Credit	DR or CR	Balance
June	1	Balance	✔			CR	5 0 0 00
	30		CPJ2	5 0 0 00			– 0 –

Purchases Discounts   Acct. No. 511

Date 2012	Explanation	Post. Ref.	Debit	Credit	DR or CR	Balance
June 30		CPJ2		1 0 00	CR	1 0 00

Advertising Expense   Acct. No. 610

Date 2012	Explanation	Post. Ref.	Debit	Credit	DR or CR	Balance
June 7		CPJ2	7 5 00		DR	7 5 00

Quiz Tip

The normal balance of the accounts payable subsidiary ledger is a credit.

COMPREHENSIVE DEMONSTRATION PROBLEM WITH SOLUTION TIPS

(The forms you need are on pages 6-11 to 6-16 of the *Study Guide with Working Papers*.)

a. Journalize, record, and post the following transactions as needed to the sales, purchases, cash receipts, cash payments, and general journals. All terms are 2/10, n/30 on both sales and purchases.

b. Prepare a schedule of accounts receivable and accounts payable.

		2013	
CRJ	July	2	Walter Lantz invested $8,000 in the business.
PJ		3	Purchased $2,000 merchandise from Patel & Sons, their invoice No. 756.
SJ		4	Sold merchandise on account to Panda Co., invoice No. 1—$300.
SJ		5	Sold merchandise on account to Buzzard Co., invoice No. 2—$600.
CR		6	Cash sale—$400.
GJ		8	Issued credit memorandum No. 1 to Panda Co. for defective merchandise—$100.
		9	Purchased $1,150 merchandise from Black Brothers, their invoice No. 2014.
		10	Return $400 defective merchandise to Patel & Sons.
CRJ		11	Received cheque from Panda Co. for invoice No. 1 less returns and discount.
		12	Paid amount owing to Black Brothers, Chq. 101.
CRJ		16	Cash sale—$500.
SJ		19	Sold merchandise on account to Panda Co.—$550, invoice No. 3.
		22	Purchased $1,800 merchandise from Black Brothers, their invoice No. 2092.
		24	Purchased $1,700 store display equipment from Adkins & Co., their invoice No. 1762.
		26	Paid amount due to Adkins & Co., Chq. 102.
		29	Wrote Chq. 103 for $250 to City News for ad.
		31	Chq. 104 to Fern Supplies for cash purchase. Invoice 2178—$640.00.

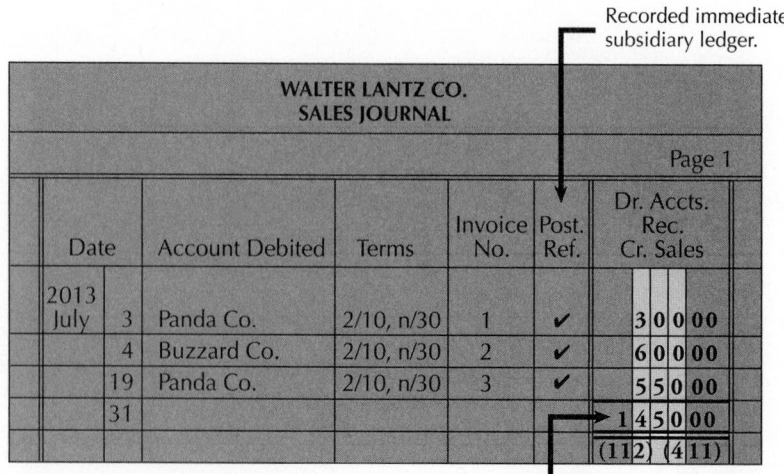

Recorded immediately in subsidiary ledger.

WALTER LANTZ CO. SALES JOURNAL

Page 1

Date		Account Debited	Terms	Invoice No.	Post. Ref.	Dr. Accts. Rec. Cr. Sales
2013 July	3	Panda Co.	2/10, n/30	1	✔	3 0 0 00
	4	Buzzard Co.	2/10, n/30	2	✔	6 0 0 00
	19	Panda Co.	2/10, n/30	3	✔	5 5 0 00
	31					1 4 5 0 00
						(112) (411)

Total posted at end of month to general ledger accounts.

Record in subsidiary ledger immediately.

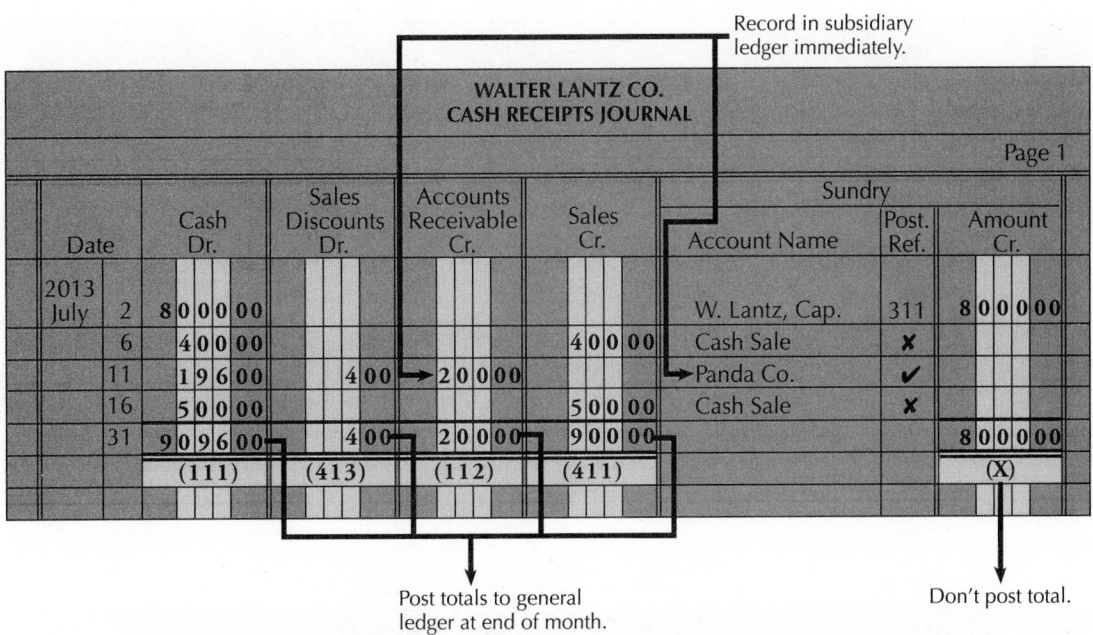

WALTER LANTZ CO.
CASH RECEIPTS JOURNAL

Page 1

Date	Cash Dr.	Sales Discounts Dr.	Accounts Receivable Cr.	Sales Cr.	Sundry Account Name	Post. Ref.	Amount Cr.
2013 July 2	8 0 0 0 00				W. Lantz, Cap.	311	8 0 0 0 00
6	4 0 0 00			4 0 0 00	Cash Sale	✗	
11	1 9 6 00	4 00	2 0 0 00		Panda Co.	✔	
16	5 0 0 00			5 0 0 00	Cash Sale	✗	
31	9 0 9 6 00	4 00	2 0 0 00	9 0 0 00			8 0 0 0 00
	(111)	(413)	(112)	(411)			(X)

Post totals to general ledger at end of month.

Don't post total.

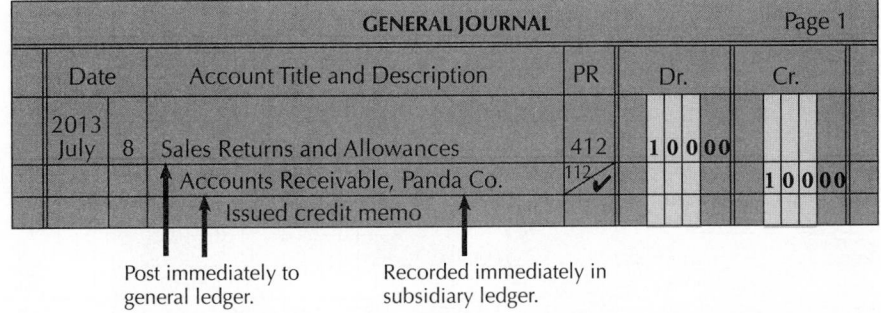

	Date	Account Title and Description	PR	Dr.	Cr.
	2013 July 8	Sales Returns and Allowances	412	1 0 0 00	
		Accounts Receivable, Panda Co.	112 ✔		1 0 0 00
		Issued credit memo			

GENERAL JOURNAL — Page 1

Post immediately to general ledger.

Recorded immediately in subsidiary ledger.

Accounts receivable subsidiary ledger usually contains accounts with debit balances

Accounts Receivable Subsidiary Ledger

Buzzard Co.

Date	PR	Debit	Credit	Dr. Balance
2013 July 4	SJ1	6 0 0 00		6 0 0 00

Panda Co.

Date	PR	Debit	Credit	Dr. Balance
2013 July 4	SJ1	3 0 0 00		3 0 0 00
8	GJ1		1 0 0 00	2 0 0 00
11	CRJ1		2 0 0 00	– 0 –
19	SJ1	5 5 0 00		5 5 0 00

General Ledger

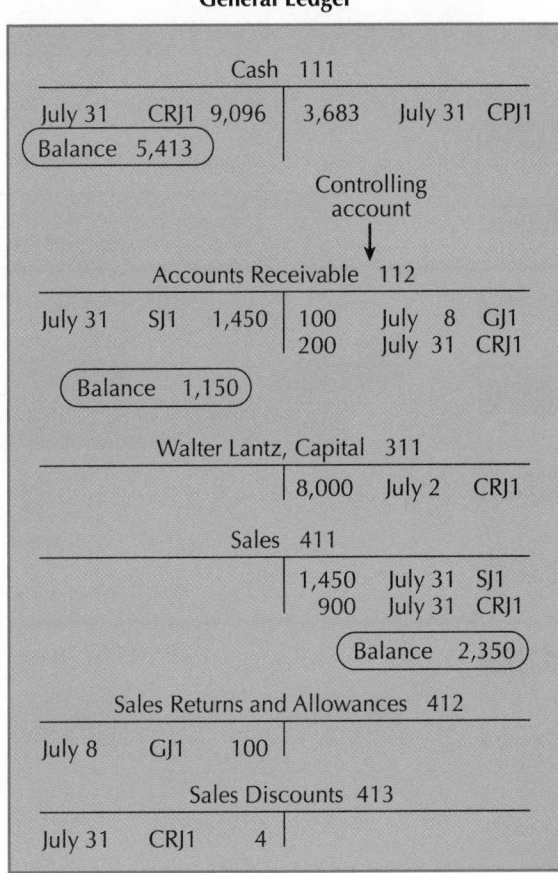

Cash 111

July 31	CRJ1	9,096	3,683	July 31	CPJ1

Balance 5,413

Controlling account

Accounts Receivable 112

July 31	SJ1	1,450	100	July 8	GJ1
			200	July 31	CRJ1

Balance 1,150

Walter Lantz, Capital 311

	8,000	July 2	CRJ1

Sales 411

	1,450	July 31	SJ1
	900	July 31	CRJ1

Balance 2,350

Sales Returns and Allowances 412

July 8	GJ1	100	

Sales Discounts 413

July 31	CRJ1	4	

WALTER LANTZ CO.
PURCHASES JOURNAL

Page 1

	Date	Accounts Credited	Date of Invoice	Invoice Number	Terms	Post. Ref.	Accounts Receivable Cr.	Purchases Dr.	Sundry Dr. Account	Post. Ref.	Amount
2013 July	5	Patel & Sons	July 5	756	2/10, N/30	✔	2 0 0 0 00	2 0 0 0 00			
	9	Black Brothers	July 7	2014	2/10, N/30	✔	1 1 5 0 00	1 1 5 0 00			
	22	Black Brothers	July 21	2092	2/10, N/30	✔	1 8 0 0 00	1 8 0 0 00			
	24	Adkins & Co.	July 24	1762	2/10, N/30	✔	1 7 0 0 00		Equipment	141	1 7 0 0 00
							6 6 5 0 00	4 9 5 0 00			1 7 0 0 00
							(211)	(555)			

Don't post this!

WALTER LANTZ CO.
CASH PAYMENT JOURNAL

Page 1

	Date	Chq. No.	Accounts Debited	Post. Ref.	Sundry Dr.	Accounts Payable Dr.	Purchases Dr.	Purchases Discount Cr.	Cash Cr.
2013 July	12	101	Black Brothers	✔		1 1 5 0 00		2 3 00	1 1 2 7 00
	26	102	Adkins & Co.	✔		1 7 0 0 00		3 4 00	1 6 6 6 00
	29	103	City News - Adv.	601	2 5 0 00				2 5 0 00
	31	104	Fern Supplies				6 4 0 00		6 4 0 00
			Monthly Totals		2 5 0 00	2 8 5 0 00	6 4 0 00	5 7 00	3 6 8 3 00
					(X)	(211)	(555)	(558)	(111)

Total is not posted.

WALTER LANTZ CO.
GENERAL JOURNAL

Page 1

	Date	Account Title and Description	PR	Dr.	Cr.
2013 July	10	Accounts Payable—Patel & Sons	211 ✔	4 0 0 00	
		Purchases Returns & Allowances	556		4 0 0 00
		Return of Goods—See Inv. 756			

WALTER LANTZ Co.
Accounts Payable Ledger

Patel & Sons

Date		Explanation	PR	Debit	Credit	Cr. Balance
2013 July	5		PJ1		2 0 0 0 00	2 0 0 0 00
	10		GJ1	4 0 0 00		1 6 0 0 00

Black Brothers

Date		Explanation	PR	Debit	Credit	Cr. Balance
2013 July	9		PJ1		1 1 5 0 00	1 1 5 0 00
	12		CPJ1	1 1 5 0 00		– 0 –
	22		PJ1		1 8 0 0 00	1 8 0 0 00

Adkins & Co.

Date		Explanation	PR	Debit	Credit	Cr. Balance
2013 July	24		PJ1		1 7 0 0 00	1 7 0 0 00
	26		CPJ1	1 7 0 0 00		– 0 –

General Ledger

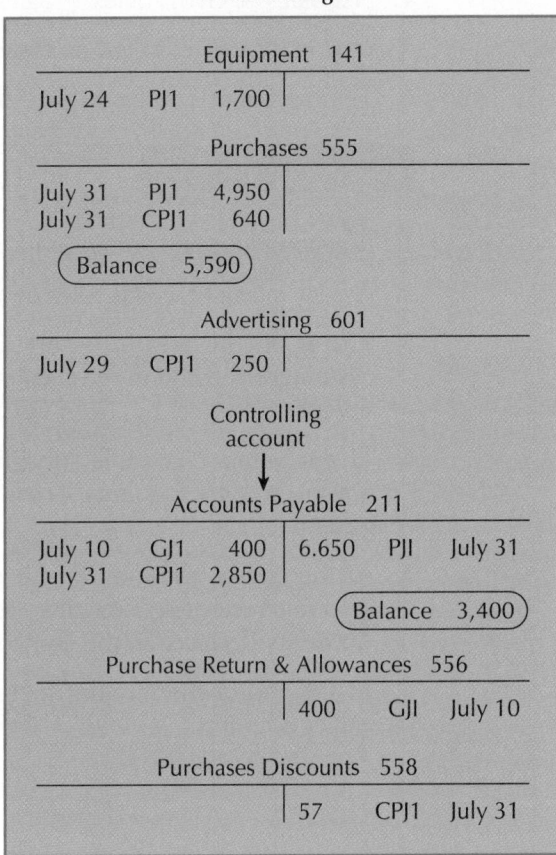

Equipment 141

July 24	PJ1	1,700	

Purchases 555

July 31	PJ1	4,950	
July 31	CPJ1	640	

(Balance 5,590)

Advertising 601

July 29	CPJ1	250	

Controlling
account
↓

Accounts Payable 211

July 10	GJ1	400	6.650	PJI	July 31
July 31	CPJ1	2,850			

(Balance 3,400)

Purchase Return & Allowances 556

			400	GJI	July 10

Purchases Discounts 558

			57	CPJ1	July 31

The controlling accounts (Accounts Receivable and Accounts Payable) at the end of the month equal the sum of the accounts receivable and accounts payable subsidiary ledger.

WALTER LANTZ CO. SCHEDULE OF ACCOUNTS RECEIVABLE JULY 31, 2013	
Buzzard Co.	$ 600 00
Panda Co.	550 00
Total Accounts Receivable	$1 150 00

WALTER LANTZ CO. SCHEDULE OF ACCOUNTS PAYABLE JULY 31, 2013	
Patel & Sons	$ 1 600 00
Black Brothers	1 800 00
	$3 400 00

SUMMARY OF KEY POINTS

Learning Unit 6-1

1. A periodic inventory system records the cost of ending inventory at the end of each accounting period.

2. A perpetual inventory system keeps a continual update of inventory.

3. Sales Returns and Allowances and Sales Discounts are contra-revenue accounts.

4. Net Sales = Gross Sales − Sales Returns and Allowances − Sales Discounts.

5. Discounts are not taken on freight or goods returned.

6. The discount period is shorter than the credit period.

Learning Unit 6-2

1. A general journal is often used with special journals.

2. A sales journal records sales on account.

3. The ✔ in the posting reference column of the sales journal means that a customer's account in the accounts receivable ledger (or the accounts receivable subsidiary ledger) has been updated (or recorded) during the month.

4. The accounts receivable subsidiary ledger, organized in alphabetical order, is not in the same book as Accounts Receivable, the controlling account in the general ledger.

5. At the end of the month, the total of all customers' ending balances in the accounts receivable subsidiary ledger should be equal to the ending balance in Accounts Receivable, the controlling account in the general ledger.

6. At the end of the month, the totals of the sales journal are posted to general ledger accounts.

1. When a credit memorandum is issued, the result is that Sales Returns and Allowances is increasing and Accounts Receivable is decreasing. When we record this in a general journal, we assume that all parts of the transaction will be posted to the general ledger and recorded in the subsidiary ledger when the entry is journalized.

Learning Unit 6-4

1. The cash receipts journal records receipt of cash from any source.

2. Post each item in the sundry column to record the credit part of a transaction that does not occur frequently. Never post the *total* of sundry. Post items in the sundry column to the general ledger when entered.

3. A ✔ in the posting reference column of the cash receipts journal means that the accounts receivable subsidiary ledger has been updated (recorded) with a credit.

4. An ✗ in the cash receipts journal posting reference column means no posting was necessary since the totals of these columns will be posted at the end of the month.

5. Cross-footing means proving that the total of debits and the total of credits are equal in the special journal, thus verifying the accuracy of recording.

6. A schedule of accounts receivable is a listing of the ending balances of customers in the accounts receivable subsidiary ledger. This total should be the same balance as found in the controlling account, Accounts Receivable, in the general ledger.

Learning Unit 6-5

1. Purchases are merchandise for resale. Purchases are expenses.

2. Purchases Returns and Allowances and Purchases Discounts are contra-expense accounts.

3. "F.O.B. shipping point" means that the purchaser of the goods is responsible for covering the shipping costs. If the terms were "F.O.B. destination," the seller would be responsible for covering the shipping costs until the goods reached their destination.

4. Purchases discounts are not taken on freight.

Learning Unit 6-6

1. The steps for buying merchandise from a company may include:
   a. The requesting department prepares a purchase requisition.
   b. The purchasing department prepares a purchase order.
   c. The seller receives the order and prepares a sales invoice (a purchase invoice for the buyer).
   d. The buyer receives the goods and prepares a receiving report.
   e. The accounting department verifies and approves the invoice for payment.

2. The purchases journal records the buying of merchandise or other items on account.

3. The accounts payable subsidiary ledger, organized in alphabetical order, is not in the same book as Accounts Payable, the controlling account in the general ledger.

4. A debit memorandum (issued by the buyer) indicates that the amount owed from a previous purchase is being reduced because some goods were defective or not up to a specific standard and thus were returned or an allowance was requested. On receiving the debit memorandum, the seller should issue a credit memorandum.

Learning Unit 6-7

1. All payments by cheque are recorded in the cash payments journal.

2. At the end of the month, the schedule of accounts payable, a list of ending amounts owed to individual creditors, should equal the ending balance in Accounts Payable, the controlling account in the general ledger.

3. Trade discounts are deductions off the list price that have nothing to do with early payments (cash discounts). Invoice amounts are recorded after the trade discount is deducted. Cash discounts are calculated on the cost after deducting any trade discounts.

KEY TERMS

Accounts payable subsidiary ledger   A book or file that contains the names of the creditors in alphabetical order and the amounts owed from purchases on account (p. 270)

Accounts receivable subsidiary ledger   A book or file that contains the individual records of amounts owed by various credit customers, usually in alphabetical order (p. 251)

Cash payments journal (cash disbursements journal)   A special journal that records all transactions involving payment by cheque (p. 275)

Cash receipts journal   A special journal that records all transactions involving the receipt of cash from any source (p. 259)

Controlling account   (AP) The account in the general ledger that summarizes or controls a subsidiary ledger. *Example:* The Accounts Payable account in the general ledger is the controlling account for the accounts payable subsidiary ledger. After postings are complete, it shows the total amount owed from purchases made on account. (p. 278)

Controlling account (AR) The Accounts Receivable account in the general ledger, after postings are complete, shows the total amount of money owed to a firm. This figure is broken down in the accounts receivable subsidiary ledger, where it indicates specifically who owes the money. (p. 251)

Credit memorandum   A piece of paper sent by the seller to a customer who has returned merchandise previously purchased on credit. The credit memorandum indicates to the customer that the seller is reducing the amount owed by the customer. (p. 278)

Credit period   Length of time allowed for payment of goods sold on account (p. 249)

Cross-footing The process of proving that the total debit columns of a special journal are equal to the total columns of that journal (p. 261)

Debit memorandum   A memo issued by a purchaser to a seller, indicating that some purchases returns and allowances have occurred and therefore the purchaser now owes less money on account (p. 270)

Discount period A period during which a customer can take a cash discount to encourage early payment of bills. The discount period is shorter than the credit period. (p. 249)

F.O.B. "Free on board," which means without shipping charge to the buyer up to a specified location. The seller bears the cost up to the specified location and the buyer bears the cost from that location to the actual destination. (p. 266)

F.O.B. destination *Seller* pays or is responsible for the cost of freight to the destination or purchaser's location (p. 266)

F.O.B. shipping point *Purchaser* pays or is responsible for the shipping costs from the seller's shipping point to the purchaser's location (p. 266)

Gross sales The revenue earned from the sale of merchandise to customers. It has a credit balance. (p. 263)

Invoice approval form The accounting department uses this form in checking the invoice and finally approving it for recording and payment. (p. 269)

Merchandise Goods brought into a store for resale to customers (p. 247)

Net sales Gross sales less sales returns and allowances and less sales discounts (p. 249)

Net purchases Gross purchases less purchase returns and allowances and purchase discounts (p. 266)

Purchase invoice The seller's sales invoice, which is sent to the purchaser (p. 268)

Purchase order A form used in business to place an order to buy goods from a seller (p. 268)

Purchase requisition A form used within a business by the requesting department asking the purchasing department of the business to buy specific goods (p. 268)

Purchases Merchandise for resale. It is an expense. (p. 264)

Purchases Discounts A contra-expense account in the general ledger that records discounts offered by suppliers of merchandise for prompt payment of purchases by buyers. Normally has a credit balance. (p. 266)

Purchases journal A multicolumn special journal that records the buying of merchandise or other items on account (p. 270)

Purchases Returns and Allowances A contra-expense account with a credit balance in the ledger that records the amount of defective or unacceptable merchandise returned to suppliers and/or price reductions given for defective items sold (p. 265)

Receiving report A business form used to notify purchasing and accounting of the ordered goods received, indicating the quantities and specific condition of the goods (p. 269)

Retailer Merchant who buys goods from wholesalers or manufacturers for resale to customers (p. 247)

Sales discount Cash discount granted to customers for payments made within a specific period of time. A contra-revenue account is used to record sales discounts granted. (p. 249)

Sales invoice A bill sent to a customer reflecting a sale, usually on credit (p. 252)

Sales journal A special journal used to record only sales made on account (p. 252)

Sales Returns and Allowances A contra-revenue account that records price adjustments and allowances granted on merchandise that is defective and has been returned. It has a debit balance. (p. 248)

Schedule of accounts receivable A list of the customers, in alphabetical order, that have an outstanding balance in the accounts receivable subsidiary ledger. This total should be equal to the balance of the Accounts Receivable controlling account in the general ledger at the end of the month. (p. 262)

Special journal A journal used to record similar groups of transactions. *Example:* the sales journal, which records all sales on account (p. 251)

Subsidiary ledger A ledger that contains accounts of a single type. *Example:* the accounts receivable subsidiary ledger, which records all customers that purchase goods on account (p. 251)

Sundry Accounts Miscellaneous accounts column(s) in a special journal, which records transactions that do not occur often (p. 259)

Wholesalers Those who buy goods from suppliers and manufacturers for sale to retailers (p. 247)

Summary of How to Post and Record Single-Column Sales Journal

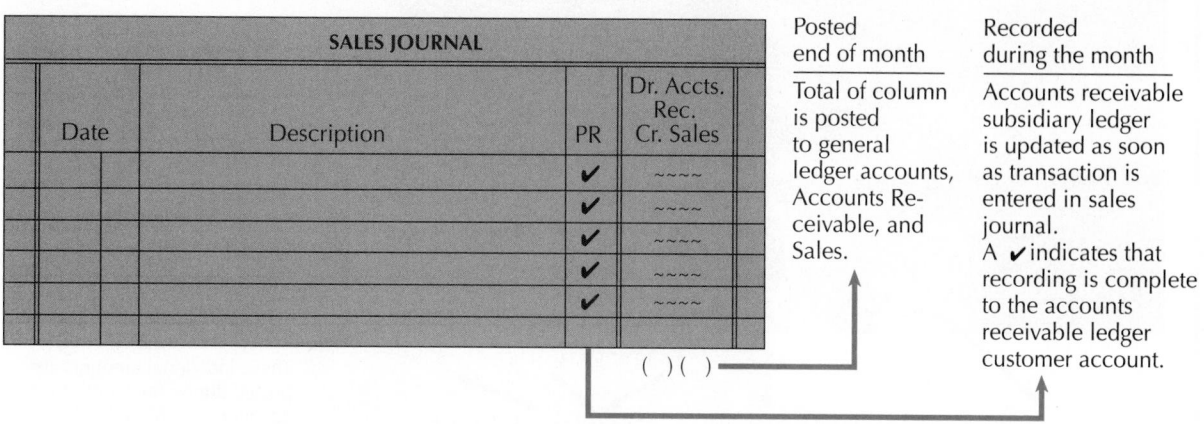

SALES JOURNAL						
Date		Description		PR	Dr. Accts. Rec. Cr. Sales	
				✔	~~~~	
				✔	~~~~	
				✔	~~~~	
				✔	~~~~	
				✔	~~~~	

Posted end of month
Total of column is posted to general ledger accounts, Accounts Receivable, and Sales.

( ) ( )

Recorded during the month
Accounts receivable subsidiary ledger is updated as soon as transaction is entered in sales journal.
A ✔ indicates that recording is complete to the accounts receivable ledger customer account.

Recording a Credit Memo in a General Journal

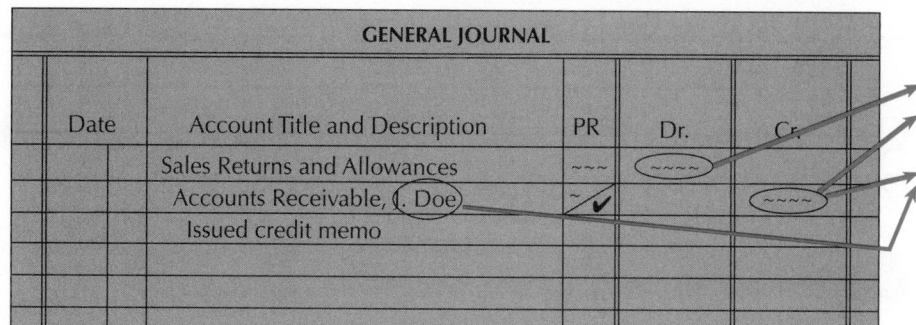

GENERAL JOURNAL				
Date	Account Title and Description	PR	Dr.	Cr.
	Sales Returns and Allowances	~~~	~~~~	
	Accounts Receivable, J. Doe	~ ✔		~~~~
	Issued credit memo			

Posted when transaction entered
Three postings:
1. Post to SRA in general ledger.
2. Post to asset account in general ledger.
3. Record in J. Doe account in accounts receivable ledger.

Multicolumn Purchases Journal

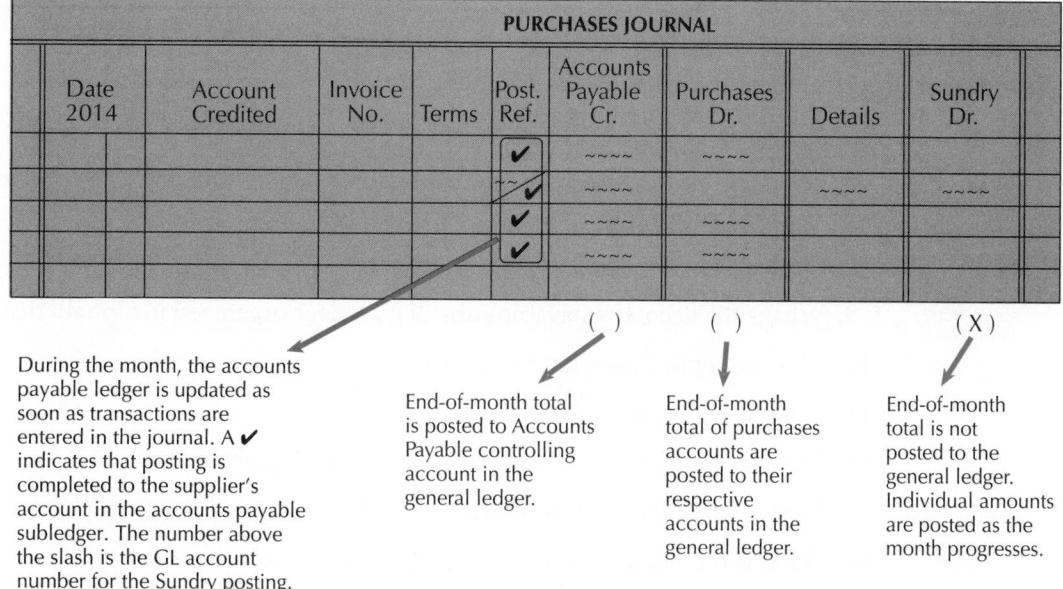

PURCHASES JOURNAL									
Date 2014		Account Credited	Invoice No.	Terms	Post. Ref.	Accounts Payable Cr.	Purchases Dr.	Details	Sundry Dr.
					✔	~~~~	~~~~		
					~~/✔	~~~~		~~~~	~~~~
					✔	~~~~	~~~~		
					✔	~~~~	~~~~		

( ) ( ) (X)

During the month, the accounts payable ledger is updated as soon as transactions are entered in the journal. A ✔ indicates that posting is completed to the supplier's account in the accounts payable subledger. The number above the slash is the GL account number for the Sundry posting.

End-of-month total is posted to Accounts Payable controlling account in the general ledger.

End-of-month total of purchases accounts are posted to their respective accounts in the general ledger.

End-of-month total is not posted to the general ledger. Individual amounts are posted as the month progresses.

(continued)

Cash Payments Journal without GST

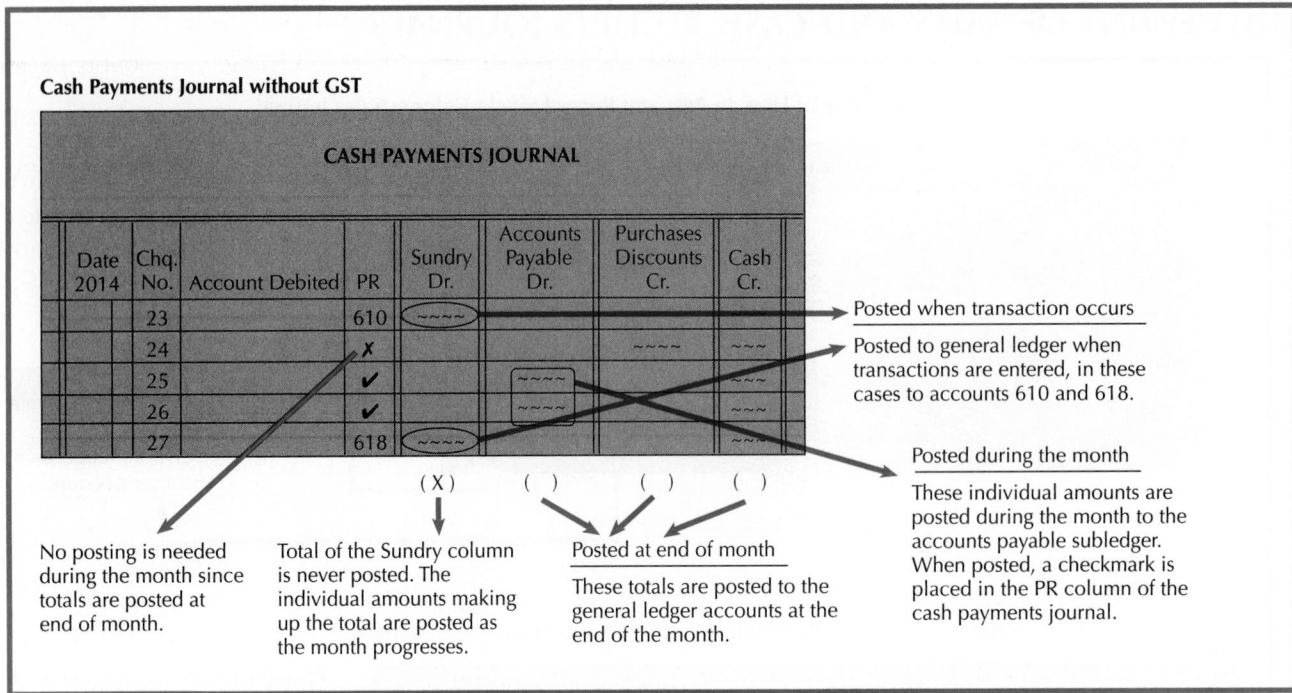

Date 2014	Chq. No.	Account Debited	PR	Sundry Dr.	Accounts Payable Dr.	Purchases Discounts Cr.	Cash Cr.
	23		610	~~~~			
	24		✗		~~~~	~~~	
	25		✔		~~~~		~~~
	26		✔		~~~~		~~~
	27		618	~~~~			~~~
				(X)	( )	( )	( )

Posted when transaction occurs

Posted to general ledger when transactions are entered, in these cases to accounts 610 and 618.

Posted during the month

These individual amounts are posted during the month to the accounts payable subledger. When posted, a checkmark is placed in the PR column of the cash payments journal.

No posting is needed during the month since totals are posted at end of month.

Total of the Sundry column is never posted. The individual amounts making up the total are posted as the month progresses.

Posted at end of month

These totals are posted to the general ledger accounts at the end of the month.

QUESTIONS, CLASSROOM DEMONSTRATION EXERCISES, EXERCISES, AND PROBLEMS

Discussion Questions and Critical Thinking/Ethical Case

1. Explain the purpose of a contra-revenue account.

2. What is the normal balance of sales discounts?

3. Give two examples of contra-revenue accounts.

4. What is the difference between a discount period and a credit period?

5. Explain the terms (a) 2/10, n/30; (b) n/10, EOM.

6. If special journals are used, what purpose will a general journal serve?

7. Compare and contrast the controlling account Accounts Receivable with the accounts receivable subsidiary ledger.

8. Explain how to calculate net purchases.

9. Why is the accounts payable subsidiary ledger organized in alphabetical order?

10. When is a purchases journal used?

11. What is an invoice? What purpose does it serve?

12. Explain the difference between F.O.B. shipping point and F.O.B. destination.

13. Explain the relationship between a purchase requisition and a purchase order.

14. What is the normal balance of the Purchase Discounts account?

15. When a seller issues a credit memorandum, what accounts will be affected?

16. Explain the main difference between a cash receipts journal and a cash payments journal.

17. When is the Sundry column of the cash payments journal posted?

18. Why would the purchaser issue a debit memorandum?

19. Explain the purpose of a schedule of accounts receivable or accounts payable.

20. Amy Jak is the National Sales Manager of Rowe Co. In order to get sales up to the projection for the old year, Amy asked the accountant to put the first two weeks of sales in January back into December. Amy told the accountant that this secret would be between them. Should Amy move the new sales into the old sales year? You make the call. Write down your specific recommendations to Amy.

MyAccountingLab

Make the grade with MyAccountingLab! The exercises and problems marked in green can be found on MyAccountingLab at **www.myaccountinglab.com**. You can practise them as often as you want, and many of them feature step-by-step guided solutions to help you find the right answer. You can also find working papers for selected problems in the Multimedia Library on MyAccountingLab.

Classroom Demonstration Exercises

(The forms you need are on pages 6-17 and 6-21 of the *Study Guide with Working Papers*.)

Set A

Overview

Recording transactions
① ⑤ (10 min)

1. Complete the following table for Sales, Sales Returns and Allowances, Sales Discounts, Purchases, and Purchases Discounts:

Accounts Affected	Category	↑ ↓	Rules	Temporary or Permanent

Calculating Net Sales and Purchases

Net sales and net purchases
① ⑤ (10 min)

2. Given the following, calculate net sales and net purchases:

Gross sales	$30	Gross purchases	$64
Sales returns and allowances	8	Purchase returns and allowance	7
Sales discounts	2	Purchase discounts	3

Sales Journal and General Journal

Sales transactions
① ③ (10 min)

3. Beside each of the three transactions below the box, enter the number of any of the following five treatments that apply. (More than one number can be used.)

> 1. Journalize into sales journal.
> 2. Record immediately to subsidiary ledger.
> 3. Post totals from sales journal at end of month to general ledger.
> 4. Journalize in general journal.
> 5. Record and post immediately to subsidiary and general ledger.

a. _____ Sold merchandise for cash to Ree Co., invoice No. 1—$50.

b. _____ Sold merchandise on account to Flynn Co., invoice No. 2—$1,000.

c. _____ Issued credit memorandum No. 1 to Flynn Co. for defective merchandise—$25.

Purchases Journal, General Journal, Recording, and Posting

Purchases transactions
5 6 (10 min)

4. For each of the three journal entries below, indicate which of these procedures should be used (more than one number can be used).

1. Journalize in purchases journal.
2. Record immediately in subsidiary ledger.
3. Post totals from purchases journal (except Sundry total) at the end of the month to general ledger.
4. Journalize in general journal.
5. Immediately record in subsidiary ledgers and post to the general ledger.

    a. Bought merchandise on account from Also Co., invoice No. 12, $20.
    b. Bought equipment on account from Jones Co., invoice No. 13, $40.
    c. Issued debit memo No. 1 to Also Co. for merchandise returned, $4, from invoice No. 12.

Recording Transactions in Special Journals

Journalizing sales and purchases
1 2 6 7 (10 min)

5. Indicate in which of these five journals each transaction described below will be journalized:

1. SJ	**4.** CPJ
2. PJ	**5.** GJ
3. CRJ	

_____ **a.** Issued credit memo No. 2, $13.

_____ **b.** Cash sales, $20.

_____ **c.** Received cheque from Blue Co., $50, less 3% discount.

_____ **d.** Bought merchandise on account from Mel Co., $35, 1/10, n/30, invoice No. 20.

_____ **e.** Cash purchase, $15.

_____ **f.** Issued debit memo to Mel Co., $15 for merchandise returned from invoice No. 20.

Schedule of accounts payable
7 (10 min)

6. From the following, prepare a schedule of accounts payable for AVE Co. for May 31, 2012:

Accounts Payable Subsidiary Ledger				**General Ledger**			
Bloss Co.				Accounts Payable			
5/25 CPJ1 10	5/19 PJ1 50			5/31 CPJ 10	5/31 PJ1 110		
Rowe Co.							
	5/8 PJ1 60						

Recording Transactions in Special Journals

Journalizing transactions
1 2 3 4 5 6 7 (15 min)

7. Journalize the following transactions:

_____ **a.** Issued credit memo No. 2 to Rose, $50.

_____ **b.** Cash sales, $210

_____ **c.** Received cheque from Tran Co., $90, less 3% discount.

      d. Bought merchandise on account from Mel Co., $50, 1/10, n/30, invoice No. 20.

      e. Cash purchase, $25

      f. Issued debit memo to Mel Co., $15 for merchandise returned from invoice No. 20.

Schedule of accounts payable
7 (10 min)

8. From the following, prepare a schedule of accounts payable for AVE Co. for May 31, 2012:

Accounts Payable Subsidiary Ledger		**General Ledger**	
Jones Co.		Accounts Payable	
5/25 GJ1 20	5/19 GJ1 60	5/31 GJ1 10	5/31 GJ1 120
Ring Co.			
	5/8 GJ1 70		

Business transactions of both the buyer and the seller
1 5 (10 min)

9. Lois Long received $300 of merchandise from Blue Co. What would be the journal entry on the books of both the buyer and the seller?

Set B

Calculating Net Sales and Net Purchases

Net sales and net purchases
1 5 7 (10 min)

1. Given the following, calculate net sales and net purchases:

Gross sales	$50	Gross purchases	$46
Sales returns and allowances	8	Purchase returns and allowance	4
Sales discounts	2	Purchase discounts	2

Credit Memorandum

Analyzing a return transaction
3 (10 min)

2. Draw a transaction analysis box for the following credit memorandum: Issued credit memorandum to Bob Corp. for defective merchandise—$100.

Sales, Cash Receipts, and General Journals

Sales transactions
1 2 3 4 (10 min)

3. Beside each of the five transactions below the box, enter the number of any of the following six treatments that apply. (A number can be used more than once.)

> **1.** Journalize into sales journal.
> **2.** Journalize into cash receipts journal.
> **3.** Record immediately to subsidiary ledger.
> **4.** Totals of special journals will be posted at end of month (except Sundry column).
> **5.** Post to general ledger immediately.
> **6.** Journalize into general journal.

  a. _____ Sold merchandise on account to Moore Co., invoice No. 9—$70.

  b. _____ Sold merchandise on account to Ally Co., invoice No. 10—$30.

  c. _____ Received cheque from Moore Co.—$70 less 2% discount.

  d. _____ Cash Sales—$400.

  e. _____ Issued credit memorandum No. 2 to Ally Co. for defective merchandise—$10.

4. From the following, prepare a schedule of accounts receivable for Blue Co. for May 31, 2012.

Accounts Receivable Subsidiary Ledger

General Ledger

Bon Co.

5/6 SJ1 90	

Accounts Receivable

5/31 SJ1 140	5/31 CRJ1 10

Peke Co.

5/20 SJ1 20	10 5/27 CRJ1

Green Co.

5/8 SJ1 30	

5. Complete the following table:

		Account
A cost	↔	a. _____
A contra-cost	↔	b. _____
A contra-cost discount	↔	c. _____
Opposite of accounts receivable ledger	↔	d. _____
Cost of freight to seller	↔	e. _____

Purchases Journal, General Journal, Recording, and Posting

6. For each of the three journal entries below, indicate which of these procedures should be used (more than one number can be used).

1. Record to accounts payable subsidiary ledger.
2. Record in the general journal.
3. Post to the general ledger.
   a. Bought merchandise on account from Also Co., invoice No. 12, $40.
   b. Bought equipment on account from Jone Co., invoice No. 13, $75.
   c. Issued debit memo No. 1 to Also Co. for merchandise returned, $7, from invoice No. 12.

7. Pete Morse returned $300 of merchandise to Logan Co. What would be the journal entry on the books of both the buyer and the seller?

8. Jeans Co. paid the cost of freight, $100. Journalize the transaction.

(The forms you need are on pages 6-22 to 6-24 of the *Study Guide with Working Papers.*)

Recording and posting from the sales journal
② ④ **(10 min)**

6-1. From the sales journal below, record in the accounts receivable subsidiary ledger and post to the general ledger accounts as appropriate.

SALES JOURNAL				
				P. 1
Date	Account Debited	Invoice No.	PR	Dr. Accts. Receivable Cr. Sales
2013 April 18	Kevin Stone Co.	1		600 00
19	Bill Valley Co.	2		900 00
	Total			1500 00

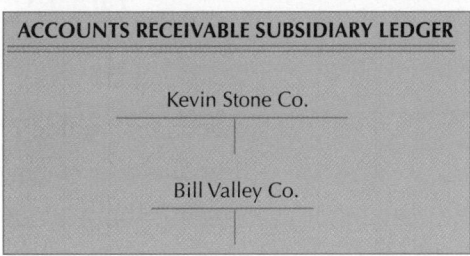

ACCOUNTS RECEIVABLE SUBSIDIARY LEDGER

Kevin Stone Co.

Bill Valley Co.

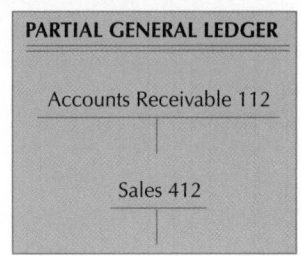

PARTIAL GENERAL LEDGER

Accounts Receivable 112

Sales 412

Journalizing, recording, and posting sales and cash receipts journal; schedule of accounts receivable
① ② ③ ④ **(20 min)**

6-2. From the following transactions for Edna Co., when appropriate, journalize, record, post, and prepare a schedule of accounts receivable. Use the same journal headings (all page 1) and chart of accounts that Art's Wholesale Clothing used in the text (use Edna Cares, Capital). You will have to set up your own accounts receivable subsidiary ledger and partial general ledger as needed. All sales terms are 2/10, n/30.

2014
June 2 Edna Cares invested $5,000 in the business.
3 Sold merchandise on account to Boston Co., invoice No. 218, $700.
3 Sold merchandise on account to Gary Co., invoice No. 219, $1,100.
6 Cash sale, $200.
9 Issued credit memorandum No. 24 to Boston Co. for defective merchandise, $200.
10 Received cheque from Boston Co. for invoice No. 218 less returns and discount.
16 Cash sale, $400.
17 Sold merchandise on account to Boston Co., invoice No. 220, $600.

Calculating net purchases
⑤ ⑥ ⑦ **(5 min)**

6-3. From the following facts, calculate what Ann Frost must pay Blue Co. for the purchase of a dining-room set. Sale terms are 2/10, n/30.

a. Sales ticket price before tax, $4,000—dated April 5.

b. Returned one defective chair for credit of $400 before any taxes on April 8.

c. Paid bill on April 13.

Journalizing, recording, and
posting a debit memorandum
6 (15 min)

6-4. On July 8, 2014, Aster Co. issued debit memorandum No. 1 for $400 to Reel Co. for merchandise returned from invoice No. 312. Your task is to journalize, record, and post this transaction as appropriate for Reel Co. Use the same account numbers as found in the text for Art's Wholesale Clothing Company. The general journal page is page 1.

Journalizing, recording, and
posting a cash payments journal
7 (20 min)

6-5. Journalize, record, and post when appropriate the following transactions into the cash payments journal (page 2) for Morgan's Clothing. Use the same headings as found in the text (page 276). All purchases discounts are 2/10, n/30.

Accounts Payable Subsidiary Ledger

Name	Balance	Invoice No.
B. Foss	$ 400	488
A. James	1,000	522
J. Ranch	900	562
B. Swanson	200	821

Partial General Ledger

Account	Balance
Cash 110	$3,000
Accounts Payable 210	2,500
Purchases Discounts 511	
Advertising Expense 610	

2013
April   2   Issued cheque No. 20 to A. James Company in payment of its March 29 invoice No. 522.

         9   Issued cheque No. 21 to Flott Advertising in payment of its advertising bill, $100, no discount.

     16   Issued cheque No. 22 to B. Foss in payment of its March 26 invoice No. 488.

6-6. From Exercise 6-5, prepare a schedule of accounts payable and verify that the total of the schedule equals the amount in the controlling account.

6-7. Angie Rase bought merchandise with a list price of $4,000. Angie was entitled to a 30% trade discount as well as a 3% cash discount. What was Angie's actual cost of buying this merchandise after the cash discount?

Group A Problems

(The forms you need are on pages 6-25 to 6-38 of the *Study Guide with Working Papers.*)

Multicolumn journal:
journalizing and posting to
general ledger and recording to
accounts receivable subsidiary
ledger and preparing a schedule
of accounts receivable
1 2 3 (40 min)

6A-1. Rita Hayle has opened Food on the Go, a wholesale grocery and pizza company, in Edmonton. The following transactions occurred in June:

2013
June   1   Sold grocery merchandise to Joe Kase Co. on account, $400, invoice No. 702.

        4   Sold pizza merchandise to Sue Moore Co. on account, $600, invoice No. 703.

        8   Sold grocery merchandise to Long Co. on account, $700, invoice No. 704.

June 11 Issued credit memorandum No. 34 to Joe Kase for $150 worth of grocery merchandise returned because of spoilage.

15 Sold pizza merchandise to Sue Moore Co. on account, $180, invoice No. 705.

18 Sold grocery merchandise to Long Co. on account, $300, invoice No. 706.

25 Sold pizza merchandise to Joe Kase Co. on account, $1,200, invoice No. 707.

Required

a. Journalize the transactions in the appropriate journals.

b. Record in the accounts receivable subsidiary ledger and post to the general ledger as appropriate.

c. Prepare a schedule of accounts receivable.

6A-2. Mark Peaker owns Peaker's Sneaker Shop of Dartmouth. (In your working papers, balances as of May 1 are provided for the accounts receivable and general ledger accounts.) The following transactions occurred in May:

2012

May 1 Mark Peaker invested an additional $12,000 in the sneaker store.

4 Sold $900 worth of merchandise on account to B. Dale, sales invoice No. 160, terms 1/10, n/30.

4 Sold $500 worth of merchandise on account to Ron Lester, sales invoice No. 161, terms 1/10, n/30.

8 Sold $200 worth of merchandise on account to Jim Zon, sales invoice No. 162, terms 1/10, n/30.

11 Received cash from B. Dale in payment of May 4 transaction, sales invoice No. 160, less discount.

21 Sold $3,000 worth of merchandise on account to Pam Pry, sales invoice No. 163, terms 1/10, n/30.

22 Received cash payment from Ron Lester in payment of May 4 transaction, sales invoice No. 161.

22 Collected cash sales, $3,000.

25 Issued credit memorandum No. 31 to Pam Pry for $2,000 worth of merchandise returned from May 21 sales on account.

25 Collected cash sales, $7,000.

28 Received cash from Pam Pry in payment of May 21 sales invoice No. 163. (Don't forget about the credit memo and discount.)

28 Sold sneaker rack equipment for $300 cash. (Beware.)

29 Sold merchandise, priced at $4,000, on account to Ron Lester, sales invoice No. 164, terms 1/10, n/30.

31 Issued credit memorandum No. 32 to Ron Lester for $700 worth of merchandise returned from May 29 transaction, sales invoice No. 164.

Required

a. Journalize the transactions.

b. Record in the accounts receivable subsidiary ledger and post to general ledger as needed.

c. Prepare a schedule of accounts receivable.

Check Figure

Schedule of Accounts
Receivable $3,230.00

Comprehensive problem:
recording transactions in sales,
cash receipts, and general
journals; recording in accounts
receivable subsidiary ledger and
posting to general ledger;
preparing a schedule of accounts
receivable
①②③④ (70 min)

(No GST or PST applied)

Check Figure

Schedule of Accounts
Receivable $5,700.00

6A-3. Ernie Costello recently opened a sporting goods shop in Brantford. As the bookkeeper of his shop, journalize, record, and post when appropriate the following transactions (account numbers are: Store Supplies, 115; Store Equipment, 121; Accounts Payable, 210; Purchases, 510):

2014

June 2 Bought merchandise on account from Aster Co., invoice No. 442, dated June 2, terms 2/10, n/30, $700.

3 Bought store equipment from Norton Co., invoice No. 502, dated June 3, $4,000.

10 Bought merchandise on account from Rolo Co., invoice No. 401, dated June 9, terms 2/10, n/30, $1,400.

13 Bought store supplies on account from Aster Co., invoice No. 519, dated June 13, $900.

6A-4. Wendy Jones operates a wholesale computer centre in Whitehorse. All transactions requiring the payment of cash are recorded in the cash payments journal (page 5). The account balances as of May 1, 2013, are as follows:

Accounts Payable Ledger

Name	Balance
Alvin Co.	$1,200
Henry Co.	600
Soy Co.	800
Xon Co.	1,400

Partial General Ledger

Account	Number	Balance
Cash	110	$17,000
Delivery Truck	150	—
Accounts Payable	210	4,000
Computer Purchases	510	—
Computer Purchases Discount	511	—
Rent Expense	610	—
Utilities Expense	620	—

Required

a. Journalize the following transactions.

b. Record in the accounts payable ledger and post to the general ledger as appropriate.

c. Prepare a schedule of accounts payable.

2013

May 3 Paid half the amount owed Henry Co. from previous purchases of computers on account, less a 2% purchases discount, cheque No. 21.

3 Bought a used delivery truck for $12,000 cash, cheque No. 22, payable to Bill Ring Co.

7 Bought computer merchandise from Lectro Co., cheque No. 23, $3,900.

17 Bought additional computer merchandise from Pulse Co., cheque No. 24, $800.

24 Paid Xon Co. the amount owed less a 2% purchases discount, cheque No. 25.

27 Paid rent expense to King's Realty Trust, cheque No. 26, $2,000.

	May	28	Paid utilities expense to Stone Utility Co., cheque No. 27, $300.
		31	Paid half the amount owed Soy Co., no discount, cheque No. 28.

Group B Problems

(The forms you need are on pages 6-25 to 6-38 of the *Study Guide with Working Papers.*)

Multicolumn journal: journalizing and posting to general ledger, recording in accounts receivable subsidiary ledger, and preparing a schedule of accounts receivable

❶❷❸ (40 min)

6B-1. The following transactions occurred for Food on the Go of Edmonton for the month of June:

2013
June 3 Sold grocery merchandise to Joe Kase Co. on account, $800, invoice No. 1.
4 Sold pizza merchandise to Sue Moore Co. on account, $550, invoice No. 2.
7 Sold grocery merchandise to Long Co. on account, $900, invoice No. 3.
11 Issued credit memorandum No. 1 to Joe Kase for $160 worth of grocery merchandise returned because of spoilage.
14 Sold pizza merchandise to Sue Moore Co. on account, $700, invoice No. 4.
18 Sold grocery merchandise to Long Co. on account, $250, invoice No. 5.

Check Figure

Schedule of Accounts Receivable $3,040.00

Required

a. Journalize the transactions in the appropriate journals.
b. Record in the accounts receivable subsidiary ledger and post to the general ledger as appropriate.
c. Prepare a schedule of accounts receivable.

Comprehensive problem: recording transactions in sales, cash receipts, and general journals; recording in accounts receivable subsidiary ledger and posting to general ledger; preparing a schedule of accounts receivable

❶❷❸❹ (70 min)

6B-2. (In your working papers, all the beginning balances needed are provided for the accounts receivable subsidiary and general ledgers.) The following transactions occurred for Peaker's Sneaker Shop of Dartmouth:

2012
May 1 Mark Peaker invested an additional $14,000 in the sneaker store.
3 Sold $2,000 worth of merchandise on account to B. Dale, sales invoice No. 60, terms 1/10, n/30.
4 Sold $900 worth of merchandise on account to Ron Lester, sales invoice No. 61, terms 1/10, n/30.
8 Sold $600 worth of merchandise on account to Jim Zon, sales invoice No. 62, terms 1/10, n/30.
11 Received cash from B. Dale in payment of May 3 transaction, sales invoice No. 60, less discount.
18 Sold $4,000 worth of merchandise on account to Pam Pry, sales invoice No. 63, terms 1/10, n/30.
21 Received cash payment from Ron Lester in payment of May 4 transaction, sales invoice No. 61.
22 Collected cash sales, $6,000.
25 Issued credit memorandum No. 1 to Pam Pry for $500 worth of merchandise returned from May 18 sale.

Check Figure

Schedule of Accounts Receivable $8,000.00

May	25	Received cash from Pam Pry in payment of May 18 sales invoice No. 63. (Don't forget about the credit memo and discount.)
	28	Collected cash sales, $12,000.
	28	Sold sneaker rack equipment for $200 cash. (Beware.)
	29	Sold $6,000 worth of merchandise on account to Ron Lester, sales invoice No. 64, terms 1/10, n/30.
	31	Issued credit memorandum No. 32 to Ron Lester for $800 worth of merchandise returned from May 29 transaction, sales invoice No. 64.

Required

a. Journalize the transactions in the appropriate journals.

b. Record and post as appropriate.

c. Prepare a schedule of accounts receivable.

Journalizing, recording, and posting a purchases journal

5 6 (30 min)

6B-3. (GST/HST is not involved in this problem.) From the following transactions of Ernie Costello's sporting goods shop of Brantford, journalize in the purchases journal and record and post as appropriate:

Check Figure

Total of Payables Column
$9,400.00

2014

June	2	Bought merchandise on account from Rolo Co., invoice No. 400, dated June 2, terms 2/10, n/30, $1,800.
	3	Bought store equipment from Norton Co., invoice No. 518, dated June 2, $6,000.
	9	Bought merchandise on account from Aster Co., invoice No. 411, dated June 9, terms 2/10, n/30, $400.
	13	Bought store supplies on account from Aster Co., invoice No. 415, dated June 13, $1,200.

Journalizing, recording, and posting a cash payments journal with GST; preparing a schedule of accounts payable

7 (45 min)

6B-4. Wendy Jones of Whitehorse has hired you as her bookkeeper to record the following transactions in the cash payments journal. She would like you to record and post as appropriate and supply her with a schedule of accounts payable. (Beginning balances are in the *Study Guide with Working Papers* and in Problem 6A-4.)

Check Figure

Total of Schedule of Accounts Payable $1,900.00

2013

May	3	Bought a used delivery truck for $10,000 cash, cheque No. 21, payable to Randy Rosse Co.
	3	Paid half the amount owed Henry Co. from previous purchases of computer merchandise on account, less a 5% purchases discount, cheque No. 22.
	7	Bought computer merchandise from Jane Co. for $900 cash, cheque No. 23.
	17	Bought additional computer merchandise from Jane Co., cheque No. 24, $1,000.
	24	Paid Xon Co. the amount owed less a 5% purchases discount, cheque No. 25.
	27	Paid rent expense to Regan Realty Trust, cheque No. 26, $3,000.
	28	Paid half the amount owed Soy Co., no discount, cheque No. 27.
	31	Paid utilities expense to County Utility, cheque No. 28, $425.

(The forms you need are on pages 6-39 to 6-53 of the *Study Guide with Working Papers*.)

Multicolumn journal:
journalizing and posting to the general ledger, recording in the accounts receivable ledger, and preparing a schedule of accounts receivable

① ② ③ (50 min)

Check Figure

Schedule of Accounts Receivable $7,855.00

6C-1. The following transactions occurred for Lodge Co. of St. Albert for the month of July:

2013
July

2　Sold upholstery merchandise to Joan Timkins Co. on account, $1,600, invoice No. 115, terms: net 30 days.

5　Sold carpet merchandise to Chris Cowan Co. on account, $825, invoice No. 116, terms: net 30 days.

9　Sold upholstery merchandise to Cross & Co. on account, $1,950, invoice No. 117, terms: net 30 days.

12　Issued credit memorandum No. 1 to Joan Timkins Co. for $400 worth of merchandise returned because of faulty colouring match.

15　Sold carpet merchandise to Chris Cowan Co. on account, $925, invoice No. 118, terms: net 30 days.

19　Sold upholstery merchandise to Cross & Co. on account, $930, invoice No. 119, terms: net 30 days.

23　Sold carpet merchandise to Joan Timkins Co. on account, $2,025, invoice No. 120, terms: net 30 days.

Required

a. Journalize the transactions in the appropriate journals.

b. Record in the accounts receivable ledger and post to the general ledger as appropriate.

c. Prepare a schedule of accounts receivable.

Comprehensive problem:
recording transactions into sales, cash receipts, and general journals; recording to accounts receivable and posting to general ledger; preparing a schedule of accounts receivable

① ② ③ ④ (70 min)

Check Figure

Schedule of Accounts Receivable $6,084.60

6C-2. (In your working papers, all the beginning balances needed are provided for the accounts receivable and general ledger.) The following transactions occurred for Bedford Sausage Supply Co.:

2014
Sept.

2　Karen Blum, owner, invested an additional $15,000 in the business.

3　Sold $1,850 worth of merchandise on account to Petra's Meat Market, sales invoice No. 460, terms 1/10, n/30.

5　Sold $825 worth of merchandise on account to Chapman's Deli, sales invoice No. 461, terms 1/10, n/30.

8　Sold $930 worth of merchandise on account to Valemont Variety Meats Co., sales invoice No. 462, terms 1/10, n/30.

12　Received cash from Petra's Meat Market in payment of September 3 transaction, sales invoice No. 460, less discount.

19　Sold $1,500 worth of merchandise on account to Discount Meats, sales invoice No. 463, terms 1/10, n/30.

22　Received cash payment from Chapman's Deli in payment of September 3 transaction, sales invoice No. 461.

23　Collected cash sale, $638.

23　Issued credit memorandum No. 101 to Discount Meats for $300 worth of merchandise returned from September 19 sales on account.

25　Received cash from Discount Meats in payment of September 19 sales invoice No. 463. (Don't forget about the credit memo and discount.)

Sept.	25	Collected cash sales, $813.
	26	Sold meat cooling equipment for $900 cash. (Beware.)
	29	Sold $1,620 worth of merchandise on account to Chapman's Deli, sales invoice No. 464, terms 1/10, n/30.
	30	Issued credit memorandum No. 102 to Chapman's Deli for $420 worth of merchandise returned from September 29 transaction, sales invoice No. 464.

Required

a. Journalize the transactions in the appropriate journals.

b. Record and post as appropriate.

c. Prepare a schedule of accounts receivable.

Journalizing, recording, and posting a purchases journal
⑤⑥ (30 min)

Check Figure

Total of Purchases Column
$2,655.00

6C-3. Mae Chu recently opened an imported foods store in Richmond. As the bookkeeper of her store, journalize, record, and post when appropriate the following transactions (account numbers are: Store Supplies, 115; Store Equipment, 141; Accounts Payable, 210; Purchases, 510):

2014

May	5	Bought merchandise on account from Convey Co., invoice No. 751, dated May 2, terms 2/10, n/30, $915.
	6	Bought store equipment from Reliable Co., invoice No. 1202, dated May 5, $5,180.
	9	Bought merchandise on account from Brendan Co., invoice No. 401, dated May 6, terms 1/10, n/30, $1,740.
	16	Bought store supplies on account from Convey Co., invoice No. 823 dated May 16, $785.

Journalizing, recording, and posting a purchases journal, as well as recording the issuing of a debit memorandum and preparing a schedule of accounts payable
⑦⑪ (45 min)

Check Figure

Total of Schedule of Accounts Payable $21,053.00

6C-4. Farber's Fabric Co. of Yellowknife uses a purchases journal (page 21) and a general journal (page 32) to record the following transactions (continued from July).

2012

August	3	Purchased fabric for resale from European Import Fabrics Co., invoice No. 653, dated August 2, terms net 15 days, $1,362.
	7	Purchased merchandise on account from Eddyn Co., invoice No. 250, dated August 7, terms 2/10, n/60, $920.
	10	Purchased merchandise on account from Forward Co., invoice No. 1124, dated August 7, terms 1/10, n/60, $1,626.
	13	Purchased store supplies on account from Lavoy Co., invoice No. 712, dated August 10, $2,680.
	14	Issued debit memo No. 8 to Eddyn Co. for merchandise returned, $160, from invoice No. 250.
	17	Purchased office equipment on account from Reliant Co., invoice No. 873, dated August 14, $2,610.
	24	Purchased additional store supplies on account from Lavoy Co., invoice No. 816, dated August 24, terms 2/10, n/30, $725.
	28	Purchased fabric for resale from European Import Fabrics Co., invoice No. 713, dated August 27, terms net 15 days, $2,740.

The fabric store has decided to keep a purchases journal. The account balances as of August 1, 2012, are as follows:

Accounts Payable Ledger

Name	Balance
Eddyn Co.	$ 800
European Import	3,100
Forward Co.	1,500
Lavoy Co.	500
Reliant Co.	2,650

Partial General Ledger

Account	Number	Balance
Store Supplies	130	$ —
Office Equipment	180	—
Accounts Payable	220	8,550
Purchases	500	86,340
Purchases Returns and Allowances	510	1,374

Required

a. Journalize the transactions.

b. Post and record as appropriate.

c. Prepare a schedule of accounts payable.

On-the-job Training

(The forms you need are on page 6-54 of the *Study Guide with Working Papers*.)

The Schedule of Accounts Receivable and the controlling account must match and the trial balance must balance
① ③ (30 min)

T-1. The bookkeeper of Floore Company records credit sales in a sales journal and returns in a general journal. The bookkeeper did the following:

1. Recorded an $18 credit sale as $180 in the sales journal.

2. Correctly recorded a $40 sale in the sales journal but posted it to B. Blue's account as $400 in the accounts receivable ledger.

3. Made an addition error in determining the balance of J. B. Window Co. in the accounts receivable ledger.

4. Posted a sales return that was recorded in the general journal to the Sales Returns and Allowance account and the Accounts Receivable account but forgot to record it to the B. Katz Co.

5. Added the total of the sales column incorrectly.

6. Posted a sales return to the Accounts Receivable account but not to the Sales Returns and Allowances account. Accounts receivable ledger was recorded correctly.

Could you inform the bookkeeper in writing as to when each error will be discovered?

Posting to the general ledger and the subsidiary ledger
①②③④⑤⑥⑦

T-2. Jeff Ryan completed an Accounting I course and was recently hired as the bookkeeper of Spring Co. The special journals shown on page 306 have not been posted, nor are "Dr." and "Cr." used on the column headings. Please assist Jeff by posting to the general ledger and recording in the subsidiary ledger. (Only post or record the amounts since no chart of accounts is provided.) Make some written recommendations on how a new computer system may lessen the need for posting.

SALES JOURNAL		
Account	PR	
Blue Co.		4 8 0 0 00
Jon Co.		5 6 0 0 00
Roff Co.		6 4 0 0 00
Totals		16 8 0 0 00

PURCHASES JOURNAL		
Account	PR	
Ralph Co.		4 0 0 0 00
Sos Co.		6 0 0 0 00
Jingle Co.		8 0 0 0 00
Totals		18 0 0 0 00

GENERAL JOURNAL		
Sales Returns and Allowances	1 6 0 0 00	
Accounts Receivable, Jon Co.		1 6 0 0 00
Customer returned merchandise		
Accounts Payable, Jingle Co.	8 0 0 00	
Purchases Returns and Allowances		8 0 0 00
Returned defective merchandise		

CASH RECEIPTS JOURNAL				Sundry		
Cash	Sales Discount	Accounts Receivable	Sales	Account Name	PR	Amount
4 7 0 4 00	9 6 00	4 8 0 0 00		Blue Co.		
1 9 6 0 00	4 0 00	2 0 0 0 00		Jon Co.		
5 0 0 0 00			5 0 0 0 00	Sales		
20 0 0 0 00				Notes Payable		20 0 0 0 00
3 1 3 6 00	6 4 00	3 2 0 0 00		Roff Co.		
4 6 0 0 00			4 6 0 0 00	Sales		
39 4 0 0 00	2 0 0 00	10 0 0 0 00	9 6 0 0 00	Totals		20 0 0 0 00

CASH PAYMENTS JOURNAL					
Account	PR	Sundry	Accounts Payable	Purchases Discounts	Cash
Sos Co.			3 0 0 0 00	6 0 00	2 9 4 0 00
Salaries Expense		2 6 0 0 00			2 6 0 0 00
Jingle Co.			4 0 0 0 00	8 0 00	3 9 2 0 00
Salaries Expense		2 6 0 0 00			2 6 0 0 00
Totals		5 2 0 0 00	7 0 0 0 00	1 4 0 00	12 0 6 0 00

CONTINUING PROBLEM

Comprehensive problem:
journalizing and posting to the
general and subsidiary ledgers
①②③④⑤⑥⑦ (120 min)

A month has elapsed since Precision Computer Centre's year-end. Tony Freedman will use four specialized journals for recording business transactions in the month of September. To assist you in recording the transactions, the Schedule of Accounts Receivable as of August 31 and the Schedule of Accounts Payable as of August 31 are shown below. An updated chart of accounts with the current balance listed for each account is provided on page 309.

The partial September transactions are as follows:

2013

Sept. 3 Sold $700 worth of merchandise to Taylor Golf on credit, sales invoice No. 12680; terms are 2/10, n/30.

5 Paid amount due to Staples, $100, cheque No. 242.

5 Bought merchandise on account from Multi Systems, purchase order No. 4010, $450; terms are 3/10, n/30.

6 Bought office supplies on account from Staples, purchase order No. 4011, $250; terms are n/30.

9 Received from Taylor Golf balance owing as of August 31.

10 Sold $3,000 worth of merchandise on account to Anthony Pitale, sales invoice No. 12681; terms are 2/10, n/30.

10 Purchased merchandise on account from Computer Connection, purchase order No. 4012, $500; terms are 1/30, n/60.

10 Collected $12,000 for cash sales for the week of September 10.

13 Paid Multi Systems re: September 5 purchase, less discount, cheque No. 243.

13 Received West Bell phone bill for September, $70; terms n/30.

13 Received and paid City Electric bill for September, $80, cheque No. 244.

16 Remitted outstanding amount payable to Automated Payroll Service for September wages, $1,810.18, cheque No. 245.

17 Issued debit memorandum No. 10 to Computer Connection for merchandise returned from purchase order No. 4012, $100.

17 Paid net amount due to Computer Connection, less discount, cheque No. 246.

17 Collected balance in full from invoice No. 12681, Anthony Pitale.

23 Sold $4,000 worth of merchandise on account to Vita Needle, sales invoice No. 12682; terms are 4/10, n/30.

23 Paid Alpha Office Co. the amount due from the end of August, cheque No. 247.

25 Paid for office supplies, $50, cheque No. 248.

27 Issued credit memorandum to Taylor Golf for $400 worth of merchandise returned, invoice No. 12680.

27 Wrote cheque No. 249 to Able Holdings Inc. for September, October, and November rent, $1,200.00.

30 Sold $1,600 worth of merchandise to Anthony Pitale, invoice No. 12683; terms 2/10, n/30.

30 Collected full payment from Vita Needle, invoice No. 12682.

30 Wrote cheque No. 250 to Automated Payroll Service for September wages, $3,740.20.

Sept. 30 Paid amount due to West Bell Canada as of August 31 plus the September phone bill received September 13, cheque No. 251. Total $216.

Schedule of Accounts Receivable
Precision Computer Centre
August 31, 2013

Taylor Golf	$2,500.00
Carson Engineering	6,240.00
Total Amount Due	$8,740.00

Schedule of Accounts Payable
Precision Computer Centre
August 31, 2013

Alpha Office Co.	$ 420.00
City Newspaper	375.00
Staples	100.00
West Bell Canada	146.00
Total Amount Payable	$1,041.00

Assignment

(See pages 6-55 to 6-63 in your *Study Guide with Working Papers*.)

1. Journalize the transactions in the appropriate journals (cash receipts, sales, cash payments, purchases, or general journal).
2. Record in the accounts receivable subsidiary ledger and accounts payable subsidiary ledger and post to the general ledger as appropriate. A partial general ledger is included in the *Study Guide with Working Papers*.
3. Prepare a schedule of accounts receivable and a schedule of accounts payable as of September 30, 2013.

	PRECISION COMPUTER CENTRE CHART OF ACCOUNTS AND CURRENT BALANCES AS OF 8/31/2013	Debit Balance	Credit Balance
Account #	Account Name		
1000	Cash	1 1 9 5 00	
1020	Accounts Receivable	8 7 4 0 00	
1025	Prepaid Rent		
1030	Supplies	4 5 0 00	
1040	Merchandise Inventory	7 1 0 0 00	
1080	Computer Shop Equipment	3 8 0 0 00	
1081	Accumulated Amortization, Computer Shop Equipment		9 9 00
1090	Office Equipment	1 0 5 0 00	
1091	Accumulated Amortization, Office Equipment		2 0 00
2000	Accounts Payable		1 0 4 1 00
2030	Other Amounts Payable		1 8 1 0 18
3000	T. Freedman, Capital		7 4 0 6 00
3010	T. Freedman, Withdrawals		
3020	Income Summary	2 0 1 5 00	
4000	Service Revenue		
4010	Sales		2 0 1 4 9 82
4020	Sales Returns and Allowances		
4030	Sales Discounts		
5010	Advertising Expense	4 8 0 00	
5020	Rent Expense	4 0 0 00	

5030	Utilities Expense	9 5 00	
5040	Phone Expense	1 4 6 00	
5050	Supplies Expense		
5060	Insurance Expense		
5070	Postage Expense	2 5 00	
5080	Amortization Expense, Computer Shop Equipment		
5090	Amortization Expense, Office Equipment		
5100	Miscellaneous Expense	1 0 00	
5110	Wages Expense	5 0 2 0 00	
5120	Payroll Benefits Expense	0 00	
5130	Interest Expense		
5140	Bad Debts Expense		
5600	Purchases		
5610	Purchases Returns and Allowances		
5620	Purchases Discounts		
5630	Freight-In		
	Totals	3 0 5 2 6 00	3 0 5 2 6 00

MyAccountingLab

Instructions and data files for completing this Computer Workshop assignment can be found in the Multimedia Library on MyAccountingLab at www.myaccountinglab.com.

Computer Workshops

Style and Sorval

Depending on the goals your instructor has set for the course you are taking, you may be asked to complete one or more of the computer workshops created especially for Chapter 6. If you need to complete any of the workshops, you will obtain all necessary details from the MyAccountingLab website.

There are a total of four workshops available. For each company, Style and Sorval, there are two versions—one using Simply Accounting Pro® and the other using QuickBooks Premier®. The choice will depend to a large extent on which software is available to you in your college's lab, on your own laptop, or other computer, as well as the preference, knowledge, and experience of your instructor. Before beginning, be sure to get clear directions as to which workshop you are to complete.

You need to obtain several files from the MyAccountingLab website before you begin. (Please also see the added details on page 136 at the end of Chapter 3.)

1. The instruction files that describe each company and the details of the assignment.

2. Data sets that have been carefully crafted for you so you may begin each workshop with minimal bother. All of these data sets are downloaded in compressed format, and will need to be Restored by the software before you can work on them.

3. A Word file that sets forth in detail the step-by-step instructions you need to complete the Style assignment, one for each of the software programs. Help files also exist for the Sorval workshops, but only if they are provided by your instructor.

7 Banking Procedures and Control of Cash

THE BIG PICTURE

What do Microsoft, PricewaterhouseCoopers, General Motors, Grant Thornton, and IBM have in common?

One surprising answer is a (relatively) small company from the Vancouver area called Colligo Networks Inc. Each of the above companies (and many others as well) is connected to this Canadian innovator either because it uses Colligo's product or is a partner in assisting Colligo to develop and then launch innovative software solutions.

So what exactly does this company's product do? Company president Barry Jinks explains that Colligo Networks has developed software to enhance collaboration in the workplace. The software places a shell of organization around what could otherwise be a very disorganized scenario. The company noticed that laptop computers and tablet PCs were outselling desktop computers, but there was an obvious problem with that: Portable devices are potentially less connected than their "hard-wired" cousins. This makes collaboration more of a challenge, especially when a local wireless network is unavailable, or unreliable, or when no Internet connection is available.

Like many really great ideas, it looks obvious in hindsight, but with able help from Brent Bolleman, chief strategy officer and founder, Colligo Networks was able to develop their software to make it both possible and reliable for employees to collaborate in doing their daily tasks. So much so that it is likely that

thousands of dollars of savings are realized for each worker each month because of the time savings the software allows.

One of the challenging aspects of public accounting is the coordination of teams who need to run audits and other assignments in an orderly and efficient way. Colligo's solution must offer real benefits because it is used by some of the best-known names in professional accounting circles. But you don't need to take their word for it—the company has won several awards, and not just local ones either. How about these:

Named to 2013 "Ready to Rocket" list
VP Marketing wins Stevie® Award for Women in Business
PC Magazine – Editor's Choice Award (score of 4.5 out of 5)
PC Magazine – Award for Technical Excellence
Best of Microsoft Tech-Ed finalist, 2007

This list is certainly impressive, but the really important awards are those bestowed on the company by its customers. Here is where Colligo really shines. At last count, the company's customer base included many Fortune 500 companies in more than 50 countries. Visit the company's website to see the impressive list of corporate logos representing the organizations Colligo does business with. Now that's an award you can take to the bank!

Speaking of banks—read on!

1 Depositing, writing, and endorsing cheques for a chequing account (p. 311)
2 Reconciling a bank statement (p. 316)
3 Establishing and replenishing a petty cash fund; setting up an auxiliary petty cash record (p. 329)
4 Establishing and replenishing a change fund (p. 333)
5 Handling transactions involving cash short and over (p. 333)

The internal control policies of a company will depend on things such as number of employees, company size, sources of cash, and usage of the Internet.

In the first five chapters of this book, we analyzed the accounting cycle for businesses that perform personal services (e.g., word processing or legal services). In this chapter, we turn our attention to Becca's Jewellery Store, a merchandising company that earns revenue by selling goods (or merchandise) to customers. When Becca's business began to increase, she became concerned that she was not monitoring the business's cash closely. She understood that a business with good **internal control systems** safeguards cash. Cash is the asset that is most easily stolen, lost, or mishandled. Therefore, it is important to protect all cash receipts and to control cash payments so that payments are made only for authorized business purposes.

After studying the situation carefully, Becca began a series of procedures that were to be followed by all company employees. The new company policies that Becca's Jewellery Store would put into place are as follows:

1.   Responsibilities and duties of employees will be divided. For example, the person receiving the cash, whether at the register or by opening the mail, will not record this information into the accounting records. The accountant will not be handling the cash receipts.

2.   All cash receipts of Becca's Jewellery Store will be deposited into the bank the same day they arrive except for unusual items such as a post-dated cheque which should be kept on file then deposited on the date it becomes negotiable.

3.   All cash payments will be made by cheque (except petty cash, which is discussed later in this chapter).

4.   Employees' jobs will be rotated. This change allows workers to become acquainted with the work of others as well as to prepare for a possible changeover of jobs or to cover for employee absenteeism.

5.   Becca Baker will sign all cheques after receiving authorization to pay from the departments concerned.

6.   At time of payment, all supporting invoices or documents will be stamped paid. The stamp will show when the invoice or document is paid as well as the number of the cheque used.

7.   All cheques will be prenumbered. Periodically, the number of the cheques that were issued and the numbers of the blank cheque forms remaining should be verified to make sure that all cheque numbers are accounted for. This change will control the use of cheques and make it difficult to use a cheque fraudulently without it being revealed at some point.

8.   Monthly bank statements will be sent to and reconciled by someone other than the employees who handle, record, or deposit the cash.

Learning Unit 7-1

Bank Procedures, Chequing Accounts, and Bank Reconciliation

1 Depositing, writing, and endorsing cheques for a chequing account

Becca knew that a chequing account is one of the most useful and common banking services available, but she had many questions and decisions to make. She wanted to know about account options, monthly service charges, cheque printing charges, minimum balance requirements, interest paid on the account, availability of automatic teller machines (ATMs), and debit cards. Before Becca's Jewellery opened on April 1, 2013, she met with the manager at her local Royal Bank to discuss opening and using a chequing account for the company.

OPENING A CHEQUING ACCOUNT

A signature card is another safeguard.

The bank manager gave Becca a signature card to fill out. The bank uses the **signature card** to verify the authenticity of the signature on all cheques. Because Becca would be signing all the cheques for her company, she was the only person who needed to sign the card.

After Becca completed the initial paperwork, she received a set of cheques and deposit slips. A **deposit slip** is a form that is used when making deposits in a bank or credit union. When filling out a deposit slip, you list the total amount of currency, coins, and cheques that you are depositing (see Figure 7-1). You list each cheque you are depositing individually.

When a deposit is completed, the depositor receives a copy of the deposit as a receipt or proof of the transaction. The deposit should also be recorded on the current cheque stub. The bank manager told Becca that she could give the deposits to a bank teller or she could use an automated teller machine (ATM). The ATM could also be used for withdrawing cash, transferring funds, or paying bills. For decades, ATM cards could be used only at ATM machines, but in recent years, they took on another function, a debit feature. As a **debit card**, the card carries a Visa or MasterCard logo and can be used anywhere Visa or MasterCard is accepted. The amount of the purchase paid for with a debit card is deducted directly from your chequing account.

When a bank credits your account, it is increasing the balance.

Often, Becca makes her deposits after business hours, when the bank is closed. At those times, she puts the deposit into a sealed bag (provided by the bank) and places the bag in the night depository. The bank will credit Becca's account when the deposit is processed. Becca plans to make all business payments by written cheque (except petty cash) and deposit all money received (cash and cheques) in the bank account.

Many chequing accounts earn interest. For our purposes, however, we assume that the chequing account for Becca's Jewellery Store does not pay interest. Also, we assume that the chequing account has a monthly service charge but no individual charge for cheques written.

CHEQUE ENDORSEMENT

Endorsements can be made by using a rubber stamp instead of a handwritten signature.

Cheques have to be *endorsed* (signed) by the person to whom the cheque is made payable before they can be deposited or cashed. **Endorsement** is the signing or stamping of one's name at the top right side on the back of the cheque. This signature means that the payee has transferred the right to deposit or cash the cheque to someone else (the bank). The bank can then collect the money from the person or company that issued the cheque.

Three different types of endorsement can be used (see Figure 7-2). The first is a *blank endorsement*. A blank endorsement does not specify that a particular person or firm must endorse it. It can be further endorsed by someone else. The bank will pay the last person who signs the cheque. This type of endorsement is not very safe. If the cheque is lost, the person who finds it can sign it and get the money.

The second type of endorsement is a *full endorsement*. The person or company signing (or stamping) the back of the cheque indicates the name of the company or the person to whom the cheque is to be paid. Only the person or company named in the endorsement can transfer the cheque to someone else.

The regulations require the endorsement to be within the top 3.8 cm (1½ inches) to speed up the cheque-clearing process.

Restrictive endorsements, the third type of endorsement, are the safest for businesses. Becca's Jewellery Store stamps the back of the cheque so that it must be deposited in the firm's account. This stamp limits any further use of the cheque.

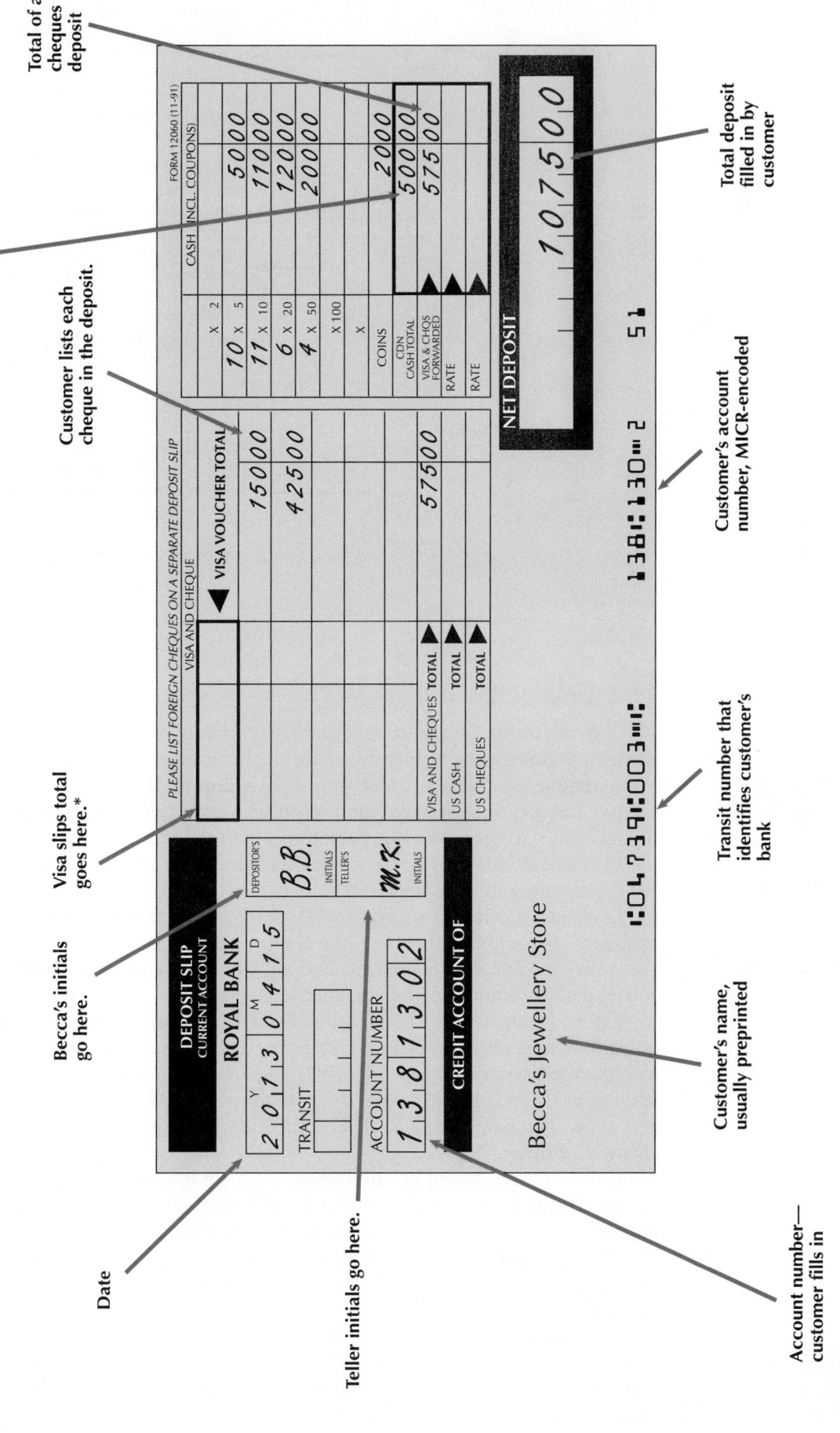

Figure 7-1 A Deposit Slip Example (This deposit is not part of the reconciliation that follows.)

Figure 7-2
Types of Cheque Endorsement

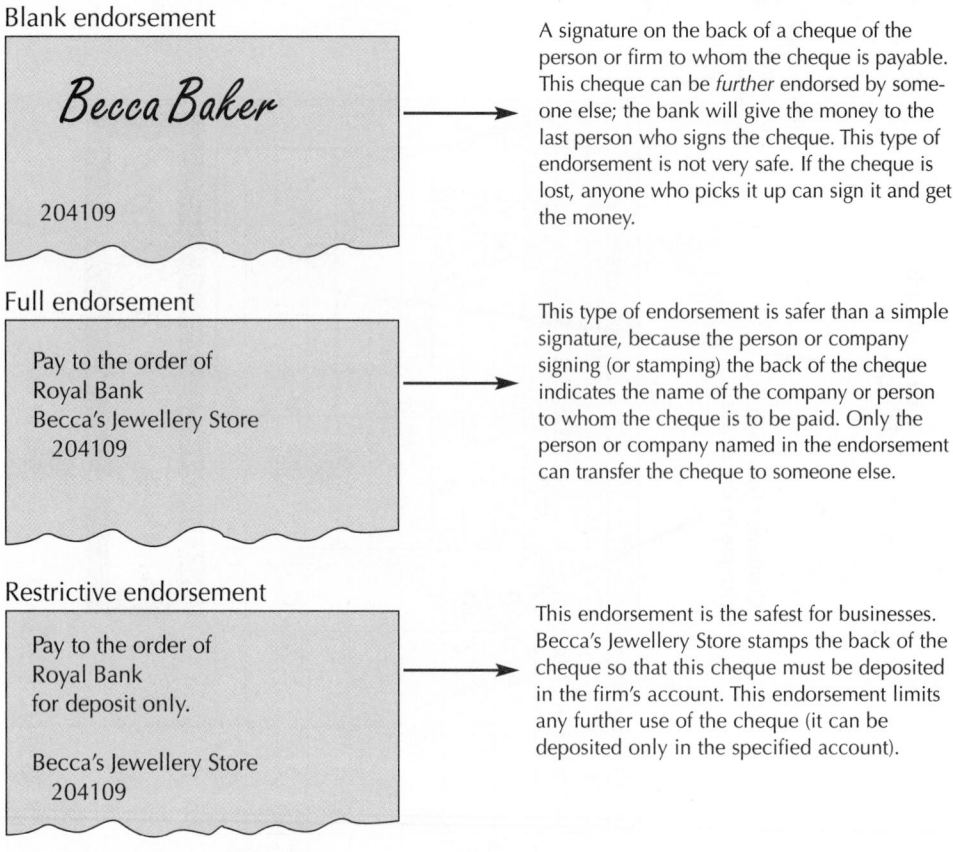

Blank endorsement

Becca Baker

204109

A signature on the back of a cheque of the person or firm to whom the cheque is payable. This cheque can be *further* endorsed by someone else; the bank will give the money to the last person who signs the cheque. This type of endorsement is not very safe. If the cheque is lost, anyone who picks it up can sign it and get the money.

Full endorsement

Pay to the order of
Royal Bank
Becca's Jewellery Store
204109

This type of endorsement is safer than a simple signature, because the person or company signing (or stamping) the back of the cheque indicates the name of the company or person to whom the cheque is to be paid. Only the person or company named in the endorsement can transfer the cheque to someone else.

Restrictive endorsement

Pay to the order of
Royal Bank
for deposit only.

Becca's Jewellery Store
204109

This endorsement is the safest for businesses. Becca's Jewellery Store stamps the back of the cheque so that this cheque must be deposited in the firm's account. This endorsement limits any further use of the cheque (it can be deposited only in the specified account).

THE CHEQUEBOOK

When Becca opened her business's chequing account, she received cheques. These cheques could be used to buy things for the business or to pay bills or salaries.

A **cheque** is a written order signed by a **drawer** (the person who writes the cheque) instructing a **drawee** (the person who pays the cheque) to pay a specific sum of money to the **payee** (the person to whom the cheque is payable). Figure 7-3 shows a cheque issued by Becca's Jewellery Store. Becca Baker is the drawer, Royal Bank is the drawee, and Ziegler Wholesalers is the payee.

Look at the cheque in Figure 7-3. Notice that certain things, such as the company's name and address and the cheque number, are preprinted. You should also notice the line drawn after the amount, which is to fill up the empty space and ensure that the amount cannot be changed.

Figure 7-3 includes a cheque stub. The cheque stub is used to record transactions, and it is kept for future reference. The information found on the stub includes the beginning balance ($3,441), the amount of any deposits ($0), the total amount in the account ($3,441), the amount of the cheque being written ($580), and the ending balance ($2,861). The cheque stub should be filled out before the cheque is written.

If the written amount on the cheque does not match the amount expressed in figures, Royal Bank may pay the amount written in words, return the cheque unpaid, or contact the drawer to see what was meant.

Many companies use cheque-writing machines to type out the information on the cheque. These machines prevent people from making fraudulent changes on handwritten cheques.

During the same time period, in-company records must be kept for all transactions affecting Becca's Jewellery Store's chequebook balance. Figure 7-4 shows these records. Note that the bank deposits ($6,446) minus the cheques written ($2,529) give an ending chequebook balance of $3,917.

Drawer: One who writes the cheque.

Drawee: One who pays money to payee.

Payee: One to whom the cheque is payable.

Banking on the Internet is expanding rapidly.

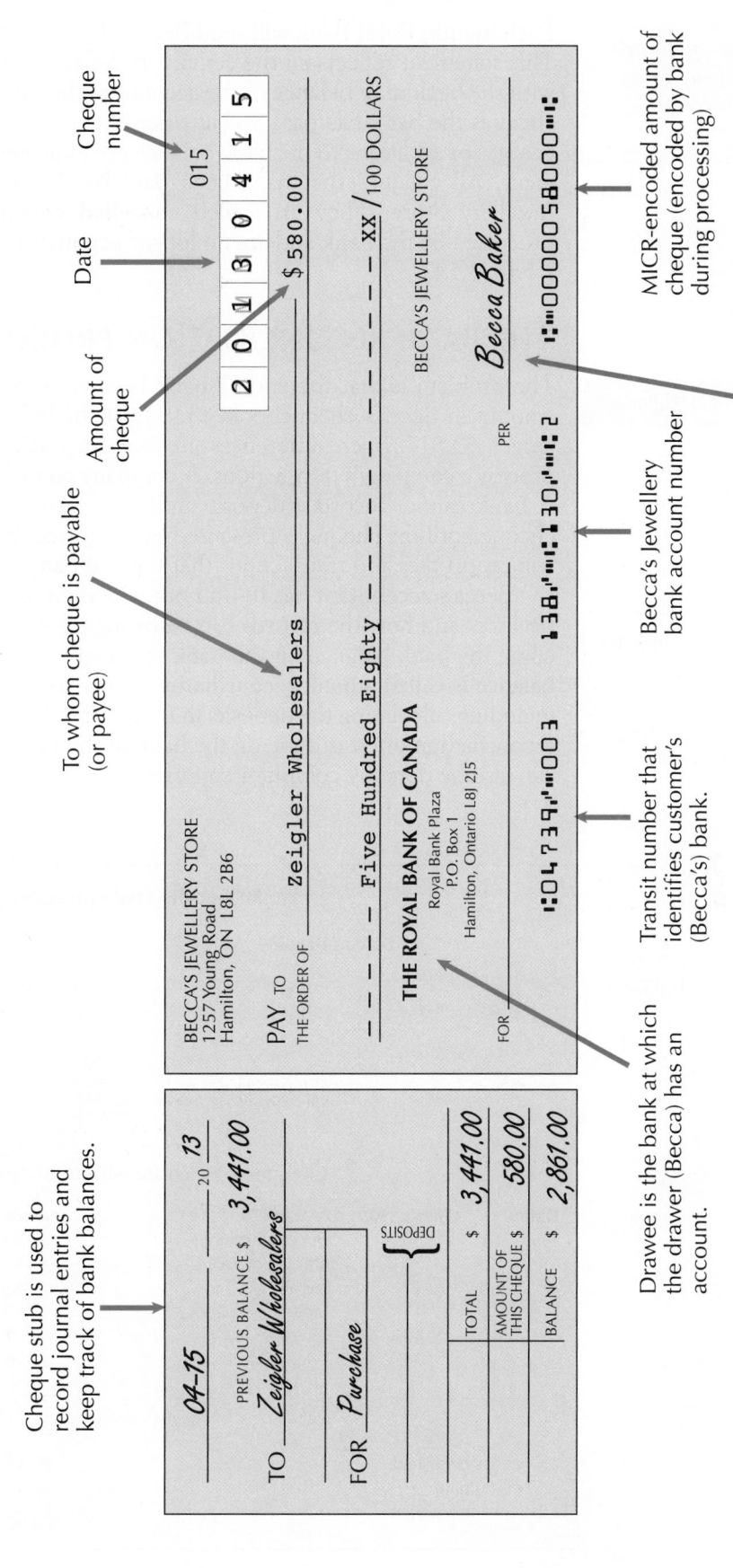

Cheque stub is used to record journal entries and keep track of bank balances.

To whom cheque is payable (or payee)

Amount of cheque

Date

Cheque number

MICR-encoded amount of cheque (encoded by bank during processing)

Signature of drawer (same as on the signature card), or one who orders the bank to pay a sum of money

Becca's Jewellery bank account number

Transit number that identifies customer's (Becca's) bank.

Drawee is the bank at which the drawer (Becca) has an account.

Figure 7-3   A Typical Cheque and Cheque Stub

MONTHLY RECORDKEEPING: THE BANK'S STATEMENT OF ACCOUNT AND IN-COMPANY RECORDS

Figure 7-5 shows one format for a bank statement. Different banks use different formats.

Each month, Royal Bank will send Becca's Jewellery Store a Statement of Account. This statement reflects all the activity in the account during that period. It begins with the beginning balance of the account at the start of the month, along with the cheques the bank has paid and any deposits received (see Figure 7-5). Any other charges or additions to the bank balance are indicated by codes found on the statement. All cheques that have been paid by the bank are sent back to Becca's Jewellery Store. They are called **cancelled cheques** because they have been processed by the bank and are no longer negotiable. The ending balance in Figure 7-5 is $3,592.

THE BANK RECONCILIATION PROCESS

2 Reconciling a bank statement

The problem is that the ending bank balance of $3,592 does not agree with the amount in Becca's chequebook, $3,917, or the balance in the cash amount in the ledger, $3,917. Such differences are caused partly by the time a bank takes to process a company's transactions. A company records a transaction when it occurs. A bank cannot record a deposit until it receives the funds, and it cannot pay a cheque until the cheque is presented by the payee. In addition, the bank statement will report fees and transactions that the company did not know about.

Becca's accountant has to find out why there is a $325 difference between the balances and how the records can be brought into balance. The process of reconciling the bank balance on the bank statement versus the company's chequebook balance is called a **bank reconciliation**. Bank reconciliations involve several steps, including calculating the deposits in transit and the outstanding cheques. The bank reconciliation often is done on the back of the **bank statement** (see Figure 7-6). It can also be done by computer software.

Online banking and computer software have made the reconciliation process even easier.

Figure 7-4
Transactions
(In-Company Records)
Affecting Chequebook
Balance

Bank Deposits Made for April

Date of Deposit		Amount	Received from
April	1	$5,000	Becca Baker, Capital
	4	340	Jennifer Leung
	15	89	Mary Figueroa
	26	117	Carl Jones
	30	900	Cash Sales
	Total deposits for month:	$6,446	

Cheques Written for Month of April

Date		Cheque No.	Payment To:	Amount	Description
April	1	10	Quality Insurance	$ 500	Insurance paid in advance
	5	11	ABC Wholesalers	400	Merchandise
	8	12	Payroll	800	Salaries
	10	13	Times Newspaper	100	Advertising
	10	14	Verizon	99	Telephone
	15	15	Zeigler Wholesalers	580	Merchandise
	15		ATM Withdrawal	50	Postage
			Total amount of cheques written:	$2,529	

Cheques deposited	$6,446
Cheques paid	− 2,529
Balance in account	$3,917

ROYAL BANK

BECCA'S JEWELLERY STORE
1257 Young Road
Hamilton ON L8L 2B6

ACCOUNT
NUMBER   138   130   2

CLOSING
PERIOD   4/30/13

Address Correction on Reverse Side ☐

CHEQUING ACCOUNT							
On	Your Balance Was	No.	We Subtracted Cheques Totalling	Less Service Charge	No.	We Added Deposits Of	Making Your Present Balance
4/1	0	6	1,949.00	5.00	4	5,546.00	3,592.00

Date	Cheques • Withdrawals • Payment		Deposits • Interest • Advances	Balance
4/1			5,000.00	5,000.00
4/3	500.00			4,500.00
4/4			340.00	4,840.00
4/9	400.00			4,440.00
4/9	800.00			3,640.00
4/13	100.00			3,540.00
4/13	99.00			3,441.00
4/15			89.00	3,530.00
4/15	50.00 ATM			3,480.00
4/26			117.00	3,597.00
4/30	5.00 SC			3,592.00

Figure 7-5   Bank Statement

Deposits in Transit

Deposits in transit. **These unrecorded deposits could result if a deposit were placed in a night depository on the last day of the month.**

In comparing the list of deposits received by the bank with the chequebook, the accountant notices that a deposit made on April 28 for $900 was not on the bank's statement. The accountant realizes that to prepare this statement, the bank included information about Becca's Jewellery Store only up to April 26. This deposit made by Becca was not shown on the monthly bank statement because it arrived at the bank after the statement was printed. Thus, timing becomes a consideration in the reconciliation process. Deposits not yet added to the bank balance are called **deposits in transit**. This deposit needs to be added to the bank balance shown on the bank statement. Becca's chequebook is not affected, because the deposit has already been added to its balance. The bank has no way of knowing that the deposit is coming until it receives it.

Outstanding Cheques

Cheque No. 15 is outstanding.

Cheques outstanding are cheques drawn by the depositor but not yet presented to the bank for payment by the payee.

The first thing the accountant does when the bank statement is received is put the cheques in numerical order (1, 2, 3, etc.). In doing so, the accountant notices that one payment was not made by the bank and cheque No. 15 was not returned by the bank.

Becca's books showed that this cheque had been deducted from the chequebook balance. The **outstanding cheque**, however, had not yet been presented to the bank for payment or deducted from the bank balance. When this cheque does reach the bank, the bank will reduce the amount of the balance.

Service Charges

Becca's accountant also notices a bank **service charge** of $5. Becca's book balance will be lowered by $5.

Figure 7-6
Bank Reconciliation Using the
Back of the Bank Statement

CHEQUES OUTSTANDING			
NUMBER	AMOUNT		1. Enter balance shown on this statement
15	580 | 00		3,592 | 00
			2. If you have made deposits since the date of this statement add them to the above balance
			900 | 00
			3. SUBTOTAL
			4,492 | 00
			4. Deduct total of cheques outstanding
			580 | 00
			5. ADJUSTED BALANCE This should agree with your chequebook
TOTAL OF CHEQUES OUTSTANDING	580 | 00		3,912 | 00 *

TO VERIFY YOUR CHEQUING BALANCE

1. Sort cheques by number or by date issued and compare with your cheque stubs and prior outstanding list. Make certain all cheques paid have been recorded in your chequebook. If any of your cheques were not included with this statement, list the numbers and amounts under "CHEQUES OUTSTANDING."

2. Deduct the Service Charge as shown on the statement from your chequebook balance.

3. Review copies of charge advices included with this statement and check for proper entry in your chequebook.

IF THE ADJUSTED BALANCE DOES NOT AGREE WITH YOUR CHEQUEBOOK BALANCE, THE FOLLOWING SUGGESTIONS ARE OFFERED FOR YOUR ASSISTANCE.
- Recheck additions and subtractions in your chequebook and figures to the left.
- Make certain chequebook balances have carried forward properly.
- Verify deposits recorded on statement against deposits entered in chequebook.
- Compare amount on each chequebook stub.

*Note the $5 service charge is included

Not Sufficient Funds

An **NSF (not sufficient funds)** cheque is a cheque that has been returned because the drawer did not have enough money in its account to pay the cheque. Accountants are continually on the lookout for NSF cheques. An NSF cheque means less money in the chequing account than was thought. Becca will have to (1) lower the chequebook balance and (2) try to collect the amount from the customer. The bank would notify Becca's Jewellery of an NSF cheque (or other deductions) by a **debit memorandum**. Think of a <u>de</u>bit memorandum as a <u>dedu</u>ction from the depositor's balance.

If the bank acts as a collecting agent for Becca's Jewellery, say in collecting notes, it will charge Becca a small fee and the net amount collected will be added to Becca's bank balance. The bank will send Becca a **credit memorandum** verifying the increase in her company's balance.

A journal entry is also needed to bring the ledger accounts of Cash and Service Charge expense up to date. Any adjustment to the chequebook balance results in a journal entry. The entry in Figure 7-7 was made to accomplish this step:

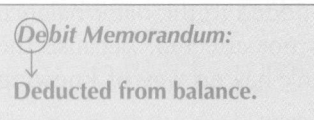

Debit Memorandum:

Deducted from balance.

Credit memorandum:
Added to balance.

Figure 7-7
Service Charge
Journalized

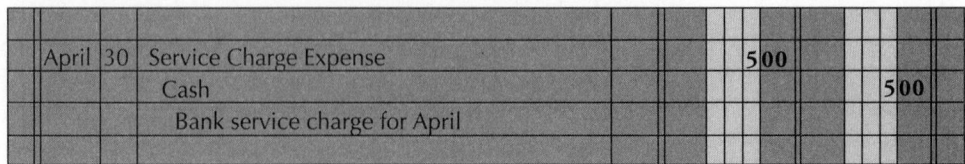

April	30	Service Charge Expense				5|00			
		Cash						5|00	
		Bank service charge for April							

It is important for Becca to prepare a bank reconciliation when she receives her bank statement every month as part of the cash control procedure. It verifies the amount of cash in her chequing account. Another important reason to do a bank reconciliation is that it may uncover irregularities such as employee theft of funds.

Here are step-by-step instructions for preparing a bank reconciliation:

1. **Prepare a list of deposits in transit.** Compare the deposits listed on your bank statement with the bank deposits shown in your general ledger cash account. On your bank reconciliation, list any deposits that have not appeared on (called "clearing") the bank statement. Also, take a look at the bank reconciliation you prepared last month. Did all of last month's deposits in transit show up on this month's bank statement? If not, you need to find out why not.

2. **Prepare a list of outstanding cheques.** In your general ledger cash account, mark each cheque that cleared the bank statement this month. On your bank reconciliation, list all the recorded cheques that did not clear. Also, take a look at the bank reconciliation you prepared last month. Did any cheques outstanding from last month still not clear the bank? If so, be sure they are on your list of outstanding cheques this month. If a cheque is several months old and still has not cleared the bank, you may want to investigate further, and either replace it, or correct the company's book balance by making an adjusting entry.

3. **Record any bank charges or credits.** Take a close look at your bank statement. Are all special charges made by the bank recorded in your books? If not, record them now as if you had just written a cheque for that amount. By the same token, any credits made to your account by the bank should be recorded as well. Post the entries to your general ledger.

4. **Compute the cash balance per your books.** This should be the general ledger balance.

5. **Enter bank balance on the reconciliation.** At the top of the bank reconciliation statement, enter the ending balance from the bank statement.

6. **Total the deposits in transit.** Add up the deposits in transit and enter the total on the reconciliation. Add the total deposits in transit to the bank balance to arrive at a subtotal.

7. **Total the outstanding cheques.** Add up the outstanding cheques, and enter the total on the reconciliation.

8. **Compute the balance per the reconciliation.** Subtract the total outstanding cheques from the subtotal in step 6. The result should equal the balance shown in your general ledger.

Before we look at a more comprehensive bank reconciliation, let's look at trends in banking.

TRENDS IN BANKING

In the past, banking took place on the main street of your town or on a nearby highway. The branches were open 9 a.m. to 3 p.m. Monday to Thursday. They were probably open 9 a.m. to 6 p.m. on Friday and possibly 9 a.m. to noon on Saturday. These times were not always convenient for people who worked full time.

Until recently, most people, even those who heard a lot about online banking, probably hadn't tried it. Many people still pay bills by mail and deposit cheques at a nearby branch, much the way their parents did.

Many financial institutions have developed or are developing ways to transfer funds electronically, without the use of paper cheques. Such systems are called **electronic funds transfers (EFT)**. Most EFTs are established to save money and avoid theft.

Financial institutions use powerful computer networks to automate millions of daily transactions. Today, banks are able to use computer technology to give you the option of bypassing the time-consuming, paper-based aspects of traditional banking so that you can manage your finances more quickly and efficiently.

Automatic teller machines (ATMs), the first step toward online banking, were first installed into banks about 35 years ago. Customers could now make deposits, withdraw money, and obtain account balances without having to stand in line during the times that the bank was open. Customers are able to use an ATM in banks, supermarkets, malls, and possibly even at your institution's student centre.

Call centres were the next major step forward for banks. Customers could telephone the centre using either a toll-free number or local number and find information about their accounts without leaving home.

The latest development in banking is Internet, or online, banking. Most of the large banks offer fully secure, fully functional online banking for free or for a small fee. Some smaller banks offer limited access; for instance, you may be able to view your account balance and history but may not be able to initiate transactions online. As more customers use the banks' sites, fully functional online banking will probably become as common as automated teller machines.

With a debit card and personal identification number (PIN), you can use an automated teller machine (ATM) to withdraw cash, make deposits, or transfer funds between accounts. Some ATMs charge a fee if you are not a member of the ATM network or are making a transaction at a remote location. Not all ATMs will accept deposits.

Retail purchases can also be made with a debit card. You enter your PIN or sign for the purchase. Some banks that issue debit cards are charging customers a fee for a debit card purchase made with a PIN. Although a debit card looks like a credit card, the money for the purchase is transferred directly from your bank account to the store's account. The purchase will be shown on your bank statement.

Immediately call the card issuer when you suspect a debit card may be lost or stolen. Most companies have toll-free numbers and a 24-hour service to deal with such emergencies. Although federal law limits your liability for a stolen credit card, your liability for unauthorized use of your ATM or debit card can be much greater—depending on how quickly you report the loss. Also, it is important to remember that when you use a debit card, federal law does not give you the right to stop payment. You must resolve the problem with the seller.

If you don't mind forgoing the teller window, a virtual bank or e-bank, such as ING Direct, may save you some money. Virtual banks are not as common in Canada as they are in the United States, but these "banks without bricks" are probably going to become more common here in the next few years. They exist entirely online and offer much of the same range of services and adhere to the same regulations as your corner bank. Virtual banks pass the money that they save on overhead, such as buildings and tellers, along to you in the form of higher yields and lower fees. Banking is available everywhere, all the time. Your finances are at your fingertips.

Advantages of Online Banking

Customers who use online banking services enjoy many advantages. They can do almost everything from the comfort of their own homes at convenient times and without standing in long lines.

◆ **Convenience.** Unlike your corner site, online banks never close. They are available 24 hours a day, seven days a week.

◆ **Availability.** If you are out of province or even out of the country when a money problem arises, you can log on instantly to your online bank and take care of business, 24/7.

◆ **Transaction speed.** Online bank sites generally execute and confirm transactions as quickly or even faster than ATM processing speeds.

◆ **Efficiency.** You can access and manage all of your bank accounts, including RSPs and TDs, from one secure site.

- **Effectiveness.** Many online banking sites now offer sophisticated tools to help you manage all of your assets more effectively. Most of these tools are compatible with money managing programs such as Quicken®, QuickBooks®, and Simply Accounting®.
- **Internal control:** The nearly instantaneous access to a business's banking records means that a bank reconciliation can be done at any time during the month. Many businesses do complete a reconciliation monthly, but performing this task more often (say weekly) means that any errors are caught quickly, improving safety over this vital asset.

Disadvantages of Online Banking

Although online banking has many advantages, it also has disadvantages.

- **Start-up may take time.** In order to register for your bank's online program, you will probably have to provide some personal identification and sign a form at a bank branch.
- **Learning curve.** Banking sites can be difficult to navigate at first. Plan to invest time to read the tutorials in order to become comfortable in your virtual lobby.
- **Bank site changes.** Even the largest banks periodically upgrade their online programs, adding new features in unfamiliar places. In some cases, you may need to re-enter account information.
- **The trust thing.** For many people, the biggest hurdle to online banking is learning to trust it. Did my transaction go through? Did I push the transfer button once or twice? Best bet: always print the transaction receipt and keep it with your bank records until it shows up on your personal site or your bank statement.

When problems arise, it is usually much easier to sort them out face to face rather than having to use e-mail or the telephone. Perhaps, the biggest problem with online banking is security. It is important to keep passwords safe and to be aware of fake e-mails arriving in your inbox. These e-mails pretend to be from your bank and attempt to obtain account details from you that can then be used to steal your money. This kind of fraud is called **phishing**.

Fraudulent practices can happen at cash registers when you make a purchase or at restaurants when you pay with a credit card and the waiter is out of your sight. Skimming at ATMs can be much more damaging because of the number of accounts and the amount of money that can be quickly accessed. Card-based purchases—online, debit, and credit—are convenient for consumers. For example, tens of thousands of ATM machines are swipe-based. The large number of ATMs contributes to the skimming problem. In a way, we've become victims of the convenience we demand.

Here are some tips to help you avoid becoming a skimming victim.

- Keep your PIN safe. Don't give it to anyone.
- Watch out for people who try to "help" you at an ATM.
- Look at the ATM before using it. If it doesn't look right, don't use it.
- If an ATM has any unusual signage, don't use it. No bank would hang a sign that says, "Swipe your ATM here before inserting it in the card reader"or something to that effect.
- If your card is not returned after the transaction or after pressing cancel, immediately contact the institution that issued the card.
- Check your statement promptly to be sure no unusual withdrawals appear on it.

Electronic Integration

This topic, while definitely related to banking, is a much more involved matter than just banking. Your instructor might suggest that the class skip this topic entirely, or that you read it as background information only.

The basic idea of **electronic integration** is that a business that needs, for instance, to purchase some supplies can accomplish the entire task without creating a single piece of paper. If the purchase is large enough, it can request possible suppliers to quote prices using the Internet (and possibly a link to a trade association). Once a suitable supplier has been identified, a *purchase order (PO)* can be sent to that supplier using the business's accounting software. (A purchase order is an enforceable document that serves to protect the vendor and the purchaser, and includes relevant details such as quantity, price, dates, and shipping details.)

Once the PO is received by the supplier (which is virtually instantaneous over the Internet), the order is picked from the supplier's warehouse or place of business, and packaged for shipment. The freight company (think FedEx, Purolator, etc.) is also contacted by the supplier, and arrangements are made to pick up the boxes and deliver them to the purchaser. This pickup also is handled over the Internet, and usually permits the shipping charges to be known accurately so they can be included in the invoice without delay.

Possibly even before the ordered goods are shipped, the vendor's computer accounting software prepares an invoice for the purchaser. Often this is as easy as converting the PO to an invoice, which is quickly done because the details are usually identical. The invoice, once approved, is sent along to the purchaser's computer—again using the Internet—and it is received soon after being sent.

This invoice, once received by the purchaser, is entered into their accounting records—often automatically. Once the goods are received, and the quantities verified, the invoice is approved for payment. Here is where banking gets involved.

Once approved for payment (say, in 10 days' time), the accounting software generates an electronic payment on the chosen day and sends this to both the supplier (or vendor) and their own bank. The electronic payment causes the purchaser's bank account to be lowered by the amount of the transfer, and the supplier's bank account to go up by the same amount.

Note that all the above happens without any paper being printed. Actually, some printing often does take place; but if so, it is done locally, and no paper needs to be sent through the mail, as was once universal.

Note also that the process is so automated that significant savings are realized for both the purchaser and the supplier. Of course, expensive investments need to be made up front, in things like a computer system, appropriate software, and training for the people who will make it all work; but the general response in the business world is that these costs are worth it. And the large investment is only needed if a company wants to send electronic payments. Even very small businesses can receive these modern funds transfers quickly and easily.

Some of you are probably thinking that this form of electronic integration is available only to the largest companies. Well, it did start out that way, but recent advances in computer software, and especially in the financial structure of electronic processing and money transfers, is making it easy for small and especially medium-sized companies to take advantage of the many cost-saving features of such integration.

Electronic integration needs to be implemented with rather strict controls in place to prevent errors and fraud. The swiftness of processing requires every company to examine and approve each transaction. Most of the accounting software that facilitates this way of conducting business does have many basic controls built in, so it does not need to be reinvented for each new business.

What does the future hold? Almost certainly this time- and cost-saving concept will continue to be adopted by many additional companies. Already, inexpensive computer accounting software packages such as Simply Accounting® and QuickBooks® contain many of the necessary features, and more updates are added annually. Expect to see electronic integration become almost universal within a few years.

International Banking

Canadian business students need to become aware that banking has an international dimension. It is becoming normal to receive money from or send money to a business entity in another country. For many decades, banks have made it possible to move money around our planet, but until recently it has been neither simple nor cheap nor instantaneous.

One of the main features of modern banking that supports the movement of funds on an international basis is **S.W.I.F.T. codes**. These codes were developed to allow most of the world's banks to be identified in an unambiguous way, so that funds can be sent between them quickly and accurately, using special forms designed to ensure excellent controls. These forms are often sent over the Internet, and are most often encoded to ensure privacy as well as accuracy.

Cheque Truncation (safekeeping)

Some banks do not return cancelled cheques to the depositor but use a procedure called **cheque truncation** or **safekeeping**. The bank holds a cancelled cheque for a specific period of time (usually 90 days) and then keeps a microfilm copy handy and destroys the original. Some credit unions do not send back cheques. Instead, the cheque date, number, and amount are listed on the bank statement. Others attach a photocopy sheet of all the cheques they have paid. If the customer needs a copy of a cheque, the bank will provide the cheque or a photocopy for a small fee. (Photocopies are accepted as evidence by Canada Revenue Agency for appeals, tax returns, and audits.)

Truncation cuts down on the amount of "paper" that is returned to both business and individual customers and thus provides substantial cost savings. It is estimated that more than 5 million cheques are written each day in Canada.

Example of a More Comprehensive Bank Statement

The bank reconciliation of Becca's Jewellery was not as complicated as it is for many companies, even using today's computer technology. Let's look at a reconciliation for Matty's Supermarket (Figures 7-8 and 7-9), which is based on the following:

Matty's cash account balance		$13,176.84
Bank balance		23,726.04
Leased space to Subway—EFT receipt		8,456.00
Leased space to Dunkin' Donuts—EFT receipt		3,616.12
Matty pays a supplementary health insurance payment each month by electronic transfer		1,444.00
Deposits in transit 6/30		6,766.52
Cheques outstanding		
Chq. # 738	$1,144.00	
739	1,277.88	
740	332.00	
741	812.56	
742	1,834.12	
Cheque # 734 was overstated in Company's Books		1,440.00

Note in Figure 7-9 that each adjustment to Matty's chequebook is the reconciliation process that would result in general journal entries.

Figure 7-8
Bank Statement for Matty's
Supermarket

ROYAL BANK
1 Left Street
Marblehead, NS B0T 6A4

ACCOUNT STATEMENT

Matty's Supermarket
20 Sullivan St.
Marblehead, NS B0T 7X3

Chequing Account: 775800061

Chequing Account Summary as of 6/30/12

Beginning Balance	Total Deposits	Total Withdrawals	Service Charge	Ending Balance
$26,224.48	$17,410.56	$19,852.00	$57.00	$23,726.04

Chequing Account Transactions

Deposits	Date	Amount
Deposit	6/05	4,000.00
Deposit	6/05	448.00
Deposit	6/08	778.40
EFT leasing: Dunkin' Donuts	6/18	3,616.12
EFT leasing: Subway	6/27	8,456.00
Interest	6/30	112.04

Charges	Date	Amount
Service charge: Cheque printing	6/30	57.00
EFT: Blue Cross/Blue Shield	6/21	1,444.00
NSF	6/21	208.00

Cheques			Daily Balance				
Number	Date	Amount	Date	Balance		Date	Balance
401	6/07	400.00	5/31	26,224.48		6/18	21,267.00
733	6/13	12,000.00	6/05	30,672.48		6/21	19,615.00
734	6/13	600.00	6/07	30,272.48		6/27	28,071.00
735	6/11	400.00	6/09	30,050.88		6/30	23,726.04
736	6/18	400.00	6/11	30,650.88			
737	6/29	4,400.00	6/13	18,050.88			

Figure 7-9
Bank Reconciliation
for Matty's Supermarket

MATTY'S SUPERMARKET
Bank Reconciliation as of June 30, 2012

General ledger balance			Bank balance		
Matty's general ledger balance		$13,176.84	Bank balance		$23,726.04
Add:			Add:		
EFT leasing: Dunkin' Donuts			Deposits in transit, 6/30		6,766.52
	$3,616.12				$30,492.56
EFT leasing: Subway					
	8,456.00				
Interest	112.04				
Error: Overstated					
Cheque No. 734	1,440.00	$13,624.16			
		$26,801.00			
Deduct:			Deduct:		
Service charge	57.00		Outstanding cheques:		
NSF cheque	208.00		No. 738	$1,144.00	
EFT health insurance			No. 739	1,277.88	
payment	1,444.00	1,709.00	No. 740	332.00	
			No. 741	812.56	
			No. 742	1,834.12	5,400.56
Reconciled balance		$25,092.00	Reconciled balance		$25,092.00

LEARNING UNIT 7-1 REVIEW

AT THIS POINT you should be able to:

◆ Define and explain the need for a deposit slip. (p. 312)

◆ List as well as compare and contrast the three common types of cheque endorsement. (pp. 312–314)

◆ Explain the structure of a cheque. (p. 314)

◆ Define and state the purpose of a bank statement. (p. 316)

◆ Explain deposits in transit, cheques outstanding, service charge, and NSF. (pp. 317–318)

◆ Explain the difference between a debit memorandum and a credit memorandum. (p. 318)

◆ Explain how to do a bank reconciliation. (p. 319)

◆ Explain electronic funds transfer and cheque truncation. (pp. 319 and 323)

◆ Explain the advantages and disadvantages of online banking. (pp. 320–321)

Self-Review Quiz 7-1A

(The forms you need are on page 7-1 of the *Study Guide with Working Papers*.)

Indicate, by placing an X under it, the heading that describes the appropriate action for each of the following situations:

Situation	Add to Bank Balance	Deduct from Bank Balance	Add to Chequebook Balance	Deduct from Chequebook Balance
1. Cheque printing charge				
2. Deposits in transit				
3. NSF cheque				
4. A $50 cheque written and recorded by the company as $60				
5. Proceeds of a note collected by the bank				
6. Cheque outstanding				
7. Forgot to record direct deposit payroll payment				

Solution to Self-Review Quiz 7-1A

Quiz Tip
Deposits in transit are added to the bank balance, while cheques outstanding are subtracted from the bank balance.

Situation	Add to Bank Balance	Deduct from Bank Balance	Add to Chequebook Balance	Deduct from Chequebook Balance
1				X
2	X			
3				X
4			X	
5			X	
6		X		
7				X

Self-Review Quiz 7-1B

Maximum value from this review question will be obtained only when you make an honest attempt to complete it before looking at the solution provided.

KELLY'S TRAIL RIDES OPENING BANK RECONCILIATION MAY 31, 2014			
Balance per Bank Statement—May 29, 2014			$8,543.86
Add: Deposit in Transit			1,253.48
			9,797.34
Less: Outstanding Cheques:	Chq. No.	Amount	
	814	78.30	
	852	579.42	
	854	1,084.00	
	858	341.75	2,083.47
			$7,713.87
Balance per General Ledger—Account 1111			$7,756.37
Less: Bank Charges for May			42.50
			$7,713.87

KELLY'S TRAIL RIDES

Period	Source	Date	Description	Reference	Posting Sequence	Debits	Credits	Dr. Balance
6	GL-JE	Jun 1, 2014	Opening Balance					7,756.37
6	GL-JE	Jun 2, 2014	Syd Jenkins Tack Shop	CHQ 859	6-01		1,840.60	5,915.77
6	GL-JE	Jun 2, 2014	Municipal Utility Co.	CHQ 860	6-01		278.32	5,637.45
6	GL-JE	Jun 3, 2014	Deposit—CHRA	3827C	6-02	2,580.00		8,217.45
6	GL-JE	Jun 3, 2014	Atkin's Repairs	CHQ 861	6-03		650.00	7,567.45
6	GL-JE	Jun 6, 2014	Deposit—NS Group	3828C	6-04	3,295.00		10,862.45
6	GL-JE	Jun 6, 2014	Kelly Dean	CHQ 862	6-05		2,000.00	8,862.45
6	GL-JE	Jun 6, 2014	Chapperal Books	CHQ 863	6-05		245.75	8,616.70
6	GL-JE	Jun 6, 2014	NSF—R. Burke—CHRA	Royal DM	6-06		415.00	8,201.70
6	GL-JE	Jun 6, 2014	NSF Service Charge	Royal DM	6-06		25.00	8,176.70
6	GL-JE	Jun 6, 2014	MKP Properties	CHQ 864	6-07		1,465.50	6,711.20
6	GL-JE	Jun 9, 2014	Mary K. Madsen	CHQ 865	6-07		975.00	5,736.20
6	GL-JE	Jun 9, 2014	Bank Charges for May	ADJ 418	6-07		42.50	5,693.70
6	GL-JE	Jun 9, 2014	Deposit—KOH Group	3829C	6-08	4,250.00		9,943.70
6	GL-JE	Jun 10, 2014	Sandy's Quick Mart	CHQ 866	6-09		153.56	9,790.14
6	GL-JE	Jun 10, 2014	Canadian Map Company	CHQ 867	6-09		386.48	9,403.66
6	GL-JE	Jun 10, 2014	Merv Stringer	CHQ 868	6-09		845.00	8,558.66
6	GL-JE	Jun 10, 2014	Hunter Wholesale Co.	CHQ 869	6-09		218.60	8,340.06
6	GL-JE	Jun 13, 2014	Deposit—Manyberries	3830C	6-10	6,200.00		14,540.06
6	GL-JE	Jun 13, 2014	Mary K. Madsen	CHQ 870	6-11		1,140.00	13,400.06
6	GL-JE	Jun 13, 2014	Receiver General	CHQ 871	6-11		1,847.37	11,552.69
6	GL-JE	Jun 13, 2014	Renown Circulation	CHQ 872	6-11		74.50	11,478.19
6	GL-JE	Jun 13, 2014	Kelly Dean	CHQ 873	6-11		1,800.00	9,678.19
6	GL-JE	Jun 16, 2014	Deposit—Tanks a Lot	3831C	6-12	2,400.00		12,078.19
6	GL-JE	Jun 17, 2014	Carolyn Wolfsun	CHQ 874	6-13		750.00	11,328.19
6	GL-JE	Jun 17, 2014	Kendall Trailer Repairs	CHQ 875	6-14		1,547.50	9,780.69
6	GL-JE	Jun 20, 2014	Deposit—OFLR Group	3832C	6-15	3,865.00		13,645.69
6	GL-JE	Jun 20, 2014	Mary K. Madsen	CHQ 876	6-16		875.00	12,770.69
6	GL-JE	Jun 23, 2014	RBC—Loan Principal	Royal DM	6-17		745.20	12,025.49
6	GL-JE	Jun 23, 2014	RBC—Loan Interest	Royal DM	6-17		415.82	11,609.67
6	GL-JE	Jun 23, 2014	County Phone Company	CHQ 877	6-18		204.10	11,405.57
6	GL-JE	Jun 23, 2014	K. Simpson Feeds	CHQ 878	6-18		2,487.35	8,918.22
6	GL-JE	Jun 23, 2014	Bo Franklin	CHQ 879	6-18		377.43	8,540.79
6	GL-JE	Jun 23, 2014	Deposit—Acadian Group	3833C	6-20	2,545.00		11,085.79
6	GL-JE	Jun 23, 2014	Kelly Dean	CHQ 880	6-21		2,500.00	8,585.79
6	GL-JE	Jun 23, 2014	Phillip Madsen	CHQ 881	6-21		645.00	7,940.79
6	GL-JE	Jun 24, 2014	Covington Supplies Co.	CHQ 882	6-22		1,525.00	6,415.79
6	GL-JE	Jun 24, 2014	Bragg Creek High School	CHQ 883	6-22		250.00	6,165.79
6	GL-JE	Jun 24, 2014	OK Corral	CHQ 884	6-22		624.35	5,541.44
6	GL-JE	Jun 27, 2014	Deposit—Finchly Group	3834C	6-23	4,275.00		9,816.44
6	GL-JE	Jun 27, 2014	Deposit—Sundry Cash Sales	3834C	6-23	1,800.00		11,616.44
6	GL-JE	Jun 30, 2014	Mary K. Madsen	CHQ 885	6-24		1,150.00	10,466.44
6	GL-JE	Jun 30, 2014	Bearly's Bridles	CHQ 886	6-24		537.00	9,929.44
6	GL-JE	Jun 30, 2014	George Early Foods	CHQ 887	6-25		1,107.30	8,822.14
6	GL-JE	Jun 30, 2014	Riopan Milling	CHQ 888	6-25		2,176.64	6,645.50
6	GL-JE	Jun 30, 2014	Deposit—Epcor Group	3835C	6-26	5,250.00		11,895.50
6	GL-JE	Jun 30, 2014	Joan Fairfax—Salary	CHQ 889	6-27		2,156.44	9,739.06
6	GL-JE	Jun 30, 2014	Curly Adams—Salary	CHQ 890	6-27		1,984.23	7,754.83
6	GL-JE	Jun 30, 2014	Kelly Dean	CHQ 891	6-27		2,200.00	5,554.83

The above is a detailed printout of the bank account (account number 1111) for Kelly's Trail Rides. It looks a bit different from a hand-posted ledger account because it has been printed by accounting software, but the two versions are essentially the same. Note that this version shows somewhat more detail—a description and reference, for example.

ROYAL BANK OF CANADA

411 MAIN STREET
BRAGG CREEK
ALBERTA   T8M 4G6

Account Statement

Account No.	422-627-8

KELLY'S TRAIL RIDES
RR#5
Bragg Creek
Alberta T8J 6N3

Period	
From	To
29-May-14	28-Jun-14

Enclosures	Page
28	1

Date	Transaction Description	Details Cheques	Deposits	Cheques & Debits	Deposits & Credits	Balance
	Balance Forward					8,543.86
May 30	Deposit				1,253.48	9,797.34
	Cheque	854		1,084.00		8,713.34
May 31	Cheque	852		579.42		8,133.92
Jun 2	Cheque	859		1,840.60		6,293.32
Jun 3	Deposit		3827C		2,580.00	8,873.32
Jun 3	Cheque	858		341.75		8,531.57
Jun 6	Deposit		3828C		3,295.00	11,826.57
	Cheque	860		278.32		11,548.25
	NSF R. Burke	DM		415.00		11,133.25
	NSF S/C	DM		25.00		11,108.25
Jun 7	Cheque	862		2,000.00		9,108.25
Jun 8	Cheque	861		650.00		8,458.25
	Cheque	863		245.75		8,212.50
Jun 9	Deposit		3829C		4,250.00	12,462.50
	Cheque	865		975.00		11,487.50
	Cheque	864		1,465.50		10,022.00
Jun 10	Cheque	868		845.00		9,177.00
Jun 13	Deposit		3830C		6,200.00	15,377.00
	Cheque	867		386.48		14,990.52
Jun 14	Cheque	866		153.56		14,836.96
	Cheque	869		218.60		14,618.36
Jun 15	Cheque	870		1,140.00		13,478.36
Jun 16	Deposit		3831C		2,400.00	15,878.36
	Cheque	873		1,800.00		14,078.36
Jun 17	Cheque	872		74.50		14,003.86
Jun 20	Deposit		3832C		3,865.00	17,868.86
	Cheque	871		1,847.37		16,021.49
	Cheque	876		875.00		15,146.49
Jun 23	Error in Jun 20 Deposit		CM		100.00	15,246.49
	Cheque	875		1,547.50		13,698.99
	Loan Principal	DM		745.20		12,953.79
	Loan Interest	DM		415.82		12,537.97
Jun 23	Deposit		3833C		2,545.00	15,082.97
	Cheque	877		204.10		14,878.87
	Cheque	878		2,487.35		12,391.52
Jun 24	Service Charges	DM		52.00		12,339.52
	Cheque	880		2,500.00		9,839.52
Jun 27	Deposit		3834C		6,075.00	15,914.52
	Cheque	881		645.00		15,269.52
	Cheque	874		750.00		14,519.52
Jun 30	Cheque	885		1,150.00		13,369.52
	Cheque	882		1,525.00		11,844.52
	Cheque	884		624.35		11,220.17

Solution to Self-Review Quiz 7-1B

Please be certain you have made an attempt at the quiz before looking at this solution.

KELLY'S TRAIL RIDES BANK RECONCILIATION JUNE 30, 2014			
Balance per Bank Statement—June 30, 2014			$11,220.17
Add: Deposit in Transit			5,250.00
			16,470.17
Less: Outstanding Cheques:	Chq. No.	Amount	
	814	78.30	
	879	377.43	
	883	250.00	
	886	537.00	
	887	1,107.30	
	888	2,176.64	
	889	2,156.44	
	890	1,984.23	
	891	2,200.00	10,867.34
			$ 5,602.83
Balance per General Ledger—Account 1111			$ 5,554.83
Add: Error in June 20 Deposit			100.00
			5,654.83
Less: Bank Charges—June 24—Bank Statement			52.00
			$ 5,602.83

Learning Unit 7-2
The Establishment of Petty Cash and Change Funds

> Petty cash is an asset on the balance sheet.

> Petty cash is an asset that is established by drawing a new cheque. The Petty Cash account is debited only when established unless the amount of the petty cash fund is changed.

3 Establishing and replenishing a petty cash fund; setting up an auxiliary petty cash record

Becca realized how time-consuming and expensive it would be to write cheques for small amounts to pay for postage, small supplies, delivery charges, and so on. What was needed was a **petty cash fund**. It was estimated that, for any given month, Becca's Jewellery would need a fund of $60 to cover small expenditures. A cheque payable to the order of the *custodian* (one of Becca's employees responsible for overseeing the fund) was drawn and cashed to establish the fund. The cash was placed in a small metal box with a simple lock, which gave control of the fund to the custodian. A payment out of the fund was made only when a receipt or other supporting documentation was presented by the person requesting the money.

Similarly, Becca established a change fund to make cash transactions with customers more convenient. This unit will explain how to manage petty cash and change funds.

SETTING UP THE PETTY CASH FUND

Shown here is the transaction analysis chart for the establishment of a $60 petty cash fund, which would be entered in the general journal (or the cash disbursements journal, as described in Chapter 6) on May 1, 2013.

1 Accounts Affected	2 Category	3 ↑↓	4 Rules
Petty Cash	Asset	↑	Dr.
Cash (cheques)	Asset	↓	Cr.

			GENERAL JOURNAL				Page 1
	Date		Account Title and Description	PR	Dr.	Cr.	
2013 May	1		Petty Cash		60 00		
			Cash			60 00	
			Establishment of Petty Cash Fund				

The cheque for $60 is made payable to the custodian, Ted Sullivan, who endorses the cheque, cashes it, and uses the cash to operate the petty cash fund.

Note the new asset called *Petty Cash*; this new asset was created by writing cheque No. 16, thereby reducing the asset Cash. In reality, the total assets stay the same; what has occurred is a shift from the asset Cash (cheque No. 16) to a new asset account called Petty Cash.

The Petty Cash account is not debited or credited again if the size of the fund is not changed. If the $60 fund is used up very quickly, the fund should be increased. If the fund is too large, the Petty Cash account should be reduced.

But who is responsible for controlling the petty cash fund? Becca gives her office manager, Ted Sullivan, the responsibility and the authority to make payments from the petty cash fund. In other companies, the cashier or secretary may be in charge of petty cash.

MAKING PAYMENTS FROM THE PETTY CASH FUND

Ted Sullivan has the responsibility for filling out a **petty cash voucher** for each cash payment made from the petty cash fund.

Note that the voucher (shown in Figure 7-11) when completed will include:

1. The voucher number (which will be in sequence): 1
2. The date: May 2
3. The person or organization to whom the payment was made: Al's Cleaners
4. The amount of payment: $3.00
5. The reason for payment: cleaning
6. The signature of the person who approved the payment: Ted Sullivan
7. The signature of the person who received the payment from petty cash: Becca Baker
8. The account to which the expense will be charged: 619

Vouchers in box
+ Cash in box
―――――――――――
= Original amount placed in petty cash

The completed vouchers are placed in the petty cash box. No matter how many vouchers Ted Sullivan fills out, *the total of (1) the vouchers in the box and (2) the cash on hand should equal the original amount of petty cash with which the fund was established ($60).*

Assume that at the end of May the following items are documented by petty cash vouchers in the petty cash box as having been paid by Ted Sullivan:

2013
May   2   Cleaning package, $3.00
         6   Postage stamps, $9.00
         8   First-aid supplies, $15.00
         9   Delivery expense, $6.00

Figure 7-11
Petty Cash Voucher

> Petty Cash Voucher No. 1
>
> Date: May 2, 2013   Amount: $3.00
> Paid To: Al's Cleaners
> For: Cleaning Package
>
>   Approved By: *Ted Sullivan*
>
>   Payment Received By: *Becca Baker*
>
> Debit Account No.: 619

It is always a good idea to use Petty Cash Vouchers, but some companies think that the small amount of cash "at risk" is not large enough to require such formal controls. Such companies may not use these vouchers, and instead let the receipt submitted stand in for a formal voucher.

May   14   Delivery expense, $15.00
       27   Postage stamps, $6.00

Think of the auxiliary petty cash record as a worksheet that gathers information for the journal entry.

Ted records this information in the **auxiliary petty cash record** shown in Figure 7-12. It is not a special journal but an aid to Ted—an auxiliary record that is not essential but is quite helpful as part of the petty cash system. You may want to think of the auxiliary petty cash record as an optional worksheet. Let's look at how to replenish the petty cash fund.

How to Replenish the Petty Cash Fund

No postings will be done from the auxiliary book; it is not a journal. At some point, the summarized information found in the auxiliary petty cash record will be used as a basis for a journal entry in the cash payments journal and eventually posted to appropriate ledger accounts to reflect up-to-date balances.

Remember—the only time that the account *Petty Cash* is debited is when it is set up initially, or increased in amount at some later date. Never debit *Petty Cash* during replenishment.

The expenses of $54 (see Figure 7-12) are recorded in the general journal, debited to the appropriate accounts (Figure 7-13), and a new cheque, No. 17 for $54, is cashed and the proceeds given to Ted Sullivan for the petty cash fund. The petty cash box once again holds $60 cash. The old vouchers that were used are stamped to indicate they have been processed and the fund replenished. The expenses recorded in the general journal to cover the replenishment of the petty cash fund will subsequently be posted to the ledger.

Note that in the replenishment process, the debits in the general journal (Figure 7-13) are a summary of the totals of expenses (except sundry) or other items from the auxiliary petty cash record. Posting of these specific expenses will ensure that the expenses will not be understated on the income statement. The credit to cash is where we draw a cheque for $54 to put money back in the petty

Date 2013	Voucher No.	Description	Receipts	Payments	Postage Expense	Delivery Expense	Sundry Account	Sundry Amount
May 1		Establishment	60 00					
2	1	Cleaning		3 00			Cleaning	3 00
6	2	Postage		9 00	9 00			
8	3	First Aid		15 00			Misc.	15 00
9	4	Delivery		6 00		6 00		
14	5	Delivery		15 00		15 00		
27	6	Postage		6 00	6 00			
		Total	60 00	54 00	15 00	21 00		18 00

Figure 7-12 Auxiliary Petty Cash Record

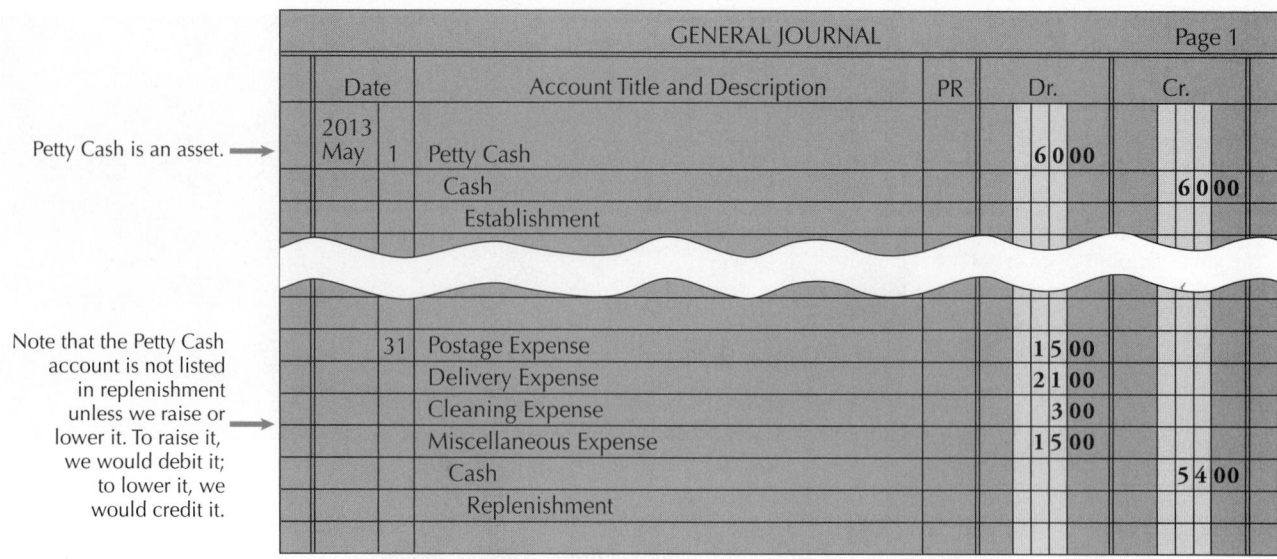

Petty Cash is an asset. →

Note that the Petty Cash account is not listed in replenishment unless we raise or lower it. To raise it, we would debit it; to lower it, we would credit it. →

GENERAL JOURNAL — Page 1

Date		Account Title and Description	PR	Dr.	Cr.
2013 May	1	Petty Cash		60 00	
		Cash			60 00
		Establishment			
	31	Postage Expense		15 00	
		Delivery Expense		21 00	
		Cleaning Expense		3 00	
		Miscellaneous Expense		15 00	
		Cash			54 00
		Replenishment			

Figure 7-13 Establishment and Replenishment of Petty Cash Fund

cash box. The $60 in the box now agrees with the petty cash account balance. *The end result is that our petty cash box is filled, and we have justified which accounts the petty cash money was spent for. Think of replenishment as a single, summarizing entry.*

> A new cheque is written in the replenishment process, which is payable to the custodian, cashed by Sullivan, and the cash placed in the petty cash box.

Remember, if at some point the petty cash fund is to be greater than $60, a cheque can be written that will increase Petty Cash and decrease Cash. If the Petty Cash account balance is to be reduced, we can credit or reduce Petty Cash. However, for our present purpose, Petty Cash will remain at $60.

The auxiliary petty cash record after replenishment would look as shown in Figure 7-14. (Keep in mind that no postings are made from the auxiliary book.)

Figure 7-15 may help you put the sequence together.

Before concluding this unit, let's look at how Becca will handle setting up a change fund and at problems with cash shortages and overages.

AUXILIARY PETTY CASH RECORD

Date 2013	Voucher No.	Description	Receipts	Payments	Postage Expense	Delivery Expense	Sundry Account	Sundry Amount
May 1		Establishment	60 00					
2	1	Cleaning		3 00			Cleaning	3 00
6	2	Postage		9 00	9 00			
8	3	First Aid		15 00			Misc.	15 00
9	4	Delivery		6 00		6 00		
14	5	Delivery		15 00		15 00		
27	6	Postage		6 00	6 00			
		Totals	60 00	54 00	15 00	21 00		18 00
		Ending Balance		6 00				
			60 00	60 00				
		Ending Balance	6 00					
31		Replenishment	54 00					
31		Balance (New)	60 00					

Figure 7-14 Recording Replenishment in the Petty Cash Record

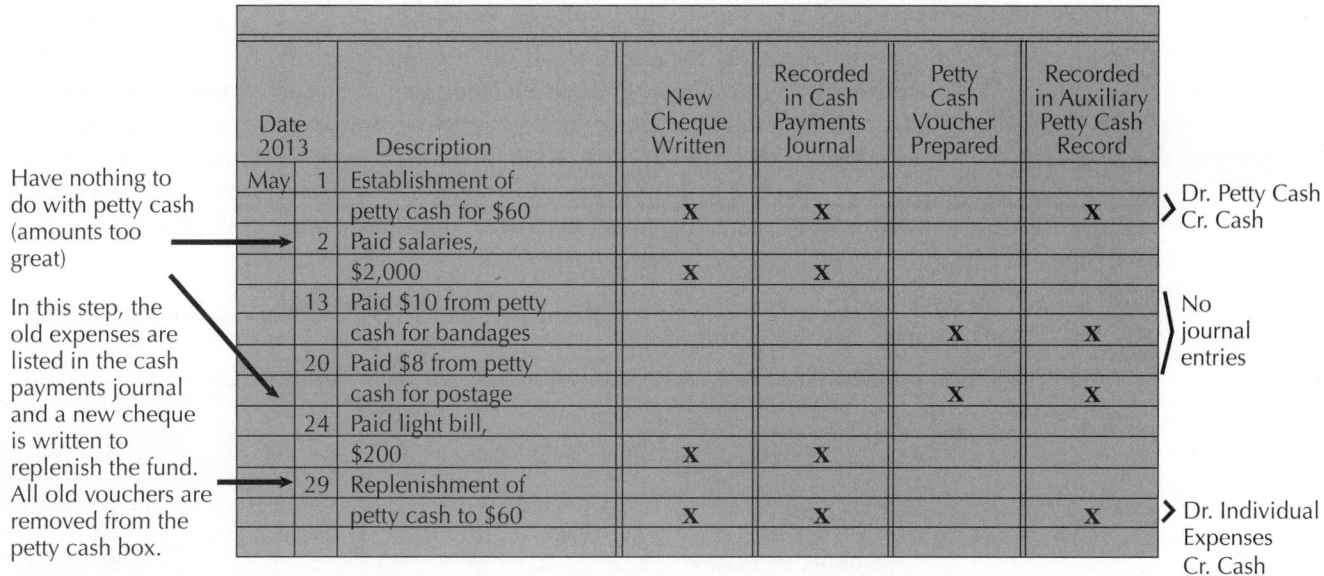

Have nothing to do with petty cash (amounts too great)

In this step, the old expenses are listed in the cash payments journal and a new cheque is written to replenish the fund. All old vouchers are removed from the petty cash box.

Date 2013		Description	New Cheque Written	Recorded in Cash Payments Journal	Petty Cash Voucher Prepared	Recorded in Auxiliary Petty Cash Record	
May	1	Establishment of petty cash for $60	X	X		X	} Dr. Petty Cash Cr. Cash
	2	Paid salaries, $2,000	X	X			
	13	Paid $10 from petty cash for bandages			X	X	} No journal entries
	20	Paid $8 from petty cash for postage			X	X	
	24	Paid light bill, $200	X	X			
	29	Replenishment of petty cash to $60	X	X		X	} Dr. Individual Expenses Cr. Cash

Figure 7-15 Steps Involving Petty Cash

4 Establishing and replenishing a change fund

Change fund is an asset on the balance sheet.

SETTING UP A CHANGE FUND AND INSIGHT INTO CASH SHORT AND OVER

If a company like Becca's Jewellery expects to have many cash transactions occurring, it may be a good idea to establish a **change fund** or float. This is a fund that is placed in the cash register drawer and used to make change for customers who pay cash. Becca decides to put $120 in the change fund, made up of various denominations of bills and coins. Let's look at a transaction analysis chart for this sort of procedure.

1 Accounts Affected	2 Category	3 ↑↓	4 Dr./Cr.
Change Fund	**Asset**	↑	**Dr.**
Cash	**Asset**	↓	**Cr.**

At the close of the business day, Becca will place the balance of the change fund back in the safe in the office. She will set up the change fund (the same amount of $120) in the appropriate denominations for the next business day. She will deposit the *remainder* of the cash taken in for the day in the bank.

Now let's look at how to record errors that are made in making change, called *cash short and over*.

5 Handling transactions involving cash short and over

Beginning change fund
+ Cash register total
= Cash should have on hand
− Counted cash
= Shortage or overage of cash

Cash Short and Over

In a local pizza shop, the total sales for the day did not match the amount of cash on hand. Errors often happen in making change. To record and summarize the differences in cash, an expense account called **Cash Short and Over** is used. This account will record both overages (too much money) and shortages (not enough money). Let's first look at the account (in T account form).

Cash Short and Over	
Dr.	Cr.
Shortage	Overage

For one example of how other income items are shown, see page 591.

All shortages will be recorded as debits and all overages will be recorded as credits. This account is temporary. If the ending balance of the account is a debit (a shortage), it is considered a miscellaneous expense that would be reported on the income statement. If the balance of the account is a credit (an overage), it is considered as other income (or reduction of expense) reported on the income statement. Let's look at how the Cash Short and Over account could be used to record shortages or overages in sales as well as in the petty cash process.

Example 1: Shortages and Overages in Sales

On December 5, the pizza shop rang up sales of $560 for the day but had only $530 in cash.

1 Accounts Affected	2 Category	3 ↑↓	4 Dr./Cr.
Cash	Asset	↑	Debit $530
Cash Short and Over	Expense	↑	Debit $30
Sales	Revenue	↑	Credit $560

The journal entry would be as follows:

Dec.	5	Cash		530 00		
		Cash Short and Over		30 00		
		Sales			560 00	
		Cash shortage				

Note that the shortage of $30 is a debit and would be recorded on the income statement as a miscellaneous expense.

What would the entry look like if the pizza shop showed a $50 overage?

1 Accounts Affected	2 Category	3 ↑↓	4 Dr./Cr.
Cash	Asset	↑	Debit $610
Cash Short and Over	Expense	↓	Credit $50
Sales	Revenue	↑	Credit $560

The journal entry would be as follows:

Dec.	5	Cash		610 00		
		Cash Short and Over			50 00	
		Sales			560 00	
		Cash overage				

Note that the Cash Short and Over account would be reported as other income on the income statement if it had a credit balance at year end. Now let's look at how to use this Cash Short and Over account to record petty cash transactions.

Example 2: Cash Short and Over in Petty Cash

A local computer company had established a $200 petty cash fund. Today, November 30, the petty cash box had $160 in vouchers as well as $32 in coin and currency. What would be the journal entry to replenish petty cash?

Assume the vouchers were made up of $90 for postage and $70 for supplies expense. If you add up the vouchers and cash in the box, cash is short by $8.

1 Accounts Affected	2 Category	3 ↑↓	4 Dr./Cr.
Postage Expense	Expense	↑	Debit $90
Supplies Expense	Expense	↑	Debit $70
Cash Short and Over	Expense	↑	Debit $8
Cash	Asset	↓	Credit $168

The journal entry would be as follows:

Nov.	8	Postage Expense		90 00		
		Supplies on Hand		70 00		
		Cash Short and Over		8 00		
		Cash			1 68 00	
		Replenish petty cash				

If there had been an overage, the cash short and over would be a credit as other income. If an auxiliary petty cash record is used to record the cash short and over, it would be recorded as a payment of $8 under the category of payments in the sundry column. The Solution to Self-Review Quiz 7-2 shows how a fund shortage would be recorded in the auxiliary record.

LEARNING UNIT 7-2 REVIEW

AT THIS POINT you should be able to:

◆ State the purpose of a petty cash fund. (p. 329)
◆ Prepare a journal entry to establish a petty cash fund. (p. 330)
◆ Prepare a petty cash voucher. (p. 330)
◆ Explain the relationship of the auxiliary petty cash record to the petty cash process. (p. 331)
◆ Prepare a journal entry to replenish Petty Cash to its original amount. (p. 332)
◆ Explain why individual expenses are debited in the replenishment process. (p. 331)
◆ Explain how a change fund is established. (p. 333)
◆ Explain how Cash Short and Over could be a miscellaneous expense. (p. 333)

Self-Review Quiz 7-2

(The forms you need are on pages 7-1 and 7-2 of the *Study Guide with Working Papers*.)

As the custodian of the petty cash fund, it is your task to prepare entries to establish the fund on October 1, 2013, as well as to replenish the fund on October 31. Please keep an auxiliary petty cash record.

2013
Oct.   1   Establish petty cash fund for $90, cheque No. 8.
         4   Voucher 1, delivery expense, $21.
         8   Voucher 2, delivery expense, $15.

Cheques to establish and replenish Petty Cash would be made out to the custodian.

Oct.	11	Voucher 3, office repair expense, $24.
	18	Voucher 4, general expense, $12.
	29	Replenishment of petty cash fund, $78, cheque No. 108. (cheque would be payable to the custodian)

Solution to Self-Review Quiz 7-2

GENERAL JOURNAL						Page 6	
Date		Account Title and Description	PR	Dr.		Cr.	
2013 Oct.	1	Petty Cash		90 00			
		Cash				90 00	
		Establishment, Cheque No. 8					

	29	Delivery Expense		36 00			
		General Expense		12 00			
		Office Repair Expense		24 00			
		Cash Short and Over		6 00			
		Cash				78 00	
		Replenishment, Cheque No. 108					

Quiz Tip

How to calculate shortage: $21 + $15 + $24 + $12 = $72 in vouchers replenished with $78 cheque; thus a $6 shortage.

Note that the amount for cash short and over was entered into the auxiliary petty cash record.

AUXILIARY PETTY CASH RECORD

Date 2013		Voucher No.	Description	Receipts	Payments	Delivery Expense	General Expense	Sundry	
								Account	Amount
Oct.	1		Establishment	90 00					
	4	1	Delivery		21 00	21 00			
	8	2	Delivery		15 00	15 00			
	11	3	Repairs		24 00			Office Repairs	24 00
	18	4	General		12 00		12 00		
	31	5	Fund shortage		6 00			Cash S & O	6 00
			Totals	90 00	78 00	36 00	12 00		30 00
			Ending Balance		12 00				
				90 00	90 00				
	31		Ending Balance	12 00					
	31		Replenishment	78 00					
Nov.	1		Balance (New)	90 00					

Subway now requires all of its franchisees to submit their weekly sales and inventory reports electronically using new point-of-sale (POS) touch-screen cash registers. With the new POS registers, clerks use a touch screen to punch in the number and type of items bought. Franchisees can quickly reconfigure prices and products to match new promotions. Not only is this POS method faster than using the old cash registers, but it also allows franchisees to view every transaction as it occurs—from their own back office computers or even from home. Also, individual POS terminals within the restaurant are linked, so franchisees are able to see consolidated data quickly.

SUBWAY

COUNTING DOWN THE CASH

Comprehensive question regarding internal controls
① ② ③ ④ (20 min)

The transition to electronic reporting and networked POS terminals, however, has not been without bumps, as Stan can testify. About six months before the deadline for all Subway franchisees to "go electronic," Stan attended a heated meeting on the topic at his local chapter of the North American Association of Subway Franchisees (NAASF). The NAASF is an independent organization of franchisees that serves as an advisory council on Subway policies and issues of common concern. Everyone seemed to be talking at once.

"I don't trust these machines. What am I supposed to do when the system crashes?" complained one man.

"Yeah, and I don't like the idea of a bunch of kids knowing more about how to run the software than I do," said one older franchisee.

"Don't be so quick to assume that our sandwich artists will love POS," one woman said. "I overheard one of my employees say to another, 'POS means Peeking Over Shoulders.' These young kids we hire have more reason to be resistant than we do!"

"I'll say they do!" rejoined Jay Harden, the president of Stan's local NAASF. "Employee theft is one of the largest problems that we face as franchisees. I, for one, really welcome the cash control we get with POS."

Stan had to agree with Jay. Training staff to record every sale and record it correctly is a critical

component of a cash business like Subway. In Stan's view, the POS machines would make that training only easier. Cash control is built into the new system, which also provides the owners with information that will help them spot problems—such as employee theft—and track trends. Of course, thought Stan, the chore of counting down the cash at the end of a shift remained. No matter what type of computer program you install, cash still must be counted down and reconciled with the register tape at the end of each shift.

As the voices rung louder around him, Stan thought about what had happened that day when Ellen closed out her cash register drawer. He had spent hours figuring out a discrepancy between the cash in the drawer and the register tape. Ellen had forgotten to void a mistaken entry for $99.99. Stan had first suspected that she had made a huge error in counting change.

Thinking of errors in counting brought him back to the topic of the meeting. Stan raised his hand to speak. "One thing that concerns me is the potential for accounting errors. I still have to key in data from the POS into my QuickBooks® accounting software. Every time I have to re-enter data, the potential for error multiplies."

"That shows some foresight, Stan," Jay Harden said. "We're actually exploring computer programs that will feed the data directly from the POS into our accounting programs."

Even some of the technophobes and POS skeptics in the group had to agree that that would be a great idea.

DISCUSSION QUESTIONS

1. What is an advisory council? Why do you think franchisees need one?
2. Why do you think some small business owners fear computerization?
3. How would Stan catch a discrepancy in the Cash account? How would he record a loss?
4. Why does Subway invest time, money, and effort in investigating new cash handling systems such as its new POS terminals?

Chapter Assignments

SUMMARY OF KEY POINTS

Learning Unit 7-1

1. Restrictive endorsement limits any further negotiation of a cheque.

2. Cheque stubs are filled out first before a cheque is written.

3. The payee is the person to whom the cheque is payable. The drawer is the one who orders the bank to pay a sum of money. The drawee is the bank where the drawer has an account.

4. The process of reconciling the bank statement balance with the company's cash balance is called bank reconciliation. The timing of deposits, when the bank statement was issued, and other factors often result in differences between the bank statement balance and the balance shown in the general ledger account.

5. Deposits in transit are added to the bank balance.

6. Cheques outstanding are subtracted from the bank balance.

7. NSF means that an account has insufficient funds to pay a cheque; therefore, the amount is not included in the recipient's bank balance and the chequing account balance is lowered.

8. When a bank debits your account, an amount is deducted from your balance. A credit to the account is an increase in your balance.

9. All adjustments to the chequebook balance require journal entries.

Learning Unit 7-2

1. Petty Cash is an asset found on the balance sheet.

2. The Auxiliary Petty Cash Record is an auxiliary book; thus no postings are done from this book. Think of it as an optional worksheet.

3. When a petty cash fund is established, the amount is entered as a debit to Petty Cash and a credit to Cash in the cash payments journal.

4. At the time of replenishment of the petty cash fund, all expenses are debited (by category) and a credit to Cash (a new cheque) results. This replenishment, when journalized and posted, updates the ledger from the journal.

5. The only time the Petty Cash account is used is to establish the fund to begin with or to bring the fund to a higher or lower level. If the petty cash level is deemed sufficient, all replenishments will debit specific expenses and credit Cash, and a new cheque will be written. The asset, Petty Cash account balance, will remain unchanged.

6. A change fund is an asset that is used to make change for customers on cash sales.

7. Cash Short and Over is an account that is either a miscellaneous expense or a miscellaneous income, depending on whether the ending balance is a shortage (a debit) or an overage (a credit).

KEY TERMS

Automated teller machine (ATM) A machine that permits customers to perform banking transactions without the assistance of a bank teller (p. 320)

Auxiliary petty cash record   A supplementary record for summarizing petty cash information (p. 331)

Bank reconciliation   The process of reconciling the chequebook balance with the bank balance given on the bank statement (p. 316)

Bank statement   A report sent by a bank to a customer indicating the previous balance, individual cheques processed, individual deposits received, service charges, other sundry items, and ending bank balance (p. 316)

Cancelled cheques   Cheques that have been processed by a bank and are no longer negotiable (p. 316)

Cash Short and Over   The account that records cash shortages and overages. If the ending balance is a debit, it is recorded on the income statement as a miscellaneous expense; if it is a credit, it is recorded as miscellaneous income. (p. 333)

Change fund   A fund made up of various denominations of bills and coins that is used to make change for customers (p. 333)

Cheque   A form used to indicate a specific amount of money that is to be paid by the bank to a named person or company (p. 314)

Cheque truncation   Procedure whereby cheques are not returned to the drawer with the bank statement but are instead kept at the bank for a certain length of time before being first transferred to microfilm and then destroyed (p. 323)

Credit memorandum   Increase in depositor's balance (p. 318)

Debit card   Similar to a credit card, but funds are deducted immediately from the cardholder's bank account (p. 312)

Debit memorandum   Decrease in depositor's balance (p. 318)

Deposit slip   Form provided by a bank for use in recording deposits of money or cheques into a bank account (p. 312)

Deposits in transit   Deposits that were made by customers of a bank but did not reach or were not processed by the bank before the preparation of the bank statement (p. 317)

Drawee   Bank with which the drawer has an account (p. 314)

Drawer   Person who writes a cheque (p. 314)

Electronic funds transfer (EFT)   An electronic system that transfers funds without the use of paper cheques (p. 319)

Electronic integration   Close connection between companies' business records that greatly expedites business transactions—including funds transfer (p. 322)

Endorsement   *Blank*—could be further endorsed. *Full*—restricts further endorsement to only the person or company named. *Restrictive*—restricts any further endorsement. (p. 312)

Internal control systems   Systems of procedures and methods to control a firm's assets as well as monitor its operations (p. 311)

NSF (not sufficient funds)   Notation indicating that a cheque has been written on an account that lacks sufficient funds to pay it (p. 318)

Outstanding cheques   Cheques written by a company or person that were not received or not processed by the bank before the preparation of the bank statement (p. 317)

Payee   The person or company the cheque is payable to (p. 314)

Petty cash fund   A fund (source) that allows payment of small cash amounts without the writing of cheques (p. 329)

Petty cash voucher   A petty cash form to be completed when money is taken out of petty cash (p. 330)

Phishing   Using fake e-mails that look official and attempt to obtain personal information regarding online banking in order to steal funds (p. 321)

Safekeeping   See *Cheque truncation* (p. 323)

Service charge   The fee charged by banks or other financial institutions to manage your bank account, such as receiving deposits and processing cheques (p. 317)

Signature card   A form signed by a bank customer that the bank uses to verify signature authenticity on all cheques (p. 312)

S.W.I.F.T. codes   Numerical codes that identify banks worldwide, allowing safe and speedy transfer of funds (p. 323)

BLUEPRINT OF A BANK RECONCILIATION

General Ledger Cash Balance			Balance per Bank		
Ending Balance per Books		$XXX	Ending Bank Statement Balance (last figure on bank statement)		$XXX
Add:			Add:		
Recording of errors that understate balance	XXX		Deposits in transit (amount not yet credited by bank)	XXX	
Proceeds of notes collected by bank or other items credited (added) by bank but not yet updated in chequebook	XXX		Bank errors	XXX	
		XXX			XXX
Deduct:			Deduct:		
Recording of errors that overstate balance	XXX		List of outstanding cheques (amount not yet debited by bank)	XXX	
Service charges	XXX		Bank errors	XXX	
Printing charges	XXX				
NSF cheques, or other items debited (charged) by bank but not yet updated in chequebook	XXX				XXX
		XXX			
Reconciled G/L Balance (Adjusted Balance)		$XXX	Reconciled Bank Balance (Adjusted Balance)		$XXX

QUESTIONS, CLASSROOM DEMONSTRATION EXERCISES, EXERCISES, AND PROBLEMS

Discussion Questions and Critical Thinking/Ethical Case

1. What is the purpose of internal control?

2. What is the advantage of having preprinted deposit slips?

3. Explain the difference between a blank endorsement and a restrictive endorsement.

4. Explain the difference between payee, drawer, and drawee.

5. Why should cheque stubs be filled out first, before the cheque itself is written?

6. A bank statement is sent twice a month. True or false? Please explain.

7. Explain the end product of a bank reconciliation.

8. Why are cheques outstanding subtracted from the bank balance?

9. An NSF cheque results in a bank's issuing the depositor a credit memorandum. Agree or disagree. Support your response.

10. Why do adjustments to the chequebook balance in the reconciliation process need to be journalized?

11. What is EFT?

12. What are the major advantages and disadvantages of online banking?

13. What is meant by cheque truncation or safekeeping?

14. Petty cash is a liability. Accept or reject.

15. Explain the relationship of the auxiliary petty cash record to the cash payments journal.

16. At time of replenishment, why are the totals of individual expenses debited?

17. Explain the purpose of a change fund.

18. Explain how Cash Short and Over can be a miscellaneous expense.

19. Albert Ray, the bookkeeper of Logan Co. of Richmond, received a bank statement from Logan's bank. Albert noticed a $200 mistake made by the bank in the company's favour. Albert called his supervisor, who said that as long as it benefits the company, he should not tell the bank about the error. You make the call. Write your specific recommendations to Albert.

MyAccountingLab

Make the grade with MyAccountingLab! The exercises and problems marked in green can be found on MyAccountingLab at www.myaccountinglab.com. You can practise them as often as you want, and many of them feature step-by-step guided solutions to help you find the right answer. You can also find working papers for selected problems in the Multimedia Library on MyAccountingLab.

Classroom Demonstration Exercises

(The forms you need are on pages 7-3 and 7-4 in the *Study Guide with Working Papers*.)

Set A

Bank Reconciliation

Preparing a bank reconciliation
② (10 min)

1. Indicate which of the actions (**1** through **4**) listed below must be taken when doing a bank reconciliation for each of the six situations (**a** through **f**) described below and on the following page.

    1. Add to bank balance

    2. Deduct from bank balance

    3. Add to general ledger Cash balance

    4. Deduct from general ledger Cash balance

____ **a.** $12 bank service charge

____ **b.** $300 deposit in transit

_____ c. $162 NSF cheque

_____ d. A $15 cheque was written and recorded as $25

_____ e. Bank collected a $1,000 note less a $50 collection fee

_____ f. Cheque No. 111 for the amount of $88 was outstanding

Journal Entries in Reconciliation Process

Recording items from the bank reconciliation
2 (5 min)

2. Which of the transactions in question 1 above would require a journal entry?

Bank Reconciliation

Bank reconciliation
2 (10 min)

3. From the following, construct a bank reconciliation for Woody Co. as of May 31, 2013.

G/L Cash balance	$1,869.60	Outstanding cheques	427.80
Bank statement balance	1,951.20	Bank service charge	13.80
Deposits in transit	271.20	NSF cheque	61.20

Petty Cash

Setting up the petty cash fund and recording petty cash expenses
3 (10 min)

4. Indicate which of the actions (**1** through **4**) listed would be necessary for each of the situations (**a** through **f**) described below.

1. New cheque written
2. Recorded in general journal
3. Petty cash voucher prepared
4. Recorded in auxiliary petty cash record

_____ a. Established petty cash

_____ b. Paid $1,000 bill for repairs

_____ c. Paid $2 for bandages from petty cash

_____ d. Paid $30 for stamps from petty cash

_____ e. Paid electricity bill, $250

_____ f. Replenished petty cash

Replenishment of Petty Cash

Replenishing the petty cash fund
3 (15 min)

5. Petty cash was originally established with $20. During the month, $5 was paid out for bandages and $6 for stamps. During replenishment, the custodian discovered that the balance in petty cash was $8. Record, using a general journal entry, the replenishment of petty cash back to $20.

Increasing Petty Cash

Increasing the Petty Cash account
3 (10 min)

6. In question 5 above, if the custodian decided to raise the level of petty cash to $30, what would be the journal entry to replenish (use a general journal entry)?

Set B

Bank Reconciliation

Preparing a bank reconciliation
2 (10 min)

1. Indicate which of the actions (**1** through **4**) listed below must be taken when doing a bank reconciliation for each of the six situations (**a** through **f**) described on the following page.

1. Add to bank balance
2. Deduct from bank balance
3. Add to general ledger Cash balance
4. Deduct from general ledger Cash balance

_____ **a.** $15 bank service charge

_____ **b.** $725 deposit in transit

_____ **c.** $36 NSF cheque

_____ **d.** A $78 cheque was written and recorded as $87

_____ **e.** Bank collected a $5,000 note less a $50 collection fee

_____ **f.** Cheque No. 113 for the amount of $360 was outstanding

Journal Entries in Reconciliation Process

2. Which of the transactions in question 1 above would require a journal entry?

Bank Reconciliation

3. From the following, construct a bank reconciliation for Marx Co. as of June 30, 2013.

G/L Cash balance	$28,724	Deposit in transit	1,714
Bank statement balance	29,840	NSF cheque	600
Outstanding cheque	3,454	Bank service charge	24

Petty Cash

4. Indicate which of the actions (**1** through **4**) listed would be necessary for each of the situations (**a** through **f**) described below.

1. New cheque written

2. Recorded in general journal

3. Petty cash voucher prepared

4. Recorded in auxiliary petty cash record

_____ **a.** Established petty cash for $200

_____ **b.** Paid telephone bill, $135

_____ **c.** Paid $10 to employee A for $10 highway toll from petty cash

_____ **d.** Paid $7.80 for stamps from petty cash

_____ **e.** Replenished petty cash

_____ **f.** Increased original petty cash fund to $300

Replenishment of Petty Cash

5. Petty cash was originally established with $60. During the month, $10 was paid out for parking; $15 for postage; and $25 for emergency purchase of office supplies. During replenishment, the custodian discovered that the balance in petty cash was $8. Record, using a general journal entry, the replenishment of petty cash back to $60.

Increasing Petty Cash

6. In question 5 above, if the custodian decided to raise the level of petty cash to $100, what would be the journal entry to replenish?

Exercises

(The forms you need are on pages 7-4 and 7-5 of the *Study Guide with Working Papers*.)

7-1. From the following information, construct a bank reconciliation for Faith Co. as of July 31, 2013. Then prepare journal entries if needed.

Recording items from the bank reconciliation

2 (5 min)

Bank reconciliation

2 (10 min)

Setting up the petty cash fund and recording petty cash expenses

3 (10 min)

Replenishing the petty cash fund

3 (15 min)

Increasing the petty cash account

3 (10 min)

Bank reconciliation

2 (15 min)

Ending G/L Cash balance	$445
Ending bank statement balance	300
Deposits (in transit)	200
Outstanding cheques	95
Bank service charge (debit memo)	15
NSF: Judith Wall's cheque returned	25

Establishing and replenishing petty cash
❸ (15 min)

7-2. In general journal form, prepare journal entries to establish a petty cash fund on July 2 and replenish it on July 31.

2012

July   2   A $100 petty cash fund is established.

      31   At the end of the month, $12 cash plus the following paid vouchers exist: donations expense, $20; postage expense, $18; office supplies expense, $25; miscellaneous expense, $25.

Cash shortage in replenishment
❸ (15 min)

7-3. If, in Exercise 7-2, cash on hand was $11, prepare the entry to replenish the petty cash on July 31.

Cash overage in replenishment
❸ (15 min)

7-4. If, in Exercise 7-2, cash on hand was $13, prepare the entry to replenish the petty cash on July 31.

Calculating cash shortage in a change fund
❺ (15 min)

7-5. At the end of the day, the clerk for Pete's Variety Shop noticed an error in the amount of cash he had. Total cash sales from the sales tape were $1,200 while the total cash in the till was $1,156. Pete also keeps a $30 change fund in his shop. Prepare an appropriate general journal entry to record the cash sales as well as reveal the cash shortage.

Group A Problems

(The forms you need are on pages 7-6 to 7-11 of the *Study Guide with Working Papers*.)

Preparing a bank reconciliation, including collection of a note
❷ (20 min)

> **Check Figure**
>
> Reconciled balance $6,410

7A-1. Rose Company in Drumheller received a bank statement from TD Canada Trust indicating a bank balance of $7,100. Based on Rose's G/L cash account, the balance was $5,700. Your task is to prepare a bank reconciliation for Rose Company as of July 31, 2014, from the following information (journalize entries as needed):

  a. Cheques outstanding: No. 122, $800; No. 130, $1,000.

  b. Deposits in transit, $1,110.

  c. Rose Company forgot to record a $33 gasoline purchase made with a debit card.

  d. Bank service charge, $60.

  e. TD Canada Trust collected a note for Rose, $810, less a $7 collection fee.

Preparing a bank reconciliation with an NSF cheque, using the back of a bank statement
❷ (40 min)

> **Check Figure**
>
> Reconciled balance $5,270

7A-2. From the bank statement on the next page and the items below, please (1) complete the bank reconciliation for Rick's Deli of Regina found on the reverse of the bank statement and (2) journalize the appropriate entries as needed.

  a. A deposit of $2,000 is in transit.

  b. Rick's Deli has an ending G/L cash balance of $5,600.

  c. Cheques outstanding: No. 111, $600; No. 119, $1,200; No. 121, $330

  d. Jim Rice's cheque for $300 bounced because of lack of sufficient funds.

Relationship to auxiliary petty cash record
❸ (30 min)

7A-3. The transactions on page 345 occurred in April and were related to the general journal and petty cash fund of Merry Co. of Lennoxville:

Account Statement

BANK OF SASKATCHEWAN
10050–101 Street
Regina, Saskatchewan
S4J 6E2

03749

RICK'S DELI
8811–102 Street
Regina, SK
S4S 3G6

Account No.
241 673 6

Period	
From	To
Feb 01/15	Feb 28/15

Enclosures	Page
7	1

Date	Transaction Description		Cheques & Debits	Deposits & Credits	Balance
Feb 01	Balance Forward				6,000.00
Feb 02	Cheque -	108	90.00		
Feb 03	Cheque -	114	210.00		5,700.00
Feb 10	Deposit			300.00	
Feb 10	Cheque -	116	150.00		5,850.00
Feb 13	Deposit			600.00	6,450.00
Feb 16	Cheque -	113	600.00		5,850.00
Feb 20	Deposit			300.00	
Feb 20	NSF Returned Item		300.00		5,850.00
Feb 23	Deposit			1,200.00	7,050.00
Feb 24	Cheque -	117	1,200.00		5,850.00
Feb 26	Deposit			180.00	6,030.00
Feb 27	Cheque -	118	600.00		
Feb 28	Service Charge		30.00		5,400.00

No. of Debits	Total Amount	No. of Credits	Total Amount
8	3,180.00	5	2,580.00

2013
April 1 Issued cheque No. 14 for $100 to establish a petty cash fund.
       5 Paid $15 from petty cash for postage, voucher No. 1.
       8 Paid $20 from petty cash for office supplies, voucher No. 2.
      16 Paid $18 from petty cash for office supplies, voucher No. 3.
      23 Paid $14 from petty cash for postage, voucher No. 4.
      26 Paid $9 from petty cash for local church donation, voucher No. 5 (this is a miscellaneous payment).
      29 Issued cheque No. 15 to Roy Kloon to pay for office equipment, $700.

Check Figure

Cash replenishment $76

The chart of accounts includes Cash, 100; Petty Cash, 120; Office Equipment, 130; Postage Expense, 610; Office Supplies Expense, 620; Miscellaneous Expense, 630. The headings of the auxiliary petty cash records are as follows:

AUXILIARY PETTY CASH RECORD								
							Category of Payments	
								Sundry	
Date 2013	Voucher No.	Description	Receipts	Payments	Postage Expense	Office Supplies Expense	Account	Amount

Required

1. Record the appropriate entries in the general journal as well as in the auxiliary petty cash record as needed.
2. Be sure to replenish the petty cash fund on April 30 (cheque No. 16).

7A-4.

Establishing and replenishing petty cash, including handling a cash shortage

3 4 5 (40 min)

7A-4. From the following, record the transactions in Logan's auxiliary petty cash record and general journal.

2012

Oct. 1 A cheque was drawn (No. 444) payable to Roberta Floss, petty cashier, to establish a $150 petty cash fund.
  5 Paid $24 for postage stamps, voucher No. 1.
  9 Paid $12 for delivery charges on goods for resale, voucher No. 2.
  12 Paid $10 for donation to a mission (Miscellaneous Expense), voucher No. 3.
  15 Paid $9 for postage stamps, voucher No. 4.
  16 Paid $18 for delivery charges on goods for resale, voucher No. 5.
  26 Purchased computer supplies from petty cash for $25, voucher No. 6.
  29 Paid $14 for postage, voucher No. 7.
  30 Drew cheque No. 618 to replenish petty cash and cover a $3 shortage.

Check Figure

Cash replenishment $115

7A-5. Shown on pages 347 and 348 are the following for Casing Suppliers Ltd. of Oakville:

a. General ledger printout for March 2015.
b. Bank reconciliation as of February 28, 2015.
c. Bank statement for March 2015.

Preparing a bank reconciliation

2 (75 min)

Required

Prepare a bank reconciliation at March 31, 2015.

Check Figure

Reconciled balance
$3,236.76

Group B Problems

(The forms you need are on pages 7-6 to 7-11 of the *Study Guide with Working Papers*.)

Preparing a bank reconciliation, including collection of a note

2 (20 min)

7B-1. As the bookkeeper of Rose Company of Drumheller, you received the bank statement from TD Canada Trust indicating a balance of $5,820. The ending chequebook balance was $6,321. Prepare the bank reconciliation for Rose Company as of July 31, 2014, and prepare journal entries as needed based on the following:

a. Deposits in transit, $2,875.
b. Bank service charges, $24.
c. Cheques outstanding: No. 111, $478; No. 115, $1,147.
d. TD Canada Trust collected a note for Rose, $1,770, less a $12 collection fee.
e. NSF cheque, $525.
f. Rose Company records cheque No. 107 as $900 to pay the month's rent. The cancelled cheque and bank statement show the actual cheque was $800.
g. The bank made an error by deducting a cheque for $560 issued by another business.

Check Figure

Reconciled balance $7,630

Preparing a bank reconciliation with an NSF cheque, using the back side of a bank statement.

2 (40 min)

7B-2. Based on the account statement on page 349, (1) complete the bank reconciliation for Rick's Deli of Regina found on the reverse of the bank statement and (2) journalize the appropriate entries as needed.

Casing Suppliers Ltd.
General Ledger Listing as of March 31, 2015

Period	Source	Date	Description	Reference	Posting Entry	Debits	Credits	Net Balance	Dr./Cr.
			1050 Royal Bank - Chequing		Balance Forward			4,741.34	Dr.
3	GL-GJ	2-Mar-15	WESTERN PROPERTIES LTD.	CHQ 3525	3 - 1		1,498.00	3,243.34	Dr.
3	GL-GJ	2-Mar-15	WALLY PIERCE - Deposit	1241	3 - 2	6,425.48		9,668.82	Dr.
3	GL-GJ	3-Mar-15	SANDY NESS - Deposit	1242	3 - 3	3,164.17		12,832.99	Dr.
3	GL-GJ	3-Mar-15	CARSON WHOLESALE INC.	CHQ 3526	3 - 4		3,614.85	9,218.14	Dr.
3	GL-GJ	4-Mar-15	QUICK COMPUTER REPAIRS LTD.	CHQ 3527	3 - 5		136.00	9,082.14	Dr.
3	GL-GJ	4-Mar-15	NIVENS QUALITY UPHOLSTERING	CHQ 3528	3 - 6		1,510.00	7,572.14	Dr.
3	GL-GJ	4-Mar-15	ALLEN MURRAY - Deposit	1243	3 - 7	8,742.00		16,314.14	Dr.
3	GL-GJ	5-Mar-15	A.F. KINGSLEY, ACCOUNTANT	CHQ 3529	3 - 8		749.00	15,565.14	Dr.
3	GL-GJ	6-Mar-15	BRENDA KELLY - Deposit	1244	3 - 9	1,756.25		17,321.39	Dr.
3	GL-GJ	6-Mar-15	EVANS CONTRACTING LTD.	CHQ 3530	3 - 10		5,248.95	12,072.44	Dr.
3	GL-GJ	6-Mar-15	CORRINTHIAN CONSULTING CO.	CHQ 3531	3 - 11		2,850.00	9,222.44	Dr.
3	GL-GJ	6-Mar-15	NANCY SNYDER	CHQ 3532	3 - 12		1,500.00	7,722.44	Dr.
3	GL-GJ	6-Mar-15	CITY PHONE COMPANY	CHQ 3535	3 - 13		168.45	7,553.99	Dr.
3	GL-GJ	9-Mar-15	LYCOS UTILITIES INC.	CHQ 3536	3 - 14		318.96	7,235.03	Dr.
3	GL-GJ	9-Mar-15	CASEY VALENCE	CHQ 3537	3 - 15		418.50	6,816.53	Dr.
3	GL-GJ	9-Mar-15	STATIONERY DEPOT LTD.	CHQ 3538	3 - 16		641.30	6,175.23	Dr.
3	GL-GJ	10-Mar-15	JAMIE DUPRE	CHQ 3539	3 - 17		365.00	5,810.23	Dr.
3	GL-GJ	11-Mar-15	WAN TSUI - Deposit	1245	3 - 18	1,616.82		7,427.05	Dr.
3	GL-GJ	11-Mar-15	LARRY MURDOCH - Salary	CHQ 3540	3 - 19		1,645.20	5,781.85	Dr.
3	GL-GJ	11-Mar-15	FREDA WANDERLING - Salary	CHQ 3541	3 - 20		1,586.45	4,195.40	Dr.
3	GL-GJ	12-Mar-15	RBC - Loan Interest	01 - 21	3 - 21		368.40	3,827.00	Dr.
3	GL-GJ	12-Mar-15	K CARDINAL - Deposit	1246	3 - 22	6,475.20		10,302.20	Dr.
3	GL-GJ	13-Mar-15	JAMISON SUPPLIERS LTD.	CHQ 3542	3 - 23		2,167.10	8,135.10	Dr.
3	GL-GJ	16-Mar-15	WORD WIZARDS LTD.	CHQ 3543	3 - 27		742.00	7,393.10	Dr.
3	GL-GJ	16-Mar-15	Canada Revenue Agency	CHQ 3544	3 - 28		1,684.52	5,708.58	Dr.
3	GL-GJ	16-Mar-15	RBC - Loan Repayment	01 - 24	3 - 29		3,000.00	2,708.58	Dr.
3	GL-GJ	16-Mar-15	JOY AMITY - Deposit	1247	3 - 30	648.00		3,356.58	Dr.
3	GL-GJ	16-Mar-15	THOMAS HUNT - Insurance	CHQ 3546	3 - 31		1,014.58	2,342.00	Dr.
3	GL-GJ	17-Mar-15	PEARSON HIGH SCHOOL ADVERT.	CHQ 3547	3 - 32		125.00	2,217.00	Dr.
3	GL-GJ	17-Mar-15	THE LOCAL TIMES	CHQ 3548	3 - 37		682.45	1,534.55	Dr.
3	GL-GJ	18-Mar-15	RBC - New cheques ordered	01 - 29	3 - 38		35.30	1,499.25	Dr.
3	GL-GJ	20-Mar-15	LINDA FRANKLIN - Deposit	1248	3 - 39	2,846.54		4,345.79	Dr.
3	GL-GJ	20-Mar-15	GRADY PURBOO - Deposit	1249	3 - 44	1,867.95		6,213.74	Dr.
3	GL-GJ	23-Mar-15	LARRY MURDOCH - Salary	CHQ 3549	3 - 45		1,645.20	4,568.54	Dr.
3	GL-GJ	23-Mar-15	FREDA WANDERLING - Salary	CHQ 3550	3 - 46		1,586.45	2,982.09	Dr.
3	GL-GJ	24-Mar-15	CRISPIN ROBICHAUD	CHQ 3551	3 - 47		1,256.75	1,725.34	Dr
3	GL-GJ	26-Mar-15	KEN CHARLES - Deposit	1250	3 - 48	1,648.65		3,373.99	Dr.
3	GL-GJ	27-Mar-15	WANDA GRIERSON - Deposit	1251	3 - 49	6,746.90		10,120.89	Dr.
3	GL-GJ	27-Mar-15	OREST FELDMAN - Deposit	1252	3 - 51	1,648.80		11,769.69	Dr.
3	GL-GJ	27-Mar-15	TIM EWASIUK - Deposit	1253	3 - 52	2,548.33		14,318.02	Dr.
3	GL-GJ	27-Mar-15	GRAHAM DENMANN	CHQ 3552	3 - 56		4,516.84	9,801.18	Dr.
3	GL-GJ	30-Mar-15	STILL PRODUCTIONS COMPANY	CHQ 3553	3 - 57		1,648.75	8,152.43	Dr.
3	GL-GJ	30-Mar-15	BRYANT WHOLESALE SUPPLIERS LTD	CHQ 3554	3 - 58		6,745.14	1,407.29	Dr.
3	GL-GJ	30-Mar-15	AGENCY RESTAURANT	CHQ 3555	3 - 62		158.76	1,248.53	Dr.
3	GL-GJ	30-Mar-15	COMPACT DESIGNS LTD.	CHQ 3556	3 - 65		253.60	994.93	Dr.
3	GL-GJ	31-Mar-15	AMY FIELDING - Deposit	1254	3 - 66	2,866.38		3,861.31	Dr.

Casing Suppliers Ltd.
Bank Reconciliation
February 28, 2015

Balance per Bank Statement				5,183.83
Add: Deposit in Transit				3,640.58
				8,824.41
Less: Outstanding Cheques:	3496		53.18	
	3523		1,685.25	
	3524		2,344.64	4,083.07
Balance per General Ledger				4,741.34

BANKING PROCEDURES AND CONTROL OF CASH

ROYAL BANK OF CANADA

Centreville Branch
Suite 410, Ambrose Gardens
Oakville, ON
M4W 7H2

CASING SUPPLIERS LTD.
1840 Rochester Road
Oakville, ON
M7J 4D6

Account Statement

Account No.
765-432-8

Period	
From	To
Mar 1/15	Mar 31/15

Enclosures	Page
29	1

Date		Transaction Description	Cheques & Debits	Deposits & Credits	Balance
Feb 28	Balance Forward				5,183.83
Mar 02	Deposit			3,640.58	8,824.41
Mar 02	Cheque	3524	2,344.64		6,479.77
Mar 02	Cheque	3525	1,498.00		4,981.77
Mar 02	Cheque	3523	1,685.25		3,296.52
Mar 02	Deposit			6,425.48	9,722.00
Mar 03	Deposit			3,164.17	12,886.17
Mar 04	Cheque	3526	3,614.85		9,271.32
Mar 04	Cheque	3527	136.00		9,135.32
Mar 04	Deposit			8,742.00	17,877.32
Mar 09	Cheque	3532	1,500.00		16,377.32
Mar 09	Cheque	3530	5,248.95		11,128.37
Mar 09	Deposit			1,756.25	12,884.62
Mar 09	Cheque	3529	749.00		12,135.62
Mar 09	Loan Interest Payment		368.40		11,767.22
Mar 10	Cheque	3528	1,510.00		10,257.22
Mar 11	Cheque	3536	318.96		9,938.26
Mar 11	Cheque	3531	2,850.00		7,088.26
Mar 11	Cheque	3535	168.45		6,919.81
Mar 11	Cheque	3538	641.30		6,278.51
Mar 11	Deposit			1,616.82	7,895.33
Mar 12	Cheque	3537	418.50		7,476.83
Mar 12	Deposit			6,475.20	13,952.03
Mar 12	Cheque	3541	1,586.45		12,365.58
Mar 12	Cheque	3540	1,645.20		10,720.38
Mar 16	Cheque	3542	2,167.10		8,553.28
Mar 16	Cheque	3543	742.00		7,811.28
Mar 16	Cheques Ordered		35.30		7,775.98
Mar 17	Cheque	3544	1,684.52		6,091.46
Mar 17	Cheque	3546	1,014.58		5,076.88
Mar 18	Cheque	3548	682.45		4,394.43
Mar 18	Deposit			648.00	5,042.43
Mar 18	Loan Principal Payment		3,000.00		2,042.43
Mar 20	Deposit			2,846.54	4,888.97
Mar 20	NSF Cheque - Joy Amity		648.00		4,240.97
Mar 20	NSF Service Charge		20.00		4,220.97
Mar 20	Deposit			1,867.95	6,088.92
Mar 22	Cheque	3550	1,586.45		4,502.47
Mar 24	Interest Earned			86.20	4,588.67
Mar 24	Cheque	3549	1,645.20		2,943.47
Mar 25	Cheque	3551	1,256.75		1,686.72
Mar 26	Deposit			1,648.65	3,335.37
Mar 27	Cheque	3552	4,516.84		(1,181.47)
Mar 27	Deposit			6,746.90	5,565.43
Mar 27	Deposit			1,648.80	7,214.23
Mar 30	Cheque	3553	1,648.75		5,565.48
Mar 30	Deposit			2,548.33	8,113.81
Mar 30	Bank Service Charge		42.75		8,071.06
Mar 30	Cheque	3555	158.76		7,912.30

BANK OF SASKATCHEWAN
10050–101 Street
Regina, Saskatchewan
S4J 6E2

03749

RICK'S DELI
8811–102 Street
Regina, SK
S3A 3G6

Account Statement

Account No.
241 673 6

Period	
From	To
Apr 01/15	Apr 30/15

Enclosures	Page
7	1

Date	Transaction Description		Cheques & Debits	Deposits & Credits	Balance
Apr 01	Balance Forward				718.00
Apr 02	Cheque -	108	12.00		
Apr 03	Cheque -	114	36.00		670.00
Apr 10	Deposit			40.00	
Apr 10	Cheque -	115	20.00		690.00
Apr 16	Deposit			80.00	770.00
Apr 17	Cheque -	113	80.00		690.00
Apr 20	Deposit			40.00	
Apr 20	NSF Returned Item		40.00		690.00
Apr 23	Deposit			160.00	850.00
Apr 24	Cheque -	117	160.00		690.00
Apr 27	Deposit			24.00	714.00
Apr 28	Cheque -	109	80.00		
Apr 30	Service Charge		2.00		632.00

No. of Debits	Total Amount	No. of Credits	Total Amount
8	430.00	5	344.00

Check Figure

Reconciled balance $756

a. Cheques outstanding: No. 110, $80; No. 116, $160; No. 118, $52.

b. A deposit of $416 is in transit.

c. The chequebook balance of Rick's Deli shows an ending balance of $798.

d. Jim Rice's cheque for $40 bounced because of lack of sufficient funds.

Establishment and replenishment of petty cash

Relationship to auxiliary petty cash record

3 (30 min)

Check Figure

Cash replenishment $48

7B-3. From the following transactions, (1) record the entries as needed in the general journal of Merry Co. of Lennoxville as well as the auxiliary petty cash record and (2) replenish the petty cash fund on April 30 (cheque No. 6).

2013

April 1 Issued cheque No. 4 for $80 to establish a petty cash fund.

5 Paid $9 from petty cash for postage, voucher No. 1.

8 Paid $12 from petty cash for office supplies, voucher No. 2.

16 Paid $9 from petty cash for office supplies, voucher No. 3.

23 Paid $6 from petty cash for postage, voucher No. 4.

26 Paid $12 from petty cash for local charity donation, voucher No. 5 (this is a miscellaneous payment).

29 Issued cheque No. 5 to Roy Kloon to pay for office equipment, $800.

Chart of accounts includes: Cash, 100; Petty Cash, 120; Office Equipment, 130; Postage Expense, 610; Office Supplies Expense, 620; Miscellaneous Expense, 630. Use the same headings as in Problem 7A-3.

7B-4. From the following, record the transactions in Logan's auxiliary petty cash record and general journal:

2012

Oct.   1   Roberta Floss, the petty cashier, cashed a cheque, No. 444 to establish a $100 petty cash fund.

        5   Paid $18 for postage stamps, voucher No. 1.

        9   Paid $12 for delivery charges on goods for resale, voucher No. 2.

        15   Paid $10 for donation to a homeless shelter (Miscellaneous Expense), voucher No. 3.

        15   Paid $14 for postage stamps, voucher No. 4.

        16   Paid $5 for delivery charges on goods for resale, voucher No. 5.

        26   Purchased computer supplies from petty cash for $7, voucher No. 6.

        29   Paid $4 for postage, voucher No. 7.

        30   Drew cheque No. 618 to replenish petty cash and cover a $3 shortage.

7B-5. Shown on pages 351 and 352 are the following for Casing Suppliers Ltd. of Oakville:

a. General ledger listing for March 2015

b. Bank reconciliation as of February 28, 2015

c. Bank statement for March 2015

Required

Prepare a bank reconciliation as of March 31, 2015.

Group C Problems

(The forms you need are on pages 7-12 to 7-18 of the *Study Guide with Working Papers*.)

7C-1. Graham Company of Moncton received a bank statement from Royal Bank indicating a bank balance of $7,483. Based on Graham's cheque stubs, the ending chequebook balance was $6,919. Your task is to prepare a bank reconciliation for Graham Company as of May 31, 2013, from the following information (please journalize entries as needed):

a. Cheques outstanding: No. 354, $297; No. 356, $512; No. 347, $684.

b. Deposits in transit, $1,381.

c. Bank service charge, $39.

d. Royal Bank collected a note for Graham, $734, less a $14 collection fee.

e. Notice was received that a cheque from Harry Pride, a customer, was returned NSF, $151.

f. Bank recorded new cheques purchase, $78.

7C-2. From the following July 28, 2014, bank statement (p. 353), (1) complete a bank reconciliation for The Fresh Flower Shop of Halifax and (2) journalize the appropriate entries as needed.

a. A deposit of $2,122 is in transit.

b. The Fresh Flower Shop has an ending chequebook balance of $5,111.

c. Cheques outstanding: No. 231, $298; No. 245, $509; No. 246, $76; No. 247, $237.

d. Jane Yates's cheque for $225 bounced because of non-sufficient funds.

Casing Suppliers Ltd.
General Ledger Listing as of March 31, 2015

Period	Source	Date	Description	Reference	Posting Entry	Debits	Credits	Net Balance	Dr./Cr.
			1050 Royal Bank - Chequing		Balance Forward			4,328.94	Dr.
3	GL-GJ	2-Mar-15	WESTERN PROPERTIES LTD.	CHQ 2325	3 - 1		1,746.20	2,582.74	Dr.
3	GL-GJ	2-Mar-15	WALLY PIERCE - Deposit	942	3 - 2	6,186.42		8,769.16	Dr.
3	GL-GJ	2-Mar-15	SANDY NESS - Deposit	943	3 - 3	3,460.84		12,230.00	Dr.
3	GL-GJ	2-Mar-15	CARSON WHOLESALE INC.	CHQ 2326	3 - 4		3,477.16	8,752.84	Dr.
3	GL-GJ	5-Mar-15	QUICK COMPUTER REPAIRS LTD.	CHQ 2327	3 - 5		145.00	8,607.84	Dr.
3	GL-GJ	5-Mar-15	NIVENS QUALITY UPHOLSTERING	CHQ 2328	3 - 6		1,645.00	6,962.84	Dr.
3	GL-GJ	6-Mar-15	ALLEN MURRAY - Deposit	944	3 - 7	8,819.00		15,781.84	Dr.
3	GL-GJ	6-Mar-15	A.F. KINGSLEY, ACCOUNTANT	CHQ 2329	3 - 8		856.00	14,925.84	Dr.
3	GL-GJ	6-Mar-15	BRENDA KELLY - Deposit	945	3 - 9	1,614.25		16,540.09	Dr.
3	GL-GJ	6-Mar-15	EVANS CONTRACTING LTD.	CHQ 2330	3 - 10		5,584.15	10,955.94	Dr.
3	GL-GJ	6-Mar-15	CORRINTHIAN CONSULTING CO.	CHQ 2331	3 - 11		2,786.50	8,169.44	Dr.
3	GL-GJ	6-Mar-15	NANCY SNYDER	CHQ 2332	3 - 12		1,650.00	6,519.44	Dr.
3	GL-GJ	6-Mar-15	CITY PHONE COMPANY	CHQ 2335	3 - 13		166.42	6,353.02	Dr.
3	GL-GJ	9-Mar-15	LYCOS UTILITIES INC.	CHQ 2336	3 - 14		342.72	6,010.30	Dr.
3	GL-GJ	9-Mar-15	CASEY VALENCE	CHQ 2337	3 - 15		505.70	5,504.60	Dr.
3	GL-GJ	9-Mar-15	STATIONERY DEPOT LTD.	CHQ 2338	3 - 16		668.62	4,835.98	Dr.
3	GL-GJ	9-Mar-15	JAMIE DUPRE	CHQ 2339	3 - 17		376.00	4,459.98	Dr.
3	GL-GJ	10-Mar-15	WAN TSUI - Deposit	946	3 - 18	3,417.25		7,877.23	Dr.
3	GL-GJ	10-Mar-15	LARRY MURDOCH - Salary	CHQ 2340	3 - 19		1,864.20	6,013.03	Dr.
3	GL-GJ	10-Mar-15	FREDA WANDERLING - Salary	CHQ 2341	3 - 20		1,714.55	4,298.48	Dr.
3	GL-GJ	11-Mar-15	RBC - Loan Interest	01 - 21	3 - 21		326.42	3,972.06	Dr.
3	GL-GJ	11-Mar-15	K CARDINAL - Deposit	947	3 - 22	5,846.84		9,818.90	Dr.
3	GL-GJ	13-Mar-15	JAMISON SUPPLIERS LTD.	CHQ 2342	3 - 23		3,459.21	6,359.69	Dr.
3	GL-GJ	16-Mar-15	WORD WIZARDS LTD.	CHQ 2343	3 - 27		972.00	5,387.69	Dr.
3	GL-GJ	16-Mar-15	Canada Revenue Agency	CHQ 2344	3 - 28		1,742.36	3,645.33	Dr.
3	GL-GJ	16-Mar-15	RBC - Loan Repayment	01 - 24	3 - 29		2,000.00	1,645.33	Dr.
3	GL-GJ	16-Mar-15	JOY AMITY - Deposit	948	3 - 30	952.00		2,597.33	Dr.
3	GL-GJ	16-Mar-15	THOMAS HUNT - Insurance	CHQ 2346	3 - 31		753.24	1,844.09	Dr.
3	GL-GJ	17-Mar-15	PEARSON HIGH SCHOOL ADVERTISING	CHQ 2347	3 - 32		150.00	1,694.09	Dr.
3	GL-GJ	17-Mar-15	THE LOCAL TIMES	CHQ 2348	3 - 37		682.45	1,011.64	Dr.
3	GL-GJ	18-Mar-15	RBC - New cheques ordered	01 - 29	3 - 38		35.30	976.34	Dr.
3	GL-GJ	19-Mar-15	LINDA FRANKLIN - Deposit	949	3 - 39	2,456.38		3,432.72	Dr.
3	GL-GJ	20-Mar-15	GRADY PURBOO - Deposit	950	3 - 44	1,964.25		5,396.97	Dr.
3	GL-GJ	21-Mar-15	LARRY MURDOCH - Salary	CHQ 2349	3 - 45		1,864.20	3,532.77	Dr.
3	GL-GJ	23-Mar-15	FREDA WANDERLING - Salary	CHQ 2350	3 - 46		1,714.55	1,818.22	Dr.
3	GL-GJ	24-Mar-15	CRISPIN ROBICHAUD	CHQ 2351	3 - 47		1,256.75	561.47	Dr.
3	GL-GJ	25-Mar-15	KEN CHARLES - Deposit	951	3 - 48	1,906.72		2,468.19	Dr.
3	GL-GJ	27-Mar-15	WANDA GRIERSON - Deposit	952	3 - 49	3,868.46		6,336.65	Dr.
3	GL-GJ	27-Mar-15	OREST FELDMAN - Deposit	953	3 - 51	2,842.66		9,179.31	Dr.
3	GL-GJ	27-Mar-15	TIM EWASIUK - Deposit	954	3 - 52	2,442.91		11,622.22	Dr.
3	GL-GJ	27-Mar-15	GRAHAM DENMANN	CHQ 2352	3 - 56		4,458.78	7,163.44	Dr.
3	GL-GJ	30-Mar-15	STILL PRODUCTIONS COMPANY	CHQ 2353	3 - 57		1,594.34	5,569.10	Dr.
3	GL-GJ	30-Mar-15	BRYANT WHOLESALE SUPPLIERS LTD	CHQ 2354	3 - 58		5,840.60	−271.50	Cr.
3	GL-GJ	30-Mar-15	AGENCY RESTAURANT	CHQ 2355	3 - 62		162.70	−434.20	Cr.
3	GL-GJ	31-Mar-15	COMPACT DESIGNS LTD.	CHQ 2356	3 - 65		268.45	−702.65	Cr.
3	GL-GJ	31-Mar-15	AMY FIELDING - Deposit	955	3 - 66	3,148.62		2,445.97	Dr.

Casing Suppliers Ltd.
Bank Reconciliation
February 28, 2015

Balance per Bank Statement			5,183.83	
Add: Deposit in Transit			2,856.32	
			8,040.15	
Less: Outstanding Cheques:	2296	87.26		
	2323	1,457.50		
	2324	2,166.45	3,711.21	
Balance per General Ledger			4,328.94	

ROYAL BANK OF CANADA

Account Statement

Centreville Branch
Suite 410, Ambrose Gardens
Oakville, ON
L4W 7H2

CASING SUPPLIERS LTD.
1840 Rochester Road
Oakville, ON
L7J 4D6

Account No.
765-432-8

Period	
From	To
Mar 1/15	Mar 31/15

Enclosures	Page
29	1

Date		Transaction Description	Cheques & Debits	Deposits & Credits	Balance
Feb 28		Balance Forward			5,183.83
Mar 02		Deposit		2,856.32	
Mar 02		Cheque	2324	2,166.45		5,873.70
Mar 02		Cheque	2325	1,746.20		
Mar 02		Cheque	2323	1,457.50		
Mar 02		Deposit			6,186.42	8,856.42
Mar 03		Deposit			3,460.84	12,317.26
Mar 04		Cheque	2326	3,477.16		8,840.10
Mar 06		Cheque	2327	145.00		
Mar 06		Deposit			8,819.00	17,514.10
Mar 06		Cheque	2332	1,650.00		15,864.10
Mar 09		Cheque	2330	5,584.15		
Mar 09		Deposit			1,614.25	
Mar 09		Cheque	2329	856.00		
Mar 09		Loan Interest Payment		326.42		10,711.78
Mar 10		Cheque	2328	1,645.00		9,066.78
Mar 10		Cheque	2336	342.72		
Mar 10		Cheque	2331	2,786.50		
Mar 10		Cheque	2335	166.42		
Mar 10		Cheque	2338	668.62		
Mar 10		Deposit			3,417.25	8,519.77
Mar 11		Cheque	2337	505.70		
Mar 11		Deposit			5,846.84	
Mar 12		Cheque	2341	1,714.55		
Mar 12		Cheque	2340	1,864.20		10,282.16
Mar 13		Cheque	2342	3,459.21		6,822.95
Mar 16		Cheque	2343	972.00		
Mar 16		Cheques Ordered		35.30		5,815.65
Mar 17		Cheque	2344	1,742.36		
Mar 17		Cheque	2346	753.24		3,320.05
Mar 18		Cheque	2348	682.45		
Mar 18		Deposit			952.00	
Mar 18		Loan Principal Payment		2,000.00		1,589.60
Mar 19		Deposit			2,456.38	4,045.98
Mar 20		NSF Cheque - Joy Amity		952.00		
Mar 20		NSF Service Charge		20.00		
Mar 20		Deposit			1,964.25	5,038.23
Mar 23		Cheque	2350	1,714.55		3,323.68
Mar 23		Interest Earned			86.20	3,409.88
Mar 24		Cheque	2349	1,864.20		1,545.68
Mar 25		Cheque	2351	1,256.75		288.93
Mar 26		Deposit			1,906.72	2,195.65
Mar 27		Cheque	2352	4,458.78		
Mar 27		Deposit			3,868.46	
Mar 27		Deposit			2,842.66	4,447.99
Mar 30		Cheque	2353	1,594.34		
Mar 30		Deposit			2,442.91	
Mar 31		Bank Service Charge		34.76		5,261.80
Mar 31		Cheque	2355	162.70		5,099.10

Date	Transaction Description		Cheques & Debits	Deposits & Credits	Balance
Jul 01	Balance Forward				2,824.00
Jul 02	Cheque -	241	385.00		2,439.00
Jul 03	Cheque -	240	410.00		2,029.00
Jul 10	Deposit			1,712.00	
Jul 10	Cheque -	243	250.00		3,491.00
Jul 14	Deposit			950.00	4,441.00
Jul 15	Cheque -	242	1,214.00		3,227.00
Jul 16	Deposit			225.00	3,452.00
Jul 21	NSF Returned Item		225.00		3,227.00
Jul 22	Deposit			1,260.00	4,487.00
Jul 24	Cheque -	248	1,410.00		3,077.00
Jul 25	Deposit			780.00	3,857.00
Jul 28	Cheque -	1126	607.00		
Jul 29	Service Charge		12.00		3,238.00

BANK OF INDUSTRY AND COMMERCE
48 JAMES STREET
HALIFAX, NOVA SCOTIA
B4T 2L0

08179

THE FRESH FLOWER SHOP
121 SPRING GARDEN ROAD
HALIFAX, NS
B5H 3E6

Account Statement

Account No.
914 817 2

Period
From Jun 29/14
To Jul 28/14

Enclosures 7
Page 1

No. of Debits	Total Amount	No. of Credits	Total Amount
8	4,513.00	5	4,927.00

e. Cheque No. 241 for utilities expense was entered in the cash payments journal as $358.

f. The cheque for $607 shown by the bank as paid on July 28 was actually a cheque of the Active Automotive Repair. This error will be corrected by the bank next month. The bank apologized for the error.

Relationship to auxiliary petty
cash record
③ (30 min)

Check Figure
Cash replenishment $178

7C-3. The following transactions occurred in March and were related to the general journal and petty cash fund of Samuel & Co. of St. John's.

2013

March 1 Issued cheque No. 314 for $200 to establish a petty cash fund.

5 Paid $45 from petty cash for postage, voucher No. 1.

8 Paid $39 from petty cash for office supplies, voucher No. 2.

18 Paid $27 from petty cash for office supplies, voucher No. 3.

25 Paid $47 from petty cash for postage, voucher No. 4.

26 Paid $20 from petty cash to support a student walk event, voucher No. 5 (this is a miscellaneous payment).

29 Issued cheque No. 315 to Klondike Office Equipment to pay for office equipment, $1,890.

The chart of accounts includes Cash, 100; Petty Cash, 105; Office Equipment, 170; Postage Expense, 645; Office Supplies Expense, 640; Miscellaneous Expense, 630. The headings of the auxiliary petty cash records are the same as for Problem 7A-3.

Required

1. Record the appropriate entries in the general journal and the auxiliary petty cash record as needed.

2. Be sure to replenish the petty cash fund on March 31 (cheque No. 316).

7C-4. From the following, record the transactions in Caron Co.'s auxiliary petty cash record and general journal.

2012

Oct.   1   A cheque was drawn, No. 772, payable to Herb Kiriak, petty cashier, to establish a $250 petty cash fund.

       5   Paid $41 for postage stamps, voucher No. 1.

       9   Paid $16 for delivery charges on goods for resale, voucher No. 2.

     12   Gave $30 donation to a church (Miscellaneous Expense), voucher No. 3.

     15   Paid $57 for postage stamps, voucher No. 4.

     16   Paid $13 for delivery charges on goods for resale, voucher No. 5.

     26   Purchased computer supplies from petty cash for $19, voucher No. 6.

     29   Paid $32 for postage, voucher No. 7.

     31   Drew cheque No. 813 to replenish petty cash (a $4 shortage was apparent when the cash was balanced).

7C-5. Shown below and on pages and 355 and 356 are the following for Northern Energy Consulting of Sinclair:

a. Bank reconciliation completed as of March 31, 2014 (see below)

b. Bank statement for March 29 to April 29, 2014

c. General ledger listing for April 2014

Required

Reconcile the Balance per Bank Statement ($9,199.21) with the Balance per General Ledger ($5,648.15).

NORTHERN ENERGY CONSULTING BANK RECONCILIATION MARCH 31, 2014			
Balance per Bank Statement			7,036.42
Add: Deposits in Transit		540.00	
		1,245.00	1,785.00
			8,821.42
Less: Outstanding cheques:			
	205	89.14	
	206	950.00	
	207	133.45	
	208	1,250.00	
	209	672.30	3,094.89
Balance per General Ledger			**5,726.53**

BANK OF ALBERTA
105 STREET BRANCH
4525–105 STREET
SINCLAIR, ALBERTA
T1Y 4P8

NORTHERN ENERGY CONSULTING
5477–134 AVE.
SINCLAIR, ALBERTA
T2S 4G7

Account Statement

Account No.		
2361-445-99		

Period		
From		To
Mar 29/14		Apr 29/14

Enclosures	Page
14	50

Date	Transaction Description		Cheques & Debits	Deposits & Credits	Balance
	Balance Forward				7,036.42
Mar 29	Error Correction		540.00		6,496.42
	Loan Proceeds			540.00	7,036.42
	Deposit			540.00	7,576.42
Apr 01	Deposit			1,245.00	8,821.42
	Cheque	0209	672.30		8,149.12
	Cheque	0205	89.14		8,059.98
	Cheque	0207	133.45		7,926.53
	Cheque	0210	208.25		7,718.28
	Cheque	0212	207.45		7,510.83
	NSF Returned		425.00		7,085.83
Apr 05	NSF Charge		15.00		7,070.83
Apr 05	Deposit			1,745.00	8,815.83
	Cheque	0208	1,250.00		7,565.83
	Cheque	0211	124.15		7,441.68
Apr 08	Deposit			428.00	7,869.68
Apr 08	Deposit			856.00	8,725.68
Apr 09	Deposit			968.27	9,693.95
	Cheque	0206	950.00		8,743.95
	Cheque	0213	642.00		8,101.95
	Cheque	0214	164.25		7,937.70
Apr 15	Deposit			254.36	8,192.06
	Cheque	0217	1,746.80		6,445.26
	Cheque	0218	1,254.35		5,190.91
Apr 15	Deposit			418.74	5,609.65
Apr 16	Deposit			366.05	5,975.70
Apr 19	Deposit			284.67	6,260.37
Apr 19	Deposit			200.60	6,460.97
Apr 19	Deposit			1,987.00	8,447.97
	Cheque	0215	65.70		8,382.27
Apr 20	Bank Service Charge		34.20		8,348.07
Apr 23	Deposit			502.46	8,850.53
Apr 26	Deposit			1,007.28	9,857.81
Apr 26	Loan Interest		37.50		9,820.31
	Loan Payment		317.50		9,502.81
	Cheque	0216	362.00		9,140.81
Apr 29	Interest Earned			58.40	9,199.21

No. of Debits	20	Total Amount Debits	9,239.04	Total Fees	34.20
No. of Credits	16	Total Amount Credits	11,401.83	Interest Paid	37.50

Date: May 12, 2014 2:34 pm   NORTHERN ENERGY CONSULTING   Page: 1
G/L listing for account   1100
                                                  General Ledger Listing as of April 30, 2014

Period	Source	Date	Description	Reference	Posting Entry	Debits	Credits	Net Balance
			1100 Bank of Alberta - Chequing					5,726.53
4	GL-GJ	01-Apr-14	ALBERTA PHONE CO.	CHQ 0210	4 - 1		208.25	5,518.28
4	GL-GJ	01-Apr-14	MAXIM OFFICE SUPPLIES	CHQ 0211	4 - 2		124.15	5,394.13
4	GL-GJ	02-Apr-14	CANADA POST	CHQ 0212	4 - 3		207.45	5,186.68
4	GL-GJ	02-Apr-14	HANDI PRINT AND GRAPHICS	CHQ 0213	4 - 4		642.00	4,544.68
4	GL-GJ	05-Apr-14	CITY TRUCK STOPS - Deposit	LT204	4 - 5	1,745.00		6.289.68
4	GL-GJ	08-Apr-14	PERFORMANCE OIL CHANGE - Deposit	LT298	4 - 6	428.00		6,717.68
4	GL-GJ	08-Apr-14	AUTO ROW SALES & SERVICE - Deposit	LT299	4 - 7	856.00		7,573.68
4	GL-GJ	08-Apr-14	SINCLAIR UTILITY	CHQ 0214	4 - 8		164.25	7,409.43
4	GL-GJ	08-Apr-14	KENYA COFFEE COMPANY	CHQ 0215	4 - 9		65.70	7,343.73
4	GL-GJ	09-Apr-14	THE CO-OPS OF MONTANA - Deposit	LT300	4 - 10	968.27		8,312.00
4	GL-GJ	09-Apr-14	RED'S GAS BAR - Deposit	LT303	4 - 11	254.36		8,566.36
4	GL-GJ	15-Apr-14	W/CANADA TRUCK STOPS - Deposit	LT296	4 - 12	418.74		8,895.10
4	GL-GJ	15-Apr-14	CITY NEWSPAPER	CHQ 0216	4 - 13		326.00	8,659.10
4	GL-GJ	15-Apr-14	CANADA REVENUE AGENCY - GST	CHQ 0217	4 - 14		1,746.80	6,912.30
4	GL-GJ	15-Apr-14	CANADA REVENUE AGENCY	CHQ 0218	4 - 15		1,254.35	5,657.95
4	GL-GJ	16-Apr-14	SUPER SAVE SERVICE - Deposit	LT290	4 - 16	366.05		6.024.00
4	GL-GJ	19-Apr-14	CARLY'S TRUCK WASH - Deposit	LT301	4 - 17	284.67		6,308.67
4	GL-GJ	19-Apr-14	APRIL'S MART - Deposit	LT302	4 - 18	200.60		6,509.27
4	GL-GJ	19-Apr-14	ELDORADO PETROLEUM - Deposit	LT295	4 - 19	1,987.00		8,496.27
4	GL-GJ	23-Apr-14	WEYBURN REFINERY	CHQ 0219	4 - 20		2,488.16	6,008.11
4	GL-GJ	23-Apr-14	TRI-CITY GAS - Deposit	LT305	4 - 21	502.46		6,510.57
4	GL-GJ	26-Apr-14	BENNY'S AUTO REPAIR - Deposit	LT306	4 - 22	1,007.28		7,517.85
4	GL-GJ	26-Apr-14	B OF A LOAN PAYMENT	4 - 23	4 - 23		317.50	7,200.85
4	GL-GJ	26-Apr-14	B OF A LOAN INTEREST	4 - 24	4 - 24		37.50	7,162.85
4	GL-GJ	26-Apr-14	LESLEY TRIPP - Salary	CHQ 0220	4 - 25		1,450.00	5,712.85
4	GL-GJ	26-Apr-14	ANDREW GALVOIR - Salary	CHQ 0221	4 - 26		1,220.00	4,492.85
4	GL-GJ	29-Apr-14	EDISON TUNE-UPS ALBERTA - Deposit	LT307	4 - 27	1,155.30		5,648.15

On-the-job Training

(The forms you need are on pages 7-19 to 7-20 of the *Study Guide with Working Papers*.)

Replenishing the petty cash fund and increasing the petty cash account

③ (15 min)

T-1. Karen Johnson, the accountant of Hoop Co. of Nelson, has appointed Jim Pool as the petty cash custodian. The following transactions occurred in November:

2013

Nov. 25 Cheque No. 441 was written and cashed to establish a $50 petty cash fund.
      26 Paid $8.50 delivery charge for goods purchased for resale.
      28 Purchased office supplies for $12 from petty cash.
      29 Purchased postage stamps for $15 from petty cash.

On December 3, Jim received the following internal memo:

To:	Jim Pool
From:	Karen Johnson
Re:	Petty Cash

Jim, I'll need $5 for postage stamps. By the way, I noticed that our petty cash account seems to be too low. Increase its size to $100 please.

Help Jim replenish petty cash on December 3 by providing him with a general journal entry. Support your answer and indicate whether Karen was correct.

T-2. Ginger Company of Bathurst has a policy of depositing all receipts and making all payments by cheque. On receiving the bank statement, Bill Free, a new bookkeeper, is quite upset that the balance in cash in the ledger is $4,209.50 while the ending bank balance is $4,440.50. Bill is convinced that the bank has made an error. Based on the following facts, is Bill's concern warranted? What other suggestions could you offer Bill in the bank reconciliation process?

a. The November 30 cash receipts, $611, had been placed in the bank's night depository after banking hours and consequently did not appear on the bank statement as a deposit.

b. Two debit memoranda and a credit memorandum were included with the returned cheques. None of the memoranda had been recorded at the time of the reconciliation. The first debit memorandum covered a $130 NSF cheque written by Abby Ellen. The second was a $6.50 debit memorandum for service charges. The credit memorandum was for $494 and represented the proceeds less a $6 collection fee from a $500 non-interest-bearing note collected for Ginger Company by the bank.

c. It was also found that cheques No. 942 for $71.50 and No. 947 for $206.50, both written and recorded on November 28, were not among the cancelled cheques returned.

d. Bill found that cheque No. 899 was correctly drawn for $1,094 as payment for a new cash register. However, this cheque had been recorded as though it were for $1,148.

e. The October bank reconciliation showed two cheques outstanding on September 30, No. 621 for $152.50 and No. 630 for $179.30. Cheque No. 630 was paid and returned with the November bank statement but cheque No. 621 was not.

T-3. On March 2, 2013, the accountant for Bergen Carpet Co. of Edmonton was injured in a skiing accident and was advised not to return to work for six weeks. The owners of the company are anxious to ensure that the company's bank statement is reconciled and have asked you to perform this task. You are presented with the following information:

a. Bank reconciliation prepared by the regular accountant at January 31, 2013:

Bergen Carpet Co.
Bank Reconciliation
January 31, 2013

Balance per Bank Statement		$ 8,364.02
Add: Deposit in Transit		2,576.03
		10,940.05
Less: Outstanding Cheques		
No. 417	$ 28.30	
419	1,043.25	
423	1,722.30	2,793.85
Balance per General Ledger		$ 8,146.20

b. General ledger listing of Bank Account (#110) for the month of February (see page 358).
c. Bank statement from the Royal Bank for the period ending February 26, 2013 (see page 359).

Required

Prepare the necessary reconciliation and any journal entries needed at February 28, 2013.

<table>
<tr><td colspan="11">Date: 11 Mar. 2013 11:06 am
G/L Listing</td><td colspan="2" align="center">BERGEN CARPET CO.
General Ledger Listing as of 28 Feb 2013</td><td align="right">Page: 1</td></tr>
</table>

```
G/L listing for account     [ 110]    to  [  110]
for department              [      ]   to  [ 222 ] ,
for fiscal period           [2] 0      [  2 ] ,
sorted by                   [ Account    ] .

Last posting sequence number:  4

Acct.  Dept.
```

Pd	Srce	Date	Description	Reference	Posting Entry	Batch Entry	Debits	Credits	Net Change/ Balance
	110	Bank							8,146.20
2	GL-GJ	01 Feb 13	KING PROPERTY	CHQ 404	2 - 1	2 - 1		974.15	
2	GL-GJ	01 Feb 13	SANDRA SMYTHE - Deposit	1007	2 - 2	2 - 2	8,145.38		
2	GL-GJ	04 Feb 13	INGRID LUNDREN - Deposit	1008	2 - 3	2 - 3	909.50		
2	GL-GJ	04 Feb 13	CAMPUS COPY SHOPPE	CHQ 424	2 - 4	2 - 4		133.75	
2	GL-GJ	04 Feb 13	BENJAMIN YEE	02 - 05	2 - 5	2 - 5	4,381.65		
2	GL-GJ	05 Feb 13	LITEMORE NEON SIGNS	CHQ 425	2 - 6	2 - 6		80.25	
2	GL-GJ	05 Feb 13	NORM & JANET TAYLOR - Deposit	1009	2 - 7	2 - 7	969.01		
2	GL-GJ	06 Feb 13	NAME - IT!	CHQ 426	2 - 9	2 - 9		240.75	
2	GL-GJ	06 Feb 13	JERRY SIMON - Deposit	1011	2 - 10	2 - 10	2,782.00		
2	GL-GJ	07 Feb 13	SAXONY WOOL MILLS	CHQ 427	2 - 11	2 - 11		4,559.11	
2	GL-GJ	07 Feb 13	QUALITY CARPET COMPANY	CHQ 428	2 - 12	2 - 12		6,829.28	
2	GL-GJ	07 Feb 13	JODY ARCHER	CHQ 429	2 - 13	2 - 13		25.00	
2	GL-GJ	08 Feb 13	CITY PHONE COMPANY	CHQ 430	2 - 14	2 - 14		121.75	
2	GL-GJ	08 Feb 13	CITY UTILITY COMPANY	CHQ 431	2 - 15	2 - 15		111.14	
2	GL-GJ	08 Feb 13	JOE'S GAS BAR	CHQ 432	2 - 16	2 - 16		94.66	
2	GL-GJ	08 Feb 13	WOOD'S STATIONERY	CHQ 433	2 - 17	2 - 17		1,091.40	
2	GL-GJ	04 Feb 13	CASH	CHQ 434	2 - 18	2 - 18		100.00	
2	GL-GJ	08 Feb 13	IVY LEUNG - Deposit	1012	2 - 19	2 - 19	2,169.96		
2	GL-GJ	08 Feb 13	EMILY BERGEN - Salary	CHQ 435	2 - 20	2 - 20		697.35	
2	GL-GJ	08 Feb 13	JAMES BERGEN - Salary	CHQ 436	2 - 21	2 - 21		697.35	
2	GL-GJ	08 Feb 13	RBC/TERMPLAN LOAN PAYMENT	02 - 22	2 - 22	2 - 22		601.87	
2	GL-GJ	08 Feb 13	RBC/DEMAND LOAN INTEREST	02 - 23	2 - 23	2 - 23		695.20	
2	GL-GJ	13 Feb 13	PAT HARPER - Deposit	1013	2 - 27	2 - 27	404.46		
2	GL-GJ	13 Feb 13	CITY LIGHTING	CHQ 437	2 - 29	2 - 29		112.50	
2	GL-GJ	13 Feb 13	FREDDY DUNCAN	CHQ 438	2 - 30	2 - 30		2,010.40	
2	GL-GJ	13 Feb 13	RECEIVER GENERAL FOR CANADA	CHQ 439	2 - 31	2 - 31		993.04	
2	GL-GJ	15 Feb 13	VOID	CHQ 440	2 - 32	2 - 32	0.00		
2	GL-GJ	18 Feb 13	WILSON INSURANCE AGENCY	CHQ 441	2 - 33	2 - 33		802.50	
2	GL-GJ	18 Feb 13	COMMUNITY CALENDAR	CHQ 442	2 - 34	2 - 34		246.10	
2	GL-GJ	18 Feb 13	STANDARD NEWS	CHQ 443	2 - 35	2 - 35		909.50	
2	GL-GJ	18 Feb 13	T C CHURCHILL - Deposit	1015	2 - 36	2 - 36	3,610.18		
2	GL-GJ	18 Feb 13	RBC/LOAN PROCESSING CHARGE	02 - 37	2 - 37	2 - 37		40.00	
2	GL-GJ	25 Feb 13	BEATRICE DAY - Deposit	1016	2 - 38	2 - 38	4,068.68		
2	GL-GJ	25 Feb 13	JOAN ANDERSON - Deposit	02 - 44	2 - 44	2 - 44	2,569.07		
2	GL-GJ	25 Feb 13	EMILY BERGEN - Salary	CHQ 444	2 - 46	2 - 46		697.35	
2	GL-GJ	25 Feb 13	JAMES BERGEN - Salary	CHQ 445	2 - 47	2 - 47		697.35	
2	GL-GJ	24 Feb 13	BOB JONES	CHQ 446	2 - 49	2 - 49		240.00	
2	GL-GJ	26 Feb 13	MICHEL ROBICHAUD - Deposit	02 - 53	2 - 53	2 - 53	3,456.10		
2	GL-GJ	26 Feb 13	JUDY CARMICHAEL - Deposit	1022	2 - 54	2 - 54	1,218.20		
2	GL-GJ	28 Feb 13	DMJ CONSTRUCTION - Deposit	02 - 55	2 - 55	2 - 55	1,786.90		
2	GL-GJ	28 Feb 13	FREDDY DUNCAN	CHQ 447	2 - 56	2 - 56		1,950.90	
2	GL-GJ	28 Feb 13	GEORGE BETTS	CHQ 448	2 - 57	2 - 57		1,213.20	
2	GL-GJ	28 Feb 13	GREENBRIAR RESTAURANT	CHQ 449	2 - 58	2 - 58		76.15	9,429.09

Acct 110 - Balance, Feb 28, 2013   17,575.29

Account Statement

Account No.	124-629-7

Period	
From	To
Jan 27/13	Feb 26/13

Enclosures	Page
	1

BERGEN CARPET CO.
BAY 215
10620 - 104 AVENUE
EDMONTON AB
T5J 3G2

Date	Transaction Description		Cheques & Debits	Deposits & Credits	Balance
	Balance Forward				8,364.02
Jan 28	Deposit			2,576.03	10,940.05
Jan 28	Cheque -	404	974.15		
	Cheque -	419	1,043.25		8,922.65
Jan 29	Cheque -	423	1,722.30		7,200.35
Jan 30	Cheque -	424	133.75		7,066.60
Feb 01	Deposit			8,145.38	15,211.98
Feb 04	Deposit			5,291.15	
	Cheque -	434	100.00		20,403.13
Feb 05	Deposit			969.01	21,372.14
Feb 06	Deposit			2,782.00	
	Cheque -	425	80.25		
	Loan Payment - Principal		601.87		
	Loan Interest		695.20		22,776.82
Feb 07	Cheque -	430	121.75		
	Cheque -	436	697.35		
	Cheque -	435	697.35		21,260.37
Feb 08	Deposit			2,169.96	
	Cheque -	431	111.14		23,319.19
Feb 10	Cheque -	433	1,091.40		
	Cheque -	432	94.66		
	Cheque -	428	6,829.28		
	Cheque -	426	240.75		15,063.10
Feb 13	Deposit			404.46	
	Loan Management Fee		40.00		
	Cheque -	438	2,010.40		
	Cheque -	427	4,559.11		
	Cheque -	437	112.50		8,745.55
Feb 18	Deposit			3,610.18	12,355.73
Feb 18	Deposit			4,068.68	
	Cheque -	429	25.00		16,399.41
Feb 18	Cheque -	441	802.50		15,596.91
Feb 18	Cheque -	442	246.10		
	NSF Returned		404.46		14,946.35
Feb 21	NSF Charge		15.00		14,931.35
Feb 24	Cheque -	444	697.35		
	Cheque -	445	697.35		13,536.65
Feb 25	Deposit			2,569.07	
	Cheque -	439	993.04		15,112.68
Feb 26	Deposit			4,674.30	
	Cheque -	446	240.00		
	Service Charge		18.45		19,528.53

No. of Debits	Total Amount	No. of Credits	Total Amount
30	26,095.71	11	37,260.22

CONTINUING PROBLEM

Recording and posting
transactions; preparing a trial
balance; and preparing a bank
reconciliation
② ③ (60 min)

Following is a list of transactions for the month of October. Petty Cash Account (1010) and Miscellaneous Expense Account (5100) have been added to the chart of accounts.

Assignment

(See pages 7-21 to 7-29 in your *Study Guide with Working Papers*.)

1. Record the transactions in appropriate journals or petty cash format.
2. Post the transactions to the general ledger accounts.
3. Prepare a trial balance.

2013

Oct.	1	Paid cleaning contract for October, November, and December, $900, cheque No. 252.
	4	Established a petty cash fund for $100, cheque No. 253.
	4	Collected $3,600 from a cash customer for building three systems.
	4	Invoiced (invoice No. 12684) and received $1,600 from Anthony Pitale.
	8	Purchased $25 worth of stamps, using petty cash voucher No. 101.
	8	Withdrew $2,000 (cheque No. 254) for personal use.
	9	Purchased $22 worth of supplies, using petty cash voucher No. 102.
	11	Paid the newspaper carrier $10, using petty cash voucher No. 103.
	15	Paid the amount due for October phone bill to West Bell Canada, $65, cheque No. 255.
	15	Paid the amount due for the October electric bill to City Electric, $95, cheque No. 256.
	22	Performed computer services for Taylor Golf; billed the client $4,200, invoice No. 12685.
	25	Paid $20 for computer paper, using petty cash voucher No. 104.
	28	Took $15 out of petty cash for lunch, voucher No. 105.
	29	Replenished the petty cash, cheque No. 257. Coin and currency in drawer $8.

Since Tony was so busy trying to close his books, he forgot to reconcile the May, June, and July bank statements. What follows on pages 361 and 362 is a list of all deposits and cheques written for these three months (each entry is identified by chapter, transaction date, or transaction letter) and bank statements for May through July. Reconciliations for August and September are not part of this problem.

Chapter	Transaction	Payor/Payee	Amount
		DEPOSITS	
1	(a)	Tony Freedman	$4,500
1	(f)	Cash customer	250
1	(g)	Cash customer	200
1	(i)	Taylor Golf	1,200
2	(p)	Cash customer	900
3	July 5	Tonya Parker Jones	325
3	July 8	Summer Lipe	220
3	July 12	Jeannine Sparks	850
3	July 26	Mike Hammer	140

Chapter	Transaction	Cheque No.	Payor/Payee	Amount
		CHEQUES		
1	(b)	201	Multi Systems, Inc.	$1,200
1	(c)	202	Office Furniture, Inc.	600
1	(e)	203	Capital Management	400
1	(j)	204	Tony Freedman	100
2	(l)	205	Insurance Protection, Inc.	150
2	(m)	206	Office Depot	200
2	(n)	207	Computer Edge Magazine	1,400
2	(q)	208	City Electric	85
2	(r)	209	Canada Post	50
3	July 3	210	Capital Management	1,200
3	July 10	211	West Bell Canada	155
3	July 15	212	Computer Connection	200
3	July 17	213	Multi Systems, Inc.	1,200

BANK STATEMENT

Royal Bank of Canada 322 Glen Avenue, Edmonton, AB T5P 2T9

Precision Computer Centre   Statement Date: May 21, 2013

Cheques Paid:

Date paid	Number	Amount
5-5	201	1,200.00
5-7	202	600.00
5-14	203	400.00

Total 3 cheques paid for $2,200.00

Ending Balance on May 21—$3,950.00

Deposits and Credits:

Date received	Amount
5-3	4,500.00
5-10	250.00
5-20	200.00
5-21	1,200.00
Total Deposits	**$6,150.00**

Received Statement May 28, 2013.

BANK STATEMENT

Royal Bank of Canada 322 Glen Avenue, Edmonton, AB T5P 2T9

Precision Computer Centre   Statement Date: June 18, 2013

Cheques Paid:

Date paid	Number	Amount
6-2	204	100.00
6-7	205	150.00
6-9	206	200.00
6-16	207	1,400.00
6-21	208	85.00

Total 5 cheques paid for $1,935.00

Beginning balance on May 21—$3,950.00

Deposits and Credits:

Date received	Amount
6-11	900.00

Total Deposits $900.00

Ending balance on June 18 —$2,915.00

Received Statement June 28, 2013.

Received Statement July 28, 2013.

Assignment

Compare Precision Computer Centre's deposits and cheques with the bank statements, and complete a bank reconciliation as of July 31.

Computer Workshops

Mona and Mikes

Depending on the goals your instructor has set for the course you are taking, you may be asked to complete one or more of the computer workshops created especially for Chapter 7. If you need to complete any of the workshops, you will obtain all necessary details from the MyAccountingLab website.

There are a total of four workshops available. For each company, Mona and Mikes, there are two versions—one using Simply Accounting Pro® and the other using QuickBooks Premier®. The choice will depend to a large extent on which software is available to you in your college's lab, on your own laptop, or other computer, as well as the preference, knowledge, and experience of your instructor. Before beginning, be sure to get clear directions as to which workshop you are to complete. Please note that special, time-limited versions of both Simply Accounting® and QuickBooks® are available at no charge from each company's website. Your instructor might handle this for you, but it is easy to obtain the software and set it up yourself by visiting www.intuit.ca (QuickBooks®) or www.simply-accounting.com (Simply Accounting®).

You need to obtain several files from the MyAccountingLab website before you begin. (Please also see the added details on page 136 at the end of Chapter 3.)

1. The instruction files that describe each company and the details of the assignment.
2. Data sets that have been carefully crafted for you so you may begin each workshop with minimal bother. All of these data are downloaded in compressed format, and will need to be restored by the software before you can work on them.
3. A Word file that sets forth in detail the step-by-step instructions you need to complete the Mona assignment (one for each of the software programs). Help files also exist for the Mikes workshops, but these are available for student use only if they are provided by your instructor.

8 Payroll Procedures

The Employees' Perspective

THE BIG PICTURE

How many jobs do you expect to have in your lifetime? Recent projections suggest that Canadians will have, on average, eight jobs and three careers over a lifetime. And many demographers suspect that the numbers will be much higher for today's college graduates.

Christie Digital is doing their bit to change that. The Kitchener, Ontario–based company has an employee turnover rate of only 1%—and president and CEO Gerry Remers is working to keep it that way.

The company is the world's largest supplier of digital projection equipment, having installed more than 75,000 projectors worldwide. It's a high-growth industry, and Remers knows that in order to continue to grow the company, he needs to retain his talented team of technical experts.

Selected as one of Canada's 10 Best Employers in Canada in 2010, Christie Digital offers one of the best benefits programs in the country, competitive salaries, and bonuses to retain staff. The company also has an on-site fitness facility, extensive on-site educational and training programs, and a fully qualified chef who makes tasty and nutritious meals for the company cafeteria.

With 751 employees worldwide, Christie Digital is a fairly small company. But managing the payroll of a business of this size is still a daunting task. Could you do it?

In this chapter, you'll learn how to calculate hourly wages—both regular and overtime. You'll also learn the basic rules and procedures for making payroll deductions, such as withholding taxes and paying employees. After learning all of this, you may want to see if there are any openings at Christie. It may just be the last job you'll ever want.

Sources: Based on information from Christie Digital's website (www.christiedigital.com) and "Christie Digital Sharpens Image," *Financial Post,* October 2006 and June 2010.

	1 Calculating gross pay, routine deductions, and net pay for an employee (p. 365)
Learning	**2** Recording a typical payroll from a summary (p. 374)
Objectives	**3** Preparing a company's payroll summary (p. 374)
	4 Maintaining an individual's earnings record (p. 378)

Becoming an expert in the subject of payroll and related issues can take a long time because:

1. There are many federal and provincial laws that affect payroll and they change periodically.
2. Sometimes employers and employees view each other with suspicion in matters concerning payroll. This requires special care to get the figures correct.
3. The actual computation and payment of a payroll is quite detailed, leaving room for a number of mistakes to occur.

In Canada today, a company has two common alternatives to processing a payroll manually:

◆ Use a computer with appropriate software, such as Simply Accounting® or QuickBooks®.

◆ Contract with a payroll service (either an independent service or one connected with a chartered bank).

Either alternative is attractive to medium- or large-sized companies. Some smaller companies continue to process their payroll manually, thus avoiding the costs of the more sophisticated alternatives. Programs such as Simply Accounting® or QuickBooks® also can help in processing a payroll for smaller companies with simple payroll needs.

In this chapter, we will examine the details of a payroll for ABC Company for the first week in March. We will stress those things that affect individual employees. The next chapter examines the same subject from the employer's point of view.

In this chapter and the next, many deductions, maximum amounts, and minimum amounts are obtained from Canada Revenue Agency's recently published figures. Students should be aware that these will change at least annually. Your instructor may supply you with the most up-to-date figures, but remember that you should concentrate on learning the principles involved, not on matching the exact figures illustrated in this chapter and the next.

The tables that are included in the appendices at the end of this chapter for CPP and EI have been somewhat condensed to save space. If you use these condensed tables, your figures will differ by a few cents from the "official" tables. This is not a problem for classroom use, but you should not use the textbook tables for any real-world payroll taxes.

Learning Unit 8-1

Important Laws and How They Affect Payroll

1 Calculating gross pay, routine deductions, and net pay for an employee

A number of laws and regulations at the federal and provincial levels govern payroll. We will look at several of them here.

MINIMUM WAGE LAWS

Every province has a law that sets the lowest hourly wage that can legally be paid to an employee. The actual **minimum wage laws** vary somewhat from province to province and have a very small effect on the subject of payroll.

However, such laws also set out the maximum number of hours an employee can be asked to work per day and per week before an *overtime* premium must be paid. A typical requirement (and the one we shall adopt) is that employees who work more than 8 hours on any day or 40 hours in a week must be paid at time-and-a-half for the overtime hours. If Janet Johnson worked 4 hours on Monday, 8 hours on Tuesday, 11 hours on Wednesday, 8 hours on Friday, and 4 hours on Saturday, she would have worked only 35 hours during the week but would have earned 3 hours of overtime premium because she worked 11 hours on Wednesday.

Now suppose that Janet worked the following hours during a sample week:

Monday	7 hours
Tuesday	8 hours
Wednesday	11 hours
Thursday	8 hours
Friday	7 hours
Saturday	4 hours
Total	45 hours for the week

If Janet's hourly rate were $10 per hour, her gross wages for the week would be computed as follows:

Regular time	40 h @ $10.00/h	$400
Overtime	5 h @ $15.00/h	75
Total earnings		$475

Note that the three hours of overtime worked on Wednesday are included in the total overtime of five hours.

Sometimes employers arrive at the same total by a slightly different calculation:

Regular rate	45 h @ $10.00/h	$450
Overtime rate (or premium)	5 h @ $5.00/h	25
Total earnings		$475

This second approach stresses the cost of overtime. A manager can more easily recognize the added cost of asking employees to work longer hours. We will use the first approach in this chapter since it reflects the point of view of the employee.

FEDERAL AND PROVINCIAL INCOME TAX

The federal and provincial governments each require employees to pay a tax based on the income that they earn. The details of our income tax system are not covered here, but we need to know a few essentials:

1. Taxes are *calculated* once a year: Employees must file a tax return by April 30 for the year ended on the previous December 31. However, the tax is *collected* from employees by payroll deductions each pay period.

2. In all provinces and territories in Canada (except Quebec), income tax must be determined and deducted by using the method called **TONI** (Tax on Income). Prior to TONI, provinces and territories typically based their income tax on the amount of federal tax. Since this percentage was easily determined for each province, only a single amount had to be looked up (or computed) for each employee per pay period. Because many provinces have introduced their own rules for income tax, this procedure no longer works, and now two amounts need to be looked up per employee per pay period; however, these amounts can then be combined for all other purposes.

These two deductions can be looked up in tables contained in a booklet called *Payroll Deductions Tables* (T4032). There is a separate booklet for each province and territory, and they can be obtained from **Canada Revenue Agency (CRA)**. You can pick up a copy from a local federal building, phone to have a copy delivered (1-800-959-2221), or go on the Internet and obtain the booklets and tables that way (www.cra-arc.gc.ca). The government also distributes the tables in electronic form. From the same website, you can download and use Tables on Disk (TOD). In this chapter, we will refer you to the printed tables, since this is arguably the clearest procedure, but in the business world, one or more of the other approaches may work better.

Appendices 8-1F and 8-1P at the end of this chapter reproduce portions of the June 30, 2010, Ontario tables* for student use. The complete tables include sections for biweekly, semi-monthly, monthly, and other pay periods. These have not been reproduced because we are restricting our coverage to a weekly pay period. The procedures for other pay periods are nearly identical.

Please take a brief look at the federal tables (see pages 398 through 411). Notice that there are ranges of earnings shown on the left and various deduction figures in the 11 columns to the right of the earnings amounts. These deduction amounts get smaller as the claim code categories increase from 0 to 10. Each employee's **claim code** is determined by filling in **TD1 forms**. Since TONI has been introduced, there are now two TD1 forms to be completed by each new employee. The federal TD1 form is shown in Figure 8-1. Each province also has its own TD1 form, and the most current example from Ontario is shown as part b of Figure 8-1. In both the federal and provincial forms, only the first page is illustrated, as this contains most of the important information needed to determine a Total Claim Amount, which is then compared to a table (shown as part c of Figure 8-1) in order to choose a claim code for an employee. Notice that there are similarities as well as differences between the two TD1 forms. Each begins with a Basic personal amount, although these amounts are different, and also lists several specific factors that help calculate the Total Claim Amount. The federal form includes as item 2 a "Child amount," which the provincial form does not, and many of the specific amounts differ between the two forms as well. Students will be especially interested to note that the treatment of tuition, and especially textbooks, differs a lot between the two forms. Also worthy of mentioning is that page 2 of these forms contains a section that allows an employee to ask that some additional amount of tax be deducted each pay period. Such a request might seem strange at first, but many taxpayers work two or sometimes three jobs at the same time, and if no extra amounts of tax were deducted, they would end up paying a significant amount of extra tax when they file their tax return each year. This is because our Canadian tax laws, like most other countries, state that the rate of tax you pay goes up as the total amount you earn gets higher.

Despite the differences, the intent of the forms is the same—to calculate a dollar amount, which, when compared to a table (see part c of Figure 8-1), will arrive at a claim code number, which ranges from 1 through 10. It is this claim code number that governs how much tax an employer deducts from each employee when calculating a payroll. This procedure may seem very complicated, and it can be a bit hard to understand, but most employers will assist their employees in completing these forms if asked, so a full understanding of all of the many implications is probably not necessary. Certainly for the purposes of this text, we can say that the completion of both TD1 forms is the responsibility of each employee, and leave it at that. Do note, however, that the more dollar amounts entered into each form (for dependents, tuition, etc.), the higher the Total Claim Amount will be, and

> The employer is not responsible for verifying the claims made by employees on their TD1 forms, except that obviously incorrect TD1 forms should be investigated, possibly with the help of a local tax service office.

---

*These tables were effective as of January 1, 2010, and include the changes made necessary by the introduction of the Ontario Health Premium. Note that this is not the same as the Employer Health Tax. The new tables (see the end of this chapter) include the new premium already—no special steps are necessary.

Canada Revenue Agency Agence du revenu du Canada	**2010 PERSONAL TAX CREDITS RETURN**	TD1

Your employer or payer will use this form to determine the amount of your tax deductions.
Read the back before completing this form. Complete this form based on the best estimate of your circumstances.

Last name	First name and initial(s)	Date of birth (YYYY/MM/DD)	Employee number
JOHNSON	JANET	1966/03/12	N/A

Address including postal code	For non-residents only – Country of permanent residence	Social insurance number
602, 805 Fifth Street, Any City, Ontario M1X 2X2		1 1 1 2 2 2 3 3 3

1. Basic personal amount – Every resident of Canada can claim this amount. If you will have more than one employer or payer at the same time in 2010, see "More than one employer or payer at the same time" on the next page. If you are a non-resident, see "Non-residents" on the next page.

10,382

2. Child amount – Either parent (but not both), may claim $2,101 for each child born in 1993 or later that resides with both parents throughout the year. Any unused portion can be transferred to that parent's spouse or common-law partner. If the child does not reside with both parents throughout the year, the parent who is entitled to claim the "Amount for an eligible dependant" on line 8 may also claim $2,101 for that same child.

3. Age amount – If you will be 65 or older on December 31, 2010, and your net income for the year from all sources will be $32,506 or less, enter $6,446. If your net income for the year will be between $32,506 and $75,480 and you want to calculate a partial claim, get the TD1-WS, *Worksheet for the 2010 Personal Tax Credits Return,* and complete the appropriate section.

4. Pension income amount – If you will receive regular pension payments from a pension plan or fund (excluding Canada Pension Plan, Quebec Pension Plan, Old Age Security, or Guaranteed Income Supplement payments), enter $2,000 or your estimated annual pension income, whichever is less.

5. Tuition, education, and textbook amounts (full time and part time) – If you are a student enrolled at a university or college, or an educational institution certified by Human Resources and Skills Development Canada, and you will pay more than $100 per institution in tuition fees, complete this section. If you are enrolled full time, or if you have a mental or physical disability and are enrolled part time, enter the total of the tuition fees you will pay, plus $400 for each month that you will be enrolled, plus $65 per month for textbooks. If you are enrolled part time and do not have a mental or physical disability, enter the total of the tuition fees you will pay, plus $120 for each month that you will be enrolled part time, plus $20 per month for textbooks.

6. Disability amount – If you will claim the disability amount on your income tax return by using Form T2201, *Disability Tax Credit Certificate,* enter $7,239.

7. Spouse or common-law partner amount – If you are supporting your spouse or common-law partner who lives with you, and whose net income for the year will be less than $10,382, enter the difference between $10,382 and his or her estimated net income for the year. If your spouse's or common-law partner's net income for the year will be more than $10,382, you cannot claim this amount.

8. Amount for an eligible dependant – If you do not have a spouse or common-law partner and you support a dependent relative who lives with you, and whose net income for the year will be less than $10,382, enter the difference between $10,382 and his or her estimated net income. If your eligible dependant's net income for the year will be $10,382 or more, you cannot claim this amount.

9. Caregiver amount – If you are taking care of a dependant who lives with you, whose net income for the year will be $14,422 or less, and who is either your or your spouse's or common-law partner's:
• parent or grandparent (aged 65 or older), or
• relative (aged 18 or older) who is dependent on you because of an infirmity, enter $4,223.
  If the dependant's net income for the year will be between $14,422 and $18,645 and you want to calculate a partial claim, get the TD1-WS, and complete the appropriate section.

10. Amount for infirm dependants age 18 or older – If you support an infirm dependant age 18 or older who is your or your spouse's or common-law partner's relative, who lives in Canada, and whose net income for the year will be $5,992 or less, enter $4,223. You cannot claim an amount for a dependant you claimed on line 9. If the dependant's net income for the year will be between $5,992 and $10,215 and you want to calculate a partial claim, get the TD1-WS, and complete the appropriate section.

11. Amounts transferred from your spouse or common-law partner – If your spouse or common-law partner will not use all of his or her age amount, pension income amount, tuition, education and textbook amounts, disability amount or child amount on his or her income tax return, enter the unused amount.

12. Amounts transferred from a dependant – If your dependant will not use all of his or her **disability amount** on his or her income tax return, enter the unused amount. If your or your spouse's or common-law partner's dependent child or grandchild will not use all of his or her **tuition, education, and textbook amounts** on his or her income tax return, enter the unused amount.

13. TOTAL CLAIM AMOUNT – Add lines 1 through 12.
Your employer or payer will use this amount to determine the amount of your tax deductions.

$10,382

Continue on the next page →

TD1 E (10)   (Vous pouvez obtenir ce formulaire en français à **www.arc.gc.ca/formulaires** ou au **1-800-959-3376**.)

Canada

Figure 8-1 (a)   Federal TD1 Form, Page 1

2010 ONTARIO
PERSONAL TAX CREDITS RETURN

TD1ON

Your employer or payer will use this form to determine the amount of your provincial tax deductions.
Read the back before completing this form. Complete this form based on the best estimate of your circumstances.

Last name	First name and initial(s)	Date of birth (YYYY/MM/DD)	Employee number
Address including postal code		For non-residents only – Country of permanent residence	Social insurance number

1. Basic personal amount – Every person employed in Ontario and every pensioner residing in Ontario can claim this amount. If you will have more than one employer or payer at the same time in 2010, see the section called "Will you have more than one employer or payer at the same time?" on the next page.

8,943

2. Age amount – If you will be 65 or older on December 31, 2010, and your net income from all sources will be $32,506, or less, enter $4,366. If your net income for the year will be between $32,506 and $61,613 and you want to calculate a partial claim, get the TD1ON-WS, *Worksheet for the 2010 Ontario Personal Tax Credits Return,* and complete the appropriate section.

3. Pension income amount – If you will receive regular pension payments from a pension plan or fund (excluding Canada Pension Plan, Quebec Pension Plan, Old Age Security, or Guaranteed Income Supplement payments), enter $1,237, or your estimated annual pension income, whichever is less.

4. Tuition and education amounts (full time and part time) – If you are a student enrolled at a university, college, or educational institution certified by Human Resources and Skills Development Canada, and you will pay more than $100 per institution in tuition fees, complete this section. If you are enrolled full time, or if you have a mental or physical disability and are enrolled part time, enter the total of the tuition fees you will pay, plus $481 for each month that you will be enrolled. If you are enrolled part time and do not have a mental or physical disability, enter the total of the tuition fees you will pay, plus $144 for each month that you will be enrolled part time.

5. Disability amount – If you will claim the disability amount on your income tax return by using Form T2201, *Disability Tax Credit Certificate*, enter $7,225.

6. Spouse or common-law partner amount – If you are supporting your spouse or common-law partner who lives with you, and whose net income for the year will be $759 or less, enter $7,594. If his or her net income for the year will be between $759 and $8,353 and you want to calculate a partial claim, get the TD1ON-WS, and complete the appropriate section.

7. Amount for an eligible dependant – If you do not have a spouse or common-law partner and you support a dependent relative who lives with you, and whose net income for the year will be $759 or less, enter $7,594. If his or her net income for the year will be between $759 and $8,353 and you want to calculate a partial claim, get the TD1ON-WS, and complete the appropriate section.

8. Caregiver amount – If you are taking care of a dependant who lives with you, whose net income for the year will be $14,421 or less, and who is either your or your spouse's or common-law partner's:
- parent or grandparent (aged 65 or older), or
- relative (aged 18 or older) who is dependent on you because of an infirmity, enter $4,216.
  If the dependant's net income for the year will be between $14,421 and $18,637 and you want to calculate a partial claim, get the TD1ON-WS, and complete the appropriate section.

9. Amount for infirm dependants age 18 or older – If you are supporting an infirm dependant aged 18 or older who is your or your spouse's or common-law partner's relative, who lives in Canada, and whose net income for the year will be $5,992 or less, enter $4,215. You cannot claim an amount for a dependant you claimed on line 8. If the dependant's net income for the year will be between $5,992 and $10,207 and you want to calculate a partial claim, get the TD1ON-WS, and complete the appropriate section.

10. Amounts transferred from your spouse or common-law partner – If your spouse or common-law partner will not use all of his or her age amount, pension income amount, tuition and education amounts, or disability amount on his or her income tax return, enter the unused amount.

11. Amounts transferred from a dependant – If your dependant will not use all of his or her **disability amount** on his or her income tax return, enter the unused amount. If your or your spouse's or common-law partner's dependent child or grandchild will not use all of his or her **tuition and education amounts** on his or her income tax return, enter the unused amount.

12. TOTAL CLAIM AMOUNT – Add lines 1 through 11.
Your employer or payer will use your claim amount to determine the amount of your provincial tax deductions.

Continue on the next page ➜

TD1ON E (10)

(Vous pouvez obtenir ce formulaire en français à **www.arc.gc.ca/formulaires** ou au **1-800-959-3376**.)

Canadä

Figure 8-1 (b) Provincial TD1 ON Form, Page 1

Chart 1 – Tableau 1
2010 federal claim codes – Codes de demande fédéraux pour 2010

Total claim amount ($) Montant total de la demande ($)		Claim code Code de demande	Total claim amount ($) Montant total de la demande ($)			Claim code Code de demande
No claim amount – Nul		0	20,302.01	–	22,286.00	7
Minimum	– 10,382.00	1	22,286.01	–	24,270.00	8
10,382.01	– 12,366.00	2	24,270.01	–	26,254.00	9
12,366.01	– 14,350.00	3	26,254.01	–	28,238.00	10
14,350.01	– 16,334.00	4	28,238.01	and over – et plus		X
16,334.01	– 18,318.00	5	The employer must do a manual calculation of tax. L'employeur doit faire le calcul manuel de l'impôt.			
18,318.01	– 20,302.00	6	No withholding – Aucune retenue			E

Chart 2 – Tableau 2
2010 Ontario claim codes – Codes de demande de l'Ontario pour 2010

Total claim amount ($) Montant total de la demande ($)		Claim code Code de demande	Total claim amount ($) Montant total de la demande ($)			Claim code Code de demande
No claim amount – Nul		0	18,578.01	–	20,505.00	7
Minimum	– 8,943.00	1	20,505.01	–	22,432.00	8
8,943.01	– 10,870.00	2	22,432.01	–	24,359.00	9
10,870.01	– 12,797.00	3	24,359.01	–	26,286.00	10
12,797.01	– 14,724.00	4	26,286.01	and over – et plus		X
14,724.01	– 16,651.00	5	The employer must do a manual calculation of tax. L'employeur doit faire le calcul manuel de l'impôt.			
16,651.01	– 18,578.00	6	No withholding – Aucune retenue			E

Figure 8-1 (c)   Federal and Ontario Claim Codes

this leads to a higher claim code as well. As you will see, a higher claim code leads to a reduced amount of federal and provincial tax being deducted, which is as it should be.

Janet Johnson's TD1 forms show that she is claiming only the Basic Personal Amount as her Total Claim Amount. Many if not most Canadians will do the same, generally because they are single, or, if married, their spouse also works. If you compare Janet's Total Claim Amount with the chart shown as part c of Figure 8-1, you will see that she has a claim code of 1 for both the federal and provincial tax deduction. The great majority of Canadian employees will also have the same Claim Code for federal and provincial purposes, but as time goes by, this might change as differences between the two tax systems become more pronounced. Naturally, this will depend to a large extent on which province you are working in, but in any event, there is only a minor difference in looking up the amount of tax to be deducted—you just need to be careful to look in the column that corresponds to the claim code arrived at using the federal TD1 and its provincial counterpart. This is a good place to emphasize that everyone should be careful, in looking up tax deduction amounts, that they ignore the first column, labelled as Claim Code 0. This column is not used too often, as it deals almost exclusively with non-resident employees, a subject that is not covered in our discussion of payroll topics.

Employees do not have to fill out a new TD1 each time the tax laws change, unless they are claiming a new type of exemption (such as an education deduction or start supporting a new dependant). The old TD1 figures are automatically updated by most accounting software programs, and even the government tables (such as those at the end of the chapter) automatically include the effects of **indexing**—the automatic increases in claim amounts to include inflation.

Notice that the procedure for deducting income tax is not very precise. The actual tax that Janet will have to pay for the year will depend on dozens of factors, some of them quite personal (such as whether she has paid any allowable medical fees during the taxation year, or whether she has charitable donations or medical expenses). The purpose of the deduction tables is to ensure that wage earners pay about as much tax as they would owe on their earnings for the week. Sometimes employees have to pay extra tax when they file their annual tax returns, but usually they get a refund. This is because the tables tend to ignore many allowable tax deductions.

In our example on page 366, Janet will have $33.85 deducted as federal income tax (from Appendix 8-1F) and $19.40 as provincial income tax (from Appendix 8-1P). This is a total of $53.25, and it is this total amount that will be used in the steps that follow. Remember that while you must look up (or compute) two amounts, they are combined for all further steps in the payroll process.

In practice, there are several modifications sometimes made to the amount of income tax deducted. Some employees (perhaps because they have more than one place of employment) ask that additional income tax be deducted. There is a place on the TD1 form to request this, and it is a fairly common event in determining income tax deduction amounts. There are also several less common reasons why the actual deduction for income tax may differ from the amounts in the official tables. A detailed study of these adjustments is not considered to be a part of this book.

In an effort to conserve resources, the government has begun to publish the various tables of deductions in computer-readable format. Your instructor may arrange to supply you with a copy, or make a copy available for the duration of the course.

You may also use the Internet to access these tables. Set your browser to: www.cra-arc.gc.ca/payroll.

CANADA OR QUEBEC PENSION PLAN

In the mid-1960s, the **Canada and Quebec Pension Plans** were introduced. Their purpose was to provide a pension benefit (as well as certain other benefits) for Canadians at retirement. The law requires a deduction of 4.95% from the earnings of each taxpayer in Canada who is at least 18 years of age but not 70 years or older and who is not in receipt of a disability or retirement pension from CPP. (The first $67.30 of earnings in a week are not subject to this deduction. Likewise, earnings in excess of $47,200 per year are not subject to the 4.95% levy.)

It is possible to compute the necessary deduction for the Canada Pension Plan (CPP) for each employee, but the federal government has provided detailed tables in the booklet *Payroll Deductions Tables (T4032)* to make this unnecessary (see Appendix 8-2 and Learning Unit 8-2). As you can see, Janet Johnson will have a CPP deduction of $20.18—($475 − $67.30) × 0.0495—made from her wages this pay period. The federal government maintains a precise record of the CPP payments made by each Canadian because the benefits that we will receive are related to the contributions we make plus the amounts contributed by our employers on our behalf—by law, the same amount as is deducted. There are more details on this in the next chapter. Remember that the tables shown in Appendix 8-2 as well as Appendix 8-3 are not as precise as the actual tables as supplied by the CRA, so expect to see minor differences in the amounts deducted for CPP (and EI—see the following page).

Payroll periods can be:

Weekly: 52 pay periods/year
Biweekly: 26 pay periods/year
Semi-monthly: 24 pay periods/year
Monthly: 12 pay periods/year

Recently, Human Resources Development Canada has been sending a summary of CPP contributions made to each worker in Canada.

EMPLOYMENT INSURANCE PLAN

The EI deduction rate is subject to change from year to year. However, the $43,200 maximum insurable earnings is fixed until it is changed by legislation.

It is a requirement for virtually all employees, regardless of age, to participate in Canada's **Employment Insurance (EI) plan**. (There are a number of exceptions.) This plan entitles workers to a certain level of income if they become unemployed. The details are very complex and a full discussion of the plan is beyond the scope of this text.

In each pay period, an amount of 1.73% is deducted from an employee's wages. This deduction applies only to the first $43,200 per year. Fortunately, the deductions are rather straightforward for most employees and can be found in the same booklet as the CPP deductions (see Appendix 8-3 at the end of this chapter). In Janet Johnson's case, she will have an EI deduction of $8.23 (approximately $475.00 × 0.0173) made from her wages for this week.

CPP AND EI: SOME ADDITIONAL INFORMATION

Students should be aware that unique CPP deduction tables are supplied for weekly, biweekly, semi-monthly, and monthly pay periods. In calculating the CPP deduction per pay period, there is no maximum contribution per period—just an annual upper limit ($2,163.15 for 2010).

The EI deduction, however, is different. A single table is used for all pay periods. As shown at the bottom of any EI table, there is a maximum deduction for each annual period. Since the maximum insurable earning is $43,200, the annual maximum premium is $747.36 ($43,200 × 0.0173).

WORKERS' COMPENSATION PLANS

In all provinces, workers' incomes are protected in the event of an injury that occurs on the job. Since the cost of this **workers' compensation** is typically paid by the employer, no deductions are made from employees' wages. We will not pursue this matter further in this chapter, except to note that computer programs such as Simply Accounting® and QuickBooks® need to know what rate to use (the rate varies by category of employment and from province to province) in order to calculate payroll expenses properly.

VARIOUS UNION AGREEMENTS

Most unions operate under laws that are enacted provincially or federally. In many businesses, workers have been organized into bargaining units, or unions. Normally, the union and the employer agree that **union dues** are to be deducted from the employees' wages and forwarded to the union treasurer, usually monthly. In our example, the ABC Company does not have unionized employees and therefore no deductions are shown.

OTHER DEDUCTIONS

Other deductions are sometimes made from an employee's earnings. Details will vary from one employer to another, but the following deductions are common in Canada:

1. Medical and dental insurance premiums
2. Company pension plan—current service
3. Company pension plan—past service
4. Charitable donations

5. Canada Savings Bonds installments
6. Parking charges
7. Social fund charges
8. Repayment of loans or advances
9. Long-term income replacement premiums
10. Life insurance premiums
11. Garnishees

LEARNING UNIT 8-1 REVIEW

AT THIS POINT you should be able to:
- Calculate regular and overtime earnings. (p. 366)
- Explain the purpose of a TD1 form. (p. 367)
- Determine income tax deductions given a completed TD1 form and total earnings. (p. 371)
- Determine a deduction for CPP from tables supplied. (p. 371)
- Determine a deduction for EI from tables supplied. (p. 372)
- Explain the operation of maximum deductions for both CPP and EI. (p. 372)
- Describe in general terms the nature of certain other routine deductions. (p. 372)

Self-Review Quiz 8-1

(The forms you need are on page 8-1 of the *Study Guide with Working Papers*.)

Using the tables in Appendices 8-1, 8-2, and 8-3, determine the gross pay and deductions for income tax, CPP, and EI for Norma Fry, a single taxpayer (claim code 1) who worked 42 hours last week at a wage rate of $12 per hour.

Solution to Self-Review Quiz 8-1

Gross pay:
40 h @ $12/h		$480.00
2 h @ $18/h (overtime)		36.00
Gross pay		$516.00

Deductions:
Income tax (from Appendices 8-1F and 8-1P)*	$61.60	
CPP (from Appendix 8-2)	22.16	
EI (from Appendix 8-3)	8.92	
Total deductions		92.68
Net pay ($516 – $92.68)		$423.32

*Federal amount = $40.05; provincial amount = $21.55.

Learning Unit 8-2

A Typical Payroll

2 Recording a typical payroll from a summary

To keep things simple, we assume no carry-forward balances into the month of March. In reality, there would usually be such balances (tax, CPP, and EI payable, for example).

The ABC Company has six employees to be paid for the first week of March 2013. They are listed below, together with the number of hours each worked and their rates of pay:

Name	Hours	Rate
Janet Johnson	45	$ 10/h
Peter Black	42	18/h
John Chernochan	44	17/h
Tony Chui	41	12/h
Beth Madora	38	15/h
Elaine Dumont, Manager	40	900/wk

Employees are paid weekly at the ABC Company. The **payroll summary** in Figure 8-2 has been prepared based upon tables and calculations covered earlier in this chapter. Don't worry if the summary appears a bit complicated—we will deal with each column in turn. Note that all deductions are based on the 2010 rates shown in the appendices to this chapter.

THE PAYROLL SUMMARY IN DETAIL

3 Preparing a company's payroll summary

Many medium- to large-sized companies use a computer to help prepare their payroll. The data output from a computerized payroll are often remarkably similar to the illustrations in this chapter.

Claim code 0 is used for non-resident taxpayers. Be careful using the tax tables—you can always ignore the first deduction column when using this textbook.

A. Claim Code The law requires all employees to complete and sign TD1 exemption forms at the beginning of employment and whenever there is a change in the employee's circumstances. As shown in Figure 8-1, this form allows employees to specify their exemption status so that an appropriate amount of income tax can be deducted. The claim code for each employee is shown in this column. You can see that four of the employees are claiming a claim code of 1, resulting in the maximum **income tax deduction** at their earnings level. The other two employees (John and Elaine) presumably have dependants, who allow each of them to specify a higher claim code, with a lower income tax deduction at that earnings level. New TD1 forms can be filed at any time, and until new forms are filed the old claim code continues. If a form is not filed, each employee is treated as if he or she has a claim code of 1.

B. Hours Worked Each employee may work a different number of hours in each week. Remember that *overtime rates* will apply to hours in excess of 40 per week or 8 in one day. Notice also that Elaine's hours are shown even though she is not paid according to the number of hours that she worked. It is typical to record the hours worked daily by each employee. A weekly total is then transferred to this column in the payroll summary.

C. Rate of Pay The rates of pay are as set out above. Notice that all employees except Elaine are paid on an hourly basis. Elaine, as manager, receives a weekly salary, but this fact does not change subsequent payroll steps.

D. Regular Earnings Regular earnings are computed based upon regular hours per week—or, as in Elaine's case, a salary.

E. Overtime Earnings The segregation of overtime earnings helps the ABC Company to control this expensive use of employees' time. A common practice is to hire an additional employee when this figure becomes too high.

F. Gross Pay Each employee earns a total amount per week. It is this figure that governs the legally required deductions.

G, H, I. Income Tax Deductions From Appendices 8-1F and 8-1P, we have already seen that Janet's income tax deduction totals $53.25. Make sure that you can find the amounts deducted for the other employees in Appendices 8-1F and 8-1P.

Figure 8-2
Payroll Summary

ABC Company
Payroll Summary Sheet
For the Week Ending March 7, 2013

Employee Name	Claim Code*	Total Hrs. Reg.	Total Hrs. O/T	Reg. Rate Pay/Hr.	Earnings Regular	Earnings Overtime	Earnings Gross Pay
Janet Johnson	1	40	5	10.00	400 00	75 00	475 00
Peter Black	1	40	2	18.00	720 00	54 00	774 00
John Chernochan	4	40	4	17.00	680 00	102 00	782 00
Tony Chui	1	40	1	12.00	480 00	18 00	498 00
Beth Madora	1	38	0	15.00	570 00	0 00	570 00
Elaine Dumont	3	40	–	900/wk	900 00	0 00	900 00
					3750 00	249 00	3999 00
	(A)	(B)		(C)	(D)	(E)	(F)

Deductions								
Memo Only FIT	Memo Only PIT	Total Tax	CPP	EI	Medical	Charitable	Net Pay	Chq. No.
33 85	19 40	53 25	20 16	8 23	0 00	5 00	388 36	1407
75 60	39 10	114 70	34 93	13 39	18 00	5 00	587 18	1408
62 40	35 10	97 50	35 33	13 55	38 00	5 00	592 62	1409
37 25	20 80	58 05	21 29	8 61	0 00	5 00	405 05	1410
47 60	24 20	71 80	24 83	9 85	18 00	5 00	440 52	1411
92 95	47 65	140 60	41 09	15 57	38 00	5 00	659 74	1412
		535 90	177 63	69 20	112 00	30 00	3074 27	
(G)	(H)	(I)	(J)	(K)	(L)	(M)	(N)	(O)

* We are assuming that the claim codes are the same for federal and provincial tax deduction purposes.
This is not always true and will depend on the details of each employee's Federal and Provincial TD-1 forms.

Note that there is no need to total columns G and H. Only the I column total is used below.

J. CPP Deduction   Appendix 8-2 is the source for these CPP deductions.

K. EI Deduction   See Appendix 8-3 to trace each employee's EI deduction.

L. Medical Deduction   The law regarding medical deductions varies from one province to another. Some provinces do not require a deduction for provincial health care plans. In our example, a deduction is required for each household. This explains why no deductions are made from Janet's and Tony's wages. We may assume that they are covered by their spouses' deductions.

M. Charitable Deduction   Each employee has agreed to a weekly deduction to support a charitable cause—perhaps Operation Eyesight.

N. Net Pay   This is each employee's gross pay less all deductions, often known as *take-home pay.*

O. Cheque Number   A cheque is issued to each employee for the exact amount due. When the cheques are issued, their numbers are written here.

LEARNING UNIT 8-2 REVIEW

AT THIS POINT you should be able to:

◆ Calculate earnings, deductions, and net pay for an employee. (pp. 374–375)

◆ Describe the preparation of a payroll summary. (pp. 374–375)

◆ Explain the purpose of each column in a payroll summary. (pp. 374–375)

Self-Review Quiz 8-2

(The forms you need are on page 8-1 of the *Study Guide with Working Papers*.)

If a new employee, Robert Meade, begins employment next week, calculate his gross and net pay assuming a TD1 claim code of 3, 40 hours worked, a wage of $11/h, and no medical or charitable deduction.

Solution to Self-Review Quiz 8-2

Did you calculate a net pay of $380.43? Details are:

Gross pay: 40 h @ $11/h		$440.00
Deductions:		
Income tax (from Appendices 8-1F and 8-1P)*	$33.55	
CPP (from Appendix 8-2)	18.42	
EI (from Appendix 8-3)	7.60	
Medical	0.00	
Charitable	0.00	
Total deductions		59.57
Net pay ($440.00 − $59.57)		$380.43

*Federal tax = $20.80; provincial tax = $12.75.

Learning Unit 8-3

Recording and Payment

The details in Figure 8-2 are used to make the journal entry shown below, which records the payroll for the first week in March for the ABC Company:

	2013					
	March	7	Salaries and Wages Expense	3 9 9 9 00		
			Income Taxes Payable		5 3 5 90	
			CPP Payable		1 7 7 63	
			EI Payable		6 9 20	
			Medical Plan Payable		1 1 2 00	
			Charitable Contributions Payable		3 0 00	
			Salaries and Wages Payable		3 0 7 4 27	
			To record payroll for first week in March			

Some companies keep track of different salary or wage expenses separately. For instance, it is useful to separate Elaine's salary from the wages of the other workers. The owners can then separate the cost of management from the cost of labour. It is also useful to further break down the labour cost into more detail. Consider the additional information available to the owners if we assume that Tony and Beth are sales personnel. The debit to Sales Wages Expense would be $1,068

($498 + $570). Instead of the single debit of $3,999 to an account called Salaries and Wages Expense, we would now have three debits:

	2013							
	March	7	Management Salaries Expense		9 0 0 00			
			Sales Wages Expense		1 0 6 8 00			
			Wages Expense		2 0 3 1 00			

(The credit side of the entry would not change.)

If we assume that the ABC Company uses this more detailed method, then the entry would be posted to the ledger accounts summarized as follows (opening balances are ignored):

Management Salaries Expense	Sales Wages Expense	Wages Expense
900.00	1,068.00	2,031.00
Expense on the Income Statement	Expense on the Income Statement	Expense on the Income Statement

Income Taxes Payable	CPP Payable	EI Payable
535.90	177.63	69.20
Liability on the Balance Sheet	Liability on the Balance Sheet	Liability on the Balance Sheet

Medical Plan Payable	Charitable Donations Payable	Salaries and Wages Payable
112.00	30.00	3,074.27
Liability on the Balance Sheet	Liability on the Balance Sheet	Liability on the Balance Sheet

Figure 8-3 summarizes the main elements of the payroll process.

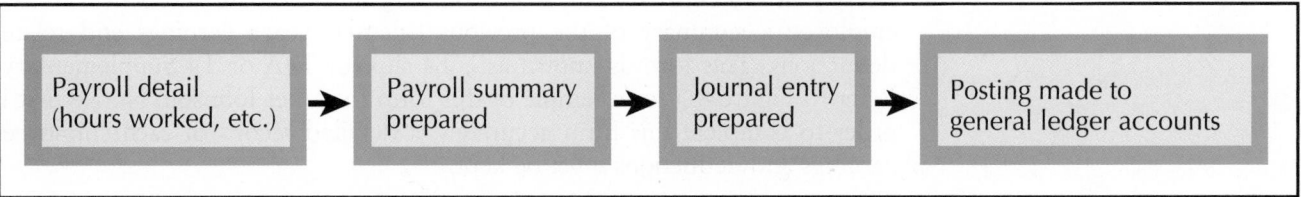

Figure 8-3 The Payroll Recording and Posting Process

LAST STEP DIRECTLY AFFECTING EMPLOYEES

From the employees' point of view, the best part of the payroll process is receiving their net pay each week. The ABC Company writes a cheque to each employee in payment of his or her weekly *take-home pay* (see columns N and O, Figure 8-2). As each cheque is written, it is recorded in the *cash disbursements journal*, as shown in Figure 8-4.

When the cash disbursements journal is posted, the balance in the Salaries and Wages Payable account will be reduced to zero. The exact same thing will be true when all of the general journal entries are posted if a cash disbursements journal is not used. This is as it should be since the amount recorded as payable, $3,074.27, has been paid by cheques numbered 1407–1412 and the amount remaining to be paid is nil. Please remember that the cash disbursements journal is posted at the

CASH DISBURSEMENTS JOURNAL									
Date 2013	Chq. No.	Accounts Payment To:	PR	Sundry Dr.	Accounts Payable Dr.	Salaries and Wages Payable Dr.	Purchases Discount Cr.	Cash Cr.	
Mar. 8	1407	Janet Johnson				388 36		388 36	
	1408	Peter Black				587 98		587 98	
	1409	John Chernochan				592 62		592 61	
	1410	Tony Chui				405 05		405 05	
	1411	Beth Madora				440 52		440 52	
	1412	Elaine Dumont				659 74		659 74	

Figure 8-4 Cash Disbursements Journal (also called Cash Payments Journal)

end of the month. The general journal may be posted more often than once a month. It is only after the cheques have been issued, recorded, and posted that the balance in the Salaries and Wages Payable account will be zero.

Most companies pay their employees by cheque although, in a very few cases, companies pay out actual cash. Many large companies transfer wages directly to their employees' bank accounts. Some companies have a separate bank account on which they issue their payroll cheques. The main reason for this practice is to simplify the payment process and reconciliation of bank accounts, especially when the number of employees is large.

EMPLOYEE EARNINGS RECORD

4 Maintaining an individual's earnings record

In order to meet legal requirements, the ABC Company must keep a separate record of each employee's earnings. This **employee earnings record** is essential for the following reasons:

1. Every year (by February 28), ABC Company must prepare and deliver to each employee a summary of the previous calendar year's earnings and related deductions. This form is known as a **T4 slip** (or **T4A** or **T4 Supplementary**). Refer to Figure 8-5 for a sample of this form for Janet Johnson. Notice that in order to complete this form accurately, a detailed record of each employee's earnings and deductions must be kept.

2. When an employee leaves his or her employment for any reason, a special form is required to comply with the employment insurance laws. This form is called a **Record of Employment**.

3. In deducting CPP, it is necessary to keep deducting only as long as an employee's earnings are below a certain level. CPP is payable up to a maximum of $2,163.15 for 2010. Therefore, it is necessary to stop making deductions when this amount is reached. For EI there is no maximum per pay period, but the total per year cannot exceed $747.36 (for 2010).

Figure 8-7 shows a partial employee earnings record for Janet Johnson for the latest year. Each employee will have his or her own earnings record. Such records are often part of a computer file.

Figure 8-5
T4 Slip

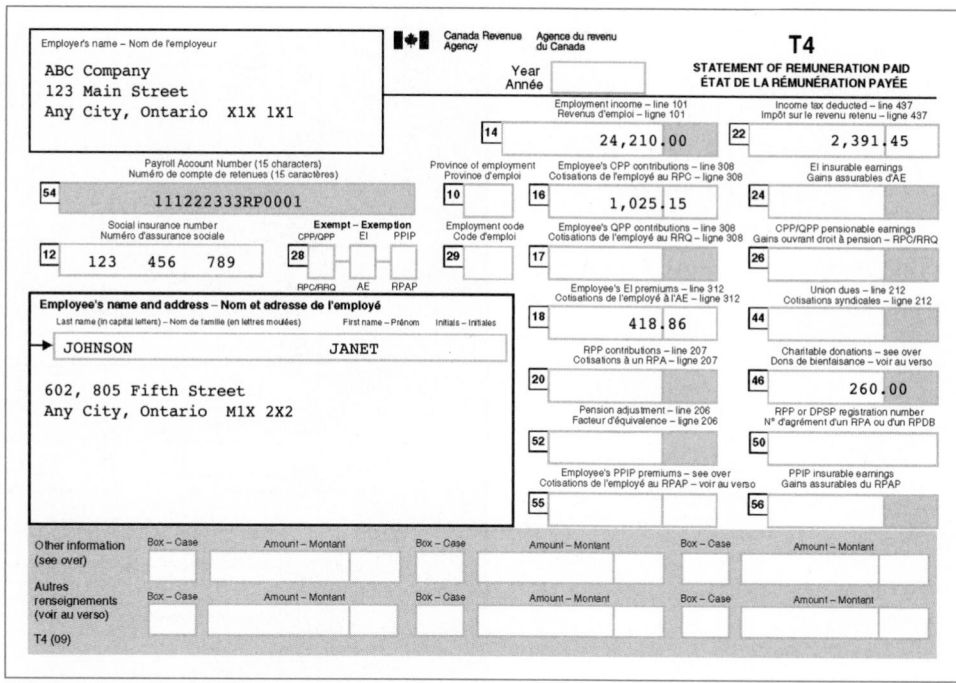

Source: Revenue Canada. Reproduced with permission of the Minister of Public Works and Government Services Canada, 2010.

LEARNING UNIT 8-3 REVIEW

AT THIS POINT you should be able to:

◆ Record a payroll from a payroll summary. (pp. 376–377)
◆ Break down gross wages into more detail. (pp. 376–377)
◆ Post the entry recording the payroll into appropriate ledger accounts. (p. 377)
◆ Demonstrate the payment of net pay to employees by cheque. (pp. 377–378)
◆ Record the cheques to employees in the cash disbursements journal. (p. 378)
◆ Illustrate the employee's earnings record. (p. 381)
◆ Describe the Record of Employment form. (p. 378)
◆ State the upper limit of EI and CPP deductions. (p. 378)

Self-Review Quiz 8-3

(The forms you need are on page 8-1 of the *Study Guide with Working Papers*.)

Indicate whether the following statements are true or false:

1. All payroll registers are special journals. This means no payroll entry is ever needed.
2. Income Tax Payable is a liability on the balance sheet.
3. Salaries and Wages Expense has a normal balance of a debit.
4. Employee earnings records are optional for an employer.
5. The Record of Employment form must be completed annually for each employee.
6. All wages must be paid by cheque.
7. Cheques paying wages must be recorded in the cash disbursements journal.

Figure 8-6 Employee Earnings Record

Name of Employee	**Janet Johnson**		ABC Company	Employee Address:
Social Insurance Number	**123 456 789**		Employee Earnings Record	**602, 805 Fifth Street**
Date of Birth	**03/12/84**		for the Calendar Year 2013	**Any City, Ontario M1X 2X2**

Week	Net Claim Code	Rate of Pay	Hours Worked	Earnings			Deductions					Net Pay	Chq. No.
				Regular	Overtime	Gross Pay	IT	CPP	EI	Medical	Charitable		
1	1	$10/h	40	400 00		400 00	35 05	16 44	6 91		5 00	336 60	1061
2			40	400 00		400 00	35 05	16 44	6 91		5 00	336 60	1102
3			42	400 00	30 00	430 00	42 40	17 93	7 43		5 00	357 24	1150
4			43	400 00	45 00	445 00	45 90	18 67	7 71		5 00	367 72	1194
5			40	400 00		400 00	35 05	16 44	6 91		5 00	336 60	1237
6			46	400 00	90 00	490 00	56 55	20 90	8 47		5 00	399 08	1291
7			40	400 00		400 00	35 05	16 44	6 91		5 00	336 60	1322
8			41	400 00	15 00	415 00	38 40	17 19	7 19		5 00	347 22	1368
9			45	400 00	75 00	475 00	53 25	20 16	8 23		5 00	388 36	1407
10			40	400 00		400 00	35 05	16 44	6 91		5 00	336 60	1451
11			40	400 00		400 00	35 05	16 44	6 91		5 00	336 60	1490
49		$12/h	46	480 00	108 00	588 00	74 80	25 73	10 16		5 00	472 31	3021
50			40	440 00		440 00	44 95	18 42	7 60		5 00	364 03	3191
51			48	480 00	144 00	624 00	82 00	27 51	10 79		5 00	498 70	3154
52			40	480 00	36 00	516 00	61 60	22 16	8 92		5 00	418 32	3214
Totals for the Year				21480 00	2730 00	24210 00	2392 45	1025 15	418 86		260 00	20113 54	

Solution to Self-Review Quiz 8-3

1. False
2. True
3. True
4. False
5. False. The Record of Employment is required only when an employee leaves.
6. False. Cash or automatic bank transfers are also normal.
7. True, in general, although other possibilities exist, such as special payroll journals or even the general journal (for very small companies).

Like every Subway restaurant owner, Stan needs to keep a master file of important employee information. This file contains every employee's name, address, phone number, social insurance number, rate of pay, hours worked per week, and other forms.

Stan employs two part-time "sandwich artists" and no full-time managers—yet. If his sales continue to be high, he'll need to hire someone to manage operations so that he can spend more time analyzing the financials—with Lila's help—and growing his business. A majority of restaurants hire mostly part-timers with a core of full-time employees, but the numbers vary from restaurant to restaurant. Benefits vary too. Stan, for instance, plans to offer health and dental benefits when he hires a manager. He knows what a great incentive these benefits are with health costs so high. He pays his sandwich artists, Rashid and Ellen, the minimum wage since they both have less than a year's experience. However, he's talking to Mariah Washington about creating some incentives to keep them motivated. If Rashid and Ellen are with him for a full year, they'll see a nice raise in their biweekly paycheques.

Stan must record all this vital information and report it to the various provincial and federal authorities. In addition, Stan includes total payroll expenses on the weekly sales and inventory report, which he submits electronically to headquarters from his POS screen.

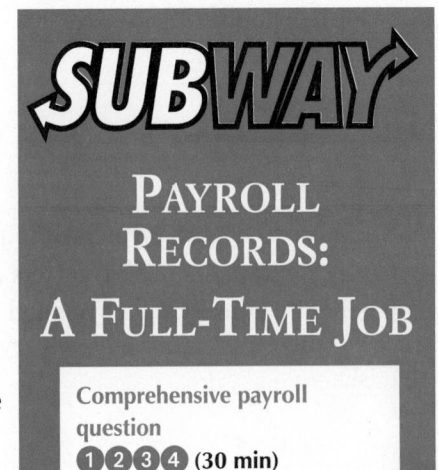

SUBWAY

PAYROLL RECORDS: A FULL-TIME JOB

Comprehensive payroll question
①②③④ (30 min)

Scheduling workers and keeping payroll records are the bane of Stan's existence. These tasks are incredibly time-consuming. He was pleased to hear, then, at the last meeting of his local North American Association of Subway Franchisees (NAASF) that the new point of sale (POS) terminals will soon offer an electronic scheduling package.

"Wow! That will really help," said Stan cheerfully to another franchisee. "No more differently coloured ink just to keep track of who will work when! Now I can plan around Rashid and Ellen's exam schedules without a hassle. Scheduling might just become my favourite module in the new system."

"Sure," said Javier Gonzalez, another owner. "Now you can concentrate on payroll records. What fun!"

"*Ay. Que lata,*" Stan groaned. What a drag!

DISCUSSION QUESTIONS

1. What payroll records does Stan need to keep for his Subway restaurant?
2. What other information might Stan want so as to schedule working hours for each employee?
3. How does the payroll register help Stan prepare the payroll? Consult the process outlined on pages 376–377.

Chapter Assignments

Learning Unit 8-1

1. The minimum-wage law sets the lowest hourly wage that can be paid to an employee and establishes the maximum number of hours per day and per week that an employee may work before an overtime premium must be paid.

2. Employers may calculate overtime pay separately from regular pay in order to highlight the cost of having employees work overtime.

3. Each pay period, employees are required to pay federal and provincial income tax and to contribute to the Canada Pension Plan and the Employment Insurance plan according to their level of earnings. The amount to be deducted for each employee is found in tables published by the federal government. Tables on Diskette (TOD) can also be used.

4. A TD1 form specifies the claim code for each employee. This in turn governs the income tax deducted each pay period. There are separate TD1 forms for both federal and provincial use.

5. CPP and EI have a maximum contribution of $2,163.15 per year and $747.36 per year, respectively. (These maximums will change annually.)

6. Other deductions (e.g., union dues or company-related matters) may also be made from an employee's earnings.

Learning Unit 8-2

1. Each pay period, a payroll summary is prepared. It includes the following information for each employee: claim code; rate of pay; hours worked; regular earnings; overtime earnings; gross pay; income tax deductions; CPP deduction; EI deduction; other deductions such as medical and charitable; net pay; and cheque number.

2. Gross pay determines the level of deductions.

3. Gross pay less deductions equals net, or take-home, pay.

Learning Unit 8-3

1. The payroll register is completed each pay period and provides basic data for recording the payroll.

2. The Salaries and Wages Expense entry is made and posted to ledger accounts. In addition to summarizing the deductions payable, the ledger accounts are used to classify wage expenses by type.

3. Each payroll cheque written is recorded in the cash disbursements journal (or the general journal). Journal amounts or totals are posted to the general ledger monthly.

4. Employers must maintain an employee earnings record for each employee. The source of the information summarized here is the payroll register.

5. Each year, employers must prepare and deliver to each employee a T4 or T4A form that summarizes the employee's earnings and deductions for the calendar year.

6. When an employee leaves, is laid off, or is terminated, the employer must complete a Record of Employment form.

KEY TERMS

Canada and Quebec Pension Plans   Provide a retirement benefit for all Canadians who contribute to the plans during their employment years. Requires a payroll deduction from each employee until a yearly maximum is reached. (The maximum that we are using is $2,163.15, but a new maximum is used each year.) (p. 371)

Canada Revenue Agency (CRA)   Canada Revenue Agency is the body that oversees the collection of income tax as well as CPP and EI. Formerly called Canada Customs and Revenue Agency (CCRA), the Customs function is now part of another federal agency. (p. 367)

Claim code   A number from 0 to 10 that determines the amount of income tax deducted each pay period. The appropriate claim code is based on information provided by the employee when completing a TD1 form. (p. 368)

Employee earnings record   A page, or sheet, or computer file that records and totals the details concerning an employee's earnings, deductions, net pay, and identification details for a calendar year. Used in preparing T4 slips. (p. 378)

Employment Insurance (EI) plan   A plan to which all employees must contribute and which provides a certain level of income for those workers who are unemployed. Contributions are made up to a maximum of $747.36 for 2010 (based on 1.73 percent of the maximum insurable earnings of $43,200). (p. 372)

Income tax deductions   The amount withheld from employees' wages each period and sent (on behalf of the employees) to the federal government. The amount of the deduction is determined by tables published by the federal government, customized for each province. (p. 374)

Indexing   A procedure whereby the personal exemption claim amounts are increased each year by the government to allow for the effects of inflation. (p. 371)

Minimum wage laws   Laws that govern the lowest wage legally payable in a province. Such a law also states the province's rules about overtime premiums and maximum weekly working hours. (p. 366)

Other deductions   Most employees have a variety of items for which a deduction is required. The exact type and amount of these deductions will vary a great deal from one employer to another. Common examples are union dues and provincial health care premiums. (p. 372)

Payroll summary   Sometimes known as the payroll journal or payroll register, this document lists in considerable detail the income, deductions, net pay, and other information for each employee for a given pay period. A total for all employees per category is always shown. This summary forms the basis for posting to appropriate ledger accounts. (p. 374)

Record of Employment   Special form to be completed for each employee at the end of his or her employment. Used in helping to determine the level of employment insurance payments a taxpayer is eligible for. (p. 378)

TD1 forms   Forms completed by an employee upon commencement of employment (and periodically thereafter) that set out the deductions claimed by the employee. A claim code determined by this form affects the amount of income tax deducted. There are separate federal and provincial forms. (p. 367)

TONI   Tax on Income is a way of determining provincial income-tax deductions. Instead of being a percentage of federal tax, each province bases its amount of income tax on the amount of income earned by a taxpayer. (p. 366)

T4 slip or T4A or T4 Supplementary   A special form issued annually to each employee summarizing annual earnings and deductions and used by an employee as a basic document in filing an annual income tax return. (p. 378)

Union dues   Fees deducted from an employee's wages and forwarded to the union treasurer, usually monthly. (p. 372)

Workers' Compensation   Provincial plans, paid by employers, designed to assist employees who are injured. (p. 372)

BLUEPRINT FOR RECORDING, POSTING, AND PAYING THE PAYROLL

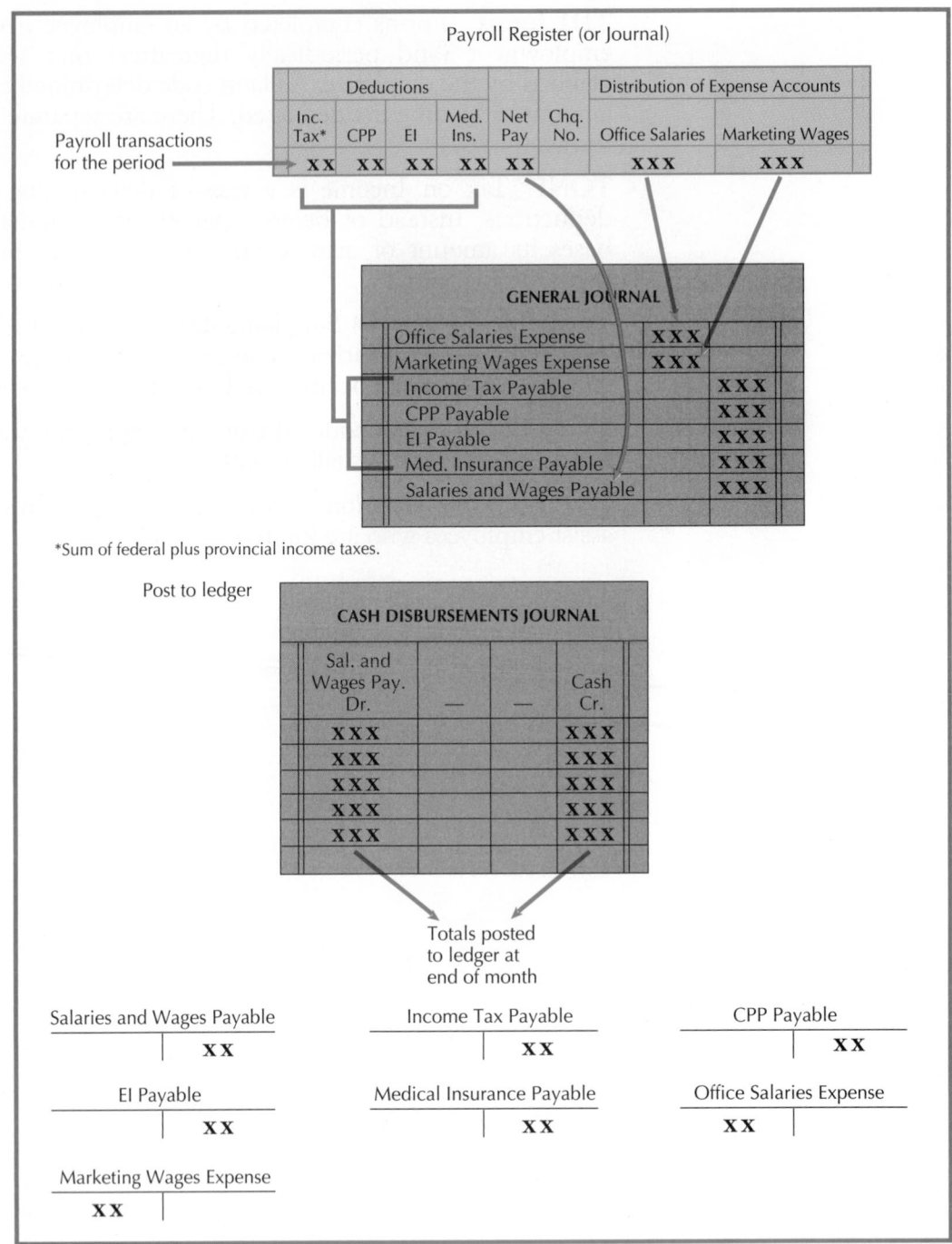

*Sum of federal plus provincial income taxes.

QUESTIONS, CLASSROOM DEMONSTRATION EXERCISES, EXERCISES, AND PROBLEMS

Discussion Questions and Critical Thinking/Ethical Case

1. Explain how overtime is usually calculated.

2. Define and state the purpose of completing a T4 Supplementary.

3. Usually, claiming more credits on a TD1 results in receiving more money per paycheque. Please comment.

4. All payroll registers must be special journals. True or false?

5. Define and state the purpose of the Canada and Quebec Pension Plans.

6. The employer doesn't have to contribute to the Canada Pension Plan. Agree or disagree?

7. Explain how federal and provincial income tax withholdings are determined.

8. What is a calendar year?

9. Define the purpose of an income-tax deduction.

10. What purposes does the employee earnings record serve?

11. Explain the differences in determining CPP and EI deductions.

12. Draw a diagram showing how the following relate: (a) weekly payroll, (b) payroll register, (c) individual earnings, (d) journal entries, (e) cash disbursements journal.

13. If you earned $80,000 this year, you would pay more CPP than your brother, who earned $60,000. Agree or disagree, and explain your answer.

14. Russ Todd works for a delicatessen. As the bookkeeper, Russ has been asked by the owner to keep two separate books for sales tax. The owner has asked Russ to hire someone on the weekends to punch in false tapes that can be submitted to the provincial government. These tapes would show low sales and thus less liability for sales-tax payments. You make the call. Write down your specific recommendations to Russ.

Make the grade with MyAccountingLab! The exercises and problems marked in green can be found on MyAccountingLab at www.myaccountinglab.com. You can practise them as often as you want, and many of them feature step-by-step guided solutions to help you find the right answer. You can also find working papers for selected problems in the Multimedia Library on MyAccountingLab.

Classroom Demonstration Exercises

(The forms you need are on page 8-2 of the *Study Guide with Working Papers*.)

Set A
Calculating Gross Earnings

Calculating wages overtime
1 (10 min)

1. Calculate the total wages earned (assume an overtime rate of time-and-a-half over 40 hours):

Employee	Hourly Rate	No. of Hours Worked
a. Marina Lizunova	$10	37
b. Jill Jones	12	50

CPP and EI

Calculating CPP and EI
1 (15 min)

2. Pete Martin, married and claiming code 1, has cumulative earnings before this weekly pay period of $48,700. Assuming that he is paid $1,200 this week, what will his deduction be for CPP and EI?

Net Pay

Calculating net pay
1 (15 min)

3. Calculate Pete's net pay from question 2 above. Income tax is $247.25 and supplemental health insurance is $40.

Payroll Register

The payroll summarized
3 (10 min)

4. For each of the six items listed below, indicate which of these three descriptions applies:
   a. Total of gross pay—comes from distribution of expense accounts
   b. A deduction
   c. Net pay

   1. Office Salaries Expense and Wages Expense
   2. CPP Payable
   3. EI Payable
   4. Federal Income Tax Payable
   5. Medical Insurance Payable
   6. Salaries and Wages Payable

Payroll Account

Categorizing accounts
3 (15 min)

5. Indicate for each of the accounts listed below and on the following page which of the following apply:
   a. An asset
   b. A liability
   c. An expense

    d. Appears in the income statement

    e. Appears on the balance sheet

        1. CPP Payable

        2. Office Salaries Expense

        3. Federal Income Tax Payable

        4. EI Payable

        5. Salaries and Wages Payable

Set B

Calculating Gross Earnings

Calculating wages with overtime
① (10 min)

1. Calculate the total wages earned (assume an overtime rate of time-and-a-half over 40 hours):

Employee	Hourly Rate	No. of Hours Worked
a. Kay Drost	$18	48
b. Anton Mandryk	20	35

CPP and EI

Calculating CPP and EI
① (15 min)

2. Kelvin Chu, married and claiming code 3, has cumulative earnings before this weekly pay period of $29,400. Assuming that he is paid $980 this week, what will his deduction be for CPP and EI?

Net Pay

Calculating net pay
① (15 min)

3. Calculate Kelvin's net pay from question 2 above. Income tax is $179.70 and supplemental health insurance is $25.

Payroll Register

The payroll summarized
③ (10 min)

4. For each of the six items listed below, indicate which of these three descriptions applies:

    a. Total of gross pay—comes from distribution of expense accounts

    b. A deduction

    c. Net pay

        1. Salaries Payable

        2. Parking Payable

        3. EI Payable

        4. Provincial Income Tax Payable

        5. Pension Payable

        6. Salaries Expense

Payroll Account

Categorizing accounts
③ (15 min)

5. Indicate for each of the accounts listed below which of the following apply:

    a. An asset

    b. A liability

    c. An expense

    d. Appears in the income statement

    e. Appears on the balance sheet

        1. Canada Savings Bond Payable

        2. Office Salaries Expense

        3. Federal Income Tax Payable

        4. Cash

        5. Salaries and Wages Payable

(The forms you need are on page 8-3 of the *Study Guide with Working Papers*.)

Calculating wages with overtime
1 (15 min)

8-1. Calculate the total wages earned for each employee (assume an overtime rate of time-and-a-half over 40 hours):

Employee	Hourly Rate	Hours Worked
Jean Knott	$13.20	36
Abe Janzen	15.00	44
Mike Toth	16.00	46

Calculating net pay
1 **3** (20 min)

8-2. Compute the net pay for each employee for the first week of February using the tables in the text.

Employee	Status	Claim Code	This Week's Pay
Ben Smith	Married	4	$610
May Cheung	Single	1	820

The only deductions are for income tax, CPP, and EI.

Categorizing accounts
3 (10 min)

8-3. Complete the table.

	Account Category	Dr./Cr.	Financial Statement on Which Account Appears
CPP Payable			
Income Tax Payable			
Medical Insurance Payable			
Wages and Salaries Payable			
Office Salaries Expense			
Marketing Wages Expense			

Payroll register and the journal entry
3 (10 min)

8-4. The following weekly payroll journal entry was prepared by Moore Co. Explain from which columns of the payroll register the data have come.

Jan.	7	Shop Expense	6 0 0 0 00		
		Factory Wages Expense	4 0 0 0 00		
		CPP Payable			4 8 5 00
		EI Payable			1 7 3 00
		Income Tax Payable			3 6 0 0 00
		Union Dues Payable			2 1 0 00
		Salaries and Wages Payable			5 5 2 2 00

Paying the payroll
3 (15 min)

If you are a student from a province other than Ontario, you may be supplied by your instructor with provincial tax tables. Otherwise, please use the tax tables supplied in the appendices at the end of this chapter.

8-5. From Exercise 8-4, prepare the entries in the cash disbursements journal to record payment of the payroll, given the following data for January 7:

Employee	Employee's Net Pay	Cheque No.
Nina Smith	$2,050	111
Jean Logan	1,329	112
Fred Singer	2,143	113

(The forms you need are on pages 8-4 to 8-10 of the *Study Guide with Working Papers*.)

Calculating gross earnings with overtime

① **(20 min)**

Check Figure

Tony Lee Gross Earnings
$832.00

8A-1. From the following information, please complete the chart for gross earnings for the week. (Assume an overtime rate of time-and-a-half over 40 hours.)

Employee	Hourly Rate	Number of Hours Worked	Gross Earnings
Stephen Post	$10.00	44	
Jean Nicola	11.50	36	
Maria Cardinal	12.00	42	
Tony Lee	16.00	48	

Completing a payroll register

①② **(30 min)**

Check Figure

Net Pay $2,911.18

8A-2. Nickels Company of Windsor has five salaried employees. Your task is to record the following information for the last week of March in a payroll register.

Employee	Department	Claim Code	Weekly Salary
Jenny Quan	Sales	3	$820
Frank Sloan	Sales	1	580
Alberta Nobel	Office	2	980
Jeremy Gold	Office	4	605
Nancy James	Sales	1	740

Assume that each employee contributes $10 per week for union dues.

Completing a payroll register and journalizing the payroll entry

①②③④ **(50 min)**

Check Figure

Net Pay $2,494.98

8A-3. The bookkeeper for Pinto Co. of Peterborough gathered the following data from employee earnings records as well as daily time cards. Your task is (1) to complete a payroll register on November 5 and (2) to journalize the appropriate entry to record the weekly payroll.

Assumptions

1. Income tax (federal and provincial), CPP, and EI are from tables at the end of this chapter (see Appendices 8-1 to 8-3).
2. Each employee contributes $20 per week for health insurance.
3. Overtime is paid at a rate of time-and-a-half over 40 hours per week, or 8 hours in any given day.

Employee	Claim Code	M	T	W	T	F	Hourly Rate	Dept.	Cum. CPP Before This Payroll
Mary Cardinal*	1	6	4	8	12	7	$23	Sales	$2,094.12
Bill Smith	3	7	9	11	9	4	15	Office	1,201.46
Joe Kingle*	2	8	10	7	12	10	24	Sales	2,135.60
Anita Tsui	4	8	8	6	8	8	12	Office	579.00

*Both of these employees exceeded the EI maximum last pay period.

Completing a payroll register,
journalizing, posting, and
recording the payment of
net pay
1 2 3 (50 min)

8A-4. Brenda Oakes, the accountant for Byscane Co. of Shelburne, has gathered the following data for the September 23 weekly payroll:

Employee	Net Claim Code	Salary	Cheque. No.	Cum. CPP Before This Payroll	Department
Jim Ryan	5	$ 820	47	$1,059.80	Factory
Emma LaPierre	1	975	48	2,108.42	Office
Jean Arnold	3	1,140	49	1,722.80	Factory
Bob Sylvan*	4	1,260	50	2,128.68	Office

*This employee has been paid more than $43,200 already this year.

Assumptions

1. Income taxes, CPP, and EI are calculated from tables in the text.
2. Union dues are $8 per week.
3. Medical coverage is $14 per week (except for Bob, whose wife pays the family premium).

Required

a. Prepare a payroll register for September 23.
b. Journalize and post the payroll entry.
c. Record the payment of the payroll on September 26 to each employee using a cash disbursements journal.

Group B Problems

(The forms you need are on pages 8-4 to 8-10 of the *Study Guide with Working Papers*.)

8B-1. From the following information, complete the chart for gross earnings for the week. (Assume an overtime rate of time-and-a-half over 40 hours.)

	Hourly Rate	Number of Hours Worked	Gross Earnings
Stephen Post	$11.50	42	
Jean Nicola	12.75	40	
Maria Cardinal	14.00	38	
Tony Lee	16.00	52	

8B-2. Nickels Company of Windsor has five salaried employees. Your task is to record the following information in a payroll register for the last week of March.

Employee	Department	Claim Code	Weekly Salary
Jenny Quan	Office	1	$765
Frank Sloan	Sales	2	430
Alberta Nobel	Office	3	965
Jeremy Gold	Office	1	575
Nancy James	Sales	4	410

Assume that each employee contributes $12 per week for union dues.

Completing the payroll register
and journalizing the payroll entry
❶❷❸❹ (50 min)

8B-3. The bookkeeper for Pinto Co. of Peterborough gathered the following data from employee earnings records as well as daily time cards. Your task is (1) to complete a payroll register on November 5 and (2) to journalize the appropriate entry to record the payroll.

Employee	Claim Code	Daily Time M	T	W	T	F	Hourly Rate	Dept.	Cum. CPP Before This Payroll
Mary Cardinal*	2	8	6	9	10	8	$22	Sales	$2,130.46
Bill Smith	4	9	10	9	10	7	14	Office	1,380.00
Joe Kingle*	3	8	10	12	8	9	25	Sales	2,163.15
Anita Tsui	1	9	7	8	10	8	12	Office	942.54

*Both of these employees exceed the EI maximum this pay period.

Assumptions

1. Income taxes, CPP, and EI are from tables at the end of this chapter. (See Appendices 8-1 to 8-3.)
2. Each employee contributes $12 per week for health insurance.
3. Overtime is paid at a rate of time-and-a-half over 40 hours per week or over 8 hours in any day.

Check Figure

Net Pay $2,687.03

Payroll register completion,
journalizing, posting, and paying
the payroll
❶❷❸ (50 min)

8B-4. Brenda Oakes, the accountant for Byscane Co. of Shelburne, has gathered the following data for the September 23 payroll:

Employee	Net Claim Code	Salary	Cheque. No.	Cum. CPP Before This Payroll	Department
Jim Ryan	4	$ 790	57	$1,692.40	Factory
Emma LaPierre	1	960	58	1,871.42	Office
Jean Arnold	1	980	59	1,879.66	Office
Bob Sylvan*	2	1,160	60	2,112.48	Factory

*This employee has been paid $44,200 already this year.

Assumptions

1. Income taxes, CPP, and EI are calculated from tables in the text.
2. Union dues are $11 per week.
3. Medical coverage is $26 per week (except for Bob, whose wife pays the family premium).

Required

a. Prepare a payroll register on September 23.
b. Journalize and post the payroll entry.
c. Record the payment of the payroll on September 25 to each employee using a cash disbursements journal.

Check Figure

Net Pay $2,859.92

(The forms you need are on pages 8-11 to 8-20 of the *Study Guide with Working Papers*.)

Calculating gross earnings with overtime
1 (20 min)

Check Figure

Erika Hance Gross Earnings $791.00

8C-1. From the following data, calculate the gross earnings for each of the five employees who are entitled to time-and-a-half for the greater of any hours exceeding 40 for the week or 8 in any given day.

Employee	M	T	W	T	F	S	Total Hours	Hourly Rate
A. Al Topping	6	8	8	9	8	5	44	$22.00
B. Barb Frank	6	7	8	8	7	5	41	20.00
C. Amos Ng	8	7	8	10	8	—	41	12.00
D. Carl Holdman	9	6	8	11	7	6	47	16.00
E. Erika Hance	8	7	9	13	8	6	51	14.00

Completing the payroll register
1 2 (30 min)

Check Figure

Net Pay $2,836.74

8C-2. The employees mentioned in Problem 8C-1 work for Waylon Company of Thunder Bay. Complete a payroll register for the second week of February using the gross earnings you obtained in answering 8C-1. Cheque numbers begin at 1424. Assume the following additional information:

Employee	Claim Code	Union Dues	Medical Plan
A	2	$16	$32.00
B	1	16	48.00
C	3	16	32.00
D	4	16	32.00
E	1	16	48.00

Completing the payroll register (alternative problem)
1 2 (40 min)

Check Figure

Net Pay $2,748.78

8C-3. (Alternative to 8C-2) Assume the following gross earnings for the employees of Waylon Company of Thunder Bay for the third week of February. Other information remains the same as in 8C-2. Cheque numbers begin at 1443. Complete the payroll register for the third week of February.

Employee	Gross Earnings
A	$978.00
B	800.00
C	680.00
D	792.00
E	558.00

Recording the payroll entry
3 (10 min)

8C-4. Refer to the payroll register that you completed in 8C-2. Prepare the journal entry necessary to record the payroll for the second week of February.

Recording the payroll entry (alternative problem)
3 (10 min)

8C-5. (Alternative to 8C-4) Refer to the payroll register you completed in 8C-3. Prepare the journal entry necessary to record the payroll for the third week of February.

Completing the payroll register and journalizing the payroll entry
1 2 3 (40 min)

8C-6. The payroll clerk for the Marlin Company of Armstrong assembled the following data for the company's five employees before suddenly becoming quite ill. You have been approached to complete the payroll register so that the employees can receive their cheques in a timely fashion. You must (1) complete the payroll register for the week ending October 20 and (2) prepare the entry necessary to record the payroll. Hours in excess of 40 in any given week are paid at time-and-a-half.

| Employee | Claim Code | \multicolumn{6}{c}{Daily Time} | Rate | Dept. | CPP to Date | Union Dues | Medical |
		M	T	W	T	F	S					
Fred Mora	2	—	8	8	10	12	5	$24.00	Sales	$2,126.12	$8	$22
Pat Samuels	1	9	—	7	10	7	8	20.00	Sales	1,084.59	8	40
Emilia Leung	3	8	9	8	9	8	6	13.50	Admin.	692.30	8	22
Keith Jones	5	8	8	8	8	8	—	16.00	Admin.	727.40	8	40
David Jarvic*	1	9	8	7	11	8	8	1,400.00*	Mgr.	2,163.15	—	40

* Weekly salary, no overtime. This employee has already earned $58,800 so far this year.

Comprehensive payroll problem—completing payroll registers, journalizing payrolls, and recording cheques issued
❶❷❸ (75 min)

Check Figure

Net Pay $5,771.66

8C-7. Comet Engineering of Delta is a consulting firm that employs four professional staff, two casual clerks, and you as office manager (accountant). Everyone except the clerks is paid a weekly salary. The clerks are paid an hourly rate and receive time-and-a-half for hours worked in excess of 8 per day or 40 per week. Using the information below, complete the payroll register for the week ending August 20; make the necessary entry to record the payroll for that week; and record the issuance of cheques to each employee. Daily hours for the clerks are shown at the end.

Employee	Claim Code	Rate or Salary	Life Ins.	Disab.	Med.	Donations	CPP to Date	Chq. No.
Donna Alvarez	3	$1,640.00	$19	$32	$36.00	$25.00	$2,146.18	574
Joan Kemp	4	1,490.00	12	28	36.00	25.00	2,163.15	575
John Harper	1	1,290.00	10	24	18.00	18.00	1,630.72	576
Tim Culver	2	1,340.00	8	25	36.00	18.00	984.37	577
May Silver	1	18.00	—	—	18.00	—	645.23	578
Joe Polemko	4	15.00	—	—	36.00	5.00	1,020.84	579
Yourself	2	875.00	6	18	18.00	5.00	823.65	580

Hourly employees worked:

	M	T	W	T	F	S	Total
May Silver	8	8	9	10	5	8	48
Joe Polemko	10	8	12	8	5	—	43

Hourly workers receive time-and-a-half rate for more than 40 hours in a week, or more than 8 hours in any given day. Two of the employees (Donna Alvarez and Joan Kemp) reached the EI maximum the last pay period.

On-the-job Training

(The forms you need are on page 8-21 of the *Study Guide with Working Papers*.)

T-1. Small Co., a sole proprietorship based in Truro, has two employees, Jim Roy and Janice Alter. The owner of Small Co. is Bert Ryan. During the current pay period, Jim has worked 48 hours and Janice 56. The reason for these extra hours is that both Jim and Janice worked their regular 40-hour work week plus Jim worked 8 extra hours on Sunday while Janice worked 8 extra hours on Saturday as well as Sunday. Their contract with Small Co. is that they are each paid an hourly rate of $14 per hour with all hours over 40 per week to be at time-and-a-half and all hours on Sunday to be paid at double time. Bert, the owner, believes he is also entitled to a salary since he works many hours. He plans to pay himself $750 per week.

As the accountant of Small Co., calculate the gross pay for Jim and Janice and offer some advice to Bert regarding his salary.

T-2. Marcy Moore recently moved to your city from another large Canadian centre. She was employed as an engineer by a large oil company and was rather well paid. She now works as a senior engineer for a newly established consulting firm. When she moved in October, Marcy had contributed the yearly maximum CPP premiums of $2,163.15 as well as the limit of $747.36 for EI while employed at the oil company. She feels that is unfair of her new employer to continue to deduct CPP and EI from her salary. She has heard that you are taking an accounting course and has asked you for your opinion.

What advice can you give her?

Comprehensive problem:
recording and posting
transactions, including preparing
the payroll register and preparing
a trial balance

1 2 3 (120 min)

CONTINUING PROBLEM

In preparing for next year, Tony Freedman has hired two employees to work on an hourly basis assisting with some troubleshooting and repair work.

Assume the following details:

a. The following accounts have been added to the chart of accounts: Wages Expense, 5110; Income Taxes Payable, 2020; CPP Payable, 2030; EI Payable, 2040; and Wages Payable, 2010.

b. CPP is deducted according to the tables in Appendix 8-2.

c. EI is deducted according to Appendix 8-3.

d. Both employees have claim codes of 1.

e. Each employee earns $20 an hour and is paid time-and-a-half for hours worked in excess of 40 weekly.

Assignment

(See pages 8-22 to 8-35 in your *Study Guide with Working Papers*.)

1. Record the partial transactions listed below in the appropriate journal and post to the general ledger.
2. Prepare a payroll register.
3. Prepare a trial balance as of November 30, 2013.

Nov. 1 Billed Vita Needle Company $6,800, invoice No. 12686, for services rendered.

4 Billed Accu Pac, Inc. $3,900, invoice No. 12687, for services rendered.

5 Purchased new shop benches, $1,400 on account from System Design Furniture (invoice No. 8771) (purchase order No. 4013).

8 Paid the two employees' wages: Lance Klumm, 38 hours, and Aurelle Hall, 42 hours (cheques No. 258 and No. 259).

11 Received the phone bill, $150.

12 Collected $500 of the amount due from Taylor Golf.

15 Paid the two employees' wages: Lance Klumm, 34 hours, and Aurelle Hall, 36 hours (cheques No. 260 and No. 261).

18 Collected $800 of the amount due from Taylor Golf.

19 Purchased a fax machine for the office from Multi Systems Inc. on credit, $450 (invoice No. 1784) (purchase order No. 4014).

22 Paid the two employees' wages: Lance Klumm, 32 hours and Aurelle Hall, 35 hours (cheques No. 262 and No. 263).

25 Collected half of the amount due from Vita Needle Company re Nov. 1 transaction.

29 Paid the two employees wages: Lance Klumm, 38 hours, and Aurelle Hall, 44 hours (cheques No. 264 and No. 265).

29 Rent expired for October and November, $800.

Schedule of Accounts Receivable
Precision Computer Centre
October 31, 2013

Carson Engineering	$ 6,240.00
Antony Pitale	1,600.00
Taylor Golf	4,500.00
Total Amount Due	$12,340.00

Schedule of Accounts Payable
Precision Computer Centre
October 31, 2013

City Newspaper	$375.00
Staples	250.00
Total Amount Payable	$625.00

Appendix 8-1F—Federal Taxes

Federal tax deductions
Effective January 1, 2010
Weekly (52 pay periods a year)
**Also look up the tax deductions
in the provincial table**

Retenues d'impôt fédéral
En vigueur le 1er janvier 2010
Hebdomadaire (52 périodes de paie par année)
**Cherchez aussi les retenues d'impôt
dans la table provinciale**

Pay Rémunération		Federal claim codes/Codes de demande fédéraux										
		0	1	2	3	4	5	6	7	8	9	10
From Less than		Deduct from each pay										
De Moins de		Retenez sur chaque paie										
	232	*	.00									
232 -	234	30.10	.15									
234 -	236	30.35	.40									
236 -	238	30.65	.70									
238 -	240	30.90	1.00									
240 -	242	31.20	1.25									
242 -	244	31.50	1.55									
244 -	246	31.75	1.80									
246 -	248	32.05	2.10									
248 -	250	32.30	2.40									
250 -	252	32.60	2.65									
252 -	254	32.90	2.95	.05								
254 -	256	33.15	3.20	.35								
256 -	258	33.45	3.50	.65								
258 -	260	33.70	3.75	.90								
260 -	262	34.00	4.05	1.20								
262 -	264	34.30	4.35	1.45								
264 -	266	34.55	4.60	1.75								
266 -	268	34.85	4.90	2.05								
268 -	270	35.10	5.15	2.30								
270 -	272	35.40	5.45	2.60								
272 -	274	35.70	5.75	2.85								
274 -	276	35.95	6.00	3.15								
276 -	278	36.25	6.30	3.45								
278 -	280	36.50	6.55	3.70								
280 -	282	36.80	6.85	4.00								
282 -	284	37.10	7.15	4.25								
284 -	286	37.35	7.40	4.55								
286 -	288	37.65	7.70	4.85								
288 -	290	37.90	7.95	5.10								
290 -	292	38.20	8.25	5.40								
292 -	294	38.50	8.55	5.65								
294 -	296	38.75	8.80	5.95	.25							
296 -	298	39.05	9.10	6.25	.50							
298 -	300	39.30	9.35	6.50	.80							
300 -	302	39.60	9.65	6.80	1.05							
302 -	304	39.90	9.95	7.05	1.35							
304 -	306	40.15	10.20	7.35	1.65							
306 -	308	40.45	10.50	7.65	1.90							
308 -	310	40.70	10.75	7.90	2.20							
310 -	312	41.00	11.05	8.20	2.45							
312 -	314	41.30	11.35	8.45	2.75							
314 -	316	41.55	11.60	8.75	3.05							
316 -	318	41.85	11.90	9.05	3.30							
318 -	320	42.10	12.15	9.30	3.60							
320 -	322	42.40	12.45	9.60	3.85							
322 -	324	42.70	12.75	9.85	4.15							
324 -	326	42.95	13.00	10.15	4.45							
326 -	328	43.25	13.30	10.45	4.70							
328 -	330	43.50	13.55	10.70	5.00							
330 -	332	43.80	13.85	11.00	5.25							
332 -	334	44.10	14.15	11.25	5.55							
334 -	336	44.35	14.40	11.55	5.85	.10						
336 -	338	44.65	14.70	11.85	6.10	.40						
338 -	340	44.90	14.95	12.10	6.40	.65						

*You normally use claim code "0" only for non-resident employees. However, if you have non-resident employees who earn less than the minimum amount shown in the "Pay" column, you may not be able to use these tables. Instead, refer to the "Step-by-step calculation of tax deductions" in Section "A" of this publication.

*Le code de demande «0» est normalement utilisé seulement pour les non-résidents. Cependant, si la rémunération de votre employé non résident est inférieure au montant minimum indiqué dans la colonne «Rémunération», vous ne pourrez peut-être pas utiliser ces tables. Reportez-vous alors au «Calcul des retenues d'impôt, étape par étape» dans la section «A» de cette publication.

This table is available on TOD   D-1   **Vous pouvez obtenir cette table sur TSD**

Federal tax deductions
Effective January 1, 2010
Weekly (52 pay periods a year)
**Also look up the tax deductions
in the provincial table**

Retenues d'impôt fédéral
En vigueur le 1er janvier 2010
Hebdomadaire (52 périodes de paie par année)
**Cherchez aussi les retenues d'impôt
dans la table provinciale**

Pay / Rémunération		Federal claim codes/Codes de demande fédéraux										
		0	1	2	3	4	5	6	7	8	9	10
From Less than / De Moins de		Deduct from each pay / Retenez sur chaque paie										
340 - 344		45.35	15.40	12.55	6.80	1.10						
344 - 348		45.90	15.95	13.10	7.35	1.65						
348 - 352		46.45	16.50	13.65	7.95	2.20						
352 - 356		47.00	17.05	14.20	8.50	2.75						
356 - 360		47.60	17.65	14.75	9.05	3.35						
360 - 364		48.15	18.20	15.35	9.60	3.90						
364 - 368		48.70	18.75	15.90	10.15	4.45						
368 - 372		49.25	19.30	16.45	10.75	5.00						
372 - 376		49.80	19.85	17.00	11.30	5.55						
376 - 380		50.40	20.45	17.55	11.85	6.10	.40					
380 - 384		50.95	21.00	18.15	12.40	6.70	.95					
384 - 388		51.50	21.55	18.70	12.95	7.25	1.50					
388 - 392		52.05	22.10	19.25	13.55	7.80	2.10					
392 - 396		52.60	22.65	19.80	14.10	8.35	2.65					
396 - 400		53.20	23.25	20.35	14.65	8.90	3.20					
400 - 404		53.75	23.80	20.95	15.20	9.50	3.75					
404 - 408		54.30	24.35	21.50	15.75	10.05	4.30					
408 - 412		54.85	24.90	22.05	16.35	10.60	4.90					
412 - 416		55.40	25.45	22.60	16.90	11.15	5.45					
416 - 420		56.00	26.05	23.15	17.45	11.70	6.00	.30				
420 - 424		56.55	26.60	23.75	18.00	12.30	6.55	.85				
424 - 428		57.10	27.15	24.30	18.55	12.85	7.10	1.40				
428 - 432		57.65	27.70	24.85	19.15	13.40	7.70	1.95				
432 - 436		58.20	28.25	25.40	19.70	13.95	8.25	2.50				
436 - 440		58.80	28.85	25.95	20.25	14.50	8.80	3.10				
440 - 444		59.35	29.40	26.55	20.80	15.10	9.35	3.65				
444 - 448		59.90	29.95	27.10	21.35	15.65	9.90	4.20				
448 - 452		60.45	30.50	27.65	21.95	16.20	10.50	4.75				
452 - 456		61.00	31.05	28.20	22.50	16.75	11.05	5.30				
456 - 460		61.60	31.65	28.75	23.05	17.30	11.60	5.90	.15			
460 - 464		62.15	32.20	29.35	23.60	17.90	12.15	6.45	.70			
464 - 468		62.70	32.75	29.90	24.15	18.45	12.70	7.00	1.25			
468 - 472		63.25	33.30	30.45	24.75	19.00	13.30	7.55	1.85			
472 - 476		63.80	33.85	31.00	25.30	19.55	13.85	8.10	2.40			
476 - 480		64.40	34.45	31.55	25.85	20.10	14.40	8.70	2.95			
480 - 484		64.95	35.00	32.15	26.40	20.70	14.95	9.25	3.50			
484 - 488		65.50	35.55	32.70	26.95	21.25	15.50	9.80	4.05			
488 - 492		66.05	36.10	33.25	27.55	21.80	16.10	10.35	4.65			
492 - 496		66.60	36.65	33.80	28.10	22.35	16.65	10.90	5.20			
496 - 500		67.20	37.25	34.35	28.65	22.90	17.20	11.50	5.75	.05		
500 - 504		67.75	37.80	34.95	29.20	23.50	17.75	12.05	6.30	.60		
504 - 508		68.30	38.35	35.50	29.75	24.05	18.30	12.60	6.85	1.15		
508 - 512		68.85	38.90	36.05	30.35	24.60	18.90	13.15	7.45	1.70		
512 - 516		69.40	39.45	36.60	30.90	25.15	19.45	13.70	8.00	2.25		
516 - 520		70.00	40.05	37.15	31.45	25.70	20.00	14.30	8.55	2.85		
520 - 524		70.55	40.60	37.75	32.00	26.30	20.55	14.85	9.10	3.40		
524 - 528		71.10	41.15	38.30	32.55	26.85	21.10	15.40	9.65	3.95		
528 - 532		71.65	41.70	38.85	33.10	27.40	21.70	15.95	10.25	4.50		
532 - 536		72.20	42.25	39.40	33.70	27.95	22.25	16.50	10.80	5.05		
536 - 540		72.80	42.85	39.95	34.25	28.50	22.80	17.10	11.35	5.65		
540 - 544		73.35	43.40	40.55	34.80	29.10	23.35	17.65	11.90	6.20	.45	
544 - 548		73.90	43.95	41.10	35.35	29.65	23.90	18.20	12.45	6.75	1.05	
548 - 552		74.45	44.50	41.65	35.90	30.20	24.50	18.75	13.05	7.30	1.60	
552 - 556		75.00	45.05	42.20	36.50	30.75	25.05	19.30	13.60	7.85	2.15	
556 - 560		75.60	45.65	42.75	37.05	31.30	25.60	19.85	14.15	8.45	2.70	

Federal tax deductions
Effective January 1, 2010
Weekly (52 pay periods a year)
**Also look up the tax deductions
in the provincial table**

Retenues d'impôt fédéral
En vigueur le 1er janvier 2010
Hebdomadaire (52 périodes de paie par année)
**Cherchez aussi les retenues d'impôt
dans la table provinciale**

Pay / Rémunération		Federal claim codes/Codes de demande fédéraux										
From / De	Less than / Moins de	0	1	2	3	4	5	6	7	8	9	10
		Deduct from each pay / Retenez sur chaque paie										
560	568	76.40	46.45	43.60	37.90	32.15	26.45	20.70	15.00	9.25	3.55	
568	576	77.55	47.60	44.75	39.00	33.30	27.55	21.85	16.10	10.40	4.65	
576	584	78.65	48.70	45.85	40.10	34.40	28.70	22.95	17.25	11.50	5.80	.05
584	592	79.80	49.85	46.95	41.25	35.50	29.80	24.05	18.35	12.65	6.90	1.20
592	600	80.90	50.95	48.10	42.35	36.65	30.90	25.20	19.45	13.75	8.05	2.30
600	608	82.00	52.05	49.20	43.50	37.75	32.05	26.30	20.60	14.85	9.15	3.40
608	616	83.15	53.20	50.35	44.60	38.90	33.15	27.45	21.70	16.00	10.25	4.55
616	624	84.25	54.30	51.45	45.70	40.00	34.30	28.55	22.85	17.10	11.40	5.65
624	632	85.40	55.45	52.55	46.85	41.10	35.40	29.65	23.95	18.25	12.50	6.80
632	640	86.50	56.55	53.70	47.95	42.25	36.50	30.80	25.05	19.35	13.60	7.90
640	648	87.60	57.65	54.80	49.10	43.35	37.65	31.90	26.20	20.45	14.75	9.00
648	656	88.75	58.80	55.95	50.20	44.50	38.75	33.05	27.30	21.60	15.85	10.15
656	664	89.85	59.90	57.05	51.30	45.60	39.90	34.15	28.45	22.70	17.00	11.25
664	672	90.95	61.05	58.15	52.45	46.70	41.00	35.25	29.55	23.85	18.10	12.40
672	680	92.10	62.15	59.30	53.55	47.85	42.10	36.40	30.65	24.95	19.20	13.50
680	688	93.20	63.25	60.40	54.70	48.95	43.25	37.50	31.80	26.05	20.35	14.60
688	696	94.35	64.40	61.50	55.80	50.10	44.35	38.65	32.90	27.20	21.45	15.75
696	704	95.45	65.50	62.65	56.90	51.20	45.50	39.75	34.05	28.30	22.60	16.85
704	712	96.55	66.65	63.75	58.05	52.30	46.60	40.85	35.15	29.45	23.70	18.00
712	720	97.70	67.75	64.90	59.15	53.45	47.70	42.00	36.25	30.55	24.80	19.10
720	728	98.80	68.85	66.00	60.30	54.55	48.85	43.10	37.40	31.65	25.95	20.20
728	736	99.95	70.00	67.10	61.40	55.70	49.95	44.25	38.50	32.80	27.05	21.35
736	744	101.05	71.10	68.25	62.50	56.80	51.05	45.35	39.65	33.90	28.20	22.45
744	752	102.15	72.20	69.35	63.65	57.90	52.20	46.45	40.75	35.00	29.30	23.60
752	760	103.30	73.35	70.50	64.75	59.05	53.30	47.60	41.85	36.15	30.40	24.70
760	768	104.40	74.45	71.60	65.90	60.15	54.45	48.70	43.00	37.25	31.55	25.80
768	776	105.55	75.60	72.70	67.00	61.30	55.55	49.85	44.10	38.40	32.65	26.95
776	784	106.65	76.70	73.85	68.10	62.40	56.65	50.95	45.25	39.50	33.80	28.05
784	792	107.80	77.85	74.95	69.25	63.50	57.80	52.10	46.35	40.65	34.90	29.20
792	800	109.45	79.50	76.65	70.95	65.20	59.50	53.75	48.05	42.30	36.60	30.85
800	808	111.15	81.20	78.35	72.60	66.90	61.15	55.45	49.70	44.00	38.25	32.55
808	816	112.80	82.85	80.00	74.30	68.55	62.85	57.10	51.40	45.65	39.95	34.20
816	824	114.50	84.55	81.70	75.95	70.25	64.50	58.80	53.05	47.35	41.65	35.90
824	832	116.20	86.25	83.35	77.65	71.90	66.20	60.50	54.75	49.05	43.30	37.60
832	840	117.85	87.90	85.05	79.35	73.60	67.90	62.15	56.45	50.70	45.00	39.30
840	848	119.55	89.60	86.75	81.05	75.30	69.60	63.85	58.15	52.40	46.70	41.00
848	856	121.25	91.30	88.45	82.75	77.00	71.30	65.55	59.85	54.10	48.40	42.70
856	864	122.95	93.00	90.15	84.45	78.70	73.00	67.25	61.55	55.80	50.10	44.40
864	872	124.65	94.75	91.85	86.15	80.40	74.70	68.95	63.25	57.55	51.80	46.10
872	880	126.35	96.45	93.55	87.85	82.10	76.40	70.65	64.95	59.25	53.50	47.80
880	888	128.05	98.15	95.25	89.55	83.80	78.10	72.35	66.65	60.95	55.20	49.50
888	896	129.80	99.85	96.95	91.25	85.50	79.80	74.05	68.35	62.65	56.90	51.20
896	904	131.50	101.55	98.65	92.95	87.20	81.50	75.75	70.05	64.35	58.60	52.90
904	912	133.20	103.25	100.35	94.65	88.90	83.20	77.50	71.75	66.05	60.30	54.60
912	920	134.95	105.00	102.15	96.40	90.70	84.95	79.25	73.50	67.80	62.05	56.35
920	928	136.70	106.75	103.90	98.15	92.45	86.70	81.00	75.25	69.55	63.85	58.10
928	936	138.45	108.50	105.65	99.95	94.20	88.50	82.75	77.05	71.30	65.60	59.85
936	944	140.20	110.25	107.40	101.70	95.95	90.25	84.50	78.80	73.05	67.35	61.60
944	952	142.00	112.05	109.15	103.45	97.70	92.00	86.30	80.55	74.85	69.10	63.40
952	960	143.75	113.80	110.95	105.20	99.50	93.75	88.05	82.30	76.60	70.85	65.15
960	968	145.50	115.55	112.70	106.95	101.25	95.50	89.80	84.05	78.35	72.65	66.90
968	976	147.25	117.30	114.45	108.75	103.00	97.30	91.55	85.85	80.10	74.40	68.65
976	984	149.00	119.05	116.20	110.50	104.75	99.05	93.30	87.60	81.85	76.15	70.40
984	992	150.80	120.85	117.95	112.25	106.50	100.80	95.10	89.35	83.65	77.90	72.20
992	1000	152.55	122.60	119.75	114.00	108.30	102.55	96.85	91.10	85.40	79.65	73.95

Federal tax deductions
Effective January 1, 2010
Weekly (52 pay periods a year)
**Also look up the tax deductions
in the provincial table**

Retenues d'impôt fédéral
En vigueur le 1er janvier 2010
Hebdomadaire (52 périodes de paie par année)
**Cherchez aussi les retenues d'impôt
dans la table provinciale**

Pay / Rémunération		Federal claim codes/Codes de demande fédéraux										
		0	1	2	3	4	5	6	7	8	9	10
From / De	Less than / Moins de	Deduct from each pay / Retenez sur chaque paie										
1000 -	1012	154.75	124.80	121.95	116.20	110.50	104.75	99.05	93.30	87.60	81.85	76.15
1012 -	1024	157.40	127.45	124.55	118.85	113.10	107.40	101.70	95.95	90.25	84.50	78.80
1024 -	1036	160.00	130.05	127.20	121.50	115.75	110.05	104.30	98.60	92.85	87.15	81.40
1036 -	1048	162.65	132.70	129.85	124.15	118.40	112.70	106.95	101.25	95.50	89.80	84.05
1048 -	1060	165.30	135.35	132.50	126.75	121.05	115.30	109.60	103.85	98.15	92.45	86.70
1060 -	1072	167.95	138.00	135.15	129.40	123.70	117.95	112.25	106.50	100.80	95.05	89.35
1072 -	1084	170.60	140.65	137.75	132.05	126.30	120.60	114.90	109.15	103.45	97.70	92.00
1084 -	1096	173.20	143.25	140.40	134.70	128.95	123.25	117.50	111.80	106.05	100.35	94.60
1096 -	1108	175.85	145.90	143.05	137.35	131.60	125.90	120.15	114.45	108.70	103.00	97.25
1108 -	1120	178.50	148.55	145.70	139.95	134.25	128.50	122.80	117.05	111.35	105.65	99.90
1120 -	1132	181.15	151.20	148.35	142.60	136.90	131.15	125.45	119.70	114.00	108.25	102.55
1132 -	1144	183.80	153.85	150.95	145.25	139.50	133.80	128.10	122.35	116.65	110.90	105.20
1144 -	1156	186.40	156.45	153.60	147.90	142.15	136.45	130.70	125.00	119.25	113.55	107.80
1156 -	1168	189.05	159.10	156.25	150.55	144.80	139.10	133.35	127.65	121.90	116.20	110.45
1168 -	1180	191.70	161.75	158.90	153.15	147.45	141.70	136.00	130.25	124.55	118.85	113.10
1180 -	1192	194.35	164.40	161.55	155.80	150.10	144.35	138.65	132.90	127.20	121.45	115.75
1192 -	1204	197.00	167.05	164.15	158.45	152.70	147.00	141.30	135.55	129.85	124.10	118.40
1204 -	1216	199.60	169.65	166.80	161.10	155.35	149.65	143.90	138.20	132.45	126.75	121.00
1216 -	1228	202.25	172.30	169.45	163.75	158.00	152.30	146.55	140.85	135.10	129.40	123.65
1228 -	1240	204.90	174.95	172.10	166.35	160.65	154.90	149.20	143.45	137.75	132.05	126.30
1240 -	1252	207.55	177.60	174.75	169.00	163.30	157.55	151.85	146.10	140.40	134.65	128.95
1252 -	1264	210.20	180.25	177.35	171.65	165.90	160.20	154.50	148.75	143.05	137.30	131.60
1264 -	1276	212.80	182.85	180.00	174.30	168.55	162.85	157.10	151.40	145.65	139.95	134.20
1276 -	1288	215.45	185.50	182.65	176.95	171.20	165.50	159.75	154.05	148.30	142.60	136.85
1288 -	1300	218.10	188.15	185.30	179.55	173.85	168.10	162.40	156.65	150.95	145.25	139.50
1300 -	1312	220.75	190.80	187.95	182.20	176.50	170.75	165.05	159.30	153.60	147.85	142.15
1312 -	1324	223.40	193.45	190.55	184.85	179.10	173.40	167.70	161.95	156.25	150.50	144.80
1324 -	1336	226.00	196.05	193.20	187.50	181.75	176.05	170.30	164.60	158.85	153.15	147.40
1336 -	1348	228.65	198.70	195.85	190.15	184.40	178.70	172.95	167.25	161.50	155.80	150.05
1348 -	1360	231.30	201.35	198.50	192.75	187.05	181.30	175.60	169.85	164.15	158.45	152.70
1360 -	1372	233.95	204.00	201.15	195.40	189.70	183.95	178.25	172.50	166.80	161.05	155.35
1372 -	1384	236.60	206.65	203.75	198.05	192.30	186.60	180.90	175.15	169.45	163.70	158.00
1384 -	1396	239.20	209.25	206.40	200.70	194.95	189.25	183.50	177.80	172.05	166.35	160.60
1396 -	1408	241.85	211.90	209.05	203.35	197.60	191.90	186.15	180.45	174.70	169.00	163.25
1408 -	1420	244.50	214.55	211.70	205.95	200.25	194.50	188.80	183.05	177.35	171.65	165.90
1420 -	1432	247.15	217.20	214.35	208.60	202.90	197.15	191.45	185.70	180.00	174.25	168.55
1432 -	1444	249.80	219.85	216.95	211.25	205.50	199.80	194.10	188.35	182.65	176.90	171.20
1444 -	1456	252.40	222.45	219.60	213.90	208.15	202.45	196.70	191.00	185.25	179.55	173.80
1456 -	1468	255.05	225.10	222.25	216.55	210.80	205.10	199.35	193.65	187.90	182.20	176.45
1468 -	1480	257.70	227.75	224.90	219.15	213.45	207.70	202.00	196.25	190.55	184.85	179.10
1480 -	1492	260.35	230.40	227.55	221.80	216.10	210.35	204.65	198.90	193.20	187.45	181.75
1492 -	1504	263.00	233.05	230.15	224.45	218.70	213.00	207.30	201.55	195.85	190.10	184.40
1504 -	1516	265.60	235.65	232.80	227.10	221.35	215.65	209.90	204.20	198.45	192.75	187.00
1516 -	1528	268.25	238.30	235.45	229.75	224.00	218.30	212.55	206.85	201.10	195.40	189.65
1528 -	1540	270.90	240.95	238.10	232.35	226.65	220.90	215.20	209.45	203.75	198.05	192.30
1540 -	1552	273.55	243.60	240.75	235.00	229.30	223.55	217.85	212.10	206.40	200.65	194.95
1552 -	1564	276.20	246.25	243.35	237.65	231.90	226.20	220.50	214.75	209.05	203.30	197.60
1564 -	1576	278.80	248.85	246.00	240.30	234.55	228.85	223.10	217.40	211.65	205.95	200.20
1576 -	1588	281.70	251.75	248.90	243.15	237.45	231.70	226.00	220.30	214.55	208.85	203.10
1588 -	1600	284.80	254.85	252.00	246.30	240.55	234.85	229.10	223.40	217.65	211.95	206.25
1600 -	1612	287.95	258.00	255.15	249.40	243.70	237.95	232.25	226.50	220.80	215.05	209.35
1612 -	1624	291.05	261.10	258.25	252.55	246.80	241.10	235.35	229.65	223.90	218.20	212.45
1624 -	1636	294.20	264.25	261.35	255.65	249.90	244.20	238.50	232.75	227.05	221.30	215.60
1636 -	1648	297.30	267.35	264.50	258.75	253.05	247.30	241.60	235.90	230.15	224.45	218.70
1648 -	1660	300.40	270.45	267.60	261.90	256.15	250.45	244.70	239.00	233.25	227.55	221.85

Federal tax deductions
Effective January 1, 2010
Weekly (52 pay periods a year)
**Also look up the tax deductions
in the provincial table**

Retenues d'impôt fédéral
En vigueur le 1er janvier 2010
Hebdomadaire (52 périodes de paie par année)
**Cherchez aussi les retenues d'impôt
dans la table provinciale**

Pay / Rémunération		Federal claim codes/Codes de demande fédéraux										
		0	1	2	3	4	5	6	7	8	9	10
From / De	Less than / Moins de	Deduct from each pay / Retenez sur chaque paie										
1660	1676	304.05	274.10	271.25	265.55	259.80	254.10	248.35	242.65	236.90	231.20	225.45
1676	1692	308.20	278.25	275.40	269.70	263.95	258.25	252.50	246.80	241.05	235.35	229.65
1692	1708	312.40	282.45	279.55	273.85	268.10	262.40	256.70	250.95	245.25	239.50	233.80
1708	1724	316.55	286.60	283.75	278.00	272.30	266.55	260.85	255.10	249.40	243.65	237.95
1724	1740	320.70	290.75	287.90	282.15	276.45	270.70	265.00	259.30	253.55	247.85	242.10
1740	1756	324.85	294.90	292.05	286.35	280.60	274.90	269.15	263.45	257.70	252.00	246.25
1756	1772	329.00	299.05	296.20	290.50	284.75	279.05	273.30	267.60	261.85	256.15	250.45
1772	1788	333.20	303.25	300.35	294.65	288.90	283.20	277.50	271.75	266.05	260.30	254.60
1788	1804	337.35	307.40	304.55	298.80	293.10	287.35	281.65	275.90	270.20	264.45	258.75
1804	1820	341.50	311.55	308.70	302.95	297.25	291.50	285.80	280.10	274.35	268.65	262.90
1820	1836	345.65	315.70	312.85	307.15	301.40	295.70	289.95	284.25	278.50	272.80	267.05
1836	1852	349.80	319.85	317.00	311.30	305.55	299.85	294.10	288.40	282.65	276.95	271.25
1852	1868	354.00	324.05	321.15	315.45	309.70	304.00	298.30	292.55	286.85	281.10	275.40
1868	1884	358.15	328.20	325.35	319.60	313.90	308.15	302.45	296.70	291.00	285.25	279.55
1884	1900	362.30	332.35	329.50	323.75	318.05	312.30	306.60	300.90	295.15	289.45	283.70
1900	1916	366.45	336.50	333.65	327.95	322.20	316.50	310.75	305.05	299.30	293.60	287.85
1916	1932	370.60	340.65	337.80	332.10	326.35	320.65	314.90	309.20	303.45	297.75	292.05
1932	1948	374.80	344.85	341.95	336.25	330.50	324.80	319.10	313.35	307.65	301.90	296.20
1948	1964	378.95	349.00	346.15	340.40	334.70	328.95	323.25	317.50	311.80	306.05	300.35
1964	1980	383.10	353.15	350.30	344.55	338.85	333.10	327.40	321.70	315.95	310.25	304.50
1980	1996	387.25	357.30	354.45	348.75	343.00	337.30	331.55	325.85	320.10	314.40	308.65
1996	2012	391.40	361.45	358.60	352.90	347.15	341.45	335.70	330.00	324.25	318.55	312.85
2012	2028	395.60	365.65	362.75	357.05	351.30	345.60	339.90	334.15	328.45	322.70	317.00
2028	2044	399.75	369.80	366.95	361.20	355.50	349.75	344.05	338.30	332.60	326.85	321.15
2044	2060	403.90	373.95	371.10	365.35	359.65	353.90	348.20	342.50	336.75	331.05	325.30
2060	2076	408.05	378.10	375.25	369.55	363.80	358.10	352.35	346.65	340.90	335.20	329.45
2076	2092	412.20	382.25	379.40	373.70	367.95	362.25	356.50	350.80	345.05	339.35	333.65
2092	2108	416.40	386.45	383.55	377.85	372.10	366.40	360.70	354.95	349.25	343.50	337.80
2108	2124	420.55	390.60	387.75	382.00	376.30	370.55	364.85	359.10	353.40	347.65	341.95
2124	2140	424.70	394.75	391.90	386.15	380.45	374.70	369.00	363.30	357.55	351.85	346.10
2140	2156	428.85	398.90	396.05	390.35	384.60	378.90	373.15	367.45	361.70	356.00	350.25
2156	2172	433.00	403.05	400.20	394.50	388.75	383.05	377.30	371.60	365.85	360.15	354.45
2172	2188	437.20	407.25	404.35	398.65	392.90	387.20	381.50	375.75	370.05	364.30	358.60
2188	2204	441.35	411.40	408.55	402.80	397.10	391.35	385.65	379.90	374.20	368.45	362.75
2204	2220	445.50	415.55	412.70	406.95	401.25	395.50	389.80	384.10	378.35	372.65	366.90
2220	2236	449.65	419.70	416.85	411.15	405.40	399.70	393.95	388.25	382.50	376.80	371.05
2236	2252	453.80	423.85	421.00	415.30	409.55	403.85	398.10	392.40	386.65	380.95	375.25
2252	2268	458.00	428.05	425.15	419.45	413.70	408.00	402.30	396.55	390.85	385.10	379.40
2268	2284	462.15	432.20	429.35	423.60	417.90	412.15	406.45	400.70	395.00	389.25	383.55
2284	2300	466.30	436.35	433.50	427.75	422.05	416.30	410.60	404.90	399.15	393.45	387.70
2300	2316	470.45	440.50	437.65	431.95	426.20	420.50	414.75	409.05	403.30	397.60	391.85
2316	2332	474.60	444.65	441.80	436.10	430.35	424.65	418.90	413.20	407.45	401.75	396.05
2332	2348	478.80	448.85	445.95	440.25	434.50	428.80	423.10	417.35	411.65	405.90	400.20
2348	2364	482.95	453.00	450.15	444.40	438.70	432.95	427.25	421.50	415.80	410.05	404.35
2364	2380	487.10	457.15	454.30	448.55	442.85	437.10	431.40	425.70	419.95	414.25	408.50
2380	2396	491.25	461.30	458.45	452.75	447.00	441.30	435.55	429.85	424.10	418.40	412.65
2396	2412	495.40	465.45	462.60	456.90	451.15	445.45	439.70	434.00	428.25	422.55	416.85
2412	2428	499.60	469.65	466.75	461.05	455.30	449.60	443.90	438.15	432.45	426.70	421.00
2428	2444	503.75	473.80	470.95	465.20	459.50	453.75	448.05	442.30	436.60	430.85	425.15
2444	2460	508.20	478.25	475.40	469.65	463.95	458.20	452.50	446.75	441.05	435.30	429.60
2460	2476	512.85	482.90	480.00	474.30	468.60	462.85	457.15	451.40	445.70	439.95	434.25
2476	2492	517.45	487.50	484.65	478.95	473.20	467.50	461.75	456.05	450.30	444.60	438.90
2492	2508	522.10	492.15	489.30	483.60	477.85	472.15	466.40	460.70	454.95	449.25	443.50
2508	2524	526.75	496.80	493.95	488.20	482.50	476.75	471.05	465.35	459.60	453.90	448.15
2524	2540	531.40	501.45	498.60	492.85	487.15	481.40	475.70	469.95	464.25	458.50	452.80

This table is available on TOD   D-5   Vous pouvez obtenir cette table sur TSD

Appendix 8-1P—Ontario Tax Tables

Ontario provincial tax deductions
Effective January 1, 2010
Weekly (52 pay periods a year)
**Also look up the tax deductions
in the federal table**

Retenues d'impôt provincial de l'Ontario
En vigueur le 1er janvier 2010
Hebdomadaire (52 périodes de paie par année)
**Cherchez aussi les retenues d'impôt
dans la table fédérale**

Pay / Rémunération			Provincial claim codes/Codes de demande provinciaux										
		0	1	2	3	4	5	6	7	8	9	10	
From / De	Less than / Moins de	Deduct from each pay / Retenez sur chaque paie											
	266	*	.00										
266 -	268	12.75	.20										
268 -	270	12.85	.40										
270 -	272	12.95	.60										
272 -	274	13.05	.75										
274 -	276	13.15	.95										
276 -	278	13.20	1.15										
278 -	280	13.30	1.35										
280 -	282	13.40	1.55										
282 -	284	13.50	1.70										
284 -	286	13.60	1.90	.05									
286 -	288	13.70	2.10	.20									
288 -	290	13.80	2.30	.40									
290 -	292	13.90	2.45	.60									
292 -	294	14.00	2.65	.80									
294 -	296	14.05	2.85	1.00									
296 -	298	14.15	3.05	1.15									
298 -	300	14.25	3.25	1.35									
300 -	302	14.35	3.40	1.55									
302 -	304	14.45	3.60	1.75									
304 -	306	14.55	3.80	1.90									
306 -	308	14.65	4.00	2.10									
308 -	310	14.75	4.15	2.30									
310 -	312	14.80	4.35	2.50									
312 -	314	14.90	4.55	2.65									
314 -	316	15.00	4.75	2.85									
316 -	318	15.10	4.90	3.05									
318 -	320	15.20	5.10	3.25									
320 -	322	15.30	5.30	3.45									
322 -	324	15.40	5.50	3.60									
324 -	326	15.50	5.70	3.80	.05								
326 -	328	15.60	5.85	4.00	.25								
328 -	330	15.65	6.05	4.20	.45								
330 -	332	15.75	6.25	4.35	.65								
332 -	334	15.85	6.45	4.55	.80								
334 -	336	15.95	6.60	4.75	1.00								
336 -	338	16.05	6.80	4.95	1.20								
338 -	340	16.15	7.00	5.10	1.40								
340 -	342	16.25	7.20	5.30	1.55								
342 -	344	16.35	7.35	5.50	1.75								
344 -	346	16.45	7.55	5.70	1.95								
346 -	348	16.50	7.75	5.90	2.15								
348 -	350	16.60	7.95	6.05	2.30								
350 -	352	16.70	8.00	6.25	2.50								
352 -	354	16.80	8.10	6.45	2.70								
354 -	356	16.90	8.20	6.65	2.90								
356 -	358	17.00	8.30	6.80	3.10								
358 -	360	17.10	8.40	7.00	3.25								
360 -	362	17.20	8.50	7.20	3.45								
362 -	364	17.30	8.60	7.40	3.65								
364 -	366	17.35	8.70	7.55	3.85	.10							
366 -	368	17.45	8.80	7.75	4.00	.30							
368 -	370	17.55	8.85	7.95	4.20	.45							
370 -	372	17.65	8.95	8.05	4.40	.65							
372 -	374	17.75	9.05	8.15	4.60	.85							

*You normally use claim code "0" only for non-resident employees. However, if you have non-resident employees who earn less than the minimum amount shown in the "Pay" column, you may not be able to use these tables. Instead, refer to the "Step-by-step calculation of tax deductions" in Section "A" of this publication.

*Le code de demande «0» est normalement utilisé seulement pour les non-résidents. Cependant, si la rémunération de votre employé non résidant est inférieure au montant minimum indiqué dans la colonne «Rémunération», vous ne pourrez peut-être pas utiliser ces tables. Reportez-vous alors au «Calcul des retenues d'impôt, étape par étape» dans la section «A» de cette publication.

This table is available on TOD   E-1   **Vous pouvez obtenir cette table sur TSD**

Ontario provincial tax deductions
Effective January 1, 2010
Weekly (52 pay periods a year)
**Also look up the tax deductions
in the federal table**

Retenues d'impôt provincial de l'Ontario
En vigueur le 1er janvier 2010
Hebdomadaire (52 périodes de paie par année)
**Cherchez aussi les retenues d'impôt
dans la table fédérale**

Pay Rémunération		Provincial claim codes/Codes de demande provinciaux										
		0	1	2	3	4	5	6	7	8	9	10
From Less than De Moins de		Deduct from each pay Retenez sur chaque paie										
374 - 378		17.90	9.20	8.25	4.85	1.15						
378 - 382		18.10	9.40	8.45	5.25	1.50						
382 - 386		18.25	9.60	8.65	5.60	1.90						
386 - 390		18.65	9.95	9.05	6.20	2.45	.20	.20	.20	.20	.20	.20
390 - 394		19.10	10.40	9.45	6.80	3.10	.45	.45	.45	.45	.45	.45
394 - 398		19.50	10.85	9.90	7.45	3.70	.70	.70	.70	.70	.70	.70
398 - 402		19.95	11.25	10.30	8.05	4.30	.90	.90	.90	.90	.90	.90
402 - 406		20.35	11.70	10.75	8.65	4.95	1.20	1.15	1.15	1.15	1.15	1.15
406 - 410		20.80	12.10	11.20	9.30	5.55	1.80	1.40	1.40	1.40	1.40	1.40
410 - 414		21.25	12.55	11.60	9.75	6.15	2.40	1.65	1.65	1.65	1.65	1.65
414 - 418		21.65	12.95	12.05	10.15	6.80	3.05	1.90	1.90	1.90	1.90	1.90
418 - 422		22.10	13.40	12.45	10.60	7.40	3.65	2.10	2.10	2.10	2.10	2.10
422 - 426		22.50	13.85	12.90	11.00	8.00	4.25	2.35	2.35	2.35	2.35	2.35
426 - 430		22.95	14.25	13.30	11.45	8.65	4.90	2.60	2.60	2.60	2.60	2.60
430 - 434		23.35	14.70	13.75	11.90	9.25	5.50	2.85	2.85	2.85	2.85	2.85
434 - 438		23.80	15.10	14.20	12.30	9.85	6.10	3.10	3.10	3.10	3.10	3.10
438 - 442		24.25	15.55	14.60	12.75	10.50	6.75	3.30	3.30	3.30	3.30	3.30
442 - 446		24.65	15.95	15.05	13.15	11.10	7.35	3.60	3.55	3.55	3.55	3.55
446 - 450		25.10	16.40	15.45	13.60	11.70	7.95	4.25	3.80	3.80	3.80	3.80
450 - 454		25.50	16.85	15.90	14.00	12.15	8.60	4.85	4.05	4.05	4.05	4.05
454 - 458		25.95	17.25	16.30	14.45	12.60	9.20	5.45	4.30	4.30	4.30	4.30
458 - 462		26.35	17.70	16.75	14.90	13.00	9.80	6.10	4.50	4.50	4.50	4.50
462 - 466		26.80	18.10	17.20	15.30	13.45	10.45	6.70	4.75	4.75	4.75	4.75
466 - 470		27.25	18.55	17.60	15.75	13.85	11.05	7.30	5.00	5.00	5.00	5.00
470 - 474		27.65	18.95	18.05	16.15	14.30	11.65	7.95	5.25	5.25	5.25	5.25
474 - 478		28.10	19.40	18.45	16.60	14.70	12.30	8.55	5.50	5.50	5.50	5.50
478 - 482		28.50	19.85	18.90	17.00	15.15	12.90	9.15	5.70	5.70	5.70	5.70
482 - 486		28.75	20.05	19.15	17.25	15.40	13.35	9.60	5.85	5.75	5.75	5.75
486 - 490		28.95	20.25	19.30	17.45	15.55	13.70	9.95	6.20	5.75	5.75	5.75
490 - 494		29.10	20.45	19.50	17.65	15.75	13.90	10.35	6.60	5.75	5.75	5.75
494 - 498		29.30	20.65	19.70	17.80	15.95	14.10	10.70	7.00	5.75	5.75	5.75
498 - 502		29.50	20.80	19.90	18.00	16.15	14.25	11.10	7.35	5.75	5.75	5.75
502 - 506		29.70	21.00	20.05	18.20	16.35	14.45	11.45	7.75	5.75	5.75	5.75
506 - 510		29.90	21.20	20.25	18.40	16.50	14.65	11.85	8.10	5.75	5.75	5.75
510 - 514		30.05	21.40	20.45	18.55	16.70	14.85	12.25	8.50	5.75	5.75	5.75
514 - 518		30.25	21.55	20.65	18.75	16.90	15.00	12.60	8.85	5.75	5.75	5.75
518 - 522		30.45	21.75	20.80	18.95	17.10	15.20	13.00	9.25	5.75	5.75	5.75
522 - 526		30.65	21.95	21.00	19.15	17.25	15.40	13.35	9.60	5.85	5.75	5.75
526 - 530		30.80	22.15	21.20	19.35	17.45	15.60	13.70	10.00	6.25	5.75	5.75
530 - 534		31.00	22.30	21.40	19.50	17.65	15.75	13.90	10.35	6.65	5.75	5.75
534 - 538		31.20	22.50	21.60	19.70	17.85	15.95	14.10	10.75	7.00	5.75	5.75
538 - 542		31.40	22.70	21.75	19.90	18.00	16.15	14.30	11.10	7.40	5.75	5.75
542 - 546		31.55	22.90	21.95	20.10	18.20	16.35	14.45	11.50	7.75	5.75	5.75
546 - 550		31.75	23.10	22.15	20.25	18.40	16.55	14.65	11.90	8.15	5.75	5.75
550 - 554		31.95	23.25	22.35	20.45	18.60	16.70	14.85	12.25	8.50	5.75	5.75
554 - 558		32.15	23.45	22.50	20.65	18.80	16.90	15.05	12.65	8.90	5.75	5.75
558 - 562		32.35	23.65	22.70	20.85	18.95	17.10	15.20	13.00	9.25	5.75	5.75
562 - 566		32.50	23.85	22.90	21.00	19.15	17.30	15.40	13.40	9.65	5.90	5.75
566 - 570		32.70	24.00	23.10	21.20	19.35	17.45	15.60	13.75	10.00	6.30	5.75
570 - 574		32.90	24.20	23.25	21.40	19.55	17.65	15.80	13.90	10.40	6.65	5.75
574 - 578		33.10	24.40	23.45	21.60	19.70	17.85	16.00	14.10	10.75	7.05	5.75
578 - 582		33.25	24.60	23.65	21.80	19.90	18.05	16.15	14.30	11.15	7.40	5.75
582 - 586		33.45	24.75	23.85	21.95	20.10	18.20	16.35	14.50	11.55	7.80	5.75
586 - 590		33.65	24.95	24.05	22.15	20.30	18.40	16.55	14.65	11.90	8.15	5.75
590 - 594		33.85	25.15	24.20	22.35	20.45	18.60	16.75	14.85	12.30	8.55	5.75

This table is available on TOD E-2 **Vous pouvez obtenir cette table sur TSD**

Ontario provincial tax deductions
Effective January 1, 2010
Weekly (52 pay periods a year)
**Also look up the tax deductions
in the federal table**

Retenues d'impôt provincial de l'Ontario
En vigueur le 1er janvier 2010
Hebdomadaire (52 périodes de paie par année)
**Cherchez aussi les retenues d'impôt
dans la table fédérale**

Pay / Rémunération			Provincial claim codes/Codes de demande provinciaux										
			0	1	2	3	4	5	6	7	8	9	10
From De	Less than Moins de		Deduct from each pay / Retenez sur chaque paie										
594	-	602	34.10	25.45	24.50	22.65	20.75	18.90	17.00	15.15	12.85	9.10	5.75
602	-	610	34.50	25.80	24.90	23.00	21.15	19.25	17.40	15.50	13.60	9.85	6.10
610	-	618	34.85	26.20	25.25	23.40	21.50	19.65	17.75	15.90	14.00	10.60	6.85
618	-	626	35.25	26.55	25.65	23.75	21.90	20.00	18.15	16.25	14.40	11.35	7.60
626	-	634	35.65	26.95	26.00	24.15	22.25	20.40	18.50	16.65	14.80	12.10	8.40
634	-	642	36.00	27.30	26.40	24.50	22.65	20.75	18.90	17.05	15.15	12.90	9.15
642	-	650	36.40	27.70	26.75	24.90	23.00	21.15	19.30	17.40	15.55	13.65	9.90
650	-	658	36.75	28.05	27.15	25.25	23.40	21.50	19.65	17.80	15.90	14.05	10.65
658	-	666	37.15	28.45	27.50	25.65	23.75	21.90	20.05	18.15	16.30	14.40	11.40
666	-	674	37.50	28.85	27.90	26.00	24.15	22.30	20.40	18.55	16.65	14.80	12.15
674	-	682	37.90	29.20	28.25	26.40	24.55	22.65	20.80	18.90	17.05	15.15	12.90
682	-	690	38.25	29.60	28.65	26.75	24.90	23.05	21.15	19.30	17.40	15.55	13.65
690	-	698	38.75	30.05	29.10	27.25	25.40	23.50	21.65	19.75	17.90	16.00	14.15
698	-	706	39.60	30.90	30.00	28.10	26.25	24.35	22.50	20.60	18.75	16.90	15.00
706	-	714	40.45	31.75	30.85	28.95	27.10	25.20	23.35	21.50	19.60	17.75	15.85
714	-	722	41.50	32.80	31.90	30.00	28.15	26.25	24.40	22.55	20.65	18.80	16.90
722	-	730	42.70	34.00	33.05	31.20	29.35	27.45	25.60	23.70	21.85	19.95	18.10
730	-	738	43.85	35.20	34.25	32.40	30.50	28.65	26.75	24.90	23.00	21.15	19.30
738	-	746	44.95	36.30	35.35	33.45	31.60	29.75	27.85	26.00	24.10	22.25	20.35
746	-	754	45.65	37.00	36.05	34.20	32.30	30.45	28.55	26.70	24.80	22.95	21.10
754	-	762	46.35	37.70	36.75	34.90	33.00	31.15	29.25	27.40	25.50	23.65	21.80
762	-	770	47.10	38.40	37.45	35.60	33.70	31.85	29.95	28.10	26.25	24.35	22.50
770	-	778	47.80	39.10	38.15	36.30	34.40	32.55	30.70	28.80	26.95	25.05	23.20
778	-	786	48.50	39.80	38.85	37.00	35.10	33.25	31.40	29.50	27.65	25.75	23.90
786	-	794	49.20	40.50	39.55	37.70	35.85	33.95	32.10	30.20	28.35	26.45	24.60
794	-	802	49.90	41.20	40.30	38.40	36.55	34.65	32.80	30.90	29.05	27.20	25.30
802	-	810	50.60	41.90	41.00	39.10	37.25	35.35	33.50	31.60	29.75	27.90	26.00
810	-	818	51.30	42.60	41.70	39.80	37.95	36.05	34.20	32.35	30.45	28.60	26.70
818	-	826	52.00	43.35	42.40	40.50	38.65	36.80	34.90	33.05	31.15	29.30	27.40
826	-	834	52.70	44.05	43.10	41.25	39.35	37.50	35.60	33.75	31.85	30.00	28.15
834	-	842	53.45	44.75	43.80	41.95	40.05	38.20	36.30	34.45	32.60	30.70	28.85
842	-	850	54.15	45.45	44.50	42.65	40.80	38.90	37.05	35.15	33.30	31.40	29.55
850	-	858	54.85	46.15	45.25	43.35	41.50	39.60	37.75	35.85	34.00	32.15	30.25
858	-	866	55.55	46.90	45.95	44.05	42.20	40.35	38.45	36.60	34.70	32.85	30.95
866	-	874	56.30	47.60	46.65	44.80	42.90	41.05	39.15	37.30	35.45	33.55	31.70
874	-	882	57.00	48.30	47.35	45.50	43.60	41.75	39.90	38.00	36.15	34.25	32.40
882	-	890	57.70	49.00	48.10	46.20	44.35	42.45	40.60	38.70	36.85	35.00	33.10
890	-	898	58.40	49.75	48.80	46.90	45.05	43.20	41.30	39.45	37.55	35.70	33.80
898	-	906	59.10	50.45	49.50	47.65	45.75	43.90	42.00	40.15	38.30	36.40	34.55
906	-	914	59.85	51.15	50.20	48.35	46.50	44.60	42.75	40.85	39.00	37.10	35.25
914	-	922	60.55	51.90	50.95	49.10	47.20	45.35	43.45	41.60	39.75	37.85	36.00
922	-	930	62.05	53.35	52.40	50.55	48.65	46.80	44.95	43.05	41.20	39.30	37.45
930	-	938	64.75	56.10	55.15	53.30	51.40	49.55	47.65	45.80	43.90	42.05	40.20
938	-	946	65.65	56.95	56.05	54.15	52.30	50.40	48.55	46.70	44.80	42.95	41.05
946	-	954	66.40	57.70	56.75	54.90	53.00	51.15	49.30	47.40	45.55	43.65	41.80
954	-	962	67.10	58.45	57.50	55.65	53.75	51.90	50.00	48.15	46.25	44.40	42.55
962	-	970	67.85	59.15	58.25	56.35	54.50	52.60	50.75	48.85	47.00	45.15	43.25
970	-	978	68.60	59.90	58.95	57.10	55.20	53.35	51.50	49.60	47.75	45.85	44.00
978	-	986	69.30	60.65	59.70	57.80	55.95	54.10	52.20	50.35	48.45	46.60	44.70
986	-	994	70.05	61.35	60.45	58.55	56.70	54.80	52.95	51.05	49.20	47.35	45.45
994	-	1002	70.80	62.10	61.15	59.30	57.40	55.55	53.65	51.80	49.95	48.05	46.20
1002	-	1010	71.50	62.85	61.90	60.00	58.15	56.30	54.40	52.55	50.65	48.80	46.90
1010	-	1018	72.25	63.55	62.60	60.75	58.90	57.00	55.15	53.25	51.40	49.50	47.65
1018	-	1026	73.00	64.30	63.35	61.50	59.60	57.75	55.85	54.00	52.15	50.25	48.40
1026	-	1034	73.70	65.00	64.10	62.20	60.35	58.45	56.60	54.75	52.85	51.00	49.10

This table is available on TOD   E-3   Vous pouvez obtenir cette table sur TSD

Ontario provincial tax deductions
Effective January 1, 2010
Weekly (52 pay periods a year)
**Also look up the tax deductions
in the federal table**

Retenues d'impôt provincial de l'Ontario
En vigueur le 1er janvier 2010
Hebdomadaire (52 périodes de paie par année)
**Cherchez aussi les retenues d'impôt
dans la table fédérale**

Pay Rémunération		Provincial claim codes/Codes de demande provinciaux										
		0	1	2	3	4	5	6	7	8	9	10
From Less than De Moins de		Deduct from each pay Retenez sur chaque paie										
1034 - 1046		74.60	65.95	65.00	63.15	61.25	59.40	57.50	55.65	53.75	51.90	50.05
1046 - 1058		75.70	67.05	66.10	64.25	62.35	60.50	58.60	56.75	54.85	53.00	51.15
1058 - 1070		76.80	68.15	67.20	65.35	63.45	61.60	59.70	57.85	55.95	54.10	52.25
1070 - 1082		77.90	69.25	68.30	66.40	64.55	62.70	60.80	58.95	57.05	55.20	53.30
1082 - 1094		79.00	70.35	69.40	67.50	65.65	63.80	61.90	60.05	58.15	56.30	54.40
1094 - 1106		80.10	71.45	70.50	68.60	66.75	64.90	63.00	61.15	59.25	57.40	55.50
1106 - 1118		81.20	72.55	71.60	69.70	67.85	66.00	64.10	62.25	60.35	58.50	56.60
1118 - 1130		82.30	73.60	72.70	70.80	68.95	67.05	65.20	63.35	61.45	59.60	57.70
1130 - 1142		83.40	74.70	73.80	71.90	70.05	68.15	66.30	64.45	62.55	60.70	58.80
1142 - 1154		84.50	75.80	74.90	73.00	71.15	69.25	67.40	65.55	63.65	61.80	59.90
1154 - 1166		85.60	76.90	76.00	74.10	72.25	70.35	68.50	66.60	64.75	62.90	61.00
1166 - 1178		86.70	78.00	77.10	75.20	73.35	71.45	69.60	67.70	65.85	64.00	62.10
1178 - 1190		87.80	79.10	78.20	76.30	74.45	72.55	70.70	68.80	66.95	65.10	63.20
1190 - 1202		88.95	80.20	79.30	77.40	75.55	73.65	71.80	69.90	68.05	66.20	64.30
1202 - 1214		90.30	81.30	80.35	78.50	76.65	74.75	72.90	71.00	69.15	67.25	65.40
1214 - 1226		91.60	82.40	81.45	79.60	77.75	75.85	74.00	72.10	70.25	68.35	66.50
1226 - 1238		92.90	83.50	82.55	80.70	78.85	76.95	75.10	73.20	71.35	69.45	67.60
1238 - 1250		94.25	84.60	83.65	81.80	79.90	78.05	76.20	74.30	72.45	70.55	68.70
1250 - 1262		95.55	85.70	84.75	82.90	81.00	79.15	77.30	75.40	73.55	71.65	69.80
1262 - 1274		96.85	86.80	85.85	84.00	82.10	80.25	78.40	76.50	74.65	72.75	70.90
1274 - 1286		98.20	87.90	86.95	85.10	83.20	81.35	79.50	77.60	75.75	73.85	72.00
1286 - 1298		99.50	89.10	88.05	86.20	84.30	82.45	80.55	78.70	76.85	74.95	73.10
1298 - 1310		100.80	90.40	89.25	87.30	85.40	83.55	81.65	79.80	77.95	76.05	74.20
1310 - 1322		102.15	91.70	90.60	88.40	86.50	84.65	82.75	80.90	79.05	77.15	75.30
1322 - 1334		103.45	93.05	91.90	89.65	87.60	85.75	83.85	82.00	80.10	78.25	76.40
1334 - 1346		104.75	94.35	93.25	91.00	88.75	86.85	84.95	83.10	81.20	79.35	77.50
1346 - 1358		106.10	95.65	94.55	92.30	90.05	87.95	86.05	84.20	82.30	80.45	78.60
1358 - 1370		107.40	97.00	95.85	93.60	91.35	89.10	87.15	85.30	83.40	81.55	79.70
1370 - 1382		108.70	98.30	97.20	94.95	92.70	90.45	88.25	86.40	84.50	82.65	80.75
1382 - 1394		110.90	100.45	99.35	97.10	94.85	92.60	90.35	88.35	86.45	84.60	82.70
1394 - 1406		114.25	103.80	102.70	100.45	98.20	95.95	93.70	91.45	89.60	87.75	85.85
1406 - 1418		115.55	105.15	104.00	101.75	99.50	97.30	95.05	92.80	90.70	88.80	86.95
1418 - 1430		116.90	106.45	105.35	103.10	100.85	98.60	96.35	94.10	91.85	89.90	88.05
1430 - 1442		118.70	108.00	106.85	104.60	102.35	100.10	97.85	95.65	93.40	91.20	89.30
1442 - 1454		120.80	109.60	108.45	106.20	103.95	101.75	99.50	97.25	95.00	92.75	90.65
1454 - 1466		122.90	111.20	110.05	107.85	105.60	103.35	101.10	98.85	96.60	94.35	92.10
1466 - 1478		125.00	112.80	111.70	109.45	107.20	104.95	102.70	100.45	98.20	95.95	93.70
1478 - 1490		127.10	114.40	113.30	111.05	108.80	106.55	104.30	102.05	99.80	97.55	95.30
1490 - 1502		129.15	116.00	114.90	112.65	110.40	108.15	105.90	103.65	101.40	99.15	96.95
1502 - 1514		131.25	117.70	116.50	114.25	112.00	109.75	107.50	105.25	103.05	100.80	98.55
1514 - 1526		133.35	119.80	118.35	115.85	113.60	111.35	109.10	106.90	104.65	102.40	100.15
1526 - 1538		135.45	121.90	120.45	117.50	115.20	113.00	110.75	108.50	106.25	104.00	101.75
1538 - 1550		137.55	124.00	122.50	119.60	116.85	114.60	112.35	110.10	107.85	105.60	103.35
1550 - 1562		139.60	126.05	124.60	121.70	118.75	116.20	113.95	111.70	109.45	107.20	104.95
1562 - 1574		141.70	128.15	126.70	123.80	120.85	117.95	115.55	113.30	111.05	108.80	106.55
1574 - 1586		143.80	130.25	128.80	125.85	122.95	120.05	117.15	114.90	112.65	110.40	108.20
1586 - 1598		145.90	132.35	130.85	127.95	125.05	122.10	119.20	116.50	114.25	112.05	109.80
1598 - 1610		147.95	134.40	132.95	130.05	127.10	124.20	121.30	118.35	115.90	113.65	111.40
1610 - 1622		150.05	136.50	135.05	132.15	129.20	126.30	123.35	120.45	117.55	115.25	113.00
1622 - 1634		152.15	138.60	137.15	134.20	131.30	128.40	125.45	122.55	119.60	116.85	114.60
1634 - 1646		154.25	140.70	139.25	136.30	133.40	130.45	127.55	124.65	121.70	118.80	116.20
1646 - 1658		156.35	142.80	141.30	138.40	135.50	132.55	129.65	126.70	123.80	120.90	117.95
1658 - 1670		158.40	144.85	143.40	140.50	137.55	134.65	131.75	128.80	125.90	122.95	120.05
1670 - 1682		160.50	146.95	145.50	142.60	139.65	136.75	133.80	130.90	128.00	125.05	122.15
1682 - 1694		162.60	149.05	147.60	144.65	141.75	138.85	135.90	133.00	130.05	127.15	124.25

This table is available on TOD   E-4   **Vous pouvez obtenir cette table sur TSD**

Ontario provincial tax deductions
Effective January 1, 2010
Weekly (52 pay periods a year)
Also look up the tax deductions
in the federal table

Retenues d'impôt provincial de l'Ontario
En vigueur le 1er janvier 2010
Hebdomadaire (52 périodes de paie par année)
Cherchez aussi les retenues d'impôt
dans la table fédérale

Pay / Rémunération		Provincial claim codes/Codes de demande provinciaux										
		0	1	2	3	4	5	6	7	8	9	10
From / De	Less than / Moins de	Deduct from each pay / Retenez sur chaque paie										
1694 -	1710	165.05	151.50	150.00	147.10	144.20	141.25	138.35	135.45	132.50	129.60	126.65
1710 -	1726	167.80	154.25	152.80	149.90	146.95	144.05	141.15	138.20	135.30	132.35	129.45
1726 -	1742	170.60	157.05	155.60	152.70	149.75	146.85	143.90	141.00	138.10	135.15	132.25
1742 -	1758	173.40	159.85	158.40	155.45	152.55	149.60	146.70	143.80	140.85	137.95	135.05
1758 -	1774	176.15	162.65	161.15	158.25	155.35	152.40	149.50	146.55	143.65	140.75	137.80
1774 -	1790	178.95	165.40	163.95	161.05	158.10	155.20	152.25	149.35	146.45	143.50	140.60
1790 -	1806	181.75	168.20	166.75	163.80	160.90	158.00	155.05	152.15	149.20	146.30	143.40
1806 -	1822	184.55	171.00	169.50	166.60	163.70	160.75	157.85	154.95	152.00	149.10	146.15
1822 -	1838	187.30	173.75	172.30	169.40	166.45	163.55	160.65	157.70	154.80	151.85	148.95
1838 -	1854	190.10	176.55	175.10	172.20	169.25	166.35	163.40	160.50	157.60	154.65	151.75
1854 -	1870	192.90	179.35	177.90	174.95	172.05	169.10	166.20	163.30	160.35	157.45	154.50
1870 -	1886	195.65	182.15	180.65	177.75	174.85	171.90	169.00	166.05	163.15	160.25	157.30
1886 -	1902	198.45	184.90	183.45	180.55	177.60	174.70	171.75	168.85	165.95	163.00	160.10
1902 -	1918	201.25	187.70	186.25	183.30	180.40	177.50	174.55	171.65	168.70	165.80	162.90
1918 -	1934	204.05	190.50	189.00	186.10	183.20	180.25	177.35	174.40	171.50	168.60	165.65
1934 -	1950	206.80	193.25	191.80	188.90	185.95	183.05	180.15	177.20	174.30	171.35	168.45
1950 -	1966	209.60	196.05	194.60	191.65	188.75	185.85	182.90	180.00	177.10	174.15	171.25
1966 -	1982	212.40	198.85	197.40	194.45	191.55	188.60	185.70	182.80	179.85	176.95	174.00
1982 -	1998	215.15	201.60	200.15	197.25	194.35	191.40	188.50	185.55	182.65	179.75	176.80
1998 -	2014	217.95	204.40	202.95	200.05	197.10	194.20	191.25	188.35	185.45	182.50	179.60
2014 -	2030	220.75	207.20	205.75	202.80	199.90	197.00	194.05	191.15	188.20	185.30	182.40
2030 -	2046	223.55	210.00	208.50	205.60	202.70	199.75	196.85	193.90	191.00	188.10	185.15
2046 -	2062	226.30	212.75	211.30	208.40	205.45	202.55	199.65	196.70	193.80	190.85	187.95
2062 -	2078	229.10	215.55	214.10	211.15	208.25	205.35	202.40	199.50	196.60	193.65	190.75
2078 -	2094	231.90	218.35	216.90	213.95	211.05	208.10	205.20	202.30	199.35	196.45	193.50
2094 -	2110	234.65	221.10	219.65	216.75	213.80	210.90	208.00	205.05	202.15	199.25	196.30
2110 -	2126	237.45	223.90	222.45	219.55	216.60	213.70	210.75	207.85	204.95	202.00	199.10
2126 -	2142	240.25	226.70	225.25	222.30	219.40	216.50	213.55	210.65	207.70	204.80	201.90
2142 -	2158	243.05	229.50	228.00	225.10	222.20	219.25	216.35	213.40	210.50	207.60	204.65
2158 -	2174	245.80	232.25	230.80	227.90	224.95	222.05	219.15	216.20	213.30	210.35	207.45
2174 -	2190	248.60	235.05	233.60	230.65	227.75	224.85	221.90	219.00	216.05	213.15	210.25
2190 -	2206	251.40	237.85	236.40	233.45	230.55	227.60	224.70	221.80	218.85	215.95	213.00
2206 -	2222	254.15	240.60	239.15	236.25	233.30	230.40	227.50	224.55	221.65	218.75	215.80
2222 -	2238	256.95	243.40	241.95	239.05	236.10	233.20	230.25	227.35	224.45	221.50	218.60
2238 -	2254	259.75	246.20	244.75	241.80	238.90	235.95	233.05	230.15	227.20	224.30	221.40
2254 -	2270	262.55	249.00	247.50	244.60	241.70	238.75	235.85	232.90	230.00	227.10	224.15
2270 -	2286	265.30	251.75	250.30	247.40	244.45	241.55	238.65	235.70	232.80	229.85	226.95
2286 -	2302	268.10	254.55	253.10	250.15	247.25	244.35	241.40	238.50	235.55	232.65	229.75
2302 -	2318	270.90	257.35	255.85	252.95	250.05	247.10	244.20	241.30	238.35	235.45	232.50
2318 -	2334	273.65	260.10	258.65	255.75	252.80	249.90	247.00	244.05	241.15	238.20	235.30
2334 -	2350	276.45	262.90	261.45	258.55	255.60	252.70	249.75	246.85	243.95	241.00	238.10
2350 -	2366	279.25	265.70	264.25	261.30	258.40	255.45	252.55	249.65	246.70	243.80	240.90
2366 -	2382	282.05	268.50	267.00	264.10	261.20	258.25	255.35	252.40	249.50	246.60	243.65
2382 -	2398	284.80	271.25	269.80	266.90	263.95	261.05	258.15	255.20	252.30	249.35	246.45
2398 -	2414	287.60	274.05	272.60	269.65	266.75	263.85	260.90	258.00	255.05	252.15	249.25
2414 -	2430	290.40	276.85	275.35	272.45	269.55	266.60	263.70	260.80	257.85	254.95	252.00
2430 -	2446	293.15	279.60	278.15	275.25	272.30	269.40	266.50	263.55	260.65	257.70	254.80
2446 -	2462	295.95	282.40	280.95	278.05	275.10	272.20	269.25	266.35	263.45	260.50	257.60
2462 -	2478	298.75	285.20	283.75	280.80	277.90	274.95	272.05	269.15	266.20	263.30	260.35
2478 -	2494	301.50	288.00	286.50	283.60	280.70	277.75	274.85	271.90	269.00	266.10	263.15
2494 -	2510	304.30	290.75	289.30	286.40	283.45	280.55	277.60	274.70	271.80	268.85	265.95
2510 -	2526	307.10	293.55	292.10	289.15	286.25	283.35	280.40	277.50	274.55	271.65	268.75
2526 -	2542	309.90	296.35	294.85	291.95	289.05	286.10	283.20	280.30	277.35	274.45	271.50
2542 -	2558	312.65	299.10	297.65	294.75	291.80	288.90	286.00	283.05	280.15	277.20	274.30
2558 -	2574	315.45	301.90	300.45	297.50	294.60	291.70	288.75	285.85	282.95	280.00	277.10

This table is available on TOD   E-5   Vous pouvez obtenir cette table sur TSD

Appendix 8-2—Simulated Canada Pension Plan Contributions

Students are advised to use this table for classroom purposes only. Although accurate for 2010, it has fewer categories of pay amounts than the official table.

Pay From	~	To	CPP	Pay From	~	To	CPP	Pay From	~	To	CPP	Pay From	~	To	CPP	Pay From	~	To	CPP
-	~	67.30	-	134.01	~	135.00	3.33	206.01	~	207.00	6.89	278.01	~	279.00	10.45	350.01	~	351.00	14.02
67.31	~	67.61	0.01	135.01	~	136.00	3.38	207.01	~	208.00	6.94	279.01	~	280.00	10.50	351.01	~	352.00	14.07
67.62	~	67.83	0.02	136.01	~	137.00	3.43	208.01	~	209.00	6.99	280.01	~	281.00	10.55	352.01	~	353.00	14.12
67.84	~	68.04	0.03	137.01	~	138.00	3.47	209.01	~	210.00	7.04	281.01	~	282.00	10.60	353.01	~	354.00	14.17
68.05	~	68.25	0.04	138.01	~	139.00	3.52	210.01	~	211.00	7.09	282.01	~	283.00	10.65	354.01	~	355.00	14.22
68.26	~	68.47	0.05	139.01	~	140.00	3.57	211.01	~	212.00	7.14	283.01	~	284.00	10.70	355.01	~	356.00	14.27
68.48	~	68.68	0.06	140.01	~	141.00	3.62	212.01	~	213.00	7.19	284.01	~	285.00	10.75	356.01	~	357.00	14.32
68.69	~	68.89	0.07	141.01	~	142.00	3.67	213.01	~	214.00	7.24	285.01	~	286.00	10.80	357.01	~	358.00	14.36
68.90	~	69.10	0.08	142.01	~	143.00	3.72	214.01	~	215.00	7.29	286.01	~	287.00	10.85	358.01	~	359.00	14.41
69.11	~	70.00	0.11	143.01	~	144.00	3.77	215.01	~	216.00	7.34	287.01	~	288.00	10.90	359.01	~	360.00	14.46
71.01	~	72.00	0.21	144.01	~	145.00	3.82	216.01	~	217.00	7.39	288.01	~	289.00	10.95	360.01	~	361.00	14.51
72.01	~	73.00	0.26	145.01	~	146.00	3.87	217.01	~	218.00	7.43	289.01	~	290.00	11.00	361.01	~	362.00	14.56
73.01	~	74.00	0.31	146.01	~	147.00	3.92	218.01	~	219.00	7.48	290.01	~	291.00	11.05	362.01	~	363.00	14.61
74.01	~	75.00	0.36	147.01	~	148.00	3.97	219.01	~	220.00	7.53	291.01	~	292.00	11.10	363.01	~	364.00	14.66
75.01	~	76.00	0.41	148.01	~	149.00	4.02	220.01	~	221.00	7.58	292.01	~	293.00	11.15	364.01	~	365.00	14.71
76.01	~	77.00	0.46	149.01	~	150.00	4.07	221.01	~	222.00	7.63	293.01	~	294.00	11.20	365.01	~	366.00	14.76
77.01	~	78.00	0.50	150.01	~	151.00	4.12	222.01	~	223.00	7.68	294.01	~	295.00	11.25	366.01	~	367.00	14.81
78.01	~	80.00	0.58	151.01	~	152.00	4.17	223.01	~	224.00	7.73	295.01	~	296.00	11.30	367.01	~	368.00	14.86
80.01	~	81.00	0.65	152.01	~	153.00	4.22	224.01	~	225.00	7.78	296.01	~	297.00	11.35	368.01	~	369.00	14.91
81.01	~	82.00	0.70	153.01	~	154.00	4.27	225.01	~	226.00	7.83	297.01	~	298.00	11.39	369.01	~	370.00	14.96
82.01	~	83.00	0.75	154.01	~	155.00	4.32	226.01	~	227.00	7.88	298.01	~	299.00	11.44	370.01	~	371.00	15.01
83.01	~	84.00	0.80	155.01	~	156.00	4.37	227.01	~	228.00	7.93	299.01	~	300.00	11.49	371.01	~	372.00	15.06
84.01	~	85.00	0.85	156.01	~	157.00	4.42	228.01	~	229.00	7.98	300.01	~	301.00	11.54	372.01	~	373.00	15.11
85.01	~	86.00	0.90	157.01	~	158.00	4.46	229.01	~	230.00	8.03	301.01	~	302.00	11.59	373.01	~	374.00	15.16
86.01	~	87.00	0.95	158.01	~	159.00	4.51	230.01	~	231.00	8.08	302.01	~	303.00	11.64	374.01	~	375.00	15.21
87.01	~	88.00	1.00	159.01	~	160.00	4.56	231.01	~	232.00	8.13	303.01	~	304.00	11.69	375.01	~	376.00	15.26
88.01	~	89.00	1.05	160.01	~	161.00	4.61	232.01	~	233.00	8.18	304.01	~	305.00	11.74	376.01	~	377.00	15.31
89.01	~	90.00	1.10	161.01	~	162.00	4.66	233.01	~	234.00	8.23	305.01	~	306.00	11.79	377.01	~	378.00	15.35
90.01	~	91.00	1.15	162.01	~	163.00	4.71	234.01	~	235.00	8.28	306.01	~	307.00	11.84	378.01	~	379.00	15.40
91.01	~	92.00	1.20	163.01	~	164.00	4.76	235.01	~	236.00	8.33	307.01	~	308.00	11.89	379.01	~	380.00	15.45
92.01	~	93.00	1.25	164.01	~	165.00	4.81	236.01	~	237.00	8.38	308.01	~	309.00	11.94	380.01	~	381.00	15.50
93.01	~	94.00	1.30	165.01	~	166.00	4.86	237.01	~	238.00	8.42	309.01	~	310.00	11.99	381.01	~	382.00	15.55
94.01	~	95.00	1.35	166.01	~	167.00	4.91	238.01	~	239.00	8.47	310.01	~	311.00	12.04	382.01	~	383.00	15.60
95.01	~	96.00	1.40	167.01	~	168.00	4.96	239.01	~	240.00	8.52	311.01	~	312.00	12.09	383.01	~	384.00	15.65
96.01	~	97.00	1.45	168.01	~	169.00	5.01	240.01	~	241.00	8.57	312.01	~	313.00	12.14	384.01	~	385.00	15.70
97.01	~	98.00	1.49	169.01	~	170.00	5.06	241.01	~	242.00	8.62	313.01	~	314.00	12.19	385.01	~	386.00	15.75
98.01	~	99.00	1.54	170.01	~	171.00	5.11	242.01	~	243.00	8.67	314.01	~	315.00	12.24	386.01	~	387.00	15.80
99.01	~	100.00	1.59	171.01	~	172.00	5.16	243.01	~	244.00	8.72	315.01	~	316.00	12.29	387.01	~	388.00	15.85
100.01	~	101.00	1.64	172.01	~	173.00	5.21	244.01	~	245.00	8.77	316.01	~	317.00	12.34	388.01	~	389.00	15.90
101.01	~	102.00	1.69	173.01	~	174.00	5.26	245.01	~	246.00	8.82	317.01	~	318.00	12.38	389.01	~	390.00	15.95
102.01	~	103.00	1.74	174.01	~	175.00	5.31	246.01	~	247.00	8.87	318.01	~	319.00	12.43	390.01	~	391.00	16.00
103.01	~	104.00	1.79	175.01	~	176.00	5.36	247.01	~	248.00	8.92	319.01	~	320.00	12.48	391.01	~	392.00	16.05
104.01	~	105.00	1.84	176.01	~	177.00	5.41	248.01	~	249.00	8.97	320.01	~	321.00	12.53	392.01	~	393.00	16.10
105.01	~	106.00	1.89	177.01	~	178.00	5.45	249.01	~	250.00	9.02	321.01	~	322.00	12.58	393.01	~	394.00	16.15
106.01	~	107.00	1.94	178.01	~	179.00	5.50	250.01	~	251.00	9.07	322.01	~	323.00	12.63	394.01	~	395.00	16.20
107.01	~	108.00	1.99	179.01	~	180.00	5.55	251.01	~	252.00	9.12	323.01	~	324.00	12.68	395.01	~	396.00	16.25
108.01	~	109.00	2.04	180.01	~	181.00	5.60	252.01	~	253.00	9.17	324.01	~	325.00	12.73	396.01	~	397.00	16.30
109.01	~	110.00	2.09	181.01	~	182.00	5.65	253.01	~	254.00	9.22	325.01	~	326.00	12.78	397.01	~	398.00	16.34
110.01	~	111.00	2.14	182.01	~	183.00	5.70	254.01	~	255.00	9.27	326.01	~	327.00	12.83	398.01	~	399.00	16.39
111.01	~	112.00	2.19	183.01	~	184.00	5.75	255.01	~	256.00	9.32	327.01	~	328.00	12.88	399.01	~	400.00	16.44
112.01	~	113.00	2.24	184.01	~	185.00	5.80	256.01	~	257.00	9.37	328.01	~	329.00	12.93	400.01	~	401.00	16.49
113.01	~	114.00	2.29	185.01	~	186.00	5.85	257.01	~	258.00	9.41	329.01	~	330.00	12.98	401.01	~	402.00	16.54
114.01	~	115.00	2.34	186.01	~	187.00	5.90	258.01	~	259.00	9.46	330.01	~	331.00	13.03	402.01	~	403.00	16.59
115.01	~	116.00	2.39	187.01	~	188.00	5.95	259.01	~	260.00	9.51	331.01	~	332.00	13.08	403.01	~	404.00	16.64
116.01	~	117.00	2.44	188.01	~	189.00	6.00	260.01	~	261.00	9.56	332.01	~	333.00	13.13	404.01	~	405.00	16.69
117.01	~	118.00	2.48	189.01	~	190.00	6.05	261.01	~	262.00	9.61	333.01	~	334.00	13.18	405.01	~	406.00	16.74
118.01	~	119.00	2.53	190.01	~	191.00	6.10	262.01	~	263.00	9.66	334.01	~	335.00	13.23	406.01	~	407.00	16.79
119.01	~	120.00	2.58	191.01	~	192.00	6.15	263.01	~	264.00	9.71	335.01	~	336.00	13.28	407.01	~	408.00	16.84
120.01	~	121.00	2.63	192.01	~	193.00	6.20	264.01	~	265.00	9.76	336.01	~	337.00	13.33	408.01	~	409.00	16.89
121.01	~	122.00	2.68	193.01	~	194.00	6.25	265.01	~	266.00	9.81	337.01	~	338.00	13.37	409.01	~	410.00	16.94
122.01	~	123.00	2.73	194.01	~	195.00	6.30	266.01	~	267.00	9.86	338.01	~	339.00	13.42	410.01	~	411.00	16.99
123.01	~	124.00	2.78	195.01	~	196.00	6.35	267.01	~	268.00	9.91	339.01	~	340.00	13.47	411.01	~	412.00	17.04
124.01	~	125.00	2.83	196.01	~	197.00	6.40	268.01	~	269.00	9.96	340.01	~	341.00	13.52	412.01	~	413.00	17.09
125.01	~	126.00	2.88	197.01	~	198.00	6.44	269.01	~	270.00	10.01	341.01	~	342.00	13.57	413.01	~	414.00	17.14
126.01	~	127.00	2.93	198.01	~	199.00	6.49	270.01	~	271.00	10.06	342.01	~	343.00	13.62	414.01	~	415.00	17.19
127.01	~	128.00	2.98	199.01	~	200.00	6.54	271.01	~	272.00	10.11	343.01	~	344.00	13.67	415.01	~	416.00	17.24
128.01	~	129.00	3.03	200.01	~	201.00	6.59	272.01	~	273.00	10.16	344.01	~	345.00	13.72	416.01	~	417.00	17.29
129.01	~	130.00	3.08	201.01	~	202.00	6.64	273.01	~	274.00	10.21	345.01	~	346.00	13.77	417.01	~	418.00	17.33
130.01	~	131.00	3.13	202.01	~	203.00	6.69	274.01	~	275.00	10.26	346.01	~	347.00	13.82	418.01	~	419.00	17.38
131.01	~	132.00	3.18	203.01	~	204.00	6.74	275.01	~	276.00	10.31	347.01	~	348.00	13.87	419.01	~	420.00	17.43
132.01	~	133.00	3.23	204.01	~	205.00	6.79	276.01	~	277.00	10.36	348.01	~	349.00	13.92	420.01	~	421.00	17.48
133.01	~	134.00	3.28	205.01	~	206.00	6.84	277.01	~	278.00	10.40	349.01	~	350.00	13.97	421.01	~	422.00	17.53

Maximum CPP contributions for the 2010 year total $2,163.15. This will probably increase from year to year.

Students are advised to use this table for classroom purposes only. Although accurate for 2010, it has fewer categories of pay amounts than the official table.

Pay From	To	CPP	Pay From	To	CPP	Pay From	To	CPP	Pay From	To	CPP	Pay From	To	CPP
422.01 ~	423.00	17.58	495.01 ~	496.00	21.20	636.01 ~	638.00	28.20	782.01 ~	784.00	35.43	1,120.01 ~	1,125.00	52.23
423.01 ~	424.00	17.63	496.01 ~	497.00	21.25	638.01 ~	640.00	28.30	784.01 ~	786.00	35.53	1,125.01 ~	1,130.00	52.48
424.01 ~	425.00	17.68	497.01 ~	498.00	21.29	640.01 ~	642.00	28.40	786.01 ~	788.00	35.63	1,130.01 ~	1,135.00	52.73
425.01 ~	426.00	17.73	498.01 ~	499.00	21.34	642.01 ~	644.00	28.50	788.01 ~	790.00	35.72	1,135.01 ~	1,140.00	52.97
426.01 ~	427.00	17.78	499.01 ~	500.00	21.39	644.01 ~	646.00	28.60	790.01 ~	792.00	35.82	1,140.01 ~	1,145.00	53.22
427.01 ~	428.00	17.83	500.01 ~	502.00	21.47	646.01 ~	648.00	28.70	792.01 ~	794.00	35.92	1,145.01 ~	1,150.00	53.47
428.01 ~	429.00	17.88	502.01 ~	504.00	21.57	648.01 ~	650.00	28.79	794.01 ~	796.00	36.02	1,150.01 ~	1,155.00	53.72
429.01 ~	430.00	17.93	504.01 ~	506.00	21.67	650.01 ~	652.00	28.89	796.01 ~	798.00	36.12	1,155.01 ~	1,160.00	53.96
430.01 ~	431.00	17.98	506.01 ~	508.00	21.77	652.01 ~	654.00	28.99	798.01 ~	800.00	36.22	1,160.01 ~	1,165.00	54.21
431.01 ~	432.00	18.03	508.01 ~	510.00	21.86	654.01 ~	656.00	29.09	800.01 ~	805.00	36.39	1,165.01 ~	1,170.00	54.46
432.01 ~	433.00	18.08	510.01 ~	512.00	21.96	656.01 ~	658.00	29.19	805.01 ~	810.00	36.64	1,170.01 ~	1,175.00	54.71
433.01 ~	434.00	18.13	512.01 ~	514.00	22.06	658.01 ~	660.00	29.29	810.01 ~	815.00	36.89	1,175.01 ~	1,180.00	54.95
434.01 ~	435.00	18.18	514.01 ~	516.00	22.16	660.01 ~	662.00	29.39	815.01 ~	820.00	37.13	1,180.01 ~	1,185.00	55.20
435.01 ~	436.00	18.23	516.01 ~	518.00	22.26	662.01 ~	664.00	29.49	820.01 ~	825.00	37.38	1,185.01 ~	1,190.00	55.45
436.01 ~	437.00	18.28	518.01 ~	520.00	22.36	664.01 ~	666.00	29.59	825.01 ~	830.00	37.63	1,190.01 ~	1,195.00	55.70
437.01 ~	438.00	18.32	520.01 ~	522.00	22.46	666.01 ~	668.00	29.69	830.01 ~	835.00	37.88	1,195.01 ~	1,200.00	55.94
438.01 ~	439.00	18.37	522.01 ~	524.00	22.56	668.01 ~	670.00	29.78	835.01 ~	840.00	38.12	1,200.01 ~	1,205.00	56.19
439.01 ~	440.00	18.42	524.01 ~	526.00	22.66	670.01 ~	672.00	29.88	840.01 ~	845.00	38.37	1,205.01 ~	1,210.00	56.44
440.01 ~	441.00	18.47	526.01 ~	528.00	22.76	672.01 ~	674.00	29.98	845.01 ~	850.00	38.62	1,210.01 ~	1,215.00	56.69
441.01 ~	442.00	18.52	528.01 ~	530.00	22.85	674.01 ~	676.00	30.08	850.01 ~	855.00	38.87	1,215.01 ~	1,220.00	56.93
442.01 ~	443.00	18.57	530.01 ~	532.00	22.95	676.01 ~	678.00	30.18	855.01 ~	860.00	39.11	1,220.01 ~	1,225.00	57.18
443.01 ~	444.00	18.62	532.01 ~	534.00	23.05	678.01 ~	680.00	30.28	860.01 ~	865.00	39.36	1,225.01 ~	1,230.00	57.43
444.01 ~	445.00	18.67	534.01 ~	536.00	23.15	680.01 ~	682.00	30.38	865.01 ~	870.00	39.61	1,230.01 ~	1,235.00	57.68
445.01 ~	446.00	18.72	536.01 ~	538.00	23.25	682.01 ~	684.00	30.48	870.01 ~	875.00	39.86	1,235.01 ~	1,240.00	57.92
446.01 ~	447.00	18.77	538.01 ~	540.00	23.35	684.01 ~	686.00	30.58	875.01 ~	880.00	40.10	1,240.01 ~	1,245.00	58.17
447.01 ~	448.00	18.82	540.01 ~	542.00	23.45	686.01 ~	688.00	30.68	880.01 ~	885.00	40.35	1,245.01 ~	1,250.00	58.42
448.01 ~	449.00	18.87	542.01 ~	544.00	23.55	688.01 ~	690.00	30.77	885.01 ~	890.00	40.60	1,250.01 ~	1,255.00	58.67
449.01 ~	450.00	18.92	544.01 ~	546.00	23.65	690.01 ~	692.00	30.87	890.01 ~	895.00	40.85	1,255.01 ~	1,260.00	58.91
450.01 ~	451.00	18.97	546.01 ~	548.00	23.75	692.01 ~	694.00	30.97	895.01 ~	900.00	41.09	1,260.01 ~	1,265.00	59.16
451.01 ~	452.00	19.02	548.01 ~	550.00	23.84	694.01 ~	696.00	31.07	900.01 ~	905.00	41.34	1,265.01 ~	1,270.00	59.41
452.01 ~	453.00	19.07	550.01 ~	552.00	23.94	696.01 ~	698.00	31.17	905.01 ~	910.00	41.59	1,270.01 ~	1,275.00	59.66
453.01 ~	454.00	19.12	552.01 ~	554.00	24.04	698.01 ~	700.00	31.27	910.01 ~	915.00	41.84	1,275.01 ~	1,280.00	59.90
454.01 ~	455.00	19.17	554.01 ~	556.00	24.14	700.01 ~	702.00	31.37	915.01 ~	920.00	42.08	1,280.01 ~	1,285.00	60.15
455.01 ~	456.00	19.22	556.01 ~	558.00	24.24	702.01 ~	704.00	31.47	920.01 ~	925.00	42.33	1,285.01 ~	1,290.00	60.40
456.01 ~	457.00	19.27	558.01 ~	560.00	24.34	704.01 ~	706.00	31.57	925.01 ~	930.00	42.58	1,290.01 ~	1,295.00	60.65
457.01 ~	458.00	19.31	560.01 ~	562.00	24.44	706.01 ~	708.00	31.67	930.01 ~	935.00	42.83	1,295.01 ~	1,300.00	60.89
458.01 ~	459.00	19.36	562.01 ~	564.00	24.54	708.01 ~	710.00	31.76	935.01 ~	940.00	43.07	1,300.01 ~	1,305.00	61.14
459.01 ~	460.00	19.41	564.01 ~	566.00	24.64	710.01 ~	712.00	31.86	940.01 ~	945.00	43.32	1,305.01 ~	1,310.00	61.39
460.01 ~	461.00	19.46	566.01 ~	568.00	24.74	712.01 ~	714.00	31.96	945.01 ~	950.00	43.57	1,310.01 ~	1,315.00	61.64
461.01 ~	462.00	19.51	568.01 ~	570.00	24.83	714.01 ~	716.00	32.06	950.01 ~	955.00	43.82	1,315.01 ~	1,320.00	61.88
462.01 ~	463.00	19.56	570.01 ~	572.00	24.93	716.01 ~	718.00	32.16	955.01 ~	960.00	44.06	1,320.01 ~	1,325.00	62.13
463.01 ~	464.00	19.61	572.01 ~	574.00	25.03	718.01 ~	720.00	32.26	960.01 ~	965.00	44.31	1,325.01 ~	1,330.00	62.38
464.01 ~	465.00	19.66	574.01 ~	576.00	25.13	720.01 ~	722.00	32.36	965.01 ~	970.00	44.56	1,330.01 ~	1,335.00	62.63
465.01 ~	466.00	19.71	576.01 ~	578.00	25.23	722.01 ~	724.00	32.46	970.01 ~	975.00	44.81	1,335.01 ~	1,340.00	62.87
466.01 ~	467.00	19.76	578.01 ~	580.00	25.33	724.01 ~	726.00	32.56	975.01 ~	980.00	45.05	1,340.01 ~	1,345.00	63.12
467.01 ~	468.00	19.81	580.01 ~	582.00	25.43	726.01 ~	728.00	32.66	980.01 ~	985.00	45.30	1,345.01 ~	1,350.00	63.37
468.01 ~	469.00	19.86	582.01 ~	584.00	25.53	728.01 ~	730.00	32.75	985.01 ~	990.00	45.55	1,350.01 ~	1,355.00	63.62
469.01 ~	470.00	19.91	584.01 ~	586.00	25.63	730.01 ~	732.00	32.85	990.01 ~	995.00	45.80	1,355.01 ~	1,360.00	63.86
470.01 ~	471.00	19.96	586.01 ~	588.00	25.73	732.01 ~	734.00	32.95	995.01 ~	1,000.00	46.04	1,360.01 ~	1,365.00	64.11
471.01 ~	472.00	20.01	588.01 ~	590.00	25.82	734.01 ~	736.00	33.05	1,000.01 ~	1,005.00	46.29	1,365.01 ~	1,370.00	64.36
472.01 ~	473.00	20.06	590.01 ~	592.00	25.92	736.01 ~	738.00	33.15	1,005.01 ~	1,010.00	46.54	1,370.01 ~	1,375.00	64.61
473.01 ~	474.00	20.11	592.01 ~	594.00	26.02	738.01 ~	740.00	33.25	1,010.01 ~	1,015.00	46.79	1,375.01 ~	1,380.00	64.85
474.01 ~	475.00	20.16	594.01 ~	596.00	26.12	740.01 ~	742.00	33.35	1,015.01 ~	1,020.00	47.03	1,380.01 ~	1,385.00	65.10
475.01 ~	476.00	20.21	596.01 ~	598.00	26.22	742.01 ~	744.00	33.45	1,020.01 ~	1,025.00	47.28	1,385.01 ~	1,390.00	65.35
476.01 ~	477.00	20.26	598.01 ~	600.00	26.32	744.01 ~	746.00	33.55	1,025.01 ~	1,030.00	47.53	1,390.01 ~	1,395.00	65.60
477.01 ~	478.00	20.30	600.01 ~	602.00	26.42	746.01 ~	748.00	33.65	1,030.01 ~	1,035.00	47.78	1,395.01 ~	1,400.00	65.84
478.01 ~	479.00	20.35	602.01 ~	604.00	26.52	748.01 ~	750.00	33.74	1,035.01 ~	1,040.00	48.02	1,400.01 ~	1,405.00	66.09
479.01 ~	480.00	20.40	604.01 ~	606.00	26.62	750.01 ~	752.00	33.84	1,040.01 ~	1,045.00	48.27	1,405.01 ~	1,410.00	66.34
480.01 ~	481.00	20.45	606.01 ~	608.00	26.72	752.01 ~	754.00	33.94	1,045.01 ~	1,050.00	48.52	1,410.01 ~	1,415.00	66.59
481.01 ~	482.00	20.50	608.01 ~	610.00	26.81	754.01 ~	756.00	34.04	1,050.01 ~	1,055.00	48.77	1,415.01 ~	1,420.00	66.83
482.01 ~	483.00	20.55	610.01 ~	612.00	26.91	756.01 ~	758.00	34.14	1,055.01 ~	1,060.00	49.01	1,420.01 ~	1,425.00	67.08
483.01 ~	484.00	20.60	612.01 ~	614.00	27.01	758.01 ~	760.00	34.24	1,060.01 ~	1,065.00	49.26	1,425.01 ~	1,430.00	67.33
484.01 ~	485.00	20.65	614.01 ~	616.00	27.11	760.01 ~	762.00	34.34	1,065.01 ~	1,070.00	49.51	1,430.01 ~	1,435.00	67.58
485.01 ~	486.00	20.70	616.01 ~	618.00	27.21	762.01 ~	764.00	34.44	1,070.01 ~	1,075.00	49.76	1,435.01 ~	1,440.00	67.82
486.01 ~	487.00	20.75	618.01 ~	620.00	27.31	764.01 ~	766.00	34.54	1,075.01 ~	1,080.00	50.00	1,440.01 ~	1,445.00	68.07
487.01 ~	488.00	20.80	620.01 ~	622.00	27.41	766.01 ~	768.00	34.64	1,080.01 ~	1,085.00	50.25	1,445.01 ~	1,450.00	68.32
488.01 ~	489.00	20.85	622.01 ~	624.00	27.51	768.01 ~	770.00	34.73	1,085.01 ~	1,090.00	50.50	1,450.01 ~	1,455.00	68.57
489.01 ~	490.00	20.90	624.01 ~	626.00	27.61	770.01 ~	772.00	34.83	1,090.01 ~	1,095.00	50.75	1,455.01 ~	1,460.00	68.81
490.01 ~	491.00	20.95	626.01 ~	628.00	27.71	772.01 ~	774.00	34.93	1,095.01 ~	1,100.00	50.99	1,460.01 ~	1,465.00	69.06
491.01 ~	492.00	21.00	628.01 ~	630.00	27.80	774.01 ~	776.00	35.03	1,100.01 ~	1,105.00	51.24	1,465.01 ~	1,470.00	69.31
492.01 ~	493.00	21.05	630.01 ~	632.00	27.90	776.01 ~	778.00	35.13	1,105.01 ~	1,110.00	51.49	1,470.01 ~	1,475.00	69.56
493.01 ~	494.00	21.10	632.01 ~	634.00	28.00	778.01 ~	780.00	35.23	1,110.01 ~	1,115.00	51.74	1,475.01 ~	1,480.00	69.80
494.01 ~	495.00	21.15	634.01 ~	636.00	28.10	780.01 ~	782.00	35.33	1,115.01 ~	1,120.00	51.98	1,480.01 ~	1,485.00	70.05

Maximum CPP contributions for the 2010 year total $2,163.15. This will probably increase from year to year.

Appendix 8-3—Simulated Employment Insurance Premium Calculations

Any number of pay periods a year — Page 1 of 2

Students are advised to use this table for classroom purposes only. Although accurate for 2010, it has fewer categories of Insurable Earnings than the official table.

Insurable Earnings From	To	EI Premium	Insurable Earnings From	To	EI Premium	Insurable Earnings From	To	EI Premium	Insurable Earnings From	To	EI Premium	Insurable Earnings From	To	EI Premium
– ~	0.68	0.01	32.98 ~	33.50	0.58	104.51 ~	105.50	1.82	176.51 ~	177.50	3.06	248.51 ~	249.50	4.31
0.69 ~	1.13	0.02	33.51 ~	34.50	0.59	105.51 ~	106.50	1.83	177.51 ~	178.50	3.08	249.51 ~	250.50	4.33
1.14 ~	1.59	0.02	34.51 ~	35.50	0.61	106.51 ~	107.50	1.85	178.51 ~	179.50	3.10	250.51 ~	251.50	4.34
1.60 ~	2.04	0.03	35.51 ~	36.50	0.62	107.51 ~	108.50	1.87	179.51 ~	180.50	3.11	251.51 ~	252.50	4.36
2.05 ~	2.49	0.04	36.51 ~	37.50	0.64	108.51 ~	109.50	1.89	180.51 ~	181.50	3.13	252.51 ~	253.50	4.38
2.50 ~	2.95	0.05	37.51 ~	38.50	0.66	109.51 ~	110.50	1.90	181.51 ~	182.50	3.15	253.51 ~	254.50	4.39
2.96 ~	3.40	0.05	38.51 ~	39.50	0.67	110.51 ~	111.50	1.92	182.51 ~	183.50	3.17	254.51 ~	255.50	4.41
3.41 ~	3.85	0.06	39.51 ~	40.50	0.69	111.51 ~	112.50	1.94	183.51 ~	184.50	3.18	255.51 ~	256.50	4.43
3.86 ~	4.31	0.07	40.51 ~	41.50	0.71	112.51 ~	113.50	1.95	184.51 ~	185.50	3.20	256.51 ~	257.50	4.45
4.32 ~	4.77	0.08	41.51 ~	42.50	0.73	113.51 ~	114.50	1.97	185.51 ~	186.50	3.22	257.51 ~	258.50	4.46
4.78 ~	5.22	0.09	42.51 ~	43.50	0.74	114.51 ~	115.50	1.99	186.51 ~	187.50	3.24	258.51 ~	259.50	4.48
5.23 ~	5.68	0.09	43.51 ~	44.50	0.76	115.51 ~	116.50	2.01	187.51 ~	188.50	3.25	259.51 ~	260.50	4.50
5.69 ~	6.13	0.10	44.51 ~	45.50	0.78	116.51 ~	117.50	2.02	188.51 ~	189.50	3.27	260.51 ~	261.50	4.52
6.14 ~	6.59	0.11	45.51 ~	46.50	0.80	117.51 ~	118.50	2.04	189.51 ~	190.50	3.29	261.51 ~	262.50	4.53
6.60 ~	7.04	0.12	46.51 ~	47.50	0.81	118.51 ~	119.50	2.06	190.51 ~	191.50	3.30	262.51 ~	263.50	4.55
7.05 ~	7.49	0.13	47.51 ~	48.50	0.83	119.51 ~	120.50	2.08	191.51 ~	192.50	3.32	263.51 ~	264.50	4.57
7.50 ~	7.95	0.13	48.51 ~	49.50	0.85	120.51 ~	121.50	2.09	192.51 ~	193.50	3.34	264.51 ~	265.50	4.58
7.96 ~	8.40	0.14	49.51 ~	50.50	0.87	121.51 ~	122.50	2.11	193.51 ~	194.50	3.36	265.51 ~	266.50	4.60
8.41 ~	8.86	0.15	50.51 ~	51.50	0.88	122.51 ~	123.50	2.13	194.51 ~	195.50	3.37	266.51 ~	267.50	4.62
8.87 ~	9.31	0.16	51.51 ~	52.50	0.90	123.51 ~	124.50	2.15	195.51 ~	196.50	3.39	267.51 ~	268.50	4.64
9.32 ~	9.77	0.17	52.51 ~	53.50	0.92	124.51 ~	125.50	2.16	196.51 ~	197.50	3.41	268.51 ~	269.50	4.65
9.78 ~	10.22	0.17	53.51 ~	54.50	0.93	125.51 ~	126.50	2.18	197.51 ~	198.50	3.43	269.51 ~	270.50	4.67
10.23 ~	10.68	0.18	54.51 ~	55.50	0.95	126.51 ~	127.50	2.20	198.51 ~	199.50	3.44	270.51 ~	271.50	4.69
10.69 ~	11.13	0.19	55.51 ~	56.50	0.97	127.51 ~	128.50	2.21	199.51 ~	200.50	3.46	271.51 ~	272.50	4.71
11.14 ~	11.59	0.20	56.51 ~	57.50	0.99	128.51 ~	129.50	2.23	200.51 ~	201.50	3.48	272.51 ~	273.50	4.72
11.60 ~	12.04	0.20	57.51 ~	58.50	1.00	129.51 ~	130.50	2.25	201.51 ~	202.50	3.49	273.51 ~	274.50	4.74
12.05 ~	12.50	0.21	58.51 ~	59.50	1.02	130.51 ~	131.50	2.27	202.51 ~	203.50	3.51	274.51 ~	275.50	4.76
12.51 ~	12.95	0.22	59.51 ~	60.50	1.04	131.51 ~	132.50	2.28	203.51 ~	204.50	3.53	275.51 ~	276.50	4.77
12.96 ~	13.41	0.23	60.51 ~	61.50	1.06	132.51 ~	133.50	2.30	204.51 ~	205.50	3.55	276.51 ~	277.50	4.79
13.42 ~	13.86	0.24	61.51 ~	62.50	1.07	133.51 ~	134.50	2.32	205.51 ~	206.50	3.56	277.51 ~	278.50	4.81
13.87 ~	14.32	0.24	62.51 ~	63.50	1.09	134.51 ~	135.50	2.34	206.51 ~	207.50	3.58	278.51 ~	279.50	4.83
14.33 ~	14.77	0.25	63.51 ~	64.50	1.11	135.51 ~	136.50	2.35	207.51 ~	208.50	3.60	279.51 ~	280.50	4.84
14.78 ~	15.23	0.26	64.51 ~	65.50	1.12	136.51 ~	137.50	2.37	208.51 ~	209.50	3.62	280.51 ~	281.50	4.86
15.24 ~	15.68	0.27	65.51 ~	66.50	1.14	137.51 ~	138.50	2.39	209.51 ~	210.50	3.63	281.51 ~	282.50	4.88
15.69 ~	16.14	0.28	66.51 ~	67.50	1.16	138.51 ~	139.50	2.40	210.51 ~	211.50	3.65	282.51 ~	283.50	4.90
16.15 ~	16.59	0.28	67.51 ~	68.50	1.18	139.51 ~	140.50	2.42	211.51 ~	212.50	3.67	283.51 ~	284.50	4.91
16.60 ~	17.05	0.29	68.51 ~	69.50	1.19	140.51 ~	141.50	2.44	212.51 ~	213.50	3.68	284.51 ~	285.50	4.93
17.06 ~	17.50	0.30	69.51 ~	70.50	1.21	141.51 ~	142.50	2.46	213.51 ~	214.50	3.70	285.51 ~	286.50	4.95
17.51 ~	17.96	0.31	70.51 ~	71.50	1.23	142.51 ~	143.50	2.47	214.51 ~	215.50	3.72	286.51 ~	287.50	4.97
17.97 ~	18.41	0.31	71.51 ~	72.50	1.25	143.51 ~	144.50	2.49	215.51 ~	216.50	3.74	287.51 ~	288.50	4.98
18.42 ~	18.87	0.32	72.51 ~	73.50	1.26	144.51 ~	145.50	2.51	216.51 ~	217.50	3.75	288.51 ~	289.50	5.00
18.88 ~	19.32	0.33	73.51 ~	74.50	1.28	145.51 ~	146.50	2.53	217.51 ~	218.50	3.77	289.51 ~	290.50	5.02
19.33 ~	19.78	0.34	74.51 ~	75.50	1.30	146.51 ~	147.50	2.54	218.51 ~	219.50	3.79	290.51 ~	291.50	5.03
19.79 ~	20.23	0.35	75.51 ~	76.50	1.31	147.51 ~	148.50	2.56	219.51 ~	220.50	3.81	291.51 ~	292.50	5.05
20.24 ~	20.69	0.35	76.51 ~	77.50	1.33	148.51 ~	149.50	2.58	220.51 ~	221.50	3.82	292.51 ~	293.50	5.07
20.70 ~	21.14	0.36	77.51 ~	78.50	1.35	149.51 ~	150.50	2.60	221.51 ~	222.50	3.84	293.51 ~	294.50	5.09
21.15 ~	21.60	0.37	78.51 ~	79.50	1.37	150.51 ~	151.50	2.61	222.51 ~	223.50	3.86	294.51 ~	295.50	5.10
21.61 ~	22.05	0.38	79.51 ~	80.50	1.38	151.51 ~	152.50	2.63	223.51 ~	224.50	3.88	295.51 ~	296.50	5.12
22.06 ~	22.51	0.39	80.51 ~	81.50	1.40	152.51 ~	153.50	2.65	224.51 ~	225.50	3.89	296.51 ~	297.50	5.14
22.52 ~	22.96	0.39	81.51 ~	82.50	1.42	153.51 ~	154.50	2.66	225.51 ~	226.50	3.91	297.51 ~	298.50	5.16
22.97 ~	23.42	0.40	82.51 ~	83.50	1.44	154.51 ~	155.50	2.68	226.51 ~	227.50	3.93	298.51 ~	299.50	5.17
23.43 ~	23.87	0.41	83.51 ~	84.50	1.45	155.51 ~	156.50	2.70	227.51 ~	228.50	3.94	299.51 ~	300.50	5.19
23.88 ~	24.33	0.42	84.51 ~	85.50	1.47	156.51 ~	157.50	2.72	228.51 ~	229.50	3.96	300.51 ~	301.50	5.21
24.34 ~	24.78	0.42	85.51 ~	86.50	1.49	157.51 ~	158.50	2.73	229.51 ~	230.50	3.98	301.51 ~	302.50	5.22
24.79 ~	25.24	0.43	86.51 ~	87.50	1.51	158.51 ~	159.50	2.75	230.51 ~	231.50	4.00	302.51 ~	303.50	5.24
25.25 ~	25.69	0.44	87.51 ~	88.50	1.52	159.51 ~	160.50	2.77	231.51 ~	232.50	4.01	303.51 ~	304.50	5.26
25.70 ~	26.15	0.45	88.51 ~	89.50	1.54	160.51 ~	161.50	2.79	232.51 ~	233.50	4.03	304.51 ~	305.50	5.28
26.16 ~	26.60	0.46	89.51 ~	90.50	1.56	161.51 ~	162.50	2.80	233.51 ~	234.50	4.05	305.51 ~	306.50	5.29
26.61 ~	27.06	0.46	90.51 ~	91.50	1.57	162.51 ~	163.50	2.82	234.51 ~	235.50	4.07	306.51 ~	307.50	5.31
27.07 ~	27.51	0.47	91.51 ~	92.50	1.59	163.51 ~	164.50	2.84	235.51 ~	236.50	4.08	307.51 ~	308.50	5.33
27.52 ~	27.97	0.48	92.51 ~	93.50	1.61	164.51 ~	165.50	2.85	236.51 ~	237.50	4.10	308.51 ~	309.50	5.35
27.98 ~	28.42	0.49	93.51 ~	94.50	1.63	165.51 ~	166.50	2.87	237.51 ~	238.50	4.12	309.51 ~	310.50	5.36
28.43 ~	28.88	0.50	94.51 ~	95.50	1.64	166.51 ~	167.50	2.89	238.51 ~	239.50	4.13	310.51 ~	311.50	5.38
28.89 ~	29.33	0.50	95.51 ~	96.50	1.66	167.51 ~	168.50	2.91	239.51 ~	240.50	4.15	311.51 ~	312.50	5.40
29.34 ~	29.79	0.51	96.51 ~	97.50	1.68	168.51 ~	169.50	2.92	240.51 ~	241.50	4.17	312.51 ~	313.50	5.41
29.80 ~	30.24	0.52	97.51 ~	98.50	1.70	169.51 ~	170.50	2.94	241.51 ~	242.50	4.19	313.51 ~	314.50	5.43
30.25 ~	30.70	0.53	98.51 ~	99.50	1.71	170.51 ~	171.50	2.96	242.51 ~	243.50	4.20	314.51 ~	315.50	5.45
30.71 ~	31.15	0.54	99.51 ~	100.50	1.73	171.51 ~	172.50	2.98	243.51 ~	244.50	4.22	315.51 ~	316.50	5.47
31.16 ~	31.61	0.54	100.51 ~	101.50	1.75	172.51 ~	173.50	2.99	244.51 ~	245.50	4.24	316.51 ~	317.50	5.48
31.62 ~	32.06	0.55	101.51 ~	102.50	1.76	173.51 ~	174.50	3.01	245.51 ~	246.50	4.26	317.51 ~	318.50	5.50
32.07 ~	32.52	0.56	102.51 ~	103.50	1.78	174.51 ~	175.50	3.03	246.51 ~	247.50	4.27	318.51 ~	319.50	5.52
32.53 ~	32.97	0.57	103.51 ~	104.50	1.80	175.51 ~	176.50	3.04	247.51 ~	248.50	4.29	319.51 ~	320.50	5.54

Students are advised to use this table for classroom purposes only. Although accurate for 2010, it has fewer categories of pay amounts than the official table.

Insurable Earnings From	To	EI Premium	Insurable Earnings From	To	EI Premium	Insurable Earnings From	To	EI Premium	Insurable Earnings From	To	EI Premium	Insurable Earnings From	To	EI Premium
320.51 ~	321.50	5.55	436.51 ~	438.50	7.57	582.56 ~	584.50	10.10	728.51 ~	730.50	12.62	946.51 ~	949.50	16.40
321.51 ~	322.50	5.57	438.51 ~	440.50	7.60	584.51 ~	586.50	10.13	730.51 ~	733.50	12.66	949.51 ~	954.50	16.47
322.51 ~	323.50	5.59	440.51 ~	442.50	7.64	586.51 ~	588.50	10.16	733.51 ~	736.50	12.72	954.51 ~	959.50	16.56
323.51 ~	324.50	5.61	442.51 ~	444.50	7.67	588.51 ~	590.50	10.20	736.51 ~	739.50	12.77	959.51 ~	964.50	16.64
324.51 ~	325.50	5.62	444.51 ~	446.50	7.71	590.51 ~	592.50	10.23	739.51 ~	742.50	12.82	964.51 ~	969.50	16.73
325.51 ~	326.50	5.64	446.51 ~	448.50	7.74	592.51 ~	594.50	10.27	742.51 ~	745.50	12.87	969.51 ~	974.50	16.82
326.51 ~	327.50	5.66	448.51 ~	450.50	7.78	594.51 ~	596.50	10.30	745.51 ~	748.50	12.92	974.51 ~	979.50	16.90
327.51 ~	328.50	5.67	450.51 ~	452.50	7.81	596.51 ~	598.50	10.34	748.51 ~	751.50	12.98	979.51 ~	984.50	16.99
328.51 ~	329.50	5.69	452.51 ~	454.50	7.85	598.51 ~	600.50	10.37	751.51 ~	754.50	13.03	984.51 ~	989.50	17.08
329.51 ~	330.50	5.71	454.51 ~	456.50	7.88	600.51 ~	602.50	10.41	754.51 ~	757.50	13.08	989.51 ~	994.50	17.16
330.51 ~	331.50	5.73	456.51 ~	458.50	7.91	602.51 ~	604.50	10.44	757.51 ~	760.50	13.13	994.51 ~	999.50	17.25
331.51 ~	332.50	5.74	458.51 ~	460.50	7.95	604.51 ~	606.50	10.48	760.51 ~	763.50	13.18	999.51 ~	1,004.50	17.33
332.51 ~	333.50	5.76	460.51 ~	462.50	7.98	606.51 ~	608.50	10.51	763.51 ~	766.50	13.23	1,004.51 ~	1,009.50	17.42
333.51 ~	334.50	5.78	462.51 ~	464.50	8.02	608.51 ~	610.50	10.54	766.51 ~	769.50	13.29	1,009.51 ~	1,014.50	17.51
334.51 ~	335.50	5.80	464.51 ~	466.50	8.05	610.51 ~	612.50	10.58	769.51 ~	772.50	13.34	1,014.51 ~	1,019.50	17.59
335.51 ~	336.50	5.81	466.51 ~	468.50	8.09	612.51 ~	614.50	10.61	772.51 ~	775.50	13.39	1,019.51 ~	1,024.50	17.68
336.51 ~	337.50	5.83	468.51 ~	470.50	8.12	614.51 ~	616.50	10.65	775.51 ~	778.50	13.44	1,024.51 ~	1,029.50	17.77
337.51 ~	338.50	5.85	470.51 ~	472.50	8.16	616.51 ~	618.50	10.68	778.51 ~	781.50	13.49	1,029.51 ~	1,034.50	17.85
338.51 ~	339.50	5.86	472.51 ~	474.50	8.19	618.51 ~	620.50	10.72	781.51 ~	784.50	13.55	1,034.51 ~	1,039.50	17.94
339.51 ~	340.50	5.88	474.51 ~	476.50	8.23	620.51 ~	622.50	10.75	784.51 ~	787.50	13.60	1,039.51 ~	1,044.50	18.03
340.51 ~	341.50	5.90	476.51 ~	478.50	8.26	622.51 ~	624.50	10.79	787.51 ~	790.50	13.65	1,044.51 ~	1,049.50	18.11
341.51 ~	342.50	5.92	478.51 ~	480.50	8.30	624.51 ~	626.50	10.82	790.51 ~	793.50	13.70	1,049.51 ~	1,054.50	18.20
342.51 ~	343.50	5.93	480.51 ~	482.50	8.33	626.51 ~	628.50	10.86	793.51 ~	796.50	13.75	1,054.51 ~	1,059.50	18.29
343.51 ~	344.50	5.95	482.51 ~	484.50	8.36	628.51 ~	630.50	10.89	796.51 ~	799.50	13.81	1,059.51 ~	1,064.50	18.37
344.51 ~	345.50	5.97	484.51 ~	486.50	8.40	630.51 ~	632.50	10.93	799.51 ~	802.50	13.86	1,064.51 ~	1,069.50	18.46
345.51 ~	346.50	5.99	486.51 ~	488.50	8.43	632.51 ~	634.50	10.96	802.51 ~	805.50	13.91	1,069.51 ~	1,074.50	18.55
346.51 ~	347.50	6.00	488.51 ~	490.50	8.47	634.51 ~	636.50	10.99	805.51 ~	808.50	13.96	1,074.51 ~	1,079.50	18.63
347.51 ~	348.50	6.02	490.51 ~	492.50	8.50	636.51 ~	638.50	11.03	808.51 ~	811.50	14.01	1,079.51 ~	1,084.50	18.72
348.51 ~	349.50	6.04	492.51 ~	494.50	8.54	638.51 ~	640.50	11.06	811.51 ~	814.50	14.06	1,084.51 ~	1,089.50	18.81
349.51 ~	350.50	6.06	494.51 ~	496.50	8.57	640.51 ~	642.50	11.10	814.51 ~	817.50	14.12	1,089.51 ~	1,094.50	18.89
350.51 ~	352.50	6.08	496.51 ~	498.50	8.61	642.51 ~	644.50	11.13	817.51 ~	820.50	14.17	1,094.51 ~	1,099.50	18.98
352.51 ~	354.50	6.12	498.51 ~	500.50	8.64	644.51 ~	646.50	11.17	820.51 ~	823.50	14.22	1,099.51 ~	1,104.50	19.06
354.51 ~	356.50	6.15	500.51 ~	502.50	8.68	646.51 ~	648.50	11.20	823.51 ~	826.50	14.27	1,104.51 ~	1,109.50	19.15
356.51 ~	358.50	6.18	502.51 ~	504.50	8.71	648.51 ~	650.50	11.24	826.51 ~	829.50	14.32	1,109.51 ~	1,114.50	19.24
358.51 ~	360.50	6.22	504.51 ~	506.50	8.75	650.51 ~	652.50	11.27	829.51 ~	832.50	14.38	1,114.51 ~	1,119.50	19.32
360.51 ~	362.50	6.25	506.51 ~	508.50	8.78	652.51 ~	654.50	11.31	832.51 ~	835.50	14.43	1,119.51 ~	1,124.50	19.41
362.51 ~	364.50	6.29	508.51 ~	510.50	8.81	654.51 ~	656.50	11.34	835.51 ~	838.50	14.48	1,124.51 ~	1,129.50	19.50
364.51 ~	366.50	6.32	510.51 ~	512.50	8.85	656.51 ~	658.50	11.37	838.51 ~	841.50	14.53	1,129.51 ~	1,134.50	19.58
366.51 ~	368.50	6.36	512.51 ~	514.50	8.88	658.51 ~	660.50	11.41	841.51 ~	844.50	14.58	1,134.51 ~	1,139.50	19.67
368.51 ~	370.50	6.39	514.51 ~	516.50	8.92	660.51 ~	662.50	11.44	844.51 ~	847.50	14.64	1,139.51 ~	1,144.50	19.76
370.51 ~	372.50	6.43	516.51 ~	518.50	8.95	662.51 ~	664.50	11.48	847.51 ~	850.50	14.69	1,144.51 ~	1,149.50	19.84
372.51 ~	374.50	6.46	518.51 ~	520.50	8.99	664.51 ~	666.50	11.51	850.51 ~	853.50	14.74	1,149.51 ~	1,154.50	19.93
374.51 ~	376.50	6.50	520.51 ~	522.50	9.02	666.51 ~	668.50	11.55	853.51 ~	856.50	14.79	1,154.51 ~	1,159.50	20.02
376.51 ~	378.50	6.53	522.51 ~	524.50	9.06	668.51 ~	670.50	11.58	856.51 ~	859.50	14.84	1,159.51 ~	1,164.50	20.10
378.51 ~	380.50	6.57	524.51 ~	526.50	9.09	670.51 ~	672.50	11.62	859.51 ~	862.50	14.90	1,164.51 ~	1,174.50	20.23
380.51 ~	382.50	6.60	526.51 ~	528.50	9.13	672.51 ~	674.50	11.65	862.51 ~	865.50	14.95	1,174.51 ~	1,184.50	20.41
382.51 ~	384.50	6.63	528.51 ~	530.50	9.16	674.51 ~	676.50	11.69	865.51 ~	868.50	15.00	1,184.51 ~	1,194.50	20.58
384.51 ~	386.50	6.67	530.51 ~	532.50	9.20	676.51 ~	678.50	11.72	868.51 ~	871.50	15.05	1,194.51 ~	1,204.50	20.75
386.51 ~	388.50	6.70	532.51 ~	534.50	9.23	678.51 ~	680.50	11.76	871.51 ~	874.50	15.10	1,204.51 ~	1,214.50	20.92
388.51 ~	390.50	6.74	534.51 ~	536.50	9.26	680.51 ~	682.50	11.79	874.51 ~	877.50	15.15	1,214.51 ~	1,224.50	21.10
390.51 ~	392.50	6.77	536.51 ~	538.50	9.30	682.51 ~	684.50	11.82	877.51 ~	880.50	15.21	1,224.51 ~	1,234.50	21.27
392.51 ~	394.50	6.81	538.51 ~	540.50	9.33	684.51 ~	686.50	11.86	880.51 ~	883.50	15.26	1,234.51 ~	1,244.50	21.44
394.51 ~	396.50	6.84	540.51 ~	542.50	9.37	686.51 ~	688.50	11.89	883.51 ~	886.50	15.31	1,244.51 ~	1,254.50	21.62
396.51 ~	398.50	6.88	542.51 ~	544.50	9.40	688.51 ~	690.50	11.93	886.51 ~	889.50	15.36	1,254.51 ~	1,264.50	21.79
398.51 ~	400.50	6.91	544.51 ~	546.50	9.44	690.51 ~	692.50	11.96	889.51 ~	892.50	15.41	1,264.51 ~	1,274.50	21.96
400.51 ~	402.50	6.95	546.51 ~	548.50	9.47	692.51 ~	694.50	12.00	892.51 ~	895.50	15.47	1,274.51 ~	1,284.50	22.14
402.51 ~	404.50	6.98	548.51 ~	550.50	9.51	694.51 ~	696.50	12.03	895.51 ~	898.50	15.52	1,284.51 ~	1,294.50	22.31
404.51 ~	406.50	7.02	550.51 ~	552.50	9.54	696.51 ~	698.50	12.07	898.51 ~	901.50	15.57	1,294.51 ~	1,304.50	22.48
406.51 ~	408.50	7.05	552.51 ~	554.50	9.58	698.51 ~	700.50	12.10	901.51 ~	904.50	15.62	1,304.51 ~	1,314.50	22.65
408.51 ~	410.50	7.08	554.51 ~	556.50	9.61	700.51 ~	702.50	12.14	904.51 ~	907.50	15.67	1,314.51 ~	1,324.50	22.83
410.51 ~	412.50	7.12	556.51 ~	558.50	9.64	702.51 ~	704.50	12.17	907.51 ~	910.50	15.73	1,324.51 ~	1,334.50	23.00
412.51 ~	414.50	7.15	558.51 ~	560.50	9.68	704.51 ~	706.50	12.21	910.51 ~	913.50	15.78	1,334.51 ~	1,344.50	23.17
414.51 ~	416.50	7.19	560.51 ~	562.50	9.71	706.51 ~	708.50	12.24	913.51 ~	916.50	15.83	1,344.51 ~	1,354.50	23.35
416.51 ~	418.50	7.22	562.51 ~	564.50	9.75	708.51 ~	710.50	12.27	916.51 ~	919.50	15.88	1,354.51 ~	1,364.50	23.52
418.51 ~	420.50	7.26	564.51 ~	566.50	9.78	710.51 ~	712.50	12.31	919.51 ~	922.50	15.93	1,364.51 ~	1,374.50	23.69
420.51 ~	422.50	7.29	566.51 ~	568.50	9.82	712.51 ~	714.50	12.34	922.51 ~	925.50	15.99	1,374.51 ~	1,384.50	23.87
422.51 ~	424.50	7.33	568.51 ~	570.50	9.85	714.51 ~	716.50	12.38	925.51 ~	928.50	16.04	1,384.51 ~	1,394.50	24.04
424.51 ~	426.50	7.36	570.51 ~	572.50	9.89	716.51 ~	718.50	12.41	928.51 ~	931.50	16.09	1,394.51 ~	1,404.50	24.21
426.51 ~	428.50	7.40	572.51 ~	574.50	9.92	718.51 ~	720.50	12.45	931.51 ~	934.50	16.14	1,404.51 ~	1,414.50	24.38
428.51 ~	430.50	7.43	574.51 ~	576.50	9.96	720.51 ~	722.50	12.48	934.51 ~	937.50	16.19	1,414.51 ~	1,424.50	24.56
430.51 ~	432.50	7.47	576.51 ~	578.50	9.99	722.51 ~	724.50	12.52	937.51 ~	940.50	16.24	1,424.51 ~	1,434.50	24.73
432.51 ~	434.50	7.50	578.51 ~	580.50	10.03	724.51 ~	726.50	12.55	940.51 ~	943.50	16.30	1,434.51 ~	1,444.50	24.90
434.51 ~	436.50	7.53	580.51 ~	582.50	10.06	726.51 ~	728.50	12.59	943.51 ~	946.50	16.35	1,444.51 ~	1,454.50	25.08

To obtain deductions for amounts over $1454.50, (or to calculate exact deductions), multiply the earnings amount by 0.0173

Note - Yearly maximum employee premiums are $747.36 (maximum insurable earnings are $43,200)

9 The Employer's Tax Responsibilities

Principles and Procedures

THE BIG PICTURE

When a Canadian thinks of coffee, it is often our homegrown Tim Hortons that springs to mind. But there is another coffee company that we readily identify with—Starbucks. According to the company's latest numbers on their Canadian website, there are around 1,000 company or licensed stores in Canada, and the number has been growing steadily—despite recent store closings in the United States and elsewhere (in Australia, almost three-quarters of their stores were closed).

At last count, at least eight books have been written about the Starbucks success story. Some call it luck; some good management; others cite that old business maxim: location, location, location. But all agree to some extent that a major ingredient in the Starbucks coffee story is their employees and how they are treated.

Whether they are part-time baristas—the front-line employees who pull espresso for your cappuccino—or full-time financial executives, Starbucks employees are all partners in the enterprise. Partners are all eligible for a long list of benefits, including these listed on the Canadian website:

- Competitive pay
- Insurance coverage: health, dental, vision, drugs, disability, and life
- Bonuses
- Paid time off
- Retirement savings plan
- Stock options
- Adoption assistance
- Domestic partner benefits
- Emergency financial aid
- Child- and elder-care support services
- A free 454-gram bag of coffee each week.

A recent study compared Starbucks' job satisfaction rate of 82% with the 50% average for all companies. It seems like its policies pay off big-time.

Truth to tell, the company has also faced some challenging legal battles relating to its employees. In addition to contending with unions and such, some legal issues have centred on the share of tips that shift managers can take home—and in that case, it was a legal challenge started not by the company but by employees.

Whatever the challenges, Starbucks continues to try to treat its partners with respect and dignity. There is a major cost to this, of course. All those benefits are expensive, and each one needs to be properly accounted for. This chapter covers how to account for many of the benefits that companies like Starbucks encounter each and every pay period, including our uniquely Canadian CPP, EI, and, in most places, WCB.

Sources: Principally, Starbucks' Canadian website (www.starbucks.ca), with background material from other Internet locations such as the U.S. website (www.starbucks.com), Wikipedia articles relating to Starbucks, and others. Use your search engine to choose from hundreds of related sites.

Learning Objectives

1. How to calculate and record the employer's expenses associated with payroll (p. 414)
2. How employers remit and record their employees' deductions to the Canada Revenue Agency (p. 418)
3. Employers' annual responsibilities for filing the T4 Summary form (p. 422)

Detailed information about how a business must deal with payroll remittances can be found by downloading form (or file) T4001, Employer's Guide—Payroll Deductions and Remittances from the CRA website:

www.cra-arc.gc.ca

In the previous chapter, we examined how ABC Company calculates its weekly payroll and maintains a record of each employee's earnings. In Canada, many employers must remit to the government monthly the totals deducted from their employees in the previous month. Certain employers (those who have more than $15,000 to remit monthly) must send in their withholdings more often, while some very small employers may now remit only every quarter (only if there are withholdings of less than $1,000 per month). In the balance of this chapter, we will assume an employer who remits monthly.

An important fact in our country is that employers share the total cost of CPP and EI with their employees. The cost of workers' compensation is borne by the employer alone. The employer's share of these payments is considered an expense of doing business and is accounted for as such. In this chapter, we will examine how this expense is calculated and illustrate the forms that need to be completed (and sent to the government) as part of the payroll process. We will also examine the accounting procedures that must be followed.

Learning Unit 9-1

Employer's Expenses Associated with Payroll

If you take over another employer's business, you must still obtain a new identification number (unless the business is a corporation).

While the remittance cheque goes to the federal government, a part of the tax deducted is forwarded to the provinces.

Employers must apply for a remittance number (called a **business number**) in order to handle their responsibilities for payroll correctly. A special form called a Request for a Business Number (Form RC1(E)) must be submitted, which asks the employer to answer several questions about the business's operations. Once this form is processed, the employer is issued a permanent unique identification number. This number is used to ensure that the amounts of money sent (we often say *remitted*) to the government each month are recorded correctly; that is, in the right company's account. The same number is also used for GST/HST remittances and other purposes.

The actual amount sent to the federal government (concerning payroll) each month depends on three deductions taken from employees' wages:

1. Income tax (total of federal plus provincial)
2. Canada (or Quebec) Pension Plan
3. Employment Insurance

Notice that the income tax amount is sent by the employer, but it is not an expense because the employees are paying it.

A simple **remittance formula** can be used to ensure that the correct figure is remitted each period:

Income tax deducted × 1.0	= $XXX.XX
CPP deducted × 2.0	= XXX.XX
EI deducted × 2.4	= XXX.XX
Total	= $XXX.XX

We will soon see in more detail how this formula works. Before we look at the details, however, a word of caution: the employer should ensure that the required remittance is made by the due date (usually the 15th day of the month following the payroll deductions). Failure to remit on time usually results in a penalty of 10% of the amount due over $500. This penalty is harsh and should be avoided. Not only is the amount high, but it is not deductible as a business expense for tax purposes.

HOW TO CALCULATE EMPLOYER'S REMITTANCE

1 How to calculate and record the employer's expenses associated with payroll

Some provinces levy higher tax rates than others. As this is written, a single taxpayer earning $2,000 weekly will have the following amounts deducted for provincial tax:

In Ontario—$204.40
In Alberta—$162.35

Note that federal tax rates are the same for all taxpayers.

Income Tax

Remember that all employees pay an amount of income tax based upon their level of earnings. We saw in Chapter 8 that the ABC Company deducted income tax from each employee's earnings. This amount must now be sent to the government. Notice that the amount sent is exactly the same as the amount deducted since the employer does not contribute to the employee's tax. This part of the required remittance is therefore quite simple: Each month employers must send in the exact amount of income tax deducted from employees in the previous month. In our simple formula, that is why we multiply by 1.0—the result is exactly the amount deducted.

Canada (Quebec) Pension Plan

Almost all employees contribute an amount every pay period to CPP (at least until the maximum is reached). In Canada, the employer must match the employee's contribution to CPP. This means that the amount of CPP remitted is exactly double the amount deducted. In our simple formula, that is why we multiply by 2.0—the result is double the amount deducted.

If an employee commences a job with a new employer partway through a calendar year, the deduction of CPP is calculated without regard to the CPP already paid while employed by the former company. If the employee pays more than the yearly maximum, then a refund of CPP contributions can be claimed by the individual when he or she files an income tax return for the year. The employer's share is not refundable and cannot be recovered.

Employment Insurance

Recall that employees contribute an amount every pay period for Employment Insurance. Employers also contribute to EI by paying an amount that is 140% of the deductions made from employees' wages. The effect is that the employer must remit 2.4 times the amount deducted from the employees. In our simple formula, that is why we multiply by 2.4—1.0 for the employees' deduction, plus 1.4 for the employer's share. This 1.4 employer's portion can be reduced if the employer has an approved wage-loss replacement plan, but in this chapter, we are assuming no reduction. Also note that the rules for overpayment of EI are almost exactly the same as for CPP: the employee can recover his or her overpayment at tax time while there is no refund to an employer.

In Chapter 8, the employer made the following journal entry for the payroll in the first week in March:

GENERAL JOURNAL

2013 Date		Account Titles and Description	PR	Dr.	Cr.
Mar	7	Management Salaries Expense		900 00	
		Sales Wages Expense		1068 00	
		Wages Expense		2031 00	
		Income Taxes Payable			535 90
		CPP Payable			177 63
		EI Payable			69 20
		Medical Plan Payable			112 00
		Charitable Contributions Payable			30 00
		Salaries and Wages Payable			3074 27
		To record payroll for the first week in March			

ABC Company must now make the following additional entry to record its liability correctly:

GENERAL JOURNAL

2013 Date		Account Titles and Description	PR	Dr.	Cr.
Mar	7	Employee Benefits Expense		274 51	
		CPP Payable (1 × 177.63)			177 63
		EI Payable (1.4 × 69.20)			96 88
		To record employer portion of CPP and			
		EI for week 1, March			

Note: This expense—employee benefits expense—is also known by many different names—payroll taxes expense, for example. Some employers separate it into EI and CPP portions, but this is not usually necessary.

After the above entry is posted, the following T accounts would be changed as shown:

Employee Benefits Expense	CPP Payable	EI Payable
274.51*	177.63** 177.63*	69.20** 96.88*
Expense on the Income Statement	Liability on the Balance Sheet	Liability on the Balance Sheet

*New entry made above.
**Original entry from Chapter 8.

Students should be aware that employers sometimes share or pay entirely for the cost of other employee benefits, such as extended health care, long-term disability insurance, and dental plans. These costs would also be recorded by journal entry at the same time CPP and EI are recorded. For example, if ABC Company agreed it would charge its employees only half the cost of health care, it would make the following entry instead of the one illustrated previously:

GENERAL JOURNAL					
					Page 4
2013 Date		Account Titles and Description	PR	Dr.	Cr.
Mar	7	Employee Benefits Expense		330 51	
		CPP Payable			177 63
		EI Payable			96 88
		Medical Plan Payable*			56 00
		To record employer's portion of CPP, EI,			
		and medical insurance for week 1, March			

*Note that the employees' deductions would go down by 50%.

Workers' Compensation

Most companies are also required to bear another expense related to salaries and wages: workers' compensation. This expenditure is typically paid to a provincial government (usually its Workers' Compensation Board, or **WCB** for short) once or several times per year, depending on how large the employer is, how many employees it has, the salaries/wages earned, and the likelihood of injury while on the job. Naturally, the rates charged are higher for relatively risky tasks such as steelworking, and a lot lower for most office workers. Assuming for this illustration that ABC Company in the province of Ontario has an average WCB rate of 2.5%, the company would make an additional journal entry for the first payroll to record the amount payable to the WCB of Ontario. Please note that the amounts payable will not go to the federal government along with income taxes, CPP, and EI, but will instead be paid to the provincial WCB at a time that differs a lot among the provinces. We will assume that ABC Company will remit these payments once every three months. Here is the entry the company would make for the first payroll in March:

GENERAL JOURNAL					
2013 Date		Account Titles and Description	Post. Ref.	Dr.	Cr.
Mar	7	WCB Expense		99 98	
		Accrued WCB Payable (a current liability)			99 98
		To record WCB expense for this payroll			

The company would make a similar entry for each payroll, based on 2.5% of the amounts earned by the employees, but we will not show these entries for each of the four payrolls in March. The actual payment of WCB amounts is covered later in the chapter (see page 424).

LEARNING UNIT 9-1 REVIEW

AT THIS POINT you should be able to:

◆ Explain one purpose of form RC1(E). (p. 413)

◆ Calculate the employer's share of CPP and EI. (p. 414)

◆ Explain when employee deductions must be remitted. (p. 414)

◆ Journalize the employer's employee benefits expense, including Workers' Compensation Board. (p. 416)

◆ Post the above journal entry to appropriate ledger accounts (p. 416)

Self-Review Quiz 9-1

(The forms you need are on page 9-1 of the *Study Guide with Working Papers*.)

Given the following journal entry for the payroll totals of the second week in March 2013, prepare the entry to record ABC Company's portion of CPP and EI:

GENERAL JOURNAL

2013 Date		Account Titles and Description	PR	Dr.	Cr.
Mar	14	Management Salaries Expense		900 00	
		Sales Wages Expense		1068 00	
		Wages Expense		2067 00	
		Income Taxes Payable			543 60
		CPP Payable			179 42
		EI Payable			69 80
		Medical Plan Payable			112 00
		Charitable Contributions Payable			30 00
		Salaries and Wages Payable			3100 18
		To record payroll for week 2 in March			

Solution to Self-Review Quiz 9-1

GENERAL JOURNAL

2013 Date		Account Titles and Description	PR	Dr.	Cr.
Mar	13	Employee Benefits Expense		277 14	
		CPP Payable (1 × 179.42)			179 42
		EI Payable (1.4 × 69.80)			97 72
		To record employer portion of CPP and			
		EI for week 2, March			

Learning Unit 9-2

Completing the Monthly Remittance Form

Income tax × 1
+ CPP × 2
+ EI × 2.4 = Amount remitted

CPP × 1
+ EI × 1.4 = Employer's expense

Most smaller companies are required to remit the total amounts due with respect to their payrolls each month by the 15th of the following month. Payment may be made at most financial institutions in Canada or a cheque can be mailed, as long as it reaches the government by the appropriate deadline.

We have already seen the ABC Company's entries for the first two weeks in March*. Let us assume the following payroll data for the third and fourth weeks:

GENERAL JOURNAL					
2013 Date	**Account Titles and Description**	**Post. Ref.**	**Dr.**	**Cr.**	
Mar 21	Management Salaries Expense		900 00		
	Sales Wages Expense		1068 00		
	Wages Expense		2145 00		
	Income Taxes Payable			557 30	
	CPP Payable			183 27	
	EI Payable			71 17	
	Medical Plan Payable			112 00	
	Charitable Contributions Payable			30 00	
	Salaries and Wages Payable			3159 26	
	To record payroll for week 3, March—new data				

GENERAL JOURNAL					
2013 Date	**Account Titles and Description**	**Post. Ref.**	**Dr.**	**Cr.**	
Mar 28	Management Salaries Expense		900 00		
	Sales Wages Expense		1068 00		
	Wages Expense		2120 00		
	Income Taxes Payable			553 70	
	CPP Payable			182 04	
	EI Payable			70 74	
	Medical Plan Payable			112 00	
	Charitable Contributions Payable			30 00	
	Salaries and Wages Payable			3164 52	
	To record payroll for week 4, March—new data				

After posting, the relevant liability T accounts would appear as shown:

		Income Taxes Payable	CPP Payable	EI Payable
Week 1:	Employees	535.90*	177.63*	69.20*
	Employer		177.63**	96.88**
Week 2:	Employees	543.60*	179.42*	69.80*
	Employer		179.42**	97.72**
Week 3:	Employees	557.30*	183.27*	71.17*
	Employer		183.27**	99.64**
Week 4:	Employees	553.70*	182.04*	70.74*
	Employer		182.04**	99.04**
Balance (March)		2,190.50	1,444.72	674.19

*Original payroll entry.

**Benefits entry. (Week 1 amounts from Chapter 8. Weeks 2, 3, and 4 amounts from this chapter. See page 419 for weeks 3 and 4.)

GENERAL JOURNAL

2013 Date		Account Titles and Description	Post. Ref.	Dr.	Cr.
Mar	21	Employee Benefits Expense		282 91	
		CPP Payable (1 × 183.27)			183 27
		EI Payable (1.4 × 71.17)			99 64
		To record employer portion of CPP and			
		EI for the third week of March—new data			

GENERAL JOURNAL

2013 Date		Account Titles and Description	Post. Ref.	Dr.	Cr.
Mar	28	Employee Benefits Expense		281 08	
		CPP Payable (1 × 182.04)			182 04
		EI Payable (1.4 × 70.74)			99 04
		To record employer portion of CPP and			
		EI for the fourth week of March—new data			

Since these liability accounts contain the total amounts due, ABC Company can complete a required **(Monthly) Remittance Form (PD7A)**.

ABC Company will issue a cheque for $4,309.41, dated April 15, payable to Canada Revenue Agency (CRA), specifically to the Receiver General. This cheque will be entered in the cash disbursements journal in April. When this cheque is entered, the following accounts will be affected:

GENERAL JOURNAL

2013		Account Titles and Description	Post. Ref.	Dr.	Cr.
April	15	Income Taxes Payable		2190 50	
		CPP Payable		1444 72	
		EI Payable		674 19	
		Cash			4309 41
		To record payment of withholdings			

After these amounts are posted, the liability accounts at the end of March will all be paid.

Remember that by April 15 there will be two new weekly payrolls (in April) to contend with, so the ledger accounts may not ever have a balance of exactly zero. The amount payable at the end of any month, however, will be accurate when all postings have been made.

So far in these chapters, we have been illustrating the use of three separate liability accounts, as is obvious from the journal entry above. Many companies prefer to operate a single account called, not surprisingly, Due to CRA. While some detail may be obscured by using just one account, it is true that a single cheque is written each month, so this practice is justified.

Students will recall that employers sometimes pay part or all of the cost of other benefits. These costs are not sent to the CRA; instead, they are remitted (usually monthly) to the provincial health care plan, the Workers' Compensation Board authority, and/or private insurance companies that provide the benefits. These details of payroll are handled in a manner similar to the remittance to the CRA and are not illustrated here.

LEARNING UNIT 9-2 REVIEW

AT THIS POINT you should be able to:

♦ Explain the balances in the following ledger accounts before the monthly remittance to the CRA is made. (p. 418)

    a. Income tax payable

    b. CPP payable

    c. EI payable

♦ Issue and record the cheque that would accompany form PD7A. (p. 419)

♦ Explain how the balances in the ledger accounts listed in **a.** to **c.** above would change after posting the remittance cheque. (p. 419)

Self-Review Quiz 9-2

(The forms you need are on pages 9-1 and 9-2 of the *Study Guide with Working Papers*.)

Given the two semi-monthly payrolls for June 2012, summarized by the journal entries below, answer the following:

1. What journal entries would be made to record the employer's share of CPP and EI for the month?

2. Post the original entries and the entries that you suggested in question 1 to the T accounts shown. (Not all T accounts are shown; ignore the ones not shown.)

3. What amount would the employer remit to the CRA by the 15th of July 2012?

Here are the semi-monthly journal entries:

		GENERAL JOURNAL			
	Date	Account Titles and Description	Post. Ref.	Dr.	Cr.
2012					
Jun	15	Sales Salaries Expense		2 8 5 0 00	
		Office Salaries Expense		3 2 4 0 00	
		Income Taxes Payable			1 2 8 2 40
		CPP Payable			2 8 4 12
		EI Payable			1 0 5 36
		Salaries and Wages Payable			4 4 1 8 12
		To record payroll data for the first half			
		of the month			

GENERAL JOURNAL

Date		Account Titles and Description	Post. Ref.	Dr.	Cr.
2012					
Jun	30	Sales Salaries Expense		2 85 000	
		Office Salaries Expense		3 17 500	
		Income Taxes Payable			1 27 1 80
		CPP Payable			2 80 90
		EI Payable			1 04 25
		Salaries and Wages Payable			4 3 68 05
		To record payroll data for the second half			
		of the month			

Here are the T accounts to use in question 2 of Self-Review Quiz 9-2 (opening balances are ignored):

Income Tax Payable	**CPP Payable**	**EI Payable**

Solutions to Self-Review Quiz 9-2

1.

GENERAL JOURNAL

Date		Account Titles and Description	Post. Ref.	Dr.	Cr.
2012					
Jun	15	Employee Benefits Expense		4 3 1 62	
		CPP Payable			2 84 12
		EI Payable (105.36 × 1.4)			1 47 50
		To record benefits expense for the			
		first half of the month			

GENERAL JOURNAL

Date		Account Titles and Description	Post. Ref.	Dr.	Cr.
2012					
Jun	30	Employee Benefits Expense		4 2 6 85	
		CPP Payable			2 80 90
		EI Payable (104.25 × 1.4)			1 45 95
		To record benefits expense for the			
		second half of the month			

2. Your T accounts should appear as follows:

Income Tax Payable	CPP Payable	EI Payable
1,282.40	284.12	105.36
1,271.80	284.12	147.50
2,554.20 Balance	280.90	104.25
	280.90	145.95
	1,130.04 Balance	503.06 Balance

3. The employer would remit $4,187.30, calculated as follows:

Income Tax Payable (balance)	$2,554.20
CPP Payable (balance)	1,130.04
EI Payable (balance)	503.06
	$4,187.30

Learning Unit 9-3

Employer's Annual T4 Summary

3 Employers' annual responsibilities for filing the T4 Summary form

Every year, employers are required to file an annual return called a **T4 Summary** (see Figure 9-1). This return summarizes the information provided to employees on their T4 slips (see Chapter 8, Figure 8-5).

		Deductions		
Employee Name	**Total Wages**	**Income Tax**	**CPP**	**EI**
Janet Johnson	$ 24,210.00	2,392.45	1,025.15	418.86
Peter Black	41,700.00	6,847.65	1,890.94	721.40
John Chernochan	38,620.00	2,745.16	1,738.44	668.14
Tony Chui	31,480.00	4,157.30	1,385.06	554.64
Beth Madora	35,090.00	4,747.52	1,563.71	607.06
Elaine Dumont	48,086.00	6,851.16	2,163.15	747.36
Casual employees (Total)	20,696.00	1,765.34	501.96	358.06
Totals	$239,882.00	29,506.58	10,268.41	4,075.52

Careful, accurate work helps ensure that the filing of the T4-T4A Summary is not an unpleasant task.

It is important to note that the form illustrated in Figure 9-1 is completed for a calendar year. Even if the fiscal year ends on September 30, the T4 Summary must be filed for the calendar year (January 1 to December 31). The deadline for submitting this form to the government and the T4 forms to the employees is February 28 each year for the calendar year ended the previous December 31.

The completion of this form can be a difficult task because any errors made during the year in completing the payroll register, and any errors made in preparing the employees' individual T4 slips, will be discovered in this final step. The totals shown for CPP, EI, and income tax as illustrated in the table above must also agree with the totals remitted according to the monthly PD7A form or any deficiency remitted.

It is not unusual to find intelligent, hard-working, successful employers who find this aspect of payroll processing very difficult. Some computer firms selling payroll software are successful because they promise employers relief from the manual balancing procedures each February 28. In actual fact, the task is not too difficult—provided the payroll register is completed with neatness and accuracy and all subsequent steps are done with care.

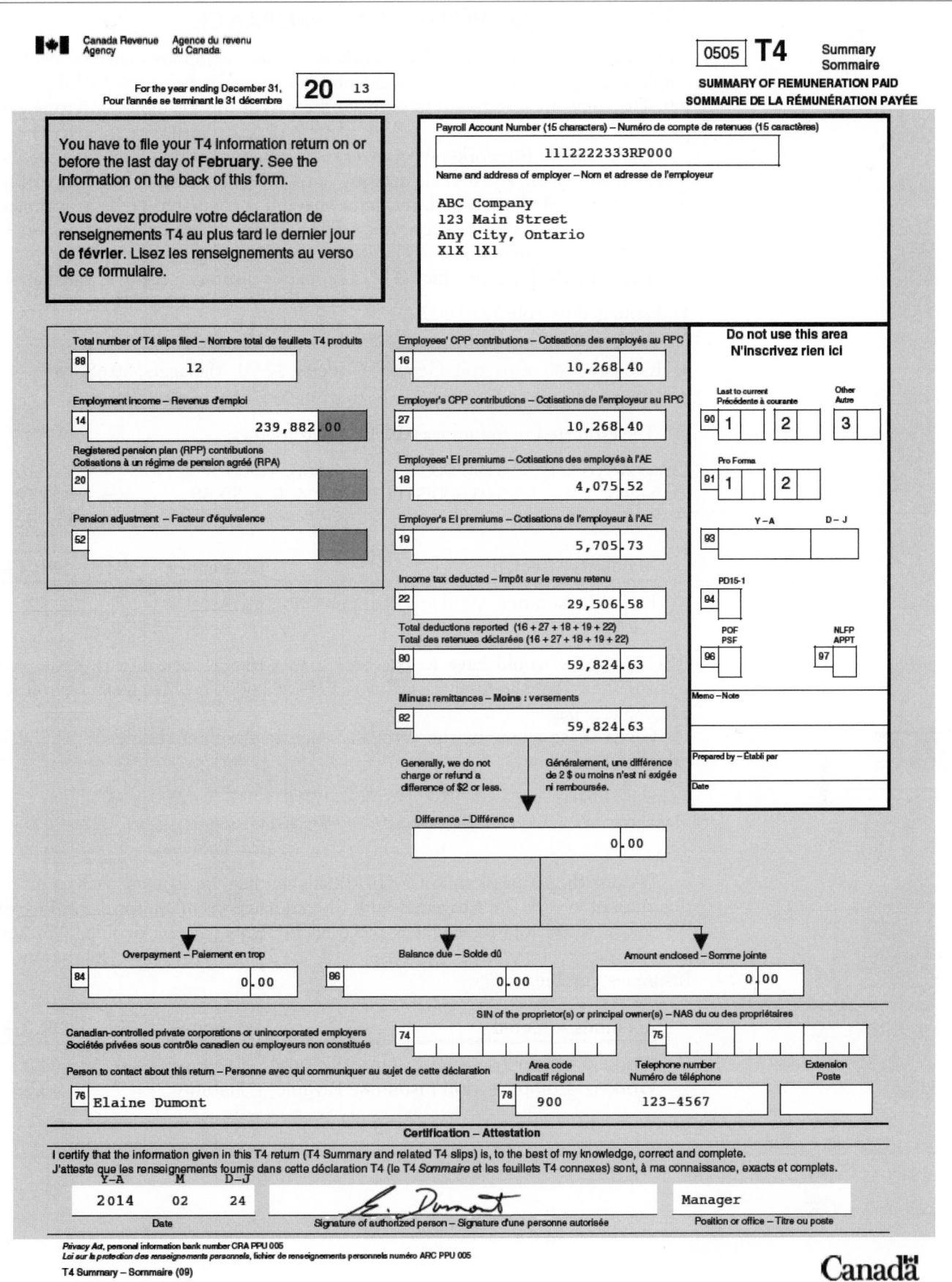

Figure 9-1 Summary of Remuneration Paid

Source: Canada Revenue Agency. Reproduced with permission of the Minister of Public Works and Government Services Canada, 2002.

WORKERS' COMPENSATION INSURANCE

ABC Company is required to have workers' compensation insurance to insure its employees against losses due to accidental injury or death incurred while on the job. The company is required to estimate the cost of this insurance and to pay the premium in advance.

The premium for workers' compensation insurance is based on the total estimated gross payroll, and in that company's province, the rate is calculated per $100 of weekly payroll. At year-end, the actual payroll is compared with the estimated payroll, and ABC will either receive credit for overpayment or be responsible for paying additional premiums.

These are the facts on which ABC Company's insurance cost was calculated:

1. Estimated payroll: $230,000.
2. Two grades of workers: General Workers and Managers.
3. Rate per $100 of payroll: General Workers, $2.90; Managers, $0.68.
4. Estimated payroll: General Workers, $190,000; Managers, $40,000.

The estimated premium was calculated as follows:

General Workers: $190,000/$100 = 1,900; 1,900 × $2.90 = $5,510
Managers: $40,000/$100 = 400; 400 × $0.68 = 272
Total Estimated Premium: $5,782

Accounts Affected	Category	↑↓	DR./CR.
Prepaid Insurance, Worker's Compensation	Asset	↑	Dr.
Cash	Asset	↓	Cr.

ABC Company would have to pay $5,782 in advance. At the end of the year, records show that the total payroll was $239,882.00. The Manager's payroll was $48,086 (see page 422).

Given those amounts, the company's actual premium should be $5,889.06, calculated as follows:

General Workers: $191,796/$100 = 1,918; 1,918 × $2.90 = $5,562.08
Managers: $48,086/$100 = 481; 481 × $0.68 = 326.98
Total Premium: $5,889.06

Because the actual premium is $107.06 higher than the estimate, ABC must pay this amount in early 2014 together with the estimated premium for the 2014 year.

The $107.06 adjustment takes place on December 31 by debiting Workers' Compensation Insurance Expense and crediting Workers' Compensation Insurance Payable.

Accounts Affected	Category	↑↓	DR./CR.
Workers' Compensation Insurance Expense	Expense	↑	Dr.
Workers' Compensation Insurance Payable	Liability	↑	Cr.

LEARNING UNIT 9-3 REVIEW

AT THIS POINT you should be able to:

◆ Describe the process of filing an annual T4 Summary. (p. 422)
◆ Illustrate the completion of the T4 Summary. (p. 423)
◆ Calculate workers' compensation insurance. (p. 424)

Self-Review Quiz 9-3

(The form you need is on page 9-2 of the *Study Guide with Working Papers*.)

Respond true or false to the following:

1. A T4 Summary must be filed each year by February 28.
2. A T4 Summary is sent to each employee by February 28 each year.
3. The completion of the T4 forms can be a difficult task.
4. The total of the individual amounts on all T4 Supplementary forms must equal the totals on the T4 Summary.

Solutions to Self-Review Quiz 9-3

1. True   2. False   3. True   4. True

"As an employer, Stan, what are your tax responsibilities?" asked Angel Tavarez, president of the local Kiwanis Club. They were at one of the luncheons sponsored by the club every month, and Stan had been asked to join a discussion on the Role of Small Business in Our Local Economy. Fortunately, Angel had told the panelists the questions in advance so Stan had his answers ready.

"Well, of course, I pay provincial and federal government taxes myself. I also have to file provincial and federal withholding taxes for each of my two employees. I have to withhold federal and provincial income taxes as well as CPP and EI for each of them. I pay workers' compensation premiums too," said Stan.

"That's strange," said a voice from the audience. "My brother-in-law has a Subway restaurant in the U.S. and he pays city taxes as well as state and federal taxes. What's going on here?"

"Naturally, the situation is slightly different for Subway owners in different locations—and certainly in different countries," said Stan confidently. "Some U.S. cities have city income taxes. Different states have different regulations about workers' compensation, as well, just as different provinces do."

"Oh, right," said the voice, sounding embarrassed.

"So, Stan, how often do you have to pay taxes," asked Angel Tavarez, shifting the topic diplomatically.

Stan picked up a piece of chalk and drew twelve large circles on the blackboard. Then he wrote the word "ASPIRIN" in each of the circles. A murmur of "Huhs" and "Whats" went around the room.

"The average employee working for a company pays tax once a year on April 30 and has

SUBWAY
HOLD THE LETTUCE, WITHHOLD THE TAXES

Payroll tax responsibilities
❶❷❸ **(30 min)**

one big tax headache. As an employer," Stan said, "I file tax returns on a monthly basis, so I have twelve big tax headaches a year! Each month I complete Form PD7A, the Employer's Monthly Remittance Report, to report and pay payroll taxes to the CRA. Along with that, I have to deposit the tax money into a chartered bank once a month. In addition, I have to file the T4 Summary at the end of each year. Then, for each employee, I must give them a T4 slip . . . ."

"Stan," Angel interrupted, "I'm afraid time is running out for your segment of the panel discussion. We'll move on to Pamela Pudelle who is going to tell us about advertising her new pet-grooming parlour."

Stan suppressed a chuckle as a woman who looked amazingly like a poodle took the microphone. Later, during the reception, he tapped Angel on the shoulder and said, "Sorry I went over my time limit."

"You didn't really go over," said Angel, "but you were getting a little too technical for the audience."

While Stan was sorry to have let the discussion veer off course, he felt a burst of pride. Who would have thought a year ago that he would be willing—and able—to expound on the tax burden of a small business owner!

DISCUSSION QUESTIONS

1. What are the taxes called federal and provincial income taxes? How much do they cost Stan?
2. Why is Stan classified as a monthly depositor of withholdings?
3. Assume Stan owed $2,069.90 in total withholdings for March. When would it be due? What would happen if that day were Sunday?

Chapter Assignments

SUMMARY OF KEY POINTS

1. The employer's remittance to the CRA includes (a) income tax (employees' deductions), (b) CPP (both employees' and employer's shares), and (c) EI (again, both employees' and employer's shares).

2. The employee benefits expense is made up of both CPP (same amount as deducted from employees) and EI (1.4 times the amount deducted from employees).

3. Journal entries are made to record the payroll and then to record the employer's share of CPP and EI.

4. Employers sometimes share or pay entirely for the cost of other employee benefits (health care, insurance, etc.). These costs would also be recorded by journal entry at the same time as CPP and EI. Workers' compensation is paid entirely by the employer.

Learning Unit 9-2

1. Employers must complete form PD7A and submit it with their remittance to the CRA by the 15th day of the month following the month in which the salary payment was made. (Larger employers remit more often.)

2. A significant penalty is paid by any employer remitting after the due date.

3. Employers sometimes pay part or all of the costs of health care, insurance plans, etc., on behalf of their employees. These costs are not sent to the CRA; instead, they are remitted (usually monthly) to the provincial health care plan and/or private companies that provide the benefits.

Learning Unit 9-3

1. Once every year, by February 28, employers must file an annual T4 Summary (for the previous calendar year) with the federal government.

2. On or before the same date, each employee must be given a copy of his or her individual earnings summary form (T4 Supplementary). This form summarizes all relevant payroll information for each employee for the previous calendar year.

3. Unless care is taken in preparing the payroll records throughout the year, the completion of the T4 forms can be a challenging task.

4. Workers' compensation is a business expense for all companies having employees. An estimated amount is usually paid early in the calendar year. The exact amount is then calculated more precisely after the year's details of payroll are known. This results in a refund or additional payment.

KEY TERMS

Business number A number given by the federal government that uniquely identifies each employer who is required to forward deductions made from employees. Used to keep track of the exact remittance each employer sends on behalf of its employees. (p. 413)

(Monthly) Remittance Form (PD7A) A form used to identify the employer and the amounts of money sent to the CRA periodically on behalf of employees. (p. 419)

Remittance formula A formula that can be used to double-check the amount of money being sent in each month on behalf of the employees. Computed as:

$$
\begin{array}{lll}
\text{Income tax deducted} \times 1.0 & = & \text{XXX.XX} \\
\text{CPP deducted} \times 2.0 & = & \text{XX.XX} \\
\text{EI deducted} \times 2.4 & = & \underline{\text{XX.XX}} \\
\text{Total} & & \underline{\underline{\text{XXX.XX}}} \quad \text{(p. 413)}
\end{array}
$$

T4 Summary A form sent to the federal government once each year showing the totals of income tax, CPP, and EI deducted from all employees during the last calendar year. The totals on this form must agree exactly with the totals submitted on the various T4 Supplementary forms (see entry below). (p. 422)

T4 Supplementary A form given to each employee by February 28 every year that gives the totals of wages earned, income tax, CPP, and EI deducted, and other similar information for the past calendar year. Total of all T4 Supplementary slips must agree with the totals reported on the T4 Summary (see entry above). (Refer to p. 379 in Chapter 8.)

WCB expense The cost to the employer of insuring employees against accidents in the workplace. (p. 416)

BLUEPRINT OF THE TAX CALENDAR

A Sampling of Dates Involving Employer's Tax Responsibilities

January 15 (and the 15th of each month)	PD7A form	Remit the monthly amount to the CRA. Remember the formula: $1 \times$ tax deducted + $2 \times$ CPP deducted + $\underline{2.4 \times \text{EI deducted}}$ = Total amount to be remitted
February 28	T4 form	Complete these forms and send or deliver them to all persons employed during the year.
February 28	T4 Summary	Send this form, together with copies of the individual T4 forms, to the government. The totals on this form must match the sum of all individual T4 slips and, as well, must agree with the employer's accounting records.

Certain other forms may be required throughout the year, although they are not subject to an exact timetable:

	RC1 form	Every employer needs to obtain a permanent number that permits the government to keep an accurate record of funds remitted. Since this number is permanent, employers will need to submit this form only once.
	Record of Employment	Whenever an employee ceases his or her employment, this form must be completed and a copy given to the former employee within one week. A copy goes to the government to assist in the fair and efficient administration of the Employment Insurance Act.

Questions, classroom demonstration exercises, exercises, and problems

Discussion Questions and Critical Thinking/Ethical Case

1. What makes up employee benefits expense?

2. All employers must remit their payroll deductions once a month (by the 15th of the following month). Please comment.

3. The only payroll-related costs borne by employers are CPP and EI. Please comment.

4. An RC1 form must be submitted annually by all employers. True or false?

5. Why could failure to remit employees' deductions on time be costly?

6. Each employer doubles the amount of income tax deducted from employees each month when remitting to the CRA. True or false?

7. Which of the following accurately summarizes the correct formula for determining the monthly remittance to the CRA? (IT = income tax.)
   a. $(2 \times IT) + (2.4 \times CPP) + (2 \times EI)$
   b. $(1 \times IT) + (2 \times CPP) + (2.4 \times EI)$
   c. $(1 \times IT) + (2.4 \times CPP) + (2 \times EI)$
   d. $(2 \times IT) + (2 \times CPP) + (2.4 \times EI)$

8. A remittance form (PD7A) must be sent to the federal government once every pay period. True or false?

9. Why do some computer firms do good business selling payroll software to employers?

10. Employers must complete their T4 Summaries no later than two months after the end of their fiscal year. True or false?

11. Abby Ross works in the Payroll Department for Lange Co. as a junior accountant. Abby also is going to school for an advanced degree in accounting. After work each day, she uses the company's photocopy machine to make extra copies of her assignments. Should she be photocopying personal material on a company machine? You make the call. Write down your specific recommendations to Abby.

Make the grade with MyAccountingLab! The exercises and problems marked in green can be found on MyAccountingLab at www.myaccountinglab.com. You can practise them as often as you want, and many of them feature step-by-step guided solutions to help you find the right answer. You can also find working papers for selected problems in the Multimedia Library on MyAccountingLab.

Classroom Demonstration Exercises

(The forms you need are on page 9-3 of the *Study Guide with Working Papers*.)

Set A

Employee benefits expense
① (15 min)

1. The Fisher Company had two employees for the week ended July 24. On the basis of the following information, prepare a general journal entry to record the employee benefits expense for that payroll.

			Deductions		
Employee	*Salary*	*IT*	*CPP*	*EI*	*Net Pay*
Brett Pym	900	165	41	16	678
Carmen Flynn	1,000	176	46	18	760

Calculating amounts to remit to CRA
② (15 min)

2. Assume that the Fisher Company (see above) had five payrolls in the month of July, all identical to the one shown above. What amount would the company send to the CRA in August to meet its legal obligation for payroll remittance?

CPP and EI deductions
① (30 min)

3. For the payroll week ending on October 9 (the 41st payroll period of the year), the three following employees had gross earnings as indicated. Each had been employed at the same salary since January 1:

Beth Hudson	$1,100
John Wong	975
Ida Hastings	850

Without using tables, compute the amount of CPP and EI to be deducted from each employee for payroll No. 41.

CPP and EI deductions
① (30 min)

4. Fred Blake has agreed to work for the Cummings Foundation at a total annual salary of $54,000. He is uncertain whether he should be paid biweekly or semi-monthly and has asked for your assistance. Calculate the typical deductions for CPP and EI that must be taken from Fred's salary under either alternative. Will the choice affect the total EI or CPP Fred pays during the year?

Employee benefits expense
① (15 min)

1. The Chan Company had two employees for the biweekly pay period ending July 23. On the basis of the following information, prepare a general journal entry to record the employee benefits expense for that payroll.

Employee	Salary	IT	CPP	EI	Net Pay
			Deductions		
Art Ellen	2,500	532	117	43	1,808
Dixie Holmes	1,500	195	68	26	1,211

Calculating amounts to remit to CRA
② (15 min)

2. Assume that the Chan Company (see above) had two payrolls in the month of July, all identical to the one shown above. What amount would the company send to the CRA in August to meet its legal obligation for payroll remittance?

CPP and EI deductions
① (30 min)

3. For the payroll week ending on September 30 (the 39th payroll period of the year), the three following employees had gross earnings as indicated. Each had been employed at the same salary since January 1:

Marvin Bay	$1,200
Alana Drost	980
Kelvin Chin	800

Without using tables, compute the amount of CPP and EI to be deducted from each employee for payroll No. 39.

CPP and EI deductions
① (30 min)

4. Ainsley Howard has agreed to work for the Parsons Foundation at a total annual salary of $48,000. She is uncertain whether she should be paid biweekly or semi-monthly and has asked for your assistance. Calculate the typical deductions for CPP and EI that must be taken from Ainsley's salary under either alternative. Will the choice affect the total EI or CPP Ainsley pays during the year?

Exercises

(The forms you need are on page 9-4 of the *Study Guide with Working Papers*.)

Recording employee benefits expense
① (15 min)

9-1. From the following information, prepare a general journal entry to record the employee benefits expense for Jones Company for the weekly payroll of July 9:

Employee	Total Salary	Tax	CPP	EI	Net Pay
			Deductions		
Troy Ness	900	183	41	16	660
Jay Young	600	95	26	10	469
Tim Wyatt	800	152	36	14	598

Recording employee benefits expense
① (20 min)

9-2. From the following information, prepare a general journal entry to record the employee benefits expense of Windsor Company for the monthly payroll for April:

Employee	Total Salary	Tax	CPP	EI	Net Pay
			Deductions		
Bert Lamont	2,500	368	109	43	1,980
Joan Quan	2,300	337	99	40	1,824
Mark Totem	1,700	191	70	29	1,410
Jean Dzurko	1,800	208	75	31	1,486

9-3. What amount will the Windsor Company send to the CRA in the month of May (for the April payroll)? See Exercise 9-2 above.

9-4. For the first two weeks of March, the Star Company had payroll details as shown below:

Employee	Hours	Rate	Total Pay	Deductions			Net Pay
				Tax	CPP	EI	
Pam Tifford	80	16	1,280	198	57	22	1,003
Isaac Gold	70	17	1,190	180	52	21	937
Bob Boudreau	80	14	1,120	162	49	19	890

Prepare the general journal entry to record the employee benefits expense for the two-week period.

9-5. For the last two weeks in March, the Star Company had the following payroll details:

Employee	Hours	Rate	Total Pay	Deductions			Net Pay
				Tax	CPP	EI	
Pam Tifford	75	16	1,200	171	53	21	955
Isaac Gold	85	17	1,445	241	65	25	1,114
Jim Francis	80	14	1,120	154	49	19	898

Prepare the general journal entry to record the employee benefits expense for the last two-week period.

9-6. There are only four payroll weeks in March. Calculate the total remittance that Star Company would make to the CRA in the month of April based on its March payroll activities. Refer to Exercises 9-4 and 9-5.

9-7. For this exercise, please assume a province that has three rates for worker's compensation: General Office Workers, $1.75 per $100; Sales Staff, $2.55 per $100; Management Personnel, $1.20 per $100.

   In the above province, DSK Enterprises operates a business that has workers in each of these categories. The company has projected the following salary expense for each category of employee for the 2014 calendar year:

General Office Worker	$254,000
Sales Staff	$347,000
Management Personnel	$418,000

Required

a. Calculate the WCB premium that DSK would submit to its provincial WCB for the 2014 year.

b. Given that actual salary expenses turned out to be as shown below, calculate the refund or added premium that the company receives from, or has to send to, its WCB early in January 2015.

General Office Worker	$249,800
Sales Staff	$354,600
Management Personnel	$416,000

(The forms you need are on pages 9-5 to 9-10 of the *Study Guide with Working Papers*.)

Recording Employee Benefits Expense and subsequent entries
① ② (40 min)

9A-1. The payroll register for Rice Company of Sackville is summarized below for the month of April 2012:

Employee	Total Salary	Tax	CPP	EI	Medical	Union Dues	Net Pay	Chq. No.
					Deductions			
Bob Roberts	3,100	438	139	54	28	21	2,420	474
Robin Case	2,750	461	122	48	56	21	2,042	475
Bailey Tropp	2,400	342	104	42	56	21	1,835	476
Ishma Blumen	2,650	345	117	46	56	21	2,065	477
	10,900	1,586	482	190	196	84	8,362	

Check Figure

Employee Benefits Expense
$944.00

The union dues are remitted to the treasurer of the union by the 10th day of the next month. Rice Company matches its employees' contributions to the medical plan. Assume that the information in the above table has been recorded and cheques No. 474 to 477 were issued.

Required

a. Record the company's benefits expense, assuming no such entry was made when cheques No. 474 to No. 477 were recorded.

b. In May, the Rice Company issued the following three cheques:

   1. May 10, 2012, to the Employees' Union, cheque No. 495.
   2. May 15, 2012, to the CRA, cheque No. 502.
   3. May 20, 2012, to the Provincial Health Care Insurance Company, cheque No. 531.

   How much was each cheque for?

c. What journal entries would be made to record the three cheques in **b.** above?

Recording Employee Benefits Expense and subsequent calculations
① ② (30 min)

9A-2. Gibraltor Co. of Sussex recorded the following payroll details in its payroll journal for the month of March 2013:

Employee	Total Salary	Tax	CPP	EI	LTD	Medical	Union Dues	Net Pay	Chq. No.
						Deductions			
Fred Jones	3,200	465	144	55	35	32	28	2,441	716
May George	2,600	401	114	45	52	58	28	1,902	717
Bren Morley	2,700	328	119	47	52	32	28	2,094	718
Joyce Fisher	2,400	288	104	42	35	-	28	1,903	719
Pat Sailer	2,300	233	99	40	35	32	28	1,833	720
	13,200	1,715	580	229	209	154	140	10,173	

Union dues are remitted by the end of the following month to the employees' union treasurer. Employees pay 100% of the long-term disability (LTD). Gibraltor Co. matches its employees' contributions to the medical plan and remits by the 20th of the following month.

a. Assume that there was no employee benefits expense recognized as the payroll register was recorded. Give the general journal entry necessary to record this employee benefits expense for March 2013.

b. List the cheques, together with their amounts and dates, that Gibraltor Co. would issue in April 2013 with respect to the above payroll data.

Recording Employee Benefits
Expense—a more comprehensive
example
1 **2** (45 min)

9A-3. The Candy Co. of Lethbridge pays its workers twice each month. Data for the two pay periods on June 2013 are shown below:

First half of June 2013:

Employee	Total Salary	Deductions					Net Pay	Chq. No.
		Tax	CPP	EI	Union	Chari-table		
Ann Wyatt	1,600	198	72	28	12	15	1,275	312
Jim Elliott	1,520	205	68	26	12	15	1,194	313
Bren Stairs	1,245	144	54	22	12	15	998	314
Becky Holmes	1,306	169	57	23	12	15	1,030	315
	5,671	716	251	99	48	60	4,497	

Second half of June 2013:

Employee	Total Salary	Deductions					Net Pay	Chq. No.
		Tax	CPP	EI	Union	Chari-table		
Ann Wyatt	1,640	208	74	28	12	15	1,303	387
Jim Elliott	1,520	205	68	26	12	15	1,194	388
Bren Stairs	1,245	144	54	22	12	15	998	389
Becky Holmes	1,492	192	67	26	12	15	1,180	390
	5,897	749	263	102	48	60	4,675	

Union dues must be remitted to the union treasurer by the 15th of the following month. Candy Co. matches the employees' charitable contributions to Save the Children Canada on a 2-to-1 basis. Donations are mailed to this organization semi-annually. A cheque will be sent for the first half of the year on July 5, 2013. Employee deductions for Charitable have remained consistent since January 1, 2013.

Required

a. Assuming that the payroll register has been posted, but no entries have been made for employee benefits expense for June, make the two journal entries that are necessary to record this expense of Candy Co. for June 2013.

b. Give details of the various cheques that will be issued in July 2013 based on Candy Co.'s payroll activities for the year so far.

9A-4. The Ripcord Parachute Club of Burlington employs three people and pays them on a weekly basis. Payroll data for the four weeks in February 2012 are shown below:

Week 1—February

Employee	Sal.	Deductions						Net Pay	Chq. No.
		Tax	CPP	EI	LTD	Pen.	Med.		
Phil Lesage	800	135	36	14	17	41	16	541	205
Linda Barry	800	121	36	14	17	41	10	561	206
Howard Post	1,000	179	46	17	17	52	16	673	207

Week 2—February

Employee	Sal.	Deductions						Net Pay	Chq. No.
		Tax	CPP	EI	LTD	Pen.	Med.		
Phil Lesage	900	169	41	16	17	48	16	593	216
Linda Barry	800	121	36	14	17	41	10	561	217
Howard Post	1,000	179	46	17	17	52	16	673	218

Week 3—February

Employee	Sal.	Deductions						Net Pay	Chq. No.
		Tax	CPP	EI	LTD	Pen.	Med.		
Phil Lesage	900	169	41	16	17	48	16	593	221
Linda Barry	800	121	36	14	17	41	10	561	222
Howard Post	1,000	179	46	17	17	52	16	673	223

Week 4—February

Employee	Sal.	Deductions						Net Pay	Chq. No.
		Tax	CPP	EI	LTD	Pen.	Med.		
Phil Lesage	900	169	41	16	17	48	16	593	244
Linda Barry	800	121	36	14	17	51	10	551	245
Howard Post	1,250	267	59	22	17	63	16	806	246

Check Figure

Cheque to CRA in March is $3,388.40

Recording Employee Benefits Expense—multiple periods

Assumptions

Employees pay 100% of the cost of long-term disability (LTD). Employees contribute just over 5% of their salary to the pension plan; the employer contributes 6% of the employees' salary to the plan. Medical cost is split 50/50 by employees and employer. All payroll-related deductions are paid on the 15th of March, 2012.

Required

a. While recording in the payroll journal for February, the Ripcord Parachute Club bookkeeper did not record any expense for employee benefits. Give the four journal entries that should be made for the month to record this expense.

Posting routine entries for a monthly period

b. Post the entries from the payroll journal and the entries in **a.** above to the T accounts shown as follows. (You may ignore the accounts that are not shown.)

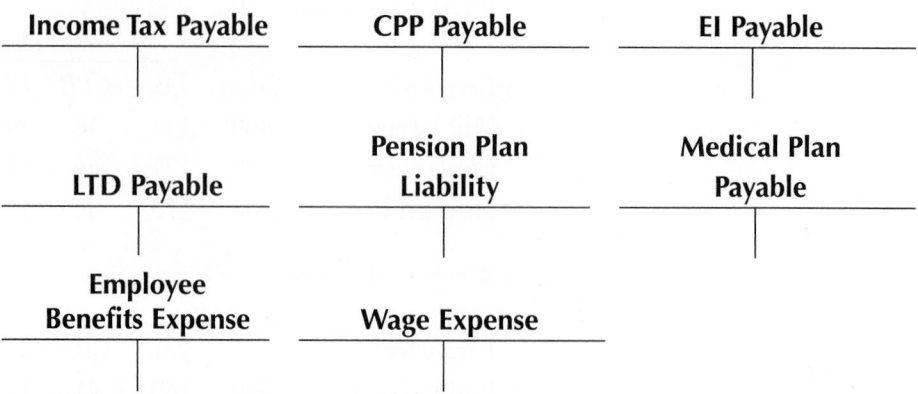

Income Tax Payable	CPP Payable	EI Payable

LTD Payable	Pension Plan Liability	Medical Plan Payable

Employee Benefits Expense	Wage Expense

Calculating remittances

1 2 (60 min)

c. List the cheques and the amounts of the cheques that will be issued on March 15 for the February payroll.

Group B Problems

(The forms you need are on pages 9-5 to 9-10 of the *Study Guide with Working Papers*.)

Recording Employee Benefits Expense and subsequent entries

1 2 (40 min)

9B-1. The payroll register for Rice Company of Sackville is summarized below for the month of April 2012:

				Deductions				
Employee	Total Salary	Tax	CPP	EI	Med-ical	Union Dues	Net Pay	Chq. No.
Bob Roberts	3,250	468	146	56	35	18	2,527	662
Robin Case	2,800	467	124	48	62	18	2,081	663
Bailey Tropp	2,450	347	107	42	62	18	1,874	664
Ishma Blumen	2,800	366	124	48	62	18	2,182	665
	11,300	1,648	501	194	221	72	8,664	

The union dues are remitted to the treasurer of the union by the 10th day of the next month. Rice Company matches its employees' contributions to the medical plan. Assume that the information in the above table has been recorded and cheques No. 662 to No. 665 were issued.

Required

a. Record the company's benefits expense, assuming no such entry was made when cheques No. 662 to No. 665 were recorded.

b. In May, Rice Company issued the following three cheques:

1. May 10, to the Employees' Union, cheque No. 681.
2. May 15, to the CRA, cheque No. 698.
3. May 20, to the Provincial Health Care Insurance Company, cheque No. 713.

How much was each cheque for?

c. What entries would be made to record the three cheques in **b.** above?

9B-2. Gibraltor Co. of Sussex recorded the following payroll details in its payroll journal for the month of March, 2013:

				Deductions					
Employee	Total Salary	Tax	CPP	EI	LTD	Med-ical	Union Dues	Net Pay	Chq. No.
Fred Jones	3,350	502	151	58	42	36	21	2,540	716
May George	2,800	442	124	48	68	61	21	2,036	717
Bren Morley	2,900	361	129	50	42	36	21	2,261	718
Joyce Fisher	2,500	298	109	43	68	—	21	1,961	719
Pat Sailer	2,500	268	109	43	68	36	21	1,955	720
	14,050	1,871	622	242	288	169	105	10,753	

Union dues are remitted by the end of the following month to the employees' union treasurer. Employees pay 100% of the long-term disability (LTD). Gibraltor Co. matches its employees' contributions to the medical plan and remits by the 20th of the following month.

Required

a. Assume that there was no employee benefits expense recognized as the payroll register was recorded. Give the general journal entry necessary to record this employee benefits expense for March 2013.

b. List the cheques, together with their amounts and dates, that Gibraltor Co. would issue in April 2013 with respect to the above payroll data.

9B-3. The Candy Co. of Lethbridge pays its workers twice each month. Data for the two pay periods on June 2013 are shown below:

First half of June 2013:

				Deductions				
Employee	Total Salary	Tax	CPP	EI	Union	Chari-table	Net Pay	Chq. No.
Ann Wyatt	1,640	208	74	28	11	16	1,303	312
Jim Elliott	1,565	215	70	27	11	16	1,226	313
Bren Stairs	1,300	156	57	22	11	16	1,038	314
Becky Holmes	1,508	198	67	26	11	16	1,190	315
	6,013	777	268	103	44	64	4,757	

Second half of June 2013:

				Deductions				
Employee	Total Salary	Tax	CPP	EI	Union	Chari-table	Net Pay	Chq. No.
Ann Wyatt	1,640	208	74	28	11	16	1,303	387
Jim Elliott	1,595	223	72	28	11	16	1,245	388
Bren Stairs	1,300	156	57	22	11	16	1,038	389
Becky Holmes	1,610	215	72	28	11	16	1,268	390
	6,145	802	275	106	44	64	4,854	

Union dues must be remitted to the union treasurer by the 15th of the following month. Candy Co. matches the employees' charitable contributions to Save the Children Canada on a 2-to-1 basis. Donations are mailed to this organization semi-annually. Deductions from all employees to May 31 this year have totalled $580. A cheque will be sent for the first half of the year on July 5, 2013.

Required

a. Assuming that the payroll register has been posted, but no entries have been made for employee benefits expense for June, make the two journal entries that are necessary to record this expense for Candy Co. for June 2013.

b. Give details of the various cheques that will be issued in July 2013 based on Candy Co.'s payroll activities for the year so far.

9B-4. The Ripcord Parachute Club of Burlington employs three people and pays them on a weekly basis. Payroll data for the four weeks in February 2012 are shown below:

Week 1—February

| | | | Deductions | | | | | Net | Chq. |
Employee	Sal.	Tax	CPP	EI	LTD	Pen.	Med.	Pay	No.
Phil Lesage	975	130	45	17	18	49	18	698	205
Linda Barry	900	145	41	16	18	46	12	622	206
Howard Post	1,125	204	52	19	18	59	18	755	207

Week 2—February

| | | | Deductions | | | | | Net | Chq. |
Employee	Sal.	Tax	CPP	EI	LTD	Pen.	Med.	Pay	No.
Phil Lesage	975	130	45	17	18	49	18	698	215
Linda Barry	950	156	44	16	18	48	12	656	216
Howard Post	1,125	204	52	19	18	59	18	755	217

Week 3—February

| | | | Deductions | | | | | Net | Chq. |
Employee	Sal.	Tax	CPP	EI	LTD	Pen.	Med.	Pay	No.
Phil Lesage	975	130	45	17	18	49	18	698	221
Linda Barry	950	156	44	16	18	48	12	656	222
Howard Post	1,185	216	55	21	18	61	18	796	223

Week 4—February

| | | | Deductions | | | | | Net | Chq. |
Employee	Sal.	Tax	CPP	EI	LTD	Pen.	Med.	Pay	No.
Phil Lesage	1,000	148	46	17	18	51	18	702	244
Linda Barry	950	125	44	16	18	48	12	687	245
Howard Post	1,185	206	55	21	18	61	18	806	246

Assumptions

Employees pay 100% of the cost of long-term disability (LTD). Employees contribute just over 5% of their salary to the pension plan; the employer contributes 6% of the employees' salary to the plan. Medical cost is split 50/50 by employees and employer. All payroll-related deductions are paid on the 15th of March, 2012.

Required

a. While recording the payroll journal in February 2012, the bookkeeper for the Ripcord Parachute Club did not record any expense for employee benefits. Give the four journal entries that should be made for the month to record this expense.

Recording Employee Benefits
Expense—multiple periods

<table>
<tr><td>Posting routine entries for a
monthly period</td><td>**b.** Post the entries from the payroll journal and the entries in **a.** above to the T accounts shown below. (You may ignore the accounts that are not shown.)</td></tr>
</table>

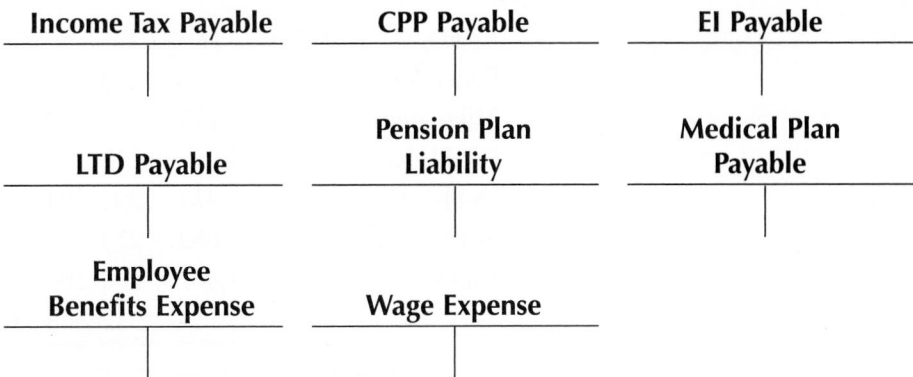

Income Tax Payable	CPP Payable	EI Payable

LTD Payable	Pension Plan Liability	Medical Plan Payable

Employee Benefits Expense	Wage Expense

Calculating remittances

 **(60 min)**

c. List the cheques and the amounts of the cheques that will be issued on March 15, 2009, for the February 2009 payroll.

Group C Problems

(The forms you need are on pages 9-10 to 9-15 of the *Study Guide with Working Papers*.)

Recording benefits expense and computing and entering cheques issued re payroll

(45 min)

9C-1. The payroll register for Bawlf Hardware Co. of Creston for the month of May 2012 is shown below:

Employee	Salary	Deductions						Net Pay	Chq. No.
		IT	CPP	EI	Health	LTD	Union		
Jake Jacobson	2,800	396	124	48	32	48	21	2,131	514
Mary Hind	2,350	294	102	41	51	42	21	1,799	515
Kyle Good	2,200	245	94	38	32	40	21	1,730	516
Lily Chau	2,750	332	122	48	51	47	21	2,129	517
Roy Verhagen	2,100	213	90	36	51	38	21	1,651	518
	12,200	1,480	532	211	217	215	105	9,440	

Union dues must be submitted to the treasurer of the union by the 20th day of the next month. Bawlf Hardware matches the employees' contributions to the LTD plan, and the total must be sent to the insurance company by the 10th of the month following the payroll. Assume that all payroll information except benefits has been recorded and cheques No. 514 to No. 518 were issued.

Check Figure

Employee Benefits Expense for CPP and EI—$827.40

Required

a. Record Bawlf's benefits expense for the month of May 2012.

b. In June 2012 Bawlf Hardware issued the following three cheques:

1. Cheque No. 543, June 10, to ABC Insurance Company for the LTD
2. Cheque No. 551, June 15, to the CRA for employee deductions
3. Cheque No. 567, June 15, to the Hardware Employees Union, Local 471, for union dues

How much was each cheque for?

c. What entry would be made in the general journal to record each cheque in **b.** above?

9C-2. Counterpoint Counselling Co. of Edmonton recorded the following details in its professional payroll journal for July 2014:

Employee	Salary	IT	CPP	EI	Char.	Life Ins.	Assn. Dues	Health	Net Pay	Chq. No.
							Deductions*			
Paula Amer	5,250	1,126	245	91	25	36	42	102	3,583	1274
Mike Steeves	5,700	1,275	268	99	50	39	42	102	3,825	1275
Pat MeIvor	4,990	1,096	233	86	40	32	42	67	3,394	1276
Debbie Chan	6,200	1,475	292	104	60	44	42	102	4,081	1277
Boris Hecht	6,600	1,682	214	62	75	48	42	67	4,410	1278
Kim Gere	6,150	1,462	290	106	55	43	42	102	4,050	1279
	34,890	8,116	1,542	548	305	242	252	542	23,343	

*Some of the deductions reflect the fact that annual maximums were reached by July 31, 2014.

Counterpoint matches the charitable donation of each employee and forwards the total on the 25th of each month to the Canadian Centre for Counselling Research. Association dues are sent to the Provincial Counsellors Society on the 20th of each month. Life insurance premiums are remitted to ABCD Insurance Company Ltd. by the 20th day of the following month. Health insurance premiums are remitted to the Provincial Health Care Organization by the 15th of the next month, at the same time as the employee deductions are sent to the CRA.

Required

a. Give the general journal entry necessary to complete the recording of this payroll, assuming no entry was made for benefits or related expenses when the payroll was recorded.

b. List the cheques, along with their amounts and dates, that Counterpoint would issue in the month of August 2014 with respect to this payroll.

9C-3. Refer to Problem 8C-2 (page 394).

Required

a. Give the general journal entry necessary to recognize all payroll benefits expense arising from that payroll, given the entry you made in Chapter 8.

9C-4. Refer to Problem 8C-3 (page 394).

Required

a. Give the general journal entry necessary to recognize all payroll benefits expenses arising from that payroll, given the entry you made in Problem 8C-3.

Recording benefits expense and
related liabilities for two pay
periods, plus calculating details
of payroll benefits cheques to be
issued

1 2 (45 min)

9C-5. Munchkin Bakery Co. of Timmins pays its employees every two weeks. (26 pay periods each year). There are two pay periods for March of 2013, and the details for each payroll are shown below:

March 15 Payroll

Employee	Total Salary	IT	CPP	EI	Health	Union	Net Pay	Chq. No.
			Deductions					
Holly Wilson	1,850	304	85	32	26	7	1,396	358
Reg Black	1,300	165	58	22	26	7	1,022	359
Amos Troy	1,350	167	60	23	48	7	1,045	360
Bernie Dyck	1,075	135	47	19	48	7	819	361
Cindy Nishimura	1,500	208	68	26	26	7	1,165	362
Totals	7,075	979	318	122	174	35	5,447	

March 29 Payroll

Employee	Total Salary	IT	CPP	EI	Health	Union	Net Pay	Chq. No.
			Deductions					
Holly Wilson	1,850	304	85	32	26	7	1,396	386
Reg Black	1,300	165	58	22	26	7	1,022	387
Amos Troy	1,350	167	60	23	48	7	1,045	388
Bernie Dyck	1,150	151	50	20	48	7	874	389
Cindy Nishimura	1,500	208	68	26	26	7	1,165	390
Totals	7,150	995	321	123	174	35	5,502	

Union dues must be remitted to the union treasurer by the 28th of the following month, while health premiums are matched by Munchkin and remitted to the provincial treasurer by the 10th of the month following. A cheque is sent to the CRA by the 15th of each following month as well.

Required

a. Assuming that the payroll register has been journalized, but no other related entries made, prepare the two journal entries necessary to record the benefits expense for March 2013.

b. Give the details of all cheques that Munchkin will issue in April 2013 with respect to payroll deductions.

Recording benefits expense and
related liabilities for five pay
periods in a month, plus
calculating details of payroll
benefits cheques to be issued

① ② (90 min)

9C-6. The Grierson Auto Repair Company pays each of its employees weekly every Friday. During the month of May 2014, there were five pay periods, which are detailed as follows. (Note that employees pay 100% of the cost of health and dental plans.)

Week 1–May 2, 2014

| | Weekly | | | | Deductions | | | Net | Chq. |
Employee	Earnings	IT	CPP	EI	Union Dues	Health Plan	Dental Plan	Pay	No.
Hal Dyer	760.00	122.40	34.29	13.15	6.52	15.80	12.85	554.99	1475
Carol James	805.00	117.50	36.52	13.93	6.52	11.69	12.85	605.99	1476
LeRoy Cohen	882.00	160.30	40.33	15.26	6.52	11.69	12.85	635.05	1477
Peter Tsui	926.00	160.45	42.51	16.02	6.52	15.80	12.85	671.85	1478
Wendy Sage	742.00	118.45	33.40	12.84	6.52	15.80	12.85	542.14	1479
Weekly Totals	4,115.00	679.10	187.05	71.20	32.60	70.78	64.25	3,010.02	

Week 2–May 9, 2014

| | Weekly | | | | Deductions | | | Net | Chq. |
Employee	Earnings	IT	CPP	EI	Union Dues	Health Plan	Dental Plan	Pay	No.
Hal Dyer	738.00	118.60	33.20	12.77	6.52	15.80	12.85	538.26	1512
Carol James	756.00	108.75	34.09	13.08	6.52	11.69	12.85	569.02	1513
LeRoy Cohen	896.00	161.40	41.02	15.50	6.52	11.69	12.85	647.02	1514
Peter Tsui	908.00	159.70	41.61	15.71	6.52	15.80	12.85	655.81	1515
Wendy Sage	725.00	115.60	32.56	12.54	6.52	15.80	12.85	529.13	1516
Weekly Totals	4,023.00	664.05	182.48	69.60	32.60	70.78	64.25	2,939.24	

Week 3–May 16, 2014

| | Weekly | | | | Deductions | | | Net | Chq. |
Employee	Earnings	IT	CPP	EI	Union Dues	Health Plan	Dental Plan	Pay	No.
Hal Dyer	785.00	125.90	35.53	13.58	6.52	15.80	12.85	574.82	1577
Carol James	734.00	113.65	33.00	12.70	6.52	11.69	12.85	543.59	1578
LeRoy Cohen	456.00	154.00	19.24	7.89	6.52	11.69	12.85	243.81	1579
Peter Tsui	856.00	164.20	39.04	14.81	6.52	15.80	12.85	602.78	1580
Wendy Sage	748.00	117.15	33.69	12.94	6.52	15.80	12.85	549.05	1581
Weekly Totals	3,579.00	674.90	160.50	61.92	32.60	70.78	64.25	2,514.05	

Week 4–May 23, 2014

| | Weekly | | | | Deductions | | | Net | Chq. |
Employee	Earnings	IT	CPP	EI	Union Dues	Health Plan	Dental Plan	Pay	No.
Hal Dyer	830.00	131.60	37.75	14.36	6.52	15.80	14.50	609.47	1604
Carol James	758.00	108.75	34.19	13.11	6.52	11.69	14.50	569.24	1605
LeRoy Cohen	902.00	163.90	41.32	15.60	6.52	11.69	14.50	648.47	1606
Peter Tsui	835.00	132.10	38.00	14.45	6.52	15.80	14.50	613.63	1607
Wendy Sage	756.00	116.50	34.09	13.08	6.52	15.80	14.50	555.51	1608
Weekly Totals	4,081.00	652.85	185.35	70.60	32.60	70.78	72.50	2,996.32	

Week 5–May 30, 2014

| | Weekly | | | | Union | Health | Dental | Net | Chq. |
| | | | | | Deductions | | | | |
Employee	Earnings	IT	CPP	EI	Dues	Plan	Plan	Pay	No.
Hal Dyer	752.00	118.47	33.89	13.01	6.52	15.80	14.50	549.81	1638
Carol James	736.00	113.65	33.10	12.73	6.52	11.69	14.50	543.81	1639
LeRoy Cohen	884.00	160.30	40.43	15.29	6.52	11.69	14.50	635.27	1640
Peter Tsui	932.00	162.40	42.80	16.12	6.52	15.80	14.50	673.86	1641
Wendy Sage	758.00	119.62	34.19	13.11	6.52	15.80	14.50	554.26	1642
Weekly Totals	4,062.00	674.44	184.41	70.26	32.60	70.78	72.50	2,957.01	

Required

a. Assuming that the payroll register has been journalized, but no other related entries have been made, prepare the five journal entries necessary to record the benefits expense for May 2014.

b. Give the details of all cheques that Grierson will issue in June 2014 with respect to payroll deductions.

On-the-job Training

(The forms you need are on page 9-15 of the *Study Guide with Working Papers*.)

Calculating employer's expenses
1 2 (30 min)

T-1. The Tidy Tax Return Co. employs 50 extra people for the period February 1 through April 30 each year in order to process a large volume of tax returns. Each employee receives $10 per hour and works 40 hours a week (for 14 weeks). Early in May, all 50 additional workers are laid off.

A personnel service has offered to supply the needed 50 workers at a cost of $12 per hour. The managers of Tidy Tax Return Co. are not sure whether to accept the new offer.

Please prepare a memo to the management outlining the advantages of using the personnel service bureau and also the advantages of continuing with the present arrangement. Do not restrict your answer to financial considerations only.

CONTINUING PROBLEM

Preparing and recording journal
entries and the payroll registry;
posting; and filing the T4
Summary
1 2 3 (150 min)

Because it is the end of the calendar year, Tony Freedman knows that, in addition to recording the normal entries for December 2013, he will need to complete certain tasks that relate to payroll. Specifically, he will need to prepare T4 slips for his two employees, and then complete the T4 Summary for the year (remember that he has had employees for only two months).

Assignment

(See pages 9-16 to 9-32 in your *Study Guide with Working Papers*.)

Nov.	30	Record the employer's share of payroll benefits for the previous month of November. Refer to the work that you completed for the end of November (Chapter 8) for the details you need to complete this task.
Dec.	6	Paid the two employees their wages: L. Klumm, 43 hours, and A. Hall, 34 hours (cheques No. 266 and No. 267).
	9	Received the balance of the amount due from Vita Needle Company, November 1, 2010, invoice No. 12685.
	10	Received invoice No. 4668 from *City Newspaper* re advertising seasonal specials, due in 30 days, $480.
	11	Received December telephone bill from West Bell Canada, $165.
	13	Paid the two employees their wages: L. Klumm, 40 hours, and A. Hall, 42 hours (cheques No. 268 and No. 269).
	13	Paid telephone bill received November 9, $150 (cheque No. 270).
	13	Collected amount owing by Accu Pac, Inc., re November 4 invoice No. 12687.
	13	Purchased the remaining goods for resale of a friend's computer sales operation for cash, $7,000 (cheque No. 271).
	13	Paid amount due to CRA re November wages, $1,692.56 (cheque No. 272).
	16	Paid amount due to System Design Furniture re November 4 purchase (its invoice No. 8771), $1,400 (cheque No. 273).
	17	Paid amount due to Multi Systems for November 19 purchase (its invoice No. 1784), $450 (cheque No. 274).
	17	Purchased on account from Alpha Office Co., supplies totalling $318, its invoice No. 8161 (purchase order No. 4015), due within 30 days.
	20	Paid the two employees their wages: L. Klumm, 34 hours, and A. Hall, 36 hours (cheques No. 275 and No. 276).
	20	Billed Carson Engineering Corp. for major project involving 28 of its computers, $8,750, invoice No. 12688.
	23	Paid overdue utilities bill for November and December, $486, to City Electric (cheque No. 277).
	24	Paid the two employees their wages to noon today: L. Klumm, 32 hours, and A. Hall, 38 hours (cheques No. 278 and No. 279). Because of seasonal factors, these are their final cheques this calendar year (office closed until January 2, 2014).
	30	Received $5,495 cash from Augustana Co. for services. Invoice No. 12689.
	31	Record the employer's share of payroll benefits for the month of December. Refer to the details of your payroll journal in order to complete this task.

Pete's Market
Completing Payroll Requirements

Estimated time 2 hours

This Mini Practice Set will aid in putting the pieces of payroll together. In this project, you are the bookkeeper and will have the responsibility of recording payroll in the payroll register, paying the payroll, recording the employer's tax responsibilities, and making payment according to the CRA's requirements.

Pete's Market, owned by Pete Reel, is located at 33 Riel Drive, Your Town, Ontario, M5W 2A4. His business number is 12345 6789 RP. The following are the employees of Pete's Market, along with their salaries, exemptions, etc.

Weekly Salaries

Date	Name	Claim Code	Weekly Salary
Sept. 7, 2018	Fred Flynn	5	$1,190
Sept. 14, 2018	Fred Flynn	5	1,190
Sept. 21, 2018	Fred Flynn	5	1,265
Sept. 28, 2018	Fred Flynn	5	1,265

Note: Fred Flynn receives a salary increase September 17, 2018.

Sept. 7, 2018	Mary Jones	1	$1,265
Sept. 14, 2018	Mary Jones	1	1,265
Sept. 21, 2018	Mary Jones	1	1,265
Sept. 28, 2018	Mary Jones	1	1,265

Note: On September 21, 2018, Mary reaches her CPP maximum of $2,163.15. Deduct only $34.67 CPP for Mary in that payroll, then no further CPP is deducted in September. Also note that Mary reached her maximum deduction for EI in August, so no EI deduction is made from her pay in September.

Sept. 7, 2018	Lilly Vron	1	$940
Sept. 14, 2018	Lilly Vron	1	940
Sept. 21, 2018	Lilly Vron	1	940
Sept. 28, 2018	Lilly Vron	3	940

Source deductions payable at August 31, 2018 (employer portion already recorded):

CPP Payable	EI Payable	Income Taxes Payable
$1,576.80	$592.08	$3,268.75

Required

(The forms you need are on pages 9-29 to 9-32 of the *Study Guide with Working Papers*.)

Using the general journal and payroll register provided, complete the following for the month of September 2018:

2018
Sept.

7 Complete payroll register for September 7 payroll, journalize payroll entry, and journalize entry for all employer's expenses related to payroll.

7 Transfer cash for September 7 payroll net pay from operating account to payroll account.

14 Process payroll (follow the same procedures as for September 7 payroll).

14 Transfer cash for September 14 payroll net pay from operating account to payroll account.

14 Pay CRA for prior month's source deductions payable.

21 Process payroll for September 21. Note change in Fred Flynn's salary.

21 Transfer cash for September 21 payroll net pay from operating account to payroll account.

28 Process payroll for September 28. Note change in Lilly Vron's claim code.

28 Transfer cash for September 28 payroll net pay from operating account to payroll account.

Verdunn Company

Payroll Project

Verdunn Company has four salaried employees as well as a couple of hourly workers who receive overtime at 1.5 times their normal rate for any hours over 40 in a week. On the payroll register (provided in the *Study Guide with Working Papers*), record the employees' payroll for the month of February of the current year. You may use current deduction tables found on the CRA website, since the text only has weekly deduction tables (or, you might use the proper formula to calculate the CPP and EI instead of using tables, but you will need the tables for the tax deductions). A solution to this comprehensive problem is available to instructors based on the rules for the province of Ontario, so you may be asked to use that province's tax tables for completing the exercise. On the other hand, your instructor may ask you to use the tables for another province—in which case a slightly different solution will be needed to assure your answers match exactly. Be sure you know what the requirements are before proceeding.

Use the following data:

Employee	Net Claim Code	Hours Worked, or Biweekly Salary (first two weeks of February)	Hours Worked, or Biweekly Salary (last two weeks of February)
Adams, Taylor	1	$ 1,245	$ 1,245
Evans, Chelsea	3	1,475	1,525
Johnson, Quinn	2	1,550	1,550
Winston, Jameel	4	980	1,050
Chan, Jeffery*	1	Wk1 – 38, Wk2 – 43	Wk3 – 42, Wk 4 – 45
Lovejoy, Katherine**	2	Wk1 – 42, Wk2 – 35	Wk3 – 40, Wk 4 – 46

*Rate is $14.00 per hour   **Rate is $16.00 per hour

Each employee contributes $16 biweekly to a supplementary health insurance plan and $11 biweekly to group insurance. This small company is sponsoring a young man in Africa to get an education, and each of the six employees agree to have $5.00 deducted from his or her payroll each pay period. The employer matches contributions to the supplemental health plan, remits exactly the group insurance premiums deducted, and doubles the charitable deductions, making the necessary payments by the 15th of the following month. Jeffery Chan has worked at the company only since mid-January and does not become eligible to participate in either the supplemental health or the group insurance until the coming April payroll. He has agreed to the charitable deduction, however.

Journalize the following:
(The blank forms you need are on pages 9-33 to 9-40 of the *Study Guide with Working Papers*.)

1. The payroll for the biweekly pay periods ending February 14 and February 28 of the current year. Remember to use biweekly CPP and Income Tax deduction tables. The EI tables are not sensitive to the payroll period being used. You can calculate both CPP and EI if that is easier.

2. Employee benefits expense resulting from each payroll.

3. Payment of net pay to employees on February 14 and February 28. (Cheques 370-375 and then 419-424)

4. Remittance to the Receiver General (Cheque 465) on March 15.

5. Remittance to Ontario Supplementary Medical (Cheque 466) on March 15.

6. Remittance of group insurance to Mayfair Financial (Cheque 467) on March 15.

7. Remittance to African Educational Fund (Cheque 468) on March 15.

Once the journals are complete, post all necessary amounts to appropriate GL accounts using the account forms provided in the *Study Guide with Working Papers*. Except for the Cash account, all opening balances have been removed for simplicity.

For the first two items above, use the General Journal (forms provided in the *Study Guide with Working Papers*). All cheques should be recorded using a Cash Payments Journal (also provided in the *Study Guide with Working Papers*).

Thanks to Imelda Engels in Cranbrook, BC, for the inspiration and much of the detail for this assignment.

10 Special Journals with Taxes

THE BIG PICTURE

Suppose you live near Toronto and want to buy an iPod to listen to music, plus record lectures from time to time. Your college bookstore has a fall special at $199.99, but you will need to pay an additional 13% for HST, bringing your total cost to about $226.00. Another option for you is to search the web for an e-tailer from outside of Ontario that sells the identical iPod and get it for $16 cheaper because only GST gets charged. This happens because the e-tailer does not charge you the Ontario sales tax. At the moment in Canada, that is how the rules work. (If the online merchant was from Ontario, then the HST would apply.)

Note that you must still pay the GST at 5% because that is standard across Canada. Not only the rate is the same, but the rules as to what gets taxed are also identical. So it seems safe to say that your savings are real, and a distinct advantage goes to the non-Ontario Internet-based merchant.

At least if we are talking about an iPod, there is an actual physical item to attract the attention of the taxation authorities. But suppose instead you needed to purchase a special software program for your laptop. You could buy it from your bookstore (let's assume a cost of $100 there) or you could download it from another Internet-based company that has its sales office in Australia for a cost of only $75. In this case, you do not need to pay the HST because no physical object gets shipped. In most cases, you are permitted to download the software, and that download includes all the documentation, help files, and, of course, the program itself. This sort of transaction has taxation authorities very worried because even if they pass laws making these sales taxable, the real question is how they could ever find out about them to initiate the taxation process.

In the United States, recent studies show that annually the various state and local governments missed out on collecting more than US$25 billion. This is a real problem for some state governments because the latest figures also disclose that, on average, states rely on sales tax revenue for about one-third of their total tax revenue. The shortfall is expected to grow as e-commerce continues to be a bigger part of our economic life. Recent changes to how sales taxes are computed and collected may have changed this somewhat, and we will not have reliable numbers for a while yet.

It is no wonder then that the issue of taxing Internet purchases has pitted brick-and-mortar retailers against their rivals in cyberspace. Consider also that there are many e-tailers based outside Canada who will cheerfully send merchandise to Canada, and modern transportation companies can get a shipment from, say, California to Edmonton in less than 48 hours—even 24 hours at a much higher cost.

Despite all the changes that are sure to come, you still need to know how to account for sales taxes and the GST. Even if these taxes may decline as a percentage, they are still a vitally important aspect of the commercial life of our nation and will stay that way for your working lifetime. Our example company in this chapter, Chou's Toy Shop, must collect both provincial sales tax and GST, so you will learn how to do the accounting for what becomes a liability on Chou's books. We also address how merchants use special journals to record all of their transactions, including all appropriate taxes, to make their record-keeping go more smoothly and efficiently.

Sources: Donald Bruce and William F. Fox, "State and Local Sales Tax Revenue Losses from E-Commerce: Estimates as of July 2004" (The University of Tennessee Center for Business and Economic Research), 4 (2004), and Walter J. Baudier, "Internet Sales Taxes from Borders to Amazon: How Long Before All of Your Purchases Are Taxed?" *Duke Law and Technology Review*, 2006 Rev 0005. Accessed August 2007 at www.law.duke.edu/journals/dltr/articles/2006dltr0005.html.

1 Recording sales that include PST, GST, or HST in the sales journal (p. 449)

2 Creating, recording, and posting a credit memorandum for returned sales when PST, GST, or HST is included (p. 451)

3 Recording cash received using a cash receipts journal when PST, GST, or HST is included (p. 459)

4 Preparing schedules of accounts receivable and accounts payable, and balancing to control accounts (pp. 464 and 474)

5 Journalizing purchase transactions that include GST or HST in the purchases journal (p. 465)

6 Creating, recording, and posting a debit memorandum for purchase returns when GST or HST is included (p. 468)

7 Recording cash paid out in the cash payments journal when GST or HST is included (p. 469)

Chapter 6 introduced the topic of Special Journals and how using them can simplify and speed up the work that bookkeepers and accountants need to do, whether this be daily, weekly, or monthly. This chapter builds on that material and expands it to cover how special journals must be designed and used to account for taxes. After all, and as much as we all may regret it, taxes are a reality in the business world and are not going to go away any time soon. Before working through a comprehensive example, we first present separate sections showing how taxes are included in each of the four main journals: Sales, Cash Receipts, Purchases, and Cash Payments. We will also show how both Sales and Purchase returns are recorded and posted correctly when taxes are included.

INTRODUCTION TO GST AND HST

With very few exceptions, all Canadians and Canadian companies must pay either GST (currently 5%) or HST (currently mostly 13%) on their purchases, including most services, such as legal fees. Since businesses both pay GST/HST and collect GST/HST from their customers, this is a subject that is essential for anyone who plans to make all or part of a career in bookkeeping or accounting.

Some of the things that Canadians buy are not subject to GST/HST. Financial services such as insurance and bank fees are not taxed, and neither are most food products. One often-mentioned example is the fact that if a Canadian buys one or two doughnuts, GST/HST is applied because they are considered a snack. However, if that same Canadian buys a half-dozen of the identical doughnuts, they are considered a foodstuff and are exempt! Some find this situation amusing, but the reality is that if exemptions are to be allowed from GST/HST rates, then definitions need to be in place to ensure that the tax is applied consistently. No doubt some changes will be made to the list of taxable items as time goes on and political priorities change. Two classes of taxable items that have often been mentioned as possibly subject to change are textbooks (indeed, books in general) and clothing (especially for children). While these changes may take place, they are details easily managed by accountants, if the accountants have a proper understanding of how the tax is supposed to work and the methods used to account for it. This chapter will cover all the critical details to ensure that students are capable of carrying out their duties involving this set of taxes.

As you read this, it is likely true for most students that they have never known Canada without the GST. The **Goods and Services Tax (GST)** was introduced in 1991, with the **Harmonized Sales Tax (HST)** coming into effect in 1997. These two taxes are essentially identical, apart from the difference in rates, and, as you will discover, are accounted for in the same way. In five provinces (Nova Scotia, New Brunswick, Ontario, British Columbia, and Newfoundland and Labrador), HST has replaced a combination of GST and a Provincial Sales Tax (PST).

The trend toward HST now appears to be unstoppable, with the possible exception of Alberta, Nunavut, Yukon, and the Northwest Territories, which have no PST to replace. Provinces moving to HST have made a sharing agreement with the federal government that provides, among many other things, that the tax will be administered by the federal government, and most of the provinces will receive 8/13 (8%) of the tax, with the federal portion equalling 5/13 (5%). This means that the same 5% GST is paid by all Canadians, and in addition an extra 8% is also added on in four of the provinces (Nova Scotia is 10%). For this edition, we illustrate HST at 13% for the most part, but have also included some material that refers to GST at 5%. Depending on where you are studying this chapter, your instructor may alter any of the problems to ensure that your educational experience is as realistic as possible.

Since some provinces still collect a PST, this chapter will illustrate, explain, and present test material on this form of taxation, since it is a fact that many students will face PST as a reality in their routine bookkeeping and accounting duties. We cover PST in Learning Unit 1, along with GST/HST on sales, since PST is applied only at the retail level, and it is accounted for in much the same way as GST/HST is collected.

Since PST is generally considered a retail tax, businesses do not pay (technically, they receive an exemption from) PST on their purchases. From time to time, a business will pay some minor amount of PST, mostly because it is too much trouble to apply for an exemption. An example is the occasional purchase of minor office supplies for cash. Regular purchases of office supplies are often done by phone or e-mail with a familiar supplier, and that business relationship is likely to include having a sales tax exemption certificate or number on file—so no PST gets charged in most cases involving office supplies. However, from time to time some "critical" office supply item needs to be replaced—often by a staff member on his or her lunch break—and so PST gets charged. In this chapter, we do not take the time to fully explain or illustrate this process, since almost by definition it is a minor matter for most businesses. Most companies just write off this tax as an expense, often including it as part of the cost of office supplies or whatever. A very few companies might charge the PST to a separate expense account—PST on Purchases, for example—but it hardly seems a useful procedure in most cases.

Learning Unit 10-1

Chou's Toy Shop: Seller's View of a Merchandising Company

1 Recording sales that include PST, GST, or HST in the sales journal

There is no PST in Alberta, Nunavut, the Northwest Territories, or the Yukon.

PROVINCIAL SALES TAX COLLECTED

Continuing the same company introduced in Chapter 6, Chou must collect PST from his customers and send it to the province. Sales tax payable represents a liability to Chou's business.

Assume that Chou's business is located in a province that charges an 8% sales tax. Remember from Chapter 6 that Chou's sales on July 18 were $3,000. Chou must figure out the PST on the sales. For this purpose, let's assume that there were only two sales on that date: the cash sale ($1,800) and the charge sale ($1,200).

The PST on the cash sale is calculated as follows:

$$\$1,800 \times 0.08 = \$144 \text{ tax}$$

$$\$1,800 + \$144 \text{ tax} = \$1,944 \text{ cash received from customer}$$

Here is how the PST on the charge sale is computed:

$$\$1{,}200 \times 0.08 = \$96 \text{ tax}$$

$$\$96 \text{ tax} + \$1{,}200 \text{ charge} = \$1{,}296 \text{ Total Accounts Receivable}$$

This is how it would be recorded:

Accounts Affected	Category	↑↓	Rules	T Account Update
Cash	**Asset**	↑	**Dr.**	Cash Dr. 1,944 | Cr.
Accounts Receivable	**Asset**	↑	**Dr.**	Accounts Receivable Dr. 1,296 | Cr.
Sales Tax Payable	**Liability**	↑	**Cr.**	Sales Tax Payable Dr. | Cr. 144 / 96
Sales	**Revenue**	↑	**Cr.**	Sales Dr. | Cr. 3,000

Date		Account Titles and Description	PR	Dr.	Cr.
July	18	Cash		1944 00	
		Accounts Receivable		1296 00	
		Sales Tax Payable			240 00
		Sales			3000 00
		July 18 Sales			

Notice that the amount of Sales does not change when sales tax is collected. It is still $3,000.

Later in this chapter, we will show you how to record a credit memorandum with sales tax. Notice that in either case (cash or credit), it is the customer who pays the PST, not Chou's business.

Also note that only a very small business would use the General Journal to record sales that include PST. Most would use a Special Journal (the Sales Journal) to record such sales. We illustrate this below.

Let's look at how Munroe Menswear Company, a retailer, handles PST at 8% on a sale made to Jones. Figure 10-1 shows Munroe's Sales Journal.

Also, a new account, **Provincial Sales Tax (PST) Payable**, must be created. This account is a liability account in the general ledger with a credit balance. The customer owes Munroe the sale amount plus the tax.

Sales Tax Payable
| XXX
A liability in the general ledger

Keep in mind that if sales discounts are available, they are not normally calculated on the sales tax. The discount is on the selling price less any returns before the tax. For example, if Jones receives a 2% discount, he pays the following:

$5,000 × 0.02 = $100 savings →

$5,400	Total owed (tax is $400)
− 100	Savings (discount)
$5,300	Amount paid

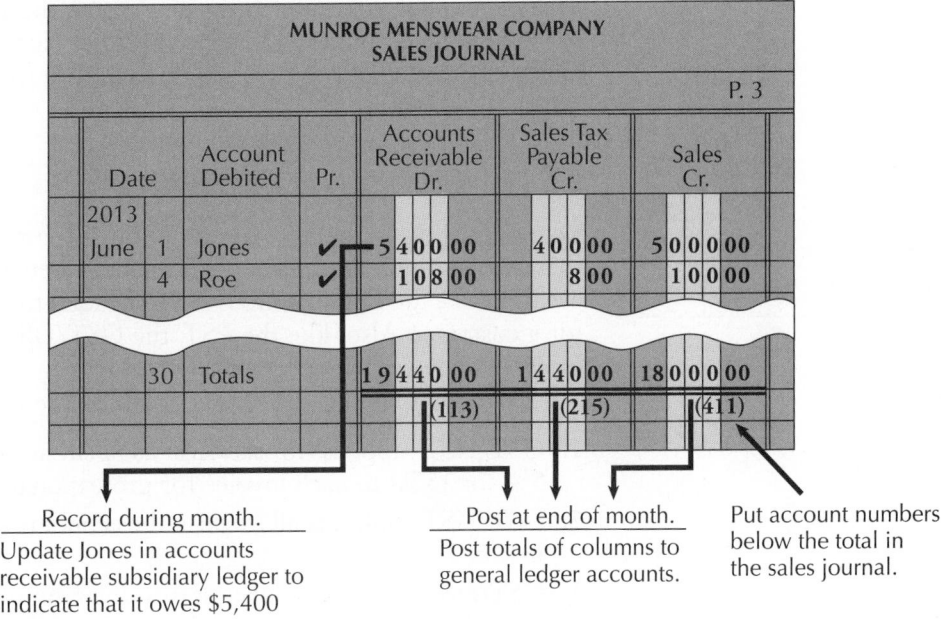

Figure 10-1
Munroe Sales Journal

MUNROE MENSWEAR COMPANY
SALES JOURNAL

P. 3

Date		Account Debited	Pr.	Accounts Receivable Dr.	Sales Tax Payable Cr.	Sales Cr.
2013 June	1	Jones	✔	5 4 0 0 00	4 0 0 00	5 0 0 0 00
	4	Roe	✔	1 0 8 00	8 00	1 0 0 00
	30	Totals		1 9 4 4 0 00	1 4 4 0 00	1 8 0 0 0 00
				(113)	(215)	(411)

Record during month.
Update Jones in accounts receivable subsidiary ledger to indicate that it owes $5,400 to Munroe.

Post at end of month.
Post totals of columns to general ledger accounts.

Put account numbers below the total in the sales journal.

2 Creating, recording, and posting a credit memorandum for returned sales when PST, GST, or HST is included

THE CREDIT MEMORANDUM WITH PROVINCIAL SALES TAX

Figure 10-1 above shows the sales journal for Munroe Menswear Company. Remember, since Munroe is a retail company, its customers must pay PST if they are in a province that charges PST. Let's assume that on June 8 Roe returns $50 worth of the $100 worth of merchandise he bought earlier in the month. Let's analyze and journalize the credit memo that Munroe issued. Keep in mind that the customer is no longer responsible for paying for either the returned merchandise or the 8% tax on it.

Accounts Affected	Category	↑↓	Rules	T Account Update			
Sales Returns and Allowances	Revenue (Contra)	↑	Dr.	**Sales Returns and Allowances**			
				Dr.	Cr.		
				50			
Provincial Sales Tax Payable ($8 tax on $100) ($4 tax on $50)	Liability	↓	Dr.	**Provincial Sales Tax Payable**			
				Dr.	Cr.		
				4.00			
Accounts Receivable, Roe	Asset	↓	Cr.	**Accounts Rec.**		**Roe**	
				Dr.	Cr.	Dr.	Cr.
					54	108	54

June	8	Sales Returns and Allowances	5 0 00		
		Provincial Sales Tax Payable	4 00		
		Accounts Receivable, Roe		5 4 00	
		Issued credit memo			

SPECIAL JOURNALS WITH TAXES   451

This journal entry requires three postings to the general ledger and one recording for Roe in the accounts receivable subsidiary ledger. Note that since Roe returned half of his merchandise, he was able to reduce what he pays for PST by half (from $8 to $4).

HOW COMPANIES RECORD GST AND HST

Similarities and differences between PST and GST

Before illustrating the normal accounting treatment of the GST/HST, notice that there are both similarities and differences between the GST and PST (covered earlier). Like the PST, the GST/HST is added to the total of each invoice prepared for a customer. Also, like the PST, the GST/HST must be remitted to the appropriate taxing authority periodically.

However, there are also a few notable differences:

1. GST/HST applies to services as well as goods (e.g., a lawyer will add 5% (or 13%) to each invoice for professional services).
2. GST/HST applies at all levels in the economy—not just the retail level, as in the case of PST.
3. GST/HST is paid by businesses to their suppliers as well as collected by them from their customers. The difference between the tax collected from customers and the tax paid to suppliers is the amount sent to (or recovered from) the federal government each period.
4. GST/HST might result in a business's receiving a refund in some periods. Since GST/HST is payable on large asset purchases (e.g., a delivery van), a business may claim this amount against the GST/HST it owes. In the long run, if a business is successful, it should remit more GST/HST than it receives as a refund; however, in a particular period it may be eligible to receive a refund.

GST/HST COLLECTED ON SALES

Note: There are more similarities with than differences from the bookkeeping procedures described previously.

To illustrate the basic accounting treatment for **GST/HST collected**, we will refer to an example you have already seen. Figure 6-3 (sales invoice) showed what an invoice would look like before GST/HST. Figure 10-2 shows the same invoice with HST added.

You should notice two things about this invoice. First, HST is added at 13% (GST would be added at 5%) of the total price of the goods. Second, the invoice shows a registration (or business) number. Each business in Canada (*except*

Figure 10-2
Sales Invoice with HST

Sales Invoice No. 1		Art's Wholesale Clothing Co.
		1528 Belle Avenue
		Toronto, Ontario M5A 2L4

Sold to: Hal's Clothing
     91 Century Avenue
     Winnipeg, MB R2C 4X7

Date: April 2, 2013
Your purchase order No: 430
Ship via: Acme Truck Co.

Shipped to: Same
Terms: 2/10, n/30

Quantity	Description	Unit Price	Total
20	Men's dress shirts—code 16B	$20.00	$400.00
10	Ladies' designer jeans—code 18C	15.00	150.00
50	Baseball caps—code 22D	5.00	250.00
	Subtotal		$800.00
	Add:	HST	104.00
		TOTAL	$904.00

Business No. 109309799

very small ones) must be registered for GST/HST by the federal government and use the number in all its dealings with the federal government.

This invoice is recorded in the sales journal of Art's Wholesale Clothing Company. The main difference is that now the bookkeeping task is made slightly longer because of the need to keep track of the HST. Figure 6-2 on page 253 showed the sales journal before HST. Figure 10-3 shows how this new invoice, and some others not illustrated individually, are recorded with HST. Posting to the various ledger accounts is also illustrated.

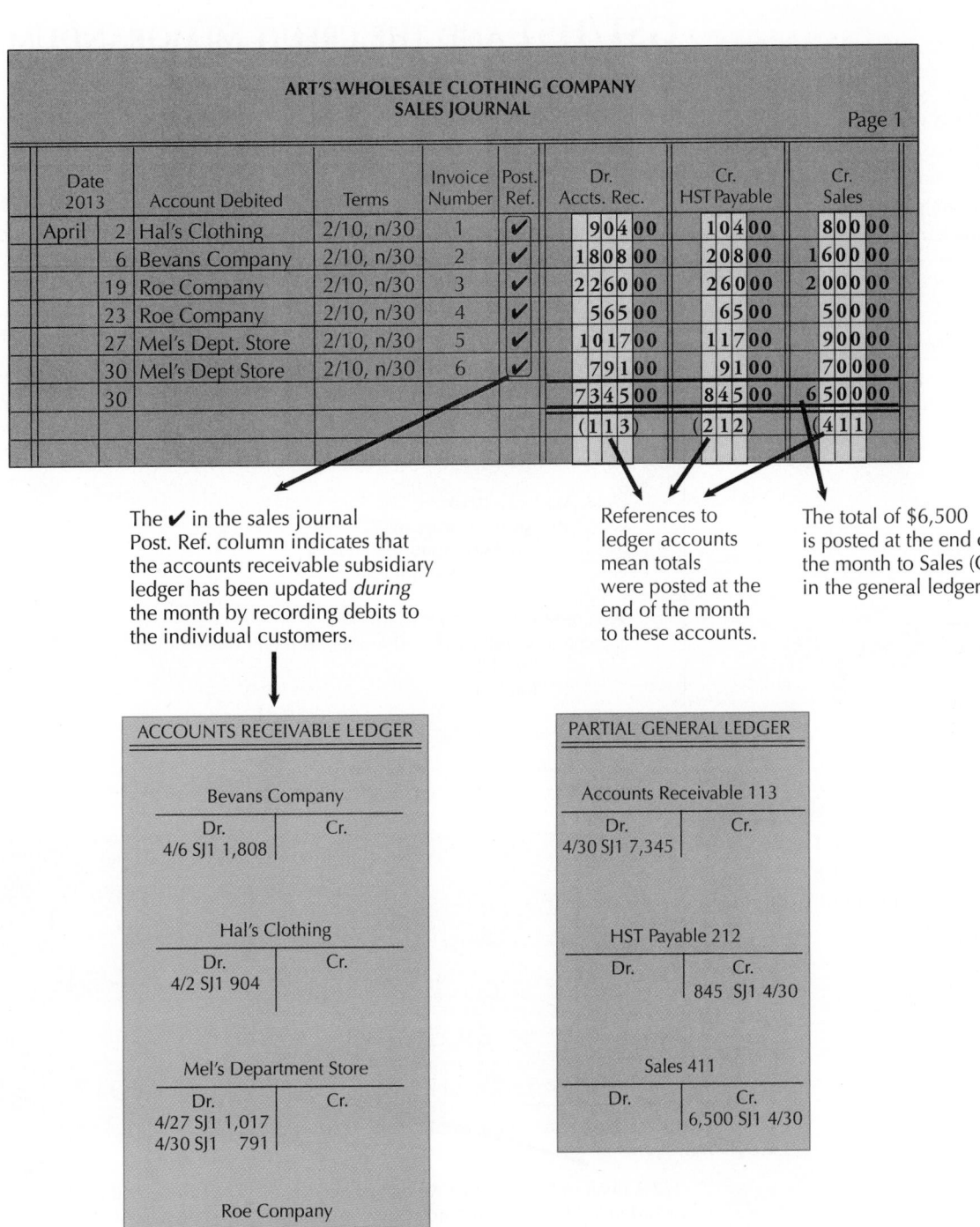

Figure 10-3 Sales Journal and Postings with HST

The total invoice amounts are recorded during the month in the individual customers' accounts in the accounts receivable subsidiary ledger. This process is identical to the pre-GST/HST method except that the totals are higher.

At the end of the month, instead of posting a single amount as *both* a credit (to Sales) and a debit (to Accounts Receivable), there are three totals to post. A new account is now required—HST payable, #212. This is a liability account in the general ledger with a credit balance. Notice that the totals of the two credits (Sales and HST) equal the single debit (Accounts Receivable).

GST/HST AND THE CREDIT MEMORANDUM

As you already know, a business occasionally finds it necessary to issue a customer a **credit memorandum** (often called a credit note). The pre-HST form of a credit memorandum is shown in Figure 6-4 on page 255. The new form of credit memorandum is shown in Figure 10-4.

As before, we will assume that the volume of credit notes is low and that Art's Wholesale uses the general journal to record these notes. The journal entry will appear as shown in Figure 10-5.

> The credit memorandum with HST is very similar to an invoice with HST except that the amounts are opposite in meaning and effect, and often smaller.

Figure 10-4 Credit Memorandum with HST

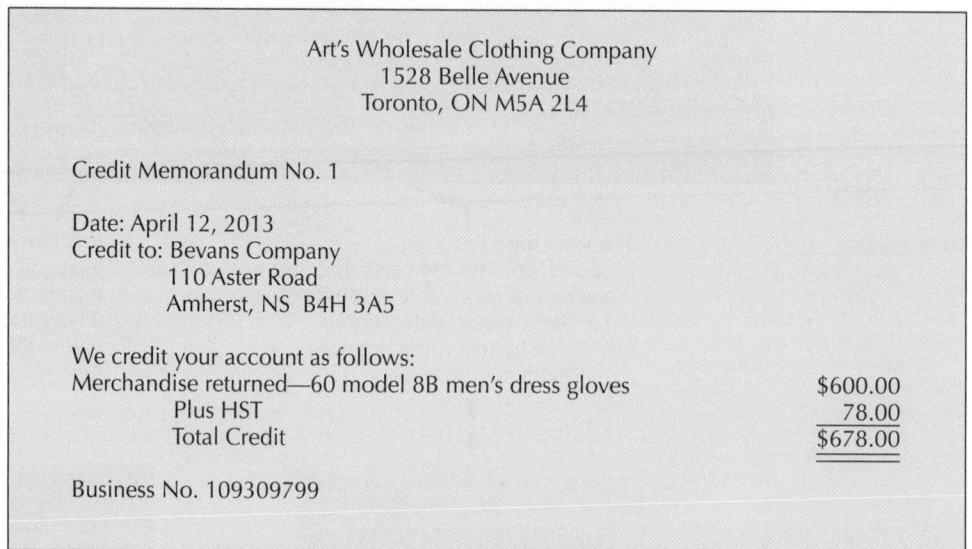

Art's Wholesale Clothing Company
1528 Belle Avenue
Toronto, ON M5A 2L4

Credit Memorandum No. 1

Date: April 12, 2013
Credit to: Bevans Company
110 Aster Road
Amherst, NS B4H 3A5

We credit your account as follows:
Merchandise returned—60 model 8B men's dress gloves ... $600.00
Plus HST ... 78.00
Total Credit ... $678.00

Business No. 109309799

Figure 10-5
Postings for the Credit Memorandum with HST

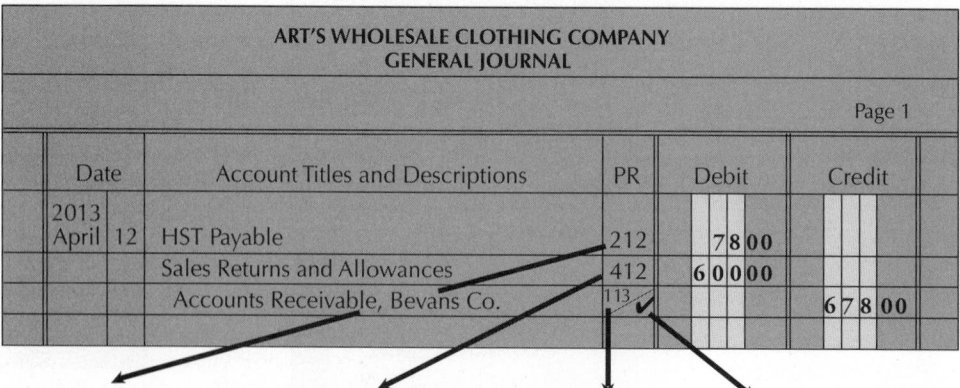

ART'S WHOLESALE CLOTHING COMPANY
GENERAL JOURNAL

Page 1

Date		Account Titles and Descriptions	PR	Debit	Credit
2013 April	12	HST Payable	212	78 00	
		Sales Returns and Allowances	412	600 00	
		Accounts Receivable, Bevans Co.	113 ✔		678 00

212 A debit of $78 is recorded in HST Payable, account 212 in the general ledger. When this is done, the account number is placed in the PR column of the journal.

412 A debit of $600 is recorded in Sales Returns and Allowances, account 412 in the general ledger. When this is done, the account number is placed in the PR column of the journal.

113 The credit of $678 is posted to Accounts Receivable, the controlling account in the general ledger. When this is done, the account number (113) is placed in the PR column of the journal, above the /.

✔ The checkmark indicates that $678 has been recorded as a credit in the account of Bevans Company in the accounts receivable ledger.

Remember that the $78 debit posting will reduce the amount of HST owed to the federal government and must be taken into account when preparing a cheque for the amount owed at period-end. The customer, Bevans Company, now receives a credit totalling $678. This includes the extra 13% for HST. Since the original invoice included this 13% tax as an addition, it is proper that any refund for returned or damaged goods also include the 13% tax. The amount owed to Art's Wholesale by Bevans Company is reduced by $678.

PROVINCIAL SALES TAX WITH GST/HST

In many provinces (not in Ontario, British Columbia, Nova Scotia, New Brunswick, Newfoundland and Labrador, or Alberta), when a sale is made to a customer at the retail level, PST is added to the invoice. Since 1991, it has been necessary to also add GST to these invoices. A typical invoice in a province with a 8% PST might look like Figure 10-6.

In provinces that charge HST, the invoice would look like Figure 10-2.

SALES INVOICE WITH PST AND GST/HST

The Munroe Menswear Company would record this invoice along with other invoices for June 2014 in its sales journal. This recording and posting process is illustrated in Figure 10-7. Note that, apart from the addition of one more column (for the GST), this is similar to the illustration shown in Figure 10-3.

It is worth repeating that if sales discounts are available, they are usually taken on the *sales amount only*, not the GST/HST or PST. If Jones receives a 2% discount on invoice No. 1420 (see Figure 10-6), it would pay the following amount:

Original sales amount of invoice No. 1420	$1,500
Less: 2% discount	30
	1,470
Plus: PST as originally computed	120
Plus: GST as originally computed	75
Amount paid	$1,665

> No sales discount is taken on GST/HST or PST amounts because the monies are collected on behalf of the government.

Figure 10-6
Sales Invoice with PST and GST

> Assume the PST rate in this province is 8%.

Munroe Menswear Company
147 Main Street
Saskatoon, Saskatchewan
S8A 2G7

To: Jones Company
228 Market Street
Saskatoon, Saskatchewan
S8J 2P2

Invoice # 1420
June 01, 2014

10 Company Blazers with logo @ $150.00 each		$1,500.00
	PST @ 8%	120.00
		1,620.00
	GST @ 5%	75.00
	Total	$1,695.00

Business No. 142716491

Figure 10-7
Munroe's Sales
Journal
with GST

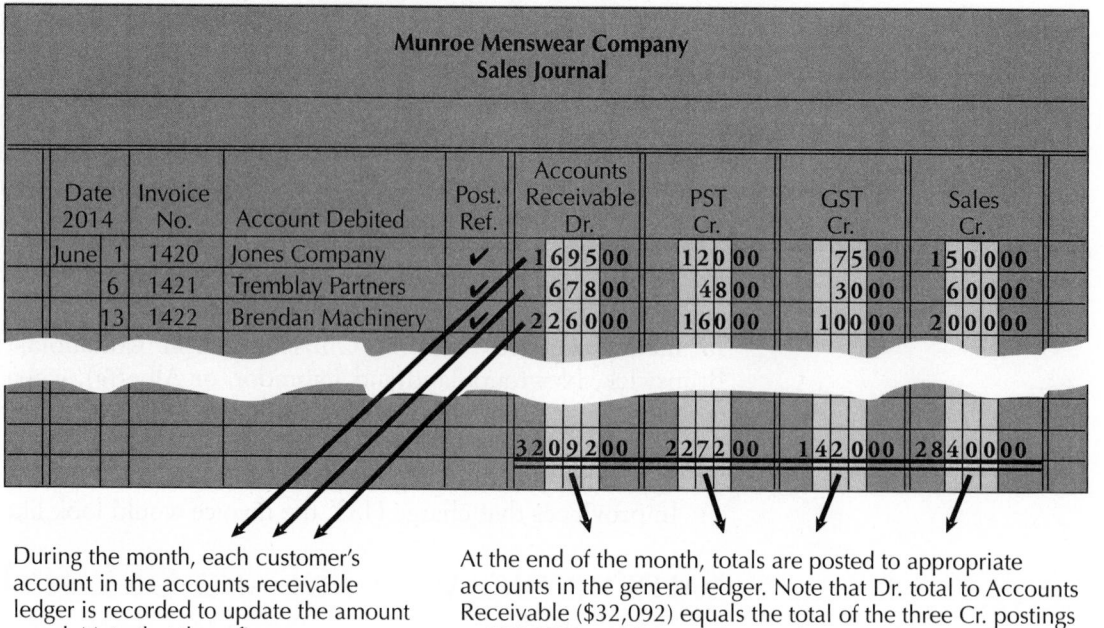

Date 2014		Invoice No.	Account Debited	Post. Ref.	Accounts Receivable Dr.	PST Cr.	GST Cr.	Sales Cr.
June	1	1420	Jones Company	✔	1 6 9 5 00	1 2 0 00	7 5 00	1 5 0 0 00
	6	1421	Tremblay Partners	✔	6 7 8 00	4 8 00	3 0 00	6 0 0 00
	13	1422	Brendan Machinery	✔	2 2 6 0 00	1 6 0 00	1 0 0 00	2 0 0 0 00
					3 2 0 9 2 00	2 2 7 2 00	1 4 2 0 00	2 8 4 0 0 00

During the month, each customer's account in the accounts receivable ledger is recorded to update the amount owed. Note that these figures include the PST and GST.

At the end of the month, totals are posted to appropriate accounts in the general ledger. Note that Dr. total to Accounts Receivable ($32,092) equals the total of the three Cr. postings to PST, GST, and Sales ($2,272 + $1,420 + $28,400 = $32,092).

CREDIT MEMORANDUM WITH PST AND GST/HST

Let us assume that Jones receives permission to return some of the goods billed on invoice No. 1420 (Figure 10-6). This results in a credit memorandum (or credit note) being prepared by Munroe Menswear Company. This credit memo would appear as shown in Figure 10-8.

The credit memo would be recorded by Munroe Company in its general journal (unless there was a large number of returns, in which case a special journal could be used). The entry to record credit note No. 104 is as shown in Figure 10-9.

This entry is posted in a similar fashion to the entry in Figure 10-5. The only change is that there is also a posting of a debit to PST Payable (account number 210) as well as to GST Collected (account number 212).

> The credit memorandum with PST and GST is very similar to an invoice with PST and GST except that the amounts are opposite in meaning and effect, and often smaller.

Figure 10-8
Credit Memo with PST and GST

Munroe Menswear Company
147 Main Street
Saskatoon, Saskatchewan
S8A 2G7

To: Jones Company
228 Market Street
Saskatoon, Saskatchewan
S8J 2P2

Credit Memo # 104
July 15, 2014

Returned 2 Blazers—Ref. Invoice 1420, June 1, 2014—@ $150.00 each

	$300.00
PST @ 8%	24.00
	324.00
GST @ 5%	15.00
Total	$339.00

Business No. 142716491

Figure 10-9
Recording Credit Memo
with PST and GST

MUNROE MENSWEAR COMPANY
GENERAL JOURNAL

Page 1

	Date		Account Titles and Descriptions	PR	Debit	Credit
2014 July		15	Sales Returns and Allowances	412	3 0 0 00	
			GST Collected	212	1 5 00	
			PST Payable	210	2 4 00	
			Accounts Receivable, Jones Co.	113 ✔		3 3 9 00
			To record credit memo number 104			

LEARNING UNIT 10-1 REVIEW

AT THIS POINT you should be able to:

♦ Explain the basics of GST/HST and PST added to sales invoices in Canada. (pp. 449–454)

♦ Explain, journalize, and post an invoice that includes both GST/HST and PST. (pp. 455–456)

♦ Explain, journalize, and post a credit memorandum that includes both GST and PST. (pp. 456–457)

Self-Review Quiz 10-1

(The forms you need are on pages 10-1 and 10-2 of the *Study Guide with Working Papers*.)

Journalize the following transactions in the sales journal or the general journal for Moss Company. Post to the accounts receivable and general ledger accounts as appropriate. Use the same journal headings and general ledger account numbers that were used in Figures 10-7 and 10-9.

2012
May   1   Sold merchandise to Jane Company, invoice No. 101—$400 plus PST $32 plus GST $20—total $452.00. Terms 2/10, n/30

4   Sold merchandise to Ralph Company, invoice No. 102—$3,000 plus PST $240 plus GST $150—total $3,390.00. Terms 2/10, n/30

21   Issued credit memorandum No. 4 to Ralph Company, $500 plus PST $40 plus GST $25—total $565.00. Reason—defective goods

Solution to Self-Review Quiz 10-1

MOSS COMPANY
SALES JOURNAL

Page 1

Date 2012		Account Debited	Invoice Number	Post. Ref.	Accts. Rec. Dr.	PST Payable Cr.	GST Collected Cr.	Sales Cr.
May	1	Jane Company	101	✔	4 5 2 00	3 2 00	2 0 00	4 0 0 00
	4	Ralph Company	102	✔	3 3 9 0 00	2 4 0 00	1 5 0 00	3 0 0 0 00
					3 8 4 2 00	2 7 2 00	1 7 0 00	3 4 0 0 00
					(1 1 2)	(2 1 0)	(2 1 2)	(4 1 1)

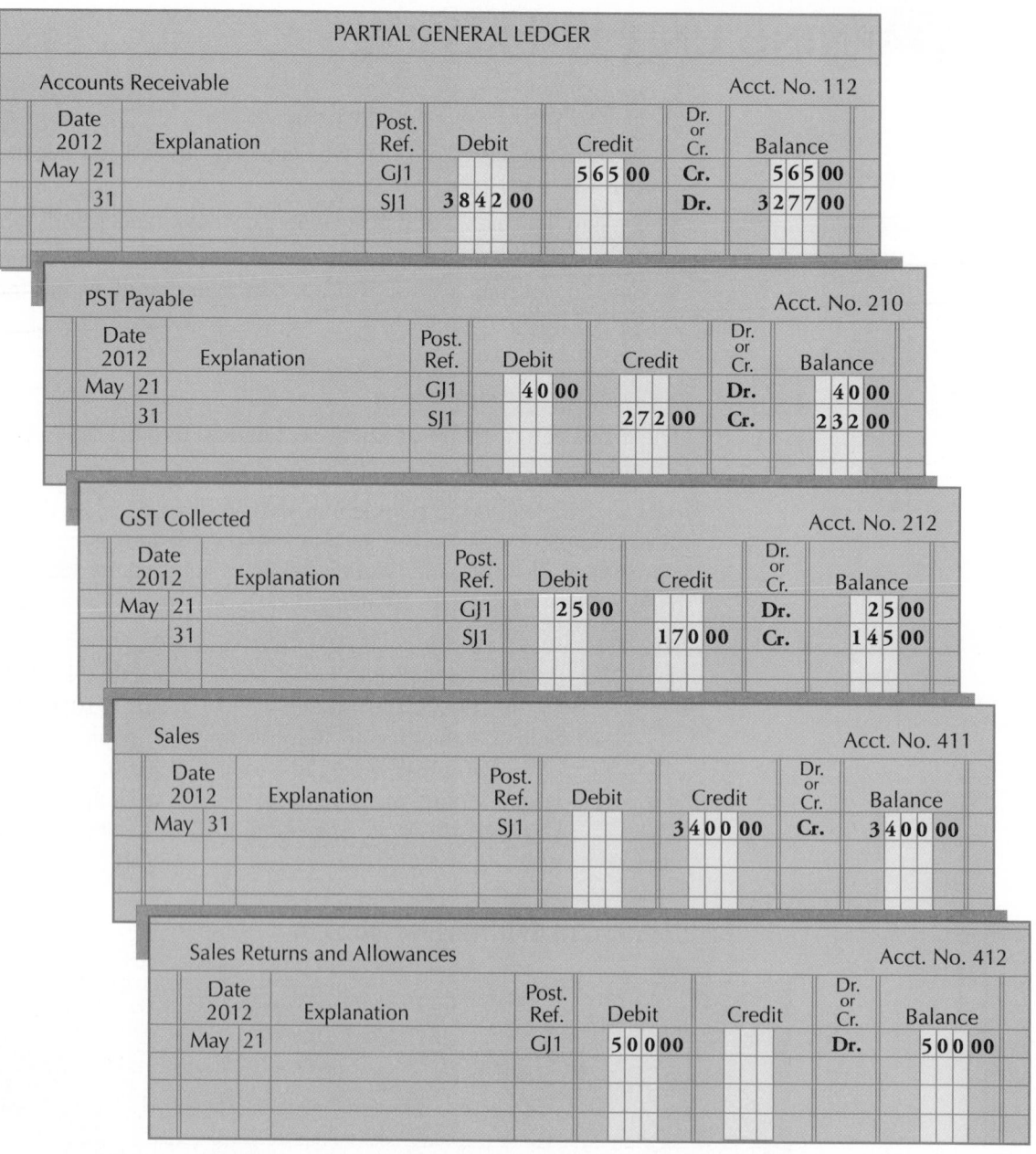

MOSS COMPANY
GENERAL JOURNAL

Date		Account Titles and Descriptions	Post. Ref.	Debit	Credit
2012 May	21	Sales Returns and Allowances	412	500 00	
		GST Collected	212	25 00	
		PST Payable	210	40 00	
		Accounts Receivable, Ralph Co.	112 ✓		565 00
		To record credit memo No. 4			

PARTIAL GENERAL LEDGER

Accounts Receivable — Acct. No. 112

Date 2012		Explanation	Post. Ref.	Debit	Credit	Dr. or Cr.	Balance
May	21		GJ1		565 00	Cr.	565 00
	31		SJ1	3842 00		Dr.	3277 00

PST Payable — Acct. No. 210

Date 2012		Explanation	Post. Ref.	Debit	Credit	Dr. or Cr.	Balance
May	21		GJ1	40 00		Dr.	40 00
	31		SJ1		272 00	Cr.	232 00

GST Collected — Acct. No. 212

Date 2012		Explanation	Post. Ref.	Debit	Credit	Dr. or Cr.	Balance
May	21		GJ1	25 00		Dr.	25 00
	31		SJ1		170 00	Cr.	145 00

Sales — Acct. No. 411

Date 2012		Explanation	Post. Ref.	Debit	Credit	Dr. or Cr.	Balance
May	31		SJ1		3400 00	Cr.	3400 00

Sales Returns and Allowances — Acct. No. 412

Date 2012		Explanation	Post. Ref.	Debit	Credit	Dr. or Cr.	Balance
May	21		GJ1	500 00		Dr.	500 00

PARTIAL ACCOUNTS RECEIVABLE LEDGER

NAME Jane Company
ADDRESS 1218 Broadview Avenue, Toronto, ON M5X 2A1

Date 2012	Explanation	Post. Ref.	Debit	Credit	Dr. Balance
May 1		SJ1	4 5 2 00		4 5 2 00

NAME Ralph Company
ADDRESS 1300 Marine Drive, West Vancouver, BC V6P 9B6

Date 2012	Explanation	Post. Ref.	Debit	Credit	Dr. Balance
May 4		SJ1	3 3 9 0 00		3 3 9 0 00
21		GJ1		5 6 5 00	2 8 2 5 00

Learning Unit 10-2
Cash Receipts Journal and Schedule of Accounts Receivable

3 Recording cash received using a cash receipts journal when PST, GST, or HST is included

Besides the sales journal, another special journal often used in a merchandising operation is the cash receipts journal. The cash receipts journal records the receipt of cash (or cheques) from any source. The number of columns a cash receipts journal will have depends on how frequently certain types of transactions occur. For example, in the cash receipts journal for Art's Wholesale, the accountant has developed the headings shown in Figure 10-10. Note that a column for HST (on cash sales only) has been included. HST on credit sales is recorded in the sales journal as already described. Below each heading is a description of the purpose of that column and when to update the accounts receivable ledger as well as the general ledger.

The following transactions occurred in April for Art's Wholesale and affected the cash receipts journal:

2013
April 1 Art Newner invested $8,000 in the business.
       5 Received cheque from Hal's Clothing for payment of invoice No. 1 less discount.
       12 Cash sales for first half of April, $900 plus HST.
       16 Received cheque from Bevans Company in settlement of invoice No. 2 less returns and discount.
       22 Received cheque from Roe Company for payment of invoice No. 3 less discount.
       26 Sold store equipment, $500.
       30 Cash sales for second half of April, $1,200 plus HST.

Figure 10-11 shows the cash receipts journal for the end of April along with the recordings to the accounts receivable ledger and posting to the general ledger. Study the diagram; we will review it in a moment.

Figure 10-10 Cash Receipts Journal with HST

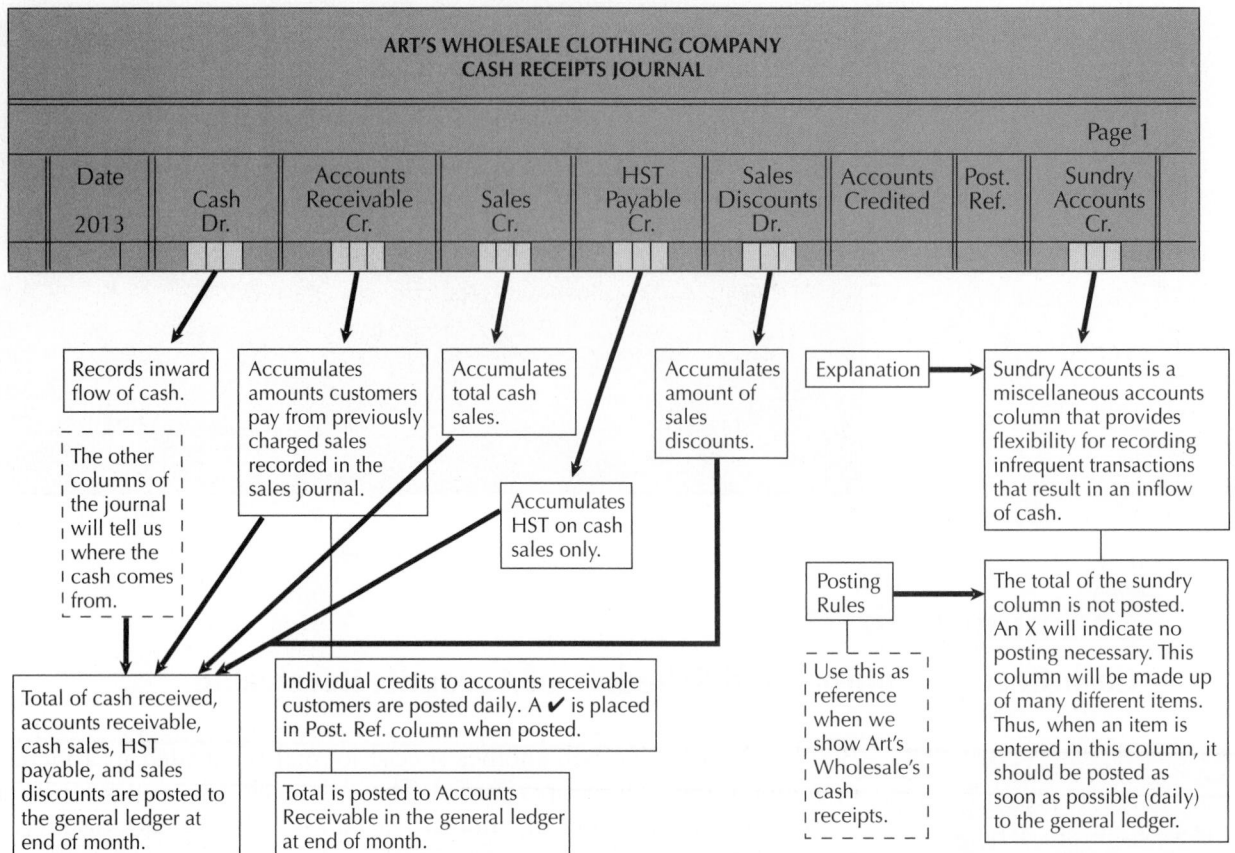

JOURNALIZING, RECORDING, AND POSTING FROM THE CASH RECEIPTS JOURNAL

On April 5, Art's Wholesale received a cheque from Hal's Clothing for payment of invoice No. 1 less discount. Remember, it was in the sales journal that this transaction was first recorded (Figure 10-3). At that time, we updated the accounts receivable ledger, indicating that Hal's Clothing owed Art $904. Since Hal's Clothing is paying within the 10-day discount period, Art's Wholesale offers a $16 sales discount ($800 × 0.02). (Remember, all credit sales carried terms of 2/10, n/30.)

Now, when payment is received, Art's Wholesale updates the cash receipts journal (see page 461) by entering the date (April 5), cash debit of $888, sales discounts debit of $16, credit to accounts receivable of $904, and which account name (Hal's Clothing) is to be credited. The terms of sale indicate that Hal's Clothing is entitled to the discount and no longer owes Art's Wholesale the $904 balance. *As soon as this line is entered into the cash receipts journal, Art's Wholesale will update the ledger account of Hal's Clothing.* Note, in the accounts receivable ledger of Hal's Clothing, how the date (April 5), posting reference (CRJ1), and credit amount ($904) account are recorded. The balance in Hal's accounts receivable ledger is zero. The last step of this transaction is to go back to the cash receipts journal and put a ✔ in the posting reference column.

In studying this cash receipts journal, note that:

1. All totals of cash receipts in the journal columns except sundry were posted to the general ledger at the end of the month.
2. Art Newner, Capital, and Store Equipment were posted to the general ledger when entered in the sundry column. It is assumed that the equipment account had a beginning balance of $4,000 in the general ledger. There is no HST on the owner's capital contribution.

> The last step is to put a checkmark in the PR column of the cash receipts journal to show the accounts receivable ledger is up to date.

Figure 10-11 Cash Receipts Journal and Posting with HST

CASH RECEIPTS JOURNAL

Page 1

Date 2013	Cash Dr.	Accounts Receivable Cr.	Sales Cr.	HST Collected Cr.	Sales Discount Dr.	Accounts Credited	PR	Sundry Accounts Cr.
April 1	8000 00					Art Newner, Capital	311	8000 00
5	888 00	904 00			16 00	Hal's Clothing	✔	
12	1017 00		900 00	117 00		Cash Sales	✗	
16	1110 00	1130 00			20 00	Bevans Company	✔	
22	2220 00	2260 00			40 00	Roe Company	✔	
26	565 00			65 00		Store Equipment	121	500 00
30	1356 00		1200 00	156 00		Cash Sales	✗	
30	15156 00	4294 00	2100 00	338 00	76 00			8500 00
	(111)	(113)	(411)	(212)	(413)			(X)

Totals posted to general ledger at end of month   Total not posted

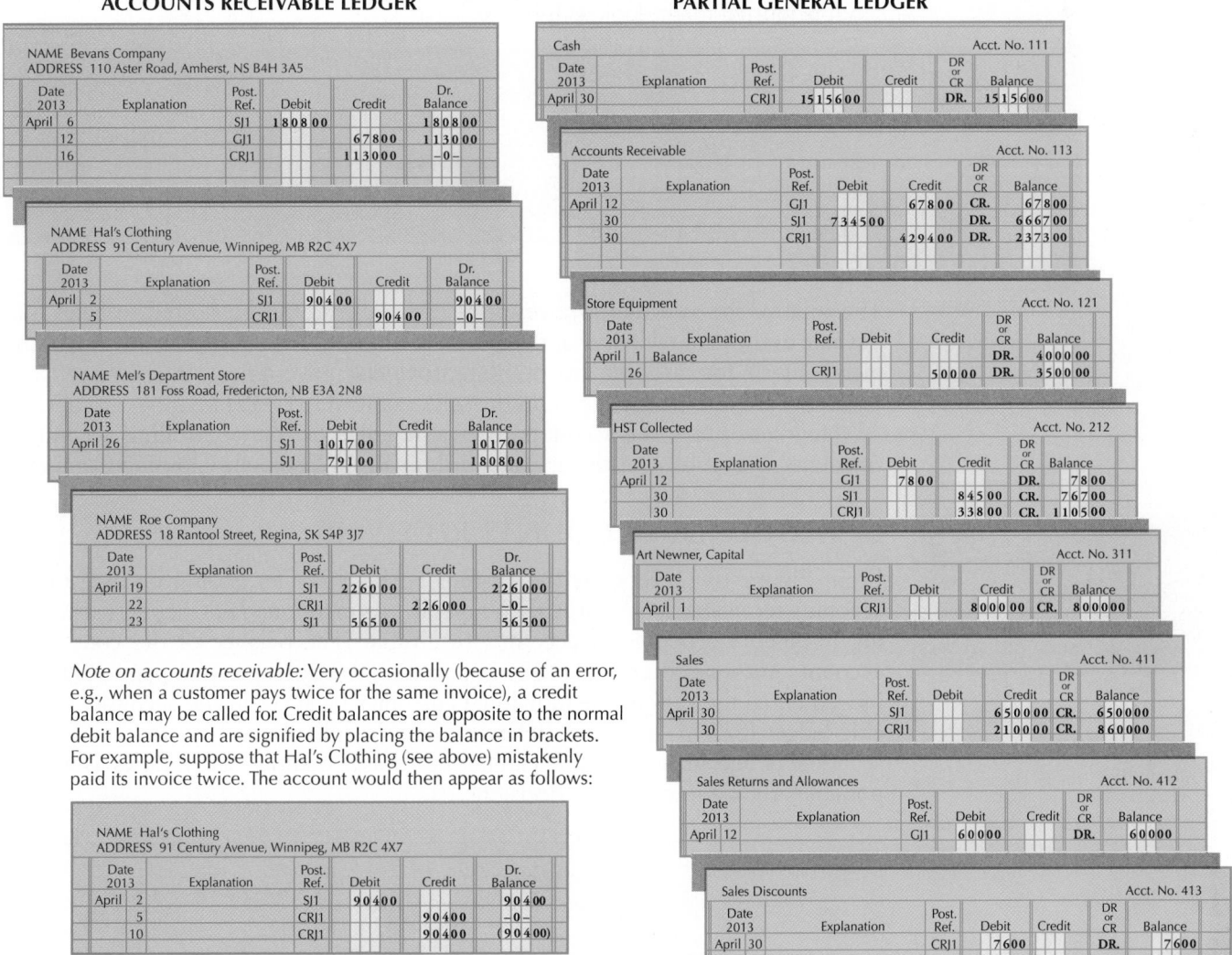

ACCOUNTS RECEIVABLE LEDGER

NAME Bevans Company
ADDRESS 110 Aster Road, Amherst, NS B4H 3A5

Date 2013	Explanation	Post. Ref.	Debit	Credit	Dr. Balance
April 6		SJ1	1808 00		1808 00
12		GJ1		678 00	1130 00
16		CRJ1		1130 00	–0–

NAME Hal's Clothing
ADDRESS 91 Century Avenue, Winnipeg, MB R2C 4X7

Date 2013	Explanation	Post. Ref.	Debit	Credit	Dr. Balance
April 2		SJ1	904 00		904 00
5		CRJ1		904 00	–0–

NAME Mel's Department Store
ADDRESS 181 Foss Road, Fredericton, NB E3A 2N8

Date 2013	Explanation	Post. Ref.	Debit	Credit	Dr. Balance
April 26		SJ1	1017 00		1017 00
		SJ1	791 00		1808 00

NAME Roe Company
ADDRESS 18 Rantool Street, Regina, SK S4P 3J7

Date 2013	Explanation	Post. Ref.	Debit	Credit	Dr. Balance
April 19		SJ1	2260 00		2260 00
22		CRJ1		2260 00	–0–
23		SJ1	565 00		565 00

Note on accounts receivable: Very occasionally (because of an error, e.g., when a customer pays twice for the same invoice), a credit balance may be called for. Credit balances are opposite to the normal debit balance and are signified by placing the balance in brackets. For example, suppose that Hal's Clothing (see above) mistakenly paid its invoice twice. The account would then appear as follows:

NAME Hal's Clothing
ADDRESS 91 Century Avenue, Winnipeg, MB R2C 4X7

Date 2013	Explanation	Post. Ref.	Debit	Credit	Dr. Balance
April 2		SJ1	904 00		904 00
5		CRJ1		904 00	–0–
10		CRJ1		904 00	(904 00)

PARTIAL GENERAL LEDGER

Cash   Acct. No. 111

Date 2013	Explanation	Post. Ref.	Debit	Credit	DR or CR	Balance
April 30		CRJ1	15156 00		DR.	15156 00

Accounts Receivable   Acct. No. 113

Date 2013	Explanation	Post. Ref.	Debit	Credit	DR or CR	Balance
April 12		GJ1		678 00	CR.	678 00
30		SJ1	7345 00		DR.	6667 00
30		CRJ1		4294 00	DR.	2373 00

Store Equipment   Acct. No. 121

Date 2013	Explanation	Post. Ref.	Debit	Credit	DR or CR	Balance
April 1	Balance				DR.	4000 00
26		CRJ1		500 00	DR.	3500 00

HST Collected   Acct. No. 212

Date 2013	Explanation	Post. Ref.	Debit	Credit	DR or CR	Balance
April 12		GJ1	78 00		DR.	78 00
30		SJ1		845 00	CR.	767 00
30		CRJ1		338 00	CR.	1105 00

Art Newner, Capital   Acct. No. 311

Date 2013	Explanation	Post. Ref.	Debit	Credit	DR or CR	Balance
April 1		CRJ1		8000 00	CR.	8000 00

Sales   Acct. No. 411

Date 2013	Explanation	Post. Ref.	Debit	Credit	DR or CR	Balance
April 30		SJ1		6500 00	CR.	6500 00
30		CRJ1		2100 00	CR.	8600 00

Sales Returns and Allowances   Acct. No. 412

Date 2013	Explanation	Post. Ref.	Debit	Credit	DR or CR	Balance
April 12		GJ1	600 00		DR.	600 00

Sales Discounts   Acct. No. 413

Date 2013	Explanation	Post. Ref.	Debit	Credit	DR or CR	Balance
April 30		CRJ1	76 00		DR.	76 00

3. The cash sales were not posted when entered (hence the X to show no posting is needed). The sales and cash totals are posted at the end of the month.
4. A ✔ means information was recorded daily to the accounts receivable ledger.
5. The Accounts Credited column describes each transaction.

We can prove the accuracy of recording transactions of the cash receipts journal by totalling the columns with debit balances and the columns with credit balances. Cross-footing is done before the totals are posted. Also, if a bookkeeper were using more than one page for the cash receipts journal, the balances on the bottom of one page would be brought forward to the top of the next page. This verifying of totals would result in less work when trying to find journalizing or posting errors at a later date. Let's see how to cross-foot the cash receipts journal of Art's Wholesale (Figure 10-11).

Proving the cash receipts journal

Debit Columns	= Credit Columns
Cash + Sales Discounts	**= Accounts Receivable + Sales + Sundry + HST**
$15,156 + $76	= $4,294 + $2,100 + $8,500 + $338
$15,232	**= $15,232**

Now let's take a moment to see what PST would look like in the cash receipts journal of a business that would need to record sales tax as well as HST. A typical cash receipts journal might look as follows:

CASH RECEIPTS JOURNAL

Page 1

Date 2010	Cash Dr.	Accounts Receivable Cr.	Sales Cr.	PST Payable Cr.	HST Payable Cr.	Sales Discounts Dr.	Accounts Credited	Post. Ref.	Sundry Accounts Cr.

The total of sales tax payable would be posted to Sales Tax Payable in the general ledger at the end of the month.

The total of the sales tax as a result of cash sales would be posted to Sales Tax Payable in the general ledger at the end of the month. It represents a liability of the merchant to forward the tax to the provincial government. Remember, cash discounts are not usually taken on the sales tax (or GST/HST).

Now let's prove the accounts receivable ledger to the controlling account—Accounts Receivable—at the end of April for Art's Wholesale Clothing Company.

SCHEDULE OF ACCOUNTS RECEIVABLE

4 Preparing schedules of accounts receivable and accounts payable, and balancing to control accounts

From Figure 10-11, let's list the customers that have an ending balance in the accounts receivable ledger of Art's Wholesale. As mentioned in Chapter 6, this listing is called a schedule of accounts receivable. The balance of the controlling account, Accounts Receivable ($2,373), in the general ledger (see page 461) does indeed equal the sum of the individual customer balances in the accounts receivable ledger ($2,373) as shown below in the schedule of accounts receivable. The schedule of accounts receivable can help forecast potential cash inflows as well as possible credit and collection decisions.

Schedule is listed in alphabetical order.

Art's Wholesale Clothing Company
Schedule of Accounts Receivable
April 30, 2013

Mel's Department Store	$1,808.00
Roe Company	565.00
Total Accounts Receivable	$2,373.00

AT THIS POINT you should be able to:

◆ Journalize, record, and post, transactions with sales tax using a cash receipts journal. (pp. 459–462)

◆ Prepare a schedule of accounts receivable. (p. 462)

Self-Review Quiz 10-2

(The forms you need are on pages 10-3 to 10-5 of the *Study Guide with Working Papers*.)

Journalize, cross-foot, record, and post when appropriate, the following transactions into the cash receipts journal of Moore Co. Use the same headings as for Art's Wholesale.

Accounts Receivable Ledger

Name	Balance	Invoice No.
Irene Welch	$565	1
Chantel Simard	226	2

Partial General Ledger

Account	Account No.	Balance
Cash	110	$600
Accounts Receivable	120	791
Store Equipment	130	600
HST Collected	212	91
Sales	410	700
Sales Discounts	420	—

2013

May 3 Received cheque from Irene Welch for invoice No. 1 less 2% discount.
7 Cash sales collected, $400 plus HST of $20.
14 Received cheque from Chantel Simard for invoice No. 2 less 2% discount.
20 Sold store equipment at cost, $300 (plus HST).

Solution to Self-Review Quiz 10-2

MOORE COMPANY
CASH RECEIPTS JOURNAL

Page 2

Date 2013	Cash Dr.	Accounts Receivable Cr.	Sales Cr.	HST Collected Cr.	Sales Discounts Dr.	Description of Receipt	Post. Ref.	Sundry Accounts Cr.
May 3	555 00	565 00			10 00	Irene Welch	✔	
7	452 00		400 00	52 00		Cash Sales	✗	
14	222 00	226 00			4 00	Chantel Simard	✔	
20	339 00			39 00		Store Equipment	130	300 00
31	1 568 00	791 00	400 00	91 00	14 00			300 00
	(110)	(120)	(410)	(212)	(420)			(X)

Cross-footing: $1,582.00 = $1,582.00

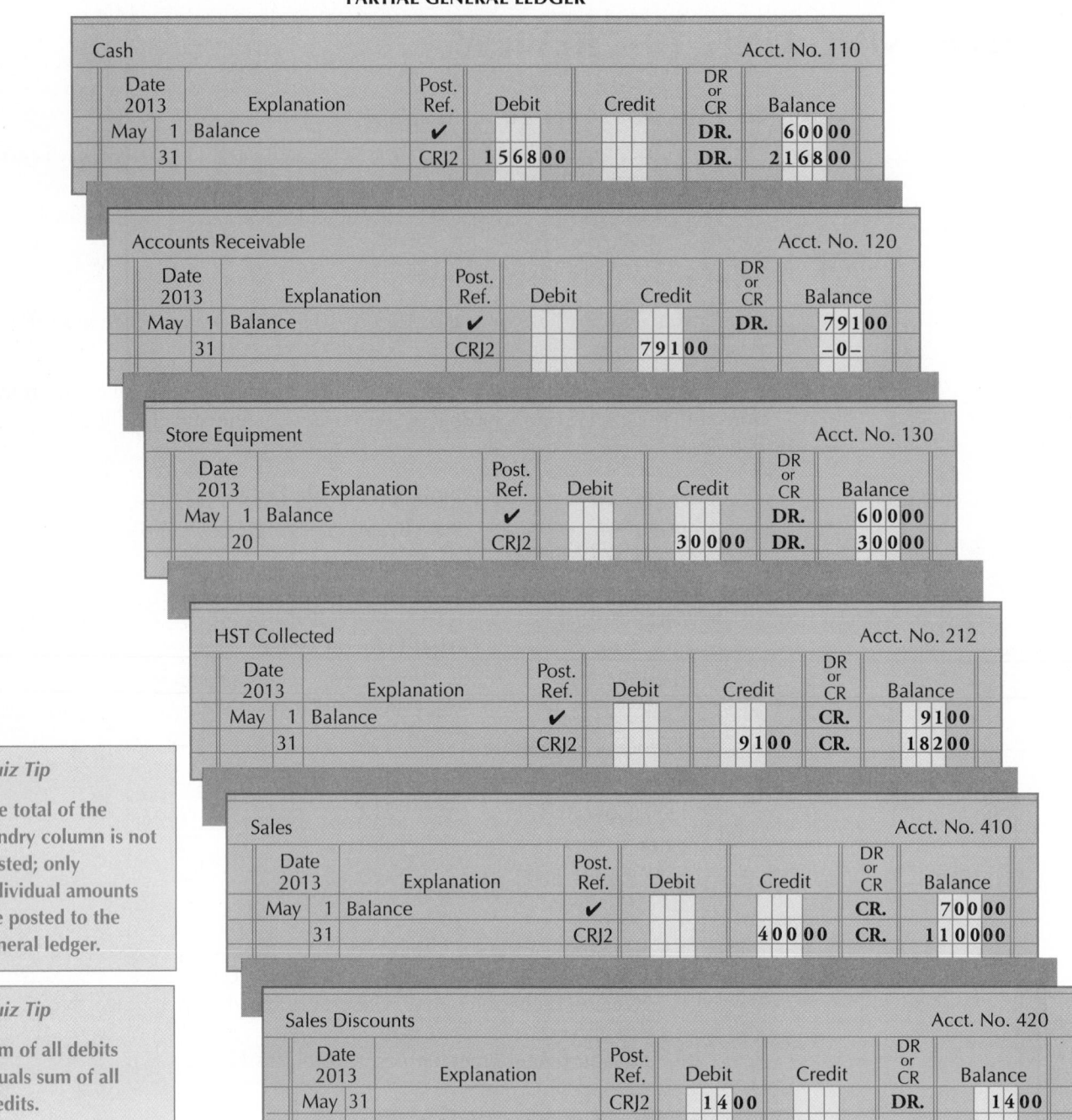

Cash — Acct. No. 110

Date 2013		Explanation	Post. Ref.	Debit	Credit	DR or CR	Balance
May	1	Balance	✔			DR.	6 00 00
	31		CRJ2	1 5 68 00		DR.	2 1 68 00

Accounts Receivable — Acct. No. 120

Date 2013		Explanation	Post. Ref.	Debit	Credit	DR or CR	Balance
May	1	Balance	✔			DR.	7 91 00
	31		CRJ2		7 91 00		– 0 –

Store Equipment — Acct. No. 130

Date 2013		Explanation	Post. Ref.	Debit	Credit	DR or CR	Balance
May	1	Balance	✔			DR.	6 00 00
	20		CRJ2		3 00 00	DR.	3 00 00

HST Collected — Acct. No. 212

Date 2013		Explanation	Post. Ref.	Debit	Credit	DR or CR	Balance
May	1	Balance	✔			CR.	9 1 00
	31		CRJ2		9 1 00	CR.	1 82 00

Sales — Acct. No. 410

Date 2013		Explanation	Post. Ref.	Debit	Credit	DR or CR	Balance
May	1	Balance	✔			CR.	7 00 00
	31		CRJ2		4 00 00	CR.	1 1 00 00

Sales Discounts — Acct. No. 420

Date 2013		Explanation	Post. Ref.	Debit	Credit	DR or CR	Balance
May	31		CRJ2	1 4 00		DR.	1 4 00

Quiz Tip

The total of the Sundry column is not posted; only individual amounts are posted to the general ledger.

Quiz Tip

Sum of all debits equals sum of all credits.

ACCOUNTS RECEIVABLE LEDGER

NAME Irene Welch
ADDRESS 10 Rong Road, Timmins, ON P4N 4M3

Date 2013		Explanation	Post. Ref.	Debit	Credit	Dr. Balance
May	1	Balance	✔			5 2 5 00
	3		CRJ2		5 2 5 00	–0–

NAME Chantel Simard
ADDRESS 9017 Robitaille Road, Montreal, QC H1K 4R3

Date 2013		Explanation	Post. Ref.	Debit	Credit	Dr. Balance
May	1	Balance	✔			2 1 0 00
	14		CRJ2		2 1 0 00	–0–

Learning Unit 10-3
GST/HST Paid on Purchases

5 Journalizing purchase transactions that include GST or HST in the purchases journal

OVERVIEW

In the previous learning unit, we learned that GST or HST collected on sales needs to be sent to the federal government periodically. No surprises here—this is very similar to PST. However, the GST/HST is what we refer to as a value-added tax. Without getting overly technical, each business in effect adds a net tax to the "improvement" in value that it adds to the goods and/or services it provides or sells. If a company buys some merchandise (to resell) for $1,000 and actually sells it for $1,500, then the GST/HST is applicable only to the $500 difference.

While that is true, the tax works in the following manner:

◆ First, the business charges the GST at 5% on the selling price of $1,500. This would amount to $75 (5% × $1,500) (covered in Learning Unit 10-1).

◆ Second, the business pays the 5% GST on the $1,000 for which the merchandise was purchased. This amounts to $50 (5% × $1,000) (covered in this learning unit).

◆ Companies remit the net difference between the GST that they collect on sales and the GST that they pay on purchases.

◆ Finally, the tax sent to the federal government in the case of 5% GST is only $25 (5% × $500 or $75 less $50) because the business gets a credit for the tax it paid on the purchase.

Summary
5% GST collected on sale of merchandise: 5% × $1,500.00 = $75
5% GST paid on purchase of merchandise: 5% × $1,000.00 = $50
Net tax to be remitted (5% of difference of $500.00) $25

If HST were involved instead of GST, the Summary would look like this:

HST collected	$195
HST paid	130
HST to remit	$ 65

Businesses do not keep track of GST/HST separately on each item of inventory they sell, of course. However, the above example makes it plain that companies must keep track of the total GST/HST that they pay so they can claim a refund when they calculate the tax that they must periodically send to the federal government.

This learning unit details the accounting tasks that must be handled properly to record GST/HST accurately.

RECORDING PURCHASES WITH GST/HST

Note: Recording purchases with GST is very similar to recording purchases with no GST—just one extra column is needed.

In the above learning units, we discussed purchases and cash payments without GST/HST. In Figure 6-8 on page 268 of Chapter 6, a typical purchase order was illustrated. Many companies have not changed their purchase orders to include GST/HST since it is now the law for GST/HST to be included even if the purchase order says nothing. Other companies may refer to the fact that the specified price does not include GST/HST. They expect that 5% GST or 13% HST will be added. Still other companies specify and calculate the tax. These companies produce a purchase order that would look like the one shown below in Figure 10-12 (assuming HST at 13%).

When the supplier fills the purchase order, an invoice will be prepared that includes GST/HST. In Figure 6-9 on page 269, a sales invoice before HST was illustrated. The same sales invoice incorporating HST is shown in Figure 10-13. Note that HST is charged on the shipping charges as well as the amount charged for the goods.

This invoice is recorded (as others) by the purchaser in a manner similar to the original example shown earlier in Chapter 6. The major change is that now the

Figure 10-12
Purchase Order with HST

Purchase Order No. 41
Art's Wholesale Clothing Company
1528 Belle Avenue
Toronto, Ontario M5A 2L4

Purchased From: Abby Blake Company
12 Foster Road
Quebec City, QC G1M 4H3

Date: April 1, 2013
Shipped VIA: Freight truck
Terms: 2/10, n/60
FOB: Quebec City

Quantity	Description	Unit Price	Total
100	Ladies' Jackets Code 14-0	$50	$5,000.00
		Add HST	650.00
		Total Price before Shipping	$5,650.00

Purchase order number must appear on all invoices.

Art's Wholesale
By: Bill Joy

Figure 10-13
Sales Invoice with HST

Sales Invoice No. 228
Abby Blake Company
12 Foster Road
Quebec City, QC G1M 4H3

Sold to: Art's Wholesale
Clothing Co.
1528 Belle Avenue
Toronto, ON
M5A 2L4

Date: April 1, 2013
Shipped VIA: Freight truck
Terms: 2/10, n/60
Your Order No: 41
FOB: Quebec City

Quantity	Description	Unit Price	Total
100	Ladies' Jackets Code 14-0	$50	$5,000.00
	Freight		50.00
	Sub-total		$5,050.00
	HST (13%)		656.50
	Total		$5,706.50
	Business No. 142714982		

Figure 10-14
Purchases Journal
with HST

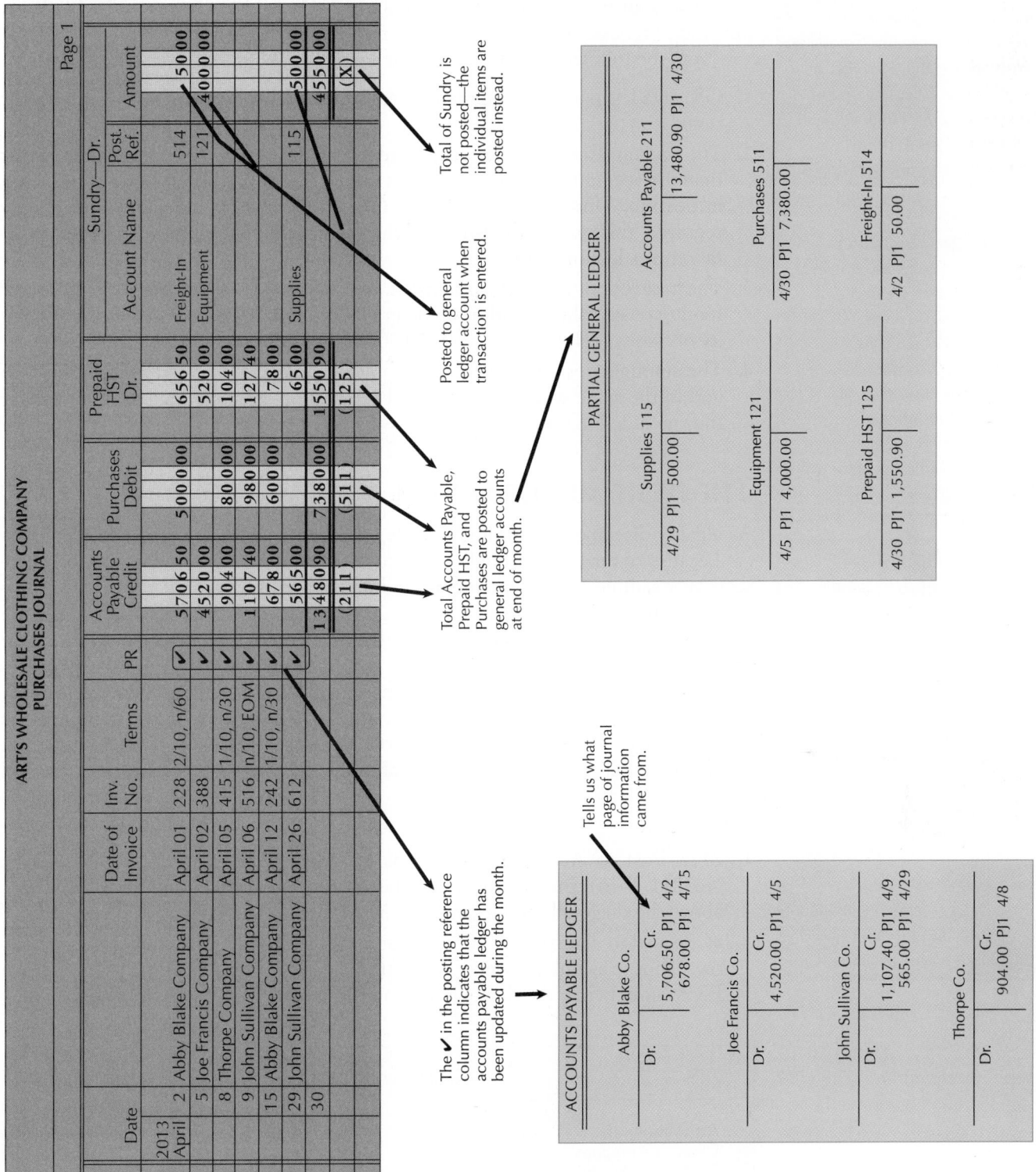

ART'S WHOLESALE CLOTHING COMPANY
PURCHASES JOURNAL

Page 1

Date		Account Name	Date of Invoice	Inv. No.	Terms	PR	Accounts Payable Credit	Purchases Debit	Prepaid HST Dr.	Sundry—Dr.		
										Account Name	Post. Ref.	Amount
2013 April	2	Abby Blake Company	April 01	228	2/10, n/60	✔	5706 50	5000 00	656 50	Freight-In	514	50 00
	5	Joe Francis Company	April 02	388		✔	4520 00		520 00	Equipment	121	4000 00
	8	Thorpe Company	April 05	415	1/10, n/30	✔	904 00	800 00	104 00			
	9	John Sullivan Company	April 06	516	n/10, EOM	✔	1107 40	980 00	127 40			
	15	Abby Blake Company	April 12	242	1/10, n/30	✔	678 00	600 00	78 00			
	29	John Sullivan Company	April 26	612		✔	565 00		65 00	Supplies	115	500 00
	30						13 480 90	7380 00	1550 90			4550 00
							(211)	(511)	(125)			(X)

Total of Sundry is not posted—the individual items are posted instead.

Posted to general ledger account when transaction is entered.

Total Accounts Payable, Prepaid HST, and Purchases are posted to general ledger accounts at end of month.

The ✔ in the posting reference column indicates that the accounts payable ledger has been updated during the month.

Tells us what page of journal information came from.

ACCOUNTS PAYABLE LEDGER

Abby Blake Co.

Dr.	Cr.
	5,706.50 PJ1 4/2
	678.00 PJ1 4/15

Joe Francis Co.

Dr.	Cr.
	4,520.00 PJ1 4/5

John Sullivan Co.

Dr.	Cr.
	1,107.40 PJ1 4/9
	565.00 PJ1 4/29

Thorpe Co.

Dr.	Cr.
	904.00 PJ1 4/8

PARTIAL GENERAL LEDGER

Accounts Payable 211

	13,480.90 PJ1 4/30

Purchases 511

4/30 PJ1 7,380.00	

Freight-In 514

4/2 PJ1 50.00	

Supplies 115

4/29 PJ1 500.00	

Equipment 121

4/5 PJ1 4,000.00	

Prepaid HST 125

4/30 PJ1 1,550.90	

6 Creating, recording, and posting a debit memorandum for purchase returns when GST or HST is included

purchases journal has one additional column—**Prepaid HST**. Figure 10-14 shows how the purchases journal would appear with HST included.

Note the following while you review Figure 10-14:

1. GST/HST is paid on equipment purchases as well as on purchases of goods for resale.

2. The account (number 125) used to record GST/HST on purchases is different than the account used to record sales (recall that account number 212 was used in Learning Unit 10-2 for recording GST/HST on sales). While not absolutely required, this procedure can make the preparation of the periodic governmental returns less of a burden.

3. The basic operation of the purchases journal is much the same as before. Cross-footing reveals that the addition of an HST column has not disturbed the equality of debits (7,380 + 4,550 + 1550.90 = 13,480.90) and credits (13,480.90).

4. The amounts posted to the accounts payable ledger are posted at the same time and in the same way as previously. The amounts are now higher, of course, as they include HST at 13%.

THE DEBIT MEMORANDUM

As already discussed, from time to time, purchased goods are returned to suppliers because of insufficient quality, defective manufacturing, and the like. We have seen an example of a **debit memorandum**, which is prepared when goods are returned (refer to Figure 6-12 on page 272). When GST/HST is charged on the original purchase, it must also be added to the debit memorandum, as shown in Figure 10-15.

Recording this debit memorandum is usually done in the general journal, although a specialized journal could be used if a large number of debit memos were common in a given business. Art's Wholesale Clothing Company would record the debit memorandum (illustrated in Figure 10-15) in its general journal (see Figure 10-16).

The four postings are:

1. 211—Post to Accounts Payable as a debit in the general ledger account No. 211. When this is done, place the account number, 211, in the PR column, above the diagonal on the same line as Accounts Payable.

2. ✔ Record to Thorpe Co. in the accounts payable ledger to show that we don't owe Thorpe as much money. When this is done, place a ✔ in the journal in the PR column below the diagonal line on the same line as Accounts Payable.

Figure 10-15
Debit Memorandum with HST

Debit Memorandum		No. 1

Art's Wholesale
Clothing Company
1528 Belle Avenue
Toronto, ON M5A 2L4

To: Thorpe Company   April 9, 2013
    3 Access Road
    Fredericton, NB E3B 4T3

WE DEBIT your account as follows:

Quantity		Unit Cost	Total
20	Men's Hats Code 827—defective brims	$10.00	$200.00
	Add HST @ 13%		26.00
	Total Adjustment		$226.00

Figure 10-16
Posting the Debit Memo
with HST

		GENERAL JOURNAL				
						Page 1
Date		Account Titles and Description	PR	Dr.	Cr.	
2013 April	9	Accounts Payable, Thorpe Company	211/ ✓	2 2 6 00		
		Purchases, Returns and Allowances	513		2 0 0 00	
		Prepaid HST	125		2 6 00	
		To record debit memo No. 1				

A debit memorandum with GST/HST is very similar to a supplier's invoice with GST/HST except that the amounts are opposite in meaning and effect, and often smaller.

3. 513—Post to Purchases Returns and Allowances as a credit in the general ledger (account No. 513). When this is done, place the account number, 513, in the posting reference column of the journal on the same line as Purchases Returns and Allowances (if equipment was returned that was not merchandise for resale, we would credit Equipment and not Purchases Returns and Allowances).

4. 125—Post to Prepaid HST as a credit. This acts to increase the amount of GST/HST owed to the federal government because it decreases the amount that is claimable to offset the liability recorded in account 212 (see Learning Objective 10-2 for details of this account).

The Cash Payments Journal

7 Recording cash paid out in the cash payments journal when GST or HST is included

The addition of HST does not alter the fact that Art's Wholesale will record all payments made by cash (or most likely by cheque) in a cash payments journal. However, as you probably suspect, this journal now has a separate column for Prepaid HST, which the original illustration shown in Figure 6-13 on page 276 did not have.

Trace the following cash disbursements through Figure 10-17. The following (revised) transactions affected the cash disbursements journal:

Note that even though the cash payments journal has a column for HST, it is never used when paying a regular supplier. The GST/HST on these purchases is recorded when the original entries are made in the Purchases Journal. Do not record the GST/HST on these purchases twice!

April   2   Issued cheque No. 101 to Pete Blum for insurance paid in advance, $900. (**Note:** Insurance is not subject to GST/HST.)
5   Issued cheque No. 102 to Joe Francis Company in payment of its April 2 invoice No. 388.
9   Issued cheque No. 103 to Flo Co. for merchandise purchased for cash $800 plus HST $104, total $904.
12   Issued cheque No. 104 to Thorpe Company in payment of its April 6 invoice No. 415, less the return and discount.
26   Issued cheque No. 105, $700 salaries paid.

In tracing the cash payments to the payments journal, a few points may be of interest:

1. There is no HST on the insurance payment of $900. Insurance premiums are classified as financial services and no HST is paid on these services.

2. Similarly, no HST is paid on salaries of $700 on April 26.

3. HST does not affect the $6 purchase discount allowed when payment is made to the Thorpe Company on April 12. This discount is calculated only on the $600 (net) purchase, not on the $678 that is the total amount payable because of the extra 13% HST. The actual amount paid is $672 because the $678 is reduced by $6 due to the allowed purchase discount.

Figure 10-17 Cash Payments Journal and Posting with HST

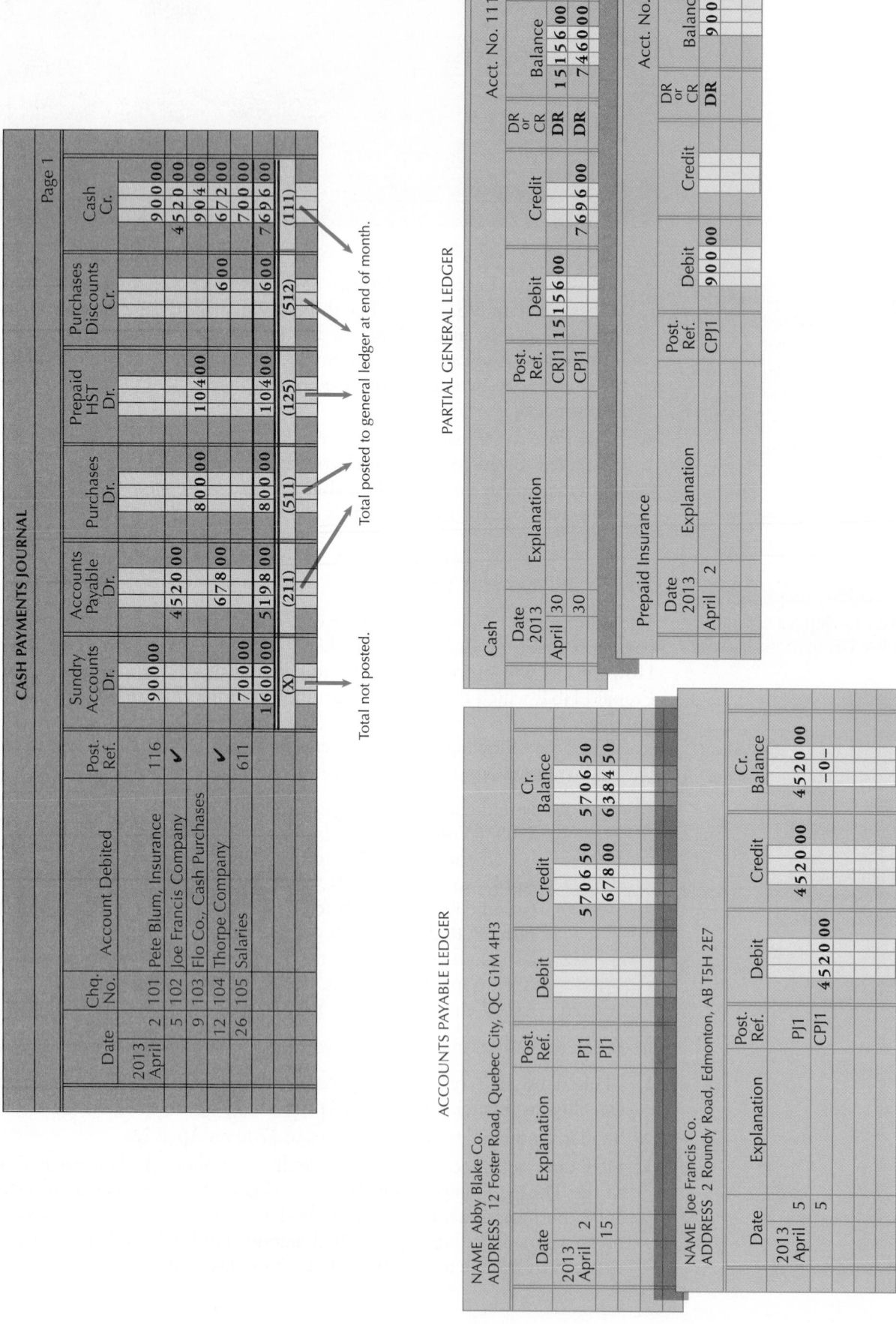

CASH PAYMENTS JOURNAL   Page 1

Date	Chq. No.	Account Debited	Post. Ref.	Sundry Accounts Dr.	Accounts Payable Dr.	Purchases Dr.	Prepaid HST Dr.	Purchases Discounts Cr.	Cash Cr.
2013 April 2	101	Pete Blum, Insurance	116	900 00					900 00
5	102	Joe Francis Company	✓		4520 00				4520 00
9	103	Flo Co., Cash Purchases				800 00	104 00		904 00
12	104	Thorpe Company			678 00			6 00	672 00
26	105	Salaries	611	700 00					700 00
				1600 00	5198 00	800 00	104 00	6 00	7696 00
				(X)	(211)	(511)	(125)	(512)	(111)

Total not posted.

Total posted to general ledger at end of month.

PARTIAL GENERAL LEDGER

Cash   Acct. No. 111

Date	Explanation	Post. Ref.	Debit	Credit	DR or CR	Balance
2013 April 30		CRJ1	15156 00		DR	15156 00
30		CPJ1		7696 00	DR	7460 00

Prepaid Insurance   Acct. No. 116

Date	Explanation	Post. Ref.	Debit	Credit	DR or CR	Balance
2013 April 2		CPJ1	900 00		DR	900 00

ACCOUNTS PAYABLE LEDGER

NAME Abby Blake Co.
ADDRESS 12 Foster Road, Quebec City, QC G1M 4H3

Date	Explanation	Post. Ref.	Debit	Credit	Cr. Balance
2013 April 2		PJ1		5706 50	5706 50
15		PJ1		678 00	6384 50

NAME Joe Francis Co.
ADDRESS 2 Roundy Road, Edmonton, AB T5H 2E7

Date	Explanation	Post. Ref.	Debit	Credit	Cr. Balance
2013 April 5		PJ1		4520 00	4520 00
5		CPJ1	4520 00		-0-

Figure 10-17 Cash Payments Journal and Posting with HST (continued)

Controlling account

Prepaid HST   Acct. No. 125

Date 2013	Explanation	Post. Ref.	Debit	Credit	DR or CR	Balance
April 9		GJ1		2 6 00	CR	2 6 00
30		PJ1	1 5 5 0 90		DR	1 5 2 4 90
30		CPJ1	1 0 4 00		DR	1 6 2 8 90

Accounts Payable   Acct. No. 211

Date 2013	Explanation	Post. Ref.	Debit	Credit	DR or CR	Balance
April 9		GJ1	2 2 6 00		DR	2 2 6 00
30		PJ1		1 3 4 8 0 90	CR	1 3 2 5 4 90
30		CPJ1	5 1 9 8 00		CR	8 0 5 6 90

Purchases   Acct. No. 511

Date 2013	Explanation	Post. Ref.	Debit	Credit	DR or CR	Balance
April 30		PJ1	7 3 8 0 00		DR	7 3 8 0 00
30		CPJ1	8 0 0 00		DR	8 1 8 0 00

Purchases Discounts   Acct. No. 512

Date 2013	Explanation	Post. Ref.	Debit	Credit	DR or CR	Balance
April 30		CPJ1		6 00	CR	6 00

Salaries   Acct. No. 611

Date 2013	Explanation	Post. Ref.	Debit	Credit	DR or CR	Balance
April 26		CPJ1	7 0 0 00		DR	7 0 0 00

NAME John Sullivan Co.
ADDRESS 18 Print Street, Regina, SK S4P 2A6

Date	Explanation	Post. Ref.	Debit	Credit	Cr. Balance
2013 April 9		PJ1		1 1 0 7 40	1 1 0 7 40
26		PJ1		5 6 5 00	1 6 7 2 40

NAME Thorpe Company
ADDRESS 3 Access Road, Fredericton, NB E3B 4T3

Date	Explanation	Post. Ref.	Debit	Credit	Cr. Balance
2013 April 8		PJ1		9 0 4 00	9 0 4 00
9		GJ1	2 2 6 00		6 7 8 00
12		CPJ1	6 7 8 00		– 0 –

Note on Accounts Payable balance: Very occasionally (perhaps because of the return of defective goods after they have been paid for), a debit balance may be called for on Accounts Payable. Debit balances are opposite to the normal credit balance and are signified by placing the balance in brackets. For example, suppose we get a credit note from Joe Francis Co. for $420.00 after we have paid off its account completely. The account would then appear as follows:

NAME Joe Francis Co.
ADDRESS 2 Roundy Road, Edmonton, AB T5H 2E7

Date	Explanation	Post. Ref.	Debit	Credit	Cr. Balance
2013 April 5		PJ1		4 5 2 0 00	4 5 2 0 00
5		CPJ1	4 5 2 0 00		– 0 –
13		GJ4	4 5 2 00		(4 5 2 00)

SPECIAL JOURNALS WITH TAXES   471

Schedule of Accounts Payable

Notice that it is not difficult to prepare a schedule of accounts payable at month-end from Figure 10-17. This schedule would look like:

Art's Wholesale Clothing Company
Schedule of Accounts Payable
April 30, 2010

Abby Blake Co.	$6,384.50
John Sullivan Co.	1,672.40
Total Accounts Payable	$8,056.90

If you refer again to Figure 10-17, you can see that $8,056.90 is exactly the balance in account 211—Accounts Payable. Hence, the subsidiary ledger accounts are in agreement with the controlling account in the general ledger. As always, if the total of the individual accounts in the accounts payable ledger does not agree with the controlling account, it will be necessary to double-check all postings and the mathematical computations of balances in each supplier's account to find the difference. Also, be sure that any entries made in the general journal are posted to the general ledger accounts.

LEARNING UNIT 10-3 REVIEW

AT THIS POINT you should be able to:

◆ Describe the nature of the GST/HST. (p. 465)

◆ Record the GST/HST on purchases. (p. 466)

◆ Record the GST/HST on returned purchases. (p. 468)

◆ Record the GST/HST on other cash payments. (p. 469)

◆ Prepare a schedule of accounts payable at period-end. (p. 472)

Self-Review Quiz 10-3

(The forms you need are on pages 10-6 and 10-7 of the *Study Guide with Working Papers*.)

Journalize the following transactions in the purchases journal (page 2) or general journal (page 1) for Munroe Co. Post or record to the accounts payable ledger and general ledger accounts as appropriate. Use the same journal headings as we used for Art's Wholesale Clothing Company.

2014
May 5 Bought merchandise on account from Flynn Co., invoice No. 512, dated May 2, terms 1/10, n/30, $900 plus GST $45. Total $945.

6 Bought merchandise from John Butler Company, invoice No. 403, dated May 6, terms n/10, EOM, $1,000 plus GST $50. Total $1,050.

13 Issued debit memo No. 1 to Flynn Co. for merchandise returned, $300, from invoice No. 512, plus GST $15. Total $315.

16 Purchased $400 worth of equipment on account from John Butler Company, invoice No. 413, dated May 16, plus GST $20. Total $420.

Solution to Self-Review Quiz 10-3

MUNROE CO.
PURCHASES JOURNAL

Page 2

Date	Description	Inv. No.	Terms	PR	Accounts Payable Credit	Purchases Debit	GST Prepaid Debit	Sundry—Debit Account Name	Post. Ref.	Amount
2014 May 5	Flynn Co.	512	1/10, n/30	✔	945 00	900 00	45 00			
6	John Butler Co.	403	n/10, EOM	✔	1050 00	1000 00	50 00			
16	John Butler Co.	413		✔	420 00		20 00	Equipment	121	400 00
31					2415 00	1900 00	115 00			400 00
					(212)	(512)	(125)			(X)

MUNROE CO.
GENERAL JOURNAL

Page 1

Date	Account Titles and Description	PR	Dr.	Cr.
2014 May 13	Accounts Payable, Flynn Co.	212 ✔	315 00	
	Purchases Returns and Allowances	513		300 00
	GST Prepaid	125		15 00

ACCOUNTS PAYABLE LEDGER

NAME Flynn Co.
ADDRESS 15 Foss Avenue, Quebec City, QC G1L 2W4

Date		Explanation	Post. Ref.	Debit	Credit	Cr. Balance
2014 May	5		PJ2		9 4 5 00	9 4 5 00
	13		GJ1	3 1 5 00		6 3 0 00

NAME John Butler Co.
ADDRESS 18 Reed Road, Winnipeg, MB R2B 8G6

Date		Explanation	Post. Ref.	Debit	Credit	Cr. Balance
2014 May	6		PJ2		1 0 5 0 00	1 0 5 0 00
	16		PJ2		4 2 0 00	1 4 7 0 00

PARTIAL GENERAL LEDGER

Equipment   Acct. No. 121

Date		Explanation	Post. Ref.	Debit	Credit	Dr or Cr	Balance
2014 May	16		PJ2	4 0 0 00		DR	4 0 0 00

GST Prepaid   Acct. No. 125

Date		Explanation	Post. Ref.	Debit	Credit	Dr or Cr	Balance
2014 May	13		GJ1		1 5 00	Cr	1 5 00
	31		PJ2	1 1 5 00		Dr	1 0 0 00

Accounts Payable   Acct. No. 212

Date		Explanation	Post. Ref.	Debit	Credit	Dr or Cr	Balance
2014 May	13		GJ1	3 1 5 00		Dr	3 1 5 00
	31		PJ2		2 4 1 5 00	Cr	2 1 0 0 00

Purchases   Acct. No. 512

Date		Explanation	Post. Ref.	Debit	Credit	Dr or Cr	Balance
2014 May	31		PJ2	1 9 0 0 00		Dr	1 9 0 0 00

Purchase Returns and Allowances   Acct. No. 513

Date		Explanation	Post. Ref.	Debit	Credit	Dr or Cr	Balance
2014 May	13		GJ1		3 0 0 00	Cr	3 0 0 00

Chapter Assignments

COMPREHENSIVE DEMONSTRATION PROBLEM WITH SOLUTION TIPS—INCLUDING HST AT 13%

(The forms you need are on pages 10-8 to 10-10 of the *Study Guide with Working Papers*.)

Record the following transactions in special or general journals. Record and post as appropriate.

Note: All credit sales are 2/10, n/30. All merchandise purchased on account has 3/10, n/30 credit terms.

	2012		
CRJ	March	1	J. Ling invested $3,000 in the business.
PJ		2	Purchased merchandise on account from Case Co., $600 plus HST, invoice No. 222.
SJ		2	Sold merchandise on account to Balder Co., $500 plus HST, invoice No. 1.
CRJ		6	Sold $2,000 worth of merchandise plus HST for cash.
CPJ		6	Paid Case Co. for previous purchases on account, cheque No. 1.
SJ		8	Sold merchandise on account to Lewis Co., $1,000 plus HST, invoice No. 2.
CRJ		9	Received payment from Balder for invoice No. 1.
GJ		12	Issued a credit memorandum to Lewis Co. for $200 plus HST for faulty merchandise.
CRJ		13	Received payment from Lewis Co.
PJ		16	Purchased merchandise on account from Noone Co., $1,000 plus HST, invoice No. 555.
PJ		19	Purchased equipment on account from Case Co., $300 plus HST, invoice No. 226.
GJ		20	Issued a debit memorandum to Noone Co. for $500 plus HST for defective merchandise.
CPJ		20	Paid salaries, $300, cheque No. 2. (No HST on salaries!)
CPJ		23	Paid Noone balance owed, cheque No. 3.
CPJ		27	Paid Bowler Co. $400 plus HST for advertising, cheque No. 4.

Record accounts receivable subsidiary ledger immediately.

**J. LING CO.
SALES JOURNAL** Page 1

Date 2012	Inv. No.	Customer's Name	Terms	Post. Ref.	Accounts Receivable Dr.	HST Collected Cr.	Sales Cr.
Mar. 2	1	Balder Co.	2/10, n/30	✔	565 00	65 00	500 00
8	2	Lewis Co.	2/10, n/30	✔	1130 00	130 00	1000 00
31					1695 00	195 00	1500 00
					(112)	(225)	(410)

Total posted at end of month to these accounts

J. LING CO.
CASH RECEIPTS JOURNAL

Date 2012		Cash Dr.	Accounts Receivable Cr.	Sales Cr.	HST Collected Cr.	Sales Discounts Dr.	Description of Receipt	Post. Ref.	Sundry Cr.
Mar.	1	3 000 00					J. Ling, Capital	310	3 000 00
	6	2 260 00		2 000 00	260 00		Cash Sales	✗	
	9	555 00	565 00			10 00	Balder Co.	✔	
	13	888 00	904 00			16 00	Lewis Co.	✔	
	31	6 703 00	1 469 00	2 000 00	260 00	26 00			3 000 00
		(111)	(112)	(410)	(225)	(430)			(X)

J. LING CO.
PURCHASES JOURNAL

Date 2012		Account Credited	Date of Inv.	Inv. No.	Terms	PR	Accounts Payable Cr.	Purchases Dr.	Prepaid HST Dr.	Sundry Dr. Account	PR	Amount
Mar.	2	Case Co.	Mar. 2	222	3%10, Net 30	✔	678 00	600 00	78 00			
	16	Noone Co.	Mar. 16	555	3%10, Net 30	✔	1 130 00	1 000 00	130 00			
	19	Case Co.	Mar. 17	226	3%10, Net 30	✔	339 00		39 00	Equipment	116	300 00
	31						2 147 00	1 600 00	247 00			300 00
							(210)	(510)	(114)			(X)

J. LING CO.
CASH PAYMENTS JOURNAL

Date 2012		Chq. No.	Account Debited	Post. Ref.	Sundry Dr.	Accounts Payable Dr.	Prepaid HST Dr.	Purchases Dr.	Purchases Discount Cr.	Cash Cr.
Mar.	6	1	Case Co.	✔		678 00			18 00	660 00
	20	2	Salaries	610	300 00					300 00
	23	3	Noone Co.	✔		565 00			15 00	550 00
	27	4	Bowler Co.	601	400 00		52 00			452 00
	31				700 00	1 243 00	52 00		33 00	1 962 00
					(X)	(210)	(114)		(530)	(111)

GENERAL JOURNAL					Page 1
Date	Account Titles and Description	PR	Dr.	Cr.	
2012 Mar. 12	Sales Returns and Allowances	420	2 0 0 00		
	HST Collected	225	2 6 00		
	Accounts Receivable, Lewis Co.	112 ✓		2 2 6 00	
	Issued credit memo (including HST)	225			
20	Accounts Payable, Noone Co.	210 ✓	5 6 5 00		
	Purchases Returns and Allowances	520		5 0 0 00	
	HST Prepaid	114		6 5 00	
	Issued debit memo				

↑ Record and post immediately to subsidiary and general ledgers.

ACCOUNTS RECEIVABLE SUBSIDIARY LEDGER

Balder Co.

Date	PR	Dr.	Cr.	Dr. Bal.
2012 3/2	SJ1	565		565
3/9	CRJ1		565	—

Lewis Co.

Date	PR	Dr.	Cr.	Dr. Bal.
2012 3/8	SJ1	1,130		1,130
3/12	GJ1		226	904
3/13	CRJ1		904	0

ACCOUNTS PAYABLE SUBSIDIARY LEDGER

Case Co.

Date	PR	Dr.	Cr.	Cr. Bal.
2012 3/2	PJ1		678	678
3/6	CPJ1	678		—
3/19	PJ1		339	339

Noone Co.

Date	PR	Dr.	Cr.	Cr. Bal.
2012 3/16	PJ1		1,130	1,130
3/20	GJ1	565		565
3/23	CPJ1	565		0

GENERAL LEDGER

Cash 111

3/31 CRJ1 6,703	1,962 3/31 CPJ1
Balance 4,741	

HST Collected 225

3/12 GJ 26	195 3/31 SJ1
	260 3/31 CRJ1
	429 Balance

Accounts Receivable 112

3/31 SJ1 1,695	226 3/12 GJ1
	1,469 3/31 CRJ1

Sales 410

	1,500 3/31 SJ1
	2,000 3/31 CRJ1
	3,500 Balance

HST Prepaid 114

3/31 PJ1 247	65 3/20 GJ1
3/31 CPJ1 52	
Balance 234	

Sales Returns and Allowances 420

3/12 GJ1 200	

Equipment 116

3/19 PJ1 300	

Sales Discounts 430

3/31 CRJ1 26	

Accounts Payable 210

3/20 GJ1 565	2,147 3/31 PJ1
3/31 CPJ1 1243	
	339 Balance

Purchases 510

3/31 PJ1 1,600	

J. Ling, Capital 310

	3,000 3/1 CRJ1

Purchases Ret. and Allow. 520

	500 3/20 GJ1

Advertising 601

3/27 CPJ1 400	

Purchases Discounts 530

	33 3/31 CPJ1

Salaries Expense 610

3/20 CPJ1 300	

Summary of Solution Tips

Learning Unit 10-2—Seller	Learning Unit 10-3—Buyer
Sales journal	Purchases journal
Cash receipts journal	Cash payments journal
Accounts receivable subsidiary ledger	Accounts payable subsidiary ledger
Sales (Cr.)	Purchases (Dr.)
Sales Returns and Allowances (Dr.)	Purchase Returns and Allowances (Cr.)
Sales Discounts (Dr.)	Purchases Discounts (Cr.)
Accounts Receivable (Dr.)	Accounts Payable (Cr.)
GST(HST) Collected (Cr.)	GST(HST) Prepaid (Dr.)
Issue a credit memo	Receive a credit memo
or	or
Receive a debit memo	Issue a debit memo
Schedule of accounts receivable	Schedule of accounts payable

When Do I Do What? — A Step-by-Step Walk-Through of This Comprehensive Demonstration Problem

Transaction   What to Do Step by Step

2012

March

1 *Money received:* Record in cash receipts journal. Post immediately to J. Ling, Capital since it is in Sundry. There is no HST on cash to or from an owner.

2 *Bought merchandise on account:* Record in purchases journal. Record to Case Co. immediately in the accounts payable subsidiary ledger. Total is $678, including HST.

2 *Sale on account:* Record in sales journal. Record immediately to Balder Co. in accounts receivable subsidiary ledger. Place a ✓ in PR column of sales journal when subsidiary is updated. Total is $565, including HST.

6 *Money in:* Record in cash receipts journal. No posting needed (put an X in PR column.) Note that total includes $260 of HST.

6 *Money out:* Record in cash payments journal. Save $18 ($600 × 0.03), which is a Purchases Discount. Record immediately to Case Co. in accounts payable subsidiary ledger (the full amount of $678).

8 *Sale on account:* Record in sales journal. Update immediately to Lewis in accounts receivable subsidiary ledger. Total to include HST.

9 *Money in:* Record in cash receipts journal. Since Balder paid within 10 days, they get a $10 discount. Record immediately to Balder in the accounts receivable subsidiary ledger the full amount of $565. Cash is $565 − $10 = $555.

12 *Returns:* Record in general journal. Seller issues credit memo resulting in higher sales returns and customers owing less. All postings and recordings are done immediately. Note the HST amount of $26 ($200 × 0.13).

13 *Money in:* Record in cash receipts journal:

$$\$1,000 - \$200 \text{ returns} = \begin{array}{r} \$800 \\ \times\, 0.02 \\ \hline \$\quad 16 \text{ discount} \end{array}$$

Record the $904 ($1,130 − $226) immediately to Lewis in the accounts receivable subsidiary ledger. Cash received is $904 less $16 = $888.

16 *Buy now, pay later:* Record in purchases journal. Record immediately to Noone Co. in the accounts payable subsidiary ledger. Note HST at 13%.

March 19 *Buy now, pay later:* Record in purchases journal under Sundry. This is not merchandise for resale, but HST still applies. Record and post immediately.

20 *Returns:* Record in general journal. Buyer issues a debit memo, reducing its accounts payable because of Purchases Returns and Allowances. Post and record immediately. HST is included at 13%.

20 *Salaries:* Record in cash payments journal, Sundry column. There is no HST on salaries.

23 *Money out:* Record in cash payments journal. Save 3% ($15), a purchases discount. Record immediately in accounts payable subsidiary ledger, reducing Noone by $565.

27 *Money out:* Record in cash payments journal. (No discount is mentioned.) Debit advertising expense in the Sundry Accounts column and post immediately. Note the HST amount of $52 that is entered in the Prepaid HST column. Total amount paid is $400 + 13%, or $452.

At the end of the month: Post totals (except Sundry) of special journals to the general ledger.

Note: In this problem, at the end of the month: (1) Accounts Receivable in the general ledger, the controlling account, has a zero balance as does each title in the accounts receivable subsidiary ledger. (2) The balance in Accounts Payable (the controlling account) is $339. In the accounts payable subsidiary ledger, Case is owed $339. The sum of the subsidiary ledger accounts does equal the balance in the controlling account at the end of the month.

SUMMARY OF KEY POINTS

Learning Unit 10-1

1. Recording GST/HST in the sales journal requires the addition of one new column. Other procedures are not changed.

2. Often both PST and GST will appear on the same invoice. Recording this in the sales journal requires the use of two extra columns, but again, the basic procedures are little changed.

3. When a sales discount is allowed, it is taken on the pre-PST and pre-GST/HST amount only, not on the total invoice.

4. Recording a credit memorandum with PST and GST/HST requires an extra line in the general journal for each. The credit to the customer's account includes the invoice amount plus PST and GST/HST.

Learning Unit 10-2

1. The cash receipts journal records receipt of cash from any source.

2. The sundry column records the credit part of a transaction that does not occur frequently. Never post the *total* of sundry. Post items in the sundry column to the general ledger when entered.

3. A ✔ in the posting reference column of the cash receipts journal means that the accounts receivable subsidiary ledger has been updated (recorded) with a credit.

4. An ✗ in the cash receipts journal posting-reference column means no posting was necessary since the totals of these columns will be posted at the end of the month.

5. Cross-footing means proving that the total of debits and the total of credits are equal in the special journal, thus verifying the accuracy of recording.

6. A schedule of accounts receivable is a listing of the ending balances of customers in the accounts receivable subsidiary ledger. This total should be the same balance as found in the controlling account, Accounts Receivable, in the general ledger.

Learning Unit 10-3

1. GST/HST is paid on most purchases of goods and services in Canada. It is very important for businesses to keep proper track of the GST/HST that they pay because they can deduct this from the GST/HST otherwise payable on their own sales.

2. All payments by cheque are recorded in the cash payments journal. Record any GST/HST paid on cash purchases in this journal as well.

3. At the end of the month, the schedule of accounts payable, a list of ending amounts owed to individual creditors, must equal the ending balance in Accounts Payable, the controlling account in the general ledger.

4. Trade discounts are deductions off the list price that have nothing to do with early payments (cash discounts). Invoice amounts are recorded after the trade discount is deducted. Cash discounts are not taken on trade discounts.

5. Cash discounts are not taken on GST/HST amounts.

6. A separate column is added to the purchases journal and to the cash payments journal to record the GST/HST on items purchased either on account or for cash.

7. When a debit note is issued for a purchases return or allowance, the GST/HST is always added to the total. When the debit note is recorded in the general journal, the GST/HST amount is credited to the same account as that used to track the GST/HST amounts paid for the period. This increases the amount owed to the federal government. Other postings are done in the same way as described earlier.

Key terms

Credit memorandum   A document sent by the seller to a customer who has returned merchandise previously purchased on credit. The credit memorandum indicates to the customer that the seller is reducing the amount owed by the customer. The total will include GST/HST (or even PST) if that was charged on the original invoice (p. 454)

Debit memorandum   A memo issued by a purchaser to a seller, indicating that some purchases returns and allowances have occurred and therefore the purchaser now owes less money on account. The total will include GST or HST if that was charged on the original invoice (p. 468)

Goods and Services Tax (GST)   A "value added" tax introduced in Canada in 1991. It is added to most sales of goods and services. Currently it is calculated at 5%. (p. 448)

GST/HST collected   The tax amount billed to customers and due to be sent to the federal government. It is a liability account with a credit balance. See also the next chapter for a fuller explanation of the net amount payable. (p. 452)

Harmonized Sales Tax (HST)   A 13% tax identical to GST, collected in Ontario, British Columbia, Nova Scotia (now 15%), New Brunswick, and Newfoundland and Labrador. It replaces both the PST and GST in those five provinces. (p. 448)

Prepaid GST/HST   An asset account used to accumulate the GST/HST paid (or payable) to suppliers on goods or services purchased. It is an asset because it can be deducted from the amount otherwise payable to the federal government. This is sometimes shown with current liabilities (but is still a debit-balance account) (p. 468)

Provincial Sales Tax (PST) Payable   A liability account in the general ledger that accumulates the amount of provincial sales tax owed. It has a credit balance. (p. 450)

BLUEPRINT OF SALES AND CASH RECEIPTS JOURNALS

Posting and Recording: Multicolumn Sales Journal

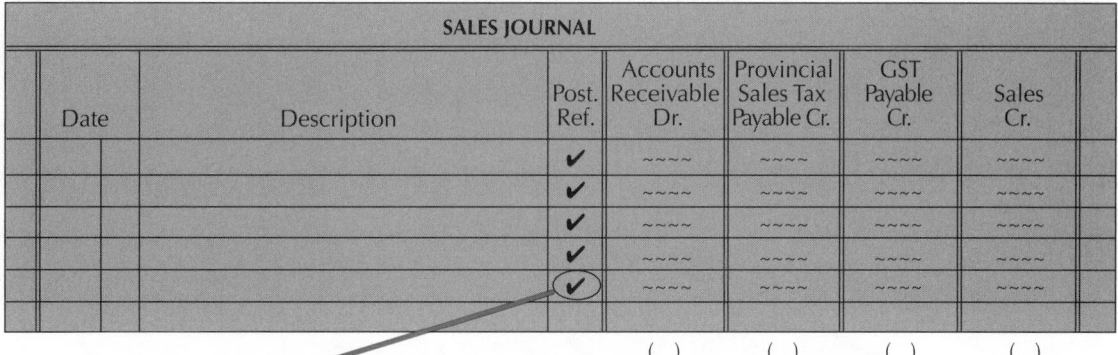

During the month, the accounts receivable ledger is updated as soon as transactions are entered in the journal. A checkmark indicates that recording is completed to the customer's account in the accounts receivable subledger.

End of month total is posted to Accounts Receivable control account in the general ledger.

End of month totals of both taxes payable are posted to their respective accounts in the general ledger.

End of month total of sales is posted to the general ledger.

Recording a Credit Memo with Sales Tax and GST/HST in a General Journal

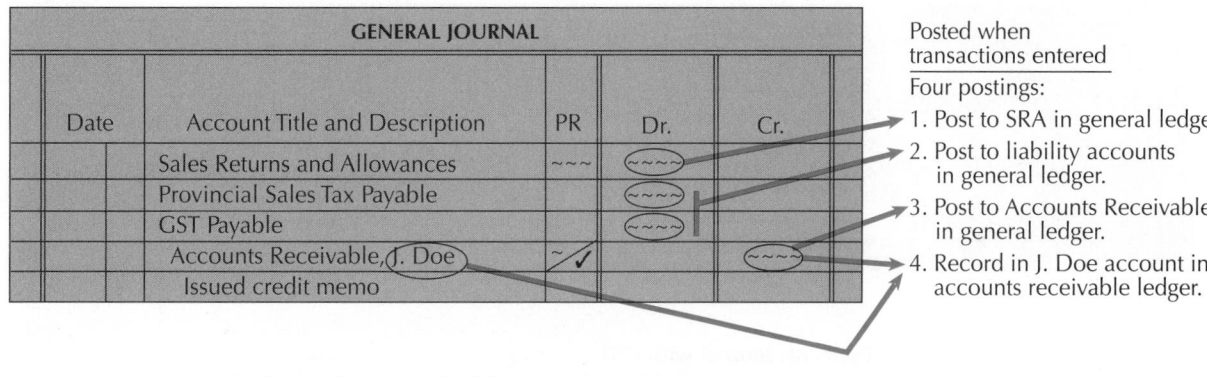

Posted when transactions entered

Four postings:

1. Post to SRA in general ledger.
2. Post to liability accounts in general ledger.
3. Post to Accounts Receivable in general ledger.
4. Record in J. Doe account in accounts receivable ledger.

Cash Receipts Journal with PST and GST/HST

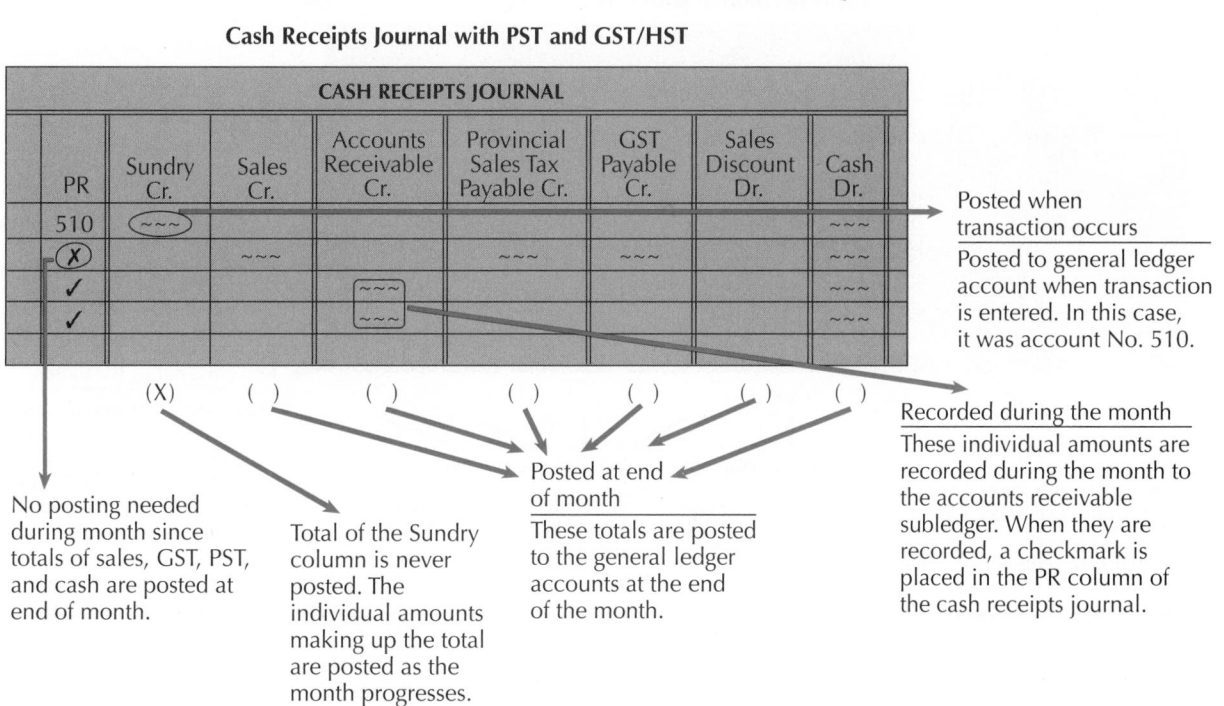

Posted when transaction occurs

Posted to general ledger account when transaction is entered. In this case, it was account No. 510.

Recorded during the month

These individual amounts are recorded during the month to the accounts receivable subledger. When they are recorded, a checkmark is placed in the PR column of the cash receipts journal.

No posting needed during month since totals of sales, GST, PST, and cash are posted at end of month.

Total of the Sundry column is never posted. The individual amounts making up the total are posted as the month progresses.

Posted at end of month

These totals are posted to the general ledger accounts at the end of the month.

Multicolumn Purchases Journal

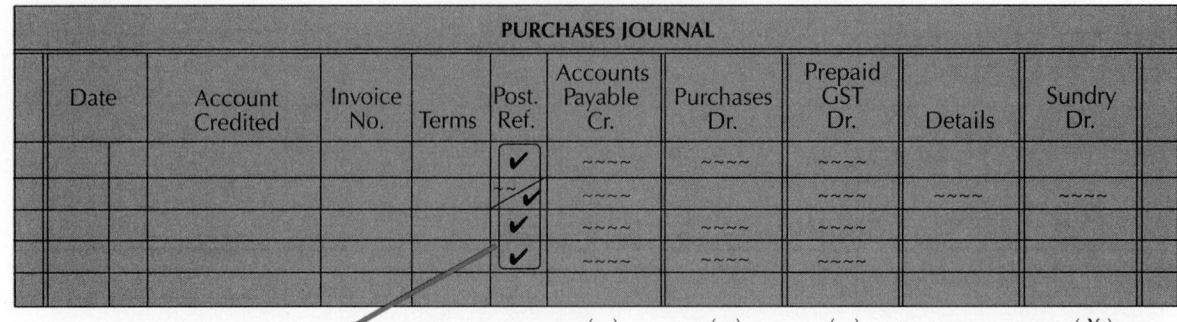

PURCHASES JOURNAL

Date	Account Credited	Invoice No.	Terms	Post. Ref.	Accounts Payable Cr.	Purchases Dr.	Prepaid GST Dr.	Details	Sundry Dr.
				✔	~~~		~~~		
				~~/✔	~~~		~~~	~~~	~~~
				✔	~~~	~~~			
				✔	~~~	~~~	~~~		

( )   ( )   ( )   (X)

During the month, the accounts payable ledger is updated as soon as transactions are entered in the journal. A ✔ indicates that recording is completed to the supplier's account in the accounts payable subledger. The number above the slash is the GL account number for the Sundry posting.

End-of-month total is posted to Accounts Payable controlling account in the general ledger.

End-of-month totals of both GST and purchases accounts are posted to their respective accounts in the general ledger.

End-of-month total is not posted to the general ledger. Individual amounts are posted as the month progresses.

Recording a Debit Memo with GST in the General Journal

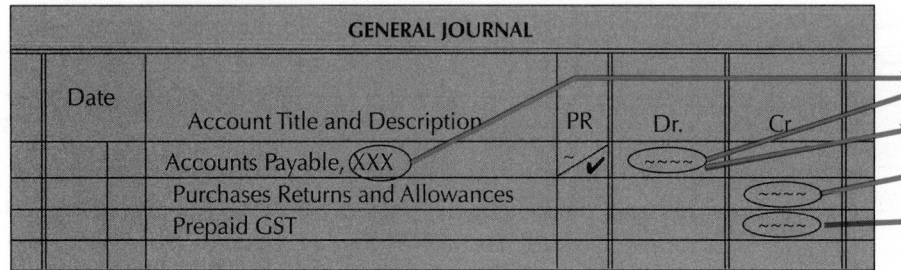

GENERAL JOURNAL

Date	Account Title and Description	PR	Dr.	Cr.
	Accounts Payable, (XXX)	~/✔	(~~~)	
	Purchases Returns and Allowances			(~~~)
	Prepaid GST			(~~~)

Posted when transaction entered

Four postings:
1. Record to XXX in accounts payable ledger.
2. Post to Accounts Payable in general ledger.
3. Post to Purchases Returns and Allowances in general ledger.
4. Post to asset account in general ledger.

Cash Payments Journal with GST

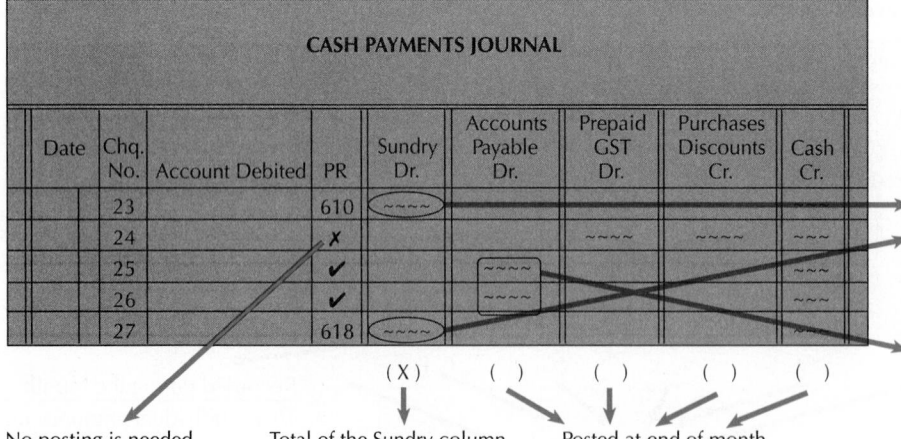

CASH PAYMENTS JOURNAL

Date	Chq. No.	Account Debited	PR	Sundry Dr.	Accounts Payable Dr.	Prepaid GST Dr.	Purchases Discounts Cr.	Cash Cr.
	23		610	(~~~)				
	24		✗			~~~	~~~	~~~
	25		✔		~~~			~~~
	26		✔		~~~			~~~
	27		618	(~~~)				

(X)   ( )   ( )   ( )   ( )

Posted when transaction occurs

Posted to general ledger when transactions are entered, in these cases to accounts 610 and 618.

Recorded during the month

These individual amounts are recorded during the month to the accounts payable subledger. When recorded, a checkmark is placed in the PR column of the cash payments journal.

No posting is needed during the month since totals of purchases, GST, PST, and cash are posted at end of month.

Total of the Sundry column is never posted. The individual amounts making up the total are posted as the month progresses.

Posted at end of month

These totals are posted to the general ledger accounts at the end of the month.

QUESTIONS, CLASSROOM DEMONSTRATION EXERCISES, EXERCISES, AND PROBLEMS

Discussion Questions and Critical Thinking/Ethical Case

1. Explain how PST differs from GST/HST.

2. What is the normal balance of the Sales Discounts account?

3. What is a value-added tax?

4. (Tricky) Why doesn't the purchase requisition generally mention GST/HST?

5. Explain why a retail business includes a column for PST in its Sales Journal, but does not include a similar column in its Purchase Journal.

6. What effect on the liability account "PST Collected" does a credit memorandum have?

7. State the differences between a cash receipts journal and a cash payments journal. Assume taxes are included, and give a brief comment on each difference.

8. When a seller issues a credit memorandum with both PST and GST included, what accounts are affected?

9. Sales discounts are taken on GST or PST amounts. Agree or disagree and say why.

10. In any given reporting period (assume a month) a successful business will always owe some GST or HST. Agree or disagree and explain your answer.

11. Why would a purchaser issue a debit memorandum? Wouldn't it include any PST?

12. Explain the relationship between a purchases journal and a cash payments journal with respect to the extra column(s) needed to account for taxes.

13. State why it is so important for firms to keep track of the GST/HST that they pay each period.

14. Why does GST/HST on a debit note act to increase the net amount of GST/HST payable?

15. Spring Co. bought merchandise from All Co. with terms 2/10, n/30. Joanne Ring, the bookkeeper, forgot to pay the bill within the first 10 days. She went to Mel Ryan, Head Accountant, who told her to backdate the cheque so it would look as though the bill was paid within the discount period. Joanne told Mel that she thought they could get away with it. Should Joanne and Mel backdate the cheque to take advantage of the discount? You make the call. Write down your specific recommendations to Joanne.

Make the grade with MyAccountingLab! The exercises and problems marked in green can be found on MyAccountingLab at **www.myaccountinglab.com**. You can practise them as often as you want, and many of them feature step-by-step guided solutions to help you find the right answer. You can also find working papers for selected problems in the Multimedia Library on MyAccountingLab.

Classroom Demonstration Exercises

(The forms you need are on pages 10-11 and 10-12 of the *Study Guide with Working Papers*.)

Set A

Overview

Categorizing accounts
1 2 5 6 (10 min)

1. Complete the following table for Sales, Sales Returns and Allowances, and Sales Discounts, PST Collected, and HST Collected.

Accounts Affected	Category	↑ ↓	Rules	Temporary or Permanent

Calculating Net Sales

Net sales
1 2 (10 min)

2. Given the following, calculate net sales:

Gross sales	$100
PST rate	8%
GST rate	5%
Sales returns and allowances	12
Sales discounts	2%

Credit Memorandum

Analyzing a return transaction
2 (10 min)

3. Draw a transaction analysis box for the following credit memorandum: Issued credit memorandum to North Corp. for defective merchandise—$315, including GST.

Calculating net purchases
5 6 (10 min)

4. Calculate net purchases from the following: Purchases, $100; Purchase Returns and Allowances, $12; Purchase Discounts, $2; and GST on Purchases, $5.

Sales and Cash Receipts Journal

Analyzing transactions
1 2 (10 min)

5. Beside each of the four transactions at the top of the next page, enter the number of any of the following six treatments that apply. (A number can be used more than once.)

1. Journalize into sales journal.
2. Journalize into cash receipts journal.
3. Record immediately to subsidiary ledger.
4. Totals of special journals will be posted at end of month (except Sundry column).
5. Post to general ledger immediately.
6. Journalize into general journal.

a. _____ Sold merchandise on account to Ally Co., invoice No. 10—$40, plus GST.

b. _____ Received cheque from Moore Co.—$105, including GST, less 2% discount.

c. _____ Cash Sales—$100, plus GST.

d. _____ Issued credit memorandum No. 2 to Ally Co. for defective merchandise—$20, plus GST.

Schedule of accounts receivable
4️⃣ (10 min)

6. From the following, prepare a schedule of accounts receivable for Blue Co. for May 31, 2012.

Accounts Receivable Subsidiary Ledger	General Ledger
Bon Co.	**Accounts Receivable**
5/6 SJ1 105 |	5/31 SJ1 252 | 5/31 CRJ1 21
Peke Co.	
5/20 SJ1 63 | 21 5/27 CRJ1	
Green Co.	
5/8 SJ1 84 |	

Set B

Overview

Categorizing accounts
1️⃣2️⃣5️⃣6️⃣ (10 min)

1. Complete the following table for Purchases, Purchases Returns and Allowances, Purchases Discounts, and GST on Purchases.

Accounts Affected	Category	↑ ↓	Rules	Temporary or Permanent

Calculating Net Purchases

Net purchases
5️⃣ (10 min)

2. Given the following, calculate net purchases:

Gross purchases	$400
Purchases returns and allowances	24
Purchases discounts	5
GST on purchases	20

Return of merchandise
1️⃣2️⃣5️⃣6️⃣ (10 min)

3. Pete Morse returned $300 of merchandise to Logan Co. The original sale was for $1,000 of merchandise, plus PST of $80 (8%) and GST of $50 (5%). What entry would the buyer (Morse) and seller (Logan) make regarding this return?

Purchases Journal, General Journal, Recording, and Posting

Analyzing transactions
5️⃣6️⃣ (10 min)

4. For each of the three journal entries at the top of the next page, indicate which of these procedures should be used (more than one number can be used).

1. Journalize in purchases journal.
2. Record immediately in subsidiary ledger.
3. Post totals from purchases journal (except Sundry total) at the end of the month to general ledger.
4. Journalize in general journal.
5. Immediately record in subsidiary ledgers and post to the general ledger.

a. Bought merchandise on account from Also Co., invoice No. 12, $200.00 + 13% HST.
b. Bought equipment on account from Jones Co., invoice No. 13, $400.00 + 13% HST.
c. Issued debit memo No. 1 to Also Co. for merchandise returned, $40.00 + 13% HST, from invoice No. 12.

Recording Transactions in Special Journals

Categorizing transactions
1 2 5 6 (10 min)

5. Indicate in which of these five journals each transaction described below will be journalized:

1.	SJ	**4.**	CPJ
2.	PJ	**5.**	GJ
3.	CRJ		

_____ a. Issued credit memo No. 2, $130 + 5% GST.

_____ b. Cash sales, $200 + 5% GST.

_____ c. Received cheque from Blue Co., $420, less 3% discount. Invoice had GST at 5%.

_____ d. Bought merchandise on account from Mel Co., $350 + 5% GST, 1/10, n/30, invoice No. 20.

_____ e. Cash purchase, $150 + 5% GST.

_____ f. Issued debit memo to Mel Co., $150 for merchandise returned from invoice No. 20. Remember the GST!

Schedule of accounts payable
4 (10 min)

6. From the following, prepare a schedule of accounts payable for AVE Co. for May 31, 2012:

Accounts Payable Subsidiary Ledger

Bloss Co.

5/25	CPJ1	21	5/19	PJ1	105

Rowe Co.

			5/8	PJ1	126

General Ledger

Accounts Payable

5/31	CPJ	21	5/31	PJ1	231

Exercises

(The forms you need are on pages 10-13 to 10-17 of the *Study Guide with Working Papers*.)

Recording and posting from the sales journal
1 (15 min)

10-1. From the sales journal below, record in the accounts receivable subsidiary ledger and post to the general ledger accounts as appropriate.

					SALES JOURNAL					

P. 1

Date		Account Debited	Invoice No.	PR	Accts. Receivable Dr.	GST Collected Cr.	Sales Cr.
2013 April	19	Kevin Stone Co.	1		630 00	30 00	600 00
	20	Bill Valley Co.	2		945 00	45 00	900 00
					1575 00	75 00	1500 00

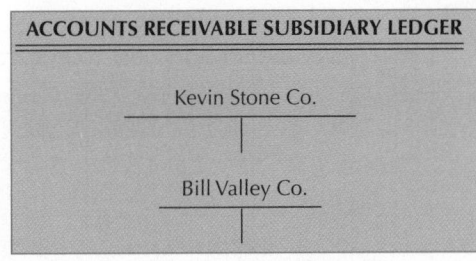

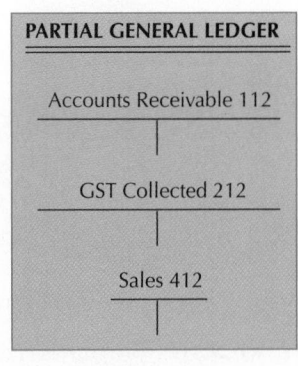

ACCOUNTS RECEIVABLE SUBSIDIARY LEDGER

Kevin Stone Co.

Bill Valley Co.

PARTIAL GENERAL LEDGER

Accounts Receivable 112

GST Collected 212

Sales 412

Journalizing, recording, and posting that includes credit memorandum

1 2 (15 min)

10-2. Journalize, record, and post when appropriate the following transactions into the sales journal (same headings as Exercise 10-1) and general journal (page 1). All sales carry terms of 2/10, n/30.

2013
May 17 Sold merchandise on account to Ronald Co., invoice No. 147, $1,200, plus 5% GST.
18 Sold merchandise on account to Bass Co., invoice No. 148, $1,900, plus 5% GST.
21 Issued credit memorandum No. 12 to Bass Co. for defective merchandise, $700, plus 5% GST.

Use the following account numbers: Accounts Receivable, 112; GST Collected, 225; Sales, 411; Sales Returns and Allowances, 412.

Journalizing transaction into cash receipts journal

3 (15 min)

10-3. From Exercise 10-2, journalize the receipt of a cheque from Ronald Co. for payment of invoice No. 147 on May 25, 2013, in the cash receipts journal. Use the same headings as for Walter Lantz Co. (on page 283 of Chapter 6).

Journalizing, recording, and posting sales and cash receipts journal; schedule of accounts receivable

1 2 3 4 (45 min)

10-4. From the following transactions for Edna Co., when appropriate, journalize, record, post, and prepare a schedule of accounts receivable. Use the same journal headings (all page 1) and chart of accounts that Art's Wholesale Clothing used in the text (use Edna Cares, Capital). You will have to set up your own accounts receivable subsidiary ledger and partial general ledger as needed. All sales terms are 2/10, n/30.

2014
June 2 Edna Cares invested $5,000 in the business.
3 Sold merchandise on account to Boston Co., invoice No. 218, $700, plus 13% HST.
3 Sold merchandise on account to Gary Co., invoice No. 219, $1,100, plus 13% HST.
6 Cash sale, $200, plus 13% HST.
9 Issued credit memorandum No. 24 to Boston Co. for defective merchandise, $200, plus 13% HST.
10 Received cheque from Boston Co. for invoice No. 218 less returns and discount.
16 Cash sale, $400, plus 13% HST.
17 Sold merchandise on account to Boston Co., invoice No. 220, $600, plus 13% HST.

10-5. From the accompanying purchases journal, record in the accounts payable subsidiary ledger and post to general ledger accounts as appropriate.

									Sundry—Dr.		
PURCHASES JOURNAL											**Page 1**
Date	Account Credited	Date of Invoice	Terms	Post. Ref.	Accounts Payable Credit	GST Prepaid Dr.	Purchases Debit		Account	PR	Amount
2014 June 3	Barr Co.	June 3	1/10, n/30		42000	2000	40000				
6	Jess Co.	June 6	n/10, EOM		84000	4000	80000				
9	Rey Co.	June 9			63000	3000			Equipment		60000

Recording in the accounts payable subsidiary ledger and posting to the general ledger from a purchases journal
④⑤ (15 min)

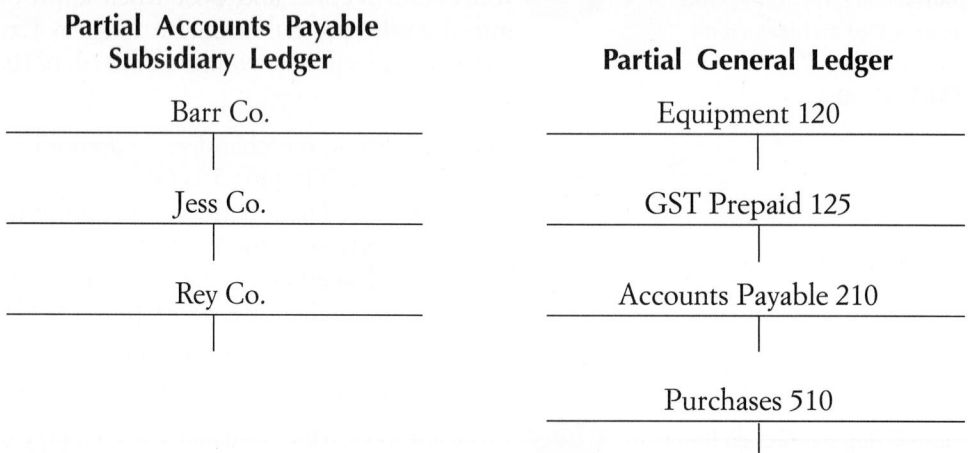

Partial Accounts Payable Subsidiary Ledger

Barr Co.

Jess Co.

Rey Co.

Partial General Ledger

Equipment 120

GST Prepaid 125

Accounts Payable 210

Purchases 510

Journalizing, recording, and posting a debit memorandum
⑥ (15 min)

10-6. On July 8, 2014, Aster Co. issued debit memorandum No. 1 for $400 to Reel Co. for merchandise returned from invoice No. 312, which originally included GST at 5%. Your task is to journalize, record, and post this transaction as appropriate. Use the same account numbers as found in the text for Art's Wholesale Clothing Company. The general journal page is page 1.

Journalizing, recording, and posting a cash payments journal
⑦ (20 min)

10-7. Journalize, record, and post when appropriate the following transactions into the cash payments journal (page 2) for Morgan's Clothing. Use the same headings as found in the text for Art's Wholesale Clothing Company (page 276 of Chapter 6). All purchases discounts are 2/10, n/30, and the amounts shown include GST at 5%.

Accounts Payable Subsidiary Ledger

Name	Balance	Invoice No.
B. Foss	$ 420	488
A. James	1,050	522
J. Ranch	945	562
B. Swanson	210	821

Partial General Ledger

Account	Balance
Cash 110	$3,000
GST Prepaid 125	
Accounts Payable 210	2,625
Purchases Discounts 511	
Advertising Expense 610	

2013

April   2   Issued cheque No. 20 to A. James Company in payment of its March 29 invoice No. 522.

9   Issued cheque No. 21 to Flott Advertising in payment of its advertising bill, $100, plus GST at 5%, no discount.

16   Issued cheque No. 22 to B. Foss in payment of its March 26 invoice No. 488.

Schedule of accounts payable
4 **(10 min)**

10-8 From Exercise 10-7, prepare a schedule of accounts payable and verify that the total of the schedule equals the amount in the controlling account.

Group A Problems

(The forms you need are on pages 10-18 to 10-44 of the *Study Guide with Working Papers*.)

Comprehensive problem: using GST and PST in recording transactions in sales, cash receipts, and general journals; recording in accounts receivable subsidiary ledger and posting to general ledger; cross-footing and preparing a schedule of accounts receivable
1 2 3 4 **(90 min)**

10A-1. Bill Murray opened Bill's Cosmetic Market in London on April 1. Bill offers no sales discount, and 8% PST and 5% GST is charged on all cosmetic sales. The following transactions occurred in April:

2013
April   2   Bill Murray invested $6,000 in the cosmetic market from his personal savings account.

5   From the cash register tapes, lipstick cash sales were $5,000 plus taxes.

5   From the cash register tapes, eyeshadow cash sales were $2,000 plus taxes.

8   Sold lipstick on account to Alice Koy Co., $300, sales invoice No. 1001, plus taxes.

9   Sold eyeshadow on account to Marika Sanchez Co., $1,000, sales invoice No. 1002, plus taxes.

12   Issued credit memorandum No. 10 to Alice Koy Co. for $150 for lipstick returned. (Be sure to reduce taxes payable for Bill's.)

19   Marika Sanchez Co. paid half the amount owed from sales invoice No. 1002, dated April 9.

22   Sold lipstick on account to Jeff Tong Co., $500, sales invoice No. 1003, plus taxes.

23   Sold eyeshadow on account to Rusty Neal Co., $800, sales invoice No. 1004, plus taxes.

23   Issued credit memorandum No. 11 to Jeff Tong Co. for $200 (plus taxes) for lipstick returned from sales invoice No. 1003, dated April 22.

26   Cash sales taken from the cash register tape showed:
1.   Lipstick—$1,000 + taxes
2.   Eyeshadow—$3,000 + taxes

29   Sold lipstick on account to Marika Sanchez Co., $400, sales invoice No. 1005, plus taxes.

30   Received payment from Marika Sanchez Co. of sales invoice No. 1005, dated April 29.

Check Figure

Schedule of Accounts
Receivable $1,977.50

Required

a. Journalize the above in the sales journal, cash receipts journal, or general journal.

b. Record in the accounts receivable subsidiary ledger and post to the general ledger when appropriate.

c. Prepare a schedule of accounts receivable for the end of April 2013.

Comprehensive problem: using HST in recording transactions in sales, cash receipts, and general journals; recording in accounts receivable and posting to general ledger; cross-footing and preparing a schedule of accounts receivable

① ② ③ ④ (90 min)

10A-2. Mary Parker owns Parker's SCUBA Shop of Bathurst. (In your *Study Guide with Working Papers*, balances as of April 1 are provided for the accounts receivable and general ledger accounts.) In Mary's province, it is necessary to add HST of 13% to arrive at the final invoice amount. The following transactions occurred in April:

2014

April	1	Mary Parker invested an additional $15,000 in the business.
	3	Sold $500 worth of merchandise (plus 13% HST) on account to J. Simpson, sales invoice No. 614, terms 2/10, n/30.
	7	Sold $1,200 worth of merchandise (plus HST) on account to R. Langley, sales invoice No. 615, terms 2/10, n/30.
	8	Sold $300 worth of merchandise (plus HST) on account to J. Fellowes, sales invoice No. 616, terms 2/10, n/30.
	11	Received cash from J. Simpson in payment of April 3 transaction, sales invoice No. 614, less discount.
	14	Sold $2,000 worth of merchandise (plus HST) on account to Phyllis Leung, sales invoice No. 617, terms 2/10, n/30.
	15	Received cash, less discount, from R. Langley in payment of April 7 transaction, sales invoice No. 615.
	18	Collected cash sales, $1,600 (plus HST).
	18	Issued credit memorandum No. 101 to Phyllis Leung for $500 (plus HST) worth of merchandise returned from April 14 sales.
	21	Received payment from Roland Doncaster of the amount due from previous month, $904.00.
	22	Received cash from Phyllis Leung in payment of April 14 sales invoice No. 617. (Don't forget about the credit memo, HST, and discount.)
	25	Collected cash sales, $4,000 (plus necessary HST).
	28	Sold merchandise priced at $5,000 (plus HST), on account, to Roland Doncaster, sales invoice No. 618, terms 2/10, n/30.
	29	Issued credit memorandum No. 102 to Roland Doncaster for $800 worth of merchandise (plus HST) returned from April 28 transaction, sales invoice No. 618.

Check Figure

Schedule of Accounts Receivable $7,090.75

Required

a. Journalize the transactions.

b. Record in the accounts receivable ledger and post to the general ledger as needed.

c. Prepare a schedule of accounts receivable as of April 30.

Journalizing, recording, and posting a purchases journal, as well as recording a debit memorandum and preparing a schedule of accounts payable

④ ⑤ ⑥ (45 min)

10A-3. Mabel's Natural Food Store of Cold Lake uses a purchases journal (page 10) and a general journal (page 2) to record the following transactions (continued from April):

2012

May	8	Purchased merchandise on account from Aton Co., invoice No. 400, dated May 7, terms 2/10, n/60, $600, plus 5% GST.
	11	Purchased merchandise on account from Broward Co., invoice No. 120, dated May 11, terms 2/10, n/60, $1,200, plus GST.
	14	Purchased store supplies on account from Midden Co., invoice No. 510, dated May 14, $700, plus GST.
	15	Issued debit memo No. 8 to Aton Co. for merchandise returned, $400 (plus GST) from invoice No. 400.

Check Figure

Total Schedule of Accounts Payable $6,310.50

May 18 Purchased office equipment on account from Relar Co., invoice No. 810, dated May 18, $560, plus GST.

25 Purchased additional store supplies on account from Midden Co., invoice No. 516, dated May 25, terms 2/10, n/30, $650, plus GST.

The food store has decided to use a separate column for the purchases of supplies in the purchases journal, which also has a separate column for GST.

Required

a. Journalize the transactions.

b. Post and record as appropriate.

c. Prepare a schedule of accounts payable as of May 31, 2012.

Accounts Payable Ledger

Name	Balance
Aton Co.	$ 420
Broward Co.	630
Midden Co.	1,260
Relar Co.	525

Partial General Ledger

Account	Number	Balance
Store Supplies	110	$ —
Prepaid GST	112	471
Office Equipment	120	—
Accounts Payable	210	2,835
Purchases	510	16,000
Purchases Returns and Allowances	512	—

Journalizing, recording, and posting a cash payments journal with GST; preparing a schedule of accounts payable

4 7 (45 min)

10A-4. Wendy Jones operates a wholesale computer centre in Whitehorse. All transactions requiring the payment of cash are recorded in the cash payments journal (page 5). The account balances as of May 1, 2013, are as follows:

Accounts Payable Ledger

Name	Balance	GST Included
Alvin Co.	$1,260	$60
Henry Co.	630	30
Soy Co.	840	40
Xon Co.	1,470	70

Check Figure

Total of Schedule of Accounts Payable $1,995.00

Partial General Ledger

Account	Number	Balance
Cash	110	$17,000
Prepaid GST	132	920
Delivery Truck	150	—
Accounts Payable	210	4,200
Computer Purchases	510	—
Computer Purchases Discount	511	—
Rent Expense	610	—
Utilities Expense	620	—

Required

a. Journalize the following transactions.

b. Record in the accounts payable ledger and post to the general ledger as appropriate.

c. Prepare a schedule of accounts payable.

2013

May	3	Paid half the amount owed Henry Co. from previous purchases of computers on account, less a 2% purchases discount, cheque No. 21.
	3	Bought a delivery truck for $8,000 cash, plus GST of $400, cheque No. 22, payable to Bill Ring Co.
	7	Bought computer merchandise from Lectro Co., cheque No. 23, $3,900, plus GST.
	17	Bought additional computer merchandise from Pulse Co., cheque No. 24, $800, plus GST.
	24	Paid Xon Co. the amount owed less a 2% purchases discount, cheque No. 25.
	27	Paid rent expense to King's Realty Trust, cheque No. 26, $2,000, plus GST.
	28	Paid utilities expense to Stone Utility Co., cheque No. 27, $300, plus GST.
	31	Paid half the amount owed Soy Co., no discount, cheque No. 28.

Comprehensive review problem with GST (or HST): all special journals and the general journal; schedules of accounts payable and accounts receivable

①②③④⑤⑥⑦ (120 min)

10A-5. Abby Ellen owns Abby's Toy House in Halifax. As her newly hired accountant, your task is to:

a. Journalize the transactions for the month of March.

b. Record in subsidiary ledgers and post to the general ledger as appropriate.

c. Total, rule, and cross-foot the journals.

d. Prepare a schedule of accounts receivable and a schedule of accounts payable, as of March 31, 2013.

Note: Please substitute HST at 13% for GST at 5% if your instructor so directs.

Check Figures

Total of Schedule of Accounts Receivable $7,980.00 (GST 5%) or $8,588.00 (HST 13%)

Total of Schedule of Accounts Payable $9,450.00 (GST 5%) or $10,170.00 (HST 13%)

The following is the partial chart of accounts for Abby's Toy House:

Assets	Revenue
110 Cash	410 Toy Sales
112 Accounts Receivable	412 Sales Returns and Allowances
114 Prepaid Rent	414 Sales Discounts
116 Prepaid GST/HST	
121 Delivery Truck	**Cost of Goods**
	510 Toy Purchases
Liabilities	512 Purchases Returns and Allowances
210 Accounts Payable	514 Purchases Discounts
218 GST/HST Payable	
	Expenses
Owner's Equity	610 Salaries Expense
310 A. Ellen, Capital	612 Cleaning Expense

2013

March 1 Abby Ellen invested $10,000 in the toy store.

1 Paid three months' rent in advance, cheque No. 1, $3,000, plus GST.

1 Purchased merchandise from Earl Miller Company on account, $4,000, plus GST. Invoice No. 410, dated March 1, terms 2/10, n/30.

4 Sold merchandise to Bill Burton on account, $1,000, plus GST. Invoice No. 1, terms 2/10, n/30.

6 Sold merchandise to Jim Rex on account, $700, plus GST. Invoice No. 2, terms 2/10, n/30.

8 Purchased merchandise from Earl Miller Co. on account, $1,200, plus GST. Invoice No. 415, dated March 8, terms 2/10, n/30.

8 Sold merchandise to Bill Burton on account, $600, plus GST. Invoice No. 3, terms 2/10, n/30.

11 Paid cleaning service $300, plus GST. Cheque No. 2.

11 Paid Earl Miller Co. invoice No. 410, dated March 1, cheque No. 3.

12 Jim Rex returned merchandise that cost $300 (before GST) to Abby's Toy House. Abby issued credit memorandum No. 1 to Jim Rex for $300, plus GST.

12 Purchased merchandise from Minnie Katz on account, $4,000, plus GST. Invoice No. 311, dated March 12, terms 1/15, n/60.

13 Sold $1,300 (plus GST) worth of toy merchandise for cash.

15 Paid salaries, $600, cheque No. 4.

15 Returned merchandise to Minnie Katz in the amount of $1,000, plus GST. Abby's Toy House issued debit memorandum No. 1 to Minnie Katz.

15 Sold merchandise for cash, $4,000, plus GST.

15 Received payment from Jim Rex, invoice No. 2 (less returned merchandise), less discount.

18 Bill Burton paid invoice No. 1.

18 Sold toy merchandise to Amy Rose on account, $4,000, plus GST. Invoice No. 4, terms 2/10, n/30.

19 Purchased delivery truck on account from Sam Katz's Garage, $3,000, plus GST. Invoice No. 111, dated March 19 (no discount).

March 22 Sold to Bill Burton merchandise on account, $900, plus GST. Invoice No. 5, terms 2/10, n/30.
22 Paid Minnie Katz balance owed, cheque No. 5.
22 Sold toy merchandise on account to Amy Rose, $1,100, plus GST. Invoice No. 6, terms 2/10, n/30.
25 Purchased toy merchandise, $600, plus GST. Cheque No. 6.
26 Purchased toy merchandise from Woody Smith on account, $4,800, plus GST. Invoice No. 211, dated March 26, terms 2/10, n/30.
26 Bill Burton paid invoice No. 5, dated March 22.
26 Amy Rose paid invoice No. 6, dated March 22.
28 Abby invested an additional $5,000 in the business.
28 Purchased merchandise from Earl Miller Co., $1,400, plus GST. Invoice No. 436, dated March 26, terms 2/10, n/30.
29 Paid Earl Miller Co. invoice No. 436, cheque No. 7.
29 Sold merchandise to Bonnie Flow Company on account, $3,000, plus GST. Invoice No. 7, terms 2/10, n/30.

Group B Problems

(The forms you need are on pages 10-18 to 10-44 of the *Study Guide with Working Papers*.)

Comprehensive problem: using sales taxes in recording transactions in sales, cash receipts, and general journals; recording in accounts receivable subsidiary ledger and posting to general ledger; preparing a schedule of accounts receivable

①②③④⑤⑥⑦ (90 min)

Check Figure

Schedule of Accounts Receivable $2,203.50

10B-1. Bill's Cosmetic Market of Brandon began operating in April. There is 8% PST and 5% GST on all cosmetic sales. Bill offers no discounts. The following transactions occurred in April:

2013
April 2 Bill Murray invested $10,000 in the cosmetic market from his personal account.
3 From the cash register tapes, lipstick cash sales were $5,000 plus taxes.
4 From the cash register tapes, eyeshadow cash sales were $3,000 plus taxes.
5 Sold lipstick on account to Alice Koy Co., $400, sales invoice No. 1001, plus taxes.
9 Sold eyeshadow on account to Marika Sanchez Co., $900, sales invoice No. 1002, plus taxes.
16 Issued credit memorandum No. 30 to Alice Koy Co. for lipstick returned, $200. (Be sure to reduce taxes payable.)
18 Marika Sanchez Co. paid half the amount owed from sales invoice No. 1002, dated April 9.
19 Sold lipstick on account to Jeff Tong Co., $600 sales invoice No. 1003, plus taxes.
22 Sold eyeshadow on account to Rusty Neal Co., $1,000, sales invoice No. 1004, plus taxes.
23 Issued credit memorandum No. 31 to Jeff Tong Co. for $300 (plus taxes), for lipstick returned from sales invoice No. 1003, dated April 20.
26 Sold lipstick on account to Marika Sanchez Co., $900, sales invoice No. 1005, plus taxes.
29 Cash sales taken from the cash register tape showed:
   1. Lipstick—$4,000 + taxes
   2. Eyeshadow—$2,000 + taxes
30 Received payment from Marika Sanchez Co. of sales invoice No. 1005, dated April 26.

Required

a. Journalize, record, and post as appropriate.

b. Prepare a schedule of accounts receivable for the end of April 2013.

Comprehensive problem: using sales taxes in recording transactions in sales, cash receipts, and general journals; recording in accounts receivable subsidiary ledger and posting to general ledger; preparing a schedule of accounts receivable

❶❷❸❹ (90 min)

Check Figure

Schedule of Accounts Receivable $8,333.75

10B-2. Mary Parker owns Parker's SCUBA Shop in Bathurst. (In your *Study Guide with Working Papers*, balances as of April 1 are provided for the accounts receivable and general ledger accounts.) In Mary's province, it is necessary to add HST of 13% to the sales total to arrive at the final invoice amount. The following transactions occurred in April:

2014

April	1	Mary Parker invested an additional $14,000 in the business.
	4	Sold $800 worth of merchandise (plus HST at 13%) on account to J. Simpson, sales invoice No. 614, terms 2/10, n/30.
	4	Sold $1,600 worth of merchandise (plus HST) on account to R. Langley, sales invoice No. 615, terms 2/10, n/30.
	8	Sold $600 worth of merchandise (plus HST) on account to J. Fellowes, sales invoice No. 616, terms 2/10, n/30.
	11	Received cash from J. Simpson in payment of April 4 transaction, sales invoice No. 614, less discount (pre-HST amount).
	14	Sold $3,000 worth of merchandise (plus HST) on account to Phyllis Leung, sales invoice No. 617, terms 2/10, n/30.
	18	Received cash payment from R. Langley in payment of April 4 transaction, sales invoice No. 615.
	18	Collected cash sales, $2,500 (plus HST).
	21	Issued credit memorandum No. 101 to Phyllis Leung for $900 (plus HST) of merchandise returned from April 14 sales on account.
	21	Received payment from Roland Doncaster of the amount due from the previous month, $904.00.
	21	Received cash from Phyllis Leung in payment of April 14 sales invoice No. 617. (Don't forget the credit memo, HST, and discount.)
	22	Collected cash sales, $3,200 plus HST.
	25	Sold merchandise priced at $6,000 (plus HST) on account to Roland Doncaster, sales invoice No. 618, terms 2/10, n/30.
	29	Issued credit memorandum No. 102 to Roland Doncaster for $1,000 worth of merchandise (plus HST) returned from April 25 transaction, sales invoice No. 618.

Required

a. Journalize the transactions.

b. Record in the accounts receivable ledger and post to the general ledger as needed.

c. Prepare a schedule of accounts receivable as of April 30, 2014.

Journalizing, recording, and posting a purchases journal with GST, as well as recording the issuing of a debit memorandum and preparing a schedule of accounts payable

4 5 6 (45 min)

10B-3. As the accountant of Mabel's Natural Food Store of Cold Lake, (1) journalize the following transactions in the purchases (page 10) or general journal (page 2), (2) record and post as appropriate, and (3) prepare a schedule of accounts payable as of May 31, 2012. Beginning balances are in your *Study Guide with Working Papers.*

2012
May   8   Purchased merchandise on account from Broward Co., invoice No. 420, dated May 7, terms 2/10, n/60, $500, plus 5% GST.

11   Purchased merchandise on account from Aton Co., invoice No. 400, dated May 11, terms 2/10, n/60, $900, plus GST.

14   Purchased store supplies on account from Midden Co., invoice No. 510, dated May 11, $800, plus GST.

15   Issued debit memo No. 7 to Aton Co. for merchandise returned, $400, plus GST (from invoice No. 400).

18   Purchased office equipment on account from Relar Co., invoice No. 810, dated May 18, $750, plus GST.

25   Purchased additional store supplies on account from Midden Co., invoice No. 516, dated May 22, terms 2/10, n/30, $850, plus GST.

10B-4. Wendy Jones of Whitehorse has hired you as her bookkeeper to record the following transactions in the cash payments journal. She would like you to record and post as appropriate and supply her with a schedule of accounts payable as of May 31, 2013. (Beginning balances are in your *Study Guide with Working Papers* and in Problem 10A-4.)

2013
May   3   Bought a delivery truck for $8,000 cash, plus GST, cheque No. 21, payable to Randy Rosse Co.

3   Paid half the amount owed Henry Co. from previous purchases of computer merchandise on account, less a 5% purchases discount, cheque No. 22.

7   Bought computer merchandise from Jane Co. for $900 cash, plus GST, cheque No. 23.

17   Bought additional computer merchandise from Jane Co., cheque No. 24, $1,000, plus GST.

24   Paid Xon Co. the amount owed less a 5% purchases discount, cheque No. 25.

27   Paid rent expense to Regan Realty Trust, cheque No. 26, $3,000, plus GST.

28   Paid half the amount owed Soy Co., no discount, cheque No. 27.

31   Paid utilities expense to County Utility, cheque No. 28, $425, plus GST.

Comprehensive review problem with GST (or HST): all special journals and the general journal; schedules of accounts payable and accounts receivable

1 2 3 4 5 6 7 (120 min)

10B-5. As the new accountant for Abby's Toy House in Halifax, your task is to:

a. Journalize the transactions for the month of March.

b. Record in subsidiary ledgers and post to the general ledger as appropriate.

c. Total, rule, and cross-foot the journals.

d. Prepare a schedule of accounts receivable and a schedule of accounts payable as of March 31, 2013.

Note: Please substitute HST at 13% for GST at 5% if your instructor so directs.

(Use the same chart of accounts as in Problem 10A-5. Your *Study Guide with Working Papers* has all the forms you need to complete this problem.)

2013	
March 1	Abby invested $8,000 in the new toy store.
1	Paid two months' rent in advance, cheque No. 1, $1,000, plus GST.
1	Purchased merchandise from Earl Miller Company, invoice No. 410, dated March 1, terms 2/10, n/30; $6,000, plus GST.
4	Sold merchandise to Bill Burton on account, $1,600, plus GST. Invoice No. 1, terms 2/10, n/30.
6	Sold merchandise to Jim Rex on account, $800, plus GST, invoice No. 2, terms 2/10, n/30.
7	Purchased merchandise from Earl Miller Company, $800, plus GST. Invoice No. 415, dated March 7, terms 2/10, n/30.
9	Sold merchandise to Bill Burton on account, $700, plus GST. Invoice No. 3, terms 2/10, n/30.
9	Paid cleaning service, $400, plus GST, cheque No. 2.
10	Jim Rex returned merchandise that cost $200 (plus GST) to Abby. Abby issued credit memorandum No. 1 to Jim Rex for $200, plus GST.
10	Purchased merchandise from Minnie Katz, $7,000, plus GST. Invoice No. 311, dated March 9, terms 1/15, n/60.
11	Paid Earl Miller Co. invoice No. 410, dated March 1, cheque No. 3.
13	Sold $1,500 (plus GST) worth of toy merchandise for cash.
15	Paid salaries, $700, cheque No. 4.
15	Returned merchandise to Minnie Katz in the amount of $500, plus GST. Abby issued debit memorandum No. 1 to Minnie Katz.
15	Sold merchandise for cash, $4,800, plus GST.
15	Received payment from Jim Rex for invoice No. 2 (less returned merchandise) less discount.
18	Bill Burton paid invoice No. 1.
18	Sold toy merchandise to Amy Rose on account, $6,000, plus GST. Invoice No. 4, terms 2/10, n/30.
19	Purchased delivery truck on account from Sam Katz's Garage, $2,500, plus GST. Invoice No. 111, dated March 19 (no discount).
21	Sold merchandise on account to Bill Burton, $2,000, plus GST. Invoice No. 5, terms 2/10, n/30.
22	Paid Minnie Katz balance owed, cheque No. 5.
22	Sold toy merchandise on account to Amy Rose, $2,000, plus GST. Invoice No. 6, terms 2/10, n/30.
26	Purchased toy merchandise, $800, plus GST, cheque No. 6.
26	Purchased toy merchandise from Woody Smith on account, $5,900, plus GST. Invoice No. 211, dated March 26, terms 2/10, n/30.
26	Bill Burton paid invoice No. 5, dated March 21.
26	Amy Rose paid invoice No. 6, dated March 22.
27	Abby invested an additional $3,000 in the business.
28	Purchased merchandise from Earl Miller Co., $4,200, plus GST. Invoice No. 436, dated March 26, terms 2/10, n/30.
29	Paid Earl Miller Co. invoice No. 436, cheque No. 7.
29	Sold merchandise to Bonnie Flow Company on account, $3,200, plus GST. Invoice No. 7, terms 2/10, n/30.

Check Figures

Total of Schedule of Accounts Receivable $10,395.00 (GST 5%) or $11,187.00 (HST 13%)

Total of Schedule of Accounts Payable $9,660.00 (GST 5%) or $10,396.00 (HST 13%)

(The forms you need are on pages 10-45 to 10-76 of the *Study Guide with Working Papers*.)

Multicolumn sales journal: use of sales tax; journalizing and posting to the general ledger and recording in accounts receivable ledger; and preparing a schedule of accounts receivable

6 7 (45 min)

Check Figure

Schedule of Accounts Receivable $37,432.50

10C-1. In September, the following transactions occurred for Forrest Equipment Supply of Regina (your *Study Guide with Working Papers* have balances as of September 1 for certain general ledger and accounts receivable ledger accounts):

2014

Sept. 2 Sold merchandise to Ray Fortuna on account, $9,500, invoice No. 703, plus 5% PST.

5 Sold merchandise to Wilma Jorge on account, $3,000, invoice No. 704, plus 5% PST.

8 Sold merchandise to Cassie Ho on account, $15,800, invoice No. 705, plus 5% PST.

9 Issued credit memorandum No. 14 to Ray Fortuna for $1,200 for defective merchandise returned from September 2 transaction. (Be careful to record the reduction in PST payable as well.)

12 Sold merchandise to Wilma Jorge on account, $4,650, invoice No. 706, plus 5% PST.

Required

a. Journalize the transactions in the appropriate journals.

b. Record in the accounts receivable ledger and post to the general ledger as appropriate.

c. Prepare a schedule of accounts receivable as of September 30, 2014.

Comprehensive problem: using sales taxes in recording transactions into sales, cash receipts, and general journals; recording in accounts receivable and posting to general ledger; and preparing a schedule of accounts receivable

1 2 3 4 (90 min)

Check Figure

Schedule of Accounts Receivable $17,311.60

10C-2. Royce's Communication Sales Co. began operating in August. Royce's offers no discounts (all terms are net 30 days), and 8% PST and 5% GST is charged on all sales. The following transactions occurred in August:

2013

Aug. 1 Royce Lamoureux invested $32,000 in Royce's Communication Sales Co. from his personal account.

2 From the cash register tapes, cellular cash sales were $5,400 plus taxes.

6 From the cash register tapes, radio cash sales were $8,150 plus taxes.

7 Sold cellular equipment on account to Kelly's Real Estate Co., $4,260, sales invoice No. 1201, plus taxes.

9 Sold radio equipment on account to Well's Hotshot Service Co., $3,100, sales invoice No. 1202, plus taxes.

13 Issued credit memorandum No. 1 to Kelly's Real Estate Co. for cellular equipment returned, $800. (Be sure to reduce taxes payable.)

16 Well's Hotshot Service Co. paid half the amount owed from sales invoice No. 1202, dated August 9.

20 Sold cellular equipment on account to Mountain Explorations Co., $5,770, sales invoice No. 1203, plus taxes.

20 Received proceeds of loan from the Business Development Bank of Canada, $50,000.

22 Sold radio equipment on account to Walkin's Safety Supply Co., $5,820. Sales invoice No. 1204, plus taxes.

Aug. 23 Issued credit memorandum No. 2 to Mountain Explorations Co. for $1,420 for equipment returned from sales invoice No. 1203, dated August 20. Remember to include taxes!

26 Received payment of net amount due from Kelly's Real Estate Co. on sales invoice No. 1201, less the credit allowed.

27 Cash sales taken from the cash register tape showed:
1. Cellular—$8,400 + taxes
2. Radio—$7,600 + taxes

30 Sold cellular equipment on account to Well's Hotshot Service Co., $5,150 sales invoice, No. 1205, plus taxes.

31 Received balance from Well's Hotshot Service Co. for sales invoice No. 1202, dated August 9.

Required

a. Journalize, record, and post as appropriate.

b. Prepare a schedule of accounts receivable for the end of August.

Comprehensive problem: using HST in recording transactions in sales, cash receipts, and general journals; recording in accounts receivable and posting to the general ledger; and preparing a schedule of accounts receivable
①②③④ (90 min)

10C-3. Martha Worth owns and operates Rarity Collectibles Shop in St. John's. (In your *Study Guide with Working Papers*, balances as of January 1 are provided for the accounts receivable and general ledger accounts.) In this province, it is necessary to add HST of 13% to the sales total to arrive at the final invoice amount. The following transactions occurred in January:

2014

Jan. 2 Martha Worth invested $42,000 in the business.

3 Sold $2,600 worth of merchandise (plus HST) on account to Starcraft Reproductions, sales invoice No. 344, terms 2/10, n/30.

6 Sold $3,200 worth of merchandise (plus HST) on account to Burgess Fancys, sales invoice No. 345, terms 2/10, n/30.

8 Sold $3,800 worth of merchandise (plus HST) on account to Hard-To-Find Co., sales invoice No. 346, terms 2/10, n/30.

10 Received cash from Starcraft Reproductions in payment of January 3 transaction, sales invoice No. 344, less discount.

14 Sold $2,480 worth of merchandise (plus HST) on account to Georgina's Collections, sales invoice No. 347, terms 2/10, n/30.

16 Received cash payment from Burgess Fancys in payment of January 6 transaction, sales invoice No. 345.

17 Collected cash sales, $4,125 plus HST.

20 Issued credit memorandum No. 10 to Georgina's Collections for $500 worth of merchandise (plus HST) returned from January 14 sales on account.

21 Received cash from Georgina's Collections in payment of January 14 sales invoice No. 347. (Don't forget about the credit memo, HST, and discount.)

24 Collected cash sales, $4,720, plus HST.

27 Sold merchandise priced at $6,000 (plus HST) on account to Perfect Sales Co., sales invoice No. 348, terms 2/10, n/30.

31 Issued credit memorandum No. 11 to Perfect Sales Co. for $1,200 (plus HST) of merchandise returned from January 27 transaction, sales invoice No. 348.

> **Check Figure**
>
> Schedule of Accounts Receivable $14,371.34

Required

a. Journalize the transactions.

b. Record in the accounts receivable ledger and post to the general ledger as needed.

c. Prepare a schedule of accounts receivable as of January 31, 2014.

Journalizing, recording, and posting a purchases journal with GST, as well as recording the issuing of a debit memorandum and preparing a schedule of accounts payable

4 5 6 (45 min)

10C-4. Farber's Fabric Co. of Yellowknife uses a purchases journal (page 21) and a general journal (page 32) to record the following transactions (continued from July). The GST rate is 5%:

2012
August 3   Purchased fabric for resale from European Import Fabrics Co., invoice No. 653, dated August 2, terms net 15 days, $1,362 plus GST.

7   Purchased merchandise on account from Eddyn Co., invoice No. 250, dated August 7, terms 2/10, n/60, $920, plus GST.

10   Purchased merchandise on account from Forward Co., invoice No. 1124, dated August 7, terms 1/10, n/60, $1,626, plus GST.

13   Purchased store supplies on account from Lavoy Co., invoice No. 712, dated August 13, $2,680, plus GST.

14   Issued debit memo No. 8 to Eddyn Co. for merchandise returned, $160, plus GST, from invoice No. 250.

17   Purchased office equipment on account from Reliant Co., invoice No. 873, dated August 14, $2,610, plus GST.

24   Purchased additional store supplies on account from Lavoy Co., invoice No. 816, dated August 24, terms 2/10, n/30, $725, plus GST.

28   Purchased fabric for resale from European Import Fabrics Co., invoice No. 713, dated August 27, terms net 15 days, $2,740, plus GST.

Check Figure

Total of Schedule of Accounts Payable $22,053.15

The fabric store has decided to keep a separate column for the purchases of supplies in the purchases journal and also has a separate column for GST. The account balances as of August 1, 2012, are as follows:

Accounts Payable Ledger

Name	Balance
Eddyn Co.	$ 840
European Import	3,255
Forward Co.	1,575
Lavoy Co.	525
Reliant Co.	2,730

Partial General Ledger

Account	Number	Balance
Store Supplies	130	$ —
Prepaid GST	142	2,795
Office Equipment	180	—
Accounts Payable	220	8,925
Purchases	500	86,340
Purchases Returns and Allowances	510	1,374

Required

a. Journalize the transactions.

b. Post and record as appropriate.

c. Prepare a schedule of accounts payable as of August 31, 2012.

Journalizing, recording, and posting a cash payments journal with GST; preparing a schedule of accounts payable

4 7 (60 min)

Check Figure

Total of Schedule of Accounts Payable $2,261.18

10C-5. Jim Stokes owns and operates a welding supplies company in Fort Liard. All transactions requiring the payment of cash are recorded in the cash payments journal (page 45). The account balances as of May 1, 2014, are as follows:

Accounts Payable Ledger

Name	Balance	GST Included
Dominion Gases Co.	$1,454.25	$ 69.25
Glover Gauges Co.	865.23	41.20
Marker Gloves Co.	1,812.95	86.33
Prism Accessories Co.	3,869.17	184.25
Vertal Rod Co.	2,434.06	115.91

Partial General Ledger

Account	Number	Balance
Cash	100	$22,941.18
Prepaid GST	145	2,418.12*
Delivery Truck	170	—
Accounts Payable	200	10,435.66
Welding Purchases	500	56,422.29
Welding Purchases Discounts	510	506.20
Rent Expense	670	3,730.00
Utilities Expense	690	1,204.66

*Will not agree with the amounts included in the accounts payable balances.

Required

a. Journalize the following transactions.

b. Record in the accounts payable ledger and post to the general ledger as appropriate.

c. Prepare a schedule of accounts payable as of May 31, 2014.

2014

May 1 Paid half the amount owed Dominion Gases Co. from previous purchases on account, less a 2% purchases discount, cheque No. 464.

2 Bought a delivery truck for $21,400 cash, plus GST of $1,070, cheque No. 465, payable to City Truck Sales Co.

5 Paid the amount owing to Glover Gauges Co., cheque No. 466.

6 Bought welding merchandise (cash purchase) from Vericon Canada Co., cheque No. 467, $1,846, plus GST.

13 Paid the balance due to Prism Accessories Co. after deducting a 5% discount as per usual terms for this company, cheque No. 468.

19 Bought additional welding merchandise (cash purchase) from Pulse Co., cheque No. 469, $850, plus GST.

23 Paid Marker Gloves Co. the amount owed less a 2% purchases discount, cheque No. 470.

27 Paid rent expense to Abbott Properties Co., cheque No. 471, $1,720, plus GST.

May 29 Paid utilities expense to Stony Plain Utility Co., cheque No. 472, $364, plus GST.

30 Paid $900.00 to Vertal Rod Co., no discount, cheque No. 473.

Comprehensive review problem with GST (or, optionally, HST): all special journals and the general journal, schedules of accounts payable, and accounts receivable

①②③④⑤⑥⑦ (140 min)

10C-6. Betty Cardinal runs Cardinal's Book Shop in a downtown location. As her newly hired accountant, your task is to do the following (substituting HST at 13% for GST at 5% if your instructor so directs):

a. Journalize the transactions for the month of October.

b. Record to subsidiary ledgers and post to the general ledger as appropriate.

c. Total, rule, and cross-foot the journals.

d. Prepare a schedule of accounts receivable and a schedule of accounts payable as of October 31, 2013.

The following is the partial chart of accounts for Cardinal's Book Shop:

Check Figures

Total of Schedule of Accounts Receivable $7,839.30 (GST 5%) or $8,436.58 (HST 13%)

Total of Schedule of Accounts Payable $28,728.00 (GST 5%) or $30,916.80 (HST 13%)

Assets	Revenue
110 Cash	410 Book Sales
120 Accounts Receivable	412 Sales Returns and Allowances
135 Prepaid Rent	414 Sales Discounts
138 Prepaid GST/HST	
180 Delivery Truck	**Cost of Goods**
	510 Book Purchases
Liabilities	512 Purchases Returns and Allowances
210 Accounts Payable	514 Purchases Discounts
218 GST/HST Payable	
	Expenses
Owner's Equity	615 Cleaning Expense
310 B. Cardinal, Capital	650 Salaries Expense

2013

Oct. 1 Betty Cardinal invested $20,000 in the bookstore.

1 Paid three months' rent in advance, cheque No. 121, $2,700, plus GST.

3 Purchased merchandise from Milligan Book Company on account, $4,270, plus GST. Invoice No. 410, dated October 2, terms 2/10, n/30.

3 Sold merchandise to First City Library on account, $2,465, plus GST. Invoice No. 781, terms 2/10, n/30.

7 Sold merchandise to District College on account, $3,160, plus GST. Invoice No. 782, terms 2/10, n/30.

8 Purchased merchandise from Milligan Book Co. on account, $2,940, plus GST. Invoice No. 415, dated October 8, terms 2/10, n/30.

8 Sold merchandise to First City Library on account, $1,856, plus GST. Invoice No. 783, terms 2/10, n/30.

8 Paid cleaning service $280, plus GST, cheque No. 122.

11 District College returned merchandise that cost $312 (before GST) to Cardinal's Book Shop. Cardinal issued credit memorandum No. 1 to District College for $312, plus GST.

11 Purchased merchandise from Winnipeg Book Supply on account, $1,852, plus GST. Invoice No. 311, dated October 8, terms 1/15, n/60.

11 Paid Milligan Book Co. invoice No. 410, dated October 2, cheque No. 123.

Oct. 14 Sold $2,420, plus GST, worth of book merchandise for cash.

15 Paid salaries, $920, cheque No. 124.

15 Returned merchandise to Winnipeg Book Supply in the amount of $362 plus GST. Cardinal's Book Shop issued debit memorandum No. 18 to Winnipeg Book Supply.

15 Sold merchandise for cash, $1,047, plus GST.

15 Received payment from District College, invoice No. 782 (less returned merchandise), less discount.

18 First City Library paid invoice No. 781.

18 Sold book merchandise to Rural Bookmobile Co. on account, $2,484, plus GST. Invoice No. 784, terms 2/10, n/30.

21 Purchased delivery truck on account from Suburban Auto Sales Co., $18,600, plus GST. Invoice No. 111, dated October 19 (no discount).

22 Sold merchandise to First City Library on account, $2,694, plus GST. Invoice No. 785, terms 2/10, n/30.

22 Paid Winnipeg Book Supply balance owed, cheque No. 125.

25 Sold book merchandise on account to Rural Bookmobile Co., $2,412, plus GST. Invoice No. 786, terms 2/10, n/30.

25 Purchased used book merchandise for cash, $3,200, plus GST, cheque No. 126.

28 Purchased book merchandise from Smithsonian Book Co. on account, $5,820, plus GST. Invoice No. 211, dated October 25, terms 2/10, n/30.

28 Sold merchandise for cash, $940, plus GST.

29 First City Library paid invoice No. 785, dated October 22.

29 Rural Bookmobile Co. paid invoice No. 786, dated October 25.

30 Betty invested an additional $12,000 in the business.

30 Purchased merchandise from Milligan Book Co., $3,120 plus GST. Invoice No. 436, dated October 26, terms 2/10, n/30.

31 Paid Milligan Book Co. invoice No. 436, cheque No. 127.

31 Sold merchandise to Flower & Company on account, $3,126, plus GST. Invoice No. 787, terms 2/10, n/30.

On-the-job Training

(The forms you need are on pages 10-77 and 10-78 of the *Study Guide with Working Papers*.)

Cash discounts

5 7 (20 min)

Hint: $R = \frac{I}{PT}$

T-1. Angie Co. bought merchandise for $1,000 with credit terms of 2/10, n/30. Because of the bookkeeper's incompetence, the 2% cash discount was missed. The bookkeeper told Pete Angie, the owner, not to get excited. After all, it was a $20 discount that was missed—not hundreds of dollars. Act as Mr. Angie's assistant and show the bookkeeper that his $20 represents a sizeable equivalent interest cost. In your calculation, assume a 360-day year. Make some written recommendations so that this will not happen again.

T-2. Ronald Howard has been hired by Green Company to help reconstruct the sales journal, general journal, and cash receipts journal, which were recently destroyed in a fire. The owner of Green has supplied him with the data shown below. Enter the entries into the reconstructed sales journal, general journal, and cash receipts journal. (Don't worry about dates, invoice numbers, etc.) What written recommendation should Ron make so that reconstruction will not be needed in the future?

Accounts Receivable Subsidiary Ledger

P. Bond

Balance	100	150	CRJ
SJ	150	Entitled to 2% discount	

M. Raff

Balance	200	
SJ	100	

J. Smooth

Balance	300	1,000	GJ
SJ	2,000	1,000	CRJ
SJ	1,000	500	GJ
		Entitled to 1% discount	

R. Venner

Balance	200	400	CRJ
SJ	400		

Partial General Ledger

Cash

12,737	

Accounts Receivable

Balance	800	1,000	GJ
SJ	3,650	500	GJ
		1,550	CRJ

Shelving Equipment

Balance	200	200	CRJ

M. Rang, Capital

	1,000	Balance
	5,000	(Additional investment this month)

Sales

	800	Balance
	6,000	CRJ ← 5,000
	3,650	SJ and 1,000

Sales Discounts

CRJ	13	

Sales Returns and Allowances

GJ	1,000	
GJ	500	

CONTINUING PROBLEM

Recording sales and purchases with HST transactions

4 6 7 (60 min)

Tony Freedman was very happy to see the progress made by using the specialized journals. Effective January 1, 2014, the company obtains an HST number* and so begins to charge HST at 13% on all sales made. The company also pays HST from January 1 on all purchases. The special journals used in Tony's company have been modified to include columns for HST, and these can be found in the *Study Guide with Working Papers*, pages 10-79 to 10-92.

The partial January transactions are as follows:

2014

Jan.	3	Received cheque from Carson Engineering Corp. for amount outstanding.
	3	Wrote cheque No. 280 to Able Holdings for December, January, and February rent, $1,200 (HST exempt).
	3	Bought merchandise on account from Computer Connection (purchase order No. 4016), $2,500, plus HST, terms 3/10, n/30.
	3	Paid amount due to Staples (cheque No. 281).
	3	Sold $900, plus HST, worth of merchandise to Taylor Golf on credit, sales invoice No. 12690; terms are 2/10, n/30.
	3	Collected $5,085, including HST, for cash sales for the week of January 3.
	6	Bought merchandise on account from Multi Systems (purchase order No. 4017), $300, plus HST; terms are 3/10, n/30.
	6	Bought office supplies on account from Staples (purchase order No. 4018), $200, plus HST; terms are n/30.
	9	Issued debit memorandum No. 11 to Computer Connection for merchandise returned from purchase order No. 4016, $300 (remember the HST).
	9	Paid *City Newspaper* amount owing from December 31, cheque No. 282.
	10	Received electric bill for January, $250, plus HST.
	10	Received from Taylor Golf balance owing as of December 31.
	10	Purchased merchandise on account from Computer Connection (purchase order No. 4019), $500, plus HST, terms are 1/30, n/60.
	10	Paid West Bell Canada December 11 bill, cheque No. 283.
	10	Sold $3,500, plus HST, worth of merchandise on account to Digital Prints Co., invoice 12691, terms are 2/10, n/30.
	10	Collected $13,560, including HST, for cash sales for the week of January 10.
	13	Paid net amount due to Computer Connection (purchase order No. 4016), less discount, cheque No. 284.
	13	Paid amount due to CRA re December wages, cheque No. 285.
	13	Received January phone bill, $110, plus HST.
	13	Paid Multi Systems re January 6 purchase, less discount, cheque No. 286.
	17	Collected $15,820, including HST, for cash sales for the week of January 17.

---

* Please ignore the fact that in Alberta there is only GST at 5%. This makes the Continuing Problem more relevant to a greater number of students.

17	Paid Alpha Office Co. the amount owing from December, cheque No. 287.
23	Sold $4,000, plus HST, worth of merchandise on account to Noel Aberhart, sales invoice No. 12692; terms are 4/10, n/30.
24	Collected $13,560, including HST, for cash sales for the week of January 24.
27	Issued credit memorandum to Digital Prints Co. for $400 worth of merchandise returned (remember the HST), invoice No. 12691.
27	Collected amount owing (less discount) from Noel Aberhart, invoice No. 12692.
30	Sold $1,600, plus HST, worth of merchandise to Anthony Pitale, invoice No. 12693; terms 2/10, n/30.
30	Collected full payment from Digital Prints (remember the credit memorandum), invoice No. 12691.
31	Collected $12,430, including HST, for cash sales for the week of January 31.
31	Wrote cheque No. 288 to Automated Payroll Service for January covering January wages, $8,740.20. Tony has decided to spend his time doing repairs and making sales rather than preparing payroll records like he did in November and December. The company issues cheques to all employees weekly but obtains one cheque monthly from Tony's company for wages, benefits, and its own charges at month-end.

Schedule of Accounts Receivable
Precision Computer Centre
December 31, 2013

Anthony Pitale	$ 1,600.00
Taylor Golf	3,200.00
Carson Engineering	14,990.00
Total Amount Due	$19,790.00

Schedule of Accounts Payable
Precision Computer Centre
December 31, 2013

Alpha Office Co.	$ 318.00
City Newspaper	855.00
Staples	250.00
West Bell Canada	165.00
Total Amount Payable	$1,588.00

Assignment

(See pages 10-79 to 10-92 in your *Study Guide with Working Papers*.)

1. Journalize the transactions in the appropriate journals (cash receipts, sales, cash payments, purchases, or general journal).
2. Record in the accounts receivable subsidiary ledger and accounts payable subsidiary ledger and post to the general ledger as appropriate. A partial general ledger is included in the *Study Guide with Working Papers*.
3. Prepare a schedule of accounts receivable, and a schedule of accounts payable as of January 31, 2014.

Computer Workshops

Mars and Abby; Mills and Adora

Depending on the goals your instructor has set for the course you are taking, you may be asked to complete one or more of the computer workshops created especially for Chapter 10. If you need to complete any of the workshops, you will obtain all necessary details from the Multimedia Library on the MyAccountingLab website.

There are a total of eight workshops available for Chapter 10. For each of the workshops, there are two versions—one using Simply Accounting Pro® and the other using QuickBooks Premier®. The choice will depend to a large extent on which software is available to you in your college's lab, on your own laptop, or other computer, as well as the preference, knowledge, and experience of your instructor. Before beginning, be sure to get clear directions as to which workshop you are to complete. In this chapter, it is recommended that students complete the Mars (or Mills) workshop before attempting the Abby (or Adora) workshop. They are designed so that the details covered in the Mars (and Mills) workshops are reinforced in the subsequent one.

You need to obtain several files from the MyAccountingLab website before you begin. (Please also see the added details on page 134 at the end of Chapter 3.)

1. The instruction files that describe each company and the details of the assignment.
2. Data sets that have been carefully crafted for you so you may begin each workshop with minimal bother. All of these data sets are downloaded in compressed format, and will need to be restored by the software before you can work on them.
3. A Word file that sets forth in detail the step-by-step instructions you need to complete the Mars/Abby assignments, one for each of the software programs. Help files also exist for the Mills/Adora workshops, but only if they are provided by your instructor.

11

The Synoptic (Combined) Journal

THE BIG PICTURE

What's the strangest thing that's ever happened to you on the job? No matter how sensible your last part-time, summer, or full-time job appeared to be, there was probably a time when life at work became a little odd—just downright weird.

For a number of Canadians, weird jobs are their bread and butter. Take bee tamer Jim Rogers: His job is to capture and relocate swarms of bees that leave their hives and take up new residences in Calgary neighbourhoods. While homeowners panic, Rogers keeps his cool and focuses on getting the swarm—generally comprising an old queen bee and up to 30,000 worker and drone bees—escorted to a safer home outside of the city.

Fellow Calgarian Megan Evans balances her life as a mother and a sculptor with another more dangerous vocation that has audiences across North America shuddering. Evans, on the other hand, can't permit herself even the slightest of shivers. She's a sword swallower—one of only five women in the world who make a living by sliding swords and other long, pointed objects down their esophaguses. Her hands need to be steady for the job. One wrong move during a performance could puncture her esophagus, which comes with a 50% risk of death.

Evans claims that staying calm, focused, and overcoming her gag reflex is the key to her work, which she suggests could be done by any reasonably healthy person with good posture. Regular visits to a chiropractor help keep her in shape for her performances.

Canadian chiropractor Dan Martin may agree with the importance of chiropractic care, but he won't be accepting Evans for an appointment anytime soon. Dr. Martin's patients are almost exclusively of the four-legged variety. Horses, dogs, and cats all benefit from his care. In the nine years since his practice was expanded to include animals, more than 1,000 horses have been adjusted under his careful hands, as well as numerous family pets.

Whether a bee tamer or a pet chiropractor, these Canadians have one thing in common: They are all service providers. As such, their success depends on their ability to increase customer numbers and satisfaction. To that end, they would rather spend their time marketing to or serving clients than posting entries to several special accounting journals. In fact, because service providers have fewer transactions than merchandisers or manufacturers, the special journals we introduced in the last two chapters are less appropriate for their needs.

In this chapter, you will learn to use a *synoptic journal* that replaces all special journals and the general journal. It is similar to an accounting worksheet and can be used in a spreadsheet format on a computer. In addition to learning how to keep a synoptic journal, you will learn the difference between using the cash basis, modified cash basis, or accrual basis of accounting.

Sound complicated? Don't worry. There's nothing weird about it. It's safer than sword-swallowing and a whole bunch more fun than a swarm of angry bees!

Source: Information from Jayne Creighton, "All in a Day's Work: 10 Weird Jobs," *Alberta Venture Magazine*, January/February 2001.

Learning Objectives	**1** Defining methods of accounting: accrual basis, cash basis, and modified cash basis (p. 511)
	2 Recording, journalizing, and posting transactions for a synoptic journal of a professional service company using a modified-cash-basis of accounting (p. 512)
	3 Recording, journalizing, and posting transactions for a synoptic journal of a merchandising company using the accrual basis of accounting (p. 518)

In the first 10 chapters of this text, we have used general journals and special journals to record business transactions. Over the years, many students have asked how to set up journals for starting their own small businesses. They have felt that the general journals were too simple and the special journals were too detailed.

The solution is a **synoptic (combined) journal**, a special journal that replaces the general journal and other special journals. It has the same basic features as other special journals. Synoptic journals are an option for small businesses that do not have many transactions. Lawyers, doctors, dentists, and other professionals may use a synoptic journal, which may be modified in many ways to suit their individual needs. If the volume of transactions increases, more specialized journals may be required. For example, if a company adds bookkeepers to its accounting department, management must be prepared to provide a system of dividing the work to be done. This division of labour may play an important part in determining the types of special journals that are needed.

Before we begin this subject, however, we need to understand the difference between the cash basis of accounting and the accrual basis of accounting.

In the chapters so far, we have been using the **accrual basis of accounting**, which is based on the *matching principle*. The matching principle says that you record revenue when it is earned (not when the money actually comes in), and you record expenses when they are incurred in producing revenue (not when they are paid).

In the **cash basis of accounting**, revenue is recorded when cash is received, and expenses are recorded when they are paid.

Companies choose the accrual basis because they want to show earned revenue along with the expenses that were incurred to earn that revenue. They can do so with the accrual basis but not always with the cash basis. However, service companies sometimes use the cash basis because it is simpler and more convenient, and provides enough information for the decisions they need to make.

Let's look at the difference between the accrual and cash basis with the following example. John Mills earned real estate commissions of $100,000, of which he received $60,000 in cash. Expenses were $25,000, of which $10,000 was paid in cash.

1 Defining methods of accounting: accrual basis, cash basis, and modified cash basis

> **Accrual accounting**
> - **Revenue is recorded when earned.**
> - **Expenses are recorded when incurred.**
>
> **Cash accounting**
> - **Cash receipts are recorded when received.**
> - **Cash payments are recorded when paid.**

> **Many service companies will use the cash method if they have no inventories.**

Comparison of Cash Basis with Accrual Basis for the Month of July 2013

Cash Basis		*Accrual Basis*	
Revenue (received)	$60,000	Revenue (earned)	$100,000
Expenses (paid)	10,000	Expenses (incurred)	25,000
Net income	$50,000	Net income	$ 75,000

Note that net income differs according to which system is used. Keep in mind that all revenue and expenses will show up eventually if the cash basis is used but not in this accounting period.

Now let's look at the record-keeping needs of a dentist, Dr. Gail Duncan. She wants to use a modified-cash-basis system of accounting because of its simplicity and convenience.

Learning Unit 11-1

Synoptic Journal: A Modified Cash System for a Service Company

2 Recording, journalizing, and posting transactions for a synoptic journal of a professional service company using a modified cash basis of accounting

Dr. Duncan's accountant has informed her that keeping strictly to a cash-basis system is difficult to do. The reason is that, because of tax regulations, Dr. Duncan's accountant would be distorting financial reports by using a strictly cash system. She feels that the best system for a dentist is a combination of the cash and accrual methods. This combination is known as the **modified-cash-basis (hybrid) method**. Under this method, Dr. Duncan will record professional fees only when cash is received and record expenses only when paid in cash. To satisfy the Canada Revenue Agency, an adjustment for amounts accrued at year-end is required before financial statements are prepared (not illustrated here). The following exceptions, however, are an attempt to reflect income clearly and minimize distortion of the financial reports:

1. Long-lived assets (equipment, building, etc.) are treated the same under cash and accrual accounting. This means that the amount paid for equipment in one year may not be treated as an expense of just that period; Dr. Duncan will be amortizing or allocating the cost of her dental equipment over a period of years.

2. Insurance premiums and purchases of a large amount of supplies are treated the same under cash and accrual accounting. This means that the amount consumed or used up is shown as an expense in the current year and the amount on hand is carried over into the next accounting period.

> Dentists can't charge the entire cost of dental equipment to the year in which it was purchased for cash.

> Only the supplies *used up* are shown as an expense.

These exceptions require adjusting entries (which we saw before under accrual accounting) when the modified cash basis is used.

Two types of personal services might use a modified cash basis. They are:

1. Professional services—lawyers, doctors, dentists, accountants, consultants, and so on

2. Business services—real estate, insurance, software support, and so on

CHART OF ACCOUNTS

The chart of accounts for Dr. Duncan is provided in Figure 11-1. Note that, unlike a chart of accounts on the accrual basis, there are no categories for Accounts Receivable, Accounts Payable, or Salaries Payable (these are added at year-end by the accountant). This chart of accounts does have titles for handling the exceptions (e.g., Accumulated Amortization, Prepaid Insurance). There is no Supplies account under assets since Dr. Duncan is not buying a large amount of supplies and thus all can be shown as Dental Supplies Expense without distorting the financial reports.

> Special journals like the synoptic are purchased at specialty office stationery stores. Their cost can be quite high—even higher than some of the more inexpensive computer accounting software (but not Simply Accounting® or QuickBooks®).

The transactions that occurred for the month of November are listed on pages 513–514. We will show you the recording of these transactions in the synoptic journal (or combined journal)—a special journal that will replace the general journal and save journalizing and posting labour. The synoptic journal has the same basic features as the other special journals that we introduced in Chapters 6 and 10. Remember, each business will design the headings of the synoptic journal to fit its individual needs. It is not unusual to find such journals with a total of 24 columns or even more—although we will be keeping things at a more manageable size in this

Figure 11-1
Chart of Accounts

**Dr. Duncan
Chart of Accounts**

Assets
111 Cash
113 Petty Cash Fund
131 Prepaid Insurance
141 Office Furniture
142 Accumulated Amortization,
       Office Furniture
151 Dental Equipment
152 Accumulated Amortization,
       Dental Equipment
161 Auto
162 Accumulated Amortization, Auto

Liabilities
211 Due to Canada Revenue Agency
212 Other Payroll Deductions Payable
213 Notes Payable

Owner's Equity
311 G. Duncan, Capital
312 G. Duncan, Withdrawals
313 Income Summary

Revenue
411 Professional Fees

Expenses
511 Automobile Expense
512 Rent Expense
513 Salaries Expense
514 Telephone Expense
515 Amortization Expense,
       Office Furniture
516 Amortization Expense,
       Dental Equipment
517 Amortization Expense, Auto
518 Miscellaneous Expense
519 Insurance Expense
520 Dental Supplies Expense
521 Payroll Tax Expense

textbook. Accounts that are used most often are the ones that should have special columns. This will save time when journalizing and posting.

Another important point is that, to keep things simple, GST is not included in the earlier examples in this chapter but is covered at the end of Learning Unit 11-2.

Transactions for Dr. Duncan

2013
Nov.   1   Paid $700 office rent for November, cheque No. 61.
       1   Received cheques totalling $3,000 from patients for dental work.
       5   Paid telephone bill, $80, cheque No. 62.
       5   Issued cheque No. 63 to Bill Blan Insurance Agency for premium on insurance for three years, $900.
       5   Purchased dental supplies from Roe Suppliers, $450, cheque No. 64.
       8   Received cheques from patients, $1,600.
       8   Calculated current cash balance.
      12   Issued cheque No. 65 to Moe Gas for automobile expenses charged during October, $280.
      12   Dr. Duncan withdrew $500 for personal use, cheque No. 66.
      15   Issued cheque No. 67 to V. P. Suppliers Company for dental supplies charged during October, $650.
      15   Paid office salaries for the period November 1 to November 15, $3,000, cheque No. 68.
      15   Cash receipts from patients totalled $2,800 for the week.
      15   Calculated current cash balance.
      18   Collected $800 from insurance companies for patients' accounts.
      19   Purchased dental supplies from J. Labs, $500, cheque No. 69.
      22   Cash receipts for the week totalled $2,900.

Nov. 22 Calculated current cash balance.

26 Issued cheque No. 70 for charitable contributions, $300.

26 Purchased dental supplies from J. Labs, $300, cheque No. 71.

29 Received cheques from patients' insurance companies totalling $3,300.

29 Paid office salaries for the period November 15 to November 30, $2,250, cheque No. 72.

29 Calculated current cash balance and cross-footed journal.

RECORDING TRANSACTIONS IN THE SYNOPTIC JOURNAL

The synoptic journal for Dr. Duncan is shown in Figure 11-2. Note that the bank balance can be calculated at any time. For example, in the explanation column, note the beginning balance of $9,500. On November 8, the current balance was calculated as follows:

Beginning balance	$ 9,500
+ Deposits	4,600
− Cheques written	2,130
Ending balance	$11,970 (Recorded in explanation column, probably by using pencil, not ink)

Figure 11-2 The Synoptic Journal

DR. DUNCAN
SYNOPTIC JOURNAL

Month: November

Cash Deposits Dr.	Cheques Cr.	Chq. No.	Date 2013	Explanation	Post. Ref.	Sundry Dr.	Sundry Cr.	Professional Fees Cr.	Dental Supplies Expense Dr.
				Cash Balance 9,500					
	700 00	61	Nov. 1	Rent Expense	512	700 00			
3000 00			1	Professional Fees	X			3000 00	
	80 00	62	5	Telephone Expense	514	80 00			
	900 00	63	5	Prepaid Insurance	131	900 00			
	450 00	64	5	Roe Supplies	X				450 00
1600 00			8	Professional Fees 11,970	X			1600 00	
	280 00	65	12	Auto Expense	511	280 00			
	500 00	66	12	G. Duncan, Withdr.	312	500 00			
	650 00	67	15	V.P. Suppliers	X				650 00
	3000 00	68	15	Salaries Expense	513	3000 00			
2800 00			15	Professional Fees 10,340	X			2800 00	
800 00			18	Professional Fees	X			800 00	
	500 00	69	19	J. Labs	X				500 00
2900 00			22	Professional Fees 13,540	X			2900 00	
	300 00	70	26	Miscellaneous Expense	518	300 00*			
	300 00	71	26	J. Labs	X				300 00
3300 00			29	Professional Fees	X			3300 00	
	2250 00	72	29	Salaries Expense 13,990	513	2250 00			
14400 00	9910 00					8010 00		14400 00	1900 00
(111)	(111)					(X)		(411)	(520)

$24,310 = $24,310

*For tax purposes, Dr. Duncan's advisor may reclassify this item.

As we have seen with other special journals, this synoptic journal is proved in the following way:

	Dr.	Cr.
Cash	$14,400	$ 9,910
Sundry	8,010	
Professional Fees		14,400
Dental Supplies Expense	1,900	
	$24,310	$24,310

POSTING THE SYNOPTIC JOURNAL

Since this is a modified cash system, there are no subsidiary ledgers for accounts receivable or accounts payable. Companies using a modified cash basis may keep information about any receivables or payables in an informal memorandum record until cash is received or paid. During the month, items entered into the Sundry column can be updated in the general ledger. At the end of the month, the totals of Cash, Professional Fees, and Dental Supplies Expense would be posted to the general ledger. The account numbers are shown at the bottom of the columns of the synoptic journal to indicate that the totals were posted. The X means that no posting is necessary. The total of the Sundry column is not posted because the various items making up the total are posted individually.

RECORDING PAYROLL DEDUCTIONS AND EMPLOYER'S PAYROLL TAX EXPENSE

In Chapters 8 and 9, we studied payroll, with the payroll register recording gross pay, deductions, and net pay. From the payroll register, a general journal entry was prepared to record the payroll. We also discussed using a general journal to record the employer's payroll tax expense before it was paid (for CPP and EI). The record-keeping involved in paying an employee will be quite similar in a synoptic journal using the cash-basis method, but recording the employer's payroll tax expense will change.

Why? In the cash-basis method of accounting, the company's share of both CPP and EI will not be recorded until paid. Under accrual accounting, we recorded them when they were incurred, not when they were paid.

Let's look at Figure 11-3, the partially completed synoptic journal on page 516 and explain each entry. For simplicity, we are ignoring the remittance requirements and monthly reports that we covered in the payroll chapters.

a. Bill Smith's gross salary of $3,500 is recorded as a salary expense and the deductions for income tax, CPP, and EI are listed as liabilities until the employer makes the remittance. Note that the cheque is written for $2,606.09 (net pay). The same procedure is followed for Joe Ring. (His net pay is $2,566.54.)

b. June 8. The remittance to the Canada Revenue Agency is assumed to have been made. This means that the employer pays the CPP and EI deducted from the employees as well as the company's matching share along with the income tax also deducted from the employees' paycheques.

Figure 11-3 Partially Completed Synoptic Journal

SYNOPTIC JOURNAL

Royal Bank		Chq. No.	Date 2013		Account or Explanation	Post. Ref.	Sundry		Professional Fees Cr.	Salary Expense Dr.	Payroll Deductions		
Deposits Dr.	Cheques Cr.						Dr.	Cr.			Income Tax Payable Cr.	CPP Payable Cr.	EI Payable Cr.
(A)	2606 09	33	May	1	Bill Smith—April salary	X				3500 00	675 60	158 81	59 50
	2566 54	34		1	Joe Ring—April salary	X				3300 00	528 45	148 91	56 10
(B)	2096 93	50	June	8	Canada Revenue Agency								
					Income Tax Payable	211	1204 05						
					CPP Payable	212	307 72						
					EI Payable	213	115 60						
					Payroll Tax Expense	521	469 56*						

*Calculated as [($307.72 × 1) + ($115.60 × 1.4)] = $469.56.

516   CHAPTER 11

Note: The payroll tax expense is now being recorded for the employer's share of CPP and EI, since it is now being *paid*. Note that the cheque amount is for $2,096.93, which includes the following:

Income tax payable	1,204.05
CPP payable	307.72
Payroll tax expense—CPP	307.72
EI payable	115.60
Payroll tax expense—EI ($115.60 × 1.4)	161.84
	2,096.93

The end result is to reduce the liabilities owed as well as record the employer's share of CPP and EI as payroll tax expense (also called employee benefits expense). When the remittance is actually made to the Canada Revenue Agency, the following entry is made in the synoptic journal:

	Dr.	Cr.
Income tax payable	XXX.XX	
CPP payable	XX.XX	
EI payable	XX.XX	
Payroll tax expense	XX.XX	
Cash		XXX.XX

Some employers keep separate expense accounts for the various employee benefits expenses, such as CPP, EI, health insurance, and the like, but this often provides too much unnecessary information.

In summary, sometimes companies will record the expense portion of CPP and EI when the *payroll* is paid, instead of when the remittance is made. If this is the case, when the remittance is made, the synoptic journal will record this entry:

	Dr.	Cr.
Income tax payable	XXX.XX	
CPP payable	XX.XX	
EI payable	XX.XX	
Cash		XXX.XX

When a company has more than a few employees, it will often maintain a payroll journal (as described in Chapters 8 and 9) in addition to its synoptic/combined journal. This is more than acceptable because otherwise the synoptic journal would be taken up with several rows of space devoted to each employee. Bear in mind, however, that it is becoming unusual for a company to have both types of journals because any company with more than a few employees will probably be using a computer, together with appropriate software, such as Simply Accounting® or QuickBooks®.

LEARNING UNIT 11-1 REVIEW

AT THIS POINT you should be able to:

◆ Explain the modified cash basis of accounting. (p. 512)

◆ Journalize transactions in a synoptic journal. (pp. 512–514)

◆ Calculate the current bank balance of a synoptic journal. (pp. 513–514)

◆ Prove a synoptic journal. (p. 515)

◆ Explain how to record payroll as well as payroll tax expense in a synoptic journal. (pp. 515–517)

Learning Unit 11-2

Synoptic Journal for Art's Wholesale Clothing Company

3 Recording, journalizing, and posting transactions for a synoptic journal of a merchandising company using the accrual basis of accounting

In Chapters 6 and 10, we developed the sales journal, cash receipts journal, purchases journal, cash payments journal, and general journal for Art's Wholesale Clothing Company. Many small businesses that are concerned with saving journalizing, recording, and posting labour, however, are not concerned about division of labour (having a different bookkeeper working on each special journal) since they have only one bookkeeper. Such businesses may want the advantages provided by special journals but would like to reduce the number of journals needed. This unit will develop a synoptic journal, a book of original entry that dispenses with the special journals yet gains their advantages in journalizing, recording, and posting for a company that uses an accrual accounting approach. (In order to focus on the basics of the synoptic journal, payroll details are not described at this point.)

Our goal in this unit is to place all the special journals for Art's Wholesale in the following synoptic journal:

SYNOPTIC JOURNAL																
								Month: April								Page 1
				Sundry		Cash		Accts. Rec.		Accts. Pay.		Sales	Sales Disc.	Purchases	Pur. Disc.	
Date	Explanation	Cheque No.	Post. Ref.	Dr.	Cr.	Dr.	Cr.	Dr.	Cr.	Dr.	Cr.	Cr.	Dr.	Dr.	Cr.	

Note that since Art's business uses *accrual* accounting, we now have columns for accounts receivable and accounts payable.

If Art decided to use the synoptic journal, he and the accountant would go over the chart of accounts. They would be concerned with setting up columns in the synoptic journal for accounts in which transactions would occur frequently. On the basis of their analysis, Art and the accountant agreed to set up the following special columns in an **accrual accounting synoptic journal**.

◆ **Cash Dr.**   This column records increases in cash.
◆ **Cash Cr.**   This column records decreases in cash.
◆ **Accounts Receivable Dr.**   This column records amounts to be received from sales on account.

- **Accounts Receivable Cr.**   This column records amounts paid by customers from past sales on account.
- **Accounts Payable Dr.**   This column reflects amounts paid to creditors.
- **Accounts Payable Cr.**   This column reflects amounts owed to creditors.
- **Sales Cr.**   This column records all sales made for cash or on account.
- **Sales Discounts Dr.**   This column records the amounts of discounts taken by customers.
- **Purchases Dr.**   All purchases of merchandise for resale are recorded in this column.
- **Purchases Discounts Cr.**   This column records the amounts of discounts Art receives by paying for purchases before the discount period expires.
- **Sundry Dr., Cr.**   These two columns record transactions that do not occur very frequently. If a transaction occurs and no special columns are set up to record part or all of it, it can be recorded in the Sundry columns.

Figure 11-4 (starting on page 520) shows the completed synoptic journal for the month of April for Art's Wholesale Clothing Company (we will go over the recordings and postings in a moment).

The synoptic journal for April can be proved as follows:

Checking the accuracy of the synoptic journal

Account Title	Dr.	Cr.
Sundry	$ 6 7 5 0 00	$ 8 7 0 0 00
Cash	14 3 2 4 00	6 9 9 4 00
Accounts Receivable	6 5 0 0 00	4 4 0 0 00
Accounts Payable	4 8 0 0 00	11 9 3 0 00
Sales		8 6 0 0 00
Sales Discounts	7 6 00	
Purchases	8 1 8 0 00	
Purchases Discounts		6 00
Totals	$40 6 3 0 00	$40 6 3 0 00

RECORDING AND POSTING THE SYNOPTIC JOURNAL

The recording and posting rules that we learned for Art's special journals will hold true for the synoptic journal. Here are some key points:

1. ✔ Record in accounts receivable or accounts payable subsidiary ledgers daily. SJ1 (Synoptic Journal, page 1) will be placed in the PR column of the ledger account when information from the journal is updated in the ledger.
2. **Sundry** Update the general ledger account on a daily basis. Use the ledger account number as a posting reference.
3. **X** in the PR column indicates no posting since the total is posted at the end of the month. An X below the total means that the total of the column is not posted.

End of Month

The total of each column (except Sundry) will be posted to the general ledger at the end of the month. Note that the account number from the ledger is placed at the bottom of the column in the synoptic journal, indicating that the total was posted to that account.

Figure 11-4
Synoptic Journal
Completed

ART'S WHOLESALE CLOTHING COMPANY
SYNOPTIC JOURNAL

Date	Explanation	Chq. No.	Post. Ref.	Sundry Dr.	Sundry Cr.	Cash Dr.	Cash Cr.
2013 Apr. 1	Art Newner, Cap.		311		8000 00	8000 00	
2	Prepaid Insurance	101	116	900 00			900 00
2	Hal's Clothing		✔				
2	Freight-In, Abby Blake		514 ✔	50 00			
5	Equip., Joe Francis		121 ✔	4000 00			
5	Hal's Clothing		✔			784 00	
6	Thorpe Co.		✔				
6	Bevans Co.		✔				
6	J. Francis Co.	102	✔				4000 00
9	J. Sullivan Co.		✔				
9	Purchases	103	✗				800 00
9	Pur. R&A, Thorpe Co.		514 ✔		200 00		
12	Thorpe Co.	104	✔				594 00
12	Sales R&A, Bevans Co.		412 ✔	600 00			
13	Abby Blake Co.		✔				
13	Cash Sales		✗			900 00	
16	Bevans Co.		✔			980 00	
19	Roe Co.		✔				
23	Roe Co.		✔			1960 00	
23	Roe Co.		✔				
27	Supplies, J. Sullivan		115 ✔	500 00			
27	Store Equipment		121		500 00	500 00	
27	Salaries Expense	105	611	700 00			700 00
27	Mel's Department Store		✔				
30	Mel's Department Store		✔				
30	Cash Sales		✗			1200 00	
	Totals			6750 00	8700 00	14324 00	6994 00
				(X)	(X)	(111)	(111)

Note the following when a synoptic journal is used:

1. Charge *and* cash sales are recorded in the sales column.
2. Purchases returns, sales returns, etc., are recorded in Sundry since no general journal is used with a synoptic journal.
3. Adjusting and closing entries will be recorded in the Sundry columns.

Whether Art's Wholesale uses a synoptic journal or a set of special journals, the schedule of accounts receivable and accounts payable will be the same, as will the trial balance.

To sum up, the synoptic journal is an option for small businesses that do not have many transactions. Lawyers, doctors, dentists, and other professionals may use a synoptic journal, which may be modified in many ways to suit their individual needs.

As the business grows, the volume of transactions may increase, possibly creating the need for more-specialized journals or a computerized set of records rather than just the synoptic journal. For example, if a company adds bookkeepers to its accounting department, management must be prepared to provide a system of dividing the work to be done. This division of labour may play an important part in determining the types of special journals that are needed.

Before stating the objectives of this unit, let's look at a sample of how a synoptic journal might look if it included either Provincial Sales Tax Payable and GST

> **Adjusting and closing entries could be recorded in the Sundry columns of a synoptic journal.**

> **It is possible to use an electronic spreadsheet running on a computer to "build" a synoptic journal in computer form. This idea is workable but of doubtful value since a variety of low-cost, full-featured accounting programs are available. Many small businesses use Simply Accounting® or QuickBooks®.**

Month: April

Accounts Receivable Dr.	Accounts Receivable Cr.	Accounts Payable Dr.	Accounts Payable Cr.	Sales Cr.	Sales Discounts Dr.	Purchases Dr.	Purchases Discounts Cr.
800 00				800 00			
			5050 00			5000 00	
			4000 00				
	800 00				16 00		
			800 00			800 00	
1600 00				1600 00			
		4000 00					
			980 00			980 00	
						800 00	
		200 00					
		600 00					6 00
	600 00						
			600 00			600 00	
				900 00			
	1000 00				20 00		
2000 00				2000 00			
	2000 00				40 00		
500 00				500 00			
			500 00				
900 00				900 00			
700 00				700 00			
				1200 00			
6500 00	**4400 00**	**4800 00**	**11930 00**	**8600 00**	**76 00**	**8180 00**	**6 00**
(113)	(113)	(211)	(211)	(411)	(413)	(511)	(512)

SYNOPTIC JOURNAL

Page 1

Cash and sundry would be located here.	Accts. Rec. Dr.	Accts. Rec. Cr.	Sales Cr.	Sales R&A Dr.	Accts. Pay. Dr.	Accts. Pay. Cr.	Sales Tax Payable Cr.	Pur. Dr.	Sup. Dr.	Office Equip. Dr.

Payable or HST Payable. In Figure 11-5 (starting on page 522), notice at the end of the month that we will still post the totals of Accounts Receivable, Sales, Sales Tax Payable, and GST Payable to the general ledger. In provinces where HST is used, HST Payable would replace both the Sales Tax Payable and GST Payable columns. Keep in mind that GST Payable, HST Payable, and Sales Tax Payable are liabilities shown on the balance sheet. Also bear in mind that the principles of recording PST and GST/HST have not changed at all from Chapter 10, where we covered them in detail. The main difference is that now we are including both collections and remittances in the same journal.

Another point worth stressing is that in the modern business world, there is less need to study the large synoptic journal with a lot of intensity. If a large synoptic journal is necessary because of complex transactions (or a large volume of transactions), a computer and some inexpensive software perhaps provide a better

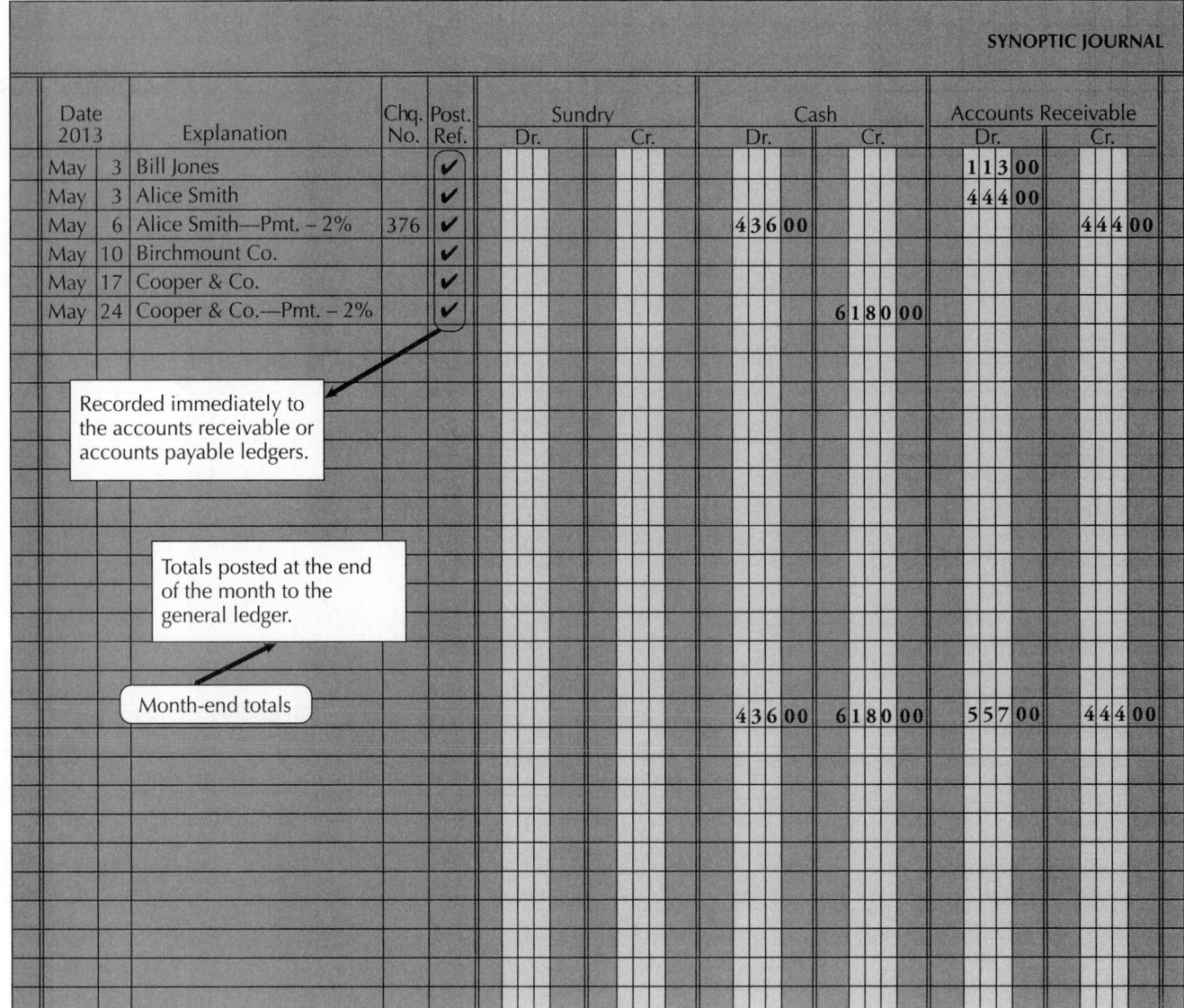

Figure 11-5   Synoptic Journal with Sales Tax and GST

solution. Remember that a knowledge of manual bookkeeping and accounting procedures means that a computerized system can be more useful and efficient.

If a retail company has many sales returns and allowances as well as purchases, the synoptic journal heading in Figure 11-5 could be designed.

LEARNING UNIT 11-2 REVIEW

AT THIS POINT you should be able to:

◆ Journalize transactions in the synoptic journal for a merchandise company. (pp. 518–519)

◆ Explain how to record and post the synoptic journal. (p. 519)

◆ Compare special journals (cash payments, receipts, etc.) and the synoptic journal. (p. 520)

◆ Explain how sales tax and GST/HST could be recorded in a synoptic journal. (p. 521)

	Month: April								
Accounts Payable		GST		Sales	Sales Discounts	Purchases	Purchases Discounts	Sales Tax	
Dr.	Cr.	Dr.	Cr.	Cr.	Dr.	Dr.	Cr.	Cr.	
			5 00	100 00				8 00	
			20 00	400 00				32 00	
					8 00				
	1155 00	55 00				1100 00			
	6300 00	300 00				6000 00			
6300 00							120 00		
6300 00	7455 00	355 00	25 00	500 00	8 00	7100 00	120 00	40 00	

Self-Review Quiz 11-2

(The form you need is on page 11-1 of the *Study Guide with Working Papers*.)

On the basis of the synoptic journal presented in this unit, classify each of the following statements as true or false.

1. Synoptic journals are less efficient than other types of special journals.
2. The total of the Cash column is posted daily.
3. The total of the Sundry column is not posted.
4. The total of the Sales column is not posted.
5. All synoptic journals have the same headings.
6. Synoptic journals cannot be proved.
7. Subsidiary ledgers are posted from the Cash column.
8. The synoptic journal is used for large companies.
9. A dentist could use a synoptic journal.
10. A lawyer will always use a synoptic journal.

Solution to Self-Review Quiz 11-2

1. False	2. False	3. True	4. False	5. False
6. False	7. False	8. False	9. True	10. False

Chapter Assignments

SUMMARY OF KEY POINTS

Learning Unit 11-1

1. A company with inventory will not use the cash method.

2. The modified cash system is used because federal and provincial requirements make a strictly cash-basis system difficult to implement without distorting the financial reports.

3. The modified cash system will require adjustments for amortization, insurance premiums, and large amounts of supplies purchased. Adjustments often will be recorded in the Sundry columns of the synoptic journal and additional adjustments can be made at year-end.

4. No accounts for accounts payable or accounts receivable are used in the chart of accounts for a modified cash system. Companies use *memoranda* to keep track of receivables or payables until money is received or paid.

5. The bank balance (cash balance) can be determined at any time when a synoptic journal is used.

6. A synoptic journal can be proved by cross-footing the totals to verify that total debits equal total credits.

7. The payroll tax expense for the employer using a cash-basis system is recorded when the remittance is made. In the cash-basis system, no *liability* accounts exist for Due to Canada Revenue Agency or other payroll taxes payable; you record them when *paid* as part of the remittance to the CRA.

Learning Unit 11-2

1. A synoptic journal for Art's Wholesale replaces the individual special journals (SJ, CRJ, PJ, CPJ, GJ).

2. Many small companies use a synoptic journal.

3. A synoptic journal on an accrual basis uses columns for accounts receivable and accounts payable. Subsidiary ledgers will be recorded during the month. The total of the Sundry columns is not posted.

4. Adjusting and closing entries will be recorded in the Sundry columns.

KEY TERMS

Accrual accounting synoptic journal   A special journal that combines the features of the sales, cash payments, cash receipts, purchases, and general journals (p. 518)

Accrual basis of accounting   An accounting method in which revenue is recorded when earned and expenses are recorded when incurred (p. 511)

Cash basis of accounting   An accounting method in which revenue is recorded when cash is received and expenses are recorded when they are paid (p. 511)

Modified-cash-basis (hybrid) method The accounting method that records revenue when cash is received and expenses when they are paid. Adjustments to long-lived assets, as well as insurance premiums and amounts of supplies on hand are required by provincial and federal laws so that financial reports will not be distorted. (p. 512)

Synoptic (combined) journal A special journal that combines the features of the sales, cash payments, cash receipts, purchases, and sometimes general journals. (p. 511)

BLUEPRINT OF A TYPICAL CHART OF ACCOUNTS FOR A LAWYER USING A MODIFIED CASH BASIS (INCLUDING PAYROLL)

Assets

No Accounts Receivable account	Royal Bank	111
	Petty Cash	112
	Office Supplies	113
	Prepaid Insurance	114
	Office Equipment	115
	Accumulated Amortization, Office Equipment	116
	Automobiles	117
	Accumulated Amortization, Automobiles	118

Liabilities

No Accounts Payable account	Income Tax Payable	211
	CPP Payable	212
	EI Payable	213
	Bank Loan Payable	214

Owner's Equity

J. Smith, Capital	311
J. Smith, Withdrawals	312
Income Summary	313

Revenue

Recorded only when cash is received ←

Professional Fees	411

Expenses

Amortization Expense, Office Equipment	511	For adjustments so that the financial reports will not be distorted
Amortization Expense, Automobiles	512	
Insurance Expense	513	
Office Supplies Expense	514	
Dues	515	
Postage	516	
Payroll Tax Expense	517	→ Records the tax expense for the employer when the CPP, EI, and income tax are remitted
Rent Expense	518	
Salary Expense	519	
Telephone Expense	520	
Miscellaneous Expense	521	

QUESTIONS, CLASSROOM DEMONSTRATION EXERCISES, EXERCISES, AND PROBLEMS

Discussion Questions and Critical Thinking/Ethical Case

1. All companies with inventory must use the cash basis of accounting. Agree or disagree.

2. Why does the strictly cash basis tend to distort financial reports?

3. List three adjustments that may result when using a modified cash system.

4. Explain how a company can change its method of accounting.

5. A modified cash system has an accounts receivable and an accounts payable ledger. Agree or disagree. Please support your answer.

6. Explain how a cash balance can be calculated during the month when a synoptic journal is used.

7. How is a synoptic journal proved?

8. Explain why there are no accounts for Due to Canada Revenue Agency or other payroll taxes payable in the chart of accounts in the cash basis method.

9. What purpose would an informal memorandum serve when dealing with accounts payable and accounts receivable in a modified cash system?

10. Explain when the Payroll Tax Expense account will be updated in a modified cash system.

11. Explain how using a synoptic journal for an accrual-basis company will aid in reducing the number of special journals needed.

12. If a company is expanding, a synoptic journal could be efficient. Please respond.

13. Angel Blythe, the bookkeeper of Aster Co., also collects the payment of invoices by customers. Angel noticed that Rume Co. paid the April 10 invoice twice. Angel, who is in need of extra cash, does not plan to inform Rume Co. of the double payment. Do you agree with Angel's decision? You make the call. Write down your specific recommendations to Angel.

MyAccountingLab

Make the grade with MyAccountingLab! The exercises and problems marked in green can be found on MyAccountingLab at www.myaccountinglab.com. You can practise them as often as you want, and many of them feature step-by-step guided solutions to help you find the right answer. You can also find working papers for selected problems in the Multimedia Library on MyAccountingLab.

Classroom Demonstration Exercises

(The forms you need are on page 11-1 of the *Study Guide with Working Papers*.)

Set A

Accounts Needing Adjustment

Preparing transactions in a modified cash system
2 (10 min)

1. Spencer Fly Fishing Company uses the modified-cash-basis system. Give three examples of accounts that might need adjusting entries.

Payment of Payroll

Recording payroll transactions using the accrual basis of accounting method
3 (10 min)

2. Mel Blanc uses the accrual accounting approach. Mel paid his employees May 30. The deductions were income tax, $360; CPP, $169; EI, $71.

   1. Assuming the company accountant enters transactions into the synoptic journal daily, when would Payroll Tax Expenses be entered?

   2. What is the total amount of Payroll Tax Expenses for this pay period?

Combined Journal Headings

Identifying which column to use in an accrual basis of accounting approach

3 (10 min)

3. Match the following partial list of column headings for Mia Frezell's synoptic journal. Use only one number for each letter.

1. Cash Dr.
2. Accounts Payable Dr.
3. Purchases Discounts Cr.
4. Sundry Cr.
5. Purchases Dr.

_____ **a.** Records purchases made on account or with cash.
_____ **b.** Records amounts paid to creditors.
_____ **c.** Records sales made for cash.
_____ **d.** Records the amounts of supplier discounts taken by Frezell.
_____ **e.** Records amounts for the infrequent purchase of vehicles.

Recording in Subsidiary Ledgers

Subsidiary ledgers under the accrual basis of accounting

3 (10 min)

4. Indicate which of the following transactions would result in a recording to a subsidiary ledger. The company uses a synoptic journal with an accrual accounting approach.

May 3, 2013

a. Gail Stephens took a purchases discount of $35 when paying invoice No. 204, dated April 27.
b. Paid freight on April 19 purchase.
c. Sold $295 worth of merchandise on account, invoice No. 599.
d. Gail Stephens paid weekly salaries May 7, $1,343.

Set B

Accounts Needing Adjustment

Preparing transactions in the modified cash basis of accounting

2 (10 min)

1. Which of the following titles may require adjusting entries when using the modified cash basis?

	Yes	No
Cash	_____	_____
Accounts Receivable	_____	_____
Equipment	_____	_____
Supplies	_____	_____
Accounts Payable	_____	_____
Salaries Payable	_____	_____
Accumulated Amortization	_____	_____
Prepaid Insurance	_____	_____

Payment of Payroll

Recording payroll transactions using the accrual basis of accounting

3 (10 min)

2. Mel Blanc uses a modified-cash-basis system. His company's payroll records show deductions for income tax, $266; CPP, $59; and EI, $22. Please record the necessary entry for the remittance of source deductions to the CRA.

Combined Journal Headings

Identifying the column to use in the accrual basis of accounting

3 (10 min)

3. Match the partial list of column headings for Pete Moore's synoptic journal on the next page to the statements following the list. Use only one number for each letter.

1. Cash Cr.
2. Accounts Payable Cr.
3. Sales Discounts Dr.
4. Sundry Dr./Cr.
5. Sales Cr.

_____ a. Reflects amounts owed to creditors.
_____ b. Records the amounts of discounts taken by customers.
_____ c. Records transactions that do not occur very often.
_____ d. Records sales made for cash or on account.
_____ e. Records decreases in cash.

Recording in Subsidiary Ledgers

Subsidiary ledgers under the accrual basis of accounting method
3 (10 min)

4. Indicate which of the following transactions would result in a recording to a subsidiary ledger. The company uses a synoptic journal with an accrual accounting approach.

a. Pete Daving invested $20,000 in the business.
b. Sold $1,300 worth of merchandise to French Co. on account.
c. Cash sales, $200.
d. Received half the amount owed by French from sales on account in **b**.

Exercises

(The forms you need are on page 11-2 of the *Study Guide with Working Papers*.)

Identifying adjustment titles for a modified cash system
2 (10 min)

11-1. In a modified cash system, which of the following titles may need adjustments?
◆ Cash
◆ Supplies
◆ Prepaid Insurance
◆ Equipment
◆ Bank Loan Payable
◆ Bill Thom, Capital
◆ Bill Thom, Withdrawals
◆ Commission Sales
◆ Salary Expense

Posting a synoptic journal using the accrual approach
3 (15 min)

11-2. Avon Company uses a synoptic journal with the following headings:

Sundry	Dr./Cr.
Accounts Receivable	Dr./Cr.
Accounts Payable	Dr./Cr.
Commission Sales	Cr.
Salary Expense	Dr.
Cash	Dr./Cr.

a. How can the balance of cash be determined at any point in the month?
b. Which column total will not be posted?
c. Do you think Avon Company has subsidiary ledgers? Please explain.
d. Which columns will be used to record the payment of advertising expense?

11-3. Listed as follows are the accounts used by Dr. Jonson, who keeps his records on a strictly cash basis. As his accountant, which titles do you think could be added to use a modified cash system? Assume that a large amount of supplies is bought.

Cash; Bank Loan Payable; L. Jonson, Capital; L. Jonson, Withdrawals; Professional Fees; Auto Expense; Rent Expense; Office Furniture Expense; Insurance Expense; Medical Supplies Expense.

11-4. Using the headings of the synoptic journal for Dr. Duncan (Figure 11-2), indicate when postings would occur.

2013
May   3   Nick Olden invested $4,000 in his dental business.
       7   Paid three months' insurance premiums, $1,200.
      14   Received cheques from patients, $900.
      17   Paid office salaries, $1,550.

11-5. Using the headings of the synoptic journal for Art's Wholesale (Figure 11-4), indicate when recordings and postings would occur.

2013
May   3   Joe Davis invested $12,000 in the business.
       6   Bought $600 worth of merchandise for cash.
       7   Cash sale, $600.
      21   Received $400 less a 3% discount from Alvie Corp. from past sale on account.

Group A Problems

(The forms you need are on pages 11-3 to 11-11 of the *Study Guide with Working Papers*.)

11A-1. Ann Kuhl, M.D., of Canmore, uses the following chart of accounts:

Chart of Accounts

Assets	Revenue
111 Alberta Bank	411 Professional Fees
112 Prepaid Insurance	
113 Medical Supplies	**Expenses**
121 Medical Equipment	511 Rent Expense
122 Accumulated Amortization, Medical Equipment	512 Donation Expense
	513 Salaries Expense
123 Office Furniture	514 Medical Supplies Expense
124 Accumulated Amortization, Office Furniture	515 Amortization Expense, Medical Equipment
125 Auto	516 Amortization Expense, Office Furniture
126 Accumulated Amortization, Auto	517 Amortization Expense, Automobile
	518 Insurance Expense
Liabilities	519 Telephone Expense
211 Bank Loan Payable	610 Cleaning Expense
	611 Miscellaneous Expense
Owner's Equity	
311 A. Kuhl, Capital	
312 A. Kuhl, Withdrawals	
313 Income Summary	

Check Figure

Cross-footing $21,865

The headings of the synoptic journal are as follows:

				Post. Ref.	Sundry Dr.	Sundry Cr.	Medical Supplies Dr.	A. Kuhl, Withdrawals Dr.	Cleaning Expense Dr.	Prof. Fees Cr.	Chq. No.	Alberta Bank Dr.	Alberta Bank Cr.
	Date	Explanation											

Page 1

Required

a. Journalize the transactions listed below in the synoptic journal.

b. Prove the synoptic journal.

Transactions

2012

May 1 Dr. Kuhl deposited $7,000 in the practice.

4 Paid rent for the month to Foster Realty, $900, cheque No. 1.

8 Bought medical equipment from Ace Supply Co., $1,500, cheque No. 2.

11 Bought medical supplies from Lone Co., $700, cheque No. 3.

15 Received payment for patient services, $3,500.

17 Bought additional medical supplies from Lone Co., $1,200, cheque No. 4.

18 Dr. Kuhl withdrew $1,625 for personal use, cheque No. 5.

21 Paid Al's Janitorial Service, $300, cheque No. 6.

22 Received payment for patient services, $1,900.

25 Paid for postage stamps, $40 (miscellaneous expense), cheque No. 7.

30 Paid salaries for month, $2,400, cheque No. 8.

30 Paid Al's Janitorial Service, $400, cheque No. 9.

31 Dr. Kuhl withdrew $400 for personal use, cheque No. 10.

11A-2. The following is the chart of accounts for Nathan Fox:

Journalizing transactions of a modified cash system into a synoptic journal with headings for payroll deductions, as well as recording payroll tax expense

2 (40 min)

Check Figure

Cross-footing $24,111.40

Chart of Accounts

Assets
111 Bank of Regina
112 Prepaid Insurance
113 Medical Supplies
121 Office Equipment
122 Accumulated Amortization, Office Equipment

Liabilities
211 Due to CRA
212 Other Payroll Deductions Payable

Owner's Equity
311 N. Fox, Capital
312 N. Fox, Withdrawals
313 Income Summary

Revenue
411 Professional Fees

Expenses
511 Rent Expense
512 Medical Supplies Expense
513 Salaries Expense
514 Payroll Tax Expense
515 Telephone Expense
516 Amortization Expense, Office Equipment
517 Insurance Expense
518 Cleaning Expense
519 Miscellaneous Expense

The headings of Nathan Fox's synoptic journal are as follows:

			Post. Ref.	Bank of Regina Dr.	Bank of Regina Cr.	Chq. No.	Prof. Fees Cr.	Sal. Exp. Dr.	Payroll Deductions Income Tax Payable Cr.	Payroll Deductions CPP Payable Cr.	Payroll Deductions EI Payable Cr.	Med. Sup. Dr.	Sundry Dr.	Sundry Cr.
	Date	Explanation												

Required

a. Journalize the following transactions listed in the synoptic journal (beginning balances are provided in the working papers).

b. Prove the synoptic journal.

Transactions

2014

May   1   Received $3,000 for patient services.

         2   Issued cheque No. 480 to Lane Drug for medical supplies, $600.

         5   Issued cheque No. 481 to A. Realty to pay three months' insurance premiums, $1,200.

         9   Received cheque for patient services, $4,500.

      15   Issued the following payroll cheques to his staff:

Employee	Cheque No.	Gross Pay	IT	CPP	EI	Net Pay
Abby Slat	482	$ 700	$50	$31	$12	$ 607
Jane Reeves	483	600	26	26	10	538
Bob Swan	484	500	5	21	9	465
		$1,800	$81	$78	$31	$1,610

      19   Issued cheque No. 485 to Lane Drug for medical supplies, $400.

      26   Nathan Fox withdrew $1,700 for personal use, cheque No. 486.

      27   Fox made the necessary remittance to the CRA from payroll of May 15, cheque No. 487. (Don't forget Fox's share of CPP and EI.)

11A-3. Debra Clark, a recent graduate of a medical school, has decided to open her own office in Sudbury. Based on the advice of her accountant, she will use a synoptic journal. The following is the chart of accounts for Dr. Clark's office:

In margin: Journalizing and proving a synoptic journal; recording transactions using an accrual basis of accounting
3 (30 min)

Chart of Accounts

Assets
111 Cash
112 Accounts Receivable
113 Prepaid Insurance
121 Office Equipment

Liabilities
211 Accounts Payable

Owner's Equity
311 D. Clark, Capital
312 Income Summary

Revenue
411 Medical Fees

Expenses
511 Telephone Expense
512 Cleaning Expense
513 Utilities Expense
514 Wages Expense

The headings of Dr. Clark's synoptic journal are:

SYNOPTIC JOURNAL														
										Month			Page 1	
Date	Explanation	Chq. No.	Post. Ref.	Sundry Dr.	Sundry Cr.	Cash Dr.	Cash Cr.	Accounts Receivable Dr.	Accounts Receivable Cr.	Accounts Payable Dr.	Accounts Payable Cr.	Office Equip. Dr.	Medical Fees Cr.	

Required

a. Record the following transactions in the synoptic journal. Complete the Post. Ref. column as if you were recording and posting.

b. Prove the synoptic journal.

Check Figure

Total, Sundry column
Dr. $2,060

2013

July	2	Debra Clark invested $7,000 cash and $4,000 worth of office equipment in the practice.
	2	Paid insurance on the office for one year in advance, $1,700, cheque No. 1.
	9	Purchased office equipment on account from Smith Stationery Co., $400.
	12	Purchased office equipment on account from Vole Stationery Co., $700.
	16	Completed vaccination of each child at Salem Elementary School, $3,000 on account.
	16	Received $1,900 cash for medical fees earned.
	19	Performed a complete examination for Alvin Ray's son, $75 on account.
	22	Paid Smith Stationery one-half the amount owed from July 9 transaction, cheque No. 2.
	26	Paid telephone bill, $90, cheque No. 3.
	29	Paid utilities, $170, cheque No. 4.
	30	Paid Toby Cleaning Co. for cleaning service performed, $100, cheque No. 5.
	30	Paid one-half the amount owed Vole Stationery Company from July 12 transaction, cheque No. 6.

Journalizing, recording, and posting a synoptic journal used to record transactions utilizing the accrual basis of accounting

3 (60 min)

11A-4. (GST at 5% and PST at 7% [not cumulative] are involved in this problem.) Buzzy Sullivan opened a dry-cleaning store that also sold accessories. The following is the chart of accounts for Buzzy's Cleaning Company of Dauphin.

Check Figure

Total of Sundry column
Dr. $2,400

Chart of Accounts

Assets
111 Cash
112 Accounts Receivable
113 Prepaid Insurance
115 Prepaid GST
121 Cleaning Equipment

Liabilities
211 Accounts Payable
212 Bank Loan Payable
215 GST Payable
217 PST Payable

Owner's Equity
311 B. Sullivan, Capital
312 B. Sullivan, Withdrawals
313 Income Summary

Revenue
411 Cleaning Revenue
412 Sales Discounts
413 Accessory Sales

Cost of Goods Sold
511 Purchases
512 Purchases Returns and Allowances
513 Purchases Discounts

Expenses
611 Utilities Expense
612 Advertising Expense
613 Cleaning Supplies Expense

Here are the transactions for the month of January:

2012

Jan.	3	Buzzy Sullivan invested $8,000 cash in the business.
	9	Paid a five-year insurance policy in advance, $1,500 (no taxes), cheque No. 1.

Jan.   9   Purchased merchandise on account from Role Company, $900, plus GST.
      12   Cleaned shirts for cash, $650, plus PST and GST.
      16   Cleaned suits on account for Pete Daley, $200, plus PST and GST.
      19   Purchased cleaning equipment on account from Ral Co., $900, plus GST.
      20   Borrowed $6,000 from National Bank.
      23   Cleaned shirts for Pete Daley for $50, plus PST and GST on account.
      26   Received entire payment from Pete Daley for January 16 transaction less a 2% discount.
      26   Purchased merchandise on account from Fresh Air Co., $250, plus GST.
      26   Cleaned slacks on account for Alice Small, $15, plus PST and GST.
      27   Paid amount due to Role Company less a 2% discount for January 9 transaction, cheque No. 2.
      27   Returned $100 worth of cleaning equipment to Ral Company for faulty workmanship. (Remember the GST.)
      30   Paid Fresh Air Co. the amount due on the January 26 purchase less a 10% discount, cheque No. 3.
      30   Cash sales, $800, plus PST and GST.
      30   Received amount due from Alice Small on the January 26 transaction, less a 20% sales discount.

Required

a. Set up accounts in the general ledger (some accounts may not be used in January).

b. Set up accounts in the accounts payable and accounts receivable ledgers as needed.

c. Journalize the above transactions.

d. Record in the accounts payable and accounts receivable ledgers as appropriate.

e. Post to the general ledger as appropriate.

f. Prove that the sum of the subsidiary ledgers is equal to the controlling account balance.

g. Prove the synoptic journal.

The headings of the synoptic journal of Buzzy's Cleaning Company will be as follows:

BUZZY'S CLEANING COMPANY
SYNOPTIC JOURNAL

Date	Explanation	Chq. No.	Post. Ref.	Sundry		Cash		Accts. Rec.		Accts. Pay.		GST		Clean. Revenue	Sales Disc.	Pur.	Pur. Disc.	PST Payable
				Dr.	Cr.	Dr.	Cr.	Dr.	Cr.	Dr.	Cr.	Dr.	Cr.	Cr.	Dr.	Dr.	Cr.	Cr.

Group B Problems

(The forms you need are on pages 11-3 to 11-11 of the *Study Guide with Working Papers*.)

Journalizing transactions of a modified cash system in a synoptic journal
2 **(30 min)**

11B-1. Using the chart of accounts for Dr. Kuhl from Problem 11A-1, record the following transactions in the synoptic journal and then prove the journal:

2012
May 1 Dr. Kuhl deposited $9,000 in the practice.
    4 Paid rent for the month to Jane Jones Realty, $700, cheque No. 1.
    8 Bought medical supplies from Able Co., $750, cheque No. 2.
    11 Bought medical equipment from Jane's Supply, $4,000, cheque No. 3.
    15 Received payment for patient services, $3,000.
    18 Bought additional medical supplies from Able Co., $910, cheque No. 4.
    21 Dr. Kuhl withdrew $790 for personal use, cheque No. 5.
    22 Paid Ron's Janitorial Service, $500, cheque No. 6.
    25 Received payment for patient services, $5,400.
    25 Paid for postage stamps, $30 (miscellaneous expense), cheque No. 7.
    30 Paid salaries for the month, $1,600, cheque No. 8.
    30 Paid Ron's Janitorial Service, $300, cheque No. 9.
    31 Dr. Kuhl withdrew $1,300 for personal use, cheque No. 10.

Journalizing transactions of a
modified cash system in a
synoptic journal with headings
for payroll deductions, and
recording payroll tax expenses
2 (40 min)

11B-2. Using the chart of accounts for Nathan Fox from Problem 11A-2, record the following transactions in the synoptic journal and then prove the journal. (Beginning balances are in your *Study Guide with Working Papers*.)

2014
May 2 Received $4,000 for patient services.
    2 Issued cheque No. 563 to Lane Drug for medical supplies, $700.
    5 Issued cheque No. 564 to J. Realty to pay three months' insurance premiums, $1,650.
    9 Received payment for patient services, $3,000.
    15 Issued the following payroll cheques:

Check Figure

Cross-footing $24,042.00

Employee	Cheque No.	Gross Pay	IT	CPP	EI	Net Pay
Abby Slat	565	$ 900	$ 94	$ 41	$16	$ 749
Jane Reeves	566	800	70	36	14	680
Bob Swan	567	600	26	26	10	538
		$2,300	$190	$103	$40	$1,967

    19 Issued cheque No. 568 to Lane Drug for medical supplies, $900.
    26 Nathan Fox withdrew $400 for personal use, cheque No. 569.
    27 Fox sent cheque to CRA relating to payroll of May 13, cheque No. 570. (Don't forget Fox's share of CPP and EI.)

Journalizing and proving a
synoptic journal; recording
transactions using an accrual
basis of accounting
3 (30 min)

11B-3. Using the chart of accounts for Debra Clark from Problem 11A-3, journalize the following transactions and prove the synoptic journal. Fill in the Post. Ref. column as if you were actually recording and posting to the ledger.

2013
July 2 Debra Clark invested $6,000 cash and $4,000 worth of office equipment in the practice.

Check Figure

Total of Sundry column
Dr. $1,430

July	2	Paid insurance on the office for one year in advance, $1,200, cheque No. 1.
	9	Purchased office equipment on account from Smith Stationery Co., $1,400.
	12	Completed physical examinations on each child at Simcoe Elementary School, $2,000 on account.
	16	Received $700 cash for medical fees earned.
	19	Performed a complete examination for Alvin Ray's son, $200 on account.
	22	Paid Smith Stationery one-half the amount owed from July 9 transaction, cheque No. 2.
	26	Paid telephone bill, $95, cheque No. 3.
	29	Paid utilities, $60, cheque No. 4.
	30	Paid Toby Cleaning Co. for cleaning service performed, $75, cheque No. 5.

Journalizing, recording, and posting a synoptic journal used to record transactions utilizing the accrual basis of accounting

③ (60 min)

11B-4. (GST at 5% and PST at 8% [not cumulative] are involved in this problem.) Buzzy Sullivan opened a dry-cleaning store in Thunder Bay that also sold accessories. The chart of accounts and synoptic journal headings for Buzzy's Cleaning Company are given in Problem 11A-4. Here are the transactions for the month of January:

2012

Jan.	3	Buzzy Sullivan invested $6,000 cash in the business.
	6	Paid for a five-year company insurance policy in advance, $1,200, cheque No. 101 (no GST or PST).
	9	Purchased merchandise on account from Role Company, $700, plus GST.
	12	Cleaned shirts for cash, $950, plus GST and PST.
	16	Cleaned suits on account for Pete Daley, $500, plus GST and PST.
	16	Purchased cleaning equipment on account from Ral Co., $600, plus GST.
	20	Borrowed $4,000 from National Bank.
	23	Cleaned shirts on account for P. Daley, $50, plus GST and PST.
	23	Received entire payment from P. Daley, less a 2% discount, from January 16 transaction.
	26	Purchased merchandise on account from Fresh Air Co., $90 plus GST.
	26	Cleaned silk blouse on account for Alice Small, $20, plus GST and PST.
	27	Paid Role Company the amount due (less a 2% discount) because of merchandise that was purchased on January 9, cheque No. 102.
	27	Returned $200 worth of cleaning equipment to Ral Company for faulty workmanship. (Remember the GST.)
	30	Paid Fresh Air Co. the amount due (less a 10% discount) on the purchases made on account on January 26, cheque No. 103.
	30	Cash sales, $700, plus GST and PST.

Your task is to journalize, record, post, and prove the synoptic journal for the cleaning company. See Problem 11A-4 for detailed requirements.

Check Figure

Total of Sundry column
Dr. $1,800

(The forms you need are on pages 11-12 to 11-21 of the *Study Guide with Working Papers*.)

Journalizing transactions of a modified cash system into a synoptic journal

2 (30 min)

Check Figure

Cross-footing $41,435.00

11C-1. Using a chart of accounts similar to that for Problem 11A-1, record the following transactions for Jennifer Reid, Physiotherapist, of Bathurst, in her synoptic journal and then prove the journal:

2014

May 2 Ms. Reid deposited $18,000 in the practice.
2 Paid rent for the month to Abby Glenn Realty, $800, cheque No. 341.
9 Bought supplies from Perkins Co., $680, cheque No. 342.
12 Bought exercise equipment from Atlas Supply, $8,100, cheque No. 343.
13 Received cash from patients, $4,550.
16 Bought additional supplies from Perkins Co., $920, cheque No. 344.
20 Ms. Reid withdrew $900 for personal use, cheque No. 345.
23 Paid Rockford Janitorial Service, $420, cheque No. 346.
23 Received payment for patient services, $3,850.
26 Paid for postage stamps, $75 (miscellaneous expense), cheque No. 347.
27 Paid salary to Brenda Curtis for month, $1,820, cheque No. 348.
29 Paid Rockford Janitorial Service, $420, cheque No. 349.
30 Ms. Reid withdrew another $900 for personal use, cheque No. 350.

Journalizing transactions of a modified cash system in a synoptic journal with headings for payroll deductions, and recording payroll tax expenses.

2 (40 min)

Check Figure

Cross-footing $40,398.20

11C-2. Using a chart of accounts similar to that for Problem 11A-2, record the following transactions for Sandy Williams, Dentist, in the synoptic journal and then prove the journal. (Beginning balances are given in your *Study Guide with Working Papers*.)

2012

June 1 Received $4,820 from patients.
4 Issued cheque No. 230 to Walkins Drug for dental supplies, $780.
5 Issued cheque No. 231 to Game Agencies to pay six months' insurance premiums, $2,400.
8 Received cheques from patients, $3,910.
15 Issued the following payroll cheques:

Employee	Cheque No.	Gross Pay	IT	CPP	EI	Net Pay
Ted Forth	232	$ 800	$ 70	$ 36	$14	$ 680
Carol Hahn	233	900	94	41	16	749
Ed Birch	234	700	50	31	12	607
Kim Shaw	235	1,100	135	51	19	895
		$3,500	$349	$159	$61	$2,931

19 Issued cheque No. 236 to Walkins Drug for dental supplies, $1,340.
26 Dr. Williams withdrew $2,400 for personal use, cheque No. 237.
29 Issued the following payroll cheques:

Employee	Cheque No.	Gross Pay	IT	CPP	EI	Net Pay
Ted Forth	238	$ 850	$ 83	$ 39	$15	$ 713
Carol Hahn	239	900	94	41	16	749
Ed Birch	240	700	50	31	12	607
Kim Shaw	241	1,100	135	51	19	895
		$3,550	$362	$162	$62	$2,964

June 29 Dr. Williams sent the remittance cheque to CRA for the payrolls of June 15 and 29, cheque No. 242. (Don't forget Dr. Williams' share of CPP and EI.)

Journalizing and proving a synoptic journal; recording transactions using an accrual basis of accounting
3 (30 min)

Check Figure

Total of Sundry column Dr. $6,177.00

11C-3. Using a chart of accounts similar to that for Problem 11A-3, journalize the following transactions for Dave Wong, Optometrist, of Sarnia, and prove the synoptic journal. Fill in the Post. Ref. column as if you were actually recording and posting to the ledger.

2013
April 1 Dr. Wong invested $12,000 cash and $36,000 worth of optical equipment in the practice.
       2 Paid insurance premium for one year in advance, $5,600, cheque No. 761.
       5 Purchased office equipment on account from Adobe Stationery Co., $4,170.
      12 Completed optical examinations on each child at Eastside Elementary School, $4,120 on account.
      16 Received $2,850 cash for professional fees earned.
      19 Performed a complete optical examination for Ms. Rachel Flemming, a famous film star, $400 on account.
      22 Paid Adobe Stationery one-half the amount owed from April 5 transaction, cheque No. 762.
      26 Paid telephone bill, $87, cheque No. 763.
      26 Paid utilities, $140, cheque No. 764.
      29 Paid Neally Cleaning Co. for services performed, $350, cheque no. 765.
      30 Received the first payment from Eastside Elementary School, $2,000.

Journalizing, recording, and posting a synoptic journal used to record transactions utilizing the accrual basis of accounting
3 (60 min)

Check Figure

Total of Sundry column Dr. $9,560.00

11C-4. (GST at 5% and PST at 7% [not cumulative] are involved in this problem.) Freda Schragge opened an appliance repair shop in Duncan that also sold accessories. The chart of accounts for her shop is shown on page 540. Here are the transactions for the month of October:

2012
Oct. 1 Freda Schragge invested $14,000 cash in the business.
      9 Paid First City Agency Co. for a three-year insurance policy in advance, $1,860, cheque No. 101 (no GST or PST).
     12 Purchased merchandise on account from Colter & Co., $1,680, plus GST.
     12 Repaired appliances for five customers for cash, $670, plus GST and PST.
     15 Sold accessories for cash, $650, plus GST and PST.
     15 Repaired appliances on account for Vince Lombardi, $940, plus GST and PST.
     16 Freda withdrew $700 for personal expenses, cheque No. 102.
     19 Purchased repair equipment on account from Sattrap Co., $7,000, plus GST.

	Oct.	22	Borrowed $10,000 from National Bank.
		22	Repaired appliances on account for Vince Lombardi, $280, plus GST and PST.
		23	Sold accessories for cash, $920, plus GST and PST.
		23	Received payment from Vince Lombardi for October 15 transaction less a 2% discount.
		25	Purchased merchandise on account from Apex Company, $840, plus GST.
		26	Cleaned stove on account for J. Fresnel, $80, plus GST and PST.
		26	Paid Colter & Co. for merchandise purchased on October 12 less a 2% discount, cheque No. 103.
		29	Returned $200 worth of repair equipment to Sattrap Co. because of faulty workmanship. (Remember the GST.)
		30	Paid Apex Company the amount owed (less a 5% discount) for the purchases made on account on October 25, cheque No. 104.
		31	Repairs made for cash, $620, plus GST and PST.

Chart of Accounts

Assets
111 Cash
112 Accounts Receivable
113 Prepaid Insurance
115 Prepaid GST
121 Repair Equipment

Liabilities
211 Accounts Payable
212 Bank Loan Payable
215 GST Payable
217 PST Payable

Owner's Equity
311 F. Schragge, Capital
312 F. Schragge, Withdrawals
315 Income Summary

Revenue
411 Appliance Sales
412 Sales Discounts
413 Repairs Revenue

Cost of Goods Sold
511 Purchases
512 Purchases Returns and Allowances
513 Purchases Discounts

Expenses
611 Utilities Expense
612 Advertising Expense
613 Supplies Expense

The headings for the synoptic journal should look like this:

FREDA'S APPLIANCE REPAIR AND SALES
SYNOPTIC JOURNAL

Date	Explanation	Chq. No.	Post. Ref.	Sundry		Cash		Accts. Rec.		Accts. Pay.		GST Paid/Coll.	Appl. Sales	Repairs Revenue	Sales Disc.	Pur.	Pur. Disc.	PST Payable
				Dr.	Cr.	Dr.	Cr.	Dr.	Cr.	Dr.	Cr.	(Dr.) or Cr.	Cr.	Cr.	Dr.	Dr.	Cr.	Cr.

Your task is to journalize, record, post, and prove the business's synoptic journal for October 2012.

(The form you need is on pages 11-22 and 11-23 of the *Study Guide with Working Papers*.)

Preparing a chart of accounts and synoptic journal for a modified cash basis of accounting system
❷ (30 min)

T-1. Jeff Smith has been running his business on a strictly cash basis. At a party over the weekend, he met an accountant who told him that his business should use a modified cash system. Jeff has brought you his chart of accounts so that you may revise it as well as lay out a synoptic journal. Using the following chart of accounts for Jeff Smith, design a synoptic journal for him. Allow columns for payroll deductions.

Chart of Accounts

Assets	Revenue
111 Cash	411 Professional Fees
113 Petty Cash	
	Expenses
Liabilities	511 Insurance Expense
211 Bank Loan Payable	512 Furniture Expense
	514 Medical Equipment Expense
Owner's Equity	515 Medical Supplies Expense
311 J. Smith, Capital	516 Salary Expense
312 J. Smith, Withdrawals	517 Telephone Expense
313 Income Summary	518 Miscellaneous Expense

Preparing a chart of accounts and synoptic journal for an accrual basis of accounting system
❸ (30 min)

T-2. Margie Henley is about to open a dry-cleaning shop. She has hired you to design a synoptic journal for her shop. It will definitely be a small business with a limited number of transactions that are not too complicated. After analyzing Margie's company, you develop the following chart of accounts:

1. Cash
2. Accounts Receivable
3. Equipment
4. Accounts Payable
5. Cleaning Revenue
6. Wage Expense
7. Supplies Expense
8. Miscellaneous Expense

Margie has asked you to provide her, as soon as possible, with a justification for your design of the parts of the synoptic journal. Be prepared to support the synoptic journal that you present to her. Label all headings of the journal in terms of debits and credits. What titles are missing from the chart of accounts?

CONTINUING PROBLEM

Tony Freedman has decided to use a combined journal for the Precision Computer Centre, beginning with February 2014.

Assignment

(See pages 11-24 to 11-32 in your *Study Guide with Working Papers*.)

Record the transactions listed below in the synoptic journal of the Precision Computer Centre; then post as necessary to the required ledger accounts and prepare a trial balance as of February 28:

Feb.   3   Billed Vita Needle for services performed, invoice No. 12694, $1,300, plus HST.

4   Paid West Bell Canada the balance owed on the phone bill received in January, $110, plus HST, cheque No. 289.

7   Received the utility bill for the month, $290, plus HST, due in 30 days.

11   Collected balance in full from Taylor Golf, $900, plus HST, sales invoice No. 12690.

14   Paid for advertising with West Bell Canada, $800, plus HST, cheque No. 290.

14   Sold to Anthony Pitale goods worth $1,150, sales invoice No. 12695, terms 2/10, n/30, plus HST.

14   Paid January electric bill, $282.50, cheque No. 291.

21   Paid insurance premium for the year beginning March 1, 2014, to Willow Agency, cheque No. 292, $1,846. (Dr. Prepaid Insurance).

24   Collected $1,700, plus HST, on sale of goods for cash.

25   Paid Universal Sales for supplies, $286, plus HST, cheque No. 293.

28   Paid Automated Payroll Service for wages and related costs for February, $6,109.00, cheque No. 294.

Journalizing and proving a synoptic journal; recording transactions using an accrual basis of accounting; posting to the general ledger; and preparing a trial balance

(3) **(90 min)**

12 Preparing a Worksheet for a Merchandising Company

THE BIG PICTURE

If you look around your accounting class, you'll see the results of successful inventory management all around you. The brand-name running shoes classmates are wearing, the cell phones they check text messages on during breaks, the watches they check to see whether class is coming to an end—all these are products that merchandising companies have to carefully manage as part of their inventory.

The need to move products quickly has resulted in a new emphasis on supply chain management. Specialists in this area talk about "just-in-time" inventory management and "increasing inventory velocity."

A hallmark of today's hyperactive economy is that we even consider the notion that inventory has a *speed*. Yet with the lifespan of a computer component or trendy leather handbag now measured in weeks, speed to market can matter more than product features or quality. Hence, inventory is more likely to be zipping around the world via overnight air express than gathering dust in a warehouse.

This is all good news for the air express companies, which are the beneficiaries and enablers of a wired, global economy. Picking up and delivering packages is just part of the total menu of products and services that the top four global express companies—Federal Express, United Parcel Service, DHL Worldwide Express, and TNT International—now offer. These companies have evolved to meet business needs; they are faster and more sophisticated, with round-the-clock operations around the globe.

The DHL Air Express hub in Brussels, Belgium, operates 24 hours a day, moving inventory from one aircraft to another. Everything is in perpetual motion: cell phones, running shoes, and watches are whisked from one aircraft to another, making the transition from supplier to store in a matter of hours. The hub is so busy that DHL's parent company, Deutsche Post World Net, moved its European hub to Leipzig, Germany, and expanded capacity. The Leipzig hub began operating in 2008; it cost more than 300 million euros and generated 10,000 jobs in the region.

This emphasis on keeping inventory in motion calls for a more up-to-date way to track inventory costs. In this chapter's appendix on MyAccountingLab.com, we introduce a method of accounting for inventory called, appropriately, the *perpetual method*. It requires more accounting effort than the *periodic method*, which is explained in this chapter. However, the perpetual method has an important advantage: Key accounts of Merchandise Inventory and Cost of Goods Sold will always provide current information to managers about their investment in inventory and the cost of the merchandise sold to customers.

Sources: Information from Lara L. Sowinski, "This Isn't Your Father's Express Shipper," *World Trade*, July 2000, pp. 52–55; Andrew Tanzer, "Warehouses That Fly," *Forbes*, October 13, 1999, pp. 120–124; Vanessa Drucker, "B2B Boom," *Global Finance*, April 2000, pp. 46–48; Anonymous, "New Offerings: DHL Considers an IPO After Buyback of Stake Daily Investing Report," *The Atlanta Constitution*, December 14, 1999, p. F6; Council of Supply Chain Management Professionals website, www.cscmp.org; Anonymous, "Green Light for Construction of the DHL Hub in Leipzig," Deutsche Post World Net website, www.dpwn.de/dpwn?skin=hi&check=yes&lang=de_EN&xmlFile=2001081, May 20, 2005, accessed September 14, 2007, and June 2010.

1 Figuring adjustments for merchandise inventory, unearned rent, supplies used, insurance expired, amortization expense, and salaries accrued (pp. 542–544 and 547–549)

2 Preparing a worksheet for a merchandising company (pp. 545 and 551–553)

In Chapters 6 and 10, we discussed the special journals and subsidiary ledgers of a merchandising company. Appendix material on MyAccountingLab.com provides an introduction to perpetual inventory. Now our attention will shift to recording adjustments and completing a worksheet for a merchandising company. Learning Unit 12-1 will introduce two new adjustments that we have not yet discussed, Merchandise Inventory and Unearned Rent. Learning Unit 12-2 will show how to complete the worksheet with these new adjustments, while the Chapter 12 appendix, located on MyAccountingLab.com, shows worksheets for a perpetual system.

Learning Unit 12-1

Adjustments for Merchandise Inventory and Unearned Rent

1 Figuring adjustments for merchandise inventory, unearned rent, supplies used, insurance expired, amortization expense, and salaries accrued

An important item in a merchandising company worksheet and financial records is *Merchandise Inventory*. This means the goods that a company has available to sell to customers. There are several ways of keeping track of the cost of goods sold and the quantity of inventory that a company has on hand. At the end of Auxiliary Chapter 19 (which is on MyAccountingLab.com), another system, called a **perpetual inventory system**, will be discussed. In this system, businesses with large inventories can have current information about inventory on hand and the actual cost of goods sold. Most such companies use a computer to keep track of their inventory records.

In this chapter, we will discuss the **periodic inventory system** in which the balance of the inventory account is updated only at the end of the accounting period. This system is used by smaller companies that sell a variety of merchandise with low unit prices. The number of companies using this system of accounting for inventory is still significant but is declining. This decline is due to the increasing availability of computers and software that together encourage the use of the more useful and informative perpetual system.

Let's take the merchandise inventory of Art's Wholesale Clothing Company as an example. Let's assume Art's Wholesale started the year with $19,000 worth of merchandise; this is called **beginning merchandise inventory** or simply **beginning inventory**. During the period, the cost of beginning inventory does not change; instead, all purchases of merchandise are recorded in the Purchases account. During the period, $52,000 worth of merchandise was purchased and recorded in the Purchases account.

At the end of the period, the company takes a physical count of the merchandise in stock; this amount is **ending merchandise inventory** or simply **ending inventory** and is calculated on an inventory sheet as shown in Figure 12-1.

This $4,000, which is the ending inventory for this period, will be the beginning inventory for the next period.

When the income statement is prepared, the cost of goods sold section will require two distinct numbers for inventory. The beginning inventory adds to the cost of goods sold, while the ending inventory reduces the cost of goods sold.

Cost of goods sold
  Beginning inventory
+ Net purchases
− Ending inventory
= Cost of goods sold

Figure 12-1
Ending Inventory Sheet

ART'S WHOLESALE CLOTHING COMPANY ENDING INVENTORY SHEET AS OF DECEMBER 31, 2013			
Amount	Explanation	Unit Cost	Total
20	Ladies' Jackets code 14-0	$50	$1,000
10	Men's Hats code 827	10	100
90	Men's Shirts code 423	10	900
100	Ladies' Blouses code 481	20	2,000
			$4,000
Counted by _____ Checked and priced by _____			

Remember that the two figures for beginning and ending inventory were calculated months apart. Thus they cannot merely be combined to come up with one inventory figure; that would not be accurate.

ADJUSTMENT FOR MERCHANDISE INVENTORY

Adjusting the Merchandise Inventory account is a two-step process because we want to keep both beginning inventory and ending inventory amounts separate; we cannot simply combine them. So the first step deals with beginning merchandise inventory.

> First adjustment transfers amount in beginning inventory from Merchandise Inventory to Income Summary.

Given: Beginning Inventory, $19,000   Our first adjustment removes the beginning inventory amount from the asset account (Merchandise Inventory) and transfers it to Income Summary. We do this by crediting Merchandise Inventory for $19,000 and debiting Income Summary for the same amount. This is shown below in T account form and on a transaction analysis chart:

> Note that Income Summary has no normal balance of debit or credit.

Merchandise Inventory 114

Bal. 19,000 | Adj. 19,000

Income Summary 313

Adj. 19,000 |

(A)

Accounts Affected	Category	↑↓	Rules
Income Summary	Equity	N/A	Dr.
Merchandise Inventory	Asset	↓	Cr.

(The adjusting entries would be first entered on the worksheet and then formally recorded in the general journal, then posted.)

The second step is to enter the amount of ending inventory ($4,000) in the Merchandise Inventory account. This is done to record the amount of goods on hand at the end of the period as an asset and to reduce the cost of goods sold (since we have not sold this inventory yet). To do this, we debit Merchandise Inventory for $4,000 and credit Income Summary for the same amount. This is shown below in T account form and on a transaction analysis chart:

> Second adjustment updates inventory account with a figure for ending inventory.

Merchandise Inventory 114

Bal. 19,000 | Adj. 19,000
Adj. 4,000 |

Income Summary 313

Adj. 19,000 | Adj. 4,000

(B)

Accounts Affected	Category	↑↓	Rules
Merchandise Inventory	Asset	↑	Dr.
Income Summary	Equity	N/A	Cr.

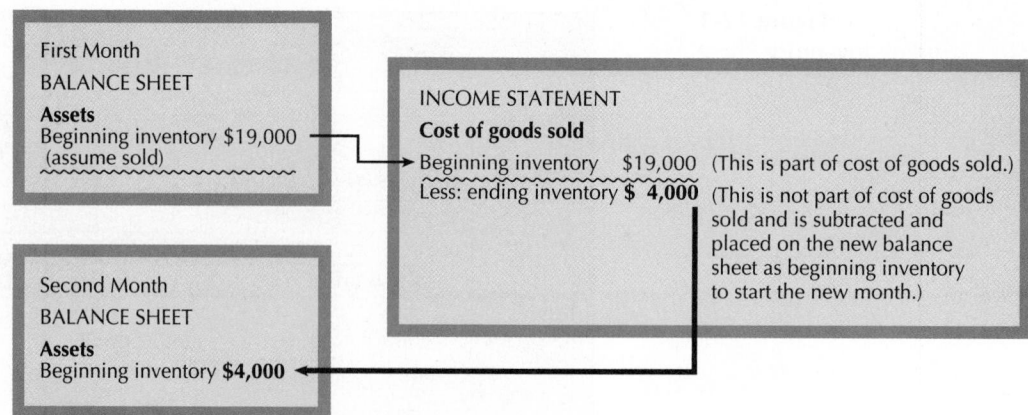

Note: If freight-in were involved, it would have been added to the net cost of purchases.

Let's look at how this process or method of recording merchandise inventory is reflected in the balance sheet and income statement (see Figure 12-2). Note that the $19,000 worth of beginning inventory is assumed sold and is shown on the income statement as part of the cost of goods sold. The ending inventory of $4,000 has not been sold and reduces the cost of goods sold on the income statement. The ending inventory for this period becomes the next period's beginning inventory. When the income statement is prepared, we will need a figure for beginning inventory as well as a figure for ending inventory.

The second adjustment we will discuss in this unit concerns an account that we have never dealt with before, Unearned Rent.

ADJUSTMENT FOR UNEARNED RENT

A new account that we have not seen before is a liability called Unearned Rent. This account records the amount collected for rent before the service has been provided (renting the space). For example, Art's Wholesale is subletting some unneeded space to Jesse Company for $200 per month. Jesse Company sends Art a cheque for $600 for three months' rent paid in advance. This unearned rent ($600) is also often called Rent Received in Advance. Regardless of the actual name, it is a liability on the balance sheet because Art's Wholesale owes Jesse Company three months' worth of occupancy.

When Art's Wholesale fulfills a portion of the rental agreement (when Jesse Company has been in the space for a period of time), this liability account will be reduced and the account called Rental Income will be increased because Art's Wholesale will have earned the rent. Rental Income is another type of revenue for Art's Wholesale in addition to its revenue earned from sales of merchandise.

There are other types of unearned revenue besides unearned rent—examples would be subscriptions for magazines, legal fees collected before the work is performed, and season tickets to the local symphony. The key point is that revenue, under accrual accounting, is recognized when it is *earned*, whether money is received then or not. Here Art's Wholesale collected cash in advance for a service that it has not performed yet. Thus a liability called Unearned Rent is the result. Art's Wholesale may have the cash, but no Rental Income is recorded until it is *earned*.

In the next learning unit, we will show how to record the adjustment to Rental Income when the worksheet is completed.

Received cash for renting space in future

Cash	A	↑	Dr.
Unearned Rent	Liab.	↑	Cr.

The adjustment when rental income is earned

Unearned Rent	Liab.	↓	Dr.
Rental Income	Other Rev.	↑	Cr.

LEARNING UNIT 12-1 REVIEW

AT THIS POINT you should be able to:

◆ Define the periodic method of inventory accounting. (p. 542)

◆ Explain why beginning and ending inventory are two separate figures in the cost of goods sold section on the income statement. (pp. 542–543)

◆ Show how to calculate a figure for ending inventory. (p. 544)

◆ Explain why unearned rent is a liability account. (p. 544)

Self-Review Quiz 12-1

(The form you need is on page 12-1 in the *Study Guide with Working Papers*.)

Given the following, prepare the two adjusting entries for Merchandise Inventory on 12/31/13:

Merchandise Inventory, 01/01/13	$ 8,000
Purchases	9,000
Purchases Returns and Allowances	3,000
Merchandise Inventory, 12/31/13	4,000
Cost of Goods Sold	10,000
Unearned Magazine Subscriptions	5,000

Solution to Self-Review Quiz 12-1

> **Quiz Tip**
>
> Note that Unearned Magazine Subscriptions is a liability and not involved in the adjustment for Merchandise Inventory.

	2013					
	Dec.	31	Income Summary	8 0 0 0 00	
			Merchandise Inventory		8 0 0 0 00
		31	Merchandise Inventory	4 0 0 0 00	
			Income Summary		4 0 0 0 00
			To record opening and		
			closing inventories		

Learning Unit 12-2

Completing the Worksheet

2 Preparing a worksheet for a merchandising company

In this unit, we prepare a worksheet for Art's Wholesale Clothing Company. For convenience, we reproduce the company's chart of accounts in Figure 12-3.

Figure 12-4 shows the trial balance that was prepared on December 31, 2013, from the general ledger of Art's Wholesale. (*Note:* It is recorded directly in the first two columns of the worksheet.)

In looking at the trial balance, we see many new titles that have appeared since we completed a trial balance for a service company back in Chapter 5. Let's look specifically at these new titles in the summary in Table 12-1.

Figure 12-3
Art's Wholesale Clothing
Company Chart of Accounts

Chart of Accounts

Assets 100–199
111 Cash
112 Petty Cash
113 Accounts Receivable
114 Merchandise Inventory
115 Supplies
116 Prepaid Insurance
121 Store Equipment
122 Accumulated Amortization,
     Store Equipment

Liabilities 200–299
211 Accounts Payable
212 Salaries Payable
213 Income Tax Payable
214 CPP Payable
215 EI Payable
218 Unearned Rent
220 Mortgage Payable

Owner's Equity 300–399
311 Art Newner, Capital
312 Art Newner, Withdrawals
313 Income Summary

Revenue 400–499
411 Sales
412 Sales Returns and Allowances
413 Sales Discounts
414 Rental Income

Cost of Goods Sold 500–599
511 Purchases
512 Purchases Discounts
513 Purchases Returns and
     Allowances
514 Freight-In

Expenses 600–699
611 Salaries Expense
612 Payroll Tax Expense
613 Amortization Expense,
     Store Equipment
614 Supplies Expense
615 Insurance Expense
616 Postage Expense
617 Miscellaneous Expense
618 Interest Expense
619 Cleaning Expense
620 Delivery Expense

TABLE 12-1 Summary of New Account Titles

Title	Category	Report(s) Found on	Normal Balance	Temporary/ Permanent
Petty Cash	Asset	Balance sheet	Dr.	Permanent
Merchandise Inventory* (Beginning)	Asset	Balance sheet prior period	Dr.	Permanent
	Expense	Income statement of current period		
Income Tax Payable	Liability	Balance sheet	Cr.	Permanent
CPP Payable	Liability	Balance sheet	Cr.	Permanent
EI Payable	Liability	Balance sheet	Cr.	Permanent
Unearned Rent**	Liability	Balance sheet	Cr.	Permanent
Mortgage Payable	Liability	Balance sheet	Cr.	Permanent
Sales	Revenue	Income statement	Cr.	Temporary
Sales Returns and Allowances	Revenue (contra)	Income statement	Dr.	Temporary
Sales Discounts	Revenue (contra)	Income statement	Dr.	Temporary
Purchases	Expense	Income statement	Dr.	Temporary
Purchases Discounts	Expense (contra)	Income statement	Cr.	Temporary
Purchases Returns and Allowances	Expense (contra)	Income statement	Cr.	Temporary
Freight-In	Expense	Income statement	Dr.	Temporary
Payroll Tax Expense	Expense	Income statement	Dr.	Temporary
Postage Expense	Expense	Income statement	Dr.	Temporary
Interest Expense	Expense	Income statement	Dr.	Temporary

*The ending inventory of the current period is a contra-expense on the income statement and will be an asset on the balance sheet for next period.
**Referred to as Unearned Revenue.
Note: Students may benefit from a brief look at the Blueprint on page 591.

Figure 12-4
Trial Balance Section
of the Worksheet

ART'S WHOLESALE CLOTHING COMPANY
WORKSHEET
FOR THE YEAR ENDED DECEMBER 31, 2013

	Trial Balance	
	Dr.	Cr.
Cash	12 9 20 00	
Petty Cash	1 00 00	
Accounts Receivable	14 5 00 00	
Merchandise Inventory	19 0 00 00	
Supplies	8 00 00	
Prepaid Insurance	9 00 00	
Store Equipment	4 0 00 00	
Accumulated Amortization, Store Equip.		4 0 00 00
Accounts Payable		17 9 00 00
Income Tax Payable		1 2 40 00
CPP Payable		2 60 00
EI Payable		2 00 00
Unearned Rent		6 00 00
Mortgage Payable		2 3 20 00
Art Newner, Capital		7 9 05 00
Art Newner, Withdrawals	8 6 00 00	
Income Summary		
Sales		95 0 00 00
Sales Returns and Allowances	9 50 00	
Sales Discounts	6 70 00	
Purchases	52 0 00 00	
Purchases Discounts		8 60 00
Purchases Returns and Allowances		6 80 00
Freight-In	4 50 00	
Salaries Expense	11 7 00 00	
Payroll Tax Expense	4 2 00 00	
Postage Expense	2 5 00	
Miscellaneous Expense	3 0 00	
Interest Expense	3 0 00 00	
	127 3 65 00	127 3 65 00

Note the following:

1. **Mortgage Payable** is a liability account that records the increases and decreases in the amount of debt owed on a mortgage. We will discuss this more in the next chapter when financial reports are prepared.

2. *Interest Expense* represents a non-operating expense for Art's Wholesale and thus is categorized as "miscellaneous expense." The interest would be a regular expense if it were incurred for business purposes. We will also be looking at this in the next chapter.

3. **Unearned Revenue** is a liability account that records receipt of payment for goods and services in advance of delivery. Unearned Rent is a particular example of this general type of account.

Adjustments We have already discussed Adjustments A and B (page 543), which make up the two-step process involved in adjusting Merchandise Inventory at the end of the accounting period. Now we will go on to show T accounts and transaction analysis charts for some more adjustments that need to be made at this point in a merchandising firm, just as they do in a service company.

Adjustment C: Rental Income Earned by Art's Wholesale, $200   A month ago, Cash was increased by $600, as was a liability, Unearned Rent. Art's Wholesale received payment in advance but had not earned the rental income. Now, since $200 has been earned, the liability is reduced and Rental Income can be recorded for the $200.

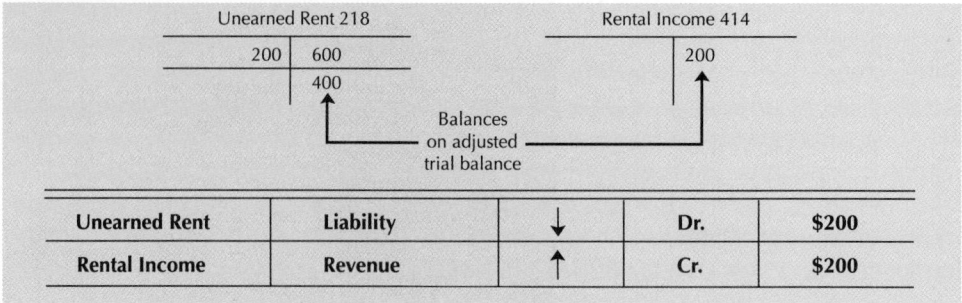

Unearned Rent	Liability	↓	Dr.	$200
Rental Income	Revenue	↑	Cr.	$200

Adjustment D: Supplies Used Up, $500 $500 worth of supplies has been used up; thus there is a need to increase Supplies Expense and decrease the asset, Supplies.

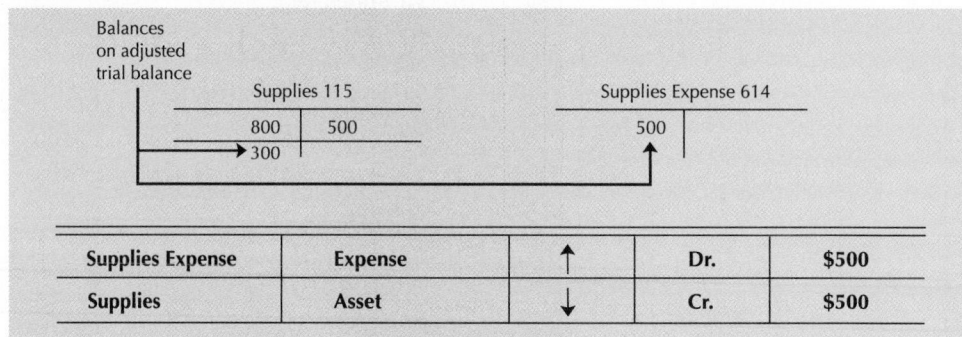

Supplies Expense	Expense	↑	Dr.	$500
Supplies	Asset	↓	Cr.	$500

Adjustment E: Insurance Expired, $300   Since $300 worth of insurance has expired, Insurance Expense is increased by $300 and the asset, Prepaid Insurance is decreased by $300.

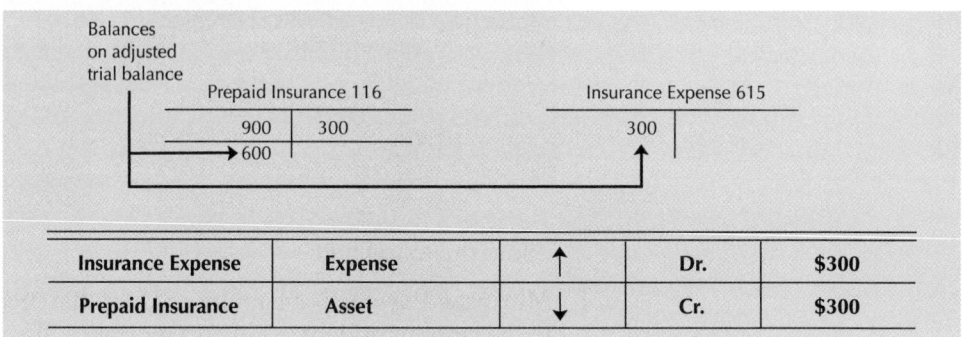

Insurance Expense	Expense	↑	Dr.	$300
Prepaid Insurance	Asset	↓	Cr.	$300

Adjustment F: Amortization Expense, $50   When amortization is taken, Amortization Expense and Accumulated Amortization are both increased by $50. Note that the cost of the store equipment remains the same.

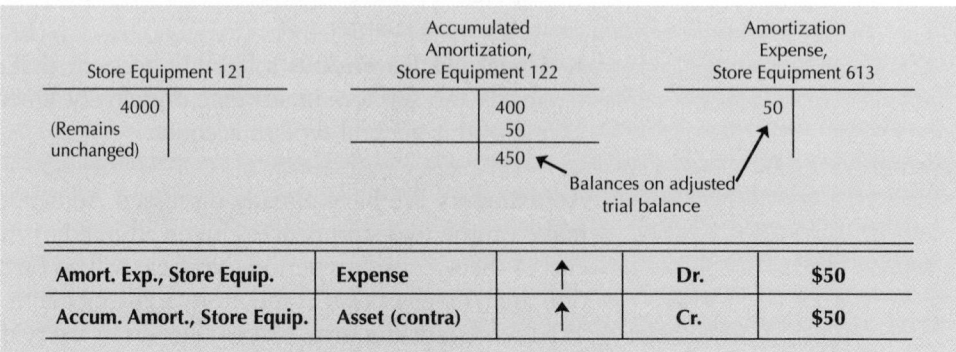

Amort. Exp., Store Equip.	Expense	↑	Dr.	$50
Accum. Amort., Store Equip.	Asset (contra)	↑	Cr.	$50

Adjustment G: Salaries Accrued, $600 The $600 in Salaries Accrued causes an increase in Salaries Expense and Salaries Payable.

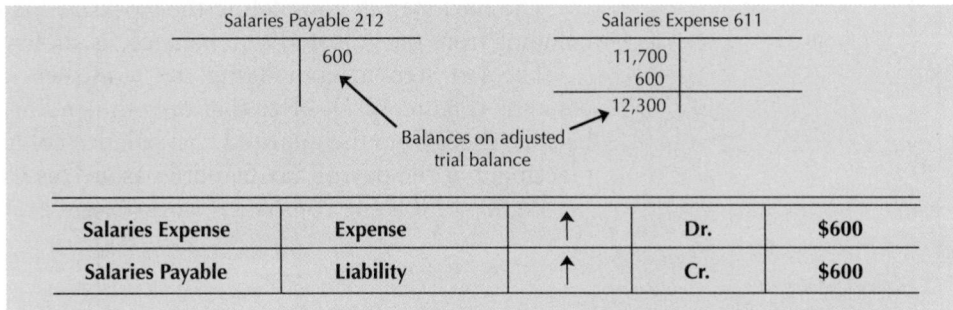

| Salaries Expense | Expense | ↑ | Dr. | $600 |
| Salaries Payable | Liability | ↑ | Cr. | $600 |

Figure 12-5
Worksheet with Three
Sections Completed

Figure 12-5 shows the worksheet with the adjustments and adjusted trial balance columns filled out. Note that the adjustment numbers in Income Summary from

	Trial Balance		Adjustments		Adjusted Trial Balance	
	Dr.	Cr.	Dr.	Cr.	Dr.	Cr.
Cash	12 9 2 0 00				12 9 2 0 00	
Petty Cash	1 0 0 00				1 0 0 00	
Accounts Receivable	14 5 0 0 00				14 5 0 0 00	
Merchandise Inventory	19 0 0 0 00		(B) 4 0 0 0 00	(A) 19 0 0 0 00	4 0 0 0 00	
Supplies	8 0 0 00			(D) 5 0 0 00	3 0 0 00	
Prepaid Insurance	9 0 0 00			(E) 3 0 0 00	6 0 0 00	
Store Equipment	4 0 0 0 00				4 0 0 0 00	
Accumulated Amortization, Store Equip.		4 0 0 00		(F) 5 0 00		4 5 0 00
Accounts Payable		17 9 0 0 00				17 9 0 0 00
Income Tax Payable		1 2 4 0 00				1 2 4 0 00
CPP Payable		2 6 0 00				2 6 0 00
EI Payable		2 0 0 00				2 0 0 00
Unearned Rent		6 0 0 00	(C) 2 0 0 00			4 0 0 00
Mortgage Payable		2 3 2 0 00				2 3 2 0 00
Art Newner, Capital		7 9 0 5 00				7 9 0 5 00
Art Newner, Withdrawals	8 6 0 0 00				8 6 0 0 00	
Income Summary			(A) 19 0 0 0 00	(B) 4 0 0 0 00	19 0 0 0 00	4 0 0 0 00
Sales		95 0 0 0 00				95 0 0 0 00
Sales Returns and Allowances	9 5 0 00				9 5 0 00	
Sales Discounts	6 7 0 00				6 7 0 00	
Purchases	52 0 0 0 00				52 0 0 0 00	
Purchases Discounts		8 6 0 00				8 6 0 00
Purchases Returns and Allowances		6 8 0 00				6 8 0 00
Freight-In	4 5 0 00				4 5 0 00	
Salaries Expense	11 7 0 0 00		(G) 6 0 0 00		12 3 0 0 00	
Payroll Tax Expense	4 2 0 00				4 2 0 00	
Postage Expense	2 5 00				2 5 00	
Miscellaneous Expense	3 0 00				3 0 00	
Interest Expense	3 0 0 00				3 0 0 00	
	127 3 6 5 00	127 3 6 5 00				
Rental Income				(C) 2 0 0 00		2 0 0 00
Supplies Expense			(D) 5 0 0 00		5 0 0 00	
Insurance Expense			(E) 3 0 0 00		3 0 0 00	
Amortization Expense, Store Equipment			(F) 5 0 00		5 0 00	
Accrued Salaries				(G) 6 0 0 00		6 0 0 00
			24 6 5 0 00	24 6 5 0 00	132 0 1 5 00	132 0 1 5 00

beginning and ending inventory are also carried over to the adjusted trial balance and are *not* combined.

The next step in completing the worksheet is to fill out the income statement columns from the adjusted trial balance, as shown in Figure 12-6.

The last step in completing the worksheet is to fill out the balance sheet columns (Figure 12-7). Note that only the ending inventory is carried over to the balance sheet from the adjusted trial balance column. Take time also to look at the placement of the payroll tax liabilities as well as Unearned Rent on the worksheet.

Figure 12-8 is the completed worksheet.

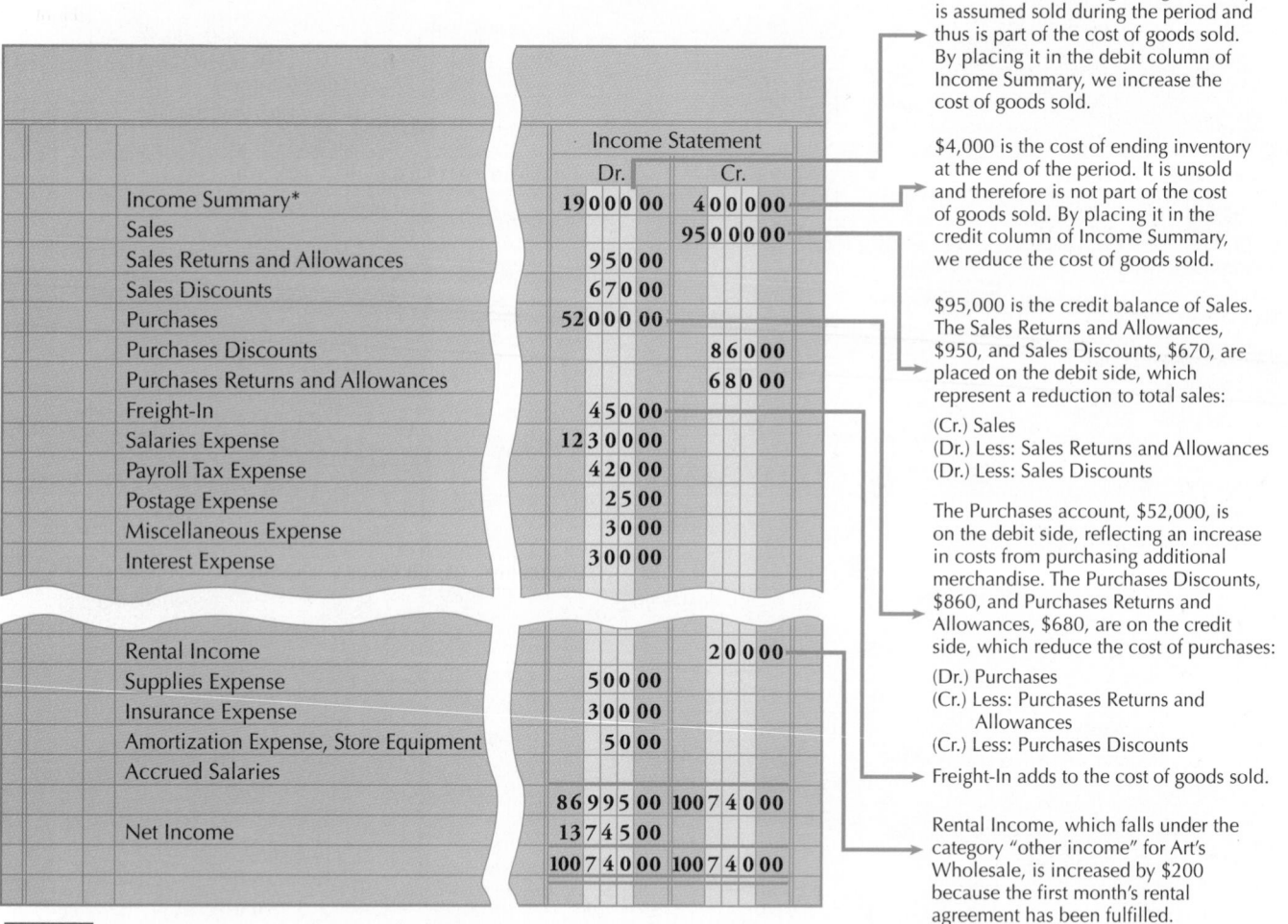

	Income Statement	
	Dr.	Cr.
Income Summary*	19 000 00	4 000 00
Sales		95 000 00
Sales Returns and Allowances	9 50 00	
Sales Discounts	6 70 00	
Purchases	52 000 00	
Purchases Discounts		8 60 00
Purchases Returns and Allowances		6 80 00
Freight-In	4 50 00	
Salaries Expense	12 300 00	
Payroll Tax Expense	4 20 00	
Postage Expense	25 00	
Miscellaneous Expense	30 00	
Interest Expense	3 00 00	
Rental Income		2 00 00
Supplies Expense	5 00 00	
Insurance Expense	3 00 00	
Amortization Expense, Store Equipment	50 00	
Accrued Salaries		
	86 995 00	100 740 00
Net Income	13 745 00	
	100 740 00	100 740 00

$19,000 worth of beginning inventory is assumed sold during the period and thus is part of the cost of goods sold. By placing it in the debit column of Income Summary, we increase the cost of goods sold.

$4,000 is the cost of ending inventory at the end of the period. It is unsold and therefore is not part of the cost of goods sold. By placing it in the credit column of Income Summary, we reduce the cost of goods sold.

$95,000 is the credit balance of Sales. The Sales Returns and Allowances, $950, and Sales Discounts, $670, are placed on the debit side, which represent a reduction to total sales:

(Cr.) Sales
(Dr.) Less: Sales Returns and Allowances
(Dr.) Less: Sales Discounts

The Purchases account, $52,000, is on the debit side, reflecting an increase in costs from purchasing additional merchandise. The Purchases Discounts, $860, and Purchases Returns and Allowances, $680, are on the credit side, which reduce the cost of purchases:

(Dr.) Purchases
(Cr.) Less: Purchases Returns and Allowances
(Cr.) Less: Purchases Discounts

Freight-In adds to the cost of goods sold.

Rental Income, which falls under the category "other income" for Art's Wholesale, is increased by $200 because the first month's rental agreement has been fulfilled.

*Remember, we do not combine the $19,000 and $4,000 in Income Summary. When we prepare the cost of goods sold section for the formal financial report, we will need both a beginning and an ending figure for inventory.

Figure 12-6 Income Statement Section of the Worksheet

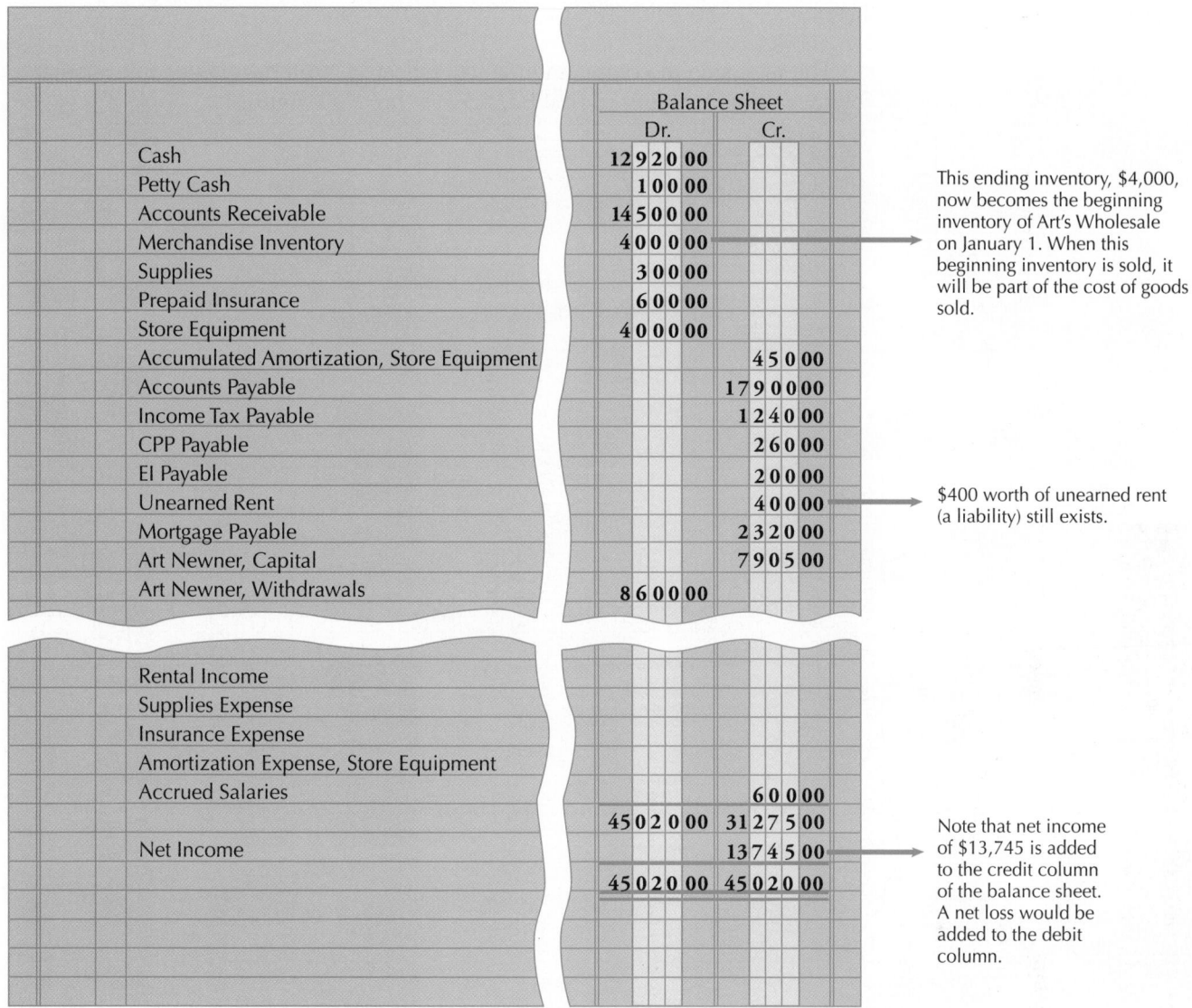

				Balance Sheet	
				Dr.	Cr.
Cash				12 9 2 0 00	
Petty Cash				1 00 00	
Accounts Receivable				14 5 0 0 00	
Merchandise Inventory				4 0 0 0 00	
Supplies				3 0 0 00	
Prepaid Insurance				6 0 0 00	
Store Equipment				4 0 0 0 00	
Accumulated Amortization, Store Equipment					4 5 0 00
Accounts Payable					17 9 0 0 00
Income Tax Payable					1 2 4 0 00
CPP Payable					2 6 0 00
EI Payable					2 0 0 00
Unearned Rent					4 0 0 00
Mortgage Payable					2 3 2 0 00
Art Newner, Capital					7 9 0 5 00
Art Newner, Withdrawals				8 6 0 0 00	
Rental Income					
Supplies Expense					
Insurance Expense					
Amortization Expense, Store Equipment					
Accrued Salaries					6 0 0 00
				45 0 2 0 00	31 2 7 5 00
Net Income					13 7 4 5 00
				45 0 2 0 00	45 0 2 0 00

This ending inventory, $4,000, now becomes the beginning inventory of Art's Wholesale on January 1. When this beginning inventory is sold, it will be part of the cost of goods sold.

$400 worth of unearned rent (a liability) still exists.

Note that net income of $13,745 is added to the credit column of the balance sheet. A net loss would be added to the debit column.

Figure 12-7 Balance Sheet Section of the Worksheet

Figure 12-8 Completed Worksheet

ART'S WHOLESALE CLOTHING COMPANY WORKSHEET FOR YEAR ENDED DECEMBER 31, 2013

Account	Trial Balance Dr.	Trial Balance Cr.	Adjustments Dr.	Adjustments Cr.	Adjusted Trial Balance Dr.	Adjusted Trial Balance Cr.	Income Statement Dr.	Income Statement Cr.	Balance Sheet Dr.	Balance Sheet Cr.
Cash	12 920 00				12 920 00				12 920 00	
Petty Cash	100 00				100 00				100 00	
Accounts Receivable	14 500 00				14 500 00				14 500 00	
Merchandise Inventory	19 000 00		(B) 4 000 00	(A) 19 000 00	4 000 00				4 000 00	
Supplies	800 00			(D) 500 00	300 00				300 00	
Prepaid Insurance	900 00			(E) 300 00	600 00				600 00	
Store Equipment	4 000 00				4 000 00				4 000 00	
Accumulated Amortization, Store Equipment		400 00		(F) 50 00		450 00				450 00
Accounts Payable		17 900 00				17 900 00				17 900 00
Income Tax Payable		1 240 00				1 240 00				1 240 00
CPP Payable		260 00				260 00				260 00
EI Payable		200 00				200 00				200 00
Unearned Rent		600 00	(C) 200 00			400 00				400 00
Mortgage Payable		2 320 00				2 320 00				2 320 00
Art Newner, Capital		7 905 00				7 905 00				7 905 00
Art Newner, Withdrawals	8 600 00				8 600 00				8 600 00	
Income Summary			(A) 19 000 00	(B) 4 000 00	19 000 00	4 000 00	19 000 00	4 000 00		
Sales		95 000 00				95 000 00		95 000 00		
Sales Returns and Allowances	950 00				950 00		950 00			
Sales Discounts	670 00				670 00		670 00			
Purchases	52 000 00				52 000 00		52 000 00			
Purchases Discounts		860 00				860 00		860 00		
Purchases Returns and Allowances		680 00				680 00		680 00		
Freight-In	450 00				450 00		450 00			
Salaries Expense	11 700 00		(G) 600 00		12 300 00		12 300 00			
Payroll Tax Expense	420 00				420 00		420 00			
Postage Expense	25 00				25 00		25 00			
Miscellaneous Expense	30 00				30 00		30 00			
Interest Expense	300 00				300 00		300 00			
	127 365 00	127 365 00								
Rental Income				(C) 200 00		200 00		200 00		
Supplies Expense			(D) 500 00		500 00		500 00			
Insurance Expense			(E) 300 00		300 00		300 00			
Amortization Expense, Store Equipment			(F) 50 00		50 00		50 00			
Accrued Salaries				(G) 600 00		600 00				600 00
			24 650 00	24 650 00	132 015 00	132 015 00	86 995 00	100 740 00	45 020 00	31 275 00
Net Income							13 745 00			13 745 00
							100 740 00	100 740 00	45 020 00	45 020 00

LEARNING UNIT 12-2 REVIEW

AT THIS POINT you should be able to:

◆ Complete adjustments for a merchandising company. (pp. 547–551)
◆ Complete a worksheet. (pp. 549–552)

Self-Review Quiz 12-2

(The form you need is a blank, fold-out worksheet at the end of the *Study Guide with Working Papers*.)

From the trial balance shown here, complete a worksheet for Ray Company. Additional data includes: (a) and (b) On December 31, 2012, ending inventory was calculated as $200; (c) storage fees earned, $516; (d) rent expired, $100; (e) amortization expense, office equipment, $60; (f) salaries accrued, $200.

RAY COMPANY TRIAL BALANCE DECEMBER 31, 2012		
	Trial Balance	
Account Titles	Dr.	Cr.
Cash	2 4 8 6 00	
Merchandise Inventory	8 2 4 00	
Prepaid Rent	1 1 5 2 00	
Prepaid Insurance	6 0 00	
Office Equipment	2 1 6 0 00	
Accumulated Amortization, Office Equipment		5 6 0 00
Unearned Storage Fees		2 5 1 6 00
Accounts Payable		1 0 0 00
B. Ray, Capital		1 9 3 2 00
Income Summary	—	—
Sales		1 1 0 4 0 00
Sales Returns and Allowances	5 4 6 00	
Sales Discounts	2 1 6 00	
Purchases	5 2 5 6 00	
Purchases Returns and Allowances		1 6 8 00
Purchases Discounts		1 0 2 00
Salaries Expense	2 0 1 6 00	
Insurance Expense	1 3 9 2 00	
Utilities Expense	9 6 00	
Plumbing Expense	2 1 4 00	
	1 6 4 1 8 00	1 6 4 1 8 00

Quiz Tip

The ending inventory of $200 becomes next year's beginning inventory.

Solution to Self-Review Quiz 12-2

The solution is shown on page 554.

RAY COMPANY
WORKSHEET
FOR YEAR ENDED DECEMBER 31, 2012

Account Titles	Trial Balance Dr.	Cr.	Adjustments Dr.	Cr.	Adjusted Trial Balance Dr.	Cr.	Income Statement Dr.	Cr.	Balance Sheet Dr.	Cr.
Cash	2486 00				2486 00				2486 00	
Merchandise Inventory	824 00		(B) 2000 00	(A) 824 00	2000 00				2000 00	
Prepaid Rent	1152 00			(D) 100 00	1052 00				1052 00	
Prepaid Insurance	60 00				60 00				60 00	
Office Equipment	2160 00				2160 00				2160 00	
Accum. Amort., Office Equipment		560 00		(E) 60 00		620 00				620 00
Unearned Storage Fees		2516 00	(C) 516 00			2000 00				2000 00
Accounts Payable		100 00				100 00				100 00
B. Ray, Capital		1932 00				1932 00				1932 00
Income Summary			(A) 824 00	(B) 2000 00	824 00	2000 00	824 00	2000 00		
Sales		11040 00				11040 00		11040 00		
Sales Returns and Allowances	546 00				546 00		546 00			
Sales Discounts	216 00				216 00		216 00			
Purchases	5256 00				5256 00		5256 00			
Purchases Returns and Allowances		168 00				168 00		168 00		
Purchases Discounts		102 00				102 00		102 00		
Salaries Expense	2016 00		(F) 200 00		2216 00		2216 00			
Insurance Expense	1392 00				1392 00		1392 00			
Utilities Expense	96 00				96 00		96 00			
Plumbing Expense	214 00				214 00		214 00			
	16418 00	16418 00								
Storage Fees Earned				(C) 516 00		516 00		516 00		
Rent Expense			(D) 100 00		100 00		100 00			
Amortization Expense, Equipment			(E) 60 00		60 00		60 00			
Accrued Salaries				(F) 200 00		200 00				200 00
			1900 00	1900 00	16878 00	16878 00	10926 00	12026 00	5958 00	4852 00
Net Income							1106 00			1106 00
							12026 00	12026 00	5958 00	5958 00

SUMMARY OF KEY POINTS

Learning Unit 12-1

1. The periodic inventory system updates the record of goods on hand only at the end of the accounting period. This system is used by companies with a variety of merchandise with low unit prices.

2. In the periodic inventory system, additional purchases of merchandise during the accounting period will be recorded in the Purchases account. The amount of beginning inventory will remain unchanged during the accounting period. At the end of the period, a new figure for ending inventory will be calculated.

3. At the end of the accounting period, beginning inventory is added to the cost of goods sold, while ending inventory reduces the cost of goods sold.

4. The perpetual inventory system keeps a continuous record of inventory. It is used by companies with a low volume of sales and high unit prices and often utilizes a computer system.

5. Unearned Revenue is a liability account that accumulates revenue that has not been earned yet, although the cash has been received. It represents a liability to the seller until the service or product is performed or delivered.

Learning Unit 12-2

1. Two important adjustments in the accounting for a merchandising company deal with the Merchandise Inventory account and with the Unearned Revenue account (unearned rent).

2. Figures for beginning and ending inventory on the Income Summary line on the worksheet are never combined; they are also carried over separately to the adjusted trial balance and income statement columns of the worksheet. In the balance sheet column, the figure for ending inventory becomes the beginning inventory figure for the new accounting period.

3. When a company delivers goods or services for which it has been paid in advance, an adjustment is made to reduce the liability account Unearned Revenue and to increase a revenue account.

KEY TERMS

Beginning merchandise inventory (beginning inventory) The cost of goods on hand in a company at the beginning of an accounting period (p. 542)

Ending merchandise inventory (ending inventory) The cost of goods that remain unsold at the end of the accounting period. It is an asset on the balance sheet. (p. 542)

Mortgage Payable A liability account showing the amount owed on a mortgage (p. 547)

Periodic inventory system An inventory system that, at the end of each accounting period, calculates the cost of the unsold goods on hand by taking the cost of each unit times the number of units of each product on hand (p. 542)

Perpetual inventory system An inventory system that keeps continual track of each type of inventory by recording units on hand at the beginning, units purchased and sold, and the balance after each sale or purchase (p. 542)

Unearned Revenue A liability account that records receipt of payment for goods or services in advance of delivery. When the goods or services are delivered, an adjustment is made to reduce Unearned Revenue and increase earned revenue. (The example we used in this chapter is Unearned Rent.) (p. 547)

BLUEPRINT OF A WORKSHEET FOR A MERCHANDISING COMPANY

WORKSHEET

Account Titles	Adjustments Dr.	Adjustments Cr.	Adjusted Trial Balance Dr.	Adjusted Trial Balance Cr.	Income Statement Dr.	Income Statement Cr.	Balance Sheet Dr.	Balance Sheet Cr.
Cash			X				X	
Petty Cash			X				X	
Accounts Receivable			X				X	
Merchandise Inventory	X-E	X-B	X-E				X-E	
Supplies			X				X	
Equipment			X				X	
Accumulated Amortization, Store Equipment				X				X
Accounts Payable				X				X
Income Tax Payable				X				X
CPP Payable				X				X
EI Payable				X				X
Unearned Sales				X				X
Mortgage Payable				X				X
A. Flynn, Capital				X				X
A. Flynn, Withdrawals			X				X	
Income Summary*	X-B	X-E	X-B	X-E	X-B	X-E		
Sales				X		X		
Sales Returns and Allowances			X		X			
Sales Discounts			X		X			
Purchases			X		X			
Purchases Returns and Allowances				X		X		
Purchases Discounts				X		X		
Freight-In			X		X			
Salaries Expense			X		X			
Payroll Tax Expense			X		X			
Insurance Expense			X		X			
Amortization Expense			X		X			
Accrued Salaries				X				X
Rental Income				X		X		

*Note that the figures for beginning inventory (X-B) and ending inventory (X-E) are never combined on the Income Summary line of the worksheet. When the formal income statement is prepared, two distinct figures for inventory will be used to explain and calculate cost of goods sold. Beginning inventory adds to cost of goods sold; ending inventory reduces cost of goods sold.

QUESTIONS, CLASSROOM DEMONSTRATION EXERCISES, EXERCISES, AND PROBLEMS

Discussion Questions and Critical Thinking/Ethical Case

1. When would a company consider using a periodic inventory system?

2. What is the function of the Purchases account?

3. A low-volume, high-unit-price inventory requires a company to use a periodic inventory system. Accept or reject this statement and support your answer.

4. Explain why unearned revenue is a liability account.

5. In a periodic system of inventory, the balance of beginning inventory will remain unchanged during the period. True or false?

6. What is the purpose of an inventory sheet?

7. Why do many unearned revenue accounts have to be adjusted?

8. Explain why figures for beginning and ending inventory are not combined on the Income Summary line of the worksheet.

9. Jim Heary is the custodian of petty cash. Jim, who is short of personal cash, decided to pay his home electrical and telephone bills from petty cash. He plans to pay it back next month. Do you believe Jim should do this? You make the call. Write down your specific recommendations to Jim.

MyAccountingLab

Make the grade with MyAccountingLab! The exercises and problems marked in green can be found on MyAccountingLab at www.myaccountinglab.com. You can practise them as often as you want, and many of them feature step-by-step guided solutions to help you find the right answer. You can also find working papers for selected problems in the Multimedia Library on MyAccountingLab.

Classroom Demonstration Exercises

(The forms you need are on page 12-2 of the *Study Guide with Working Papers*.)

Set A

Adjustment for Merchandise Inventory

Journalizing adjustments for merchandise inventory
1 (10 min)

1. Given the following, journalize the adjusting entries for merchandise inventory. Note that ending inventory has a balance of $18,000.

Merchandise Inventory 114	Income Summary 313
60,000	

Adjustment for Unearned Fees

2. a. Given the following, journalize the adjusting entry. By December 31, 2014, $210 worth of the unearned dog-walking fees were earned.

Unearned Dog-Walking Fees 225	Earned Dog-Walking Fees 441
900 12/1/14	5,000 12/1/14

b. What is the account category of unearned dog-walking fees?

3. Match each of the six items listed below with one of the following locations:

1. Located on the Income Statement debit column of the worksheet
2. Located on the Income Statement credit column of the worksheet
3. Located on the Balance Sheet debit column of the worksheet
4. Located on the Balance Sheet credit column of the worksheet

_____ **a.** Beginning Merchandise Inventory
_____ **b.** Sales Returns and Allowances
_____ **c.** Accrued Salaries
_____ **d.** Sales
_____ **e.** Ending Merchandise Inventory
_____ **f.** Accounts Receivable

Merchandise Inventory Adjustment on Worksheet

4. Given beginning merchandise inventory of $2,000 and ending merchandise inventory of $50, what would be the adjusting entries?

Income Summary on the Worksheet

5.

	Adjustments		Adjusted Trial Balance		Income Statement	
	Dr.	Cr.	Dr.	Cr.	Dr.	Cr.
Income Summary	A	B	C	D	E	F

Given a figure for Beginning Inventory of $400 and a $900 figure for Ending Inventory, place these numbers on the Income Summary line of this partial worksheet.

Set B

Adjustment for Merchandise Inventory

1. Given the following, journalize the adjusting entries for merchandise inventory. Note that ending inventory has a balance of $17,000.

Merchandise Inventory 114	Income Summary 313
60,000	

Adjustment for Unearned Fees

2. a. Given the following, journalize the adjusting entry. By December 31, 2014, $300 worth of the unearned dog-walking fees were earned.

Unearned Dog-Walking Fees 225	Earned Dog-Walking Fees 441
650 12/1/14	4,000 12/1/14

b. What is the account category of unearned dog-walking fees?

The Income Statement and Balance Sheet columns of a worksheet
2 (10 min)

3. Match each of the six items listed at the bottom with one of the following locations:

1. Located on the Income Statement debit column of the worksheet
2. Located on the Income Statement credit column of the worksheet
3. Located on the Balance Sheet debit column of the worksheet
4. Located on the Balance Sheet credit column of the worksheet

_____ **a.** Ending Merchandise Inventory
_____ **b.** Unearned Rent
_____ **c.** Sales Discounts
_____ **d.** Purchases
_____ **e.** Rental Income
_____ **f.** Petty Cash

Merchandise Inventory Adjustment on Worksheet

Adjustments for merchandise inventory
1 (10 min)

4. Adjustment column of a worksheet:

Merchandise Inventory
Income Summary

Explain what the letters A and B represent. Why are the letters A and B never combined?

Income Summary on the Worksheet

Adjustments for merchandise inventory
2 (10 min)

5.

	Adjustments		Adjusted Trial Balance		Income Statement	
	Dr.	Cr.	Dr.	Cr.	Dr.	Cr.
Income Summary	A	B	C	D	E	F

Given a figure for Beginning Inventory of $500 and a $700 figure for Ending Inventory, place these numbers on the Income Summary line of this partial worksheet.

Exercises

(The forms you need are on page 12-3 of the *Study Guide with Working Papers*.)

Categorizing account titles
1 (10 min)

12-1. Indicate the normal balance and category of each of the following accounts:

a. Purchases Returns and Allowances
b. Merchandise Inventory (beginning of period)
c. Freight-In
d. Payroll Tax Expense
e. Purchases Discounts
f. Sales Discounts
g. CPP Payable
h. Unearned Revenue

Calculating net sales, cost of goods sold, gross profit, and net income

① (15 min)

12-2. From the following, calculate **a.** net sales, **b.** cost of goods sold, **c.** gross profit, and **d.** net income:

Data Sales, $22,000; Sales Discounts, $500; Sales Returns and Allowances, $250; Beginning Inventory, $650; Net Purchases, $13,200; Ending Inventory, $510; Operating Expenses, $3,600.

Unearned revenue

① (10 min)

12-3. Allan Co. had the following balances on December 31, 2012:

Cash	Unearned Janitorial Service Revenue
2,100	600

Janitorial Service Revenue
7,200

The accountant for Allan has asked you to make an adjustment since $400 worth of janitorial services have just been performed for customers who had paid in advance. Construct a transaction analysis chart.

Calculating cost of goods sold

①② (15 min)

12-4. Lesan Co. purchased merchandise costing $400,000. Calculate the cost of goods sold under the following different situations:

a. Beginning inventory of $40,000 and no ending inventory
b. Beginning inventory of $50,000 and a $60,000 ending inventory
c. No beginning inventory and a $30,000 ending inventory

Preparing a worksheet

② (20 min)

12-5. Prepare a worksheet from the following information:

(A and B) Merchandise Inventory—ending	$13
(C) Store Supplies on Hand	4
(D) Amortization on Store Equipment	4
(E) Accrued Salaries	2

MOORE CO.
TRIAL BALANCE
DECEMBER 31, 2012

	Dr.	Cr.
Cash	8 00	
Accounts Receivable	5 00	
Merchandise Inventory	11 00	
Store Supplies	10 00	
Store Equipment	20 00	
Accumulated Amortization, Store Equipment		6 00
Accounts Payable		5 00
J. Moore, Capital		34 00
Income Summary	—	—
Sales		64 00
Sales Returns and Allowances	9 00	
Purchases	23 00	
Purchases Discounts		3 00
Freight-In	3 00	
Salaries Expense	10 00	
Advertising Expense	13 00	
Totals	112 00	112 00

Group A Problems

(The forms you need are on page 12-4 of the *Study Guide with Working Papers.*)

Calculating net sales, cost of goods sold, gross profit, and net income

❶ (30 min)

12A-1. On the basis of the accounts listed below, calculate:

a. Net sales
b. Cost of goods sold
c. Gross profit
d. Net income

Accounts Payable	$ 6,000
Operating Expenses	2,000
J. Jensen, Capital	19,400
Purchases	4,450
Freight-In	80
Ending Merchandise Inventory, December 31, 2013	1,250
Sales	10,210
Accounts Receivable	1,489
Cash	756
Purchases Discounts	142
Sales Returns and Allowances	275
Beginning Merchandise Inventory, January 1, 2013	1,565
Purchases Returns and Allowances	251
Sales Discounts	394

Check Figure

Net Income $3,089

Comprehensive problem: Completing a worksheet for a merchandising company

❶❷ (60 min)

12A-2. From the following trial balance, complete a worksheet for Jim's Hardware of Halifax:

Check Figure

Net Income $1,989

JIM'S HARDWARE TRIAL BALANCE DECEMBER 31, 2012		
	Dr.	Cr.
Cash	786 00	
Accounts Receivable	1152 00	
Merchandise Inventory	600 00	
Prepaid Insurance	684 00	
Store Equipment	2160 00	
Accumulated Amortization, Store Equipment		660 00
Accounts Payable		516 00
Jim Spool, Capital		1632 00
Income Summary	—	—
Sales		11040 00
Sales Returns and Allowances	546 00	
Sales Discounts	216 00	
Purchases	5256 00	
Purchases Discounts		168 00
Purchases Returns and Allowances		102 00
Wages Expense	1716 00	
Rent Expense	792 00	
Telephone Expense	114 00	
Miscellaneous Expense	96 00	
	14118 00	14118 00

Assumptions

a. and b. Ending inventory on December 31 is calculated at $315
c. Insurance expired, $150
d. Amortization expense on store equipment, $60
e. Accrued wages, $90

12A-3. The owner of Waltz Company in Fairview has asked you to prepare a worksheet from the following trial balance and additional data:

WALTZ COMPANY
TRIAL BALANCE
DECEMBER 31, 2014

	Dr.	Cr.
Cash	5 4 0 8 00	
Petty Cash	2 4 0 00	
Accounts Receivable	2 5 1 2 00	
Beginning Merchandise Inventory, January 1	5 0 9 2 00	
Prepaid Rent	6 1 6 00	
Office Supplies	9 4 4 00	
Office Equipment	9 2 8 0 00	
Accumulated Amortization, Office Equipment		7 6 0 0 00
Accounts Payable		5 9 6 4 00
K. Waltz, Capital		5 4 7 6 00
K. Waltz, Withdrawals	4 8 0 0 00	
Income Summary	—	—
Sales		5 2 4 8 4 00
Sales Returns and Allowances	9 6 00	
Sales Discounts	2 4 0 0 00	
Purchases	2 9 3 1 6 00	
Purchases Discounts		1 6 00
Purchases Returns and Allowances		3 4 8 00
Office Salaries Expense	7 4 0 8 00	
Insurance Expense	2 4 0 0 00	
Advertising Expense	8 0 0 00	
Utilities Expense	5 7 6 00	
	7 1 8 8 8 00	7 1 8 8 8 00

Additional Data

a. and **b.** Ending merchandise inventory on December 31, $1,805
c. Office supplies used up, $210
d. Rent expired, $195
e. Amortization expense on office equipment, $550
f. Office salaries earned but not paid, $310

Comprehensive problem:
Completing a worksheet with
payroll and unearned revenue

1 2 (60 min)

12A-4. From the following trial balance and additional data, complete the worksheet for Ron's Wholesale Clothing Company of Winnipeg.

RON'S WHOLESALE CLOTHING COMPANY TRIAL BALANCE DECEMBER 31, 2013		
	Dr.	Cr.
Cash	4 4 6 0 00	
Petty Cash	3 0 0 00	
Accounts Receivable	7 5 0 0 00	
Merchandise Inventory	9 0 0 0 00	
Supplies	1 0 0 0 00	
Prepaid Insurance	8 5 0 00	
Store Equipment	2 5 0 0 00	
Accumulated Amortization, Store Equipment		1 5 0 0 00
Accounts Payable		10 6 3 5 00
Income Tax Payable		1 0 6 0 00
CPP Payable		1 0 8 00
EI Payable		1 5 0 00
Unearned Storage Fees		3 5 7 00
Ron Win, Capital		12 5 0 0 00
Ron Win, Withdrawals	4 3 0 0 00	
Income Summary	—	—
Sales		45 0 0 0 00
Sales Returns and Allowances	1 4 7 5 00	
Sales Discounts	1 3 3 5 00	
Purchases	26 0 0 0 00	
Purchases Discounts		5 5 0 00
Purchases Returns and Allowances		4 0 0 00
Freight-In	2 2 5 00	
Salaries Expense	12 0 0 0 00	
Payroll Tax Expense	4 2 0 00	
Interest Expense	8 9 5 00	
	72 2 6 0 00	72 2 6 0 00

Additional Data

a. and **b.** Ending merchandise inventory on December 31, $6,000

c. Supplies on hand, $400

d. Insurance expired, $600

e. Amortization expense on store equipment, $400

f. Storage fees earned, $176

Group B Problems

(The forms you need are on page 12-4 of the *Study Guide with Working Papers*.)

Calculating net sales, cost of
goods sold, gross profit, and net
income

1 (30 min)

12B-1. From the following accounts, calculate **a.** net sales, **b.** cost of goods sold, **c.** gross profit, and **d.** net income.

Sales Discounts	$ 500
Purchases Returns and Allowances	64
Beginning Merchandise Inventory, January 1, 2013	79

	$	
Sales Returns and Allowances	$	191
Purchases Discounts		42
Cash		3,895
Accounts Receivable		441
Sales		3,950
Ending Merchandise Inventory, December 31, 2013		75
Freight-In		41
Purchases		1,152
R. Roland, Capital		1,950
Operating Expenses		895
Accounts Payable		129

Comprehensive problem:
Completing a worksheet for a merchandising company
①② (60 min)

12B-2. As the accountant for Jim's Hardware of Halifax, you have been asked to complete a worksheet from the following trial balance as well as additional data.

JIM'S HARDWARE
TRIAL BALANCE
DECEMBER 31, 2012

	Dr.	Cr.
Cash	9 60 00	
Accounts Receivable	1 60 0 00	
Merchandise Inventory	7 36 00	
Prepaid Insurance	1 1 12 00	
Store Equipment	3 2 00 00	
Accumulated Amortization, Store Equipment		1 68 0 00
Accounts Payable		1 40 8 00
J. Spool, Capital		2 57 6 00
Income Summary	—	—
Sales		14 80 0 00
Sales Returns and Allowances	7 2 8 00	
Sales Discounts	6 88 00	
Purchases	7 0 88 00	
Purchases Discounts		2 40 00
Purchases Returns and Allowances		2 48 00
Wages Expense	2 3 04 00	
Rent Expense	1 84 0 00	
Telephone Expense	5 52 00	
Miscellaneous Expense	1 44 00	
	20 95 2 00	20 95 2 00

Additional Data

a. and b. Cost of ending inventory on December 31, $480

c. Insurance expired, $112

d. Amortization expense on store equipment, $90

e. Accrued wages, $150

12B-3. From the following, complete a worksheet for Waltz Company of Fairview.

WALTZ COMPANY TRIAL BALANCE DECEMBER 31, 2014		
	Dr.	Cr.
Cash	3 8 0 0 00	
Petty Cash	1 0 0 00	
Accounts Receivable	3 4 0 0 00	
Merchandise Inventory	5 2 0 4 00	
Prepaid Rent	1 2 0 0 00	
Office Supplies	1 3 6 0 00	
Office Equipment	9 6 8 0 00	
Accumulated Amortization, Office Equipment		4 0 4 0 00
Accounts Payable		7 9 6 4 00
K. Waltz, Capital		5 4 7 6 00
K. Waltz, Withdrawals	5 0 0 0 00	
Income Summary	—	—
Sales		5 2 4 6 2 00
Sales Returns and Allowances	1 1 6 00	
Sales Discounts	2 2 0 0 00	
Purchases	2 9 2 9 6 00	
Purchases Discounts		1 2 0 8 00
Purchases Returns and Allowances		1 3 5 0 00
Office Salaries Expense	7 4 0 8 00	
Insurance Expense	2 2 0 0 00	
Advertising Expense	8 0 0 00	
Utilities Expense	7 3 6 00	
	7 2 5 0 0 00	7 2 5 0 0 00

Additional Data

a. and **b.** Ending merchandise inventory on December 31, $1,600
c. Office supplies on hand, $470
d. Rent expired, $600
e. Amortization expense on office equipment, $250
f. Salaries accrued, $180

Comprehensive problem:
Completing a worksheet with
payroll and unearned revenue
1 2 (60 min)

12B-4. From the following trial balance and additional data, complete the worksheet for Ron's Wholesale Clothing Company of Winnipeg.

Check Figure

Net Income $3,636

RON'S WHOLESALE CLOTHING COMPANY
TRIAL BALANCE
DECEMBER 31, 2013

	Dr.	Cr.
Cash	2 600 00	
Petty Cash	30 00	
Accounts Receivable	3 000 00	
Beginning Merchandise Inventory, January 1	3 600 00	
Supplies	270 00	
Prepaid Insurance	180 00	
Store Equipment	1 000 00	
Accumulated Amortization, Store Equipment		496 00
Accounts Payable		4 590 00
Income Tax Payable		590 00
CPP Payable		74 00
EI Payable		100 00
Unearned Storage Fees		350 00
Ron Win, Capital		2 734 00
Ron Win, Withdrawals	1 800 00	
Income Summary	—	—
Sales		19 400 00
Sales Returns and Allowances	560 00	
Sales Discounts	480 00	
Purchases	8 600 00	
Purchases Discounts		240 00
Purchases Returns and Allowances		160 00
Freight-In	100 00	
Salaries Expense	6 000 00	
Payroll Tax Expense	194 00	
Interest Expense	320 00	
	28 734 00	28 734 00

Additional Data

a. and b. Ending merchandise inventory on December 31, $3,950
c. Supplies on hand, $50
d. Insurance expired, $55
e. Amortization expense on store equipment, $100
f. Storage fees earned, $115

Group C Problems

(The forms you need are on page 12-5 of the *Study Guide with Working Papers*.)

Calculating net sales, cost of
goods sold, gross profit, and net
income
1 (30 min)

12C-1. On the basis of the accounts listed below, calculate:

a. Net sales
b. Cost of goods sold
c. Gross profit
d. Net income

Accounts Payable	$ 3,800
Operating Expenses	1,150
P. Juarez, Capital	12,460
Purchases	6,785
Freight-In	157
Ending Merchandise Inventory, December 31, 2012	1,670
Sales	13,730
Accounts Receivable	2,675
Cash	1,456
Purchases Discounts	262
Sales Returns and Allowances	208
Beginning Merchandise Inventory, January 1, 2012	1,940
Purchases Returns and Allowances	466
Sales Discounts	424

**Comprehensive problem:
Completing a worksheet for a
merchandising company**

1 2 (75 min)

12C-2. From the following trial balance and additional data, complete a worksheet for Corocan Tile Company of Cranbrook for the 12-month period ending October 31, 2013.

**COROCAN TILE COMPANY
TRIAL BALANCE
OCTOBER 31, 2013**

	Dr.	Cr.
Cash	171040	
Petty Cash	20000	
Accounts Receivable	431670	
Beginning Merchandise Inventory, November 1	1346700	
Supplies	73300	
Prepaid Insurance	91400	
GST Prepaid	74852	
Tile Cutting Equipment	782000	
Accumulated Amortization, Equipment		175555
Accounts Payable		1678240
GST Collected		167358
Income Tax Payable		177100
CPP Payable		24620
EI Payable		37380
Winnie Corocan, Capital		639544
Winnie Corocan, Withdrawals	633800	
Income Summary	—	—
Sales		6906673
Sales Returns and Allowances	138824	
Sales Discounts	71542	
Purchases	4277264	
Purchases Discounts		88230
Purchases Returns and Allowances		51286
Freight-In	42570	
Salaries Expense	1587000	
Payroll Taxes Expense	142600	
Interest Expense	61424	
	9945986	9945986

Additional Data

a. and **b.** Ending merchandise inventory on October 31, $11,416

c. Supplies on hand, $357.10

d. Insurance expired, $609.33

e. Amortization expense on equipment for the year ending October 31, 2013, is calculated assuming a life of six years, residual value of $1,500, straight-line method.

f. Advertising bill received, $500, plus GST of $25.00

g. Employees had worked for 62 hours at an average of $18 per hour at fiscal year-end but will receive this pay in November.

Comprehensive problem: Completing a worksheet

❶❷ (75 min)

12C-3. The owner of Patel Antique Clock Company of Churchill has asked you to prepare a worksheet from the following trial balance and additional data:

Check Figure

Net Income $6,681.87

PATEL ANTIQUE CLOCK COMPANY TRIAL BALANCE MAY 31, 2014		
	Dr.	Cr.
Cash	762 40	
Petty Cash	150 00	
Accounts Receivable	2715 96	
Beginning Clock Inventory, June 1	10766 42	
Repair Supplies	624 30	
Prepaid Insurance	753 76	
GST Prepaid	696 12	
Clock Repair Equipment	4300 00	
Accumulated Amortization, Repair Equipment		1480 00
Accounts Payable		8686 92
GST Collected		912 48
Income Tax Payable		1155 40
CPP Payable		167 70
EI Payable		278 60
Mike Patel, Capital		5566 08
Mike Patel, Withdrawals	4380 00	
Income Summary	—	—
Sales		57014 08
Sales Returns and Allowances	267 10	
Sales Discounts	176 42	
Purchases	30488 92	
Purchases Discounts		277 44
Purchases Returns and Allowances		512 86
Freight-In	1096 33	
Salaries Expense	13475 00	
Payroll Taxes Expense	1276 40	
Advertising Expense	721 68	
Rent Expense	2788 00	
Utilities Expense	612 75	
	76051 56	76051 56

Additional Data

a. and b. Ending clock inventory on May 31, 2014, $12,488.92

c. Supplies on hand at May 31 totalled $376.40

d. Insurance expired, $502.51

e. Amortization expense on equipment for the year ending May 31, 2014, is calculated using the straight-line method, 10-year life with a residual value of $600.

f. Advertising bill received, $300, plus GST of $15

g. Employees had worked but not been paid for 43.5 hours at $12 per hour at year-end.

Comprehensive problem:
Completing a worksheet with
payroll and unearned revenue
❶ ❷ (75 min)

12C-4. From the following trial balance and additional data, complete the worksheet for Gwendolyn's Archery Sales Company of Moncton.

Check Figure

Net Income $3,943.73

GWENDOLYN'S ARCHERY SALES COMPANY
TRIAL BALANCE
APRIL 30, 2013

	Dr.	Cr.
Cash	2 4 6 7 93	
Petty Cash	7 5 00	
Accounts Receivable	7 6 4 82	
Beginning Merchandise Inventory, May 1	1 7 3 6 8 44	
Supplies on Hand	8 9 6 26	
Prepaid Insurance	1 1 5 8 20	
GST Prepaid	1 4 5 8 76	
Equipment	8 9 7 5 00	
Accumulated Amortization, Equipment		5 7 6 2 14
Accounts Payable		2 1 4 7 9 50
GST Collected		2 4 4 4 70
Income Tax Payable		9 7 4 70
CPP Payable		3 6 7 12
EI Payable		1 9 0 08
Gwen Sterling, Capital		1 1 3 7 3 06
Gwen Sterling, Withdrawals	8 4 5 0 00	
Income Summary	—	—
Sales		7 8 4 2 2 76
Sales Returns and Allowances	4 6 7 13	
Sales Discounts	4 7 2 38	
Purchases	5 6 3 8 1 58	
Purchases Discounts		7 8 2 40
Purchases Returns and Allowances		1 3 2 8 37
Freight-In	3 7 6 82	
Salaries Expense	1 4 7 6 2 80	
Payroll Taxes Expense	1 8 1 2 61	
Advertising Expense	2 5 7 2 84	
Rent Expense	3 7 2 0 00	
Utilities Expense	9 4 4 26	
	1 2 3 1 2 4 83	1 2 3 1 2 4 83

Additional Data

a. and **b.** Ending merchandise inventory on April 30, 2013, $26,407.30

c. Supplies on hand at end of April, $412.68

d. A calculation showed that $531.40 of prepaid insurance was the correct amount at year-end.

e. Amortization expense on equipment for the year ending April 30, 2013, was calculated using the straight-line method, seven-year life with a residual value of $450.

f. Utilities bill received, $110, plus GST of $5.50

g. At year-end, employees had worked but not been paid for a total of 120 hours at an average of $14 per hour.

(The forms you need are on page 12-6 of the *Study Guide with Working Papers*.)

Professional fees on the accrual basis
1 (20 min)

T-1. Kim Andrews prepared the following income statement on a cash basis for Ed Sloan, M.D.:

ED SLOAN, M.D. INCOME STATEMENT FOR YEAR ENDED DECEMBER 31, 2012	
Professional Fees Earned	5 0 0 0 0 00
Expenses	1 8 0 0 0 00
Net Income	3 2 0 0 0 00

Ed Sloan has requested information from Kim as to what his professional fees earned would be under the accrual-basis system of accounting. Kim has asked you to provide Dr. Sloan with this information, basing it on the following facts that Kim ignored in the original preparation of the financial report:

	2011	2012
Accrued Professional Fees	$4,200	$5,300
Unearned Professional Fees	6,200	4,250

Merchandise inventory in relation to net income/loss
1 (20 min)

T-2. Abby Jay is having a difficult time understanding the relationships among sales, cost of goods sold, gross profit, and net income for a merchandising company. As the accounting lab tutor, you have been asked to sit down with Abby and explain how to calculate the missing amounts in each situation listed below. Keep in mind that each situation is a distinct and separate business problem.

	Sales	Beginning Inventory	Purchases	Ending Inventory	Cost of Goods Sold	Gross Profit	Expense	Net Income or Loss
Sit. 1	320,000	200,000	160,000	?	260,000	?	80,000	?
Sit. 2	380,000	140,000	?	180,000	200,000	?	100,000	80,000
Sit. 3	480,000	200,000	?	160,000	?	220,000	140,000	80,000
Sit. 4	?	160,000	280,000	140,000	?	160,000	140,000	?
Sit. 5	440,000	160,000	260,000	?	240,000	?	100,000	?
Sit. 6	280,000	120,000	?	140,000	160,000	?	?	40,000
Sit. 7	?	160,000	200,000	120,000	?	160,000	?	−20,000
Sit. 8	320,000	?	200,000	140,000	?	160,000	?	40,000

Recording adjustments and
completing a worksheet
1 2 (60 min)

CONTINUING PROBLEM

Another six months have passed and the fiscal year has concluded for Precision Computer Centre. Tony Freedman wants to make the necessary adjustments to his company's accounts in order to prepare accurate financial statements at July 31, 2014.

Assignment

(The worksheet you require is at the end of the *Study Guide with Working Papers*.)

To prepare the necessary adjustments, use the trial balance shown on the next page and the information below.

Complete the 10-column worksheet for the 12 months ended July 31, 2014.

Inventory

Tony took inventory at the end of July and determined that there was $17,400 worth of merchandise left in stock on July 31.

Amortization of Computer Equipment

Computer depreciates at $33 a month—purchased May 6, 2013.

Computer workstations depreciate at $20 per month—purchased July 17, 2013.

Shop benches depreciate at $25 per month—purchased November 5, 2013.

Amortization of Office Equipment

Office equipment depreciates at $10 per month—purchased May 16, 2013.

Fax machine depreciates at $10 per month—purchased November 19, 2013.

Remember: If any long-term asset is purchased in the first 15 days of the month, Freedman will record amortization for the full month. If an asset is purchased later than the 15th, he will not record amortization in the month when it was purchased.

Additional Information

Rent for 6 months, at $400 per month, has expired.

Supplies on hand at year-end amounted to $530.

A portion of the insurance paid for in February has expired. Remember that the entire premium was debited to Prepaid Insurance.

The balance in Unearned Service Revenue (account 2050) was received from a new customer on June 1, 2014. It represents a prepayment to cover all necessary service on 10 computers for the 12 months ending May 31, 2015.

PRECISION COMPUTER CENTRE
TRIAL BALANCE AS OF JULY 31, 2014

Account #	Account Name	Debit Balance	Credit Balance
1000	Cash	3 9 5 7 4 72	
1010	Petty Cash	1 0 0 00	
1020	Accounts Receivable	2 1 6 2 0 00	
1025	Prepaid Rent	2 4 0 0 00	
1030	Supplies	1 8 6 0 52	
1035	Prepaid Insurance	1 8 4 6 00	
1040	Merchandise Inventory	7 1 0 0 00	
1080	Computer Shop Equipment	5 2 0 0 00	
1081	Accumulated Amortization, Computer Shop Equipment		9 9 00
1090	Office Equipment	1 5 0 0 00	
1091	Accumulated Amortization, Office Equipment		2 0 00
2000	Accounts Payable		4 3 6 2 00
2010	Wages Payable		
2015	Due to CRA		
2050	Unearned Service Revenue		4 8 0 0 00
2060	HST Payable		3 1 4 9 83
2066	HST Recoverable	2 8 1 8 64	
3000	T. Freedman, Capital		7 4 0 6 00
3010	T. Freedman, Withdrawals	1 8 7 3 5 00	
3020	Income Summary		
4000	Service Revenue		9 6 8 0 6 00
4010	Sales		1 4 6 4 4 8 00
4020	Sales Returns and Allowances	1 3 5 0 00	
4030	Sales Discounts	5 9 0 00	
4050	Service Contracts Sold		
5010	Advertising Expense	2 7 1 6 37	
5015	Cleaning Expense	9 0 0 00	
5020	Rent Expense	2 4 0 0 00	
5030	Utilities Expense	2 4 8 2 15	
5040	Phone Expense	1 9 8 0 04	
5050	Supplies Expense	2 8 6 00	
5060	Insurance Expense		
5070	Postage Expense	1 7 6 11	
5080	Amortization Expense, Computer Shop Equipment		
5090	Amortization Expense, Office Equipment		
5100	Miscellaneous Expense	1 4 3 12	
5110	Wages Expense	7 7 9 6 4 89	
5120	Payroll Benefits Expense	8 3 5 37	
5140	Bad Debts Expense		
5600	Purchases	6 8 4 1 4 06	
5610	Purchases Returns and Allowances		8 2 2 18
5620	Purchases Discounts		2 4 5 80
5630	Freight-In	1 1 6 5 82	
	Totals	2 6 4 1 5 8 81	2 6 4 1 5 8 81

13

Completion of the Accounting Cycle for a Merchandising Company

THE BIG PICTURE

For Canadian entrepreneurs Chris Emery and Larry Finnson, success has been sweet. Chocolate-coated, cashew-crunchy, graham-wafer sweet, that is.

The two Winnipeg natives are the founders of Krave's Candy Co., which sells a confection called Clodhoppers—clusters of cashews, graham wafers, and chocolate available in several flavours.

The idea for Clodhoppers came from a favourite recipe of Emery's grandmother. Realizing that there was nothing like it in the marketplace, Emery and Finnson launched Krave's Candy Co. in 1996. Success came rapidly, with sales growing from $59,000 in the first year of operations to well over $5 million five years later.

Smart marketing is one of the reasons for the company's quick success. Rather than spending money on television advertising, Emery and Finnson decided to promote their product by giving away free samples so potential buyers would know how good the confection tasted. The strategy helped the company get into such stores as Zellers and Shoppers Drug Mart.

The two thirty-somethings learned from their mistakes as well as from their early successes. They originally packed their product in plastic jars, like those used for peanut butter. However, the packaging didn't look as good as that of competitors and the product had a tendency to settle over time, making it look like customers weren't getting their money's worth.

In early 1998, the company changed its packaging to a classy black carton with gold embossed lettering. The new packaging helped get the product into Canadian Wal-Mart stores, which had previously declined to carry the product. In 2001, after giving away free Clodhoppers in 400 American Wal-Mart stores, the company signed a deal to supply all 2,600 stores in the Wal-Mart USA chain.

While it remains to be seen whether Clodhoppers will ever be as popular as other well-known chocolates, such as Turtles or After Eights, one thing is certain: The future for these two Manitoba natives will continue to be as sweet as a Winnipeg winter is cold.

When merchandise companies like Krave's Candy Co. plan for the future, they need to analyze past results. At the end of each fiscal year, they close their books and generate financial reports that give them accurate information on such key accounts as *selling expenses* (such as the money Krave's Candy spends on advertising), *administrative expenses* (including salaries for Krave's Candy's 15 employees) and *cost of goods sold* (including the cost of the candy ingredients as well as packaging materials). Only by looking at the complete cycle of accounting information can Emery and Finnson plan their continued expansion.

In this chapter, you'll learn the steps involved in completing the accounting cycle for a merchandising company—from preparing financial statements to completing reversing entries. However, you won't learn the recipe for Clodhoppers candy. That's a company secret.

Sources: Information from Krave's Candy website, www.clodhoppers.tv; Myron Love, "Winnipeg Candy Manufacturer Scores Major Wal-Mart sale," *Food in Canada*, March 2001; Geoff Kirbyson, "Success Sweet for Krave's: City Candy Company Strikes DQ Deal for Clodhopper Blizzard," *Winnipeg Free Press*, November 30, 2000; Casey Mahood, "Managing Media and Marketing Makeover: Clodhoppers Stepping Out," *The Globe and Mail*, January 7, 2000.

1 Preparing financial statements for a merchandising company (pp. 574–577)
2 Recording adjusting and closing entries (pp. 581–584)
3 Preparing a post-closing trial balance (pp. 584–586)
4 Dealing with reversing entries (pp. 587–589)

In this chapter, we discuss the steps involved in completing the accounting cycle for a merchandising company: preparing financial statements, journalizing and posting adjusting and closing entries, preparing a post-closing trial balance, and reversing entries. First, we will deal with preparing financial statements at the close of the accounting cycle.

Learning Unit 13-1
Preparing Financial Statements

1 Preparing financial statements for a merchandising company

As we discussed in Chapter 5, when we were dealing with a service company rather than a merchandising company, the three financial statements can be prepared from the worksheet. Let's begin by looking at how Art's Wholesale Clothing Company prepares the income statement.

THE INCOME STATEMENT

Art is interested in knowing how well his business performed for the year ended December 31, 2013. What were its net sales? Were there many returns of goods from dissatisfied customers? What was the cost of the goods brought into the store versus the selling price received? How many goods were returned to suppliers? What is the cost of the goods that have not been sold? What was the cost of the freight-in? The income statement in Figure 13-1 is prepared from the income statement columns of the worksheet. (Review it first, and then we will explain each section of the income statement and where the information came from on the worksheet.)

Note that there are no debit or credit columns on the formal income statement—the inside columns on financial reports are used for subtotalling, not for debit and credit.

Note also that the income statement is broken down into several sections. Remembering the sections can help you make sense of the statement and set it up correctly on your own. Basically what it presents is this:

Net Sales
– **Cost of Goods Sold**
= **Gross Profit**
– **Operating Expenses**
= **Net Income from Operations**
+ **Other Income**
– **Other Expenses**
= **Net Income**

Let's take these sections one at a time and see where the figures come from on the worksheet.

ART'S WHOLESALE CLOTHING COMPANY
INCOME STATEMENT
FOR YEAR ENDED DECEMBER 31, 2013

Revenue				
Gross Sales				$95 000 00
Less: Sales Ret. and Allow.		$ 95 000		
Sales Discounts		67 000		1 620 00
Net Sales				93 380 00
Cost of Goods Sold				
Merchandise Inventory, 1/1/13			19 000 00	
Purchases	$52 000 00			
Less: Pur. Discounts	$ 86 000			
Pur. Ret. and Allow.	68 000	1 54 000		
Net Purchases		50 46 000		
Add: Freight-In		45 000		
Net Cost of Purchases			50 91 000	
Cost of Goods Available for Sale			69 91 000	
Less: Merch. Inv., 12/31/13			4 00 000	
Cost of Goods Sold				65 91 000
Gross Profit				27 47 000
Operating Expenses				
Salaries Expense			12 30 000	
Payroll Tax Expense			42 000	
Amort. Exp., Store Equip.			5 000	
Supplies Expense			50 000	
Insurance Expense			30 000	
Postage Expense			2 500	
Miscellaneous Expense			3 000	
Total Operating Expenses				13 625 00
Net Income from Operations				13 845 00
Other Income				
Rental Income			20 000	
Other Expenses				
Interest Expense			30 000	10000
Net Income				$13 745 00

ART'S WHOLESALE CLOTHING COMPANY
PARTIAL WORKSHEET
FOR YEAR ENDED DECEMBER 31, 2013

	Income Statement	
	Dr.	Cr.
Income Summary	19 00 000	4 00 000
Sales		95 00 000
Sales Returns and Allowances	95 000	
Sales Discounts	67 000	
Purchases	52 000 00	
Purchases Discounts		86 000
Purchases Returns and Allowances		68 000
Freight-In	45 000	
Salaries Expense	12 30 000	
Payroll Tax Expense	42 000	
Postage Expense	2 500	
Miscellaneous Expense	3 000	
Interest Expense	30 000	
Rental Income		20 000
Supplies Expense	50 000	
Insurance Expense	30 000	
Amortization Expense, Store Equip.	5 000	
Accrued Salaries		
	86 995 00	100 74 000
Net Income	13 745 00	
	100 74 000	100 74 000

Figure 13-1
Partial Worksheet and Income Statement

Revenue Section

Net Sales The first major category of the income statement shows net sales. The figure here of $93,380 is *not* found on the worksheet—the accountant must take the individual amounts for gross sales, sales returns and allowances, and sales discounts found on the worksheet and *combine* them to arrive at a figure for net sales. Thus, although the worksheet has the individual components, it is not until the formal income statement that these individual amounts are summarized in one figure for net sales.

Sales
− Sales Returns and Allowances
− Sales Discounts
= Net Sales

Cost of Goods Sold Section

On the worksheet, we separate figures for Merchandise Inventory. The $19,000 represents the beginning inventory of the period while the $4,000, calculated from an inventory sheet, is the ending inventory. Note on the financial report that the cost of goods sold section uses two separate figures for inventory. Remember in the periodic system that goods brought in during the accounting period are added to the Purchases account, not to the Merchandise Inventory account.

Beginning Inventory
+ Net Cost of Purchases
− Ending Inventory
= Cost of Goods Sold

 Note that the following numbers are not found on the worksheet but are shown on the formal income statement (they are combined by the accountant in preparing the income statement):

- ◆ **Net Purchases:** $50,460 (Purchases − Purchases Discounts − Purchases Returns and Allowances)
- ◆ **Net Cost of Purchases:** $50,910 (Net Purchases + Freight-In)
- ◆ **Cost of Goods Available for Sale:** $69,910 (Beginning Inventory + Net Cost of Purchases)
- ◆ **Cost of Goods Sold:** $65,910 (Cost of Goods Available for Sale − Ending Inventory)

Gross Profit

The figure for gross profit ($27,470) is arrived at by subtracting cost of goods sold from net sales ($93,380 − $65,910). The gross profit figure of $27,470 is not found by itself on the worksheet but, like others we have discussed, it is calculated by the accountant from separate figures on the worksheet.

Net Sales
− Cost of Goods Sold
= Gross Profit

Operating Expenses Section

The total of the operating expenses does not appear on its own on the worksheet; to get this figure of $13,625, the accountant adds up all the expenses on the worksheet that resulted from doing business.

 Many companies break expenses down into those directly related to the selling activity of the company (**selling expenses**) and those related to administrative or office activity (**administrative expenses** or **general expenses**). Here's a sample list broken down into these two categories:

Operating Expenses

Selling Expenses	*Administrative Expenses*
Sales Salaries Expense	Rent Expense
Delivery Expense	Office Salaries Expense
Advertising Expense	Utilities Expense
Amortization Expense,	Supplies Expense
Store Equipment	Amortization Expense,
Insurance Expense	Office Equipment
Total Selling Expenses	Total Administrative Expenses

Other Income (or Other Revenue) Section

This section will record any **other income** or revenue besides revenue from sales. For example, Art's Wholesale makes a profit from subletting a portion of a building and earning rental income of $200 and that income goes in this section.

Other Expenses Section

This section will record **other expenses**, non-operating expenses—those not related to the main operating activities of the business. For example, Art's Wholesale has paid or owes $300 interest on money it has borrowed.

STATEMENT OF OWNER'S EQUITY

> Statement of owner's equity is the same for a merchandising business as for a service firm.

The information used to complete the statement of owner's equity comes from the balance sheet columns of the worksheet. Keep in mind that the capital account in the ledger should be checked to see if any additional investments have occurred during the period. Note in the following diagram that the worksheet aids in this. The ending figure of $13,050 for Art Newner, Capital, will be carried over to the balance sheet, which is the final report we will look at in this chapter.

> Any additional investment by the owner would be added to his or her beginning capital amount. The illustration at the right does not show this however.

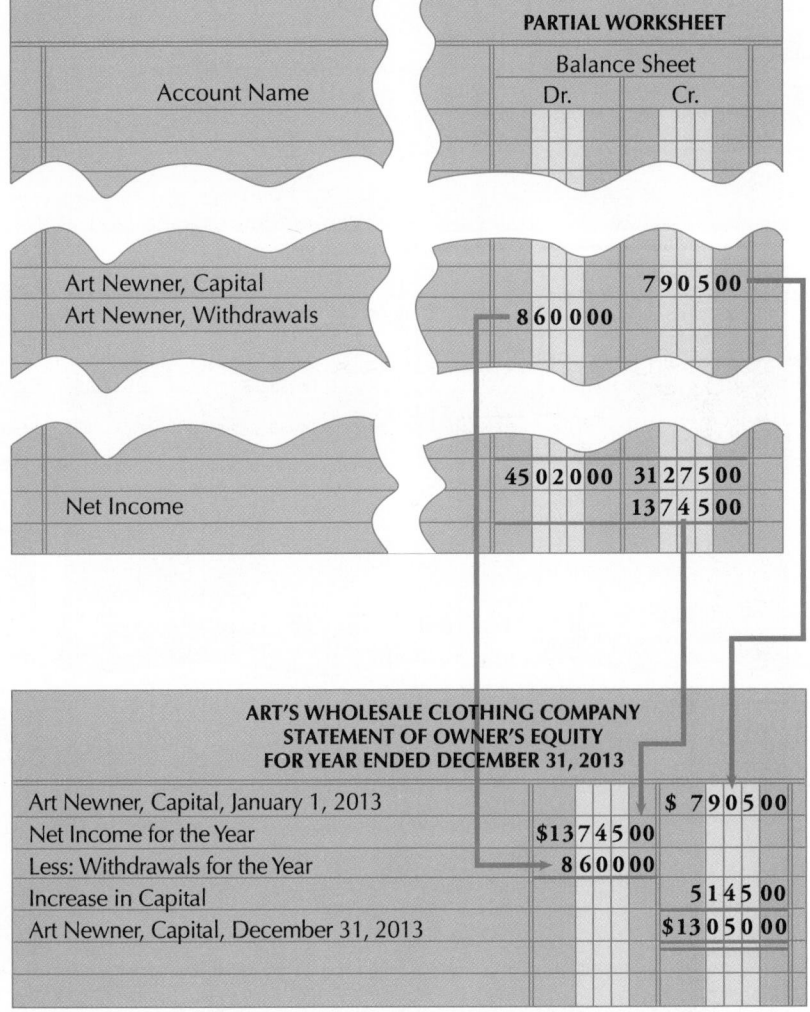

THE BALANCE SHEET

Figure 13-2 shows how a worksheet is used to aid in the preparation of a **classified balance sheet**. A classified balance sheet breaks down the assets and liabilities into

ART'S WHOLESALE CLOTHING COMPANY
WORKSHEET
FOR YEAR ENDED DECEMBER 31, 2013

	Balance Sheet	
	Dr.	Cr.
Cash	12 920 00	
Petty Cash	100 00	
Accounts Receivable	14 500 00	
Merchandise Inventory	4 000 00	
Supplies	300 00	
Prepaid Insurance	600 00	
Store Equipment	4 000 00	
Accum. Amort., Store Equipment		45 0 00
Accounts Payable		17 900 00
Income Tax Payable		1 24 0 00
CPP Payable		26 0 00
EI Payable		20 0 00
Unearned Rent		40 0 00
Mortgage Payable		2 32 0 00
Accrued Salaries		6 00 00
	45 020 00	31 275 00
Net Income		13 745 00
	45 020 00	45 020 00

ART'S WHOLESALE CLOTHING COMPANY
CLASSIFIED BALANCE SHEET
DECEMBER 31, 2013

Assets

Current Assets		
Cash	$12 920 00	
Petty Cash	100 00	
Accounts Receivable	14 500 00	
Merchandise Inventory	4 000 00	
Supplies	300 00	
Prepaid Insurance	600 00	
Total Current Assets		$32 420 00
Capital Assets		
Store Equipment	4 000 00	
Less: Accumulated Amortization	45 0 00	3 55 0 00
Total Assets		$35 970 00

Liabilities

Current Liabilities		
Accounts Payable	$17 900 00	
Income Tax Payable	1 24 0 00	
CPP Payable	26 0 00	
EI Payable	20 0 00	
Accrued Salaries	6 00 00	
Mortgage Payable (current portion)	32 0 00	
Unearned Rent	40 0 00	
Total Current Liabilities		$20 920 00
Long-Term Liabilities		
Mortgage Payable (net of current portion)		2 000 00
Total Liabilities		22 920 00

Owner's Equity

Art Newner, Capital		13 050 00
Total Liabilities and Owner's Equity		$35 970 00

Note: The figure of $13,050 for Art Newner, Capital, comes from the statement of owner's equity.

Figure 13-2 Partial Worksheet and Balance Sheet

more detail. Classified balance sheets provide management, owners, creditors, and suppliers with more information about the company's ability to pay current and long-term debts. They also provide a more complete financial picture of the firm.

The categories on the classified balance sheet are as follows.

Current assets are defined as cash and assets that will be converted into cash or used up during the normal operating cycle of the company or one year, whichever is longer. (Think of the **operating cycle** as the time period it takes a company to buy and sell merchandise and then collect accounts receivable.)

Accountants list current assets in order of how easily they can be converted into cash (this is called *liquidity*). In most cases, Accounts Receivable can be turned into cash more quickly than Merchandise Inventory—for example, it can be quite difficult to sell an outdated computer in a computer store or to sell last year's model car this year.

Capital assets are long-lived assets used in the production or sale of goods or services. Art's Wholesale has only one capital asset, store equipment; other capital assets could include buildings and land. The assets are usually listed in order of how long they will last; the longest-lived assets are listed first. Land would usually be the first asset listed (and land is never amortized). Note that we still show the cost of the asset less its accumulated amortization.

Mortgage payable	$2,320
Current portion	– 320
Long-term	$2,000

Current liabilities are the debts or obligations of Art's Wholesale that must be paid within one year or one operating cycle. The order of listing accounts in this section is not always the same—many times companies will list their liabilities in the order in which they expect to pay them off. Note that the current portion of the mortgage, $320 (that portion due within one year), is listed toward the end of the list since that is paid off over the year.

Long-term liabilities are debts or obligations not due and payable for a comparatively long period, usually for more than one year. For Art's Wholesale, there is only one long-term liability—Mortgage Payable. The long-term portion of the mortgage is listed here; the current portion, due within one year, is listed under Current Liabilities.

The current portion of a long-term liability is the amount of principal to be repaid during the next year. Do not include any interest to be paid next year.

A classified balance sheet (when examined along with the income statement) can provide management, owners, creditors, and suppliers with more information about the company's ability to pay debts, both current and long-term. As well, it provides a more complete financial picture of the firm than a standard balance sheet would.

LEARNING UNIT 13-1 REVIEW

AT THIS POINT you should be able to:

- ◆ Prepare a detailed income statement from the worksheet. (pp. 574–577)
- ◆ Explain the difference between selling and administrative expenses. (p. 576)
- ◆ Explain which columns of the worksheet are used in preparing a statement of owner's equity. (p. 577)
- ◆ Prepare a classified balance sheet from a worksheet. (pp. 577–579)
- ◆ Explain as well as compare current assets and capital assets. (p. 579)
- ◆ Using Mortgage Payable as an example, explain the difference between current and long-term liabilities. (p. 579)

Self-Review Quiz 13-1

(The forms you need are on pages 13-2 and 13-3 of the *Study Guide with Working Papers*.)

Using the worksheet from Self-Review Quiz 12-2 (page 554), prepare in proper form (1) an income statement, (2) a statement of owner's equity, and (3) a classified balance sheet for Ray Company.

Solutions to Self-Review Quiz 13-1

Quiz Tip

Note that the cost of goods sold has separate figures for beginning inventory and ending inventory.

1.

RAY COMPANY INCOME STATEMENT FOR YEAR ENDED DECEMBER 31, 2012				
Revenue				
Sales				$110400 0
Less: Sales Returns and Allowances		$ 5460 0		
Sales Discounts		2160 0	762 00	
Net Sales				1027800
Cost of Goods Sold				
Merchandise Inventory, 1/1/12			82400	
Purchases		$52560 0		
Less: Pur. Ret. and Allowances	$ 1680 0			
Purchases Discounts	1020 0	2700 0		
Net Purchases			49860 0	
Cost of Goods Available for Sale			58100 0	
Less: Merchandise Inv., 12/31/12			2000 0	
Cost of Goods Sold				561000
Gross Profit				466800
Operating Expenses				
Salaries Expense			221600	
Insurance Expense			139200	
Utilities Expense			9600	
Plumbing Expense			21400	
Rent Expense			10000	
Amortization Expense, Equipment			6000	
Total Operating Expenses				407800
Net Income from Operations				59000
Other Income				
Storage Fees				51600
Net Income				$ 110600

2.

RAY COMPANY STATEMENT OF OWNER'S EQUITY FOR YEAR ENDED DECEMBER 31, 2012	
B. Ray, Capital, 1/1/12	$ 193200
Net Income for the Year	110600
B. Ray, Capital, 12/31/12	$ 303800

3.

RAY COMPANY BALANCE SHEET DECEMBER 31, 2012		
Assets		
Current Assets		
Cash	$2 4 8 6 00	
Merchandise Inventory	2 0 0 00	
Prepaid Rent	1 0 5 2 00	
Prepaid Insurance	6 0 00	
Total Current Assets		$3 7 9 8 00
Capital Assets		
Office Equipment	$2 1 6 0 00	
Less: Accumulated Amortization	6 2 0 00	1 5 4 0 00
Total Assets		$5 3 3 8 00
Liabilities		
Current Liabilities		
Accounts Payable	$ 1 0 0 00	
Accrued Salaries	2 0 0 00	
Unearned Storage Fees	2 0 0 0 00	
Total Liabilities		$2 3 0 0 00
Owner's Equity		
B. Ray, Capital		3 0 3 8 00
Total Liabilities and Owner's Equity		$5 3 3 8 00

Learning Unit 13-2

Journalizing and Posting Adjusting and Closing Entries; Preparing the Post-Closing Trial Balance

> **2** Recording adjusting and closing entries

JOURNALIZING AND POSTING ADJUSTING ENTRIES

From the worksheet of Art's Wholesale, repeated here as Figure 13-3 for your convenience, the adjusting entries can be journalized from the adjustments column and posted to the ledger. Keep in mind that the adjustments have been recorded only on the worksheet, not in the journal or in the ledger—at this point the journal does not reflect adjustments, and the ledger still contains only unadjusted amounts.

ART'S WHOLESALE CLOTHING COMPANY
WORKSHEET
FOR YEAR ENDED DECEMBER 31, 2013

Account	Trial Balance Dr.	Trial Balance Cr.	Adjustments Dr.	Adjustments Cr.	Adjusted Trial Balance Dr.	Adjusted Trial Balance Cr.	Income Statement Dr.	Income Statement Cr.	Balance Sheet Dr.	Balance Sheet Cr.
Cash	12920 00				12920 00				12920 00	
Petty Cash	100 00				100 00				100 00	
Accounts Receivable	14500 00				14500 00				14500 00	
Merchandise Inventory	19000 00		(B)4000 00	(A)19000 00	4000 00				4000 00	
Supplies	800 00			(D)500 00	300 00				300 00	
Prepaid Insurance	900 00			(E)300 00	600 00				600 00	
Store Equipment	4000 00				4000 00				4000 00	
Accum. Amort., Store Equipment		400 00		(F) 50 00		450 00				450 00
Accounts Payable		17900 00				17900 00				17900 00
Income Tax Payable		1240 00				1240 00				1240 00
CPP Payable		260 00				260 00				260 00
EI Payable		200 00				200 00				200 00
Unearned Rent		600 00	(C)200 00			400 00				400 00
Mortgage Payable		2320 00				2320 00				2320 00
Art Newner, Capital		7905 00				7905 00				7905 00
Art Newner, Withdrawals	8600 00				8600 00				8600 00	
Income Summary			(A)19000 00	(B)4000 00	19000 00	4000 00	19000 00	4000 00		
Sales		95000 00				95000 00		95000 00		
Sales Returns and Allowances	950 00				950 00		950 00			
Sales Discounts	670 00				670 00		670 00			
Purchases	52000 00				52000 00		52000 00			
Purchases Discounts		860 00				860 00		860 00		
Purchases Returns and Allowances		680 00				680 00		680 00		
Freight-In	450 00				450 00		450 00			
Salaries Expense	11700 00		(G)600 00		12300 00		12300 00			
Payroll Tax Expense	420 00				420 00		420 00			
Postage Expense	25 00				25 00		25 00			
Miscellaneous Expense	30 00				30 00		30 00			
Interest Expense	300 00				300 00		300 00			
	127365 00	127365 00								
Rental Income				(C) 200 00		200 00		200 00		
Supplies Expense			(D)500 00		500 00		500 00			
Insurance Expense			(E)300 00		300 00		300 00			
Amortization Expense, Store Equip.			(F) 50 00		50 00		50 00			
Accrued Salaries				(G) 600 00		600 00				600 00
			24650 00	24650 00	132015 00	132015 00	86995 00	100740 00	45020 00	31275 00
Net Income							13745 00			13745 00
							100740 00	100740 00	45020 00	45020 00

Figure 13-3   Completed Worksheet

The journalized and posted adjusting entries are shown below. Note that the liability Unearned Rent is reduced by $200 and Rental Income has increased by $200.

ART'S WHOLESALE CLOTHING COMPANY
GENERAL JOURNAL

Page 2

Date 2013		Account Titles and Description	Post. Ref.	Dr.	Cr.
		Adjusting Entries			
Dec.	31	Income Summary	313	19 000 00	
		Merchandise Inventory	114		19 000 00
		Transferred beginning inventory			
		to Income Summary			
	31	Merchandise Inventory	114	4 000 00	
		Income Summary	313		4 000 00
		Records cost of ending inventory			
	31	Unearned Rent	218	2 00 00	
		Rental Income	414		2 00 00
		Rental income earned			
	31	Supplies Expense	614	5 00 00	
		Supplies	115		5 00 00
		Supplies consumed			
	31	Insurance Expense	615	3 00 00	
		Prepaid Insurance	116		3 00 00
		Insurance expired			
	31	Amortization Exp., Store Equipment	613	5 0 00	
		Acc. Amortization, Store Equipment	122		5 0 00
		Amortization on equipment			
	31	Salaries Expense	611	6 00 00	
		Accrued Salaries	212		6 00 00
		Accrued salary			

Partial Ledger

Merchandise Inventory 114		Accum. Amort., Store Equipment 122		Income Summary 313		Amort. Expense, Store Equipment 613	
19,000	19,000		400	19,000	4,000	50	
4,000			50				

Supplies 115		Accrued Salaries 212		Rental Income 414		Supplies Expense 614	
800	500		600		200	500	

Prepaid Insurance 116		Unearned Rent 218		Salaries Expense 611		Insurance Exp. 615	
900	300	200	600	11,700		300	
				600			

JOURNALIZING AND POSTING CLOSING ENTRIES

In Chapter 5, we discussed the closing process for a service company. The goals of closing have not changed. They are to clear all temporary accounts in the ledger to zero and to update capital in the ledger to its latest balance. A merchandising company will also use the worksheet and the following steps to complete the closing process:

1. Close all balances in the income statement credit column of the worksheet, *except* Income Summary, by debits. Then credit the total to the Income Summary account.
2. Close all balances in the income statement debit column of the worksheet, *except* Income Summary, by credits. Then debit the total to the Income Summary account.
3. Transfer the balance of the Income Summary account to the Capital account.
4. Transfer the balance of the owner's Withdrawal account to the Capital account.

Let's look now at the journalized closing entries in Figure 13-4. When these entries are posted, all the temporary accounts will have zero balances in the ledger and the Capital account will be updated with a new balance.

Let's take a moment to look at the Income Summary account in T account form as it would exist after step 2 above:

Income Summary 313

Adj.	19,000	4,000	Adj.
Clos.	67,995	96,740	Clos.
	86,995	100,740	
Net income → Clos.	13,745		

Note that Income Summary before the closing process contains the adjustments for Merchandise Inventory. Sometimes accountants include the inventory adjustments as part of the closing. This is not illustrated in this text; *it is not very important which procedure is used*, just that it is made accurately. The end result is that the net income of $13,745 is closed to the Capital account.

THE POST-CLOSING TRIAL BALANCE

3 Preparing a post-closing trial balance

The post-closing trial balance (often referred to as an opening trial balance) shown on page 586 is prepared from the general ledger. Note first that all temporary accounts have been closed and thus are not shown on this post-closing trial balance. Note also that the ending inventory figure of the last accounting period, $4,000, becomes the beginning inventory figure on January 1, 2014.

Figure 13-4
General Journal

ART'S WHOLESALE CLOTHING COMPANY
GENERAL JOURNAL

Page 2

Date		Account Titles and Description	Post. Ref.	Dr.	Cr.
2013		Closing Entries			
Dec.	31	Sales	411	95 0 0 0 00	
		Rental Income	414	2 0 0 00	
		Purchases Discounts	512	8 6 0 00	
		Purchases Returns and Allowances	513	6 8 0 00	
		Income Summary	313		96 7 4 0 00
		To transfer credit account balances			
		on income statement column of			
		worksheet to Income Summary			
	31	Income Summary	313	67 9 9 5 00	
		Sales Returns and Allowances	412		9 5 0 00
		Sales Discounts	413		6 7 0 00
		Purchases	511		52 0 0 0 00
		Freight-In	514		4 5 0 00
		Salaries Expense	611		12 3 0 0 00
		Payroll Tax Expense	612		4 2 0 00
		Postage Expense	616		2 5 00
		Miscellaneous Expense	617		3 0 00
		Interest Expense	618		3 0 0 00
		Supplies Expense	614		5 0 0 00
		Insurance Expense	615		3 0 0 00
		Amortization Expense, Store Equip.	613		5 0 00
		To transfer all expenses and other			
		debit balances in the income			
		statement column of the worksheet			
		to Income Summary			
	31	Income Summary	313	13 7 4 5 00	
		A. Newner, Capital	311		13 7 45 00
		To transfer net income to			
		Capital from Income Summary			
	31	A. Newner, Capital	311	8 6 0 0 00	
		A. Newner, Withdrawals	312		8 6 0 0 00
		Closes withdrawals to			
		Capital account			

Notice that the adjustments to inventory are not included in these closing entries although some accountants do include them here.

Quiz Tip

Note in the first closing entry that the four account titles (now listed as debits) were found on the worksheet as credits in the Income Statement column.

ART'S WHOLESALE CLOTHING COMPANY POST-CLOSING TRIAL BALANCE DECEMBER 31, 2013		
	Dr.	Cr.
Cash	12 9 2 0 00	
Petty Cash	1 0 0 00	
Accounts Receivable	14 5 0 0 00	
Merchandise Inventory	4 0 0 0 00	
Supplies	3 0 0 00	
Prepaid Insurance	6 0 0 00	
Store Equipment	4 0 0 0 00	
Accumulated Amortization, Store Equipment		4 5 0 00
Accounts Payable		17 9 0 0 00
Income Tax Payable		1 2 4 0 00
CPP Payable		2 6 0 00
EI Payable		2 0 0 00
Accrued Salaries		6 0 0 00
Unearned Rent		4 0 0 00
Mortgage Payable		2 3 2 0 00
Art Newner, Capital		13 0 5 0 00
	36 4 2 0 00	36 4 2 0 00

LEARNING UNIT 13-2 REVIEW

AT THIS POINT you should be able to:

◆ Journalize and post adjusting entries for a merchandising company. (pp. 581–583)

◆ Explain the relationship of the worksheet to the adjusting and closing process. (p. 581)

◆ Complete the closing process for a merchandising company. (p. 584–585)

◆ Prepare a post-closing trial balance and explain why ending Merchandise Inventory is not a temporary account. (p. 584 and 586)

Self-Review Quiz 13-2

(The form you need is on page 13-4 of the *Study Guide with Working Papers*.)

Using the worksheet from Self-Review Quiz 12-2 (page 554), journalize the closing entries.

Solution to Self-Review Quiz 13-2

	Date		Account Titles and Description	PR	Dr.	Cr.
			Closing			
	Dec.	31	Sales		11 04 00 00	
			Storage Fees Earned		5 16 00	
			Purchases Returns and Allowances		1 68 00	
			Purchases Discounts		1 02 00	
			Income Summary			11 82 6 00
		31	Income Summary		10 09 6 00	
			Sales Returns and Allowances			5 46 00
			Sales Discounts			2 16 00
			Purchases			5 25 6 00
			Salaries Expense			2 21 6 00
			Insurance Expense			1 39 2 00
			Utilities Expense			96 00
			Plumbing Expense			2 14 00
			Rent Expense			1 00 00
			Amortization Expense, Equipment			60 00
		31	Income Summary		1 10 6 00	
			B. Ray, Capital			1 10 6 00

Page 2

Learning Unit 13-3

Reversing Entries *(Optional Section)*

4 Dealing with reversing entries

Reversing entries are not mandatory.

Now that we have completed the accounting cycle for Art's Wholesale Clothing Company, let's look at an optional way of handling some adjusting entries—it is called making reversing entries. **Reversing entries** are general journal entries that are the opposite of adjusting entries. Reversing entries help reduce potential errors and simplify the record-keeping process. Let's look at how Art's bookkeeper handles the closing entry for salaries at the end of the year (see Figure 13-5).

Note that the permanent account, Accrued Salaries carries a $600 balance over to the new accounting period. *Remember:* The $600 was an expense of the prior year.

Figure 13-5
Closing Entries

	Adjusting Journal Entry			**T Account Update**	
(1) On December 31, after adjusting entry for $600 of salaries incurred but not paid was journalized and posted	2013 Dec. 31 Salaries Expense 31 Accrued Salaries	6 00 00	6 00 00	**Salaries Expense** 11,700 600	**Accrued Salaries** 600

	Closing Journal Entry (partial)			**T Account Update**	
(2) On December 31, after closing entries have been journalized and posted	2013 Dec. 31 Income Summary 31 Salaries Expense	XXX	12 30 0 00	**Salaries Expense** 11,700 600 │ 12,300 Bal. –0–	**Accrued Salaries** 600

On January 8 of the new year (2014), the payroll to be paid is $2,000. If the optional reversing entry is *not* used, the bookkeeper makes the following journal entry:

2014				
Jan.	8	Accrued Salaries	600 00	
	8	Salaries Expense	1 400 00	
	8	Cash		2 000 00

Salaries Expense	Accrued Salaries	Cash
1,400		600	600		2,000

To do this, the bookkeeper has to refer to the adjustment on December 31 to determine how much of the $2,000 of salary is indeed a new salary expense and what portion was shown in the old year although not paid then. It is easy to see how errors can result if the bookkeeper pays the payroll but forgets about the adjustment in the previous year. For this reason, reversing entries can help avoid errors.

Figure 13-6 shows the four steps the bookkeeper would take if reversing entries were used. Note that steps 1 and 2 are the same whether the accountant uses reversing entries or not.

Note that the balance of Salaries Expense is indeed only $1,400, the *true* expense in the new year. Reversing results in switching the adjustment on the first day of the new period. Also note that each of the accounts ends up with the same balance no matter which method is chosen. However, using a reversing entry for salaries allows the accountant to make the normal entry when it is time to pay salaries.

One should be careful with reversing entries since not all adjustments can be reversed. Here is a list of the types of adjustments that can be reversed:

1. When there is an increase in an asset account (no previous balance)
   Example: Interest Receivable
                        Interest Income
   (Interest earned but not collected: We will cover this in later chapters.)

Figure 13-6   Reversing Entries

(1)
On December 31, adjustment for salary was recorded.

Salaries Expense	Accrued Salaries
11,700		600
600		

(2)
Closing entry on December 31

Salaries Expense	Accrued Salaries
11,700	12,300		600
600		

(3)
On January 1 (first day of the following fiscal period), reverse adjusting entry was made for salary on December 31. (This means "flipping" adjustment.)

2014				
Jan.	1	Accrued Salaries	600 00	
		Salaries Expense		600 00

Salaries Expense	Accrued Salaries
	600	600	600

By doing this, the liability is reduced to zero. We know it will be paid in this new period, but the salaries expense has a credit balance of $600 until the payroll is paid. When the payroll of $2,000 is paid, the following happens:

(4)
Paid payroll, $2,000

2014				
Jan.	8	Salaries Expense	2 000 00	
		Cash		2 000 00

Salaries Expense	Cash
2,000	600		2,000

2. When there is an increase in a liability account (no previous balance)

Example: Wages Expense
   Accrued Wages

Except in the case of businesses in their first year of operation, accounts such as Accumulated Amortization or Inventory will have previous balances and thus will *not* be reversed. As we progress in the course, we will take time to review whether reversing takes place or not.

The increasing use of computers in accounting has changed the role and purpose of reversing entries somewhat. Most accounting software packages allow users to establish recurring entries that can be entered into the accounting records more or less automatically each month. Also, many accounting programs permit a given entry to be automatically reversed in the next period by simply checking a box on a screen.

In this text, we are continuing to illustrate reversing entries as being done manually. Students are encouraged to discover what features are present in the software they are using (or have access to) that modify the nature, purpose, and usefulness of reversing entries.

LEARNING UNIT 13-3 REVIEW

AT THIS POINT you should be able to:
- ◆ Explain the purpose of reversing entries. (p. 587)
- ◆ Complete a reversing entry. (p. 588)
- ◆ Explain when reversing entries can be used. (pp. 588–589)

Self-Review Quiz 13-3

(The form you need is on page 13-4 of the *Study Guide with Working Papers*.)

Explain which of the following situations could be reversed:

1.

Supplies Expense	
200	

Supplies	
800	200

2.

Wages Expense	
3,000	
200	

Accrued Wages	
	200

3.

Sales	
	4,000
	50

Unearned Sales	
50	200

Solution to Self-Review Quiz 13-3

1. Not reversed—Asset, Supplies is decreasing, not increasing.
2. Reversed—Liability is increasing and no previous balance exists.
3. Not reversed—Liability is decreasing and a previous balance exists.

SUMMARY OF KEY POINTS

Learning Unit 13-1

1. The formal income statement can be prepared from the income statement columns of the worksheet.

2. There are no debit or credit columns on the formal income statement.

3. The cost of goods sold section has a figure for beginning inventory and a separate figure for ending inventory.

4. Operating expenses could be broken down into selling and administrative expenses.

5. The ending figure for capital is not found on the worksheet. It comes from the statement of owner's equity.

6. A classified balance sheet breaks assets down into current and capital. Liabilities are broken down into current and long-term.

Learning Unit 13-2

1. The information for journalizing adjusting and closing entries can be obtained from the worksheet.

2. In the closing process, all temporary accounts will be zero and the capital account is brought up to its new balance.

3. Inventory is not a temporary account. The ending inventory, along with other permanent accounts, will be listed in the post-closing trial balance.

Learning Unit 13-3

1. Reversing entries are optional and could aid in reducing potential errors and also simplify the record-keeping process.

2. The reversing entry "flips" the adjustment on the first day of the new fiscal period. Thus, the bookkeeper need not look back at what happened in the old year when recording the current year's transactions.

3. Reversing entries are used only if (a) assets are increasing and have no previous balance or (b) liabilities are increasing and have no previous balance.

KEY TERMS

Administrative expenses (general expenses)   Expenses such as general office expenses that are incurred indirectly in the selling of goods (p. 576)

Capital assets   Long-lived assets such as buildings or land that are used in the production or sale of goods or services (p. 579)

Classified balance sheet   A balance sheet that categorizes assets as current or capital and groups liabilities as current or long-term (p. 577)

Current assets   Assets that can be converted into cash or used within one year or the normal operating cycle of the business, whichever is longer (p. 579)

Current liabilities Obligations that will come due within one year or within the operating cycle, whichever is longer (p. 579)

Long-term liabilities   Obligations that are not due or payable for a long time, usually for more than a year (p. 579)

Operating cycle   Average time it takes to buy and sell merchandise and then collect accounts receivable (p. 579)

Other expenses   Non-operating expenses that do not relate to the main operating activities of the business; they appear in a separate section on the income statement. One example given in the text is Interest Expense—interest owed on money borrowed by the company. (p. 577)

Other income   This includes any revenue other than revenue from sales and appears in a separate section on the income statement. Examples would be Rental Income and Storage Fees. (p. 577)

Reversing entries   Year-end optional bookkeeping technique in which certain adjusting entries are reversed or switched on the first day of the new accounting period so that transactions in the new period can be recorded without referring to prior adjusting entries (p. 587)

Selling expenses   Expenses directly related to the sale of goods (p. 576)

BLUEPRINT OF FINANCIAL STATEMENTS

(1) INCOME STATEMENT				
Revenue				
Sales				$ XXX
Less: Sales Ret. and Allow.			$ XXX	
Sales Discounts			XXX	XXX
Net Sales				XXXX
Cost of Goods Sold				
Merchandise Inventory, 1/1/10			XXX	
Purchases		$XXX		
Less: Pur. Ret. and Allow.	$XXX			
Purchases Discounts	XXX	XXX		
Net Purchases		XXX		
Add: Freight-In		XXX		
Net Cost of Purchases			XXX	
Cost of Goods Available for Sale			XXXX	
Less: Merch. Inv., 12/31/10			XXX	
Cost of Goods Sold				XXXX
Gross Profit				XXXX
Operating Expenses				
~~			XXX	
~~			XXX	
~~			XXX	
Total Operating Expenses				XXX
Net Income from Operations				XXX
Other Income				
Rental Income			XXX	
Storage Fees Income			XXX	
Total Other Income				XXX
Other Expenses				
Interest Expense			XXX	XXX
Net Income				$ XXX

(2) STATEMENT OF OWNER'S EQUITY		
Beginning Capital		$XXX
Additional Investments		XXX
Total Investment		XXX
Net Income*	$XXX	
Less: Withdrawals	XXX	
Increase (Decrease) in Capital		XXX
Ending Capital		$XXX

*From the income statement.

(3) BALANCE SHEET			
Assets			
Current Assets			
Cash		$ XXXX	
Accounts Receivable		XXXX	
Merchandise Inventory		XXXX	
Prepaid Insurance		XXX	
Total Current Assets			$ XXXX
Capital Assets			
Store Equipment	$XXXX		
Less: Accumulated Amortization	XXX	XXXX	
Office Equipment	XXXX		
Less: Accumulated Amortization	XXX	XXXX	
Total Capital Assets			XXXX
Total Assets			$XXXX
Liabilities			
Current Liabilities			
Accounts Payable		$XXX	
Accrued Salaries		XXX	
Income Taxes Payable		XXX	
Unearned Revenue		XX	
Mortgage Payable (current portion)		XX	
Total Current Liabilities			$ XXX
Long-Term Liabilities			
Mortgage Payable			XXX
Total Liabilities			XXXX
Owner's Equity			
Capital*			XXXX
Total Liabilities and Owner's Equity			$XXXX

*From statement of owner's equity.

Questions, Classroom Demonstration Exercises, Exercises, and Problems

Discussion Questions and Critical Thinking/Ethical Case

1. Which columns of the worksheet aid in the preparation of the income statement?

2. Explain the components of cost of goods sold.

3. Explain how operating expenses can be broken down into different categories.

4. What is the difference between current assets and capital assets?

5. What is an operating cycle?

6. Why journalize adjusting entries after the formal reports have been prepared?

7. Explain the steps in closing for a merchandising company.

8. Temporary accounts could appear on a post-closing trial balance. Agree or disagree with this statement.

9. What is the purpose of using reversing entries? Are they mandatory? When should they be used?

10. Janet Flynn, owner of Reel Company, plans to apply for a bank loan at Canadian National Bank. Since the company has a lot of debt on its balance sheet, Janet does not plan to show the loan officer the balance sheet. She plans only to take the income statement. Do you feel that this is a sound financial move by Janet? You make the call. Write down your specific recommendations to Janet.

MyAccountingLab

Make the grade with MyAccountingLab! The exercises and problems marked in green can be found on MyAccountingLab at **www.myaccountinglab.com**. You can practise them as often as you want, and many of them feature step-by-step guided solutions to help you find the right answer. You can also find working papers for selected problems in the Multimedia Library on MyAccountingLab.

Classroom Demonstration Exercises

(The forms you need are on page 13-5 of the *Study Guide with Working Papers.*)

Set A
Calculate Net Sales

The revenue section of the income statement

1 (5 min)

1. From the following, calculate net sales:

Purchases	$100
Gross Sales	180
Sales Returns and Allowances	5
Sales Discounts	2
Operating Expenses	15

Calculate Cost of Goods Sold

The cost of goods sold section of the income statement

1 (5 min)

2. From the following, calculate cost of goods sold:

Freight-In	$ 5
Beginning Inventory	20
Ending Inventory	15
Net Purchases	50

Calculate Gross Profit and Net Income

Gross profit and net income on the income statement

1 (10 min)

3. Using Classroom Demonstration Exercises 1 and 2, calculate:
   a. Gross profit
   b. Net income or net loss

Classification of Accounts

Analyzing accounts for the Balance Sheet

1 2 (15 min)

4. Indicate in which of the following four categories each of the 10 accounts listed below belongs:
   a. Current assets
   b. Capital assets
   c. Current liabilities
   d. Long-term liabilities

_____ **1.** Merchandise Inventory	_____ **6.**	Mortgage Payable (Not Current)
_____ **2.** Unearned Rent	_____ **7.**	Income Tax Payable
_____ **3.** Prepaid Insurance	_____ **8.**	Accumulated Amortization
_____ **4.** CPP Payable	_____ **9.**	EI Payable
_____ **5.** Store Equipment	_____ **10.**	Petty Cash

Reversing Entries

Preparing a reversing entry

4 (10 min)

5.

December 31, 2012

Salary Expense		Accrued Salaries	
900	1,200 closing		300 Adj.
Adj. 300			

   a. On January 1, 2013, prepare a reversing entry. On January 8, 2013, journalize the entry to record the payment of salary expense, $900.
   b. What will be the balance in Salary Expense on January 8 (after posting)?

Set B

Calculate Net Sales

The revenue section of the income statement

1 (5 min)

1. From the following, calculate net sales:

Purchases	$ 90
Gross Sales	280
Sales Returns and Allowances	15
Sales Discounts	5
Operating Expenses	25

Calculate Cost of Goods Sold

The cost of goods sold section of the income statement

1 (5 min)

2. From the following, calculate cost of goods sold:

Freight-In	$ 6
Beginning Inventory	12
Ending Inventory	4
Net Purchases	66

Calculate Gross Profit and Net Income

Gross profit and net income on the income statement

1 (10 min)

3. Using Classroom Demonstration Exercises 1 and 2, calculate:

a. Gross profit

b. Net income or net loss

Classification of Accounts

Analyzing accounts for the balance sheet

1 **2** (15 min)

4. Indicate in which of the following four categories each of the 10 accounts listed below belongs:

a. Current assets

b. Capital assets

c. Current liabilities

d. Long-term liabilities

_____ 1. Petty Cash	_____ 6. Mortgage Payable (Current)
_____ 2. Accounts Receivable	_____ 7. Accrued Wages
_____ 3. Prepaid Rent	_____ 8. Accumulated Amortization
_____ 4. WCB Payable	_____ 9. Computer Equipment
_____ 5. Store Supplies	_____ 10. Unearned Rent

Reversing Entries

Preparing a reversing entry

4 (10 min)

5.

December 31, 2012

Salary Expense		Accrued Salaries	
800	1,200 closing		400 Adj.
Adj. 400			

a. On January 1, 2013, prepare a reversing entry. On January 8, 2013, journalize the entry to record the payment of salary expense, $800.

b. What will be the balance in Salary Expense on January 8 (after posting)?

Exercises

(The forms you need are on pages 13-6 and 13-7 of the *Study Guide with Working Papers*.)

Preparing cost of goods sold section

1 (15 min)

13-1. From the following account information, prepare an income statement cost of goods sold section in proper form: Freight-In, $300; Merchandise Inventory, 12/31/14, $9,000; Purchases Discounts, $900; Merchandise Inventory, 12/1/14, $4,000; Purchases, $58,000; Purchases Returns and Allowances, $1,100.

13-2. Give the category, the classification, and the report(s) on which each of the following appears (e.g., **Cash**—asset, current asset, balance sheet):

    a. Accrued Salaries
    b. Accounts Payable
    c. Mortgage Payable
    d. Unearned Legal Fees
    e. Income Tax Payable
    f. Office Equipment
    g. Land

13-3. From the following partial worksheet, journalize the closing entries of December 31 for A. Slow Co.

A. SLOW CO. WORKSHEET FOR YEAR ENDED DECEMBER 31, 2013

Account Titles	Income Statement Dr.	Income Statement Cr.	Balance Sheet Dr.	Balance Sheet Cr.
Cash			193 00	
Merchandise Inventory			450 00	
Prepaid Advertising			561 00	
Prepaid Insurance			30 00	
Office Equipment			1080 00	
Accum. Amort., Office Equip.				210 00
Accounts Payable				258 00
A. Slow, Capital				966 00
Income Summary	362 00	450 00		
Sales		5520 00		
Sales Returns and Allowances	223 00			
Sales Discounts	108 00			
Purchases	2628 00			
Purchases Returns and Allow.		34 00		
Purchases Discounts		51 00		
Salaries Expense	1083 00			
Insurance Expense	696 00			
Utilities Expense	48 00			
Plumbing Expense	57 00			
Advertising Expense	15 00			
Amort. Expense, Office Equip.	30 00			
Accrued Salaries				75 00
	5250 00	6055 00	2314 00	1509 00
Net Income	805 00			805 00
	6055 00	6055 00	2314 00	2314 00

13-4. From the worksheet in Exercise 13-3, prepare the assets section of a classified balance sheet.

13-5. On December 31, 2013, $300 of salaries has been accrued. (Salaries before accrued amount totalled $26,000.) The next payroll to be paid will be on February 3, 2014, for $6,000. Do the following:

    a. Journalize and post the adjusting entry (use T accounts).
    b. Journalize and post the reversing entry on January 1.
    c. Journalize and post the payment of the payroll. Cash has a balance of $15,000 before the payment of payroll on February 3, 2014.

(The forms you need are on pages 13-8 to 13-25 of the *Study Guide with Working Papers.*)

Preparing an income statement from a worksheet
1 (40 min)

13A-1. Prepare a formal income statement from the following partial worksheet for Porter's Pants Co. of Hantsport.

Account Titles	PORTER'S PANTS CO. PARTIAL WORKSHEET FOR YEAR ENDED DECEMBER 31, 2012	
	Income Statement	
	Dr.	Cr.
Income Summary	3 7 0 00	2 6 0 00
Sales		2 8 0 0 00
Sales Returns and Allow.	1 1 9 00	
Sales Discounts	6 4 00	
Purchases	8 7 0 00	
Purchases Returns and Allow.		1 6 7 00
Purchases Discounts		1 2 9 00
Freight-In	1 0 2 00	
Salaries Expense	3 0 0 00	
Insurance Expense	2 0 0 00	
Advertising Expense	1 5 5 00	
Rental Income		2 0 0 00
Rent Expense	2 1 5 00	
Amortization Exp., Store Equip.	2 0 0 00	
Accrued Salaries		
	2 5 9 5 00	3 5 5 6 00
Net Income	9 6 1 00	
	3 5 5 6 00	3 5 5 6 00

Check Figure

Net Income from operations $761

Check Figure (for P13A-2)

Total Assets $18,340

13A-2. Prepare a statement of owner's equity and a classified balance sheet from the partial worksheet for James Company of Penticton (page 598). ***Note:*** Of the Mortgage Payable, $200 is due within one year.

Completing the worksheet; preparing financial reports; journalizing adjusting and closing entries
1 2 (90 min)

13A-3. a. Complete the partial worksheet for Jay's Supplies of Sarnia (p. 599).

b. Prepare an income statement, a statement of owner's equity, and a classified balance sheet. ***Note:*** The amount of the mortgage due the first year is $800.

c. Journalize the adjusting and closing entries.

Check Figure (for P13A-3)

Net Income $4,340

Comprehensive problem: preparing the worksheet; preparing financial reports; journalizing and posting adjusting and closing entries; preparing a post-closing trial balance; journalizing a reversing entry
1 2 3 4 (150 min)

13A-4. Using the ledger balances and additional data shown on the next two pages, do the following for Callahan Lumber of Hinton for the year ended December 31, 2013:

a. Prepare the worksheet.

b. Prepare the income statement, statement of owner's equity, and balance sheet.

c. Journalize and post adjusting and closing entries. (Be sure to put beginning balances in the ledger first.)

d. Prepare a post-closing trial balance.

e. Journalize the reversing entry for wages.

Check Figure

Net Income $4,841

JAMES COMPANY
WORKSHEET
FOR YEAR ENDED DECEMBER 31, 2014

Account Titles	Balance Sheet	
	Dr.	Cr.
Cash	8 5 0 0 00	
Petty Cash	9 0 00	
Accounts Receivable	1 3 5 0 00	
Merchandise Inventory	4 0 0 0 00	
Supplies	3 2 5 00	
Prepaid Insurance	5 0 0 00	
Store Equipment	2 8 0 0 00	
Accum. Amort., Store Eq.		7 0 0 00
Automobile	1 7 0 0 00	
Accum. Amort., Auto		2 2 5 00
Accounts Payable		2 8 0 0 00
Taxes Payable		2 4 0 0 00
Unearned Rent		8 5 0 0 00
Mortgage Payable		4 5 0 0 00
H. James, Capital		7 4 0 0 00
H. James, Withdrawals	1 0 0 00	
Accrued Salaries		6 0 0 00
	1 9 3 6 5 00	2 3 0 7 5 00
Net Loss	3 7 1 0 00	
	2 3 0 7 5 00	2 3 0 7 5 00

Additional Data (for Problem 13A-4)

Account No.

No.	Account	Amount
110	Cash	$ 1,680
111	Accounts Receivable	960
112	Merchandise Inventory	4,550
113	Lumber Supplies	269
114	Prepaid Insurance	218
121	Lumber Equipment	3,000
122	Accumulated Amortization, Lumber Equipment	490
220	Accounts Payable	1,160
221	Accrued Wages	—
330	J. Callahan, Capital	7,352
331	J. Callahan, Withdrawals	3,000
332	Income Summary	—
440	Sales	22,800
441	Sales Returns and Allowances	200
550	Purchases	14,800
551	Purchases Discounts	285
552	Purchases Returns and Allowances	300
660	Wages Expense	2,480
661	Advertising Expense	400
662	Rent Expense	830
663	Amortization Expense, Lumber Equipment	—
664	Lumber Supplies Expense	—
665	Insurance Expense	—

JAY'S SUPPLIES
WORKSHEET
FOR YEAR ENDED DECEMBER 31, 2013

Account Titles	Trial Balance Dr.	Trial Balance Cr.	Adjustments Dr.	Adjustments Cr.	
Cash	2000 00				
Accounts Receivable	3000 00				
Merchandise Inventory	11000 00		(B) 10400 00	11000 00	(A)
Prepaid Insurance	1880 00			500 00	(E)
Equipment	3400 00				
Accum. Amort., Equipment		1080 00		400 00	(D)
Accounts Payable		5080 00			
Unearned Training Fees		2120 00	(C) 320 00		
Mortgage Payable		1200 00			
P. Jay, Capital		10560 00			
P. Jay, Withdrawals	4280 00				
Income Summary			(A) 11000 00	10400 00	(B)
Sales		9580 00			
Sales Returns and Allowances	3200 00				
Sales Discounts	2600 00				
Purchases	63600 00				
Purchases Returns and Allow.		1360 00			
Purchases Discounts		320 00			
Freight-In	2680 00				
Advertising Expense	11400 00				
Rent Expense	10000 00				
Salaries Expense	13600 00				
	132640 00	132640 00			
Training Fees Earned				320 00	(C)
Amort. Exp., Equipment			(D) 400 00		
Insurance Expense			(E) 500 00		
			22620 00	22620 00	

Additional Data (for Problem 13A-4)

a. and b. Merchandise inventory, December 31 $5,420
c. Lumber supplies on hand, December 31 $ 110
d. Insurance expired $ 120
e. Amortization for the year $ 300
f. Accrued wages on December 31 $ 125

(The forms you need are on pages 13-8 to 13-25 of the *Study Guide with Working Papers*.)

Preparing an income statement from a worksheet

1 (40 min)

13B-1. From the partial worksheet shown below, prepare a formal income statement.

PORTER'S PANTS CO.
PARTIAL WORKSHEET
FOR YEAR ENDED DECEMBER 31, 2012

Account Titles	Income Statement	
	Dr.	Cr.
Income Summary	3 00 00	2 95 00
Sales		41 00 00
Sales Returns and Allowances	1 45 00	
Sales Discounts	1 75 00	
Purchases	20 00 00	
Purchases Returns and Allowances		1 75 00
Purchases Discounts		85 00
Freight-In	50 00	
Salaries Expense	3 60 00	
Insurance Expense	2 75 00	
Advertising Expense	1 65 00	
Rental Income		2 30 00
Rent Expense	2 25 00	
Amortization Exp., Store Equipment	1 15 00	
Accrued Salaries		
	38 10 00	48 85 00
Net Income	10 75 00	
	48 85 00	48 85 00

Preparing a statement of owner's equity and a classified balance sheet from a worksheet

1 (40 min)

Completing the worksheet; preparing financial reports; journalizing adjusting and closing entries

1 **2** (90 min)

13B-2. From the partial worksheet for James Company of Penticton shown on page 601, complete:

a. Statement of owner's equity

b. Classified balance sheet

Note: Of the Mortgage Payable, $3,000 is due within one year.

13B-3. Using the information provided on the partial worksheet for Jay's Supplies of Sarnia shown on page 602, your task is to:

a. Complete the worksheet.

b. Prepare the income statement, statement of owner's equity, and classified balance sheet. The amount of the mortgage due the first year is $800.

c. Journalize the adjusting and closing entries.

JAMES COMPANY WORKSHEET FOR YEAR ENDED DECEMBER 31, 2014		
	Balance Sheet	
Account Titles	Dr.	Cr.
Cash	2500 00	
Petty Cash	50 00	
Accounts Receivable	1300 00	
Merchandise Inventory	4250 00	
Supplies	344 00	
Prepaid Insurance	600 00	
Store Equipment	18000 00	
Accum. Amort., Store Eq.		750 00
Automobile	2500 00	
Accum. Amort., Auto		500 00
Accounts Payable		3450 00
Taxes Payable		2100 00
Unearned Rent		11000 00
Mortgage Payable		8000 00
H. James, Capital		10500 00
H. James, Withdrawals	4000 00	
Accrued Salaries		100 00
	33544 00	36400 00
Net Loss	2856 00	
	36400 00	36400 00

Comprehensive problem: preparing the worksheet; preparing financial reports, journalizing and posting adjusting and closing entries; preparing a post-closing trial balance; journalizing reversing entry

①②③④ (150 min)

13B-4. From the following ledger balances and additional data on page 602, do the following for Callahan Lumber of Hinton:

a. Prepare the worksheet.

b. Prepare the income statement, statement of owner's equity, and balance sheet.

c. Journalize and post adjusting and closing entries. (Be sure to put beginning balances in the ledger first.)

d. Prepare a post-closing trial balance.

e. Journalize the reversing entry for wages.

Check Figure

Net Income $3,480

Account No.

110	Cash	$ 1,140
111	Accounts Receivable	1,270
112	Merchandise Inventory	5,600
113	Lumber Supplies	260
114	Prepaid Insurance	117
121	Lumber Equipment	2,600
122	Accumulated Amortization, Lumber Equipment	340
220	Accounts Payable	1,330
221	Accrued Wages	—
330	J. Callahan, Capital	7,562
331	J. Callahan, Withdrawals	3,500
332	Income Summary	—
440	Sales	23,000
441	Sales Returns and Allowances	400
550	Purchases	14,700

JAY'S SUPPLIES
WORKSHEET
FOR YEAR ENDED DECEMBER 31, 2013

Account Titles	Trial Balance Dr.	Trial Balance Cr.	Adjustments Dr.	Adjustments Cr.
Cash	3 0 0 0 00			
Accounts Receivable	3 0 0 0 00			
Merchandise Inventory	11 7 0 0 00		(B) 8 0 0 0 00	11 7 0 0 00 (A)
Prepaid Insurance	1 0 0 0 00			3 5 0 00 (E)
Equipment	5 0 0 0 00			
Accum. Amort., Equipment		1 9 0 0 00		5 0 0 00 (D)
Accounts Payable		2 1 0 0 00		
Unearned Training Fees		1 4 5 0 00	(C) 4 0 0 00	
Mortgage Payable		2 4 0 0 00		
P. Jay, Capital		27 7 5 0 00		
P. Jay, Withdrawals	4 0 0 0 00			
Income Summary			(A) 11 7 0 0 00	8 0 0 0 00 (B)
Sales		100 8 0 0 00		
Sales Returns and Allowances	4 1 0 0 00			
Sales Discounts	2 8 0 0 00			
Purchases	70 0 0 0 00			
Purchases Returns and Allow.		2 0 0 0 00		
Purchases Discounts		1 4 0 0 00		
Freight-In	2 7 0 0 00			
Advertising Expense	8 0 0 0 00			
Rent Expense	8 5 0 0 00			
Salaries Expense	16 0 0 0 00			
	139 8 0 0 00	139 8 0 0 00		
Training Fees Earned				4 0 0 00 (C)
Amortization Exp., Equipment			(D) 5 0 0 00	
Insurance Expense			(E) 3 5 0 00	
			20 9 5 0 00	20 9 5 0 00

Additional Data (for Problem 13B-4)

551	Purchases Discounts	$ 440
552	Purchases Returns and Allowances	545
660	Wages Expense	2,390
661	Advertising Expense	400
662	Rent Expense	840
663	Amortization Expense, Lumber Equipment	—
664	Lumber Supplies Expense	—
665	Insurance Expense	—

Additional Data

a. and b.	Merchandise inventory, December 31	$4,700
c.	Lumber supplies on hand, December 31	$ 80
d.	Insurance expired	$ 70
e.	Amortization for the year	$ 460
f.	Accrued wages on December 31	$ 165

(The forms you need are on pages 13-26 to 13-43 of the *Study Guide with Working Papers*.)

13C-1. From the partial worksheet shown below, prepare a formal income statement for Kate's Pie and Kite Shop of Yarmouth:

KATE'S PIE AND KITE SHOP
PARTIAL WORKSHEET
FOR THE YEAR ENDED SEPTEMBER 30, 2012

Account Titles	Income Statement Dr.	Income Statement Cr.
Income Summary	4 2 5 7 82	5 4 7 7 26
Sales		5 3 5 6 8 25
Sales Returns and Allowances	8 3 4 50	
Sales Discounts	3 4 4 75	
Purchases	2 1 4 5 8 34	
Purchases Returns and Allowances		5 5 8 30
Purchases Discounts		2 3 8 76
Freight-In	4 7 1 58	
Rental Income		1 8 0 0 00
Advertising Expense	1 3 5 2 50	
Amortization Expense, Equipment	8 7 5 00	
Cleaning Expense	2 4 0 0 00	
Insurance Expenses	3 6 8 75	
Rent Expense	7 2 0 0 00	
Salaries Expense	1 1 4 5 8 60	
Utilities Expense	2 5 4 2 60	
	5 3 5 6 4 44	6 1 6 4 2 57
Net Income	8 0 7 8 13	
	6 1 6 4 2 57	6 1 6 4 2 57

13C-2. Using the information provided on the partial worksheet of Toronto's Castell Ceramics Co. shown on page 604, complete:

   a. Statement of owner's equity

   b. Classified balance sheet

   Note: Of the Mortgage Payable, $1,800 is due within one year.

13C-3. From the partial worksheet of Mikolaski Modern Design Company of Brandon, shown on page 605, your task is to:

   a. Complete the worksheet.

   b. Prepare the income statement, statement of owner's equity, and a classified balance sheet. The amount of the mortgage due the first year is $3,600.

   c. Journalize the adjusting and closing entries.

	CASTELL CERAMICS CO. PARTIAL WORKSHEET FOR YEAR ENDED AUGUST 31, 2014	Balance Sheet	
Account Titles		Dr.	Cr.
Petty Cash		75 00	
Cash		11538 62	
Accounts Receivable		18976 30	
Merchandise Inventory		22766 28	
Supplies on Hand		1268 75	
Prepaid Insurance		875 40	
Prepaid GST		2137 64	
Cutting Equipment		18760 00	
Accumulated Amortization, Cutting Equipment			7250 00
Delivery Van		21875 00	
Accumulated Amortization, Delivery Van			4780 00
Accounts Payable			27648 36
GST Collected			2874 62
Unearned Rent			1750 00
Chattel Mortgage Payable, Van			15742 37
B. Castell, Capital			42675 98
B. Castell, Withdrawals		14670 00	
Accrued Salaries			860 00
Net Income			9361 66
		112942 99	112942 99

Comprehensive problem: preparing the worksheet; preparing financial reports; journalizing and posting adjusting and closing entries; preparing a post-closing trial balance; journalizing reversing entry

①②③④ (180 min)

Check Figure

Net Income $3,868

13C-4. Using the ledger balances and additional data shown below and on the next two pages, do the following for Brennan Sales Co. as of December 31, 2012:

a. Prepare the worksheet.

b. Prepare the income statement, statement of owner's equity, and balance sheet.

c. Journalize and post adjusting and closing entries. (Be sure to put beginning balances in the ledger first.)

d. Prepare a post-closing trial balance.

e. Journalize the reversing entry for wages.

Account No.

1100	Cash	$	720
1110	Accounts Receivable		1,620
1120	Merchandise Inventory		5,910
1130	Supplies		430
1140	Prepaid Insurance		238
1150	Prepaid GST		647
1210	Equipment		8,500
1220	Accumulated Amortization, Equipment		1,640

MIKOLASKI MODERN DESIGN COMPANY
WORKSHEET
FOR YEAR ENDED NOVEMBER 30, 2013

Account Titles	Trial Balance Dr.	Trial Balance Cr.	Adjustments Dr.	Adjustments Cr.
Cash in Bank	3465 78			
Petty Cash	50 00			
Accounts Receivable	11575 20			
Merchandise Inventory	16479 22		(B)25672 44	16479 22 (A)
Prepaid Insurance	765 85			257 75 (E)
Prepaid GST	1653 45			
Equipment	21575 00			
Accum. Amortization, Equipment		14762 40		1357 60 (D)
Building	28700 00			
Accum. Amortization, Building		21653 70		647 82 (D)
Accounts Payable		8400 00		
Mortgage Payable		11446 52		
Unearned Rent		2400 00	(C) 800 00	
GST Collected		2167 85		
L. Mikolaski, Capital		32420 22		
L. Mikolaski, Withdrawals	16450 00			
Income Summary			(A) 16479 22	25672 44 (B)
Sales		77327 56		
Sales Discounts and Allowances	358 92			
Purchases	42649 04			
Purchases Returns and Allowances		455 72		
Purchases Discounts		576 22		
Freight-In	632 88			
Advertising Expense	1245 00			
Cleaning Expense	2605 60			
Repair Expense	876 20			
Salaries Expense	21575 60			
Utilities Expense	952 45			
	171610 19	171610 19		
Rental Income Earned				800 00 (C)
Amort. Exp., on Equip. and Building			(D) 2005 42	
Insurance Expense			(E) 257 75	
			45214 83	45214 83

Additional Data (for Problem 13C-4)

2200	Accounts Payable	$ 1,660
2210	Accrued Wages	—
2220	GST Collected	897
3300	W. Brennan, Capital	12,012
3310	W. Brennan, Withdrawals	4,700
3320	Income Summary	—
4400	Sales	31,000
4410	Sales Returns and Allowances	630
5500	Purchases	18,400
5510	Purchases Discounts	730
5520	Purchases Returns and Allowances	276
6600	Wages Expense	4,530
6610	Advertising Expense	690

Additional Data (for Problem 13C-4)

6620	Rent Expense	$1,200
6630	Amortization Expense, Equipment	—
6640	Supplies Expense	—
6650	Insurance Expense	—

a. and b.	Merchandise inventory, December 31	$4,875
c.	Supplies on hand, December 31	$ 190
d.	Insurance expired	$ 68
e.	Amortization for the year	$ 750
f.	Accrued wages on December 31	$ 395
g.	Advertising bill received—due next year (add Prepaid GST of $10)	$ 200

On-the-job Training

(The forms you need are on pages 13-44 to 13-45 of the *Study Guide with Working Papers*.)

Reconstructing an income statement
❶❷ (60 min)

T-1. Chan Company recently had most of its records destroyed in a fire. The information for 2014 was discovered by the bookkeeper.

CHAN COMPANY
GENERAL JOURNAL

Page 2

2014 Date		Description	PR	Dr.	Cr.
Dec.	31	Income Summary	312	3 6 3 0 00	
		Sales Returns and Allowances	420		1 4 0 00
		Sales Discounts	430		3 0 00
		Purchases	500		2 4 0 0 00
		Delivery Expense	600		9 0 00
		Salaries Expense	610		8 4 0 00
		Rent Expense	620		3 0 00
		Office Supplies Expense	630		5 0 00
		Advertising Expense	640		1 0 00
		Amortization Exp., Store Equipment	650		4 0 00
	31	Sales	410	5 5 4 2 00	
		Purchases Discounts	510	1 2 0 00	
		Purchases Returns and Allowances	520	1 0 0 00	
		Income Summary	312		5 7 6 2 00
	31	Income Summary	312	1 7 3 2 00	
		J. Chan, Capital	310		1 7 3 2 00

Beg. Inv. $1,400
End. Inv. 1,000

Assist the bookkeeper in reconstructing an income statement for 2014.

Preparing a classifed balance sheet
❶❷ (60 min)

T-2. Hope Lang, a junior accountant, has the December 31, 2012, trial balance of Gregot Company sitting on her desk. Attached is a memo from her supervisor requesting that a classified balance sheet be prepared. Hope gathers the following data:

a. A physical inventory at December 31 showed $70,000 on hand.

b. The cost of office supplies on hand was $600.

c. Insurance unexpired was $750.

d. Amortization (straight-line) is based on a 25-year life.

Using the following trial balance of Gregot Co., assist Hope with this project. *Hint:* Ending figure for capital is $105,850.

GREGOT COMPANY TRIAL BALANCE DECEMBER 31, 2012		
	Dr.	Cr.
Cash	11 000 00	
Accounts Receivable	38 000 00	
Inventory, January 1	80 000 00	
Prepaid Insurance	2 000 00	
Office Supplies	1 000 00	
Land	17 500 00	
Building	50 000 00	
Accumulated Amortization, Building		10 000 00
Notes Payable		40 000 00
Accounts Payable		30 000 00
G. Gregot, Capital		98 400 00
G. Gregot, Withdrawals	13 000 00	
Income Summary	—	
Retail Sales		32 900 00
Sales Returns and Allowances	21 000 00	—
Sales Discounts	8 000 00	
Purchases	215 500 00	
Purchases Returns and Allowances		11 600 00
Purchases Discounts		4 000 00
Transportation-In	5 000 00	
Advertising Expense	2 500 00	
Wage Expense	55 000 00	
Utilities Expense	3 500 00	
	523 000 00	523 000 00

CONTINUING PROBLEM

Journalizing and posting adjusting entries; preparing the financial statements from a worksheet

1 **2** (60 min)

Using the worksheet in Chapter 12 for Precision Computer Centre, journalize and post the adjusting entries and prepare the financial statements.

(See pages 13-46 to 13-55 in your *Study Guide with Working Papers*.)

The Corner Dress Shop

This Mini Practice Set will help you review all the key concepts of the accounting cycle for a merchandising company along with the integration of payroll.

Betty Loeb took over the business now known as The Corner Dress Shop on January 1, 2013. Betty purchased the business name and all assets except cash from her aunt Marion, who had run it for over 10 years. Certain liabilities were assumed by Betty's new business as part of the deal.

You are the bookkeeper of The Corner Dress Shop and have gathered the following information. It is your task to complete the accounting cycle for March 2013.

The Corner Dress Shop
Trial Balance
February 28, 2013

	Debits	Credits
Cash	30,905.28	
Petty Cash	50.00	
Accounts Receivable	8,291.85	
Office Supplies	624.30	
Prepaid Rent	1,800.00	
Prepaid Insurance	1,000.00	
GST Prepaid	436.34	
Inventory	8,309.00	
Computer and Office Equipment	5,000.00	
Acc. Amort.—Computer & Office Equipment		261.12
Computer Software	739.00	
Acc. Amort.—Computer Software		61.58
Delivery Truck	12,000.00	
Acc. Amort.—Delivery Truck		340.00
Accounts Payable		4,788.99
Income Taxes Payable		1,233.35
EI Payable		376.18
CPP Payable		810.30
Medical Plan Payable		112.00
Charitable Donations Payable		180.00
GST Collected		2,313.65
Rent Received in Advance		600.00
Betty Loeb, Capital		48,078.80
Betty Loeb, Withdrawals	7,300.00	
Sales		59,865.05
Cost of Goods Sold	19,073.38	
Wages Expense	18,120.00	
EI Expense	438.87	
CPP Expense	810.30	
Insurance Expense	200.00	
Rent Expense	1,800.00	
Amort. Expense—Computer & Office Equipment	261.12	
Amort. Expense—Software	61.58	
Amort. Expense—Delivery Truck	340.00	
Accounting Expense	1,460.00	
	119,021.02	119,021.02

Balances in subsidiary ledgers as of February 28:

Accounts Receivable*		Accounts Payable*	
Ronald Co.	$5,538.00	Blew Co.	$2,543.77
Sally's Store	2,753.85	Dresses by Shelley	1,510.22
		Silk Magic	735.00

*Includes 5% GST.

Payroll is paid monthly and employee claim codes are unchanged.

The payroll register for January and February is provided on page 611. In March, salaries are as follows (all deductions are the same unless indicated):

Mel Case	$1,960	New income tax = $124.05 ($70.50 + $53.55)
Jane Holl	2,900	For CPP and EI use 0.0495 and 0.0173
Jackie Moore	4,300	respectively (remember no CPP on amounts less than $291.67 in a month).

Required

(The forms you need are on pages 13-58 to 13-79 of the *Study Guide with Working Papers*.)

a. Set up a general ledger, accounts receivable ledger, accounts payable ledger, auxiliary petty cash record, and payroll register. (Before beginning, be sure to update the ledger accounts on the basis of information given in the trial balance for February 28.)

b. Journalize all transactions during March. Your instructor may ask you to use an inventory ledger and the perpetual method. The practice set can be completed using either method of accounting for inventory. If no specific method is indicated, use the periodic method and change the name of the "Cost of Goods Sold" account to "Purchases."

c. Prepare the payroll register for March.

d. Update the accounts payable and accounts receivable subsidiary ledgers for March.

e. Post to the general ledger.

f. Prepare a trial balance on a worksheet and complete the worksheet as of March 31, 2013.

g. Prepare an income statement, statement of owner's equity, and classified balance sheet.

h. Journalize the adjusting and closing entries.

i. Post the adjusting and closing entries to the ledger.

j. Prepare a post-closing trial balance.

The chart of accounts for The Corner Dress Shop is as follows:

Chart of Accounts

Assets
1110 Cash
1115 Petty Cash
1120 Accounts Receivable
1135 Office Supplies
1140 Prepaid Rent
1145 Prepaid Insurance
1150 GST Prepaid
1210 Inventory
1330 Computer and Office Equipment
1335 Acc. Amort.—Computer & Office Equipment
1340 Computer Software
1345 Acc. Amort.—Computer Software
1350 Delivery Truck
1355 Acc. Amort.—Delivery Truck

Liabilities
2100 Accounts Payable
2200 Accrued Wages
2330 Income Taxes Payable
2335 EI Payable
2340 CPP Payable
2350 Medical Plan Payable
2360 Charitable Donations Payable
2400 GST Collected
2500 Rent Received in Advance

Owner's Equity
3110 Betty Loeb, Capital
3120 Betty Loeb, Withdrawals

Revenue
4110 Sales
4140 Sales Discounts
4150 Sales Returns & Allowances

Cost of Goods Sold
5040 Cost of Goods Sold
5140 Purchases Discounts
5150 Purchases Returns and Allowances

Expenses
5400 Wages Expense
5430 EI Expense
5440 CPP Expense
5500 Postage Expense
5510 Insurance Expense
5520 Cleaning Expense
5530 Rent Expense
5540 Delivery Expense
5550 Amort. Expense—Computer and Office Equipment
5560 Amort. Expense—Software
5570 Amort. Expense—Delivery Truck
5590 Accounting Expense
5595 Miscellaneous Expense

Transactions

2013
March 1   Paid rent cheque No. 121 to Smithstone Realty, $900.00 + GST of 5%.

4   Purchased merchandise from Jones Company, invoice No. JC 59087:
CT-01   50 @ $10 each + GST
CY-01   50 @ $10 each + GST

4   Paid $6 from petty cash fund for doughnuts, voucher No. 01 (miscellaneous expense, NO GST).

4   Sold merchandise on account to Morris Company, invoice No. CD 1081:
PO-01   5 @ $39.99 each + GST
PO-02   5 @ $39.99 each + GST
SK-01   6 @ $89 each + GST

5   Paid Dresses by Shelley $1,510.22 (invoice No. DS 12895), cheque No. 122.

PAYROLL JOURNAL—JANUARY

Employee	Federal Claim	Provincial Claim	Gross Earnings	Cumulative CPP	IT—Fed	IT—Prov	IT—Total
Mel Case	4	4	1860 00	–	57 90	38 05	95 95
Jane Holl	1	1	2900 00	–	263 50	124 45	387 95
Jackie Moore	3	3	4300 00	–	496 00	253 45	749 45
							1233 35
Totals			9060 00				

JANUARY (continued)

	Deductions			Net Pay	Cheque No.
CPP	EI	Health	Charitable		
77 63	32 18	28 00	20 00	1606 24	
129 11	50 17	42 00	30 00	2260 77	
198 41	74 39	42 00	40 00	3195 75	
405 15	156 74	112 00	90 00	7062 75	

PAYROLL JOURNAL—FEBRUARY

Employee	Federal Claim	Provincial Claim	Monthly Salary	Cumulative CPP	IT—Fed	IT—Prov	IT—Total
Mel Case	4	4	1860 00	77 63	57 90	38 05	95 95
Jane Holl	1	1	2900 00	129 11	263 50	124 45	387 95
Jackie Moore	3	3	4300 00	198 41	496 00	253 45	749 45
							1233 35
Totals			9060 00				

FEBRUARY (continued)

	Deductions			Net Pay	Cheque No.
CPP	EI	Health	Charitable		
77 63	32 18	28 00	20 00	1606 24	
129 11	50 17	42 00	30 00	2260 77	
198 41	74 39	42 00	40 00	3195 75	
405 15	156 74	112 00	90 00	7062 75	

March 5 Received payment from Ronald Company, $5,538.00 (invoice No. CD 1078).

7 Paid $12.60 from petty cash fund for postage, voucher No. 02.

8 Paid Blew Company $2,543.77, cheque No. 123 (invoice No. BC 1795).

8 Received payment from Sally's Store (invoice No. CD 1076), $2,753.85.

11 Paid $5 for delivery expense from petty cash fund, voucher No. 03.

12 Received amount due from Morris Company, less 2% discount.

March 12   Purchased from Dresses by Shelley, invoice No. DS 12947:
              CD-01   75 @ $19 each + GST
              CD-02   75 @ $19 each + GST
       12   Paid cleaning service $300 + GST, cheque No. 124 (cheque was issued to Cleaners Inc.).
       13   Purchased from Blew Company, invoice No. BC 1896:
              DI-01   20 @ $48 each + GST
              DS-01   20 @ $80 each + GST
              PO-01   75 @ $12.50 each + GST
              PO-02   75 @ $12.50 each + GST
       15   Sold to Bing Company, invoice No. CD 1082:
              SD-01   5 @ $29.99 each + GST
       15   Paid CRA for income tax, CPP, and EI for February, cheque No. 125. (**Note:** Record as a compound entry in the cash payments journal.)
       15   Paid CRA for GST due (net) end of February, cheque No. 126.*
       15   Paid the Government of Ontario for medical premiums due for the month of February, cheque No. 127.
       18   Cash sales, summarized on invoice No. CD 1083:
              CD-01   30 @ $59.95 each + GST
              CD-02   45 @ $59.95 each + GST
              CT-01   15 @ $30 each + GST
              CY-01   21 @ $30 each + GST
              DI-01   10 @ $150 each + GST
              DS-01   6 @ $250 each + GST
              SK-01   4 @ $89 each + GST
              WD-01   5 @ $750 each + GST
       18   Paid Jones Company amount owed (invoice No. JC 59087), cheque No. 128.
       19   Bing Company returns dresses purchased on invoice No. CD 1082. Credit memo No. 001 was issued.
       19   Paid Dresses by Shelley amount due, less 2% discount (invoice No. DS 12947), cheque No. 129.
       20   Betty Loeb withdrew $1,000 for her personal use, cheque No. 130.
       21   Sold to Sally's Store, invoice No. CD 1084:
              DI-01   10 @ $150 each + GST
              CD-01   10 @ $59.95 each + GST
       26   Purchased from Dresses by Shelley, invoice No. DS 13062:
              CD-01   50 @ $19 each + GST
              CD-02   50 @ $19 each + GST
       28   Paid $10 from the petty cash fund for first aid emergency, voucher No. 04.
       29   Recorded and paid employees, cheques No. 131, No. 132, and No. 133 (cash payments journal).
       29   Issued cheque to Jane Holl for replenishment of petty cash fund, cheque No. 134 (compound entry in cash payments journal).

---

*Two steps are usually needed here. Step 1 (done in the G/L) is to transfer the debit balance in the GST Prepaid account to the GST Collected liability account. The net credit balance, then, is reduced by posting the cheque (recorded in the cash payments journal) that pays this net amount (step 2).

Additional Data

a. and **b.** Ending merchandise inventory is $13,424.

c. Rental income earned, $300 (one month's rent from subletting. Received in advance in February).

d. Amortization (straight-line):

Delivery truck	Residual value = $1,800, expected life of 5 years
Computer	Residual value = $ 300, expected life of 3 years
Computer Software	Residual value = $ 0, expected life of 2 years

e. One month of insurance has expired.

Accounting for Bad Debts

THE BIG PICTURE

Remember back in Chapter 5 where you learned about closing the books? Pretty boring and tedious, right? But necessary all the same—or is it?

Canadian accounting software innovator Q.W. Page Associates doesn't think so, and has a Technical Award of Excellence from *PC Magazine* to back it up.

Its accounting software, NewViews, has become something of a legend because it broke so many rules when it first hit the market. NewViews was designed to combine in a single package a lot of the features formerly available only in a spreadsheet (think Excel) or a database (think Access). Combining these features into what was already an excellent accounting software solution is what earned the company its major award.

How does this relate to not closing the books? The closing process is the accountant's answer to separating a business's lifetime of transactions into yearly "volumes," so that, for example, annual income statements can easily be produced. What Q.W. Page realized is that so long as you are careful to date each transaction correctly, the computer itself can generate annual financial statements with

a minimum of fuss and bother. So why close the books at all?

You can well imagine the reaction of professional accountants everywhere when an upstart small company from Aurora, Ontario, dared to suggest that 500 years of accounting history and practice was no longer needed! Despite a lot of skepticism, the product took hold, and it is used today by companies all over the world, and not just small ones. Customers really like the flexibility in reporting that the product offers, as well as its leading-edge innovation.

One thing NewViews handles with comparative ease is recognizing situations in which one or more customers cannot pay what they owe. While unpleasant, this is a business reality and needs to be handled properly and efficiently. This chapter will provide details so that when you are faced with the need to record such events, you will find it easy to do. Read on.

Source: Q.W. Page Associates Inc. website, www.qwpage.com, accessed September 14, 2007, and June 4, 2010; personal knowledge and training in NewViews of the Canadian author of this book.

1 Using the Bad Debts Expense account and the Allowance for Doubtful Accounts account to record bad debts (pp. 615–617)

2 Using the income statement approach and the balance sheet approach to estimate the amount of bad debts expense (pp. 618–621)

3 Preparing an aging of accounts receivable (p. 620)

4 Writing off an account using the Allowance for Doubtful Accounts account (pp. 622–623)

5 Using the direct write-off method (pp. 623–624)

All companies (Internet-based or not) that sell goods or services on account will eventually have to face the problem of not being able to collect some of the money owed them. Some of the questions that we will be dealing with in this chapter are at what point accounts receivable turn into bad debts (or uncollectible accounts), how and what to charge them to, and how to write them off.

The question of bad debts is important to a company because it affects its credit policy. If a company extends credit too easily, it may end up with too many uncollectible accounts. On the other hand, if the credit policy is too strict, the company will end up losing customers to other firms with easier credit policies—that could mean a loss in profit just as uncollectible debts do.

In the first learning unit, we will look at how bad debts are recorded in the accrual system of accounting.

Learning Unit 14-1

Accrual Accounting and Recording Bad Debts

1 Using the Bad Debts Expense account and the Allowance for Doubtful Accounts account to record bad debts

As we discussed in earlier chapters, in the accrual system of accounting, it is important to match earned revenue with expenses that have been incurred in producing revenue during an accounting period. In a merchandising firm, for example, it is important to match cost of goods sold with revenue earned by the sale of those goods. One expense that is incurred as a result of sales on credit or on account is bad debts expense. The problem is that at the time the sale occurs, one doesn't know whether or not it is going to be uncollectible—this may not be known until much later, possibly a year or so. So how can sales be matched with expenses (in this case, bad debts expense) on the books?

One way to do this is to estimate at the end of the year what percentage of sales already made will turn out to be bad debts. There are several ways of arriving at the percentage, which we will discuss in a later unit, but for the moment, let's say that Abby Ellen Company estimates that 1.6% of its sales of $100,000 for the year 2013 will not be collectible; that means the company expects not to collect $1,600 of the $100,000 owed it from sales made on account.

To handle this situation, we need to introduce two accounts that we haven't dealt with before, Bad Debts Expense and Allowance for Doubtful Accounts. **Bad Debts Expense** is an expense account whose normal balance is a debit; it is a temporary account that is closed to Income Summary at year's end. **Allowance for Doubtful Accounts** is a contra-asset account that accumulates the expected amount of bad debts as of a given date; its normal balance is a credit. It is a permanent account that is *not* closed to Income Summary at the end of the year.

In the case of Abby Ellen Company, an adjustment is made debiting Bad Debts Expense and crediting Allowance for Doubtful Accounts in the amount of $1,600 at the end of 2013. This is the portion of $100,000 owed Abby Ellen that it anticipates will be uncollectible. The journal entry is shown below, along with a transaction analysis chart:

	2013							
	Dec.	31	Bad Debts Expense		1 6 0 0 00			
			Allowance for Doubtful Accounts				1 6 0 0 00	
			Record estimate of bad debts					

Will go on income statement as an operating expense and eventually be closed to Income Summary.

Will go on balance sheet as a reduction of Accounts Receivable. The normal balance of the allowance account is a credit. It will not be closed at the end of the period.

1 Accounts Affected	2 Category	3 ↑↓	4 Rules
Bad Debts Expense	Expenses	↑	Dr.
Allowance for Doubtful Accounts	Asset (Contra)	↑	Cr.

Accounts Receivable
− Allowance for Doubtful Accounts
= Net Realizable Value

We will do write-offs in Learning Unit 14-3. This is only an introductory example.

Think of the Allowance for Doubtful Accounts as a reservoir that is filled before bad debts occur. When the customers' bills are declared uncollectible, this reservoir will be drained. Abby Ellen Company estimates that, out of its $100,000 of credit sales, $1,600 will prove to be uncollectible, but it does not know at this time which accounts will be uncollectible. The allowance account is subtracted from Accounts Receivable, leaving a **net realizable value** of $98,400. Net realizable value is the amount Abby Ellen Company expects to collect. When an account is written off, the net realizable value doesn't change because both the Accounts Receivable and the Allowance for Doubtful Accounts are reduced.

Figure 14-1 shows a partial balance sheet to illustrate how the Allowance for Doubtful Accounts relates to Accounts Receivable.

At some point, a customer's bill must be written off as uncollectible. Let's look at how Abby Ellen Company would write off the account of Jones Moore on June 5, 2014. (The sale was made in 2013.)

WRITING OFF AN ACCOUNT DEEMED UNCOLLECTIBLE

Remember, at the end of 2013, Abby made an adjusting entry increasing Bad Debts Expense (debit) and filling the Allowance for Doubtful Accounts (credit) with the estimate of accounts receivable that would not be collectible.

ABBY ELLEN COMPANY PARTIAL BALANCE SHEET DECEMBER 31, 2013			
Assets			
Current Assets			
Cash			$ 51 4 0 0 00
Accounts Receivable	$100 0 0 0 00		
Less: Allowance for Doubtful Accounts	1 6 0 0 00		98 4 0 0 00
Merchandise Inventory			200 0 0 0 00
Total Current Assets			$349 8 0 0 00

Figure 14-1
Partial Balance Sheet

Now, on June 6, 2014, Jones Moore's account is deemed to be uncollectible in the amount of $200 and the following journal entry is recorded to write off this account:

	2014 June	6	Allowance For Doubtful Accounts		2 0 0 00	
			Accounts Receivable, J. Moore			2 0 0 00
			Writing off J. Moore account			

The bad debts expense was recorded in the old year when credit sales were earned.

Note that we did *not* debit the account Bad Debts Expense since the estimate for this account was made on December 31, 2013 (and applies to that year, not to 2014). When that estimate was made, we did not know which customers' accounts would turn out to be uncollectible, and thus we recorded the estimate in the Allowance for Doubtful Accounts. Now that this debt is identified as uncollectible, we *reduce* or *drain* the allowance account (and reduce the controlling account, Accounts Receivable) and also update the accounts receivable ledger. Note that the customer's account in the subsidiary ledger will be credited just as the controlling account is.

LEARNING UNIT 14-1 REVIEW

AT THIS POINT you should be able to:

◆ Define and explain the purpose of Bad Debts Expense and Allowance for Doubtful Accounts. (pp. 615–616)

◆ Explain why the subsidiary ledger account cannot be updated at the time the Bad Debts Expense is estimated. (p. 617)

◆ Prepare an adjusting entry for Bad Debts Expense. (p. 616)

◆ Explain net realizable value. (p. 616)

◆ Prepare a partial balance sheet showing the relationship between the Allowance for Doubtful Accounts and Accounts Receivable. (p. 616)

◆ Prepare a journal entry to write off a customer's debt in a year following the sale. (p. 617)

Self-Review Quiz 14-1

(The form you need is on page 14-1 of the *Study Guide with Working Papers*.)

Respond true or false to the following:

1. The Bad Debts Expense account should be updated only when the customer's debt is declared to be uncollectible.

2. The Allowance for Doubtful Accounts is a contra-asset account on the balance sheet.

3. Bad Debts Expense is part of cost of goods sold.

4. Net realizable value equals Accounts Receivable less Allowance for Doubtful Accounts.

5. When a customer's debt is written off as uncollectible, the account Allowance for Doubtful Accounts is credited.

Quiz Tip

The Allowance account fills with a credit and drains with a debit.

Solution to Self-Review Quiz 14-1

1. False   **2.** True   **3.** False   **4.** True   **5.** False

Learning Unit 14-2

The Allowance Method: Two Approaches to Estimating the Amount of Bad Debts Expense

2 Using the income statement approach and the balance sheet approach to estimate the amount of bad debts expense

As we said earlier, at the end of the year, a company estimates the percentage of the year's sales that will turn out to be uncollectible accounts, or bad debts. How do we arrive at this estimate? In this learning unit, we will look at two approaches to making an annual estimate of Bad Debts Expense. Figure 14-2 presents an overview. Don't memorize it; we will be covering it step by step.

THE INCOME STATEMENT APPROACH

Bad debts expense is based on a percentage of the dollar volume of net credit sales on the income statement.

Abby Ellen Company uses the **income statement approach** at the end of the year to calculate how much bad debts expense will be associated with this year's sales. On the basis of the past several years, the company has averaged bad debts expense of 1% of net credit sales. From the following facts, let's prepare an adjusting entry to record the bad debts expense that is based on a percentage of net credit sales.

2016	Dr.	Cr.
Sales (all credit)		$95,000
Sales Returns and Allowances	$10,000	
Sales Discounts	5,000	
Accounts Receivable	7,000	
Allowance for Doubtful Accounts		100

Analysis:
Sales	$95,000
– SRA	10,000
– SD	5,000
Net Credit Sales	$80,000

1 Accounts Affected	2 Category	3 ↑↓	4 Rules
Bad Debts Expense	Operating Expenses	↑	Dr.
Allowance for Doubtful Accounts	Asset (Contra)	↑	Cr.

2016					
Dec.	31	Bad Debts Expense	80000		
		Allowance for Doubtful Accounts		80000	
		Record estimate of bad debts			
		(0.01 × $80,000)			

When posted, the allowance account is as follows:

Allowance for Doubtful Accounts

Dr.	Cr.
	100 → Balance *before* adjustment
	800 → Adjustment
	900 → New balance

Figure 14-2
Two Approaches to Estimating
Amount of Bad Debts Expense

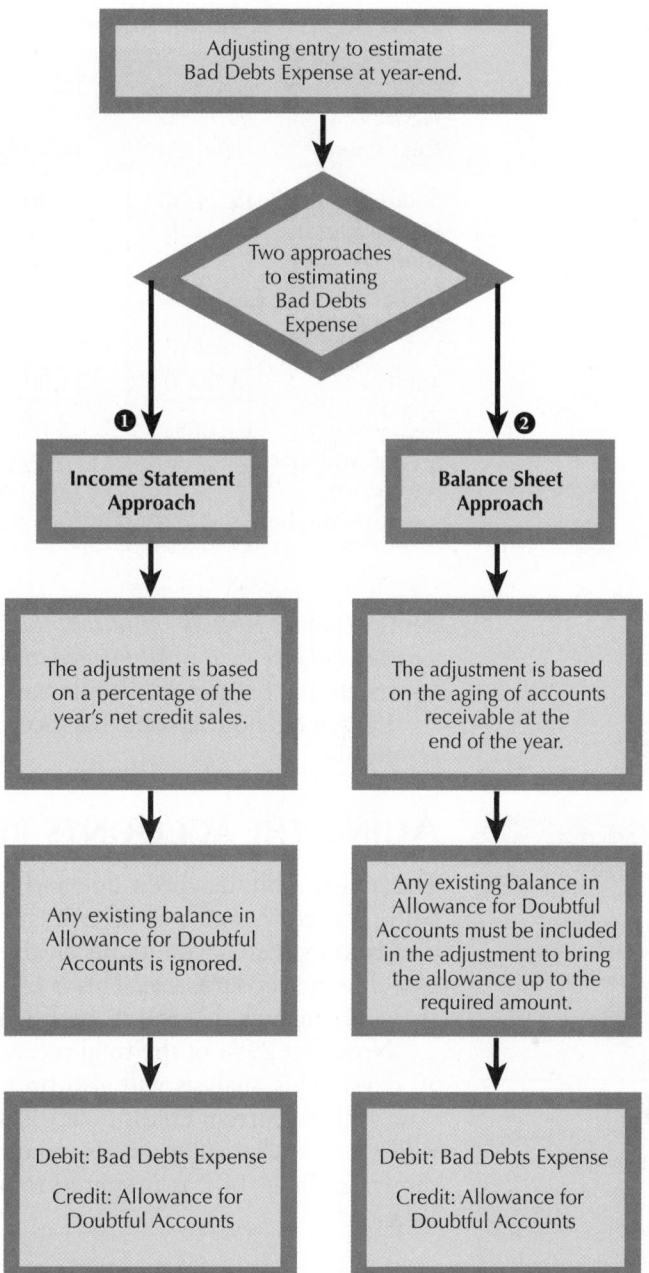

Beginning balance in the
allowance account represents
potential bad debts from
previous periods.

Why? The balance in the Allowance for Doubtful Accounts is ignored since this approach calculates the amount of bad debts expense *for the year* based on a percentage of net credit sales. This approach emphasizes the matching requirements of the income statement. The $100 in the allowance account represents a carryover of potential bad debts from prior years. Thus, the total of $900 represents total potential uncollectible accounts of several periods of sales. If, over the years, the estimate for bad debts expense has been inaccurate, an adjusting entry can be made in the current year's bad debts expense. If this happens, the company may re-evaluate its percentage and use a higher or lower percentage as necessary.

THE BALANCE SHEET APPROACH

In the income statement approach, the estimate for the bad debts expense used a percentage of net credit sales from the income statement as the basis for the adjusting entry. The **balance sheet approach**, on the other hand, uses accounts receivable on the balance sheet as its basis in preparing the adjusting entry to estimate bad

TABLE 14-1 Aging of Accounts Receivable

Name of Customer	Total Balance	Not Yet Due	Days Past Due			
			1–30	31–60	61–90	Over 90
Sarah Elliot	$ 100	$ 100				
Joshua Karras	30			$ 30		
Alan Ledbury	160	160				
John Sullivan	180				$160	$ 20
Sheri Missan	80	80				
Others	6,450	3,260	$2,000	840	40	310
Totals	$7,000	$3,600	$2,000	$870	$200	$330
Percentage of total (rounded to nearest whole number)	100%	51% $\left(\dfrac{\$3,600}{\$7,000}\right)$	29% $\left(\dfrac{\$2,000}{\$7,000}\right)$	12% $\left(\dfrac{\$870}{\$7,000}\right)$	3% $\left(\dfrac{\$200}{\$7,000}\right)$	5% $\left(\dfrac{\$330}{\$7,000}\right)$

debts expense. *Keep in mind that the adjusting entry will take into consideration the existing balance in the Allowance for Doubtful Accounts.* (In the income statement approach, the balance in the allowance account was ignored.)

Let's look now at one balance sheet approach—the aging of the accounts receivable.

3 Preparing an aging of accounts receivable

AGING THE ACCOUNTS RECEIVABLE

Aging classifies uncollected amounts for individual customers according to days past due.

The longer a bill has been due and not paid, the more likely it is not going to be paid. Therefore, one way of estimating the amount of bad debts for the year just past is to look at Accounts Receivable and analyze it according to how many days past due the accounts are. This is called **aging the accounts receivable**. Table 14-1 shows an analysis that the Abby Ellen Company did on December 31, 2016.

Today, with the computer, an analysis of Accounts Receivable can be completed quickly.

Note that 29% of the total receivables for Abby Ellen is past due from one to 30 days. (This analysis will also provide feedback to the credit department as to how well the current credit policy is working.) Now let's look at how the company will estimate what allowance is required to meet probable bad debts. The schedule shown in Table 14-2 is prepared to assist the company in calculating the needed balance.

TABLE 14-2 Balance Required to Meet Probable Bad Debts and Adjusting Entry

	Amount	Estimated Percentage Considered to Be Bad Debts Expense	Amount Needed in Allowance for Doubtful Accounts to Cover Estimated Bad Debts Expense
Not yet due	**$3,600**	3%	($3,600 × 0.03) $108
Days past due			
1–30	2,000	4%	80
31–60	870	10%	87
61–90	200	20%	40
Over 90	330	50%	165
Total accounts receivable	$7,000		
		Total balance required in Allowance for Doubtful Accounts	$480
		Less current balance	−100
		Adjusting entry	$380

In this schedule, Abby Ellen Company has applied a sliding scale of percentages (3, 4, 10, 20, 50), based on *previous experience*, to the total amount of receivables due in each time period. For example, of the $200 overdue by 61–90 days, 20% (or $40) will probably never be paid. Looking at this schedule reveals that Abby Ellen Company needs $480 to cover estimated bad debts. *Currently,* the balance in the allowance account is $100. Thus, to reach a balance of $480, we must adjust the balance of the account by the following adjusting journal entry:

<table>
<tr><td>The balance in the Allowance for Doubtful Accounts is not ignored.</td><td></td><td></td><td></td></tr>
</table>

2016 Dec.	31	Bad Debts Expense	3 8 0 00	
		Allowance for Doubtful Accounts		3 8 0 00
		Record estimate of bad debts		

Bad Debts Expense		Allowance for Doubtful Accounts	
Dr.	Cr.	Dr.	Cr.
380			100 Beginning Balance
			380 Adjustment
			480 New balance in account

Some companies that consider aging too time-consuming may estimate bad debts on the basis of a percentage of total Accounts Receivable.

The desired balance of $480 is now reached. If the Allowance had a *debit* balance of $100 before the adjustment, the amount of the adjusting entry would be $580 credit to Allowance for Doubtful Accounts to arrive at the $480 balance. Once again, the adjustment *must* consider the *existing balance* in the allowance account before the adjusting entry is prepared.

LEARNING UNIT 14-2 REVIEW

AT THIS POINT you should be able to:
- Explain the two approaches to estimating Bad Debts Expense. (pp. 618–621)
- Explain why the balance in Allowance for Doubtful Accounts is ignored when an adjusting entry for bad debts is prepared in the income statement approach. (p. 619)
- Show how to prepare an aging of accounts receivable. (p. 620)
- Explain how the aging of accounts receivable is used to arrive at the balance required in Allowance for Doubtful Accounts. (p. 621)

Self-Review Quiz 14-2

(The form you need is on page 14-1 of the *Study Guide with Working Papers*.)

From the following, prepare an adjusting journal entry for bad debts expense for (1) the income statement approach and (2) the balance sheet approach.

Allowance for Doubtful Accounts		Income Statement Approach
Dr.	Cr.	Net Sales: $160,000
	400	1% of Net Sales

Balance Sheet Approach		Percentage Considered Bad Debts
Not yet due	$4,000	4
Days past due		
1–30	3,000	5
31–60	400	10
Over 60	5,000	30

Solution to Self-Review Quiz 14-2

(1)	Dec.	31	Bad Debts Expense		1 6 0 0 00	
			Allowance for Doubtful Accounts			1 6 0 0 00
			(0.01 × $160,000)			
(2)		31	Bad Debts Expense		1 4 5 0 00	
			Allowance for Doubtful Accounts			1 4 5 0 00
			$4,000 × 0.04 = $ 160			
			3,000 × 0.05 = 150			
			400 × 0.10 = 40			
			5,000 × 0.30 = 1,500			
			$1,850			

Quiz Tip

Note allowance adjusted:
$1,850 − $400 = $1,450

Learning Unit 14-3
Writing Off Uncollectible Accounts

4 Writing off an account using the Allowance for Doubtful Accounts account

This unit will look at two ways to write off uncollectible accounts: one using the Allowance for Doubtful Accounts, the other using the direct write-off method.

WRITING OFF AN ACCOUNT USING THE ALLOWANCE FOR DOUBTFUL ACCOUNTS

Let's assume that on March 18, 2017, the Abby Ellen Company determines that the account of Jill Sullivan for $900 is uncollectible. (The sale to Jill Sullivan was made in 2015.) This means that this Accounts Receivable amount should no longer be considered an asset and should be written off. The following journal entry reduces Allowance for Doubtful Accounts and reduces the Accounts Receivable controlling account as well as the accounts receivable subsidiary ledger.

2017					
Mar.	18	Allowance for Doubtful Accounts		9 0 0 00	
		Accounts Receivable, Jill Sullivan			9 0 0 00
		Wrote off Sullivan account			

Note the following key points:

1. This journal entry does *not* affect any expenses. Remember, Bad Debts Expense is *not* affected when an account is finally written off under this method. The estimate for bad debts expense was recorded in previous years before the bad debt actually occurred.

2. If more than one customer is written off, a compound entry can be used, debiting Allowance for Doubtful Accounts for the total and crediting each individual account.

3. The net realizable value of Accounts Receivable is unchanged. Let's prove this:

	Balances before the Write-Off		*Balances after the Write-Off*
Accounts Receivable	$12,000	$900 write-off →	$11,100
Less: Allowance for Doubtful Accounts	2,000	$900 drain →	1,100
Estimated realizable value (what to expect to collect)	$10,000	No change →	$10,000

Let's look now at what would happen on the books of Abby Ellen Company if Jill Sullivan should pay part or all of the debt in the future.

Let's assume that Jill Sullivan is able to pay off half of her debt and sends a cheque to Abby Ellen Company on February 2, 2018. (Keep in mind the fact that her account was written off on March 18, 2017, and the original sale was made in 2015.) To record this, Abby Ellen Company reverses, in part, the entry that was made to write off the account in the amount expected to be recovered and records the amount received from Jill. The following are the journal entries to record the recovery of $450 out of the original amount of $900:

2018				
Feb.	2	Accounts Receivable, Jill Sullivan	450 00	
		Allowance for Doubtful Accounts		450 00
		Restores collectible portion		
	2	Cash	450 00	
		Accounts Receivable, Jill Sullivan		450 00
		Records payment received		

Reinstates the account

Records the amount received

The reason we record both a debit and a credit to Accounts Receivable is that it provides a clear picture of the transactions involving Jill Sullivan. If the company is considering giving credit again to Jill Sullivan, these previous records could be of assistance in determining how much credit, if any, should be extended. Note how the first entry partially reinstates the account and the second entry records the cash received. In fact, the second entry would be made in the cash receipts journal.

Let's now look at another method of handling bad debts expense, the direct write-off method.

THE DIRECT WRITE-OFF METHOD

5 Using the direct write-off method

The direct write-off method does not fulfill the matching principle.

When a company cannot reasonably estimate its bad debts expense, it may use the **direct write-off method**. Using this method, an account that is determined to be uncollectible would be directly written off to this year's Bad Debts Expense account without regard to when the original sale was made. In this method, the

Allowance for Doubtful Accounts is not used since no adjustment is needed at the end of the year to estimate bad debts expense. Let's replay the Jill Sullivan write-off as well as the recovery so that we can make comparisons between the Allowance for Doubtful Accounts method and the direct write-off method. In the recovery, we will see a new account title, Bad Debts Recovered. Think of it as a revenue account found in the Other Income section of an income statement.

<table>
<tr><td>2017
Mar.</td><td>18</td><td>Bad Debts Expense</td><td></td><td>9 0 0 00</td><td></td></tr>
<tr><td></td><td></td><td>Accounts Receivable, Jill Sullivan</td><td></td><td></td><td>9 0 0 00</td></tr>
<tr><td></td><td></td><td>Wrote off account</td><td></td><td></td><td></td></tr>
</table>

<table>
<tr><td>2018
Feb.</td><td>2</td><td>Accounts Receivable, Jill Sullivan</td><td></td><td>4 5 0 00</td><td></td></tr>
<tr><td></td><td></td><td>Bad Debts Recovered</td><td></td><td></td><td>4 5 0 00</td></tr>
<tr><td></td><td></td><td>Restores collectible portion</td><td></td><td></td><td></td></tr>
<tr><td></td><td>2</td><td>Cash</td><td></td><td>4 5 0 00</td><td></td></tr>
<tr><td></td><td></td><td>Accounts Receivable, Jill Sullivan</td><td></td><td></td><td>4 5 0 00</td></tr>
<tr><td></td><td></td><td>Records payment received</td><td></td><td></td><td></td></tr>
</table>

Writing off Jill Sullivan on March 18, 2017: Note that Allowance for Doubtful Accounts is not used.

Recovery of half the amount owed by Jill Sullivan on February 2, 2018: Note that Bad Debts Recovered replaces Allowance for Doubtful Accounts.

On the balance sheet, Accounts Receivable is recorded at gross. No allowance account or realizable amount is used.

Bad Debts Recovered	Other Revenue	↑	Cr.

In the direct write-off method, when the amount is written off, Allowance for Doubtful Accounts is not used. Rather, the debit is to Bad Debts Expense. On the recovery in years following the sale, instead of crediting Allowance for Doubtful Accounts, the direct method credits **Bad Debts Recovered** (an account in the Other Revenue category). This in effect increases the revenue and puts the Accounts Receivable back on the books. If recovery is made in the same year (let's say, on May 2), you just reverse the entry you made to write off the account:

<table>
<tr><td>2017
May</td><td>2</td><td>Accounts Receivable, Jill Sullivan</td><td></td><td>4 5 0 00</td><td></td></tr>
<tr><td></td><td></td><td>Bad Debts Expense</td><td></td><td></td><td>4 5 0 00</td></tr>
</table>

INSIGHT INTO INCOME TAX REGULATIONS

For tax purposes, the law permits the bad debt reserve method of deducting bad debts. Since the direct write-off method does vary from generally accepted accounting principles, tax law follows the *CICA Handbook* and allows the deduction of an annual reserve.

Students should also be aware that the GST/HST rules permit "recovery" of any GST or HST on an amount written off. Details of how to accomplish this are beyond the scope of this textbook, but industrious and inquisitive students will be able to find details on the Internet.

LEARNING UNIT 14-3 REVIEW

AT THIS POINT you should be able to:

◆ Write off an account using the Allowance for Doubtful Accounts method. (pp. 623–624)

◆ Explain why net realizable value is unchanged after a write-off is complete. (p. 623)

◆ Prepare journal entries to recover entire or partial amounts that were once declared uncollectible. (p. 623)

◆ Explain the direct write-off method and prepare appropriate journal entries for write-off and recovery. (pp. 623–624)

Self-Review Quiz 14-3

(The form you need is on page 14-1 of the *Study Guide with Working Papers*.)

Respond true or false to the following:

1. When an account is written off using the Allowance for Doubtful Accounts method in a period following the sale, the result is a debit to Bad Debts Expense and a credit to Accounts Receivable.
2. The direct write-off method will sometimes use the Allowance for Doubtful Accounts account.
3. When an account is written off (using the Allowance for Doubtful Accounts method), net realizable value is unchanged.
4. Bad Debts Recovered is an asset.
5. A debit balance in Allowance for Doubtful Accounts indicates that the estimate for Bad Debts Expense was too low.

Solution to Self-Review Quiz 14-3

1. False   **2.** False   **3.** True   **4.** False   **5.** True

SUMMARY OF KEY POINTS

Learning Unit 14-1

1. If accrual accounting is used, bad debts expense should be recognized in the year in which the sale was made even though the actual write-off may not yet have taken place.

2. Bad debts expense is an expense found on the income statement.

3. The Allowance for Doubtful Accounts is a contra-asset account found on the balance sheet that accumulates the amount of estimated uncollectibles before they are actually written off.

4. Net realizable value equals Accounts Receivable minus Allowance for Doubtful Accounts.

5. When an account is written off, the Allowance for Doubtful Accounts is debited and Accounts Receivable is credited (along with the subsidiary ledger account).

Learning Unit 14-2

1. The two approaches to estimating bad debts expense are the income statement approach and the balance sheet approach.

2. The income statement approach estimates bad debts expense on the basis of a percentage of net sales. (Some companies use credit sales; some use total sales.) The balance is ignored in Allowance for Doubtful Accounts when the bad debts expense is estimated from sales of the period.

3. The balance sheet approach estimates the balance required in Allowance for Doubtful Accounts by aging the accounts receivable. The balance in the allowance account will have to be adjusted based on the anticipated default rate determined by the aging of the receivables.

Learning Unit 14-3

> After the write-off, net realizable value is unchanged.

1. When an account is written off (using the allowance account) in years following the sale, the result is to debit Allowance for Doubtful Accounts and credit Accounts Receivable. Do not debit Bad Debts Expense as it has already been debited in the year in which the sale was made.

2. When an uncollectible account has been written off and is now recovered, the entry reverses the original write-off by debiting Accounts Receivable and crediting Allowance for Doubtful Accounts. Then the cash received is debited to the Cash account and credited to Accounts Receivable.

3. The direct write-off method will recognize the bad debts expense only when the customer account is declared uncollectible. The direct method does *not* use the Allowance for Doubtful Accounts account since no estimate is made for bad debts. This method does not follow the matching principle in accrual accounting.

4. Bad Debts Recovered is classified as Other Revenue when a customer account is reinstated after being written off in the direct method.

BLUEPRINT SUMMARY OF RECORDING BAD DEBTS EXPENSE, WRITE-OFFS, AND RECOVERY

Situation	Allowance for Doubtful Accounts Method		Direct Write-Off Method
Adjusting entry is made to record estimated uncollectible accounts.	*A. Income Statement Approach*	*B. Balance Sheet Approach*	None

	Bad Debts Expense XX
	  Allowance for Doubtful Accounts XX
		Bad Debts Expense XX
		  Allowance for Doubtful Accounts XX	

	Based on percentage of net sales Balance in allowance account is ignored.	Aging of Accounts Receivable determines amount needed in allowance account. Balance in allowance account is adjusted.	

Receivable is determined to be uncollectible.	Allowance for Doubtful Accounts XX
	  Accounts Receivable XX
		Allowance for Doubtful Accounts XX
		  Accounts Receivable XX
			Bad Debts Expense XX
			  Accounts Receivable XX

Bad debts are recovered.	Accounts Receivable XX
	  Allowance for Doubtful Accounts XX
	Cash XX
	  Accounts Receivable XX
		Accounts Receivable XX
		  Allowance for Doubtful Accounts XX
		Cash XX
		  Accounts Receivable XX
			Accounts Receivable XX
			  Bad Debts Recovered* XX
			Cash XX
			  Accounts Receivable XX

Bal. sheet updated.	Shows net realizable value.		Does not show net realizable value.

*Used if recovery is not in the same year as the write-off.

KEY TERMS

Aging the accounts receivable The procedure of classifying accounts of individual customers by age group where age is the number of days elapsed since the due date (p. 620)

Allowance for Doubtful Accounts A contra-asset account that is subtracted from the Accounts Receivable. This account accumulates the *expected* amount of uncollectibles as of a given date. (p. 615)

Bad Debts Expense The operating expense account that estimates the amount of credit sales in a given accounting period that will probably not be collectible when the allowance method is used. For the direct write-off method, this account would be the actual amount written off. (p. 615)

Bad Debts Recovered When an account receivable has been written off and is recovered, this account, which is in the Other Revenue category, is credited in the direct write-off method if the recovery is in a year *following* the write-off. (p. 624)

Balance sheet approach A method used to calculate the amount *required* in Allowance for Doubtful Accounts to cover expected uncollectibles. This method is based on the Accounts Receivable account and the aging process. The adjustment to Allowance for Doubtful Accounts will bring the new balance of that account to the new required level. (p. 619)

Direct write-off method The method of writing off uncollectibles when it is determined that an account is uncollectible, thus not using the Allowance for Doubtful Accounts account. This method does not follow the matching principle of accrual accounting. (p. 623)

Income statement approach A method that estimates the amount of bad debts expense that will result on the basis of a percentage of net credit sales for the period. The amount of the expected bad debts is added to the existing balance of Allowance for Doubtful Accounts. (p. 618)

Net realizable value The amount (Accounts Receivable – Allowance for Doubtful Accounts) that is expected to be collected. (p. 616)

QUESTIONS, CLASSROOM DEMONSTRATION EXERCISES, EXERCISES, AND PROBLEMS

Discussion Questions and Critical Thinking/Ethical Case

1. Explain the matching principle in relationship to recording bad debts expense.

2. What is the purpose of the Allowance for Doubtful Accounts account?

3. What is net realizable value?

4. When an account receivable is written off, Bad Debts Expense must be debited. True or false? Discuss.

5. Explain why Allowance for Doubtful Accounts is a contra-asset account.

6. Recording bad debts expense is a closing entry. True or false? Defend your position.

7. The income statement approach used to estimate bad debts is based on Accounts Receivable on the balance sheet. Accept or reject. Why?

8. In which approach is the balance of Allowance for Doubtful Accounts considered when the estimate of bad debts expense is made? Explain.

9. Why would a company age its accounts receivable?

10. Using the Allowance for Doubtful Accounts method, what journal entries would be made to write off an account as well as to later record the recovery of the receivable?

11. Why doesn't net realizable value change when an account is written off using the allowance account?

12. What is the purpose of using the direct write-off method?

13. Explain the purpose of the Bad Debts Recovered account.

14. Pete Sazich, the accountant for Moore Company, believes that all bad debts will be eliminated if credit transactions are done by credit card. He also believes that the cost of credit card charges should be added on to the price of the goods. Pete feels that in the future the allowance method will be totally eliminated. You make the call. Write a letter stating your opinion regarding this matter to Pete's boss.

MyAccountingLab

Make the grade with MyAccountingLab! The exercises and problems marked in green can be found on MyAccountingLab at **www.myaccountinglab.com**. You can practise them as often as you want, and many of them feature step-by-step guided solutions to help you find the right answer. You can also find working papers for selected problems in the Multimedia Library on MyAccountingLab.

Classroom Demonstration Exercises

(The forms you need are on pages 14-2 and 14-3 of the *Study Guide with Working Papers*.)

Set A

Categorizing Accounts

Analyzing transactions
1 (5 min)

1. **a.** Complete the following transactional analysis chart:

Accounts Affected	Account Category	↓ ↑	Rules of Dr. and Cr.
Bad Debts Expense			
Allowance for Doubtful Accounts			

b. On which financial statement will each title be recorded?

Allowance Method

Allowance for doubtful accounts is a contra-asset account
2 (10 min)

2. Explain under which method the balance in the Allowance account is ignored. Give an example.

Journalize Adjusting Entries for Income Statement and Balance Sheet Approaches

Journalizing adjusting entries for bad debts
2 (15 min)

3. Given that the balance in the Allowance for Doubtful Accounts is $300 credit, prepare adjusting entries for bad debts based on the following assumptions:

   a. Bad debts are to be 5% of net credit sales, or $700.

   b. Bad debts should be $600 on the basis of the aging of Accounts Receivable.

Writing Off Uncollectible Accounts and Reinstatement—Allowance Method

The allowance for doubtful accounts method
4 (15 min)

4. Journalize entries for the following situations (assume allowance method):

   Situation 1: Wrote off Mia Kaminsky as a bad debt two years after the sale for $100.

   Situation 2: Reinstated Mia Kaminsky, who sent in her past due amount.

Writing Off an Uncollectible Account and Reinstatement—Direct Write-Off Method

The direct write-off method
5 (15 min)

5. Journalize entries for the following situations (assume direct write-off method).

   Situation 1: Wrote off Mia Kaminsky as a bad debt two years after the sale of $100.

   Situation 2: Reinstated Mia Kaminsky, who sent in her past due amount two years after it had been written off.

Set B

Categorizing Accounts

Analyzing transactions
1 (5 min)

1. a. Complete the following transactional analysis chart:

Accounts Affected	Account Category	↓	↑	Rules of Dr. and Cr.
Bad Debts Expense				
Accounts Receivable				

   b. On which financial statement will each title be recorded?

   c. Which account is temporary? Which account is permanent?

Allowance Method

Two approaches to making an estimate of bad debts: the income statement approach and the balance sheet approach
2 (15 min)

2. Complete the table:

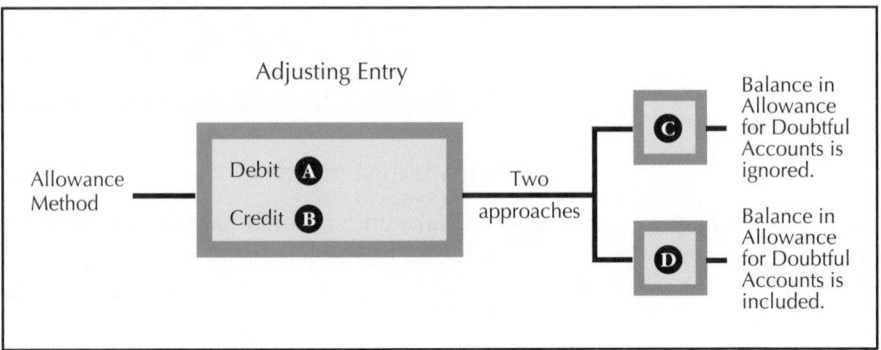

Journalize Adjusting Entries for Income Statement and Balance Sheet Approaches

Journalizing adjusting entries for bad debts
2 (15 min)

3. Given that the balance in the Allowance for Doubtful Accounts is $100 credit, prepare adjusting entries for bad debts based on the following assumptions:

   a. Bad debts are to be 5% of net credit sales, or $400.

   b. Bad debts should be $400 on the basis of the aging of Accounts Receivable.

Writing Off Uncollectible Accounts and Reinstatement— Allowance Method

The allowance for doubtful accounts method
4 (15 min)

4. Journalize entries for the following situations (assume allowance method):

   Situation 1: Wrote off Bill Allen as a bad debt two years after the sale for $50.

   Situation 2: Reinstated Bill Allen, who sent in his past due amount.

Writing Off an Uncollectible Account and Reinstatement— Direct Write-Off Method

The direct write-off method
1 (20 min)

5. Journalize entries for the following situations (assume direct write-off method).

   Situation 1: Wrote off Bill Allen as a bad debt two years after the sale of $50.

   Situation 2: Reinstated Bill Allen, who sent in his past due amount two years after it had been written off.

Exercises

(The forms you need are on pages 14-4 and 14-5 of the *Study Guide with Working Papers*.)

Preparing a partial balance sheet with Allowance for Doubtful Accounts
1 (20 min)

14-1. Robson Co. has requested that you prepare a partial balance sheet on December 31, 2012, from the following: Cash, $115,000; Petty Cash, $60; Accounts Receivable, $60,000; Bad Debts Expense, $40,000; Allowance for Doubtful Accounts, $12,000; Merchandise Inventory, $18,000.

Calculating bad debts expense with the income statement approach
2 (20 min)

14-2. Given the information in the T accounts below, journalize the adjusting entry on December 31, 2012, for bad debts expense, which is estimated to be 4% of net sales. The income statement approach is used.

Accounts Receivable	Sales	Sales Returns and Allowances
30,000		110,000	500	

Sales Discounts	Allowance for Doubtful Accounts
9,500		5,000

Calculating bad debts expense using the balance sheet approach
2 (20 min)

14-3. Assuming that in Exercise 14-2 the balance sheet approach is used, prepare a journalized adjusting entry for bad debts expense. Aging of accounts receivable indicates that an $8,000 balance in the allowance account will be needed to cover bad debts.

Journalizing adjustment for bad
debts as well as reinstatement by
allowance method; comparison
with direct write-off method
2 4 5 (20 min)

14-4. The Austin Co., which uses an Allowance for Doubtful Accounts, had the
following transactions in 2013 and 2014:

2013
Dec.   31   Recorded Bad Debts Expense of $12,000.

2014
Apr.   1   Wrote off Angie Ring account of $4,000 as uncollectible.
June   3   Wrote off Mike Catuc account of $3,000 as uncollectible.

2014
Aug.   7   Recovered $500 from Mike Catuc.

   a. Journalize the transactions. (The Austin Co. uses the income statement
   approach to estimate bad debts.)
   b. Journalize how Austin Co. would record the Mike Catuc bad debt situation if the direct write-off method were used.

Journalizing adjustments for bad
debts expense on the basis of
(1) percentage of sales, (2) aging
of accounts receivable with
balance of Allowance for
Doubtful Accounts a debit
balance
3 4 (20 min)

14-5. Rowe Company had credit sales of $200,000 during 2014. The balance in the
Allowance for Doubtful Accounts is a $1,000 debit balance. Journalize the
bad debts expense for December 31, using each of the following methods:

   a. Bad debts expense is estimated at 0.5% of credit sales.
   b. The aging of accounts receivable indicates that $2,200 will be required in
   Allowance for Doubtful Accounts account to cover bad debts expense.

Group A Problems

(The forms you need are on pages 14-6 to 14-10 of the *Study Guide with Working
Papers*.)

The income statement approach:
journalizing bad debts expense
and writing off accounts
1 2 (25 min)

14A-1. Yuen Co. of Windsor has requested that you prepare journal entries from
the following (this company uses the Allowance for Doubtful Accounts
method based on the income statement approach).

2012
Dec.   31   Recorded Bad Debts Expense of $13,000.

2013
Jan.   7   Wrote off Gene Smore's account of $800 as uncollectible.
Mar.   5   Wrote off Paul Jane's account of $600 as uncollectible.
July   9   Recovered $300 from Paul Jane.
Aug.   19   Wrote off Bob Seager's account of $1,300 as uncollectible.
       23   Wrote off Jill Neuman's account of $750 as uncollectible.
Nov.   19   Recovered $400 from Bob Seager.

Check Figure

Aug. 23
Dr. Allowance for
   Doubtful Accounts $750
Cr. Accounts Receivable,
   Jill Neuman $750

The balance sheet approach:
aging analysis and journalizing of
bad debts expense
1 2 (30 min)

14A-2. Given the additional data in the table below:

   a. Prepare the adjusting journal entry for bad debts expense on
   December 31, 2013.
   b. Prepare a partial balance sheet on December 31, 2013, showing how
   net realizable value is calculated.
   c. If the balance in Allowance for Doubtful Accounts was a $300 debit
   balance, journalize the adjusting entry for bad debts expense on
   December 31, 2013.

Balances: Cash, $30,000; Accounts Receivable, $152,000; Allowance for
Doubtful Accounts, $300 credit; Inventory, $12,000.

Additional Data

Alvie Co.
December 31, 2013

	Amount	Estimated Percentage Considered to Be Bad Debts Expense	Estimated Amount Needed in Allowance for Doubtful Accounts
Not yet due	$130,000	1	_____
0–60	9,000	5	_____
61–180	8,000	20	_____
Over six months	5,000	40	_____
	$152,000		

The direct write-off method
2 5 (25 min)

Check Figure

Dec. 8
Dr. Bad Debts Expense $285
Cr. Accounts Receivable,
   J. Miller $285

14A-3. T. J. Rack Company of Hope uses the direct write-off method for recording Bad Debts Expense. At the beginning of 2014, Accounts Receivable has a $119,000 balance. Journalize the following transactions for T.J. Rack:

2014
Mar.   11   Wrote off S. Rose's account for $1,800.
Apr.   14   Wrote off P. Soy's account for $750.

2015
Nov.   6   P. Soy paid bad debt of $750 that was written off April 14, 2014.
Dec.   8   Wrote off J. Miller's account as uncollectible, $285.
Dec.   11   Wrote off D. Lovejoy's account for $375 due from sales made on account in 2013.

Journalizing and posting adjustments for bad debts expense and write-offs and recovery based on balance sheet approach; preparing partial balance sheet
2 4 (60 min)

Check Figure

Total Current Assets $272,360

14A-4. Simon Company of Bathurst completed the following transactions:

2013
Jan.   8   Sold merchandise on account to Ray's Supply, $1,500.
        15   Wrote off the account of Pete Runnels as uncollectible because of his death, $600.
Mar.   15   Received $400 from Roland Co., whose account had been written off in 2011. The account was reinstated and the collection recorded.
Apr.   9   Received 10% of the $4,000 owed by Lane Drug. The remainder was written off as uncollectible.
June   14   The account of Mel's Garage was reinstated for $1,200 (amount received). The account was written off three years ago.
Oct.   18   Prepared a compound entry to write the following accounts off as uncollectible: Jane's Diner, $200; Keen Auto, $400; Ralph's Hardware, $600.
Nov.   12   Sold merchandise on account to J.B. Rug, $1,900.
Dec.   31   On the basis of an aging of accounts receivable, it was estimated that $7,000 will be uncollectible out of a total of $160,000 in Accounts Receivable.
        31   Closed Bad Debts Expense to Income Summary.

Additional Data

	Account No.	Balance	Dr./Cr.
Allowance for Doubtful Accounts	114	$4,100	Cr.—Jan. 1, 2013
Income Summary	312	—	
Bad Debts Expense	612	—	

Required

a. Journalize the transactions.

b. Post to Allowance for Doubtful Accounts, Income Summary, or Bad Debts Expense as needed. (Be sure to record the beginning balance in the allowance account in your workbook.)

c. Prepare a current assets section of the balance sheet. Ending balances needed: Cash, $13,000; Accounts Receivable, $160,000; Office Supplies, $2,110; Merchandise Inventory, $103,000; Prepaid Rent, $1,250; and your calculated balance for Allowance for Doubtful Accounts.

Group B Problems

(The forms you need are on pages 14-6 to 14-10 of the *Study Guide with Working Papers*.)

The income statement approach: journalizing bad debts expense and writing off accounts

❶❷ (25 min)

Check Figure

Aug. 23
Dr. Allowance for
   Doubtful Accounts $950

Cr. Accounts Receivable,
   Jim O'Reilly $950

14B-1. Yuen Co. of Windsor has requested that you prepare journal entries from the following (this company uses the Allowance for Doubtful Accounts method based on the income statement approach):

2012
Dec. 31   Recorded bad debts expense of $14,800.

2013
Jan.   8   Wrote off Woody Tree's account of $1,200 as uncollectible.
Mar.   5   Wrote off Jim Lantz's account of $600 as uncollectible.
July   9   Recovered $600 from Jim Lantz.
Aug. 20   Wrote off Mabel Hest's account of $750 as uncollectible.
      23   Wrote off Jim O'Reilly's account of $950 as uncollectible.
Nov. 19   Recovered $500 from Mabel Hest.

The balance sheet approach: aging analysis and journalizing of bad debts expense

❶❷ (30 min)

Check Figure

Net Realizable Value
$166,000

14B-2. Given the information below, and assuming the following balances: Cash, $42,000; Accounts Receivable, $173,000; Allowance for Doubtful Accounts, $400 credit; Inventory, $12,000,

a. Prepare on December 31, 2013, the adjusting journal entry for bad debts expense.

b. Prepare a partial balance sheet on December 31, 2013, showing how net realizable value is calculated.

c. If the balance in Allowance for Doubtful Accounts were a $400 debit balance, journalize the adjusting entry for bad debts expense on December 31, 2013.

Additional Information

Alvie Co.
December 31, 2013

	Amount	Estimated Percentage Considered to Be Bad Debts Expense	Estimated Amount Needed in Allowance for Doubtful Accounts
Not yet due	$150,000	2	_____
0–60	10,000	6	_____
61–180	9,000	20	_____
Over six months	4,000	40	_____
	$173,000		

14B-3. T.J. Rack Company of Hope uses the direct write-off method for recording bad debts expense. At the beginning of 2014, Accounts Receivable has an $88,000 balance. Journalize the following transactions for T. J. Rack:

2014

Mar. 11 Wrote off Jill Diamond's account for $1,950.

Apr. 14 Wrote off Buffy Hall's account for $900.

2015

Nov. 6 Buffy Hall paid debt of $900 that was written off April 14, 2014.

Dec. 10 Wrote off Joe Francis's account as uncollectible, $880.

      15 Wrote off Joe Martin's account for $410 from sales made on account in 2013.

Journalizing and posting
adjustments for bad debts
expense and write-offs and
recovery based on balance sheet
approach; partial balance sheet
prepared
2 4 (60 min)

14B-4. Simon Company of Bathurst completed the following transactions:

2013

Jan. 8 Sold merchandise on account to Lowe's Supply, $1,900.

      15 Wrote off the account of Kevin Reese as uncollectible because of his death, $700.

Mar. 14 Received $300 from J. James, whose account had been written off in 2012. The account was reinstated and the collection recorded.

Apr. 9 Received 20% of the $5,000 owed by Long Drug. The remainder was written off as uncollectible.

June 13 The account of Morse's Garage was reinstated for $3,100 (amount received). The account was written off three years ago.

Oct. 18 Prepared a compound entry to write the following accounts off as uncollectible: Sal's Diner, $800; Ring Auto, $1,300; Neel's Hardware, $800.

Nov. 12 Sold merchandise on account to Able Roy, $1,950.

Dec. 31 On the basis of an aging of Accounts Receivable, it was estimated that $8,000 would be uncollectible out of a total of $170,000 in Accounts Receivable.

      31 Closed Bad Debts Expense to Income Summary.

Additional Data

	Account No.	Balance	Dr./Cr.
Allowance for Doubtful Accounts	114	$3,300	Cr.—Jan. 1, 2013
Income Summary	312	—	
Bad Debts Expense	612	—	

Required

a. Journalize the transactions.

b. Post to Allowance for Doubtful Accounts, Income Summary, or Bad Debts Expense as needed.

c. Prepare a current assets section of the balance sheet. Ending balances needed: Cash, $24,000; Accounts Receivable, $170,000; Office Supplies, $3,000; Merchandise Inventory, $94,000; Prepaid Rent, $1,200; and your calculated balance for Allowance for Doubtful Accounts.

(The forms you need are on pages 14-11 to 14-16 of the *Study Guide with Working Papers*.)

The income statement approach: journalizing bad debts expense and writing off accounts
1 2 (25 min)

Check Figure

Aug. 27
Dr. Allowance for
    Doubtful Accounts $525
Cr. Accounts Receivable,
    Ellen Watt $525

14C-1. Redtail Co. of Waltham has requested that you prepare journal entries from the following (this company uses the Allowance for Doubtful Accounts method based on the income statement approach):

2012
Dec. 31 Recorded bad debts expense of $11,200.

2013
Jan.   8 Wrote off Helen Jamison's account of $850 as uncollectible.
Mar.   5 Wrote off Rob Hart's account of $400 as uncollectible.
July   9 Recovered $200 from Rob Hart.
Aug. 20 Wrote off Brian Brisk's account of $1,640 as uncollectible.
      27 Wrote off Ellen Watt's account of $525 as uncollectible.
Nov. 19 Recovered $700 from Brian Brisk.

The balance sheet approach: aging analysis and journalizing of bad debts expense
1 2 (30 min)

Check Figure

Net Realizable Value
$102,200

14C-2. Given the additional information presented below,

  a. Prepare on December 31, 2014, the adjusting journal entry for bad debts expense.

  b. Prepare a partial balance sheet on December 31, 2014, showing how net realizable value is calculated.

  c. If the balance in Allowance for Doubtful Accounts were a $500 debit balance, journalize the adjusting entry for bad debts expense on December 31, 2014.

Additional Information

Dominion Company
December 31, 2014

	Amount	*Estimated Percentage Considered to Be Bad Debts Expense*	*Estimated Amount Needed in Allowance for Doubtful Accounts*
Not yet due	$76,000	1	_____
0–30	12,000	2	_____
31–60	8,000	6	_____
61–180	4,000	13	_____
Over six months	6,000	30	_____
	$106,000		

Balances: Cash, $16,400; Accounts Receivable, $106,000; Allowance for Doubtful Accounts, $700 credit; Inventory, $53,700.

The direct write-off method

2 **5** (25 min)

Check Figure

Dec. 6
Dr. Bad Debts Expense $418
Cr. Accounts Receivable,
    S. Lowe $418

Journalizing and posting adjustments for bad debts expense and write-offs and recovery based on balance sheet approach; preparing partial balance sheet

2 **4** (60 min)

Check Figure

Total Current Assets $265,022

14C-3. Camping Equipment Company of Waterloo uses the direct write-off method for recording bad debts expense. At the beginning of 2012, Accounts Receivable has an $86,700 balance. Journalize the following transactions for the company:

2012
Mar.   23   Wrote off F. Robichaud's account for $1,280.
June   7   Wrote off K. Cheung's account for $915.

2013
Aug.   16   K. Cheung paid bad debt of $915 that was written off June 7, 2012.
Dec.   6   Wrote off S. Lowe's account as uncollectible, $418.
       17   Wrote off R. Patel's account for $316 due from sales made on account in 2011.

14C-4. Prospecting Supply Company of Edson completed the following transactions:

2013
Jan.   8   Sold merchandise on account to May Expeditions, $4,160.
Feb.   19   Wrote off the account of Avery Fischer as uncollectible because of his death, $624.
Mar.   15   Received $600 from Maximum Co.; account had been written off in 2008. The account was reinstated and the collection recorded.
Apr.   5   Received 25% of the $6,400 owed by Airborne Surveys. The remainder was written off as uncollectible.
July   19   The account of Hallicrafter Explorations was reinstated for $3,000 (amount received). The account was written off three years ago.
Oct.   29   Prepared a compound entry to write the following accounts off as uncollectible: Corbett Co., $275; Quark Co., $654; Lonely Expeditions, $247.
Nov.   14   Sold merchandise on account to Partridge Surveys, $4,280.
Dec.   31   Based on an aging of accounts receivable, it was estimated that $6,850 would be uncollectible out of a total of $142,000 in Accounts Receivable.
       31   Closed Bad Debts Expense to Income Summary.

Additional Data as of 01/01/2013:

	Account No.	Balance	Dr./Cr.
Allowance for Doubtful Accounts	1124	$6,150	Cr.—Jan. 1, 2013
Income Summary	3100	—	
Bad Debts Expense	6125	—	

Required

a. Journalize the transactions.

b. Post to Allowance for Doubtful Accounts, Income Summary, or Bad Debts Expense as needed. (Be sure to record the beginning balance in the allowance account in your *Study Guide with Working Papers*.)

c. Prepare a current assets section of the balance sheet. Ending balances needed: Cash, $16,742; Accounts Receivable, $142,000; Office Supplies, $2,630; Merchandise Inventory, $107,000; Prepaid Rent, $3,500; and your calculated balance for Allowance for Doubtful Accounts.

(The forms you need are on page 14-17 of the *Study Guide with Working Papers*.)

Preparing an aging of accounts receivable

3 (20 min)

T-1. Joan Myers, the newly hired bookkeeper of Lyon Company, has until 5 p.m. today to prepare an analysis on December 31, 2013, of accounts receivable by age as well as record the entry for bad debts expense. Assist Joan, who has found the following invoices and balances scattered on her desk. Terms of all sales are n/30.

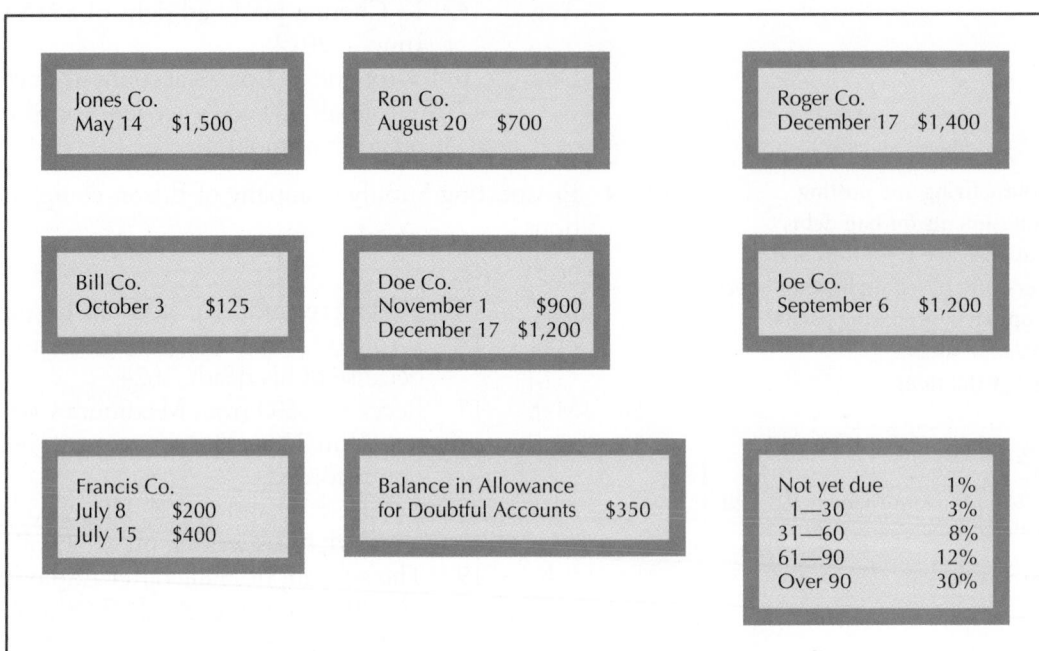

Jones Co. May 14 $1,500	Ron Co. August 20 $700	Roger Co. December 17 $1,400
Bill Co. October 3 $125	Doe Co. November 1 $900 December 17 $1,200	Joe Co. September 6 $1,200
Francis Co. July 8 $200 July 15 $400	Balance in Allowance for Doubtful Accounts $350	Not yet due 1% 1—30 3% 31—60 8% 61—90 12% Over 90 30%

Writing off an account

2 4 5 (20 min)

T-2.

September 30, 2013

To: Al Jones

From: Peter Flynn, President

Re: Bad Debts

At a party last night, a friend of mine told me that we should not be using the direct write-off method. He told me that it doesn't fulfill the matching principle of accounting. Give me your arguments to support or reject this information.

CONTINUING PROBLEM

At the end of the fiscal year, the Precision Computer Centre has a $21,620 balance in Accounts Receivable. Here is a current schedule of accounts receivable:

Precision Computer Centre
Schedule of Accounts Receivable
July 31, 2014

Taylor Golf	$ 6,270
Vita Needle	10,610
Accu Pac	1,450
Fortune Consulting	3,290
Total	$21,620

Assignment

(See page 14-18 in your *Study Guide with Working Papers*.)

Although Accu Pac's account is not 90 days past due, Freedman has determined that it is necessary to provide for one-half of that balance because the business has closed. Of the remaining balances, 5% may become bad debts at some future point.

Calculate the necessary allowance at the end of the company's fiscal year; then make the necessary journal entry to record it. Please use a new account, 1022—Allowance for Doubtful Accounts.

State what changes would have been made to the annual financial statements that were based on the information given in the Chapter 12 Continuing Problem if the entries covering bad debts transactions had been made at that time.

Suppose that later in the year (assume November 30, 2014), it was obvious that the entire Accu Pac account was uncollectible and must be completely written off. Show the journal entry you would make to record this event. What effect would this have on the net income for the fiscal year ending July 31, 2015?

15 Accounting for Property, Plant, Equipment, and Intangible Assets

THE BIG PICTURE

Imagine a company that started business in Canada about 75 years ago. Assume that the company's business is something that needs a lot of electric power—smelting aluminum, for example.

Further consider that the company built not one, or even two, but three power-generating dams on a major Canadian river. The cost was, for that time and place, enormous, say $400,000,000 in total.

Now, put yourself in the place of an accountant back in the 1930s who has the job of deciding how the company will spread the cost of the dams over the many dozens of years they will allow electricity to be generated and used by the company to produce aluminum. How many years would you suggest? Twenty? Thirty? Forty? Perhaps fifty or more? If you chose 50 years, even as a young accountant, you would have long retired by the time the dams were fully written off. But let's agree that 50 years is a good number. That's only 2% per year, so that should get the job done, right?

Well, the job did get done, and after a 50-year period, the dams are what accountants refer to as fully amortized. They have a book value of zero.

But wait a minute! The three dams that once cost $400,000,000 to construct, and that have a "book value" of zero, would now cost $4,000,000,000 if they needed to be duplicated more than 50 years later. And here's the thing: The dams are just as good in the year 2011 as they were in 1935! Note that the generators themselves are replaced every decade or so, and we are not thinking about those, just the dams themselves.

So accountants are really crazy, right? Actually, some experts think this is true, but the process described above (which is loosely based on a real Canadian company) agrees in every respect with generally accepted accounting principles.

Accounting for assets with long lives, and satisfying every person who wants to understand financial statements, is a real challenge. In our example, the company's dams are shown on the balance sheet at a nominal value of one dollar, while their true economic value is in the billions. Can this be both true and generally accepted? Yes, it can!

You see, accounting for amortization of property, plant, and equipment is more about matching historical costs with income than it is about placing a proper value on a particular asset. This chapter has more details.

Does seem kind of strange, though.

1 Calculating the cost of an asset (p. 641)
2 Calculating amortization using one of four methods: straight-line, units of production, declining balance, and sum of the years' digits (p. 644)
3 Calculating amortization for tax purposes using capital cost allowance (p. 647)
4 Explaining the difference between capital expenditures and revenue expenditures (p. 652)
5 Journalizing entries for discarding, selling, or exchanging plant assets (p. 654)
6 Explaining amortization and how it applies to intangible assets (p. 659)
7 Considering some complexities in accounting for capital assets (p. 661)

In Chapter 13 we classified assets as either current or long term. Current assets are used up in a company's operations or converted into cash within one year or one accounting cycle, whichever is longer. Long-term assets, such as plant and equipment, provide benefits to a company for more than one year or one accounting cycle. Types of long-term assets include property (such as land), plant (such as buildings), and equipment (such as trucks and tools). Another classification of assets is called **intangible assets**. These assets are rights owned by a business that do not involve a *physical* object. Examples are patents or franchises. Intangible assets are also considered long-term assets.

In this chapter, we look at how to calculate a long-term asset's overall cost and its **amortization** (amortization being the allocation of the cost of the asset to the income statement over its lifetime). We also show how to record expenditures involved in improving or repairing an asset and how to account for the disposal of these assets. Note that in Canada the term "depreciation" is often used as a substitute for "amortization."

Learning Unit 15-1
Cost of Property, Plant, and Equipment

1 Calculating the cost of an asset

The cost of property, plant, and equipment is not just the price one pays to buy it. One must also include the cost involved in getting it into position and in condition for use in the company. Thus, the cost of a machine includes freight, assembly, and all other costs that are needed to get the machine up and ready to run.

For example, Smith Company ordered a machine with a list price of $20,000 with terms of 3/10, n/30. A freight charge of $1,500 covered transportation to the railroad station. Smith Company paid $250 to transport the machine from the railroad station to corporate headquarters. Total costs of assembling and installation amounted to $700. In addition, Smith Company purchased a special concrete foundation for $900 to keep the machine from tilting when operational. Assume that the asset was paid for within the discount period. The life of the machine is expected to be 15 years.

Entries to record freight, assembly, installation, and so forth would be made as a debit to the Machinery account and as a credit to Cash.

The $22,750 cost of the asset will be spread over the years the machine helps Smith Company produce revenue. This example is one of the matching principle. Notice, however, that all these additional costs were reasonable and necessary to get the machine *ready for use*. If the buyer causes negligence, illegal acts, or gross inefficiencies to occur, these acts would be charged to an expense and not to the cost of the asset.

Cost of the machine will be matched with revenue.

List price	$20,000
Less: Cash discount (0.03 × $20,000)	600
Net purchase price	19,400
Freight	1,500
Transportation from railroad station	250
Assembly and installation	700
Special foundation	900
Total cost of machine	$22,750

> Note that cash discount is deducted in arriving at total cost of the machine. If PST were involved, it would be added to the cost of the asset.

> GST/HST is not considered part of an asset's cost. It is refundable.

Let's look now at how to record the cost of land.

LAND AND LAND IMPROVEMENTS

> Land does not depreciate, because it has an unlimited life.

When land (which has unlimited useful life) is purchased, many incidental costs are usually considered part of the *cost* of the land. These costs include surveying, commissions to attorneys and real estate brokers, title searches, grading, draining, and clearing the property. Any special one-time assessment made for paving a street or installing sewers should be charged to cost of land, because it adds "permanent value" to the land.

Now let's look at some items related to land that will not be added to the cost of land. **Land Improvements** is an asset account that records improvements to land that have a *limited* useful life. Some examples are driveways, fences, shrubbery, paving of parking lots, and sprinkler systems. These improvements are subject to amortization, and thus we need an account that is kept separate from the Land account, which does *not* depreciate.

BUILDINGS

The cost of buying a building would include the purchase price and all the cost of repairs and other expenses to get the building *ready for use.* For construction of a new building, the cost would include all reasonable and necessary payments for labour, insurance, building permits, architect's fees, legal fees, and so on to get the building ready for use.

If a building and land are purchased for one lump-sum payment, the cost must be separated (allocated) for each, because land will not depreciate, but buildings will.

LEARNING UNIT 15-1 REVIEW

AT THIS POINT you should be able to:

♦ Explain how to classify property, plant, and equipment. (p. 641)
♦ Calculate the cost of an asset. (p. 642)
♦ Explain the difference between land and land improvements. (p. 642)

Self-Review Quiz 15-1A

(The forms you need for both quizzes are on page 15-1 of the *Study Guide with Working Papers.*)

Respond true or false to the following:

1. Land does not depreciate.

2. Total cost of acquiring an asset cannot include cost of freight.

3. Land improvements are not subject to amortization.

4. A cash discount is added to list price.

5. PST is added to cost of an asset.

6. GST is part of the cost of an asset.

Solution to Self-Review Quiz 15-1A

1. True

2. False

3. False

4. False

5. True

6. False

Self-Review Quiz 15-1B

KNL Company opened a new branch office in Dartmouth, purchasing some land in order to construct a new company building. The following expenditures were encountered in the process of getting the new building ready to move in:

	Cost of building site	$136,500
____	Removal cost for old condemned structure on lot	38,000
____	Survey fee	11,400
____	Lawyer's fee for handling lot purchase	5,680
____	Special municipal levy for sewer improvements	74,600
____	Cost to level site ready for building	25,000
____	Paid real estate agent re services for purchase	9,500
____	Contract price for construction of building	427,000
____	Salary of company director of construction during the building process	84,775
____	Building permit and municipal inspections	4,800
____	Constructing and paving parking lot for building	69,500
____	Landscaping expenses for building grounds	35,000

Required

For each of the expenditures listed, place one of three possible letters in front of each: L means Land; I means Land Improvements; B means Building.

Solution to Self-Review Quiz 15-1B

L	Cost of building site	$136,500
L	Removal cost for old condemned structure on lot	38,000
L	Survey fee	11,400
L	Lawyer's fee for handling lot purchase	5,680
L	Special municipal levy for sewer improvements	74,600
L	Cost to level site ready for building	25,000
L	Paid real estate agent re services for purchase	9,500
B	Contract price for construction of building	427,000
B	Salary of company director of construction during the building process	84,775
B	Building permit and municipal inspections	4,800
I	Constructing and paving parking lot for building	69,500
I	Landscaping expenses for building grounds	35,000

Learning Unit 15-2

Amortization Methods

2 Calculating amortization using one of four methods: straight-line, units of production, declining balance, and sum of the years' digits

Now that you know which long-term assets are depreciable, let's look at different methods for computing amortization. If you want to check any of the concepts of amortization we discussed in Chapter 4, take a moment to refer back to page 141.

When a company calculates its periodic amortization expense, different methods will produce significantly different results. Thus, the method of amortization chosen will affect the net income for current as well as future periods as well as the **book value** (cost of asset less accumulated amortization) of the asset on the balance sheet.

Let's assume that Melvin Company purchased a truck on January 1, 2013, for $20,000, with a **residual (salvage) value** of $2,000 and an estimated life of five years. The following are the four common amortization methods that Melvin Company could use:

Think 1. Determine cost. 2. Determine life (years, units). 3. Determine residual value. 4. Choose a method.

1. Straight-line method
2. Units-of-production method
3. Double-declining-balance method
4. Sum-of-the-years'-digits method (an optional section)

STRAIGHT-LINE METHOD

The **straight-line method** is simple to use, because it allocates the cost of the asset (less residual value) evenly over its estimated useful life. (At the time an asset is acquired, an estimate is made of its usefulness or **useful life** in terms of number of years it will last, amount of output expected, and so forth.) Let's look at how Melvin Company calculates its amortization expense for each of the estimated five years of usefulness using the straight-line method. Take a moment to read the key points in the parentheses in the accompanying table.

The formula is

$$\frac{\text{Cost} - \text{Residual Value}}{\text{Service Useful Life in Years}} = \frac{\$20,000 - \$2,000}{5} = \$3,600$$

End of Year:	Cost of Delivery Truck	Yearly Amortization Expense*	Accumulated Amortization, End of Year	Book Value, End of Year (Cost − Accum. Amort.)
1 (2013)	$20,000	$3,600	$ 3,600	$16,400
2 (2014)	20,000	3,600	7,200	12,800
3 (2015)	20,000	3,600	10,800	9,200
4 (2016)	20,000	3,600	14,400	5,600
5 (2017)	20,000	3,600	18,000	2,000
	↑	↑	↑	↑
	(Cost of truck doesn't change.)	(Note that amortization expense is the same each year.)	(Accumulated amortization increases by $3,600 each year.)	(Book value each year is lowered by $3,600 until residual value of $2,000 is reached.)

*The amortization rate is 100% ÷ 5 years = 20%. The 20% is then multiplied times the cost minus the residual value.

UNITS-OF-PRODUCTION METHOD

With the **units-of-production method** it is assumed that *passage of time* does not determine the amount of amortization taken. Amortization expense is based on *use,* be it total estimated kilometres, tonnes hauled, or estimated units of production (e.g., the number of shoes a machine could produce in its expected useful life). The following table shows the calculations that Melvin Company makes for its truck using the units-of-production method. ***Note:*** For this example the truck is assumed to have an estimated life of 90,000 kilometres.

The formula is

$$\frac{\text{Cost} - \text{Residual Value}}{\text{Estimated Units of Production}} = \frac{\$20,000 - \$2,000}{90,000 \text{ kilometres}} = \$0.20 \text{ per km}$$

$$(\$0.20) \times (\text{Number of Kilometres Driven}) = \text{Amortization Expense for Period}$$

End of Year:	Cost of Delivery Truck	Kilometres Driven in Year	Yearly Amortization Expense	Accumulated Amortization, End of Year	Book Value, End of Year (Cost – Accum. Amort.)
1 (2013)	$20,000	30,000	$6,000	$ 6,000	$14,000
2 (2014)	20,000	21,000	4,200	10,200	9,800
3 (2015)	20,000	15,000	3,000	13,200	6,800
4 (2016)	20,000	5,000	1,000	14,200	5,800
5 (2017)	20,000	19,000	3,800	18,000	2,000
		↑	↑		↑
		(After 5 years, truck has been driven 90,000 kilometres.)	(Amorization expense is directly related to number of kilometres driven.)		(Residual value of $2,000 is reached.)

DOUBLE-DECLINING-BALANCE METHOD

The **double-declining-balance method** is an accelerated method in which a larger amortization expense is taken in earlier years and smaller amounts in later years. For this reason it is called an **accelerated amortization method**. This method depreciates at twice the straight-line rate, which is why it is called the *double-declining-balance method.

A key point in this method is that *residual value* is *not* deducted from cost in the calculations, and the asset cannot be depreciated below its residual value. To calculate amortization, take the following steps:

1. Calculate the straight-line rate and double it:

$$\frac{100\%}{\text{Useful Life}} \times 2$$

2. At the *end of each year* multiply the rate times the book value of the asset at the beginning of the year.

Let's look at how Melvin Company calculates the amortization on its truck using this method. Be sure to note the $592 in year 5 of amortization expense. We could not take more than the $592 or we would have depreciated the asset below the residual value.

End of Year:	Cost	Accumulated Amortization, Beg. of Year	Book Value Beg. of Year (Cost – Acc. Amort.)	Amort. Exp. (Book Value Beg. of Year × Rate)	Accumulated Amortization, End of Year	Book Value, End of Year (Cost – Acc. Amort.)
1 (2013)	$20,000		$20,000	$8,000 ($20,000 × 0.40)	$ 8,000	$12,000 (20,000 – 8,000)
2 (2014)	20,000	$ 8,000	12,000	4,800 (12,000 × 0.40)	12,800	7,200 20,000 – (8,000 + 4,800)
3 (2015)	20,000	12,800	7,200	2,880 (7,200 × 0.40)	15,680	4,320
4 (2016)	20,000	15,680	4,320	1,728 (4,320 × 0.40)	17,408	2,592
5 (2017)	20,000 ↑ (Original cost remains the same.)	17,408	2,592	592 ↑ (Amortization is limited to $592, because the asset cannot depreciate below the residual value.)	18,000	2,000 ↑ (The book value now equals the residual value.)

OPTIONAL SECTION: SUM-OF-THE-YEARS'-DIGITS METHOD

The **sum-of-the-years'-digits method** places more amortization expense in the early years rather than in the later years to match revenue and expenses better, because an asset's productivity may be reduced in later years. To use it, you multiply cost minus residual times a certain fraction. This fraction is made up of the following:

1. The *denominator.* The denominator is based on how many years the asset is likely to last (say five). You then add the sum of the digits of five years (1 + 2 + 3 + 4 + 5), which equals 15; 15 is the denominator. (The formula to use for the denominator is $N(N + 1)/2$, where N stands for number of years of useful life [in our case, five years]. In our case, the formula would give $5(5 + 1)/2 = 15$.)

2. The *numerator.* The years in reverse order are the numerator (in our case, 5, 4, 3, 2, 1).

Thus, in year 1 the fraction would be $\frac{5}{15}$, in year 2, $\frac{4}{15}$, in year 3, $\frac{3}{15}$, in year 4, $\frac{2}{15}$, in year 5, $\frac{1}{15}$. In each year you would multiply this fraction times cost minus the residual to find the amortization expense. This process is shown in the following table.

End of Year:	Cost Minus Residual Value	×	Fraction for Year	=	Yearly Amortization Expense	Accumulated Amortization, End of Year	Book Value, End of Year (Cost – Accum. Amort.)
1 (2013)	$18,000 (20,000 – 2,000)	×	$\frac{5}{15}$	=	$6,000	$ 6,000	$14,000 ($20,000 – $6,000)
2 (2014)	18,000	×	$\frac{4}{15}$	=	4,800	10,800	9,200
3 (2015)	18,000	×	$\frac{3}{15}$	=	3,600	14,400	5,600
4 (2016)	18,000	×	$\frac{2}{15}$	=	2,400	16,800	3,200
5 (2017)	18,000 ↑ (Fraction for year is multiplied by cost minus residual.)	×	$\frac{1}{15}$	=	1,200 ↑ (Amortization expense in first year is highest.)	18,000 ↑ (Each year amortization accumulates by a smaller amount.)	2,000 ↑ (Book value goes down each year until residual is reached.)

Take a moment to make sure you see how the figures for these calculations are arrived at before moving on to the next method.

Now let's look at how Melvin Company could handle amortization calculations for partial years (if it bought a truck on May 4, 2013).

AMORTIZATION FOR PARTIAL YEARS

When depreciating for partial years, we assume that for any asset purchased before the 15th of the month, amortization is calculated for a full month. After the 15th of the month, the amortization is disregarded for the month.

STRAIGHT-LINE METHOD   For Melvin Company, if the truck was purchased on May 4, 2013, amortization expense would be calculated as follows for the 2013 year:

$$\frac{\$20,000 - \$2,000}{5 \text{ Years}} \times \frac{8}{12} = \$2,400$$

We use 8 because the truck was bought on May 4. Do not count the first four months of the year in the calculation of amortization. The following year the full yearly amortization would be taken.

UNITS-OF-PRODUCTION METHOD   The units-of-production method would not be affected, because amortization is based on usage, not passage of time.

DOUBLE-DECLINING-BALANCE METHOD   Because Melvin Company has the benefit of the truck for eight months, the company's amortization for the 2013 year would be:

$$(\$20,000 \times 0.40) \times \frac{8}{12}$$

In year 2 and in future years the annual rate of 40% is multiplied times the *current* book value.

SUM-OF-THE-YEARS'-DIGITS METHOD (OPTIONAL SECTION)   If the truck is bought on May 4, 2013, the company would take amortization of eight months or $4,000 ($18,000 \times \frac{5}{15}) \times \frac{8}{12}$. In the following year, Melvin Company would take amortization of the last four months of the first year and the first eight months of the second year. Let's look at the calculation for year 2014:

$$\text{Year 2014} = (\$18,000 \times \tfrac{5}{15}) \times \tfrac{4}{12} + (\$18,000 \times \tfrac{4}{15}) \times \tfrac{8}{12}$$

— Amortization completed from 2013 year first.

AMORTIZATION FOR TAX PURPOSES: CAPITAL COST ALLOWANCE

3 Calculating amortization for tax purposes using capital cost allowance

So far in this chapter, we have described how a business might amortize its capital assets for the purpose of preparing its annual financial statements. When preparing their financial statements, Canadian Tire, Loblaws, Tim Hortons, and most businesses in Canada generally choose one of the four amortization methods that were illustrated earlier. According to GAAP rules, each company can select which method it wants to use; but, having chosen it, it is not permitted to change methods unless it has a very good reason, and then it must also provide details of the effects of the change when it is made.

The choice of which method to use can be very important. If a company wants to present a very healthy income statement in its early years (e.g., to make it easier to get financing), it might choose the straight-line method, and take the view that its assets will last a long time. This method will result in the lowest charge for amortization in the early years. Other companies might consider that many of their assets are "used up" more rapidly in the early years, and therefore adopt one of the accelerated methods, such as double-declining-balance or, in a very few cases, sum-of-the-years'-digits. Sometimes a company operating in Canada will be related to a "parent" corporation in, for example, the United States, and may have little choice but to use the amortization method dictated by its parent.

You might be thinking that many businesses would choose the amortization method that gives the lowest net income in the early years, because this results in the least amount of income tax being paid. If this is what you think, congratulations! Your logic is impressive, and in many countries throughout the world, your deduction would be correct. But it is not true in Canada, and here's why.

Very simply, the amortization method used for financial statements cannot be used for taxation purposes.* Instead, Canadian tax laws and regulations permit only one method for calculating how much of a deduction for "amortization" a business can make when calculating its taxable income for a year. That method is called **capital cost allowance** (CCA), and it can be a complex procedure in some situations.

For most business situations, however, CCA is reasonably straightforward. Each business asset is assigned to one of a set of "classes." Each class has its own rate that governs two things: the maximum amount that can be deducted in a year when computing taxable income and the resulting tax. Most taxpayers agree that the classes are generally "fair," in that the rates are higher for assets that have a shorter useful life. Take a look at the partial list below to see whether you agree:

Concrete buildings	5%	(Class 3)
Wooden buildings	10%	(Class 6)
General business assets	20%	(Class 8)
Airplanes	25%	(Class 9)
Trucks, cars, and busses	30%	(Class 10)
Computer software	100%	(Class 12)
Computers (2004–2007)	45%	(Class 45)
Computers (2007 and newer)	55%	(Class 50)

Note that CCA regulations are very detailed, and the above short list is just a general guide. It should not be used as any sort of legal guideline. You should also be aware that the government periodically adjusts the classes and/or rates to either reflect changed business realities (hence the new rate for computers at 55%, up from 45% in 2004 and 30% prior to that) or incentives to encourage investments in socially desirable projects such as "green" power-generating technology (Class 43.1 is where you can find a list of assets falling into this category).

Once it is decided which class an asset falls into, it is quite simple to calculate the maximum amount a business may deduct when calculating its taxable income. In many ways, the CCA method operates like the double-declining-balance method described earlier in this chapter. We will examine an example of this shortly, but first you should understand the "half-year rule."

You will find a little bit of history helpful at this point. In the past, many taxpaying businesses timed major capital asset purchases so that they occurred just prior to the company's year-end. This was because, according to the tax laws of the time, as long as an asset was purchased at any time during the fiscal year, a full year's worth of CCA could be deducted. Over time, the tax authorities realized that some ordinary Canadians saw this loophole as unfair, and so the *half-year rule* was implemented. This rule limits the CCA deductible for the first year of most assets purchased to one-half of the amount it would be otherwise. For instance, if an asset falls into Class 8 (20%), only 10% can be claimed in the first year. As another example, if computer hardware was purchased, only half of the new 55% rate would be permitted in the first year.

Just as with the double-declining-balance method, each year's CCA is simply based on that class's balance from the previous year, multiplied by the stated rate, plus whatever amount is allowed on new assets added during the year. Let's look at a simple example.

---

*The opposite is permitted, however. It is not unusual for a smaller Canadian company to adopt the CCA method as its method of amortization. That is one of the reasons for including the topic of CCA in this chapter.

Assume that Simple Company has a fiscal year that ends on July 31, and that this company purchased 10 new computers that cost $20,000 before GST on May 15, 2013. We will ignore for now the possibility that there were previous purchases of other Class 50 assets, and show how the company would calculate the maximum CCA (based on the rate of 55%) that the tax laws allow for this new purchase.

Note: For taxation years 2010 and 2011, the 2009 federal budget allows 100% write off of computers, etc. This is a temporary measure that affects only these two years.

Class 50—55%

Additions for 2013	$20,000	
Maximum 2013 capital cost allowance:		
(1/2 × 55% × $20,000)	$ 5,500	(half-year rule)
Balance remaining at July 31, 2013*	$14,500	
Maximum 2014 capital cost allowance:		
(55% × $14,500)	$ 7,975	(no half-year rule)
Balance remaining at July 31, 2014*	$ 6,525	(etc.)

*Tax regulations refer to these amounts as **undepreciated capital cost** (UCC).

Several times in the above material, we referred to "maximum CCA" for a given year. The reason we are this precise is that under certain circumstances, a business may choose not to claim all the CCA it is allowed in one year. A common example is when the company has lost money for the year, and therefore does not need to claim CCA in calculating how much tax is owing. This is a major difference between amortization and CCA. Generally, amortization is charged to match revenue and expenses, and a loss is not an acceptable reason to suspend charging amortization. CCA is totally optional, and is deducted only if a company calculates that it is a good idea.

Often this decision can be quite complex. Will a company always defer charging CCA if it suffers a loss? The answer depends a lot on whether the company anticipates a major turnaround in its financial results in the next few years. If profits are anticipated, the company might elect to charge CCA in the year of the loss (even if this is not necessary to minimize that year's tax payable). The effect is to increase the current year's taxable loss so this larger amount can then be carried forward to offset even larger profits in the next few (profitable) years.

Though the topic of income taxation can become a major headache, relax! It is not the purpose of this text to make you an expert. Most of the professional accounting bodies in Canada insist on at least two full courses on taxation for their graduates.

That said, to give you a clearer awareness of how the CCA system operates, let's look at a slightly more complex example of how CCA is handled. Assume that Robust Company has a fiscal year that ends on September 30, 2013, and that during the year that ends on that date, the company made the following asset purchases:

- *Class 8—20%.* During the year, Robust Company purchased general business assets (desks and other office furniture, let's say) totalling $12,000 before GST. Remember that we do not need to know the exact date of all the purchases; all purchases made in the same year are treated exactly the same for CCA purposes. This may not be true for amortization calculations.

- *Class 10—30%.* During the year the company traded in a delivery van that had once cost $28,000 for a new delivery van with a list price of $40,000. The van that was traded in had a net book value of $12,000, and its UCC was $14,000. The company got a trade-in allowance of $18,000, meaning they paid a net amount of $22,000 for the new van. All the persons involved in this deal agree that the true value of the old van was about $15,000, and also that the cash purchase price of the new van was probably $37,000 (note that the "difference" is still $22,000 before GST).

- *Class 12—100%.* During the year, Robust Company also purchased computer software (cost was $4,000 before GST) to analyze sales data.

- *Class 50—55%.* Several computers were purchased throughout the year. The company spent $9,800 on these new machines, before GST. They also donated to a local charity five older computers that had a net book value of $865 (no cash changed hands for this).

Table 15-1 shows how the company would calculate the maximum CCA deductible for the 2013 fiscal year.

TABLE 15-1   Calculation of Maximum CCA Deductible for 2013 Fiscal Year

Robust Company
Schedule of Capital Cost Allowance
For the Year Ending September 30, 2013

	Class 8 20%	Class 10 30%	Class 12 100%	Class 50 50%	Total
Undepreciated capital cost, September 30, 2012*	34,600	87,500	2,500	17,286	141,886
Additions	12,000	22,000	4,000	9,800	47,800
Balances before CCA	46,600	109,500	6,500	27,086	189,686
CCA for the year:					
On beginning UCC	6,920	26,250	2,500	9,507	45,177
On additions	1,200	3,300	2,000	2,695	9,195
2013 maximum CCA	8,120	29,550	4,500	12,202	54,372
Undepreciated capital cost, September 30, 2013**	38,480	79,950	2,000	14,884	135,314

Note: The additions for Class 10 are simply the cash difference paid for the new van. Also note that the donation of the computers has no effect on the calculations, since no cash changed hands.
*These numbers are invented for this table.
**These numbers will be carried forward to next year.

Bear in mind that $54,372 is the maximum Robust Company can claim for 2013. If it does not claim the maximum, the carry-forward UCC will be adjusted to reflect only the amounts claimed in 2013.

When preparing its tax return for 2013, Robust Company will make a simple calculation, adding back to net income any amortization deducted on its financial statements (since that amount is not deductible for tax purposes), then deducting the CCA claimed up to $54,372—the maximum allowable for the year.

Many technical and highly detailed rules govern how CCA is applied, and even the experts do not always have the same perspective on a given set of facts. Learning about the details of CCA can be rewarding, but it is usually only attempted by students who plan to pursue a career in accounting.

LEARNING UNIT 15-2 REVIEW

AT THIS POINT you should be able to:

◆ Explain and calculate four methods of amortization. (pp. 644–646)
◆ Calculate amortization for partial years. (p. 647)
◆ Explain and calculate capital cost allowance for tax purposes. (pp. 647–650)

Self-Review Quiz 15-2

(The forms you need are on pages 15-2 and 15-3 of the *Study Guide with Working Papers*.)

From the following facts complete amortization schedules for the **a.** straight-line, **b.** units-of-production, **c.** declining-balance, and **d.** sum-of-the-years'-digits (optional) methods.

Cost of equipment	$40,000
Residual value	7,000
Service life	5 years
Estimated units of output	20,000
Units produced in year 1:	8,000
2:	2,000
3:	5,000
4:	2,800
5:	2,200

Solution to Self-Review Quiz 15-2

a.

End of Year:	Cost of Equipment	Yearly Amortization Expense	Accumulated Amortization, End of Year	Book Value, End of Year (Cost – Acc. Amort.)
1	$40,000	$6,600	$ 6,600	$33,400 ($40,000 – $6,600)
2	40,000	6,600	13,200	26,800
3	40,000	6,600	19,800	20,200
4	40,000	6,600	26,400	13,600
5	40,000	6,600	33,000	7,000 ← Book value now equals residual value.

b.

End of Year:	Cost of Equipment	Units of Output in Year	Yearly Amortization Expense	Accumulated Amortization, End of Year	Book Value, End of Year

$$\frac{\$40,000 - \$7,000}{20,000 \text{ units}} = \$1.65 \text{ per unit}$$

End of Year:	Cost of Equipment	Units of Output in Year	Yearly Amortization Expense	Accumulated Amortization, End of Year	Book Value, End of Year
1	$40,000	8,000	$13,200 (8,000 × $1.65)	$13,200	$26,800
2	40,000	2,000	3,300	16,500	23,500
3	40,000	5,000	8,250	24,750	15,250
4	40,000	2,800	4,620	29,370	10,630
5	40,000	2,200	3,630	33,000	7,000

c.

End of Year:	Cost	Accumulated Amortization, Beg. of Year	Book Value Beg. of Year (Cost – Acc. Amort.)	Amort. Exp. (B.V. Beg. of Year × Rate)	Acc. Amort., End of Year	Book Value, End of Year (Cost – Acc. Amort.)
1	$40,000	—	$40,000	$16,000 ($40,000 × 0.40)	$16,000	$24,000 ($40,000 – $16,000)
2	40,000	$16,000	24,000	9,600 ($24,000 × 0.40)	25,600	14,400 ($40,000 – $25,600)
3	40,000	25,600	14,400	5,760	31,360	8,640
4	40,000	31,360	8,640	→1,640	33,000	7,000

Rate is 40%.

$$\frac{100\%}{5 \text{ Years}} = \frac{1.00}{5}$$

$$= 0.20 = 20\%$$

$$2 \times 20\% = 40\%$$

Only $1,640 could be taken so that book value would not go below residual value.

d. (optional)

End of Year:	Cost Less Residual × Rate = Yearly Amortization Expense	Accumulated Amortization, End of Year	Book Value, End of Year
1	$33,000 \times \frac{5}{15} = \$11,000$	$11,000	$29,000 ($40,000 − $11,000)
2	$33,000 \times \frac{4}{15} = \$8,800$	$19,800	$20,200
3	$33,000 \times \frac{3}{15} = \$6,600$	$26,400	$13,600
4	$33,000 \times \frac{2}{15} = \$4,400$	$30,800	$ 9,200
5	$33,000 \times \frac{1}{15} = \$2,200$	$33,000	$ 7,000

Learning Unit 15-3

Capital and Revenue Expenditures and Disposal of Plant Assets

4 Explaining the difference between capital expenditures and revenue expenditures

Now that we have seen amortization calculations, let's look at capital and revenue expenditures and the disposal of plant assets.

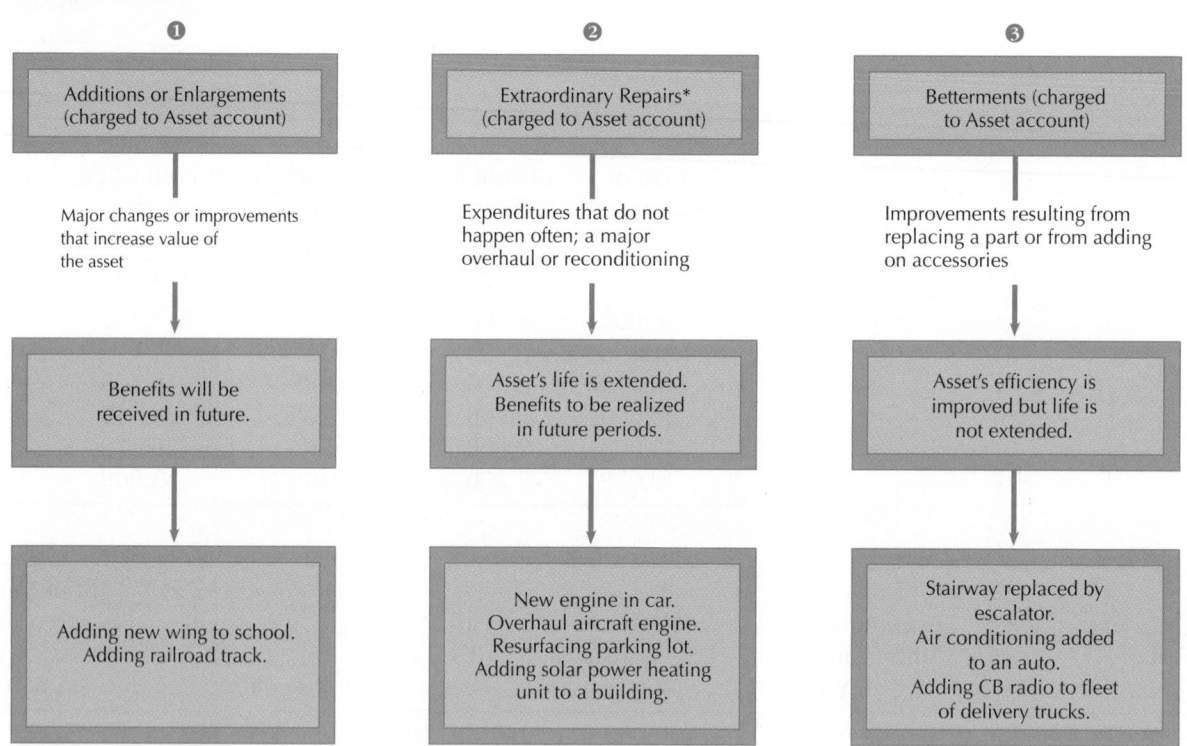

*In some cases, a repair will replace a worn or damaged part of an asset with a part that is significantly better or longer-lasting. An example is replacing a wooden fence with a concrete one. When this happens, Canadian GAAP rules insist that the "repair" be apportioned between the part that is a repair (charged to expense) and the amount that is a betterment (charged as an asset).

Figure 15-1   Three Categories of Capital Expenditures

CAPITAL EXPENDITURES

Capital expenditures include the original cost of an asset as well as payments that improve on or enlarge existing assets. Capital expenditures may be broken down into three categories: additions or enlargements, extraordinary repairs, and betterments. The differences among these three categories are based on whether the change will add to the value of the asset, extend the life of the asset, or only improve its efficiency. For example, adding a new wing to a school building will increase the value of the asset, so it is categorized as an **addition** or **enlargement.** Overhauling an aircraft engine definitely extends the life of the asset, so it is categorized as an **extraordinary repair.** Adding a CB radio to a fleet of delivery trucks improves the efficiency of the asset but does not extend its life, so it is categorized as a **betterment**. These three categories are shown in the chart in Figure 15.1.

It may be a little difficult at first to see the difference between betterments and extraordinary repairs. Betterments do not extend the life of the asset; the cost of a betterment is debited to the asset account. Extraordinary repairs do extend the life of the asset.

The following is an example of how to analyze and record an extraordinary repair to a machine that has a cost of $20,000, has no residual value, and has an estimated life of 10 years.

Machine			Accumulated Amortization, Machine	
Dr.	Cr.		Dr.	Cr.
20,000				16,000
				(after 8 years)

> **Additions or enlargements and betterments are charged to the asset account. An amount seen as "normal repairs" is charged to expense.**

Note that after eight years the book value of the machine is $4,000 ($20,000 – $16,000). On March 30, a major overhaul of the machine is completed for $3,000. It is believed that this overhaul will extend the machine's life by three years. Thus, the journal entry to record this extraordinary repair is as shown in Figure 15-2.

Because the machine's life is extended by three years, the owner can now take five years of amortization. The new annual amortization of $1,400 (instead of $2,000) is calculated as follows:

Book value before extraordinary repair	$4,000
Extraordinary repair	3,000
New book value	$7,000 ÷ 5 years = $1,400 per year

If the machine had an estimated residual value at the end of year 5, it would be subtracted from the new book value.

REVENUE EXPENDITURES

Another type of expenditure occurs after an asset has been acquired. *Revenue expenditures* are payments made for ordinary maintenance of an asset or unnecessary or unreasonable situations. These expenditures occur on a regular basis and are recorded as expenses. Examples include changing oil and greasing a car, replacing windowpanes, replacing tires on a truck, repainting a car, and adding a sun roof. When an expenditure is treated as a revenue expenditure, it is recorded on the income statement as an expense and thus reduces net income in the period in which it occurred. Now let's turn our attention to the disposal of certain plant assets.

Figure 15-2
Overhaul Extends Asset's Life

				Dr.	Cr.
Mar.	30	Machine		3 0 0 0 00	
		Cash			3 0 0 0 00
		To record extraordinary repair			

DISPOSAL OF PLANT ASSETS

5 Journalizing entries for discarding, selling, or exchanging plant assets

We now move on to the basic accounting procedures followed when disposing of plant assets in the following ways:

a. Discarding plant assets

b. Selling plant assets

c. Exchanging for similar plant assets

We present a different example for each category (**a**, **b**, or **c**). It is important to remember that amortization is recorded up until the date a plant asset is disposed of. Take time to compare journal entries to T accounts in each example.

A. DISPOSAL BY DISCARDING PLANT ASSETS A company discards a plant asset when it is no longer operational (e.g., machinery or a truck that no longer works). That also means that no other company is willing to buy or exchange something for the asset.

SITUATION 1: NO GAIN OR LOSS Boulder Company is disposing of a $7,000 truck with no residual value that has been fully amortized (remember that it is possible to keep using a fully depreciated asset, but in this case the asset—the truck—is no longer in working order). Because the asset has been fully depreciated, it is not necessary to bring any amortization up to date before getting rid of it.

The journal entry shown in Figure 15-3 is made after disposing of the truck.

Figure 15-3
Disposing of the Fully Amortized Truck

Accumulated Amortization, Truck	7 0 0 0 00	
Truck		7 0 0 0 00

Here is how the ledger for these accounts would look after posting:

Truck			Accumulated Amortization, Truck	
Dr.	Cr.		Dr.	Cr.
7,000	7,000		7,000	7,000

Therefore, the truck and the accumulated amortization associated with it are off the books. Note that no gain or loss occurs here.

SITUATION 2: LOSS ON DISPOSAL Moore Company disposed of a partially amortized truck. The truck, costing $6,000, was considered worthless (amortization of $5,000 to date). Because nothing is received for this asset that has a book value of $1,000, the difference between the cost of the truck and the accumulated amortization is a loss. The Loss on Disposal account is categorized as Other Expense on the income statement. Let's look at the journal entry for this loss on disposal (Figure 15-4) and see how the ledger would look after posting.

Figure 15-4
Loss on Disposal of Truck

Loss on Disposal of Plant Asset	1 0 0 0 00	
Accumulated Amortization, Truck	5 0 0 0 00	
Truck		6 0 0 0 00

Truck			Accumulated Amortization, Truck			Loss on Disposal of Plant Asset	
Dr.	Cr.		Dr.	Cr.		Dr.	Cr.
6,000	6,000		5,000	5,000		1,000	

SITUATION 3: LOSS FROM FIRE Missan Company received a cheque for $500 from an insurance company, settling a claim on a machine costing $1,500 that was damaged by fire before the end of its useful life. The balance in Accumulated Amortization was $900. Figure 15-5 shows the journal entry Missan Company records when it receives the $500 cheque:

Figure 15-5
Loss from Fire

Cash			500 00		
Loss from Fire			100 00		
Accumulated Amortization, Machinery			900 00		
Machinery				1500 00	

A loss from the fire amounts to $100; the book value of the machine was $600 ($1,500 – $900), and the amount received from the insurance company was $500. Here is how the ledger would look after posting:

Machinery		Accumulated Amortization, Machinery		Loss from Fire	
Dr.	Cr.	Dr.	Cr.	Dr.	Cr.
1,500	1,500	900	900	100	

Now our attention turns to situations when assets could be sold rather than discarded.

B. DISPOSAL BY SELLING PLANT ASSETS

SITUATION 4: GAIN ON SALE Mason Company sold a truck costing $7,000 for $1,500 cash. The balance in Accumulated Amortization is $6,000.

To see whether this sale results in a gain or a loss, Mason Company must calculate whether the amount of cash received is greater or less than the book value of the truck. If the amount received is greater than the book value, the company realizes a gain. A gain on the sale of a plant asset is categorized as Other Income on the income statement. Let's look at the calculation:

Cost of truck	$7,000	Amount received	$1,500
Less accumulated amortization	6,000	Less book value	1,000
Book value	$1,000	Gain on sale	$ 500

Because the sale results in a gain, the journal entry in Figure 15-6 is made.

Figure 15-6
Gain on Sale of Truck

Cash			1500 00		
Accumulated Amortization, Truck			6000 00		
Truck				7000 00	
Gain on Sale of Plant Asset				500 00	

Here is what the ledger would look like after posting:

Truck		Accumulated Amortization, Truck	
Dr.	Cr.	Dr.	Cr.
7,000	7,000	6,000	6,000

Gain on Sale of Plant Asset	
Dr.	Cr.
	500

SITUATION 5: LOSS ON SALE Let's assume that in the previous situation Mason Company receives only $900 cash for the truck.

Now let's look at the calculation Mason Company does to see whether the sale results in a loss or a gain:

Cost of truck	$7,000
Less accumulated amortization	–6,000
Book value	1,000
Amount received	– 900
Loss on sale	$ 100

When price is less than book value, the company realizes a loss. Because Mason's truck has a book value of $1,000 and the cash received is $900, the end result is a loss of $100 on the sale of the plant asset. This entry is categorized as Other Expense on the income statement. Figure 15-7 shows the journal entry prepared by Mason to record this loss.

Figure 15-7
Loss on Sale of Truck

Cash	9 0 0 00	
Accumulated Amortization, Truck	6 0 0 0 00	
Loss on Sale of Plant Asset	1 0 0 00	
Truck		7 0 0 0 00

Here is what the ledger would look like after posting:

Truck			Accumulated Amortization, Truck	
Dr.	Cr.		Dr.	Cr.
7,000	7,000		6,000	6,000

Loss on Sale of Plant Asset	
Dr.	Cr.
100	

The final category of disposal is exchanging a plant asset rather than discarding or selling.

C. DISPOSAL BY EXCHANGING FOR SIMILAR PLANT ASSETS

SITUATION 6: LOSS ON EXCHANGE VTR Company trades its old machine costing $19,000 for a new one with a cash price of $22,000 less a trade-in allowance of $2,000. Accumulated Amortization of the old machine has a balance of $16,000. A **trade-in allowance** is given when you are buying a new car, for example, and trade in your old one for a sum of money that is applied to the price of the new car. A loss on exchange will result if the book value of the old machine is greater than what is received for the trade-in allowance. Let's look at how VTR calculates its loss on this machine exchange.

Step 1 Calculate the book value of the old machine:

Cost	$19,000
– Accumulated amortization	16,000
Book value	$ 3,000

Step 2 Compare the book value of the old machine with the trade-in:

$3,000	Book value of old machine
2,000	Trade-in
$1,000	Loss

Because the book value of the old machine is $3,000 and VTR receives only a $2,000 trade-in, the result is a $1,000 loss. Figure 15-8 shows the journal entry prepared by VTR.

Figure 15-8
Loss on Exchange of
Machinery

Machinery	22 0 0 0 00		
Loss on Exchange of Machinery	1 0 0 0 00		
Accumulated Amortization, Machinery	16 0 0 0 00		
Machinery		19 0 0 0 00	
Cash		20 0 0 0 00	

The entry puts on the books the cost of the new machine. It also records the loss on the exchange, the removal of the old machine, and the related accumulated amortization. Note that cash is reduced by $20,000 (cash price less trade-in). Here is what the ledger would look like after posting:

Machinery (Old)		Accumulated Amortization, Machinery	
Dr.	Cr.	Dr.	Cr.
19,000	19,000	16,000	16,000

Machinery (New)		Loss on Exchange of Machinery	
Dr.	Cr.	Dr.	Cr.
22,000		1,000	

SITUATION 7: EXCHANGING TANGIBLE CAPITAL ASSETS—COMMERCIAL SUBSTANCE
Section 3831 of the *CICA Handbook* makes a distinction between how to account for exchanges of business assets depending on whether the transaction has or does not have "Commercial Substance." Frankly, it is difficult to imagine any "arm's-length" exchange of tangible assets that does not have Commercial Substance, because if the exchange does not have any, why bother with it?

The formal definition of Commercial Substance is that the business entity's predicted future cash flows from the newly acquired asset differ in amount, risk, or timing from the cash flows that would have been recorded if the entity had kept the asset that was given up. Apart from a very few "arranged" transactions between business entities that may be related to each other, it is hard to imagine an actual example of an exchange that does not have Commercial Substance.

If one asset is exchanged for another, and there is Commercial Substance, the accounting proceeds exactly as already described. The fair value of the asset given up is compared to its book value, and the resulting gain or loss is recognized. This change in value is quite easy to follow when the asset involved is (let's say) an older vehicle that was traded in for a newer one. It is also easy to trace the exchange of a whole factory in Italy for a different factory in Quebec, though the amounts involved are probably much larger.

In the unlikely event that you come across an exchange without Commercial Substance, no gain or loss is recorded, and the new asset is recorded at the book value of the asset given up. Since such transactions are very rare, we have not included any examples here.

LEARNING UNIT 15-3 REVIEW

AT THIS POINT you should be able to:

◆ Compare and contrast capital and revenue expenditures. (pp. 652–653)

◆ Prepare journal entries to record discarding, selling, or exchanging plant assets. (pp. 654–657)

Self-Review Quiz 15-3A

(The forms you need are on page 15-3 of the *Study Guide with Working Papers*.)

Respond true or false to the following:

1. In selling a plant asset, a gain results if cash received is greater than the book value of the asset sold.
2. A loss on exchange of equipment can result if the book value of the old equipment is less than the trade-in allowance.
3. Revenue expenditures extend the useful life of an asset.
4. Putting an air conditioner in a truck is an example of a betterment.

Solution to Self-Review Quiz 15-3A

1. True
2. False
3. False
4. True

Self-Review Quiz 15-3B

(The forms you need to complete this Self-Review Quiz are found on page 15-3 of the *Study Guide with Working Papers*.)

Germain Construction purchased a front-end loader several years ago at a cost of $58,000. On March 15, 2013, it sold this old machine in readiness for purchase of a newer model. The new purchase has not yet taken place. The balance in the Accumulated Amortization account for the old machine was $41,200 at the time of the sale.

Please make two different journal entries to record the sale of the old machine. For your first entry, assume the sale price to be $12,000. For your second entry, assume that the sale was for twice that amount, $24,000.

Solution to Self-Review Quiz 15-3B

Assuming a sale price of $12,000:

a.

		GENERAL JOURNAL				Page 1
Date		Account Titles and Descriptions	PR	Debit	Credit	
2013 Mar. 15		Cash		12 00 0 00		
		Accumulated Amortization—Loader		41 2 0 0 00		
		Loss on sale of loader		4 8 0 0 00		
		Loader			58 0 0 0 00	
		To record sale of loader				

Assuming a sale price of $24,000:

b.

	GENERAL JOURNAL				Page 1
Date	Account Titles and Descriptions	PR	Debit	Credit	
2013 Mar. 15	Cash		24 0 0 0 00		
	Accumulated Amortization—Loader		41 2 0 0 00		
	Loader			58 0 0 0 00	
	Gain on sale of loader			7 2 0 0 00	
	To record sale of loader				

Learning Unit 15-4

Natural Resources and Intangible Assets

Another type of long-term asset is natural resources. Natural resources consist of natural assets such as oil, coal, or timber. The acquisition of oil wells or timber is recorded at cost, and as the oil or timber or coal is extracted from the earth, the allocation of that cost occurs through a process known as **depletion**. Depletion is similar to the units-of-production method of amortization, discussed earlier in the chapter, and is listed as an operating expense on the income statement.

Let's take the example of a coal deposit. If a coal deposit has 200,000 tonnes available and was purchased for $200,000, the depletion per tonne is $1. Thus, if 91,000 tonnes were removed from the deposit in 2014, the depletion charge that year would be recorded as shown in Figure 15-9.

Figure 15-9
Depletion of Long-Term Asset

2014 Dec. 31	Depletion of Coal Deposit		91 0 0 0 00	
	Accumulated Depletion, Coal			91 0 0 0 00

Accumulated Depletion is a contra-asset on the balance sheet.

Coal Deposit
Dr.	Cr.
200,000	

(on balance sheet)

Accumulated Depletion, Coal
Dr.	Cr.
	91,000

(on balance sheet)

Depletion of Coal Deposit
Dr.	Cr.
91,000	

(on income statement)

INTANGIBLE ASSETS AND THE CONCEPT OF IMPAIRMENT

6 Explaining amortization and how it applies to intangible assets

Intangible assets are long-lived assets that have no physical existence but do represent valuable legal rights and monetary relationships that benefit a company. (In fact, Prepaid Insurance, Notes, and Accounts Receivable are intangible, but they are classified as *current* assets.) We are looking at intangible assets classified in the *long-term* asset section. Examples include patents, copyrights, franchises, and goodwill. Intangible assets are recorded at cost on the balance sheet and usually have no contra-accounts.

The process of allocating the cost of an intangible asset over all the periods it provides benefits is called *amortization*. The expense incurred in acquiring these assets is **amortized**; that means it is written off over a fixed number of years. **Amortization expense** is an operating expense on the income statement.

PATENTS A **patent** is an exclusive right to the owner to sell or produce his or her discovery or invention. Let's assume that on January 1, 2013, a patent costing $100,000 is amortized over 10 years. The adjusting entry shown in Figure 15-10 is made.

> A patent is good for 20 years but is amortized for a shorter period.

Figure 15-10
Amortizing a Patent

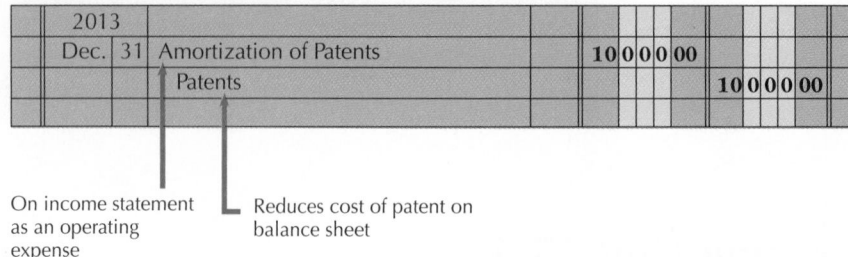

	2013					
	Dec.	31	Amortization of Patents		10 0 0 0 00	
			Patents			10 0 0 0 00

On income statement as an operating expense

Reduces cost of patent on balance sheet

COPYRIGHTS **Copyrights** are exclusive rights granted to owners by the federal government to publish artistic, literary, or musical work. In Canada a copyright is generally granted for the life of the creator and for 50 years thereafter. Certain works are treated differently; for instance, a musical recording is protected for 50 years from the date the recording was made. The cost of the copyright is recorded as a cost and amortized over its expected useful life in an account called Amortization Expense, Copyrights.

FRANCHISES A **franchise** is the result of someone purchasing an exclusive privilege or right to sell a manufacturer's product or a service in a specifically defined geographical location. Subway restaurants, for example, are franchises. The useful life of many franchises are indefinite and thus not amortized.

GOODWILL When all or part of a business is purchased, the difference between the price paid and the value of the identifiable assets is called goodwill. **Goodwill** occurs when the expected rate of future earnings is greater than the rate of earnings for the industry standard. Some considerations that may cause goodwill could include brand names, business location, and a reputation for excellent service. It is not easy to pinpoint the exact amount of goodwill in each accounting period. Thus, in the accounting profession it is agreed not to record goodwill until a company is bought or sold. According to generally accepted accounting principles (GAAP), goodwill is not amortized because the goodwill of companies increases in value. However, if for some reason the value of goodwill is impaired, this decrease in value is recorded in the year in which it takes place by writing down the amount of goodwill by a debit to Loss on Goodwill and a credit to Goodwill.

LEARNING UNIT 15-4 REVIEW

AT THIS POINT you should be able to:

- Define depletion and accumulated depletion and indicate their normal balances and on which financial reports they are located. (p. 659)
- Explain amortization. (p. 660)
- Discuss how a patent is amortized. (p. 660)
- Explain the life of a copyright. (p. 660)
- Define and explain how goodwill is calculated. (p. 660)

Self-Review Quiz 15-4

(The forms you need are on page 15-3 of the *Study Guide with Working Papers*.)

Respond true or false to the following:

1. Intangible assets are depleted, not amortized.
2. A copyright lasts for 25 years.
3. The cost of a franchise must be amortized over 40 years.
4. Goodwill represents excess earning power for a company.

Solution to Self-Review Quiz 15-4

1. False
2. False
3. False
4. True

Learning Unit 15-5
Complex Cases in Accounting for Capital Assets

7 Considering some complexities in accounting for capital assets

Like most topics in accounting, capital assets can have a few challenging aspects. The purpose here is to make you aware of some of these, but not provide details to the extent that you become expert in handling them. Your instructor may advise you to ignore this section entirely.

SITE RESTORATION COSTS

With the current emphasis on the environment, it is becoming rather common for businesses (especially those in the mining sector) to commit to restoring a particular site to the condition they found it in when development began. This commitment is usually made for legal reasons, though in some cases public relations plays a major part. A company that commits to restoring a property to a certain pre-development condition may find that this can be an expensive undertaking.

Since the costs of restoring a property will be incurred years or even decades in the future, it is difficult, if not impossible, to predict with any accuracy what these costs will be. Even if it is possible, calculating these future cash outflows in current values is a major challenge, because such calculations will be based on future interest or discount rates that will not be precise.

Nevertheless, Canadian GAAP rules insist that companies attempt to ascertain an annual expense amount that approximates a fair annual expense to be charged against income for this new reality. The *CICA Handbook* (in Section 3110, "Asset Retirement Obligations") provides more than 20 pages of guidance to Canadian accountants on this very complex topic.

ASSETS ACQUIRED BY LEASE

Many companies arrange to lease various assets instead of purchasing them. For many years now, Canadian GAAP rules have attempted to remove this distinction from Canadian companies' financial statements. Basically, there should be little difference in how the purchased assets and leased assets are accounted for. This is because, legal issues aside, most leases on major capital assets are really not much different from outright ownership.

Accountants in Canada must, of course, treat a true rental agreement as the annual expense it is; fortunately, these contracts are easy to identify by their comparatively short-term nature. The rules set out by the *CICA Handbook* (in Section 3065, "Leases") make it possible for professional accountants to make a judgment about what is and what is not a capital lease.

When a lease is determined to be capital in nature, GAAP require the asset to be set up much like a purchased asset. This means that it is subject to the same levels of amortization as similar assets in the same company, or similar assets in other companies in the same industry. The accounting for leased capital assets itself is not too difficult, but the *Handbook* rules for determining the nature of a capital lease can be a real challenge in some cases.

WRITING DOWN GOODWILL

Earlier in this chapter we mentioned that goodwill is recorded only if a company was purchased. We also mentioned the fact that it is not written off, on the understanding that, in most well-run companies, goodwill will generally increase in value.

Of course, not all companies are well run. What should accountants do when it becomes apparent that goodwill has suffered a permanent decline in value? Once again, the *CICA Handbook* comes to the rescue. Section 3062, starting in paragraph 25, discusses this "impairment loss" and assists Canadian accountants in determining and then recording any loss in value of this particular intangible capital asset. The Section also discusses how to handle similar "impairment losses" on other intangible capital assets, providing guidance on how to record these economic events.

IMPAIRMENT OF TANGIBLE LONG-TERM ASSETS

Not only does the *CICA Handbook* cover how to account for declines in value for intangible capital assets, it also (in Section 3063) details how to account for the possible **impairment** of major assets or groups of assets that have tangible form.

In previous years, the assumption has always been that tangible assets, once purchased, are kept on the company's books, and amortized over the years (almost) without regard to any sort of market price considerations. Accountants who followed this assumption obeyed this "cost principle" in all but a very few circumstances. In the current *Handbook*, Section 3063 overturns this assumption and now requires Canadian accountants to record any measurable and permanent impairment in the listed value of tangible assets.

While the rationale for writing down the value of impaired assets is obvious, it is not always as easy to measure such declines; as a result, Section 3063 provides more than a dozen pages of complex assistance to allow accountants to handle these write-downs in a fair, consistent, and predictable manner. The Section also details how accountants are to handle changes to future amortization charges, as these charges will certainly change on the basis of the revised asset values.

SELF-CONSTRUCTED CAPITAL ASSETS

It is common for a company to commission the construction of one or more of its major capital assets. Quite commonly, this is a building, a head office, or sometimes a factory. When this happens, the company must collect the various costs incurred in the project, and debit these to the cost of the asset. This is clear enough when it comes to materials and labour, but there are certain other costs that should be included as well.

One of these elusive costs is the amount paid for supervision. Often it is not easy to determine what amount to charge to the asset account for these costs, but a fair and reasonable determination must be made to ensure that the new asset's cost includes an allocation of supervision and other "overhead" costs. Note that this can be a very important issue in determining the company's net income, since the choice is between writing the cost off in one year if it is considered a normal expense *or* including it in the asset's cost and writing it off over many years.

Another large cost of self-constructed assets is interest. A project such as constructing a new factory is usually a multiyear undertaking. During this time, most companies borrow money to finance the project. The *CICA Handbook* (Section 3061) permits a company to "capitalize" the interest paid on these loans up until the point that the asset goes into service. After this, the interest is written off as an expense of the period.

FINAL THOUGHTS

The above list of complexities relating to capital assets is certainly not complete, and it will no doubt expand as business complexities increase. Once again, the purpose of this section is not to make you into a sophisticated accountant who can easily deal with such detailed issues. Rather, it is to introduce the reality that there are many tough choices to be made in accounting for capital assets, and to help you know when you need to call upon professional assistance.

SUMMARY OF KEY POINTS

Learning Unit 15-1

1. The total cost of an asset includes all expenditures that are reasonable and necessary in acquiring it and getting it into position and in condition for use in the company.

2. Cash discounts are deducted from the cost of an asset.

3. Incidental costs related to the purchase of land and special costs that add a permanent value are added to the cost of land.

4. The Land Improvements account records improvements to land that have a limited useful life (such as driveways or fences). This account is subject to amortization.

5. The cost of buying a building would include purchase price and all costs of repairs and other expenses to get the building ready for use. When constructing a new building, the cost would include all payments necessary to get the building ready for use.

Learning Unit 15-2

In this unit we look at four different amortization methods.

1. Straight-line method:
   a. Amortization expense is the same each year.
   b. Book value each year is lowered until residual value is reached.

2. Units-of-production method:
   a. Amortization expense is directly related to output or usage of asset.
   b. Assets cannot be amortized below residual value.

3. Double-declining-balance method:
   a. Residual value is not deducted from cost.
   b. Amortization expense is book value at beginning of year times rate.
   c. Asset cannot amortize below residual value.

4. Sum-of-the-years'-digits method (optional section):
   a. Fraction for the year is multiplied times cost less residual value.
   b. Amortization in year 1 is highest.

5. Amortization can be taken for partial years. If an asset is purchased in the first 15 days of the month, the whole month is considered in the amortization calculation.

6. CCA is for tax reporting, whereas the other four amortization methods are used for financial reports.

Learning Unit 15-3

1. Capital expenditures include the original cost of an asset and three categories of additional payments:
   a. *Additions or enlargements:* major changes or improvements that increase the value of an asset
   b. *Extraordinary repairs:* extend the life of the asset
   c. *Betterments:* improvements that increase efficiency but do not extend the life of an asset

Additions or enlargements and betterments are charged to the asset account, as are extraordinary repairs.

2. After an asset is acquired, the expenditures for ordinary maintenance and unnecessary or unreasonable situations that do not try to extend useful life are treated as expenses of the current period and are called *revenue expenditures*.

3. A plant asset can be disposed of by discarding, selling, or exchanging it.

4. The Loss on Disposal account appears as Other Expense on the income statement.

5. A gain on sale of an asset occurs if the cash received is greater than the book value of the asset. Such a gain appears as Other Income on the income statement.

6. When a plant asset is exchanged, loss occurs when the trade-in allowance is less than the book value of the asset.

7. In an exchange of similar assets without commercial substance, the *CICA Handbook* states that gains are to be absorbed into the cost of the new asset.

Learning Unit 15-4

1. Natural resources, such as oil, coal, or timber, will deplete over a period of time as resources are extracted. Depletion expense is listed as an operating expense on the income statement.

2. Accumulated depletion is a contra-asset on the balance sheet.

3. Intangible assets, such as patents, copyrights, franchises, and goodwill, are also used up over a period of years. Amortization is the process of estimating and recording the charges as these intangible assets are used up.

4. Amortization expenses are operating expenses on the income statement.

5. A patent is good for 20 years; a copyright is granted for the life of the creator and 50 years thereafter.

6. The cost of obtaining a franchise is usually not amortized.

7. Because it is not easy to put a price on goodwill in each accounting period, it is not until a company is bought or sold that a cost is placed on goodwill. Goodwill is not amortized but impairment could result if a loss in value is incurred.

Learning Unit 15-5

1. Accounting for assets with relatively long lives sometimes becomes quite challenging. This may require that professional accounting assistance be obtained for issues like the following.

2. Site restoration costs are now required to be estimated and charged to expense annually when necessary.

3. Leased assets may just be a minor legal document away from being essentially an asset purchase. The *CICA Handbook* requires the lease to be accounted for as a purchase whenever the lease is not clearly a rental agreement.

4. Accounting for goodwill when it has been purchased is in one way simpler than before. If there has been no impairment of its value, no accounting entries are needed; otherwise it should be written down to its impaired value.

5. Impairment of other long-term assets is also now grounds for accounting for the impairment. This is a recent change to the long-established rule that assets are carried at their actual cost.

6. Self-constructed assets need to include all costs necessary to their completion. Things such as supervision and interest charges are sometimes a challenge to identify exactly, and may require expert accounting advice to be completed correctly.

KEY TERMS

Accelerated amortization method   More amortization taken in early years of an asset's life; decreasing amounts in later years (p. 645)

Additions or **enlargements**   Major changes or improvements that increase the value of an asset (such as adding a new wing to a school) (p. 653)

Amortization expense   An operating expense on the income statement relating to intangible assets (pp. 641, 660)

Amortize   To charge a portion of an expenditure over a fixed number of years. Those assets with indefinite lives are not subject to amortization (p. 660)

Betterments   Improvements that increase the efficiency of an asset by adding accessories or replacing parts (p. 653)

Book value   Cost of asset less accumulated amortization (p. 644)

Capital cost allowance   The government-permitted method of computing the maximum amount of amortization that can be deducted from business net income in one year (p. 648)

Capital expenditures   Original cost of an asset as well as additions or enlargements, extraordinary repairs, and betterments (p. 653)

Copyright   The exclusive right that is granted by the federal government to sell and reproduce literary, musical, or artistic works for a period of time (p. 660)

Depletion   Amount of natural resources that has been exhausted by mining, pumping, and so forth for a period of time (p. 659)

Double-declining-balance method   An accelerated amortization method that uses up to twice the straight-line rate times book value of asset to calculate amortization expense. Residual value is not subtracted from the cost of an asset in determining amortization. (p. 645)

Extraordinary repairs   Infrequent expenditures that extend an asset's life (such as a new engine in a car) (p. 653)

Franchise   A right granted by business or government to produce or sell goods in a specific geographic region (examples are Subway and Holiday Inn) (p. 660)

Goodwill   When a business is purchased, the difference between the price paid and the value of the identifiable assets is goodwill. Goodwill may depend on brand names, business location, service, or other elements; it is a valuable asset that plays an important part in the expected rate of future earnings of a business. (p. 660)

Impairment   Value of an asset that decreases and is written off or taken over a period of time (p. 662)

Intangible assets   Assets having no physical substance (such as patents or franchises) (p. 641)

Land Improvements   An asset account that records improvements made to land. Such improvements have a limited life and are subject to amortization (an example is a driveway or fences). (p. 642)

Patent   An exclusive right to sell or produce one's discovery or invention. A patent is good for 20 years. (p. 660)

Residual (salvage) value   The anticipated amount of the asset's cost that will be recovered when the asset is sold, traded in, or scrapped (p. 644)

Straight-line method   Method that allocates an equal amount of amortization over an asset's period of usefulness (p. 644)

Sum-of-the-years'-digits method   An accelerated method that allocates amortization each period of an asset's life by multiplying a fraction for that period times cost less residual value (p. 646)

Trade-in allowance   A value received when one asset is traded in on the purchase of another asset. For example, when you buy a new car you may trade in your old car for an amount of money that is applied toward the purchase of the new car. (p. 656)

Undepreciated capital cost   The total of capital expenditures recorded but not yet claimed as capital cost allowance. This amount is carried forward to be available as a CCA deduction in future years. (p. 649)

Units-of-production method   An amortization method that is based on usage and not on time. An example of units of production is the numbers of shoes a machine could produce in its expected useful life. (p. 645)

Useful life   At the time an asset is acquired, an estimate is made of its usefulness in terms of years, output, and so forth. (p. 644)

BLUEPRINT OF KEY ACCOUNTS

Review of Key Accounts				
Account	**Category***	↑	**Normal Balance**	**Financial Report Found on**
Equipment	Plant Asset	Dr.	Dr.	Balance Sheet
Buildings	Plant Asset	Dr.	Dr.	Balance Sheet
Land	Plant Asset	Dr.	Dr.	Balance Sheet
Loss on Disposal of Plant Asset	Other Expense	Dr.	Dr.	Income Statement
Loss from Fire	Other Expense	Dr.	Dr.	Income Statement
Gain on Sale of Plant Asset	Other Income	Cr.	Cr.	Income Statement
Loss on Exchange of Machinery	Other Expense	Dr.	Dr.	Income Statement
Depletion of Coal Deposit	Operating Expense	Dr.	Dr.	Income Statement
Accumulated Depletion	Contra-Asset	Cr.	Cr.	Balance Sheet
Coal Deposit	Natural Resource	Dr.	Dr.	Balance Sheet
Patents	Intangible Asset	Dr.	Dr.	Balance Sheet
Amortization Expense	Operating Expense	Dr.	Dr.	Income Statement
Copyrights, Franchises, or Goodwill	Intangible Assets	Dr.	Dr.	Balance Sheet
Loss of Goodwill	Other Expense	Dr.	Dr.	Income Statement

*We use Plant Assets to represent property, plant, and equipment.

QUESTIONS, CLASSROOM DEMONSTRATION EXERCISES, EXERCISES, AND PROBLEMS

Discussion Questions and Critical Thinking/Ethical Case

1. What types of payment are considered "reasonable and necessary" when determining the cost of an asset?

2. What is the purpose of the Land Improvements account?

3. What is the difference between revenue and capital expenditures?

4. What are four methods of calculating amortization? Briefly explain the key points of each.

5. What is the purpose of the CCA system?

6. A betterment is a revenue expenditure. True or false? Please explain.

7. Which method of amortization does *not* deduct residual value in its calculation?

8. When a plant asset is sold, a loss results if the cash received is greater than book value. Agree or disagree? Please explain.

9. A loss on an exchange of plant assets occurs when the book value of the old machine is more than the trade-in allowance. True or false?

10. Explain how the CCA tax method treats the recording of exchanges of plant assets that result in a loss.

11. What is the purpose of the Accumulated Depletion account?

12. List and describe three intangible assets.

13. Pete went to an auto dealer to buy a new Jeep. The salesperson told Pete that cars really appreciate in value. He cited antique cars as a perfect example. The dealer went on to tell Pete that buying a car represents some great tax savings. He told Pete that leasing is getting less and less popular. Should Pete buy a new car? You make the call. Write down your recommendations to Pete.

MyAccountingLab

Make the grade with MyAccountingLab! The exercises and problems marked in green can be found on MyAccountingLab at www.myaccountinglab.com. You can practise them as often as you want, and many of them feature step-by-step guided solutions to help you find the right answer. You can also find working papers for selected problems in the Multimedia Library on MyAccountingLab.

Classroom Demonstration Exercises

(The forms you need are on pages 15-4 to 15-5 of the *Study Guide with Working Papers*.)

Set A

Cost of Property, Plant, and Equipment

The total cost of a machine
1 (5 min)

1. Calculate the total cost of the machine given the following:

List price	$3,000
Cash discount	6%
Freight	$60
Assembly	$200
Special foundation	$60

Straight-Line Method

Yearly amortization using the straight-line method
2 (10 min)

2. Lee Ring amortizes his truck by the straight-line method. Calculate the yearly amortization expense given the following:

Cost	$7,000
Residual value	$2,000
Estimate of useful life	5 years

Book Value

Book value of the asset—cost of asset less accumulated amortization
2 (10 min)

3. If a machine had a cost of $6,000 with an accumulated amortization of $500, what would be its book value?

Units-of-Production Method

Amortization expense directly related to use—the units-of-production method
2 (10 min)

4. If Lee Ring (Classroom Demonstration Exercise 2) amortized his truck by the units-of-production method, calculate the first year's amortization based on the following: cost, $7,000; residual value, $2,000. Estimated mileage is 50,000 kilometres. The truck was driven 7,000 kilometres in year 1.

Double-Declining-Balance Method

Double-declining-balance amortization is an accelerated method
2 (10 min)

5. If Lee Ring (Classroom Demonstration Exercise 2) amortized his truck by the double-declining-balance method, calculate the amortization expense for year 1.

Sum-of-the-Years'-Digits Method (Optional)

Sum-of-the-years'-digits method places more amortization expense in the early years
2 (10 min)

6. If Lee Ring (Classroom Demonstration Exercise 2) amortized his truck by the sum-of-the-years'-digits method, calculate the first year's amortization. Round the answer to the nearest dollar.

Capital and Revenue Expenditures

The difference between capital and revenue expenditures
4 (5 min)

7. Identify each situation as a capital expenditure or revenue expenditure.

Situation	Capital Expenditure		Revenue Expenditure
		Betterment/ Extraordinary	
	Addition	Repair	
a. New car engine replaced			
b. New air-conditioning filters			
c. New roof			
d. New addition on prep school			

Loss and Gains

8. Complete the following:

	Account	Category	Financial Statement Found On:
a.	Gain on Sale of Plant Assets		
b.	Accumulated Depletion		
c.	Loss on Disposal of Plant Assets		

Exchange with Loss

Book value, loss, and journalizing the exchange
5 (15 min)

9. Lee Co. traded in an old machine costing $20,000 for a new machine for a cash price of $19,000 with a trade-in allowance of $6,000. Accumulated Amortization on the old machine was $11,000.
   a. What is the book value of the old machine? What is the loss?
   b. Provide a journal entry to record the exchange.

Exchange with Gain

Trade-in with gain; journalizing the gain
5 (15 min)

10. Assume in Exercise 9 the trade-in value was $10,000. Prepare a journal entry to record the exchange.

Set B

Cost of Property, Plant, and Equipment

The total cost of a machine
1 (5 min)

1. Calculate the total cost of the machine given the following:

List price	$2,000
Cash discount	5%
Freight	$50
Assembly	$150
Special foundation	$50

Straight-Line Method

Yearly amortization using the straight-line method
2 (10 min)

2. Mel Jones amortizes his truck by the straight-line method. Calculate the yearly amortization expense given the following:

Cost	$6,000
Residual value	$1,000
Estimated useful life	10 years

Book Value

Book value of the asset—cost of asset less accumulated amortization
2 (10 min)

3. If a machine had a cost of $4,000 with an accumulated amortization of $1,000, what would be its book value?

Units-of-Production Method

Amortization expense directly related to use—the units-of-production method
2 (10 min)

4. If Mel Jones (Classroom Demonstration Exercise 2) amortized his truck by the units-of-production method, calculate the first year's amortization based on the following: cost $6,000; residual value $1,000. Estimated mileage is 100,000 kilometres. The truck was driven 8,000 kilometres in year 1.

Double-Declining-Balance Method

Double-declining-balance amortization is an accelerated method
2 (10 min)

5. If Mel Jones (Exercise 2) amortized his truck by the double-declining-balance method, calculate the amortization expense for year 1.

Sum-of-the-Years'-Digits Method (Optional)

Sum-of-the-years'-digits method places more amortization expense in the early years
2 (10 min)

6. If Mel Jones (Classroom Demonstration Exercise 2) amortized his truck by the sum-of-the-years'-digits method, calculate the first year's amortization. Round the answer to the nearest dollar.

Capital and Revenue Expenditures

The difference between capital and revenue expenditures
4 (5 min)

7. Identify each situation as a capital expenditure or revenue expenditure.

Situation	Capital Expenditure		Revenue Expenditure
	Addition	Betterment/ Extraordinary Repair	
a. New tires			
b. New air-conditioning for a car			
c. New car engine			
d. New addition on school			

Loss and Gains

Analyzing loss and gains of plant assets
5 (5 min)

8. Complete the following:

	Account	Category	Financial Statement Found On:
a. Accumulated Amortization			
b. Loss on Disposal of Plant Assets			
c. Gain on Sale of Plant Assets			

Exchange with Loss

Book value, loss, and journalizing the exchange
5 (15 min)

9. Pete Co. traded in an old machine costing $10,000 for a new machine for a cash price of $13,000 with a trade-in allowance of $3,000. Accumulated Amortization on the old machine was $6,000.
 a. What is the book value of the old machine? What is the loss?
 b. Provide a journal entry to record the exchange.

Exchange with Gain

Trade-in with gain; journalizing the gain
5 (15 min)

10. Assume in Classroom Demonstration Exercise 9 the trade-in value was $5,000. Prepare a journal entry to record the exchange.

Exercises

(The forms you need are on pages 15-6 to 15-9 of the *Study Guide with Working Papers.*)

The total cost of a machine
1 (15 min)

15-1. Mack Company incurred the following expenditures to buy a new machine:
 ◆ Invoice, $30,000 less 10% cash discount
 ◆ Freight charges, $500
 ◆ Assembly charges, $1,400
 ◆ Special base to support machine, $505
 ◆ Machine dropped and repaired, $350

What is the actual cost of the machine?

Amortization methods
2 (30 min)

15-2. From the following, prepare amortization schedules for the first two years for **a.** straight-line, **b.** units-of-production, **c.** double-declining-balance at twice the straight-line rate, and **d.** sum-of-the-years'-digits (optional) methods.

 ◆ Machine purchased on January 1, $1,440
 ◆ Residual value, $240

- ◆ Estimated useful life, 5 years
- ◆ Total estimated output, 600 units
- ◆ Output year 1, 100 units
- ◆ Output year 2, 200 units

Amortization schedules
2 (30 min)

15-3. Larson Co., whose accounting period ends on December 31, purchased a machine for $6,800 on January 1 with an estimated residual value of $800 and estimated useful life of 10 years. Prepare amortization schedules for the current as well as the following year using **a.** straight-line, **b.** double-declining-balance at twice the straight-line rate, and **c.** sum-of-the-years'-digits (optional) methods.

Book value, loss, and journalizing
the exchange
5 (30 min)

15-4. A machine that cost $9,000 with $3,900 of accumulated amortization was traded in for a similar machine having a $5,800 cash price. An $800 trade-in was offered by the seller.

- **a.** Calculate the book value of the old machine.
- **b.** Calculate the loss on the exchange.
- **c.** Prepare the journal entry for the exchange.
- **d.** Calculate the cost basis of the new equipment if the income tax method (CCA) is used. Assume accumulated amortization and total CCA taken before the exchange are equal.

Amortization of an intangible
asset—a pattern
6 (10 min)

15-5. On May 1, 2014, Osgood Company bought a patent at a cost of $5,000. It is estimated that the patent will give Osgood a competitive advantage for 10 years. Record in general journal form amortization for 2014 and 2015. (Assume December 31 is the end of the accounting period for Osgood.)

Capital cost allowance—
amortization for tax purposes
3 (10 min)

15-6. Pultzer Company bought a light general-purpose truck for $18,000 on March 8, 2013. This Class 10 asset had an UCC of $41,000 from 2012. Calculate the maximum CCA allowed for 2013 for this asset class.

Group A Problems

(The forms you need are on pages 15-10 to 15-15 of the *Study Guide with Working Papers*.)

Journalizing asset transactions
1 4 (30 min)

15A-1. Record the following transactions into the general journal of Orange Company of Surrey.

2012
Feb.   6   Purchased land for $90,000. The $90,000 included legal fees of $6,000.

17   Orange Company decided to pave the parking lot for $5,400.

Mar.   23   Purchased a building for $90,000, putting down 30% and mortgaging the remainder.

30   Bought equipment for $32,000. Freight and assembly were an additional $4,000.

May   11   Added a new wing for $175,000 to building that was purchased on March 23.

June   15   Performed ordinary repair work on equipment purchased March 30, $750, to maintain its normal operations.

July   3   Bought a truck for $14,000.

Oct.   15   Added a hydraulic loader to truck, $2,200.

Nov.   30   Truck purchased in July was brought in for grease and oil, $33.

Dec.   28   Overhauled truck's motor for $900, extending its life by more than one year.

Dec.   31   Changed tires on truck, $325.

15A-2. On January 1, 2014, a machine was installed at Moncton's Lavy Factory at a cost of $58,000. Its estimated residual value at the end of its estimated life of four years is $18,000. The machine is expected to produce 80,000 units with the following production schedule:

- 2014: 12,000 units
- 2015: 27,000 units
- 2016: 15,000 units
- 2017: 26,000 units

Complete amortization schedules for **a.** straight-line, **b.** units-of-production, **c.** double-declining-balance at twice the straight-line rate, and **d.** sum-of-the-years'-digits (optional) methods.

Amortization of equipment

2 (60 min)

Check Figure

b. Book Value End of Year 2015
$1,722.50

15A-3. On June 13, 2013, Cook Company of Brandon bought equipment for $4,080. Its estimated life is four years with a residual value of $240. Prepare amortization schedules for 2013, 2014, and 2015 for **a.** straight-line, **b.** double-declining-balance at twice the straight-line rate, and **c.** sum-of-the-years'-digits (optional) methods.

Journalizing entries for discarding, selling, or exchanging equipment

5 (60 min)

15A-4. Journalize the following transactions for the Robe Company of Yorktown and below each entry show all calculations:

2014

Jan.   3 Sold a truck for $1,250 that cost $6,750 and had accumulated amortization of $6,100.

Feb.   10 A machine costing $3,200 with accumulated amortization of $2,450 was destroyed in a fire. The insurance company settled the claim for $300.

May   2 Traded in a machine costing $19,400 with $16,500 of accumulated amortization for a new machine costing $25,100 with a trade-in allowance of $2,700. Note that amortization is up to date. The loss is to be recognized.

Check Figure

May 2: Loss on trade-in
$200 Dr.

July   8 Traded in a machine costing $40,000 with $34,000 of accumulated amortization (which is up to date) for a new machine for a cash price of $45,000 and a trade-in allowance of $8,000.

Sept. 12 A truck costing $7,000 and fully amortized was disposed of.

Group B Problems

(The forms you need are on pages 15-10 to 15-15 of the *Study Guide with Working Papers*.)

Journalizing asset transactions

1 4 (30 min)

15B-1. Journalize the following transactions for Orange Company of Surrey.

2012

Apr.   3 Purchased a machine for $89,500 along with an additional charge for freight and assembly of $1,500.

10 Purchased land at a cost of $22,000. The $22,000 included legal fees of $2,500.

16 Purchased a building for $90,000, putting down 10% and mortgaging the remainder.

30 At a cost of $1,900, cleared and graded the land purchased on April 10 (the additional cost considered as part of the cost of land).

Check Figure

May 8:

Dr. Building $2,900
Cr. Cash $2,900

May   1 Performed regular maintenance work on machinery, $160, to maintain its normal operations.

8 Painted the building purchased on April 16, $2,900. Painting was necessary to have the building ready for proper use.

May 29 Purchased a second airplane for company business, $65,000.
June 27 Installed a hydraulic loader on a truck at a cost of $2,900.
July 30 First airplane's engine was overhauled for $7,900.
Sept. 28 Building is completely renovated at a cost of $30,000, which will extend its life by 10 years.

Amortization of a machine
❷ (60 min)

Check Figure

b. Book Value End of Year 2017 $9,000

15B-2. On January 1, 2014, Lavy Factory of Moncton installed a new machine at a cost of $117,000. Its estimated residual value at the end of its estimated life of four years is $9,000. The machine is expected to produce 90,000 units with the following production schedule:

◆ 2014: 11,000 units   ◆ 2016: 11,000 units
◆ 2015: 9,000 units   ◆ 2017: 59,000 units

Complete amortization schedules for **a.** straight-line, **b.** units-of-production, **c.** double-declining-balance at twice the straight-line rate, and **d.** sum-of-the-years'-digits (optional) methods.

Amortization of equipment
❷ (60 min)

Check Figure

b. Book Value End of Year 2015 $1,562.40

15B-3. On April 5, 2013, Cook Company of Brandon bought equipment for $6,200. Its estimated life is five years with a residual value of $200. Prepare amortization schedules for 2013, 2014, and 2015 for **a.** straight-line, **b.** double-declining-balance at twice the straight-line rate, and **c.** sum-of-the-years'-digits (optional) methods.

Journalizing entries for discarding, selling, or exchanging equipment
❺ (60 min)

15B-4. Journalize the following transactions for the Robe Company of Yorktown and below each entry show all calculations:

2014
Jan. 2 Sold a truck for $3,600 that cost $12,800 and had accumulated amortization of $10,900.

Check Figure

May 9: Loss on Trade-in $150 Dr.

Feb. 6 A machine costing $4,000 with accumulated amortization of $3,390 was destroyed in a fire. The insurance company settled the claim for $150.

May 9 Traded in a machine costing $18,500 with $15,750 of accumulated amortization (which is up to date) for a new machine costing $26,200 with a trade-in allowance of $2,600. The loss is to be recognized.

July 10 Traded in a machine costing $39,500 with $35,700 of accumulated amortization (amortization is up to date) for a new machine for a cash price of $44,000 and a trade-in allowance of $11,500.

Sept. 12 A truck costing $11,000 and fully amortized was disposed of.

Group C Problems

(The forms you need are on pages 15-16 to 15-22 of the *Study Guide with Working Papers*.)

Journalizing asset transactions
❶ ❹ (60 min)

Check Figure

Apr 30:

Dr. Metalworking Machinery $11,400
    Metal Lathe $8,775
Cr. Wages Expense $20,175

15C-1. The O'Hannigan Company of Edmonton made the following transactions relating to property, plant, and equipment during 2012. Use the company's General Journal to record the following transactions:

2012
Jan. 26 Purchased land and a building for $780,000. In addition to this actual purchase amount, the total cost of the purchase included legal fees of $6,800, an appraisal fee of $3,600, a survey certificate of $4,200, and GST of $39,730. One cheque (No. 4772) for the total of the amounts listed ($834,330) was issued to Humboldt and Lim, Barristers and

Solicitors. The appraisal determined that 40% of the total purchase price was for the land, while the rest was for the building.

Mar. 14 Purchased a new metal lathe from Hanover Ltd. of Germany. The purchase price was 265,000 euros, which at the current exchange rate equates to $347,400 Canadian. Wrote cheque No. 4816 to cover this purchase. Delivery is expected in mid-April. The company wants to keep the cost of this major asset separate from all other machinery.

Mar. 22 Purchased four used metalworking machines from Parmar and Sons, Auctioneers in Grande Cache. Total purchase price was $146,500, plus GST of $7,325 (cheque No. 4907). Mainland Transport will deliver the four machines in three days.

Mar. 27 The four machines mentioned above were delivered, and Mainland Transport requested and got a cheque for the freight—$4,885, plus GST of $244.25 (cheque No. 4988).

Apr. 2 Eastern Renovations Ltd. completed an extensive renovation of the building purchased Jan. 26. Wrote cheque No. 5033 —$57,500, plus GST of $2,875 for the job, which got the building ready for occupancy.

Apr. 5 Wrote cheque No. 5079 for $5,000, plus GST of $250, to McReady Concrete Ltd. to pay for concrete bases for the four machines purchased at auction, as well as for the new German lathe expected to arrive next week. Estimated that 70% of this cost is for the concrete base for the lathe, while the rest is for concrete bases for the other four machines.

Apr. 9 Wrote cheque No. 5122 to Liberty Millwrights for installing the four machines purchased at auction—$8,600, plus GST of $430.

Apr. 12 Intercontinental Brokers Ltd. faxed an invoice that covered: import duties on the metal lathe ($7,300); transportation charges from Germany to Edmonton ($24,550); GST charges on the purchase price plus duties and transportation totalling $28,693; plus its own fee for handling the entire importation process ($3,000, plus GST of $150). It requested that a cheque be prepared to cover all of these amounts (except the lathe purchase price, which was paid separately), and cheque No. 5185 was prepared, signed, and delivered in the amount of $63,693.

Apr. 20 Another cheque to Liberty Millwrights for installing the German lathe—$14,000, plus GST of $700 (cheque No. 5336).

Apr. 30 The company's controller calculated that of the total payroll for April, $11,400 was paid to employees who worked on calibrating and doing final adjustments on the four auction machines. The controller also calculated that a further $8,775 represented wages to calibrate, adjust, and program the computer-controlled feature of the new lathe. Up to this point, all wages have been debited to Wages Expense.

June 19 Purchased a computer-controlled module to replace a manual part on one of the machines bought at auction. Cheque No. 5472 to Lifetime Maximum Machinery Ltd. was for $12,600, which included installation, testing and 5% GST. This greatly expands the capability and speed of the machine to which it is attached.

July 13 A careless employee stripped the drive gear assembly of the new German lathe. Repairs cost $8,000, plus GST of $400, payable to Action Machinery Ltd. (cheque No. 5504). Such repairs, while unfortunate, are far from unusual, and are expected to happen occasionally.

Oct. 23 Paid (cheque No. 5709) Acme Roofing Ltd. $60,000, plus GST of $3,000 for emergency installation of a new metal roof, because a storm destroyed the old, shingled roof. After careful consideration, it was determined that one-third of the cost of the new roof represents ordinary repairs, while the balance is considered the cost of a major roof improvement.

Amortization of machine
2 **(90 min)**

15C-2. At the end of month three of its fiscal year, on March 29, 2013, the Abrahmson Company of Winnipeg purchased a new wave-soldering machine that complies with the standards needed to fabricate parts for space exploration. The new machine cost $80,000, plus GST of $4,000, and is expected to last for five years, with a salvage value of $20,000 at that time. Each year the machine is capable of producing 5,000 square metres of printed circuit board (PCB) at maximum capacity. Planned output for the five-year period is as follows:

Check Figure

b. Amort. Expense 2018
$2,268 (Rounding)

2013 (9 months only) 2,800 m^2
2014 (12 months) 4,200 m^2
2015 (12 months) 4,600 m^2
2016 (12 months) 4,800 m^2
2017 (12 months) 4,000 m^2
2018 (3 months only) 800 m^2

This company has a policy of taking amortization in any year proportional to the number of months the equipment is used (or how many square metres of board are produced).

Required

Complete an amortization schedule for **a.** straight-line, **b.** units-of-production, **c.** double-declining-balance at two times the rate used in **a.** above, and **d.** optionally, sum-of-the-years'-digits methods. Be certain to include the amounts to be amortized for each of the six years ending in 2013 through 2018.

Capital cost allowance
1 3 **(60 min)**

15C-3. Refer to Problem 15C-2. Assume the identical set of facts, but in addition pretend that the machine falls into a new CCA class for taxation purposes. Let's say it falls into Class 44, which has a rate of 60%.
   a. Calculate the maximum allowable CCA that the company will be permitted to claim for each of the five taxation years of 2013 through 2017.
   b. Assuming that the company claims the maximum CCA each year, what is the unamortized capital cost for this asset at the end of 2017 after the CCA for that year is claimed?
   c. Assume that in 2018 the machine is not sold, but remains idle after producing the final production run of 800 square metres of PCBs by March 31 of that year. How much CCA can the company claim in the 2018 taxation year?

Check Figure

UCC December 31, 2016
$3,584

Capital cost allowance schedule
1 3 **(60 min)**

15C-4. The Montreal Music Company Ltd. has a fiscal year that ends March 31. As of March 31, 2012, the company had the following unamortized capital costs (UCC) in each of its four categories as shown here:

Buildings	Class 6	10% rate	UCC—$452,072
Office Equipment	Class 8	20% rate	UCC—$120,644
Vehicles	Class 10	30% rate	UCC—$378,906
Computers	Class 50	55% rate	UCC—$46,403

During the year ending March 31, 2012, the company had the following transactions involving these assets:

- *Buildings.* No transactions.
- *Office equipment.* Purchased a total of $16,400 (net of GST), and hauled office equipment that had once cost $6,000 to the recycle centre.
- *Vehicles.* Purchased two new delivery vans for a combined total cost of $54,000 (net of GST), and traded in an older car used by the sales manager for a new model with a list price of $32,800. The traded-in car had cost $24,000, had a net book value of $12,580, and was given a trade-in price of $14,800. Newspapers at the time of the trade-in had several ads regarding the exact new model purchased for an offering price of $29,999, and the cheque written (before GST) was for $14,900.
- *Computers.* New computers with operating systems were added at a total cost (before GST) of $23,450. Four older computers with a net book value of $1035 were donated to a local school. No cash changed hands for this donation.

Required

Prepare a CCA schedule for the company for the March 31, 2013 year. Assume that the company wants to take the maximum CCA available for the year.

Amortization

① ② (90 min)

Check Figure

b. Net Book Value June 30, 2016

$350,000

15C-5. Eastern Press Company of Regina has a fiscal year that ends on June 30 each year. On March 12, 2012, the company purchased a new high-speed printing press at a total cost of $875,000 before GST. The company has a policy that such assets are amortized on a monthly basis commencing the month after they are purchased. While the press is expected to last for 10 years, when it will have a value of $100,000, it is far more likely that it will be made obsolete for Eastern Press Company in four years, when it could be sold for $350,000.

Required

Assuming that the four-year term is the most likely, generate amortization schedules for 2012 through 2016 (that's 5 fiscal years) for the new press, assuming three methods of amortization:

- Straight-line
- Double-declining-balance (at two times the straight-line rate)
- (Optional) Sum-of-the-years'-digits

Your schedules should clearly show the amortization charged for each year, as well as the net book value at the end of each year.

Disposal of capital assets

① ⑤ (45 min)

Check Figure

Mar 5:

Dr. Accum. Amort.— Computers $2,710
Loss on Theft of Laptop $1,540
Cr. Computer Equipment $4,250

15C-6. The Kingsly Company of Wabamun had disposals of various capital assets for its latest fiscal year, which ended December 31, 2013 (all amounts are net of GST):

a. *Feb. 23, 2013:* Sold for $2,000 a large drafting table with all accompanying fittings that had cost $11,300 and had accumulated amortization of $8,680.

b. *Mar. 5, 2013:* A laptop computer that had cost $4,250 a couple of years ago, and that had accumulated amortization of $2,710, was stolen from the car of a company officer. No insurance is maintained on assets like this, and police had a good laugh when asked about the chances of its being found.

c. *Apr. 23, 2013:* An old forklift that had originally cost $18,600 and with accumulated amortization of $12,570 (to the end of March 2013) was traded in on a new unit with somewhat greater capacity. The new unit had a selling price of $34,000, and the old forklift was given a trade-in price of $9,500. Since the company takes no amortization in the month of purchase, but a full month's in the month of disposal, the amortization amount of $83 needs to be recorded in April 2013 before recording the purchase/trade-in.

d. *Oct. 12, 2013:* A movie producer from California wrote a cheque for $200,000 (plus GST of $10,000) for an old coal-crushing machine that had been fully amortized eight years previously. (Net book value is now zero.) The crusher had cost $1,600,000 in 1972, but was too old and underpowered to function in a modern mining operation. The machine is to be a main prop in a forthcoming movie filmed mainly in Alberta. The film company assumed financial responsibility for dismantling and moving the large machine.

Required

Record the above disposals in general journal format. Please also record any necessary adjustments as indicated in each item **a.** to **d.**

On-the-job Training

(The forms you need are on page 15-23 of the *Study Guide with Working Papers*.)

Repairing or disposing of an asset
❷ (30 min)

T-1. On August 2, 2013, Hope Co. purchased a customized light truck for $96,000 cash. On August 6, special shelving was added to the truck for $6,000. The truck has a useful life of six years with a trade-in value of $12,000 and is amortized by the straight-line method. On January 4, 2016, Hope Co. was trying to decide whether to overhaul the truck at a cost of $15,000 or buy a new truck for $100,000 and depreciate it using CCA rules. Overhauling the truck would increase its useful life by two years, and residual value would remain at $12,000.

As the accountant of Hope Co., you have been called into a meeting with Mr. Reynolds, the vice-president, to further discuss this matter. Bring all your data with you, along with a written recommendation regarding the financial aspects of the two possibilities.

Amortization for financial reports
❷ (20 min)

T-2.

MEMO

To: Hal Owen

From: Pete Sanchez

Re: Decision on general-purpose truck

We need your help deciding which amortization method would be best for us to use. I'm thinking that we should use the CCA rules instead of the straight-line method for both financial and tax purposes. We could save lots of dollars! Could you verify my decision (or not) and work up the numbers for me based on the following:

Cost:	$20,000
Life:	5 years
Residual:	$5,000

Statement of Cash Flows

THE BIG PICTURE

When you walk into a lululemon athletica store, the first sound you hear might be the trickling of water from a fountain or the soothing melody of a meditation CD. The stores project an atmosphere of peace and calm that befits a store selling yoga-inspired clothing. But the sound that most people associate with lululemon these days is less a spiritual "Ohmm" and more the cheerful *cha-ching!* of the cash register.

Founded by Chip Wilson in Vancouver in 2000, the athletic clothing store has taken North America by storm, with its fashions appearing in top magazines and television shows. Stores have opened in Japan and Australia, and the company went public in 2007. Shares sold originally for about $30, dropping to a low of below $6 in late summer of 2009. Much of that loss has been made up, and the shares are currently about $40 in late 2010. The shares did reach a high of more than $50 at one point. Sales revenues were $148 million in 2007, and the 2010 figures show the company closing in on half a billion. Profits likewise have soared—from $8 million in 2007 to a 2010 amount of $58 million.

All of this activity has undoubtedly had a positive effect on lululemon's cash flow, which is an interesting and important part of running any business. A statement of cash flows is something that accountants use that discloses the sources and uses of cash. It provides invaluable information about the cash flow of a company that is not available from other financial statements.

So when you walk into lululemon and put $100 down on a pair of "boogie pants," know that somewhere—someplace—there is an accountant keeping track of your money.

Just so long as they're eyeing the bottom line, and not eyeing...

Well, you get the idea.

In preceding chapters we analyzed as well as prepared three financial statements. Let's quickly review the purposes of each statement.

- *Income statement:* Shows the results of the company's operations for a given period. The net income or loss results in an increase or decrease to retained earnings.
- *Statement of retained earnings:* Summarizes the changes in retained earnings of a company during a period of time.
- *Balance sheet:* Shows the end-of-period financial position of a company at a particular date.

1 **Understanding the purpose of a statement of cash flows**

Simply Accounting® and QuickBooks® recalculate each account as the transaction is recorded and saved. This feature allows any financial statement, including the statement of cash flows, to be prepared at any point in time.

In this chapter, we turn our attention to a fourth major financial statement that is used to better understand the operating, investing, and financing activities of a company. It is called the **statement of cash flows**, and it summarizes the sources and uses of cash by a company during an accounting period. It is easy to compute the change in cash balance by looking at the comparative balance sheet, but just the change in total cash tells us nothing about specific cash transactions. The statement of cash flows not only shows in detail the sources and uses of cash; it also gives readers of the financial statements a good basis for judging the possible future cash flows. Internal users of the financial statements (such as management) can also benefit by understanding how to read the statement of cash flows.

Learning Unit 16-1
Statement of Cash Flows: Indirect Method

We use as our example in this chapter the Zabel Corporation, which sells soccer equipment and supplies. To prepare a statement of cash flows, we need to obtain information from the other financial statements prepared for the company: the income statement, the statement of retained earnings, and the balance sheet. These statements are shown in Figures 16-1, 16-2, and 16-3. Note that the balance sheet shown in Figure 16-3 is slightly different from the ones we have shown in the past. This one is a **comparative balance sheet**, which shows figures from two separate years side by side. We discuss this type of statement in more detail in Chapter 17, which is located on MyAccountingLab at www.myaccountinglab.com.

The statement of cash flows consists of three main sections: (1) net cash flows from operating activities, (2) net cash flows from investing activities, and (3) net cash flows from financing activities. Some of the complexities of this statement are beyond the scope of this text, but the following paragraphs contain a few examples of transactions reported in each of the three sections.

Transactions with customers, vendors, and employees are *operating activities.*

Operating activities include selling products or services to customers. **Cash inflows** from operating activities include cash collected from customers. **Cash outflows** from operating activities include paying for merchandise inventory, salaries, rent, and other such expenses.

Figure 16-1
Income Statement of
Zabel Corporation

ZABEL CORPORATION INCOME STATEMENT FOR YEAR ENDED DECEMBER 31, 2013		
Sales		$190 000 00
Cost of Goods Sold		106 000 00
Gross Profit		$ 84 000 00
Operating Expenses:		
Salary Expense	$ 51 040 00	
Insurance Expense	7 200 00	
Rent Expense	3 600 00	
Amortization Expense	11 000 00	
Miscellaneous Expense	1 200 00	
Total Operating Expenses		74 040 00
Net Income		$ 9 960 00

Figure 16-2
Statement of Retained
Earnings of Zabel Corporation

ZABEL CORPORATION STATEMENT OF RETAINED EARNINGS FOR YEAR ENDED DECEMBER 31, 2013		
Retained Earnings, January 1, 2013		$ 38 140 00
Net Income for the Year	$ 9 960 00	
Less: Cash Dividends	8 000 00	
Increase in Retained Earnings		1 960 00
Retained Earnings, December 31, 2013		$ 40 100 00

> Transactions involving the purchase or sale of plant assets are *investing activities*.

Investing activities include such things as purchase or sale of plant and equipment, buying stocks and bonds (of other companies), and making loans to other businesses or individuals.

Financing activities include raising money by issuing stocks and bonds, repurchasing of the company's shares, and paying cash dividends to the shareholders.

A fourth classification reported on the statement of cash flows is called **noncash investing and financing activities**, which includes such transactions as issuing shares of stock in exchange for assets such as land and buildings. Although cash is not involved, the event is reported because no other financial statement specifically discloses the transaction. If the stock was issued for cash (financing activity, a cash increase) and if we used the cash proceeds to purchase land and a building (investing activity, a cash decrease), the event would be disclosed on the statement of cash flows in two separate sections. Because our example is a noncash transaction, it can be reported on the statement of cash flow as a footnote or on a separate schedule listing such transactions.

CASH FLOWS FROM OPERATING ACTIVITIES: INDIRECT METHOD

> **2** Preparing the operating activities section of the statement of cash flows using the indirect method

> **4** Preparing a statement of cash flows

A business needs a positive cash flow to survive. A company's ability to raise money from financing activities (issuing shares, bonds, or long-term notes) is often tied to its success in generating cash flow from its operations. The operating activities section of the statement of cash flows is therefore of great importance to potential investors and creditors.

This section introduces a procedure known as the **indirect method** of reporting cash flows from operating activities. Note that the distinction between the indirect method and the direct method (discussed in the next learning unit) applies only to the operating activities section of the statement of cash flows.

Figure 16-3
Comparative Balance
Sheet for Zabel Corporation

ZABEL CORPORATION
COMPARATIVE BALANCE SHEET
AS OF DECEMBER 31, 2013, AND DECEMBER 31, 2012

Assets	2013	2012	Increase (Decrease)
Current Assets:			
Cash	$ 2 900 00	$ 2 480 00	$ 420 00
Accounts Receivable	19 560 00	14 720 00	4 840 00
Merchandise Inventory	30 000 00	32 000 00	(2 000 00)
Prepaid Insurance	600 00	400 00	200 00
Total Current Assets	$ 53 060 00	$ 49 600 00	$ 3 460 00
Plant and Equipment:			
Office Equipment	$ 96 000 00	$ 66 000 00	$ 30 000 00
Accum. Amort., Office Equipment	(37 200 00)	(26 200 00)	(11 000 00)
Total Plant and Equipment	$ 58 800 00	$ 39 800 00	$ 19 000 00
Total Assets	$111 860 00	$ 89 400 00	$ 22 460 00
Liabilities			
Current Liabilities:			
Notes Payable—Short Term (used to purchase inventory)	$ 17 400 00	$ 14 800 00	$ 2 600 00
Accounts Payable	360 00	460 00	(100 00)
Total Current Liabilities	$ 17 760 00	$ 15 260 00	$ 2 500 00
Long-Term Liabilities:			
Long-Term Note Payable	$ 28 000 00	$ 20 000 00	$ 8 000 00
Total Liabilities	$ 45 760 00	$ 35 260 00	$ 10 500 00
Shareholders' Equity			
Common Shares, $10 par	$ 11 000 00	$ 10 000 00	$ 1 000 00
Share Capital in Excess of Par	15 000 00	6 000 00	9 000 00
Retained Earnings	40 100 00	38 140 00	1 960 00
Total Shareholders' Equity	$ 66 100 00	54 140 00	$ 11 960 00
Total Liabilities and Shareholders' Equity	$111 860 00	$ 89 400 00	$ 22 460 00

In the indirect method we are converting the net income on the income statement from the accrual basis to the cash basis. As we have been learning throughout this text, businesses normally report their net income on the accrual basis, which places the primary emphasis on *when* the revenues are earned and *when* the expenses are incurred.

The indirect method's name comes from the way we view the income statement. We begin with the bottom line of the income statement and work backward until we have computed net cash flow from operating activities. We begin the operating activities section with the net income as reported on the income statement (see Figure 16-4) and convert it from the accrual basis to the cash basis. Figure 16-4 shows how the net cash flows from operating activities are computed for the Zabel Corporation using the indirect method.

In this example, the first item to be added to the net income is Amortization Expense. The amortization is *added back* to net income because it was subtracted out as an expense on the income statement to derive the $9,960 net income. You will recall that when amortization is recorded, the entry involves a debit to Amortization Expense and a credit to Accumulated Amortization. Neither of these accounts

ZABEL CORPORATION STATEMENT OF CASH FLOWS (INDIRECT METHOD) FOR YEAR ENDED DECEMBER 31, 2013		
Cash Flows from Operating Activities:		
Net Income from Operations	$ 9 960 00	
Add (deduct) Items to Convert Net Income from		
Accrual Basis to Cash Basis:		
Amortization Expense	11 000 00	
Increase in Accounts Receivable	(4 840 00)	
Decrease in Merchandise Inventory	2 000 00	
Increase in Prepaid Insurance	(1 200 00)	
Increase in Notes Payable (Short Term)	2 600 00	
Decrease in Accounts Payable	(1 000 00)	
Net Cash Provided by Operating Activities		$20 420 00

involves cash. Because amortization is therefore a "noncash" expense, it is added back to net income when using the indirect method. Next, each of the current assets and current liabilities is examined to determine its effect on cash flow.

The aid sheet shown in Figure 16-5 is useful for remembering whether to add or subtract a given item on the statement of cash flows. Alternatively, some instructors prefer the simple opposite effect/same effect approach. For current assets, cash flow has the *opposite effect*, whereas for current liabilities, the cash flow has the *same effect.* For example, the increase in Accounts Receivable (a current asset) must be subtracted, whereas the increase in Short-Term Notes Payable (a current liability) would be added.

Figure 16-5
Aid Sheet for Converting from
Accrual Basis to Cash Basis

	Add to Net Income If This Account Has:	Deduct from Net Income If This Account Has:
Current Assets	DECREASED	INCREASED
Current Liabilities	INCREASED	DECREASED

After each of the items is listed with its proper sign, the entire list is combined with net income to compute the net cash provided by operating activities of $20,420. The term *net cash provided* by operating activities is commonly used if the result is positive, whereas *net cash used* in operating activities indicates that the result is negative. As you might imagine, the goal is to have a strong positive cash flow from operating activities. A negative operating cash flow cannot be tolerated for long. Investors and creditors would hesitate to provide funds to a firm that cannot generate a positive cash flow from its operating activities.

CASH FLOWS FROM INVESTING ACTIVITIES

The cash flows from investing activities section of the statement of cash flows includes (1) the purchase and sale of other companies' stocks and bonds, (2) the buying and disposal of plant assets, and (3) making loans to other parties. We analyze the noncurrent accounts to find these activities. For example, the following transactions would be recorded in this section:

1. Sale or purchase of equipment
2. Sale or purchase of land
3. Cash spent to invest in other companies' stocks and bonds
4. Cash received from sales of shares or bond investments
5. Loaning cash to borrowers

On the balance sheet for Zabel Corporation, we see an increase in plant and equipment from 2012 to 2013 of $30,000. Thus, the cash outflow for equipment would be reported as shown in Figure 16-6.

Figure 16-6
Cash Outflow for Equipment

Cash Flows from Investing Activities:		
Purchase of Plant Asset	$(30 0 0 0 00)	
Net Cash Flows Used in Investing Activities		$(30 0 0 0 00)

CASH FLOWS FROM FINANCING ACTIVITIES

The cash flows from financing activities section of the statement of cash flows records transactions such as the following:

1. Issuance of long-term notes and bonds
2. Issuance of common shares
3. Repurchasing company shares
4. Payment of cash dividends
5. Retirement of bonds

From the comparative balance sheet for Zabel Corporation, we see that the Long-Term Notes Payable account increased by $8,000. This increase is shown as a source (increase) of cash, because an increase in Long-Term Notes Payable means that more cash has been borrowed and therefore has been received by the business. Also, note that the issuance of $10,000 of common shares has *increased* the cash flows, whereas the payment of $8,000 in dividends results in a *decrease* in cash flows. The end result is that net cash provided by financing activities has increased by $10,000, as shown in Figure 16-7.

Figure 16-7
Net Cash Flows Provided by Financing Activities

Cash Flows from Financing Activities:		
Issuance of Long-Term Note	$ 8 0 0 00	
Issuance of Common Shares	10 0 0 0 00	
Payment of Dividends	(8 0 0 0 00)	
Net Cash Flows Provided by Financing Activities		$10 0 0 0 00

To arrive at net change in cash for the overall statement, we perform the following calculation:

Net Cash Provided by Operating Activities	$ 20,420
– Cash Flow Used by Investing Activities	(30,000)
+ Net Cash Provided by Financing Activities	10,000
= Net Increase in Cash	$ 420

Figure 16-8 shows all three sections together in the statement of cash flows.

Note that at the bottom of the statement of cash flows, the cash has increased by $420 (just as is shown for cash on the comparative balance sheet), but this report gives us a complete breakdown of just what caused the cash to increase by $420.

The statement of cash flows is helpful in evaluating, comparing, and predicting future cash flows. By dividing this report into three sections, creditors as well as investors can judge how cash flows from operations compared with those from investing or financing activities. For example, in the case of Zabel Corporation, an investor or a creditor can see a substantial reduction in cash in one area (investing) that is offset by an increase in cash from the other areas (operating and financing).

Figure 16-8
Statement of Cash Flows—
Indirect Method

ZABEL CORPORATION STATEMENT OF CASH FLOWS (INDIRECT METHOD) FOR YEAR ENDED DECEMBER 31, 2013		
Net Cash Flows from Operating Activities		
Net Income	$ 9 960 00	
Add (Deduct) Items to Convert Net Income		
from Accrual Basis to Cash Basis:		
Amortization Expense	11 000 00	
Increase in Accounts Receivable	(4 840 00)	
Decrease in Merchandise Inventory	2 000 00	
Increase in Prepaid Insurance	(200 00)	
Increase in Short-Term Notes Payable	2 600 00	
Decrease in Accounts Payable	(100 00)	
Net Cash Provided by Operating Activities		$ 20 420 00
Cash Flows from Investing Activities		
Purchase of Plant Asset	$ (30 000 00)	
Net Cash Used by Investing Activities		(30 000 00)
Cash Flows from Financing Activities		
Issuance of Long-Term Note	$ 8 000 00	
Issuance of Common Shares	10 000 00	
Payment of Dividends	(8 000 00)	
Net Cash Provided by Financing Activities		10 000 00
Net Increase in Cash		$ 420 00
Beginning Balance of Cash		2 480 00
Ending Balance of Cash		$ 2 900 00

A second approach, known as the direct method, gives a more useful presentation of cash flows from operating activities. Although this method gives more understandable data, many firms think it much easier to use the indirect method to prepare the reports. Regardless of the method used, the cash flows from operating activities will be the same. The direct method is illustrated in Learning Unit 16-2.

LEARNING UNIT 16-1 REVIEW

AT THIS POINT you should be able to:

◆ Explain the components of a statement of cash flows. (pp. 680–681)

◆ Calculate net cash flows from operating activities using the indirect method. (pp. 681–683)

◆ Calculate net cash flows from investing activities. (pp. 683–684)

◆ Calculate net cash flows from financing activities. (p. 684)

◆ Prepare a complete statement of cash flows using the indirect method. (p. 685)

Self-Review Quiz 16-1

(The forms you need are on page 16-1 of the *Study Guide with Working Papers*.)

From Figure 16-9, calculate net cash flows from operating activities.

Figure 16-9
Income Statement
for Johnson Company

JOHNSON COMPANY
INCOME STATEMENT
FOR YEAR ENDED DECEMBER 31, 2013

Sales			$150 000 00
Cost of Goods Sold			90 000 00
Gross Profit			$ 60 000 00
Operating Expenses:			
Salary Expense	$40 000 00		
Amortization Expense	3 000 00		
Advertising Expense	8 000 00		
Total Operating Expenses		51 000 00	
Net Income		$ 9 000 00	

Additional Data	2010	2009
Accounts Receivable	$10 600 00	$ 4 000 00
Merchandise Inventory	10 000 00	12 000 00
Prepaid Advertising	1 400 00	3 000 00
Accounts Payable	18 000 00	15 000 00
Accrued Salaries	1 800 00	1 900 00

Solution to Self-Review Quiz 16-1

Figure 16-10
Net Cash Flows from
Operating Activities

Net Cash Flows from Operating Activities:		
Net Income		$ 9 000 00
Add (deduct) Items to Convert Net Income to Cash		
Basis from the Accrual Basis:		
Amortization Expense		3 000 00
Increase in Accounts Receivable		(6 600 00)
Decrease in Merchandise Inventory		2 000 00
Decrease in Prepaid Advertising		1 600 00
Increase in Accounts Payable		3 000 00
Decrease in Accrued Salaries		(1 000 00)
Net Cash Flow from Operating Activities		$11 900 00

Learning Unit 16-2
Statement of Cash Flows: Direct Method

3 Preparing the operating activities section of the statement of cash flows using the direct method

4 Preparing a statement of cash flows

As indicated in Learning Unit 16-1, cash flows from operating activities include the cash effects of transactions such as selling goods or services to customers and paying for merchandise inventory and operating expenses. Many accountants prefer the **direct method** of reporting the cash flows from operating activities. This approach provides useful information and is easily understood by the users of the financial statements.

The direct method requires listing major groups of operating cash receipts and cash payments. We first compute cash receipts from customers. Because most firms sell products or services on account as well as for cash, the sales figure on the income statement is not the same as total cash received. We analyze Accounts Receivable and combine its change (increase or decrease) with the sales figure from the income statement. An *increase* in Accounts Receivable results in a negative impact on cash, so the amount of the increase is *subtracted* from sales. A *decrease* in Accounts Receivable results in a positive effect on cash, so the amount of the decrease is *added* to sales. Thus, for computing cash received from customers, we can treat Accounts Receivable as we did in the indirect method by using the *opposite effect*.

The same reasoning applies to cash payments, except that because these payments are outflows of cash, any change with a *positive* cash effect is *subtracted* (because a positive effect means less cash to pay out). Any change with a *negative* cash effect is *added* (because a negative effect means more cash to pay out).

Our first example of an operating cash outflow is cash paid for merchandise inventory. We begin the computation with Cost of Goods Sold and then adjust by the change in the Merchandise Inventory account. A further adjustment is necessary to account for changes in Accounts Payable and Short-Term Notes Payable (if notes were used to pay for inventory, as in our example). Specifically, an *increase* in the balance of Merchandise Inventory means a *negative* cash effect that would be *added* in the computation of cash paid for merchandise. A *decrease* in Merchandise Inventory results in a *positive* cash effect that is *subtracted* to compute cash paid for merchandise. After adjusting for inventory changes, if Accounts Payable increased, the cash effect is positive and thus would be subtracted from the computation. If Accounts Payable decreased, the cash effect is negative and thus would be added to the calculation. The changes in Short-Term Notes Payable (assuming notes were used to pay for inventory) would be analyzed in the same way as Accounts Payable.

Cash paid for operating expenses is handled in much the same way as cash paid for merchandise inventory. Cash paid for salaries, for instance, is computed by combining the change in Salaries Payable with the amount of Salary Expense from the income statement. If Salaries Payable increased (positive cash effect), the amount of increase would be subtracted from Salary Expense. If this account decreased (negative cash effect), the amount of the decrease would be added to the Salary Expense.

For expenses involving a prepayment (such as Prepaid Insurance), the insurance expense balance would be combined with the change in Prepaid Insurance. If Prepaid Insurance increased (negative cash effect), the amount of the change would be added to insurance expense to compute cash paid for insurance. If Prepaid Insurance had decreased (positive cash effect), the amount of the change would be subtracted from insurance expense.

We now look at an example of the computation of net cash flow from operating activities. Zabel Corporation computes cash received from customers by combining the sales figure from the income statement with the change in Accounts Receivable from the comparative balance sheet (see Figures 16-1 and 16-3). Sales are $190,000, and Accounts Receivable *increased* by $4,840. Because the increase in Accounts Receivable means a negative cash effect (more of our money is currently in the pockets of our customers!), it is *subtracted* from sales to arrive at the cash collected from customers figure of $185,160. This computation is illustrated in Figure 16-11.

A second computation in Figure 16-11 shows cash paid for inventory. The Cost of Goods Sold figure is adjusted for changes in Merchandise Inventory, Accounts Payable, and Short-Term Notes Payable (if such notes are used to finance inventory). In our example, Cost of Goods Sold of $106,000 is adjusted by subtracting the decrease in Inventory ($2,000), subtracting the increase in Short-Term Notes Payable ($2,600), and adding the decrease in Accounts Payable ($100) to arrive at the Cash Paid for Inventory figure of $101,500.

Cash Paid for Insurance is also illustrated in Figure 16-11 by adding the decrease in Prepaid Insurance to the Insurance Expense to yield $7,400 for Cash Paid for Insurance.

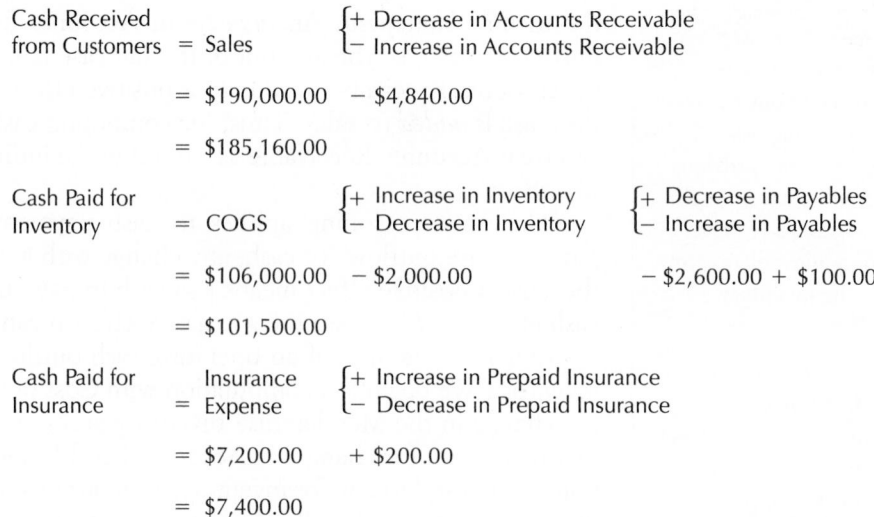

Cash Received
from Customers = Sales $\begin{cases} + \text{ Decrease in Accounts Receivable} \\ - \text{ Increase in Accounts Receivable} \end{cases}$

$\qquad$ = \$190,000.00 $\quad$ – \$4,840.00

$\qquad$ = \$185,160.00

Cash Paid for
Inventory $\quad$ = COGS $\begin{cases} + \text{ Increase in Inventory} \\ - \text{ Decrease in Inventory} \end{cases}$ $\begin{cases} + \text{ Decrease in Payables} \\ - \text{ Increase in Payables} \end{cases}$

$\qquad$ = \$106,000.00 $\quad$ – \$2,000.00 $\qquad$ – \$2,600.00 + \$100.00

$\qquad$ = \$101,500.00

Cash Paid for
Insurance $\quad$ = $\begin{matrix}\text{Insurance} \\ \text{Expense}\end{matrix}$ $\begin{cases} + \text{ Increase in Prepaid Insurance} \\ - \text{ Decrease in Prepaid Insurance} \end{cases}$

$\qquad$ = \$7,200.00 $\quad$ + \$200.00

$\qquad$ = \$7,400.00

Note: The other items on Zabel's net cash flows from operating activities section do not require any adjustment, because no changes occurred in current assets or current liabilities on the income statement figures for such items as salaries, rent, and miscellaneous expenses.

Figure 16-12 shows the complete statement of cash flows for the Zabel Corporation using the direct method. Note that the investing activities and financing activities sections are the same as in Figure 16-8, because the distinction between the indirect and direct methods applies only to the cash flows from operating activities section.

Figure 16-12
Statement of Cash Flows—
Direct Method

ZABEL CORPORATION
STATEMENT OF CASH FLOWS—DIRECT METHOD
FOR YEAR ENDED DECEMBER 31, 2013

Net Cash Flows from Operating Activities:			
Cash Received from Customers			\$185,160.00
Cash Paid for Merchandise Inventory	\$(101,500.00)		
Cash Paid for Salaries	(51,040.00)		
Cash Paid for Insurance	(7,400.00)		
Cash Paid for Rent	(3,600.00)		
Cash Paid for Miscellaneous Expenses	(1,200.00)		
Total Cash Paid for Operating Activities			(164,740.00)
Net Cash Provided by Operating Activities			\$ 20,420.00
Cash Flows from Investing Activities:			
Purchase of Plant Asset	\$(30,000.00)		
Net Cash Used by Investing Activities			(30,000.00)
Cash Flows from Financing Activities:			
Issuance of Long-Term Note	\$ 8,000.00		
Issuance of Common Shares	10,000.00		
Payment of Dividends	(8,000.00)		
Net Cash Provided by Financing Activities			10,000.00
Net Increase in Cash			\$ 420.00
Beginning Balance of Cash			2,480.00
Ending Balance of Cash			\$ 2,900.00

LEARNING UNIT 16-2 REVIEW

Self-Review Quiz 16-2

(The forms you need are on page 16-1 of the *Study Guide with Working Papers*.)

Using the data from Self-Review Quiz 16-1 on page 686, show in good form the cash flows from the operating activities section of the statement of cash flows for Johnson Company using the direct method.

Solution to Self-Review Quiz 16-2

Figure 16-13
Net Cash Flows from
Operating Activities

Net Cash Flows from Operating Activities:			
Cash Received from Customers			$143 400 00
Cash Paid for Merchandise Inventory	$85 000 00		
Cash Paid for Salaries	40 100 00		
Cash Paid for Advertising	6 400 00		
Total Cash Paid for Operating Activities		131 500 00	
Net Cash Provided by Operating Activities		$ 11 900 00	

Explanations of computations:

Cash from Customers = Sales − Increase in Accounts Receivable
Cash Paid for Inventory = COGS − Decrease in Inventory − Increase in Accounts Payable
Cash Paid for Salaries = Salary Expense + Decrease in Accrued Salaries
Cash Paid for Advertising = Advertising Expense − Decrease in Prepaid Advertising

SUMMARY OF KEY POINTS

1. In the statement of cash flows, net change in cash equals net cash from operating activities plus or minus cash from investing activities plus or minus cash from financing activities.

2. In figuring the net cash from operating activities section of the statement, it is necessary to convert the net income from the income statement from the accrual basis to the cash basis. This change affects the following accounts: Amortization Expense, Accounts Receivable, Inventory, Prepaid Expenses, Accounts Payable, and Short-Term Notes Payable. Note that we are analyzing current assets and current liabilities to see their effect on net income. This approach to computing cash flows from operating activities is known as the indirect method.

3. Cash flows from investing activities include such things as purchase and sale of stocks and bonds (of other companies), buying and selling plant assets, and lending money to other parties.

4. Cash flows from financing activities include such things as issuing and repaying long-term notes and bonds, issuing common shares, buying back a company's own common stock, and paying dividends.

1. An alternative way of preparing the net cash from operating activities section of the statement is called the direct method.

2. The direct method requires listing separately the major categories of cash inflows and outflows. The major cash inflow for most firms is the cash received from customers, which is computed by adjusting the sales figure by the change in Accounts Receivable.

3. Cash outflows under the operating activities section include cash paid for inventory, cash paid for salaries, and cash paid for other operating expenses. In each case, the appropriate income statement figure is adjusted by the changes in one or more current asset or current liability accounts.

4. Regardless of the method selected, the net cash from operating activities will be the same. Also, the distinction between the direct and indirect methods applies only to net cash from operating activities. The investing and financing sections remain the same.

KEY TERMS

Cash inflow Any increase in cash is called a cash inflow or a source of cash. When listing the total for a major section of the statement of cash flows, if cash is increased, the figure is often described as "cash provided" by operating activities (or by investing activities or financing activities). (p. 680)

Cash outflow A decrease in cash is called a cash outflow or a use of cash. When listing a total for a major section of the statement of cash flows, if cash has decreased, the figure is often described as "cash used" in operating activities (or in investing activities or financing activities). (p. 680)

Comparative balance sheet A balance sheet listing financial condition for two or more years in a side-by-side manner. This format allows the reader to make quick comparisons between the two balance sheet dates. (p. 680)

Direct method One of two methods of preparing the net cash flows from operating activities section of the statement of cash flows. Each of the major areas of sources and uses of cash for operations is detailed separately. (p. 686)

Financing activities Activities relating to raising money from investors and creditors such as the issuance of shares and bonds and long-term notes; also, repurchase of a company's own outstanding shares, and retiring bonds and notes as well as paying dividends (p. 681)

Indirect method One of two methods of preparing the net cash flows from the operating activities section of the statement of cash flows. Involves converting the accrual-basis net income figure from the income statement to the cash-basis net income. (p. 681)

Investing activities Activities such as purchase and sale of plant and equipment and placing excess cash in shares, bonds, and notes of other companies (p. 681)

Noncash investing and financing activities Transactions such as the issuance of shares in exchange for land would be listed in a footnote or a separate schedule to the statement of cash flows, because such transactions would not be reported separately on any other financial statement. (p. 681)

Operating activities Those activities most closely related to conducting the business for which the enterprise was established. Activities such as selling merchandise and services to customers, and paying salaries and other expenses needed to continue earning the operating revenue are classified as operating activities. (p. 680)

Statement of cash flows A financial report that provides a detailed breakdown of the specific increases and decreases in cash during an accounting period. It helps readers of the statement evaluate past performance as well as predict future cash flows of the business. (p. 680)

BLUEPRINT OF STATEMENT OF CASH FLOWS

INDIRECT METHOD

Net Cash Flows from Operating Activities:		
Net Income		XXX
Add (Deduct) Items to Convert Net		
Income to Cash Basis:		
Amortization Expense		XX
Increase in Accounts Receivable		(XX)
Decrease in Inventory		XX
Increase in Prepaid Expenses		(XX)
Increase in Accounts Payable		XX
Decrease in Accrued Salaries		(XX)
Net Cash Provided by Operating Activities		XXX
Cash Flows from Investing Activities:		
Purchase of Investment Securities	(XXX)	
Purchase of Equipment	(XXX)	
Sale of Land	XXX	
Cash Used by Investing Activities		(XXX)
Cash Flows from Financing Activities:		
Issuance of Common Shares	XX	
Payment of Dividends	(X)	
Cash Provided by Financing Activities		XX
Net Increase in Cash		XXX
Beginning Balance of Cash		XXX
Ending Balance of Cash		XXX

DIRECT METHOD

Net Cash Flows from Operating Activities:		
Cash Received from Customers		XXX
Cash Paid for Inventory	XXX	
Cash Paid for Salaries	XX	
Cash Paid for Insurance	X	
Cash Paid for Rent	X	
Cash Paid for Other Expenses	XX	
Total Cash Paid for Operations		XX
Net Cash Provided by Operating Activities		XXX

QUESTIONS, CLASSROOM DEMONSTRATION EXERCISES, EXERCISES, AND PROBLEMS

Discussion Questions and Critical Thinking/Ethical Case

1. List the three main sections of the statement of cash flows.

2. Explain how net cash flows from operating activities is calculated using the indirect method.

3. Explain how net cash flows from operating activities is calculated using the direct method.

4. The issuance of shares is an investing activity. Agree or disagree? Why?

5. Explain how a creditor might analyze a statement of cash flows.

6. Explain what is meant by financing activities.

7. Explain why amortization is *added* to net income when using the indirect method.

8. Risch Company each year prepares an income statement and balance sheet. Tom Martin, the controller, issued a memo to Debbie Kreiger, vice-president, that the company should prepare a statement of cash flows. Debbie called the controller and told him that she would not let a cash flows statement be published, that this type of information is for internal purposes only, and that the public has no right to these data. She said that the competition would kill them if they got this information. Do you agree with Debbie's position or with Tom's? Write your recommendation to Dave Risch, the chief executive officer.

MyAccountingLab

Make the grade with MyAccountingLab! The exercises and problems marked in green can be found on MyAccountingLab at www.myaccountinglab.com. You can practise them as often as you want, and many of them feature step-by-step guided solutions to help you find the right answer. You can also find working papers for selected problems in the Multimedia Library on MyAccountingLab.

Classroom Demonstration Exercises

(The forms you need are on page 16-2 of the *Study Guide with Working Papers.*)

Set A

Calculating Net Cash Flows from Operating Activities: Indirect Method

Calculating net cash flows—
indirect method
❶❷ (15 min)

1. The following accounts showed an increase or a decrease from the comparative balance sheet. Explain which account will be added to net income and which will be subtracted in calculating net cash flows from operating activities.
   a. Accounts Receivable: Decrease
   b. Inventory: Increase
   c. Short-Term Notes Payable: Decrease
   d. Accounts Payable: Increase

Net cash flows—indirect method
2 (20 min)

2. From the following, calculate the net cash flow from operating activities using the indirect method:

	2012	2013
Merchandise Inventory	$3,000	$3,500
Accounts Receivable	600	800
Prepaid Insurance	500	300
Accounts Payable	1,000	800
Accrued Salaries	600	800
For the year ended 2013:		
Net Income		$1,700
Amortization Expense		2,000

Calculating Net Cash Flows from Operating Activities: Direct Method

Calculating net cash flows—
direct method
3 (30 min)

3. Using the data from Classroom Demonstration Exercise 2 plus the additional information in Figure 16-14, compute net cash flows from operating activities using the direct method.

Figure 16-14
Income Statement

Sales		$ 7900 00
Cost of Goods Sold		2300 00
Gross Profit		$ 5600 00
Expenses:		
Amortization Expense	$ 600 00	
Salaries Expense	2200 00	
Insurance Expense	400 00	
Miscellaneous Expense	300 00	
Total Expenses		3500 00
Net Income		$ 2100 00

Calculating Cash Flows from Financing Activities

Cash flows from financing
activities
4 (15 min)

4. From the following, calculate net cash flows from financing activities:

Payments of dividends	$ 7,000
Issuance of common shares	2,500
Issuance of long-term note	16,000

Calculating Change in Cash

Net change in cash
4 (15 min)

5. Given the following, calculate the net change in cash:

Net cash flows from operating activities	$4,000
Net cash used by investing activities	(2,500)
Net cash provided by financing activities	900

Set B

Calculating Net Cash Flows from Operating Activities: Indirect Method

Calculating net cash flows—
indirect method
1 2 (15 min)

1. The following accounts showed an increase or a decrease from the comparative balance sheet. Explain which account will be added to net income and which will be subtracted in calculating net cash flows from operating activities.
   a. Accounts Receivable: Increase
   b. Inventory: Decrease
   c. Short-Term Notes Payable: Increase
   d. Accounts Payable: Decrease

2. From the following, calculate the net cash flow from operating activities using the indirect method:

	2012	2013
Merchandise Inventory	$2,000	$2,500
Accounts Receivable	500	700
Prepaid Insurance	400	300
Accounts Payable	1,000	600
Accrued Salaries	500	700
For the year ended 2013:		
Net Income		$1,900
Amortization Expense		500

Calculating Net Cash Flows from Operating Activities: Direct Method

3. Using the data from Classroom Demonstration Exercise 2 plus the additional information in Figure 16-15, compute net cash flows from operating activities using the direct method.

Figure 16-15
Income Statement

Sales		$ 8000 00
Cost of Goods Sold		2400 00
Gross Profit		$ 5600 00
Expenses:		
Amortization Expense	$ 500 00	
Salaries Expense	2200 00	
Insurance Expense	700 00	
Miscellaneous Expense	300 00	
Total Expenses		3700 00
Net Income		$ 1900 00

Calculating Cash Flows from Financing Activities

4. From the following, calculate net cash flows from financing activities:

Payments of dividends	$ 6,000
Issuance of common shares	2,000
Issuance of long-term note	14,000

Calculating Change in Cash

5. Given the following, calculate the net change in cash:

Net cash flows from operating activities	$3,000
Net cash used by investing activities	(1,000)
Net cash provided by financing activities	600

Exercises

(The forms you need are on page 16-3 of the *Study Guide with Working Papers*.)

16-1. Complete the following chart regarding the indirect method.

	Add to Net Income	Subtract from Net Income
?	Decrease	Increase
?	Increase	Decrease

16-2. From the following, calculate the net cash flow from operating activities (use the indirect method):

	2012	2013
Accounts Receivable	$5,900	$7,900
Prepaid Insurance	900	850
Accounts Payable	4,000	4,600
Accrued Salaries	1,200	2,200

For the year ended 2013:

Net Income	$17,000
Amortization Expense	4,000

16-3. From the following, calculate the net cash flows from operating activities (use the direct method):

Sales	$9,000
Cost of Goods Sold	4,400
Salary Expense	1,600
Insurance Expense	800
Other Expenses (all cash)	1,000

Changes in current assets and liabilities:
Accounts Receivable increased by $600.
Inventory increased by $500.
Accounts Payable increased by $100.
Accrued Salaries decreased by $200.
Prepaid Insurance decreased by $150.

16-4. For each of the following transactions, identify the appropriate section of the statement of cash flows (OA = Operating, IA = Investing, FA = Financing, and NC = Noncash).

_____ **a.** Sold merchandise to customers.
_____ **b.** Purchase of equipment.
_____ **c.** Buy shares of another corporation.
_____ **d.** Pay dividends to shareholders.
_____ **e.** Paid salaries to employees.
_____ **f.** Issue shares in exchange for equipment.

Group A Problems

(The forms you need are on pages 16-4 to 16-5 of the *Study Guide with Working Papers.*)

16A-1. From the following income statement (Figure 16-16), balance sheet (Figure 16-17), and additional data (below) for Dent Corporation, prepare a statement of cash flows using the indirect method.

Additional Data:

1. All Plant and Equipment was purchased for cash.
2. Sold additional 2,500 shares of stock for cash of $2,500.
3. A $1,400 dividend was declared and paid.
4. Short-term notes used to finance inventory.

Figure 16-16
Income Statement for
Dent Corporation

DENT CORPORATION
INCOME STATEMENT
FOR THE YEAR ENDED DECEMBER 31, 2013

Sales		$96 500 00
Cost of Goods Sold		69 100 00
Gross Profit		$27 400 00
Operating Expenses:		
Rent Expense	$ 7 500 00	
Amortization Expense	7 000 00	
Salary Expense	6 600 00	
Miscellaneous Expense	3 200 00	
Total Operating Expenses		24 300 00
Net Income		$ 3 100 00

Check Figure

Net Increase in Cash $800

Figure 16-17
Balance Sheet for
Dent Corporation

DENT CORPORATION
BALANCE SHEET
DECEMBER 31, 2013 AND 2012

Assets	2013	2012
Current Assets:		
Cash	$ 3 400 00	$ 2 600 00
Accounts Receivable, Net	5 600 00	4 500 00
Merchandise Inventory	2 200 00	2 000 00
Prepaid Rent	1 000 00	1 200 00
Total Current Assets	$12 200 00	$10 300 00
Plant and Equipment:		
Store Equipment	$58 000 00	$50 000 00
Accum. Amort., Store Equipment	(12 000 00)	(5 000 00)
Total Plant and Equipment	$46 000 00	$45 000 00
Total Assets	$58 200 00	$55 300 00
Liabilities		
Current Liabilities:		
Notes Payable—Short Term	$ 6 800 00	$ 5 200 00
Accounts Payable	4 400 00	4 800 00
Total Current Liabilities	$11 200 00	$10 000 00
Long-Term Liabilities:		
Bonds Payable	$12 500 00	$15 000 00
Total Liabilities	$23 700 00	$25 000 00
Shareholders' Equity		
Common Shares	$22 500 00	$20 000 00
Retained Earnings	12 000 00	10 300 00
Total Shareholders' Equity	$34 500 00	$30 300 00
Total Liabilities and Shareholders' Equity	$58 200 00	$55 300 00

Statement of cash flows—direct method
❶❸ (60 min)

Check Figure

Cash Paid for Inventory
$68,100

16A-2. From the financial statements and additional information provided in Problem 16A-1 for Dent Corporation, prepare a statement of cash flows using the direct method.

(The forms you need are on pages 16-4 to 16-5 of the *Study Guide with Working Papers.*)

Statement of cash flows—indirect method
① ② (60 min)

16B-1. From the following income statement (Figure 16-18), balance sheet (Figure 16-19), and additional data for Blumer Limited, prepare a statement of cash flows using the indirect method.

Additional Data:

1. All increases in Plant and Equipment were paid for in cash.
2. No dividend was declared in 2013.
3. Sold 2,000 shares of stock for cash of $2,000.

Hint: Office Equipment and Machinery are recorded at *net* on the balance sheet. Be sure to add back amortization expense to the cost of the assets in 2013 to compute the actual cost of the additional assets purchased.

Figure 16-18
Income Statement for
Blumer Limited

BLUMER LIMITED INCOME STATEMENT FOR THE YEAR ENDED DECEMBER 31, 2013			
Sales			$36 000 00
Cost of Goods Sold			25 000 00
Gross Profit			$11 000 00
Operating Expenses:			
Amortization Expense, Equipment	$	800 00	
Amortization Expense, Machinery		500 00	
Advertising Expense		660 00	
Salary Expense		1 800 00	
Miscellaneous Expense		3 600 00	
Total Operating Expenses			7 360 00
Net Income			$ 3 640 00

Check Figure

Net Increase in Cash $1500

Figure 16-19
Balance Sheet for
Blumer Limited

BLUMER LIMITED BALANCE SHEET DECEMBER 31, 2013 AND 2012		
Assets	2013	2012
Current Assets:		
Cash	$ 2 0 4 0 00	$ 5 4 0 00
Accounts Receivable, Net	2 6 8 0 00	2 9 1 0 00
Merchandise Inventory	3 2 0 0 00	2 4 3 0 00
Total Current Assets	7 9 2 0 00	5 8 8 0 00
Plant and Equipment:		
Office Equipment, Net	$ 6 0 3 0 00	$ 4 5 3 0 00
Machinery, Net	4 8 3 0 00	3 0 3 0 00
Land	1 1 8 0 00	4 8 0 00
Total Plant and Equipment	$12 0 4 0 00	$ 8 0 4 0 00
Total Assets	$19 9 6 0 00	$13 9 2 0 00
Liabilities		
Current Liabilities:		
Notes Payable—Short Term	$ 2 0 8 0 00	$ 1 9 8 0 00
Accounts Payable	1 0 0 00	1 5 0 00
Total Current Liabilities	$ 2 1 8 0 00	$ 2 1 3 0 00
Long-Term Liabilities:		
Mortgage Payable	$ 2 1 2 0 00	$ 1 7 7 0 00
Total Liabilities	$ 4 3 0 0 00	$ 3 9 0 0 00
Shareholders' Equity		
Common Shares	$ 9 5 3 0 00	$ 7 5 3 0 00
Retained Earnings	6 1 3 0 00	2 4 9 0 00
Total Shareholders' Equity	$15 6 6 0 00	$10 0 2 0 00
Total Liabilities and Shareholders' Equity	$19 9 6 0 00	$13 9 2 0 00

Statement of cash flows—direct method

1 3 (60 min)

Check Figure

Cash Received from Customers $36,230

16B-2. From the financial statements and additional information provided in Problem 16B-1 for Blumer Limited, prepare a statement of cash flows using the direct method.

(The forms you need are on pages 16-6 to 16-7 of the *Study Guide with Working Papers*.)

Statement of cash flows—indirect method
① ② (90 min)

16C-1. From the following income statement, balance sheet, and added information for Empire Company Ltd., prepare a statement of cash flows using the indirect method.

Empire Company Ltd.
Income Statement
For the Year Ended May 31, 2015

Sales		$512,520
Cost of Goods Sold		290,140
Gross Profit		222,380
Expenses:		
Advertising	$21,480	
Amortization	23,910	
Insurance	17,638	
Interest	5,030	
Miscellaneous	18,400	
Rent	36,000	
Salaries	63,402	
Total Expenses		185,860
Net Income		$ 36,520

Check Figure

Net Increase in Cash $21,910

Empire Company Ltd.
Balance Sheet
As of May 31, 2015 and 2014

Assets	2015		2014	
Current Assets:				
Cash		$ 10,580		$ 8,670
Temporary Investments		50,000		30,000
Accounts Receivable—Net		69,930		58,465
Merchandise Inventory		84,550		61,894
Prepaid Insurance		8,405		7,815
Prepaid Rent		12,000		12,000
Total Current Assets		235,465		178,844
Plant and Equipment:				
Automotive	$ 88,600		$ 72,480	
Less: Accum. Amort.	39,400	49,200	32,400	40,080
Computers and Related	42,880		37,340	
Less: Accum. Amort.	26,200	16,680	17,400	19,940
Store Equipment	146,540		138,620	
Less: Accum. Amort.	62,490	84,050	54,380	84,240
Plant and Equipment—total		149,930		144,260
Total Assets		$385,395		$323,104

Liabilities and Shareholders' Equity

Current Liabilities:		
Bank Loan Payable	22,000	19,400
Accounts Payable	86,386	78,675
Accrued Salaries	2,814	3,465
Current Portion of Auto Loan Payable	10,250	11,840
Total Current Liabilities	121,450	113,380
Long-Term Liability:		
Automotive Loan—Long-Term Portion	27,425	32,724
Total Liabilities	148,875	146,104
Shareholders' Equity		
Preferred Shares—$6.00 Nonparticipating	120,000	90,000
Common Shares	20,000	15,000
Retained Earnings	96,520	72,000
Total Shareholders' Equity	236,520	177,000
Total Liabilities and Shareholders' Equity	$385,395	$323,104

Additional Data:

1. All fixed asset additions were paid by cheque.
2. A dividend of $12,000 was paid in cash during the year.
3. Additional preferred and common shares were sold for cash.
4. There were no disposals of capital assets during the year.
5. The company defines cash as including Temporary Investments.

Statement of cash flows—direct method

① ③ (90 min)

Check Figure

Purchase of Automotive ($16,120)

16C-2. From the financial statements and added information provided in Problem 16C-1 for the Empire Company Ltd., prepare a statement of cash flows using the direct method.

On-the-job Training

(The forms you need are on page 16-8 of the *Study Guide with Working Papers*.)

Net cash flows

① ② ③ ④ (60 min)

T-1. Diane Clubb is trying to convert income statement items from an accrual basis to a cash basis. Accounts Receivable at the beginning of the year totalled $205,000. At the end of the year Accounts Receivable amounted to $240,000. On the income statement using accrual accounting, sales were $360,000. Amortization Expense is $18,000 on the accrual income statement.

Diane calculates her cash received from customers to be $305,000. Do you accept her calculation? What written recommendations could you suggest to Diane? How would she calculate the amount of cash paid for advertising if Advertising Expense was listed as $6,000 and the Prepaid Advertising account showed a decrease of $400?

Reporting cash flows from operating activities

② ④ (50 min)

T-2. Pat Kinne is trying to calculate how much cash is being paid to suppliers of her firm's inventory during 2013. Cost of Goods Sold was reported at $190,500. Pat thinks she needs more data than are provided. From the following facts, could you show Pat how to calculate cash paid to suppliers as well as explain whether this method of computation is a part of the direct method or the indirect method?

	12/31/2013	12/31/2012
Accounts Receivable	$39,000	$37,000
Merchandise Inventory	50,400	53,000
Accounts Payable	28,500	30,700
Notes Payable (used to buy Merchandise Inventory)	17,000	15,000
Accrued Salaries	11,000	11,200

Index

A

accelerated amortization method, 645, 666
account
  see also specific accounts
  categories, 148*f*
  chart of accounts. *See* chart of accounts
  contra-asset account, 142
  contra-expense account, 266
  contra-revenue account, 248
  controlling account, 251, 252, 258, 278, 462
  defined, 74
  described, 47
  nominal accounts, 188
  normal balance of an account, 51
  permanent accounts, 187–188
  real accounts, 187–188
  standard account, 47, 47*f*
  T account. *See* T account
  temporary accounts, 188
  three-column account, 101–102, 102*f*
  types of accounts, 47
accountants
  as career, 4
  managerial accountants, 5
  non-profit (governmental) accountants, 6
  private accountants, 5
  public accountants, 5
  types of, 5–6
accounting
  accrual basis of accounting, 511, 524, 615–617, 683*f*
  vs. bookkeeping, 6
  careers in accounting, 4
  cash basis of accounting, 137, 511, 512, 524, 683*f*
  defined, 5, 31
  described, 5, 6
  functions, 5
  importance of, 2

modified-cash-basis (hybrid) method, 512–517
accounting analysis, 52
accounting clerks, 4
accounting cycle
  accounting period, 92
  adjusting entries, journalizing and posting, 183–185
  analyzing and recording transactions in journal, 92–97
  blueprint of first four steps, 120*f*
  blueprint of steps 5 and 6, 164
  closing entries, journalizing and posting, 187–192
  defined, 119
  demonstration problems, 114–118, 203–211
  described, 92, 138*f*
  financial statements, preparation of, 152–154, 574–579
  mini practice set, 229–244
  post-closing trial balance, 198–199
  posting to the ledger, 101–103
  reviewed, 199–200
  steps of manual accounting cycle, 199*t*
  trial balance, preparation of, 109–112
  worksheet, preparation of. *See* worksheet
accounting equation
  after closing process, 188
  assets, 7
  balance, 9
  balance sheet, preparation of, 22
  balancing the equation, 51
  basic accounting equation, 6, 7–8, 31
  creditors, importance of, 8
  equities, 7
  expanded accounting equation, 15–18, 31, 187
  key terms in, 14–15
  liabilities, 7
  T account entries, 50–52

accounting period, 92, 119
accounting process. *See* accounting
accounting software, 268
accounting software firms, 182
accounting standards, 6
accounts payable
  controlling account, 278, 288
  debit memorandum, effect of, 270
  defined, 31
  described, 9
  schedule of accounts payable, 278, 278*f*, 472
accounts payable subsidiary ledger, 270, 278–279, 288
accounts receivable
  aging the accounts receivable, 620–621
  asset, 14
  controlling account, 251, 252, 258, 288, 462
  credit memorandum, effect of, 255
  defined, 31
  described, 14
  schedule of accounts receivable, 262, 290, 462
accounts receivable subsidiary ledger, 251–252, 252–253, 288
accrual accounting synoptic journal, 518–519, 524
accrual basis of accounting, 511, 524, 615–617, 683*f*
accrued salaries, 144–145, 146*f*, 163, 549
accumulated amortization, 142, 143, 163
Accumulated Depletion, 659
addition, 653, 666
adjusted, 139, 163
  see also adjustments
adjusting journal entries, 183–185, 184*f*, 212, 581–583
  see also adjustments
adjustments
  accrued salaries, 146*f*
  Accrued Salaries account, 144–145

adjusted trial balance, 145–148, 147f
for amortization, 141–144
bad debts, balance required to meet, 620t
balance sheet, effect on, 140
to chequebook balance, 319
described, 139
Desktop Publishing Equipment account, 141–144
income statement, effect on, 140
for inventory, 543–544
journalizing and posting adjusting entries, 183–185, 581–583
merchandising companies, 543–544, 547–550
Office Supplies account, 139–140
Prepaid Rent account, 141
purpose of, 183
reversing entries, 587–589, 588f
in synoptic (combined) journal, 520
for unearned rent, 544
on worksheet, 139–145, 146f
administrative expenses, 576, 590
aging the accounts receivable, 620–621, 628
air express companies, 541
Allowance for Doubtful Accounts, 615–616, 619, 622–623, 628
see also bad debts
allowance method, 618–621
amortization
accelerated amortization method, 645, 666
accumulated amortization, 142, 143
Accumulated Amortization account, 142
adjusting for amortization, 141–145
calculation of, 142
defined, 163
described, 141, 641
double-declining-balance method, 645, 647, 666
as expense, 142, 143
on income statement, 142
partial years, 647
straight-line amortization, 141, 644, 647, 667
sum-of-the-years'-digits method, 646–647, 647, 667
for tax purposes. See capital cost allowance
units-of-production method, 645, 647
amortization expense, 548, 660, 666
Amortization Expense account, 142

amortized, 660, 666
analysis, 5
asset accounts, 22
assets
see also specific assets
asset accounts, 22
book value, 143, 163, 644, 666
capital assets, 579, 590
contra-asset account, 142, 615
cost, 641–642
current assets, 579, 590, 687
defined, 31
described, 7
disposal of assets, 654–657
and equities, relationship between, 7
intangible assets, 641, 659–660, 666
leased assets, 661–662
life of asset, 141
liquidity, 579
long-term assets. See long-term assets
natural resources, 659
property, plant, and equipment. See property, plant, and equipment
real or permanent accounts, 187–188
rules of debit and credit, 51
shift in assets, 9, 32
useful life, 642, 644
automated teller machines (ATMs), 312, 320, 321, 338
auxiliary petty cash record, 331, 331f, 339

B

bad debts
and accrual accounting, 615–617
aging the accounts receivable, 620–621, 628
Allowance for Doubtful Accounts, 615–616, 619, 622–623, 628
allowance method, 618–621
Bad Debts Expense, 615, 628
Bad Debts Recovered, 624, 628
balance required, and adjusting entry, 620t
balance sheet approach, 619–620, 628
blueprint, 627f
and credit policy, 615
direct write-off method, 623–624, 628
estimate, 618–621, 619f

income statement approach, 618–619, 628
writing off uncollectible accounts, 616–617, 622–624
Bad Debts Expense, 615, 628
see also bad debts
Bad Debts Recovered, 624, 628
balance sheet
see also financial statements
accumulated amortization, 142
adjustments, effect of, 140
capital assets, 579
classified balance sheet, 577–579, 578f, 590
comparative balance sheet, 680, 682f, 690
current assets, 579
current liabilities, 579
defined, 31
described, 11, 12f
distinguishing the total, 12–13
dollar sign, use of, 12
elements of, 12
from expanded accounting equation, 22
heading, 12
historical cost, 141
illustration of, 22f
inventory, 544, 544f
long-term liabilities, 579
main elements of, 22–23
merchandising companies, 577–579, 578f
preparation from trial balance, 64f
preparation from worksheet, 154, 155f
preparation of, 12–13
purpose of, 680
worksheet, balance sheet section on, 148a, 550, 551f
balance sheet accounts, 52t
balance sheet approach, 619–620, 628
bank charges. See service charge
bank reconciliation
bank statement, back of, 316, 318f
blueprint, 340f
defined, 339
deposits in transit, 317, 319
described, 316
NSF (not sufficient funds), 318–319
outstanding cheque, 317, 319
sample, 325f
service charge, 317, 319
bank statement, 316, 317f, 318f, 323–324, 324f, 339

banking
  automated teller machines (ATMs),
    312, 320, 321
  bank reconciliation, 316–319
  bank statement, 317f, 318f,
    323–324, 324f
  cancelled cheques, 316, 323
  cheque, 314, 315f
  cheque stub, 314, 315f
  cheque truncation, 323
  chequebook, 314
  chequing account, 312
  credit memorandum, 318
  debit card, 312
  debit memorandum, 318
  deposit slip, 312, 313f
  drawee, 314
  drawer, 314
  electronic funds transfer (EFT),
    319
  electronic integration, 322–323
  endorsement, 312, 314f
  in-company records, 316, 316f
  international banking, 323
  monthly recordkeeping, 316
  online banking, 314, 320–322
  payee, 314
  safekeeping, 323
  signature card, 312
  statement of account, 316
  S.W.I.F.T. codes, 323
  trends in banking, 319–324
basic accounting equation, 7, 31
Baudier, Walter J., 447n
bee tamer, 510
Beesley, Warren, 182
Beesley Exhibitions Inc., 182
beginning inventory, 542, 555
beginning merchandise inventory, 542,
  555
betterment, 653, 666
blank endorsement, 312, 314f
Bolleman, Brent, 310
book of final entry, 92, 119
book of original entry, 92, 119
book value, 143, 163, 644, 666
bookkeepers, 4, 518
bookkeeping, 6, 31
The Bottom Line, 182
Bruce, Donald, 447n
buildings, 642
business entity, 6, 31
business number, 413, 427
business organization, 3, 3f
business services, 512

see also synoptic (combined)
  journal

C

calendar year, 92, 119
Canada
  banking system, 1
  financial position of, 137
  financial scandals, 2
  international accounting rules, 6
  largest reporting entity, 137
Canada Pension Plan (CPP), 371–372,
  375, 378, 385, 408t–409t, 414
Canada Revenue Agency (CRA), 141,
  367, 385, 419
Canada Savings Bonds installments,
  373
Canadian Institute of Chartered
  Accountants, 5
Canadian Public Accountability
  Board, 2
Canadian Tire, 3, 647
cancelled cheques, 316, 323, 339
capital
  account, 148a
  defined, 31
  described, 8
  ending capital, 23, 31
  ending figure for capital, 148a, 198
  real or permanent accounts,
    187–188
  transfer to, 191–192
capital assets
  see also long-term assets; property,
    plant, and equipment
  complex issues, 661–663
  defined, 579, 590
  impairment, 662
  leased assets, 661–662
  self-constructed capital assets,
    662–663
  site restoration costs, 661
  writing down goodwill, 662
capital cost allowance, 141, 163,
  647–650, 666
capital expenditures, 652f, 653, 666
careers in accounting, 4
cash
  Cash Short and Over, 333–335, 339
  change fund, 333–335
  internal control systems, 311
  meaning, in accounting, 8
  petty cash. See petty cash fund
cash account, 8
cash balance, 319

cash basis of accounting, 137, 511,
  512, 524, 683f
cash basis of accounting, modified,
  512–517
cash disbursement journal, 275–279,
  288, 377, 419
cash flow statement. See statement of
  cash flows
cash inflows, 680, 690
cash outflows, 680, 690
cash payments journal, 275–279, 276f,
  288, 292f, 469, 470f, 471f, 484f
cash receipts journal, 259–261, 259f,
  260f, 288, 291f, 459–462, 460f,
  461f, 483f
Cash Short and Over, 333–335, 339
categories of business organization, 3,
  3f
CCA classes, 649
Certified General Accountants
  Association, 5
Certified Internal Auditors (CIAs), 5
Certified Management Accountants
  (CMAs), 5
change fund, 333–335, 339
charitable donations, 372, 375
chart of accounts, 51–52, 52t, 74, 93,
  93f, 512–514, 513f, 525f, 546f
checkmark in journal, 252, 253f
cheque, 314, 315f, 339
cheque endorsement, 312, 314f
cheque number, 375
cheque stub, 314, 315f
cheque truncation, 323, 339
chequebook, 314
chequing account, 312
Chrapko, Evan, 46
Chrapko, Shane, 46
Christie Digital, 364
CICA Handbook, 624, 657, 661, 662
claim code, 367, 370f, 374, 385
classification by activity, 4–5, 4t
classified balance sheet, 577–579,
  578f, 590
classifying, 5
Clodhoppers, 573
closing, 187, 212, 213f
closing journal entries
  closing figures on worksheet, 189f
  defined, 212
  journalizing and posting, 187–192,
    189f, 584, 587f
  in synoptic (combined) journal, 520
collection decisions, 262
Colligo Networks Inc., 310

combined journal. *See* synoptic (combined) journal

"commercial substance," 657

company pension plan, 372

comparative balance sheet, 680, 682*f*, 690

compound entry, 53, 74

compound journal entry, 94, 95, 119

Computer Workshop assignments
   Atlas and Altinora, 136
   Mars and Abby, 509
   Mills and Adora, 509
   Mona and Mikes, 363
   Style and Sorval, 309
   Sullivan and Sully, 245
   Zell and Zadich, 181

contra-asset account, 142, 163, 615

contra-expense account, 266

contra-revenue account, 248

controlling account (AP), 278, 288

controlling account (AR), 251, 252, 258, 288, 462

"cooking the books," 2

copyrights, 660, 666

corporation, 3, 31

corrections
   after posting, 111
   entry posted to wrong account, 111–112
   before posting, 110–111

cost
   of asset, 641–642
   historical cost, 141
   negative cost, 246
   net cost of purchases, 576
   property, plant, and equipment, 641–642
   supervision costs, 662–663

cost of goods available for sale, 576

cost of goods sold, 542, 576

cost principle, 662

CPP deduction tables, 372

credit
   in banking, 312
   defined, 74
   described, 48
   effect of, 141
   rules of debit and credit, 51, 51*t*

credit decisions, 262

credit memorandum
   banking, 318
   defined, 288, 339, 482
   described, 255–256, 255*f*, 291*f*
   with GST/HST, 454–455, 454*f*
   with PST, 451–452

with PST and GST/HST, 456, 456*f*, 457*f*, 483*f*

credit note. *See* credit memorandum

credit period, 249, 288

credit policy, 615

creditor
   described, 7
   importance of creditors, 8

Creighton, Jayne, 510*n*

Critical Path, 46

cross-footing, 261, 288

cross-referencing, 102, 119

current assets, 579, 590, 687

current liabilities, 579, 590, 687

custodian, 329, 332

customer service, 91

D

debit
   defined, 74
   described, 48
   effect of, 141
   of petty cash fund, 331
   rules of debit and credit, 51, 51*t*

debit card, 312, 339

debit memorandum
   banking, 318
   defined, 288, 339, 482
   described, 270–272, 272*f*
   with GST/HST, 468–469, 468*f*, 469*f*, 484*f*

demonstration problems
   accounting concepts and procedures, 27
   accounting cycle, review of, 203–211
   accounting cycle, steps 1-4, 114–118
   business transactions, analyzing and recording, 69–73
   HST, 475–480
   special journals, 282–286

dental insurance premiums, 372

depletion, 659, 659*f*, 666

deposit slip, 312, 313*f*, 339

deposits in transit, 317, 319, 339

DHL Worldwide Express, 541

direct method, 686–688, 688*f*, 691, 692*f*

direct write-off method, 623–624, 628

discount
   and cost of asset, 642
   and freight, 278
   purchases discounts, 266–267
   sales discount, 289, 455, 462

sales discounts, 249, 256
   and sales tax, 278
   trade discounts, 278–279

discount period, 249, 289

disposal of plant assets, 654–657

division of labour, 518

DocSpace Company, 46

dollar sign, use of, 12, 138

double-declining-balance method, 645, 647, 666

double-entry bookkeeping, 53, 74

drawee, 314, 339

drawer, 314, 339

Drucker, Vanessa, 541*n*

Due to CRA account, 419

E

e-tailers, 246

earned revenue, 14

earnings
   overtime earnings, 374
   regular earnings, 374

Eddie Bauer, 5

EI table, 372

electronic funds transfer (EFT), 319, 339

electronic integration, 322–323, 339

Emery, Chris, 573

employee earnings record, 378, 381*f*, 385

employee payroll deductions
   federal tax deductions, 398*t*–402*t*
   Ontario tax tables, 403*t*–407*t*
   simulated Canada Pension Plan contributions, 408*t*–409*t*
   simulated Employment Insurance premium calculations, 410*t*–411*t*

employees
   payroll. *See* employee payroll deductions; payroll
   turnover, 364

Employer Health Tax, 367*n*

employer's remittances
   business number, 413
   Canada (Quebec) Pension Plan, 414
   Due to CRA account, 419
   Employment Insurance, 414–416
   income tax, 414
   (Monthly) Remittance Form (PD7A), 418–420
   remittance, calculation of, 414–416
   remittance formula, 413
   small companies, 418

synoptic (combined) journal, 515–517

T4 Summary, 422, 423*f*

tax calendar, blueprint of, 428*f*

workers' compensation, 416, 424

Employment Insurance (EI) plan, 372, 375, 378, 385, 410*t*–411*t*, 414–416

ending balance, 49, 62, 74

ending capital, 23, 31

ending inventory, 542

ending inventory sheet, 543*f*

ending merchandise inventory, 542

endorsement, 312, 314*f*, 339

enlargement, 653, 666

Enron, 2

equipment

  see also property, plant, and equipment

  adjusting for amortization, 141–145

  defined, 31

  described, 8

  historical cost, 141

  residual value, 142

  of retailer, 247

equities

  and assets, relationship between, 7

  defined, 31

  described, 7

errors

  Cash Short and Over, 333–335

  common mistakes, 110

  correction of entry posted to wrong account, 111–112

  corrections after posting, 111

  corrections before posting, 110–111

  slide, 110

  transposition, 110

  in trial balance, 110

  worksheets, use of, 138

Evans, Megan, 510

Excel, 139

exchange of business assets, 654–657

expanded accounting equation, 15–18, 31, 187

expenses

  see also specific expenses

  amortization, 142, 143

  clearing expense balances, 190–191

  contra-expense account, 266

  defined, 31

  described, 14

  nominal or temporary accounts, 188

  operating expenses, 576

  other expenses, 577, 591

  recording when incurred, 15, 96

extraordinary repair, 653, 666

F

Federal Express, 541

federal government, 137

federal income tax, 366–371

federal tax deductions, 398*t*–402*t*

financial scandals, 2

financial statements

  balance sheet. *See* balance sheet

  blueprint, 33, 75, 591*f*

  contents of, 23*t*

  income statement. *See* income statement

  interim reports, 92, 199

  for merchandising companies, 574–579

  preparation from trial balance, 63, 64*f*, 75

  preparation from worksheet, 152–154

  preparation of, 20–23

  statement of cash flows. *See* statement of cash flows

  statement of owner's equity. *See* statement of owner's equity

  statement of retained earnings, 680, 681*f*

Financial Technology Show, 182

financing activities, 681, 684–685, 684*f*, 691

Finnson, Larry, 573

fiscal year, 92, 119, 199

fixtures, 247

F.O.B., 266, 289

F.O.B. destination, 266, 289

F.O.B. shipping point, 266, 289

footings, 49, 62, 74

forecasting cash inflows, 262

Fox, William F., 447*n*

franchise, 660, 666

fraudulent practices, 321

freight charges, 266

full endorsement, 312, 314*f*

G

GAAP. *See* generally accepted accounting principles (GAAP)

gain on sale, 655

garnishees, 373

general expenses, 576

general journal, 92, 101, 119

  see also journal

general ledger, 101, 119

  see also ledger

General Motors, 5, 310

generally accepted accounting principles (GAAP), 5, 31, 647, 661

Goods and Services Tax (GST)

  see also sales taxes

  cash payments journal, 469, 470*f*, 471*f*, 484*f*

  cash receipts journal, 459–462, 460*f*, 461*f*, 483*f*

  and cost of asset, 642

  credit memorandum, 454–455, 454*f*, 456, 456*f*, 457*f*, 483*f*

  debit memorandum, 468–469, 468*f*, 469*f*, 484*f*

  defined, 482

  described, 246, 448–449

  GST/HST collected, 452–454

  Input Tax Credit, 468

  and the Internet, 447

  paid on purchases, 465–472

  Prepaid GST/HST, 468

  vs. PST, 452

  with PST, 455

  recording, 452

  recovery of amounts written off, 624

  registration, 453

  and sales discounts, 455, 462

  sales invoice, 455, 455*f*

  synoptic (combined) journal, 520–522, 522*f*

goodwill, 660, 662, 666

Government of Canada, 137

governmental accountants, 6

Grant Thornton, 310

gross pay, 374

gross profit, 576

gross sales, 247–248, 289

GST. *See* Goods and Services Tax (GST)

GST/HST collected, 452–454, 482

H

half-year rule, 648

Harmonized Sales Tax (HST)

  see also sales taxes

  cash payments journal, 469, 470*f*, 471*f*

  cash receipts journal, 459–462, 460*f*, 461*f*, 483*f*

  and cost of asset, 642

  credit memorandum, 454–455, 454*f*, 456, 456*f*, 457*f*, 483*f*

  debit memorandum, 468–469, 468*f*, 469*f*

defined, 482
described, 246, 448–449
GST/HST collected, 452–454
Input Tax Credit, 468
paid on purchases, 465–472
Prepaid HST, 468
provinces collecting HST, 449, 468
vs. PST, 452
with PST, 455
purchase order, 466, 466*f*
recording, 452
recovery of amounts written off, 624
registration, 453
and sales discounts, 455, 462
sales invoice, 455, 466, 466*f*
synoptic (combined) journal, 520–522, 522*f*
historical cost, 141, 163
hours worked, 374
HST. *See* Harmonized Sales Tax (HST)
hybrid method (modified-cash-basis), 512–517

I

IBM, 310
impairment, 662, 666
impairment loss, 662
in-company records, 316, 316*f*
income
  net income. *See* net income
  other income, 577, 591
  rental income, 544, 548
income statement
  see also financial statements
  adjustments, effect of, 140
  amortization, 142
  cost of goods sold section, 576
  defined, 31
  described, 20
  gross profit, 576
  heading, 20
  inventory, 544, 544*f*
  main elements of, 22–23
  for merchandising companies, 574–577, 575*f*
  net sales, 576
  operating expenses section, 576
  other expenses section, 577
  other income (other revenue) section, 577
  preparation from trial balance, 64*f*
  preparation from worksheet, 152, 153*f*

preparation of, 20
purposes of, 680
revenue section, 576
Sales Returns and Allowances, 248
sample, 21*f*, 681*f*
set-up, 20
worksheet, income statement section on, 148, 148a*f*, 550, 550*f*
income statement accounts, 52*t*
income statement approach, 618–619, 628
Income Summary, 188–191, 212, 543
income tax deduction, 374–375, 385
indexing, 371, 385
indirect method
  blueprint, 692*f*
  cash flows from financing activities, 684–685, 684*f*
  cash flows from investing activities, 683–684
  cash flows from operating activities, 681–683, 683*f*
  defined, 691
  described, 681–682
  sample statement of cash flows, 685*f*
inflation, 371
Input Tax Credit, 468
Institute of Internal Auditors, 5
insurance expired, 548
intangible assets, 641, 659–660, 666
Intel Corporation, 5
interest, 663
Interest Expense, 547
interim reports, 92, 119, 199
internal control, and online banking, 321
internal control systems, 311, 339
international banking, 323
International Financial Reporting Standards (IFRS), 6, 31–32
Internet
  e-tailers, and sales taxes, 246
  online banking, 314, 320–322
  opportunities on, 2
  phishing, 321, 340
  sales taxes and, 447
  travel industry, 91
interpretation, 5
inventory
  adjustments, 543–544
  on balance sheet, 544, 544*f*
  beginning merchandise inventory, 542
  cost of goods sold, 542, 576

ending inventory sheet, 543*f*
ending merchandise inventory, 542
on income statement, 544, 544*f*
just-in-time inventory management, 541
periodic inventory system, 247, 542, 555
perpetual inventory system, 247, 541, 542, 555
investing activities, 681, 683–684, 691
investments in owner's business, 8
invoice
  purchase invoice, 268–269, 289
  sales invoice, 252, 254*f*, 268, 268*f*, 289, 452–453, 452*f*, 455, 455*f*, 466, 466*f*
invoice approval form, 269, 269*f*, 289

J

Jinks, Barry, 310
journal
  analyzing and recording transactions in, 92–97
  beginning of new page, 98
  book of original entry, 92
  cash disbursement journal, 275–279, 288, 377, 419
  cash payments journal, 275–279, 276*f*, 288, 292*f*, 469, 470*f*, 471*f*, 484*f*
  cash receipts journal, 259–261, 259*f*, 260*f*, 288, 291*f*, 459–462, 460*f*, 461*f*, 483*f*
  and chart of accounts, 93, 93*f*
  checkmark in journal, 252, 253*f*
  computerized format, 93
  cross-referencing, 102
  defined, 92, 119
  described, 92–93, 93*f*
  vs. ledger, 92
  merchandising companies, 585*f*
  posting from, to the ledger, 101–102, 103*f*
  posting references (PR), 102
  purchases journal, 270, 271*f*, 289, 467*f*, 484*f*
  sales journal, 252–254, 289, 291*f*, 451*f*, 453*f*, 456*f*, 483*f*
  special journals, 250–254
  synoptic (combined) journal. *See* synoptic (combined) journal
  use of, 92
journal entries
  see also journalizing

adjusting journal entries, 183–185, 184*f*

closing journal entries, 187–192

compound journal entry, 94, 95

defined, 92, 120

gross sales, 248

merchandising companies, 247–250

recording from worksheet, 183–185

Sales Returns and Allowances, 248

service charge, 318*f*

structure of, 94

journalizing

  see also journal entries

  adjusting entries, 183–185, 184*f*

  adjusting entries for merchandising companies, 581–583

  from cash payments journal, 278–279

  from cash receipts journal, 261, 459–462, 460*f*, 461*f*

  chequebook balance, adjustments to, 319

  closing entries, 188–192, 189*f*

  closing entries for merchandising companies, 584, 587*f*

  debit memorandum, 270–272

  defined, 92, 120

  merchandising companies, 256

  transactions, 93–98

just-in-time inventory management, 541

K

Kirbyson, Geoff, 573*n*

Knowles, Paul, 91*n*

Krave's Candy Co., 573

L

land, 642

land improvements, 642, 666

laws affecting payroll, 365–373

leased assets, 661–662

ledger

  accounts payable subsidiary ledger, 270, 278–279

  accounts receivable subsidiary ledger, 251–252, 252–253

  book of final entry, 92

  complete ledger, 193*f*

  computerized format, 93

  controlling account, 251, 252

  credit memorandum, postings and recordings for, 256*f*

  defined, 74, 92

  described, 47

vs. journal, 92

  posting from cash payments journal, 278

  posting from sales journal, 253–254

  posting to the ledger, 101–102, 103*f*

  special ledgers, 251–252

  subsidiary ledgers, 251–252, 256*f*

  use of, 92

ledger accounts, 47

legal ownership (title), 267

liabilities

  see also specific liabilities

  current liabilities, 579, 590, 687

  defined, 32

  described, 7

  long-term liabilities, 579, 591

  real or permanent accounts, 187–188

  rules of debit and credit, 51

life insurance premiums, 373

liquidity, 579

Loblaws, 647

long-term assets

  see also capital assets

  blueprint of key accounts, 667*f*

  depletion, 659, 659*f*

  impairment, 662

  intangible assets, 659–660

  natural resources, 659

  property, plant, and equipment. *See* property, plant, and equipment

long-term income replacement premiums, 373

long-term liabilities, 579, 591

loss

  on disposal, 654

  on exchange, 656–657

  from fire, 655

  on sale, 655–656

Love, Myron, 573*n*

lululemon athletica, 679

M

Mahood, Casey, 573*n*

managerial accountants, 5

manufacturing companies, 4*t*, 5, 32

market value, 143

Martin, Dan, 510

MasterCard, 312

matching principle, 511

Mattel Manufacturing, 264

medical insurance premiums, 372

memorandum records, 515

merchandise, 247, 289

  see also inventory

merchandising companies

  see also inventory

  accounts payable subsidiary ledger, 270

  accounts receivable subsidiary ledger, 251–252, 252–253

  adjusting entries, journalizing and posting, 581–583

  adjustments, 543–544, 547–550

  balance sheet, 577–579, 578*f*

  buyer's view of, 264–267

  cash disbursement journal, 275–279

  cash payments journal, 275–279, 276*f*, 292*f*, 469, 470*f*, 471*f*, 484*f*

  cash receipts journal, 259–261, 259*f*, 291*f*, 459–462, 460*f*, 461*f*, 483*f*

  chart of accounts, 546*f*

  closing entries, journalizing and posting, 584, 587*f*

  credit memorandum, 255–256, 255*f*, 291*f*

  debit memorandum, 270–272, 272*f*

  defined, 32

  described, 4*t*, 5

  financial statements, blueprint of, 591*f*

  financial statements, preparation of, 574–579

  general journal, 585*f*

  income statement, 574–577, 575*f*

  invoice approval form, 269, 269*f*

  overview of journal entries, 247–250

  post-closing trial balance, 584, 586*f*

  purchase invoice, 268–269

  purchase order, 268

  purchase requisition, 268

  Purchases, 264–265

  Purchases Discounts, 266–267

  purchases journal, 270, 271*f*, 467*f*, 484*f*

  Purchases Returns and Allowances, 265

  purchasing merchandise, 268–272

  receiving report, 269

  recording purchases, 268–272

  reversing entries, 587–589, 588*f*

  sales journal, 252–254, 291*f*, 451*f*, 453*f*, 456*f*, 483*f*

  schedule of accounts payable, 278, 278*f*

  schedule of accounts receivable, 262

  seller's view of, 247–250, 449–457

  special journals, 250–254

statement of owner's equity, 577
subsidiary ledgers, 251–252
synoptic (combined) journal, 518–522
trade discounts, 278–279
worksheet, 545–550, 549f, 556f, 575f, 582f
Microsoft Corporation, 310
Mini Practice Sets
The Corner Dress Shop, 608–612
Pete's Market, 445–446
Sullivan Realty (accounting cycle), 229–244
minimum wage laws, 366, 385
modified-cash-basis (hybrid) method, 512–517, 525, 525f
(Monthly) Remittance Form (PD7A), 418–420, 427
Mortgage Payable, 547, 555
multicolumn purchases journal, 291f, 484f
multicolumn sales journal, 483f

N

National Policies, 2
natural business year, 92, 120
natural resources, 659
negative cost, 246
net cost of purchases, 576
net credit sales, 618
net income, 15, 32, 148
net loss, 15, 32, 148
net pay, 375
net purchases, 266, 289, 576
net realizable value, 616, 628
net sales, 249, 289, 576
NewViews, 614
nominal accounts, 188
non-profit accountants, 6
noncash investing and financing activities, 681, 691
normal balance, in accounts payable subsidiary ledger, 270
normal balance of an account, 51, 74, 148f
Nortel Networks Corporation, 2
NSF (not sufficient funds), 318–319, 339

O

Office Supplies account, 139–140
Office Supplies Expense account, 140, 141
online banking, 314, 320–322
Ontario Health Premium, 367n

Ontario Securities Commission, 2
Ontario tax tables, 403t–407t
operating activities, 680, 681–683, 683f, 691
operating cycle, 579, 591
operating expenses, 576
other deductions, 372–373, 385
other expenses, 577, 591
other income, 577, 591
outstanding cheque, 317, 319, 339
overtime earnings, 374
overtime premium, 366
overtime rates, 374
owner's drawing account, 15
owner's equity
defined, 32
described, 7
illustration of, 14f
statement of owner's equity. See statement of owner's equity
subdivision of, 18

P

Pappes, Valerian, 46
parking charges, 373
partial years, amortization for, 647
partnership, 3, 32
patent, 660, 667
pay rate, 374
payee, 314, 339
payroll
blueprint, 386f
Canada and Quebec Pension Plans, 371–372, 375, 414
Canada Pension Plan (CPP), 378
charitable donations, 375
cheque number, 375
claim code, 374
employee earnings record, 378, 381f
employee payroll deductions, 398–411
employer's expenses associated with payroll. See employer's remittances
Employment Insurance (EI) plan, 372, 375, 378, 414–416
federal and provincial income tax, 366–371
gross pay, 374
hours worked, 374
income tax deduction, 374–375
laws and regulations, 365–373
minimum wage laws, 366
net pay, 375

other deductions, 372–373
overtime earnings, 374
payroll cheques, 378
payroll periods, 371
payroll summary, 374–375, 375f
rate of pay, 374
Record of Employment, 378, 380f
recording a typical payroll, 374–375
recording and payment, 376–378
regular earnings, 374
synoptic (combined) journal, 515–517
T4 slip, 378, 379f
T4 Summary, 422, 423f
T4 Supplementary, 378
T4A slip, 378
union agreements, 372
workers' compensation, 372, 416, 424
writing cheques, 377–378
Payroll Deductions Tables (T4032), 367, 371
payroll summary, 374–375, 375f, 385
PC Magazine, 614
pension plan, 372
periodic inventory system, 247, 542, 555
permanent accounts, 187–188, 212
perpetual inventory system
defined, 555
described, 247, 542
key advantage of, 541
personal identification number (PIN), 320
personal income taxes, 366–371
pet chiropractor, 510
Petty Cash account, 330
petty cash fund
asset, 329
auxiliary petty cash record, 331, 331f
custodian, 329, 332
debits and, 331
defined, 339
described, 329
making payments from, 330–334
petty cash voucher, 330, 331f, 339
replenishment, 331–332, 332f
setting up, 329–330, 332f
steps involving petty cash, 333
petty cash voucher, 330, 331f, 339
phishing, 321, 340
post-closing trial balance, 198–199, 212, 584, 586f
posting

adjusting entries for merchandising companies, 581–583

from cash payments journal, 278–279

from cash receipts journal, 260*f*, 261, 459–462, 460*f*, 461*f*

chequebook balance, adjustments to, 319

closing entries for merchandising companies, 584, 587*f*

debit memorandum, 270–272

defined, 120

described, 101

to the ledger, 101–102, 103*f*

merchandising companies, 256

posting references (PR), 102, 252, 261, 460

from sales journal to general ledger, 253–254

to synoptic journal, 515, 519–522

posting references (PR), 102, 252, 261, 460

Prepaid GST/HST, 468, 482

prepaid rent, 95, 141

PricewaterhouseCoopers, 310

private accountants, 5

private insurance companies, 420

professional services, 512

see also synoptic (combined) journal

profit, gross, 576

property, plant, and equipment

see also capital assets; long-term assets

accelerated amortization method, 645

amortization methods, 644–650

buildings, 642

capital expenditures, 652*f*, 653

"commercial substance," 657

cost of, 641–642

disposal of plant assets, 654–657

double-declining-balance method, 645, 647

land and land improvements, 642

partial years, amortization for, 647

revenue expenditures, 653

straight-line amortization, 644, 647

sum-of-the-years'-digits method, 646–647, 647

units-of-production method, 645, 647

provincial health care plan, 420

provincial income tax, 366–371

provincial sales tax (PST)

see also sales taxes

cash receipts journal, 462, 483*f*

credit memorandum, 451–452, 456, 456*f*, 457*f*, 483*f*

described, 246

with GST/HST, 455

Provincial Sales Tax (PST) Payable, 449–450

and sales discounts, 455, 462

sales invoice, 455, 455*f*

synoptic (combined) journal, 520–522, 522*f*

Provincial Sales Tax (PST) Payable, 450, 482

proving

accounts receivable subsidiary ledger, 252

cash receipts journal, 261, 462

cross-footing, 261

the synoptic journal, 515

PST. *See* provincial sales tax (PST)

public accountants, 5

purchase invoice, 268–269, 289

purchase order, 268, 289, 466, 466*f*

purchase requisition, 268, 289

purchases

see also merchandising companies

defined, 289

discounts, 266–267

GST/HST paid on purchases, 465–472

net cost of purchases, 576

net purchases, 266, 289, 576

Purchases account, 264–265

Purchases Returns and Allowances, 265, 272, 289

recording purchases, 268–272

steps taken in purchasing merchandise, 268–272

Purchases account, 264–265

Purchases Discounts, 266–267, 289

purchases journal, 270, 271*f*, 289, 467*f*, 484*f*

Purchases Returns and Allowances, 265, 272, 289

Q

Quebec Pension Plan (QPP), 371–372, 375, 385, 414

QuickBooks®, 372, 680

QuickBooks® Pro, 520

Q.W. Page Associates, 614

R

rate of pay, 374

real accounts, 187–188

Receiver General, 419

receiving report, 269, 289

reconciliation process. *See* bank reconciliation

Record of Employment, 378, 380*f*, 385

recording

business transactions, 50–59

business transactions in a journal, 92–98

from cash payments journal, 278–279

from cash receipts journal, 261, 459–462, 460*f*, 461*f*

debits and credits, 50–59

described, 5

GST and HST, 452

inventory on balance sheet and income statement, 544, 544*f*

merchandising companies, 256

payroll, 376–378

purchases, 268–272

purchases with GST/HST, 466–468

replenishment in petty cash record, 332*f*

in synoptic (combined) journal, 514–515, 519–522

regular earnings, 374

regulations affecting payroll, 365–373

Remers, Gerry, 364

remittance, employer's. *See* employer's remittances

remittance formula, 413, 428

remitted, 413

Rental Income, 544, 548

repayment of loans or advances, 373

reporting, 5

see also financial statements

residual value, 142, 163, 644, 667

restrictive endorsement, 312, 314*f*

retailer, 247, 289

revenue

see also specific revenues

clearing revenue balances, 188–190

contra-revenue account, 248

defined, 32

described, 14

gross sales, 247–248

nominal or temporary accounts, 188

recording when earned, 14, 97

revenue expenditures, 653

reversing entries, 587–589, 588*f*, 591

Rogers, Jim, 510

Royal Bank of Canada, 1

rules of debit and credit, 51, 51*t*

S

safekeeping, 323
Salaries Payable, 145, 163
salary, 15, 16, 549
   see also payroll
sales
   gross sales, 247–248, 289
   net credit sales, 618
   net sales, 249, 289, 576
   sales discount, 249, 256
   Sales Returns and Allowances, 248,
      255, 270, 290
sales discount, 249, 256, 289, 455, 462
sales invoice, 252, 254*f*, 268, 268*f*, 289,
   452–453, 452*f*, 455, 455*f*, 466,
   466*f*
sales journal, 252–254, 289, 291*f*, 451*f*,
   453*f*, 456*f*, 483*f*
Sales Returns and Allowances, 248,
   255, 270, 290
sales taxes
   cash payments journal, 469, 470*f*,
      471*f*, 484*f*
   cash receipts journal, 459–462,
      460*f*, 461*f*, 483*f*
   and cost of asset, 642
   credit memorandum, 451–452,
      454–455, 456, 456*f*, 457*f*, 483*f*
   debit memorandum, 468–469, 468*f*,
      469*f*, 484*f*
   described, 246, 278, 448–449
   Goods and Services Tax (GST), 246,
      447, 448–449, 452–456
   GST/HST collected, 452–454
   Harmonized Sales Tax (HST), 246,
      448–449, 452–456
   paid on purchases, 465–472
   prepaid sales taxes, 468
   provincial sales tax (PST), 246,
      449–450
   Provincial Sales Tax (PST) Payable,
      450
   PST with GST/HST, 455
   recording purchases with
      GST/HST, 466–468
   recovery of amounts written off,
      624
   and sales discounts, 455, 462
   sales invoice with PST and
      GST/HST, 455, 455*f*
   synoptic (combined) journal,
      520–522, 522*f*
salvage value. *See* residual value
Sarbanes-Oxley Act, 2, 32

schedule of accounts payable, 278,
   278*f*, 472
schedule of accounts receivable, 262,
   290, 462
Sears, 5
self-constructed capital assets,
   662–663
selling expenses, 576, 591
service charge, 317, 318*f*, 319, 340
service company
   cash basis of accounting, 511
   defined, 32
   described, 4, 4*t*
   modified-cash-basis (hybrid)
      method, 512–517
share prices, 1
shift in assets, 9, 32
shipping and handling (S&H), 246,
   266
Shoppers Drug Mart, 573
signature card, 312, 340
Simply Accounting®, 268, 372, 520,
   680
simulated Canada Pension Plan
   contributions, 408*t*–409*t*
simulated Employment Insurance
   premium calculations, 410*t*–411*t*
single-column sales journal, 291*f*
site restoration costs, 661
skimming victims, 321
slide, 110, 120
social fund charges, 373
Society of Management Accountants
   of Canada, 5
sole proprietorship, 3, 32
Sowinski, Lara L., 541*n*
special journals
   cash disbursement journal,
      275–279, 288, 377, 419
   cash payments journal, 275–279,
      276*f*, 288, 292*f*, 469, 470*f*, 471*f*,
      484*f*
   cash receipts journal, 259–261,
      259*f*, 260*f*, 288, 291*f*, 459–462,
      460*f*, 461*f*, 483*f*
   defined, 290
   described, 251
   merchandising companies, 250–254
   purchases journal, 270, 271*f*, 289,
      467*f*, 484*f*
   sales journal, 252–254, 289, 291*f*,
      451*f*, 453*f*, 456*f*, 483*f*
   synoptic (combined) journal. *See*
      synoptic (combined) journal
special ledgers, 251–252
spreadsheet software, 139, 520

standard account, 47, 47*f*, 74
Starbucks, 412
statement of account, 316
statement of cash flows
   blueprint, 692*f*
   defined, 691
   described, 680
   direct method, 686–688, 688*f*, 691,
      692*f*
   financing activities, 681, 684–685,
      684*f*, 691
   indirect method, 681–685, 683*f*,
      685*f*, 691, 692*f*
   investing activities, 681, 683–684,
      691
   noncash investing and financing
      activities, 681, 691
   operating activities, 680, 681–683,
      683*f*, 691
statement of financial position. *See*
   balance sheet
statement of owner's equity
   see also financial statements
   defined, 32
   described, 21
   illustration of, 21*f*, 22*f*
   main elements of, 22–23
   merchandising companies, 577
   preparation from trial balance, 64*f*
   preparation from worksheet,
      152–154, 153*f*
statement of retained earnings, 680,
   681*f*
straight-line amortization, 141, 644,
   647, 667
strange jobs, 510
subsidiary ledgers
   accounts payable subsidiary ledger,
      270, 278–279, 288
   accounts receivable subsidiary
      ledger, 251–252, 256*f*, 288
   defined, 290
Subway case study, 26–27, 68, 158,
   202, 337, 383, 426
sum-of-the-years'-digits method,
   646–647, 647, 667
summarizing, 5
Sundry Accounts, 259, 278, 290
supervision costs, 662–663
supplies, 8, 32, 95, 139–140, 548
supply chain management, 541
S.W.I.F.T. codes, 323, 340
sword swallowing, 510
synoptic (combined) journal
   accrual accounting synoptic
      journal, 518–519

adjusting entries, 520
chart of accounts, 512–514, 513*f*
closing entries, 520
defined, 525
employer's payroll tax expense, 515–517
end of month, 519–522
memorandum records, 515
merchandising company, 518–522
modified-cash-basis (hybrid) method, 512–517, 525*f*
payroll deductions, 515–517
posting, 515, 519–522
proving the journal, 515
recording transactions in, 514–515, 519–522
with sales tax and GST, 520–522, 522*f*
sample, 514*f*, 516*f*, 520*f*
spreadsheet program, 520

T

T account
and accounting equation, 50–52
balancing an account, 49
balancing the equation, 51
basic parts, 47–48
credit, 48
debit, 48
defined, 74
described, 47
ending balance, 49, 62
footings, 49, 62
normal balance of an account, 51
transaction analysis, 52–58
T4 slip, 378, 379*f*, 386
T4 Summary, 422, 423*f*, 428
T4 Supplementary, 378, 386, 428
T4A slip, 378, 386
take-home pay, 375, 377
Tanzer, Andrew, 541*n*
tax calendar, 428*f*
taxation
capital cost allowance, 141, 163, 647–650, 666
CCA classes, 649
claim code, 367, 370*f*, 374
employee payroll deductions, 398–411
employer's remittances. *See* employer's remittances
employer's tax responsibilities. *See* employer's remittances
federal and provincial income tax, 366–371

federal tax deductions, 398*t*–402*t*
half-year rule, 648
income tax deduction, 374–375
Ontario tax tables, 403*t*–407*t*
Payroll Deductions Tables (T4032), 367
personal income taxes, 366–371
personal tax credits return, 368*f*, 369*f*
sales taxes. *See* sales taxes
simulated Canada Pension Plan contributions, 408*t*–409*t*
simulated Employment Insurance premium calculations, 410*t*–411*t*
T4 slip, 378, 379*f*
T4 Supplementary, 378
T4A slip, 378
tax calendar, blueprint of, 428*f*
TD1 forms, 367–370, 371
TONI, 366, 367
Total Claim Amount, 367, 370
undepreciated capital cost (UCC), 649*n*, 650, 667
and write-offs, 624
TD1 forms, 367–370, 371, 385
temporary accounts, 188, 212
three-column account, 101–102, 102*f*, 120
Tim Hortons, 412, 647
title to goods, 267
TNT International, 541
TONI, 366, 367, 385–386
trade discounts, 278–279
trade-in allowance, 656–657, 667
transaction analysis, 52–58
transaction analysis chart, 52
transactions
analyzing, 92–97
recording in journal, 92–97
transposition, 110, 120
travel industry, 91
trial balance
adjusted trial balance, 145–148, 147*f*
capital figure, 109
common mistakes, 110
correction after posting, 111
correction before posting, 110–111
correction of entry posted to wrong account, 111–112
defined, 63, 74, 109, 120
errors, 110
financial statements, preparation of, 63, 64*f*, 75
illustration of, 109*f*

not balanced, 110
post-closing trial balance, 198–199, 212, 584, 586*f*
preparation of, 109–112
summary of new account titles, 546*t*
on worksheet, 139, 547*f*
truncation, 323
trust, 321
turnover rates, 364

U

uncollectible accounts, 616–617, 622–624
undepreciated capital cost (UCC), 649*n*, 650, 667
Unearned Rent, 544
Unearned Revenue, 547, 556
union agreements, 372
union dues, 372, 386
United Parcel Service, 541
United States
financial scandals, 2
Sarbanes-Oxley Act, 2
units-of-production method, 645, 647, 667
useful life, 642, 644, 667

V

Visa, 312

W

wages. *See* payroll; salary
Wal-Mart, 573
WCB expense, 416, 428
weird jobs, 510
WestJet, 91
wholesalers, 247, 290
Wilson, Chip, 679
withdrawals, 15, 21, 32, 188, 191–192
workers' compensation, 372, 386, 416, 420, 424
worksheet
adjusted trial balance section, 145–148, 147*f*
adjustments, journalizing and posting from, 183–185, 184*f*
adjustments section, 139–145, 146*f*
balance sheet section, 148a, 550, 551*f*
chart of accounts, 546*f*
closing figures on, 189*f*
closing process, blueprint of, 213*f*
completed worksheet, sample, 552*f*, 582*f*
defined, 163

described, 138–139

financial statements, preparation of, 152–154

function of, 138

heading, 139

income statement section, 148, 148a*f,* 550, 550*f*

for merchandising company, 545–550, 549*f,* 556*f,* 575*f,* 582*f*

net income, 148

net loss, 148

recording journal entries from, 183–185

sample worksheet, 139*f,* 148b*f*

spreadsheet software, 139

trial balance section, 139, 547*f*

WorldCom, 2

write-offs

Allowance for Doubtful Accounts, use of, 622–623

blueprint, 627*f*

direct write-off method, 623–624, 628

income tax regulations, 624

introductory example, 616–617

writing down goodwill, 662

Z

Zellers, 573